S0-AIA-557

CMR

barbri®
BAR REVIEW

The Conviser Mini Review

Table of Contents

Constitutional Law
Contracts
Sales
Criminal Law
Criminal Procedure
Evidence
Real Property
Torts

celebrating over
35
YEARS
of preparing
law students
for the bar exam

THOMSON
BAR/BRI

CONSTITUTIONAL LAW

TABLE OF CONTENTS

PART 1: POWERS OF THE FEDERAL GOVERNMENT 1

I. THE JUDICIAL POWER 1
- A. ARTICLE III 1
- B. POWER OF JUDICIAL REVIEW 1
- C. FEDERAL COURTS 1
- D. JURISDICTION OF THE SUPREME COURT 1
  - 1. Original Jurisdiction 1
  - 2. Appellate Jurisdiction 1
- E. CONSTITUTIONAL AND SELF-IMPOSED LIMITATIONS ON EXERCISE OF FEDERAL JURISDICTION—"STRICT NECESSITY" 2
  - 1. No Advisory Opinions 2
  - 2. Ripeness—Immediate Threat of Harm 2
  - 3. Mootness 2
  - 4. Standing 2
  - 5. Adequate and Independent State Grounds 4
  - 6. Abstention 4
  - 7. Political Questions 4
  - 8. Eleventh Amendment Limits on Federal Courts 4

II. LEGISLATIVE POWER 5
- A. ENUMERATED AND IMPLIED POWERS 5
  - 1. Necessary and Proper "Power" 5
  - 2. Taxing Power 5
  - 3. Spending Power 5
  - 4. Commerce Power 6
  - 5. War and Related Powers 6
  - 6. Investigatory Power 6
  - 7. Property Power 7
  - 8. No Federal Police Power 7
  - 9. Bankruptcy Power 7
  - 10. Postal Power 7
  - 11. Power Over Citizenship 7
  - 12. Admiralty Power 7
  - 13. Power to Coin Money and Fix Weights and Measures 7
  - 14. Patent/Copyright Power 7
- B. DELEGATION OF LEGISLATIVE POWER 8
- C. SPEECH AND DEBATE CLAUSE—IMMUNITY FOR FEDERAL LEGISLATORS 9
- D. CONGRESSIONAL "VETO" OF EXECUTIVE ACTIONS INVALID 9

III. THE EXECUTIVE POWER 9
- A. DOMESTIC POWERS 9
  - 1. Appointment and Removal 9

2. **Pardons** 9
3. **Veto Power** 10
4. **Power as Chief Executive** 10
B. **POWER OVER EXTERNAL AFFAIRS** 10
1. **War** 10
2. **Foreign Relations** 10
3. **Treaty Power** 10
4. **Executive Agreements** 11
C. **EXECUTIVE PRIVILEGE/IMMUNITY** 12
1. **Executive Privilege** 12
2. **Executive Immunity** 12
D. **IMPEACHMENT** 12

PART 2: THE FEDERAL SYSTEM 12

IV. **RELATIVE SPHERES OF FEDERAL AND STATE POWERS** 12
A. **EXCLUSIVE FEDERAL POWERS** 12
1. **Power of States Expressly Limited** 12
2. **Inherent Federal Powers** 12
B. **EXCLUSIVE STATE POWERS** 12
C. **CONCURRENT FEDERAL AND STATE POWER—EFFECT OF SUPREMACY CLAUSE** 12
1. **Conflict Between State and Federal Laws** 12
2. **State Prevents Achievement of Federal Objective** 13
3. **Preemption** 13
D. **ABSENCE OF FEDERAL AND STATE POWERS** 13
E. **INTERSTATE COMPACT CLAUSE** 13
F. **FULL FAITH AND CREDIT CLAUSE** 13

V. **INTERSOVEREIGN LITIGATION** 13
A. **SUITS BY UNITED STATES AGAINST A STATE** 13
B. **SUITS BY A STATE AGAINST UNITED STATES** 13
C. **FEDERAL OFFICER AS DEFENDANT** 13
1. **Limitation** 13
2. **Specific Relief Against Officer** 13
D. **SUITS BY ONE STATE AGAINST ANOTHER** 14

VI. **INTERGOVERNMENTAL TAX AND REGULATION IMMUNITIES** 14
A. **FEDERAL TAXATION AND REGULATION OF STATE OR LOCAL GOVERNMENTS** 14
1. **Tax or Regulation Applying to Both State and Private Entities—Valid** 14
2. **Tax or Regulation Applying Only to States** 14
3. **Commandeering State Officials** 14
B. **STATE TAXATION AND REGULATION OF FEDERAL GOVERNMENT** 14

VII. **PRIVILEGES AND IMMUNITIES CLAUSES** 15
A. **ARTICLE IV—PRIVILEGES OF STATE CITIZENSHIP** 15
1. **Only "Fundamental Rights" Protected** 15
2. **Substantial Justification Exception** 15

3. Note—Relationship to Commerce Clause 15
B. FOURTEENTH AMENDMENT—PRIVILEGES OF NATIONAL CITIZENSHIP 16

PART 3: STATE REGULATION OR TAXATION OF COMMERCE 16

VIII. REGULATION OF FOREIGN COMMERCE 16

IX. REGULATION OF INTERSTATE COMMERCE 16
A. REGULATION OF COMMERCE BY CONGRESS 16
1. Power of Congress to Supersede or Preempt State Regulation 16
2. Power of Congress to Permit or Prohibit State Regulation 16
B. STATE REGULATION OF COMMERCE IN THE ABSENCE OF CONGRESSIONAL ACTION 16
1. Discriminatory Regulations 16
2. Nondiscriminatory Laws—Balancing Test 19
C. TWENTY-FIRST AMENDMENT—STATE CONTROL OVER INTOXICATING LIQUOR 19
1. Intrastate Regulation 19
2. Interstate Regulation 19
3. Federal Power 19

X. POWER OF STATES TO TAX INTERSTATE COMMERCE 20
A. GENERAL CONSIDERATIONS 20
1. Discriminatory Taxes 20
2. Nondiscriminatory Taxes 20
B. USE TAXES 20
1. Permissible in Buyer's State 20
2. State May Force Seller to Collect Use Tax 20
C. SALES TAXES 20
D. AD VALOREM PROPERTY TAXES 20
1. No Tax on Commodities in Course of Interstate Commerce 22
2. Tax on Instrumentalities Used to Transport Goods Interstate 22
E. PRIVILEGE, LICENSE, FRANCHISE, OR OCCUPATIONAL TAXES 22

XI. POWER OF STATES TO TAX FOREIGN COMMERCE 24

PART 4: INDIVIDUAL GUARANTEES AGAINST GOVERNMENTAL OR PRIVATE ACTION 24

XII. LIMITATIONS ON POWER AND STATE ACTION REQUIREMENT 24
A. CONSTITUTIONAL RESTRICTIONS ON POWER OVER INDIVIDUALS 24
1. Bill of Rights 24
2. Thirteenth Amendment 24
3. Fourteenth and Fifteenth Amendments 24
4. Commerce Clause 24
5. Rights of National Citizenship 25
B. STATE ACTION REQUIREMENT 25

1. **Exclusive Public Functions** 25
2. **Significant State Involvement—Facilitating Private Action** 25

XIII. RETROACTIVE LEGISLATION 26
A. **CONTRACT CLAUSE—IMPAIRMENT OF CONTRACT** 26
1. **Not Applicable to Federal Government** 26
2. **Basic Impairment Rules** 26
B. **EX POST FACTO LAWS** 26
C. **BILLS OF ATTAINDER** 26
D. **DUE PROCESS CONSIDERATIONS** 27

XIV. PROCEDURAL DUE PROCESS 27
A. **BASIC PRINCIPLE** 27
B. **IS LIFE, LIBERTY, OR PROPERTY BEING TAKEN?** 27
1. **Liberty** 27
2. **Property** 27
C. **WHAT TYPE OF PROCESS IS REQUIRED?** 27
D. **DUE PROCESS RIGHTS ARE SUBJECT TO WAIVER** 27
E. **ACCESS TO COURTS—INDIGENT PLAINTIFFS** 28

XV. THE "TAKING" CLAUSE 28
A. **IN GENERAL** 28
B. **"PUBLIC USE" LIMITATION LIBERALLY CONSTRUED** 29
C. **"TAKING" VS. "REGULATION"** 29
1. **Actual Appropriation or Physical Invasion** 29
2. **Use Restrictions** 29
3. **Remedy—"Just Compensation"** 30

XVI. INTRODUCTION TO SUBSTANTIVE DUE PROCESS AND EQUAL PROTECTION 30
A. **RELATIONSHIP BETWEEN SUBSTANTIVE DUE PROCESS AND EQUAL PROTECTION** 30
1. **Substantive Due Process** 30
2. **Equal Protection** 30
B. **WHAT STANDARD OF REVIEW WILL THE COURT APPLY?** 31
1. **Strict Scrutiny (Maximum Scrutiny)** 31
2. **Intermediate Scrutiny** 31
3. **Rational Basis (Minimal Scrutiny)** 31

XVII. SUBSTANTIVE DUE PROCESS 31
A. **CONSTITUTIONAL SOURCE—TWO CLAUSES** 31
B. **APPLICABLE STANDARDS** 32
C. **A FEW IRREBUTTABLE PRESUMPTIONS MAY BE INVALID** 32

XVIII. EQUAL PROTECTION 32
A. **CONSTITUTIONAL SOURCE** 32
B. **APPLICABLE STANDARDS** 32
C. **PROVING DISCRIMINATORY CLASSIFICATION** 32
D. **SUSPECT CLASSIFICATIONS** 32

1. Race and National Origin 32
2. Alienage Classifications 34

E. QUASI-SUSPECT CLASSIFICATIONS 35
1. Gender Classifications 35
2. Legitimacy Classifications 36

F. OTHER CLASSIFICATIONS 36

XIX. FUNDAMENTAL RIGHTS 36

A. INTRODUCTION 36

B. RIGHT OF PRIVACY 36
1. Marriage 36
2. Use of Contraceptives 36
3. Abortion 37
4. Obscene Reading Material 37
5. Keeping Extended Family Together 37
6. Rights of Parents 38
7. Intimate Sexual Conduct 38
8. Collection and Distribution of Personal Data—No Privacy Right 38

C. RIGHT TO VOTE 38
1. Restrictions on Right to Vote 38
2. Dilution of Right to Vote 38
3. Candidates and Campaigns 39

D. RIGHT TO TRAVEL 39
1. Interstate Travel 39
2. Right to International Travel 40

PART 5: FIRST AMENDMENT FREEDOMS 40

XX. FREEDOM OF SPEECH AND ASSEMBLY 40

A. GENERAL PRINCIPLES 40
1. Content vs. Conduct 40
2. Reasonableness of Regulation 41
3. Scope of Speech 41
4. Funding vs. Regulation 42

B. TIME, PLACE, AND MANNER RESTRICTIONS—REGULATION OF CONDUCT 42
1. Public Forums and Designated Public Forums 42
2. Nonpublic Forums 42

C. UNPROTECTED SPEECH—REGULATION BASED ON CONTENT 42
1. Inciting Imminent Lawless Action 43
2. Fighting Words 43
3. Obscenity 43
4. Defamatory Speech 44
5. Some Commercial Speech 44

D. PRIOR RESTRAINTS 44
1. Procedural Safeguards 45
2. Obscenity Cases 45

E. FREEDOM OF THE PRESS 46
1. Publication of Truthful Information 46

2. **Access to Trials** 46
3. **Requiring Press to Testify Before Grand Jury** 46
4. **Interviewing Prisoners** 46
5. **Business Regulation or Tax** 46
6. **Broadcasting Regulations** 46
7. **Cable Television Regulation** 46
8. **Internet Regulation** 47

XXI. FREEDOM OF ASSOCIATION AND BELIEF 47
A. **NATURE OF THE RIGHT** 47
B. **ELECTORAL PROCESS** 47
1. **Limits on Contributions** 48
2. **Limits on Expenditures** 48
3. **Compare—Regulations of Core Political Speech** 48
C. **BAR MEMBERSHIPS AND PUBLIC EMPLOYMENT** 48
1. **Restraints on Conduct** 48
2. **Loyalty Oaths** 49
3. **Disclosure of Associations** 49

XXII. FREEDOM OF RELIGION 49
A. **CONSTITUTIONAL PROVISION** 49
B. **FREE EXERCISE CLAUSE** 49
1. **No Punishment of Beliefs** 49
2. **General Conduct Regulation—No Religious Exemptions Required** 50
C. **ESTABLISHMENT CLAUSE** 50
1. **Sect Preference** 50
2. **No Sect Preference** 50

CONSTITUTIONAL LAW

PART 1: POWERS OF THE FEDERAL GOVERNMENT

I. THE JUDICIAL POWER

A. ARTICLE III

Federal judicial power extends to cases involving:

1. ***Interpretation*** of the Constitution, federal laws, treaties, and admiralty and maritime laws; and

2. ***Disputes*** between states, states and foreign citizens, and citizens of diverse citizenship.

B. POWER OF JUDICIAL REVIEW

The Supreme Court may review the constitutionality of acts of other branches of the federal government. It may also review state acts pursuant to the Supremacy Clause.

C. FEDERAL COURTS

Only Article III courts (*i.e.,* courts established by Congress pursuant to Article III) are the subject of this outline. Congress has plenary power to delineate the original and appellate jurisdiction of these courts but is bound by the standards set forth in Article III as to subject matter and party jurisdiction and the requirement of a "case or controversy." Congress can also create courts under Article I (*e.g.,* tax courts). Judges in those courts do not have life tenure as do Article III judges, and Congress may not assign to Article I courts jurisdiction over cases that have traditionally been tried in Article III courts.

D. JURISDICTION OF THE SUPREME COURT

1. Original Jurisdiction

The Supreme Court has original jurisdiction in all cases affecting ambassadors, public ministers, consuls, and those in which a state is a party, but Congress has given concurrent jurisdiction to lower federal courts in all cases except those between states.

2. Appellate Jurisdiction

The Supreme Court has appellate jurisdiction in all cases to which federal power extends, subject to congressional exceptions and regulation. Cases can come to the Court by one of two ways:

a. Writ of Certiorari—Most Cases

The Supreme Court has complete ***discretion*** to hear cases that come to it by certiorari. The cases that come by certiorari are:

1) Cases from ***state courts*** where (i) the constitutionality of a federal statute, federal treaty, or state statute is in issue, or (ii) a state statute allegedly violates federal law.

2) All cases from ***federal courts*** of appeals.

b. Appeal—Rare Cases

The Supreme Court ***must*** hear cases that come to it by appeal. These cases are confined to decisions by a three-judge federal district court panel that grants or denies injunctive relief.

E. CONSTITUTIONAL AND SELF-IMPOSED LIMITATIONS ON EXERCISE OF FEDERAL JURISDICTION—"STRICT NECESSITY"

Whether a case is "justiciable" (*i.e.,* a federal court may address it) depends on whether there is a "case or controversy." In addition to the "case or controversy" requirement, there are other limitations on federal court jurisdiction.

1. No Advisory Opinions

There must be specific ***present harm*** or threat of specific future harm. Federal courts can hear actions for declaratory relief if there is an actual dispute between parties having adverse legal interest. Complainants must show that they have engaged in (or wish to engage in) specific conduct and that the challenged action poses a ***real and immediate danger*** to their interests. However, the federal courts will not determine the constitutionality of a statute if it has never been enforced and there is no real fear that it ever will be.

2. Ripeness—Immediate Threat of Harm

A plaintiff is not entitled to review of a statute or regulation before its enforcement (*i.e.,* may not obtain a declaratory judgment) unless the plaintiff will suffer some harm or immediate threat of harm.

3. Mootness

A real controversy must exist at all stages of review. If the matter has already been resolved, the case will be dismissed as moot.

a. Exception

Controversies capable of repetition, but evading review are not moot. *Examples:* Issues concerning events of short duration (*e.g.,* abortion) or a defendant who voluntarily stops the offending practice but is free to resume.

b. Class Actions

A class representative may continue to pursue a class action after the representative's controversy has become moot if claims of other class members are still viable.

CMR Exam Tip Ripeness bars consideration of claims ***before*** they have been developed; mootness bars their consideration ***after*** they have been resolved.

4. Standing

A person must have a concrete stake in the outcome of a case.

a. Components

1) Injury

Plaintiff must show that she has been or will be ***directly*** and ***personally*** injured by the allegedly unlawful government action, which affects her rights under the Constitution or federal law. The injury need not be economic.

2) Causation

There must be a causal connection between the injury and the conduct complained of.

3) Redressability

A decision in the litigant's favor must be capable of eliminating her grievance.

Exam Tip Remember that standing just allows the plaintiff to get into court. Thus, a successful ruling on the standing issue does not mean plaintiff wins his suit; it merely means that he gets an opportunity to try it.

b. Common Standing Issues

1) Congressional Conferral of Standing
A federal statute may create new interests, injury to which may be sufficient for standing. However, Congress has no power to eliminate the case or controversy requirement and, thus, cannot grant standing to someone not having an injury.

2) Standing to Enforce Government Statutes
A plaintiff may have standing to enforce a federal statute if she is within the "***zone of interests***" Congress meant to protect.

3) Standing to Assert Rights of Others
Generally, one cannot assert the constitutional rights of others to obtain standing, but a ***claimant with standing*** in her own right may also assert the rights of a third party ***if***:

a) It is difficult for the third party to assert her own rights (*e.g.,* association may attack law requiring disclosure of membership lists, because members cannot attack law without disclosing their identities); or

b) A special relationship exists between the claimant and the third party (*e.g.,* doctor can assert patient's rights in challenging an abortion restriction).

4) Standing of Organizations
An organization has standing if (i) there is an injury in fact to members which gives them a right to sue on their own behalf, (ii) the injury is related to the organization's purpose, ***and*** (iii) individual member participation in the lawsuit is not required.

5) No Citizenship Standing
People have no standing merely as "citizens" to claim that government action violates federal law or the Constitution. The injury is too generalized.

6) Taxpayer Standing Requisites
A taxpayer has standing to litigate her tax bill, but a taxpayer generally has no standing to ***challenge government expenditures***, because the taxpayer's interest is too remote. *Exception:* Suits attacking taxing and spending measures on First Amendment ***Establishment Clause*** grounds (*e.g.,* federal expenditures to aid parochial schools).

Exam Tip For a taxpayer to have standing, the ***spending power*** must be involved. Thus, for example, there is no standing to challenge federal government grants of surplus property to religious groups.

7) Legislators' Standing
Legislators may have standing to challenge the constitutionality of government action if they have a sufficient "personal stake" in the dispute and suffer sufficient "concrete injury."

5. Adequate and Independent State Grounds

The Supreme Court will not exercise jurisdiction if the state court judgment is based on adequate and independent state law grounds—even if federal issues are involved. State law grounds are adequate if they are fully dispositive of the case. They are independent if the decision is not based on federal case interpretations of identical federal provisions. When the state court has not clearly indicated that its decision rests on state law, the Supreme Court may hear the case.

6. Abstention

a. Unsettled Question of State Law

A federal court will temporarily abstain from resolving a constitutional claim when the disposition rests on an unsettled question of state law.

b. Pending State Proceedings

Federal courts will not enjoin pending state ***criminal*** proceedings (and in some cases pending state administrative or civil proceedings involving an important state interest), except in cases of proven harassment or prosecutions taken in bad faith.

7. Political Questions

Political questions will not be decided. These are issues (i) constitutionally committed to another branch of government or (ii) inherently incapable of judicial resolution.

a. Examples of Political Questions

Challenges based on the "Republican Form of Government" Clause of Article IV, challenges to congressional procedures for ratifying constitutional amendments, and the President's conduct of foreign policy are political questions.

b. Compare—Nonpolitical Questions

Legislative apportionment, arbitrary exclusion of a congressional delegate, and production of presidential papers and communications are not political questions.

8. Eleventh Amendment Limits on Federal Courts

The Eleventh Amendment prohibits ***federal courts*** from hearing a private party's or foreign government's claims against a state government.

a. What Is Barred?

The prohibition extends to actions where the state is named as a party or where the state will have to pay retroactive damages. Similarly, the Supreme Court has held that the ***doctrine of sovereign immunity bars*** suits against a state government in state court, even on federal claims, unless the defendant state consents.

b. What Is Not Barred?

The prohibition does not extend to actions against local governments or actions by the United States or other states.

c. Exceptions

1) Certain Actions Against State Officers

The following actions can be brought against state officers in federal court despite the Eleventh Amendment: (i) actions to enjoin an officer from future conduct that violates the Constitution or federal law, even if this will require prospective payment from the state; and (ii) actions for damage against an officer personally.

2) **State Consents**
A state may consent to a suit in federal court. Such consent must be express and unequivocal.

3) **Congress Removes the Immunity**
Congress can remove Eleventh Amendment immunity as to actions created under the Fourteenth Amendment, but it must be unmistakably clear that Congress intended to remove the immunity.

II. LEGISLATIVE POWER

The federal government has limited powers. Every exercise of federal power must be traced to the Constitution.

A. ENUMERATED AND IMPLIED POWERS

Congress can exercise those powers ***enumerated*** in the Constitution plus all auxiliary powers ***necessary and proper*** to carry out all powers vested in the federal government.

1. **Necessary and Proper "Power"**
Congress has the power to make all laws necessary and proper (appropriate) for executing ***any*** power granted to ***any*** branch of the federal government.

CMR **Exam Tip** The Necessary and Proper Clause standing alone cannot support federal law. It must work in conjunction with another federal power. Thus, an answer choice that states that a law is supported by the Necessary and Proper Clause (or is valid under Congress's power to enact legislation necessary and proper) will be incorrect unless another federal power is linked to it in the question.

2. **Taxing Power**
Congress has the power to tax, and most taxes will be upheld if they bear some ***reasonable relationship to revenue production*** or if Congress has the ***power to regulate*** the activity taxed. However, neither Congress nor the states may tax exports to foreign countries.

3. **Spending Power**
Congress may spend to "provide for the common defense and general welfare." Spending may be for ***any public purpose***.

CMR **Exam Tip** The federal government can tax and ***spend*** for the general welfare; it cannot directly legislate for it. Thus, nonspending regulations cannot be supported by the General Welfare Clause.

Also recall that although the power to spend for the general welfare is broad (any public purpose), it is still limited by the Bill of Rights and other constitutional provisions.

4. Commerce Power

Congress has the ***exclusive*** power to regulate all foreign and interstate commerce. To be within Congress's power under the Commerce Clause, a federal law regulating interstate commerce must either:

(i) ***Regulate the channels*** of interstate commerce;

(ii) ***Regulate the instrumentalities*** of interstate commerce and persons and things in interstate commerce; or

(iii) ***Regulate activities that have a substantial effect*** on interstate commerce.

If Congress attempts to regulate noneconomic (*i.e.,* noncommercial) ***intrastate*** activity, the federal government must prove to the Court that the activity in fact ***affects*** interstate commerce.

5. War and Related Powers

The Constitution gives Congress power to declare war, raise and support armies, and provide for and maintain a navy.

a. Economic Regulation

Economic regulation during war and in the postwar period to remedy wartime disruptions has been upheld.

b. Military Courts and Tribunals

Congress is authorized to make rules for the government and regulation of armed forces.

1) Judicial Review

Regular federal (or state) courts have no general power to review court-martial proceedings.

2) Enemy Civilians and Soldiers

Enemy civilians and soldiers may be tried by military courts.

3) American Soldiers

Military courts have jurisdiction over ***all offenses*** committed by persons who are members of the armed services both at the time of the offense ***and*** when charged.

4) American Civilians

American civilians may be tried by military courts under martial law only if actual warfare forces the federal courts to shut down.

6. Investigatory Power

The power of Congress to investigate is implied. Investigation must be expressly or impliedly authorized by the appropriate congressional house.

7. Property Power

Congress has the power to dispose of and make rules for territories and other properties of the United States. While there is no express limitation on Congress's power to ***dispose*** of property, federal ***takings*** (eminent domain) must be for the purpose of effectuating an enumerated power under some other provision of the Constitution.

8. No Federal Police Power

Congress has no general police power. However, Congress has police power type powers over the District of Columbia, federal lands, military bases, and Indian reservations (based on its power over the capitol and its property power).

CMR **Exam Tip** If an answer choice attempts to support federal action on the basis of the police power (*e.g.*, "Congress can constitutionally act under the police power" or "the action is valid under the federal police power"), see whether the facts state that the action pertains to the District of Columbia or other federal possessions. If not, it is a wrong choice.

9. Bankruptcy Power

Congress's power to establish uniform rules for bankruptcy is nonexclusive; states may legislate in the field as long as their laws do not conflict with federal law.

10. Postal Power

The postal power is exclusive. Under the postal power, Congress may validly classify and place reasonable restrictions on use of the mails, but may not deprive any citizen or group of citizens of the general mail "privilege."

11. Power Over Citizenship

Congress may establish uniform rules of naturalization. This gives Congress plenary power over aliens.

a. Exclusion of Aliens

Aliens have no right to enter the United States and can be refused entry summarily because of their political beliefs. However, resident aliens are entitled to ***notice and a hearing*** before they can be deported.

b. Naturalization and Denaturalization

Congress has ***exclusive*** power over naturalization and denaturalization. However, Congress may not take away the citizenship of any citizen—native born or naturalized—without his consent.

12. Admiralty Power

Congress's admiralty power is plenary and exclusive unless Congress leaves maritime matters to state jurisdiction.

13. Power to Coin Money and Fix Weights and Measures

Congress has the power to coin money and fix standards for weights and measures.

14. Patent/Copyright Power

Congress has the power to control the issuance of patents and copyrights.

SOURCES OF CONGRESSIONAL POWER

Government Action	Source of Power
1. Congress enacts divorce laws for the District of Columbia.	General federal police power for D.C. (as well as military bases and federal lands).
2. Congress pays for highways.	Spending Power and Commerce Clause.
3. Federal income tax.	Taxing Power.
4. Congress conditions aid to states for medical programs on state funding of AIDS research.	Spending Power.
5. Congress adopts a tax to regulate banknotes rather than to raise revenue.	Power to coin money.
6. Congress prohibits hunting on federal lands.	Property Power.
7. Congress bars racial discrimination at places of public accommodation.	Commerce Clause.
8. Congress requires all employers, including state governments, to comply with federal minimum wage and overtime provisions.	Commerce Clause.

Note: The Amendments to the Constitution may also be a source of power (*e.g.,* the Thirteenth Amendment gives Congress power to outlaw badges of slavery; thus Congress may require a private seller to sell land to blacks as well as whites). (*See infra.*)

B. DELEGATION OF LEGISLATIVE POWER

Legislative power may generally be delegated to the executive or judicial branch as long as intelligible standards are set and the power is not uniquely confined to Congress (*e.g.,* powers to declare war, impeach).

Note: Congress may not appoint members of a body with administrative or enforcement powers (*see* III.A.1.a.2), *infra*).

CMR **Exam Tip** Although you should know that a valid delegation of legislative power requires "intelligible standards" for the delegate to follow (*see* above), in applying that rule almost anything will pass for an intelligible standard, and thus no legislative delegation has been invalidated since 1936.

C. SPEECH AND DEBATE CLAUSE—IMMUNITY FOR FEDERAL LEGISLATORS

Conduct that occurs in the regular course of the federal legislative process and the motivation behind that conduct are immune from prosecution.

Note: Immunity does not cover bribes, speeches outside Congress, or the republication in a press release or newsletter of a defamatory statement originally made in Congress.

D. CONGRESSIONAL "VETO" OF EXECUTIVE ACTIONS INVALID

A legislative veto is an attempt by Congress to overturn an executive agency action ***without*** bicameralism (*i.e.,* passage by both houses of Congress) or presentment (*i.e.,* giving the bill to the President for his signature or veto). Legislative vetoes of executive actions are invalid.

III. THE EXECUTIVE POWER

A. DOMESTIC POWERS

1. Appointment and Removal

a. Appointment Powers

The executive appoints "all ambassadors, other public ministers and consuls, justices of the Supreme Court, and all other officers of the United States whose appointments are not otherwise provided for," with advice and consent of Senate. Congress, however, may vest the appointment of ***inferior officers*** in the President alone, the courts, or the heads of departments.

1) Appointment of "Independent Counsel" (Special Prosecutor)

A special prosecutor with the limited duties of investigating a narrow range of persons and subjects is an "inferior officer," and therefore the Appointment Clause allows Congress to vest the power to appoint a special prosecutor in the judiciary.

2) No Appointments by Congress

Congress itself may ***not*** appoint members of a body with administrative or enforcement powers.

b. Removal of Appointees

1) By President

The President can remove high level, purely executive officers (*e.g.,* cabinet members) at will, without any interference by Congress. However, Congress may provide statutory limitations (*e.g.,* removal only for good cause) on the President's power to remove all other executive appointees.

2) By Congress

Congress may remove executive officers ***only*** through the impeachment process.

2. Pardons

The President may grant pardons for all federal offenses but not for impeachment or civil contempt. The pardon power cannot be limited by Congress.

3. **Veto Power**
If the President disapproves (vetoes) an act of Congress, the act may still become law if the veto is overridden by a ***two-thirds*** vote of ***each*** house.

a. **Pocket Veto**
The President has 10 days to exercise the veto power. If he fails to act within that time, the bill is automatically vetoed if Congress is not in session. If Congress is in session, the bill becomes law.

b. **Line Item Veto Unconstitutional**
The veto power allows the President only to approve or reject a bill ***in toto***; he cannot cancel part (through a line item veto) and approve other parts.

4. **Power as Chief Executive**
The President's powers over internal affairs are unsettled. Clearly the President has some power to direct subordinate executive officers, and there is a long history of Presidents issuing executive orders. Perhaps the best guide is as follows:

a. If the President acts with the express or implied authority of Congress, his authority is at its maximum and his actions likely are valid;

b. If the President acts where Congress is silent, his action will be upheld unless it usurps the power of another governmental branch or prevents another branch from carrying out its tasks; and

c. If the President acts against the express will of Congress, he has little authority, and his action likely is invalid (*e.g.*, the President has no power to refuse to spend appropriated funds when Congress has expressly mandated that they be spent).

B. POWER OVER EXTERNAL AFFAIRS

1. **War**
The President has ***no power*** to declare war but may act militarily in actual hostilities against the United States without a congressional declaration of war. However, Congress, under its power to enact a military appropriation every two years, may limit the President.

2. **Foreign Relations**
The President has paramount power to represent the United States in day-to-day foreign relations.

3. **Treaty Power**
The President has the power to enter into treaties with the consent of two-thirds of the Senate.

a. **Supreme Law**
Like other federal law, treaties are the "supreme law of the land." ***State*** laws that conflict are invalid.

b. **Conflict with Federal Laws**
A conflict between a congressional act and a valid treaty is resolved by order of adoption: ***the last in time prevails***.

c. **Conflict with Constitution**
Treaties are ***not*** co-equal with the Constitution; a treaty may not be inconsistent with the Constitution.

CMR **Exam Tip** Treaties are subject to constitutional limits. Thus, no treaty (or executive agreement) can confer on Congress authority to act in a manner inconsistent with any specific provision of the Constitution.

4. **Executive Agreements**
Executive agreements are signed by the President and the head of a foreign country. They can be used for any purpose that treaties can be used for. They do ***not*** require the consent of the Senate.

a. **Conflict with State Laws**
If a state law conflicts with an executive agreement, the agreement prevails.

b. **Conflict with Federal Laws**
If an executive agreement conflicts with a federal law, the federal law prevails over the agreement.

HIERARCHY OF U.S. LAW

United States Constitution

prevails over

Treaties and Federal Statutes
(if a conflict between these two, last in time prevails)

prevail over

Executive Agreements

prevail over

State Law

C. EXECUTIVE PRIVILEGE/IMMUNITY

1. Executive Privilege

The President has a privilege to keep certain communications secret. National security secrets are given great deference by the courts.

a. Exception

In criminal proceedings, presidential communiques will be available to the prosecution where a need for such information is demonstrated.

2. Executive Immunity

The President has ***absolute immunity*** from civil damages based on any action he took within his official responsibilities, but there is no immunity for acts that allegedly occurred before taking office. If presidential aides have exercised discretionary authority in a sensitive area, they may share in the immunity for suits brought concerning that area.

D. IMPEACHMENT

The President, Vice President, and all civil officers of the United States are subject to impeachment (the bringing of charges). Grounds include treason, bribery, high crimes, and misdemeanors. A ***majority*** vote in the House is necessary to invoke the charges of impeachment, and a ***two-thirds*** vote in the Senate is necessary to convict and remove from office.

PART 2: THE FEDERAL SYSTEM

IV. RELATIVE SPHERES OF FEDERAL AND STATE POWERS

A. EXCLUSIVE FEDERAL POWERS

1. Power of States Expressly Limited

Some powers are exclusively federal because the Constitution limits or prohibits the use of the power by states (*e.g.,* treaty power, coinage of money).

2. Inherent Federal Powers

Other powers are exclusively federal because the nature of the power itself is such that it can be exercised only by the federal government (*e.g.,* declaration of war, federal citizenship).

B. EXCLUSIVE STATE POWERS

All powers not delegated to federal government are reserved to the states. Note, however, that federal powers are given an expansive interpretation, and thus little state power is exclusive.

C. CONCURRENT FEDERAL AND STATE POWER—EFFECT OF SUPREMACY CLAUSE

Because of the Supremacy Clause, a federal law may supersede or preempt local laws.

1. Conflict Between State and Federal Laws

If a state law conflicts with federal law, the state law will be invalidated.

2. State Prevents Achievement of Federal Objective

If a state or local law prevents achievement of a federal objective, it will be invalidated. This is true even where state law was enacted for some valid purpose and not to frustrate the federal law (*e.g.,* state law providing for suspension of driver's license of persons who fail to pay off an auto accident case judgment, regardless of the person's discharge in bankruptcy, is invalid).

3. Preemption

A valid federal statute or regulation may expressly or impliedly "occupy" the entire field, thus precluding any state or local regulation ***even if the state or local regulation is nonconflicting***. Factors considered here (if there is no express preemption) are (i) comprehensiveness of the federal scheme and (ii) creation of an agency to administer the law.

D. ABSENCE OF FEDERAL AND STATE POWERS

Some powers are denied to both Congress and the states. For example, the qualifications for serving in Congress are set by the Constitution and cannot be altered by Congress or the states.

E. INTERSTATE COMPACT CLAUSE

The Interstate Compact Clause concerns agreements between states. If the agreement increases the states' power at the expense of federal power, congressional approval is required.

F. FULL FAITH AND CREDIT CLAUSE

By virtue of the Full Faith and Credit Clause, if a judgment is entitled to full faith and credit, it must be recognized in sister states (*i.e.*, a party who loses a case in New York generally may not relitigate it in New Jersey; the New Jersey courts are bound by the New York ruling). This Clause applies only if: (i) the court that rendered the judgment had ***jurisdiction*** over the parties and the subject matter; (ii) the judgment was ***on the merits***; and (iii) the judgment is ***final***.

V. INTERSOVEREIGN LITIGATION

A. SUITS BY UNITED STATES AGAINST A STATE

The United States may sue a state without its consent.

B. SUITS BY A STATE AGAINST UNITED STATES

Public policy forbids a state from suing the United States without its consent. Congress can pass legislation that permits the United States to be sued by a state in given situations.

C. FEDERAL OFFICER AS DEFENDANT

1. Limitation

A suit against a federal officer is deemed to be brought against the United States itself if the judgment sought would be satisfied out of the public treasury or would interfere with public administration and therefore is not permitted.

2. Specific Relief Against Officer

Specific relief against an officer as an individual will be granted if the officer acted ultra vires (beyond his authority).

D. SUITS BY ONE STATE AGAINST ANOTHER

One state may sue another state without the latter's consent. The Supreme Court has exclusive original jurisdiction.

VI. INTERGOVERNMENTAL TAX AND REGULATION IMMUNITIES

A. FEDERAL TAXATION AND REGULATION OF STATE OR LOCAL GOVERNMENTS

1. Tax or Regulation Applying to Both State and Private Entities—Valid

Congress may subject state and local government activities to regulation or taxation if the law or tax applies to ***both*** the public sector and the private sector (*e.g.,* minimum wage laws).

2. Tax or Regulation Applying Only to States

A federal tax or regulation that is not applicable to private businesses and that merely taxes or regulates a purely state or local governmental activity may be limited by the Tenth Amendment (*e.g.,* requiring states to either regulate radioactive waste or take title to it is beyond Congress's power).

a. Exception—Civil Rights

Congress may restrict state activities that violate civil liberties.

b. Exception—Spending Power Conditions

Congress may "indirectly" regulate states through the spending power by imposing conditions on the grant of money (*e.g.,* federal highway funds will be given only to states with a 21-year minimum age for drinking of alcohol).

CMR **Exam Tip** As a practical matter, the Court almost never strikes down on Tenth Amendment grounds a federal regulation or tax that impacts on state or local government entities. Thus, a choice on an MBE question that suggests that the Tenth Amendment will invalidate a federal action is almost always wrong.

3. Commandeering State Officials

While not specifically resting on the Tenth Amendment, the Supreme Court has held that Congress may not require state executive officials (*e.g.,* the police) to enforce federal laws because such a requirement would upset the Constitution's "dual sovereignty" structure (*i.e.,* both the states and the federal government are sovereigns).

B. STATE TAXATION AND REGULATION OF FEDERAL GOVERNMENT

A state may not directly tax federal instrumentalities without the consent of Congress. However, ***nondiscriminatory***, ***indirect*** taxes are permissible if they do not unreasonably burden the federal government (*e.g.,* state income tax on federal employees). States may not regulate the federal government or its agents while performing their federal functions.

VII. PRIVILEGES AND IMMUNITIES CLAUSES

A. ARTICLE IV—PRIVILEGES OF STATE CITIZENSHIP

The Interstate Privileges and Immunities Clause prohibits discrimination by a state ***against nonresidents***.

Note: Corporations and aliens are ***not*** protected by this clause. (In contrast, corporations and aliens are protected by the Equal Protection and Due Process Clauses of the Fourteenth Amendment, as well as the Dormant Commerce Clause, discussed *infra.*)

1. Only "Fundamental Rights" Protected

Only "fundamental rights"—those involving important ***commercial activities*** (*e.g.,* the pursuit of livelihood) and ***civil liberties***—are protected.

2. Substantial Justification Exception

The state law may be valid if the state has a substantial justification for the different treatment. In effect, the state must show that nonresidents either cause or are part of the problem that the state is attempting to solve and that there are ***no less restrictive means*** to solve the problem.

3. Note—Relationship to Commerce Clause

Although the Article IV Privileges and Immunities Clause and the Dormant Commerce Clause may apply different standards and produce different results, they tend to mutually reinforce each other. Consequently, they both have to be considered in analyzing bar exam questions.

ARTICLE IV PRIVILEGES AND IMMUNITIES CLAUSE

Invalid Discrimination

1. Statute requiring $2,500 license fee from nonresident ***commercial fishermen***, while residents paid $25.
2. Statute giving resident creditors priority over nonresident creditors to assets of foreign corporations in receivership proceedings.
3. Statute imposing a residency requirement for abortion.
4. Rule limiting bar admission to state residents.
5. Statute requiring ***private sector*** employers to give hiring preference to residents.

Discrimination Upheld

Statute requiring nonresidents to pay $225 license fee, as opposed to $30 residents' fee, for ***recreational*** hunting.

B. FOURTEENTH AMENDMENT—PRIVILEGES OF NATIONAL CITIZENSHIP

States may not deny their citizens the privileges or immunities of ***national*** citizenship (*e.g.,* the right to petition Congress for redress of grievances, the right to vote for federal officers, and the right to interstate travel). Corporations are not protected by this Clause.

PART 3: STATE REGULATION OR TAXATION OF COMMERCE

VIII. REGULATION OF FOREIGN COMMERCE

With a few minor exceptions, the power to regulate foreign commerce lies exclusively with Congress.

IX. REGULATION OF INTERSTATE COMMERCE

A. REGULATION OF COMMERCE BY CONGRESS

1. Power of Congress to Supersede or Preempt State Regulation

When Congress regulates interstate commerce, conflicting state laws are ***superseded*** and even nonconflicting state or local laws in the same field may be ***preempted***. (*See* IV.C.3., *supra.*)

2. Power of Congress to Permit or Prohibit State Regulation

Congress may permit state regulations that would otherwise violate the Commerce Clause. Likewise, Congress may prohibit state regulations that could otherwise be upheld under the Commerce Clause. Congress may ***not***, however, permit states to violate civil liberties.

B. STATE REGULATION OF COMMERCE IN THE ABSENCE OF CONGRESSIONAL ACTION

If Congress has not enacted laws regarding the subject, a state or local government may regulate local aspects of interstate commerce. To do so, however, it must ***not discriminate against*** or ***unduly burden*** interstate commerce. If it does, the state or local regulation will violate the Commerce Clause.

CMR **Exam Tip** The examiners sometimes use the terms "Dormant Commerce Clause" and "Negative Commerce Clause." These are merely descriptive terms that reflect the above idea: even where Congress has not acted, the Commerce Clause restricts state regulation of interstate commerce; states may not favor local economic interests or unduly burden interstate commerce.

1. Discriminatory Regulations

State or local regulations that discriminate against interstate commerce to protect local economic interests ***are almost always invalid*** (*e.g.,* New York cannot ban California wines or tax them at a higher rate than local wines).

a. Exception—Important State Interest

A discriminatory state or local law may be valid if it furthers an important, noneconomic state interest and there are ***no reasonable nondiscriminatory alternatives***

CMR APPROACH CHART

STATE REGULATION OF INTERSTATE COMMERCE

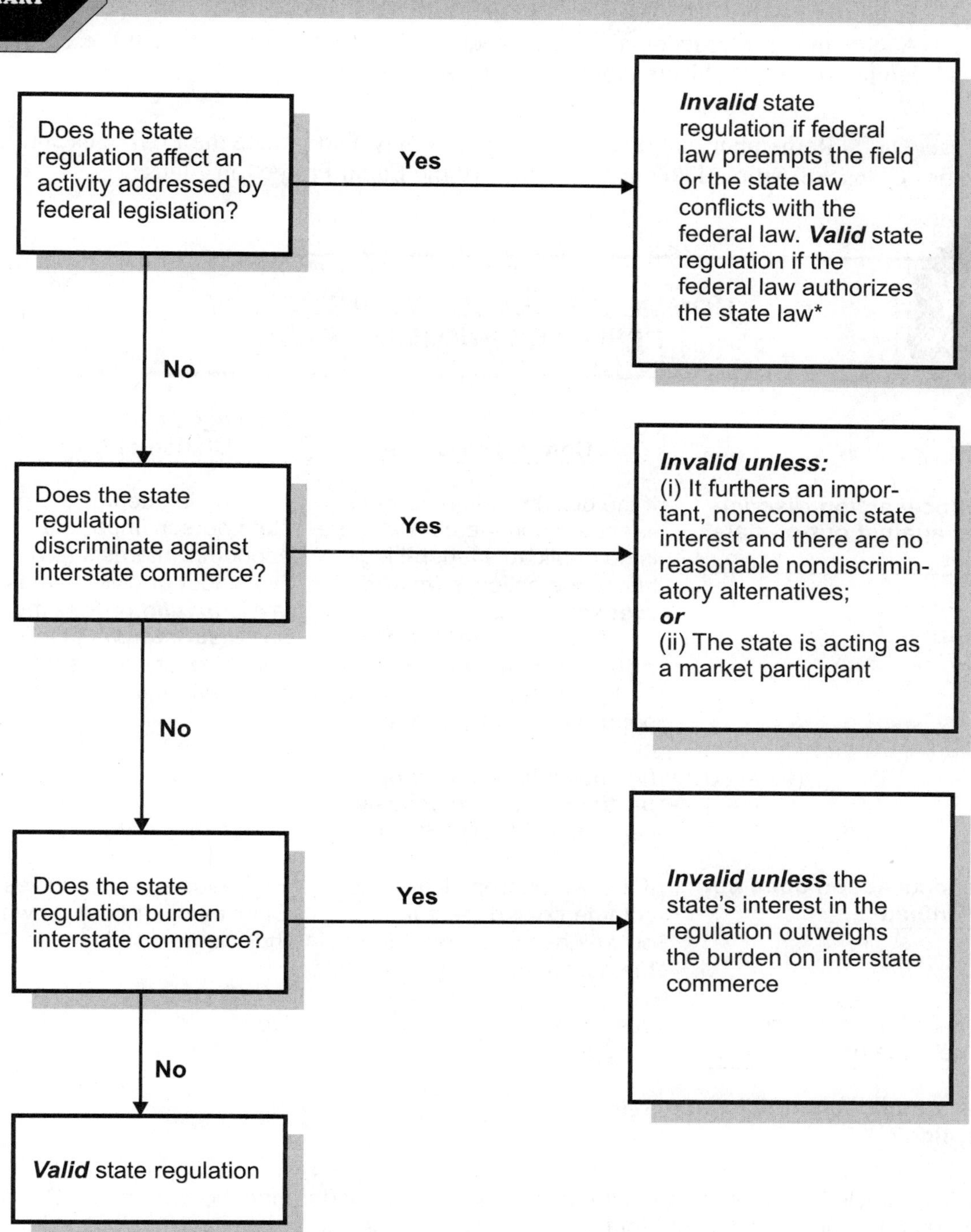
Does the state regulation affect an activity addressed by federal legislation?
Yes
Invalid state regulation if federal law preempts the field or the state law conflicts with the federal law. ***Valid*** state regulation if the federal law authorizes the state law*
No
Does the state regulation discriminate against interstate commerce?
Yes
Invalid unless:
(i) It furthers an important, noneconomic state interest and there are no reasonable nondiscriminatory alternatives;
or
(ii) The state is acting as a market participant
No
Does the state regulation burden interstate commerce?
Yes
Invalid unless the state's interest in the regulation outweighs the burden on interstate commerce
No
Valid state regulation

*Of course, Congress has no power to authorize legislation that would violate other constitutional provisions, such as the Privileges and Immunities Clause of Article IV.

available. *Example:* State could prohibit ***importation*** of live bait fish because parasites could have detrimental effect on its own fish population. However, state could not prohibit ***export*** of live bait fish when no major state interest was involved.

b. **Exception—State as "Market Participant"**
A state may prefer its own citizens when acting as a market participant (*e.g.,* when buying or selling, hiring labor, or giving subsidies).

CMR Exam Tip Remember that discriminatory laws may also violate the Privileges and Immunities Clause of Article IV (*see* chart *infra*) or the Equal Protection Clause.

CMR COMPARISON CHART

COMMERCE CLAUSE VS. ARTICLE IV PRIVILEGES AND IMMUNITIES

	Commerce Clause	Privileges and Immunities Clause of Article IV
State/local action *discriminates* against out-of-state entities	If the discrimination burdens interstate commerce and there is no applicable federal legislation, the action is ***invalid unless:*** (i) It furthers an ***important, noneconomic state interest*** and there are no reasonable nondiscriminatory alternatives; or (ii) The state is a ***market participant*** (*i.e.,* purchaser, seller, subsidizer).	If the action denies the out-of-state person important economic interests (*e.g.,* livelihood) or civil liberties, the law is ***invalid unless*** the state has a ***substantial*** justification and there are no less restrictive means.
State/local action does *not discriminate*	If the law burdens interstate commerce and the burden outweighs the state's interest in the action, the law is ***invalid***.	Privileges and Immunities Clause does not apply where there is no discrimination.
May an alien or a corporation be a plaintiff?	Yes	No
Is there a market participant exception?	Yes	No

Note: The Article IV Privileges and Immunities Clause is stronger than the Commerce Clause (no market participant exception), but it is much narrower in scope (applies only to discrimination against economic interest; does not protect corporations or aliens).

2. Nondiscriminatory Laws—Balancing Test

If a nondiscriminatory state law (*i.e.*, local and out-of-state interests are treated alike) burdens interstate commerce, it will be valid ***unless*** the burden outweighs the promotion of a legitimate local interest. The court will consider whether less restrictive alternatives are available. *Example:* Iowa statute banning trucks over 60 feet was invalid because the state showed no significant evidence of increased safety and the burden on commerce was substantial.

a. State Control of Corporations

A different standard may apply to statutes ***adopted by the state of incorporation*** regulating the ***internal governance of a corporation.*** Because of the states' long history of regulating the internal governance of corporations that they create, and because of their strong interest in doing so, even a statute that heavily impacts interstate commerce may be upheld (*e.g.,* a state may deny voting rights to persons who acquire a controlling interest in a state corporation without approval from other shareholders, despite the impact this may have on interstate commerce).

CMR Exam Tip When a bar exam question involves a state regulation that affects the free flow of interstate commerce, you should ask:

- Does the question refer to any ***federal legislation*** that might (i) ***supersede*** the state regulation or ***preempt*** the field or (ii) ***authorize*** state regulation otherwise impermissible?

- If neither of these possibilities is dispositive, does the state regulation either ***discriminate*** against interstate or out-of-state commerce or place an ***undue burden*** on the free flow of interstate commerce? If the regulation is discriminatory, it will be invalid unless (i) it furthers an important, noneconomic state interest ***and*** there are no reasonable nondiscriminatory alternatives, or (ii) the state is a market participant. If the regulation does not discriminate but burdens interstate commerce, it will be invalid if the burden on commerce outweighs the state's interest.

C. TWENTY-FIRST AMENDMENT—STATE CONTROL OVER INTOXICATING LIQUOR

1. Intrastate Regulation

State governments have wide latitude over the ***importation*** of liquor and the conditions under which it is ***sold or used*** within the state. However, regulations that constitute only an economic preference for local liquor manufacturers may violate the Commerce Clause.

2. Interstate Regulation

Liquor in interstate commerce is subject to the Commerce Clause.

3. Federal Power

Congress may regulate economic transactions involving liquor (*e.g.,* sales of alcoholic beverages) through federal commerce power (*e.g.,* antitrust laws) or by conditioning grants of money (*e.g.,* highway funds given only to states with minimum drinking age of 21).

X. POWER OF STATES TO TAX INTERSTATE COMMERCE

The same general considerations that apply to state regulation of commerce (*see supra*) apply to state taxation of commerce.

A. GENERAL CONSIDERATIONS

Congress has complete power to authorize or forbid state taxation that affects interstate commerce.

1. Discriminatory Taxes

Unless authorized by Congress, state taxes that discriminate against interstate commerce (*e.g.,* tax on out-of-state businesses higher than tax on in-state businesses) violate the Commerce Clause. Note that these taxes may also violate other constitutional provisions (*e.g.,* the Privileges and Immunities Clause of Article IV or the Equal Protection Clause).

2. Nondiscriminatory Taxes

A nondiscriminatory tax will be valid ***if*** the following requirements are met:

a. Substantial Nexus

To be valid, the tax must apply to an activity having a substantial nexus to the taxing state; *i.e.,* there must be significant or substantial activity within the taxing state. (Lack of a substantial nexus might also violate the due process requirement of minimum contacts, but substantial nexus requires more in-state connections.)

b. Fair Apportionment

To be valid, the tax must be fairly apportioned according to a rational formula. However, the taxpayer has the burden of proving unfair apportionment. (An unfairly apportioned tax may also violate equal protection.)

c. Fair Relationship

To be valid, the tax must be fairly related to the services or benefits provided by the state.

B. USE TAXES

1. Permissible in Buyer's State

Use taxes are imposed on goods purchased outside the state but used within it. They are valid.

2. State May Force Seller to Collect Use Tax

An interstate seller may be required to collect a use tax ***if*** the seller has a ***sufficient nexus*** with the taxing state (*e.g.,* maintains offices in the taxing state). Merely soliciting orders by mail and shipping orders into the state is not sufficient.

C. SALES TAXES

Sales taxes are taxes imposed on the seller of goods for sales consummated within the state. They generally do not discriminate against interstate commerce; rather, the issue usually involves whether there is a substantial nexus between the taxpayer and the taxing state or whether the tax is properly apportioned.

D. AD VALOREM PROPERTY TAXES

Ad valorem property taxes are based on the assessed value of the property in question.

STATE TAXATION OF INTERSTATE COMMERCE

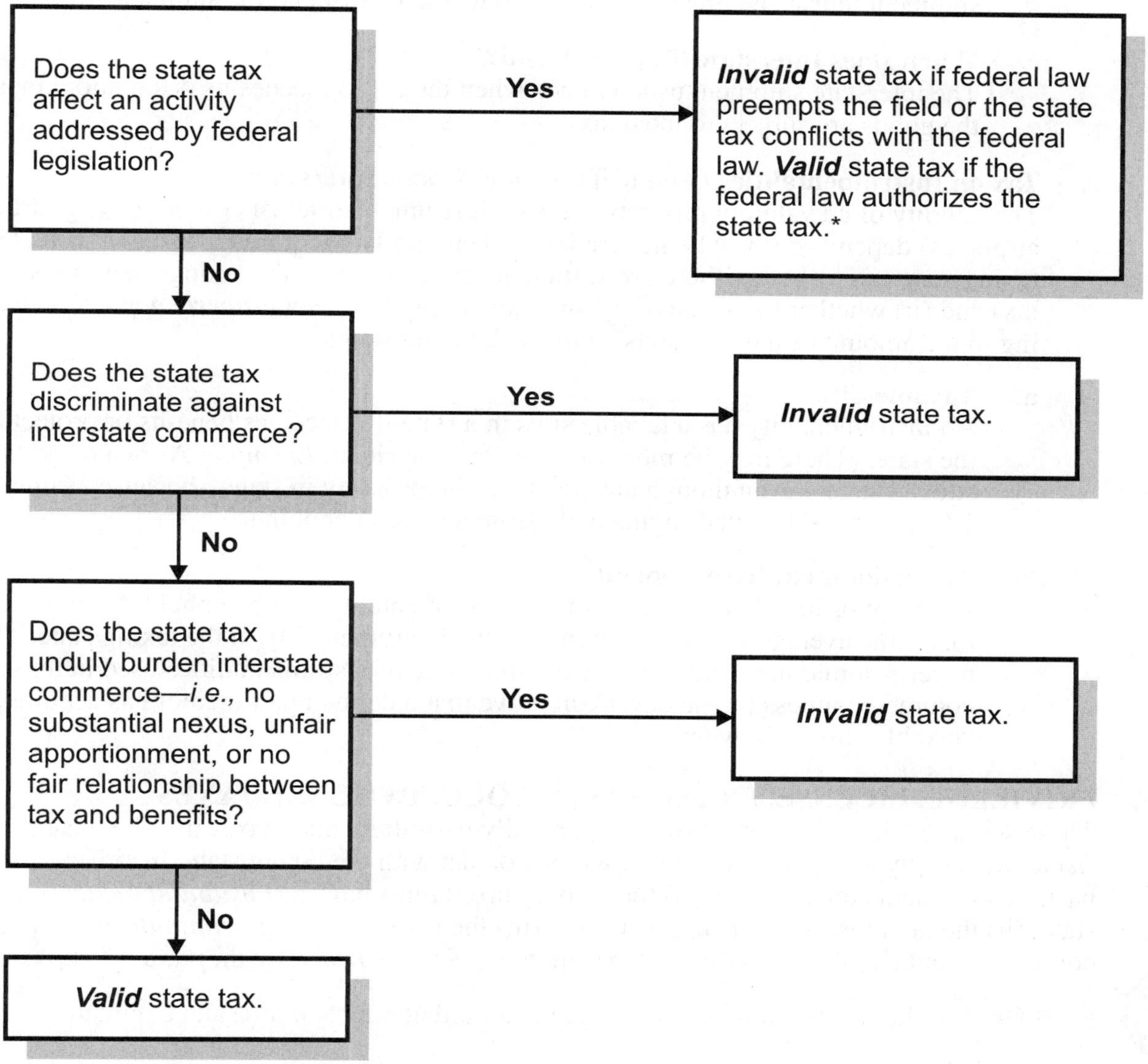

Does the state tax affect an activity addressed by federal legislation?

- **Yes** → ***Invalid*** state tax if federal law preempts the field or the state tax conflicts with the federal law. ***Valid*** state tax if the federal law authorizes the state tax.*
- **No** ↓

Does the state tax discriminate against interstate commerce?

- **Yes** → ***Invalid*** state tax.
- **No** ↓

Does the state tax unduly burden interstate commerce—*i.e.,* no substantial nexus, unfair apportionment, or no fair relationship between tax and benefits?

- **Yes** → ***Invalid*** state tax.
- **No** ↓

Valid state tax.

*Of course, Congress has no power to authorize taxes that would violate the Constitution (*i.e.,* go beyond Congress's taxing power).

1. **No Tax on Commodities in Course of Interstate Commerce**
Commodities in interstate transit are entirely ***exempt*** from state taxation.

a. **When Does Interstate Transportation Begin?**
Interstate transportation begins when the cargo (i) is delivered to an interstate carrier ***or*** (ii) actually starts its interstate journey.

b. **Effect of "Break" in Transit**
A break in the continuity of transit does not destroy the interstate character of the shipment unless the break was intended to end or suspend the shipment.

c. **When Does Interstate Shipment End?**
The interstate shipment usually ends when the cargo reaches its destination; thereafter the goods are subject to local tax.

2. **Tax on Instrumentalities Used to Transport Goods Interstate**
The validity of ad valorem property taxes on instrumentalities of commerce (*e.g.,* trucks or airplanes) depends on (i) whether the instrumentality has acquired a ***"taxable situs"*** in the taxing state (*i.e.,* whether there are sufficient "contacts" with the taxing state to justify the tax) and (ii) whether the value of the instrumentality has been ***properly apportioned*** according to the amount of the "contacts" with each taxing state.

a. **Taxable Situs**
An instrumentality has a taxable situs in a state if it receives benefits or protection from the state. (There may be more than one taxable situs). *Example:* Airplane had taxable situs in state—even though airline owned no property in state—because airline made 18 regularly scheduled flights daily from a rented depot in state.

b. **Apportionment Requirement**
A tax apportioned on the value of the instrumentality will be upheld if it fairly approximates the average physical presence of the instrumentality in the taxing state. The taxpayer's domiciliary state can tax the full value of instrumentalities used in interstate commerce unless the taxpayer can prove that a defined part thereof has acquired a "taxable situs" elsewhere.

E. PRIVILEGE, LICENSE, FRANCHISE, OR OCCUPATIONAL TAXES

These so-called doing business taxes are generally permitted. Such taxes may be measured by a flat amount or by a proportional rate based on contact with the taxing state. In either case, the basic requirements must be met: (i) the activity taxed must have a ***substantial nexus*** to the taxing state; (ii) the tax must be ***fairly apportioned***; (iii) the tax must ***not discriminate*** against interstate commerce; and (iv) the tax must ***fairly relate to services provided*** by the state.

CMR **Exam Tip** When a question involves state taxation that affects interestate commerce, you should ask:

1. Does the question refer to any federal legislation that might (i) ***forbid*** the state tax or ***preempt*** the field or (ii) ***authorize*** state taxation?

2. If neither of these possibilities is dispositive, does the state tax ***discriminate*** against or ***unduly burden*** the free flow of interstate commerce? If the state tax discriminates or is unduly burdensome (no substantial nexus, unfair apportionment, or no fair relationship), it is invalid.

STATE TAXATION OF INTERSTATE COMMERCE—SPECIFIC TYPES OF TAXES

Type	Definition	Validity Under Commerce Clause
Use Tax	Tax on goods purchased outside of the state, but used within it	Valid unless higher than sales tax.
Sales Tax	Tax on the sale of goods consummated within the state	Generally valid if there is a substantial nexus to the taxing state and the tax is properly apportioned (if more than one state can tax the sale)
Ad Valorem Tax	Tax on the assessed value of some property	*Commodities:* Valid only if property is no longer in interstate commerce. *Instrumentalities:* Valid if instrumentality has "taxable situs" in state and tax is fairly apportioned. Full tax by domiciliary state valid unless taxpayer can prove a defined part has acquired taxable situs elsewhere.
Privilege, License, Franchise, and Occupational Tax	Tax placed on some activity ("doing business" tax)	Valid if (i) substantial nexus to taxing state, (ii) fairly apportioned, (iii) does not discriminate against interstate commerce, and (iv) fairly relates to services provided by the state.

XI. POWER OF STATES TO TAX FOREIGN COMMERCE

The Import-Export Clause and the Commerce Clause greatly limit the states' power to tax foreign commerce.

PART 4: INDIVIDUAL GUARANTEES AGAINST GOVERNMENTAL OR PRIVATE ACTION

XII. LIMITATIONS ON POWER AND STATE ACTION REQUIREMENT

A. CONSTITUTIONAL RESTRICTIONS ON POWER OVER INDIVIDUALS

1. Bill of Rights

By its terms, the Bill of Rights (the first 10 amendments to the United States Constitution) limits ***federal*** power. However, the Fourteenth Amendment Due Process Clause applies almost all provisions of the Bill of Rights to states. *Exceptions:* The most notable exceptions to incorporation are: (i) the Fifth Amendment's prohibition of criminal trials without a grand jury indictment and (ii) the Seventh Amendment's right to a jury in civil cases.

2. Thirteenth Amendment

The Thirteenth Amendment prohibits slavery and involuntary servitude. Under the Thirteenth Amendment's Enabling Clause, Congress can prohibit racially discriminatory action by ***anyone*** (the government or a private citizen).

3. Fourteenth and Fifteenth Amendments

The Fourteenth Amendment prevents ***states*** from depriving any person of life, liberty, or property without due process and equal protection of law. The Fifteenth Amendment prevents both the ***federal and state governments*** from denying a citizen the right to vote on account of race or color. Generally, private conduct is not prohibited by these amendments—only where some ***state action*** is involved. (Purely private conduct may be prohibited, however, on a separate constitutional basis such as the Commerce Clause.)

a. Scope of Congressional Power Under Fourteenth Amendment

Section 5 of the Fourteenth Amendment gives Congress the power to adopt ***appropriate legislation*** to enforce the rights and guarantees provided by the Fourteenth Amendment. Under Section 5, Congress may ***not*** expand existing constitutional rights or create new ones—it may only enact laws to prevent or remedy violations of rights already recognized by the courts. To adopt a valid law, Congress must point to a history or pattern of state violation of such rights and adopt legislation that is ***congruent and proportional*** (*i.e.,* narrowly tailored) to solving the identified violation.

4. Commerce Clause

Under the broadly construed commerce power, Congress may prohibit ***private*** racial discrimination in activities that might have a substantial effect on interstate commerce.

CMR Exam Tip Since almost any activity taken cumulatively might have a substantial effect on interstate commerce, the Commerce Clause is an important basis for civil rights laws.

5. **Rights of National Citizenship**
Congress has inherent power to protect rights of citizenship (*e.g.,* rights to interstate travel, assemble, and petition Congress for redress).

B. STATE ACTION REQUIREMENT

Since the Constitution generally applies only to governmental action, to show a constitutional violation "state action" must be involved. *Note:* This concept applies to government and government officers at all levels—local, state, or federal. Note, however, that state action can be found in actions of seemingly private individuals who (i) perform exclusive public functions or (ii) have significant state involvement.

1. **Exclusive Public Functions**
Activities that are so ***traditionally*** the ***exclusive*** prerogative of the state are state action no matter who performs them.

2. **Significant State Involvement—Facilitating Private Action**
State action also exists wherever a state ***affirmatively*** facilitates, encourages, or authorizes acts of discrimination by its citizens.

CMR EXAMPLE CHART

STATE ACTION VS. NO STATE ACTION

State Action	No State Action
Public Function	
Running a town	Running a shopping mall (does not have all the attributes of a town)
Conducting an election	Holding a warehouseman's lien sale
Significant State Involvement	
Enforcing restrictive covenants prohibiting sale or lease of property through use of state courts	Granting a license and providing essential services to a private club
Leasing premises to a discriminatory lessee where state derives extra benefit from the discrimination (*i.e.,* symbiotic relationship exists)	Granting a monopoly to a utility
Allowing state official to act in discriminatory manner under "color of state law"	Heavily regulating an industry
Administering a private discriminatory trust by public officials	Granting a corporation its charter and exclusive name

Exam Tip On the bar exam, remember that the state must be "significantly involved" in the private entity; mere acquiescence by the state in private conduct is not enough. Also, states are not constitutionally required to outlaw discrimination. They are only forbidden to facilitate, encourage, or authorize it.

XIII. RETROACTIVE LEGISLATION

A. CONTRACT CLAUSE—IMPAIRMENT OF CONTRACT

The Contract Clause prohibits ***states*** from enacting any law that ***retroactively*** impairs contract rights. It does not affect contracts not yet entered into.

1. Not Applicable to Federal Government

There is no comparable clause applicable to the federal government, but flagrant contract impairment would violate the Fifth Amendment Due Process Clause.

2. Basic Impairment Rules

a. Private Contracts—Intermediate Scrutiny

State legislation that ***substantially impairs*** an existing ***private*** contract is invalid unless the legislation (i) serves an important and legitimate public interest and (ii) is a reasonable and narrowly tailored means of promoting that interest. *Example:* Imposing a moratorium on mortgage foreclosures during a severe depression did not violate the Contract Clause.

b. Public Contracts—Stricter Scrutiny

Legislation that impairs a contract to which the state is a party is tested by the same basic test, but the contract will likely receive stricter scrutiny, especially if the legislation reduces the contractual burdens on the state.

B. EX POST FACTO LAWS

The state or federal government may not pass an ex post facto law (*i.e.,* a law that ***retroactively*** alters ***criminal*** offenses or punishments in a substantially prejudicial manner for the purpose of punishing a person for some past activity). A statute retroactively alters a law in a substantially prejudicial manner if it: (i) makes criminal an act that was ***innocent when done***; (ii) prescribes ***greater punishment*** for an act than was prescribed for the act when it was done; or (iii) ***reduces the evidence*** required to convict a person of a crime than was required when the act was committed. Note that the Due Process Clauses of the Fifth and Fourteenth Amendments similarly prohibit ***courts*** from retroactively interpreting criminal laws in an unexpected and indefensible way.

Exam Tip The Ex Post Facto Clauses apply only to ***criminal*** cases. Thus, an answer choice that attempts to apply these prohibitions in a civil case (*e.g.,* regarding a denial of a professional license) is ***wrong.***

C. BILLS OF ATTAINDER

Bills of attainder are legislative acts that inflict punishment on individuals without a judicial trial. Both federal and state governments are prohibited from passing bills of attainder.

D. DUE PROCESS CONSIDERATIONS

If a retroactive law does not violate the Contracts, Ex Post Facto, or Bill of Attainder Clauses, it still must pass muster under the Due Process Clause. If the retroactive law does not relate to a fundamental right, it need only be rationally related to a legitimate government interest.

XIV. PROCEDURAL DUE PROCESS

A. BASIC PRINCIPLE

A ***fair process*** (*e.g.,* notice and a hearing) is required for a government agency to individually take a person's "life, liberty, or property." Only intentional—not negligent—deprivation of these rights violates the Due Process Clause.

B. IS LIFE, LIBERTY, OR PROPERTY BEING TAKEN?

1. Liberty

The term "liberty" is not specifically defined. It includes more than just freedom from bodily restraints (*e.g.,* it includes the right to contract and to engage in gainful employment). A deprivation of liberty occurs if a person:

a. Loses significant freedom of action; ***or***

b. Is denied a freedom provided by the Constitution or a statute.

2. Property

"Property" includes more than personal belongings and realty, but an abstract need or desire for (or a unilateral expectation of) a benefit is not enough. There must be a ***legitimate claim*** or "***entitlement***" to the benefit under state or federal law. Examples of property interests include continued attendance at public school, welfare benefits, and government employment.

Exam Tip At one time, due process protected a "right" but not a "privilege." This distinction has been rejected by the Court. Thus, an answer that uses that terminology (right versus privilege) should be discarded as a red herring. The proper terminology is "entitlement."

C. WHAT TYPE OF PROCESS IS REQUIRED?

The type and extent of required procedures are determined by a three-part balancing test, which weighs:

(i) The ***importance of the interest*** to the individual;

(ii) The value of specific ***procedural safeguards*** to that interest; and

(iii) The ***government interest*** in fiscal and administrative efficiency.

Presumably, fair procedures and an unbiased decisionmaker will always be required. Notice and chance to respond before termination of the liberty or property interest are usually required.

D. DUE PROCESS RIGHTS ARE SUBJECT TO WAIVER

As a general rule, due process rights are, presumably, subject to waiver if the waiver is ***voluntary and made knowingly***.

E. ACCESS TO COURTS—INDIGENT PLAINTIFFS

Government fees (*e.g.,* court filing fees) must be waived when imposition of a fee would deny a fundamental right to the indigent (*see infra,* for discussion of fundamental rights). Thus, for example, a marriage license or divorce court filing fee (privacy rights) or filing fee for candidates for electoral office (voting rights) must be waived. However, fees can be imposed when nonfundamental rights are involved (*e.g.,* fees for a bankruptcy discharge or review of welfare termination).

TYPE OF PROCESS REQUIRED

Interest Involved	Process Required
1. Commitment to Mental Institution	*Adults:* Prior notice and ***prior*** evidentiary hearing (except in emergency). *Children:* Prior screening by ***"neutral factfinder."*** (Parental consent alone insufficient.)
2. Welfare Benefits	Prior notice and ***prior*** evidentiary hearing.
3. Disability Benefits	Prior notice and opportunity to respond, and ***subsequent*** evidentiary hearing.
4. Public Employment (tenured or termination only "for cause")	Generally, prior notice and opportunity to respond, and ***subsequent*** evidentiary hearing.
5. Public Education (disciplinary suspension or academic dismissal)	Prior notice and opportunity to respond; ***no*** formal evidentiary hearing required.
6. Driver's License Suspension	Prior evidentiary hearing. *Exception:* Breathalizer test suspension statutes.
7. Termination of Parent's Custody Rights	Prior notice and ***prior*** evidentiary hearing.
8. Civil Forfeitures	***Prior*** notice and evidentiary hearing for ***real property; subsequent*** notice and hearing for ***personal property.***

XV. THE "TAKING" CLAUSE

A. IN GENERAL

The Fifth Amendment provides that private property may not be taken for ***public use*** without

just compensation. This rule is applicable to the states via the Fourteenth Amendment. The Taking Clause is not a source of power for taking, but rather is a limitation. "Taking" includes not only physical appropriations but also ***some*** government action that damages property or impairs its use.

B. "PUBLIC USE" LIMITATION LIBERALLY CONSTRUED

If the government's action is ***rationally related*** to a ***legitimate*** public purpose (*e.g.,* for health, welfare, safety, economic, or aesthetic reasons), the public use requirement is satisfied. Authorized takings by private enterprises are included if they redound to the public advantage (*e.g.,* railroads and public utilities).

C. "TAKING" VS. "REGULATION"

The crucial issue is whether governmental action is a ***taking*** (requiring payment of just compensation) or merely a ***regulation*** (not requiring compensation). There is no clear-cut formula for making this determination, but the following general guidelines apply:

1. Actual Appropriation or Physical Invasion

These types of action will almost always amount to a taking. *Exception:* Emergency situations.

2. Use Restrictions

a. Denial of *All* Economic Value of Land—Taking

If a government regulation denies a landowner ***all*** economic use of his land (*e.g.,* a regulation enacted after plaintiff buys his land prohibits building on the land), the regulation amounts to a taking unless principles of nuisance or property law that existed when the owner acquired the land make the use prohibitable.

1) Temporary Denials of All Economic Use

Temporarily denying an owner of all economic use of property does not constitute a per se taking. Instead, the Court will carefully examine and weigh all the relevant circumstances—the planners' good faith, the reasonable expectations of the owners, the length of the delay, the delay's actual affect on the value of the property, etc.—in order to determine whether "fairness and justice" require just compensation.

b. Decreasing Economic Value—Balancing Test

Regulations that merely decrease the value of property (*e.g.,* prohibit the most beneficial use) do not amount to a taking if they leave an ***economically viable use for the property***. The Court will consider:

(i) The ***social goals*** sought to be promoted;

(ii) The ***diminution in value*** to the owner; and

(iii) The ***owner's reasonable expectations*** regarding the property.

The more drastic the reduction in value or the less it promotes public welfare, the more likely it is to be a taking.

CMR EXAMPLE CHART

"TAKING" VS. "REGULATION"

Government Action	Characterization
1. Condemnation of land to build highway	Taking
2. Creating public access easement on private property	Taking
3. Abolishing inheritance rights	Taking
4. Zoning ordinances that merely prohibit the most beneficial use of property	Regulation
5. Ordering destruction of diseased trees	Regulation
6. Landmark ordinances	Regulation

3. Remedy—"Just Compensation"
If the regulation amounts to a taking, the government must:

(i) ***Pay*** the property owner just compensation for the property (*i.e.,* fair market value); ***or***

(ii) ***Terminate the regulation and pay*** the owner for damages that occurred while the regulation was in effect (*i.e.,* temporary taking damages).

a. "Worthless" Property
Just compensation is measured by the ***loss to the owner***, not by the gain to the taker. Thus, while property that is worthless to the owner can be the subject of a taking, no compensation need be paid when it is taken.

XVI. INTRODUCTION TO SUBSTANTIVE DUE PROCESS AND EQUAL PROTECTION

A. RELATIONSHIP BETWEEN SUBSTANTIVE DUE PROCESS AND EQUAL PROTECTION

Both substantive due process and equal protection guarantees require the Court to review the substance of a law rather than the procedures employed.

1. Substantive Due Process
Where the law limits liberty of ***all*** persons to engage in some activity, on the MBE it usually is a due process question.

2. Equal Protection
Where the law treats a ***person or class of persons*** differently from others, on the MBE it usually is an equal protection problem.

B. WHAT STANDARD OF REVIEW WILL THE COURT APPLY?

Under either guarantee, the Court is reviewing the legitimacy of governmental acts. Three standards of review are used:

1. Strict Scrutiny (Maximum Scrutiny)

Regulations affecting ***fundamental rights*** (*i.e.,* interstate travel, privacy, voting, and First Amendment rights) or involving ***suspect classifications*** (*i.e.,* race, national origin, and alienage) are reviewed under the strict scrutiny standard: The law is upheld if it is ***necessary*** to achieve a ***compelling*** government purpose. This is a difficult test to meet, and so a law examined under a strict scrutiny standard will often be invalidated—especially when there is a ***less burdensome*** alternative to achieve the government's goal.

a. Burden of Proof

The government has the burden of proof.

2. Intermediate Scrutiny

Regulations involving ***quasi-suspect classifications*** (*i.e.,* gender and legitimacy) are reviewed under the intermediate scrutiny standard: The law is upheld if it is ***substantially related*** to an ***important*** government purpose.

a. Burden of Proof

It is unclear who has burden of proof. It is probably the government.

3. Rational Basis (Minimal Scrutiny)

Regulations that do ***not*** affect fundamental rights or involve suspect or quasi-suspect classifications (most laws) are reviewed under the rational basis standard: The law is upheld if it is ***rationally related*** to a ***legitimate*** government purpose. This is a very easy standard to meet; therefore the law is usually valid—unless it is ***arbitrary*** or ***irrational***.

a. Burden of Proof

The person challenging the law has the burden of proof.

b. Classifications that Are Not Suspect or Quasi-Suspect

The rational basis standard is used to review regulations involving classifications that are ***not*** suspect or quasi-suspect, such as age, disability, and poverty.

CMR **Exam Tip** Many exam questions ask you about the standard that the Court will use to review governmental regulation. Therefore, you need to know which standard will apply in a particular case (*e.g.,* if a fundamental right is involved, strict scrutiny is applied). However, the choices may not ***name*** the standard ("strict scrutiny") but merely state it ("upheld if necessary to a compelling government interest"). Be prepared to recognize the standard by name ***or*** definition.

CMR **Exam Tip** Due process or equal protection questions also commonly test your knowledge of which party bears the burden of proof. Know the standards and their respective burdens.

XVII. SUBSTANTIVE DUE PROCESS

A. CONSTITUTIONAL SOURCE—TWO CLAUSES

The Due Process Clause of the Fifth Amendment applies to the federal government. The Due

Process Clause of the Fourteenth Amendment applies to state and local governments. The same tests are applied under each clause.

B. APPLICABLE STANDARDS

Where a ***fundamental right*** is limited, the law or action is evaluated under the ***strict scrutiny*** standard. In ***all other cases***, the ***rational basis*** standard is applied.

C. A FEW IRREBUTTABLE PRESUMPTIONS MAY BE INVALID

If facts are presumed against a person so that she cannot demonstrate that she is qualified for some important benefit or right, the "irrebuttable presumption" may be unconstitutional.

Exam Tip The Supreme Court no longer treats irrebuttable presumptions differently from other regulations or classifications. Thus, if an answer choice says "invalid because it is an irrebuttable presumption," it is probably wrong. You must consider whether it concerns a ***fundamental right*** or ***suspect or quasi-suspect class***, and judge it accordingly.

XVIII. EQUAL PROTECTION

A. CONSTITUTIONAL SOURCE

The Equal Protection Clause of the Fourteenth Amendment is limited to state action. However, grossly unreasonable discrimination by the federal government violates the Due Process Clause of the Fifth Amendment. The Court applies the same tests under either constitutional provision.

B. APPLICABLE STANDARDS

If a ***fundamental right*** or ***suspect classification*** is involved, the ***strict scrutiny*** standard is used to evaluate the regulation. If a ***quasi-suspect classification*** is involved, ***intermediate scrutiny*** is the applicable standard. If the classification does not affect a fundamental right or involve a suspect or quasi-suspect classification, the ***rational basis*** standard applies.

C. PROVING DISCRIMINATORY CLASSIFICATION

For strict or intermediate scrutiny to be applied, there must be ***intent*** on the part of the government to discriminate. Intent may be shown by:

(i) A law that is ***discriminatory on its face***;

(ii) A ***discriminatory application*** of a facially neutral law; or

(iii) A ***discriminatory motive*** behind the law.

Note: The third way to show intentional discrimination is the most difficult to prove. A discriminatory effect alone is ***not*** enough. The legislature's discriminatory motive must be shown (*e.g.,* by evidence of a history of discrimination).

D. SUSPECT CLASSIFICATIONS

Classifications are suspect if they are based on race, national origin, or alienage.

1. Race and National Origin

Classifications based on race or national origin are judged by a strict scrutiny standard.

a. School Integration

Only intentional segregation violates the Constitution. If school systems and attendance

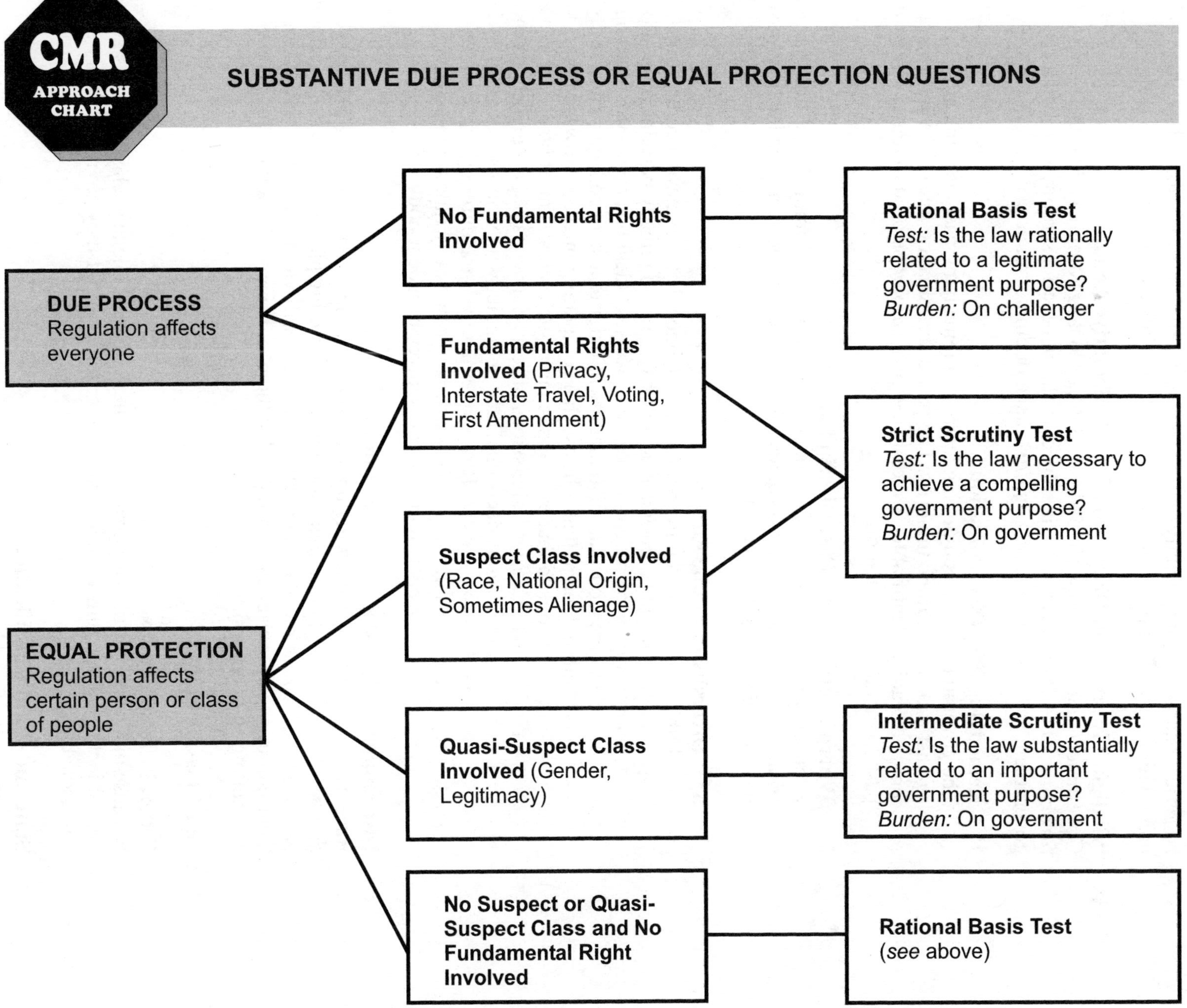
CMR
APPROACH CHART
SUBSTANTIVE DUE PROCESS OR EQUAL PROTECTION QUESTIONS
DUE PROCESS Regulation affects everyone
EQUAL PROTECTION Regulation affects certain person or class of people
No Fundamental Rights Involved
Fundamental Rights Involved (Privacy, Interstate Travel, Voting, First Amendment)
Suspect Class Involved (Race, National Origin, Sometimes Alienage)
Quasi-Suspect Class Involved (Gender, Legitimacy)
No Suspect or Quasi-Suspect Class and No Fundamental Right Involved
Rational Basis Test Test: Is the law rationally related to a legitimate government purpose? Burden: On challenger
Strict Scrutiny Test Test: Is the law necessary to achieve a compelling government purpose? Burden: On government
Intermediate Scrutiny Test Test: Is the law substantially related to an important government purpose? Burden: On government
Rational Basis Test (see above)

zones are established in a racially neutral manner, there is no violation. Thus, there is no violation if housing patterns result in racial imbalance in schools.

b. "Benign" Government Discrimination—Affirmative Action

Government action—whether by federal, state, or local governmental bodies—that ***favors*** racial or ethnic minorities is subject to the same strict scrutiny standard as is government action discriminating ***against*** racial or ethnic minorities.

1) Remedying Past Discrimination

The government has a compelling interest in remedying past discrimination against a racial or ethnic minority. The past discrimination must have been persistent and readily identifiable. A race-based plan ***cannot*** be used to remedy ***general*** past "societal discrimination."

2) Where There Was No Past Discrimination

Even where the government has not engaged in past discrimination, it may have a compelling interest in affirmative action. However, the governmental action must be ***narrowly tailored*** to that interest.

a) Diversity in Public Educations

Public colleges and universities have claimed that they have a compelling interest in having a diverse student body—not to remedy past discrimination, but rather in its own right—because a diverse student body enhances learning. The Supreme Court has held that it will defer to a state college or university's good faith judgment that it has such a compelling interest. However, the Court has also held that each applicant to such schools must be considered as an individual. Although admissions officers may consider an applicant's race in making admissions decisions, race or ethnicity may only be deemed a ***plus among a range of factors***. If race or ethnicity is the defining criterion for admission, the admission policy will not be narrowly tailored to achieving the compelling interest of ensuring a diverse student body.

c. Discriminatory Legislative Apportionment

Race can be considered in drawing up new voting districts, but it ***cannot be the predominate factor***. If a plaintiff can show that a redistricting plan was drawn up predominately on the basis of racial considerations, the plan will violate the Equal Protection Clause unless the government can show that the plan is narrowly tailored to serve a compelling state interest.

2. Alienage Classifications

a. Federal Classifications

Because of Congress's plenary power over aliens, federal alienage classifications are ***not*** subject to strict scrutiny. Such classifications are valid if they are not arbitrary and unreasonable.

b. State and Local Classifications

Generally, state/local laws on alienage are suspect classifications subject to strict scrutiny. *Examples:* It is unconstitutional for United States citizenship to be required for welfare, civil service jobs, or to become a lawyer.

1) **Exception—Participation in Self-Government Process**
If a law discriminates against alien participation in state government (*e.g.,* voting, jury service, elective office), the ***rational basis*** standard is applied. Also, the rational basis standard is used for state and local laws limiting certain non-elective offices involving important public policy (*e.g.,* police officers, probation officers, and teachers).

c. **Undocumented Aliens**
Undocumented ("illegal") aliens are ***not*** a suspect classification. Thus, state laws regarding them are subject to a "rational basis" standard. (However, denial of free public education to undocumented alien children is invalid, and more than a simple rational basis standard was used by the Court.)

E. QUASI-SUSPECT CLASSIFICATIONS

Classifications based on legitimacy and gender are "quasi-suspect."

1. Gender Classifications

Gender classifications are reviewed under the intermediate scrutiny standard: They must be ***substantially related*** to an ***important*** government purpose. The government bears the burden of showing an "exceedingly persuasive justification" for the discrimination.

a. **Women**
Intentional discrimination ***against*** women generally is invalid. Classifications ***benefiting*** women that are designed to ***remedy past discrimination*** generally are valid.

b. **Intentional Discrimination Against Men**
Intentional discrimination against men is generally invalid. However, certain laws have been found to be substantially related to an important government interest (*e.g.,* statutory rape laws, all male draft).

CMR EXAMPLE CHART

GENDER CLASSIFICATION

Classification	Status
Gender-based death benefits	Invalid
Gender-based peremptory strikes	Invalid
Alimony for women only	Invalid
State supported all-male or all-female schools	Invalid
Discriminatory minimum drinking age (women at 18, men at 21)	Invalid
Discriminatory statutory rape laws	Valid
All-male draft	Valid
Requiring American fathers (but not mothers) to prove their parentage of nonmarital children born abroad in order to obtain U.S. citizenship for them	Valid

CMR **Exam Tip** The preceding chart spells out the most likely exam candidates. In any event, remember that most gender classifications are struck down. This is particularly true if they perpetuate stereotypes of economically dependent women.

2. Legitimacy Classifications

Legitimacy classifications are also reviewed under the intermediate scrutiny standard: They must be ***substantially related*** to an ***important*** government interest. Discriminatory regulations intended to punish illegitimate children (*e.g.,* law providing a benefit to legitimate children but not to illegitimate children) are invalid. *Example:* A law allowing only legitimate children to recover from their father's estate is invalid. *But note:* A law allowing illegitimate children to recover from their father's estate only if parenthood is established before the father's death is ***valid***.

F. OTHER CLASSIFICATIONS

All other classifications are evaluated under the ***rational basis*** standard. These include age, disability, and wealth classifications. For example, mandatory retirement ages may be established; and since education is not a fundamental right, there is no denial of equal protection when wealthier children can afford to pay for access to the best state-operated schools.

CMR **Exam Tip** For the MBE, you must memorize the suspect classifications (race, national origin, and sometimes alienage), quasi-suspect classifications (gender and legitimacy), and the fundamental rights (right to interstate travel, privacy, voting, and First Amendment rights). Any other classification or any other right is ***not*** entitled to more than the rational basis test, and thus the government regulation will usually be valid. Do not let your personal feelings lead you to apply the wrong standard (and pick the wrong answer) because you think the right is important or the group is worthy.

XIX. FUNDAMENTAL RIGHTS

A. INTRODUCTION

Certain fundamental rights are protected under the Constitution. If they are denied to everyone, it is a substantive due process problem. If they are denied to some individuals but not others, it is an equal protection problem. The applicable standard in either case is strict scrutiny. Thus, government action must be ***necessary*** to protect a ***compelling*** governmental interest. (Remember that there must be no less restrictive means to achieve this goal.)

B. RIGHT OF PRIVACY

Various privacy rights including marriage, sexual relations, abortion, and childrearing are fundamental rights. Regulations affecting these rights are reviewed under the ***strict scrutiny*** standard.

1. Marriage

The right of a male and female to enter into (and, probably, to dissolve) the marriage relationship is a fundamental right. However, a statute restricting the rights of prison inmates to marry will be upheld if reasonably related to legitimate penological interests.

2. Use of Contraceptives

A state cannot prohibit distribution of nonmedical contraceptives to adults.

3. **Abortion**
The right of privacy includes the right of a woman to have an abortion without interference from the state under certain circumstances. However, normal strict scrutiny analysis cannot be applied because the state has two compelling interests here that often compete: protecting the woman's health and protecting the fetus that may become a child. In its latest abortion rights approach, the Supreme Court has adopted two basic rules: a pre-viability rule and a post-viability rule.

a. **Pre-Viability Rule—No Undue Burdens**
Before viability (a realistic possibility that the fetus could survive outside the womb), a state may adopt a regulation protecting the mother's health and the life of the fetus if the regulation does not place an "undue burden" on or substantial obstacle to the woman's right to obtain an abortion.

PRE-VIABILITY ABORTION REGULATION

No Undue Burden	Undue Burden
Requiring doctor to give woman relevant information to make ***informed consent***.	Requiring woman to ***notify spouse*** about abortion.
Requiring ***24-hour waiting period***.	Barring ***all*** partial-birth abortions.
Requiring ***parental consent*** or ***parental notice*** in order for minors to obtain an abortion, if there is a judicial bypass option.	
Requiring that abortions be performed only ***by licensed physicians***.	

b. **Post-Viability Rule—May Prohibit Abortion Unless Woman's Health Threatened**
Once the fetus is viable, the state's interest in the fetus's life can override the woman's right to choose an abortion, but the state cannot prohibit the woman from obtaining an abortion if an abortion is necessary to protect the woman's health or safety.

c. **Financing Abortions**
The government has no obligation to pay for abortions.

4. **Obscene Reading Material**
The right to privacy includes freedom to read obscene material in one's home (except for child pornography), but not the right to sell, purchase, or transport such material.

5. **Keeping Extended Family Together**
Zoning regulations that prevent family members—even extended ones—from living together are invalid. This right does ***not*** extend to unrelated people.

6. Rights of Parents

Parents have a fundamental right to make decisions concerning the care, custody, and control of their children (*e.g.,* a parent has a fundamental right to send a child to private school or to forbid visitation with grandparents).

7. Intimate Sexual Conduct

The state has no legitimate interest in making it a crime for fully consenting adults to engage in private intimate sexual conduct (*e.g.,* sodomy) that is not commercial in nature.

8. Collection and Distribution of Personal Data—No Privacy Right

The state may reasonably gather and distribute information about its citizens. Thus, there is no privacy right to prohibit the accumulation of names and addresses of patients for whom dangerous drugs are prescribed.

C. RIGHT TO VOTE

The right to vote is a fundamental right. Thus, restrictions on that right, other than on the basis of residence, age, and citizenship, are ***invalid*** unless they can pass ***strict scrutiny***.

1. Restrictions on Right to Vote

a. Residency Requirements

Reasonable time periods for residency (*e.g.,* 30 days) are valid. Note that Congress may override state residency requirements in ***presidential*** elections and substitute its own.

b. Property Ownership

Conditioning the right to vote or hold office on ownership of property is usually invalid. *Exception:* Special purpose elections (water storage districts); *see* below.

c. Poll Taxes

Poll taxes are unconstitutional.

d. Primary Elections

States may require early registration to vote in primaries. However, states cannot prohibit political parties from opening their primary elections to anyone, whether or not registered with the party.

2. Dilution of Right to Vote

a. One Person, One Vote Principle

The "one person, one vote" principle applies whenever any level of government, state or local, decides to select representatives to a governmental body by popular election from ***individual districts***.

1) Congressional Elections

States must use ***almost exact mathematical equality*** when creating congressional districts within the state. This is not true of Congress, however, when it apportions representatives among the states; Congress's good faith method for apportioning representatives commands more deference and is ***not*** subject to the precise mathematical formula as are state plans.

2) **State and Local Elections**
For state and local elections, the variance in the number of persons included within districts must not be more than a few percentage points.

3) **Exception—Appointed Officials and Officials Elected "At-Large"**
The apportionment requirement is inapplicable to officials who are appointed or elected at-large.

4) **Exception—Special Purpose Election**
The one person, one vote principle does not apply to elections of officials who do not exercise "normal governmental authority" but rather deal with matters of special interest in the community (*e.g.,* water storage districts).

b. **Gerrymandering**
Race (and presumably other suspect classifications) cannot be the predominant factor in drawing the boundaries of voting districts unless the district plan can pass muster under strict scrutiny.

3. **Candidates and Campaigns**

a. **Candidate Qualifications**

1) **Fee Must Not Preclude Indigents**
States may not charge candidates a fee that results in making it impossible for indigents to run for office.

2) **Restrictions on Ability to Be a Candidate**
A ballot access regulation must be a reasonable, nondiscriminatory means of promoting important state interests. A state may require candidates to show reasonable support to have their names placed on the ballot.

b. **Campaign Funding**
The government may allocate more public funds to the two "major" parties than to "minor" parties for political campaigns.

D. RIGHT TO TRAVEL

1. **Interstate Travel**
An individual has a fundamental right to migrate from state to state and to be treated equally after moving into a new state. However, not every restriction on the right to cross state lines is an impairment of the right to travel (*e.g.,* increased penalties for a father abandoning his children and leaving the state are valid). A problem arises when a state imposes a minimum durational residency requirement for receiving its benefits or otherwise dispenses state benefits based on the length of time a person has resided in the state. It is not clear whether the Court always reviews these regulations under the strict scrutiny standard. It may be best to just recall the examples below.

CMR EXAMPLE CHART

DURATIONAL RESIDENCY REQUIREMENT

Residency Requirement	Status
One-year residency to receive full welfare benefits	Invalid
One-year residency to receive state subsidized medical care	Invalid
One-year residency to vote in state	Invalid
Thirty-day residency to vote in state	Valid
One-year residency to get divorced	Valid

2. Right to International Travel

International travel is ***not a fundamental right***. It is, however, protected from arbitrary federal interference by the Fifth Amendment Due Process Clause; the rational basis standard applies.

PART 5: FIRST AMENDMENT FREEDOMS

The First Amendment prohibits Congress from establishing a religion or interfering with the free exercise of religion, abridging the freedoms of speech and press, or interfering with the right of assembly. These prohibitions are applicable to the states through the Fourteenth Amendment.

XX. FREEDOM OF SPEECH AND ASSEMBLY

A. GENERAL PRINCIPLES

Whenever the government seeks to regulate the freedoms of speech or assembly, the Court will weigh the great importance of speech and assembly rights against the interests or policies sought to be served by the regulation. Keep the following guidelines in mind:

1. Content vs. Conduct

Speech and assembly regulations can generally be categorized as either ***content*** regulations (regulations forbidding communication of specific ideas) or ***conduct*** regulations (regulations of the conduct associated with speaking, such as the time of the speech, sound level, etc.). Different standards are used to assess the validity of a regulation within each category.

a. **Content**
It is presumptively unconstitutional to place burdens on speech because of its content except for certain categories of speech (obscenity, defamation, etc.). Content-neutral speech regulations generally are subject to ***intermediate scrutiny***; *i.e.*, they must advance ***important*** interests unrelated to the suppression of speech and ***must not burden substantially more speech than necessary*** to further those interests.

b. **Conduct**
Conduct related to speech can be regulated by content-neutral time, place, and manner restrictions. (These rules will be discussed in detail below.) Additionally, all regulations of speech are subject to the following restrictions.

2. **Reasonableness of Regulation**
A regulation of speech or assembly is void "on its face" if it is explicitly vague or overbroad. A void regulation is totally invalid; *i.e.,* it is incapable of any application, and thus a person cannot be punished for failure to follow the regulation—even if his speech or assembly could otherwise be regulated. A regulation could be found to be void if it:

a. Is ***overbroad***, *i.e.,* it regulates ***substantially*** more speech than is necessary (*e.g.,* outlawing ***all*** First Amendment activity within an airport terminal; prohibiting ***all*** canvassers from going onto private residential property to promote ***any*** cause without first obtaining a permit);

b. Is ***vague***, *i.e.,* it does not give ***reasonable notice*** of what is prohibited (*e.g.,* a prohibition against lewd speech); or

c. Gives officials ***broad discretion*** in applying the regulation (*e.g.,* allowing issuance of parade permit based on officials' judgment about parade's effect on community welfare).

CMR **Exam Tip** As a practical matter, vagueness and overbreadth almost always go together; *i.e.,* the same regulation will violate both concepts. Thus, both terms are often found in the same alternative on the bar exam.

3. **Scope of Speech**
The freedom to speak includes the freedom ***not to speak***. Thus, the government generally cannot require people to salute the flag or display other messages with which they disagree (*e.g.,* a person need not display the motto "live free or die" on a license plate). The freedom can extend to ***symbolic acts*** undertaken to communicate an idea (*e.g.,* wearing a black armband to protest the war), although the government may regulate such conduct if it has an ***important*** interest in the regulation ***independent*** of the speech aspects of the conduct and the incidental burden on speech is no greater than necessary (*e.g.,* to facilitate a smooth draft, the government can prohibit the burning of draft cards).

a. **Mandatory Financial Support**
While the government cannot require a person to pay a fee if the ***primary purpose*** of the fee is to subsidize speech that the person finds offensive, it can require a person to pay a fee to support a ***comprehensive program*** that benefits the person, even if some of the fee is used to support speech that is offensive to the person (*e.g.,* a government employee can be forced to pay union dues even if some of the money is used to promote political views with which the employee disagrees).

4. Funding vs. Regulation
Congress has more leeway when funding speech than it does when it is regulating speech. Congress may selectively fund programs that it believes to be in the public interest while denying funding to alternative programs. However, viewpoint restrictions generally are not allowed when the government funds private speech.

B. TIME, PLACE, AND MANNER RESTRICTIONS—REGULATION OF CONDUCT

The government has power to regulate the ***conduct*** associated with speech and assembly, although the breadth of this power depends on whether the forum involved is a public forum, a designated public forum (sometimes called a limited public forum), or a nonpublic forum.

1. Public Forums and Designated Public Forums
Public property that has historically been open to speech-related activities (*e.g.*, ***streets, sidewalks, and public parks***) is called a public forum. Public property that has not historically been open to speech-related activities, but which the government has thrown open for such activities on a permanent or limited basis, by practice or policy (*e.g.*, school rooms that are open for after school use by social, civic, or recreation groups), is called a designated or limited public forum. The government may regulate speech in public forums and designated public forums with reasonable time, place, and manner regulations that:

(i) Are ***content neutral***;

(ii) Are ***narrowly tailored*** to serve a ***significant*** (important) government interest; and

(iii) Leave open ***alternative channels*** of communication.

Note: Almost every legitimate governmental interest satisfies the significant/important standard.

Exam Tip Remember that even if a regulation meets the time, place, and manner requirements above, it could still be invalid if it is overbroad, vague, or gives unfettered discretion.

a. Injunctions
Injunctions against speech in public forums are treated differently from generally applicable laws. If the injunction is content based, it must be necessary to achieve a compelling interest. If the injunction is content neutral, it must burden no more speech than is necessary to achieve a significant government interest.

2. Nonpublic Forums
Speech and assembly can be more broadly regulated in nonpublic forums (*i.e.,* government-owned forums not historically linked with speech and assembly and not held open for speech activities, such as military bases, schools while classes are in session, government workplaces, etc.). In such locations, regulations are valid if they are:

a. ***Viewpoint neutral***; and

b. ***Reasonably related to a legitimate*** government purpose.

C. UNPROTECTED SPEECH—REGULATION BASED ON CONTENT

To be valid, restrictions on the content of speech must be ***narrowly tailored*** to achieve a

compelling government interest. The government has a compelling interest in the following categories of speech, which are deemed "unprotected" speech under the First Amendment:

1. Inciting Imminent Lawless Action

Speech can be burdened if it creates a clear and present danger of imminent lawless action. It must be shown that imminent illegal conduct is ***likely*** and that the speaker intended to cause it.

2. Fighting Words

Speech can be burdened if it constitutes fighting words (personally abusive words that are likely to incite immediate physical retaliation in an average person). Words that are merely annoying are not sufficient. Note also that the Supreme Court will not tolerate fighting words statutes that are designed to punish only certain viewpoints (*e.g.,* proscribing only fighting words that insult on the basis of race, religion, or gender). However, the First Amendment does not protect "true threats," and, therefore, the Supreme Court has upheld a statute banning cross-burning when carried out with the ***intent to intimidate***.

CMR **Exam Tip** While this classification of punishable speech exists in theory, as a practical matter, statutes that attempt to punish fighting words are usually vague or overbroad. Thus, on the examination, they generally should be regarded as ***invalid***.

3. Obscenity

Obscene speech is not protected.

a. Elements

Speech is obscene if it describes or depicts sexual conduct that, taken as a whole, by the average person:

1) ***Appeals to the prurient interest*** in sex, using a ***community standard***;

2) Is ***patently offensive*** and an affront to contemporary ***community standards***; and

3) ***Lacks serious value*** (literary, artistic, political, or scientific), using a ***national reasonable person standard***.

CMR **Exam Tip** Note the two different standards used in the obscenity test: appeal to the prurient interest and offensiveness are judged by contemporary ***community*** standards (local or statewide, not necessarily national standards), while value is judged on a ***national reasonable person*** basis.

b. Standard May Be Different for Minors

The state can adopt a specific definition of obscenity applying to materials sold to minors, even though the material might not be obscene in terms of an adult audience. However, government may not prohibit the sale or distribution of material to adults merely because it is inappropriate for children.

1) Pictures of Minors

To protect minors from exploitation, the government may prohibit the sale or distribution of ***visual*** depictions of sexual conduct involving minors, even if the material would not be found obscene if it did not involve children.

2) **Compare—Simulated Pictures of Minors**
The government may not bar visual material that only appears to depict minors engaged in sexually explicit conduct, but that in fact uses young-looking adults or computer generated images.

c. **Land Use Regulations**
A land-use (or zoning) regulation may limit the location or size of adult entertainment establishments if the regulation is designed to reduce the secondary effects of such businesses (*e.g.*, rise in crime rates, drop in property values, etc.). However, regulations may not ban such establishments altogether.

d. **Liquor Regulation**
Under the Twenty-First Amendment, states have broad power to regulate intoxicating beverages. Laws relating to this power that affect free speech rights generally will not be set aside unless they are irrational.

e. **Private Possession of Obscene Material**
Private possession of obscene material ***in the home*** cannot be punished (except for possession of child pornography). However, the protection does not extend outside the home.

4. **Defamatory Speech**
Defamatory statements can be burdened. If the defamatory statement is about a ***public official*** or ***public figure*** or involves a ***public concern***, the First Amendment requires the plaintiff to prove all the elements of defamation ***plus falsity*** and some degree of ***fault***. (*See* Torts outline for detailed discussion.)

CMR **Exam Tip** The First Amendment may also play a role in certain privacy actions. (*See* Torts outline.)

5. **Some Commercial Speech**
As a general rule, commercial speech is afforded First Amendment protection if it is truthful. However, commercial speech that proposes ***unlawful activity*** or that is ***misleading or fraudulent*** may be burdened. Any other regulation of commercial speech will be upheld only if it:

a. Serves a ***substantial government interest***;

b. ***Directly advances*** that interest; and

c. Is ***narrowly tailored*** to serve that interest.

CMR **Exam Tip** "Narrowly tailored" does ***not*** require the least restrictive means of accomplishing the legislative goal; there just must be a ***reasonable*** fit between the goal and the means chosen.

D. **PRIOR RESTRAINTS**
Prior restraints prevent speech before it occurs, rather than punish it afterwards. They are rarely

allowed. The government has a heavy burden in justifying a prior restraint; it must show that some ***special societal harm*** will otherwise result.

1. Procedural Safeguards

To be valid, a system for prior restraint must provide the following safeguards:

(i) The standards must be ***narrowly drawn***, ***reasonable***, ***and definite***;

(ii) Injunction must ***promptly*** be sought; and

(iii) There must be ***prompt and final determination*** of the validity of the restraint.

A number of other cases, especially in the area of movie censorship, require that the ***government bear the burden*** of proving that the speech involved is unprotected.

VALID AND INVALID PRIOR RESTRAINTS

Valid	Invalid
Prohibiting publishing of troop movement ***in times of war***.	Prohibiting publication of *The Pentagon Papers* because it ***might*** have an effect on the Vietnam War.
Enforcing ***contractual prepublication review*** of CIA agent's writings.	Prohibiting grand jury witness from ***ever*** disclosing testimony.

2. Obscenity Cases

a. Seizures of Books and Films

Seizures of a single book or film may be made with a ***warrant*** based on probable cause, although if the item is available for sale to the public, a police officer may purchase a book or film to use as evidence without a warrant. Large-scale seizures must be ***preceded by a full scale adversary hearing*** and a judicial determination of obscenity.

b. Movie Censorship

The Court has found that time delays incident to censorship are less burdensome on movies than on other forms of expression. Thus, the Court allows the government to establish censorship boards to screen movies before they are released, as long as the procedural safeguards discussed above are followed.

E. FREEDOM OF THE PRESS

Generally, the press has ***no greater First Amendment freedom*** than does a private citizen. Thus, the concepts discussed above apply.

1. Publication of Truthful Information

Generally the press has a right to publish truthful information regarding a matter of public concern, and this right can be restricted only by a sanction that is narrowly tailored to further an interest of the highest order.

2. Access to Trials

The First Amendment guarantees the public and press a right to attend criminal (and probably civil) trials. However, the right may be ***outweighed*** by an overriding interest stated in the trial judge's findings (*e.g.,* to protect children who are victims of sex offenses). The right includes the right to be present at voir dire and at other pretrial proceedings, unless the judge makes specific findings that closure was narrowly tailored to preserve a higher value.

3. Requiring Press to Testify Before Grand Jury

Members of the press may be required to testify before grand juries.

4. Interviewing Prisoners

The First Amendment does not give journalists a right to interview specified prisoners of their choice or to inspect prison grounds.

5. Business Regulation or Tax

The press and broadcasting companies can be subjected to ***general*** business regulations or taxes but cannot be targeted for special regulation or taxes. A tax or regulation impacting on the press or a subpart of the press cannot be based on the content of a publication (*e.g.,* a tax exemption cannot be given to "medical journals") absent a compelling justification.

6. Broadcasting Regulations

Radio and television broadcasting may be more closely regulated than the press. The paramount right is the right of ***viewers and listeners*** to receive information of public concern rather than the right of broadcasters to broadcast what they please. This paramount right allows government to forbid newspaper ownership of radio stations and to prohibit indecent speech over the airwaves.

a. Fairness Doctrine

The First Amendment does not require broadcasters to accept political advertisements. However, a radio station may constitutionally be required to offer free broadcasting time to certain individuals (*e.g.,* opponents of political candidates or views endorsed by station or persons who have been personally attacked in a broadcast).

7. Cable Television Regulation

While generally regulations of newspapers are subject to strict scrutiny, and regulations of the broadcast media are subject to less critical review, regulation of cable television transmissions generally are subject to review by a standard somewhere between these two (*e.g.*, a law requiring cable operators to carry local stations is subject to "intermediate scrutiny"—because it is content-neutral (*see* A.1.a., *supra*)—and is constitutional because it serves the important interest of preserving economic viability of local broadcasters). However, content-based restrictions (*e.g.,* a law forbidding sexually oriented cable programs before 10 p.m.) are subject to strict scrutiny.

8. **Internet Regulation**
The strict standard of First Amendment scrutiny, rather than the more relaxed standard applicable to broadcast regulation, applies to regulation of the Internet.

XXI. FREEDOM OF ASSOCIATION AND BELIEF

A. NATURE OF THE RIGHT

Although the freedom of association is not mentioned explicitly in the Constitution, it is clearly implied from the rights that are explicitly noted. Pursuant to this freedom, the government may neither prohibit politically unpopular groups nor unduly burden a person's right to belong to such groups. *But note:* This right is not absolute. Infringements of the right must be justified by a ***compelling*** state interest, unrelated to the suppression of ideas, and must be the ***least restrictive means*** of protecting the government interest involved.

B. ELECTORAL PROCESS

Laws regulating elections might impact on the First Amendment freedoms of speech, assembly, and association. The Court uses a balancing test to determine whether a regulation of the electoral process is valid: If the restriction on First Amendment activity is severe, strict scrutiny is applied, but if the restriction is reasonable and nondiscriminatory, it generally will be upheld.

ELECTORAL REGULATIONS

Valid	Invalid
1. Requiring reasonable number of signatures to get on ballot.	1. Prohibiting party from endorsing or opposing candidates in a primary.
2. Requiring voter to be registered with a political party to vote in primary.	2. Regulating party selection of delegates to national convention.
3. Prohibiting campaign activity within 100 feet of a polling place (involves core political speech but is narrowly tailored).	3. Prohibiting ***any*** campaigning on election day (involves core political speech and is overbroad).
4. Prohibiting individuals from appearing on the ballot as the candidate of more than one party.	4. Requiring political parties to allow nonparty members to vote in the parties' primary elections.
	5. Prohibiting judicial candidates from announcing their views on disputed legal and political issues.

1. **Limits on Contributions**
To prevent corruption or the appearance thereof, laws may limit the amount of money that a person, group, or corporation can contribute to a ***political candidate***. However, the government may ***not*** limit the amount of money that may be spent to support or oppose a ***ballot referendum***, and there is an exception for groups or corporations formed specifically to participate in the political debate.

2. **Limits on Expenditures**
Laws may not limit the amount that a candidate or group spends on a political campaign.

3. **Compare—Regulations of Core Political Speech**
Regulation of "core political speech" (*e.g.,* electioneering, distributing campaign literature), rather than regulation of the process surrounding an election, will be upheld only if it passes muster under strict scrutiny.

C. BAR MEMBERSHIPS AND PUBLIC EMPLOYMENT

1. **Restraints on Conduct**
If a government employer seeks to fire an employee (or to terminate a relationship with an independent contractor) for speech-related conduct, one of two tests will apply depending on whether the speech involved a matter of public concern. If a matter of public concern is involved, courts must carefully balance the employee's rights as a citizen to comment on a matter of public concern against the government's interest as an employer in efficient performance of public service. If the speech did not involve a matter of public concern, the courts should give a wide degree of deference to the government employer's judgment concerning whether the speech was disruptive.

   a. **Participation in Political Campaigns**
   The federal government ***may*** prohibit federal executive branch employees from taking an active part in political campaigns.

   b. **Bans on Receiving Honoraria**
   A provision banning government employees from accepting an honorarium for making speeches, writing articles, or making appearances was held to violate the First Amendment when applied to "rank and file" employees. Such a rule deters speech within a broad category of expression by a massive number of potential speakers and, thus, can be justified only if the government can show that the employees' and their potential audiences' rights are outweighed by the necessary impact the speech would have on actual operation of the government.

   c. **Patronage**
   A public employee may not be hired, fired, promoted, transferred, etc., based on party affiliation except as to policymaking positions, where party affiliation is relevant.

   d. **Must Not Be Vague**
   A standard for conduct must not be vague (*e.g.,* a prohibition against "treasonable or seditious" utterings is vague).

2. **Loyalty Oaths**
The government may require employees to take loyalty oaths, as long as the oaths are not overbroad or vague.

a. **Overbreadth**
An oath cannot prohibit membership in the Communist Party or require abstention from advocating overthrow of the government ***as an abstract doctrine***.

b. **Vagueness**
An oath requiring employees to support the Constitution and to oppose the ***unlawful*** overthrow of the government is valid; but an oath requiring public employees to support the flag is invalid (since refusal to salute the flag on religious grounds might conflict with the oath).

3. **Disclosure of Associations**
The government may not force disclosure of every organizational membership in exchange for a government employment or other benefit; it may only inquire into those activities that are relevant to the employment or benefit sought. Even here, however, a person can exercise his Fifth Amendment right to remain silent if the disclosure would be incriminating.

XXII. FREEDOM OF RELIGION

A. CONSTITUTIONAL PROVISION
The First Amendment prohibition on establishment of religion and its protection of the free exercise of religion is applicable to the states through the Fourteenth Amendment.

B. FREE EXERCISE CLAUSE

1. **No Punishment of Beliefs**
The Free Exercise Clause prohibits government from punishing someone on the basis of her religious beliefs. For example, the Clause forbids:

(i) State governments from requiring office holders or employees to take a ***religious oath*** (the federal government is similarly restricted by Article VI);

(ii) States from ***excluding clerics*** from holding public office; and

(iii) Courts from ***declaring a religious belief to be false***.

The Supreme Court has not defined what constitutes religious belief, but it is clear that religious belief need not come from an organized religion or involve a supreme being. The Court has never held an asserted religious belief to be not religious for First Amendment purposes.

CMR **Exam Tip** Technically, the government may deny benefits to or impose a burden on someone based on her religious beliefs ***if there is a compelling interest***. However, the Supreme Court has ***never*** found an interest so compelling that it justifies such action.

2. **General Conduct Regulation—No Religious Exemptions Required**
The Free Exercise Clause cannot be used to challenge government regulation unless the regulation was ***specifically designed*** to interfere with religion (*e.g.,* a law that prohibits the precise type of animal slaughter used in a ritual by a particular religious sect is unconstitutional). Moreover, the Free Exercise Clause does ***not require religious exemptions*** from generally applicable governmental regulations that happen to burden religious conduct; *i.e.,* a law that regulates the conduct of ***all*** people can be applied to prohibit the conduct of a person despite the fact that his religious beliefs prevent him from complying with the law.

a. **Exception—Unemployment Compensation Cases**
A state cannot refuse to grant unemployment benefits to persons who quit their jobs for religious reasons (*i.e.,* the work or conditions of work conflict with tenets of the worker's religion). The worker need not even belong to a formal religious organization in such a situation, as long as the belief is sincere.

b. **Exception—Right of Amish Not to Educate Children**
The Supreme Court has granted the Amish an exemption from a law requiring compulsory school attendance until age 16, based on the Free Exercise Clause ***and*** the fundamental right to educate one's children.

CMR **Exam Tip** To summarize, the Free Exercise Clause prohibits government interference with religious ***beliefs***, but it generally does ***not*** prohibit regulation of ***conduct***. If the governmental action regulates ***general conduct***—including religious conduct—it is ***valid*** (*e.g.,* banning any use of peyote is valid even though a group's religious beliefs require its use during its ceremonies). The only exceptions to this rule are those pertaining to unemployment compensation and the education of Amish children.

C. **ESTABLISHMENT CLAUSE**
The Establishment Clause prohibits laws respecting the establishment of religion.

1. **Sect Preference**
If a government regulation or action includes a preference for one religious sect over another, it is invalid unless it is ***narrowly tailored*** to promote a ***compelling*** interest.

CMR **Exam Tip** Although you should know the standard (narrowly tailored to promote a compelling interest) for government preference of a religious sect (or sects), it is unlikely that the government could ever have a compelling interest in preferring one religious group.

2. **No Sect Preference**
If a government regulation or action contains no sect preference, it is ***valid*** under the Establishment Clause ***if*** it:

(i) Has a ***secular purpose***;

(ii) Has a ***primary effect that neither advances nor inhibits religion***; and

(iii) Does not produce ***excessive government entanglement*** with religion.

a. **Cases Unconnected to Financial Aid or Education**
A good rule of thumb here is that a law favoring or burdening religion or a specific religious group will be invalid (*e.g.,* exempting certain religious groups—traditional religions—from state registration requirement), but a law favoring or burdening a large segment of society that happens to include religious groups will be upheld (*e.g.,* a Sunday closing law).

b. **Cases Involving Financial Benefits to Religious Institutions**
The Supreme Court applies the three-part test above with greater strictness when government financial aid is going to a religiously affiliated ***grade or high school*** than it does when the aid is going to another type of religious institution.

1) **Recipient-Based Aid**
The government may give aid in the form of financial assistance to a defined class of persons as long as the class is defined without reference to religion or religious criteria. Such a program is valid even if most of the people receiving the aid use it to attend a religiously affiliated school.

2) **Aid to Colleges and Hospitals**
Aid to colleges or hospitals will be upheld as long as the government program requires the aid to be used ***for nonreligious purposes*** and the recipient so agrees.

3) **Aid to Grade Schools and High Schools**
Aid to religious grade schools and high schools is usually found to have a secular purpose, but may fail the other parts of the test. For example, if the aid significantly improves the ability of students to attend such schools, it will be deemed to have a primary effect that advances religion. And if the program has detailed administrative regulations to prevent the effect of advancement of religion, the law will be stricken for excessive government entanglement.

c. **Religious Activities in Public Schools**
School ***sponsored*** religious activity is ***invalid***, but school ***accommodation*** of religion is ***valid***. Moreover, if a public school allows members of the public and private organizations to use school property when classes are not in session, it cannot deny a religious organization permission to use the property for meetings merely because religious topics will be discussed.

CMR EXAMPLE CHART

ESTABLISHMENT CLAUSE CASES

Valid	Invalid
Nonfinancial Aid and Education Cases	
Legislature's employment of a chaplain.	Delegation of zoning power to religious organization.
Granting religious organizations exemptions from employment discrimination laws where contrary to the organization's beliefs.	Requirement that all employers grant all workers their Sabbath day off.
Christmastime display that includes religious symbols and nonreligious symbols (*e.g.,* nativity scene along with a Christmas tree or Santa).	Christmastime display of ***only*** religious symbols (*e.g.,* nativity scene or menorah only).
Recipient-Based Aid	
Tax credits for parents of ***all*** students for educational expenses.	Tax credits only to parents of ***private school*** students for educational expenses.
Tuition vouchers for poor students that can be used at participating ***public and private schools***.	
Aid to Religious Grade and High Schools	
Reimbursement to private schools ***compiling*** state-required data or ***administering*** standardized achievement tests.	Reimbursement to private schools for ***writing*** achievement tests.
Providing government employees to ***test*** private school students for health or learning problems and to ***provide*** on-site auxiliary services, such as remedial education, guidance, or job counseling.	Providing private schools with ***teachers***, or money to pay teachers, of secular classes.
Exemption from property tax for religious, charitable, ***and*** educational property.	Tax exemption ***only*** for religious associations or activities.
Transportation ***to and from school*** for all students.	
Providing all students with state-approved ***textbooks*** or lending religiously neutral instructional material (*e.g.,* computers) to private as well as public schools.	
Religious Activities in Public Schools	
Ending classes early to allow students to attend ***off-school*** religious classes.	Ending classes early to give voluntary ***in-school*** religious classes.
Allowing religious student groups to meet in unused classrooms ***as any other*** student group.	***Prayer, Bible reading, or posting Ten Commandments*** in classrooms or at school football games.
	Requiring that "***creation science***" be taught.

CONTRACTS

TABLE OF CONTENTS

I. WHAT IS A CONTRACT? 1
A. GENERAL DEFINITION 1
B. LAW GOVERNING CONTRACTS 1
C. TYPES OF CONTRACTS 1
1. Classified by Formation 1
2. Classified by Acceptance 2
3. Void, Voidable, and Unenforceable Contracts 2
D. CREATION OF A CONTRACT 2

II. MUTUAL ASSENT—OFFER AND ACCEPTANCE 2
A. IN GENERAL 2
B. THE OFFER 4
1. Promise, Undertaking, or Commitment 4
2. Terms Must Be Definite and Certain 4
3. Communication Requirement 5
C. TERMINATION OF OFFER 5
1. Termination by Acts of Parties 5
2. Termination by Operation of Law 6
D. THE ACCEPTANCE 7
1. Who May Accept 7
2. Acceptance Must Be Unequivocal 7
3. Generally Acceptance Must Be Communicated 8
E. UNILATERAL OR BILATERAL CONTRACT 10
1. Interpreting Contract as Unilateral or Bilateral 10
2. Formation Problems 10

III. CONSIDERATION 10
A. INTRODUCTION 10
B. ELEMENTS OF CONSIDERATION 11
1. Bargained-for Exchange 11
2. Legal Value Element 11
C. MUTUAL AND ILLUSORY PROMISES—REQUIREMENT OF MUTUALITY . 12
1. Examples 12
2. Right to Choose Alternative Courses 13
D. NO REQUIREMENT THAT ALL CONSIDERATION BE VALID 13
E. SUBSTITUTES FOR CONSIDERATION 13
1. Promissory Estoppel or Detrimental Reliance 13
2. Modification Under the U.C.C. 13
3. Promises to Pay Legal Obligations Barred by Law 13
4. Seal 14

IV. REQUIREMENT THAT NO DEFENSES EXIST 14
A. DEFENSES TO FORMATION 14
1. Absence of Mutual Assent 14

2. Absence of Consideration 15
3. Public Policy Defenses—Illegality of Contract 15
B. DEFENSES BASED ON LACK OF CAPACITY 15
C. DEFENSES TO ENFORCEMENT 15
1. Statute of Frauds 15
2. Unconscionability 17

V. RIGHTS AND DUTIES OF NONPARTIES TO CONTRACT 17
A. INTRODUCTION 17
B. THIRD-PARTY BENEFICIARIES 17
1. Who Is Third-Party Beneficiary? 17
2. When Does Beneficiary Acquire Contractual Rights? 17
3. Who Can Sue Whom? 18
C. ASSIGNMENT OF RIGHTS AND DELEGATION OF DUTIES 18
1. Assignment 18
2. Delegation of Duties 20
D. NOVATION DISTINGUISHED 20

VI. RULES OF CONTRACT CONSTRUCTION AND THE PAROL EVIDENCE RULE . 20
A. RULES OF CONTRACT CONSTRUCTION 20
B. PAROL EVIDENCE RULE 21
1. Exceptions 21

VII. INTERPRETATION AND ENFORCEMENT OF THE CONTRACT 21
A. INTRODUCTION 21
B. WHEN HAS A CONTRACTING PARTY'S DUTY TO PERFORM BECOME ABSOLUTE? 21
1. Distinction Between Promise and Condition 21
2. Classification of Conditions 23
3. Have the Conditions Been Excused? 24
C. HAS THE DUTY TO PERFORM BEEN DISCHARGED? 26
1. Discharge by Performance or Tender of Performance 26
2. Discharge by Condition Subsequent 26
3. Discharge by Illegality 26
4. Discharge by Impossibility, Impracticability, or Frustration 26
5. Discharge by Rescission 27
6. Partial Discharge by Modification of Contract 28
7. Discharge by Novation 28
8. Discharge by Cancellation 28
9. Discharge by Release 28
10. Discharge by Substituted Contract 28
11. Discharge by Accord and Satisfaction 28
12. Discharge by Account Stated 29
13. Discharge by Lapse 29
14. Discharge by Operation of Law 29
15. Effect of Running of Statute of Limitations 29

VIII. BREACH OF CONTRACT AND AVAILABLE REMEDIES 29
A. WHEN DOES BREACH OCCUR? 29

B. MATERIAL OR MINOR BREACH? 30
   1. Tests for Materiality 30
   2. Timeliness of Performance 30
C. REMEDIES FOR BREACH 30
   1. Damages 30
   2. Suit in Equity for Specific Performance 32
   3. Rescission and Restitution 33
   4. Quasi-Contractual Relief 33

CONTRACTS

I. WHAT IS A CONTRACT?

A. GENERAL DEFINITION

A contract is a promise or set of promises, for breach of which the law gives a remedy, or the performance of which the law in some way recognizes as a duty.

B. LAW GOVERNING CONTRACTS

Generally, contracts are governed by the common law. Contracts for the sale of ***goods*** (movable, tangible property) are governed by Article 2 of the Uniform Commercial Code ("U.C.C.") as well as the common law. In such contracts, when Article 2 conflicts with the common law, Article 2 prevails. (*See* Sales outline for more detail on Article 2.)

C. TYPES OF CONTRACTS

Contracts are classified by how they are formed and how they can be accepted.

1. Classified by Formation

Contracts may be ***express*** (formed by language, oral or written) or ***implied*** (formed by manifestations of assent other than oral or written language, *i.e.*, by conduct).

a. Quasi-Contract

Quasi-contracts are ***not contracts***, but a way to avoid unjust enrichment. Thus, even if an agreement does not qualify as a contract, under a quasi-contract, a party can recover the benefit she has conferred on the other party.

CMR EXAMPLE CHART

THEORIES OF CONTRACT LIABILITY

Theory	Description	Example
Express Contract	Promises are communicated by ***language***.	X promises to paint Y's car in return for Y's promise to pay X $100.
Implied Contract	Parties' ***conduct*** indicates that they assented to be bound.	(i) X fills her car with gas at Y's gas station. There is a contract for purchase and sale of the gas. (ii) X watches Y paint X's house, knowing that Y mistakenly thought they had an agreement for Y to be paid for it.
Quasi-Contract (Not a contract at all)	One party is ***unjustly enriched*** at the expense of the other party, so that the enriched party must pay restitution to the other party equal to the unjust enrichment.	X contracts with Y to build a house for Y. X becomes ill and is unable to continue after completing a third of the work. X cannot sue on the contract, but may recover the benefit conferred on Y.

2. Classified by Acceptance

Contracts are either ***bilateral*** or ***unilateral***. Bilateral contracts require an exchange of promises. Unilateral contracts require the exchange of an act for a promise. Under the modern view, most contracts are bilateral. Unilateral contracts are limited to two circumstances: (i) where the offeror clearly indicates that performance is the ***only manner of acceptance***; or (ii) where there is an ***offer to the public*** clearly contemplating acceptance by performance (*e.g.,* a reward offer).

3. Void, Voidable, and Unenforceable Contracts

Certain contracts may not be enforceable:

a. ***A void contract*** is one ***without any legal effect*** from the beginning (*e.g.,* an agreement to commit a crime).

b. ***A voidable contract*** is one that a party may ***elect to avoid or ratify*** (*e.g.,* a contract by a minor).

c. ***An unenforceable contract*** is one otherwise valid but for which some ***defense*** exists extraneous to formation (*e.g.,* the Statute of Frauds).

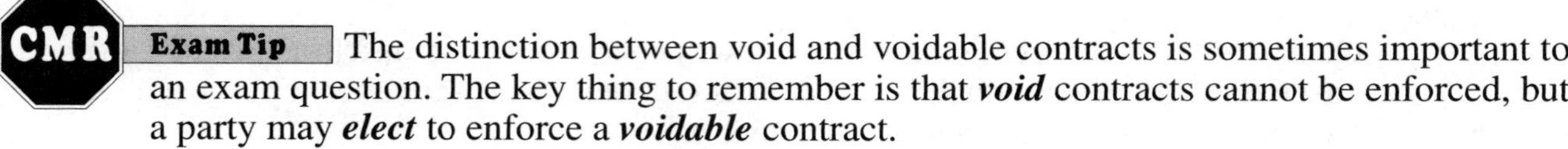

Exam Tip The distinction between void and voidable contracts is sometimes important to an exam question. The key thing to remember is that ***void*** contracts cannot be enforced, but a party may ***elect*** to enforce a ***voidable*** contract.

D. CREATION OF A CONTRACT

Three elements are required to create a contract:

1. ***Mutual assent***, *i.e.,* offer and acceptance;

2. ***Consideration*** or a substitute; and

3. ***No defenses*** to formation.

CMR **Exam Tip** Contract formation is a major topic on the exam. For any contract question, be sure that there really is an enforceable contract; *i.e.,* ***all three*** of the above elements must be present. Fact patterns sometimes greatly emphasize some elements (*e.g.,* offer and acceptance) to try to fool you into thinking that a contract has been formed, but on closer examination, you find that another element (*e.g.,* consideration) is missing. Remember to check carefully for all three elements. (Of course, if the ***facts state*** that one or more of the elements is present—or that a valid contract has been formed—don't waste your time analyzing elements already given to you.)

II. MUTUAL ASSENT—OFFER AND ACCEPTANCE

A. IN GENERAL

For an agreement to be enforced as a contract, there must be mutual assent. In other words, one party must accept the other's offer. Whether mutual assent is present will be determined by an objective standard; *i.e.,* did words or conduct manifest a present intention to contract?

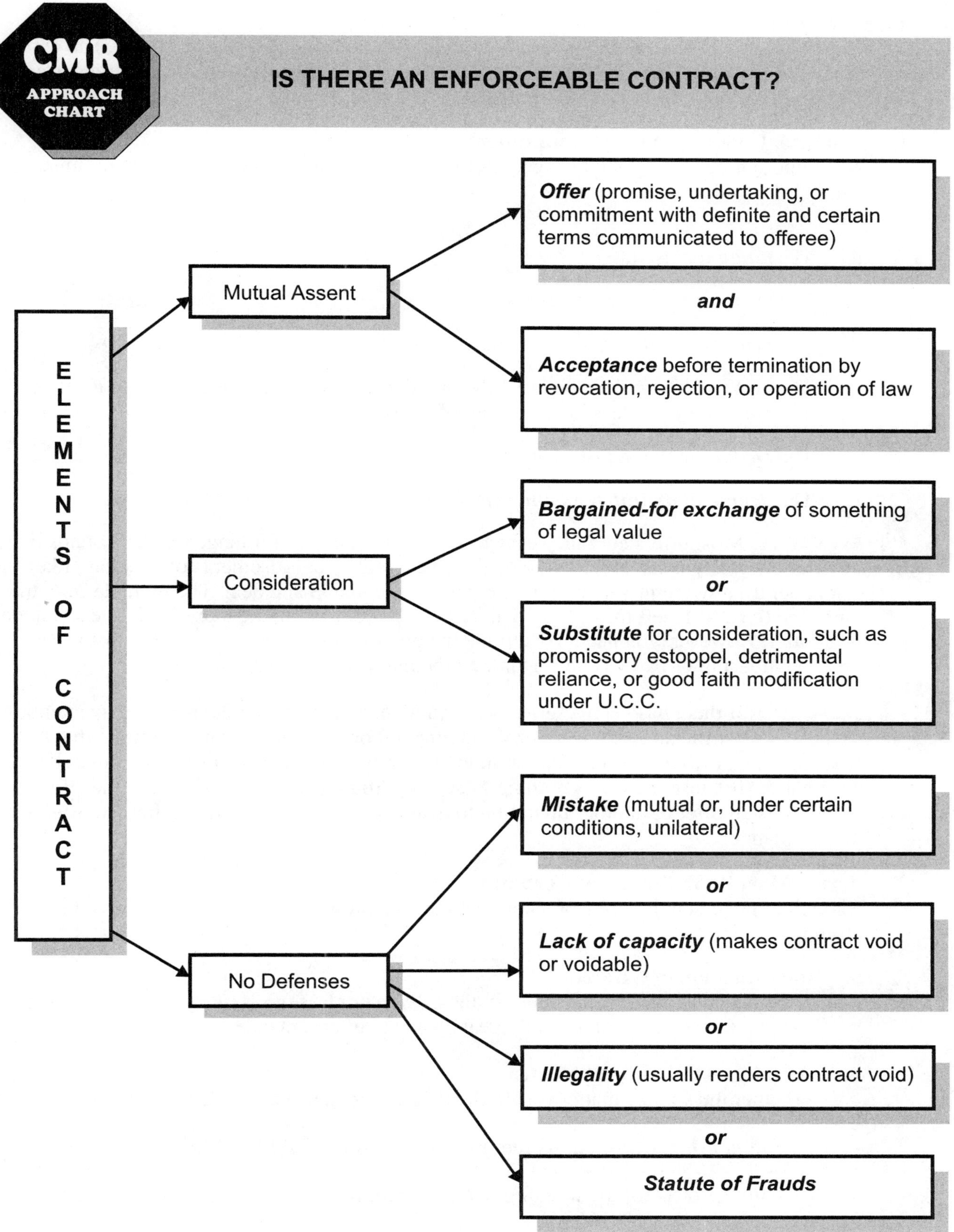
CMR
APPROACH CHART
IS THERE AN ENFORCEABLE CONTRACT?
ELEMENTS OF CONTRACT
Mutual Assent
Offer (promise, undertaking, or commitment with definite and certain terms communicated to offeree)
and
Acceptance before termination by revocation, rejection, or operation of law
Consideration
Bargained-for exchange of something of legal value
or
Substitute for consideration, such as promissory estoppel, detrimental reliance, or good faith modification under U.C.C.
No Defenses
Mistake (mutual or, under certain conditions, unilateral)
or
Lack of capacity (makes contract void or voidable)
or
Illegality (usually renders contract void)
or
Statute of Frauds

B. THE OFFER

An offer creates a power of acceptance in the offeree. To be valid, an offer must be: (i) an expression of ***promise, undertaking, or commitment*** to enter into a contract; (ii) ***definite and certain*** in its terms; and (iii) ***communicated*** to the offeree.

1. Promise, Undertaking, or Commitment

It is important to distinguish between preliminary negotiations (not offers) and promises (offers). Consider:

a. The ***language*** used;

b. The ***surrounding circumstances***;

c. The ***prior relationship*** of the parties;

d. The ***method of communication***—the broader the communicating media (*e.g.,* an advertisement), the less likely it is an offer;

e. The ***custom*** in the industry; and

f. The ***degree of definiteness and certainty*** of terms.

CMR **Exam Tip** Most offers are fairly easy to spot, but watch out for language that sounds like an offer but really is an invitation to deal. For example, advertisements often sound like offers but usually are just invitations for people to come in and deal. The more definite the language (*e.g.,* "I'll sell for . . ." or "I'll pay you $10 for . . ."), the more likely the statement is an offer. However, you need to examine the other factors (surrounding circumstances, prior relationship of parties, etc.). Don't be too hasty in your determination.

CMR **Exam Tip** If there has been a series of communications between the parties, pay attention to the legal significance, if any, of each statement. For example, if you determine that A's first statement to B is not an offer but an invitation to deal, then B's response cannot be an acceptance (because there was nothing to accept). You must then consider whether B's response is an offer or another invitation to deal. Keep checking until you find an offer and an acceptance.

2. Terms Must Be Definite and Certain

Enough of the essential terms of a contract must be provided to make it capable of being enforced.

a. Identification of Offeree

The offer must sufficiently identify the offeree or class of offerees to justify the inference that the offeror intended to create a power of acceptance.

b. Definiteness of Subject Matter

Whether the subject matter is sufficiently definite depends on the kind of contract.

(i) ***Real estate transactions*** require identification of ***land*** and ***price*** terms.

(ii) In contracts for the ***sale of goods***, the ***quantity*** must be certain or capable of being made certain. ("Requirements" and "output" offers are generally sufficient, as a good faith intendment is usually read into the contract. The subject matter is also sufficiently identified if the offer specifies a reasonable range of choices.)

(iii) In an ***employment*** contract, the ***duration*** of employment must be specified.

1) Reasonable Terms Supplied by Court

Certain ***missing*** terms may be supplied by the court if they are consistent with the parties' intent. Under the U.C.C., a reasonable price term and a reasonable time for performance may be supplied by the court.

2) Vagueness and Terms to Be Agreed on

A ***vague*** term may defeat formation of a contract unless acceptance or part performance makes the vague term clear. Formation fails if an offer provides that a material term will be agreed on at a future date.

3. Communication Requirement

The offer must be communicated to the offeree.

C. TERMINATION OF OFFER

An offer may be accepted only as long as it has not been terminated. It may be terminated by (i) an act of either party or (ii) operation of law.

1. Termination by Acts of Parties

a. Termination by Offeror—Revocation

The offeror terminates an offer if he: (i) directly communicates the revocation (*i.e.,* retraction of the offer) to the offeree; or (ii) acts inconsistently with continued willingness to maintain the offer, and the offeree receives correct information of this from a reliable source. Offers made by publication, etc., may be terminated only by use of comparable means of publication.

1) Effective When Received

Revocation is effective when received by the offeree (but publication of revocation is effective when published).

2) Offeror's Power to Revoke

Offers not supported by consideration or detrimental reliance can be revoked at will by the offeror, even if he has promised not to revoke for a certain period of time.

a) Limitations

The offeror's power to revoke is limited if:

(1) There is an ***option contract*** supported by consideration (*i.e.,* the party with the power of acceptance has paid for the offer's irrevocability);

(2) There is a ***firm offer under the U.C.C.*** (a signed writing by a merchant—*i.e.,* one who deals in goods of the kind sold or who has specialized knowledge of the business practices involved—promising to hold the offer open for some period of time);

(3) The offeree has ***detrimentally relied*** on the offer and the offeror could ***reasonably have expected*** such reliance; or

(4) In the case of a ***unilateral contract***, the offeree has embarked on performance (this is usually construed as an option contract giving the offeree reasonable time to complete performance).

b. Termination by Offeree—Rejection or Lapse of Time

1) Rejection

An offeree may reject an offer (i) expressly or (ii) by making a counteroffer (as distinguished from a mere inquiry).

CMR **Exam Tip** Remember that a counteroffer is ***both*** a rejection and a new offer. It terminates the original offer and reverses the roles of the parties: the offeree giving a counteroffer becomes the offeror of a new offer, which the other party may accept or reject. Thus, if A offers to sell his property, Blackacre, for $100,000, and B says, "I'll buy it for $90,000," what has happened? A's offer has been rejected and B has made an offer for $90,000, which A may accept or reject. B cannot later say to A, "All right, I'll take Blackacre for $100,000," and accept A's offer. It no longer exists because it was rejected. (Of course, A could accept B's new offer to buy it for $100,000.)

a) Effective when Received

A rejection is effective when received. Once an offer has been rejected, the original offer is not valid (*i.e.,* cannot be accepted); however, if the offeror restates the offer after it has been rejected, the offeree has the power to accept the new offer.

b) Rejection of Option

Rejection of an option does ***not*** terminate the offer; the offeree is still free to accept the offer within the option period ***unless*** the offeror has ***detrimentally relied*** on the offeree's rejection.

2) Lapse of Time

An offer may be terminated by the offeree's failure to accept within the time specified by the offer or within a reasonable period if no deadline was specified.

2. Termination by Operation of Law

The following events will terminate an offer:

a. ***Death or insanity of either party*** (unless the offer is of a kind the offeror could not terminate, *e.g.*, an option supported by consideration). Death or insanity need ***not*** be communicated to the other party;

b. ***Destruction*** of the proposed contract's ***subject matter***; or

c. ***Supervening illegality***.

CMR SUMMARY CHART

TERMINATION OF OFFER

	Revocation by Offeror	Rejection by Offeree	Termination by Operation of Law
When Effective	Effective when received	Effective when received	Effective when the death or insanity of either party, the destruction of the subject matter, or the supervening illegality occurs
Methods	Express revocation or implied (*e.g.,* offeree discovers offeror sold subject matter to someone else)	Express rejection, counteroffer, or lapse of reasonable time	Death or insanity of either party, destruction of subject matter, or supervening illegality
Limitations on Power to Terminate	Option contract, merchant's firm offer, detrimental reliance, beginning performance on unilateral contract	Generally cannot reject if already accepted	

D. THE ACCEPTANCE

Valid acceptance of a bilateral contract requires: (i) an ***offeree*** with the power of acceptance; (ii) ***unequivocal terms of acceptance***; and (iii) ***communication*** of acceptance.

1. Who May Accept

The person to whom the offer was addressed has the power of acceptance, as does a member of the class to whom the offer was addressed. Although the right to accept most contracts cannot be assigned, option contracts supported by consideration can be assigned to a "new" offeree.

2. Acceptance Must Be Unequivocal

a. Common Law

Acceptance must mirror the offeror's terms, neither omitting nor adding terms. Otherwise, it may be a counteroffer (*i.e.,* a rejection).

b. U.C.C. Rules

In contracts involving the sale of goods, an acceptance need ***not*** mirror the offer's terms (*i.e.,* an acceptance that deviates from the offer is ***not*** necessarily a rejection and counteroffer). Any acceptance that indicates an intention to enter into a contract is valid unless it is made conditional on the acceptance of new or different terms. Whether the offer terms or the acceptance terms govern depends on the status of the parties.

1) Nonmerchants—Terms of Offer Govern
If one of the parties is not a merchant, the terms of the offer control. The new or different terms are considered mere proposals.

2) Merchants—Acceptance Terms Usually Included
In transactions between merchants (*i.e.,* ***both*** parties are merchants), ***additional*** terms proposed in the acceptance ***become part of the contract*** unless they ***materially alter*** the agreement, the offer ***expressly limits acceptance*** to the terms of the offer, or the offeror ***objects within a reasonable time*** to the additional terms. Additional terms that materially alter the agreement do not prevent contract formation, but become part of the contract ***only if*** the offeror expressly assents to inclusion. There is a split of authority over whether ***different*** terms in the acceptance become part of the contract. Some courts treat different terms like additional terms, and they use the above test to determine whether the different terms should be part of the contract. Other courts follow the "knockout rule," which states that conflicting terms in the offer and acceptance are knocked out of the contract and the terms instead are provided by the U.C.C.

3. Generally Acceptance Must Be Communicated
Acceptance is judged on an objective standard (*i.e.,* would a reasonable person think there was an acceptance?); the offeree's subjective state of mind is irrelevant. The modern rule and the U.C.C. permit acceptance by ***any reasonable means*** unless the offeror unambiguously limits acceptance to particular means.

a. "Mailbox Rule"
Under the mailbox rule, if acceptance is by mail or similar means and properly addressed and stamped, it is ***effective at the moment of dispatch***. (If it is improperly sent, it is effective upon receipt.)

CMR Exam Tip The mailbox rule ("effective upon dispatch") applies only to ***acceptance***. It does not apply to other events in the contract setting, such as rejection or revocation.

1) Limitations on Mailbox Rule
The following limitations apply to the mailbox rule:

a) The rule does not apply if the ***offer stipulates*** that acceptance is not effective until received.

b) The rule does not apply if an ***option contract*** is involved (acceptance is effective upon receipt).

c) If the offeree sends a ***rejection and then sends an acceptance***, whichever arrives first is effective.

d) If the offeree sends an acceptance and then a rejection, the acceptance is effective (*i.e.,* the mailbox rule applies) ***unless the rejection arrives first and*** the offeror ***detrimentally relies*** on it.

EFFECT OF REJECTION OR REVOCATION ON OFFER

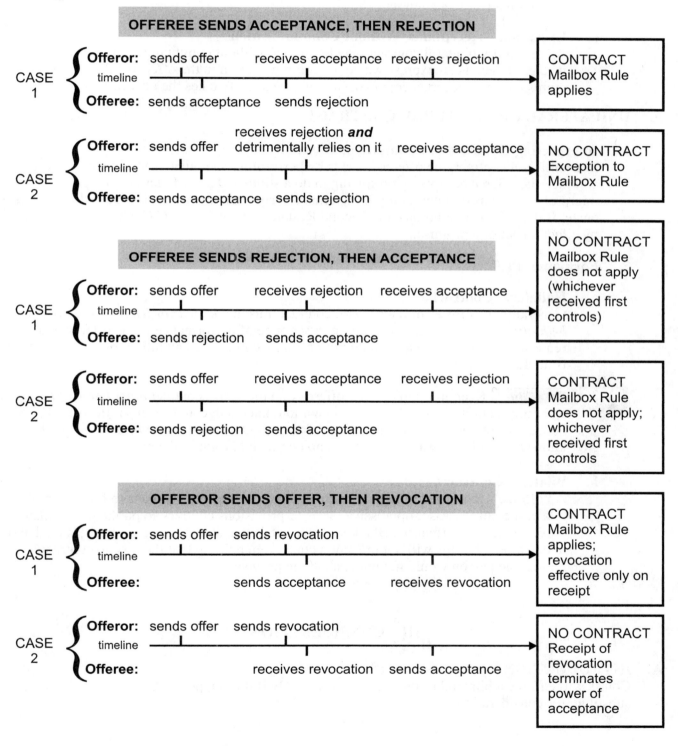

OFFEREE SENDS ACCEPTANCE, THEN REJECTION

CASE 1
- **Offeror:** sends offer — receives acceptance — receives rejection
- **Offeree:** sends acceptance — sends rejection
- Result: CONTRACT. Mailbox Rule applies

CASE 2
- **Offeror:** sends offer — receives rejection ***and*** detrimentally relies on it — receives acceptance
- **Offeree:** sends acceptance — sends rejection
- Result: NO CONTRACT. Exception to Mailbox Rule

OFFEREE SENDS REJECTION, THEN ACCEPTANCE

CASE 1
- **Offeror:** sends offer — receives rejection — receives acceptance
- **Offeree:** sends rejection — sends acceptance
- Result: NO CONTRACT. Mailbox Rule does not apply (whichever received first controls)

CASE 2
- **Offeror:** sends offer — receives acceptance — receives rejection
- **Offeree:** sends rejection — sends acceptance
- Result: CONTRACT. Mailbox Rule does not apply; whichever received first controls

OFFEROR SENDS OFFER, THEN REVOCATION

CASE 1
- **Offeror:** sends offer — sends revocation
- **Offeree:** sends acceptance — receives revocation
- Result: CONTRACT. Mailbox Rule applies; revocation effective only on receipt

CASE 2
- **Offeror:** sends offer — sends revocation
- **Offeree:** receives revocation — sends acceptance
- Result: NO CONTRACT. Receipt of revocation terminates power of acceptance

b. **Acceptance by Unauthorized Means**
An acceptance transmitted by unauthorized means is effective if it is actually received by the offeror while the offer is still in existence.

c. **"Crossing" Offers**
Since an offer is effective on receipt, offers stating the same terms that cross in the mail do not give rise to a contract.

d. **Exception—Acceptance Without Communication**
An executory bilateral contract may be formed without communication of acceptance where (i) there is an express waiver of communication in the offer; (ii) the offer requires an act as acceptance; or (iii) the offeree silently takes the offered benefits.

E. UNILATERAL OR BILATERAL CONTRACT

1. Interpreting Contract as Unilateral or Bilateral
In a unilateral contract, the offeree accepts by performing a stipulated act. In a bilateral contract, the offeree accepts by promising to do a stipulated act. Modern courts generally interpret an offer as unilateral only if its terms clearly warn that an act is required for acceptance. If the offer is ambiguous, the Second Restatement and the U.C.C. allow acceptance by either an act or a promise.

2. Formation Problems

a. **Unilateral Contracts**
Generally, the offeree of a unilateral contract must act ***with knowledge of the offer and be motivated*** by it. There is a duty to give notice of performance to the offeror if he requests notice or if the act would not normally come to his attention; otherwise, there is no duty to notify.

CMR **Exam Tip** Keep in mind that the offeree of a unilateral contract ***must know of the offer*** to accept it. If the "offeree" acts without knowledge and learns of the offer later, her acts were not an acceptance. Thus, if A finds O's watch and returns it to O without knowledge of O's reward offer, A has no contractual right to the reward.

b. **Bilateral Contracts**
An offeree's ignorance of certain contractual terms may be a defense to formation of a bilateral contract. Also, oppressive terms or provisions contrary to public policy may prevent contract formation. Blanket form recitals that state that the offeree has read and understood all terms will not prevent a court from holding that there is no contract if a reasonable person would not understand the provisions.

III. CONSIDERATION

A. INTRODUCTION
Courts will enforce a bilateral or unilateral contract only if it is supported by consideration or a substitute for consideration.

B. ELEMENTS OF CONSIDERATION

Consideration involves two elements: (i) "***bargain***"; and (ii) ***legal value***.

1. Bargained-for Exchange

The parties must exchange something. In the case of a bilateral contract, they exchange promises. In the case of a unilateral contract, they exchange a promise for an act.

a. Gift

There is no bargain involved (*i.e.,* no consideration) when one party gives a gift to another.

1) Act or Forbearance by Promisee

An act or forbearance by the promisee will be sufficient to form a bargain ***if it benefits*** the promisor.

2) Economic Benefit Not Required

If one party gives the other peace of mind or gratification in exchange for something, it may be sufficient to establish a bargain.

b. Past or Moral Consideration

A promise given in exchange for something already done does not satisfy the bargain requirement.

1) Exceptions

Where a past obligation is unenforceable because of a technical defense (*e.g.,* statute of limitations), that obligation will be enforceable ***if a new promise*** is made ***in writing*** or is ***partially performed***. Also, under the modern trend, if a past act was performed by the promisee at the promisor's ***request***, a ***new promise*** to pay for that act will be enforceable.

CMR Exam Tip Beware of questions that use the word "consideration" to refer to something already done, as in "In consideration of your having done X, I promise you $1,000." Under the general rule, this promise is not enforceable since the promise is given in exchange for past acts.

2. Legal Value Element

a. Adequacy of Consideration

In general, courts do ***not*** inquire into the adequacy or fairness of consideration. However, if something is entirely devoid of value (token consideration), it is insufficient. Sham consideration (recited in the contract, but not actually paid) may also be insufficient. Where there is a possibility of value in the thing bargained for, consideration will be found even if the value never comes into existence.

b. Legal Benefit and Legal Detriment Theories

The majority of courts require that a party incur ***detriment*** (by doing something he is not legally obligated to do or by refraining from something he has a legal right to do) to satisfy the legal value element. Under the minority rule, conferring a benefit on the other party is also sufficient.

c. **Specific Situations**

1) **Preexisting Legal Duty**
Traditionally, performing or promising to perform an existing legal duty is ***insufficient*** consideration.

a) **Exceptions**
The preexisting legal duty rule is riddled with exceptions; there is consideration if:

(i) ***New or different*** consideration is promised;

(ii) The promise is to ***ratify a voidable obligation*** (*e.g.,* a promise to ratify a minor's contract after reaching majority, a promise to go through with a contract despite the other party's fraud);

(iii) The preexisting duty is ***owed to a third person*** rather than to the promisor;

(iv) There is an ***honest dispute*** as to the duty; or

(v) There are ***unforeseen circumstances*** sufficient to discharge a party.

Any ***good faith*** agreement modifying a contract subject to the ***U.C.C.*** needs ***no consideration*** to be binding.

CMR **Exam Tip** Although payment of a smaller sum than due on an existing debt is generally ***not*** sufficient consideration for a promise by the creditor to discharge the debt, courts will attempt to avoid this result by applying the above exceptions. Thus, see if there is new or different consideration given in the facts (*e.g.,* payment ***earlier*** than required or payment in ***stock*** instead of cash); this change in performance could make the payment of a smaller amount sufficient consideration.

2) **Forbearance to Sue**
A promise to refrain from suing on a claim may constitute consideration if the claim is valid or the claimant ***in good faith*** believed the claim was valid.

C. MUTUAL AND ILLUSORY PROMISES—REQUIREMENT OF MUTUALITY

Consideration must exist on both sides of a contract (although the benefit of the consideration generally need not flow to all parties). If only one party is bound to perform, the promise is illusory and will not be enforced. Courts often supply implied promises (*e.g.,* a party must use her best efforts) to infer mutuality.

1. **Examples**
The following are common examples of contracts that satisfy the mutuality requirement:

a. Requirements and output contracts;

b. Conditional promises, unless the condition is entirely within the promisor's control;

c. Contracts where a party has the right to cancel, if that right is somehow restricted (*e.g.,* a party must give 60 days' notice);

d. Voidable promises (*e.g.,* one made by an infant);

e. Unilateral and option contracts; and

f. Gratuitous suretyship promises made before consideration flows to the principal debtor.

CMR **Exam Tip** Closely analyze the wording of contract terms; language can make a big difference here. For example, a valid requirements or output contract term will say, "all the widgets I require" or "all that you produce," but a term such as "all the widgets I want" or "all you want to sell me" is illusory.

2. Right to Choose Alternative Courses

A promise to choose one of several alternative means of performance is illusory ***unless every alternative*** involves legal detriment to the promisor. The promise will not be found illusory if: (i) at least one alternative involves legal detriment and the power to choose rests with the promisee or a third party, or (ii) a valuable alternative (*i.e.,* one involving legal detriment) is actually selected.

D. NO REQUIREMENT THAT ALL CONSIDERATION BE VALID

There is no requirement that each of the promises given as consideration be sufficient as consideration (*i.e.*, one promise may be defective and another sufficient).

E. SUBSTITUTES FOR CONSIDERATION

In some special situations, consideration as defined above is not necessary to create contractual liability. In these cases, a "substitute" for consideration will suffice.

1. Promissory Estoppel or Detrimental Reliance

Promissory estoppel is a sufficient substitute. The following elements must be present: (i) the promisor should ***reasonably expect*** her promise ***to induce action or forbearance***, (ii) of a ***definite and substantial*** character, and (iii) such action or forbearance is ***in fact induced***.

CMR **Exam Tip** A valid contract is better than an agreement that can be enforced only by promissory estoppel because some states limit recovery under promissory estoppel "as justice requires." Thus, in a question asking whether a party can prevail based on an agreement, always check first to see if there is a valid contract. Only if there is not should you consider promissory estoppel as a proper choice.

2. Modification Under the U.C.C.

Under the U.C.C., consideration is ***not*** necessary to a good faith written modification of a contract.

3. Promises to Pay Legal Obligations Barred by Law

If a legal obligation is not enforceable under law (*e.g.*, a debt barred by the statute of limitations), a new promise to fulfill the legal obligation is enforceable if in ***writing***. However, it will be enforceable only according to ***the new terms***, not the terms of the original legal obligation.

4. Seal
In many states and under the U.C.C., a seal is ***no longer a substitute*** for consideration.

IV. REQUIREMENT THAT NO DEFENSES EXIST

A. DEFENSES TO FORMATION

1. Absence of Mutual Assent

a. Mutual Mistake

A mistake by ***both parties*** is a defense if:

(i) The mistake concerns a ***basic assumption*** on which the contract was made;

(ii) The mistake has a ***material adverse effect*** on the agreed-upon exchange; and

(iii) The adversely affected party ***did not assume the risk*** of the mistake.

1) Assumption of Risk
Note that when the parties know that their assumption is doubtful (so-called conscious ignorance), mutual mistake is not a defense—the parties will be deemed to have assumed the risk that their assumption was wrong.

2) Mistake in Value Generally No Defense
A mistake in value generally goes unremedied, as courts presume parties assume the risk of determining value. *But note:* There are exceptions (such as when the parties rely on a third party to establish value).

b. Unilateral Mistake

Whether it be of identity, subject matter, or computation, a mistake by one party is generally ***insufficient*** to make a contract voidable. However, if the nonmistaken party knew or should have known of the mistake, the contract is voidable by the mistaken party.

c. Mistake by Intermediary (Transmission)

Where there is a mistake by an intermediary (*e.g.,* a telegraph company makes a mistake), the message usually will be operative ***as transmitted*** unless the party receiving the message should have been aware of the mistake.

d. Latent Ambiguity Mistakes

If the contract includes an ambiguous term, the result depends on the parties' awareness of the ambiguity:

(i) Neither party aware—no contract unless both parties intended the same meaning;

(ii) Both parties aware—no contract unless both parties intended the same meaning;

(iii) One party aware—binding contract based on what the ignorant party reasonably believed to be the meaning of ambiguous words.

Ambiguity is one area where subjective intent is taken into account.

e. Misrepresentation

If a party induces another to enter into a contract by using ***fraudulent misrepresentation*** (*e.g.,* by asserting information she knows is untrue) or by using ***nonfraudulent material misrepresentation*** (*e.g.,* by asserting information that she does not know is untrue but that would induce a reasonable person to enter into a contract), the contract is ***voidable*** by the innocent party if she ***justifiably relied*** on the misrepresentation. *Distinguish:* If there is ***fraud in the factum*** (*i.e.,* if a party is tricked into assenting without understanding the significance of her action) rather than fraudulent misrepresentation (which is a type of ***fraud in the inducement***), the contract is ***void,*** rather than voidable.

2. Absence of Consideration

If promises exchanged at the formation stage lack elements of bargain or legal detriment, no contract exists.

3. Public Policy Defenses—Illegality of Contract

If the ***consideration or subject matter*** of a contract is illegal (*e.g.,* a contract to commit a murder), the contract is void. *Exceptions:* (i) the plaintiff is unaware of the illegality while the defendant knows of the illegality; (ii) the parties are not in pari delicto (*i.e.,* one party is not as culpable as the other); or (iii) the illegality is the failure to obtain a license when the license is for revenue-raising purposes rather than for protection of the public. If only the ***purpose*** behind the contract is illegal, the contract is ***voidable*** by a party who was (i) unaware of the purpose; or (ii) aware but did not facilitate the purpose ***and*** the purpose does not involve serious moral turpitude (*e.g.,* murder).

B. DEFENSES BASED ON LACK OF CAPACITY

In most jurisdictions, ***persons under age 18*** lack capacity to contract. (Some exceptions exist, *e.g.,* contracts providing for the incapacitated party's necessities.) Upon reaching majority, the infant may affirm her contractual obligation (if there is no express disaffirmance, this will be construed as affirmance). A contract between an infant and an adult is voidable by the infant but binding on the adult. ***Insane persons*** lack capacity, although such persons may contract during a lucid interval. ***Intoxicated persons*** may also lack capacity if the other party has reason to know of the intoxication. Contracts induced by ***duress and coercion*** are voidable.

Exam Tip Duress usually requires ***more*** than one party's taking economic advantage of another (*e.g.,* by charging a high price for something the other party desperately needs).

C. DEFENSES TO ENFORCEMENT

1. Statute of Frauds

a. When Agreement Is Unenforceable

Certain agreements ***must be in writing*** (evidenced by a memorandum) to be enforced. These agreements are:

1) Promises by ***executors or administrators*** to pay estates' debts ***out of their own funds***;

2) Promises to ***answer for the debt or default of another*** (*i.e.,* to act as a surety);

3) Promises made in consideration of ***marriage***;

4) Promises creating an ***interest in land*** (but leasehold interests for one year or less generally are not subject to the Statute);

5) Promises that by their terms ***cannot be performed within one year*** (the year runs from the date of agreement, not the date of performance; lifetime contracts are not within the Statute because they could be performed within a year); and

6) Agreements for the ***sale of goods for $500 or more, except*** (i) specially manufactured goods, (ii) a written confirmation of an oral agreement between merchants, (iii) admission in pleadings or court that a contract for goods existed, or (iv) partial payment or delivery made and accepted.

CMR **Exam Tip** Statute of Frauds issues are often raised in MBE questions. Remember that the Statute does not apply to all contracts. You must check the facts to see whether the contract falls within any of the covered areas (above). An easy way to remember agreements covered by the Statute of Frauds is by using the acronym ***MY LEGS***: Marriage, (within one) Year, Land, Executor (or Administrator), Goods (for $500 or more), Surety.

b. Memorandum Requirements

The Statute is satisfied if the writing contains the following:

1) The ***identity of parties*** sought to be charged;

2) Identification of the ***contract's subject matter***;

3) ***Terms and conditions*** of the agreement;

4) Recital of the ***consideration***; and

5) The ***signature of the party to be charged*** or his agent.

CMR **Exam Tip** To be sufficient under the Statute of Frauds, something ***in writing*** must show the above items. The writing need not be a full-fledged contract, nor need it even be one piece of paper. Thus, several pieces of correspondence between the parties could be a sufficient memorandum of the agreement; a fax or a memo written on a napkin also could suffice. The key is that there is something in writing.

CMR **Exam Tip** Also note that the memorandum does ***not*** need to be signed by both parties to the contract. Only the party to be charged (*i.e.,* the person to be sued) must sign. Thus, if a fact situation has an otherwise sufficient writing that is signed by the seller but not the buyer, if the buyer is suing the seller, the writing is enough for the Statute of Frauds. However, if the seller sued the buyer, there would not be a sufficient memorandum. (*Compare:* One signature may be enough for ***merchants'*** contracts under the ***U.C.C.; See*** Sales outline.)

c. When Statute Is Not Applicable

Noncompliance with the Statute renders a contract unenforceable. The Statute is not applicable to the extent of admissions in court that a contract was formed or to the extent there was part performance. For a ***sale of goods***, part payment or acceptance and receipt of part of the goods takes the contract out of the Statute to the extent of the part payment or partial acceptance and receipt of goods. For a ***sale of land***, most jurisdictions do not apply the Statute if there is performance that unequivocally indicates that the parties contracted for the sale of land. Most jurisdictions require two of the following: payment (in whole or in part), possession, and/or valuable improvements. *Note:* In cases where it would be inequitable to allow the Statute of Frauds to defeat a meritorious claim, courts will occasionally use the doctrine of ***promissory estoppel*** to remove the contract from the Statute.

2. Unconscionability

A contract may be voidable where the clauses are so one-sided as to be unconscionable. This includes contracts with inconspicuous risk-shifting provisions (*e.g.,* disclaimers of warranty) and contracts of adhesion ("take it or leave it"). Unconscionability is tested ***at the time the contract was made***, not later (*i.e.,* the contract must have been unfair when it was entered into). The defense is often applied where one party has substantially superior bargaining power.

Exam Tip Unconscionability is seldom a good defense on the MBE. That a contract turned out badly for one party is insufficient in itself to give rise to unconscionability. Look for great differences in bargaining power (*e.g.,* big company vs. average consumer).

V. RIGHTS AND DUTIES OF NONPARTIES TO CONTRACT

A. INTRODUCTION

Nonparties to a contract may have rights or duties in connection with the contract.

B. THIRD-PARTY BENEFICIARIES

In the typical third-party beneficiary situation, A (the promisee) contracts with B (the promisor) that B will render some performance to C (the third-party beneficiary).

1. Who Is Third-Party Beneficiary?

a. Intended vs. Incidental Beneficiary

Only intended beneficiaries have contractual rights, not incidental beneficiaries. In determining if a beneficiary is intended, consider whether the beneficiary (i) is ***identified*** in the contract, (ii) ***receives performance directly*** from the promisor, or (iii) has some ***relationship with the promisee*** to indicate intent to benefit.

b. Creditor vs. Donee Beneficiary

There are two types of intended beneficiaries: (i) a creditor beneficiary—a person to whom a debt is owed by the promisee, and (ii) a donee beneficiary—a person the promisee intends to benefit gratuitously.

2. When Does Beneficiary Acquire Contractual Rights?

A third party can enforce a contract only when his rights have vested. This occurs when he (i) ***manifests assent*** to a promise in the manner requested by the parties; (ii) brings a ***suit to***

enforce the promise; or (iii) ***materially changes position*** in justifiable reliance on the promise. Prior to vesting, the promisee and promisor are free to modify or rescind the beneficiary's rights under the contract.

3. Who Can Sue Whom?

a. Third-Party Beneficiary vs. Promisor

A beneficiary may sue the promisor on the contract. The promisor may raise against the third-party beneficiary any defense that the promisor has against the promisee. Whether the promisor may use the defenses the promisee would have against the third-party beneficiary depends on whether the promisor made an absolute promise to pay or only a promise to pay what the promisee owes the beneficiary. If the promise is absolute, the promisor cannot assert the promisee's defenses; if the promise is not absolute, the promisor can assert the promisee's defenses.

b. Third-Party Beneficiary vs. Promisee

A ***creditor*** beneficiary can sue the promisee on the existing obligation between them. She may also sue the promisor, but may obtain only one satisfaction. A donee beneficiary has no right to sue the promisee unless grounds for a detrimental reliance remedy exist (*see* III.E.1., *supra*).

c. Promisee vs. Promisor

A promisee may sue the promisor both at law and in equity for specific performance if the promisor is not performing for the third person.

C. ASSIGNMENT OF RIGHTS AND DELEGATION OF DUTIES

1. Assignment

In the typical assignment situation, X (the obligor) contracts with Y (the assignor). Y assigns his right to X's performance to Z (the assignee).

a. What Rights May Be Assigned?

Generally, all contractual rights may be assigned. *Exceptions:* (i) an assignment that would ***substantially change*** the obligor's duty or risk (*e.g.*, personal service contracts where the service is unique, requirements and output contracts where the assignee will substantially vary the quantity); (ii) an assignment of future rights to ***arise from future contracts*** (not future rights in already existing contracts); and (iii) an assignment ***prohibited by law*** (*e.g.*, wage assignments).

1) Nonassignment Provisions

A clause prohibiting assignment of ***"the contract"*** will be construed as barring only delegation of the assignor's duties. A clause prohibiting assignment of ***contractual rights*** generally does not bar assignment, but merely gives the obligor the right to sue for damages. However, if the contract provides that attempts to assign ***will be void***, the parties can bar assignment. Also, if the assignee has notice of the nonassignment clause, an assignment will be ineffective.

b. What Is Necessary for an Effective Assignment?

For an assignment to be effective, the assignor must manifest an intent to immediately and completely transfer her rights. A writing is usually not required to have an effective assignment. The right being assigned must be adequately described. It is not necessary to use the word "assign"; any accepted words of transfer will suffice. A gratuitous assignment is effective; consideration is not required.

c. **Is Assignment Revocable or Irrevocable?**
An assignment for ***consideration*** is irrevocable. An assignment not for consideration is generally revocable. However, a gratuitous assignment is irrevocable if: (i) the obligor has already performed; (ii) a token chose (*i.e.,* a tangible claim, such as a stock certificate) is delivered; (iii) an assignment of a simple chose (*i.e.,* an intangible claim, such as a contract right) is put in writing; or (iv) the assignee can show detrimental reliance on the gratuitous assignment (*i.e.*, estoppel). A revocable gratuitous assignment may be terminated by: (i) the death or bankruptcy of the assignor; (ii) notice of revocation by the assignor to the assignee or the obligor; (iii) the assignor taking performance directly from the obligor; or (iv) subsequent assignment of the same right by the assignor to another.

1) **Effect of Assignment**
The effect of an assignment is to establish privity of contract between the obligor and the assignee while extinguishing privity between the obligor and the assignor.

d. **Who Can Sue Whom?**

1) **Assignee vs. Obligor**
The assignee can sue the obligor, as the assignee is the real party in interest; *i.e.,* the assignee—not the assignor—is entitled to performance under the contract. (The obligor has as a defense against the assignee any defense inherent in the contract, *e.g.,* failure of consideration and other defenses that came into existence before the obligor had knowledge of the assignment.) The obligor cannot raise by way of defense any defenses the assignor might have against the assignee.

2) **Assignee vs. Assignor**
The assignee can sue the assignor for wrongfully exercising the power to revoke in an irrevocable assignment situation. An action by the assignee against the assignor may also lie where the obligor successfully asserts a defense against the assignor in an action brought by the assignee against the obligor to enforce the obligation. The assignor will not be liable to the assignee if the obligor is incapable of performing.

e. **What Problems Exist If There Have Been Successive Assignments of Same Rights?**
If the first assignment is revocable, a subsequent assignment revokes it. If it is irrevocable, ***the first assignment will usually prevail*** over a subsequent assignment. Several exceptions exist (***if*** the second assignee has ***paid value and taken without notice*** of the first assignment): (i) the subsequent assignee gets the first judgment against the obligor; (ii) the subsequent assignee gets the first payment of a claim from the obligor; (iii) the subsequent assignee gets delivery of a token chose; (iv) the subsequent assignee is the party to a novation releasing the assignor; and (v) the subsequent assignee can proceed against the first assignee on an estoppel theory (estoppel could, of course, operate against the subsequent assignee as well).

2. Delegation of Duties

In the typical delegation situation, Y (the obligor/delegator) promises to perform for X (the obligee). Y delegates her duty to Z (the delegate).

a. What Duties May Be Delegated?

Generally, all duties may be delegated. *Exceptions:* (i) the duties involve ***personal judgment and skill***; (ii) delegation would ***change the obligee's expectancy*** (*e.g.*, requirements and output contracts); (iii) a ***special trust*** was reposed in the delegator by the other party to the contract; and (iv) there is a ***contractual restriction*** on delegation.

b. Requirements for Effective Delegation

The delegator must manifest a present intention to make a delegation. There are no special formalities to be complied with to have a valid delegation. It may be written or oral.

CMR **Exam Tip** Although "assignment" and "delegation" have precise meanings (rights are assigned and duties are delegated), on the MBE the terms are often used loosely. Thus, a question might state initially that "Y assigned his rights in the contract to X," but the facts later show that duties were also delegated.

c. Rights and Liabilities of Parties

The obligee must accept performance from the delegate of all duties that may be delegated. The delegator remains liable on the contract; thus, the obligee may sue the delegator for nonperformance by the delegate. The obligee may sue the delegate for nonperformance, but can require the delegate to perform ***only if*** there has been an ***assumption*** (*i.e.,* the delegate promises he will perform the duty delegated and this promise is supported by consideration or its equivalent). This promise creates a contract between the delegator and the delegate in which the obligee is a third-party beneficiary.

d. Terminology

Today, words assigning "the contract" or "all my rights under the contract" are usually construed as including an assumption of the duties by the assignee, unless a contrary intention appears.

D. NOVATION DISTINGUISHED

Novation substitutes a new party for an original party to the contract. It requires assent of all parties and completely releases the original party. (*See* VII.C.7., *infra.*)

VI. RULES OF CONTRACT CONSTRUCTION AND THE PAROL EVIDENCE RULE

A. RULES OF CONTRACT CONSTRUCTION

A contract is construed as a "whole," and according to the ordinary meaning of words. If there is an inconsistency between provisions, written or typed provisions prevail over printed provisions.

Ambiguities are construed against the party preparing the contract, absent evidence of the intention of the parties. Courts look to the custom and usage in a particular business and in a particular locale to determine the parties' intent when it is unclear. Courts generally will try to reach a determination that a contract is valid and enforceable.

B. PAROL EVIDENCE RULE

Evidence of ***prior or contemporaneous*** negotiations and agreements that contradict, modify, or vary contractual terms is inadmissible if the written contract is intended as a ***complete and final expression*** of the parties. A "merger clause" (recital that the contract is complete on its face) strengthens the presumption that the written document is final.

1. Exceptions

Evidence of the following is admissible: (i) ***formation defects*** (*e.g.,* fraud, duress, mistake, illegality); (ii) the existence of a ***condition precedent*** to a contract; (iii) the parties' intent regarding ***ambiguous terms***; (iv) ***consideration problems*** (*e.g.,* consideration stated in the contract was never paid); (v) a prior valid agreement which (as by mistake) is ***incorrectly reflected in the writing***; (vi) a ***collateral agreement*** if it does not contradict or vary the main contract and if it is not so closely connected as to be part of the main contract; and (vii) ***subsequent modifications***.

VII. INTERPRETATION AND ENFORCEMENT OF THE CONTRACT

A. INTRODUCTION

Two basic questions must be asked: (i) whether a present duty to perform has arisen (*i.e.,* is there an absolute promise ***or*** have all conditions been met or excused); and (ii) whether the duty to perform has been discharged. If a present duty to perform has arisen and has not been discharged, nonperformance will be a contractual breach.

B. WHEN HAS A CONTRACTING PARTY'S DUTY TO PERFORM BECOME ABSOLUTE?

1. Distinction Between Promise and Condition

a. Definitions

A ***promise*** is a commitment to do or refrain from doing something. It may be conditional or unconditional. A ***condition*** is an event the occurrence or nonoccurrence of which will create, limit, or extinguish the absolute duty to perform; it is a promise modifier.

b. Interpretation of Provision as Promise or Condition

It is not always clear whether a contract provision is a promise or a condition. The basic test is the "***intent of the parties***," as judged by the words of the agreement, the prior practices of the parties, and custom in the business. In doubtful situations, the courts prefer a promise, since a promise will support the contract.

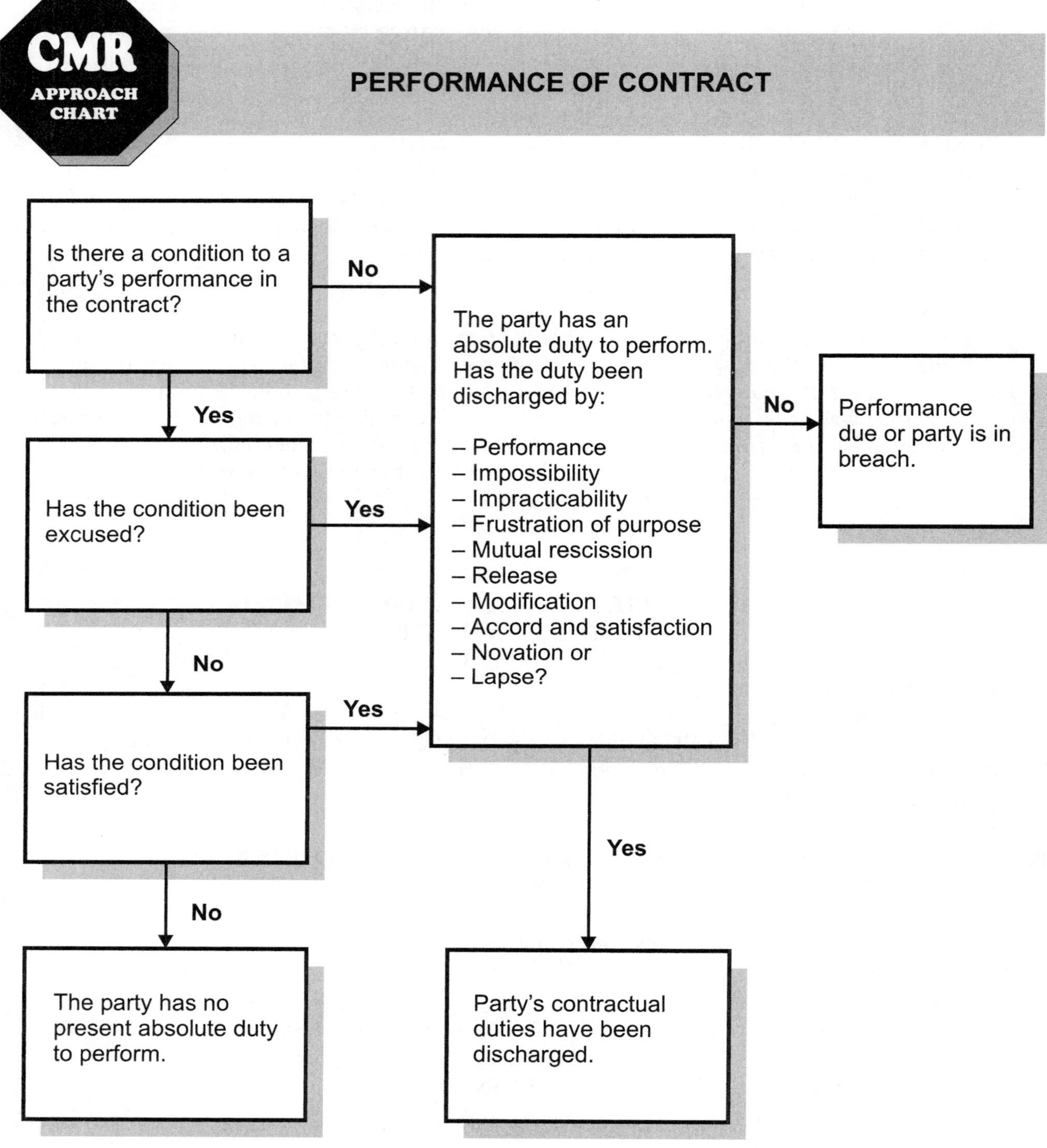
CMR
APPROACH
CHART
PERFORMANCE OF CONTRACT
Is there a condition to a party's performance in the contract?
No
Yes
Has the condition been excused?
Yes
No
Has the condition been satisfied?
Yes
No
The party has no present absolute duty to perform.
The party has an absolute duty to perform. Has the duty been discharged by:
– Performance
– Impossibility
– Impracticability
– Frustration of purpose
– Mutual rescission
– Release
– Modification
– Accord and satisfaction
– Novation or
– Lapse?
No
Performance due or party is in breach.
Yes
Party's contractual duties have been discharged.

Exam Tip The distinction between a promise and a condition is important, since the failure of a ***promise*** gives rise to a ***breach***, whereas the failure of a ***condition relieves*** a party of the obligation to perform.

c. **Condition or Promise**

A provision may be a promise for one party ***and*** a condition for the other, as in an exchange where the second party's duty to pay is conditioned on the first party's performance of her promise. A provision may also be both a promise and a condition for the same party, as where a party is under a duty to reasonably ensure that a condition comes about (*e.g.,* to secure financing).

2. Classification of Conditions

a. According to Time of Occurrence

A condition ***precedent*** is one that must occur before an absolute duty of performance arises in the other party. Conditions ***concurrent*** are those that are capable of occurring together, as where property is tendered in exchange for cash. A condition ***subsequent*** is one that cuts off an already existing duty of performance.

CMR SUMMARY CHART

CONDITIONS—TIME OF OCCURRENCE

Type	Definition	Effect of Occurrence of Condition	Example
Condition Precedent	Condition must occur before performance is due.	Performance due.	Agreement to pay $10,000 "if my house is sold by April 1." No payment unless house is sold by April 1.
Conditions Concurrent	Conditions to occur at the same time.	If one condition has occurred, performance of the other is due.	Agreement to pay $100,000 for Blackacre. Money and deed exchanged in same transaction.
Condition Subsequent	Condition cuts off already existing duty.	Duty to perform is excused.	Agreement to buy Blackacre for $100,000 unless zoning is changed. If zoning is changed, no duty to pay $100,000 or transfer deed.

CMR **Exam Tip** Theoretically, it is the plaintiff's burden to plead and prove that all conditions precedent to the defendant's duty have been performed, and it is the defendant's burden to plead and prove that a condition subsequent has cut off his duty. In practice, however, pleading rules, presumptions, and the court's discretion in the interest of justice may shift these burdens.

b. Express, Implied, and Constructive Conditions

Express conditions are those expressed in the contract. ***Implied*** conditions (called "implied in fact" conditions) are those to be inferred from evidence of the parties' intention. ***Constructive*** conditions (called "implied in law" conditions) are those read into a contract by the court ***without regard to the parties' intention*** in order to ensure that the parties receive what they bargained for. Constructive conditions may relate to the time of performance, *i.e.,* which party performs first.

3. Have the Conditions Been Excused?

A duty of performance becomes absolute when conditions are either ***performed or excused***. Conditions may be excused in several ways:

a. Excuse of Condition by Failure to Cooperate

A party who wrongfully prevents a condition from occurring will no longer be given the benefit of it.

b. Excuse of Condition by Actual Breach

An actual, material breach by one party excuses the other's duty of counterperformance. (A minor breach might suspend the duty, but will not excuse it.)

c. Excuse of Condition by Anticipatory Repudiation

Anticipatory repudiation must be unequivocal, not just an expression of doubt. It applies ***only if*** there are ***executory*** (unperformed) ***duties on both sides*** of a bilateral contract. (If the nonrepudiating party has nothing further to do at the time of repudiation—he has performed his part of the contract—he must wait until the time originally set for performance; the repudiator may change his mind up to that time.) Anticipatory repudiation gives the nonrepudiating party four alternatives:

(i) Treat the contract as totally repudiated and ***sue immediately***;

(ii) ***Suspend his own performance*** and wait until the performance is due to sue;

(iii) Treat the repudiation as an ***offer to rescind and treat the contract as discharged***; or

(iv) ***Ignore*** the repudiation and urge performance (but note that by urging the repudiating party to perform, the nonrepudiating party is ***not*** waiving the repudiation—she can still sue for breach and is excused from performing unless the repudiation is retracted).

Repudiation may be retracted until the nonrepudiating party has accepted the repudiation or detrimentally relied on it.

d. Excuse of Condition by Prospective Inability or Unwillingness to Perform

A party might have reasonable grounds to believe the other party will be unable or unwilling to perform when performance is due.

1) **Distinguish from Anticipatory Repudiation**
Prospective inability to perform merely ***raises doubts*** about performance; thus, it does not meet the unequivocality requirement of anticipatory repudiation.

2) **What Conduct Will Suffice?**
Conduct is judged according to a reasonable person standard.

3) **Effect of Prospective Failure**
The innocent party may ***suspend*** her own performance until she receives adequate assurances of performance. If these are not forthcoming, she may treat the failure as a repudiation.

4) **Retraction**
Retraction is possible, but may be ineffective if the other party has changed her position in reliance on the prospective failure.

e. **Excuse of Condition by Substantial Performance**
Where a party has almost completely performed his duties, but has breached in some minor way, the rule of substantial performance avoids forfeiture of a return performance.

1) **Application**
The rule is generally applied only where ***constructive*** conditions are involved; applying it to express conditions might defeat the express intent of the parties that performance be perfect. Substantiality of performance is judged by the same standards as materiality of breach. (*See* VIII.B.1., *infra.*) The rule is usually ***not*** applied if the breach was ***willful***.

2) **Damages Offset**
The substantially performing party may be required to pay damages to compensate the other party for the incomplete performance.

3) **Applicability of Substantial Performance to Sale of Goods**
Although the U.C.C. sets forth a "perfect tender rule," it is subject to exceptions, such as the provision for a seller's right to cure defective tender.

f. **Excuse of Condition by Divisibility of Contract**
Where a party performs one of the units of a divisible contract, she is entitled to the agreed equivalent for that unit even though she fails to perform the other units.

1) **What Is a Divisible Contract?**
Three tests must be met to find that a contract is divisible:

a) The performance of each party is divided into two or more parts under the contract;

b) The number of parts due from each party is the same; and

c) The performance of each part by one party is the agreed equivalent of the corresponding part by the other party.

2) **Installment Contracts**
Under the U.C.C., a contract that authorizes or requires delivery in separate lots is an installment contract. The buyer may declare a total breach only if defects in an installment are such as to substantially impair the value of the ***entire contract***.

g. **Excuse of Condition by Waiver or Estoppel**

1) **Estoppel Waiver**
A party may "waive" a condition by indicating that he will not insist on it. However, such a waiver may be retracted at any time unless the other party relies on the waiver and changes her position to her detriment. Upon such detrimental reliance, the waiving party is estopped from asserting the condition.

2) **Election Waiver**
If a condition is broken, the party who was to have its benefit may either terminate his liability or continue under the contract. If he chooses the latter, he is deemed to have waived the condition.

3) **Conditions that May Be Waived**
If no consideration is given for the waiver, the condition must be one that is ancillary or collateral to the main purpose of the contract. Otherwise, the waiver amounts to a gift and is thus not enforceable.

4) **Right to Damages for Failure of Condition**
Waiving a condition does ***not*** waive one's right to damages for the other's defective performance.

h. **Excuse of Condition by Impossibility, Impracticability, or Frustration**
Conditions may be excused by impossibility, impracticability, or frustration of purpose according to the tests described under discharge. (*See* C.4., *infra.*)

C. HAS THE DUTY TO PERFORM BEEN DISCHARGED?
Once it is established that there is an immediate duty to perform (either because the duty is unconditional or the condition has been satisfied or excused), that duty must be discharged.

1. **Discharge by Performance or Tender of Performance**
The duty may be discharged by complete performance or tender of performance, assuming the tendering party possesses the present ability to perform.

2. **Discharge by Condition Subsequent**
The duty may be discharged by occurrence of a condition subsequent.

3. **Discharge by Illegality**
The duty may be discharged by supervening illegality of the subject matter.

4. **Discharge by Impossibility, Impracticability, or Frustration**

a. **Discharge by Impossibility**
The duty may be discharged by impossibility (measured by an ***objective standard***—

nobody could perform according to the terms of the contract). This impossibility must arise after the contract was entered into. A party who has rendered part performance prior to the impossibility may recover in quasi-contract. Impossibility examples include: (i) ***death or physical incapacity*** of a person necessary to effectuate the contract, (ii) a subsequently enacted law rendering the contract subject matter ***illegal***, and (iii) ***subsequent destruction of the contract's subject matter*** or means of performance, as long as the promisor was not at fault and it is truly impossible to fulfill the terms of the contract at any price.

CMR **Exam Tip** A contract is ***not*** discharged by the death or incapacity of the person who was to perform the services if the services are of a kind that can be delegated. Thus, if the contract was for personal services of a ***unique*** kind (*e.g.,* the painting of a portrait by a famous artist), the death or incapacity of that person could make performance impossible, but if the services are not unique (*e.g.,* the painting of a farmer's barn), the death or incapacity of that person would ***not*** make performance impossible.

CMR **Exam Tip** Be sure to distinguish destruction of the subject matter of a contract to build from destruction of the subject matter of a contract to repair. When a ***contract to build's*** subject matter is accidentally destroyed (*e.g.,* a house that is almost finished being built is destroyed by accidental fire), the builder's performance is ***not*** discharged by impossibility because the builder is still capable of starting over and rebuilding. However, when a ***contract to repair's*** subject matter is accidentally destroyed (*e.g.,* a house getting a new roof is destroyed by accidental fire), the repairer's performance is discharged by impossibility because there is nothing left to repair.

b. Discharge by Impracticability

Modern courts will also discharge a duty because of impracticability (subjective test). Impracticability requires that a party encounter ***extreme and unreasonable*** difficulty or expense that was ***not anticipated***. A mere change in the difficulty or expense due to normal risks that could have been anticipated (*e.g.*, increase in price of raw materials) will ***not*** warrant discharge by impracticability.

c. Discharge by Frustration of Purpose

A duty may also be discharged by frustration of purpose. This requires (i) a ***supervening event***; (ii) that was ***not reasonably foreseeable*** at the time of entering into the contract; (iii) which completely or almost completely ***destroys the purpose*** of the contract; and (iv) the purpose was understood ***by both parties***.

5. Discharge by Rescission

a. Mutual Rescission

Duties may be discharged by mutual rescission, *i.e.,* where both parties expressly agree to it. The contract to be rescinded must be ***executory on both sides***. A mutual agreement to rescind will usually be enforced where a bilateral contract has been partially performed. Where the contract is unilateral, a contract to mutually rescind where only one party still has a duty to perform will be ineffective (unless there is an offer of new consideration by the nonperforming party, there are elements of promissory estoppel, or the original offeree manifests an intent to make a gift of the obligation owed her).

Mutual rescission may be made ***orally*** unless the subject matter is within the Statute of Frauds or it involves a contract for the sale of goods requiring a rescission to be in writing.

CMR **Exam Tip** Although mutual rescission generally discharges the parties to a contract, watch out for a third-party beneficiary case. Where the rights of a third-party beneficiary have ***already vested***, a contract will ***not*** be discharged by mutual rescission by the promisor and promisee.

b. **Unilateral Rescission**

Rescission may be unilateral where only one of the parties to the contract desires to rescind it. In this case, that party must have adequate legal grounds (*e.g.*, mistake, misrepresentation, or duress).

6. **Partial Discharge by Modification of Contract**

A duty may be discharged partially by modification of the contract. There must be mutual assent to the modifying agreement. Generally, consideration is necessary, although courts will usually find it where ***each party*** has limited his right to enforce the original contract. Consideration is not necessary where the modification is only a correction, or for a modification of a contract for the sale of goods.

CMR **Exam Tip** Remember this important difference between the common law and the U.C.C.—under the U.C.C. a contract modification is enforceable if made in good faith, ***even without consideration***. Of course, keep in mind that the U.C.C. applies only to contracts for the sale of goods. Modification of other contracts must be supported by consideration.

7. **Discharge by Novation**

A duty may be discharged by a novation, *i.e.*, a new contract substituting a new party for one of the parties to the original contract. Necessary elements are: (i) a previous valid contract; (ii) an agreement among all parties, including the new party; (iii) immediate extinguishment of contractual duties as between the original contracting parties; and (iv) a valid new contract.

8. **Discharge by Cancellation**

Duties may be discharged by cancellation of the original agreement.

9. **Discharge by Release**

Duties may be discharged by a release and/or covenant not to sue. The release must be in ***writing*** and supported by ***new consideration*** or ***promissory estoppel*** elements.

10. **Discharge by Substituted Contract**

There is a discharge by substituted contract where the parties to a contract enter into a second contract that expressly or impliedly ***immediately*** revokes the first contract.

11. **Discharge by Accord and Satisfaction**

a. **Accord**

An accord is an agreement in which one party to a contract agrees to accept performance different from that originally promised. Generally, an accord requires consideration. Consideration less than that of the original contract will be sufficient if it is of a different type or is to be paid to a third party (*e.g.*, an accord agreement to exchange a $500 TV set for a $700 cash debt is valid).

1) **Effect**
An accord does not discharge a contractual duty. It merely suspends the other party's right to enforce it.

2) **Partial Payment of Original Debt**
Payment of a smaller amount than is due on a claim is valid consideration if it is made in good faith and there is a ***bona fide dispute*** as to the claim. This is often accomplished by tendering a check conspicuously marked "payment in full."

b. **Satisfaction**
Satisfaction is the performance of the accord. It discharges both the accord and the original debt.

12. **Discharge by Account Stated**
Duties may be discharged by an account stated; *i.e.*, parties agree to an amount as a final balance due from one to the other as settlement of all previous transactions between them. It is necessary that there have been ***more than one prior transaction***. A writing is required only if one or more of the original transactions was subject to the Statute of Frauds.

13. **Discharge by Lapse**
Duties may be discharged by the lapse of time if each party's duty is a condition to the other's duty and neither party performs her duty.

14. **Discharge by Operation of Law**
Duties may be discharged by operation of law (*e.g.*, the contractual duty of performance is merged in a court judgment for breach of the duty; discharge in bankruptcy bars any right of action on the contract).

15. **Effect of Running of Statute of Limitations**
Where the statute of limitations on an action has run, it is generally held that an action for breach of contract may be barred.

CMR **Exam Tip** Note the difference between a discharge by lapse and the effect of a statute of limitations. Although both have to do with time and the end result may be similar, technically, lapse ***discharges*** a contract while the statute of limitations merely ***makes it unenforceable*** in court.

VIII. BREACH OF CONTRACT AND AVAILABLE REMEDIES

A. WHEN DOES BREACH OCCUR?

If (i) the promisor is under an absolute duty of performance and (ii) this duty has not been discharged, then this failure to perform in accordance with the contractual terms may be held to be a breach of contract.

B. MATERIAL OR MINOR BREACH?

A breach is material if, as a result of the breach, the nonbreaching party does not receive the substantial benefit of her bargain. If the breach is material, the nonbreaching party (i) may treat the contract as at an end (any duty of counterperformance is discharged), and (ii) has an ***immediate right*** to all remedies for breach of the entire contract, including total damages. (Note that a minor breach, if coupled with anticipatory repudiation, is treated as a material breach.)

CMR **Exam Tip** The distinction between a material and a minor breach is important. A minor breach may allow the aggrieved party to recover damages, ***but*** she still must perform under the contract. If the breach is a material one, the aggrieved party need not perform.

1. Tests for Materiality

In determining whether a breach is material or minor, courts look at:

(i) ***The amount of benefit received*** by the nonbreaching party;

(ii) ***The adequacy of compensation*** for damages to the injured party;

(iii) ***The extent of part performance*** by the breaching party;

(iv) ***Hardship*** to the breaching party;

(v) ***Negligent or willful behavior*** of the breaching party; and

(vi) ***The likelihood that the breaching party will perform*** the remainder of the contract.

The nonbreaching party must show that he was both willing and able to perform.

2. Timeliness of Performance

Failure to perform by the time stated in the contract is generally not a material breach if performance is rendered within a reasonable time. However, if the nature of the contract makes timely performance essential, or if the contract expressly provides that time is of the essence, then failure to perform on time is a material breach.

C. REMEDIES FOR BREACH

There are several remedies for breach of contract, *e.g.,* damages, specific performance, and rescission and restitution.

1. Damages

There are three kinds of damages: compensatory, nominal, and punitive. Most important for bar examination purposes are compensatory damages. The goal of compensatory damages is to put the nonbreaching party into ***as good a position*** as the party would have been in had the other party fully performed. There are two kinds of compensatory damages and the nonbreaching party may recover both: the "standard measure" (cost of a substitute) and consequential damages.

a. Standard Measure of Damages

In most cases, the standard measure of damages will be expectation damages that would permit the plaintiff to buy a substitute. In cases where expectation damages are speculative, the plaintiff may recover reliance damages (*i.e.,* the cost she has incurred by performing).

CMR **Exam Tip** Note that damages must be reasonably certain; a court will not award damages that are speculative in nature. A typical example concerns a new business that fails to open on time due to the defendant's breach. Lost profits of such businesses generally are too speculative to recover, although modern courts may allow recovery if the plaintiff can present evidence of comparable business profits.

1) **Contracts for Sale of Goods**
Damages are measured by the difference between the contract price and the market price when the seller tenders the goods or when the buyer learns of the breach. If the ***buyer breaches***, under the U.C.C. the seller may withhold delivery or stop delivery by the carrier, resell the goods and recover the difference, or recover ordinary contract damages for nonacceptance. If the buyer has already accepted the goods, or if the seller is unable to resell identified goods, the seller may recover the contract price. If the ***seller breaches***, under the U.C.C. the buyer may reject nonconforming goods, cancel, cover, recover goods identified to the contract, obtain specific performance (in some cases), or recover damages for nondelivery. If the buyer accepts the nonconforming goods, the buyer may recover the difference between the value that the goods would have had if they had been as warranted and the actual value of the goods.

2) **Contracts for Sale of Land**
Damages are measured by the difference between the contract price and fair market value.

3) **Employment Contracts**
If an employment contract is breached by the ***employer***, the measure of damages is the full contract price (less wages actually earned elsewhere after the breach); if breached by the ***employee***, the measure is whatever it costs to replace the employee. The modern view allows the employee to offset any monies due from work done to date.

4) **Construction Contracts**
If a construction contract is breached by the ***owner***, the builder will be entitled to profits that would have resulted from the contract plus any costs expended. (If the contract is breached after construction is completed, the measure is the full contract price plus interest.) If the contract is breached by the ***builder***, the owner is entitled to the cost of completion plus reasonable compensation for the delay. Most courts allow the builder to offset or recover for work performed to date to avoid unjust enrichment of the owner. (If the breach is only late performance, the owner is entitled to damages incurred because of late performance.)

5) **Contracts Calling for Installment Payments**
If a contract calls for payments in installments and a payment is not made, there is only a partial breach. The aggrieved party is limited to recovering only the missed payment, not the entire contract price. However, the contract may include an acceleration clause making the entire amount due on any late payment, in which case the aggrieved party may recover the entire amount.

b. **Consequential Damages**
Consequential damages are awarded in addition to the standard measure and will be given if a ***reasonable person*** would have foreseen at the time of entering the contract that such damages would result from the breach. Note that the plaintiff bears the burden of proving the foreseeability of damages where "special circumstances" are involved (*i.e.,* whether those special circumstances were made clear to the other party at the time of contract formation).

c. **Punitive and Nominal Damages**
Punitive damages are generally ***not*** awarded in commercial contract cases. Nominal damages (*e.g.,* $1) may be awarded where a breach is shown but ***no actual loss*** is proven.

d. **Liquidated Damages**
A liquidated damages provision will be valid if (i) damages were ***difficult to ascertain at the time the contract was formed***, and (ii) the amount agreed upon was a ***reasonable forecast*** of compensatory damages. If these requirements are met, the plaintiff will receive the liquidated damages amount even though no actual money damages have been suffered. If the liquidated damages amount is unreasonable, the courts will construe this as a penalty and will not enforce the provision.

1) **U.C.C. Rule**
Under the U.C.C., a court can consider the ***actual damages*** incurred in determining whether a liquidated damages clause is valid.

e. **Duty to Mitigate Damages**
The nonbreaching party has a duty to mitigate damages. If she does not do so, her damages will be reduced by the amount that might have been avoided by mitigation. In employment contracts, the employee is under a duty to use reasonable diligence to find a like position. In sale of goods contracts, cover must be reasonable, in good faith, and without unreasonable delay. In construction and manufacturing contracts, mitigation requires the builder or manufacturer to cease work unless completion would decrease damages, *e.g.,* finishing partly manufactured goods.

CMR **Exam Tip** Keep in mind that the duty to mitigate only reduces a recovery; it does not prohibit recovery. Thus, if a fact pattern shows a clear breach and the plaintiff does not attempt to mitigate damages, she can recover for the breach, but the recovery will be reduced by the damages that would have been avoided by mitigation.

2. **Suit in Equity for Specific Performance**
Where the legal remedy (*i.e.,* damages) is inadequate, the nonbreaching party can seek specific performance—essentially an order from the court to perform or face contempt of court charges. The legal remedy is considered inadequate when the subject matter of the contract is rare or unique.

a. **Available for Land and Unique Goods but Not for Services**
Specific performance is always available for contracts involving the sale of land (because all land is considered unique) and for contracts for the sale of unique or rare goods (*e.g.,* a unique painting or gasoline in short supply because of an embargo).

However, even where services are unique, specific performance will not be granted in a service contract because of difficulty in supervision and because the courts feel it is tantamount to involuntary servitude. *Note:* Even though a court may not be able to grant specific performance of a service contract, it may ***enjoin*** a breaching employee from working for a competitor throughout the duration of the employment contract if the services contracted for are rare or unique.

b. Equitable Defenses Available

In addition to standard contract defenses, an action for specific performance is subject to the equitable defenses of:

1) ***Laches***—a claim that the plaintiff has delayed bringing the action and that ***the delay has prejudiced the defendant***;

2) ***Unclean hands***—a claim that the party seeking specific performance is guilty of ***wrongdoing in the transaction being sued upon***; and

3) ***Sale to a bona fide purchaser***—a claim that the subject matter has been ***sold to a person who purchased for value and in good faith***.

3. Rescission and Restitution

The nonbreacher may rescind (*i.e.,* cancel) and sue for damages at law or in equity. If the nonbreacher transferred a benefit to the breacher while attempting to perform, the nonbreacher is entitled to restitution for the benefit transferred.

4. Quasi-Contractual Relief

If there is no contractual relief available under the rules discussed in this outline, quasi-contractual relief might be proper.

a. Failed Contract

Where quasi-contractual relief is used to remedy a failed contract, all that is necessary is that the failed contract ***results in unjust enrichment of one of the parties***. Even the breaching party may be able to recover in quasi-contract, as long as the breach did not involve seriously wrongful or unconscionable conduct.

b. Where No Contract Involved

Where there is no contractual relationship between the parties, quasi-contractual relief requires that:

(i) One party has ***conferred a benefit*** on the other by rendering services or expending properties;

(ii) The conferring party had a ***reasonable expectation of being compensated***;

(iii) The benefits were conferred at the express or implied ***request of the other person***; and

(iv) ***Unjust enrichment would result*** if the defendant were allowed to retain the benefits without compensating the plaintiff.

The modern rule grants relief even though the defendant, in fact, received no benefit, as long as the plaintiff expended something on the defendant's behalf. The measure of relief is the benefit received by the defendant, or the detriment suffered by the plaintiff where the plaintiff has not breached the contract and where the benefits are difficult to measure, or where the benefit measure would achieve an unfair result. Relief may exceed the proposed contract price.

CMR **Exam Tip** Always keep the quasi-contract remedy in the back of your mind. Look first for a valid contract allowing the plaintiff relief. But if there is no valid contract, a quasi-contract will provide a remedy if the plaintiff has suffered a loss or rendered services.

SALES

TABLE OF CONTENTS

I. INTRODUCTION 1
A. UNIFORM COMMERCIAL CODE GOVERNS TRANSACTIONS IN GOODS . 1
B. SUBJECT MATTER OF ARTICLE 2 1
1. Goods Associated with Realty 1
2. Merchants vs. Nonmerchants 1
3. Good Faith Requirement 1

II. FORMATION OF THE CONTRACT 2
A. IN GENERAL 2
B. OFFER AND ACCEPTANCE 2
1. Merchants' Firm Offers 2
2. Methods of Acceptance 3
3. Mirror Image Rule Abandoned—Battle of the Forms 3
4. Open Terms 3
C. AUCTIONS 5
D. DEFENSES TO FORMATION OF A CONTRACT 5
1. Statute of Frauds 5
2. Unconscionability 6

III. CONTRACT MODIFICATION 6
A. BY AGREEMENT OF THE PARTIES 6
1. Modification Without Consideration 6
2. Writing Prohibiting Oral Modification 6
3. Waiver of Writing Requirement 6
B. BY OPERATION OF LAW 6
1. Destruction or Injury to Identified Goods 6
2. Failure of Agreed-Upon Method of Transportation 6
3. Failure of Presupposed Conditions—Impracticability 6

IV. PAROL EVIDENCE RULE 7

V. PERFORMANCE OF THE CONTRACT 7
A. SELLER'S OBLIGATION OF TENDER AND DELIVERY 7
1. Noncarrier Contracts 7
2. Carrier Contracts 7
B. BUYER'S OBLIGATION TO PAY—RIGHT TO INSPECT 9
1. Delivery and Payment Concurrent Conditions 9
2. Shipment Under Reservation—Buyer Pays Prior to Receipt of Goods 9
3. Payment by Check 9
4. Installment Contracts 9
5. Buyer's Right of Inspection 9

VI. ALLOCATION OF INTEREST AND RISK OF LOSS 9
A. IDENTIFICATION 9

1. Specific, Ascertained, and Existing Goods 9
2. Crops and Unborn Animals 9
3. Other Goods 9

B. INSURABLE INTEREST 10

C. RISK OF LOSS 10
1. Risk in the Absence of Breach 10
2. Effect of Breach on Risk of Loss 10
3. Risk in "Sale or Return" and "Sale on Approval" Contracts 10

D. RULES FOR PASSAGE OF TITLE 10

VII. REMEDIES 11

A. BUYER'S REMEDIES 11
1. Acceptance 11
2. Rejection Prior to Acceptance 12
3. Revocation of Acceptance 13
4. Buyer's Right to Replevy Identified Goods 13
5. Buyer's Right to Specific Performance 13
6. Buyer's Damages 13

B. SELLER'S REMEDIES 14
1. Seller's Right to Withhold Goods 14
2. Seller's Right to Recover Goods 14
3. Seller's Right to Force Goods on Buyer and Recover Full Price—Limited 14
4. Seller's Damages 14

C. REMEDIES AVAILABLE TO BOTH BUYER AND SELLER 15
1. Right to Demand Assurances 15
2. Anticipatory Repudiation 15
3. Retraction of Repudiation 16
4. Right to Sue Third Parties 16
5. Liquidated Damages 16

D. STATUTE OF LIMITATIONS 16

VIII. WARRANTIES 16

A. TYPES OF WARRANTIES 16

B. WARRANTY OF TITLE AND AGAINST INFRINGEMENT 16
1. Warranty of Title 16
2. Warranty Against Infringement 16

C. IMPLIED WARRANTY OF MERCHANTABILITY 16

D. IMPLIED WARRANTY OF FITNESS FOR PARTICULAR PURPOSE 17

E. EXPRESS WARRANTIES 17

F. DISCLAIMER OF WARRANTIES 17
1. Express Warranties 17
2. Implied Warranties 17
3. Unconscionability 17
4. Federal Consumer Product Warranties Law of 1975 ("Magnuson-Moss") 17

G. LIMITATION OF DAMAGES FOR BREACH OF WARRANTY 17

H. WARRANTY AND THIRD PARTIES 18

I. STRICT LIABILITY 19

IX. THIRD-PARTY RIGHTS 19

A. ENTRUSTMENT 19
B. VOIDABLE TITLE 19
C. THIEF GENERALLY CANNOT PASS GOOD TITLE 19
D. FRAUDULENT RETENTION OF POSSESSION RULES 20
E. SALE OR RETURN 20

SALES

I. INTRODUCTION

A. UNIFORM COMMERCIAL CODE GOVERNS TRANSACTIONS IN GOODS

The Uniform Commercial Code ("U.C.C.") governs the sale of goods. The Code adopts much of the common law of contracts, but includes a number of modifications to the common law.

IMPORTANT DIFFERENCES BETWEEN COMMON LAW AND U.C.C.

Common Law	U.C.C.
Option contract requires consideration or promissory estoppel.	Merchant's firm offer is irrevocable without consideration.
Acceptance must be absolute and unequivocal; otherwise it will be treated as a rejection and counteroffer.	Proposal of additional terms does not constitute rejection; terms may become part of contract per battle of the forms rule.
Contracts cannot be modified without consideration.	Modifications sought in good faith are binding without consideration.
Rule of substantial performance (performance need not be perfect).	Perfect tender rule (with exceptions).

B. SUBJECT MATTER OF ARTICLE 2

U.C.C. Article 2 deals with transactions in ***goods*** (*i.e.,* all things that are movable when they are identified under the contract). It does not apply to the sale of realty or intangibles.

1. Goods Associated with Realty

"Goods associated with realty" (*e.g.*, timber, minerals, structures to be removed) fall under Article 2 if severance is to be ***made by the seller***. Growing crops fall under Article 2 regardless of who severs. Other things (mostly fixtures) that can be removed from the land without material harm to the land are within Article 2. Contracts involving the sale of things other than goods are generally governed by the common law contracts rules.

2. Merchants vs. Nonmerchants

A number of the rules under Article 2 differentiate between merchants and nonmerchants. A merchant is one who regularly deals in goods of the kind sold or who otherwise by his profession holds himself out as having special knowledge of the goods sold.

3. Good Faith Requirement

Article 2 requires all parties to act in good faith (*i.e.*, with honesty in fact and in observance of reasonable commercial standards of fair dealing).

WHEN DOES MERCHANT STATUS MATTER?

Listed below are the principal U.C.C. Article 2 sections distinguishing ***merchants*** from other buyers and sellers.

Section	Topic
2-201(2)	Statute of Frauds—merchant's confirmatory memo rule.
2-205	Merchant's firm offer.
2-207(2)	Additional terms in acceptance or confirmation—"battle of the forms" rule for merchants.
2-209(2)	Agreement excluding modification except by signed writing—form supplied by merchant.
2-312	Warranty against infringement.
2-314	Implied warranty of merchantability.
2-316(2)	Disclaimer of implied warranty of merchantability.
2-403(2)	Entrusting goods to merchant gives her power to transfer rights to buyer in ordinary course.
2-509(3)	Risk of loss in the absence of breach (noncarrier cases)—passes on buyer's receipt if seller is a merchant, otherwise on tender of delivery.

II. FORMATION OF THE CONTRACT

A. IN GENERAL

A contract for the sale of goods may be made in any manner sufficient to show agreement.

B. OFFER AND ACCEPTANCE

1. Merchants' Firm Offers

Common law offers generally are revocable unless consideration is given to keep the offer open. Article 2 modifies the common law rule for certain offers made ***by merchants***. A ***written*** offer ***signed*** by a merchant giving assurances that it will be ***held open*** will be ***irrevocable—without consideration***—for the stated time period or for a reasonable time if no period is expressly stated. The period of irrevocability may ***not exceed three months***.

2. Methods of Acceptance

An offer is construed as inviting acceptance in any reasonable manner and by any reasonable medium. Generally, an offer to buy goods for current shipment is construed as inviting acceptance ***either by a promise to ship or by prompt shipment of conforming or nonconforming*** goods.

3. Mirror Image Rule Abandoned—Battle of the Forms

Article 2 has abandoned the common law mirror image rule for acceptance. Any acceptance or written confirmation that shows an intention to contract is effective. Whether terms in the acceptance that are different from or in addition to the offered terms will be included in the contract depends on whether ***both*** parties are merchants.

a. Contracts Involving a Nonmerchant—Terms of Offer Govern

If one of the parties to the contract is not a merchant, the contract will include only the terms of the offer.

b. Contracts Between Merchants—Acceptance Terms Usually Included

If both parties to the contract are merchants, ***additional*** terms ***automatically become part*** of the contract ***unless***:

(i) They ***materially alter*** the original contract;

(ii) The offer ***expressly limits acceptance*** to the offer's terms; or

(iii) The ***offeror objects*** within a reasonable time.

CMR **Exam Tip** Recall that the U.C.C. changes the common law rule. Thus, for an offer for the purchase or sale of ***goods***, an acceptance with additional terms is still an acceptance and a contract is formed (with or without the new terms). If the offer is for something ***other*** than the sale of goods (*e.g.*, land), an acceptance proposing additional terms is a rejection and a counteroffer; no contract is formed.

Note: There is a split of authority over whether ***different*** terms in the acceptance become part of the contract. Some courts treat different terms like additional terms, and they use the above test to determine whether the different terms should be part of the contract. Other courts follow the "knockout rule," which states that conflicting terms in the offer and acceptance are knocked out of the contract and the terms instead are provided by the U.C.C.

4. Open Terms

The fact that one or more terms (including price) are left open does not prevent the formation of a contract if the parties intended such and there is a reasonable basis for giving a remedy. The ***court can supply reasonable terms*** for those that are missing.

a. Quantity

The one term that is essential (*i.e.,* that a court cannot supply) is quantity. A quantity term must be included to create a sales contract. Contracts for a seller's ***output*** or a buyer's ***requirements*** satisfy the quantity requirement because the terms usually can be determined objectively.

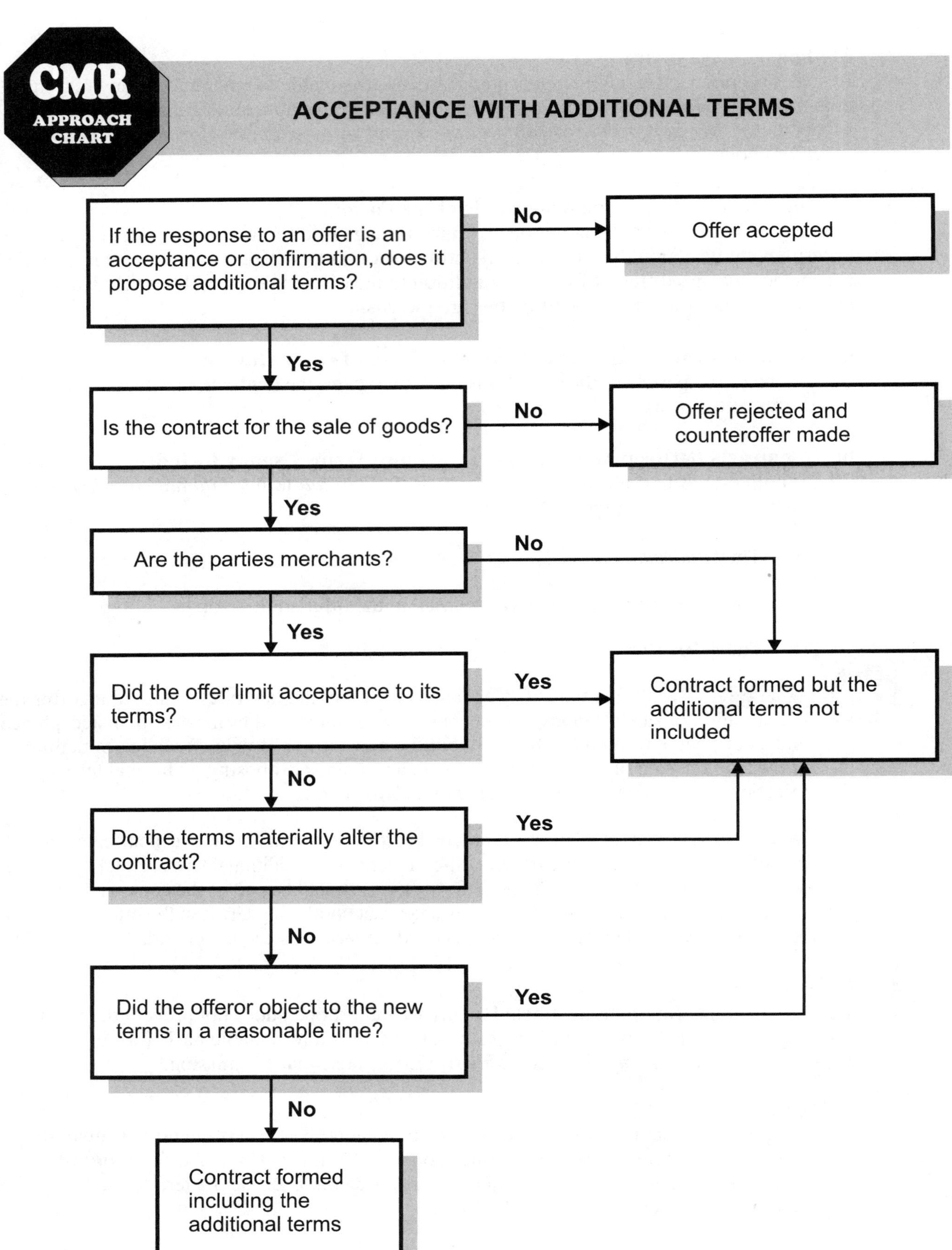
CMR
APPROACH
CHART
ACCEPTANCE WITH ADDITIONAL TERMS
If the response to an offer is an acceptance or confirmation, does it propose additional terms?
No
Offer accepted
Yes
Is the contract for the sale of goods?
No
Offer rejected and counteroffer made
Yes
Are the parties merchants?
No
Yes
Did the offer limit acceptance to its terms?
Yes
Contract formed but the additional terms not included
No
Do the terms materially alter the contract?
Yes
No
Did the offeror object to the new terms in a reasonable time?
Yes
No
Contract formed including the additional terms

C. AUCTIONS

A sale by auction is complete when the auctioneer so announces by the fall of the hammer or in another customary manner. Auctions are with reserve (*i.e.*, the goods may be withdrawn at any time before the auctioneer announces they are sold) unless explicitly offered without reserve.

D. DEFENSES TO FORMATION OF A CONTRACT

1. Statute of Frauds

Contracts for the sale of goods at a price of ***$500 or more*** (including any modifications) are not enforceable unless there is ***some writing*** that is ***signed by the party to be charged***. A writing is sufficient even though it omits or incorrectly states a term, but a ***quantity*** must be stated because the contract is not enforceable beyond the quantity of goods shown in the writing.

CMR **Exam Tip** To be sufficient for the Statute of Frauds, the writing may be informal and need not be contained in a single document. The "signature" can be any symbol meant to adopt or accept a writing. Thus, a note on a letterhead can be enough (the letterhead acts as a signature). *But remember:* A ***quantity*** must be stated in the writing.

a. Merchants—Confirmatory Memo Rule

In contracts between merchants, if one party, within a reasonable time after an oral understanding has been reached, sends a ***written*** confirmation thereof to the other party that binds the sender, it will satisfy the Statute of Frauds requirements against ***the recipient as well*** if he had reason to know of the confirmation's contents, ***unless*** he objects to its contents in writing within 10 days after it is received.

CMR **Exam Tip** For the Statute of Frauds to be satisfied (and the contract to be enforceable), you need to look carefully for a writing signed ***by the party to be charged*** (*i.e.*, sued). Often the facts of a question will show that only one party signed the memo. Check first to see if the signature is of the party you need to hold liable. If not, consider the merchants' confirmatory memo rule—it may provide the answer. Be sure, however, that the contract is between ***merchants***; if not, the rule does not apply and the signature of one party cannot bind the other.

b. When Writing Not Required

A writing is not required:

(i) If the goods are ***specially made for the buyer*** and not suitable for sale to others in the ordinary course of the seller's business, and the seller has started making them or committed for their procurement;

(ii) If the party ***admits*** in his pleading or court testimony that a contract was made; or

(iii) If the contract is ***performed*** (the goods are either received and accepted or paid for).

CMR **Exam Tip** An acronym for remembering when a writing signed by the party to be charged is ***not required*** for a sale of goods, even if for $500 or more, is SWAP: ***Specially*** made goods, ***Written confirmation*** by a merchant, ***Admission*** in court, or ***Performance***. These things take the contract out of the Statute of Frauds.

2. Unconscionability
If a contract was unconscionable when made, the court may refuse to enforce it or limit it to avoid unconscionable results. The test for unconscionability is whether, ***at the time of execution***, the contract or one of its provisions could result in unfair surprise and was oppressive to a disadvantaged party.

III. CONTRACT MODIFICATION

A. BY AGREEMENT OF THE PARTIES

At common law, contracts may not be modified without consideration. Article 2 does not follow this rule.

1. Modification Without Consideration
Contract modifications sought in ***good faith*** are binding without consideration. Contract modifications must meet the Statute of Frauds requirements if the contract ***as modified*** is within the statute.

2. Writing Prohibiting Oral Modification
A provision that a written contract cannot be modified or rescinded except by a signed writing is valid and binding.

3. Waiver of Writing Requirement
An invalid oral modification (*e.g.,* one that violates the Statute of Frauds) may serve as a ***waiver*** of a party's right to enforce the contract as written if one of the parties relied to her detriment on the modification.

B. BY OPERATION OF LAW

1. Destruction or Injury to Identified Goods
If a contract requires for its performance particular goods identified when the contract is made and, ***before risk passes to the buyer***, the goods are destroyed or damaged without the fault of either party, the contract is ***avoided***. For damaged goods, the buyer may elect to take the goods with a reduction in price. If the goods are destroyed or damaged after risk of loss has passed to the buyer, the buyer will bear the loss.

2. Failure of Agreed-Upon Method of Transportation
If the agreed-upon delivery facilities become unavailable or commercially impractical, any ***commercially reasonable*** transportation ***must*** be tendered and ***must*** be accepted.

3. Failure of Presupposed Conditions—Impracticability
A seller will be discharged from performing a sales contract under the doctrine of impracticability if:

(i) At the time the parties made their contract, a basic assumption of ***both*** parties was that a certain circumstance that would make performance extremely more burdensome would not occur; and

(ii) The circumstance does occur.

The seller is discharged only to the extent of the impracticability.

a. **Events Sufficient for Discharge**
Unforeseen wars, embargoes, and natural catastrophes will usually be sufficient if they make it extremely difficult for the seller to obtain or convert raw materials. If the event merely makes performance more expensive (*e.g.,* adds to shipping expenses), the seller usually will not be discharged.

CMR **Exam Tip** For performance under a contract to be excused, the unforeseen circumstances must have been unforeseen ***at the time the contract was made***. If the change was reasonably foreseeable (*e.g.,* a price increase), it will not excuse performance.

b. **Seller's Partial Inability to Perform**
A ***partial*** inability to perform (*e.g.,* shortage of goods) does ***not*** excuse performance; the seller must allocate the available supply among his customers.

IV. PAROL EVIDENCE RULE

The terms of a contract set forth in the confirmatory memoranda of the parties or in a writing intended as a final expression of the parties' agreement ***cannot be contradicted*** by evidence of any ***prior agreement*** or ***contemporaneous oral agreement***. Such terms, however, ***may be explained or supplemented*** by: (i) ***consistent additional terms***, (ii) ***course of dealing*** (a sequence of conduct concerning previous transactions between the parties to a transaction that may be regarded as establishing a common basis of understanding), (iii) ***usage of the trade or business***, or (iv) ***course of performance*** (repeated occasions for performance and a party has opportunity to object to performance; any performance acquiesced to is relevant in determining the meaning of the contract).

Note: There is ***no*** requirement that a contract term be ambiguous before allowing an explanation by course of dealing, usage of trade, or course of performance.

V. PERFORMANCE OF THE CONTRACT

A. SELLER'S OBLIGATION OF TENDER AND DELIVERY

The extent of the seller's obligation depends on how the goods are to be delivered.

1. **Noncarrier Contracts**
If the parties did not intend that the goods be moved by a carrier, the seller must put and hold conforming goods at the buyer's disposition for a time sufficient for the buyer to take possession. In the absence of agreement, the place of delivery is the seller's place of business, or if he has none, his residence.

2. **Carrier Contracts**
If the parties intend that a carrier be used to move the goods, the seller may be obliged to deliver the goods for shipment or to deliver them to a particular destination.

a. **Shipment Contracts—Seller Has Not Agreed to Tender at Particular Destination**
In a shipment contract, the seller need not see that the goods reach the buyer, but is only required to put the goods into the hands of a carrier, make a reasonable contract

for their shipment, promptly tender required documents, and promptly notify the buyer of the shipment.

Note: Failure to make a contract for shipment or notify the buyer is a ground for rejection of the goods by the buyer only if the failure results in a material loss or delay.

b. Destination Contracts—Seller Has Agreed to Deliver to Destination
In a destination contract, a seller is required to see that the goods reach the buyer, and is required to put and hold conforming goods at the buyer's disposition for a time sufficient for the buyer to take possession of the goods at the destination specified.

c. F.O.B. Contracts
In contracts that specify that delivery is F.O.B. ("free on board") a particular point, the ***F.O.B. point is the delivery point***. The delivery point may be the seller's place of shipment or the goods' final destination. Depending on the type of contract (shipment or destination), the seller must tender delivery in the manner described in either a. or b., above.

d. F.A.S. Contracts
In contracts that specify that delivery is F.A.S. ("free alongside"), the seller must ***deliver the goods alongside the vessel*** in the manner usual in the port of delivery or on a dock designated by the buyer, and obtain and tender a receipt for the goods.

CMR COMPARISON CHART

NONCARRIER VS. CARRIER CONTRACTS

	Noncarrier Contract	Carrier Contract
Place of Delivery	Seller's place of business	***Shipment contract:*** seller must deliver to the shipper ***Destination contract:*** seller must tender delivery of goods to the buyer at the destination
Time for Payment	Upon tender of delivery	When buyer receives the goods
When does the risk of loss shift from the seller to the buyer?	***If seller is a merchant:*** when buyer takes possession ***If seller is not a merchant:*** when seller tenders delivery	***Shipment contract:*** when goods are delivered to the shipper ***Destination contract:*** when seller tenders delivery of goods to the buyer at the destination

B. BUYER'S OBLIGATION TO PAY—RIGHT TO INSPECT

1. Delivery and Payment Concurrent Conditions

In ***noncarrier cases***, unless the contract provides otherwise, a sale is for cash and the price is due concurrently with tender of delivery. However, unless otherwise agreed, when goods are shipped ***by carrier***, the price is due only at the time and place at which the buyer receives the goods.

2. Shipment Under Reservation—Buyer Pays Prior to Receipt of Goods

In cases where there is no express provision as to payment or the contract specifies cash, and the contract is one for shipment by carrier, the seller may send the goods "under reservation" so that the buyer will be unable to get the goods from the carrier until he pays.

3. Payment by Check

Tender of payment by check is sufficient unless the seller demands legal tender and gives the buyer the time reasonably necessary to get cash. When payment is by check, payment is ***not final until the check is honored***.

4. Installment Contracts

In an installment contract (*i.e.,* goods are delivered in installments), the seller can demand payment for each installment if the price can be so apportioned, unless a contrary intent appears.

5. Buyer's Right of Inspection

Unless the contract provides otherwise, the buyer has a right to inspect the goods before she pays (except if the goods are sent C.O.D. or against documents that indicate the buyer has promised to pay without inspecting the goods).

VI. ALLOCATION OF INTEREST AND RISK OF LOSS

A. IDENTIFICATION

A buyer obtains an interest in goods under a sales contract when the goods can be "identified." Identification is a ***designation of specific goods*** as the ones to be delivered under the contract of sale. It gives the buyer an insurable interest in the goods and, in certain circumstances, the right to get the goods from the seller and the right to sue third parties for injury to them.

1. Specific, Ascertained, and Existing Goods

Identification takes place at the time the contract is made if it calls for the sale of specific and ascertained goods currently existing.

2. Crops and Unborn Animals

If a sale is of unborn animals or of crops to be harvested within 12 months (or the next harvest season), identification takes place when the young are conceived or when the crops are planted.

3. Other Goods

In other cases, identification takes place when the goods are shipped, marked, or otherwise designated by the seller as the goods to pass under the contract.

B. INSURABLE INTEREST

The buyer has an insurable interest in identified goods and may procure insurance covering goods even before the risk of their loss has passed to her. The seller ***also*** has an insurable interest in the goods as long as he has title to or a security interest in them.

C. RISK OF LOSS

1. Risk in the Absence of Breach

a. Noncarrier Cases

If the seller is a ***merchant***, risk of loss passes to the buyer only upon the buyer taking ***physical possession*** of the goods. If the seller is ***not a merchant***, risk of loss passes to the buyer upon ***tender of delivery*** (*e.g.,* the seller has goods ready for the buyer to pick up at the time and place specified in the contract).

b. Carrier Cases

In a ***shipment*** contract (*i.e.,* the seller is to ship the goods by carrier but is not required to tender delivery at a particular destination), risk of loss passes to the buyer when the goods are duly ***delivered to the carrier***. In a ***destination*** contract (*i.e.,* the seller must tender delivery of the goods at a particular destination), the risk of loss passes to the buyer when the goods are ***tendered to the buyer*** at the destination.

2. Effect of Breach on Risk of Loss

a. Defective Goods

If the goods are so defective that the buyer has a right to reject them, the risk of loss does ***not pass*** to her until the defects are cured or she accepts the goods in spite of their defects. If the buyer rightfully revokes acceptance (*see* VII.A.3., *infra*), the risk of loss is treated as having rested on the seller from the beginning for any losses not covered by the buyer's insurance.

b. Breach by Buyer

Where the seller has identified conforming goods to the contract and the buyer repudiates or otherwise breaches the contract before the risk of loss passes to her under the contract, ***any loss*** occurring within a commercially reasonable time after the seller learns of the breach falls on the buyer to the extent of any deficiency in the seller's insurance coverage.

3. Risk in "Sale or Return" and "Sale on Approval" Contracts

For purposes of risk of loss, a sale or return contract (*i.e.,* the buyer takes goods for resale but may return them if he is unable to resell them) is an ordinary sale. If the goods are returned to the seller, the risk remains ***on the buyer*** while the goods are in transit. In a sale on approval contract (*i.e.,* the buyer takes goods for use but may return them even if they conform to the contract), the risk of loss does ***not pass to the buyer until he accepts***. If the buyer decides not to take the goods, return is at the seller's risk.

D. RULES FOR PASSAGE OF TITLE

In the absence of an agreement, title passes when the seller completes his performance with respect to the physical delivery of the goods. Note that title does ***not*** control risk of loss, the seller's right to the sale price, or the buyer's right to the goods.

CMR **Exam Tip** Note that ***title*** is not a central concept under the U.C.C. It has little or nothing to do with the rights and remedies of the parties to a sales contract. Rather, the U.C.C. has replaced title with identification, insurable interest, and risk of loss. Thus, an answer choice in a sale of goods situation concerning title is probably the ***wrong*** choice.

CMR COMPARISON CHART

SALE OR RETURN VS. SALE ON APPROVAL

	Sale or Return	Sale on Approval
Defined	Buyer takes goods for resale but may return them if unable to resell.	Buyer takes goods for trial period and may return them even though they conform to the contract.
Risk of Loss	Rules for ordinary sale apply, but if goods are returned to seller, risk remains on buyer while goods are in transit.	Risk does not pass until buyer accepts goods (by failing to return them or to notify seller of intention within the required time). If buyer decides to return the goods, return is at seller's risk.
Creditor's Rights	Goods are subject to the claims of buyer's creditors while in buyer's possession.	Goods are not subject to claims of buyer's creditors until acceptance.

VII. REMEDIES

A. BUYER'S REMEDIES

The buyer's remedies depend on whether she rejects the goods prior to acceptance or revokes acceptance she has already given.

1. Acceptance

Acceptance of goods occurs when:

a. The buyer, after ***reasonable opportunity to inspect*** them, indicates to the seller that they ***conform or*** that she will keep them ***in spite of nonconformance***;

b. The buyer ***fails to reject*** them within a reasonable time after tender or delivery of the goods or ***fails to seasonably notify*** the seller of her rejection; or

c. The buyer ***does anything inconsistent*** with the seller's ownership.

2. **Rejection Prior to Acceptance**

a. **Right of Rejection Generally**
When goods that ***do not conform*** to the contract are tendered to a buyer, the buyer may either keep them (and sue for damages) or, under some circumstances, reject the goods and either cancel the contract or sue.

1) **Right of Rejection in Single Delivery Contracts**
In single delivery contracts (all goods to be delivered at once), if the goods or the tender fail to conform, the buyer may ***reject all***, ***accept all***, or ***accept any commercial units*** and reject the rest.

a) **Failure to Make Reasonable Contract with Carrier or to Notify Buyer**
The seller's failure to make a reasonable contract with a carrier or his failure to notify the buyer that the goods have been shipped are grounds for rejection ***only if material loss or delay results***.

2) **Right of Rejection in Installment Contracts**
In an installment contract (goods are delivered in installments), the buyer can reject an installment only if the nonconformity ***substantially impairs*** the value of ***that installment*** and ***cannot be cured***. The ***whole contract*** is breached if the noncomformity ***substantially impairs*** the value of the ***entire contract***.

b. **Formal Requirements for Rejection**
Rejection must be ***within a reasonable time*** after delivery or tender and before acceptance. The buyer must ***seasonably notify*** the seller. If the buyer fails to state that the goods have a particular defect ascertainable by reasonable inspection, he cannot rely on that defect to justify rejection or show the seller's breach if: (i) the seller could have ***cured*** the defect if he had been told about it; or (ii) in contracts between merchants the seller has, after rejection, ***made a request in writing*** for a full and final written statement of all defects upon which the buyer proposes to rely.

c. **Buyer's Responsibility for Goods After Rejection**
After rejection of goods in her physical possession, the buyer has an obligation to hold them with reasonable care at the seller's disposition for a time sufficient to permit the seller to remove them or give instructions as to what to do. If a seller gives no instructions within a reasonable time after notification of rejection, the buyer may ***reship*** the goods to the seller, ***store*** them for the seller's account, or ***resell*** them for the seller's account. The buyer has a security interest in rejected goods in her possession for any part of the price already paid and for expenses reasonably incurred in connection with handling the goods after rejection.

d. **Seller's Right to Cure**
Where a buyer has rejected goods because of defects, the seller may ***within the time originally provided*** for performance "cure" by:

(i) ***Giving reasonable notice*** of intention to cure; and

(ii) ***Making a new tender of conforming goods,*** which the buyer must then accept.

1) **Limited Right to Cure Beyond Original Contract Time**
There is one circumstance where a seller is allowed to cure after the original time for performance has passed: If the seller sends the buyer nonconforming goods that he reasonably believes will be acceptable to the buyer, but the buyer rejects, the seller will get a reasonable time to cure, even though the original time for performance has passed.

2) **Seller's Right to Cure in Installment Contracts**
A defective shipment in an installment contract cannot be rejected if the defect can be cured.

3. **Revocation of Acceptance**
The time of acceptance is important because it terminates the buyer's power to reject and obligates her to pay the price less any damages because of the seller's breach. However, the buyer may revoke her acceptance of goods if the defect ***substantially impairs their value*** to her ***and***: (i) she accepted them on the reasonable belief that the defect would be cured and it has not been; or (ii) she accepted them because of the difficulty of discovering defects or because of the seller's assurance that the goods conformed to the contract. Revocation of acceptance must occur ***within a reasonable time after the buyer discovers*** or should have discovered the defect ***and before any substantial change*** in the goods not caused by their own defects. A proper revocation of acceptance has the effect of rejection.

4. **Buyer's Right to Replevy Identified Goods**
In some circumstances, a buyer will want to replevy (obtain) goods in the seller's possession. The buyer may replevy ***identified, undelivered*** goods from the seller if the buyer has tendered full payment and made at least part payment and either: (i) the seller becomes ***insolvent*** within 10 days after receiving the buyer's first payment, or (ii) the goods were purchased for personal, family, or household purposes. In other cases, where the seller has failed to deliver identified goods, the buyer may replevy them from the seller if the buyer is ***unable to secure substitute goods***.

5. **Buyer's Right to Specific Performance**
The court may order specific performance "where the goods are unique or in other proper circumstances" (*e.g.,* perhaps inability to cover) even if the goods have not been identified to the contract.

6. **Buyer's Damages**

a. **For Nondelivery or upon Rejection or Revocation of Acceptance**
The buyer's basic remedy where the seller does not deliver or the buyer properly rejects or revokes acceptance of tendered goods is the difference between the ***contract price*** and either the ***market price or the cost of buying replacement goods***. (In either case, the buyer is also entitled to incidental and consequential damages less expenses saved as a result of the seller's breach.)

b. **For Accepted Goods**
If the buyer accepts goods that breach one of the seller's warranties, the buyer may recover as damages the difference between the ***value of the goods delivered*** and the

value they would have had if they had conformed to the contract plus incidental and consequential damages. To recover damages for any defect as to accepted goods, the buyer ***must***, ***within a reasonable time*** after he discovers or should have discovered the breach, ***notify*** the seller of the defect.

B. SELLER'S REMEDIES

1. Seller's Right to Withhold Goods

If the buyer fails to make a payment due on or before delivery, the seller may withhold delivery of the goods.

2. Seller's Right to Recover Goods

a. From Buyer on Buyer's Insolvency

When a seller learns that a buyer has received delivery of goods on credit while insolvent, he may reclaim the goods upon demand made within 10 days after the buyer's receipt of the goods.

b. From Bailee

The seller may stop delivery of goods in the possession of a carrier or other bailee when he discovers the buyer is insolvent. The seller may stop delivery of carload, truckload, or larger shipments of goods when the buyer breaches the contract or when the seller has a right to withhold performance pending receipt of assurances.

3. Seller's Right to Force Goods on Buyer and Recover Full Price—Limited

The seller has a right to force goods on a buyer who has not accepted them ***only if*** the seller is ***unable to resell*** the goods to others at a reasonable price or if the goods have been ***lost or damaged*** within a reasonable time after the risk of loss has passed to the buyer.

4. Seller's Damages

The Code provides three measures for damages for when the buyer wrongfully repudiates or refuses to accept conforming goods. The seller can:

(i) Recover the difference between the market price and the contract price [U.C.C. §2-708(1)];

(ii) Resell the goods and recover the difference between the contract price and the resale price [U.C.C. §2-706]; or

(iii) Recover, under a "***lost profits***" measure, the difference between the list price and the cost to the seller [U.C.C. §2-708(2)]. (Note that if the seller is a dealer, his costs would be the costs incurred in obtaining the goods from the manufacturer or another dealer, whereas if the seller is a manufacturer, his costs would be the costs of manufacturing the goods.)

The seller may also recover incidental damages.

Note: The Code provides that the lost profits measure may be used only when the other measures will not put the seller in as good a position as he would have been in if the buyer had not breached.

Example: Sara contracts to sell an original oil painting to Bob. Bob breaches. Sara sells the painting to Tom. If Sara uses one of the first two damages measures above, she should be fully compensated for Bob's breach; *i.e.,* she will recover what she would have made on the sale to Bob. However, if Sara is a retailer with an unlimited inventory and the contract was for a 19" color TV, the result would be different. If Bob refuses to take the TV—even if Sara sells it to Tom—Sara will not be in as good a position as she would have been if Bob had performed, because if Bob had performed, Sara would have sold ***two*** TV sets. Thus, in this case, the lost profits measure is appropriate to compensate Sara for the breach.

CMR **Exam Tip** Although the Code provides that the lost profits measure is used only if the other two measures do not adequately compensate the seller, this is quite often the case in commercial sales contracts. To determine whether the lost profits measure is appropriate, look at the seller's ***supply***. If the seller's supply of goods is ***unlimited*** (*i.e.,* he can obtain all the goods he can sell), then he is a ***lost volume seller***, and the lost profits measure can be used. If the seller's supply is limited (*i.e.,* he cannot obtain all the goods he can sell, as when the sale is for a unique item), the lost profits measure cannot be used, and one of the other two measures must be used instead.

a. Incidental Damages

The seller's incidental damages include such expenses as the cost of storing, shipping, and reselling the goods incurred as a result of the buyer's breach.

C. REMEDIES AVAILABLE TO BOTH BUYER AND SELLER

1. Right to Demand Assurances

If reasonable grounds for insecurity arise with respect to the performance of either party, the other may ***in writing*** demand adequate assurance of due performance. Until he receives adequate assurances, he may ***suspend his own performance***. If proper assurances are not given within a reasonable time (not over 30 days), the party seeking assurances can treat the contract as repudiated.

2. Anticipatory Repudiation

In cases where the other party's words, actions, or circumstances make it clear that he is unwilling or unable to perform, the aggrieved party may: (i) for a commercially reasonable time ***await performance*** by the other party; (ii) ***resort to any remedy for breach*** even though he has also urged the other party to perform; or (iii) ***suspend his own performance***.

CMR **Exam Tip** Be sure that you understand the difference between circumstances giving rise to a right to demand assurances and those constituting anticipatory repudiation. The right to demand assurances arises when there are ***reasonable grounds for insecurity***—something makes a party nervous that the other will not perform. Anticipatory repudiation requires much more than nervousness; there must be a ***clear indication*** that the other party is unwilling or unable to perform. Thus, for example, "I'm not going to perform" is an anticipatory repudiation, but "I'm not sure if I can perform" most likely is only a reason to demand assurances.

3. **Retraction of Repudiation**
A repudiating party may, at any time before his next performance is due, withdraw his repudiation unless the other party has canceled, materially changed his position in reliance on the repudiation, or otherwise indicated that he considers the repudiation final.

4. **Right to Sue Third Parties**
Where a third party deals with goods identified to a contract for sale so as to injure a party to the contract (*e.g.,* a negligent bailee), the seller may sue if he has either title or a security interest in the goods; the buyer may sue if the goods have been identified to the contract.

5. **Liquidated Damages**
The parties may liquidate damages at any amount that is reasonable (*i.e.,* specify in the contract what the damages will be in case of breach). Unreasonably large liquidated damages are considered penalties and are void.

D. STATUTE OF LIMITATIONS

The statute of limitations for actions for breach of a sales contract is ***four years*** from the time of breach.

VIII. WARRANTIES

A. TYPES OF WARRANTIES

Under the U.C.C., there are four types of warranties: (i) warranty of ***title*** and against infringement, (ii) implied warranty of ***merchantability***, (iii) implied warranty of ***fitness for a particular purpose***, and (iv) ***express*** warranties.

B. WARRANTY OF TITLE AND AGAINST INFRINGEMENT

1. **Warranty of Title**
Any seller of goods impliedly warrants that the title transferred is good, the transfer is rightful, and that there are no liens or encumbrances against title of which the buyer is unaware at the time of contracting.

2. **Warranty Against Infringement**
A ***merchant seller*** dealing in goods of the kind sold warrants that the goods are delivered free of any patent, trademark, copyright, or similar claims. But a buyer who furnishes specifications for the goods to the seller must hold the seller harmless against such claims.

C. IMPLIED WARRANTY OF MERCHANTABILITY

In every sale ***by a merchant*** who deals in goods of the kind sold, there is an implied warranty that the goods are merchantable. The most important test for the warranty is whether the goods are "***fit for the ordinary purposes for which such goods are used***," and a failure of such is the usual claim in a merchantability suit. As in all implied warranty cases, it makes no difference that the seller himself did not know of the defect or that he could not have discovered it.

Note: The serving of food or drink for consumption on the premises is a sale of goods subject to a warranty of merchantability.

D. IMPLIED WARRANTY OF FITNESS FOR PARTICULAR PURPOSE

The implied warranty of fitness for a particular purpose arises whenever ***any seller***, merchant or not, has reason to ***know the particular purpose*** for which the goods are to be used and that the ***buyer is relying*** on the seller's skill and judgment to select suitable goods.

E. EXPRESS WARRANTIES

Any affirmation of fact or promise made by the seller to the buyer, any description of the goods, and any sample or model creates an express warranty if the statement, description, sample, or model is part of the ***basis of the bargain*** (*i.e.,* the buyer could have relied on it).

F. DISCLAIMER OF WARRANTIES

1. Express Warranties

The Code requires that language limiting express warranties be read consistently with the warranty and to the extent they are inconsistent, the disclaimer is not given effect. The effect of this requirement is to make it, for practical purposes, extremely difficult to negate an express warranty.

2. Implied Warranties

The implied warranty of ***merchantability*** may be specifically disclaimed by mentioning "***merchantability,***" and if the disclaimer is in writing it must be ***conspicuous***. The warranty of ***fitness for a particular purpose*** may be specifically disclaimed by a ***conspicuous writing*** (it need not mention fitness for a particular purpose). These two implied warranties may also be disclaimed by one of the following general disclaimer methods: (i) language such as "as is," or "with all faults"; (ii) inspection, at least as to defects that a reasonable inspection would reveal; or (iii) course of dealing, course of performance, or usage of trade.

CMR **Exam Tip** It may seem odd that there are specific disclaimer methods, with detailed requirements, and general disclaimer methods, requiring little formality. In actual practice, it is better to use the specific disclaimers because general disclaimers may be limited by the circumstances. However, on the MBE, an "as is" or "with all faults" disclaimer will generally be as effective as a specific disclaimer.

3. Unconscionability

In addition to meeting the above requirements, disclaimers will also be tested by conscionability standards (*e.g.,* lack of bargaining power may invalidate a disclaimer).

4. Federal Consumer Product Warranties Law of 1975 ("Magnuson-Moss")

Under the Federal Consumer Product Warranties Law of 1975 [15 U.S.C. §§2301-2312], if a consumer product manufacturer or marketer issues a ***full*** written warranty, implied warranties cannot be disclaimed. If the written warranty is described as a ***limited*** warranty, implied warranties cannot be disclaimed or modified, but they may be limited to the duration of the written warranty.

G. LIMITATION OF DAMAGES FOR BREACH OF WARRANTY

Limits on damages for breach of warranty will be judged by an unconscionability test. For example, consequential damages for breach of warranty may be limited where the loss is commercial, but not, in the case of consumer goods, where the damages are for personal injury.

Damages for breach of warranty may be liquidated, but only at an amount that is reasonable in light of the anticipated or actual harm.

H. WARRANTY AND THIRD PARTIES

In most states, the seller's warranty liability extends to any natural person who is in the ***family or household*** of the buyer ***or who is a guest*** in her home if it is reasonable to expect that such person may use, consume, or be affected by the goods and he suffers ***personal injury*** because of a breach of warranty. The seller cannot escape the effect of this section by contract (*i.e.,* he cannot provide that his warranties extend only to the buyer).

CMR SUMMARY CHART

WARRANTIES

Type	How Arise	By Whom	Disclaimer
Express	By affirmation of fact, promise, description, model, or sample	Any seller	Extremely difficult to disclaim
Implied			
Warranty of Title (title is good, transfer rightful, no liens or encumbrances)	By sale of goods	Any seller	By specific language or circumstances showing seller does not claim title
Warranty of Merchantability (fit for ordinary purposes)	By sale of goods of the kind regularly sold by the merchant	Merchant only	By disclaimer mentioning "merchantability" (if written disclaimer, it must be conspicuous)*
Warranty of Fitness for Particular Purpose (fit for buyer's particular purpose)	By sale of goods where seller has reason to know of particular purpose and of buyer's reliance on seller to choose suitable goods	Any seller	By conspicuous ***written*** disclaimer*

*These may also be disclaimed by language such as "as is"; by inspection (or refusal to inspect); or by course of dealing, course of performance, or usage of trade.

I. STRICT LIABILITY

Many states have adopted a strict tort liability theory to make a manufacturer or seller of goods liable for injuries to persons or property caused by defects in goods sold. The theory allows a purchaser to recover from all sellers in the distributive chain without regard to privity of contract. It also allows an injured person who is not a purchaser to recover from the same parties. (*See* Torts outline.)

IX. THIRD-PARTY RIGHTS

A. ENTRUSTMENT

Entrusting goods to a ***merchant who deals in goods of that kind*** gives him power to transfer all rights of the entruster to ***a buyer in the ordinary course*** of business.

Example: Eric leaves his watch at a jeweler's for repair. The jeweler sells the watch to Bonnie. Bonnie gets title to the watch, and Eric's only recourse is to recover damages from the jeweler.

CMR **Exam Tip** Note that the requirements for entrustment are very specific. The merchant must be one who ordinarily deals in goods of the kind (*e.g.,* a television repair shop that only repairs televisions does not qualify). The sale must be in the ordinary course of business (*e.g.,* seizure by a creditor to satisfy a lien does not qualify). Entrustment passes only the rights of the entruster (*i.e.,* if the entruster is not the owner, ownership cannot pass).

B. VOIDABLE TITLE

Generally, if a sale is induced by fraud, the seller can rescind the sale and recover the goods (voidable title). *Exception:* The defrauded seller may not recover the goods from a ***good faith purchaser for value*** from the fraudulent buyer. Specifically, the good faith purchaser for value ***cuts off the defrauded seller's rights***, even though:

1. The seller was deceived as to the identity of the buyer;

2. The delivery was in exchange for a check later dishonored;

3. The sale was a "cash sale"; or

4. The fraudulent conduct of the buyer is punishable as larceny.

C. THIEF GENERALLY CANNOT PASS GOOD TITLE

If a thief steals goods from a true owner and then sells them to a buyer, the thief is ***unable*** to pass good title to the buyer (because the thief's title is ***void***). Therefore, in such a situation, the true owner can recover the stolen goods from the buyer, even if the buyer is a good faith purchaser for value. *Exceptions:* A thief ***can*** pass good title if: (i) the goods are ***money;*** (ii) the goods are ***negotiable instruments*** that were transferred to a holder in due course; (iii) the buyer has made ***accessions*** (*i.e.,* valuable improvements) to the goods; or (iv) the true owner is estopped from asserting title (*e.g.,* if the true owner expressly or impliedly represented that the thief had title).

D. FRAUDULENT RETENTION OF POSSESSION RULES

Retention of possession by a seller of sold goods is conclusively fraudulent (as against the seller's creditors) unless the sale is evidenced by a written bill of sale. Therefore, the seller's creditors can reach the goods while they are in the seller's hands. However, retention of possession in good faith and current course of trade by a merchant seller for a commercially reasonable time after sale or identification is not fraudulent.

The buyer has the right in certain cases to get goods from the seller even though title has not passed. This right apparently exists as against the seller's creditors as well, unless the fraudulent possession rules prevent it.

E. SALE OR RETURN

If the buyer takes goods for resale and has a right to return them ("sale or return") if they are not sold, the goods are subject to the claims of the buyer's creditors while they are in his possession.

CRIMINAL LAW

TABLE OF CONTENTS

I. JURISDICTION AND GENERAL MATTERS 1
- A. JURISDICTION 1
- B. SOURCES OF CRIMINAL LAW 1
- C. THEORIES OF PUNISHMENT 1
- D. CLASSIFICATION OF CRIMES 1
- E. VAGUENESS AND OTHER CONSTITUTIONAL LIMITATIONS 1
- F. INTERPRETATIONS OF CRIMINAL STATUTES 1
- G. MERGER 1
  - 1. Common Law 1
  - 2. Modern Law—No Merger 1
  - 3. Rules Against Multiple Convictions for Same Transaction 2

II. ESSENTIAL ELEMENTS OF A CRIME 2
- A. ELEMENTS OF A CRIME 2
- B. PHYSICAL ACT 2
  - 1. Omission as an "Act" 2
- C. MENTAL STATE 3
  - 1. Specific Intent 3
  - 2. Malice—Common Law Murder and Arson 3
  - 3. General Intent—Awareness of Factors Constituting Crime 3
  - 4. Strict Liability Offenses 4
  - 5. Model Penal Code Analysis of Fault 5
  - 6. Vicarious Liability Offenses 5
  - 7. Enterprise Liability—Liability of Corporations and Associations 5
- D. CONCURRENCE OF MENTAL FAULT WITH PHYSICAL ACT 6
- E. CAUSATION 6

III. ACCOMPLICE LIABILITY 7
- A. PARTIES TO A CRIME 7
  - 1. Common Law 7
  - 2. Modern Statutes 7
- B. MENTAL STATE—INTENT REQUIRED 7
- C. SCOPE OF LIABILITY 8
  - 1. Inability to Be Principal No Bar to Accomplice Liability 8
  - 2. Exclusions from Liability 8

IV. INCHOATE OFFENSES 10
- A. SOLICITATION 10
  - 1. Elements 10
  - 2. Defenses 10
  - 3. Merger 11
- B. CONSPIRACY 11
  - 1. Elements 11
  - 2. Liability for Co-Conspirators' Crimes 12

3. **Termination of Conspiracy** 12
4. **Defenses** 13
5. **Punishment—No Merger** 13
6. **Number of Conspiracies in Multiple Party Situations** 13

C. ATTEMPT 14
1. **Elements** 14
2. **Defenses** 14
3. **Prosecution for Attempt—Merger** 15

V. RESPONSIBILITY AND CRIMINAL CAPACITY 15

A. INSANITY 15
1. ***M'Naghten* Rule** 15
2. **Irresistible Impulse Test** 15
3. ***Durham* (or New Hampshire) Test** 15
4. **A.L.I. or Model Penal Code Test** 15
5. **Procedural Issues** 16
6. **Post-Acquittal Commitment to Mental Institution** 16
7. **Mental Condition During Criminal Proceedings** 16
8. **Diminished Capacity** 17

B. INTOXICATION 17
1. **Voluntary Intoxication** 17
2. **Involuntary Intoxication** 17
3. **Relationship to Insanity** 17

C. INFANCY 17

VI. PRINCIPLES OF EXCULPATION 18

A. JUSTIFICATION 18
1. **Self-Defense** 19
2. **Defense of Others** 19
3. **Defense of a Dwelling** 19
4. **Defense of Other Property** 19
5. **Crime Prevention** 20
6. **Use of Force to Effectuate Arrest** 20
7. **Resisting Arrest** 20
8. **Necessity** 20
9. **Public Policy** 20
10. **Domestic Authority** 21

B. EXCUSE OF DURESS 22

C. OTHER DEFENSES 22
1. **Mistake or Ignorance of Fact** 22
2. **Mistake or Ignorance of Law—No Defense** 22
3. **Consent** 22
4. **Condonation or Criminality of Victim—No Defense** 24
5. **Entrapment** 24

VII. OFFENSES AGAINST THE PERSON 24

A. ASSAULT AND BATTERY 24
1. **Battery** 24
2. **Assault** 24

B. MAYHEM 25
C. HOMICIDE 25
1. Common Law Criminal Homicides 25
2. Statutory Modification of Common Law Classification 28
3. Felony Murder 28
4. Causation 29
D. FALSE IMPRISONMENT 30
E. KIDNAPPING 30
1. Aggravated Kidnapping 30

VIII. SEX OFFENSES 30
A. RAPE 30
1. Absence of Marital Relationship 30
2. Lack of Effective Consent 30
B. STATUTORY RAPE 31
C. ADULTERY AND FORNICATION 31
D. INCEST 31
E. SEDUCTION 31
F. BIGAMY 31

IX. PROPERTY OFFENSES 31
A. LARCENY 31
1. Possession 31
2. Intent to Permanently Deprive 32
3. Abandoned, Lost, or Mislaid Property 32
4. "Continuing Trespass" Situation 32
B. EMBEZZLEMENT 32
1. Distinguish from Larceny 33
2. Fraudulent Intent 33
C. FALSE PRETENSES 33
1. "Larceny by Trick" Distinguished 33
2. The Misrepresentation Required 33
D. ROBBERY 33
1. Distinguish Larceny 34
E. EXTORTION 34
1. Distinguish Robbery 35
F. RECEIPT OF STOLEN PROPERTY 35
1. "Possession" 35
2. "Stolen" Property 35
G. THEFT 35
H. FORGERY 35
1. Fraudulently Obtaining Signature of Another 36
2. Uttering a Forged Instrument 36
I. MALICIOUS MISCHIEF 36

X. OFFENSES AGAINST THE HABITATION 36
A. BURGLARY 36
B. ARSON 37

1. **Damage Required** 37
2. **Related Offense—Houseburning** 37

XI. OFFENSES INVOLVING JUDICIAL PROCEDURE 37
A. PERJURY 37
B. SUBORNATION OF PERJURY 37
C. BRIBERY 37
D. COMPOUNDING A CRIME 37
E. MISPRISION OF A FELONY 38

CRIMINAL LAW

I. JURISDICTION AND GENERAL MATTERS

A. JURISDICTION

Generally, a state has jurisdiction over a crime if: any act constituting an element of the offense was committed in the state, an act outside the state caused a result in the state, the crime involved the neglect of a duty imposed by the law of the state, there was an attempt or conspiracy outside the state plus an act inside the state, or there was an attempt or conspiracy inside the state to commit an offense outside the state.

B. SOURCES OF CRIMINAL LAW

There is no federal common law of crimes; all federal crimes are statutory. A majority of the states retain common law crimes. The modern trend is to abolish common law crimes either expressly by statute or impliedly by the enactment of comprehensive criminal codes.

C. THEORIES OF PUNISHMENT

Theories justifying criminal punishment include incapacitation of the criminal, special deterrence of the criminal, general deterrence of others, retribution, rehabilitation, and education of the public.

D. CLASSIFICATION OF CRIMES

There are two classes of crimes: felonies and misdemeanors. Felonies are generally punishable by ***death or imprisonment for more than one year***; other crimes are misdemeanors.

E. VAGUENESS AND OTHER CONSTITUTIONAL LIMITATIONS

Due process requires that a criminal statute not be vague. There must be (i) ***fair warning*** (*i.e.,* a person of ordinary intelligence must be able to discern what is prohibited), and (ii) ***no arbitrary and discriminatory enforcement***. The Constitution places two substantive limitations on both federal and state legislatures—no ex post facto laws and no bills of attainder.

F. INTERPRETATIONS OF CRIMINAL STATUTES

Criminal statutes are construed strictly in favor of defendants. If two statutes address the same subject matter but dictate different conclusions, the more specific statute will be applied rather than the more general. The more recently enacted statute will control an older statute. Under new comprehensive codes, crimes committed prior to the effective date of the new code are subject to prosecution and punishment under the law as it existed at the time the offense was committed.

G. MERGER

1. Common Law

At common law, if a person engaged in conduct constituting both a felony and a misdemeanor, she could be ***convicted*** only of the felony. The misdemeanor merged into the felony.

2. Modern Law—No Merger

There is no longer any merger ***except*** that one who solicits another to commit a crime may not be convicted of ***both the solicitation and the completed crime*** (if the person solicited does complete it). Similarly, a person who completes a crime after attempting it may not be convicted of ***both the attempt and the completed crime***. Conspiracy, however, does not merge with the completed offense (*e.g.,* one can be convicted of both robbery and conspiracy to commit robbery).

3. Rules Against Multiple Convictions for Same Transaction

Double jeopardy prohibits trial or conviction of a person for a lesser included offense if he has been put in jeopardy for the greater offense. However, a court can impose multiple punishments at a single trial where the punishments are for two or more statutorily defined offenses specifically intended by the legislature to carry ***separate punishments***, even though the offenses arise from the same transaction and constitute the same crime.

II. ESSENTIAL ELEMENTS OF A CRIME

A. ELEMENTS OF A CRIME

A crime almost always requires proof of a physical act (actus reus) and a mental state (mens rea), and concurrence of the act and mental state. It may also require proof of a result and causation (*i.e.,* that the act caused the harmful result).

B. PHYSICAL ACT

Defendant must have either performed a ***voluntary*** physical act or failed to act under circumstances imposing a legal duty to act. An act is a ***bodily movement***.

CMR **Exam Tip** Remember that the act must be ***voluntary***. In the past, the bar examiners have set up very unlikely scenarios to test this point—*e.g.,* they have an unconscious person shoot a victim. Don't be fooled by these odd facts; if the facts tell you that the defendant was unconscious, the act was not voluntary, and thus defendant cannot be convicted of a crime based on this act. (The only exception to this rule would be if the defendant knew he was likely to become unconscious and commit the act, but this situation would have to be presented in the facts.)

1. Omission as an "Act"

Failure to act gives rise to liability only if:

(i) There is a ***specific duty to act*** imposed by law;

(ii) The ***defendant has knowledge*** of the facts giving rise to the duty to act; and

(iii) It is ***reasonably possible to perform*** the duty.

A legal duty to act can arise from a statute, contract, relationship between the defendant and the victim (*e.g.,* a parent has a duty to protect child from harm), voluntary assumption of care by the defendant for the victim, or the creation of peril for the victim by the defendant.

CMR **Exam Tip** For an omission to be a criminal act, there must be a ***duty*** to act. There is no general Good Samaritan law requiring people to help others in trouble. Thus, a defendant is not liable for the failure to help or rescue another person unless he has a duty to do so—no matter how easy it would have been to render help. Your moral outrage is not enough for a criminal conviction.

C. MENTAL STATE

1. Specific Intent

A crime may require not only the doing of an act, but also the doing of it with a specific intent or objective. The existence of a specific intent cannot be inferred from the doing of the act. The major specific intent crimes and the intents they require are as follows:

a. ***Solicitation***: Intent to have the person solicited commit the crime.

b. ***Attempt***: Intent to complete the crime.

c. ***Conspiracy***: Intent to have the crime completed.

d. ***First degree premeditated murder***: Premeditation.

e. ***Assault***: Intent to commit a battery.

f. ***Larceny and robbery***: Intent to permanently deprive the other of his interest in the property taken.

g. ***Burglary***: Intent to commit a felony in the dwelling.

h. ***Forgery***: Intent to defraud.

i. ***False pretenses***: Intent to defraud.

j. ***Embezzlement***: Intent to defraud.

CMR **Exam Tip** Never forget that attempt is a ***specific intent*** crime—even when the crime attempted is not. Thus, although murder does not require a specific intent to kill (*i.e.*, recklessly disregarding a high risk to human life would be enough), attempted murder requires the specific ***intent to kill***. Without that intent, a defendant is not guilty of attempted murder.

Examples: 1) D intends to kill V but only wounds him. D had the requisite specific intent (*i.e.*, the intent to kill) and is guilty of attempted murder.

2) D intends to scare V by shooting V's hat off his head. If D's shot kills V, D is guilty of murder; but if V is merely wounded, D is not guilty of attempted murder. (D may, of course, be guilty of battery.)

2. Malice—Common Law Murder and Arson

The intent necessary for malice crimes (common law murder and arson) sounds like specific intent, but it is not as restrictive; it requires only a reckless disregard of an obvious or high risk that the particular harmful result will occur. Defenses to specific intent crimes (*e.g.*, voluntary intoxication) do not apply to malice crimes.

3. General Intent—Awareness of Factors Constituting Crime

Almost all crimes require at least "general intent," which is an awareness of all factors constituting the crime; *i.e.*, defendant must be aware that she is acting in the proscribed way and that any required attendant circumstances exist. The defendant need not be certain that all the circumstances exist; it is sufficient that she is aware of a high likelihood that they will occur.

a. Inference of Intent from Act

A jury may infer the required general intent merely from the doing of the act.

b. Transferred Intent

The defendant can be liable under the doctrine of transferred intent where she intends the harm that is actually caused, but to a different victim or object. Defenses and mitigating circumstances may also usually be transferred. The doctrine of transferred intent applies to homicide, battery, and arson. It does not apply to attempt.

CMR Exam Tip A person found guilty of a crime on the basis of transferred intent is usually guilty of two crimes: the completed crime against the actual victim and attempt against the intended victim. Thus, if D intends to shoot and kill X, but instead shoots and kills V, D can be guilty of the murder of V (under the transferred intent doctrine) and the attempted murder of X.

c. Motive Distinguished

Motive is the reason or explanation for the crime; it is different from intent to commit the crime. Motive is immaterial to substantive criminal law.

4. Strict Liability Offenses

A strict liability or public welfare offense is one that does not require awareness of all of the factors constituting the crime; *i.e.*, the defendant can be found guilty from the mere fact that she committed the act. Common strict liability offenses are selling liquor to minors and statutory rape. Certain defenses, such as mistake of fact, are not available.

CMR SUMMARY CHART

REQUISITE INTENT FOR MAJOR CRIMES

Specific Intent	General Intent	Malice	Strict Liability
1. Solicitation	1. Battery	1. Common Law Murder	1. Statutory Rape
2. Attempt	2. Rape	2. Arson	2. Selling Liquor to Minors
3. Conspiracy	3. Kidnapping		3. Bigamy (some jurisdictions)
4. First Degree Premeditated Murder	4. False Imprisonment		
5. Assault (Attempted Battery)			
6. Larceny, Robbery			
7. Burglary			
8. Forgery			
9. False Pretenses			
10. Embezzlement			

5. **Model Penal Code Analysis of Fault**
The M.P.C. eliminates the common law distinctions between general and specific intent and adopts the following categories of intent:

a. **Purposely, Knowingly, or Recklessly**
When a statute requires that the defendant act purposely, knowingly, or recklessly, a ***subjective standard*** is used.

1) **Purposely**
A person acts purposely when his ***conscious object*** is to engage in certain conduct or cause a certain result.

2) **Knowingly**
A person acts knowingly when he is ***aware*** that his conduct is of a particular nature or ***knows*** that his conduct will necessarily or very likely cause a particular result. Knowing conduct satisfies a statute requiring willful conduct.

3) **Recklessly**
A person acts recklessly when he ***knows*** of a ***substantial and unjustifiable risk*** and ***consciously disregards*** it. Mere realization of the risk is not enough. Thus, recklessness involves both objective ("unjustifiable risk") and subjective ("awareness") elements. Unless the statute specifies a different degree of fault or is a strict liability offense, the defendant must have acted at least recklessly to be criminally liable.

CMR **Exam Tip** A criminal law question often asks you to interpret a statute. Check the language of the statute carefully for the mental state required for each material element of the crime, because whether a defendant is guilty often turns on that mental state. For example, if the statute requires that a defendant act "knowingly" (such as "knowingly selling guns to a felon"), the defendant will not be guilty if she did not have that knowledge (*e.g.,* did not know the purchaser was a felon). In interpreting a statute, also keep in mind that "willfully" is equivalent to "knowingly."

b. **Negligence**
A person acts negligently when he ***fails to be aware of a substantial and unjustifiable risk***, where such failure is a substantial deviation from the standard of care. To determine whether a person acted negligently, an ***objective standard*** is used. However, it is not just the reasonable person standard that is used in torts. The defendant must have taken a very unreasonable risk.

6. **Vicarious Liability Offenses**
A vicarious liability offense is one in which a person without personal fault may nevertheless be held liable for the criminal conduct of another (usually an employee). The trend is to limit vicarious liability to regulatory crimes and to limit punishment to fines.

7. **Enterprise Liability—Liability of Corporations and Associations**
At common law, a corporation does not have capacity to commit crimes. Under modern statutes, corporations may be held liable for an act performed by: (i) an agent of the corporation acting within the scope of his office or employment; or (ii) a corporate agent high enough in hierarchy to presume his acts reflect corporate policy.

CMR SUMMARY CHART

STATE OF MIND

Mens Rea	State of Mind Required	Objective or Subjective Test?
	Common Law	
Specific Intent	Intent to engage in proscribed conduct	Subjective
General Intent	Awareness of acting in proscribed manner	Subjective
Malice	Reckless disregard of a known risk	Subjective
Strict Liability	Conscious commission of proscribed act	Objective
	MPC Fault Standards	
Purposely	Conscious object to engage in proscribed conduct	Subjective
Knowingly	Awareness that conduct is of a particular nature or will cause a particular result	Subjective
Recklessly	Consciously disregarding a substantial known risk	Subjective
Negligently	Failure to be aware of a substantial risk	Objective

D. CONCURRENCE OF MENTAL FAULT WITH PHYSICAL ACT

The defendant must have had the intent necessary for the crime at the time he committed the act constituting the crime, and the intent must have actuated the act. For example, if D is driving to V's house to kill him, he will lack the necessary concurrence for murder if he ***accidentally*** runs V over before reaching the house.

E. CAUSATION

Some crimes (*e.g.,* homicide) require result and causation (*see* VII.C.4., *infra*).

III. ACCOMPLICE LIABILITY

A. PARTIES TO A CRIME

1. Common Law

At common law, parties to a crime included the ***principal in the first degree*** (person who actually engaged in the act or omission that constitutes the offense), ***principal in the second degree*** (person who aided, commanded, or encouraged the principal and was present at the crime), ***accessory before the fact*** (person who assisted or encouraged but was ***not present***), and ***accessory after the fact*** (person who, with knowledge that the other committed a felony, assisted him to escape arrest or punishment).

At common law, conviction of the principal was required for conviction of an accessory and the charge must have indicated the correct theory of liability (*i.e.,* as principal or accessory).

2. Modern Statutes

Most jurisdictions have abolished the distinctions between principals in the first degree and principals in the second degree or accessories before the fact. All such "parties to the crime" can be found guilty of the principal offense. For convenience, however, think of the one who actually engages in the act or omission as the principal and the other parties as accomplices.

Note: An accessory after the fact (one who assists another knowing that he has committed a felony in order to help him escape) is still treated separately. Punishment for this crime usually bears no relationship to the principal offense.

CMR SUMMARY CHART

MODERN ACCOMPLICE LIABILITY

Defendant	Conduct	Liability
Principal	Person who commits the illegal act	Liable for principal crime
Accomplice (includes common law accessory before the fact)	Person who aids or encourages principal to commit the illegal conduct	Liable for principal crime if accomplice intended to aid or encourage crime
Accessory After the Fact	Person who aids another to escape knowing that he has committed a felony	Liable for separate, less serious crime of being an accessory after the fact

B. MENTAL STATE—INTENT REQUIRED

To be guilty as an accomplice, most jurisdictions require that the person give aid, counsel, or encouragement to the principal with the ***intent*** to encourage the crime. In the absence of a statute, most courts would hold that ***mere knowledge*** that a crime will result is not enough, at least where the aid given is in the form of the sale of ordinary goods at ordinary prices (*e.g.,* a gas station attendant will not be liable for arson for knowingly selling a gallon of gasoline to an arsonist). However, procuring an illegal item or selling at a higher price because of the buyer's purpose (*e.g.,* charging the arsonist $100 for the gallon of gas) may constitute a sufficient "stake in the venture" to constitute intent.

C. SCOPE OF LIABILITY

An accomplice is responsible for the crimes he did or counseled ***and*** for any other crimes committed in the course of committing the crime contemplated to the same extent as the principal, as long as the other crimes were ***probable or foreseeable***.

1. Inability to Be Principal No Bar to Accomplice Liability

One who may not be convicted of being a principal may be convicted of being an accomplice. *Example:* At common law a woman cannot be convicted of being the principal in a rape but can be found guilty as an accomplice if she aids the principal.

2. Exclusions from Liability

a. Members of the Protected Class

Members of the class protected by a statute are excluded from accomplice liability. *Example:* A woman transported across state lines cannot be an accomplice to the crime of transporting women across state lines for immoral purposes, since she is within the class protected.

b. Necessary Parties Not Provided For

A party necessary to the commission of a crime, by statutory definition, who is not provided for in the statute is excluded from accomplice liability. *Example:* If a statute makes the sale of heroin illegal, but does not provide for punishment of the purchaser, he cannot be found guilty under the statute as an accomplice to the seller.

c. Withdrawal

A person who effectively withdraws from a crime before it is committed cannot be held guilty as an accomplice. Withdrawal must occur ***before*** the crime becomes unstoppable.

(i) ***Repudiation*** is sufficient withdrawal for mere encouragement.

(ii) ***Attempt to neutralize*** assistance is required if participation went beyond mere encouragement.

Notifying the police or taking other action to prevent the crime is also sufficient.

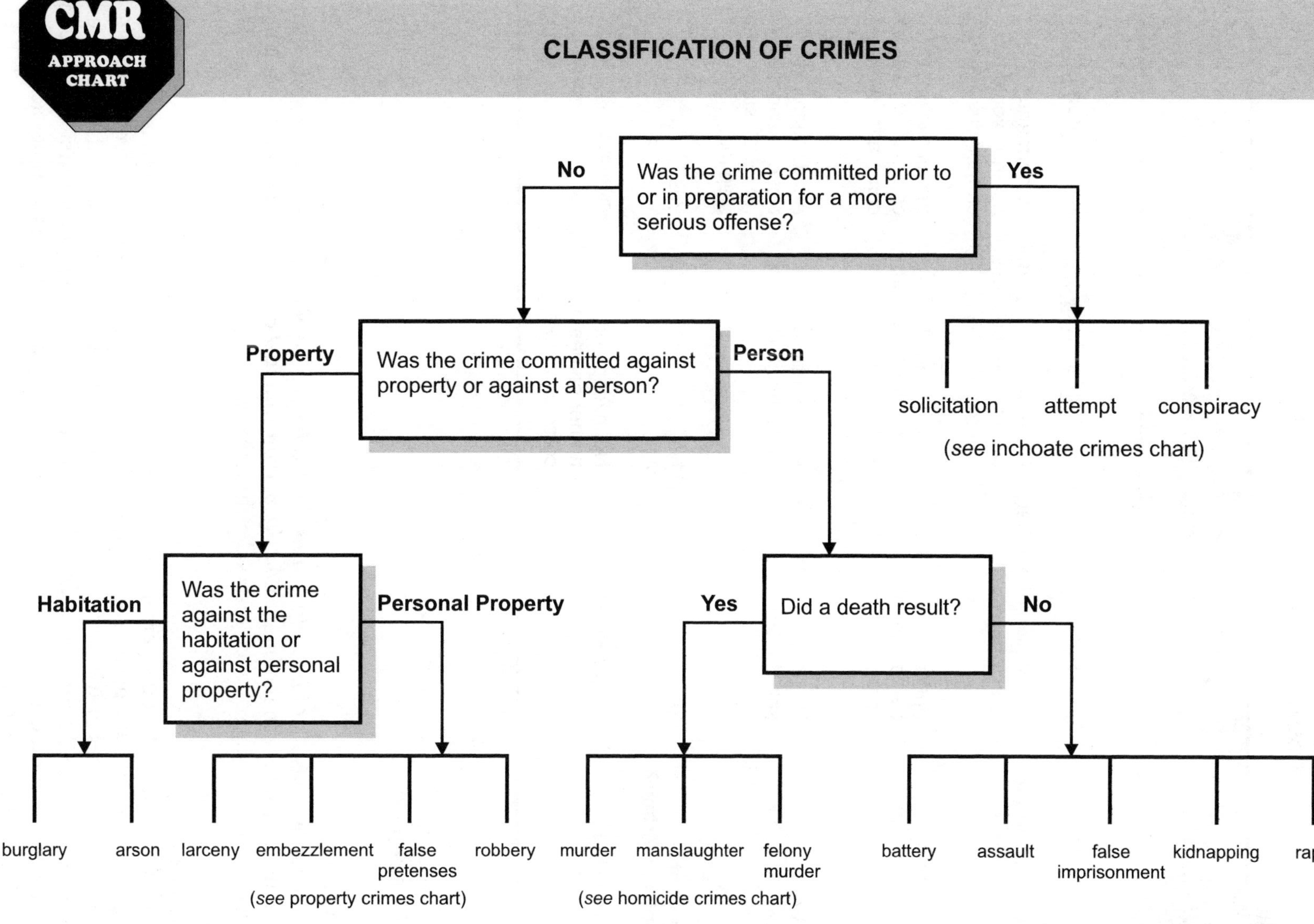
CMR APPROACH CHART
CLASSIFICATION OF CRIMES
Was the crime committed prior to or in preparation for a more serious offense?
No
Yes
solicitation
attempt
conspiracy
(see inchoate crimes chart)
Was the crime committed against property or against a person?
Property
Person
Was the crime against the habitation or against personal property?
Habitation
Personal Property
burglary
arson
larceny
embezzlement
false pretenses
robbery
(see property crimes chart)
Did a death result?
Yes
No
murder
manslaughter
felony murder
(see homicide crimes chart)
battery
assault
false imprisonment
kidnapping
rape

IV. INCHOATE OFFENSES

CMR COMPARISON CHART

INCHOATE CRIMES

	Solicitation	Conspiracy	Attempt
Culpable Conduct	Solicitation of another to commit a felony	Agreement between two or more people to commit a crime	Performance of an act that would be a crime if successful
Mental State	Specific intent that person solicited commit the crime	Specific intent to: (i) enter into agreement; and (ii) achieve objective	Specific intent to commit the particular crime attempted
Overt Act	No act (other than the solicitation)	Act in furtherance of the conspiracy	Act dangerously close to success (M.P.C.—substantial step test)
Merger into Completed Crime?	Yes	No	Yes
Withdrawal a Defense?	Generally no	No, except for further crimes of co-conspirators	Generally no

A. SOLICITATION

1. Elements

Solicitation consists of ***inciting***, ***counseling***, ***advising***, ***urging***, ***or commanding*** another to commit a crime, with the ***intent that the person solicited commit the crime***. It is not necessary that the person solicited respond affirmatively.

2. Defenses

It is not a defense that the person solicited is not convicted, nor that the offense solicited could not in fact have been successful. In most jurisdictions, it is not a defense that the solicitor renounces or withdraws the solicitation. However, it ***is a defense*** that the solicitor could not be found guilty of the completed crime because of a legislative intent to exempt her (*e.g.,* a woman cannot be found guilty of soliciting a man to transport her across state lines for immoral purposes).

3. Merger

If the person solicited commits the crime solicited, both that person and the solicitor can be held liable for that crime. If the person solicited commits acts sufficient to be liable for attempt, both parties can be liable for attempt. If the person solicited agrees to commit the crime, but does not even commit acts sufficient for attempt, both parties can be held liable for conspiracy. However, under the doctrine of merger, the solicitor ***cannot be punished for both*** the solicitation and these other offenses.

B. CONSPIRACY

A conspiracy is an agreement between two or more parties to commit a crime.

1. Elements

A conspiracy requires (i) an ***agreement*** between two or more persons; (ii) an ***intent to enter into the agreement***; and (iii) an ***intent*** by at least two persons ***to achieve the objective of the agreement***. A majority of states now also require an ***overt act***, but an act of mere preparation will suffice.

Exam Tip Conspiracy is probably the most tested inchoate crime. One important thing for you to remember is that it takes two to conspire at common law. Make sure that the facts of a question show at least two "guilty minds"—two people who intend to agree ***and*** intend that the crime be committed. Thus, if the defendant and an undercover police officer "agree" to commit a crime, there is no conspiracy at common law because only the defendant intended that the crime be committed. Similarly, if the defendant and another person "agree" but the facts show that the other person merely pretended to go along and really meant to warn the police, there is no conspiracy.

a. Agreement Requirement

The parties must agree to accomplish the same objective by mutual action. However, the agreement need not be express; it may be inferred from joint activity.

1) Implications of Requirement of Two or More Parties

A conspiracy at common law must involve a "meeting of minds" between at least two independent persons. This requirement presents the following issues:

a) Husband and Wife

At common law, a husband and wife could not conspire together, but this distinction has been abandoned in most states.

b) Corporation and Agent

There can be no conspiracy between a corporation and a single agent acting on its behalf. There is a split of authority as to whether the agents of a corporation can be deemed co-conspirators with the corporation.

c) Wharton Rule

Under the Wharton Rule, where two or more people are necessary for the commission of the substantive offense (*e.g.*, adultery, dueling), there is no crime of conspiracy unless ***more parties participate*** in the agreement than are necessary for the crime (*e.g.,* because it takes two people to commit adultery, it takes three people to conspire to commit adultery). *Exception:* The Wharton Rule does not apply to agreements with "necessary parties not provided for" by the substantive offense; both parties may be guilty of conspiracy even though both are necessary for commission of the substantive offense.

d) **Agreement with Person in "Protected Class"**
If members of a conspiracy agree to commit a crime designed to protect persons within a given class, persons within that class cannot be guilty of the crime itself or of conspiracy to commit that crime. Likewise, the nonprotected person cannot be guilty of conspiracy if the agreement was with the protected person only.

e) **Effect of Acquittal of Some Conspirators**
Under the traditional view, the ***acquittal*** of all persons with whom a defendant is alleged to have conspired precludes conviction of the remaining defendant. In some jurisdictions following the traditional view, a conviction for conspiracy against one defendant is allowed to stand when the alleged co-conspirator is acquitted in a ***separate trial***.

CMR Exam Tip Acquittal is the key here. If the defendant and others allegedly conspired and only the defendant is charged and tried (*e.g.,* the other parties are not apprehended or not prosecuted), the defendant can be convicted. But if the defendant is charged and tried and ***all the others have been acquitted***, the defendant cannot be convicted. (The acquittals show that there was no one with whom the defendant could conspire.)

f) **Model Penal Code Unilateral Approach**
Under the M.P.C. "unilateral" approach, the defendant can be convicted of conspiracy regardless of whether the other parties have all been acquitted or were only feigning agreement.

b. **Mental State—Specific Intent**
Conspiracy is a specific intent crime. Parties must have: (i) the intent to ***agree*** and (ii) the intent to ***achieve the objective*** of the conspiracy.

c. **Overt Act**
Most states require that an act in furtherance of the conspiracy be performed. An act of mere preparation is usually sufficient.

2. **Liability for Co-Conspirators' Crimes**
A conspirator may be held liable for crimes committed by other conspirators if the crimes (i) were committed ***in furtherance*** of the objectives of the conspiracy and (ii) were ***foreseeable.***

3. **Termination of Conspiracy**
The point at which a conspiracy terminates is important because acts and statements of co-conspirators are admissible against a conspirator only if they were done or made in furtherance of the conspiracy. A conspiracy usually terminates ***upon completion of the wrongful objective***. Unless agreed to in advance, acts of concealment are ***not*** part of the conspiracy. Note also that the government's defeat of the conspiracy's objective does not automatically terminate the conspiracy.

4. **Defenses**

a. **Impossibility**
Impossibility is ***not*** a defense to conspiracy.

b. **Withdrawal**
Generally, withdrawal from the conspiracy is ***not*** a defense ***to the conspiracy***, because the conspiracy is complete as soon as the agreement is made and an act in furtherance is performed. Withdrawal ***may*** be a defense to ***crimes committed in furtherance*** of the conspiracy, including the substantive target crime of the conspiracy.

1) **When Withdrawal Effective**
To withdraw, a conspirator must perform an affirmative act that notifies all members of the conspiracy of her withdrawal. Notice must be given in time for the members to abandon their plans. If she has also provided assistance as an accomplice, she must try to neutralize the assistance.

CMR **Exam Tip** Withdrawal from a conspiracy is another important test issue. You must be careful here not to let your feelings get in the way of a correct answer. Remember that a conspiracy is complete upon the agreement with the requisite intent and an overt act. Since the overt act can be a preparatory act, the conspiracy is usually complete very soon after the agreement. If the crime is complete, the defendant is ***guilty of conspiracy***—even if the facts show that she had second thoughts, told her co-conspirators that she was backing out, warned the police, hid the weapons, etc. These actions come too late; defendant is guilty of conspiracy. (Such actions may relieve defendant of criminal liability for her co-conspirators' acts after this withdrawal, but they have no effect on the crime of conspiracy.)

5. **Punishment—No Merger**
Conspiracy and the completed crime are distinct offenses; *i.e.*, there is no merger. A defendant may be convicted of and punished for both.

6. **Number of Conspiracies in Multiple Party Situations**
In complex situations, there may be a large conspiracy with a number of subconspiracies. In such situations, it is important to determine whether members of one subconspiracy are liable for the acts of another subconspiracy. The two most common situations are:

a. **Chain Relationship**
A chain relationship is a single, large conspiracy in which all parties to subagreements are interested in the single large scheme. In this case, all members are liable for the acts of the others in furtherance of the conspiracy.

b. **Hub-and-Spoke Relationship**
In a hub-and-spoke relationship a number of independent conspiracies are linked by a common member. Although the common member will be liable for all of the conspiracies, members of the individual conspiracies are not liable for the acts of the other conspirators.

C. ATTEMPT

1. Elements

Attempt is an act, done with ***intent to commit a crime***, that ***falls short of completing*** the crime.

a. Mental State

To be guilty of attempt, the defendant must intend to perform an act and obtain a result that, if achieved, would constitute a crime. Regardless of the intent necessary for the completed offense, an attempt ***always requires a specific intent*** (*i.e.,* the intent to commit the crime). *Example:* To be guilty of attempt to commit murder, defendant must have had the specific ***intent to kill*** another person, even though the mens rea for murder itself does not necessarily require a specific intent to kill.

CMR **Exam Tip** Attempt to commit a crime defined as the negligent production of a result (*e.g.,* negligent homicide) is logically impossible because a person does not intend to be negligent. Thus, there can be no attempted negligent homicide, etc.

b. Overt Act

Defendant must commit an act ***beyond mere preparation*** for the offense. Traditionally, most courts followed the "***proximity***" ***test***, which requires that the act be "dangerously close" to successful completion of the crime (*e.g.,* pointing a loaded gun at an intended victim and pulling the trigger, only to have the gun not fire or the bullet miss its mark is sufficient). However, today most state criminal codes (and the Model Penal Code) require that the act or omission constitute a "***substantial step*** in a course of conduct planned to culminate in the commission of the crime" that strongly corroborates the actor's criminal purpose.

Exam Tip Note that the overt act required for attempt is much more substantial than the overt act required for conspiracy.

2. Defenses

a. Impossibility of Success

1) Factual Impossibility No Defense

Factual impossibility (*i.e.,* that it was factually impossible for defendant to complete the intended crime) is ***not*** a defense to attempt (*e.g.,* it is not a defense to attempted robbery that the intended victim had no money with her). This includes impossibility due to mistake in attendant circumstances (*e.g.,* it is no defense to a charge of ***attempted*** receipt of stolen goods that the goods were no longer stolen because defendant purchased them from an undercover police officer).

2) Legal Impossibility Is a Defense

Legal impossibility (*i.e.,* that it is not a crime to do that which defendant intended to do) is a defense (*e.g.,* defendant going fishing in a lake in which he erroneously believed fishing was prohibited cannot be convicted of attempted violation of the fishing ordinance).

CMR **Exam Tip** On the MBE, when facts give rise to impossibility, it is usually factual impossibility and is no defense to attempt. Thus, if you are unsure how to categorize the impossibility in a particular fact pattern, your best bet is to decide that it is no defense.

b. Abandonment

Abandonment is ***not*** a defense. If defendant had the intent and committed an overt act, she is guilty of attempt despite the fact that she changed only her mind and abandoned the plan before the intended crime was completed.

3. Prosecution for Attempt—Merger

Attempt merges with the completed crime. Thus, a defendant ***cannot be found guilty of both*** attempt and the completed crime. Also, a defendant charged only with a completed crime may be found guilty of attempt, but a defendant charged only with attempt may not be convicted of the completed crime.

V. RESPONSIBILITY AND CRIMINAL CAPACITY

A. INSANITY

There are several formulations of the test to be applied to determine whether, at the time of the crime, the defendant was so mentally ill as to be entitled to acquittal.

1. *M'Naghten* Rule

Under this rule, a defendant is entitled to acquittal only if he had a mental disease or defect that caused him to either: (i) ***not know that his act would be wrong***; or (ii) ***not understand the nature and quality of his actions***. Loss of control because of mental illness is no defense.

2. Irresistible Impulse Test

Under this test, a defendant is entitled to acquittal only if, because of a mental illness, he was ***unable to control his actions or conform his conduct to the law***.

3. *Durham* (or New Hampshire) Test

Under this test, a defendant is entitled to acquittal if the ***crime was the product of his mental illness*** (*i.e.,* crime would not have been committed but for the disease). The *Durham* test is broader than either the *M'Naghten* test or the irresistible impulse test.

4. A.L.I. or Model Penal Code Test

Under the M.P.C. test (which represents the "modern trend"), a defendant is entitled to acquittal if he had a mental disease or defect, and, as a result, he ***lacked the substantial capacity*** to either:

(i) ***Appreciate the criminality*** of his conduct; or

(ii) ***Conform his conduct*** to the requirements of law.

CMR Exam Tip It is important to know these separate insanity tests because questions may ask you about a specific test (*e.g.,* "If the jurisdiction has adopted the M.P.C. test for determining insanity, what is defendant's best argument for acquittal on this ground?"). To answer this type of question, you must know the requirements for that particular test. A shorthand way to remember the test is:

M'Naghten—defendant does ***not know right from wrong***;

Irresistible Impulse—(as the name says) an ***impulse*** that defendant ***cannot resist***;

Durham—***but for the mental illness***, defendant would not have done the act;

A.L.I. or M.P.C.—***combination*** of *M'Naghten* and irresistible impulse.

5. Procedural Issues

a. Burdens of Proof

All defendants are presumed sane; the defendant must raise the insanity issue. There is a split among the jurisdictions as to whether the defendant raising the issue bears the burden of proof.

b. When Defense May Be Raised

Although the insanity defense may be raised at the arraignment when the plea is taken, the defendant need not raise it then. A simple "not guilty" at that time does not waive the right to raise the defense at some future time.

c. Pretrial Psychiatric Examination

If the defendant does ***not*** raise the insanity issue, he ***may*** refuse a court-ordered psychiatric examination to determine his competency to stand trial. If the defendant ***raises*** the insanity issue, he may ***not*** refuse to be examined by a psychiatrist appointed to aid the court in the resolution of his insanity plea.

6. Post-Acquittal Commitment to Mental Institution

In most jurisdictions, a defendant acquitted by reason of insanity may be committed to a mental institution until cured. Confinement may exceed the maximum period of incarceration for the offense charged.

7. Mental Condition During Criminal Proceedings

Under the Due Process Clause of the United States Constitution, a defendant may not be tried, convicted, or sentenced if, as a result of a mental disease or defect, he is unable (i) to understand the nature of the proceedings being brought against him; or (ii) to assist his lawyer in the preparation of his defense. A defendant may not be executed if he is incapable of understanding the nature and purpose of the punishment.

8. Diminished Capacity

Some states recognize the defense of "diminished capacity" under which defendant may assert that as a result of a mental defect short of insanity, he did not have the mental state required for the crime charged. Most states allowing the diminished capacity defense limit it to specific intent crimes, but a few states allow it for general intent crimes as well.

B. INTOXICATION

Intoxication may be caused by any substance (*e.g.,* drugs, alcohol, medicine). It may be raised whenever intoxication negates one of the elements of the crime. The law usually distinguishes between voluntary and involuntary intoxication.

1. Voluntary Intoxication

Intoxication is voluntary if it is the result of the intentional taking without duress of a substance known to be intoxicating.

a. Defense to Specific Intent Crimes

Evidence of "voluntary" intoxication may be offered by defendant only if the crime requires ***purpose*** (***intent***) ***or knowledge***, and the intoxication prevented the defendant from formulating the purpose or obtaining the knowledge. Thus, it is often a good defense to ***specific intent*** crimes. The defense is not available if the defendant purposely becomes intoxicated in order to establish the defense.

b. No Defense to Other Crimes

Voluntary intoxication is no defense to crimes involving malice, recklessness, negligence, or strict liability.

2. Involuntary Intoxication

Intoxication is involuntary only if it results from the taking of an intoxicating substance ***without knowledge*** of its nature, ***under direct duress*** imposed by another, or ***pursuant to medical advice*** while unaware of the substance's intoxicating effect. Involuntary intoxication may be treated as a mental illness, and the defendant is entitled to acquittal if she meets the jurisdiction's insanity test.

3. Relationship to Insanity

Continuous, excessive drinking or drug use may bring on actual insanity and thus a defendant may be able to claim both an intoxication defense and an insanity defense.

C. INFANCY

At common law, there could be no liability for an act committed by a child under age seven. For acts committed by a child between ages seven and 14, there was a rebuttable presumption that the child was unable to understand the wrongfulness of his acts. Children age 14 or older were treated as adults. Modern statutes often modify this and provide that no child can be convicted of a crime until a stated age is reached, usually 13 or 14. However, children can be found to be delinquent in special juvenile or family courts.

CMR SUMMARY CHART

DEFENSES NEGATING CRIMINAL CAPACITY

Defense	Elements	Applicable Crimes
Insanity	Meet applicable insanity test (*M'Naghten*, irresistible impulse, *Durham*, or M.P.C.)	Defense to ***all*** crimes
Intoxication -voluntary	Voluntary intentional taking of a substance known to be intoxicating	Defense to ***specific intent*** crime if intoxication prevents formation of required intent
-involuntary	Taking intoxicating substance without knowledge of its nature, under duress, or pursuant to medical advice	Treated as mental illness (*i.e.*, apply appropriate insanity test); may be a defense to ***all*** crimes
Infancy	Defendant under age 14 at common law; under modern statutes, defendant under age 13 or 14	*Common law:* Under age seven, absolute defense to ***all*** crimes; under 14, rebuttable presumption of defense. *Modern statutes:* Defense to adult crimes but may still be delinquent
Diminished Capacity (some states)	As a result of mental defect short of insanity, defendant did not have the required mental state to commit the crime	Most states with this defense limit it to ***specific intent*** crimes

VI. PRINCIPLES OF EXCULPATION

A. JUSTIFICATION

The justification defenses arise when society has deemed that although the defendant committed a proscribed act, she should not be punished because the circumstances justify the action.

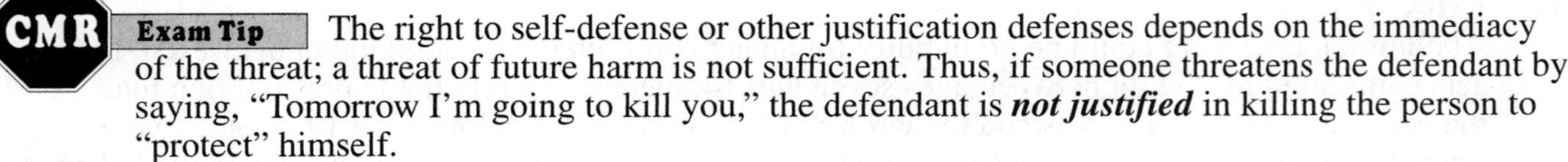

CMR Exam Tip The right to self-defense or other justification defenses depends on the immediacy of the threat; a threat of future harm is not sufficient. Thus, if someone threatens the defendant by saying, "Tomorrow I'm going to kill you," the defendant is ***not justified*** in killing the person to "protect" himself.

CMR Exam Tip It is crucial to determine the level of force that the defendant used in committing the proscribed act. As a rule of thumb, ***nondeadly force*** is justified where it appears necessary to avoid imminent injury or to retain property; ***deadly force*** is justified only to prevent death or serious bodily injury.

1. Self-Defense

a. Nondeadly Force

A person without fault may use such force as ***reasonably appears necessary*** to protect herself from the imminent use of unlawful force upon herself. There is no duty to retreat.

b. Deadly Force

A person may use deadly force in self-defense if (i) she is without fault; (ii) she is confronted with "unlawful force"; and (iii) she is threatened with imminent death or great bodily harm.

CMR **Exam Tip** If the defendant kills in self-defense but not all three of the requirements for the use of deadly force are met, some states would find the defendant guilty of manslaughter rather than murder under the "imperfect self-defense" doctrine.

1) Retreat

Generally there is no duty to retreat before using deadly force. The minority view requires retreat before using deadly force if the victim can safely do so, ***unless***: (i) the attack occurs in the victim's home, (ii) the attack occurs while the victim is making a lawful arrest, or (iii) the assailant is in the process of robbing the victim.

c. Right of Aggressor to Use Self-Defense

If one is the aggressor in the altercation, she may use force in defense of herself only if (i) she ***effectively withdraws*** from the altercation and ***communicates*** to the other her desire to do so, ***or*** (ii) the victim of the initial aggression ***suddenly escalates*** the minor fight into a deadly altercation and the initial aggressor has no chance to withdraw.

2. Defense of Others

A defendant has the right to defend others if she reasonably believes that the person assisted has the legal right to use force in his own defense. All that is necessary is the ***reasonable appearance*** of the right to use force. Generally, there need be no special relationship between the defendant and the person in whose defense she acted.

3. Defense of a Dwelling

Nondeadly force may be used to prevent or terminate what is reasonably regarded as an unlawful entry into or attack on the defender's dwelling. ***Deadly force*** may be used only to prevent a violent entry made with the intent to commit a personal attack on an inhabitant, or to prevent an entry to commit a felony in the dwelling.

Exam Tip As a practical matter, deadly force usually is justified in repelling a home invader but the basis for the right to use such force is ***not*** to protect the dwelling, but to protect the safety of the inhabitants of the dwelling.

4. Defense of Other Property

a. **Defending Possession**
Deadly force may never be used in defense of property. *Nondeadly force* may be used to defend property in one's possession from unlawful interference, but may not be used if a request to desist or refrain from the activity would suffice.

b. **Regaining Possession**
Force ***cannot*** be used to regain possession of property wrongfully taken unless the person using force is in immediate pursuit of the taker.

5. **Crime Prevention**
Nondeadly force may be used to the extent that it reasonably appears necessary to prevent a felony or serious breach of the peace. ***Deadly force*** may be used only to terminate or prevent a dangerous felony involving risk to human life.

6. **Use of Force to Effectuate Arrest**
Nondeadly force may be used by police officers if it reasonably appears necessary to effectuate an arrest. ***Deadly force*** is reasonable only if it is necessary to prevent a felon's escape ***and*** the felon threatens death or serious bodily harm.

a. **Private Persons**
A private person has a privilege to use ***nondeadly force*** to make an arrest if a ***crime was in fact committed*** and the private person has ***reasonable grounds to believe*** the person arrested has in fact committed the crime. A private person may use ***deadly force only if*** the person harmed was ***actually guilty*** of the offense for which the arrest was made.

7. **Resisting Arrest**
Nondeadly force may be used to resist an improper arrest even if a known officer is making that arrest. ***Deadly force*** may be used, however, only if the person does not know that the person arresting him is a police officer.

8. **Necessity**
It is a defense to a crime that the person ***reasonably believed*** that commission of the crime was necessary to avoid an imminent and greater injury to society than that involved in the crime. The test is objective; a good faith belief is not sufficient.

a. **Limitation—Death**
Causing the death of another person to protect property is ***never justified***.

b. **Limitation—Fault**
The defense of necessity is not available if the defendant is at fault in creating the situation requiring that he choose between two evils.

c. **Duress Distinguished**
Necessity involves pressure from natural or physical forces; duress involves a human threat (*see* B., *infra*).

9. **Public Policy**
A police officer (or one assisting him) is justified in using reasonable force against another, or in taking property, provided the officer acts pursuant to a law, court order, or process requiring or authorizing him to so act.

10. Domestic Authority
The parents of a minor child, or any person "in loco parentis" with respect to that child, may lawfully use reasonable force upon the child for the purpose of promoting the child's welfare.

CMR SUMMARY CHART

JUSTIFICATION DEFENSES

Defense	Amount of Force Allowed: Nondeadly Force	Amount of Force Allowed: Deadly Force
1. Self-Defense	If reasonably necessary to protect self	Only if threatened with death or great bodily harm
2. Defense of Others	If reasonably necessary to protect person	Only if threatened with death or great bodily harm
3. Defense of Dwelling	If reasonably necessary to prevent or end unlawful entry	Only if person inside is threatened or to prevent felony inside
4. Defense of Other Property	If reasonably necessary to defend property in one's possession (but if request to desist would suffice, force ***not*** allowed)	Never
5. Crime Prevention	If reasonably necessary to prevent felony or serious breach of peace	Only to prevent or end felony risking human life
6. Effectuate Arrest		
Police	If reasonably necessary to arrest	Only to prevent escape of felon who threatens human life
Private Person	If crime in fact committed and reasonable belief that this person committed it	Only to prevent escape of person who actually committed felony and who threatens human life
7. Resisting Arrest	If improper arrest	Only if improper arrest and defendant does not know arrester is a police officer
8. Necessity	If reasonably necessary to avoid greater harm	Never

B. EXCUSE OF DURESS

It is a defense to a crime ***other than a homicide*** that the defendant reasonably believed that another person would imminently inflict death or great bodily harm upon him or a member of his family if he did not commit the crime.

C. OTHER DEFENSES

1. Mistake or Ignorance of Fact

Mistake or ignorance of fact is relevant to criminal liability only if it shows that the defendant ***lacked the state of mind required*** for the crime; thus, it is irrelevant if the crime imposes "strict" liability.

a. Reasonableness

If mistake is offered to "disprove" a ***specific intent***, the mistake ***need not be reasonable***; however, if it is offered to disprove any other state of mind, it ***must have been reasonable*** mistake or ignorance.

CMR Exam Tip Don't confuse the defense of mistake of fact with the issue of factual impossibility, discussed earlier. Even though in both situations defendant is mistaken about certain facts, the results are different. ***Mistake*** is usually raised as a defense to a crime that has been completed; mistake of fact may negate the intent required for the crime. ***Impossibility*** arises only when defendant has ***failed*** to complete the crime because of his mistaken belief about the facts, and is being charged with an ***attempt*** to commit the crime; factual impossibility is ***not*** a defense to attempt.

2. Mistake or Ignorance of Law—No Defense

Generally, it is not a defense that the defendant believed that her activity would not be a crime, even if that belief was reasonable and based on the advice of an attorney. However, if the reliance on the attorney negates a necessary mental state element, such reliance can demonstrate that the government has not proved its case beyond a reasonable doubt.

a. Exceptions

The defendant has a defense if: (i) the statute proscribing her conduct was not published or made reasonably available prior to the conduct; (ii) there was reasonable reliance on a statute or judicial decision; or (iii) in some jurisdictions, there was reasonable reliance on official interpretation or advice.

b. Ignorance of Law May Negate Intent

If the defendant's mistake or ignorance as to a collateral legal matter proves that she lacked the state of mind required for the crime, she is entitled to acquittal. This rule applies only to those crimes in which the state of mind required involves some knowledge of the law. *Example:* A defendant cannot be found guilty of selling a gun to a known felon if she thought that the crime the buyer had been found guilty of was only a misdemeanor.

3. Consent

Unless the crime requires the lack of consent of the victim (*e.g.,* rape), consent is usually ***not*** a defense. Consent is a defense to minor assaults or batteries if there is no danger of serious bodily injury. Whenever consent may be a defense, it must be established that: (i) the consent was ***voluntarily and freely given***; (ii) the party was ***legally capable*** of consenting; and (iii) ***no fraud*** was involved in obtaining the consent.

EXCULPATORY DEFENSES

Defense	Applicable To	When Available
Justification (self-defense, defense of others, defense of property, necessity, etc.)	Usually crimes of force (*e.g.,* battery, homicide)	***Nondeadly force*** may usually be used if reasonably necessary to avoid imminent injury or to retain property; ***deadly force*** may be used only to prevent serious bodily harm
Duress	All crimes ***except*** homicide	Defendant reasonably believed that another would imminently harm him or a family member if he did not commit the crime
Mistake of fact	Crimes with a mental state element (*i.e.,* all crimes ***except*** strict liability)	For ***specific intent*** crimes, any mistake that negates intent; for other crimes, ***only reasonable mistakes***
Mistake of law	Crimes with a mental state element and statutory crimes	Mistake must negate awareness of some aspect of law that the crime requires or must be due to: statute not being reasonably available, reasonable reliance on statute or judicial interpretation, or (in some states) reasonable reliance on official advice; reliance on advice of counsel may negate mental state element
Consent	Crimes requiring lack of consent (*e.g.,* rape) and minor assaults and batteries	Applicable only if: consent is freely given, the party is capable of consenting, and no fraud was used to obtain consent
Entrapment	Most crimes, but ***not*** available if the police merely provide the opportunity to commit the crime	Criminal design originated with the police and the defendant was not predisposed to commit the crime before contact with police

4. **Condonation or Criminality of Victim—No Defense**
Forgiveness by the victim is no defense. Likewise, the nearly universal rule is that illegal conduct by the victim of a crime is no defense.

5. **Entrapment**
Entrapment exists only if (i) the ***criminal design originated with law enforcement officers*** and (ii) the defendant was ***not predisposed*** to commit the crime prior to contact by the government. Merely providing the opportunity for a predisposed person to commit a crime is not entrapment.

a. **Unavailable—If Private Inducement or If Material for Crime Provided by Government Agent**
A person cannot be entrapped by a private citizen. Under federal law, an entrapment defense cannot be based on the fact that a government agent provided an ingredient for commission of the crime (*e.g.,* ingredients for drugs), even if the material provided was contraband.

Exam Tip Entrapment is a difficult defense to establish in court and so too on the MBE. In fact, on the exam, the defendant is usually predisposed to commit the crime and thus entrapment usually is a wrong choice.

VII. OFFENSES AGAINST THE PERSON

A. ASSAULT AND BATTERY

1. **Battery**
Battery is an ***unlawful application of force*** to the person of another resulting in either ***bodily injury or an offensive touching***. Simple battery is a misdemeanor. A battery need not be intentional, and the force need not be applied directly (*e.g.,* causing a dog to attack the victim is a battery). Some jurisdictions recognize consent as a defense to simple battery and/or certain specified batteries.

a. **Aggravated Battery**
Most jurisdictions treat the following as aggravated batteries and punish them as felonies: (i) battery with a deadly weapon; (ii) battery resulting in serious bodily harm; and (iii) battery of a child, woman, or police officer.

2. **Assault**
Assault is ***either*** (i) an ***attempt to commit a battery*** or (ii) the ***intentional creation***—other than by mere words—***of a reasonable apprehension*** in the mind of the victim of ***imminent bodily harm***. If there has been an actual touching of the victim, the crime can only be battery, not assault.

a. **Aggravated Assault**
Aggravated assault (*e.g.,* with a deadly weapon or with intent to rape or maim) is treated more severely than simple assault.

CMR Exam Tip Think of assault as two separate crimes: (i) attempted battery assault—a ***specific intent*** crime (*i.e.,* defendant must intend to commit a battery), and (ii) creation of reasonable apprehension assault. Be sure to consider both types of assault in answering a question, because one may apply even though the other does not. For example, if D stops V at knifepoint and demands V's money, but was merely trying to scare V by posing as a robber and feigning a holdup (*e.g.,* as a practical joke), D has committed creation of reasonable apprehension assault but ***not*** attempted battery assault. You would not want to decide that D is not guilty of assault because you thought only about attempted battery assault.

B. MAYHEM

At common law, the felony of mayhem required either dismemberment or disablement of a bodily part. The recent trend is to abolish mayhem as a separate offense and to treat it instead as a form of aggravated battery.

C. HOMICIDE

1. Common Law Criminal Homicides

At common law, criminal homicide is divided into three categories:

a. Murder

Murder is the unlawful killing of a human being with ***malice aforethought***. Malice aforethought exists if there are no facts reducing the killing to voluntary manslaughter or excusing it (*i.e.,* giving rise to a defense) and it was committed with one of the following states of mind:

(i) Intent ***to kill***;

(ii) Intent ***to inflict great bodily injury***;

(iii) ***Reckless indifference to an unjustifiably high risk to human life*** ("abandoned and malignant heart"); or

(iv) Intent ***to commit a felony*** (felony murder).

Intentional use of a deadly weapon authorizes a permissive inference of intent to kill.

Exam Tip Homicides are emotionally charged crimes, so you must be careful not to let your emotions lead you to an incorrect answer. If a defendant killed with one of the states of mind above, he is guilty of murder; if he did not, he is not guilty of murder (although he could be guilty of other crimes). Thus, even where the facts go out of their way to paint the defendant as a completely despicable human being (*e.g.*, a mass murderer), you cannot convict him of murder when he drives into a schoolyard, killing three children, if the incident was due to defendant's fiddling with a cigarette lighter. More troublesome is the mercy killing case. If defendant intends to kill, even as an act of love, he ***is*** guilty of murder. Society does not accept compassion as a sufficient justification for the killing of a human being.

CMR APPROACH CHART

HOMICIDE CRIMES

Did defendant's acts cause the victim's death?
- No → No homicide liability
- Yes → Did the killing occur during the commission of a crime?
  - Yes → Was the crime a dangerous felony?
    - Yes → Apply felony murder rules
    - No → Apply misdemeanor manslaughter rules
  - No → Did defendant have the intent to kill or inflict great bodily harm, or recklessly disregard great risk to human life?
    - Yes → Did defendant act in response to adequate provocation?
      - Yes → Voluntary manslaughter
      - No → Murder
    - No → Did defendant act with criminal negligence?
      - Yes → Involuntary manslaughter
      - No → No homicide liability

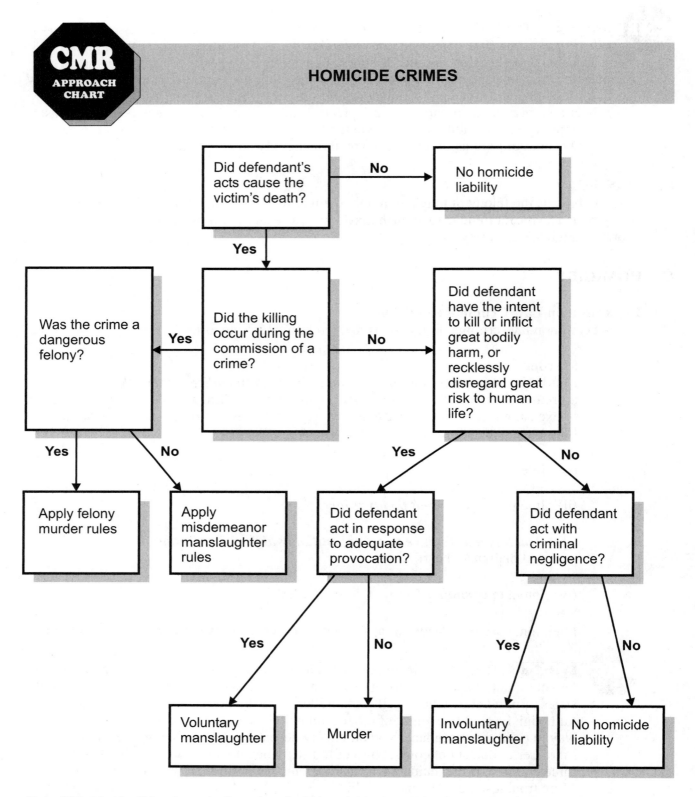

Note: This chart will lead you to the prima facie homicide that defendant committed. You must then decide whether any defenses apply.

b. Voluntary Manslaughter

Voluntary manslaughter is a killing that would be ***murder but for the existence of adequate provocation***. Provocation is adequate ***only if***:

(i) It was a provocation that would arouse ***sudden and intense passion*** in the mind of an ordinary person, causing him to lose self-control (*e.g.*, exposure to a ***threat of deadly force*** or finding your ***spouse in bed with another*** are adequate);

(ii) The defendant was ***in fact provoked***;

(iii) There was ***not sufficient time*** between provocation (or provocations) and killing for passions of a reasonable person to cool; and

(iv) The defendant ***in fact did not cool off*** between the provocation and the killing.

CMR **Exam Tip** The adequacy of provocation is a key issue in homicide questions. Be sure to consider carefully the four factors for adequate provocation and not just jump to the conclusion that there was adequate provocation because you see some signs of provocation in the fact pattern. Also note the interplay between the reasonable person standard and what actually happened to defendant. Consider:

(i) ***Sudden and intense passion*** that would cause a ***reasonable person to*** lose control—passion must be reasonable under the circumstances; defendant cannot have been set off by something that would not bother most others.

(ii) ***Defendant lost control***—even if a reasonable person would have been provoked, if defendant was not, there is no reduction to manslaughter.

(iii) ***Not enough time*** for ***reasonable person*** to cool off—this is tricky because it is hard to say how much time is needed to cool off; a lot depends on the situation, but the more time that has passed, the more likely it is that a reasonable person would have cooled off.

(iv) ***Defendant did not cool off***—this is a little easier to judge; if the facts show that defendant calmed down, there is no reduction to manslaughter.

CMR **Exam Tip** Remember that "heat of passion" is no defense to a killing, although it may ***reduce*** the killing from murder to manslaughter. Often a question will set up facts showing sufficient provocation and then ask about defendant's criminal liability. Don't be fooled by a choice "Not guilty because defendant acted in the heat of passion." The correct choice will be something like "Guilty of manslaughter, but not murder, because defendant acted in the heat of passion."

1) Imperfect Self-Defense

Some states recognize an "imperfect self-defense" doctrine under which murder may be reduced to manslaughter even though (i) the defendant was at fault in starting the altercation; or (ii) the defendant ***unreasonably*** but honestly believed in the necessity of responding with deadly force (*i.e.*, defendant's actions do not qualify for self-defense).

c. **Involuntary Manslaughter**
A killing is involuntary manslaughter if it was committed ***with criminal negligence*** (defendant was grossly negligent) or ***during the commission of an unlawful act*** (misdemeanor or felony not included within felony murder rule).

CMR **Exam Tip** Some questions refer specifically to the type of manslaughter (voluntary or involuntary), while others just say "manslaughter." If the question does not specify the type, be sure to consider both, although on the MBE, voluntary manslaughter is more often involved.

2. **Statutory Modification of Common Law Classification**
In some jurisdictions, murder is divided into degrees by statute. A murder will be second degree murder unless it comes under the following circumstances, which would make it first degree murder:

a. **Deliberate and Premeditated**
If defendant made the decision to kill in a cool and dispassionate manner and actually reflected on the idea of killing, even if only for a very brief period, it is first degree murder.

CMR **Exam Tip** First degree murder based on premeditation requires a specific intent, which may be negated by the defense of ***voluntary intoxication***. If the defendant was so intoxicated that he was unable to premeditate, he can be convicted only of second degree or common law murder, which requires only reckless indifference to human life (and for which voluntary intoxication is ***not*** a defense).

b. **Felony Murder**
If a murder is committed during the perpetration of an enumerated felony, it is first degree murder. The felonies most commonly listed include arson, robbery, burglary, rape, mayhem, and kidnapping. In these jurisdictions, other felony murders are second degree murder.

c. **Others**
Some statutes make killings performed in certain ways (*e.g.*, by torture) first degree murder.

3. **Felony Murder**
Any death caused in the ***commission of, or in an attempt to commit, a felony*** is murder. Malice is implied from the intent to commit the underlying felony.

a. **Felonies Included**
At common law, there are only a handful of felonies (*e.g.,* burglary, arson, rape, sodomy, etc.). Statutes today have created many more felonies, but the felony murder doctrine is limited to felonies that are ***inherently dangerous***.

b. **Limitations on Liability**
There are several limitations on this rule:

(i) The ***defendant must be guilty*** of the underlying felony.

(ii) The ***felony must be distinct*** from the killing itself (*e.g.*, commission of aggravated battery that causes a victim's death does not qualify as an underlying felony for felony murder liability).

(iii) ***Death must have been a foreseeable result*** of the felony (a minority of courts require only that the felony be malum in se).

(iv) The ***death must have been caused before the defendant's "immediate flight"*** from the felony ended; once the felon has reached a place of "temporary safety," subsequent deaths are not felony murder.

(v) In most jurisdictions, the defendant is ***not*** liable for felony murder when a ***co-felon*** is killed as a result of resistance from the felony victim or the police.

(vi) Under the "agency theory," the defendant is not liable for felony murder when an ***innocent party*** is killed ***unless*** the death is caused by the defendant or his "agent" (*i.e.*, an accomplice). (Under the "proximate cause" theory, the defendant may be liable when an innocent party is killed by the victim or police.)

1) Misdemeanor Manslaughter

Note that there are similar limitations on misdemeanor manslaughter. Generally, the misdemeanor must be "malum in se," or, if the misdemeanor involved is not malum in se, the death must have been a foreseeable result of the commission of the misdemeanor.

4. Causation

The defendant's conduct must be both the cause-in-fact and the proximate cause of the victim's death.

a. Cause-in-Fact

A defendant's conduct is the cause-in-fact of the result if the result would not have occurred "***but for***" the defendant's conduct.

b. Proximate Causation

A defendant's conduct is the proximate cause of the result if the result is ***a natural and probable consequence*** of the conduct, even if the defendant did not anticipate the precise manner in which the result occurred. Superseding factors break the chain of proximate causation.

c. Rules of Causation

An act that ***hastens an inevitable result*** is still the legal cause of that result. Also, ***simultaneous acts*** of two or more persons may be independently sufficient causes of a single result. A victim's preexisting weakness or fragility, even if unforeseeable, does not break the chain of causation.

d. Limitations

1) Year and a Day Rule

For a defendant to be liable for homicide, the death of the victim must occur within one year and one day from infliction of the injury or wound.

2) **Intervening Acts**
Generally, an intervening act shields the defendant from liability if the act is a coincidence or is outside the foreseeable sphere of risk created by the defendant. Note that a third party's negligent medical care and the victim's refusal of medical treatment for religious reasons are both foreseeable risks, so the defendant would be liable.

D. FALSE IMPRISONMENT

False imprisonment consists of the ***unlawful confinement*** of a person ***without his valid consent***. It is not confinement to simply prevent a person from going where she desires to go, as long as alternative routes are available to her. Note also that consent is invalidated by coercion, threats, deception, or incapacity due to mental illness, retardation, or youth.

E. KIDNAPPING

Modern statutes often define kidnapping as unlawful confinement of a person that involves either (i) some ***movement*** of the victim, or (ii) ***concealment*** of the victim in a "secret" place.

1. Aggravated Kidnapping

Aggravated kidnapping includes kidnapping for ransom, kidnapping for the purpose of committing other crimes, kidnapping for offensive purposes, and child stealing (the consent of a child to her detention or movement is not of importance because a child is incapable of giving valid consent).

VIII. SEX OFFENSES

A. RAPE

Rape is the unlawful carnal knowledge of a woman by a man, not her husband, without her effective consent. The slightest penetration is sufficient.

1. Absence of Marital Relationship

Under the traditional rule, a husband cannot rape his wife, but most states today either reject this rule entirely or reject it where the parties are estranged or separated.

2. Lack of Effective Consent

To be rape, the intercourse must be without effective consent. Lack of effective consent exists where:

(i) Intercourse is accomplished by ***actual force***;

(ii) Intercourse is accomplished by ***threats of great and immediate bodily harm***;

(iii) The victim is ***incapable of consenting*** due to unconsciousness, intoxication, or mental condition; or

(iv) The victim is ***fraudulently caused to believe that the act is not intercourse***.

Note that consent due to other types of fraud (*e.g.,* perpetrator persuading victim that he is her husband or that he will marry her) ***is*** effective.

B. STATUTORY RAPE

This is carnal knowledge of a female under the age of consent; it is not necessary to show lack of consent. A showing of reasonable mistake as to age or a showing of voluntary consent is irrelevant since statutory rape is a ***strict liability crime***.

C. ADULTERY AND FORNICATION

Adultery is committed by both parties to sexual intercourse if either is validly married to someone else. It is often required that the behavior be open and notorious. Fornication is sexual intercourse or open and notorious cohabitation by unmarried persons.

D. INCEST

Incest consists of marriage or a sexual act between closely related persons.

E. SEDUCTION

Seduction consists of inducing, by promise of marriage, an unmarried woman to engage in intercourse. The M.P.C. does not require chastity or that the female be unmarried.

F. BIGAMY

Bigamy is the common law strict liability offense of marrying someone while having another living spouse.

IX. PROPERTY OFFENSES

A. LARCENY

Larceny consists of:

(i) ***A taking*** (obtaining control);

(ii) ***And carrying away*** (asportation);

(iii) ***Of tangible personal property*** (excluding realty, services, and intangibles, but including written instruments embodying intangible rights such as stock certificates);

(iv) ***Of another*** with possession;

(v) ***By trespass*** (without consent or by consent induced by fraud);

(vi) ***With intent to permanently deprive*** that person of her interest in the property.

1. Possession

The property must be taken from the possession of another. If the ***defendant*** had possession of the property at the time of the taking, the crime is not larceny, but may be embezzlement.

a. Custody vs. Possession

Possession involves a greater scope of authority to deal with the property than does custody. Ordinarily, low level employees have only custody of an employer's property and so are guilty of larceny for taking it. A bailee, on the other hand, has a greater scope of authority over an owner's property and so is not guilty of larceny for taking it, but may be guilty of embezzlement.

2. Intent to Permanently Deprive

Generally, larceny requires that ***at the time of the taking*** defendant intended to permanently deprive a person of her property.

a. Sufficient Intent

An intent to create a substantial risk of loss, or an intent to sell or pledge the goods to the owner, is sufficient for larceny.

b. Insufficient Intent

Where the defendant believes that the property she is taking is hers or where she intends only to borrow the property or to keep it as repayment of a debt, there is no larceny.

c. Possibly Sufficient Intent

There ***may be*** larceny where the defendant intends to pay for the goods (***if*** the goods were not for sale) or intends to collect a reward from the owner (***if*** there is no intent to return the goods absent a reward).

CMR Exam Tip For a larceny question, be sure that the defendant had the intent to permanently deprive ***when she took the property***. If not, there is no larceny (unless it is a continuing trespass situation (*see* 4., *infra*)). Many questions turn on this one small point.

3. Abandoned, Lost, or Mislaid Property

Larceny can be committed with lost or mislaid property or property that has been delivered by mistake, but not with abandoned property.

4. "Continuing Trespass" Situation

If the defendant ***wrongfully*** takes property ***without*** the intent to permanently deprive (*e.g.*, without permission borrows an umbrella), and later decides to keep the property, she is guilty of larceny when she decides to keep it. However, if the original taking was ***not wrongful*** (*e.g.*, she took the umbrella thinking it was hers) and she later decides to keep it, it is not larceny.

B. EMBEZZLEMENT

Embezzlement is:

(i) The ***fraudulent***;

(ii) ***Conversion*** (*i.e.*, dealing with the property in a manner inconsistent with the arrangement by which defendant has possession);

(iii) Of ***personal property***;

(iv) Of ***another***;

(v) By a person ***in lawful possession*** of that property.

1. Distinguish from Larceny

Embezzlement differs from larceny because in embezzlement the defendant misappropriates property while it is in his rightful possession, while in larceny the defendant misappropriates property not in his possession.

2. Fraudulent Intent

Defendant must intend to defraud.

a. Intent to Restore

If the defendant intends to restore the ***exact*** property taken, it is ***not*** embezzlement. However, if the defendant intends to restore similar or substantially identical property, it is embezzlement, even if it was money that was initially taken and other money—of identical value—that he intended to return.

b. Claim of Right

As in larceny, embezzlement is not committed if the conversion is pursuant to a claim of right to the property. Whether defendant took the property openly is an important factor.

C. FALSE PRETENSES

The offense of false pretenses is:

(i) Obtaining ***title***;

(ii) To ***personal property of another***;

(iii) By an ***intentional false statement*** of past or existing ***fact***;

(iv) With ***intent to defraud*** the other.

1. "Larceny by Trick" Distinguished

If the victim is tricked—by a misrepresentation of fact—into giving up mere ***possession*** of property, the crime is larceny by trick. If the victim is tricked into giving up ***title*** to property, the crime is false pretenses.

2. The Misrepresentation Required

The victim must actually be deceived by, or act in reliance on, the misrepresentation, and this must be a major factor (or the sole cause) of the victim passing title to the defendant. A misrepresentation as to what will occur in the future is not sufficient. A false promise, even if made without the present intent to perform, is also not sufficient.

D. ROBBERY

Robbery consists of:

(i) A ***taking***;

(ii) Of ***personal property of another***;

(iii) ***From the other's person or presence*** (including anywhere in his vicinity);

(iv) ***By force or threats of immediate death or physical injury*** to the victim, a member of his family, or some person in the victim's presence;

(v) With the ***intent to permanently deprive*** him of it.

CMR Exam Tip For a defendant to be guilty of robbery, the victim must give up her property because she feels threatened. If she gives up her property for another reason (*e.g.*, she feels sorry for the defendant, or she wants the defendant to go away), the defendant will not be guilty of robbery. He may, however, be guilty of attempted robbery.

1. Distinguish Larceny

Robbery differs from larceny because robbery requires that the defendant use ***force or threats*** to obtain or retain the victim's property. Thus, pickpocketing generally would be larceny, but if the victim notices the attempt and resists, the taking would be robbery.

CMR COMPARISON CHART

PROPERTY CRIMES

Crime	Activity	Method	Intent	Title
Larceny	Taking and asportation of property from possession of another person	Without consent or with consent obtained by fraud	With intent to steal	Title does not pass
Embezzlement	Conversion of property held pursuant to a trust agreement	Use of property in a way inconsistent with terms of trust	With intent to defraud	Title does not pass
False pretenses	Obtaining title to property	By consent induced by fraudulent misrepresenta-tion	With intent to defraud	Title passes
Robbery	Taking of property from another's presence	By force or threat of force	With intent to steal	Title does not pass

E. EXTORTION

Common law extortion consists of the corrupt collection of an unlawful fee by an officer under color of office. Under modern statutes, extortion (blackmail) often consists of obtaining property ***by means of threats*** to do harm or to expose information. Under some statutes, the crime is complete when threats are made with the intent to obtain property; *i.e.,* the property need not be obtained.

1. **Distinguish Robbery**
Extortion differs from robbery because in extortion the threats may be of future harm and the taking does not have to be in the presence of the victim.

F. RECEIPT OF STOLEN PROPERTY

Receipt of stolen property consists of:

(i) Receiving ***possession and control***;

(ii) Of ***"stolen" personal property***;

(iii) ***Known*** to have been obtained in a manner constituting a criminal offense;

(iv) ***By another person***;

(v) With the ***intent to permanently deprive*** the owner of his interest in it.

1. **"Possession"**
Manual possession is not necessary. The defendant possesses the property when it is put in a location designated by her or she arranges a sale for the thief to a third person (*i.e.,* "fencing").

2. **"Stolen" Property**
The property must be stolen property ***at the time the defendant receives it***.

CMR **Exam Tip** In analyzing receipt of stolen property questions, carefully check the property's status at the time defendant receives it. If the police have already recovered the property and use it ***with the owner's permission***, it is no longer stolen, and the defendant cannot be convicted of receipt of stolen property. Note, however, that the defendant ***can*** be convicted of ***attempted*** receipt of stolen property if she intended to receive the property believing it to be stolen.

G. THEFT

Under many modern statutes, some or all of the above property offenses are combined and defined as the crime of "theft."

H. FORGERY

Forgery consists of the following:

(i) ***Making or altering*** (by drafting, adding, or deleting);

(ii) A ***writing*** with apparent legal significance (*e.g.,* a contract, not a painting);

(iii) So that it is ***false***; *i.e.,* representing that it is something that it is not, not merely containing a misrepresentation (*e.g.,* a ***fake*** warehouse receipt, but not an ***inaccurate*** real warehouse receipt);

(iv) With ***intent to defraud*** (although no one need actually have been defrauded).

1. Fraudulently Obtaining Signature of Another

If the defendant fraudulently causes a third person to sign a document that the third person does not realize he is signing, forgery has been committed. But if the third person realizes he is signing the document, forgery has not been committed even if the third person was induced by fraud to sign it.

2. Uttering a Forged Instrument

Uttering a forged instrument consists of: (i) ***offering as genuine***; (ii) an ***instrument*** that may be the subject of forgery and is ***false***; (iii) with ***intent to defraud***.

I. MALICIOUS MISCHIEF

Malicious mischief consists of:

(i) The ***malicious***;

(ii) ***Destruction*** of or damage to;

(iii) The ***property of another***.

Malice requires no ill will or hatred. It does, however, require that the damage or destruction have been ***intended or contemplated*** by the defendant.

X. OFFENSES AGAINST THE HABITATION

A. BURGLARY

Common law burglary consists of:

(i) A ***breaking*** (creating or enlarging an opening by at least minimal force, fraud, or intimidation; if defendant had the resident's consent to enter, the entry is not a breaking);

(ii) And ***entry*** (placing any portion of the body or any instrument used to commit the crime into the structure);

(iii) ***Of a dwelling*** (a structure used with regularity for sleeping purposes, even if used for other purposes such as conducting a business);

(iv) ***Of another*** (ownership is irrelevant; occupancy by someone other than defendant is all that is required);

(v) ***At nighttime***;

(vi) ***With the intent to commit a felony in the structure*** (felony need not be carried out to constitute burglary).

Modern statutes often eliminate many of the "technicalities" of common law burglary, including the requirements of a breaking, that the structure be a dwelling, that the act occur at nighttime, and that the intent be to commit a felony (*i.e.,* intent to commit misdemeanor theft is often enough).

Exam Tip The intent to commit a felony within must be present ***at the time of entry***; a later-acquired intent is not sufficient. This technicality is tested; remember it.

B. ARSON

Arson at common law consists of:

(i) The ***malicious*** (*i.e.*, intentional or with reckless disregard of an obvious risk);

(ii) ***Burning*** (requiring some damage to the structure caused by fire);

(iii) ***Of the dwelling***;

(iv) ***Of another.***

CMR **Exam Tip** Although common law arson requires a burning of a ***dwelling***, MBE questions testing on other arson issues often assume, without specifically stating, that arson extends to structures other than dwellings. Many statutes so provide.

1. Damage Required

Destruction of the structure, or even significant damage to it, is not required to complete the crime of arson. Mere blackening by smoke or discoloration by heat (scorching) is not sufficient, but mere ***charring is sufficient***.

CMR **Exam Tip** For arson, the damage must be caused by fire. An explosion is not enough unless it causes a fire.

2. Related Offense—Houseburning

The common law misdemeanor of houseburning consisted of: (i) a malicious; (ii) burning; (iii) of one's own dwelling; (iv) if the structure is situated either in a city or town, or so near to other houses as to create a danger to them.

XI. OFFENSES INVOLVING JUDICIAL PROCEDURE

A. PERJURY

Perjury is the ***intentional*** taking of a false oath (lying) in regard to a ***material matter*** (*i.e.,* one that might affect the outcome of the proceeding) in a judicial proceeding.

B. SUBORNATION OF PERJURY

Subornation of perjury consists of ***procuring or inducing*** another to commit perjury.

C. BRIBERY

Bribery at common law was the corrupt payment or receipt of anything of value for official action. Under modern statutes, it may be extended to nonpublic officials, and either the offering of a bribe or the taking of a bribe may constitute the crime.

D. COMPOUNDING A CRIME

Compounding consists of agreeing, for valuable consideration, not to prosecute another for a felony or to conceal the commission of a felony or the whereabouts of a felon. Under modern statutes, the definition refers to any crime.

E. MISPRISION OF A FELONY

At common law, misprision of a felony consisted of the failure to disclose knowledge of the commission of a felony or to prevent the commission of a felony. Under modern statutes, misprision is no longer a crime, or if it remains a crime, it requires some affirmative action in aid of the felon.

CRIMINAL PROCEDURE

TABLE OF CONTENTS

I. CONSTITUTIONAL RESTRAINTS ON CRIMINAL PROCEDURE 1
A. CONSTITUTIONAL REQUIREMENTS BINDING ON STATES 1
B. CONSTITUTIONAL RIGHTS NOT BINDING ON STATES 1

II. EXCLUSIONARY RULE 1
A. IN GENERAL—SCOPE OF RULE 1
B. LIMITATIONS ON THE RULE 2
1. Inapplicable to Grand Juries, Civil Proceedings, Internal Agency Rules, and Parole Revocation Proceedings 2
2. Good Faith Reliance on Law, Defective Search Warrant, or Clerical Error .. 2
3. Use of Excluded Evidence for Impeachment Purposes 2
4. *Miranda* Violations 2
C. HARMLESS ERROR TEST 2
D. ENFORCING THE EXCLUSIONARY RULE 2

III. FOURTH AMENDMENT 3
A. IN GENERAL 3
B. ARRESTS AND OTHER DETENTIONS 3
1. What Constitutes a Seizure? 3
2. Arrests 3
3. Other Detentions 3
4. Stop and Identify Statutes 4
5. Grand Jury Appearance 4
6. Deadly Force 4
C. EVIDENTIARY SEARCH AND SEIZURE 4
1. Governmental Conduct Required 6
2. Reasonable Expectation of Privacy 6
3. Searches Conducted Pursuant to a Warrant 7
4. Exceptions to Warrant Requirement 8
5. Administrative Inspections and Searches 11
6. Searches in Foreign Countries and at the Border 12
7. Wiretapping and Eavesdropping 13
D. METHOD OF OBTAINING EVIDENCE THAT SHOCKS THE CONSCIENCE .. 13

IV. CONFESSIONS 13
A. INTRODUCTION 13
B. FOURTEENTH AMENDMENT—VOLUNTARINESS 13
1. Harmless Error Test Applies 15
C. SIXTH AMENDMENT RIGHT TO COUNSEL 15
1. Offense Specific 15
D. FIFTH AMENDMENT PRIVILEGE AGAINST COMPELLED SELF-INCRIMINATION 15
1. *Miranda* Warnings 15
2. When Required 15

3. Right to Terminate Interrogation 16
4. Effect of Violation 17
5. Public Safety Exception 17

V. PRETRIAL IDENTIFICATION 17
A. SUBSTANTIVE BASES FOR ATTACK 17
1. Sixth Amendment Right to Counsel 17
2. Due Process Standard 17
B. THE REMEDY 17
1. Independent Source 18
2. Hearing 18

VI. PRETRIAL PROCEDURES 18
A. PRELIMINARY HEARING TO DETERMINE PROBABLE CAUSE TO DETAIN 18
B. PRETRIAL DETENTION—BAIL 18
1. Defendant Incompetent to Stand Trial 18
C. GRAND JURIES 18
1. Use of Grand Jury 18
2. Grand Jury Proceedings 19
D. SPEEDY TRIAL 20
1. Standards 20
2. When Right Attaches 20
E. PROSECUTORIAL DUTY TO DISCLOSE EXCULPATORY INFORMATION AND NOTICE OF DEFENSES 20
1. Prosecutor's Duty to Disclose Exculpatory Evidence 20
2. Notice of Alibi and Intent to Present Insanity Defense 20
F. COMPETENCY TO STAND TRIAL 20
1. Competency and Insanity Distinguished 20
2. Due Process Standard 21
3. Detention of Defendant 21
G. PRETRIAL PUBLICITY 21

VII. TRIAL 21
A. BASIC RIGHT TO A FAIR TRIAL 21
1. Right to Public Trial 21
2. Right to Unbiased Judge 21
3. Must Judge Be Lawyer? 21
4. Other Due Process Rights 21
B. RIGHT TO TRIAL BY JURY 22
1. Right to Jury Trial Only for "Serious" Offenses 22
2. Number and Unanimity of Jurors 22
3. Right to Venire Selected from Representative Cross-Section of Community . 22
4. Right to Impartial Jury 23
5. Inconsistent Verdicts 23
6. Sentence Enhancement 23
C. RIGHT TO COUNSEL 23
1. Stages at Which Applicable 23
2. Stages at Which Not Applicable 24

3. Waiver of Right to Counsel and Right to Defend Oneself ... 24
4. Indigence and Recoupment of Cost ... 24
5. Effective Assistance of Counsel ... 24
6. Conflicts of Interest ... 24
7. Right to Support Services for Defense ... 26
8. Seizure of Funds Constitutional ... 26
9. Right Limited While Testifying ... 26
D. RIGHT TO CONFRONT WITNESSES ... 26
1. Introduction of Co-Defendant's Confession ... 26
2. Hearsay ... 26
E. BURDEN OF PROOF AND SUFFICIENCY OF EVIDENCE ... 26
1. Presumptions ... 27

VIII. GUILTY PLEAS AND PLEA BARGAINING ... 27
A. TAKING THE PLEA ... 27
1. Requirement of Adequate Record ... 27
2. Remedy ... 27
B. COLLATERAL ATTACKS ON GUILTY PLEAS AFTER SENTENCE ... 27
C. PLEA BARGAINING ... 27
D. COLLATERAL EFFECTS OF GUILTY PLEAS ... 27

IX. CONSTITUTIONAL RIGHTS IN RELATION TO SENTENCING AND PUNISHMENT ... 28
A. PROCEDURAL RIGHTS IN SENTENCING ... 28
1. Capital Sentencing ... 28
B. RESENTENCING AFTER SUCCESSFUL APPEAL AND RECONVICTION ... 28
1. Exceptions ... 28
C. SUBSTANTIVE RIGHTS IN REGARD TO PUNISHMENT ... 28
1. Death Penalty ... 28
2. Status Crimes ... 29
3. Considering Defendant's Perjury ... 29
4. Imprisonment of Indigents for Nonpayment ... 29

X. CONSTITUTIONAL PROBLEMS ON APPEAL ... 29
A. NO RIGHT TO APPEAL ... 29
B. EQUAL PROTECTION AND RIGHT TO COUNSEL ON APPEAL ... 29
C. RETROACTIVITY ... 30

XI. COLLATERAL ATTACK UPON CONVICTION ... 30
A. AVAILABILITY OF COLLATERAL ATTACK ... 30
B. HABEAS CORPUS PROCEEDING ... 30

XII. RIGHTS DURING PUNISHMENT ... 30
A. RIGHT TO COUNSEL AT PAROLE AND PROBATION REVOCATION ... 30
B. PRISONERS' RIGHTS ... 30
1. Due Process ... 30
2. No Fourth Amendment Protections in Cells ... 30
3. Right of Access to Courts ... 30
4. First Amendment Rights ... 30

5. Right to Adequate Medical Care 31
C. NO RIGHT TO BE FREE FROM DISABILITIES UPON COMPLETION OF SENTENCE 31

XIII. DOUBLE JEOPARDY 31
A. WHEN JEOPARDY ATTACHES 31
B. EXCEPTIONS PERMITTING RETRIAL 31
C. SAME OFFENSE 31
1. General Rule—When Two Crimes Not the Same Offense 31
2. Cumulative Punishments for Offenses Constituting the Same Crime 31
3. Lesser Included Offenses 32
4. Conduct Used as a Sentence Enhancer 32
5. Subsequent Civil Actions 32
D. SEPARATE SOVEREIGNS 32
E. APPEALS BY PROSECUTION 32
F. COLLATERAL ESTOPPEL 33

XIV. PRIVILEGE AGAINST COMPELLED SELF-INCRIMINATION 33
A. WHO MAY ASSERT THE PRIVILEGE 33
B. WHEN PRIVILEGE MAY BE ASSERTED 33
C. METHOD FOR INVOKING PRIVILEGE 33
D. SCOPE OF PROTECTION 33
1. Testimonial but Not Physical Evidence 33
2. Compulsory Production of Documents 33
3. Seizure of Incriminating Documents 33
4. When Does Violation Occur? 33
E. PROHIBITION AGAINST BURDENS ON ASSERTION OF PRIVILEGE 34
1. Comments on Defendant's Silence 34
2. Penalties for Failure to Testify 34
F. ELIMINATION OF PRIVILEGE 34
1. Grant of Immunity 34
2. No Possibility of Incrimination 35
3. Scope of Immunity 35
G. WAIVER OF PRIVILEGE 35

XV. JUVENILE COURT PROCEEDINGS 35
A. RIGHTS THAT MUST BE AFFORDED 35
B. DOUBLE JEOPARDY 35

XVI. FORFEITURE ACTIONS 35
A. INTRODUCTION 35
B. RIGHT TO PRE-SEIZURE NOTICE AND HEARING 35
C. MAY BE SUBJECT TO EIGHTH AMENDMENT 36
1. General Rule 36
2. Compare—Nonpunitive Forfeiture 36
D. PROTECTION FOR "INNOCENT OWNER" NOT REQUIRED 36

CRIMINAL PROCEDURE

I. CONSTITUTIONAL RESTRAINTS ON CRIMINAL PROCEDURE

A. CONSTITUTIONAL REQUIREMENTS BINDING ON STATES

The first eight amendments to the U.S. Constitution apply to the federal government. Most of these rights are applicable to the states through the Due Process Clause of the Fourteenth Amendment. The following rights are binding on the states (as well as the federal government):

1. The Fourth Amendment ***prohibition against unreasonable searches and seizures***, and the ***exclusionary rule***;
2. The Fifth Amendment ***privilege against compulsory self-incrimination***;
3. The Fifth Amendment ***prohibition against double jeopardy***;
4. The Sixth Amendment right to ***speedy trial***;
5. The Sixth Amendment right to a ***public trial***;
6. The Sixth Amendment right to ***trial by jury***;
7. The Sixth Amendment right to ***confront witnesses***;
8. The Sixth Amendment right to ***compulsory process*** for obtaining witnesses;
9. The Sixth Amendment right to ***assistance of counsel*** in felony cases and in misdemeanor cases in which imprisonment is imposed; and
10. The Eighth Amendment ***prohibition against cruel and unusual punishment***.

B. CONSTITUTIONAL RIGHTS NOT BINDING ON STATES

The right to indictment by a grand jury for capital and infamous crimes has been held not to be binding on the states. It has not yet been determined whether the Eighth Amendment prohibition against excessive bail creates a right to bail. However, most state constitutions create a right to bail and prohibit excessive bail.

II. EXCLUSIONARY RULE

A. IN GENERAL—SCOPE OF RULE

The exclusionary rule is a judge-made doctrine that prohibits introduction of evidence obtained in violation of a defendant's Fourth, Fifth, and Sixth Amendment rights. Under the rule, illegally obtained evidence is inadmissible at trial, and all "fruit of the poisonous tree" (*i.e.,* evidence obtained from exploitation of the illegally obtained evidence) must also be excluded. ***Exceptions to fruit of the poisonous tree doctrine:***

(i) Evidence obtained from a ***source independent*** of the original illegality;

(ii) An ***intervening act of free will*** by the defendant (*e.g.*, defendant is illegally arrested but is released and later returns to the station to confess); and

(iii) ***Inevitable discovery;*** *i.e.*, the prosecution can show that the police would have discovered the evidence whether or not the police acted unconstitutionally.

Note: It is difficult to have live witness testimony excluded on exclusionary rule grounds. Also, a defendant may not exclude a witness's in-court identification on the ground that it is the fruit of an unlawful detention.

B. LIMITATIONS ON THE RULE

1. Inapplicable to Grand Juries, Civil Proceedings, Internal Agency Rules, and Parole Revocation Proceedings

The exclusionary rule is inapplicable to grand juries unless evidence was obtained in violation of the federal wiretapping statute. The rule is also inapplicable at parole revocation proceedings, in civil proceedings, or where evidence was obtained contrary only to agency rules.

2. Good Faith Reliance on Law, Defective Search Warrant, or Clerical Error

The exclusionary rule does not apply when police act in good faith based on (i) case law, (ii) a facially valid statute or ordinance, or (iii) a computer report containing clerical errors not made by the police. Neither does the rule apply when the police act in good faith reliance on a defective search warrant ***unless*** (i) the underlying affidavit was so lacking in probable cause that it could not reasonably be relied on, (ii) the warrant was defective on its face, (iii) the affiant lied to or misled the magistrate, or (iv) the magistrate has "wholly abandoned his judicial role."

3. Use of Excluded Evidence for Impeachment Purposes

Some illegally obtained evidence may still be used to impeach defendant's credibility if he takes the stand at trial. Specifically, an otherwise ***voluntary confession*** taken in violation of the *Miranda* requirements is admissible for impeachment purposes, and ***evidence obtained from an illegal search*** may be used by the prosecution to impeach defendant's, but not others', statements.

4. *Miranda* Violations

The Supreme Court has suggested that fruits derived from statements obtained in violation of *Miranda* might be admissible despite the exclusionary rule. (*See, e.g.,* IV.D.4.b., *infra.*)

C. HARMLESS ERROR TEST

If illegal evidence is admitted, a resulting conviction should be overturned ***on appeal*** unless the government can show beyond reasonable doubt that the error was ***harmless***. In a habeas proceeding where the petitioner claims constitutional error, he should be released if he can show that the error had a ***substantial and injurious effect or influence*** in determining the jury's verdict; if the judge is in grave doubt as to the harm, the petition must be granted.

CMR Exam Tip The harmless error standard never applies to the denial of the right to counsel ***at trial***; *i.e.,* this error is never harmless.

D. ENFORCING THE EXCLUSIONARY RULE

A defendant is entitled to have the admissibility of evidence or a confession decided as a matter of law by a judge out of the hearing of the jury. The government bears the burden of establishing the admissibility by a preponderance of the evidence. The defendant has the right to testify at a suppression hearing without his testimony's being admitted against him at trial on the issue of guilt.

III. FOURTH AMENDMENT

A. IN GENERAL

The Fourth Amendment provides that people should be free from unreasonable searches and seizures.

B. ARRESTS AND OTHER DETENTIONS

Governmental seizures of persons, including arrests, are seizures within the scope of the Fourth Amendment and so must be reasonable.

1. What Constitutes a Seizure?

A seizure occurs when a reasonable person would believe that she is not free to leave or terminate an encounter with the government.

2. Arrests

An arrest occurs when the police take a person into custody against her will for purposes of criminal prosecution or interrogation.

a. Probable Cause Requirement

An arrest must be based on probable cause—*i.e.,* trustworthy facts or knowledge sufficient for a reasonable person to believe that the suspect has committed or is committing a crime.

b. Warrant Generally Not Required Except for Home Arrests

A warrant generally is not required before arresting a person ***in a public place***. However, police generally must have a warrant to effect a nonemergency arrest of a person in his home.

3. Other Detentions

a. Investigatory Detentions (Stop and Frisk)

If police have a ***reasonable suspicion*** of criminal activity or involvement in a completed crime, supported by ***articulable facts*** (*i.e.,* not merely a hunch), they may detain a person for investigative purposes. If the police also have reasonable suspicion that the detainee is armed and dangerous, they may frisk the detainee for weapons.

1) Duration and Scope

The detention must be no longer than necessary to conduct a limited investigation to verify the suspicion. If during the detention probable cause arises, the detention becomes an arrest.

2) Property Seizures

Brief property seizures are similarly valid if based on reasonable suspicion.

b. Automobile Stops

Generally police may not stop a car unless they have at least reasonable suspicion to believe that a law has been violated. However, if ***special law enforcement needs*** are involved, the Supreme Court allows police to set up roadblocks to stop cars without individualized suspicion that the driver violated some law. To be valid, the roadblock must: (i) stop cars on the basis of some neutral, articulable standard (*e.g.,* every car); and (ii) be designed to serve purposes closely related to a particular problem related to automobiles and their mobility (*e.g.,* a roadblock to test for drunk drivers is valid because of the pervasiveness of the drunk driving problem, but a roadblock to search cars for illegal drugs is not valid because the purpose of such a checkpoint is only to detect evidence of ordinary criminal wrongdoing).

1) **Pretextual Stops**
If the police reasonably believe a driver violated a traffic law, they may stop the car, even if their ulterior motive is to investigate whether some other law—for which the police lack reasonable suspicion—has been violated.

c. **Detention to Obtain a Warrant**
If the police have probable cause to believe that a suspect has hidden drugs in his home, they may, for a reasonable time, prevent him from going into the home unaccompanied so that they can prevent him from destroying the drugs while they obtain a search warrant.

d. **Occupants of the Premises**
A valid warrant to search for contraband allows the police to detain occupants of the premises during a proper search.

e. **Station House Detentions**
Police must have full probable cause for arrest to bring a suspect to the station for questioning or fingerprinting.

4. **Stop and Identify Statutes**
Stop and identify statutes may be unconstitutionally vague for failure to clarify what will satisfy the identification requirement.

5. **Grand Jury Appearance**
Seizure of a person (by subpoena) for a grand jury appearance is not within the Fourth Amendment's protection.

6. **Deadly Force**
A police officer may not use deadly force to apprehend a suspect unless the officer has probable cause to believe that the suspect poses a significant threat of death or serious physical injury. On the other hand, a mere attempt to arrest that results in the death of a suspect is not necessarily a seizure governed by the Fourth Amendment.

C. EVIDENTIARY SEARCH AND SEIZURE

Like arrests, evidentiary searches and seizures must be reasonable to be valid under the Fourth Amendment, but here reasonableness requires a warrant except in six circumstances (*see* 4., *infra*). Evidentiary search and seizure issues should be approached using the following analytical model:

(i) Does defendant have a ***Fourth Amendment right*** (seizure by the ***government*** concerning a place or thing in which defendant had a ***reasonable expectation of privacy***)?

(ii) Did the government have a ***valid warrant*** (issued by a neutral and detached magistrate on a showing of ***probable cause*** and ***reasonably precise*** as to the place to be searched and items to be seized)?

(iii) If the police did not have a valid warrant, did they make a ***valid warrantless search and seizure***?

CMR APPROACH CHART

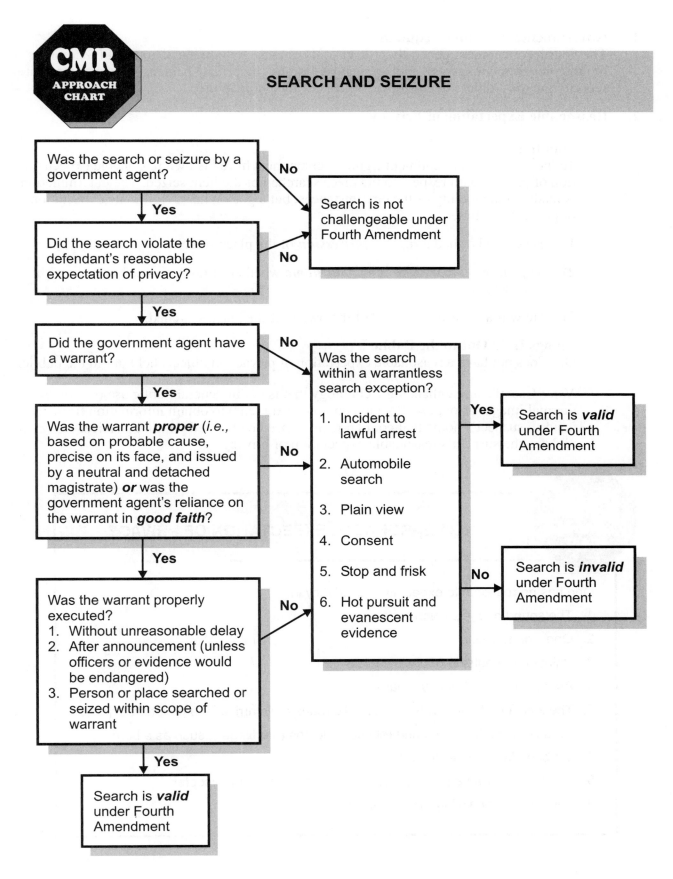

SEARCH AND SEIZURE

Was the search or seizure by a government agent?
- No → Search is not challengeable under Fourth Amendment
- Yes ↓

Did the search violate the defendant's reasonable expectation of privacy?
- No → Search is not challengeable under Fourth Amendment
- Yes ↓

Did the government agent have a warrant?
- No → Was the search within a warrantless search exception?
- Yes ↓

Was the warrant ***proper*** (*i.e.*, based on probable cause, precise on its face, and issued by a neutral and detached magistrate) ***or*** was the government agent's reliance on the warrant in ***good faith***?
- No → Was the search within a warrantless search exception?
- Yes ↓

Was the warrant properly executed?
1. Without unreasonable delay
2. After announcement (unless officers or evidence would be endangered)
3. Person or place searched or seized within scope of warrant

- No → Was the search within a warrantless search exception?
- Yes → Search is ***valid*** under Fourth Amendment

Was the search within a warrantless search exception?
1. Incident to lawful arrest
2. Automobile search
3. Plain view
4. Consent
5. Stop and frisk
6. Hot pursuit and evanescent evidence

- Yes → Search is ***valid*** under Fourth Amendment
- No → Search is ***invalid*** under Fourth Amendment

1. **Governmental Conduct Required**
The Fourth Amendment generally protects only against governmental conduct (*i.e.,* police or other government agents), and not against searches by private persons—including private security guards—unless deputized as officers of the public police.

2. **Reasonable Expectation of Privacy**

a. **Standing**
To have a Fourth Amendment right, a person must have his own reasonable expectation of privacy with respect to the place searched or the item seized. The determination is made on the totality of the circumstances, but a person has a legitimate expectation of privacy any time:

1) He owned or had a ***right to possession*** of the place searched;

2) The place searched was in fact ***his home*** whether or not he owned or had a right to possession of it; or

3) He was an ***overnight guest*** of the owner of the place searched.

b. **Things Held Out to the Public**
One does not have a reasonable expectation of privacy in objects held out to the public.

Note: Use of sense enhancing technology that is not in general public use (*e.g.,* a thermal imager as opposed to a telephoto camera lens) to obtain information from inside a suspect's home that could not otherwise be obtained without physical intrusion violates the suspect's reasonable expectation of privacy.

NO REASONABLE EXPECTATION OF PRIVACY

One has no reasonable expectation of privacy in:

1. The sound of one's voice
2. One's handwriting
3. Paint on the outside of one's vehicle
4. Account records held by a bank
5. The location of one's vehicle on public roads or its arrival at a private residence
6. Areas outside the home and related buildings ("curtilage"), such as a barn
7. Garbage left for collection
8. Land visible from a public place, even from a plane or helicopter
9. The smell of one's luggage ("sniff-test")

3. **Searches Conducted Pursuant to a Warrant**
Generally, the police must have a warrant to conduct a search unless it falls within one of the six exceptions to the warrant requirement (*see* 4., *infra*).

a. **Showing of Probable Cause**
A warrant will be issued only if there is probable cause to believe that seizable evidence will be found on the person or premises to be searched. Officers must submit to a magistrate an affidavit setting forth circumstances enabling the magistrate to make a determination of probable cause independent of the officers' conclusions.

1) **Use of Informers**
An affidavit based on an informer's tip must meet the "totality of the circumstances" test. Under this test, the affidavit may be sufficient even though the reliability and credibility of the informer or his basis for knowledge are not established. Note that the informer's identity generally need not be revealed.

2) **Going "Behind the Face" of the Affidavit**
A search warrant issued on the basis of an affidavit will be held invalid if the defendant establishes ***all three*** of the following:

(i) A ***false statement*** was included in the affidavit by the affiant (the officer applying for the warrant);

(ii) The affiant ***intentionally or recklessly*** included the false statement; ***and***

(iii) The false statement was ***material to the finding of probable cause***.

CMR **Exam Tip** This test for invalidating the affidavit is very restrictive—all three requirements for invalidity (falsehood, intentionally or recklessly included, and material to probable cause) must be met. Thus, if the affiant believed the lie, or if he intentionally included the lie but it was not material to the finding of probable cause (because there was sufficient other evidence), the affidavit is valid. Therefore, a defendant is rarely successful in challenging the affidavit.

a) **Police May Reasonably Rely on Validity of Warrant**
Evidence obtained by the police in reasonable reliance on a facially valid warrant may be used by the prosecution, despite an ultimate finding that the warrant was not supported by probable cause. (*See* II.B.2., *supra*.)

CMR **Exam Tip** This good faith exception applies ***only if the police obtained a warrant*** and it is invalid. The exception does not apply if the police failed to obtain a warrant.

b. **Warrant Must Be Precise on Its Face**
A warrant must describe with reasonable precision the place to be searched and items to be seized.

c. **Search of Third-Party Premises Permissible**
A warrant may be obtained to search premises belonging to nonsuspects, as long as there is probable cause to believe that evidence will be found there.

d. **Neutral and Detached Magistrate Requirement**
The magistrate who issues the warrant must be neutral and detached (*e.g.,* state attorney general is not neutral).

e. **Execution of Warrant**
Only the police (and not private citizens) may execute a warrant, and it must be executed without unreasonable delay. Police must knock and announce their purpose (unless the officer has reasonable suspicion, based on facts, that announcing would be dangerous or futile or would inhibit the investigation). Police may seize any contraband or fruits or instrumentalities of crime that they discover, whether or not specified in the warrant.

1) **Search of Persons Found on Searched Premises**
A warrant founded on probable cause to search for contraband authorizes the police to ***detain*** occupants of the premises during a proper search, but a search warrant does ***not*** authorize the police to ***search*** persons found on the premises who were not named in the warrant.

4. **Exceptions to Warrant Requirement**
All warrantless searches are unconstitutional unless they fit into one of six recognized exceptions to the warrant requirement.

a. **Search Incident to Lawful Arrest**
Incident to a ***lawful*** arrest, the police may search the person and areas into which he might reach to obtain weapons or destroy evidence (including the entire passenger compartment of a car). The police may also make a protective sweep of the area if they believe accomplices may be present. The search must be contemporaneous in time and place with the arrest.

1) **Lawful Arrest Requirement**
If an arrest is unlawful, any search incident to that arrest is also unlawful.

2) **Search Incident to Incarceration**
At the police station, the police may make an inventory search of the arrestee's belongings. Similarly, the police may make an inventory search of an impounded vehicle.

b. **"Automobile" Exception**
If the police have probable cause to believe that a vehicle contains fruits, instrumentalities, or evidence of a crime, they may search the whole vehicle and any container that might reasonably contain the item for which they had probable cause to search. If a warrantless search of a vehicle is valid, the police may tow the vehicle to the station and search it later.

Note: If the police have probable cause to believe that an automobile itself is contraband, they may seize it from a public place without a warrant.

VALID WARRANTLESS SEARCHES

Type of Search	Need Probable Cause?	Contemporaneousness Requirement?	Other Limitations?
1. Search Incident to Lawful Arrest	Yes (for arrest)	Yes	Lawful arrest
Search Incident to Incarceration (Inventory Search)	No	No	Established routine
2. "Automobile" Exception	Yes	No	Containers—limited to those that could contain evidence sought
3. Plain View	Yes (to believe item is evidence, contraband, etc.)	Yes	Lawfully on premises; evidence in plain view
4. Consent	No	Yes	Voluntary and intelligent consent; apparent authority to consent
5. Stop and Frisk			
Stop	No	Yes	Reasonable and articulable suspicion of criminal activity
Frisk	No	Yes	Reasonable belief that person is armed; limited to patdown of outer clothing
6. Hot Pursuit, Emergencies	No	Yes	Emergency situation—no time to get warrant

Exam Tip Note that the police have fairly broad authority to search a vehicle depending on what they are looking for. If there is probable cause to search the vehicle, the police can search the entire car and anything in it that ***might contain the evidence***. Thus, if they are looking for evidence of illegal drugs, they can look in almost anything in the car, but if they are looking for undocumented aliens, they cannot look inside a small suitcase.

1) **Passenger's Belongings**
The search may extend to packages belonging to a passenger; it is not limited to the driver's belongings.

2) **Containers Placed in Vehicle**
If the police have probable cause only to search a container in a vehicle (*e.g.*, luggage recently placed in the trunk), they may search only the container, not other parts of the vehicle.

c. **Plain View**
The police may make a warrantless seizure when they:

(i) Are ***legitimately on the premises***;

(ii) Discover ***evidence, fruits or instrumentalities*** of crime, or ***contraband***;

(iii) See such evidence in ***plain view***; and

(iv) ***Have probable cause*** to believe (*i.e.,* it must be immediately apparent) that the item is evidence, contraband, or a fruit or instrumentality of crime.

Exam Tip For this exception, be sure the police officer is legitimately on the premises (*i.e.,* where she has a lawful right to be), such as on a public sidewalk or in a home executing a warrant. If she is, anything the officer sees (or smells, hears, etc.) in plain view is admissible. Thus, if while executing a search warrant for a handgun, the officer opens a small drawer where the gun could be and sees heroin, the heroin is admissible since it was in plain view of an officer who had a right to look there.

d. **Consent**
A warrantless search is valid if the police have a ***voluntary and intelligent*** consent. Knowledge of the right to withhold consent is ***not*** a prerequisite to establishing a voluntary and intelligent consent. The scope of the search may be limited by the scope of the consent, but generally extends to all areas to which a reasonable person under the circumstance would believe it extends.

1) **Authority to Consent**
Any person with an apparent equal right to use or occupy the property may consent to a search, and any evidence found may be used against the other owners or occupants.

Exam Tip Exam questions on the validity of warrantless searches often suggest consent as a choice, especially the consent of someone other than the defendant.

Be careful to check whether the person has reasonably apparent authority to consent. For example, a homeowner parent can certainly consent to a search of the home's kitchen, and probably to a search of her son's room ***unless*** the facts strongly indicate that the parent does not have a right to go in the room (*e.g.,* always locked, only defendant has key, etc.).

e. Stop and Frisk

1) Standards
As noted above, a police officer may stop a person without probable cause for arrest if she has an ***articulable and reasonable suspicion*** of criminal activity. If the officer also reasonably believes that the person may be armed and presently dangerous, she may conduct a protective frisk.

CMR **Exam Tip** Remember that a ***stop*** is not an arrest, and thus an officer need not have probable cause. However, he must have a reason to believe that criminal activity is afoot. Thus, seeing a person pace in front of a jewelry store might justify a stop. A ***frisk*** will be justified only if the officer reasonably thinks that the suspect has a weapon.

2) Scope of Intrusion
The scope of the frisk is generally limited to a patdown of outer clothing, unless the officer has specific information that a weapon is hidden in a particular area of the suspect's clothing. An officer may also search the passenger compartment of an automobile of a detained occupant where there is a reasonable belief that the occupant is dangerous.

3) Admissibility of Evidence
During a patdown, an officer may reach into the suspect's clothing and seize any item that the officer reasonably believes, based on its "plain feel," is a ***weapon or contraband***, and such items are admissible as evidence.

4) Ordering Driver Out of Car Permissible
Once a vehicle has been properly stopped for a traffic violation, the police may order the driver out of the vehicle, even without suspicion of criminal activity. If the police then reasonably believe that the driver may be armed and dangerous, they may conduct a frisk.

f. Hot Pursuit, Evanescent Evidence, and Other Emergencies
There is no general "emergency" exception (*e.g.*, no need to investigate a fire after it has been extinguished and its cause determined). However, (i) police in hot pursuit of a fleeing felon may make a warrantless search and seizure and may even pursue the suspect into a private dwelling; (ii) police may seize without a warrant evidence likely to disappear before a warrant can be obtained; and (iii) contaminated food or drugs, children in trouble, and burning fires may justify warrantless searches and seizures.

5. Administrative Inspections and Searches
Inspectors must have a warrant for searches of private residences and commercial buildings, but the probable cause required to obtain a warrant is more lenient than for other searches: A showing of a general and neutral enforcement plan will justify issuance of a warrant.

a. **Exceptions Permitting Warrantless Searches**
The following warrantless searches have been upheld:

1) Administrative searches to ***seize spoiled or contaminated food***;

2) Administrative searches of a ***business within a highly regulated industry***;

3) ***Inventory searches of arrestees***;

4) Searches of ***airline passengers*** prior to boarding;

5) Searches of ***probationers' homes*** when there are reasonable grounds for the search;

6) Searches of ***government employees' desks and file cabinets*** where the scope is reasonable and there is a work-related need or reasonable suspicion of work-related misconduct;

7) ***Drug tests of railroad employees involved in an accident***;

8) ***Drug tests of persons seeking customs employment in positions connected to drug interdiction***; and

9) ***Drug tests of public school students who participate in extracurricular activities.***

6. **Searches in Foreign Countries and at the Border**

a. **Searches in Foreign Countries**
The Fourth Amendment does not apply to searches and seizures by United States officials in foreign countries and involving an alien, at least where the alien does not have a substantial connection to the United States. Thus, for example, the Fourth Amendment was held not to bar the use of evidence obtained in a warrantless search of an alien's home in Mexico.

b. **Searches at the Border or Its Equivalent**
No warrant is necessary for border searches. Neither citizens nor noncitizens have any Fourth Amendment rights at the border. Roving patrols inside the U.S. border may stop a vehicle for questioning of occupants if an officer ***reasonably suspects*** that the vehicle contains illegal aliens. Border officials may stop a vehicle at a fixed checkpoint inside the border for questioning of occupants even without reasonable suspicion, but to conduct a ***search***, they must have probable cause or consent.

c. **Opening International Mail**
Permissible border searches include opening of international mail when postal authorities have reasonable cause to suspect that the mail contains contraband.

d. **I.N.S. Enforcement Actions**
The I.N.S. may do a "factory survey" of the work force in a factory to determine citizenship of each employee. Moreover, even illegally obtained evidence (*i.e.*, evidence obtained in violation of the Fourth Amendment) may be used in a ***civil*** deportation hearing.

e. **Detentions**
Officials with "reasonable suspicion" that a traveler is smuggling contraband in her stomach may detain the traveler.

7. **Wiretapping and Eavesdropping**
Wiretapping (and other forms of electronic surveillance violating a reasonable expectation of privacy) constitutes a search under the Fourth Amendment. A valid warrant authorizing a wiretap may be issued if (i) there is showing of probable cause, (ii) the suspected persons involved in the conversations to be overheard are named, (iii) the warrant describes with particularity the conversations that can be overheard, (iv) the wiretap is limited to a short period of time, (v) the wiretap is terminated when the desired information has been obtained, and (vi) return is made to the court, showing what conversations have been intercepted.

a. **Exceptions**
A speaker assumes the risk that the person to whom he is talking is an informer wired for sound or taping the conversation. A speaker has no Fourth Amendment claim if he makes no attempt to keep a conversation private.

b. **Pen Registers**
Although pen registers (devices that record only phone numbers that are dialed from a phone) are not controlled by the Fourth Amendment, by statute judicial approval is required before a pen register may be used.

D. METHOD OF OBTAINING EVIDENCE THAT SHOCKS THE CONSCIENCE
Evidence obtained in a manner offending a "sense of justice" is inadmissible under the Due Process Clause. The reasonableness of searches within a person's body is determined by balancing society's need against the magnitude of the intrusion. Taking of a blood sample is usually upheld, but surgery (*e.g.*, to remove a bullet) requires great need.

IV. CONFESSIONS

A. INTRODUCTION
The admissibility of a defendant's confession (or other incriminating admission) involves analysis under the Fourth, Fifth, Sixth, and Fourteenth Amendments.

B. FOURTEENTH AMENDMENT—VOLUNTARINESS
For a self-incriminating statement to be admissible under the Due Process Clause, it must be voluntary, as determined by the totality of the circumstances. A statement will be involuntary only if there is some official compulsion (*e.g.*, a confession is not involuntary merely because it is a product of mental illness).

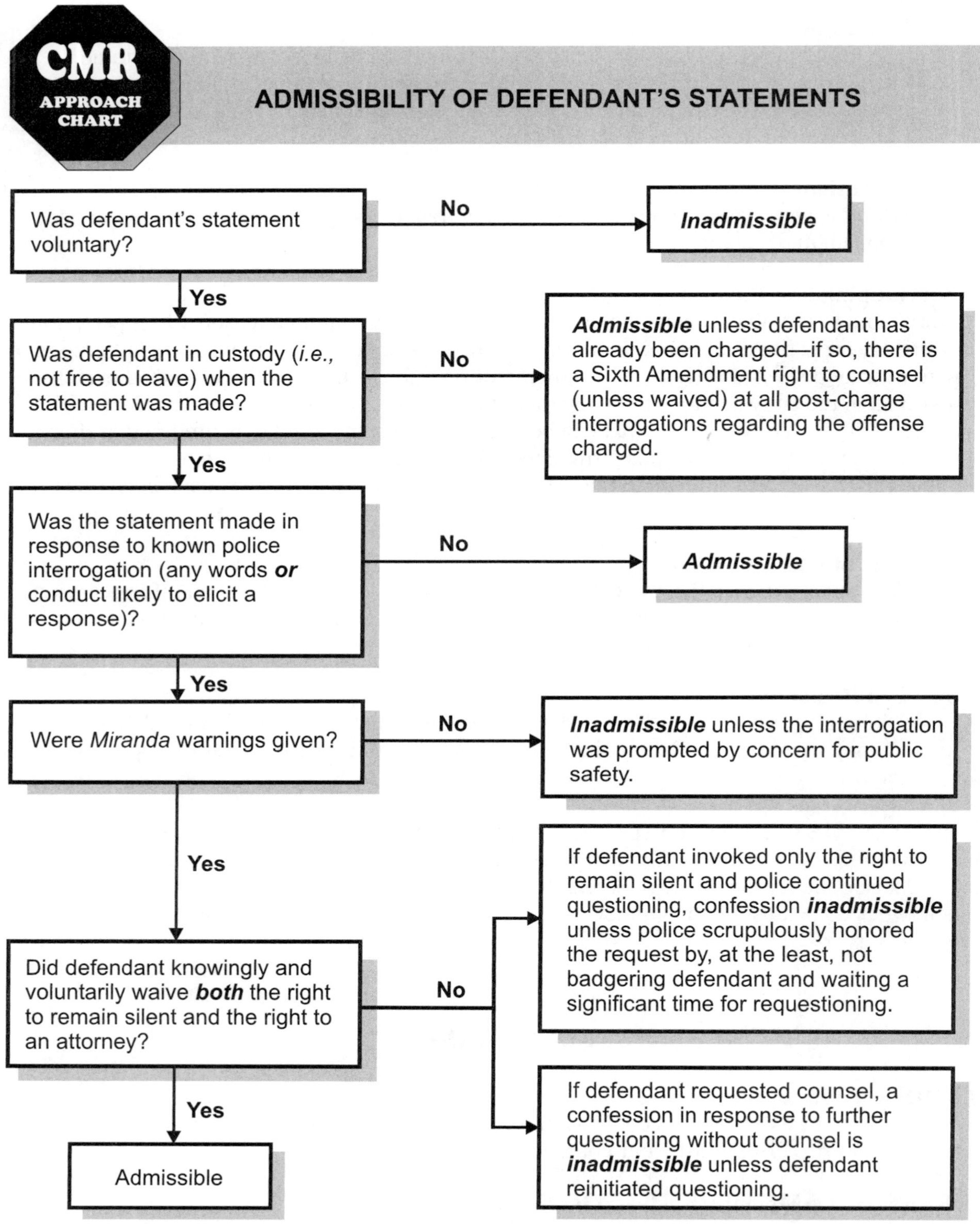
CMR
APPROACH
CHART
ADMISSIBILITY OF DEFENDANT'S STATEMENTS
Was defendant's statement voluntary?
No
Inadmissible
Yes
Was defendant in custody (i.e., not free to leave) when the statement was made?
No
Admissible unless defendant has already been charged—if so, there is a Sixth Amendment right to counsel (unless waived) at all post-charge interrogations regarding the offense charged.
Yes
Was the statement made in response to known police interrogation (any words or conduct likely to elicit a response)?
No
Admissible
Yes
Were Miranda warnings given?
No
Inadmissible unless the interrogation was prompted by concern for public safety.
Yes
Did defendant knowingly and voluntarily waive both the right to remain silent and the right to an attorney?
No
If defendant invoked only the right to remain silent and police continued questioning, confession inadmissible unless police scrupulously honored the request by, at the least, not badgering defendant and waiting a significant time for requestioning.
If defendant requested counsel, a confession in response to further questioning without counsel is inadmissible unless defendant reinitiated questioning.
Yes
Admissible

Note: Confessions obtained in violation of *Miranda* are admissible to ***impeach*** defendant's trial testimony.
And note: If inadmissible confessions are erroneously admitted into evidence, a resulting conviction need not be reversed if there is other overwhelming evidence of guilt (the "harmless error" test).

1. Harmless Error Test Applies

If an involuntary confession is admitted into evidence, the harmless error test applies; *i.e.*, the conviction need not be overturned if there is other overwhelming evidence of guilt.

C. SIXTH AMENDMENT RIGHT TO COUNSEL

The Sixth Amendment guarantees the right to the assistance of counsel in all criminal proceedings, which include all critical stages of a prosecution ***after judicial proceedings have begun*** (*e.g.,* formal charges have been filed). It prohibits the police from eliciting an incriminating statement from a defendant outside the presence of counsel after the defendant has been charged ***unless*** he has waived his right to counsel.

CMR **Exam Tip** Note that there can be no violation of the Sixth Amendment right to counsel before formal proceedings have begun. Thus, a defendant who is arrested but not yet charged does not have a Sixth Amendment right to counsel but does have a Fifth Amendment right to counsel (*see* below) under *Miranda*.

1. Offense Specific

The Sixth Amendment is offense specific. Thus, even though a defendant's Sixth Amendment rights have attached regarding the charge for which he is being held, he may be questioned regarding ***unrelated***, ***uncharged*** offenses without violating the Sixth Amendment right to counsel (although the interrogation might violate the defendant's Fifth Amendment right to counsel under *Miranda; see* below). Two offenses will be considered different if each requires proof of an additional element that the other crime does not require.

D. FIFTH AMENDMENT PRIVILEGE AGAINST COMPELLED SELF-INCRIMINATION

1. *Miranda* Warnings

For an admission or confession to be admissible under the Fifth Amendment privilege against self-incrimination, a person in custody must, prior to interrogation, be informed, in substance, that:

(i) He has the right to ***remain silent***;

(ii) Anything he says ***can be used against*** him in court;

(iii) He has the right to presence of an ***attorney***; and

(iv) If he cannot afford an attorney, one will be ***appointed*** for him if he so desires.

CMR **Exam Tip** Despite the fact that the *Miranda* warnings mention a right to counsel, the failure to give the warnings violates a defendant's ***Fifth Amendment*** right to be free from compelled self-incrimination, not his Sixth Amendment right to counsel. Thus, do not be fooled by an answer choice that states such failure is a violation of defendant's Sixth Amendment rights.

2. When Required

Anyone in the custody of the government and accused of a crime must be given *Miranda* warnings ***prior*** to interrogation by the police.

a. **Governmental Conduct**
Generally, *Miranda* warnings are necessary only if the defendant ***knows*** that he is being interrogated by a ***government agent***.

b. **Custody Requirement**
Whether a person is in custody depends on whether the person's freedom of action is denied in a significant way based on the ***objective*** circumstances (*e.g.,* an arrest constitutes custody; a routine traffic stop does not constitute custody).

c. **Interrogation Requirement**
"Interrogation" includes any words or conduct by the police that they should know would ***likely elicit a response*** from the defendant. Thus, *Miranda* warnings are not required before spontaneous statements are made by a defendant. Note that routine booking questions do not constitute interrogation.

d. **Waiver**
A suspect can waive his *Miranda* rights, but the prosecution must prove that the waiver was knowing, voluntary, and intelligent.

e. **Types of Statements**
Miranda applies to both inculpatory statements and exculpatory statements (*e.g.,* "I didn't shoot V, you did").

f. **Inapplicable at Grand Jury Hearing**
The *Miranda* requirements do not apply to a witness testifying before a grand jury, even if the witness was compelled by subpoena to be there.

3. **Right to Terminate Interrogation**
The accused may terminate police interrogation any time prior to or during the interrogation by invoking either the right to remain silent or the right to counsel.

a. **Right to Remain Silent**
If the accused indicates that he wishes to remain silent, the police must scrupulously honor this request by not badgering the accused, although the Supreme Court has allowed later questioning to occur on an unrelated crime.

b. **Right to Counsel**
If the accused ***unambiguously*** indicates that he wishes to speak to counsel, ***all questioning must cease*** until counsel has been provided unless the accused then waives his right to counsel (*e.g.*, by reinitiating questioning). The request must be specific (*i.e.*, indicate that the defendant desires assistance in dealing with interrogation). Allowing defendant to consult with counsel and then resuming interrogation after counsel has left generally does not satisfy the right to counsel—counsel must be present during the interrogation unless defendant has waived the right.

CMR **Exam Tip** Note the difference here depending on what the defendant asks: If the defendant indicates that he wishes to remain silent, the police probably may requestion him about a different crime after a break if fresh warnings are administered. If the defendant requests counsel, the police may not resume interrogating defendant until counsel is provided or the defendant initiates the questioning.

4. **Effect of Violation**
Generally evidence obtained in violation of the *Miranda* rules is inadmissible at trial under the exclusionary rule.

   a. **Use of Confession for Impeachment**
   Statements obtained in violation of the *Miranda* rules may be used to impeach the ***defendant's*** trial testimony, but may not be used as evidence of guilt.

   b. **Subsequent Valid Confession Admissible**
   The fact that a confession was obtained before *Miranda* warnings were given will not render invalid a confession made later, after *Miranda* warnings are given.

5. **Public Safety Exception**
The Supreme Court has allowed interrogation without *Miranda* warnings where it was reasonably prompted by a concern for public safety (*e.g.*, to locate a hidden gun that could have caused injury to innocent persons).

V. PRETRIAL IDENTIFICATION

A. SUBSTANTIVE BASES FOR ATTACK

1. **Sixth Amendment Right to Counsel**
A suspect has a right to the presence of an attorney at any ***post-charge*** lineup or showup. An accused does ***not*** have a right to counsel at photo identifications or when police take physical evidence, such as handwriting exemplars or fingerprints, from him.

CMR **Exam Tip** Recall that the right to counsel ***before*** trial is very limited and does not cover procedures where defendant is not personally confronted by the witness against him (as in photo identification).

2. **Due Process Standard**
A defendant can attack an identification as denying due process if the identification is ***unnecessarily suggestive*** and there is a ***substantial likelihood of misidentification***.

CMR **Exam Tip** Since a lineup does not involve compulsion to give "testimonial" evidence, a suspect's Fifth Amendment right against compelled self-incrimination does not apply. Thus, the defendant may not refuse to participate in a lineup on this basis.

B. THE REMEDY

The remedy for unconstitutional identifications is exclusion of the in-court identification and is rarely granted.

1. Independent Source

A witness may make an in-court identification despite the existence of an unconstitutional pretrial identification if the in-court identification has an independent source. The most common independent source is opportunity to observe at the time of the crime (*e.g.,* the witness viewed the defendant close up for 40 minutes during commission of the crime).

2. Hearing

Admissibility of identification evidence should be determined at a suppression hearing in the absence of the jury, but exclusion of the jury is not constitutionally required. The government bears the burden of proving that: (i) counsel was present; (ii) the accused waived counsel; or (iii) there is an independent source for the in-court identification. The defendant must prove an alleged due process violation.

VI. PRETRIAL PROCEDURES

A. PRELIMINARY HEARING TO DETERMINE PROBABLE CAUSE TO DETAIN

A defendant's liberty can be restricted only on a finding of probable cause. If probable cause has already been determined (*e.g.,* the arrest was pursuant to a warrant or a grand jury indictment), no preliminary hearing to determine probable cause need be held. If probable cause has not already been determined and there are ***significant constraints on an arrestee's liberty*** (*e.g.*, jail or bail, but not release on recognizance), a preliminary hearing to determine probable cause must be held within a reasonable time (*e.g.*, 48 hours). The hearing is an informal, nonadversarial proceeding. There is no real remedy for a denial of the hearing, but evidence discovered as a result of the unlawful detention can be excluded under the exclusionary rule.

B. PRETRIAL DETENTION—BAIL

Most state constitutions create a right to be released on bail unless the charge is a capital one. Generally, bail can be set no higher than is necessary to assure the defendant's appearance at trial. Refusal to grant bail or the setting of excessive bail may be appealed immediately; however, the Supreme Court has upheld portions of the federal Bail Reform Act that allow arrestees to be held without bail if they pose a danger or would fail to appear at trial.

CMR **Exam Tip** Since the Supreme Court has never held that the Eighth Amendment provision for bail applies to the states, the Eighth Amendment is not a very strong argument against a state's denial of bail. If, however, a state provides for bail (and most states do), arbitrary denials of bail will violate ***due process***—detainees must be given the opportunity to prove eligibility.

1. Defendant Incompetent to Stand Trial

Standards for commitment and subsequent release of defendants incompetent to stand trial must be essentially identical with those for commitment of persons not charged with a crime; otherwise there is a denial of equal protection.

C. GRAND JURIES

1. Use of Grand Jury

The Fifth Amendment right to indictment by grand jury has not been incorporated into the Fourteenth Amendment, but some state constitutions require grand jury indictment. Most states east of the Mississippi and the federal system use the grand jury as a regular part of the charging process. Western states generally charge by filing an information—a written accusation of the crime prepared and presented by the prosecutor.

2. Grand Jury Proceedings

a. Secrecy and Defendant's Lack of Access

Grand jury proceedings are conducted in secret. The defendant has ***no right*** to notice that the grand jury is considering an indictment against him, to be present and confront witnesses at the proceeding, or to introduce evidence before the grand jury.

b. No Right to Counsel or to *Miranda* Warnings

A witness subpoenaed to testify before the grand jury does not have the right to receive *Miranda* warnings, nor is he entitled to a warning that he is a "potential defendant" when called to testify before the grand jury. Witnesses have no right to have an attorney present.

c. No Right to Have Evidence Excluded

A grand jury may base its indictment on evidence that would be inadmissible at trial, and an indicted defendant may not have the indictment quashed on ground that it is based on illegally obtained evidence.

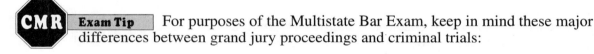

Exam Tip For purposes of the Multistate Bar Exam, keep in mind these major differences between grand jury proceedings and criminal trials:

- The "defendant" (grand jury witness) has no right to have counsel present during his grand jury testimony;
- The grand jury may consider evidence that would be excluded at the criminal trial (*e.g.,* illegally obtained evidence or hearsay); and
- The "defendant" (grand jury witness) must appear if called, although he can refuse to answer specific questions on the grounds that they may incriminate him.

d. No Right to Challenge Subpoena

There is no right to challenge a subpoena on the Fourth Amendment grounds that the grand jury lacked "probable cause"—or any reason at all—to call a witness for questioning.

e. Exclusion of Minorities

A conviction resulting from an indictment issued by a grand jury from which members of a minority group have been excluded will be reversed ***without regard*** to harmlessness of error.

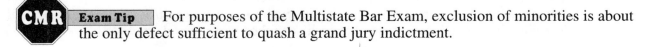

Exam Tip For purposes of the Multistate Bar Exam, exclusion of minorities is about the only defect sufficient to quash a grand jury indictment.

D. SPEEDY TRIAL

1. Standards

A determination of whether a defendant's Sixth Amendment right to a speedy trial has been violated is made by an evaluation of the ***totality of the circumstances.*** Factors considered are the length of delay, reason for delay, whether defendant asserted his right, and prejudice to defendant. The remedy for a violation of the right to speedy trial is dismissal with prejudice.

2. When Right Attaches

The right to speedy trial does not attach until defendant has been ***arrested or charged***. If defendant is charged and is incarcerated in another jurisdiction, reasonable efforts must be used to obtain the presence of defendant. Also it is a violation of the right to speedy trial to permit the prosecution to indefinitely suspend charges.

Note: The defendant does not need to know of the charges for the speedy trial rights to attach.

CMR Exam Tip When a speedy trial issue is raised in a question, first check the timing—has the defendant been arrested or charged? If not, there is no right to a speedy trial.

E. PROSECUTORIAL DUTY TO DISCLOSE EXCULPATORY INFORMATION AND NOTICE OF DEFENSES

1. Prosecutor's Duty to Disclose Exculpatory Evidence

The government has a duty to disclose material, exculpatory evidence to the defendant. Failure to disclose such evidence—whether willful or inadvertent—violates the Due Process Clause and is grounds for reversing a conviction if the defendant can prove that: (i) the evidence is ***favorable*** to him because it either impeaches or is exculpatory; and (ii) ***prejudice has resulted*** (*i.e.,* there is a ***reasonable probability*** that the result of the case would have been different if the undisclosed evidence had been presented at trial).

2. Notice of Alibi and Intent to Present Insanity Defense

If defendant is going to use an alibi or insanity defense, he must notify the prosecution. If an alibi is to be used, the defendant must give the prosecution a list of his witnesses. The prosecution must give the defendant a list of the witnesses it will use to rebut the defense. The prosecutor may not comment at trial on defendant's failure to produce a witness named as supporting the alibi or on failure to present the alibi itself.

F. COMPETENCY TO STAND TRIAL

1. Competency and Insanity Distinguished

Insanity is a defense to a criminal charge based on the defendant's ***mental condition at the time he committed the charged crime***. A defendant acquitted by reason of insanity may not be retried and convicted, although he may be hospitalized under some circumstances. ***Incompetency*** to stand trial, on the other hand, is not a defense to the charge, but rather is a bar to trial. It is based on the defendant's ***mental condition at the time of trial***. If defendant later regains his competency, he can then be tried and convicted.

2. **Due Process Standard**
A defendant is incompetent to stand trial if he either (i) lacks a rational as well as factual understanding of the charges and proceedings, or (ii) lacks sufficient present ability to consult with his lawyer with a reasonable degree of understanding. The state may place on the defendant the burden of proving incompetency by a preponderance of the evidence, but requiring the defendant to show incompetency by "clear and convincing" evidence is unconstitutional.

3. **Detention of Defendant**
A defendant who has successfully asserted the insanity defense may be confined to a mental hospital for a term longer than the maximum period of incarceration for the offense. However, the defendant cannot be indefinitely committed after regaining sanity merely because he is unable to prove himself not dangerous to others.

G. PRETRIAL PUBLICITY

Excessive pretrial publicity prejudicial to the defendant may require change of venue or retrial.

VII. TRIAL

A. BASIC RIGHT TO A FAIR TRIAL

1. **Right to Public Trial**
The Sixth and Fourteenth Amendments guarantee the right to a public trial, but the right varies with the stage of the proceeding involved.

   a. **Pretrial Proceedings**
   Preliminary probable cause hearings are presumptively open to the public and press, as are ***pretrial*** suppression hearings, although the latter may be closed to the public under limited circumstances (*e.g.,* the party seeking closure has an overriding interest likely to be prejudiced by disclosure and there is no reasonable alternative besides closure).

   b. **Trial**
   The press and public have a First Amendment right to attend the ***trial itself***, even when the defense and prosecution agree to close it. The state may constitutionally permit televising criminal proceedings over the defendant's objection.

2. **Right to Unbiased Judge**
Due process is violated if the judge is shown to have ***actual malice*** against the defendant or to have had a ***financial interest*** in having the trial result in a guilty verdict.

3. **Must Judge Be Lawyer?**
A defendant in a minor misdemeanor prosecution has no right to have the trial judge be a lawyer if upon conviction defendant has a right to trial de novo in a court with a lawyer-judge, but for serious crimes, the judge probably must be law-trained.

4. **Other Due Process Rights**
Due process is violated if:

   (i) The trial is conducted in a manner making it ***unlikely that the jury gave the evidence reasonable consideration***;

(ii) The state compels the defendant to ***stand trial in prison clothing***; or

(iii) The jury is exposed to ***influence favorable to the prosecution***.

Due process does not require the police to preserve all items that might be used as exculpatory evidence at trial, but does prohibit bad faith destruction.

B. RIGHT TO TRIAL BY JURY

1. Right to Jury Trial Only for "Serious" Offenses

There is no constitutional right to jury trial for petty offenses, but only for serious offenses. An offense is serious if imprisonment for more than six months is authorized. Also, there is no right to jury trial in juvenile delinquency proceedings.

a. Contempt

For civil contempt proceedings, there is no jury trial right. For criminal contempt proceedings, cumulative penalties totaling more than six months cannot be imposed without affording defendant the right to a jury trial. If a judge summarily imposes punishment for contempt ***during trial***, penalties may aggregate more than six months without a jury trial.

1) Probation

A judge may place a contemnor on probation for up to five years without affording him the right to jury trial, as long as revocation of probation would not result in imprisonment for more than six months.

2. Number and Unanimity of Jurors

There is no constitutional right to a jury of 12, but there must be at least six jurors to satisfy the right to a jury trial. The Supreme Court has upheld convictions that were less than unanimous, but probably would not approve an 8-4 vote for conviction. Six-person juries must be unanimous.

3. Right to Venire Selected from Representative Cross-Section of Community

A defendant has a right to have the jury selected from a representative cross-section of the community. He need only show the underrepresentation of a distinct and numerically significant group in the venire to show his jury trial right was violated. Note that a defendant does not have the right to proportional representation of all groups on his ***particular jury***.

a. Use of Peremptory Challenges for Racial and Gender-Based Discrimination

Although generally a prosecutor may exercise peremptory challenges for any reason, the Equal Protection Clause forbids the use of peremptory challenges to exclude potential jurors solely on account of their race or gender. An equal protection-based attack on peremptory strikes involves three steps: (i) The defendant must show ***facts or circumstances that raise an inference*** that the exclusion was based on race or gender. (ii) Upon such a showing, the prosecutor must come forward with a ***race-neutral explanation*** for the strike (even an unreasonable explanation is sufficient, as long as it is race-neutral). (iii) The judge then determines whether the prosecutor's explanation was the genuine reason for striking the juror, or merely a pretext for purposeful discrimination. If the judge believes that the ***prosecutor was sincere***, the strike may be upheld.

4. **Right to Impartial Jury**

a. **Right to Questioning on Racial Bias**
A defendant is entitled to questioning on voir dire specifically directed to racial prejudice whenever race is bound up in the case or he is accused of an interracial ***capital*** crime.

b. **Juror Opposition to Death Penalty**
In capital punishment cases, a state may not automatically exclude for cause all those who express a doubt or scruple about the death penalty; it must be determined whether the juror's views would prevent or substantially impair performance of his duties in accordance with his instructions and oath. A death sentence imposed by a jury from which a juror was improperly excluded is subject to automatic reversal.

c. **Juror Favoring Death Penalty**
If a jury is to decide whether a defendant is to be sentenced to death, on voir dire the defendant must be allowed to ask potential jurors if they would automatically give the death penalty upon a guilty verdict. A juror who answers affirmatively must be excluded for cause because such a juror cannot perform his duties in accordance with instructions as to mitigating circumstances.

d. **Use of Peremptory Challenge to Maintain Impartial Jury**
If a trial court refuses to exclude for cause a juror whom the court should exclude, and the defendant uses a peremptory challenge to exclude the juror, there is no constitutional violation.

5. **Inconsistent Verdicts**
Inconsistent verdicts (*e.g.,* finding defendant guilty and co-defendant innocent on the same evidence) are ***not*** reviewable.

6. **Sentence Enhancement**
If substantive law provides that a sentence may be increased beyond the statutory maximum for a crime if additional facts (other than prior conviction) are proved, proof of the facts must be ***submitted to the jury*** and proved beyond reasonable doubt; the defendant's right to jury trial is violated if the judge makes the determination. However, judges may determine the presence of sentencing factors (*i.e.*, facts) to determine whether the defendant should receive the minimum or maximum penalty available under the sentencing scheme.

C. **RIGHT TO COUNSEL**
A defendant has a right to counsel. Violation of this right ***at trial*** requires reversal. For nontrial denials, the harmless error test is applied.

1. **Stages at Which Applicable**
A defendant has a right to be represented by privately retained counsel, or to have counsel appointed for him by the state if he is indigent, at the following stages: (i) custodial police interrogation; (ii) post-indictment interrogation whether or not custodial; (iii) preliminary hearings to determine probable cause to prosecute; (iv) arraignment; (v) post-charge lineups; (vi) guilty plea and sentencing; (vii) felony trials; (viii) misdemeanor trials when imprisonment is actually imposed or when a suspended jail sentence is imposed; (ix) overnight recesses during trial; and (x) appeals as a matter of right.

CMR **Exam Tip** Remember that the right to counsel is available in misdemeanor cases only if imprisonment is actually imposed. Thus, if an exam question involves a nonfelony and defendant asks for counsel, is denied, and is convicted, whether the right to counsel has been violated depends on defendant's sentence: if he receives no imprisonment, his right has not been violated; if he receives prison time, his right has been violated.

2. Stages at Which Not Applicable

(i) Blood sampling; (ii) taking of handwriting or voice exemplars; (iii) precharge or investigative lineups; (iv) photo identifications; (v) preliminary hearings to determine probable cause to detain; (vi) brief recesses during the defendant's testimony at trial; (vii) discretionary appeals; (viii) parole and probation revocation proceedings; and (ix) post-conviction proceedings.

3. Waiver of Right to Counsel and Right to Defend Oneself

A defendant has a right to defend himself ***at trial*** if, in the judgment of the judge, his waiver is knowing and intelligent; he need not be found capable of representing himself effectively. Note that a defendant does not have a right to self-representation on appeal.

4. Indigence and Recoupment of Cost

The state generally provides counsel in close cases of indigence, but may then seek reimbursement from those convicted defendants who later become able to pay.

5. Effective Assistance of Counsel

The Sixth Amendment right to counsel includes the right to ***effective*** counsel. This right extends to the first appeal. Effective assistance of counsel is ***generally presumed***.

a. Circumstances Constituting Ineffective Assistance

An ineffective assistance claimant must show:

(i) ***Deficient performance*** by counsel; and

(ii) But for the deficiency, the ***result of the proceeding would have been different*** (*e.g.,* defendant would not have been convicted or his sentence would have been shorter).

The defendant must point out specific deficiencies and cannot base the claim on inexperience, lack of time to prepare, the gravity of the charges, the complexity of defenses, or accessibility of witnesses to counsel.

b. Circumstances Not Constituting Ineffective Assistance

Circumstances ***not*** constituting ***ineffective*** assistance include: (i) trial tactics, (ii) failure to argue frivolous issues, (iii) rejection of defendant's request for a continuance, and (iv) the failure to raise a constitutional defense that is later invalidated.

6. Conflicts of Interest

Joint representation is not per se invalid. However, if an attorney advises the trial court of a resulting conflict of interest at or before trial, and the court refuses to appoint separate counsel, the defendant is entitled to automatic reversal.

a. Conflict with Attorney

A defendant's conflict of interest with his attorney is rarely a ground for relief.

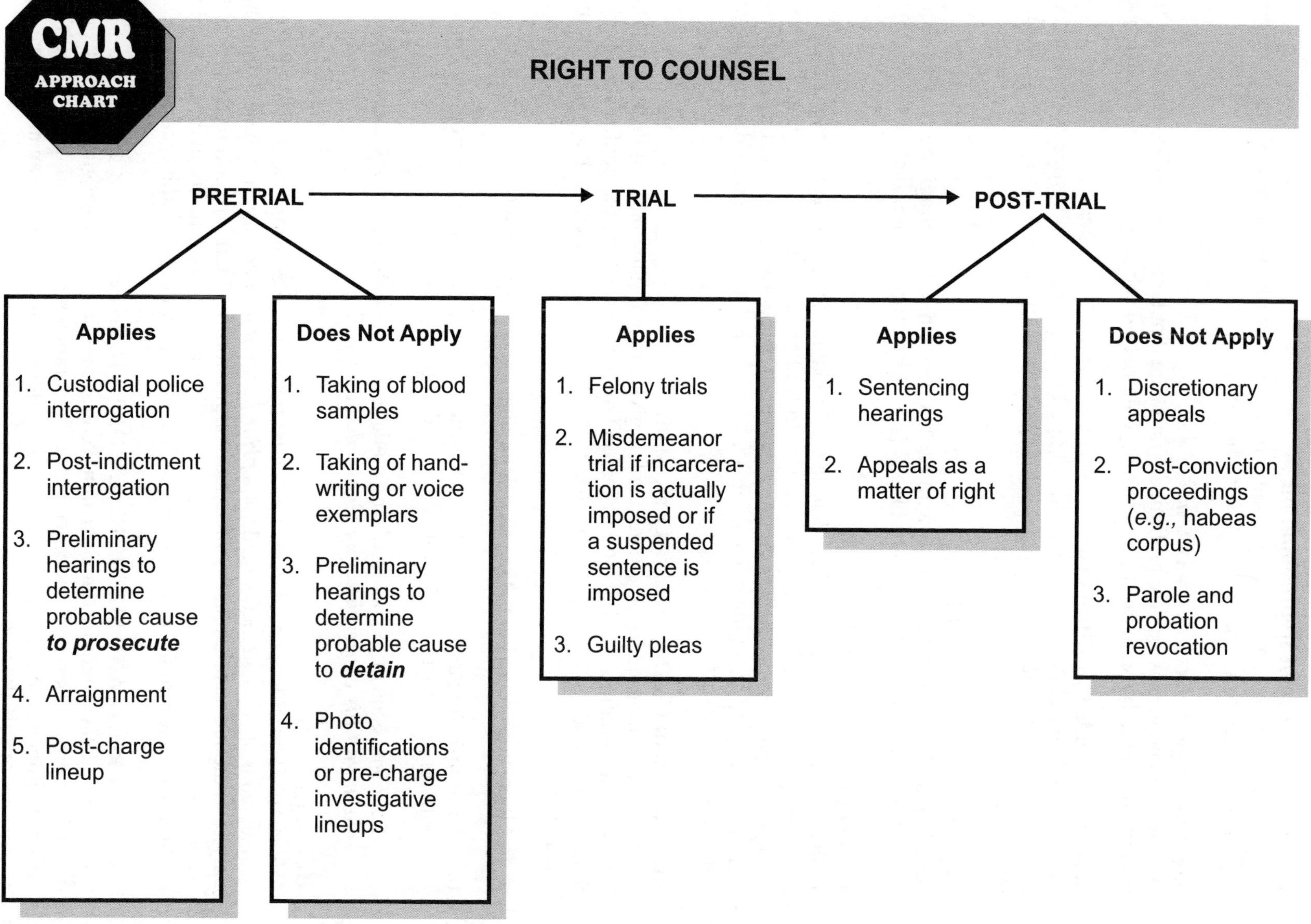
CMR
APPROACH
CHART
RIGHT TO COUNSEL
PRETRIAL
TRIAL
POST-TRIAL
Applies
1. Custodial police interrogation
2. Post-indictment interrogation
3. Preliminary hearings to determine probable cause ***to prosecute***
4. Arraignment
5. Post-charge lineup
Does Not Apply
1. Taking of blood samples
2. Taking of hand-writing or voice exemplars
3. Preliminary hearings to determine probable cause to ***detain***
4. Photo identifications or pre-charge investigative lineups
Applies
1. Felony trials
2. Misdemeanor trial if incarcera-tion is actually imposed or if a suspended sentence is imposed
3. Guilty pleas
Applies
1. Sentencing hearings
2. Appeals as a matter of right
Does Not Apply
1. Discretionary appeals
2. Post-conviction proceedings (*e.g.,* habeas corpus)
3. Parole and probation revocation

b. **No Right to Joint Representation**
A defendant has no right to be jointly represented with his co-defendants if the government can show a potential conflict of interest.

7. **Right to Support Services for Defense**
Where a defendant has made a preliminary showing that he is likely to be able to use the insanity defense, the state must provide a psychiatrist for the preparation of the defense.

8. **Seizure of Funds Constitutional**
The right to counsel does not forbid the seizure of drug money and property obtained with drug money, even where defendant was going to use such money or property to pay an attorney.

9. **Right Limited While Testifying**
A defendant has no right to consult with her attorney while testifying, and may be sequestered from her attorney during short breaks (*e.g.,* 15 minutes as opposed to overnight).

D. RIGHT TO CONFRONT WITNESSES

The Sixth Amendment grants to a defendant in a criminal prosecution the right to confront adverse witnesses. The right is not absolute: Face to face confrontation is not required when preventing such confrontation serves an important public purpose (*e.g.,* protecting child witnesses from trauma). Also, a judge may remove a disruptive defendant, and a defendant may voluntarily leave the courtroom during trial.

1. **Introduction of Co-Defendant's Confession**
If two persons are tried together and one has given a confession that implicates the other, the right of confrontation prohibits use of that statement, even where the confession interlocks with the defendant's own confession, which is admitted. However, such a statement may be admitted if:

   a. All portions referring to the other defendant can be ***eliminated***;

   b. The ***confessing defendant takes the stand*** and subjects himself to cross-examination with respect to truth or falsity of what the statement asserts; or

   c. The confession of the nontestifying co-defendant is being used ***to rebut the defendant's claim that his confession was obtained coercively***.

2. **Hearsay**
"Hearsay," if admitted, could deny a defendant the right to confront the declarant. If the hearsay consists of statements made at a ***prior judicial proceeding***, it will be admissible only if (i) the prosecution has made a good faith effort to obtain in-court testimony of the witnesses and has failed, and (ii) the defendant has had an opportunity to cross-examine the declarant as to testimony or has otherwise had an opportunity to test its accuracy.

E. BURDEN OF PROOF AND SUFFICIENCY OF EVIDENCE

The Due Process Clause requires in all criminal cases that the ***state*** prove guilt beyond a reasonable doubt. The presumption of innocence is a basic component of a fair trial. However, the state may generally impose the burden of proof upon the defendant in regard to an affirmative defense such as insanity or self-defense.

1. Presumptions
A mandatory presumption or a presumption that shifts the burden of proof to the defendant violates the Fourteenth Amendment's requirement that the state prove every element of the crime beyond a reasonable doubt.

VIII. GUILTY PLEAS AND PLEA BARGAINING

A. TAKING THE PLEA
A guilty plea is a waiver of the Sixth Amendment right to a jury trial. The judge must advise defendant personally:

(i) Of the ***nature of the charge*** to which the plea is offered;

(ii) Of the ***maximum possible penalty*** and of any ***mandatory minimum*** (but failure to explain a special parole term is not fatal);

(iii) That defendant has a ***right not to plead guilty***; and

(iv) That by pleading guilty defendant ***waives his right to a trial***.

1. Requirement of Adequate Record
A record must be made of the taking of all guilty pleas. The record must indicate that the plea was ***voluntary and intelligent***.

2. Remedy
The remedy for a failure to meet the standards for taking a plea is withdrawal of the plea and pleading anew.

B. COLLATERAL ATTACKS ON GUILTY PLEAS AFTER SENTENCE
Those pleas that are seen as an intelligent choice among defendant's alternatives are immune from collateral attack. But a plea can be set aside for (i) involuntariness (failure to meet standards for taking a plea), (ii) lack of jurisdiction, (iii) ineffective assistance of counsel, or (iv) failure to keep the plea bargain.

C. PLEA BARGAINING
A plea bargain will be enforced against the prosecutor and the defendant, but not against the judge, who does not have to accept the plea. A guilty plea is not involuntary merely because it was entered in response to the prosecution's threat to charge defendant with a more serious crime if he does not plead guilty. There is no prosecutorial vindictiveness in charging a more serious offense when defendant demands a jury trial.

D. COLLATERAL EFFECTS OF GUILTY PLEAS
A guilty plea conviction may be used as a conviction in other proceedings when relevant (*e.g.*, as the basis for sentence enhancement). However, a guilty plea neither admits the legality of incriminating evidence nor waives Fourth Amendment claims in a subsequent civil damages action.

IX. CONSTITUTIONAL RIGHTS IN RELATION TO SENTENCING AND PUNISHMENT

A. PROCEDURAL RIGHTS IN SENTENCING

A defendant has a ***right to counsel*** during sentencing. The usual sentence may be based on hearsay and uncross-examined reports (*i.e.,* defendant has ***no right to confrontation or cross-examination***). However, where a magnified sentence is based on a statute that requires new findings of fact to be made (*e.g.*, defendant is mentally ill), those facts must be found in a context that grants a right to confrontation and cross-examination.

1. Capital Sentencing

A defendant in a death penalty case must have more opportunity for confrontation than need be given a defendant in other sentencing proceedings.

B. RESENTENCING AFTER SUCCESSFUL APPEAL AND RECONVICTION

If a greater punishment is imposed on a defendant who has been reconvicted after a successful appeal than was imposed at the first trial, the judge must set forth in the record the reasons for the harsher sentence. This ensures that the defendant is not vindictively penalized for exercising his right to appeal.

1. Exceptions

A judge need not give reasons if the greater sentence was imposed upon a de novo trial or in a state that uses jury sentencing, unless the second jury was told of the first jury's sentence.

C. SUBSTANTIVE RIGHTS IN REGARD TO PUNISHMENT

The Eighth Amendment prohibits ***cruel and unusual punishment***. A penalty that is grossly disproportionate to the seriousness of the offense committed is cruel and unusual. State appellate courts do not have to compare the death sentence imposed in a case under appeal with other penalties imposed in similar cases.

1. Death Penalty

a. For Murder

The death penalty can be imposed only under a statutory scheme that gives the judge or jury reasonable discretion, full information concerning defendants, and guidance in making the decision. The statute cannot be vague. Moreover, it must allow the sentencing body to consider all mitigating evidence.

1) Based on Prior Convictions

If the death sentence is partly based on the aggravating factor of defendant's prior conviction, the sentence must be reversed if the prior conviction is invalidated.

2) Standard of Review

A death sentence that has been affected by a vague or otherwise unconstitutional factor can still be upheld, but only if all aggravating and mitigating factors involved are reweighed and death is still found to be appropriate.

b. For Rape or Felony Murder

The Eighth Amendment prohibits imposition of the death penalty for the crime of raping an adult woman, because the penalty is disproportionate to the offense. Also, the same logic precludes the death penalty for felony murder unless the felony murderer's participation was major and he acted with reckless indifference to the value of human life.

c. **Sanity Requirement**
The Eighth Amendment prohibits executing a prisoner who is insane at the time of execution, even if he was sane at the time the crime was committed.

d. **Mental Retardation**
It is cruel and unusual punishment to impose the death penalty on a person who is mentally retarded.

e. **For Minors**
The death penalty may be imposed on murderers who were 16 or older at the time they committed murder. Execution of murderers younger than 16 at the time of their crime might be forbidden.

2. **Status Crimes**
A statute that makes it a crime to have a given "status" violates the Eighth Amendment because it punishes a mere propensity to engage in dangerous behavior. However, it is permissible to make criminal specific activity related to a certain status (*e.g.,* driving while intoxicated).

3. **Considering Defendant's Perjury**
In determining the sentence, the trial judge may take into account a belief that the defendant committed perjury while testifying at trial on his own behalf.

4. **Imprisonment of Indigents for Nonpayment**
Where aggregate imprisonment exceeds the maximum period fixed by statute and results directly from involuntary nonpayment of a fine or court costs, there is an impermissible discrimination and violation of the Equal Protection Clause.

X. CONSTITUTIONAL PROBLEMS ON APPEAL

A. NO RIGHT TO APPEAL
There is no federal constitutional right to an appeal.

B. EQUAL PROTECTION AND RIGHT TO COUNSEL ON APPEAL
If an avenue of post-conviction review is provided, conditions that make the review less accessible to the poor than to the rich violate equal protection. Thus, indigents must be given counsel at state expense during a first appeal granted to all ***as a matter of right***.

In a jurisdiction using a two-tier system of appellate courts with discretionary review by the highest court, an indigent defendant need not be provided with counsel during the second, discretionary appeal.

C. RETROACTIVITY

If the Supreme Court announces a new rule of criminal procedure (*e.g.*, one not dictated by precedent) in a case on direct review, the rule must be applied to all other cases on direct review.

XI. COLLATERAL ATTACK UPON CONVICTION

A. AVAILABILITY OF COLLATERAL ATTACK

After appeal is no longer available or has proven unsuccessful, defendants may generally still attack their convictions collaterally.

B. HABEAS CORPUS PROCEEDING

An indigent has no right to appointed counsel at a habeas corpus proceeding. Petitioner has the burden of proof by ***preponderance of evidence*** to show an unlawful detention. The state may appeal the grant of a writ of habeas corpus. A defendant generally may bring a habeas petition only if the defendant is in custody. Generally, this includes anyone who has not fully served the sentence about which he wishes to complain.

XII. RIGHTS DURING PUNISHMENT

A. RIGHT TO COUNSEL AT PAROLE AND PROBATION REVOCATION

If revocation of probation also involves imposition of a new sentence, the defendant is entitled to representation by counsel in all cases in which she is entitled to counsel at trial. If, after probation revocation, an already imposed sentence of imprisonment springs into application, or if the case involves parole revocation, the right to counsel is available ***only if representation is necessary*** to a fair hearing (*e.g.*, defendant denies commission of alleged acts or issues are otherwise difficult to present and develop).

B. PRISONERS' RIGHTS

Prisoners' rights issues rarely appear on the Multistate Bar Exam, and when they do appear they usually involve the same constitutional analysis as set out in the general constitutional law outline. The most important rules peculiar to criminal procedure are:

1. Due Process

Prison regulations impinge on due process rights only if the regulations impose "***atypical and significant hardship***" in relation to the ordinary incidents of prison life.

2. No Fourth Amendment Protections in Cells

Prisoners have no reasonable expectation of privacy in their cells and so have no Fourth Amendment protection with respect to searches of their cells.

3. Right of Access to Courts

Prisoners must be given reasonable access to the courts.

4. First Amendment Rights

Prisoners' First Amendment rights of freedom of speech, association, and religion may be burdened by regulations ***reasonably related to penological interests*** (*e.g.*, running a safe and secure prison). Note that ***incoming*** mail can be broadly regulated, but outgoing mail generally cannot be regulated.

5. **Right to Adequate Medical Care**
Prisoners have a right to adequate medical care under the Eighth Amendment prohibition against cruel and unusual punishment.

C. NO RIGHT TO BE FREE FROM DISABILITIES UPON COMPLETION OF SENTENCE

A person convicted of a felony may be unable to vote in state elections, and this disability can constitutionally continue beyond the term of her sentence.

XIII. DOUBLE JEOPARDY

A. WHEN JEOPARDY ATTACHES

Under the Fifth Amendment, a person may not be retried for the same offense once jeopardy has attached. Jeopardy attaches in a jury trial at the empaneling and swearing of the jury. In bench trials jeopardy attaches when the first witness is sworn. Commencement of a juvenile proceeding bars a subsequent criminal trial for the same offense. Jeopardy generally does not attach in civil proceedings other than juvenile proceedings.

B. EXCEPTIONS PERMITTING RETRIAL

Certain exceptions permit retrial of a defendant even if jeopardy has attached:

1. A state may retry a defendant whose first trial ends in a ***hung jury***.

2. A trial may be discontinued and the defendant reprosecuted for the same offense when there is ***manifest necessity*** to abort the original trial or when termination occurs at the behest of the defendant on any ground not constituting acquittal on the merits.

3. A state may retry a defendant who has ***successfully appealed*** a conviction unless the ground for reversal was insufficient evidence to support a guilty verdict. Retrial is permitted when reversal is based on the ***weight*** (rather than sufficiency) of the evidence. However, on retrial, a defendant ***may not be tried for a greater offense*** than that for which he was convicted. A harsher sentence may be imposed for reasons other than vindictiveness for taking an appeal, but if the jury found that the death penalty was not appropriate in the first trial, a death sentence may not be imposed at the second trial.

4. Charges may be reinstated after a defendant ***breaches*** her ***plea bargain***.

C. SAME OFFENSE

1. **General Rule—When Two Crimes Not the Same Offense**
Two crimes are the same offense unless ***each crime requires proof of an additional element*** that the other does not require, even though some of the same facts may be necessary to prove both crimes.

2. **Cumulative Punishments for Offenses Constituting the Same Crime**
Even if two crimes constitute the same offense under this test, multiple punishments are

permissible if there was a ***legislative intent*** to have the cumulative punishments (*e.g.*, a defendant can be sentenced both for robbery and using a weapon during the commission of a crime if statutes so provide).

3. Lesser Included Offenses

Attachment of jeopardy for a greater offense bars retrial for lesser included offenses. Attachment of jeopardy for a lesser included offense bars retrial for greater offense, except that retrial for murder is permitted if the victim dies after attachment of jeopardy for battery. A state may continue to prosecute a charged offense despite defendant's guilty plea to a lesser included or "allied" offense stemming from the same incident.

a. Exception—New Evidence

An exception to the double jeopardy bar exists if unlawful conduct that is subsequently used to prove the greater offense (i) has not occurred at the time of prosecution for the lesser offense or (ii) has not been discovered despite due diligence.

4. Conduct Used as a Sentence Enhancer

The Double Jeopardy Clause is not violated when a person is indicted for a crime the conduct of which was already used to enhance the defendant's sentence for another crime.

5. Subsequent Civil Actions

The Double Jeopardy Clause prohibits only repetitive ***criminal*** prosecutions. Thus, a state generally is free to bring a civil action against a defendant even if the defendant has already been criminally tried for the conduct out of which the civil action arises. Similarly, the government may bring a criminal action even though the defendant has already faced civil trial for the same conduct unless it is clear from the statutory scheme that the purpose or effect of the statute is to impose a criminal penalty.

D. SEPARATE SOVEREIGNS

The constitutional prohibition against double jeopardy does not apply to trials by separate sovereigns. Thus, a person may be tried for the same conduct by both the state and federal governments or by two states, but not by a state and its municipalities.

CMR **Exam Tip** Double jeopardy questions on the MBE occasionally raise the separate sovereign issue. The rule is simple: Separate sovereigns ***can*** try a defendant for the same offense. Beware of facts that try to divert you from this easy issue (*e.g.,* statements about juries being empaneled or witnesses sworn in—things that go to attachment). Attachment does not matter if there are two separate sovereigns.

On the other hand, remember that municipalities are considered part of the state, and so both a state and its municipality ***cannot*** validly try defendant for the same offense.

E. APPEALS BY PROSECUTION

Even after jeopardy has attached, the prosecution may appeal any dismissal on defendant's motion that does not constitute an acquittal on the merits. Also, the Double Jeopardy Clause does not bar appeals by the prosecution if a successful appeal would not require a retrial. There is no bar to a government appeal of a ***sentence*** pursuant to statute permitting such review. However, if the jury fails to impose the death penalty, the prosecution may not seek the death penalty on retrial after successful appeal.

F. COLLATERAL ESTOPPEL
Under the doctrine of collateral estoppel, a defendant may not be tried or convicted of a crime if a prior prosecution by that sovereignty resulted in a factual determination inconsistent with one required for conviction.

XIV. PRIVILEGE AGAINST COMPELLED SELF-INCRIMINATION

A. WHO MAY ASSERT THE PRIVILEGE
Only natural persons may assert the privilege, not corporations or partnerships. The privilege is personal and so may be asserted by a defendant, witness, or party only if the answer to the question might tend to incriminate him.

B. WHEN PRIVILEGE MAY BE ASSERTED
A person may refuse to answer a question whenever his response might furnish a link in the chain of evidence needed to prosecute him. The privilege must be claimed in civil proceedings to prevent the privilege from being waived for a later criminal prosecution. Thus, if an individual responds to questions instead of claiming the privilege during a civil proceeding, he cannot later bar that evidence from a criminal prosecution on compelled self-incrimination grounds.

C. METHOD FOR INVOKING PRIVILEGE
A ***criminal defendant*** has a right not to take the witness stand at trial and not to be asked to do so. In any other situation, the privilege does not permit a person to avoid being sworn as a witness or being asked questions. Rather, the person must listen to the questions and specifically invoke the privilege rather than answer the questions.

D. SCOPE OF PROTECTION

1. Testimonial but Not Physical Evidence
The Fifth Amendment privilege protects only testimonial or communicative evidence and not real or physical evidence. For a suspect's communication to be considered testimonial, it must relate a factual assertion or disclose information.

2. Compulsory Production of Documents
A person served with a subpoena requiring production of documents tending to incriminate him generally has no basis in the privilege to refuse to comply, because the act of producing the documents does not involve testimonial self-incrimination.

3. Seizure of Incriminating Documents
The Fifth Amendment does not prohibit law enforcement officers from searching for and seizing documents tending to incriminate a person.

4. When Does Violation Occur?
A violation of the Self-Incrimination Clause does not occur until a person's compelled statements are used against him in a criminal case.

Exam Tip For purposes of the Multistate Bar Exam, two of the most important things to remember about the Fifth Amendment self-incrimination privilege are:

- Only ***testimonial*** evidence is protected. Thus, a defendant has no self-incrimination basis to object to a lineup or other identification procedure—even if he is asked to say certain words (*e.g.,* "Your money or your life!"). This procedure does not involve testimonial evidence; the words are used for identification purposes and not as testimony.

- Likewise, only ***compelled*** testimonial evidence is privileged. Thus, if defendant produced a writing of his own free will (*e.g.,* took incriminating notes of a meeting), the police may seize this writing, or defendant may be compelled to produce it by subpoena, because he was not compelled to make the statement originally.

E. PROHIBITION AGAINST BURDENS ON ASSERTION OF PRIVILEGE

1. Comments on Defendant's Silence

A prosecutor may not comment on a defendant's silence after being arrested and receiving *Miranda* warnings. Neither may the prosecutor comment on a defendant's failure to testify at trial. However, a defendant, upon timely motion, is entitled to have the judge instruct the jury that they may not draw an adverse inference from the defendant's failure to testify. Moreover, the judge may offer this instruction sua sponte, even over the defendant's objection.

a. Exception

A prosecutor can comment on a defendant's failure to take the stand when the comment is in response to defense counsel's assertion that defendant was not allowed to explain his side of the story.

b. Harmless Error Test Applies

When a prosecutor impermissibly comments on defendant's silence, the harmless error test applies.

2. Penalties for Failure to Testify

The state may not chill exercise of Fifth Amendment privilege against compelled self-incrimination by imposing penalties for failure to testify.

F. ELIMINATION OF PRIVILEGE

1. Grant of Immunity

A witness may be compelled to answer questions if granted adequate immunity from prosecution.

a. "Use and Derivative Use" Immunity Sufficient

"Use and derivative use" immunity guarantees that the witness's testimony and evidence located by means of the testimony will not be used against the witness. However, the witness may still be prosecuted if the prosecutor shows that the evidence to be used against the witness was derived from a source independent of the immunized testimony.

b. Immunized Testimony Involuntary

Testimony obtained by a promise of immunity is coerced and therefore involuntary. Thus, immunized testimony may not be used for impeachment of a defendant's testimony at trial. However, any immunized statements, whether true or untrue, can be used in a trial for perjury.

c. **Use of Testimony by Another Sovereign Prohibited**
Federal prosecutors may not use evidence obtained as a result of a state grant of immunity, and vice versa.

2. **No Possibility of Incrimination**
A person has no privilege against compelled self-incrimination if there is no possibility of incrimination (*e.g.*, statute of limitations has run).

3. **Scope of Immunity**
Immunity extends only to the offenses to which the question relates and does not protect against perjury committed during the immunized testimony.

G. WAIVER OF PRIVILEGE

A criminal defendant, by taking the witness stand, waives the privilege to the extent necessary to subject him to any cross-examination. A witness waives the privilege only if he discloses incriminating information.

XV. JUVENILE COURT PROCEEDINGS

A. RIGHTS THAT MUST BE AFFORDED

The following rights must be given to a child during trial of a delinquency proceeding: (i) written ***notice*** of charges, (ii) ***assistance of counsel***, (iii) ***opportunity to confront*** and cross-examine witnesses, (iv) the ***right not to testify***, and (v) the right to have "***guilt***" ***established by proof beyond reasonable doubt***.

The Supreme Court has held that there is ***no*** right to trial by jury in delinquency proceedings. Pretrial detention of a juvenile is allowed where it is found that the juvenile is a "serious risk" to society, as long as the detention is for a strictly limited time before trial may be held.

B. DOUBLE JEOPARDY

If the juvenile court adjudicates a child a delinquent, jeopardy has attached and the prohibition against double jeopardy prevents him from being tried as an adult for the same behavior.

XVI. FORFEITURE ACTIONS

A. INTRODUCTION

Actions for forfeiture are brought directly against property and are generally regarded as quasi-criminal in nature. Certain constitutional rights may exist for those persons whose interest in property would be lost by forfeiture.

B. RIGHT TO PRE-SEIZURE NOTICE AND HEARING

The owner of ***personal*** property (and others with an interest in it) is not constitutionally entitled to notice and a hearing before the property is seized for purposes of a forfeiture proceeding. A hearing is, however, required before final forfeiture of the property. Where ***real property*** is seized, notice and an opportunity to be heard is required before the seizure of the real property unless the government can prove that exigent circumstances justify immediate seizure.

C. MAY BE SUBJECT TO EIGHTH AMENDMENT

1. General Rule

The Supreme Court has held that the Excessive Fines Clause of the Eighth Amendment applies only to fines imposed as punishment; it does not apply to civil fines. Thus, ***penal*** forfeitures are subject to the Clause, but ***civil*** forfeitures are not. Even if the Clause applies, the forfeiture will not be "excessive" unless ***grossly disproportionate*** to the gravity of the offense.

2. Compare—Nonpunitive Forfeiture

a. Civil In Rem Forfeitures

Civil in rem forfeitures generally are ***not*** subject to the Excessive Fines Clause.

b. Monetary Forfeitures

Monetary forfeitures (*e.g.*, forfeiture of twice the value of illegally imported goods) brought in civil actions generally are ***not*** subject to the Eighth Amendment.

D. PROTECTION FOR "INNOCENT OWNER" NOT REQUIRED

The Due Process Clause does ***not*** require forfeiture statutes to provide an "innocent owner" defense (*e.g.*, a defense that the owner took all reasonable steps to avoid having the property used by another for illegal purposes), at least where the innocent owner ***voluntarily entrusted*** the property to the wrongdoer.

EVIDENCE

TABLE OF CONTENTS

I. GENERAL CONSIDERATIONS 1
A. SOURCES OF EVIDENCE LAW 1
B. THRESHOLD ADMISSIBILITY ISSUES 1
C. DIRECT AND CIRCUMSTANTIAL EVIDENCE 1
D. LIMITED ADMISSIBILITY 1

II. RELEVANCE 1
A. DETERMINING RELEVANCE 1
1. General Rule—Must Relate to Time, Event, or Person in Controversy 1
2. Exceptions—Certain Similar Occurrences Are Relevant 1
B. DISCRETIONARY EXCLUSION OF RELEVANT EVIDENCE 4
C. EXCLUSION OF RELEVANT EVIDENCE FOR PUBLIC POLICY REASONS . 4
1. Liability Insurance 4
2. Subsequent Remedial Measures 6
3. Settlement Offers and Withdrawn Guilty Pleas 6
4. Offers to Pay Medical Expenses 6
D. CHARACTER EVIDENCE—A SPECIAL RELEVANCE PROBLEM 7
1. Means of Proving Character 7
2. Generally Not Admissible in Civil Cases 7
3. Accused in Criminal Case—Generally Only Accused Can Initiate 7
4. Victim in Criminal Case 8
5. Specific Acts of Misconduct 8

III. JUDICIAL NOTICE 9
A. JUDICIAL NOTICE OF FACT 9
1. Facts Appropriate for Judicial Notice 9
2. Procedural Aspects of Judicial Notice 9
3. "Adjudicative" and "Legislative" Facts 9
B. JUDICIAL NOTICE OF LAW—MANDATORY OR PERMISSIVE 10

IV. REAL EVIDENCE 10
A. IN GENERAL 10
B. GENERAL CONDITIONS OF ADMISSIBILITY 10
1. Authentication 10
2. Condition of Object 10
3. Balancing Test—Legal Relevance 10
C. PARTICULAR TYPES OF REAL PROOF 10
1. Reproductions and Explanatory Real Evidence 10
2. Maps, Charts, Models, Etc. 10
3. Exhibition of Child in Paternity Suits 10
4. Exhibition of Injuries 11
5. Jury View of the Scene 11
6. Demonstrations 11

V. DOCUMENTARY EVIDENCE 11
A. IN GENERAL 11
B. AUTHENTICATION 11
1. Authentication by Pleadings or Stipulation 11
2. Evidence of Authenticity 11
3. Compare—Authentication of Oral Statements 12
4. Self-Authenticating Documents 13
C. BEST EVIDENCE RULE 13
1. Applicability of the Rule 13
2. Nonapplicability of the Rule 13
3. Definitions of "Writings," "Original," and "Duplicate" 13
4. Admissibility of Secondary Evidence of Contents 15
5. Functions of Court and Jury 15
D. PAROL EVIDENCE RULE 15
1. When the Rule Does Not Apply 15
2. Subsequent Modifications 16

VI. TESTIMONIAL EVIDENCE 16
A. COMPETENCY OF WITNESSES 16
1. Federal Rules of Competency 16
2. Modern Modifications of the Common Law Disqualifications 16
3. Dead Man Acts 17
B. FORM OF EXAMINATION OF WITNESS 17
1. Leading Questions 17
2. Improper Questions 17
3. Use of Memoranda by Witness 17
C. OPINION TESTIMONY 19
1. Opinion Testimony by Lay Witnesses 19
2. Opinion Testimony by Expert Witnesses 19
D. CROSS-EXAMINATION 21
1. Restrictions on Scope 21
2. Collateral Matters 21
E. CREDIBILITY—IMPEACHMENT 21
1. Accrediting or Bolstering 21
2. Any Party May Impeach 22
3. Impeachment Methods—Cross-Examination and Extrinsic Evidence 22
4. Impeachment on Collateral Matter 24
5. Impeachment of Hearsay Declarant 24
6. Rehabilitation 25
F. OBJECTIONS, EXCEPTIONS, AND OFFERS OF PROOF 26
1. Objections 26
2. Exceptions 27
3. Offers of Proof 27
G. TESTIMONIAL PRIVILEGES 27
1. Federal Rules—No Specific Privilege Provisions 27
2. General Considerations 27
3. Attorney-Client Privilege 28
4. Physician-Patient Privilege 29
5. Psychotherapist/Social Worker-Client Privilege 29

6. Husband-Wife Privilege 30
7. Privilege Against Self-Incrimination 31
8. Clergy or Accountant Privilege 31
9. Professional Journalist Privilege 31
10. Governmental Privileges 31
H. EXCLUSION AND SEQUESTRATION OF WITNESSES 31

VII. THE HEARSAY RULE 31
A. STATEMENT OF THE RULE 31
1. "Statement" 31
2. "Offered to Prove the Truth of the Matter" 31
3. Nonhuman Declarations 33
B. STATEMENTS THAT ARE NONHEARSAY UNDER THE FEDERAL RULES 33
1. Prior Statements by Witness 33
2. Admissions by Party-Opponent 33
C. HEARSAY EXCEPTIONS—DECLARANT UNAVAILABLE 35
1. "Unavailability" 35
2. Former Testimony 35
3. Statements Against Interest 35
4. Dying Declarations—Statements Under Belief of Impending Death 36
5. Statements of Personal or Family History 36
6. Statements Offered Against Party Procuring Declarant's Unavailability 37
D. HEARSAY EXCEPTIONS—DECLARANT'S AVAILABILITY IMMATERIAL 37
1. Present State of Mind 37
2. Excited Utterances 38
3. Present Sense Impressions 38
4. Declarations of Physical Condition 38
5. Business Records 38
6. Past Recollection Recorded 39
7. Official Records and Other Official Writings 39
8. Ancient Documents and Documents Affecting Property Interests 40
9. Learned Treatises 40
10. Reputation 40
11. Family Records 40
12. Market Reports 40
E. RESIDUAL "CATCH-ALL" EXCEPTION OF FEDERAL RULES 43
F. CONSTITUTIONAL ISSUES 43

VIII. PROCEDURAL CONSIDERATIONS 43
A. BURDENS OF PROOF 43
1. Burden of Producing Evidence 43
2. Burden of Persuasion (Proof) 43
B. PRESUMPTIONS 43
1. Effect—Shift Burden of Production 43
2. Rebutting a Presumption 44
3. Distinguish True Presumptions from Inferences and Substantive Law 44
4. Specific Presumptions 44
5. Conflicting Presumptions 45
6. Choice of Law Regarding Presumptions in Civil Actions 45

C. RELATIONSHIP OF PARTIES, JUDGE, AND JURY 45
1. Allocation of Responsibilities 45
2. Preliminary Determination of Admissibility 46

EVIDENCE

I. GENERAL CONSIDERATIONS

A. SOURCES OF EVIDENCE LAW

There are three sources of evidence law: (i) state common law and miscellaneous state statutes, (ii) comprehensive state evidence codes, and (iii) the Federal Rules of Evidence.

CMR **Exam Tip** The Federal Rules govern on the Multistate Bar Examination ("MBE"). Beware of answer choices stating the correct common law rule, rather than the Federal Rule.

B. THRESHOLD ADMISSIBILITY ISSUES

Generally, relevant evidence is admissible if it is competent. Under the Federal Rules, "relevant evidence" tends to prove (probativeness) any fact of consequence to the action (materiality). Evidence is competent if it does not violate any exclusionary rule (*e.g.,* the hearsay rule).

C. DIRECT AND CIRCUMSTANTIAL EVIDENCE

Direct evidence involves no inferences. It is testimony or real evidence that speaks directly to a material issue in the case. Circumstantial evidence is indirect and relies on inference. It is evidence of a subsidiary or collateral fact from which, alone or in conjunction with other facts, the existence of the material issue can be inferred.

D. LIMITED ADMISSIBILITY

Evidence may be admissible for one purpose but not another, or admissible against one party but not another. In these situations, the court must, upon request, restrict the evidence to its proper scope and instruct the jury accordingly.

II. RELEVANCE

CMR **Exam Tip** Relevance questions should be approached in two steps. ***Step 1***: Determine whether the evidence is relevant (*i.e.,* tends to prove or disprove a material fact). ***Step 2***: If relevant, determine whether the evidence should nonetheless be excluded based on: (i) judicial discretion (*i.e.,* probative value outweighed by prejudice, etc.), or (ii) public policy (*e.g.,* insurance, subsequent repairs).

A. DETERMINING RELEVANCE

Evidence is relevant if it tends to make the existence of any fact of consequence to the outcome of the action more probable than it would be without the evidence.

1. General Rule—Must Relate to Time, Event, or Person in Controversy

Generally, the evidence must relate to the time, event, or person involved in the ***present*** litigation; otherwise, it is not relevant.

When considering the relevance of evidence relating to a time, event, or person other than the one at issue, an important factor is its proximity in time to the current events.

2. Exceptions—Certain Similar Occurrences Are Relevant

Previous similar occurrences may be relevant if they are probative of a material issue and that probativeness outweighs the risk of confusion or unfair prejudice. The following are examples of relevant similar occurrences:

CMR
APPROACH CHART

DETERMINING ADMISSIBILITY OF EVIDENCE

STEP 1
Is the evidence ***relevant*** ?

STEP 2
Is there a proper ***foundation*** (*e.g.,* has the competency of the witness, the authenticity of the evidence, or the reliability of the scientific test been established)?

STEP 3
Is the evidence in the proper ***form*** (*e.g.,* questions are properly phrased, answers are within the requirements for lay and expert opinion, and documents comply with the best evidence rule)?

STEP 4
Is the evidence beyond the application of, or within an exception to, one of the following ***exclusionary rules*** ?

- Discretionary exclusion for prejudice (Rule 403)
- Policy-based exclusions (*i.e.,* subsequent remedial measures, settlement negotiations)
- Privilege
- Hearsay
- Parol evidence

ADMISSIBLE

a. **Causation**
Complicated issues of causation may be established by evidence concerning other times, events, or persons (*e.g.,* damage to nearby homes caused by D's blasting is relevant to prove D's blasting damaged P's home).

b. **Prior False Claims or Same Bodily Injury**
Evidence that a person has previously filed similar tort claims or has been involved in prior accidents is generally inadmissible to show the invalidity of the present claim. But evidence that the party has made previous similar false claims or claims involving the same bodily injury is usually relevant to prove that: (i) the present claim is likely to be false, or (ii) the plaintiff's condition is attributable in whole or in part to the prior injury.

c. **Similar Accidents or Injuries Caused by Same Event or Condition**
Evidence of prior accidents or injuries caused by the same event or condition is admissible to prove: (i) the ***existence*** of a dangerous condition, (ii) that the defendant had ***knowledge*** of the dangerous condition, and (iii) that the dangerous condition was the ***cause*** of the present injury.

1) **Absence of Similar Accidents**
Many courts are reluctant to admit evidence of the ***absence*** of similar accidents to show absence of negligence or lack of a defect. However, evidence of the absence of complaints is admissible to show the defendant's lack of knowledge of the danger.

d. **Previous Similar Acts Admissible to Prove Intent**
Similar conduct previously committed by a party may be introduced to prove the party's present motive or intent when such elements are relevant (*e.g.,* history of school segregation admissible to show motive for current exclusion of minorities).

e. **Rebutting Claim of Impossibility**
The requirement that prior occurrences be similar to the litigated act may be relaxed when used to rebut a claim of impossibility (*e.g.,* defendant's claim that car will not go above 50 m.p.h. can be rebutted by showing occasions when car went more than 50 m.p.h.).

f. **Sales of Similar Property**
Evidence of sales of similar personal or real property that are not too remote in time is admissible to prove value. Prices quoted in mere offers to purchase are not admissible. However, evidence of unaccepted offers by a party to the action to buy or sell the property may be used against him as an admission.

g. **Habit**
Habit describes a person's ***regular response*** to a specific set of circumstances. In contrast, character describes one's disposition in respect to general traits. Under Federal Rule 406, evidence of the habit of a person is relevant to prove that the conduct of the person on a particular occasion was in conformity with the habit.

CMR **Exam Tip** Watch for words such as ***"instinctively"*** and ***"automatically"*** in a question's fact pattern. These words indicate habit.

CHARACTER EVIDENCE VS. HABIT EVIDENCE

Character Evidence	Habit Evidence
"Sally is always in a hurry."	"Sally always takes the stairs two at a time."
"Bart is a drunk."	"Bart stops at Charlie's tavern every night after work and has exactly four beers."
"Jeff is a careless driver."	"Jeff never slows down for the YIELD sign at the end of the street."
"Lara is very conscientious about the maintenance of her car."	"Lara checks the brakes on her car every Sunday before church."

h. Industrial or Business Routine
Evidence that a particular business had an established business routine is relevant as tending to show that a particular event occurred.

i. Industry Custom as Evidence of Standard of Care
Industry custom may be offered to show adherence to or deviance from an industry-wide standard of care. However, industry custom is not conclusive on this point; *e.g.*, an entire industry may be acting negligently.

B. DISCRETIONARY EXCLUSION OF RELEVANT EVIDENCE

A trial judge has broad discretion to exclude relevant evidence if its ***probative value is substantially outweighed*** by the danger of unfair prejudice, confusion of issues, misleading the jury, undue delay, or waste of time.

CMR Exam Tip Under the Federal Rules, ***unfair surprise*** is ***not*** a valid ground upon which to exclude relevant evidence.

C. EXCLUSION OF RELEVANT EVIDENCE FOR PUBLIC POLICY REASONS

Certain evidence of questionable relevance is excluded by the Federal Rules because public policy favors the behavior involved. Subsequent repairs, for example, are not admissible to show negligence because society wishes to encourage the immediate repair of dangerous conditions. Evidence excluded for public policy reasons includes the following:

1. Liability Insurance
Evidence of insurance against liability is ***not admissible to show negligence or ability to pay*** a substantial judgment. However, it may be admissible: (i) to prove ownership or control, (ii) to impeach, or (iii) as part of an admission.

ADMISSIBILITY OF RELEVANT EVIDENCE

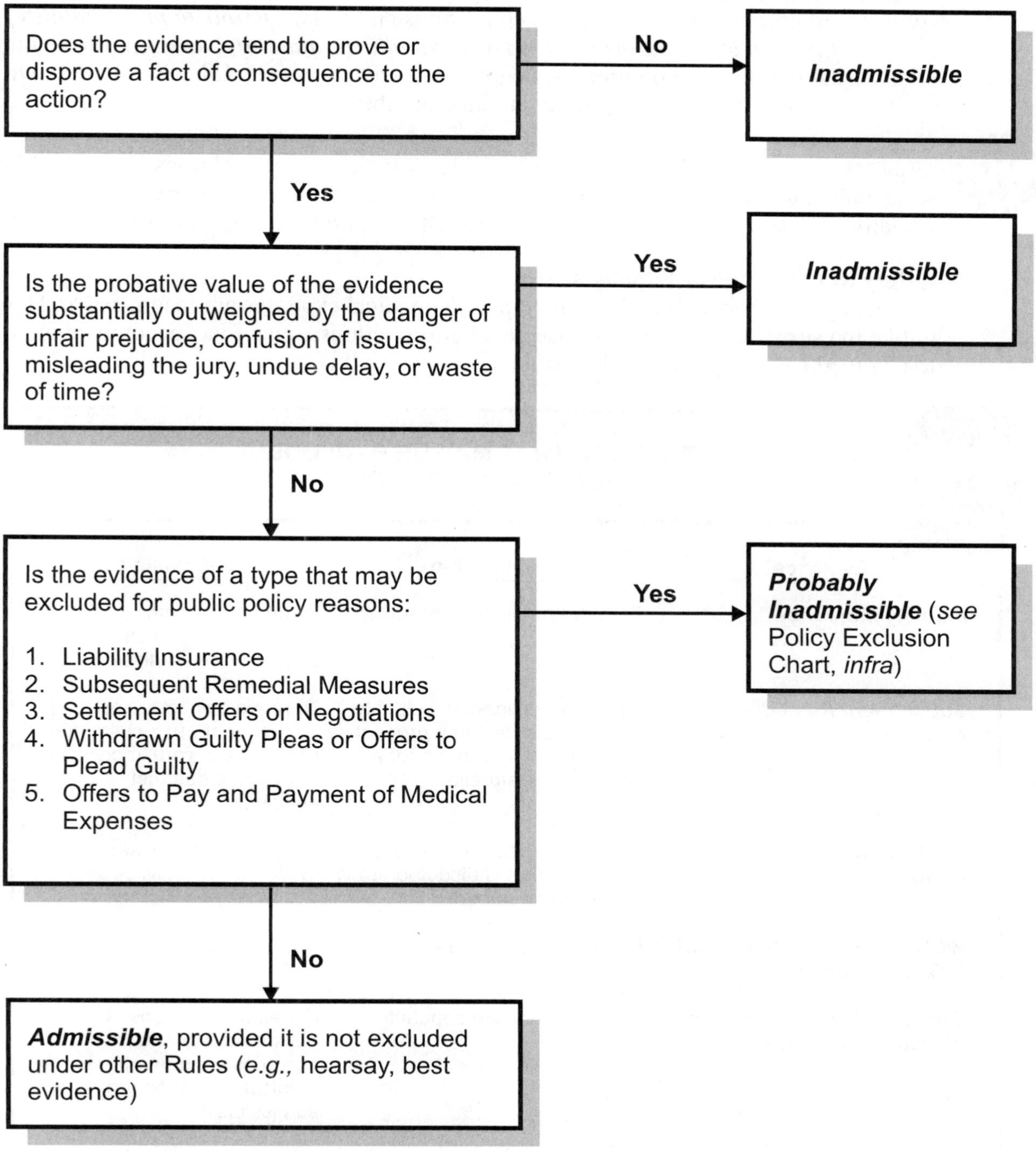

Does the evidence tend to prove or disprove a fact of consequence to the action?

- **No** → ***Inadmissible***
- **Yes** ↓

Is the probative value of the evidence substantially outweighed by the danger of unfair prejudice, confusion of issues, misleading the jury, undue delay, or waste of time?

- **Yes** → ***Inadmissible***
- **No** ↓

Is the evidence of a type that may be excluded for public policy reasons:

1. Liability Insurance
2. Subsequent Remedial Measures
3. Settlement Offers or Negotiations
4. Withdrawn Guilty Pleas or Offers to Plead Guilty
5. Offers to Pay and Payment of Medical Expenses

- **Yes** → ***Probably Inadmissible*** (*see* Policy Exclusion Chart, *infra*)
- **No** ↓

Admissible, provided it is not excluded under other Rules (*e.g.,* hearsay, best evidence)

2. Subsequent Remedial Measures
Evidence of repairs or other precautionary measures made following an injury is ***not admissible*** to prove negligence, culpable conduct, a defect in a product or its design, or a need for a warning or instruction. However, it may be admissible to: (i) prove ownership or control, (ii) rebut a claim that the precaution was not feasible, or (iii) prove that the opposing party has destroyed evidence.

3. Settlement Offers and Withdrawn Guilty Pleas
Evidence of compromises or offers to compromise is ***not admissible to prove liability for, or invalidity of, a claim that is disputed as to validity or amount***. Not even direct admissions of liability during compromise negotiations are admissible. Likewise, withdrawn guilty pleas and offers to plead guilty are inadmissible.

CMR **Exam Tip** For the exclusionary rule to apply to settlement negotiations, there must be some indication that a party is going to ***make a claim*** (although the party need not have actually filed suit). Furthermore, the claim must be ***in dispute*** as to liability or amount.

4. Offers to Pay Medical Expenses
Payment of or offers to pay the injured party's medical expenses are inadmissible. However, unlike the situation with compromise negotiations, admissions of fact accompanying offers to pay medical expenses are admissible.

CMR SUMMARY CHART

EVIDENCE THAT MAY BE EXCLUDED FOR POLICY REASONS

Evidence	Inadmissible	Admissible
Liability Insurance	To prove negligence or ability to pay	To prove ownership or control, as impeachment, or as part of an admission
Subsequent Remedial Measures	To prove negligence, culpable conduct, a defect in a product or its design, or a need for a warning or instruction	To prove ownership or control, to rebut a claim that precautions were impossible, or to prove destruction of evidence
Settlement Offers or Negotiations	To prove liability or invalidity of a claim that is disputed as to validity or amount	For all other purposes
Withdrawn Guilty Pleas and Offers to Plead Guilty	For nearly all purposes	Not admissible
Offers to Pay and Payment of Medical Expenses	To prove culpable conduct	For all other purposes (Admissions of fact accompanying an offer to pay medical expenses are admissible)

D. CHARACTER EVIDENCE—A SPECIAL RELEVANCE PROBLEM

Character evidence may be offered as substantive, rather than impeachment, evidence to: (i) prove character when it is the ***ultimate issue*** in the case, or (ii) serve as ***circumstantial evidence*** of how a person probably acted. The latter is more heavily tested and is the focus of the following discussion.

1. Means of Proving Character

Depending on the jurisdiction, the purpose of the offer, and the nature of the case, one or all of the following methods of proving character may be available:

a. Evidence of ***specific acts***;

b. ***Opinion testimony*** of a witness who knows the person; and

c. Testimony as to the person's general ***reputation*** in the community.

2. Generally Not Admissible in Civil Cases

Unless character is directly in issue (*e.g.,* defamation), evidence of character offered by either party to prove the conduct of a person in the litigated event is generally not admissible in a civil case. For example, a plaintiff in a suit involving a car accident may not introduce evidence that the defendant is usually a reckless driver to prove that she was negligent at the time in question, nor may the defendant introduce evidence that she is generally a cautious driver.

3. Accused in Criminal Case—Generally Only Accused Can Initiate

The prosecution cannot initiate evidence of bad character of the defendant merely to show that she is more likely to have committed the crime. (Although the prosecution may introduce evidence of prior misconduct for reasons other than propensity to commit the crime. *See* 5., below.) The accused, however, may introduce evidence of her good character to show her innocence of the alleged crime.

a. How Defendant Proves Character

Under the Federal Rules, a witness for the defendant may testify as to the defendant's good ***reputation*** for the trait in question and may give his personal ***opinion*** concerning that trait of the defendant.

Exam Tip Remember that a defendant does not put his character in issue merely by testifying. Taking the stand places the defendant's ***credibility*** (as opposed to character) in issue; *i.e.,* the prosecution is limited to impeachment evidence rather than substantive character evidence.

b. How Prosecution Rebuts Defendant's Character Evidence

Once the defendant opens the door by introducing character evidence, the prosecution may rebut it by:

1) ***Cross-examining the character witness*** regarding the basis for his testimony, including whether he knows or has heard of specific instances of the defendant's misconduct.

CMR **Exam Tip** ***Any*** misconduct, including prior arrests, may be inquired about while cross-examining a defendant's character witness. Remember, however, that the prosecutor is limited to inquiry of the witness; she ***may not introduce any extrinsic evidence*** of the misconduct. Be careful to distinguish asking a ***character*** witness whether he is aware of the ***defendant's*** prior arrests, which is proper, and impeaching a witness with the ***witness's*** arrests, which is improper. (*See* VI. E. 3.d., *infra.*)

2) ***Calling qualified witnesses*** to testify to the defendant's bad reputation or give their opinions of the defendant's character.

4. Victim in Criminal Case

Except in rape cases, the defendant may introduce reputation or opinion evidence of a bad character trait of the alleged crime victim when it is relevant to show the defendant's innocence. Once the defendant has introduced evidence of a bad character trait of the victim, the prosecution may counter with reputation or opinion evidence of (i) the victim's ***good*** character, or (ii) the ***defendant's*** bad character for the ***same trait***.

a. Rape Victim's Past Behavior Generally Inadmissible

In any civil or criminal proceeding involving alleged sexual misconduct, evidence offered to prove the sexual behavior or sexual disposition of the victim is generally inadmissible.

1) Exceptions in Criminal Cases

In a criminal case, a victim's sexual behavior is admissible to prove that someone other than the defendant is the source of semen, injury, or other physical evidence. Also, specific instances of sexual behavior between the victim and the accused are admissible by the prosecution for any reason and by the defense to prove consent.

2) Exceptions in Civil Cases

In a civil case, evidence of the alleged victim's sexual behavior is admissible if it is not excluded by any other rule and its probative value substantially outweighs the danger of harm to the victim and of unfair prejudice to any party. Evidence of an alleged victim's reputation is admissible only if it has been placed in controversy by the victim.

5. Specific Acts of Misconduct

Evidence of a person's other crimes or misconduct is inadmissible if offered solely to establish a criminal disposition or bad character.

a. Admissible If Independently Relevant

Evidence of other crimes or misconduct is admissible if these acts are ***relevant to some issue other than the defendant's character or disposition*** to commit the crime or act charged. Such issues include motive (*e.g.,* burn building to hide embezzlement), intent (*i.e.,* guilty knowledge, lack of good faith), absence of mistake or accident, identity (*e.g.,* stolen gun used or "signature" crimes), or common plan or scheme. In a criminal case, the prosecution must, upon request, provide reasonable notice prior to trial of the general nature of any of this type of evidence it intends to introduce.

CMR **Exam Tip** A convenient way to remember the issues for which evidence of prior acts of misconduct is admissible is through the mnemonic device "MIMIC":

Motive
Intent
Mistake (absence of)
Identity
Common plan or scheme

1) **Requirements for Admissibility**
To be admissible: (i) there must be sufficient evidence to support a jury finding that the defendant committed the prior act, ***and*** (ii) its probative value must not be substantially outweighed by the danger of unfair prejudice (or the judge, in her discretion, may exclude it).

b. **Prior Acts of Sexual Assault or Child Molestation**
Evidence of a defendant's prior acts of sexual assault or child molestation is admissible in a case where the defendant is accused of committing an act of sexual assault or child molestation. The party intending to offer this evidence must disclose it to the defendant 15 days before trial (or later with good cause).

III. JUDICIAL NOTICE

A. JUDICIAL NOTICE OF FACT

Judicial notice is the recognition of a fact as true without formal presentation of evidence.

1. **Facts Appropriate for Judicial Notice**
Courts take judicial notice of ***indisputable facts*** that are either matters of ***common knowledge*** in the community (notorious facts) or ***capable of verification*** by resort to easily accessible sources of unquestionable accuracy (manifest facts). Courts have increasingly taken judicial notice of scientific principles as a type of manifest fact.

2. **Procedural Aspects of Judicial Notice**
A party must formally request that notice be taken of a particular fact. Judicial notice may be taken for the first time on appeal. The Federal Rules provide that a judicially noticed fact is conclusive in a civil case but not in a criminal case. In a criminal case, the jury is instructed that it may, but is not required to, accept as conclusive any judicially noticed fact.

3. **"Adjudicative" and "Legislative" Facts**
The Federal Rules, and thus their requirements, govern only judicial notice of "adjudicative" facts (*i.e.,* those that relate to the particular case). "Legislative" facts (*i.e.,* those relating to legal reasoning and lawmaking), such as the rationale behind the spousal privilege, need not be of common knowledge nor capable of indisputable verification to be judicially noticed.

B. JUDICIAL NOTICE OF LAW—MANDATORY OR PERMISSIVE

Courts ***must*** take judicial notice of federal and state law and the official regulations of the forum state and the federal government. Courts ***may*** take judicial notice of municipal ordinances and private acts or resolutions of Congress or of the local state legislature. Laws of foreign countries may also be judicially noticed.

IV. REAL EVIDENCE

A. IN GENERAL

Real or demonstrative evidence is actual physical evidence addressed directly to the trier of fact. Real evidence may be direct, circumstantial, original, or prepared (demonstrative).

B. GENERAL CONDITIONS OF ADMISSIBILITY

Real evidence must be relevant and meet the following legal requirements:

1. Authentication

The object must be identified as what the proponent claims it to be, either by:

a. ***Testimony*** of a witness that she ***recognizes*** the object as what the proponent claims it is (*e.g.,* witness testifies that a gun is the one found at the crime scene); or

b. Evidence that the object has been held in a ***substantially unbroken chain of possession*** (*e.g.,* blood taken for blood-alcohol test).

2. Condition of Object

If the condition of the object is significant, it must be shown to be in substantially the same condition at trial.

3. Balancing Test—Legal Relevance

Some auxiliary policy or principle may outweigh the need to admit the real evidence. Such policies include physical inconvenience of bringing the object into the courtroom, indecency or impropriety, or undue prejudice.

C. PARTICULAR TYPES OF REAL PROOF

1. Reproductions and Explanatory Real Evidence

Relevant photographs, diagrams, maps, or other reproductions are admissible if their value is not outweighed by the danger of unfair prejudice. However, items used entirely for explanatory purposes are permitted at a trial, but are usually not admitted into evidence (*i.e.,* they are not given to the jury during its deliberations).

2. Maps, Charts, Models, Etc.

Maps, charts, models, etc., are usually admissible for the purpose of illustrating testimony, but must be authenticated (testimonial evidence that they are faithful reproductions of the object or thing depicted).

3. Exhibition of Child in Paternity Suits

In paternity suits, almost all courts permit exhibition of the child to show whether it is the race of the putative father. The courts are divided with respect to the propriety of exhibition for the purpose of proving physical resemblance to the putative father.

4. **Exhibition of Injuries**
Exhibition of injuries in a personal injury or criminal case is generally permitted, but the court has discretion to exclude this evidence if unfair prejudice would result.

5. **Jury View of the Scene**
The trial court has discretion to permit the jury to view places at issue in a civil or criminal case. The need for the view and changes in the condition of the premises are relevant considerations here.

6. **Demonstrations**
The court, in its discretion, may permit experiments or demonstrations to be performed in the courtroom. Demonstrations of bodily injury may not be allowed where the demonstrations would unduly dramatize the injury.

V. DOCUMENTARY EVIDENCE

A. IN GENERAL
Documentary evidence must be relevant in order to be admissible. In the case of writings, the authenticity of the document is one aspect of its relevancy.

B. AUTHENTICATION
As a general rule, a writing or any secondary evidence of its content will not be received in evidence unless the writing is authenticated by proof that shows that the writing is what the proponent claims it is. The proof must be ***sufficient to support a jury finding*** of genuineness.

1. **Authentication by Pleadings or Stipulation**
The genuineness of a document may be admitted by the pleadings or by stipulation.

2. **Evidence of Authenticity**
The following are examples of proper authentication:

a. **Admissions**
A writing may be authenticated by evidence that the party against whom it is offered has either admitted its authenticity or acted upon it as authentic.

b. **Eyewitness Testimony**
A writing can be authenticated by testimony of one who sees it executed or hears it acknowledged. The testimony need not be given by a subscribing witness.

c. **Handwriting Verifications**
A writing may be authenticated by evidence of the genuineness of the handwriting of the maker. This evidence may be the opinion of a ***nonexpert with personal knowledge*** of the alleged writer's handwriting or the opinion of an ***expert who has compared*** the writing to samples of the maker's handwriting. Genuineness may also be determined by the ***trier of fact through comparison of samples***.

CMR **Exam Tip** Remember that a nonexpert without personal knowledge of the handwriting cannot become familiar with it for purposes of testifying.

d. Ancient Documents

A document may be authenticated by evidence that it:

1) Is at least ***20 years old***;

2) Is in such ***condition*** as to be free from suspicion as to authenticity; and

3) Was found in a ***place*** where such a writing would likely be kept.

CMR **Exam Tip** In contrast to the rule in many jurisdictions, the ancient document provision of the Federal Rules applies to all writings, not just dispositive instruments.

e. Reply Letter Doctrine

A writing may be authenticated by evidence that it was written in response to a communication sent to the claimed author.

f. Photographs

Generally, photographs are admissible only if identified by a witness as a portrayal of certain facts relevant to the issue and verified by the witness as a correct representation of those facts. Ordinarily, it is not necessary to call the photographer to authenticate the photograph; a witness familiar with the scene is sufficient.

1) Unattended Camera—Proper Operation of Camera

If a photograph is taken when no person who could authenticate the scene is present, the photograph may be admitted upon a showing that the camera was properly operating at the relevant time and that the photograph was developed from film obtained from that camera.

g. X-Ray Pictures, Electrocardiograms, Etc.

Unlike photographs, an X-ray cannot be authenticated by testimony of a witness that it is a correct representation of the facts. It must be shown that the process used is accurate, the machine was in working order, and the operator was qualified to operate it. Finally, a custodial chain must be established to assure that the X-ray has not been tampered with.

3. Compare—Authentication of Oral Statements

When a statement is admissible only if said by a particular person (*e.g.,* admission by a party), authentication as to the ***identity of the speaker*** is required.

a. Voice Identification

A voice may be identified by the opinion of anyone who has heard the voice at ***any time***, including after litigation has begun for the sole purpose of testifying.

b. Telephone Conversations

Statements made during a telephone conversation may be authenticated by one of the parties to the call who testifies that: (i) he recognized the other party's voice; (ii) the speaker had knowledge of certain facts that only a particular person would have; (iii) he called a particular person's number and a voice answered as that person or that person's residence; or (iv) he called a business and talked with the person answering the phone about matters relevant to the business.

4. Self-Authenticating Documents
Certain writings are said to "prove themselves." Extrinsic evidence of authenticity is not required for the following: (i) certified copies of public records, (ii) official publications, (iii) newspapers and periodicals, (iv) trade inscriptions, (v) acknowledged documents, (vi) commercial paper and related documents, and (vii) certified business records.

C. BEST EVIDENCE RULE

This rule is more accurately called the "***original document rule***." To ***prove the terms*** of a writing (including a recording, photograph, or X-ray), the original writing must be produced if the terms of the writing are material. Secondary evidence of the writing (*e.g.,* oral testimony) is admissible only if the original is unavailable.

1. Applicability of the Rule
The rule applies to two classes of situations, namely where: (i) the writing is a ***legally operative or dispositive instrument***; or (ii) the ***knowledge of a witness*** concerning a fact results from having read it in the document.

2. Nonapplicability of the Rule
The best evidence rule does not apply in the following circumstances:

a. Fact to Be Proved Exists Independently of Writing
The rule does not apply where the fact to be proved has an existence independent of any writing. Many writings record details of essentially nonwritten transactions. Oral testimony of these facts may be given without the original writings recording the event.

b. Writing Is Collateral to Litigated Issue
The rule does not apply where the writing is of minor importance (*i.e.,* collateral) to the matter in controversy.

c. Summaries of Voluminous Records
The rule does not apply to summaries of voluminous records. It would be inconvenient to examine a voluminous collection of writings in court, and so the proponent may present their contents in the form of a chart or summary.

d. Public Records
The rule does not apply to copies of public records that are certified as correct or testified to as correct.

3. Definitions of "Writings," "Original," and "Duplicate"
The Federal Rules govern ***writings***, ***recordings***, ***and photographs***, and they are broadly defined. An original is the writing itself or any duplicate that is intended by the person executing it to have the same effect as an original. A duplicate is an ***exact copy*** of an original, such as a carbon copy. Duplicates are admissible in federal courts unless the authenticity of the original is challenged or unfairness would result.

BEST EVIDENCE RULE

Best Evidence Rule Applies	Best Evidence Rule Does Not Apply
Party seeks to prove the contents of a deed through witness testimony or other secondary evidence.	If D denies having made a contract with P, P may introduce secondary evidence to prove that a contract exists—but not its contents.
Party seeks to prove the contents of a contract through witness testimony or other secondary evidence.	Witness may testify that he is 30 years old and married, without producing the respective certificates.
Party seeks to prove the contents of a will through witness testimony or other secondary evidence.	Witness may testify to testimony he heard at a prior proceeding, without producing a transcript.
In breach of warranty case, a witness seeks to testify to the contents of the written warranty, which she read.	Witness may testify that he is a real estate broker without producing his license (if not material to the case).
Nurse seeks to testify regarding the content of a medical record that she read.	Nurse who took vital signs may testify to them without producing medical record.
In an obscenity or copyright trial for a book, movie, photograph, etc., party seeks to introduce a newspaper review or witness testimony.	Party may introduce chart summarizing the personnel records of 500 employees.
In a case where P claimed D defrauded her by selling her a gown she claimed was an original "Halvenchy," P seeks to testify that she found a label in the arm of the gown stating that it was made by L-Mart.	Party may introduce a certified copy of a certificate of incorporation, the original of which is on file with the secretary of state.
Radiologist seeks to testify regarding the extent of P's injuries he found in X-rays he took, without producing the X-rays.	W may testify about a plane crash she witnessed, despite the fact that the crash was captured on home video.
	P may testify that D delivered a deed to her by handing it to her.

CMR **Exam Tip** It is important to distinguish photocopies and copies made by hand. Photocopies are duplicates and, thus, are treated the same as originals. In contrast, handwritten copies are considered secondary evidence and are admissible only if the original or a duplicate is unavailable.

4. Admissibility of Secondary Evidence of Contents

If the proponent cannot produce the original writing in court, he may offer secondary evidence of its contents (handwritten copies, notes, oral testimony) if a satisfactory explanation is given for the nonproduction of the original.

a. Satisfactory Foundation

Valid excuses justifying the admissibility of secondary evidence include:

1) ***Loss or destruction*** of the original.

2) The original is in possession of a third party ***outside the jurisdiction*** and is ***unobtainable***.

3) The original is ***in the possession of an adversary*** who, after due notice, fails to produce the original.

b. No Degrees of Secondary Evidence

Upon satisfactory foundation, the Federal Rules permit a party to prove the contents of a writing by any kind of secondary evidence, thus abolishing degrees of secondary evidence.

c. Testimony or Written Admission of Party

A proponent may prove the contents of a writing, recording, or photograph through the testimony, deposition, or written admission of the party against whom it is offered, and need not account for the nonproduction of the original.

5. Functions of Court and Jury

Ordinarily, it is for the ***court*** to make determinations of fact regarding ***admissibility*** of duplicates, other copies, and oral testimony as to the contents of an original. However, the Federal Rules reserve the following questions of preliminary fact for the jury:

a. Whether the original ever existed;

b. Whether a writing, recording, or photograph produced at trial is an original; and

c. Whether the evidence offered correctly reflects the contents of the original.

D. PAROL EVIDENCE RULE

If an agreement is reduced to writing, that writing is the agreement and hence constitutes the only evidence of it. Prior or contemporaneous negotiations or agreements are merged into the written agreement, and they are inadmissible to vary the terms of the writing.

1. When the Rule Does Not Apply

The parol evidence rule does not apply to exclude evidence of prior or contemporaneous agreements in the following circumstances:

a. **Incomplete or Ambiguous Contract**
Parol evidence is admissible to complete an incomplete contract or explain an ambiguous term.

b. **Reformation of Contract**
The parol evidence rule does not apply where a party alleges facts (*e.g.,* mistake) entitling him to reformation.

c. **Challenge to Validity of Contract**
Parol evidence is admissible to show that the contract is ***void or voidable***, or was made subject to a valid ***condition precedent*** that has not been satisfied.

2. **Subsequent Modifications**
The rule applies only to negotiations prior to, or at the time of, the execution of the contract. Parol evidence is admissible to show subsequent modification or discharge of the written contract.

VI. TESTIMONIAL EVIDENCE

A. COMPETENCY OF WITNESSES

Witnesses must pass tests of basic reliability to establish their competency to give testimony, but they are generally presumed to be competent until the contrary is established. Witnesses must possess to some degree four basic testimonial attributes: the capacity to observe, to recollect, to communicate, and to appreciate the obligation to speak truthfully.

1. **Federal Rules of Competency**
The Rules do not specify any mental or moral qualifications for witness testimony beyond these two limitations:

(i) The witness must have ***personal knowledge*** of the matter about which he is to testify; and

(ii) The witness must ***declare he will testify truthfully***.

If a witness requires an interpreter, the interpreter must be qualified and take an oath to make a true translation.

2. **Modern Modifications of the Common Law Disqualifications**
Most jurisdictions and the Federal Rules have removed the common law witness disqualifications for lack of religious belief, conviction of a crime, and interest in the lawsuit.

a. **Infancy**
The competency of an infant depends on the capacity and intelligence of the particular child as determined by the trial judge.

b. **Insanity**
An insane person may testify, provided he understands the obligation to speak truthfully and has the capacity to testify accurately.

c. **Judge and Jurors**
The presiding judge may not testify as a witness. Likewise, jurors are incompetent to testify before the jury in which they are sitting.

3. **Dead Man Acts**
Most states have Dead Man Acts, which provide that a party or person interested in the event is incompetent to testify to a personal transaction or communication with a deceased, when such testimony is offered against the representative or successors in interest of the deceased. A person is "interested" if he stands to gain or lose by the judgment or the judgment may be used for or against him in a subsequent action. A predecessor in interest of the interested party is also disqualified.

CMR **Exam Tip** There is no Dead Man Act in the Federal Rules, but a state Act will apply in federal cases where state law, under the *Erie* doctrine, provides the rule of decision (*e.g.,* diversity cases).

B. **FORM OF EXAMINATION OF WITNESS**
The judge may exercise reasonable control over the examination of witnesses in order to aid the ascertainment of truth, to avoid wasting time, and to protect witnesses from harassment.

1. **Leading Questions**
Leading questions (*i.e.,* questions that suggest the answer desired) are ***generally improper on direct*** examination. However, they are permitted:

a. On cross-examination;

b. To elicit preliminary or introductory matter;

c. When the witness needs aid to respond because of loss of memory, immaturity, or physical or mental weakness; or

d. When the witness is hostile.

2. **Improper Questions**
Questions that are misleading (cannot be answered without making an unintended admission), compound (requiring a single answer to more than one question), argumentative, conclusionary, cumulative, unduly harassing or embarrassing, or that assume facts not in evidence are improper and are not permitted.

3. **Use of Memoranda by Witness**
A witness ***cannot read her testimony*** from a prepared memorandum. However, a memorandum may be used in certain circumstances.

CMR **Exam Tip** Any time you encounter an exam question in which a witness consults a writing, keep in mind the differences between refreshing and recorded recollection. The fact patterns are very similar and could be confusing if you have not thoroughly memorized the distinguishing features.

a. **Present Recollection Revived—Refreshing Recollection**
A witness may use any writing or thing for the purpose of refreshing her present

recollection. She usually may not read from the writing while she actually testifies because the writing is not authenticated and not in evidence.

b. Past Recollection Recorded—Recorded Recollection

Where a witness states that she has insufficient recollection of an event to enable her to testify fully and accurately, even after she has consulted a writing given to her on the stand, the writing itself may be ***read into evidence*** if a proper foundation is laid. The foundation must include proof that:

1) The witness at one time had ***personal knowledge*** of the facts in the writing;

2) The writing was ***made by the witness*** or under her direction, or it was ***adopted*** by the witness;

3) The writing was ***timely made*** when the matter was fresh in the witness's mind;

4) The writing is ***accurate***; and

5) The witness has ***insufficient recollection*** to testify fully and accurately.

c. Inspection and Use on Cross-Examination

Whenever a witness has used a writing to refresh her memory on the stand, an adverse party is entitled to have the writing produced at trial, to cross-examine the witness thereon, and to introduce portions relating to the witness's testimony into evidence.

PRESENT RECOLLECTION REFRESHED VS. PAST RECOLLECTION RECORDED

Present Recollection Refreshed	Past Recollection Recorded
Any writing may be used to refresh a witness's memory. (Things other than a writing may also be used, *e.g.*, a photograph.)	Only a ***writing*** that meets several ***foundational requirements*** (*e.g.*, timely made by witness; witness cannot remember the events after reading the writing) may be used.
The witness cannot read from the writing while testifying.	The writing itself is read into evidence.
There is ***no hearsay problem***, because the writing is not offered into evidence.	This is ***hearsay***, but it falls within a specific ***exception*** to the hearsay rule.

C. OPINION TESTIMONY

The general policy of the law is to prohibit admissibility of opinion evidence except in cases where the courts are sure that it will be necessary or at least helpful.

1. Opinion Testimony by Lay Witnesses

a. General Rule of Inadmissibility

Opinions by lay witnesses are generally inadmissible. However, there are many cases where no better evidence can be obtained. In most jurisdictions and under the Federal Rules, opinion testimony by a lay witness is admissible when it is: (i) rationally based on the witness's perception, (ii) helpful to a clear understanding of his testimony or helpful to the determination of a fact in issue, and (iii) not based on scientific, technical, or other specialized knowledge.

b. Situations Where Opinions of Lay Witnesses Are Admissible

An opinion of a lay witness is generally admissible with respect to:

1) The ***general appearance or condition*** of a person;

2) The ***state of emotion*** of a person;

3) Matters involving ***sense recognition***;

4) ***Voice or handwriting identification***;

5) The ***speed*** of a moving object;

6) The ***value of his own services***;

7) The ***rational or irrational nature*** of another's conduct; and

8) ***Intoxication*** of another.

c. Situations Where Opinions of Lay Witnesses Are Not Admissible

Opinions of lay witnesses are not admissible with regard to whether one acted as an agent or whether an agreement was made.

2. Opinion Testimony by Expert Witnesses

An expert may state an opinion or conclusion, provided:

(i) The ***subject matter*** is one where scientific, technical, or other specialized knowledge would ***assist the trier of fact*** (an opinion will assist the trier of fact if it is relevant and reliable);

(ii) The ***witness is qualified*** as an expert (*i.e.,* possesses special knowledge, skill, experience, training, or education);

ADMISSIBLE OPINIONS OF LAY WITNESSES

1. ***General Appearance or Condition of a Person***	"He was about 80 years old." ***or*** "She seemed ill."
2. ***State of Emotion***	"She was angry." ***or*** "He was distraught."
3. ***Matters Involving Sense Recognition***	"The suitcase was heavy." ***or*** "He smelled of garlic."
4. ***Voice or Handwriting Identification*** (Foundation required)	"It sounded like Mark." ***or*** "That's Fran's handwriting."
5. ***Speed of Moving Object***	"The truck was going very fast" or (if experienced in estimating rates of speed), "The truck was going at least 60 miles per hour."
6. ***Value of Own Services***	"My time is worth $50 per hour."
7. ***Rational or Irrational Nature of Another's Conduct***	"He was acting crazy."
8. ***Intoxication*** (Foundation may be required)	"She was slurring her words and smelled of gin. She was drunk."

(iii) The expert possesses ***reasonable probability regarding his opinion***; and

(iv) The opinion is supported by a ***proper factual basis***. The expert's opinion may be based on one or more of three possible sources of information: (i) personal observation, (ii) facts made known to the expert at trial, or (iii) facts not known personally but supplied to him outside the courtroom and of a ***type reasonably relied upon by experts*** in the particular field.

a. Opinion on Ultimate Issues

Under the Federal Rules, an expert may render an opinion as to the ultimate issue in the case. However, in a criminal case in which the defendant's mental state constitutes an element of the crime or defense, an expert may not, under the Federal Rules, state an opinion as to whether the accused did or did not have the mental state in issue.

b. Authoritative Texts and Treatises

An expert may be cross-examined concerning statements contained in any publication established as reliable authority either by the testimony of this expert or another expert, or by judicial notice. Under the Federal Rules, these texts and treatises can be used not only to impeach experts, but also as substantive evidence, subject to the following limitations:

1) An ***expert must be on the stand*** when an excerpt is read from a treatise; and

2) The relevant portion is ***read into evidence*** but is not received as an exhibit.

D. CROSS-EXAMINATION

Cross-examination of adverse witnesses is a matter of right in every trial of a disputed issue of fact, but the scope of cross-examination is frequently a matter of judicial discretion.

1. Restrictions on Scope

Cross-examination is generally limited to: (i) the scope of direct examination, including all reasonable inferences that may be drawn from it, and (ii) testing the credibility of the witness.

2. Collateral Matters

The cross-examiner is generally bound by the answers of the witness to questions concerning collateral matters. Thus, the response may not be refuted by extrinsic evidence. However, certain recognized matters of impeachment, such as bias, interest, or a conviction, may be developed by extrinsic evidence because they are sufficiently important. The trial court has considerable discretion in this area.

E. CREDIBILITY—IMPEACHMENT

Impeachment means the casting of an adverse reflection on the veracity of the witness.

1. Accrediting or Bolstering

Generally, a party may not bolster or accredit the testimony of his witness (*e.g.,* by introducing a prior consistent statement) until the witness has been impeached. However, in certain cases, a party may prove the witness made a timely complaint or a prior statement of identification. The prior identification may also serve as substantive evidence that the identification was correct.

2. Any Party May Impeach
Under the Federal Rules, a witness may be impeached by any party, including the party calling him.

Exam Tip When a question involves a party impeaching his own witness, be sure to avoid the following ***wrong answer choices*** reflecting the traditional rule, which prohibits impeaching your own witness unless the witness:

(i) Is an ***adverse party*** or identified with an adverse party;

(ii) Is ***hostile*** and affirmatively uncooperative;

(iii) Is one whom the party is ***required by law*** to call; or

(iv) Gives ***surprise testimony*** that is affirmatively harmful to the party calling him.

3. Impeachment Methods—Cross-Examination and Extrinsic Evidence
A witness may be impeached either by cross-examination (by eliciting facts from the witness that discredit his own testimony) or by extrinsic evidence (by putting other witnesses on the stand who will introduce facts discrediting his testimony). Certain grounds for impeachment require that a foundation be laid during cross-examination before extrinsic evidence can be introduced. Other grounds allow impeachment to be accomplished only by cross-examination and not by extrinsic evidence. (*Note:* The term "cross-examination" is used for convenience because it is usually an adverse witness who is impeached. But remember that a party may impeach his own witness, which would be on direct or redirect examination.) The traditional impeachment devices follow.

a. Prior Inconsistent Statements
A party may show, by cross-examination or extrinsic evidence, that the witness has, on another occasion, made statements inconsistent with his present testimony. To prove the statement by extrinsic evidence, a proper foundation must be laid and the statement must be relevant to some issue in the case.

1) Foundation for Extrinsic Evidence
Extrinsic evidence can be introduced to prove a prior inconsistent statement only if the witness is, at some point, given an opportunity to explain or deny the statement. The exception to the rule is that inconsistent statements by hearsay declarants may be used to impeach despite the lack of a foundation. Under the Federal Rules, foundation requirements may be dispensed with where the interests of justice require (*e.g.,* witness unavailable when inconsistent statement is discovered).

CMR **Exam Tip** Remember the MBE follows the Federal Rules. Under the Rules, the opportunity to explain or deny need not come before introduction of a prior inconsistent statement.

2) **Evidentiary Effect of Prior Inconsistent Statements**
Usually, prior inconsistent statements are hearsay, admissible only for impeachment purposes. If, however, the statement was made under oath at a prior proceeding, it is admissible nonhearsay and may be admitted as substantive evidence of the facts stated.

b. **Bias or Interest**
Evidence that a witness is biased or has an interest in the outcome of a suit tends to show that the witness has a motive to lie.

1) **Foundation for Extrinsic Evidence**
Before a witness can be impeached by extrinsic evidence of bias or interest, he must first be asked about the facts that show bias or interest on cross-examination.

CMR **Exam Tip** Watch for facts indicating that the foundation requirement for extrinsic evidence of bias or interest has been fulfilled. Evidence that is otherwise inadmissible (*e.g.,* arrests, liability insurance) may be introduced if relevant for these impeachment purposes, provided the proper foundation is laid.

c. **Conviction of Crime**
A witness may be impeached by proof of a ***conviction*** (arrest or indictment is not sufficient) for certain crimes. A pending review or appeal does not affect the use of a conviction for impeachment.

1) **Type of Crime**

a) **Any Crime Involving Dishonesty**
A witness may be impeached by any crime, felony or misdemeanor, involving dishonesty or false statement. The court has ***no discretion*** to bar impeachment by these crimes.

b) **Felony Not Involving Dishonesty**
A witness may also be impeached by a felony that does not involve dishonesty, but the court has ***discretion to exclude*** it if:

(1) The witness being impeached is a ***criminal defendant***, and the ***prosecution has not shown*** that the conviction's probative value outweighs its prejudicial effect; or

(2) In the case of all other witnesses, the ***court determines*** that the conviction's probative value is substantially outweighed by its prejudicial effect.

2) **Remote, Juvenile, and Constitutionally Defective Convictions Not Admissible**
Generally, if more than 10 years have elapsed since the date of conviction or the

date of release from confinement (whichever is later), the conviction is inadmissible. Juvenile convictions are similarly inadmissible. A conviction obtained in violation of the defendant's constitutional rights is invalid for all purposes, including impeachment.

3) **Effect of Pardon**
A conviction may not be used to impeach a witness if the witness has been pardoned and: (i) the pardon is based on innocence, or (ii) the person pardoned has not been convicted of a subsequent felony.

4) **No Foundation Required for Extrinsic Evidence**
A prior conviction may be shown either by cross-examination of the witness or by introducing a record of the judgment. No foundation is necessary.

d. **Specific Instances of Misconduct—Bad Acts**
Under the Federal Rules, subject to discretionary control of the trial judge, a witness may be interrogated upon cross-examination with respect to an act of misconduct only if the act is ***probative of truthfulness*** (*i.e.,* is an act of deceit or lying). However, the cross-examiner must inquire in good faith.

1) **Extrinsic Evidence Not Permitted**
Extrinsic evidence of "bad acts" to prove misconduct is not permitted. A specific act of misconduct relevant to impair credibility can be elicited only on cross-examination of the witness.

CMR **Exam Tip** Keep in mind that asking about specific instances of misconduct does not include inquiring about arrests. An arrest itself is not a bad act. Thus, it is permissible to ask a witness whether he embezzled money from his employer. It is not permissible to ask him whether he was ***arrested*** for embezzlement.

e. **Opinion or Reputation Evidence for Truth**
A witness may be impeached by showing that he has a poor reputation for truthfulness. This may include evidence of reputation in business circles as well as in the community in which the witness resides. Under the Federal Rules, an impeaching witness may state his own opinion as to the character of a witness for truth.

f. **Sensory Deficiencies**
A witness may be impeached by showing, either on cross-examination or by extrinsic evidence, that his faculties of perception and recollection were so impaired as to make it doubtful that he could have perceived those facts. A witness may also be impeached by showing that he had no knowledge of the facts to which he testified.

4. **Impeachment on Collateral Matter**
Where a witness makes a statement not directly relevant to the issue in the case, the rule against impeachment on a collateral matter applies to bar his opponent from proving the statement untrue either by extrinsic evidence or by a prior inconsistent statement.

5. **Impeachment of Hearsay Declarant**
Under the Federal Rules, the credibility of someone who does not testify but whose out-of-court

statement is introduced at trial may be attacked (and if attacked, may be supported) by evidence that would be admissible if the declarant had testified as a witness. The declarant need not be given the opportunity to explain or deny a prior inconsistent statement. In addition, the party against whom the out-of-court statement was offered may call the declarant as a witness and cross-examine him about the statement.

CMR SUMMARY CHART

METHODS OF IMPEACHMENT

Impeachment Method	Means of Proof	Foundation
Prior Inconsistent Statements	• Cross-examination • Extrinsic evidence (if not a collateral matter)	Witness must be given opportunity to explain or deny the inconsistent statement. (Exception for hearsay declarants)
Bias or Interest	• Cross-examination • Extrinsic evidence	Witness must be asked on cross-examination about facts showing bias or interest before extrinsic evidence is allowed. If these facts are admitted on cross-examination, admissibility of extrinsic evidence is within court's discretion.
Conviction of Crime—Must be a ***felony*** or crime involving ***dishonesty***	• Cross-examination • Record of judgment	None required
Specific Instances of Misconduct (Bad Acts)	• Cross-examination only	Not applicable
Opinion or Reputation for Truthfulness	• Calling other witnesses	None required
Sensory Deficiencies	• Cross-examination • Extrinsic evidence	None required

6. **Rehabilitation**

A witness who has been impeached may be rehabilitated by the following methods:

a. **Explanation on Redirect**

The witness on redirect may explain or clarify facts brought out on cross-examination.

b. Good Reputation for Truth

When the witness's character for truth and veracity has been attacked, other witnesses may be called to testify to the good reputation for truth of the impeached witness or to give their opinions as to the truthfulness of the impeached witness.

c. Prior Consistent Statement

A party may not ordinarily rehabilitate a witness by showing a prior consistent statement. This is true even when the witness has been impeached by showing a prior inconsistent statement. But if the testimony of the witness has been attacked by an express or implied charge that the witness is ***lying or exaggerating*** because of some motive, a previous consistent statement is admissible to rebut this evidence. This previous statement also is substantive evidence of the truth of its contents.

F. OBJECTIONS, EXCEPTIONS, AND OFFERS OF PROOF

1. Objections

Objections at trial should be made after the question, but before the answer, if the question calls for inadmissible matter. Otherwise, a motion to strike must be made as soon as an answer emerges as inadmissible. At a deposition, objections to the form of a question, or to a testimonial privilege, should be made when the question is asked or it may be waived. Objections based on the substance of a question or answer may be postponed until the deposition is offered in evidence.

CMR **Exam Tip** Failure to object is deemed a waiver of any ground for objection. Thus, if no objection is made, otherwise inadmissible evidence will be admitted.

a. Specificity of Objections

1) General Objections

A sustained general objection (one that does not state the grounds of the objection) will be upheld on appeal if there was any ground for the objection. An overruled general objection will be upheld on appeal unless the evidence was not admissible under any circumstances for any purpose.

2) Specific Objections

A sustained specific objection, which states the reason for the objection, will be upheld on appeal only if the ground stated was correct or if the evidence excluded was not competent and could not be made so.

b. "Opening the Door"

One who introduces evidence on a particular subject thereby asserts its relevance and cannot complain if his adversary thereafter offers evidence on the same subject.

c. Introducing Part of Transaction

Where part of a conversation, act, or writing is introduced into evidence, the adverse party may require the proponent of the evidence to introduce any other part that ought in fairness to be considered.

d. Motion to Strike—Unresponsive Answers

Examining counsel may move to strike an unresponsive answer, but opposing counsel may not.

2. **Exceptions**
It is not necessary for a party to "except" from a trial ruling in order to preserve the issue for appeal in most states.

3. **Offers of Proof**
An offer of proof may be made, disclosing the nature, purpose, and admissibility of rejected evidence, to persuade the trial court to hear the evidence and to preserve the evidence for review on appeal. It may be made by witness testimony, a lawyer's narration, or tangible evidence marked and offered.

G. TESTIMONIAL PRIVILEGES

Testimonial privileges permit one to refuse to disclose, and prohibit others from disclosing, certain confidential information in judicial proceedings.

1. **Federal Rules—No Specific Privilege Provisions**
The Federal Rules have no specific privilege provisions; privilege in federal courts is governed by common law principles as interpreted by the courts. The federal courts currently recognize the attorney-client privilege, the privilege for spousal communications, and the psychotherapist/social worker-client privilege. In ***diversity*** cases, the state law of privilege applies.

2. **General Considerations**

   a. **Persons Who May Assert Privilege**
   A privilege is personal to the holder; *i.e.,* it generally may be asserted only by the holder. Sometimes the person with whom the confidence was shared (*e.g.,* an attorney) may assert the privilege on the holder's behalf.

   b. **Confidentiality**
   To be privileged, a communication must be shown or presumed to have been made in confidence.

   c. **Comment on Privilege Forbidden**
   Neither counsel for the parties nor the judge may comment on a claim of privilege.

   d. **Waiver**
   Any privilege is waived by: (i) failure to claim the privilege; (ii) voluntary disclosure of the privileged matter by the privilege holder; or (iii) a contractual provision waiving in advance the right to claim a privilege.

CMR Exam Tip A privilege is not waived when someone wrongfully discloses information without the privilege holder's consent. Similarly, a waiver by one joint holder does not affect the right of the other holder to assert the privilege.

   e. **Eavesdroppers**
   A privilege based on confidential communications is not abrogated because it was overheard by someone whose presence is unknown to the parties. Under the modern view, in the absence of negligence by the one claiming privilege, even the eavesdropper would be prohibited from testifying.

3. Attorney-Client Privilege

Communications between an attorney and client, made during professional consultation, are privileged from disclosure. The important elements of this privilege are:

a. Attorney-Client Relationship

The client must be seeking the professional services of the attorney at the time of the communication. Disclosures made before the attorney accepts or declines the case are covered by the privilege.

1) Corporate Clients

Corporations are "clients" within the meaning of the privilege, and statements made by corporate officials or employees to an attorney are protected if the employees were authorized by the corporation to make such statements.

b. Confidential Communication

To be protected, the communication must be confidential (*i.e.,* not intended to be disclosed to third parties), but representatives of the attorney or client may be present without destroying the privilege; otherwise, communications made in the known presence and hearing of a stranger are not privileged.

1) Communications Through Agents

Communications made to third persons (*e.g.,* secretaries, messengers, accountants) are confidential and covered by the privilege if necessary to transmit information between the attorney and client.

CMR Exam Tip A favorite exam topic involves communications between a client and a doctor during an examination made at the attorney's request. Be careful—the physician-patient privilege (*infra*) does not apply because no treatment is contemplated. The attorney-client privilege will apply, however, as long as the doctor is not called as an expert witness.

2) No Privilege Where Attorney Acts for Both Parties

Where an attorney acts for both parties to a transaction, no privilege can be invoked in a lawsuit between the two parties, but the privilege can be claimed in a suit between either or both of the two parties and third persons.

c. Client Holds Privilege

The client holds the privilege, and she alone may waive it. The attorney's authority to claim the privilege on behalf of the client is presumed in the absence of contrary evidence.

d. Privilege Applies Indefinitely

The attorney-client privilege applies indefinitely. The privilege even continues to apply after the client's death.

e. When the Privilege Does Not Apply

There are three significant exceptions to the attorney-client privilege. There is no privilege:

1) If the attorney's services were sought to aid in the planning or commission of something the ***client should have known was a crime or fraud***;

2) Regarding a communication relevant to an issue between ***parties claiming through the same deceased client***; and

3) For a communication relevant to an issue of breach of duty in a ***dispute between the attorney and client***.

f. **Attorney's Work Product**
Although documents prepared by an attorney for his own use in a case are not protected by the privilege, they are not subject to discovery except in cases of necessity.

4. **Physician-Patient Privilege**
The physician-patient privilege belongs to the patient, and he may decide to claim or waive it. Confidential communications between a patient and his physician are privileged, provided that:

(i) A ***professional relationship*** exists;

(ii) The information is acquired while attending the patient in the ***course of treatment***; and

(iii) The information is ***necessary for treatment***. (Nonmedical information is not privileged.)

a. **When the Privilege Does Not Apply**
The physician-patient privilege does not apply (or is impliedly waived) if:

1) The ***patient puts his physical condition in issue*** (*e.g.,* personal injury suit);

2) The physician's assistance was sought to ***aid wrongdoing*** (*e.g.,* commission of crime or tort);

3) The communication is relevant to an issue of breach of duty in a ***dispute between the physician and patient***;

4) The patient ***agreed*** by contract (*e.g.,* insurance policy) to waive the privilege; or

5) It is a ***federal case applying the federal law of privilege***.

b. **Criminal Proceedings**
In some states, the privilege applies in both civil and criminal cases. In a number of others, it cannot be invoked in criminal cases generally. In still other states, the privilege is denied in felony cases, and in a few states, it is denied only in homicide cases.

CMR **Exam Tip** Remember that when a psychiatrist is the doctor involved, the applicable privilege is the psychotherapist-client privilege (below), which is more widely accepted in all proceedings than is the physician-patient privilege.

5. **Psychotherapist/Social Worker-Client Privilege**
The United States Supreme Court recognizes a federal privilege for communications between a psychotherapist (psychiatrist or psychologist) or licensed social worker and his client. Thus, the federal courts and virtually all of the states recognize a privilege for this type of confidential communication. In most particulars, this privilege operates in the same manner as the attorney-client privilege (*supra*).

6. Husband-Wife Privilege

There are two distinct spousal privileges.

a. Spousal Immunity

A married person whose spouse is a defendant in a ***criminal*** case may not be called as a witness by the prosecution. Moreover, a married person may not be compelled to ***testify*** against his spouse in ***any criminal proceeding***, regardless of whether the spouse is the defendant. There must be a valid marriage for the privilege to apply, and the privilege lasts only during the marriage.

1) Who Holds the Privilege

In federal court, the privilege belongs to the witness-spouse. Thus, the witness-spouse cannot be compelled to testify, but may choose to do so. (In most state courts, however, the privilege belongs to the party-spouse.)

b. Privilege for Confidential Marital Communications

In any civil or criminal case, confidential communications between a husband and wife during a valid marriage are privileged. For this privilege to apply, the ***marital relationship must exist*** when the communication is made. Divorce will not terminate the privilege, but communications after divorce are not privileged. In addition, the communication must be ***made in reliance upon the intimacy*** of the marital relationship (confidential).

c. When Neither Marital Privilege Applies

Neither privilege applies in actions between the spouses or in cases involving crimes against the testifying spouse or either spouse's children.

HUSBAND-WIFE PRIVILEGE

Spousal Immunity	Confidential Marital Communications
One spouse ***cannot be compelled to testify*** against the other spouse in any ***criminal*** proceeding.	***Communications*** made in reliance upon the intimacy of the marital relationship are privileged. The privilege applies in both ***civil and criminal*** proceedings.
Only the ***witness-spouse*** may invoke spousal immunity.	***Both spouses*** have the privilege not to disclose, and to prevent the other from disclosing, a confidential marital communication.
The privilege can be claimed ***only during marriage***, but covers information learned before and during the marriage.	The privilege ***survives the marriage***, but covers only statements made during marriage.

7. **Privilege Against Self-Incrimination**
Under the Fifth Amendment to the Constitution, a witness cannot be compelled to testify against himself. Any witness compelled to appear in a civil or criminal proceeding may refuse to give an answer that ties the witness to the commission of a crime.

8. **Clergy or Accountant Privilege**
A privilege exists for statements made to a member of the clergy or an accountant, the elements of which are very similar to the attorney-client privilege.

9. **Professional Journalist Privilege**
There is no constitutional right for a professional journalist to protect his source of information, so any privilege in this area is limited to individual state statutes on the subject.

10. **Governmental Privileges**
Official information not otherwise open to the public or the identity of an informer may be protected by a privilege for the government. No privilege exists if the identity of the informer is voluntarily disclosed by a holder of the privilege.

H. EXCLUSION AND SEQUESTRATION OF WITNESSES

Upon a party's request, the trial judge will order witnesses excluded from the courtroom. The judge may also do this on his own motion. The judge, however, may not exclude: (i) a party or a designated officer or employee of a party, (ii) a person whose presence is essential to the presentation of a party's case, or (iii) a person statutorily authorized to be present.

VII. THE HEARSAY RULE

A. STATEMENT OF THE RULE

The Federal Rules define hearsay as "a statement, other than one made by the declarant while testifying at the trial or hearing, offered in evidence to prove the truth of the matter asserted." If a statement is hearsay, and no exception to the rule applies, the evidence must be excluded upon appropriate objection. The reason for excluding hearsay is that the adverse party was denied the opportunity to cross-examine the declarant.

CMR **Exam Tip** An out-of-court statement that incorporates other hearsay ("hearsay on hearsay" or "double hearsay") is admissible only if each part of the statement falls within an exception to the rule. If any part is inadmissible, the entire statement is inadmissible.

1. **"Statement"**
For purposes of the hearsay rule, a "statement" is: (i) an oral or written assertion, or (ii) nonverbal conduct intended as an assertion (*e.g.,* nod of the head).

2. **"Offered to Prove the Truth of the Matter"**
If the out-of-court statement is introduced for any purpose other than to prove the truth of the matter asserted, there is no need to cross-examine the declarant; so the statement is not hearsay. The following out-of-court statements are ***not hearsay***:

   a. ***Verbal acts or legally operative facts*** (*e.g.,* words of contract; defamatory words);

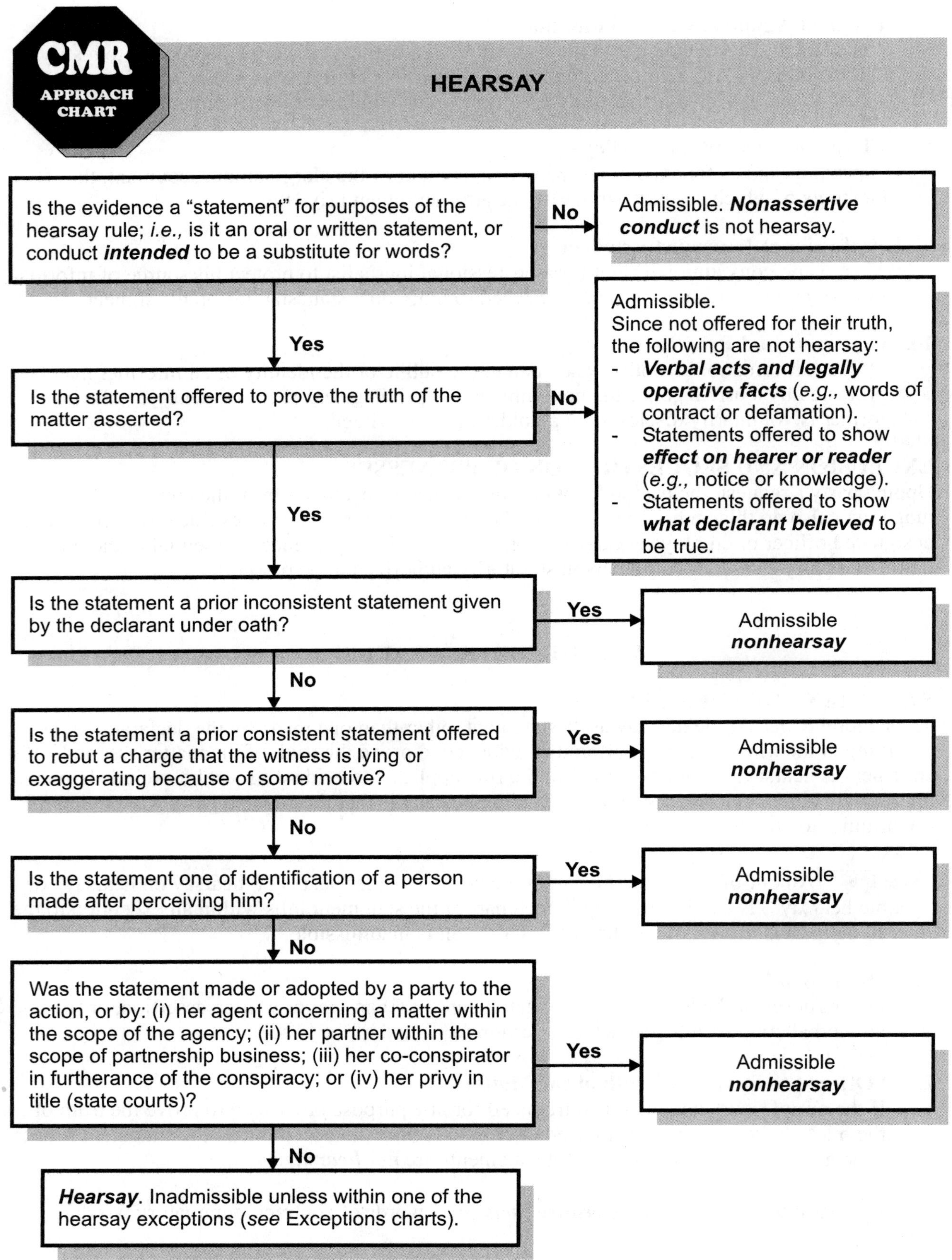
CMR
APPROACH CHART
HEARSAY
Is the evidence a "statement" for purposes of the hearsay rule; i.e., is it an oral or written statement, or conduct intended to be a substitute for words?
No
Admissible. Nonassertive conduct is not hearsay.
Yes
Is the statement offered to prove the truth of the matter asserted?
No
Admissible.
Since not offered for their truth, the following are not hearsay:
- Verbal acts and legally operative facts (e.g., words of contract or defamation).
- Statements offered to show effect on hearer or reader (e.g., notice or knowledge).
- Statements offered to show what declarant believed to be true.
Yes
Is the statement a prior inconsistent statement given by the declarant under oath?
Yes
Admissible nonhearsay
No
Is the statement a prior consistent statement offered to rebut a charge that the witness is lying or exaggerating because of some motive?
Yes
Admissible nonhearsay
No
Is the statement one of identification of a person made after perceiving him?
Yes
Admissible nonhearsay
No
Was the statement made or adopted by a party to the action, or by: (i) her agent concerning a matter within the scope of the agency; (ii) her partner within the scope of partnership business; (iii) her co-conspirator in furtherance of the conspiracy; or (iv) her privy in title (state courts)?
Yes
Admissible nonhearsay
No
Hearsay. Inadmissible unless within one of the hearsay exceptions (see Exceptions charts).

b. Statements offered to show their ***effect on the hearer or reader*** (*e.g.,* to prove notice in negligence case); and

c. Statements offered as ***circumstantial evidence of declarant's state of mind*** (*e.g.,* evidence of insanity or knowledge).

CMR **Exam Tip** Do not confuse statements offered as circumstantial evidence of declarant's state of mind, which are almost always offered as evidence of insanity or knowledge, with statements that reflect directly on declarant's state of mind, which are usually offered to establish intent. The former is not hearsay, while the latter is hearsay subject to a specific exception.

CMR **Exam Tip** In deciding whether evidence is hearsay, ask yourself whether we are relying on the declarant's credibility; *i.e.,* does it matter whether the declarant is telling the truth? If not, the evidence is not hearsay.

3. Nonhuman Declarations

There is no such thing as ***animal*** or ***machine*** hearsay; there must be an out-of-court statement by a ***person***. Thus, testimony about what a radar gun "said" or what a drug-sniffing dog did is not hearsay.

B. STATEMENTS THAT ARE NONHEARSAY UNDER THE FEDERAL RULES

Despite meeting the common law definition of hearsay, the following statements are not hearsay under the Federal Rules and are, therefore, admissible as substantive evidence:

1. Prior Statements by Witness

Under the Federal Rules, a prior statement by a witness is not hearsay if:

a. The prior statement is ***inconsistent*** with the declarant's in-court testimony and was ***given under oath*** at a prior proceeding;

b. The prior statement is ***consistent*** with the declarant's in-court testimony and is ***offered to rebut*** a charge that the witness is ***lying or exaggerating*** because of some motive (and the statement was made before any motive to lie or exaggerate arose); or

c. The prior statement is one of ***identification*** of a person made after perceiving him.

2. Admissions by Party-Opponent

An admission is a statement made or act that amounts to a prior acknowledgment by one of the parties of one of the relevant facts. Admissions of a party-opponent are not hearsay under the Federal Rules. To be an admission, the statement need not have been against the declarant's interest when made, and may even be in the form of an opinion. Personal knowledge is not required; the admission may be predicated on hearsay. The following types of admissions merit special attention.

a. Judicial and Extrajudicial Admissions

Formal judicial admissions (*e.g.,* in pleadings, stipulations, etc.) are conclusive. ***Informal*** judicial admissions made during testimony and ***extrajudicial*** (evidentiary) admissions are not conclusive and can be explained.

b. Adoptive Admissions

A party may make an admission by expressly or impliedly adopting or acquiescing in the statement of another.

1) Silence

If a reasonable person would have responded, and a party remains silent in the face of accusatory statements, his silence may be considered an implied admission. Silence is treated as an admission only if:

(i) The party ***heard and understood*** the statement;

(ii) The party was physically and mentally ***capable of denying*** the statement; and

(iii) A ***reasonable person would have denied*** the accusation.

Note that silence in the face of accusations by police in a ***criminal case*** is almost never considered an admission of a crime.

c. Vicarious Admissions

1) Co-Parties

Admissions of a party are not receivable against her co-parties merely because they happen to be joined as parties.

2) Principal-Agent

Under the Federal Rules, an agent's statements concerning any matter within the scope of her agency, made while the employment relationship exists, are not hearsay and are admissible against the principal.

3) Partners

After a partnership is shown to exist, an admission of one partner relating to matters within the scope of the partnership business is binding upon her co-partners.

4) Co-Conspirators

Admissions of one conspirator, made to a third party in furtherance of a conspiracy to commit a crime or civil wrong at a time when the declarant was participating in the conspiracy, are admissible against co-conspirators.

5) Privies in Title and Joint Tenants—State Courts Only

In most state courts, admissions of each joint owner are admissible against the other, and admissions of a former owner of real property made at the time she held title are admissible against those claiming under her (grantees, heirs, etc.). These statements are not considered admissions under the Federal Rules, but may be admissible under one of the hearsay exceptions (*e.g.,* statement against interest).

6) Preliminary Determinations

Before admitting a hearsay statement as a vicarious admission, the court must make a preliminary determination of the declarant's relationship with the party against whom the statement is offered. In making such a determination, the court

must consider the contents of the statement, but the statement alone is not sufficient to establish the required relationship.

C. HEARSAY EXCEPTIONS—DECLARANT UNAVAILABLE

There are five important exceptions to the hearsay rule that condition admissibility of the hearsay statement on the present unavailability of the declarant to testify.

1. "Unavailability"

A declarant is unavailable if he:

a. Is exempt from testifying because of ***privilege***;

b. ***Refuses to testify*** concerning the statement despite a court order;

c. Testifies to ***lack of memory*** of the subject matter of the statement;

d. Is unable to testify due to ***death or physical or mental illness***; or

e. Is ***absent*** (beyond the reach of the court's subpoena), and the proponent is unable to procure his attendance by reasonable means.

2. Former Testimony

The testimony of a now-unavailable witness, given at another hearing or deposition, is admissible if:

a. The party against whom the testimony is offered was a ***party or in privity*** (*e.g.*, grantor-grantee, life tenant-remainderman) ***with a party in the former action***;

b. The former action involved the ***same subject matter*** (causes of action need not be identical);

c. The testimony was given ***under oath***; and

d. The party against whom the testimony is offered had an ***opportunity at the prior proceeding to develop the declarant's testimony*** (*i.e.*, by direct, cross, or redirect examination).

CMR **Exam Tip** Because grand jury proceedings do not provide an opportunity for cross-examination, the ***grand jury testimony*** of an unavailable declarant is not admissible against a defendant under the former testimony exception to the hearsay rule. Be careful not to confuse this with a prior inconsistent statement given under oath by a witness currently testifying. Grand jury testimony is admissible in that case, both as impeachment and substantive evidence.

3. Statements Against Interest

The statement of a person, now unavailable as a witness, against that person's pecuniary, proprietary, or penal interest ***when made***, as well as collateral facts contained in the statement, is admissible under the statement against interest exception to the hearsay rule. The declarant must also have had personal knowledge of the facts, and must have been aware that the statement was against her interest when she made it.

a. Risk of Criminal Liability
Note that when a criminal defendant wishes to show her innocence by introducing another's statements admitting the crime, ***corroborating circumstances*** indicating the trustworthiness of the statements are required.

b. "Statement" Means Single Remark
If a person makes a declaration containing statements that are against his interest (*e.g.,* "I sold the drugs") and statements that are not (*e.g.,* "X runs the drug ring"), the exception covers only those remarks that inculpate the declarant, not the entire extended declaration.

ADMISSIONS VS. STATEMENTS AGAINST INTEREST

Admissions by Party-Opponent	Statements Against Interest
Statement need not have been against interest when made.	Statement must have been against interest when made.
Declarant need not have personal knowledge of facts.	Declarant must have personal knowledge of facts.
Declarant need not be unavailable.	Declarant must be unavailable.
Declarant must be a party.	

4. Dying Declarations—Statements Under Belief of Impending Death
In a ***homicide prosecution or a civil action***, a statement made by a now unavailable declarant is admissible if:

a. The declarant ***believed his death was imminent*** (he need not actually die); and

b. The statement concerned the ***cause or circumstances*** of what he believed to be his impending death.

CMR **Exam Tip** The bar exam will likely require you to distinguish the Federal Rule on dying declarations from the traditional rule. Beware of answer choices reflecting the traditional rule, which required that the declarant ultimately die of the injury and restricted the statement's use to homicide prosecutions.

5. Statements of Personal or Family History
Statements by a now unavailable declarant concerning births, marriages, divorces, relationship, genealogical status, etc., are admissible provided that:

a. The declarant is a ***member of the family*** in question or intimately associated with it; and

b. The statements are based on the declarant's ***personal knowledge*** of the facts or her knowledge of family reputation.

6. **Statements Offered Against Party Procuring Declarant's Unavailability**
The statement of a person (now unavailable as a witness) is admissible when offered against a party who has engaged or acquiesced in wrongdoing that ***intentionally procured the declarant's unavailability***.

CMR SUMMARY CHART

HEARSAY EXCEPTIONS—UNAVAILABILITY REQUIRED

Former Testimony	Statement made ***under oath*** at same or at other proceeding at which the party against whom it is offered had ***motive and opportunity to develop testimony***.
Statement Against Interest	Statement against declarant's ***pecuniary, proprietary, or penal interest when made***.
Dying Declaration	Statement made while declarant ***believed death was imminent, concerning the cause*** or circumstances of the impending death.
Statement of Personal or Family History	Statement of personal or family history (*e.g.*, birth, death, marriage) ***made by family member*** or one intimately associated with the family.
Statement Offered Against Party Procuring Declarant's Unavailability	Statement of unavailable declarant ***offered against party who procured*** declarant's unavailability.

D. HEARSAY EXCEPTIONS—DECLARANT'S AVAILABILITY IMMATERIAL

The following exceptions to the hearsay rule do not require that the declarant be unavailable.

1. **Present State of Mind**
A statement of a declarant's then-existing state of mind, emotion, sensation, or physical condition is admissible. It is usually offered to establish a person's intent or as circumstantial evidence that the intent was carried out. Except as to certain facts concerning the declarant's will, however, a statement of memory or belief is not admissible to prove the truth of the fact remembered or believed.

2. **Excited Utterances**
An out-of-court statement ***relating to a startling event***, made while under the stress of the excitement from the event (*i.e.*, ***before the declarant had time to reflect*** upon it), is admissible.

3. **Present Sense Impressions**
Comments made concurrently with the sense impression of an event that is not necessarily exciting may be admissible. There is little time for a calculated misstatement, and the contemporaneous nature of the statement makes it reliable.

4. **Declarations of Physical Condition**

a. **Present Bodily Condition—Admissible**
A spontaneous declaration of present bodily condition is admissible as an exception to the hearsay rule even though not made to a physician.

b. **Past Bodily Condition—Admissible If to Assist Diagnosis or Treatment**
Generally, declarations of past physical condition are inadmissible hearsay. Under the Federal Rules, however, these declarations are admissible if made to medical personnel to assist in diagnosing or treating the condition. Even declarations about the cause or source of the condition are admissible if pertinent to diagnosis or treatment.

Exam Tip Remember that, contrary to the majority state view, declarations of past physical condition made to a doctor employed to testify are ***admissible*** under the Federal Rules.

5. **Business Records**
Any writing or record made as a memorandum of any act or transaction is admissible in evidence as proof of that act or transaction. Under the Federal Rules and modern statutes, the main requirements for admissibility are as follows:

a. **"Business"**
"Business" includes every association, profession, occupation, or calling of any kind, whether or not conducted for profit.

b. **Entry Made in Regular Course of Business**
To be admissible, it must appear that the record was made in the course of a regularly conducted business activity, and that it was customary to make the type of entry involved (*i.e.*, the entrant had a duty to make the entry). Self-serving accident reports prepared primarily for litigation usually are inadmissible.

c. **Personal Knowledge**
The business record must consist of matters within the personal knowledge of the entrant or within the knowledge of someone with a ***duty*** to transmit such matters to the entrant.

Exam Tip Watch for fact patterns involving police reports containing the statements of witnesses. Generally, witnesses, or even parties, are not under a business duty to convey information to the police. Therefore, the report containing their statements cannot qualify as a business record, although it may be admissible under another exception (*see* 7., *infra*) or as an admission.

d. **Entry Made Near Time of Event**
The entry must be made at or near the time of the transaction.

e. **Authentication**
The authenticity of the record must be established. This can be accomplished by the custodian (i) ***testifying*** that the record is a business record, or (ii) ***certifying in writing*** that the record is a business record.

CMR **Exam Tip** Business records may be used to prove the nonoccurrence or nonexistence of a matter if it was the regular practice of the business to record all such matters.

6. **Past Recollection Recorded**
If the witness's memory cannot be revived, a party may introduce a memorandum that the witness made at or near the time of the event. For admissibility requirements, *see* VI.B.3.b., *supra*. The writing itself is not admissible; it must be read to the jury.

7. **Official Records and Other Official Writings**

a. **Public Records and Reports**
The following are admissible: records setting forth the activities of the office or agency; recordings of matters observed pursuant to a duty imposed by law (except police observations in criminal cases); or in civil actions and ***against the government in criminal cases***, records of factual findings resulting from an investigation authorized by law. The writing must have been made by and within the scope of the duty of the public employee, and it must have been made at or near the time of the event.

CMR **Exam Tip** Police reports that do not qualify as business records may be admitted under the public records and reports exception. Even the officer's opinions and factual (not legal) conclusions would be admissible under this exception. Be careful, however, to test the statements of others contained in the report to make sure they are admissible under a hearsay exception; otherwise, those statements will be excluded even if the report is admitted.

CMR **Exam Tip** Remember that public records and reports generally are ***not admissible against the defendant in a criminal case***. This means that investigative reports by the police, FBI, and other agencies are inadmissible in this situation.

b. **Records of Vital Statistics**
Records of vital statistics are admissible if the report was made to a public officer pursuant to requirements of law.

c. **Statement of Absence of Public Record**
Evidence in the form of a certification or testimony from the custodian of public records that she has diligently searched and failed to find a record is admissible to prove that the matter was not recorded, or inferentially that the matter did not occur.

d. Judgments

A certified copy of a judgment is always admissible proof that such judgment has been entered.

1) Prior Criminal Conviction—Felony Conviction Admissible

Under the Federal Rules, judgments of felony convictions are admissible in criminal and civil actions to prove any fact essential to the judgment. In a criminal case, however, the government may use the judgment for this purpose only against the accused; it may be used only for impeachment purposes against others.

2) Prior Criminal Acquittal—Excluded

The exclusionary rule is still applied to records of prior acquittals.

3) Judgment in Former Civil Case

A civil judgment is clearly inadmissible in a subsequent criminal proceeding and generally inadmissible in subsequent civil proceedings.

8. Ancient Documents and Documents Affecting Property Interests

Under the Federal Rules, statements in any authenticated document ***20 years old or more*** are admissible, as are statements in ***any document affecting an interest in property***, regardless of age.

9. Learned Treatises

Treatises are admissible as substantive proof under the Federal Rules if:

a. Called to the attention of, or relied upon by, an expert witness; and

b. Established as reliable authority by the testimony of that witness, other expert testimony, or judicial notice.

10. Reputation

Reputation evidence is admissible, under several exceptions to the hearsay rule, as evidence of the following: (i) character; (ii) personal or family history; (iii) land boundaries; and (iv) a community's general history.

11. Family Records

Statements of fact concerning personal or family history contained in family Bibles, jewelry engravings, genealogies, tombstone engravings, etc., are admissible.

12. Market Reports

Market reports and other published compilations are admissible if generally used and relied upon by the public or by persons in a particular occupation.

HEARSAY EXCEPTIONS—AVAILABILITY IMMATERIAL

State of Mind	Statement of ***then-existing state of mind, emotion, sensation, or physical condition***. (Usually introduced to establish ***intent***. Admissible when state of mind is a material issue or to show subsequent acts of declarant.)
Excited Utterance	Statement made while ***under stress of excitement of startling event***.
Present Sense Impression	Statement made ***concurrently with perception*** of event described.
Medical Diagnosis or Treatment	Statement made to ***medical personnel*** for the purpose of diagnosis or treatment.
Recorded Recollection	***Writing by witness who cannot now remember*** the facts, made while the facts were fresh in her mind.
Business Records or Absence Thereof	Writing made in the ***regular course of business***, consisting of matters within the ***personal knowledge*** of one with a ***business duty*** to transmit. Lack of such writing may be used to show nonoccurrence of event.
Public Records and Reports or Absence Thereof; Records of Vital Statistics	Records and reports of ***public agencies*** regarding their activities, and records of ***births, deaths, marriages,*** etc. Absence of public record is admissible to show nonexistence of matter.
Judgments	A copy of a judgment of a ***prior felony conviction*** is admissible to prove any fact essential to the judgment. In a criminal case, it may be used for this purpose only against the accused.
Ancient Documents	Documents ***20 years old*** or more.
Documents Affecting Property Interests	Statements in a document affecting an interest in a property (*e.g.,* ***deed, will***).
Learned Treatises	Statements from ***authoritative works*** admitted if called to attention of expert witness and ***established as reliable*** authority.
Reputation	Reputation evidence concerning a person's ***character***, a person's ***personal or family history***, land ***boundaries***, or a community's ***general history***.
Family Records	Statements of fact found in ***family Bibles, jewelry engravings, tombstones,*** etc.
Market Reports	Market reports and public compilations ***generally relied on by the public*** or persons of a particular occupation.

ADMISSIBLE OUT-OF-COURT STATEMENTS

NONHEARSAY

1. Nonassertive Conduct
2. Statement Not Offered for Its Truth
3. Prior Inconsistent Statement Made Under Oath
4. Prior Consistent Statement Offered to Rebut Charge that Witness Is Lying or Exaggerating
5. Prior Statement of Identification
6. Admission of Party-Opponent (including vicarious admission)

HEARSAY EXCEPTIONS

Unavailability Required

1. Former Testimony
2. Dying Declaration
3. Statement Against Interest
4. Statement of Personal or Family History
5. Statement Offered Against Party Procuring Declarant's Unavailability

Availability Immaterial

1. State of Mind
2. Excited Utterance
3. Present Sense Impression
4. Physical Condition (Medical Diagnosis or Treatment)
5. Recorded Recollection
6. Business Records or Absence Thereof
7. Public Records and Reports
8. Records of Vital Statistics
9. Judgments of Prior Convictions
10. Ancient Documents
11. Documents Affecting a Property Interest
12. Learned Treatises
13. Reputation
14. Family Records
15. Market Reports

E. RESIDUAL "CATCH-ALL" EXCEPTION OF FEDERAL RULES

For a hearsay statement that is not covered by a specific exception to be admitted, the Federal Rules provide a catch-all exception, which requires:

1. That the hearsay statement possess circumstantial guarantees of ***trustworthiness***;

2. That the statement be strictly ***necessary***; and

3. That ***notice*** be given to the adversary as to the nature of the statement.

F. CONSTITUTIONAL ISSUES

The Supreme Court has indicated that requirements of the Confrontation Clause may be met where circumstances indicate the reliability of the hearsay statement. In addition, hearsay rules and other exclusionary rules cannot be applied where such application would deprive the accused of her right to a fair trial or deny her right to compulsory process.

VIII. PROCEDURAL CONSIDERATIONS

A. BURDENS OF PROOF

The burden of proof encompasses the burden of producing or going forward with the evidence, and the burden of persuasion.

1. Burden of Producing Evidence

The party who has the burden of pleading usually has the burden of producing or going forward with evidence sufficient to make out a prima facie case (*i.e.,* create a fact question of the issue for the trier of fact). Once the party has satisfied the burden of going forward with evidence, it is incumbent upon the other side to come forward with evidence to rebut the accepted evidence.

2. Burden of Persuasion (Proof)

After the parties have sustained their burden of production of evidence, the question is whether the party with the burden of persuasion has satisfied it. The burden of persuasion for civil cases is usually by a preponderance of the evidence (more probably true than not true), although some civil cases require proof of clear and convincing evidence (high probability). The burden of persuasion for criminal cases is beyond a reasonable doubt.

B. PRESUMPTIONS

A presumption is a rule that requires that a particular inference be drawn from an ascertained set of facts. It is a form of substitute proof in that proof of the presumed fact is rendered unnecessary once evidence has been introduced of the basic fact that gives rise to the presumption.

1. Effect—Shift Burden of Production

A presumption operates, until rebutted, to shift the burden of production to the party against whom the presumption operates.

CMR **Exam Tip** Remember that a presumption ***does not shift the burden of persuasion***. The burden of persuasion remains on the same party throughout a trial.

2. **Rebutting a Presumption**
A presumption is overcome or destroyed when the adversary produces some evidence contradicting the presumed fact. Once sufficient contrary evidence is admitted, the presumption is of no force or effect.

3. **Distinguish True Presumptions from Inferences and Substantive Law**
True presumptions are the rebuttable type discussed above. Be careful not to confuse them with inferences and rules of substantive law.

    a. **Permissible Inferences**
    A permissible inference may allow the party to meet his burden of production (*e.g.*, establish a prima facie case), but does not shift the burden to the adversary. Examples include the inference of negligence arising from res ipsa loquitur, the inference that destroyed evidence was unfavorable to the spoliator, and the inference of undue influence when a will's drafter is also the principal beneficiary.

    b. **"Presumptions" in Criminal Cases**
    The presumption of innocence in criminal cases is merely a permissible inference. The burden of production never shifts to the accused.

CMR **Exam Tip** Special considerations apply when true presumptions arise in the criminal context. The judge cannot instruct the jury that it ***must*** find a presumed fact against the accused; he must instruct them that they ***may*** regard the basic facts as sufficient evidence of the presumed fact.

CMR **Exam Tip** If, in a criminal case, a presumed fact establishes guilt, is an element of the offense, or negates a defense, it must be proved beyond a reasonable doubt.

    c. **Conclusive Presumptions**
    Because it cannot be rebutted, a conclusive presumption (*e.g.*, that a child under age seven cannot commit a crime) is really a rule of substantive law.

4. **Specific Presumptions**
The following are common rebuttable presumptions:

    a. **Legitimacy**
    Every person is presumed to be legitimate.

    b. **Against Suicide**
    When cause of death is in dispute, there is a presumption in civil cases that it was not suicide.

    c. **Sanity**
    Every person is presumed sane in civil and criminal cases until the contrary is shown.

d. **Death from Absence**
If a person is unexplainably absent for a continuous period of seven years and he has not been heard from, he is presumed dead.

e. **Ownership of Car—Agent Driver**
Proof of ownership of a motor vehicle creates the presumption that the owner was the driver or that the driver was the owner's agent.

f. **Chastity**
Every person is presumed chaste and virtuous.

g. **Regularity**
It is presumed that persons acting in an official office are properly performing their duties.

h. **Continuance**
Proof of the existence of a person or condition at a given time raises a presumption that it continued for as long as it is usual with things of that nature.

i. **Mail Delivery**
A letter, properly addressed, stamped, and mailed, is presumed to have been delivered.

j. **Solvency**
A person is presumed solvent, and every debt is presumed collectible.

k. **Bailee's Negligence**
Proof of delivery of goods in good condition to a bailee and failure of the bailee to return the goods in the same condition create the presumption that the bailee was negligent.

l. **Marriage**
Upon proof of a marriage ceremony, a marriage is presumed valid.

5. **Conflicting Presumptions**
When two or more conflicting presumptions arise, the judge should apply the presumption founded on the weightier considerations of policy and logic.

6. **Choice of Law Regarding Presumptions in Civil Actions**
Under the Federal Rules, state law governs the effect of a presumption concerning a fact that is an element of a claim or defense to which, under the *Erie* doctrine, the rule of decision is supplied by state law.

C. RELATIONSHIP OF PARTIES, JUDGE, AND JURY

1. **Allocation of Responsibilities**
In our adversarial adjudicative process, the focus is on the party's responsibility to frame the issues in a litigation and to assume the burden of proving the issues he has raised. The trial judge's primary responsibility is to superintend the trial fairly. As a general rule, questions of law are for the trial judge to determine and questions of fact are for the jury.

2. Preliminary Determination of Admissibility

In most cases, the existence of some preliminary or foundational fact is an essential condition to the admissibility of proffered evidence. The Federal Rules distinguish preliminary facts to be decided by the jury from those to be decided by the judge on the ground that the former questions involve the relevancy of the proffered evidence, while the latter questions involve the competency of evidence that is relevant.

a. Preliminary Facts Decided by Jury

Examples of preliminary facts to be decided by the jury include agency, authenticity of a document, credibility of a witness, and personal knowledge.

b. Preliminary Facts Decided by Judge

Facts affecting the competency of the evidence must be determined by the trial judge. Requirements for hearsay exceptions, privileges, and expert testimony, as well as mental competence, must also be decided by the judge.

1) What Evidence May Be Considered

The Federal Rules permit the trial judge to consider any relevant evidence even though not otherwise admissible under the rules of evidence. Most state courts, however, hold that the rules of evidence apply in preliminary fact determinations as much as in any other phase of the trial; thus, only admissible evidence may be considered.

2) Presence of Jury

Whether the jury should be excused during the preliminary fact determination is generally within the discretion of the trial judge.

c. Testimony by Accused Does Not Waive Privilege Against Self-Incrimination

An accused may testify on any preliminary matter (*e.g.,* circumstances surrounding an allegedly illegal search) without subjecting herself to testifying at trial.

d. Judicial Power to Comment upon Evidence

A judge may comment on the weight of the evidence in federal courts, but generally not in state courts.

e. Power to Call Witnesses

A judge may call and interrogate witnesses on her own initiative.

f. Rulings

A trial judge has an obligation to rule promptly on counsel's evidentiary objections and, upon request, to state the grounds for her rulings.

g. Instructions on Limited Admissibility of Evidence

A judge will restrict evidence to its proper scope and instruct the jury accordingly.

REAL PROPERTY

TABLE OF CONTENTS

I. ESTATES IN LAND 1
A. PRESENT POSSESSORY ESTATES 1
1. Fee Simple Absolute 1
2. Defeasible Fees 1
3. Fee Tail 3
4. Life Estate 3
5. Estate for Years, Periodic Estate, Estate at Will, Tenancy at Sufferance 4
B. FUTURE INTERESTS 5
1. Reversionary Interests—Future Interests in Transferor 5
2. Remainders 5
3. Executory Interests 8
4. Transferability of Remainders and Executory Interests 9
5. Class Gifts 9
C. TRUSTS 10
1. Application of Rule Against Perpetuities 10
2. Creation of Trusts 10
3. Charitable Trusts 10
D. THE RULE AGAINST PERPETUITIES 10
1. When Perpetuities Period Begins to Run 12
2. "Must Vest" 12
3. "Lives in Being" 12
4. Interests Exempt from Rule 12
5. Effect of Violating Rule—Offensive Interest Stricken 12
6. The Rule in Operation—Common Pitfall Cases 12
7. Application of the Rule to Class Gifts 14
8. Statutory Reforms 14
E. THE RULE AGAINST RESTRAINTS ON ALIENATION 16
1. Types of Restraints on Alienation 16
2. Valid Restraints on Alienation 16
F. CONCURRENT ESTATES 16
1. Joint Tenancy 16
2. Tenancy by the Entirety 19
3. Tenancy in Common 19
4. Rights and Duties of Co-Tenants 19

II. LANDLORD AND TENANT 20
A. NATURE OF LEASEHOLD 20
1. Tenancies for Years 20
2. Periodic Tenancies 21
3. Tenancies at Will 21
4. Tenancies at Sufferance 21
5. The Hold-Over Doctrine 23
B. LEASES 23
C. TENANT DUTIES AND LANDLORD REMEDIES 23

1. Tenant's Duty to Repair (Doctrine of Waste) 23
2. Duty to Not Use Premises for Illegal Purpose 24
3. Duty to Pay Rent 24
4. Landlord Remedies 24

D. LANDLORD DUTIES AND TENANT REMEDIES 25
1. Duty to Deliver Possession of Premises 25
2. Quiet Enjoyment 25
3. Implied Warranty of Habitability 25
4. Retaliatory Eviction 25

E. ASSIGNMENTS AND SUBLEASES 26
1. Consequences of Assignment 26
2. Consequences of Sublease—Sublessee Not in Privity with Landlord 26
3. Covenants Against Assignment or Sublease 26
4. Assignments by Landlords 28

F. CONDEMNATION OF LEASEHOLDS 28

G. TORT LIABILITY OF LANDLORD AND TENANT 28
1. Landlord Liability 28
2. Tenant's Liability 29

III. FIXTURES 29

A. IN GENERAL 29

B. CHATTELS INCORPORATED INTO STRUCTURE 29

C. COMMON OWNERSHIP CASES 29
1. Constructive Annexation 30

D. DIVIDED OWNERSHIP CASES 30
1. Landlord-Tenant 30
2. Life Tenant and Remainderman 30
3. Licensee or Trespasser and Landlord 30

E. THIRD-PARTY CASES 30
1. Third-Party Lien on Land to Which Chattel Affixed 30
2. Third-Party Lien on Chattel Affixed to Land 30

IV. RIGHTS IN THE LAND OF ANOTHER—EASEMENTS, PROFITS, COVENANTS, AND SERVITUDES 30

A. IN GENERAL 30

B. EASEMENTS 31
1. Introduction 31
2. Creation of Easements 32
3. Scope 34
4. Termination of Easements 34
5. Compare—Licenses 35

C. PROFITS 35

D. COVENANTS RUNNING WITH THE LAND AT LAW (REAL COVENANTS) 35
1. Requirements for Burden to Run 35
2. Requirements for Benefit to Run 36
3. Specific Situations Involving Real Covenants 37
4. Remedy—Damages Only 37
5. Termination 37

E. EQUITABLE SERVITUDES 38

1. Creation 38
2. Requirements for Burden to Run 38
3. Requirements for Benefit to Run 39
4. Equitable Defenses to Enforcement 39
5. Termination 39

F. PARTY WALLS AND COMMON DRIVEWAYS 40
1. Creation 40
2. Running of Covenants 40

V. ADVERSE POSSESSION 40
A. IN GENERAL 40
B. REQUIREMENTS 40
1. Running of Statute 40
2. Open and Notorious Possession 40
3. Actual and Exclusive Possession 40
4. Continuous Possession 40
5. Hostile 41

C. DISABILITY 41
D. ADVERSE POSSESSION AND FUTURE INTERESTS 41
E. EFFECT OF COVENANTS IN TRUE OWNER'S DEED 41
F. LAND THAT CANNOT BE ADVERSELY POSSESSED 41

VI. CONVEYANCING 42
A. LAND SALE CONTRACTS 42
1. Statute of Frauds Applicable 42
2. Doctrine of Equitable Conversion 42
3. Marketable Title 42
4. Time of Performance 43
5. Tender of Performance 45
6. Remedies for Breach of Sales Contract 45
7. Seller's Liabilities for Defective Property 45
8. Real Estate Brokers 46

B. DEEDS—FORM AND CONTENT 46
1. Formalities 46
2. Defective Deeds 46
3. Fraudulent Conveyances 47
4. Description of Land Conveyed 47

C. DELIVERY AND ACCEPTANCE 47
1. Delivery—In General 48
2. Retention of Interest by Grantor or Conditional Delivery 48
3. Where Grantor Gives Deed to Third Party 48
4. Acceptance 49
5. Dedication 49

D. COVENANTS FOR TITLE AND ESTOPPEL BY DEED 49
1. Covenants in General Warranty Deed 49
2. Statutory Special Warranty Deed 50
3. Quitclaim Deeds 50
4. Estoppel by Deed 50

E. RECORDING 51

1. Recording Acts—In General 51
2. Types of Recording Acts 51
3. Who Is Protected by Recording Acts 52
4. Title Search 54
5. Effect of Recordation 54

F. WILLS—FORM AND CONTENT 55
1. Ademption 55
2. Exoneration 55
3. Lapse and Anti-Lapse Statutes 55

G. CROPS (EMBLEMENTS) 56

VII. SECURITY INTERESTS IN REAL ESTATE 56

A. TYPES OF SECURITY INTERESTS 56
1. Mortgage 56
2. Deed of Trust 56
3. Installment Land Contract 56
4. Absolute Deed 56
5. Sale-Leaseback 57

B. TRANSFERS BY MORTGAGEE AND MORTGAGOR 57
1. Transfer by Mortgagee 57
2. Transfer by Mortgagor—Grantee Takes Subject to Mortgage 58

C. POSSESSION BEFORE FORECLOSURE 58
1. Theories of Title 58
2. Mortgagor Consent and Abandonment 59
3. Risks of Mortgagee in Possession 59
4. Receiverships 59

D. FORECLOSURE 59
1. Redemption 59
2. Priorities 59
3. Proceeds of Sale 61
4. Deficiency Judgments 61

E. INSTALLMENT LAND CONTRACTS 61
1. Equity of Redemption 61
2. Restitution 61
3. Treat as a Mortgage 61
4. Waiver 61
5. Election of Remedies 61

VIII. RIGHTS INCIDENTAL TO OWNERSHIP OF LAND (NATURAL RIGHTS) 61

A. IN GENERAL 61

B. RIGHTS TO LATERAL AND SUBJACENT SUPPORT OF LAND 62
1. Lateral Support 62
2. Subjacent Support 62

C. WATER RIGHTS 62
1. Watercourses (Streams, Rivers, and Lakes) 62
2. Ground Water (Percolating Water) 63
3. Surface Waters 63

D. RIGHT IN AIRSPACE 64

E. RIGHT TO EXCLUDE—REMEDIES OF POSSESSOR 64

IX. COOPERATIVES, CONDOMINIUMS, AND ZONING 64
A. COOPERATIVES 64
B. CONDOMINIUMS 64
C. ZONING 64
1. Nonconforming Use 64
2. Special Use Permit 64
3. Variance 65
4. Unconstitutional Takings and Exactions 65

REAL PROPERTY

I. ESTATES IN LAND

A. PRESENT POSSESSORY ESTATES

A present possessory estate is an interest that gives the holder the right to present possession.

1. Fee Simple Absolute

A fee simple absolute is the largest estate recognized by law. It can be sold, divided, devised, or inherited and has an indefinite or potentially ***infinite duration***. Today, a fee simple is presumed in the absence of express contrary intent (words of inheritance are no longer necessary).

2. Defeasible Fees

Defeasible fees are fee simple estates (*i.e.,* of uncertain or potentially infinite duration) that can be terminated upon the happening of a stated event.

a. Fee Simple Determinable (and Possibility of Reverter)

A fee simple determinable terminates upon the happening of a stated event and ***automatically reverts*** to the grantor. It is created by durational language, such as "for so long as," "while," "during," or "until." A fee simple determinable can be conveyed, but the grantee takes subject to the estate's being terminated by the specified event.

Exam Tip Remember that statements of motive or purpose do not create a determinable fee. To create a fee simple determinable, words limiting the ***duration*** of the estate must be used. Watch for grants such as "for the purpose of" and "to be used for"; they are merely expressions of motive.

1) Correlative Future Interest in Grantor—Possibility of Reverter

Whenever a grantor conveys a fee simple determinable he ***automatically*** retains a possibility of reverter, which is a reversionary future interest. A possibility of reverter is transferable, descendible, and devisable.

b. Fee Simple Subject to Condition Subsequent (and Right of Entry)

A fee simple subject to a condition subsequent is an estate in which the grantor ***reserves the right to terminate*** the estate upon the happening of a stated event; *i.e.,* the estate does not automatically terminate—the grantor must take some action. The estate is created by use of conditional words, such as "upon condition that," "provided that," "but if," and "if it happens that."

1) Correlative Future Interest in Grantor—Right of Entry

The right to terminate, reserved by the grantor, is called a right of entry. It must be ***expressly reserved***; in contrast with a possibility of reverter, it does not arise automatically. Some courts hold that rights of entry are not transferable inter vivos, but most states agree they are devisable and all states agree they are descendible.

PRESENT POSSESSORY ESTATES

Present Estate	Examples	Duration	Correlative Future Interest in Grantor	Correlative Future Interest in Third Party
Fee Simple Absolute	"To A & his heirs"	Forever	None	None
Fee Simple Determinable	"To A & his heirs for so long as . . ." until . . ." while . . ." during . . ."	As long as condition is met, then ***automatically*** to grantor	Possibility of Reverter	(*See* Fee Simple Subject to an Executory Interest, below)
Fee Simple Subject to Condition Subsequent	"To A & his heirs, but if . . ." upon condition that . . ." provided that . . ."	Until happening of named event ***and*** reentry by grantor	Right of Entry	(*See* Fee Simple Subject to an Executory Interest, below)
Fee Simple Subject to an Executory Interest	"To A & his heirs for so long as . . ., and if not . . ., to B"	As long as condition is met, then to third party	(*See* Fee Simple Determinable, above)	Executory Interest
	"To A & his heirs but if . . ., to B"	Until happening of event	(*See* Fee Simple Subject to a Condition Subsequent, above)	Executory Interest
Fee Tail	"To A & the heirs of his body"	Until A and his line die out	Reversion	None (but remainder is possible)
Life Estate (may be defeasible)	"To A for life," ***or*** "To A for the life of B"	Until the end of the measuring life	Reversion	None (but see below)
	"To A for life, then to B"	Until the end of the measuring life	None	Remainder
	"To A for life, but if . . ., to B"	Until the end of the measuring life ***or*** the happening of the named event	Reversion	Executory Interest

c. **Fee Simple Subject to an Executory Interest**
If a fee simple estate terminates upon the happening of a stated event (because it is determinable or subject to a condition subsequent) and then passes to a third party rather than reverting to the grantor or giving the grantor a right to terminate, the third party has an executory interest.

Examples: 1) "To A and his heirs for so long as liquor is not sold on the premises; in that event, to B." B has an executory interest.

2) "Blackacre to XYZ Church, but if it is used for anything other than church purposes, then to B." B has an executory interest.

3. **Fee Tail**
The fee tail is an estate where ***inheritability is limited to lineal heirs***. It is created by the words "to B and the heirs of his body." Most jurisdictions have abolished the fee tail, and an attempt to create one results in a ***fee simple.***

4. **Life Estate**
A life estate is one ***measured by the life*** or lives of one or more persons. It may be created by operation of law (*e.g.,* dower) or by conveyance.

a. **Life Estates by Marital Right (Legal Life Estates)**
Dower and curtesy were the common law interests of a spouse in the real property of the other spouse. These interests could not be defeated by conveyance or by creditors. Most states have abolished dower and curtesy in favor of a statutory right to a portion of a spouse's estate.

b. **Conventional Life Estates**

1) **For Life of Grantee**
The usual life estate is measured by the life of the grantee (*e.g.*, "to B for life"). This type of life estate may be implied from language such as "to C after the life of B."

2) **Life Estate Pur Autre Vie (Life of Another)**
A life estate "pur autre vie" is measured by a life ***other than the grantee's*** (*e.g.,* "to B for the life of C"). A life estate pur autre vie also results when the ***life tenant conveys*** his life estate to another (*e.g.,* if B, the holder of a life estate, conveys his interest to D, D has a life estate for the life of B).

CMR **Exam Tip** Although a life estate is usually indefeasible (*i.e.,* it ends only when the life tenant dies), it is possible to create life estates that are defeasible in the same ways that fee estates can be defeasible. A life estate can be determinable, subject to a condition subsequent, and subject to an executory interest (*e.g.,* "to A for life so long as alcohol is not used on the premises" or "to A for life, but if A is divorced, to B").

c. **Rights and Duties of Life Tenant—Doctrine of Waste**
A life tenant is entitled to any ***ordinary*** uses and profits of the land, but cannot do anything that injures the interests of a remainderman or reversioner. A future interest holder may sue for damages or enjoin such acts.

1) **Affirmative (Voluntary) Waste—Natural Resources**
Exploitation of natural resources (*e.g.,* minerals) by a life tenant is generally limited to situations when: (i) necessary for ***repair or maintenance*** of the land; (ii) the land is ***suitable only for such use***; or (iii) it is expressly or impliedly ***permitted by the grantor***. Under the open mines doctrine, if mining was done on the land prior to the life estate, the life tenant can continue mining—but is limited to the mines already open.

2) **Permissive Waste**
Permissive waste occurs when a life tenant fails to protect or preserve the land. A life tenant is obligated to: (i) preserve the ***land and structures in a reasonable state of repair***; (ii) pay ***interest*** on mortgages (not principal); (iii) pay ***ordinary taxes*** on the land; and (iv) pay ***special assessments*** for public improvements ***of short duration*** (improvements of long duration are apportioned between the life tenant and future interest holder). A life tenant is ***not*** obliged to insure the premises for the benefit of remaindermen and is not responsible for damages caused by a third-party tortfeasor.

3) **Ameliorative Waste**
Ameliorative waste is a change that ***benefits*** the property economically. This waste was actionable at common law, but now a life tenant may alter or even demolish existing buildings if:

(i) The market value of the future interests is not diminished; and ***either***

(ii) The remaindermen do not object; ***or***

(iii) A substantial and permanent change in the neighborhood conditions (*e.g.,* change from residential to 90% industrial) has deprived the property in its current form of reasonable productivity or usefulness.

a) **Compare—Leasehold Tenant**
Leasehold tenants remain liable for ameliorative waste even if the neighborhood has changed and the market value of the premises was increased.

b) **Compare—Worthless Property**
If the land is practically worthless in its present state, the life tenant may seek a partition sale, the proceeds of which are put in trust with income paid to the life tenant.

d. **Renunciation of Life Estate**
If a life tenant who receives the estate by will or intestacy renounces his interest, the future interest following the life estate is generally accelerated so that it becomes immediately possessory.

5. **Estate for Years, Periodic Estate, Estate at Will, Tenancy at Sufferance**
These present estates are considered in the next chapter, which concerns the landlord-tenant relationship.

B. FUTURE INTERESTS

A future interest gives its holder the right or possibility of ***future*** possession of an estate. It is a ***present***, legally protected right in property.

1. Reversionary Interests—Future Interests in Transferor

a. Possibilities of Reverter and Rights of Entry

These interests are discussed *supra* in connection with defeasible fees.

CMR COMPARISON CHART

POSSIBILITY OF REVERTER VS. RIGHT OF ENTRY

	Possibility of Reverter	Right of Entry
Correlative Present Interest	Fee Simple Determinable	Fee Simple Subject to a Condition Subsequent
Example	"To A so long as alcohol is not used on the premises"	"To A on condition that if alcohol is used on the premises, O shall have the right to reenter and retake the premises"
Rights of Grantor	Estate ***automatically*** reverts to grantor upon the occurrence of the stated event	Estate does not revert automatically; ***grantor must exercise his right of entry***
Alienability	Transferable, descendible, and devisable	Descendible and devisable, but some courts hold not transferable inter vivos

b. Reversions

A reversion is the estate left in a grantor who conveys less than she owns (*e.g.*, A conveys "to B for life"; A has a reversion). It arises by operation of law; it does not have to be expressly reserved. A reversion is alienable, devisable, and inheritable. Its holder can sue for waste and for tortious damage to the reversionary interest.

CMR **Exam Tip** All reversionary interests are ***vested*** and, thus, not subject to the Rule Against Perpetuities.

2. Remainders

A remainder is a future interest ***in a third person*** that can become possessory on the ***natural expiration*** of the preceding estate. It cannot divest a prior estate, and it cannot follow a time gap after the preceding estate. A remainder must be ***expressly created*** in the instrument creating the preceding possessory estate.

Examples: 1) A conveys "to B for life and then to C and his heirs"; C has a remainder.

2) A conveys "to B for life and then to C and his heirs one day after B's death"; C does ***not*** have a remainder (because there is a gap).

Exam Tip Since a remainder cannot "cut short" a preceding estate, it can ***never follow a fee simple*** estate, which is of potentially infinite duration. Executory interests are the future interests that cut short preceding estates or follow a gap after them.

a. Indefeasibly Vested Remainder

A vested remainder is one created in an ***existing and ascertained*** person, and ***not subject to a condition precedent***. The remainderman has a right to immediate possession upon normal termination of the preceding estate. An ***indefeasibly*** vested remainder is a vested remainder that is not subject to divestment or diminution.

b. Vested Remainder Subject to Open

This is a vested remainder created in a class of persons (*e.g.,* "children") that is certain to become possessory, but is ***subject to diminution***—by the birth of additional persons who will share in the remainder as a class.

Example: A conveys "to B for life and then to the children of C." B and C are living and C has one child, D. D has a vested remainder subject to open.

c. Vested Remainder Subject to Total Divestment

This is a vested remainder that is subject to a ***condition subsequent***.

Example: A conveys "to B for life, then to C and his heirs, but if C dies unmarried, then to D and his heirs." C has a vested remainder subject to complete divestment by D's executory interest.

d. Contingent Remainder

Contingent remainders are those created in ***unborn or unascertained*** persons, or ***subject to a condition precedent***.

1) Subject to Condition Precedent

A condition is precedent if it must be satisfied before the remainderman has a right to possession.

Examples: 1) A conveys "to B for life and then to C and his heirs ***if*** C marries D." C's remainder is contingent because he must marry D before he can take possession.

2) A conveys "to B for life, then to C and his heirs if C marries D, otherwise to E and his heirs." C and E have ***alternative contingent remainders***.

Compare: A conveys "to B for life, then to C and his heirs; but if C marries D, then to E and his heirs." C has a vested remainder (because no condition precedent) subject to divestment by E's executory interest.

2) Unborn or Unascertained Persons
A remainder is contingent because until the remainderman is ascertained, no one is ready to take possession if the preceding estate ends.

Example: A conveys "to B for life and then to the children of C." If C is childless at the time, the remainder is contingent.

3) Destructibility of Contingent Remainders
At common law, a contingent remainder was destroyed if it failed to vest before or upon the termination of the preceding freehold estate.

Example: A conveys "to B for life, then to C if she reaches age 21." If B dies before C reaches age 21, C's remainder is destroyed.

Most states have abolished the destructibility rule. In those states, C's interest in the above example would be converted to an executory interest upon B's death because it will divest A's reversionary estate when C turns 21.

a) Related Doctrine of Merger
When one person acquires all of the present and future interests in land except a contingent remainder, under the common law, the contingent remainder is destroyed.

Example: X conveys "to Y for life, then to Z's children." If, before Z has any children, X purchases Y's life estate, X will have a life estate pur autre vie and a reversion. These interests merge, and the contingent remainder in Z's unborn children is destroyed.

CMR **Exam Tip** When considering whether estates merge to destroy a contingent remainder, remember that if the life estate and the next vested interest were ***created by the same instrument***, there is no merger. (This would defeat the grantor's obvious intent.) Merger ***may*** occur only as in the example above, when one person later acquires immediately successive estates.

e. Rule in Shelley's Case (Rule Against Remainders in Grantee's Heirs)
At common law, if the same instrument created a life estate in A and gave the remainder only to A's heirs, the remainder was not recognized, and A took the life estate ***and*** the remainder.

Example: A conveys "to B for life, then to C for life, then to the heirs of B." The Rule transforms the remainder in B's heirs into a remainder in B. (No merger, however, because the remainder for life in C is ***vested***.)

The Rule in Shelley's Case has been abolished in most states.

f. Doctrine of Worthier Title (Rule Against Remainders in Grantor's Heirs)
Under the Doctrine of Worthier Title ("DOWT"), a remainder in the grantor's heirs is invalid and becomes a reversion in the grantor. For example, if A grants Blackacre "to B for life, then to the heirs of A," B has a life estate, and A has a reversion. DOWT is generally treated as a rule of construction (*i.e.,* it does not apply if an intent to create a remainder in heirs has been clearly manifested). DOWT applies only to inter vivos transfers (not wills), and only if the word "heirs" is used.

CMR SUMMARY CHART

TECHNICAL RULES OF THE COMMON LAW

	Destruction of Contingent Remainders	Rule in Shelley's Case	Doctrine of Worthier Title
Rule	Contingent remainders are destroyed if not vested at time of termination of preceding estate.	A remainder in a life tenant-grantee's heirs is deemed to be in the life tenant herself.	A remainder in the grantor's heirs is ineffective, so grantor has a reversion.
Example	"To A for life, remainder to A's children who reach 21."	"To B for life, then to B's heirs."	"To B for life, then to my heirs at law."
Result	If A has no children who are at least 21 at time of her death, property reverts to grantor.	B has a fee simple.	B has a life estate; the grantor has a reversion.
Modern Status	Abolished in most jurisdictions.	Abolished in most jurisdictions.	Generally treated as rule of construction only.
Modern Result	Property reverts to grantor; A's children have springing executory interest.	B's heirs have a contingent remainder.	Grantor's heirs have a contingent remainder.

3. Executory Interests

Executory interests are future interests in third parties that either ***divest*** a transferee's preceding freehold estate ("shifting interests"), or ***follow a gap*** in possession or ***cut short*** a grantor's estate ("springing interests").

Examples: 1) In a grant from A "to B and his heirs when B marries C," B has a ***springing*** executory interest because it divests the grantor's estate.

2) In a grant from A "to B for life, then to C and his heirs, but if C predeceases B, then to D and his heirs," D has a ***shifting*** executory interest because it divests a transferee's preceding estate.

Executory interests are not considered vested and thus are subject to the Rule Against Perpetuities, but executory interests are not destructible.

CMR Exam Tip Remember that if the future interest does not follow the natural termination of the preceding estate, it must be an executory interest; only an executory interest can follow a fee simple estate.

CMR Exam Tip Where language is ambiguous, the preference is for vested remainders subject to divestment rather than contingent remainders or executory interests. Policy favors early vesting of estates.

4. Transferability of Remainders and Executory Interests

Vested remainders are fully transferable, descendible, and devisable. At common law, contingent remainders and executory interests were not transferable inter vivos, but most courts today hold that they are freely transferable. Contingent remainders and executory interests are descendible and devisable, provided survival is not a condition to the interest's taking.

CMR Exam Tip Any future interest that is transferable is subject to involuntary transfer; *i.e.,* it is reachable by creditors.

5. Class Gifts

A "class" is a group of persons having a common characteristic (*e.g.,* children, nephews). The share of each member is determined by the number of persons in the class. A class gift of a remainder may be vested subject to open (where at least one group member exists) or contingent (where all group members are unascertained).

a. When the Class Closes—The Rule of Convenience

Under the rule of convenience, in the absence of express contrary intent, a class closes (*i.e.,* no one born after that time may share in the gift) ***when some member of the class can call for distribution*** of her share of the class gift.

Examples: 1) T's will devises property to W for life, then to A's children. At the time the will is executed, A has two children, B and C. A then has another child, D. T dies. A has child E, then W dies. After W's death, A has another child, F. The class closed at W's death because it was time to make the distribution. Thus, B, C, D, and E share the property, and F is excluded.

2) T's will devises the residue of his estate "to those of A's children who attain age 21." If any of A's children is 21 at T's death, the class closes at that time. Otherwise it closes when one of A's children reaches age 21. But remember, if it had been a future gift (*i.e.,* "to A for life, then to such of A's children who attain age 21"), the class would remain open until the life tenant's death even if some of the class members had reached the stated age at T's death.

Exam Tip Recall that persons in gestation at the time the class closes are included in the class.

b. Survivorship

Survivorship of a class member to the time of closing is usually unnecessary to share in a future gift—unless survival was made an express condition (*e.g.,* "to B for life and then to his ***surviving*** children"). However, certain terms are construed to create ***implied*** survivorship conditions (*e.g.,* widow, issue, heirs, next of kin).

CMR **Exam Tip** Generally, when the instrument creating a gift of a future interest in an open class becomes effective, existing class members have a vested remainder subject to open. But watch for a condition precedent, which will prevent the remainder from vesting. For example, "to A for life, remainder to those of B's children who survive A" creates a contingent remainder in B's children even if they are in existence—and even if B is dead—because the remainder is contingent on surviving A.

C. TRUSTS

A trust is a fiduciary relationship with respect to specific property (***res***) wherein the ***trustee*** holds legal title to the property subject to enforceable equitable rights in a ***beneficiary***. The creator of a trust is the ***settlor*** who must own the property at the time of trust creation and must have had the ***intent*** to create the trust.

1. Application of Rule Against Perpetuities

The Rule Against Perpetuities applies to the equitable future interests of the beneficiaries in a private trust just as it does to "legal" future interests.

2. Creation of Trusts

A trust can be created by will (testamentary trust), inter vivos transfer of the trust res, or inter vivos declaration that the settlor is holding property in trust. All trusts of real property must be in writing. Note that a settlor may bequeath (by will) property to a trust created during his lifetime—*i.e.,* he may "pour it over" into the trust.

3. Charitable Trusts

A charitable trust must have a charitable purpose. The rules governing charitable trusts differ from those applicable to private trusts in three important ways: (i) a charitable trust must have ***indefinite beneficiaries***; (ii) it may be ***perpetual*** (the Rule Against Perpetuities does not apply); and (iii) the ***cy pres doctrine***, which allows a court to select an alternative charity when the purpose of the settlor becomes impractical or impossible, applies. Charitable trusts may be enforced by an action of the attorney general of the state.

CMR **Exam Tip** Remember that the Rule Against Perpetuities does apply to a shift from a private to charitable use or a charitable to private use.

D. THE RULE AGAINST PERPETUITIES

No interest in property is valid unless it must vest, if at all, not later than ***21 years after some life in being*** ("measuring life") at the creation of the interest. If there is ***any possibility*** the interest might vest more than 21 years after a life in being, the interest is void. The Rule applies to contingent remainders, executory interests, vested remainders subject to open (class gifts), options to purchase (not attached to a leasehold), rights of first refusal, and powers of appointment.

FUTURE INTERESTS IN TRANSFEREES

Future Interests	Example	Alienability	Subject to Rule Against Perpetuities?
Indefeasibly Vested Remainder	"To A for life, then to B."	Transferable, descendible, and devisable	No
Vested Remainder Subject to Total Divestment	"To A for life, and on A's death, to B; but if B predeceases A, then to C."	Transferable, descendible, and devisable	No
Vested Remainder Subject to Open	"To A for life, then to A's children in equal shares."	Transferable, descendible, and devisable	Yes—As long as the class remains open
Contingent Remainder	"To A for life, then to B if B marries C." ***or*** "To X for life, then to X's surviving children."	Transferable in most states (not at common law), descendible, and devisable	Yes
Shifting Executory Interest	"To A for life, remainder to B and her heirs, but if B predeceases A, then to C and his heirs."	Transferable in most states (not at common law), descendible, and devisable	Yes
Springing Executory Interest	"To X when and if he becomes a doctor." ***or*** "To X for life, then two years after X's death, to Y."	Transferable in most states (not at common law), descendible, and devisable	Yes

1. **When Perpetuities Period Begins to Run**
The time the interest is created and the perpetuities period begins to run depends on the instrument and the interest created: For interests granted by ***will***, it runs from the date of the ***testator's death***; for ***deeds***, it is the date of ***delivery***. The period runs on an ***irrevocable trust*** from the date it is ***created***; it runs on a revocable trust from the date it becomes irrevocable.

2. **"Must Vest"**
An interest vests for purposes of the Rule when it becomes: (i) possessory, or (ii) an indefeasibly vested remainder or a vested remainder subject to total divestment.

CMR **Exam Tip** In analyzing Rule Against Perpetuities problems, keep in mind that the key is when the interest ***could possibly vest***—not when it is likely to vest or even when it did. You must examine the grant as of the time of its creation and be sure that if the interest vests it will be within the period of the Rule (*i.e.,* life in being plus 21 years). If there is any possibility that it could vest beyond the period, it is void.

CMR **Exam Tip** Remember that the Rule Against Perpetuities applies ***only*** to ***contingent*** remainders, ***executory interests***, vested remainders ***subject to open***, and in most states, ***options to purchase***. Thus, the ***grantor's interests*** (reversion, possibilities of reverter, rights of entry) are safe from the Rule; you don't need to consider them.

3. **"Lives in Being"**
Unless other measuring lives are specified, one connected with the vesting of the interest is used. Any lives may be denominated measuring lives, provided they are ***human*** and of reasonable number.

4. **Interests Exempt from Rule**
Except for vested remainders subject to open, the Rule Against Perpetuities does not apply to vested interests. Thus, other vested remainders, reversions, possibilities of reverter, and rights of entry are not subject to the Rule. Moreover, there is a ***charity-to-charity*** exception to the Rule (*i.e.,* the Rule does not apply to any disposition over from one charity to another), and an exception for options to purchase ***held by a current tenant***.

5. **Effect of Violating Rule—Offensive Interest Stricken**
Violation of the Rule destroys only the offending interest. The exception is the rare case of "infectious invalidity" where the testator would probably have preferred the entire gift to fail.

6. **The Rule in Operation—Common Pitfall Cases**

   a. **Executory Interest Following Defeasible Fee**
   Generally, an executory interest that follows a defeasible fee (*e.g.,* "to A for so long as no liquor is consumed on the premises, then to B") violates the Rule Against Perpetuities, and the executory interest is stricken. (An executory interest following a defeasible fee is valid only if the condition is specific to the fee holder or expressly limited to the perpetuities period.)

Exam Tip When a void interest is stricken, the interests are classified as if the void interest were never there. For example, if G conveys "to A for as long as no liquor is consumed on the premises, then to B," B's interest would be stricken, A would have a fee simple determinable, and G would have a possibility of reverter. In contrast, if G conveys "to A, but if liquor is ever consumed on the premises then to B," B's interest and the condition are stricken, and A has a fee simple absolute.

b. Age Contingency Beyond Age Twenty-One in Open Class

A gift to an open class conditioned on members surviving beyond age 21 violates the Rule.

Example: "To X for life, then to those of X's children who attain the age of 25." The remainder in X's children violates the Rule and is void.

Some states have enacted perpetuities reform legislation that reduces such age contingencies to 21.

c. Fertile Octogenarian

A woman is conclusively presumed to be capable of bearing children, regardless of her age or medical condition. Thus, a disposition "to A for life, then to A's children for life, then to A's grandchildren in fee" is invalid as to A's grandchildren despite the fact that A is 80 years old. Some states have enacted perpetuities reform statutes that raise a presumption that women over a certain age (*e.g.,* 55) cannot bear children. Also, medical testimony regarding a woman's childbearing capacity is admissible in these states.

d. Unborn Widow or Widower

Since a person's widow or widower is not determined until his death, it may turn out to be someone who was not in being at the time of the disposition.

Example: O conveys "to A for life, then to A's widow for life, then to A's surviving ***issue*** in fee." In the absence of a statute to the contrary, the gift to A's issue is invalid, because A's widow might be a spouse who was not in being when the interest was created.

Compare: A remainder to A's ***children*** would be valid since, unlike issue, they would be determined at A's death.

Where necessary to sustain a gift, some state statutes raise a presumption that any reference to a person's spouse, widow, or widower is to a person in being at the time of the transfer.

e. Administrative Contingency

A gift conditioned on an administrative contingency (*e.g.,* admission of will to probate) violates the Rule. For example, a gift "to my issue surviving at the distribution of my estate" is invalid since the estate might be administered beyond the period of the Rule. Some state reform statutes eliminate this problem by raising a presumption that the transferor intended that the contingency should occur, if at all, within 21 years.

f. Options and Rights of First Refusal

Generally, an option to purchase or right of first refusal that is structured so that it might be exercised later than the end of the perpetuities period is void. *Exception:* The Rule Against Perpetuities does not apply to options to purchase held by the current lessee.

Example: When A conveys Blackacre to B, he includes a clause in the deed that states, "B, his heirs, and assigns promise that upon finding a ready, willing, and able buyer for Blackacre, Blackacre will be offered to A, his heirs, or assigns on the same terms." This right of first refusal can be exercised well beyond a life in being plus 21 years, and thus violates the Rule.

Exam Tip Watch for a fact pattern on the exam where a tenant has an option to purchase beyond the perpetuities period. Remember that the Rule does not apply to such an option held by a ***current*** tenant, but it does apply to a former tenant and to any party to whom the current tenant might transfer the option separately from the lease (in jurisdictions permitting such a transfer).

7. Application of the Rule to Class Gifts

a. "Bad-as-to-One, Bad-as-to-All" Rule

If the interest of any class member may vest too remotely, the whole class gift fails. For the class gift to vest, the class must be ***closed and all conditions precedent satisfied*** for every member.

b. "Gift to Subclass" Exception

Each gift to a subclass may be treated as a separate gift under the Rule.

Example: "Income to A for life, then to A's children for their lives. Upon the death of each of A's children, the corpus is to be distributed to that child's issue, per stirpes." The gifts to each of A's children's issue are considered separately. Thus, the gifts to issue of A's children living at the time of the disposition are good, but the gifts to the issue of afterborn children of A violate the Rule and are void.

c. Per Capita Gift Exception

A gift of a fixed amount to each member of a class is not treated as a class gift under the Rule.

Example: "$1,000 to each of my great-grandchildren, whether born before or after my death." This creates gifts to individuals, each of whom is judged separately under the Rule.

8. Statutory Reforms

In a number of states, statutes modify the Rule Against Perpetuities. "Wait and see" statutes determine an interest's validity upon the termination of the preceding life estate. Some states have statutes dealing with the common pitfall cases (*see supra*). Other statutes provide alternative vesting periods, and some allow court reformation of invalid interests to carry out the donor's general intent (*e.g.*, cy pres). These reforms are irrelevant for bar exam purposes unless referred to in the question.

INTERESTS UNDER THE RULE AGAINST PERPETUITIES

Valid Interests	Interests Void Under the Rule
"To A for life, then to A's children for their lives; and upon the death of the last survivor, to B." (B's interest is vested.)	"To A for life, then to A's children for their lives; and upon the death of the last survivor, to A's grandchildren." (A may have a child after this interest is created, so she could have grandchildren beyond the perpetuities period.)
"To B for life, remainder to those of B's siblings who reach age 21." (B's parents can be used as measuring lives.)	"To A for life, then to such of A's children who attain age 25." (Age contingency beyond age 21 in an open class.)
"To XYZ Orphanage for so long as it is used to house orphans; if it ceases to be so used, then to the American Red Cross." (This falls within the charity-to-charity exception.)	"To Amnesty International so long as the premises are used for Amnesty International purposes; when they cease to be so used, then to Jane Webb." (This gift passes from a charity to a private person and so does not fall within the charity-to-charity exception.)
"To A for life, and on his death to his wife, W, for life; upon W's death to A's children then living." (No unborn widow problem because the gift is to W, a life in being.)	"To A for life, then to his widow for life, then to A's surviving descendants." (Unborn widow problem.)
"To X for life, then to Y; but if at her death, Y is not survived by children, then to Z." (Y is the measuring life.)	"To M for life, then to M's children for their lives, then to M's grandchildren in fee." M is 80 years old and has had a complete hysterectomy. (Fertile octogenarian problem.)
"To A, but if alcohol is served on the premises during Z's lifetime or within 21 years of Z's death, to B." (B's interest will vest, if at all, within a life in being plus 21 years.)	"To X, but if alcohol is ever served on the premises, then to Y." (Future interest following a defeasible fee.)
"Trust income to Polo Club. At the death of the survivor of A, B, C, D, E (all babies born on this date at Obie Hospital), the trust will terminate and the corpus will be distributed to Z, his heirs, successors, or assigns." (Saving clause.)	"The residue of my estate to my descendants who are living when my estate is distributed." (Administrative contingency—here slothful executor—problem.)
"To A for life, then to A's children for their lives, then to B if B is then living, and if B is not then living, to C." (B is the measuring life. B's and C's interests will vest or fail within B's lifetime.)	"To B for life, then to such of B's children who become lawyers." (B may have a child born after the disposition who becomes a lawyer more than 21 years after B's death.)

E. THE RULE AGAINST RESTRAINTS ON ALIENATION

Generally, any restriction on the transferability of a legal (as opposed to equitable) interest is void.

1. Types of Restraints on Alienation

There are three types of restraints on alienation: (i) ***disabling*** restraints, under which attempted transfers are ineffective; (ii) ***forfeiture*** restraints, under which an attempted transfer forfeits the interest; and (iii) ***promissory*** restraints, under which an attempted transfer breaches a covenant.

a. Disabling Restraints on Legal Interests Are Void

A disabling restraint on ***any*** type of legal interest (*e.g.,* fee simple, life estate) is void.

b. All Restraints (of Whatever Type) on Fee Simple Are Void

All restraints on fee simple interests are void, even if transferability is restricted for only a short time.

2. Valid Restraints on Alienation

The following are valid restraints on alienation:

a. Forfeiture and promissory restraints on life estates;

b. Forfeiture restraints on transferability of future interests;

c. Restraints on partition by co-tenants (provided it is limited to a reasonable time);

d. Reasonable restrictions in commercial transactions;

e. Rights of first refusal; and

f. Restrictions on assignment and sublease of leaseholds (*e.g.,* requiring landlord's consent).

Exam Tip Remember the Rule Against Restraints on Alienation applies only to legal interests. Restraints on the alienation of ***equitable*** interests (*e.g.,* spendthrift clauses in trust instruments) are valid.

F. CONCURRENT ESTATES

An estate in land can be held concurrently by several persons, all of whom have the right to enjoyment and possession of the land.

1. Joint Tenancy

A joint tenancy's distinguishing feature is the ***right of survivorship***. When one joint tenant dies, the property is ***freed*** from her concurrent interest (her survivors do not succeed to it).

a. Creation

The common law requires four unities—***time, title, interest, possession***—to create a joint tenancy; *i.e.,* the interests of joint tenants must be ***equal*** in every way. They must take ***identical*** interests, at the ***same time***, by the ***same instrument***, with the ***same right***

to possession. Thus, all interests in a joint tenancy must be equal shares. If there are three joint tenants, they each own an undivided one-third interest. In a tenancy in common, by contrast, equal shares are presumed, but are not required. In a tenancy in common held by three parties, one tenant may own a two-thirds undivided interest while each of the other two tenants holds an undivided one-sixth share. In addition, modern law requires a clear expression of a right of survivorship; otherwise a conveyance to two or more persons is ***presumed to be a tenancy in common***.

CMR **Exam Tip** If the bar examiners tell you in the question that the parties are joint tenants, take it as given that they are joint tenants with right of survivorship. In this situation, ***do not*** apply the presumption that any conveyance to two or more persons is a tenancy in common. The bar examiners are not testing your knowledge of that presumption unless the fact pattern actually gives you the quoted language of the grant creating the concurrent estate and asks you about the type of tenancy involved.

b. **Severance**

Under certain circumstances, the right of survivorship is severed (*i.e.,* terminated) and a tenancy in common results.

1) **Inter Vivos Conveyance**

A voluntary or involuntary conveyance (including the execution of a mortgage in title theory states and a judicial sale to satisfy a creditor's judgment lien) by a joint tenant of her undivided interest destroys the joint tenancy. The transferee takes as a tenant in common. When there are more than two joint tenants, conveyance by one destroys the joint tenancy only to the extent of the conveyor's interest. Severance may not occur where one joint tenant does not transfer her entire interest.

a) **Judgment Liens**

Usually when a plaintiff obtains a money judgment against a defendant, that judgment becomes a lien on the defendant's real property in the county where the judgment is docketed. The lien runs with the land, burdening it until the judgment is paid or the lien expires (usually 10 years). If such a lien is acquired against a joint tenant, it does not sever the joint tenancy until it is actually sold at a foreclosure sale.

b) **Mortgages**

In most states, a mortgage is a lien on title and does not sever a joint tenancy. Severance occurs only if the mortgage is foreclosed and the property is sold.

c) **Leases**

States are split as to whether one joint tenant's lease of her interest causes a severance.

2) **Contract to Convey**

Severance results if one joint tenant contracts to convey her interest, but the courts are split on whether an executory contract by ***all*** joint tenants works a severance.

CONCURRENT OWNERSHIP

Type of Tenancy	Definition	Creation	Termination
Joint Tenancy	Each tenant has an undivided interest in the whole estate, and the surviving co-tenant has a right to the whole estate (***right of survivorship***).	"To A and B as joint tenants with the right of survivorship." (Without survivorship language, it may be construed as a tenancy in common.) Joint tenants must take: (i) identical interests; (ii) from the same instrument; (iii) at the same time; (iv) with an equal right to possess (the four unities).	The right of survivorship may be severed, and the estate converted to a tenancy in common by: a conveyance by one joint tenant, agreement of joint tenants, murder of one co-tenant by another, or simultaneous death of co-tenants. A joint tenancy can be terminated by partition (voluntary or involuntary).
Tenancy by the Entirety	Husband and wife each has an undivided interest in the whole estate and a ***right of survivorship***.	"To H and W." Most states presume a tenancy by the entirety in any joint conveyance to husband and wife where the four unities (above) are present.	The right of survivorship may be severed by divorce, mutual agreement, or execution by a joint creditor. Tenancy by the entirety cannot be terminated by involuntary partition.
Tenancy in Common	Each tenant has a distinct, proportionate, undivided interest in the property. There is ***no right of survivorship***.	"To A and B" or, sometimes, "To A and B as joint tenants." Only unity required is possession.	May be terminated by partition.

3) **Testamentary Disposition Has No Effect**
A will is ineffective to work a severance because at death the testator's interest vanishes.

4) **Effect of One Joint Tenant Murdering Another**
Conceptually, a joint tenant who murders the other joint tenant should not lose her right of survivorship. In some jurisdictions, statutes change this result; in others, a constructive trust is imposed for the decedent's estate.

2. **Tenancy by the Entirety**
A tenancy by the entirety is a ***marital*** estate akin to joint tenancy. In common law jurisdictions it arises presumptively in any conveyance to a husband and wife. Only death, divorce, ***mutual*** agreement, or execution by a joint creditor of ***both*** the husband and wife can sever a tenancy by the entirety. An individual spouse cannot convey or encumber tenancy by the entirety property. A deed or mortgage executed by only one spouse is ineffective.

3. **Tenancy in Common**
A tenancy in common is a concurrent estate with no right of survivorship. Tenants can hold different interests in the property, but each is entitled to possession of the whole. Interests are alienable, devisable, and inheritable. Today, multiple grantees are ***presumed*** to take as tenants in common, not as joint tenants.

4. **Rights and Duties of Co-Tenants**

a. **Possession**
Each co-tenant has the right to possess all portions of the property but has no right to exclusive possession of any part. A co-tenant out of possession cannot bring a possessory action unless she is "ousted" (*e.g.,* another co-tenant claims right to exclusive possession).

b. **Rents and Profits**
In most states, a co-tenant in possession has the right to retain profits from her own use of the property; *i.e.*, she need not share profits with other co-tenants absent ouster or an agreement to the contrary. She must, however, share net rents from third parties and net profits gained from exploitations of land, such as mining.

c. **Effect of One Concurrent Owner's Encumbering the Property**
A joint tenant or tenant in common may encumber her interest (*e.g.,* by mortgage or judgment lien), but may not encumber the interests of other co-tenants. If, for example, one tenant in common mortgages her interest, the mortgagee can foreclose only on the mortgaging co-tenant's interest. If a joint tenancy is involved, a mortgage (in a lien-theory state) or lien does not sever the joint tenancy, but a foreclosure sale will. Note, however, that in the case of a joint tenancy, a mortgagee or lienor runs the risk that the obligated co-tenant will die before foreclosure, extinguishing the mortgagee's or lienor's interest.

d. **Remedy of Partition**
Any co-tenant has a right to judicial partition, either in kind (physical division of land among co-tenants) or by sale and division of proceeds.

e. **Expenses for Preservation of Property—Contribution**

1) **Repairs—Contribution May Be Compelled for Necessary Repairs**
A co-tenant who pays more than her pro rata share of ***necessary*** repairs is entitled to contribution from the other co-tenants, provided she has notified the other co-tenants of the need for repairs.

2) **Improvements**
There is no right of contribution for the cost of improvements unless there is a partition.

3) **Taxes and Mortgages**
Contribution can be demanded for taxes or mortgage payments paid on the entire property. However, reimbursement to a co-tenant in sole possession is limited to the extent that expenditures exceed the rental value of her use.

f. **Duty of Fair Dealing**
A confidential relationship exists among co-tenants; *e.g.*, one co-tenant's acquisition of an outstanding title or lien that may affect the estate is deemed to be on behalf of other co-tenants. It is difficult for one co-tenant to adversely possess against other co-tenants.

II. LANDLORD AND TENANT

A. NATURE OF LEASEHOLD
A leasehold is an ***estate in land***, under which the tenant has a present possessory interest in the leased premises and the landlord has a future interest (reversion).

1. **Tenancies for Years**
A tenancy for years continues for a ***fixed*** period of time (*e.g.,* A rents to B for two years).

a. **Creation**
Tenancies for years are usually created by written leases. Under the Statute of Frauds, a writing is required if the lease is for more than one year.

b. **Termination**
A tenancy for years ends ***automatically*** at its termination date.

1) **Breach of Covenants**
In most leases, the landlord reserves a right of entry, which allows him to terminate the lease if the tenant breaches any of the lease's covenants.

a) **Failure to Pay Rent**
In many jurisdictions, a landlord may, by statute, terminate the lease upon the tenant's failure to pay the promised rent—even in the absence of a reserved right of entry.

2) **Surrender**
A tenancy for years may also terminate if the tenant surrenders the tenancy and the landlord accepts. The same formalities required for creation of the leasehold are required for surrender (*e.g.,* if unexpired term exceeds one year, surrender must be in writing).

2. **Periodic Tenancies**
A periodic tenancy continues for successive periods (*e.g.,* month-to-month) until terminated by proper notice by either party.

a. **Creation**
A periodic tenancy can be created by:

(i) ***Express agreement*** (*e.g.,* L leases to T from month-to-month);

(ii) ***Implication*** (*e.g.,* L leases to T at a rent of $100 payable monthly); or

(iii) ***Operation of law*** (*e.g.,* T remains in possession after the lease expires, and L treats it as a periodic tenancy; or the lease is invalid, but T goes into possession).

b. **Termination**
A periodic tenancy is automatically renewed until proper notice of termination is given. Usually, the notice must be one full period in advance (*e.g.,* one month's notice for a month-to-month tenancy) and timed to terminate the lease at the end of a period (*e.g.,* the usual month-to-month tenancy can end only on the 30th or 31st, not the 15th). For a year-to-year lease, six months' notice is required.

3. **Tenancies at Will**
A tenancy at will is terminable at the will of either the landlord or the tenant.

a. **Creation**
Generally, a tenancy at will must be created by an express agreement that the lease can be terminated at any time. Absent such an agreement, periodic rent payments will cause a court to treat it as a periodic tenancy. If the lease gives only the landlord the right to terminate, a similar right will be implied in favor of the tenant. However, if only the tenant has a right to terminate, a similar right will not be implied in favor of the landlord.

b. **Termination**
A tenancy at will may be terminated without notice by any party with the power to do so, or it may be terminated by operation of law (*e.g.,* for death, commission of waste, etc.).

4. **Tenancies at Sufferance**

a. **Creation**
A tenancy at sufferance arises when a tenant wrongfully remains in possession after the expiration of a lawful tenancy.

b. **Termination**
A tenancy at sufferance lasts only until the landlord takes steps to evict the tenant. No notice of termination is required.

LEASEHOLD ESTATES

Type of Leasehold	Definition	Creation	Termination
Tenancy for Years	Tenancy that lasts for some fixed period of time.	"To A for 10 years."	Terminates at the end of the stated period without either party giving notice.
Periodic Tenancy	Tenancy for some fixed period that continues for succeeding periods until either party gives notice of termination.	"To A from month to month." ***or*** "To A, with rent payable on the first day of every month." ***or*** Landlord elects to bind hold-over tenant for an additional term.	Terminates by notice from one party at least equal to the length of the time period (*e.g.,* one full month, for a month-to-month tenancy). *Exception:* Only six months' notice is required to terminate a year-to-year tenancy.
Tenancy at Will	Tenancy of no stated duration that lasts as long as both parties desire.	"To T for and during the pleasure of L." (Even though the language gives only L the right to terminate, L or T may terminate at any time.) ***or*** "To T for as many years as T desires." (Only T may terminate.)	Usually terminates after one party displays an intention that the tenancy should come to an end. May also end by operation of law (*e.g.,* death of a party, attempt to transfer interest).
Tenancy at Sufferance	Tenant wrongfully holds over after the termination of the tenancy.	B's lease expires, but B continues to occupy the premises.	Terminates when landlord evicts the tenant or elects to hold the tenant to another term.

5. The Hold-Over Doctrine

If a tenant continues in possession after his right to possession has ended, the landlord may: (i) ***evict*** him, or (ii) bind him to a ***new periodic tenancy***. Generally, the terms and conditions of the expired tenancy govern the new one. However, if the landlord notifies the tenant before the lease expires that occupancy after the termination will be at increased rent, the tenant, by holding over, is held to have acquiesced to the new terms (even if the tenant actually objected to the new terms).

CMR **Exam Tip** There are exceptions to the hold-over doctrine. Watch for situations where: (i) the tenant remains in possession for ***only a few hours*** after termination or leaves a few articles of personal property, (ii) the delay is ***not the tenant's fault*** (*e.g.,* severe illness), or (iii) it is a ***seasonal lease***. In these cases, the landlord cannot bind the tenant to a new tenancy.

B. LEASES

A lease is a contract that governs the landlord-tenant relationship. Covenants in the lease are generally independent; *i.e.,* if one party breaches a covenant, the other party can recover damages but must still perform his promises and cannot terminate the landlord-tenant relationship. The doctrines of actual and constructive eviction and the implied warranty of habitability are exceptions to this rule. Also, many states have created a statutory exception allowing the landlord to terminate the lease for the nonpayment of rent.

C. TENANT DUTIES AND LANDLORD REMEDIES

1. Tenant's Duty to Repair (Doctrine of Waste)

A tenant cannot damage (*i.e.,* commit waste on) the leased premises. The rules governing waste in the leasehold context are much like those governing waste in the life estate context.

a. Types of Waste

There are three types of waste:

1) ***Voluntary (affirmative) waste*** results when the tenant intentionally or negligently damages the premises or exploits minerals on property.

2) ***Permissive waste*** occurs when the tenant fails to take reasonable steps to protect the premises from damage from the elements. The tenant is liable for all ordinary repairs, excluding ordinary wear and tear. If the duty is shifted to the landlord (by lease or statute), the tenant has a duty to report deficiencies promptly.

3) ***Ameliorative waste*** occurs when the tenant alters the leased property, thereby increasing its value. Generally, the tenant is liable for the cost of restoration. There is a modern exception to this rule, however, which permits a tenant to make this type of change if he is a long-term tenant and the change reflects changes in the neighborhood.

b. Destruction of Premises Without Fault

If the leased premises are destroyed without the fault of either the landlord or the tenant, no waste is involved. In the absence of lease language or a statute to the contrary, neither party has a duty to restore the premises, but the tenant has a duty to continue paying rent. In most states, statutes or case law now give the tenant the option to terminate the lease in this situation, even in the presence of an explicit covenant to repair.

c. **Tenant's Liability for Covenants to Repair**
If the tenant ***specifically covenants to make repairs***, his duty will be higher than the duty implied by the law of waste. The tenant has a duty to repair even ordinary wear and tear unless ***expressly excluded***, but has no duty to repair structural failures or damage from fire or other casualty unless ***expressly included***. A tenant with a duty to repair is liable under such a covenant for all other defects, including reconstruction if the premises are destroyed.

2. **Duty to Not Use Premises for Illegal Purpose**
If the tenant uses the premises for an illegal purpose, the landlord may terminate the lease or obtain damages and injunctive relief. Occasional unlawful conduct by the tenant does not breach this duty.

3. **Duty to Pay Rent**
At common law, rent was due at the end of the leasehold term. However, leases usually contain a provision making rent payable at some other time (*e.g.,* "monthly in advance"). Most states today have statutes providing that if the leasehold terminates before the time originally agreed upon, the tenant must pay a ***proportionate amount*** of the agreed rent.

a. **Rent Deposits**
The landlord is not permitted to retain a ***security deposit*** beyond the damages actually suffered. If a rent deposit is denominated a ***"bonus,"*** the landlord can retain it after the tenant is evicted.

b. **Termination of Rent Liability—Surrender**
If a tenant effectively conveys (surrenders) his leasehold interest back to the landlord, his duty to pay rent ends.

4. **Landlord Remedies**

a. **Tenant on Premises but Fails to Pay Rent—Evict or Sue for Rent**
At common law, a breach of the lease, such as failure to pay rent, resulted only in a cause of action for money damages; a breach did not give rise to a right to terminate the lease. Most modern leases, however, give the nonbreaching party the right to terminate. Thus, if a tenant is on the premises and fails to pay rent, the landlord may bring suit for rent due or may evict the tenant under the state's ***unlawful detainer*** statute. The ***only*** issue in an unlawful detainer proceeding is whether the tenant has the right to possession; the tenant cannot raise counterclaims.

b. **Tenant Abandons—Do Nothing or Repossess**
If the tenant ***unjustifiably*** abandons the property the majority view is that the landlord has a duty to mitigate damages by seeking to relet the premises. If the landlord repossesses and/or relets, the tenant's liability depends on whether the landlord has ***accepted the surrender***. If surrender is not found, the tenant is liable for the difference between the promised rent and the fair rental value of the property (in cases of reletting, between the promised rent and the rent received from the reletting). If surrender is found, the tenant is free from any rent liability accruing after abandonment. Note that the landlord's resumption of possession for himself constitutes acceptance of surrender.

D. LANDLORD DUTIES AND TENANT REMEDIES

Subject to modification by the lease, a statute, or the implied warranty of habitability, the general rule is that a landlord has ***no duty to repair or maintain*** the premises.

1. Duty to Deliver Possession of Premises

Statutes in most states require the landlord to put the tenant in ***actual*** possession of the premises at the beginning of the leasehold term; *i.e.,* the landlord is in breach if he has not evicted a hold-over tenant by the beginning of the lease term.

2. Quiet Enjoyment

Every lease has an implied covenant that neither the landlord nor a paramount title holder (*e.g.*, a prior mortgagee who forecloses) will interfere with the tenant's quiet enjoyment and possession of the premises. This covenant may be breached in the following ways:

a. Actual Eviction

Actual eviction occurs when the landlord or a paramount title holder excludes the tenant from the ***entire*** leased premises. Actual eviction terminates the tenant's obligation to pay rent.

b. Partial Eviction

Partial actual eviction occurs when the tenant is physically excluded from only part of the leased premises. Partial eviction ***by the landlord*** relieves the tenant of the obligation to pay rent for the ***entire*** premises, even though the tenant continues in possession of the remainder. Partial eviction by a third person with paramount title results in an apportionment of rent; *i.e.,* the tenant is liable for the reasonable rental value of the portion she continues to possess.

c. Constructive Eviction

If the landlord does something (or, more often, fails to provide a service he has a legal duty to provide) that renders the property uninhabitable, the tenant may terminate the lease and seek damages. The conditions must be the result of the ***landlord's actions*** (not a neighbor's or other third party's), and the tenant ***must vacate*** the premises within a reasonable time.

3. Implied Warranty of Habitability

Most jurisdictions imply a covenant of habitability into ***residential leases***. This warranty is ***nonwaivable***. The landlord's duty is tied to standards of local housing codes. In the event of a breach, the tenant may: (i) ***terminate*** the lease; (ii) ***make repairs and offset*** the cost against future rent; (iii) ***abate the rent*** to an amount equal to the fair rental value in view of the defects; or (iv) remain in possession, pay full rent, and ***sue for damages.***

CMR **Exam Tip** Keep in mind that the implied warranty of habitability does ***not*** apply to commercial tenants—only to residential tenants.

4. Retaliatory Eviction

In many states, a landlord may not terminate a lease or otherwise penalize a tenant in retaliation for the tenant's exercise of her legal rights, including reporting housing or building code violations. Many statutes presume a retaliatory motive if the landlord acts within, for example, 90 to 180 days after the tenant exercises her rights. To overcome the presumption, the landlord must show a valid, nonretaliatory reason for his actions.

E. ASSIGNMENTS AND SUBLEASES

Absent an express restriction in the lease, a tenant may freely transfer her leasehold interest, in whole or in part. A ***complete*** transfer of the entire remaining term is an ***assignment***. If the tenant retains any part of the remaining term (other than a right to reenter upon breach), the transfer is a ***sublease***.

CMR **Exam Tip** For bar exam purposes, a transfer will be considered a sublease, rather than an assignment, only when the original tenant reserves time for herself (*e.g.,* the last month of the lease).

1. Consequences of Assignment

An assignee stands in the shoes of the original tenant in a direct relationship with the landlord; *i.e.,* the assignee and the landlord are in ***"privity of estate,"*** and each is liable to the other on all covenants in the lease that "run with the land."

a. Covenants that Run with the Land

A covenant runs with the land if the original parties to the lease so intend and if the covenant "touches and concerns" the land (benefits the landlord and burdens the tenant (or vice versa) with respect to their interests in the property).

b. Rent Covenants

Since a covenant to pay rent runs with the land, the assignee owes rent ***directly*** to the landlord. After assignment, the original tenant is no longer in privity of estate with the landlord but remains liable on the ***original contractual obligation*** to pay rent (privity of contract). If the assignee reassigns the leasehold interest, his privity of estate with the landlord ends, and he has no liability for the subsequent assignee's failure to pay rent.

2. Consequences of Sublease—Sublessee Not in Privity with Landlord

A sublessee is the tenant of the original lessee and usually pays rent to the original lessee, who then pays the landlord. A sublessee is not personally liable to the landlord for rent or for the performance of any of the covenants in the main lease unless the sublessee expressly assumes the covenants.

a. Landlord's Remedies

The landlord may terminate the main lease for nonpayment of rent or breach of other covenants if the lease so states or the power is given by statute. The sublease automatically terminates with the main lease. Also, many states allow a landlord who does not receive rent to assert a lien on personal property found on the premises; this applies to a sublessee's property as well as that of the original tenant.

b. Rights of Sublessee

A sublessee cannot enforce any covenants made by the landlord in the main lease, except a residential sublessee may be able to enforce the implied warranty of habitability against the landlord.

3. Covenants Against Assignment or Sublease

Lease covenants restricting assignment and sublease are strictly ***construed against the landlord***. (Thus, a covenant prohibiting assignment does not prohibit subleasing and vice versa.)

ASSIGNMENT VS. SUBLEASE

	Assignment by Landlord	Assignment by Tenant	Sublease by Tenant
Consent	Tenant's consent not required.	Landlord's consent may be required by lease.	Landlord's consent may be required by lease.
Privity of Estate	Assignee and tenant are in privity of estate.	Assignee and landlord are in privity of estate.	Sublessee and landlord are not in privity of estate. Original tenant remains in privity of estate with landlord.
Privity of Contract	Assignee and tenant are not in privity of contract. Original landlord and tenant remain in privity of contract.	Assignee and landlord are not in privity of contract. Original tenant and landlord remain in privity of contract.	Sublessee and landlord are not in privity of contract. Original tenant remains in privity of contract with landlord.
Liability for Covenants in Lease	Assignee liable to tenant on all covenants that run with the land.	Assignee liable to landlord on all covenants that run with the land.	Sublessee is not personally liable on any covenants in the original lease and cannot enforce the landlord's covenants.
	Original landlord remains liable on ***all*** covenants in the lease.	Original tenant remains liable for rent and ***all*** other covenants in the lease.	Original tenant remains liable for rent and ***all*** other covenants in the lease and can enforce the landlord's covenants.

a. **Waiver**

A valid covenant against assignment is considered waived if the landlord was aware of the assignment and did not object (*e.g.,* by knowingly accepting rent from the assignee). Once the landlord consents to one transfer, he waives the covenant as to future transfers unless he expressly reserves it.

b. **Transfer in Violation of Lease**

If a tenant assigns or sublets in violation of a lease provision, the transfer is not void. The landlord, however, usually may terminate the lease or sue for damages.

4. **Assignments by Landlords**

A landlord may assign the rents and reversion interest he owns. This is usually done by deed when the landlord conveys a building to a new owner. The tenants' consent is ***not*** required.

a. **Rights of Assignee Against Tenants—Attornment**

Once tenants are given reasonable notice of the assignment, they must recognize and pay rent to the new owner as their landlord. The benefit of all tenant covenants that touch and concern the land runs with the landlord's estate to the new owner.

b. **Liabilities of Assignee to Tenants**

The burden of the landlord's covenants that touch and concern the land runs with the landlord's estate to the assignee; thus, the assignee is liable for the performance of those covenants. ***The original landlord also remains liable on all of the covenants he made in the lease.***

F. CONDEMNATION OF LEASEHOLDS

If the ***entire leasehold*** is taken by eminent domain, the tenant's liability for rent is extinguished because both the leasehold and reversion have merged in the condemnor and there is no longer a leasehold estate. The lessee is entitled to compensation. However, if the taking is ***temporary*** or ***partial***, the tenant is ***not*** discharged from the rent obligation, but is entitled to compensation (*i.e.,* a share of the condemnation award) for the taking.

G. TORT LIABILITY OF LANDLORD AND TENANT

1. **Landlord Liability**

At common law, a landlord had no duty to make the premises safe. Today, there are several exceptions.

a. **Concealed Dangerous Condition (Latent Defect)**

If, at the time the lease is entered into, the landlord knows (or should know) of a dangerous condition that the tenant could not discover by reasonable inspection, the landlord must ***disclose*** (not repair) it. Otherwise, the landlord will be liable for any injuries resulting from the condition. If the tenant accepts the premises after disclosure, she assumes the risk for herself and others; the landlord is no longer liable.

b. **Public Use**

A landlord is liable for injuries to members of the public if, at the time of the lease, he:

1) Knows (or should know) of a ***dangerous condition***;

2) Has reason to believe the tenant ***may admit the public before repairing*** the condition; and

3) ***Fails to repair*** the condition.

c. Repairs
Although the landlord is not liable for injuries from dangerous conditions arising after the tenant takes possession, if ***the landlord undertakes such repairs***, he owes a duty of reasonable care. The landlord also has a duty of reasonable care in maintaining common areas (*e.g.,* halls, elevators). If the landlord covenants to repair or has a statutory duty to repair (*e.g.,* housing codes), he is liable for injuries resulting from failure to repair or negligent repair.

d. Furnished Short-Term Residence
A landlord who rents a fully furnished premises for a short period (*e.g.,* summer cottage) is under a stricter duty. He is liable for injuries resulting from ***any*** defect whether or not he knew of the defect.

e. Modern Trend—General Duty of Reasonable Care
Many courts are now holding that a landlord owes a general duty of reasonable care toward residential tenants, and will be held liable for injuries resulting from ordinary negligence if he had notice of a defect and an opportunity to repair it.

2. Tenant's Liability
The duty of care owed by a tenant, as an occupier of land, to third persons is discussed in the Torts outline.

III. FIXTURES

A. IN GENERAL
A fixture is a chattel that has been so affixed to land that it has ceased being personal property and has become part of the realty. A fixture passes with the ownership of the land.

B. CHATTELS INCORPORATED INTO STRUCTURE
When items are incorporated into the realty so that they lose their identity (*e.g.,* bricks, concrete), they are fixtures, as are items that are identifiable but whose removal would cause considerable damage (*e.g.,* plumbing, heating ducts).

C. COMMON OWNERSHIP CASES
A common ownership case is one in which the person who brings the chattel to the land owns both the chattel and the land (*e.g.*, X installs a furnace in his home). An item is a "fixture" if the objective intention of the party who made the "annexation" was to make the item part of the realty. This intention is determined by: the nature of the article; the manner of attachment; the amount of damage that would be caused by its removal; and the adaptation of the item to the use of the realty.

1. **Constructive Annexation**
An article of personal property that is so uniquely adapted to the real estate that it makes no sense to separate it (*e.g.,* keys to doors, custom curtain rods) may be considered a fixture even if it is not physically annexed to the property.

D. DIVIDED OWNERSHIP CASES

In divided ownership cases, the chattel is owned and brought to the realty by someone other than the landowner (*e.g.*, tenant, licensee, or trespasser).

1. **Landlord-Tenant**
An agreement between the landlord and tenant is controlling on whether an annexed chattel is a fixture. Absent an agreement, a tenant is deemed to lack the intent to permanently improve the property, and thus may remove his annexed chattels if removal would not damage the premises or destroy the chattel. Annexed chattels must be removed by the end of the lease term (or within a reasonable time after the termination of an indefinite tenancy) and the tenant is responsible for repairing any damage caused by the removal.

2. **Life Tenant and Remainderman**
The same rules apply in the life tenant-remainderman context as in landlord-tenant situations except that the life tenant must remove annexations before the end of his tenancy.

3. **Licensee or Trespasser and Landlord**
Licensees are treated much like tenants, whereas trespassers normally lose their annexations. Thus, absent a statute, an adverse possessor or good faith trespasser cannot remove fixtures (*e.g.*, house erroneously constructed on a parcel that possessor believed she owned).

E. THIRD-PARTY CASES

1. **Third-Party Lien on Land to Which Chattel Affixed**
Generally, the mortgagee has no greater rights than the mortgagor. Thus, chattels annexed by the mortgagor's tenant are generally not within the lien of the mortgagee ***except*** where the mortgage is made after the lease and the mortgagee is without notice of the tenant's rights.

2. **Third-Party Lien on Chattel Affixed to Land**
Suppose a landowner affixes a chattel to the land. The seller of the chattel retains a security interest in the chattel, and the landowner mortgages the land. If the landowner then defaults on both chattel and mortgage payments, as between the seller and the mortgagee, the general rule is that the first to record his interest wins. However, under the U.C.C., a seller wins if the "fixture filing" is recorded within 20 days after the chattel is affixed to the land. The seller must compensate the mortgagee for damage or repair caused by removal.

IV. RIGHTS IN THE LAND OF ANOTHER—EASEMENTS, PROFITS, COVENANTS, AND SERVITUDES

A. IN GENERAL

Easements, profits, covenants, and servitudes are ***nonpossessory*** interests in land, creating a right to ***use land possessed by someone else***.

NONPOSSESSORY INTERESTS

	Easement	License	Profit	Real Covenant/ Equitable Servitude
Definition	A grant of an interest in land that allows someone to use another's land	Permission to go onto another's land	Right to take resources from another's land	Promise to do or not to do something on the land
Example	Owner of parcel A grants owner of parcel B the right to drive across parcel A	O allows the electrician to come onto his land to fix an outlet	O allows A to come onto O's land to cut and remove timber	O conveys an adjoining parcel to A. A promises not to build a swimming pool on the property
Writing	Generally required. *Exceptions:* Less than one year Implication Necessity Prescription	Not required. *Note:* An invalid oral easement is a license	Required	Required. *Exception:* Equitable servitude may be implied from common scheme of development of residential subdivision
Termination	Stated conditions Release Merger Abandonment Estoppel Prescription End of necessity	Usually revocable at will. May be irrevocable if coupled with an interest or if licensor estopped by licensee's expenditures	Same as easement	Release Merger Condemnation Also equitable defenses may apply to enforcement of servitude

B. EASEMENTS

1. Introduction

An easement holder has the right to use another's tract of land for a special purpose (*e.g.,* to lay pipe, to access a road or lake), but has no right to possess or enjoy that land. An easement is presumed to be of ***perpetual duration*** unless the grant specifically limits the interest.

a. **Types of Easements**
Most easements are ***affirmative***, which means the holder is entitled to make affirmative use of the servient tenement. ***Negative*** easements, which entitle the holder to compel the possessor of the servient tenement to refrain from engaging in an activity on the servient estate (*e.g.*, building a structure in excess of three stories), are generally confined to only four types of easements: (i) for ***light***, (ii) for ***air***, (iii) for lateral and subjacent ***support***, and (iv) for ***flow*** of an artificial stream.

CMR **Exam Tip** Negative easements are really restrictive covenants. Thus, for exam purposes, a restriction relating to light, air, support, or flow of an artificial stream can be either a negative easement or a restrictive covenant. Restrictions relating to anything else, however, are considered restrictive covenants.

b. **Easement Appurtenant**
An easement is appurtenant when it benefits the holder in his physical use or enjoyment of another tract of land. Thus, for an easement to be appurtenant, there must be ***two tracts***: the ***dominant*** tenement (the estate benefited by the easement), and the ***servient*** tenement (the estate subject to the easement right). An easement appurtenant passes with the transfer of the benefited land, regardless of whether it is mentioned in the conveyance. The burden of the easement also passes automatically with the servient estate unless the new owner is a bona fide purchaser with no actual or constructive notice of the easement.

CMR **Exam Tip** It is important to remember that the easement appurtenant ***passes with the benefited land***. Don't be fooled by questions that make you think it must be specifically mentioned in the deed. Similarly, recall that an easement appurtenant cannot be conveyed apart from the dominant tenement (unless it is conveyed to the owner of the servient tenement to ***extinguish*** the easement).

c. **Easement in Gross**
The holder of an easement in gross acquires a right to use the servient tenement independent of his possession of another tract of land; *i.e.*, the easement benefits the holder rather than another parcel. An easement in gross for the holder's personal pleasure (*e.g.*, right to swim in the pond on Blackacre) is not transferable, but one that serves an economic or commercial interest (*e.g.*, right to erect billboards on Blackacre) is transferable.

2. **Creation of Easements**
The basic methods of creating an easement are: express grant or reservation, implication, and prescription.

a. **Express Grant**
Any easement must be in writing and signed by the holder of the servient tenement unless its duration is brief enough (commonly one year or less) to be outside a particular state's Statute of Frauds' coverage. A grant of easement must comply with all the formal requisites of a deed (*see* VI.B.1., *infra*).

b. **Express Reservation**
An easement by reservation arises when a grantor conveys title to land, but reserves the right to continue to use the tract for a special purpose.

Exam Tip Watch for fact patterns in which a grantor reserves an easement for someone else. Under the majority view, an easement can be reserved only for the ***grantor***. An attempt to reserve an easement for anyone else is ***void***.

c. **Implication**
An easement by implication is created by operation of law; it is an exception to the Statute of Frauds. Aside from the easement automatically implied with any grant of a profit (*see* C., *infra*), there are two types of easements by implication:

1) **Easement Implied from Existing Use ("Quasi-Easement")**
An easement may be implied if:

a) ***Prior to the division*** of a single tract,

b) An ***apparent and continuous*** use exists on the "servient" part,

c) That is ***reasonably necessary*** for the enjoyment of the "dominant" part, and

d) The court determines that the parties ***intended*** the use to continue after division of the land.

2) **Easement Implied Without Any Existing Use**

a) **Subdivision Plat**
When lots are sold in a subdivision with reference to a recorded plat or map that also shows streets leading to the lots, buyers of the lots have implied easements to use the streets to access their lots.

b) **Profit a Prendre**
The holder of the profit a prendre (*see* C., *infra*) has an implied easement to pass over the surface of the land and to use it as reasonably necessary to extract the product.

3) **Easement by Necessity**
An easement by necessity arises when a landowner sells a portion of his tract and by this division deprives one lot of access to a public road or utility line. The owner of the servient parcel has the right to locate the easement.

d. **Prescription**
Acquiring an easement by prescription is analogous to acquiring property by adverse possession. To acquire a prescriptive easement, the use must be:

(i) ***Open and notorious*** (*i.e.,* discoverable upon inspection);

(ii) ***Adverse*** (without the owner's permission); and

(iii) ***Continuous and uninterrupted***;

(iv) For the ***statutory period***.

Generally, prescriptive easements cannot be acquired in public land.

3. **Scope**
In the absence of specific limitations in the grant, courts assume the easement was intended to meet both present and future needs of the dominant tenement (*e.g.,* easement may widen to accommodate new, wider cars). If, however, the dominant parcel is subdivided, the lot owners will not succeed to the easement if to do so would unreasonably overburden the servient estate.

CMR **Exam Tip** When confronted with an exam question involving overuse or misuse of an easement, remember that such use ***does not terminate*** the easement. The appropriate remedy for the servient owner is an injunction against the misuse.

4. **Termination of Easements**
An easement can be terminated in the following ways:

   a. **Stated Conditions**
   The original easement grant may specify when or under what conditions the easement will terminate.

   b. **Unity of Ownership (Merger)**
   If the same person acquires ownership of both the easement and the servient estate, the dominant and servient estates merge and the easement is destroyed. Even though there may be later separation, the easement will not be automatically revived. The unity must be complete (*e.g.,* the holder of the easement must acquire an interest in the servient tenement of equal or greater duration than the duration of the easement privilege).

   c. **Release**
   An easement (including an easement in gross, which is otherwise inalienable) can be terminated by a deed of release from the owner of the easement to the owner of the servient tenement.

   d. **Abandonment**
   An easement is extinguished when its holder demonstrates by physical action (*e.g.,* building a structure that blocks access to easement on adjoining lot) an intent to permanently abandon the easement. Merely expressing a wish to abandon does not extinguish the easement; neither does mere nonuse.

   e. **Estoppel**
   Oral expressions of an intent to abandon do not terminate an easement unless in writing (release) or accompanied by action (abandonment). But if the owner of the servient estate changes his position in reasonable reliance on the representations made or conduct by the owner of the easement, the easement terminates through estoppel.

   f. **Prescription**
   To terminate an easement by prescription there must be an adverse, continuous interruption of the use for the prescription period (typically 20 years).

   g. **Necessity**
   Easements created by necessity expire as soon as the necessity ends.

h. **Condemnation and Destruction**
Condemnation of the servient estate extinguishes all easements. Courts are split as to whether easement holders are entitled to compensation. Involuntary destruction of a structure in which there is an easement extinguishes the easement; voluntary destruction of such a structure does not.

5. **Compare—Licenses**
Licenses privilege their holders to go upon the land of another. But unlike an easement, a license is not an interest in land; it is merely a privilege, ***revocable*** at the will of the licensor. A license is personal to the licensee and, thus, inalienable. Any attempt to transfer a license results in revocation by operation of law.

CMR **Exam Tip** A failed attempt to create an easement results in a license. Thus, if a grantor orally grants an easement for more than one year, it is unenforceable because it is not in writing. The grantee does not have a valid easement but does have a license.

a. **Irrevocable Licenses**
A license becomes irrevocable in the following circumstances:

1) **Estoppel**
If a licensee invests substantial amounts of money or labor in reliance on the license, the licensor is estopped to revoke. The license becomes an easement by estoppel, which lasts until the holder receives sufficient benefit to reimburse him for his expenditures.

2) **License Coupled with an Interest**
A license coupled with an interest is irrevocable as long as the interest lasts. For example, the vendee of a chattel may enter the seller's land to remove the chattel, and a future interest holder may enter and inspect the land for waste.

C. PROFITS

Profits entitle the holder of the benefit to take some resources (soil, timber, materials, fish, etc.) from the servient estate. Implied in every profit is an easement entitling the benefit holder to enter the servient estate to remove the resources. All of the rules governing creation, alienation, and termination of easements are applicable to profits. In addition, a profit may be extinguished through surcharge (misuse that overly burdens the servient estate).

D. COVENANTS RUNNING WITH THE LAND AT LAW (REAL COVENANTS)

A real covenant, normally found in a deed, is a ***written promise*** to do something on the land (*e.g.,* maintain a fence) or a promise not to do something on the land (*e.g.,* not build a multifamily dwelling). Real covenants run with the land at law, which means that subsequent owners may enforce or be burdened by the covenants.

1. **Requirements for Burden to Run**
If the following requirements are met, any successor in interest to the burdened estate will be bound by the covenant as if she had herself expressly agreed to it.

a. **Intent**
The covenanting parties must have ***intended*** that successors in interest to the covenantor be bound by the terms of the covenant. This intent may be inferred from circumstances surrounding the creation of the covenant, but is usually found in the language of the conveyance itself.

b. **Notice**
Under modern recording acts (*see* VI.E., *infra*), to be bound by a covenant, a subsequent purchaser for value must have had actual, inquiry, or record notice of the arrangement at the time of purchase.

CMR **Exam Tip** Since the notice requirement arises under the recording acts, remember that it will protect ***only purchasers for value***. Someone who does not give value may be bound by a covenant at law (not equity) even if he has no actual or constructive notice of the covenant.

c. **Horizontal Privity**
At the time the promisor entered into the covenant with the promisee, the two must have shared ***some interest*** in the land independent of the covenant (*e.g.,* grantor-grantee, landlord-tenant, mortgagee-mortgagor).

CMR **Exam Tip** Horizontal privity concerns only the ***original*** parties. Even if successors in interest are trying to enforce the covenant, you must look only to the original covenanting parties to determine horizontal privity.

d. **Vertical Privity**
To be bound, the successor in interest to the covenanting party must hold the ***entire durational interest*** held by the covenantor at the time he made the covenant.

e. **Touch and Concern**
Negative covenants touch and concern the land if they restrict the holder of the servient estate in his ***use of that parcel*** of land. Affirmative covenants touch and concern the land if they require the holder of the servient estate to ***do something***, which increases his obligations in connection with his enjoyment of the land.

2. **Requirements for Benefit to Run**
If the following three requirements are met, the promisee's successor in interest may enforce the covenant:

a. **Intent**
The covenanting parties must have ***intended*** that the successors in interest to the covenantee be able to enforce the covenant.

b. **Vertical Privity**
The benefits of a covenant run to the assignees of the ***original estate or any lesser estate***; *i.e.,* ***any*** succeeding possessory estate may enforce the benefit.

CMR **Exam Tip** Horizontal privity is not required for the benefit to run. Thus, where horizontal privity is lacking, the promisee's successors can enforce the covenant against the promisor, but not against the promisor's successors.

c. **Touch and Concern**
The benefit of a covenant touches and concerns the land if the promised performance benefits the covenantee and her successors in their use and enjoyment of the benefited land.

3. **Specific Situations Involving Real Covenants**
Generally, promises to ***pay money*** to be used in connection with the land (*e.g.,* home-owner's association fees) and covenants ***not to compete*** run with the land. Racially restrictive covenants are unenforceable.

4. **Remedy—Damages Only**
A breach of a real covenant is remedied by an award of money damages, collectible from the defendant's general assets. If an injunction is sought, the promise must be enforced as an equitable servitude (*see* below) rather than a real covenant.

5. **Termination**
As with all other nonpossessory interests, a covenant may be terminated by: (i) a written ***release***, (ii) the ***merger*** of benefited and burdened estates, or (iii) the ***condemnation*** of the burdened property.

CMR COMPARISON CHART

DISTINGUISHING CHARACTERISTICS OF REAL COVENANTS AND EQUITABLE SERVITUDES

	Real Covenants	Equitable Servitudes
Creation	Writing is ***always*** required	Writing is ***usually*** required but may arise by ***implication*** from common scheme of development of a residential subdivision
Running of Burden	Horizontal privity (shared interest in land, apart from the covenant, by ***original*** covenanting parties; *e.g.,* mortgagor-mortgagee, landlord-tenant) and vertical privity (successor holds entire interest held by covenanting party) required	No privity required
Running of Benefit	Vertical privity required	No privity required
Remedy	Damages	Injunction

E. EQUITABLE SERVITUDES

An equitable servitude is a covenant that, regardless of whether it runs with the land at law, equity will enforce against the assignees of the burdened land who have ***notice*** of the covenant. The usual remedy is an injunction.

CMR **Exam Tip** The crucial difference between real covenants and equitable servitudes is the remedy sought. If money damages are sought, you must use the real covenant analysis. If a party seeks an injunction, you must consider whether the requirements for enforcement as an equitable servitude have been met. A single promise can create both a real covenant and an equitable servitude.

1. Creation

Generally, as with real covenants, equitable servitudes are created by ***covenants*** contained in a ***writing*** that satisfies the Statute of Frauds. There is one exception: Negative equitable servitudes may be implied from a common scheme for development of a residential subdivision. Thus, if a developer subdivides land, and some deeds contain negative covenants while others do not, the negative covenants will be binding on all parcels provided there was a common scheme of development and notice of the covenants.

a. Common Scheme

Reciprocal negative servitudes will be implied only if, at the time that sales in the subdivision began, the developer had a plan that all parcels would be subject to the restriction. The scheme may be evidenced by: (i) a recorded plat, (ii) a general pattern of restrictions, or (iii) oral representations to early buyers.

CMR **Exam Tip** If the scheme arises after some lots are sold, no implied servitude can arise with respect to the lots already sold without express covenants. So remember, if Lots 1 through 5 are sold without a restrictive covenant and the deeds to Lots 6 through 50 contain one, the covenant cannot be enforced as a servitude against the owners of Lots 1 through 5.

b. Notice

To be bound by a covenant not in her deed, a grantee must have had notice of the covenants in the deeds of others in the subdivision. Notice may be ***actual*** (direct knowledge of covenants), ***inquiry*** (neighborhood appears to conform to common restrictions), or ***record*** (prior deed with covenant in grantee's chain of title).

2. Requirements for Burden to Run

A successor of the promisor is bound if:

a. The covenanting parties ***intended*** that the servitude be enforceable by and against assignees;

b. The successor of the promisor has ***actual, inquiry, or record*** notice of the servitude; and

c. The covenant ***touches and concerns*** the land (*i.e.,* it restricts the holder of the servient estate in his use of that parcel).

3. **Requirements for Benefit to Run**
The benefit of an equitable servitude runs with the land, and thus, is enforceable by the promisee's successors if: (i) the original parties so ***intended***, and (ii) the servitude ***touches and concerns*** the benefited property.

CMR **Exam Tip** In contrast to real covenants, which require vertical and horizontal privity of estate for burdens to run, and vertical privity for benefits to run, ***no privity of estate is required*** for an equitable servitude to be enforceable by and against assignees.

4. **Equitable Defenses to Enforcement**
A court will not enforce an equitable servitude if:

a. The person seeking enforcement is violating a similar restriction on his own land (***unclean hands***);

b. A benefited party ***acquiesced*** in a violation of the servitude by one burdened party;

c. A benefited party acted in such a way that a reasonable person would believe the covenant was abandoned (***estoppel***);

d. The benefited party fails to bring suit against the violator within a reasonable time (***laches***); or

e. The ***neighborhood has changed*** so significantly that enforcement would be inequitable.

5. **Termination**
Like other nonpossessory interests, an equitable servitude may be extinguished by: (i) ***written release*** from the benefit holders, (ii) ***merger*** of the benefited and burdened estates, or (iii) ***condemnation*** of the burdened property.

CMR SUMMARY CHART

CHECKLIST OF REQUIREMENTS FOR THE RUNNING OF BENEFITS AND BURDENS

	Covenants		Equitable Servitudes	
	Benefit	Burden	Benefit	Burden
Intent	✓	✓	✓	✓
Notice		✓*		✓
Touch & Concern	✓	✓	✓	✓
Horizontal Privity		✓		
Vertical Privity	✓	✓		

* Under recording acts

F. PARTY WALLS AND COMMON DRIVEWAYS

Courts will treat a wall erected partly on the property of each of two adjoining landowners as belonging to each owner to the extent it rests upon her land. Courts will also imply mutual cross-easements of support, with the result that each party can use the wall or driveway and neither party can unilaterally destroy it.

1. Creation

A ***written agreement*** is required by the Statute of Frauds for the express creation of a party wall or common driveway agreement, but an "irrevocable license" can arise from detrimental reliance on a parol agreement. Party walls and common driveways can also result from ***implication or prescription***.

2. Running of Covenants

If party wall or common driveway owners agree to be mutually responsible for maintaining the wall or driveway, the burdens and benefits of these covenants run to the successive owners of each parcel.

V. ADVERSE POSSESSION

A. IN GENERAL

Title to real property may be acquired by adverse possession. Title by adverse possession results from the operation of the statute of limitations for trespass. If an owner does not, within the statutory period, take action to eject a possessor who claims adversely to the owner, the title vests in the possessor.

B. REQUIREMENTS

1. Running of Statute

The statute of limitations begins to run when the true owner can first bring suit. Filing a suit will not stop the period from running, however; the suit must be pursued to judgment.

2. Open and Notorious Possession

Possession is open and notorious when it is the kind of use the owner would make of the land. The adverse possessor's occupation must be ***sufficiently apparent*** to put the true owner on ***notice*** that a trespass is occurring.

3. Actual and Exclusive Possession

An adverse possessor will gain title only to land she actually occupies. In some cases, actual possession of the entire parcel claimed is not necessary. If an adverse possessor actually occupies a reasonable portion of the parcel, and her occupation is under ***color of title*** to the entire parcel, then she will be deemed to have constructively possessed the ***entire*** parcel, with the same result as if she had actually occupied the entire parcel. "Exclusive" means that the possessor is not sharing with the true owner or the public. Two or more people may obtain title by adverse possession; they take title as tenants in common.

4. Continuous Possession

An adverse claimant's possession must be continuous throughout the statutory period.

Intermittent periods of occupancy are ***not*** sufficient. However, constant use by the claimant is not required as long as possession is of a type that the usual owner would make. Also, there need ***not*** be continuous possession by the same person; an adverse possessor can ***tack*** her own possession onto the periods of adverse possession of her predecessors, but privity is required.

5. **Hostile**
The hostility requirement is satisfied if the possessor enters ***without the owner's permission***. The adverse possessor's state of mind is irrelevant; *i.e.,* it does not matter whether she believes the land to be her own or knows she is trespassing. When possession starts permissively (*e.g.,* by lease), possession does not become adverse until the possessor makes clear to the true owner the fact that she is claiming "hostilely."

a. **Co-Tenants—Ouster Required**
Possession by one co-tenant is usually not adverse to his co-tenants, since each co-tenant has the right to possession of all the property. A co-tenant must oust others or make an explicit declaration that he is claiming exclusive dominion to create adverse possession.

b. **Grantor Stays in Possession—Permission Presumed**
Where a grantor stays in possession of land after her conveyance, she is presumed to be there with permission of the grantee. (Likewise, if a tenant remains in possession after the expiration of the lease, he is presumed to have permission of the landlord.)

C. DISABILITY

The statute of limitations does not begin to run if the true owner was under some disability to sue ***when the cause of action first accrued***. (Typical disabilities: minority, imprisonment, insanity.) Only the disability of the ***owner*** existing at the time the cause of action arose is considered.

D. ADVERSE POSSESSION AND FUTURE INTERESTS

The statute of limitations does not run against a holder of a future interest until the interest becomes possessory.

CMR **Exam Tip** The event or condition giving rise to a grantor's right of entry (*e.g.,* "To Grantee on condition that if alcohol is ever used on the premises, Grantor shall have the right to reenter and retake the premises") does not trigger the statute of limitations for purposes of adverse possession. The statute does not begin to run until the right is ***asserted by the grantor*** because, until that time, the grantee's continued possession of the land is proper.

E. EFFECT OF COVENANTS IN TRUE OWNER'S DEED

If an adverse possessor uses the land in violation of a restrictive covenant in the owner's deed for the limitations period, she takes free of the restriction. If, however, the possessor's use complies with such a covenant, she takes title subject to the restriction.

F. LAND THAT CANNOT BE ADVERSELY POSSESSED

Title to government-owned land and land registered under a Torrens system cannot be acquired by adverse possession.

VI. CONVEYANCING

A. LAND SALE CONTRACTS

Contracts of sale precede most transfers of land.

1. Statute of Frauds Applicable

A contract must be in writing and contain the signature of the party to be charged and the essential terms (*e.g.*, parties, description of land, price). Part performance (*e.g.*, possession, substantial improvements, payment of purchase price) can take a contract out of the statute.

2. Doctrine of Equitable Conversion

Under this doctrine, once a contract is signed, equity regards the buyer as the owner of the real property. The seller's interest (the right to the proceeds of sale) is considered personal property. The bare legal title that remains in the seller is considered to be held in trust for the buyer. The right to possession follows the bare legal title, however; thus, the seller is entitled to possession until closing.

a. Risk of Loss

If property is destroyed (without fault of either party) before closing, the majority rule places the risk on the buyer. Some states, however, have enacted the Uniform Vendor and Purchaser Risk Act, which places the risk on the seller unless the buyer has title or possession at the time of loss.

CMR Exam Tip Even though the risk of loss is on the buyer, if the property is damaged or destroyed, the seller must credit any fire or casualty insurance proceeds he receives against the purchase price the buyer is required to pay.

b. Passage of Title on Death

Under the doctrine of equitable conversion, if a party to a land sale contract dies before the contract is completed, the seller's interest passes as personal property and the buyer's interest passes as real property. Thus, if the seller dies, bare legal title passes to his heirs or devisees, but they must give up title to the buyer at closing. If the buyer dies, his heirs or devisees can demand conveyance of the land at closing.

CMR Exam Tip If the property is specifically devised by will, check to see whether the ademption rules (F.1., *infra*) change the result of the equitable conversion doctrine.

3. Marketable Title

Every contract contains an implied warranty that the seller will provide marketable title (title reasonably free from doubt) at closing. It need not be perfect title, but must be free of questions that present an unreasonable risk of litigation.

a. Defects in Record Chain of Title

Title may be unmarketable because of a defect in the chain of title (*e.g.,* variation in land description in deeds, defectively executed deed, evidence that a prior grantor lacked capacity to convey).

1) Adverse Possession

On the Multistate Bar Exam, title acquired by adverse possession is ***unmarketable***, despite the fact that most recent cases are contra.

2) **Future Interests Held by Unborn or Unascertained Parties**
While most states consider all types of future interests transferable, when a holder of a future interest is unborn or unascertained it is impossible to convey marketable title. Courts will not appoint a guardian ad litem to represent the unborn or unascertained parties for the purposes of conveying land.

b. **Encumbrances**
Generally, mortgages, liens, restrictive covenants, easements, and ***significant*** encroachments render title unmarketable. A beneficial easement, however, if visible or known to the buyer, does not impair the marketability of title.

CMR **Exam Tip** Remember that a seller has the right to satisfy a mortgage or lien at closing, with the proceeds of the sale. Thus, the buyer cannot claim title is unmarketable because it is subject to a mortgage prior to closing, if the closing will result in marketable title.

c. **Zoning Restrictions**
Zoning restrictions do not affect marketability, but an ***existing violation*** of a zoning ordinance does render title unmarketable.

d. **Time of Marketability**
If the seller has agreed to furnish title at the date of closing, the buyer cannot rescind prior to that date on grounds that the seller's title is not marketable. Note that in an installment land contract, the seller need not provide marketable title until the buyer has made his last payment.

CMR **Exam Tip** Avoid answer choices referring to the implied warranty of marketability of title if the closing has already occurred. Once the closing occurs and the deed changes hands, the seller is ***no longer liable*** on this contractual warranty. The seller is then liable only for promises made ***in the deed***.

e. **Remedy If Title Not Marketable**
The buyer must notify the seller that his title is unmarketable and give him reasonable time to cure the defects. If the seller fails to cure the defects, the buyer's remedies include rescission, damages, specific performance with abatement, and a quiet title suit. But if closing occurs, the contract and deed merge, and the seller's liability on the implied contractual warranty ends.

CMR **Exam Tip** Don't be fooled into choosing the answer that lets the seller off the hook for title defects because the contract calls for a quitclaim deed. A quitclaim deed does not in any way affect the warranty to provide marketable title.

4. **Time of Performance**
Courts presume that time is not "of the essence" in real estate contracts. Thus, the closing date is not absolutely binding, and a party late in tendering her own performance can still enforce the contract if she tenders within a reasonable time (*e.g.,* two months) after the closing date.

THE SALE OF LAND

This chart represents the chronological progression from contract through recording.

Parties Enter Into Land Sale Contract →	Time Between Contract and Closing →	Closing →	Recordation →
1. Contract must be in writing (Statute of Frauds). 2. Presumption that time is not of the essence unless so stated. 3. Implied warranty of marketability arises.	1. Buyer investigates Seller's title. If defective, Buyer must notify Seller and give him an opportunity to cure. 2. During this time, the risk of loss is on Buyer.	1. Title passes if deed is validly executed and delivered. Valid execution requires a writing signed by the grantor containing an adequate description of the parcel. Valid delivery requires intent by the grantor to immediately part with legal control. 2. When title passes, the land sale contract is extinguished (along with the implied warranty of marketability). 3. The only basis for a suit by Buyer after title passes is an express covenant, if any, in the deed. There are six possible covenants: Seisin Right to Convey Encumbrances Quiet Enjoyment Warranty Further Assurances	Buyer records deed to protect her title against a subsequent purchaser for value.

a. **When Presumption Overcome**
Time is of the essence if: (i) the ***contract*** so states, (ii) the circumstances indicate that was the parties' ***intent***, or (iii) one party gives the other ***notice*** that time is of the essence.

b. **Liability**
If time is of the essence, a party who fails to tender performance on the closing date is in breach and may not enforce the contract. Even if time is not of the essence, a party who is late in tendering performance is liable for incidental losses.

5. **Tender of Performance**
The buyer's obligation to pay and the seller's obligation to convey are ***concurrent conditions.*** Thus, neither party is in breach until the other tenders performance (even if the closing date passes). If neither party tenders performance, the closing date is extended until one of them does so.

a. **When Party's Tender Excused**
A party need not tender performance if the other party has repudiated the contract or it is impossible (*e.g.,* unmarketable title that cannot be cured) for the other party to perform.

6. **Remedies for Breach of Sales Contract**
The nonbreaching party is entitled to ***damages*** (difference between contract price and market value on date of breach, plus incidental costs) or, because land is unique, ***specific performance***. Note that if the buyer wishes to proceed despite unmarketable title, she can usually get specific performance with an abatement of the purchase price.

a. **Liquidated Damages**
Sales contracts usually require the buyer to deposit "earnest money" with the seller, and provide that if the buyer defaults in performance, the seller may retain this money as liquidated damages. Courts routinely uphold the seller's retention of earnest money if the amount appears to be reasonable in light of the seller's anticipated and actual damages.

7. **Seller's Liabilities for Defective Property**

a. **Warranty of Fitness or Quality—New Construction Only**
Contracts of sale and deeds of real property carry no implied warranty of quality or fitness for purpose. However, a majority of courts now recognize a warranty of fitness or quality in the sale of a new house.

b. **Sale of Existing Land and Buildings—Liability for Defects**
The seller of existing buildings (not new construction) may be liable to the purchaser for defects such as a leaky roof, flooding basement, or termite infestation, on any of several different theories:

1) **Misrepresentation (Fraud)**
The seller is liable for defects about which he knowingly ***or negligently*** made a false statement of fact to the buyer if the ***buyer relied*** on the statement and it ***materially affected*** the value of the property.

2) **Active Concealment**
The seller will be liable for defects, even ***without making any statements***, if he took steps to ***conceal the defects*** (*e.g.,* wallpapering over water damage).

3) **Failure to Disclose**
Most states hold a seller liable for failure to disclose defects if: (i) he ***knows*** or has reason to know of the defect; (ii) the defect is ***not apparent***, and the seller knows the buyer is unlikely to discover it upon ordinary inspection; and (iii) the defect is ***serious*** and would probably cause the buyer to reconsider the purchase if known. Factors increasing the likelihood that liability will be imposed in these cases include whether the property is a personal residence, whether the defect is dangerous, and whether the seller created the defect or made a failed attempt to repair it.

c. **Negligence**
A person may sue a builder for negligence in performing a building contract. Some courts permit the ultimate vendee to sue the builder despite lack of privity.

d. **Disclaimers of Liability**
A general disclaimer in the sales contract (*e.g.,* "property sold as is" or "with all defects") is ***not*** sufficient to overcome a seller's liability for fraud, concealment, or (in the states that recognize it) failure to disclose. If the disclaimer identifies specific types of defects (*e.g.,* "seller is not liable for any defects in the roof"), it will likely be upheld.

8. **Real Estate Brokers**
Real estate brokers are the seller's agents, but should disclose material information about the property if they have actual knowledge of it. Traditionally, agents earned their commissions when they produced a buyer who was ready, willing, and able to purchase the property. Therefore, the commission was owed regardless of whether the deal actually closed. The growing trend, however, is to award the commission only if the sale actually closes or if it fails to close because of the fault of the seller.

B. DEEDS—FORM AND CONTENT
Deeds transfer title to an interest in real property.

1. **Formalities**
A deed must be ***in writing***, be ***signed by the grantor***, and ***reasonably identify the parties and land***. Most other formalities (*e.g.,* seal, consideration, attestation, and acknowledgment) are generally unnecessary.

CMR **Exam Tip** Note that if a deed is delivered with the ***name of the grantee*** left blank, the court presumes the person taking delivery has authority to fill in the name of the grantee. If the person fills in a name, the deed is valid. If, however, the ***land description*** is left blank, the deed is void unless the grantee was explicitly given authority to fill in the description.

2. **Defective Deeds**
A ***void*** deed will be set aside by the court even if the property has passed to a bona fide purchaser, but a ***voidable*** deed will be set aside only if the property has ***not*** passed to a bona fide purchaser. Void deeds include those that are forged, were never delivered, or were obtained by fraud in the factum (*i.e.,* the grantor was deceived and did not realize that she

was executing a deed). Voidable deeds include those executed by minors or incapacitated persons, and those obtained through fraud in the inducement, duress, undue influence, mistake, and breach of fiduciary duty.

CMR **Exam Tip** Watch for a situation in which a joint owner attempts to convey property by forging the signature(s) of the other owner(s). Such a conveyance would be valid as to the interest of the owner whose signature is genuine but void as to the other owner(s). Thus, if one joint tenant executes a deed for the entire property with his own signature and the forged signature of the other joint tenant, the conveyance works a severance; the buyer would hold as a tenant in common with the joint tenant whose signature was forged.

3. Fraudulent Conveyances

Even when a deed complies with the required formalities, it may be set aside by the grantor's creditors if it was made (i) with actual intent to hinder, delay, or defraud any creditor of the grantor; or (ii) without receiving a reasonably equivalent value in exchange for the transfer and the debtor was insolvent or became insolvent as a result of the transfer. However, the deed will not be set aside as against any grantee who took in good faith and paid reasonably equivalent value.

4. Description of Land Conveyed

A description is sufficient if it provides a ***good lead*** to the identity of the property (*e.g.,* "all my land in Stockton"). If it is too indefinite, the grantor retains title (but reformation of the deed is a possible remedy). Parol evidence is generally admissible to resolve patent or latent ambiguities if the description gives a good lead, but may not be admissible where the description is inadequate.

a. Rules of Construction

Where descriptions are inconsistent or conflicting, these methods of description are given the following order of priority: natural monuments (*e.g.,* oak tree), artificial monuments (*e.g.,* stakes, buildings), courses (*e.g.,* angles), distances (*e.g.,* feet, yards), name (*e.g.,* Blackacre), and quantity (*e.g.,* 300 acres).

b. Boundary Cases

Presumptively, title to land passes to the center of a right-of-way or water boundary. This presumption can be rebutted by language in the deed. In variable boundary line cases (*i.e.,* water boundary) the ***slow and imperceptible change*** in the course of a river or stream operates to change the legal boundary; ***accretion*** (slow deposit of soil on land abutting water) belongs to the abutting owner. ***Avulsion*** (sudden change of water-course) does not change ownership rights. Fixed boundaries are not changed by encroachment of water.

c. Reformation of Deeds

A deed will be reformed if it does not represent the parties' agreement because of: (i) mutual mistake; (ii) a scrivener's error; or (iii) a unilateral mistake caused by misrepresentation or other inequitable conduct.

C. DELIVERY AND ACCEPTANCE

A deed is not effective unless it has been delivered and accepted.

CMR **Exam Tip** Remember that a deed to a dead person is void and conveys no title. The fact that the grantor was unaware of the grantee's death is irrelevant. Title remains in the grantor.

1. Delivery—In General

Delivery refers to the grantor's ***intention*** to make a deed ***presently*** effective even if possession is postponed. Delivery may be satisfied by manual delivery, notarized acknowledgment by the grantor, recording, or anything else showing the grantor's intent to deliver. Parol evidence is admissible on the issue of intent to deliver, but not to show delivery was conditional.

CMR **Exam Tip** Title passes upon delivery. It cannot be canceled or taken back. Thus, if a fact pattern has the grantee returning a deed to the grantor, this has no effect; it is not a cancellation or a reconveyance. To return title to the grantor, the grantee must draw up a new deed and deliver it to the grantor.

2. Retention of Interest by Grantor or Conditional Delivery

Retention of control or interest by the grantor (*e.g.,* right to revoke) indicates a lack of intent to pass title. Thus, if a grantor executes a deed but does not deliver it during his lifetime, no title passes. Failure to record a delivered deed does not affect the passage of title even if the parties believe that the deed is ineffective until recording.

a. Express Condition of Grantor's Death

A properly executed and delivered deed that provides that title will not pass until the grantor's death is valid and creates a future interest in the grantee.

b. Conditions Not Contained in Deed

If a deed is absolute on its face but delivered with an oral condition, the condition is disregarded and the delivery is absolute.

3. Where Grantor Gives Deed to Third Party

Here conditional delivery is permissible.

a. Transfer to Third Party with No Conditions

If the grantor gives a deed to a third party with instructions to give it to the grantee, there is a valid delivery. If the grantor fails to give instructions, the validity of the delivery depends on whether the third party could be considered the grantor's agent. If so, there is no delivery.

b. Transfer to Third Party with Conditions (Commercial Transaction)

A valid conditional delivery occurs when a grantor gives a deed to a third party with instructions to give it to the grantee when certain conditions occur (*e.g.,* if grantee pays purchase price before a certain date). Parol evidence is admissible to show that delivery is conditional. (Remember that the rule is contra where the grantor gives the deed ***directly*** to the grantee; *see supra.*)

1) Grantor's Right to Recover Deed

A grantor can revoke only if: (i) the condition has not yet occurred, and (ii) there is no enforceable written contract to convey.

2) Breach of Escrow Conditions

If a grantee wrongfully acquires the deed from the escrow holder prior to performance of the condition, title does not pass and the grantee cannot give good title to a subsequent purchaser.

3) **"Relation Back" Doctrine**
Title usually passes when the condition occurs, but if justice requires it (*e.g.*, grantor dies or becomes incompetent) and there is an enforceable contract to convey, title may "relate back" to the time when the grantor gave the deed to the third party. Rights of intervening bona fide purchasers are protected.

c. **Transfer to Third Party with Conditions (Donative Transaction)**
When a grantor gives a deed to a third party to give to a ***donee*** when a condition occurs, the main issue is whether the grantor can revoke the deed before the condition occurs. Where the condition is not the grantor's death, delivery is irrevocable and creates a springing executory interest in the donee. Where the condition is the grantor's death, most courts follow the same reasoning but some hold deeds revocable unless there is an enforceable contract to convey (*i.e.,* same as true escrow cases, above).

4. **Acceptance**
Acceptance by the grantee is required in order to complete a conveyance. Most states ***presume*** acceptance. Acceptance relates back to the date the deed was delivered into escrow (unless this would defeat the rights of intervening third parties).

5. **Dedication**
Land may be transferred to a public body (*e.g.,* city, county) by dedication. An offer may be made by written or oral statement, submission of a map or plat showing the dedication, or opening the land for public use. To be effective, a dedication must be accepted, which may be done by formal resolution, approval of map or plat, or actual assumption of maintenance or improvements.

D. COVENANTS FOR TITLE AND ESTOPPEL BY DEED

There are three types of deeds used to convey property interests other than leaseholds: the general warranty deed, the special warranty deed, and the quitclaim deed. The difference among these deeds is the scope of title assurance (*i.e.,* covenants for title).

CMR **Exam Tip** Be careful not to confuse covenants for title with real covenants (written promises to do or not do something on the land). They are completely different. Real covenants do not relate to title.

1. **Covenants in General Warranty Deed**

a. **Usual Covenants**
The following are the usual covenants for title contained in a general warranty deed.

1) **Covenant of Seisin**
The grantor covenants that she has the estate she purports to convey. She must have both title and possession at the time of the grant.

2) **Covenant of Right to Convey**
The grantor covenants that she has the authority to make the grant. Title alone will satisfy this covenant.

3) **Covenant Against Encumbrances**
The grantor covenants against the existence of physical (*e.g.,* encroachments) or title (*e.g.,* mortgages) encumbrances.

4) **Covenant for Quiet Enjoyment**
The grantor covenants that the grantee will not be disturbed in possession by a third party's ***lawful*** claim of title.

5) **Covenant of Warranty**
The grantor agrees to defend against reasonable claims of title by a third party, and to compensate the grantee for any loss sustained by the claim of superior title.

CMR **Exam Tip** The covenant for quiet enjoyment and the covenant of warranty are generally considered to be identical covenants for title.

6) **Covenant for Further Assurances**
The grantor promises to perform acts reasonably necessary to perfect title conveyed. (This covenant is ***not*** one of the usual covenants, but is frequently given.)

b. **Breach of the Covenants**
Three of the covenants (seisin, right to convey, encumbrances) are breached, if at all, at the time of conveyance. Quiet enjoyment, warranty, and further assurances are future covenants and are breached only upon disturbance of the grantee's possession.

c. **Damages and Remote Grantees**
If there are successive conveyances by general warranty deed and the last grantee is evicted by lawful claim of title, he may sue ***anyone*** up the line. Some states allow him to recover to the extent of consideration ***received*** by a defendant-covenantor. Other states limit recovery to the ***lesser*** of what he paid or what the defendant-covenantor received.

2. **Statutory Special Warranty Deed**
In many states, use of the word "grant" in a deed creates by implication two limited assurances against acts of the grantor (not her predecessors): (i) that the grantor has not conveyed the same estate or any interest therein to anyone other than the grantee; and (ii) that the estate is free from encumbrances made by the grantor.

3. **Quitclaim Deeds**
A quitclaim deed releases ***whatever interest*** the grantor has. No covenants of title are included or implied.

4. **Estoppel by Deed**
If the grantor purports to convey an estate in property that she does not then own, her subsequent acquisition of the estate will inure to the benefit of the grantee. This doctrine applies where the conveyance was by warranty deed, or where the deed purported to convey a ***particular*** estate. It is not usually applicable to quitclaim deeds.

a. **Rights of Subsequent Purchasers**
Most courts hold that title inures to the benefit of the grantee only as against the grantor. Thus, if the grantor transfers her after-acquired title to a bona fide purchaser for value ("BFP"), the BFP will prevail over the original grantee.

b. **Remedies of Grantee**
The original grantee can accept title or sue for damages for breach of covenant.

E. RECORDING

At common law, if a grantor conveyed the same property twice, the grantee first in time generally prevailed. The recording acts change that outcome under certain circumstances.

1. Recording Acts—In General

Recording acts generally protect all bona fide purchasers from ***secret*** interests previously created and provide a mechanism for "earlier" grantees to give notice through recordation. These statutes require a grantee to record his deed to put subsequent purchasers on notice of his interest. Recording is not essential to the validity of the deed between the grantor and grantee, but can be essential to protect the grantee against a BFP. Proper recordation gives ***constructive notice*** of the first conveyance to everyone, so there can be no subsequent BFPs. Any instrument creating or affecting an interest in land can be recorded, provided it is acknowledged by the grantor before a notary public.

2. Types of Recording Acts

Recording acts are in effect in every state. There are three major types, but under all three, the burden is on the subsequent taker to prove that he qualifies for protection under the statute.

a. **Notice Statutes**
Under a notice statute, a subsequent BFP (person who pays value and has no notice of the prior instrument) prevails over a prior grantee who failed to record. The key is that the subsequent purchaser had ***no actual or constructive notice at the time of the conveyance***.

Example: O conveys to A on January 1. A does not record. O conveys to B on January 15 for valuable consideration. B has no notice of the conveyance to A. B prevails over A. It is irrelevant whether A recorded after January 15 and before B recorded, because B had no notice ***at the time he took***. (This distinguishes notice and race-notice statutes.)

Exam Tip Remember that under a notice statute, the subsequent BFP is protected regardless of whether she records at all.

b. **Race-Notice Statutes**
Under a race-notice statute, a subsequent BFP is protected only if she takes without notice ***and*** records before the prior grantee.

Example: O conveys to A on January 1. A does not record. O conveys to B on January 15 for valuable consideration. B has no notice of the conveyance to A. A records on January 18. B records on January 20. A prevails over B because B did not record first.

c. **Race Statutes**
Under a pure race statute, whoever records first wins. Notice is irrelevant. Only two states have such statutes.

CMR EXAMPLE CHART

RECORDING STATUTES

Type of Statute	Typical Language
Notice	"No conveyance or mortgage of an interest in land is valid against any subsequent purchaser for value without notice thereof, unless it is recorded."
Race	"No conveyance or mortgage of an interest in land is valid against any subsequent purchaser whose conveyance is first recorded."
Race-Notice	"No conveyance or mortgage of an interest in land is valid against any subsequent purchaser for value without notice thereof whose conveyance is first recorded."

3. Who Is Protected by Recording Acts

Only BFPs are protected from the claims of a prior transferee under "notice" and "race-notice" statutes. To be a BFP, a person must be a purchaser, without notice (actual, constructive, or inquiry), and pay valuable consideration.

a. Purchasers

All statutes protect purchasers (of the fee or lesser estate). Mortgagees for value are purchasers. Donees, heirs, and devisees are ***not*** protected because they do not give value.

1) Judgment Creditors

Most states permit a plaintiff who obtains a money judgment to place a judgment lien on the defendant's real property by filing the judgment in the appropriate county office. The majority, however, hold that such a judgment creditor is not protected by the recording statute against a prior unrecorded conveyance by the defendant.

2) Purchaser from Heir

A purchaser from an heir or devisee of the record owner is protected against prior unrecorded conveyances of the record owner (now deceased).

3) Transferees from Bona Fide Purchaser—Shelter Rule

A person who takes ***from*** a BFP will prevail against any interest the transferor-BFP would have prevailed against. This is true even if the transferee had actual notice of a prior unrecorded conveyance. This rule does not, however, help a transferee who previously held title; she cannot "ship through" a BFP to get good title.

b. Without Notice

"Without notice" means the purchaser had no actual, constructive (record), or inquiry notice of a prior conveyance at the time she paid consideration and received the interest.

CMR **Exam Tip** In determining who is a bona fide purchaser for purposes of protection of the recording statutes, remember that the purchaser must be without notice ***at the time of conveyance***. It does not matter if she learns of an adverse claim after the conveyance but before recording.

1) Actual Notice

Actual notice includes knowledge obtained from any source (*e.g.,* newspaper, word-of-mouth).

2) Record Notice—Chain of Title

A subsequent purchaser is charged with notice of only those conveyances that are recorded and appear in the chain of title.

a) "Wild Deeds"

A "wild deed" is a recorded deed that is not connected to the chain of title. It does not impart constructive notice because a subsequent purchaser could not feasibly find it.

Example: A conveys Blackacre to B. B does not record. B conveys it to C, and C records. A conveys Blackacre to D. D does not have notice of C's claim.

b) Deeds Recorded Late

A deed recorded ***after*** the grantor is shown by record to have parted with title through another (subsequent) instrument is not constructive notice in most states (but is in some "race-notice" jurisdictions).

Example: A conveys to B on March 1. A conveys to C on April 1. C records on April 10. B records on April 15. C conveys to D on May 1. If D has no actual or inquiry notice of the A-B deed he will prevail. Most states would hold that B's deed was recorded late and was not in D's chain of title.

c) Deeds Recorded Before Grantor Obtained Title

There is a split of authority on whether a recorded deed, received from a grantor who had no title when conveyed but who afterwards obtains title, imparts constructive notice to subsequent purchasers. Most courts say it does not, and a BFP will win on the grounds that the deed is not in his chain of title. The minority view protects the prior grantee over the BFP on an estoppel by deed theory (*see* D.4., *supra*).

d) Deed in Chain Referring to Instrument Outside Chain

Reference to another instrument in a recorded document that is in the chain of title may impart constructive notice of the instrument referred to—even if it is unrecorded or not itself in the chain of title.

e) **Restrictive Covenants—Deeds from Common Grantor**
Courts are split on whether deeds to adjacent lots or lots in a subdivision, executed by the same grantor and containing restrictions and easements involving the subject lot, are within the chain of title of the subject lot. The better view is that they are not.

3) **Inquiry Notice**
Under certain circumstances, a purchaser is required to make reasonable inquiries. He is charged with knowledge of whatever the inquiry would have revealed, even if in fact he made none. References in recorded instruments to unrecorded transactions, unrecorded instruments in the chain of title (*e.g.,* grantor's title documents are not recorded), and possession unexplained by the record put a purchaser on inquiry notice. The mere fact that a quitclaim deed was used does not charge the purchaser with inquiry notice.

c. **Valuable Consideration**
To be protected by the recording statute, the subsequent grantee must prove that he is a purchaser, not a donee. The consideration need not be adequate, but it must be of some pecuniary value (*i.e.,* love and affection is not valuable consideration). Note that property received as security for an antecedent debt is insufficient.

CMR **Exam Tip** A purchaser is protected by a recording statute only from the time consideration is paid. Thus, even if the deed was delivered and recorded before the consideration was paid, a purchaser will not prevail over deeds recorded subsequently but before the consideration was paid.

4. **Title Search**
In a ***tract index*** jurisdiction, the searcher looks at the page indexed by block and/or lot describing the property and any instruments affecting it. In a ***grantor and grantee index*** jurisdiction, the searcher establishes a chain of title by searching back in time in the grantee-grantor index. From that point, he then searches forward in time in the grantor-grantee index to see if any grantor conveyed an interest to someone outside of the backward chain.

5. **Effect of Recordation**
Recordation gives prospective subsequent grantees constructive notice of the existence and content of recorded instruments. It also raises a presumption of valid delivery and authenticity. However, it does not validate an invalid deed or protect against interests arising by operation of law (*e.g.,* dower, title by adverse possession); to this extent, BFPs are still in jeopardy.

a. **Recorder's Mistakes**
An instrument is considered recorded when filed with the recorder's office, regardless of whether it is thereafter properly indexed. A subsequent purchaser is charged with notice of a misindexed instrument, but has a cause of action against the recorder's office.

b. **Effect of Recording Unacknowledged Instrument**
Since an unacknowledged instrument is not entitled to recordation, it does ***not*** give constructive notice. A subsequent grantee must have actual notice of a deed (*e.g.,*

discover it in a title search) to be bound by it. *Compare*: Where acknowledgment is ***defective*** for reasons ***not apparent on the face*** of the instrument, the better view is that it imparts constructive notice.

F. WILLS—FORM AND CONTENT

Another way of conveying property is by will.

1. Ademption

If property is specifically devised or bequeathed in the testator's will, but the testator no longer owns it at the time of death, the gift fails. Ademption applies only to specific bequests, which can be satisfied only by the delivery of a ***particular item***; they cannot be satisfied by money. A gift of land is always a specific devise. If the testator specifically devises property and then sells or gives away a part of that property, only that portion is adeemed; the remainder passes to the devisee.

a. Land Under Executory Contract

Most state statutes do not apply the ademption doctrine to the proceeds of a contract for sale of land that was executory at the time of the testator's death; *i.e.,* the devisee gets the proceeds in place of the land. These statutes take precedence over the equitable conversion doctrine. In addition, ademption does not apply when the contract is entered into by the representative of an incompetent testator.

b. Other Proceeds Not Subject to Ademption

When property is damaged or destroyed before the testator's death but the casualty insurance proceeds are not paid until after the testator's death, ademption does not usually apply. The beneficiary of the specific bequest takes the insurance proceeds. Similarly, ademption usually does not apply to property condemned by the government where the taking was before death but the condemnation award was paid after death.

2. Exoneration

At common law and in most states, the devisee of specific property is entitled to have the land "exonerated" by the payment of liens and mortgages from the testator's residuary estate. There is a growing trend toward abolition of the exoneration doctrine.

3. Lapse and Anti-Lapse Statutes

A lapse occurs when the beneficiary of a gift in a will ***dies before the testator***. Under the common law, if a lapse occurred, the gift was void. However, nearly all states now have statutes that prevent lapse by permitting the gift to pass to the predeceasing beneficiary's living descendants under certain circumstances. These statutes vary as to the scope of beneficiaries covered by the statute.

a. Degree of Relationship to Testator

Many of the anti-lapse statutes apply only when the named beneficiary is a descendant of the testator. Others apply if the beneficiary is more remotely related, such as a descendant of the testator's grandparent. Others apply to any relative, and still others apply to any beneficiary at all.

1) Descendants Are Substitutes

The anti-lapse statute does not save the gift for the predeceasing beneficiary's estate; rather it substitutes the beneficiary's descendants for the beneficiary. Thus, property will never pass under the anti-lapse statute to a predeceasing beneficiary's spouse.

b. **Inapplicable If Beneficiary Dead When Will Executed**
If the beneficiary is already dead when the will is executed, the anti-lapse statute usually does not apply, and the gift will lapse and fail.

c. **Application to Class Gifts**
If a class member within the coverage of an anti-lapse statute predeceases the testator leaving surviving issue, the statute will apply and the issue will take the deceased class member's share of the gift.

d. **Anti-Lapse Statute Does Not Apply If Contrary Will Provision**
The anti-lapse statute does not apply if there is a contrary will provision; *i.e.*, the gift is contingent on the beneficiary's surviving the testator.

G. CROPS (EMBLEMENTS)

Generally, the conveyance of land includes all crops growing on it. However, exceptions exist for (i) crops that have already been harvested or severed from the land, and (ii) crops planted by a tenant during the term of the tenancy. For title to crops to remain in a tenant, the tenancy must have been of ***uncertain duration*** and have terminated ***without fault*** on the part of the tenant.

VII. SECURITY INTERESTS IN REAL ESTATE

A. TYPES OF SECURITY INTERESTS

Of the five important types of security interests in real estate, the first three are the most important.

1. **Mortgage**
The debtor/notemaker is the mortgagor. The lender is the mortgagee. On default, the lender can realize on the mortgaged real estate only by having a judicial foreclosure sale conducted by the sheriff.

2. **Deed of Trust**
The debtor/notemaker is the trustor. He gives a deed of trust to a third-party trustee, who is usually closely connected to the lender (the beneficiary). On default the lender instructs the trustee to foreclose the deed of trust by sale.

3. **Installment Land Contract**
An installment purchaser obtains legal title only when the full contract price has been paid off. Forfeiture clauses, allowing the vendor upon default to cancel the contract, retake possession, and retain all money paid, are common.

4. **Absolute Deed**
An absolute deed, if given for security purposes, can be treated by the court as an "equitable" mortgage to be treated as any other mortgage (*i.e.*, creditor must foreclose by judicial action).

5. **Sale-Leaseback**
A landowner may sell her property for cash and then lease it back from the purchaser for a long period of time. Like an absolute deed, this may be treated as a disguised mortgage.

B. TRANSFERS BY MORTGAGEE AND MORTGAGOR

All parties to a mortgage or deed of trust may transfer their interests. The note and mortgage must pass to the ***same person*** for the transfer to be complete.

1. Transfer by Mortgagee

a. Transfer of Mortgage Without Note

Some states hold that the transfer of the mortgage automatically transfers the note as well, unless the mortgagee-transferor expressly reserves the rights to the note. In these states, the transferee of the mortgage can then file an equitable action and compel a transfer of the note as well. Other states hold that, since the note is the principal evidence of the debt, a transfer of the mortgage without the note is void.

b. Transfer of Note Without Mortgage

The ***note can be transferred without the mortgage***, but the mortgage will automatically follow the properly transferred note, unless the mortgagee-transferee expressly reserves the rights to the mortgage. No separate written assignment of the mortgage is necessary.

1) **Methods of Transferring the Note**
The note may be transferred either by endorsing it and delivering it to the transferee, or by a separate document of assignment. Only if the endorsement and delivery method is used can the transferee become a ***holder in due course***. To be a holder in due course of the note, the following requirements must be met:

a) The note must be ***negotiable in form*** (payable to "bearer" or "to the order of" the named payee, with a promise to pay a sum certain, and no other promises).

b) The original note must be ***endorsed*** and signed by the named payee.

c) The original note must be ***delivered*** to the transferee.

d) The transferee must take the note in ***good faith*** (no notice that it is overdue, has been dishonored, is subject to any defense by the maker) and must pay ***value*** for it.

2) **Benefits of Holder in Due Course Status**
A holder in due course takes the note free of any personal defenses of the maker (*e.g.*, failure of consideration, fraud in the inducement, waiver, estoppel, and payment), but is still subject to real defenses (*e.g.*, infancy, other incapacity, duress, illegality, fraud in the execution, forgery, discharge in insolvency, and any other insolvency).

Exam Tip Remember that if possession of the note has been transferred by the original mortgagee, any payment to that mortgagee will not count. The holder of the note can still

demand payment—even if the mortgagor had no notice of the transfer. For example, X borrows $10,000 from Y, giving Y a note secured by a mortgage on Farmacre. Later Y assigns the note to Z, but does not tell X. X pays the $10,000 to Y. Z may still demand payment of the $10,000, and may foreclose the mortgage on Farmacre if payment is not forthcoming. The payment to Y is no defense.

2. Transfer by Mortgagor—Grantee Takes Subject to Mortgage

A grantee of mortgaged property takes subject to the mortgage.

a. Assumption

If the grantee signs an assumption agreement, he becomes primarily liable to the lender, while the original mortgagor is secondarily liable as a surety. If no assumption agreement is signed, the grantee is not personally liable on the loan, and the original mortgagor remains primarily and personally liable. However, if the grantee does not pay, the loan may be foreclosed, wiping out the grantee's investment.

CMR **Exam Tip** Remember that once a grantee has assumed a mortgage, any modification of the obligation by the grantee and mortgagee discharges the original mortgagor of all liability.

b. Due-on-Sale Clauses

Due-on-sale clauses, which appear in most modern mortgages, allow the lender to demand full payment of the loan if the mortgagor transfers any interest in the property without the lender's consent.

C. POSSESSION BEFORE FORECLOSURE

When a mortgagor defaults on his debt, the mortgagee can foreclose on the mortgage. A mortgagee may wish to take possession of the property, or begin receiving the rents from the property, before foreclosure.

1. Theories of Title

The mortgagee may have a right to take possession before foreclosure, depending on the theory the state follows. Most states follow either the title or the lien theory.

a. The Lien Theory

According to the lien theory, the mortgagee is considered the ***holder of a security interest only*** and the mortgagor is deemed the owner of the land until foreclosure. The mortgagee may not have possession before foreclosure.

b. The Title Theory

Under the title theory, ***legal title is in the mortgagee*** until the mortgage has been satisfied or foreclosed, and the mortgagee is entitled to possession upon demand at any time.

c. The Intermediate Theory

In the few states that follow the intermediate theory, legal title is in the mortgagor until default, and upon default, ***legal title is in the mortgagee***. The mortgagee may demand possession when a default occurs. There is little practical difference between this theory and the title theory.

2. **Mortgagor Consent and Abandonment**
The mortgagee may take possession if the mortgagor gives consent to do so, or if the mortgagor abandons the property.

3. **Risks of Mortgagee in Possession**
Most mortgagees do not wish to take possession because of the risks of liability. These risks involve the duty to account for rents, the duty to manage the property in a prudent manner, and potential tort liability for those injured on the property.

4. **Receiverships**
Most mortgagees attempt to intercept the rents before foreclosure by getting a receiver appointed by the court to manage the property. Courts will generally appoint receivers for rental property upon showing: (i) that waste is occurring; (ii) that the value of the property is inadequate to secure the debt; and (iii) that the mortgagor is insolvent.

D. FORECLOSURE

Almost all states require foreclosure by sale, under which the property is sold to satisfy the debt in whole or part. While all states allow judicial sale, some states allow nonjudicial sale under a power of sale (usually with respect to deeds of trust). Foreclosure sales are usually conducted by auction, and the lender is permitted to bid at the sale.

1. **Redemption**

a. **Redemption in Equity**
At ***any time prior to the foreclosure sale***, the mortgagor may redeem the property by paying the amount due. If the note or mortgage contains an acceleration clause, the full balance of the note or mortgage must be paid to redeem. This right cannot be waived in the mortgage itself.

b. **Statutory Redemption**
About half the states allow the mortgagor to redeem the property for some fixed period (*e.g.*, six months) ***after the foreclosure sale*** has occurred.

2. **Priorities**
A mortgage's priority is usually determined by the time it was placed on the property. Foreclosure does not destroy any interests senior to the interest being foreclosed. It generally destroys all junior interests, but failure to include a junior interest holder in a foreclosure action results in preservation of that party's interest.

a. **Modification of Priority**
Generally, priority among mortgages follows the chronological order in which they were placed on the property. This priority may, however, be changed by: (i) the operation of the recording statute if a ***prior mortgagee fails to record***; (ii) a ***subordination agreement*** between a senior and junior mortgagee; (iii) a ***purchase money mortgage***; (iv) the ***modification of a senior mortgage*** (junior mortgage has priority over the modification); or (v) the ***granting of optional future advances*** by a mortgagee with notice of a junior lien (junior lien has priority over advances).

REAL ESTATE FINANCING AND FORECLOSURE

Financing

Buyer finances purchase of land using the land as collateral. Usually done by giving lender a mortgage on the property, although it could be done with deed of trust, installment land contract, absolute deed, or sale-leaseback.

↓

Default

Mortgagor-borrower defaults. Mortgagee has right to foreclose. Up until the foreclosure sale, borrower may redeem by paying off mortgage and accrued interest. (Equitable redemption)

↓

Foreclosure

Foreclosure must be by sale, usually judicial sale.

Proceeds distributed according to priorities of security interests.

↓

Post-Foreclosure

If proceeds of sale insufficient to satisfy debt, mortgagee can bring personal action against borrower for deficiency.

About one-half of states give borrower a right to redeem for a fixed period (*e.g.,* six months) after foreclosure by paying sale price. (Statutory redemption)

b. **Purchase Money Mortgages**
A purchase money mortgage ("PMM") is a mortgage given in exchange for funds used to purchase the property. PMMs are given either to the seller as part of the purchase price or to a third-party lender. PMMs have priority over non-PMMs executed at about the same time even if the non-PMM was recorded first. As between two PMMs, a seller's mortgage has priority over a third-party's. If there are two third-party PMMs, priority is determined by chronological order. Usually two PMMs have notice of the other's existence; thus, the recording acts are of no use in determining priority.

3. **Proceeds of Sale**
Proceeds are applied first to the expenses of the sale, attorneys' fees, and court costs; then to pay the principal and accrued interest on the foreclosed loan; next to pay off any other junior interests in the order of their priority; and finally to the mortgagor.

4. **Deficiency Judgments**
If the proceeds are insufficient to satisfy the mortgage debt, the mortgagee retains a personal cause of action against the mortgagor for the deficiency.

E. INSTALLMENT LAND CONTRACTS

Most installment contracts provide for forfeiture rather than foreclosure as the vendor's remedy for default, but courts use the following theories to avoid that harsh result:

1. **Equity of Redemption**
Several states give the contract purchaser a grace period to pay the accelerated full balance of the contract and keep the land after default.

2. **Restitution**
A number of decisions, while granting forfeiture, have required the vendor to refund to the purchaser any amount by which his payments exceed the vendor's damages.

3. **Treat as a Mortgage**
A few states treat installment contracts as mortgages, thus requiring a judicial foreclosure sale.

4. **Waiver**
Many cases hold that a vendor's pattern of accepting late payments constitutes a waiver of the right of strict performance. To reinstate strict performance, the vendor must send the purchaser a notice of his intention to do so and must allow a reasonable time for the purchaser to make up any late payments.

5. **Election of Remedies**
The vendor must choose only one remedy (damages or specific performance) and forgo all others.

VIII. RIGHTS INCIDENTAL TO OWNERSHIP OF LAND (NATURAL RIGHTS)

A. IN GENERAL

An owner of real property has the exclusive right to use and possess the surface, the airspace, and the soil of the property.

B. RIGHTS TO LATERAL AND SUBJACENT SUPPORT OF LAND

1. Lateral Support

Ownership of land includes the right to have the land supported in its ***natural state*** by adjoining land.

a. Support of Land in Natural State

A landowner is ***strictly liable*** if his excavation causes adjacent land to subside (*i.e.,* slip or cave-in).

b. Support of Land with Buildings

An adjacent landowner is strictly liable for damage to buildings caused by excavation only if it is shown that the land would have collapsed in its natural state. Otherwise, he is liable for such damage only if his excavation was done negligently.

2. Subjacent Support

An underground occupant of land (*e.g.*, a mining company) must support the surface and buildings existing on the date the subjacent estate was created. Liability for subsequently erected buildings requires negligence.

C. WATER RIGHTS

Different rules apply to watercourses, ground water, and surface waters.

1. Watercourses (Streams, Rivers, and Lakes)

There are two major systems for determining allocation of water in watercourses: the riparian doctrine and the prior appropriation doctrine.

a. Riparian Doctrine

Under this doctrine, the water belongs to those who own the land bordering the watercourse. Riparian rights attach to all contiguous tracts held by the same owner as long as one abuts the water. Riparian owners can use water only in connection with the riparian parcel.

1) Natural Flow Theory

Under this theory, a riparian owner's use resulting in substantial or material diminution of the water's quantity, quality, or velocity is enjoinable.

2) Reasonable Use Theory

Under this theory, which is the most common, all riparians share the right of "reasonable use" of the water (*i.e.*, one owner's use is not enjoinable unless it substantially interferes with the use of other riparian owners). In determining "reasonable" use, courts balance the utility of the owner's use against the gravity of the harm. Six factors are helpful in making this determination: alteration of flow; purpose of use; pollution; extent of use; destination of water taken; and miscellaneous conduct that may give rise to litigation.

3) Natural vs. Artificial Use

Under either theory, natural uses (human uses, such as consumption, gardening) prevail over artificial uses (irrigation, manufacturing).

b. **Prior Appropriation Doctrine**
Under this doctrine, individuals acquire rights by actual use. Appropriative rights are determined by priority of beneficial use. If there is a decrease in flow, priority is accorded in terms of time of appropriation. An appropriative right can be lost by abandonment.

2. **Ground Water (Percolating Water)**
Four doctrines determine rights in diffuse underground water recovered through wells.

a. **Absolute Ownership Doctrine**
This doctrine is followed by about 12 eastern states. The owner of overlying land can take all the water she wishes, for any purpose, including export.

b. **Reasonable Use Doctrine**
About 25 states follow this doctrine. It is like absolute ownership, but exporting is allowed only if it does not harm other owners who have rights in the same aquifer.

c. **Correlative Rights Doctrine**
In California, owners of overlying land own the underground water basin as joint tenants, and each is allowed a reasonable amount for his own use.

d. **Appropriative Rights Doctrine**
This doctrine is followed in some western states. Priority of use (not ownership of overlying land) is determinative.

3. **Surface Waters**
A landowner can use surface water (water without a channel that passes over land, such as rainfall, seepage, etc.) within her boundaries for any purpose she desires. Questions on surface water usually concern liability for changing natural flow by dikes, drains, etc. Liability depends on which theory the state follows:

a. **Natural Flow (Civil Law) Theory**
Under this theory, followed by half of the states, owners cannot alter natural drainage patterns. This rule has been "softened" in most states to allow "reasonable changes."

b. **Common Enemy Theory**
Under this theory, followed by most of the other states, an owner can take any protective measures to get rid of the water (*e.g.,* dikes). The rule has been modified by many courts to prohibit unnecessary damage to others' lands.

c. **Reasonable Use Theory**
There is a growing trend to apply this theory, which involves balancing the utility of the use against the gravity of the harm.

Exam Tip Remember that the above theories apply to redirecting surface water. A landowner can ***capture*** (*e.g.,* by a dam or in barrels) as much surface water as he wishes. Surface water can be diverted to any purpose on or off the land. Owners below have no cause of action unless the diversion was malicious.

D. RIGHT IN AIRSPACE

The right to airspace above a parcel is not exclusive, but the owner is entitled to freedom from excessive noise.

E. RIGHT TO EXCLUDE—REMEDIES OF POSSESSOR

The possessor of real property has the right to exclude others. His remedies for invasions include actions for:

1. ***Trespass*** (land invaded by ***tangible*** physical object);

2. ***Private nuisance*** (land invaded by ***intangibles*** such as odors or noise);

3. ***Continuing trespass*** (land repeatedly invaded by trespasser); and

4. ***Ejectment or unlawful detainer*** to remove a trespasser or tenant. This action can be joined with a demand for money damages.

IX. COOPERATIVES, CONDOMINIUMS, AND ZONING

A. COOPERATIVES

In a cooperative, title to the land and buildings is held by a corporation that leases individual apartments to its shareholders. Because of their economic interdependence and because the individual owners are regarded as tenants, a direct restraint on the alienation of an individual interest is valid.

B. CONDOMINIUMS

In a condominium, each owner owns the interior of his individual unit plus an undivided interest in the exterior and common areas. Since condominium unit ownership is treated as fee ownership, the ordinary rules against restraints on alienation apply.

C. ZONING

The state may enact statutes to reasonably control the use of land for the protection of the ***health, safety, morals, and welfare*** of its citizens. The zoning power is based on the state's police power and is limited by the Due Process and Equal Protection Clauses of the Fourteenth Amendment, and the "no taking without just compensation" clause of the Fifth Amendment. Cities and counties can exercise zoning power only if so authorized by a state enabling act. These terms should be remembered:

1. Nonconforming Use

A use that exists at the time of passage of a zoning act that does not conform to the statute cannot be eliminated at once.

2. Special Use Permit

A special use permit is one that must be obtained even though the zoning is proper for the intended use. It is often required for hospitals, funeral homes, drive-in businesses, etc.

3. **Variance**
A variance is a departure from the literal restrictions of a zoning ordinance granted by administrative action.

CMR **Exam Tip** Zoning ordinances are generally invalid if they have no reasonable relation to public welfare, are too restrictive, are discriminatory as to a particular parcel, are beyond the grant of authority, violate due process, or are racially discriminatory.

4. **Unconstitutional Takings and Exactions**
A zoning ordinance may so reduce the value of real property that it constitutes a taking under the Fifth and Fourteenth Amendments. If the ordinance constitutes a taking, the local government must pay damages to the landowner equal to the value reduction. If the ordinance regulates activity that would be considered a nuisance under common law principles, it will not be a taking even if it leaves the land with no economic value.

a. **Denial of *All* Economic Value—Taking**
A regulation that deprives the owner of ***all*** economic use of his land constitutes a taking (unless the use was prohibited by nuisance or property law when the owner acquired the property).

b. **Denial of *Nearly All* Economic Value—Balancing Test**
If a regulation leaves property with ***very little economic value***, to determine if there was a taking the court will balance: (i) the ***social goals*** of the regulation, (ii) the ***diminution in value*** of the property, and (iii) the owner's ***reasonable expectations*** for use of the property.

c. **Unconstitutional Exactions**
Local governments often demand, in exchange for zoning approval for a new project, that the landowner give up some land for a public purpose, such as street widening. However, such demands are unconstitutional under the Fifth and Fourteenth Amendments unless the government proves: (i) the government demands are ***rationally connected*** to an additional burden the project will place on public facilities or rights; and (ii) the dedication is reasonably related in ***nature*** and ***extent*** to the impact of the proposed development.

d. **Remedy**
If a regulation constitutes a taking, the government will be required either to compensate the owner for the property or to terminate the regulation and pay the owner damages for the temporary taking.

TORTS

TABLE OF CONTENTS

I. INTENTIONAL TORTS 1
- A. PRIMA FACIE CASE 1
  - 1. Act by Defendant 1
  - 2. Intent 1
  - 3. Causation 1
- B. PRIMA FACIE CASE—INTENTIONAL TORTS TO THE PERSON 1
  - 1. Battery 2
  - 2. Assault 2
  - 3. False Imprisonment 3
  - 4. Intentional Infliction of Emotional Distress 3
- C. PRIMA FACIE CASE—INTENTIONAL TORTS TO PROPERTY 4
  - 1. Trespass to Land 4
  - 2. Trespass to Chattels 5
  - 3. Conversion 5
- D. DEFENSES TO INTENTIONAL TORTS 6
  - 1. Consent 6
  - 2. Self-Defense, Defense of Others, and Defense of Property 7
  - 3. Privilege of Arrest 10
  - 4. Necessity 11
  - 5. Discipline 11

II. HARM TO ECONOMIC AND DIGNITARY INTERESTS 12
- A. DEFAMATION 12
  - 1. Defamatory Language 12
  - 2. "Of or Concerning" Plaintiff 12
  - 3. Publication 14
  - 4. Damage to Plaintiff's Reputation 14
  - 5. First Amendment Concerns 15
  - 6. Defenses to Defamation 17
  - 7. Mitigating Factors 18
- B. INVASION OF RIGHT TO PRIVACY 18
  - 1. Four Branches 18
  - 2. Causation 19
  - 3. Proof of Special Damages Unnecessary 19
  - 4. Defenses 19
  - 5. Right of Privacy—Miscellaneous 19
- C. MISREPRESENTATION 19
  - 1. Intentional Misrepresentation (Fraud, Deceit) 19
  - 2. Negligent Misrepresentation 20
- D. WRONGFUL INSTITUTION OF LEGAL PROCEEDINGS 20
  - 1. Malicious Prosecution 20
  - 2. Abuse of Process 20
- E. INTERFERENCE WITH BUSINESS RELATIONS 20
  - 1. Privileges 20

III. NEGLIGENCE 21
A. PRIMA FACIE CASE 21
B. DUTY OF CARE 21
1. Foreseeable/Unforeseeable Plaintiffs 21
2. Specific Situations 21
3. Standards of Care 22
4. Duty Regarding Negligent Infliction of Emotional Distress 26
5. Affirmative Duties to Act 27
C. BREACH OF DUTY 27
1. Custom or Usage 27
2. Violation of Statute 27
3. Res Ipsa Loquitur 27
D. CAUSATION 28
1. Actual Cause (Causation in Fact) 28
2. Proximate Cause (Legal Causation) 29
E. DAMAGES 31
1. Personal Injury 31
2. Property Damage 31
3. Punitive Damages 31
4. Nonrecoverable Items 31
5. Duty to Mitigate 31
6. Collateral Source Rule 31
F. DEFENSES TO NEGLIGENCE 31
1. Contributory Negligence 31
2. Assumption of Risk 32
3. Comparative Negligence 32

IV. LIABILITY WITHOUT FAULT (STRICT LIABILITY) 33
A. PRIMA FACIE CASE 33
B. LIABILITY FOR ANIMALS 34
1. Trespassing Animals 34
2. Personal Injuries 34
C. ULTRAHAZARDOUS OR ABNORMALLY DANGEROUS ACTIVITIES 34
D. EXTENT OF LIABILITY 34
1. Scope of Duty Owed 34
2. Defenses 34

V. PRODUCTS LIABILITY 35
A. BASIC PRINCIPLES 35
1. Theories of Liability 35
2. Common Elements 35
B. LIABILITY BASED ON INTENT 36
1. Who Can Sue? 36
2. Damages 36
3. Defenses 36
C. LIABILITY BASED ON NEGLIGENCE 36
1. Duty of Care 36
2. Breach of Duty 37
3. Causation 37

4. Nature of Damages Recoverable 37
5. Defenses 37
D. LIABILITY BASED ON STRICT TORT LIABILITY 37
1. Duty 37
2. Breach of Duty 38
3. Causation 38
4. Nature of Damages Recoverable 38
5. Defenses 38
6. Disclaimers Ineffective 38
E. IMPLIED WARRANTIES OF MERCHANTABILITY AND FITNESS 38
1. Who Can Sue? 38
2. What Constitutes Breach? 38
3. Causation 39
4. Damages 39
5. Defenses 39
6. Effect of Disclaimers 39
F. REPRESENTATION THEORIES 39
1. Express Warranty 39
2. Misrepresentation of Fact 39

VI. NUISANCE 41
A. PRIVATE NUISANCE 41
1. Substantial Interference 41
2. Unreasonable Interference 41
3. Trespass to Land Distinguished 41
B. PUBLIC NUISANCE 41
C. REMEDIES 42
1. Damages 42
2. Injunctive Relief 42
3. Abatement by Self-Help 42
D. DEFENSES 42
1. Legislative Authority 42
2. Conduct of Others 42
3. Contributory Negligence 42
4. Coming to the Nuisance 42

VII. GENERAL CONSIDERATIONS FOR ALL TORT CASES 42
A. VICARIOUS LIABILITY 42
1. Doctrine of Respondeat Superior 43
2. Independent Contractor Situations 43
3. Partners and Joint Venturers 43
4. Automobile Owner for Driver 43
5. Bailor for Bailee 44
6. Parent for Child 44
7. Tavernkeepers 44
B. PARTIES—MULTIPLE DEFENDANT ISSUES 45
1. Joint and Several Liability 45
2. Satisfaction and Release 46
3. Contribution and Indemnity 46

C. **SURVIVAL AND WRONGFUL DEATH** 47
   1. **Survival of Tort Actions** 47
   2. **Wrongful Death** 47
D. **TORTIOUS INTERFERENCES WITH FAMILY RELATIONSHIPS** 47
   1. **Husband-Wife** 47
   2. **Parent-Child** 47
   3. **Nature of Action** 47
E. **TORT IMMUNITIES** 47
   1. **Intra-Family Tort Immunities** 48
   2. **Governmental Tort Immunity** 48
   3. **Charitable Immunity** 48

TORTS

I. INTENTIONAL TORTS

A. PRIMA FACIE CASE

To establish a prima facie case of intentional tort, plaintiff must prove:

1. Act by Defendant

The act required is a ***volitional movement by*** defendant.

2. Intent

Intent may be either (i) ***specific*** (the goal in acting is to bring about specific consequences) or (ii) ***general*** (the actor knows with "substantial certainty" that these consequences will result).

a. Transferred Intent

1) General Rule

The transferred intent doctrine applies where the defendant intends to commit a tort against one person but instead (i) commits a different tort against that person, (ii) commits the same tort as intended but against a different person, or (iii) commits a different tort against a different person. In such cases, the intent to commit a certain tort against one person is transferred to the tort actually committed or to the person actually injured for purposes of establishing a prima facie case.

2) Limitations on Use of Transferred Intent

Transferred intent may be invoked only where both the tort intended and the tort that results are one of the following:

a) Assault;

b) Battery;

c) False imprisonment;

d) Trespass to land; or

e) Trespass to chattels.

CMR Exam Tip Everyone is "capable" of intent. Incapacity is not a good defense. Thus, young children and persons who are mentally incompetent will be liable for their intentional torts.

3. Causation

The result must have been legally caused by defendant's act or something set in motion by him. Causation is satisfied if defendant's conduct was a ***substantial factor*** in bringing about the injury.

B. PRIMA FACIE CASE—INTENTIONAL TORTS TO THE PERSON

1. Battery
Elements of the prima facie case:

(i) ***Harmful*** or ***offensive contact***;

(ii) To plaintiff's person;

(iii) Intent; and

(iv) Causation.

a. Harmful or Offensive Contact

1) Judged by Reasonable Person Standard
Harmfulness and offensiveness are judged by a reasonable person standard.

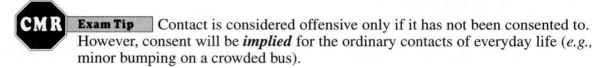

CMR Exam Tip Contact is considered offensive only if it has not been consented to. However, consent will be ***implied*** for the ordinary contacts of everyday life (*e.g.,* minor bumping on a crowded bus).

2) Direct or Indirect Contact
Contact can be direct (*e.g.,* striking plaintiff) or indirect (*e.g.,* setting a trap for plaintiff to fall into).

b. Plaintiff's Person
Plaintiff's person includes anything connected to the plaintiff (*e.g.,* clothing or a purse).

2. Assault
Elements of the prima facie case:

(i) An act by defendant creating a ***reasonable apprehension*** in plaintiff;

(ii) Of ***immediate harmful or offensive contact*** to plaintiff's person;

(iii) Intent; and

(iv) Causation.

a. Distinguish Fear
Apprehension should not be confused with fear or intimidation (*e.g.,* a weakling can cause apprehension and thus assault a bully).

b. Apparent Ability Sufficient
If defendant has the ***apparent ability*** to commit a battery, this will be enough to cause a reasonable apprehension.

c. Effect of Words
Words alone are not sufficient. For the defendant to be liable, the words must be coupled

with conduct. However, words can ***negate*** reasonable apprehension (*e.g.,* the defendant shakes her fist but states that she is not going to strike the plaintiff).

d. Requirement of Immediacy
Plaintiff must be apprehensive that she is about to become the victim of an immediate battery.

3. False Imprisonment
Elements of the prima facie case:

(i) An act or omission on the part of defendant that ***confines or restrains*** plaintiff;

(ii) To a ***bounded area***;

(iii) Intent; and

(iv) Causation.

a. Sufficient Methods of Confinement or Restraint
Sufficient acts of restraint include: (i) physical barriers, (ii) physical force, (iii) threats of force, (iv) failure to release, and (v) invalid use of legal authority.

b. Insufficient Methods of Confinement or Restraint
Insufficient acts of restraint include: (i) moral pressure and (ii) future threats.

c. Time of Confinement
It is irrelevant how short the period of the confinement is.

d. Awareness of Confinement
Plaintiff must ***know*** of the confinement or be ***harmed*** by it.

e. What Is a Bounded Area?
For an area to be "bounded," freedom of movement must be limited in all directions. There must be no ***reasonable*** means of escape ***known*** to plaintiff.

4. Intentional Infliction of Emotional Distress
Elements of the prima facie case:

(i) An act by defendant amounting to ***extreme and outrageous conduct***;

(ii) Intent or recklessness;

(iii) Causation; and

(iv) Damages—***severe*** emotional distress.

a. Extreme and Outrageous Conduct
This is conduct that transcends all bounds of decency. Conduct that is not normally outrageous may become so if:

1) It is continuous in nature;

2) It is directed toward a certain type of plaintiff (children, elderly persons, pregnant women, supersensitive adults if the sensitivities are known to defendant); or

3) It is committed by a certain type of defendant (common carriers or innkeepers may be liable even for mere "gross insults").

b. Requisite Intent
Unlike for other intentional torts, ***recklessness*** as to the effect of defendant's conduct will satisfy the intent requirement.

c. Damages
Actual damages (severe emotional distress), not nominal damages, are required. Proof of physical injury is not required. The more outrageous the conduct, the less proof of damages is required.

CMR **Exam Tip** Intentional infliction of emotional distress is the only intentional tort to the person that requires damages.

d. Causation in Bystander Cases
When the defendant intentionally causes physical harm to a third person and the plaintiff suffers severe emotional distress because of it, the plaintiff may recover by showing ***either*** the prima facie case elements of emotional distress ***or*** that (i) she was present when the injury occurred, (ii) she is a close relative of the injured person, and (iii) the defendant knew facts (i) and (ii).

CMR **Exam Tip** Intentional infliction of emotional distress is a fallback tort position. Thus, if another alternative in your exam question is a tort that will also allow plaintiff to recover, it should be chosen over this alternative.

C. PRIMA FACIE CASE—INTENTIONAL TORTS TO PROPERTY

1. Trespass to Land
Elements of the prima facie case:

(i) ***Physical invasion*** of plaintiff's ***real property***;

(ii) Intent; and

(iii) Causation.

a. Physical Invasion
The invasion may be by a person or object (*e.g.,* throwing a baseball onto plaintiff's land is a trespass). If ***intangible matter*** (*e.g.,* vibrations or odor) enters, the plaintiff may have a case for nuisance.

b. Real Property
Real property includes not only the surface, but also airspace and subterranean space for a reasonable distance.

c. Intent
Defendant need intend only to enter on that particular piece of land (he need not know that the land belonged to another).

d. Potential Plaintiffs
Anyone in actual or constructive possession of the land may maintain this action.

2. Trespass to Chattels
Elements of the prima facie case:

(i) An act by defendant that ***interferes with plaintiff's right of possession*** in a chattel;

(ii) Intent;

(iii) Causation; and

(iv) Damages.

a. Two Types of Interference
The interference may either be an intermeddling (*i.e.,* directly ***damaging*** the chattel) or a dispossession (*i.e.,* depriving plaintiff of his lawful right of ***possession*** of the chattel).

b. Damages
Actual damages—not necessarily to the chattel, but at least to a possessory right—are required.

3. Conversion
Elements of the prima facie case:

(i) An act by defendant that ***interferes with plaintiff's right of possession*** in a chattel;

(ii) The interference is ***so serious*** that it warrants requiring defendant to pay the chattel's full value;

(iii) Intent; and

(iv) Causation.

a. Acts of Conversion
Acts of conversion include wrongful acquisition (theft), wrongful transfer, wrongful detention, and substantially changing, severely damaging, or misusing a chattel.

b. Seriousness of Interference
The longer the withholding period and the more extensive the use, the more likely it is to be conversion. A less serious interference is trespass to chattels.

c. Subject Matter of Conversion
Only tangible personal property and intangibles that have been reduced to physical form (*e.g.,* a promissory note) are subject to conversion.

d. Potential Plaintiffs
Anyone with possession or the immediate right to possession of the chattel may maintain an action for conversion.

e. Remedies
Plaintiff may recover ***damages*** (fair market value at the time of conversion) ***or possession*** (replevin).

CMR COMPARISON CHART

TRESPASS TO CHATTELS VS. CONVERSION

	Trespass to Chattels	Conversion
Act by Defendant	An interference with plaintiff's right of possession of chattel (either intermeddling or dispossession)	An interference with plaintiff's right of possession so ***serious*** as to warrant that defendant pay the chattel's full value
Intent	Intent to do the act that brings about the interference	Intent to do the act that brings about the interference
Remedy	Recovery of actual damages from harm to chattel or loss of use (if dispossession, damages based on rental value)	Damage award of fair market value of chattel at time of conversion (*i.e.,* forced sale of chattel). May instead recover chattel (replevin)

D. DEFENSES TO INTENTIONAL TORTS

1. Consent
Plaintiff's consent to defendant's conduct is a defense, but the majority view is that one ***cannot*** consent to a ***criminal act***. Any consent fact pattern raises two inquiries:

(i) Was there a valid consent (*e.g.,* no fraud)?

(ii) Did the defendant stay within the boundaries of the consent (*e.g.,* not use a gun in a boxing match)?

a. **Express (Actual) Consent**
Defendant is not liable if plaintiff expressly consents to defendant's conduct. Exceptions: (i) Mistake will undo express consent ***if*** defendant knew of and took advantage of the mistake; (ii) consent induced by fraud will be invalidated if it goes to an essential matter, but not a collateral matter; and (iii) consent obtained by duress will be invalidated unless the duress is only threats of future action or future economic deprivation.

b. **Implied Consent**
Apparent consent is that which a reasonable person would infer from custom and usage or plaintiff's conduct, *e.g.,* normal contacts inherent in body-contact sports, ordinary incidental contact, etc. ***Consent implied by law*** arises where action is necessary to save a person's life or some other important interest in person or property.

c. **Capacity Required**
Individuals without capacity are deemed incapable of consent, *e.g.,* incompetents, drunken persons, and very young children.

CMR **Exam Tip** This requirement of capacity differs from the rule for the intent element of intentional torts, where incapacity is no defense; *i.e.,* everyone (even a young child) has the capacity to ***commit*** a tort, but not everyone has the capacity to ***consent*** to a tort.

d. **Exceeding Consent Given**
If defendant exceeds the scope of consent and does something substantially different, he may be liable.

2. **Self-Defense, Defense of Others, and Defense of Property**
When a question involves the defense of self, others, or property, ask the following three questions:

(i) Is the privilege available? The tort must now be or about to be committed. Already committed torts do not qualify.

(ii) Is a mistake permissible as to whether the tort being defended against (battery, trespass, etc.) is actually being committed?

(iii) Was a proper amount of force used?

CMR **Exam Tip** Keep your parties clear. In questions involving these defenses, the conduct of the defendant was prompted by the commission or apparent commission of a tort by the plaintiff. That tort is not at issue, however; the issue is whether the defendant's response itself constituted a tort against the plaintiff (usually battery, trespass to land, or trespass to chattels) or instead was privileged by one of these defenses.

a. **Self-Defense**
When a person ***reasonably believes*** that she is being or is about to be attacked, she may use such force as is reasonably necessary to protect against injury.

1) **When Is Defense Available?**

a) One need not attempt to escape, but the modern trend imposes a duty to retreat before using deadly force where this can be done safely, unless the actor is in her home.

b) Self-defense is generally not available to the initial aggressor.

c) Self-defense may extend to third-party injuries (caused while the actor was defending herself). An actor might be liable to a third person if she deliberately injured him in trying to protect herself.

2) **Is Mistake Allowed?**
A reasonable mistake as to the existence of the danger is allowed.

3) **How Much Force May Be Used?**
One may use only that force that reasonably appears to be necessary to prevent the harm (including deadly force). If more force than is reasonably necessary is used, the defense is lost.

b. Defense of Others

1) **When Is Defense Available?**
One may use force to defend another when the actor ***reasonably believes*** that the other person could have used force to defend himself.

2) **Is Mistake Allowed?**
A reasonable mistake as to whether the other person is being attacked or has a right to defend himself is permitted.

3) **How Much Force May Be Used?**
The defender may use as much force as he could have used in self-defense if the injury were threatened to him.

c. Defense of Property

1) **When Is Defense Available?**
One may use reasonable force to prevent the commission of a tort against her real or personal property. A request to desist or leave must first be made unless it clearly would be futile or dangerous. The defense does not apply once the tort has been committed; however, one may use force in ***hot pursuit*** of another who has tortiously dispossessed the owner of her chattels because the tort is viewed as still being committed.

CMR **Exam Tip** Remember that this defense is ***not available against one with a privilege***. Whenever an actor has a privilege to enter on the land of another because of necessity, recapture of chattels, etc., that privilege will ***supersede*** the privilege of the land possessor to defend her property.

2) Is Mistake Allowed?

A reasonable mistake is allowed as to whether an intrusion has occurred or whether a request to desist is required. A mistake is ***not*** allowed as to whether the entrant has a privilege (*e.g.,* necessity) that supersedes the defense of property right, unless the entrant conducts the entry so as to lead defendant to reasonably believe it is not privileged (such as by refusing to say what the necessity is).

3) How Much Force May Be Used?

Reasonable force may be used. However, one may ***not*** use force causing death or serious bodily harm unless the invasion of property also entails a serious threat of bodily harm.

CMR **Exam Tip** There is a common misperception that deadly force may be used to protect one's home. This is not strictly true. Many of the "home defense" cases are really self-defense cases. Thus, deadly force can only be used when a person, not just property, is threatened.

d. Reentry onto Land

At common law, one could use force to reenter land only when the other came into possession tortiously. Under modern law, there are summary procedures for recovering possession of real property. Hence, resort to self-help is no longer allowed.

e. Recapture of Chattels

The basic rule is the same as that for reentry of land at common law: when another's possession began lawfully (*e.g.,* a conditional sale), one may use only peaceful means to recover the chattel. Force may be used to recapture a chattel only when in hot pursuit of one who has obtained possession wrongfully, *e.g.,* by theft.

1) When Is Defense Available?

a) Timely Demand Required

A timely demand to return the chattel is first required unless clearly futile or dangerous.

b) Recovery Only from Wrongdoer

The recapture may be only from a tortfeasor or some third person who knows or should know that the chattels were tortiously obtained. One may not use force to recapture chattels in the hands of an innocent party.

c) **Entry on Land to Remove Chattel**

(1) **On Wrongdoer's Land**
When chattels are located on the land of the wrongdoer, the owner is privileged to enter on the land and reclaim them at a reasonable time and in a reasonable manner, after first making a demand for their return.

(2) **On Land of Innocent Party**
Similarly, when the chattels are on the land of an innocent party, the owner may enter and reclaim her chattel at a reasonable time and in a peaceful manner when the landowner has been given notice of the presence of the chattel and refuses to return it. (As noted above, the chattel owner's right of recapture supersedes the landowner's right to defend his property.) However, the chattel owner will be liable for any actual damage caused by the entry.

(3) **On Land Through Owner's Fault**
If the chattels are on the land of another through the owner's fault (*e.g.*, negligently letting cattle wander), there is no privilege to enter on the land. They may be recovered only through legal process.

2) **Is Mistake Allowed?**
Generally, no mistake regarding defendant's right to recapture the chattels or enter on the land is allowed. However, ***shopkeepers*** may have a privilege to detain for a reasonable period of time individuals whom they reasonably believe to be in possession of shoplifted goods.

3) **How Much Force May Be Used?**
Reasonable force, not including force sufficient to cause death or serious bodily harm, may be used to recapture chattels.

3. **Privilege of Arrest**
Depending on the facts, the actor may have a privilege to make an arrest of a third person.

a. **Invasion of Land**
The privilege of arrest carries with it the privilege to enter another's land for the purpose of effecting the arrest.

b. **Subsequent Misconduct**
Although the arrest itself may be privileged, the actor may still be liable for subsequent misconduct (*e.g.*, failing to bring the arrested party before a magistrate, unduly detaining the party in jail).

c. **Mistake**

1) **Misdemeanor**
If the arrest is for a misdemeanor, it is privileged only if for a breach of peace and if the action takes place in front of defendant.

2) **Felony**
For a felony arrest, a ***police officer*** may make a reasonable mistake. Citizens may make a reasonable mistake regarding the identity of the felon, but not regarding whether the felony occurred.

CMR COMPARISON CHART

ARRESTS WITHOUT A WARRANT

	Felony Arrest by Police Officer	Felony Arrest by Private Citizen	Misdemeanor Arrests
When Privileged	The officer must reasonably believe that a felony has been committed and that the person he arrests has committed it	The felony in fact must have been committed and the citizen must reasonably believe that the person he arrests has committed it	The misdemeanor must be a breach of peace and committed in the arresting party's presence
Force Allowed	That degree of force reasonably necessary to make the arrest; deadly force only when the suspect poses a threat of ***serious harm***	That degree of force reasonably necessary to make the arrest; deadly force only when the suspect poses a threat of ***serious harm***	That degree of force reasonably necessary to make the arrest, but ***never*** deadly force

4. **Necessity**
A person may interfere with the real or personal property of another when it is reasonably and apparently necessary to avoid threatened injury from a natural or other force and when the threatened injury is substantially more serious than the invasion that is undertaken to avert it. There are two types of necessity: (i) public—when the act is for the public good; and (ii) private—when the act is solely to benefit any person or any property from destruction or serious injury. Under private necessity, the actor must pay for any injury he causes.

CMR Exam Tip Necessity is a defense only to property torts.

5. **Discipline**
A parent or teacher may use reasonable force in disciplining children.

II. HARM TO ECONOMIC AND DIGNITARY INTERESTS

A. DEFAMATION

The law of defamation is divided into two parts: the common law elements and the constitutional requirements.

The elements of common law defamation are:

(i) ***Defamatory language***;

(ii) ***"Of or concerning"*** the plaintiff;

(iii) ***Publication*** thereof by defendant to a third person; and

(iv) Damage to plaintiff's reputation.

If the defamation involves a ***matter of public concern***, the Constitution requires the plaintiff to prove two additional elements:

(v) ***Falsity*** of the defamatory language; and

(vi) ***Fault*** on the part of defendant.

CMR **Exam Tip** In a common law case, plaintiff does not have to prove falsity as part of the prima facie case. Rather, defendant can offer truth of the statement as a defense.

1. Defamatory Language

Defamatory language is defined as language tending to adversely affect one's reputation. A statement of opinion is actionable only if it appears to be based on specific facts, and an express allegation of those facts would be defamatory. Name-calling is insufficient.

a. Inducement and Innuendo

If the statement is not defamatory on its face, plaintiff may plead additional facts as "inducement" to establish defamatory meaning by "innuendo."

b. Living Person Requirement

Any living person may be defamed. Defamation of a deceased person is not actionable. In a limited sense, a corporation, unincorporated association, or partnership may be defamed (*e.g.,* by remarks as to its financial condition, honesty, integrity, etc.).

2. "Of or Concerning" Plaintiff

The plaintiff must establish that a reasonable reader, listener, or viewer would understand that the defamatory statement referred to the plaintiff.

a. Colloquium

If the statement does not refer to plaintiff on its face, extrinsic evidence may be offered to establish that the statement refers to the plaintiff. This is known as pleading "colloquium."

COMMON LAW DEFAMATION

Does the statement at issue involve a matter of public concern? (Assume that all statements about public figures involve matters of public concern)

Yes → Go to Constitutional Defamation Chart

No ↓

Is the statement by defendant:

- ***defamatory*** (*i.e.,* does it tend to adversely affect a person's reputation)?

- ***"of or concerning"*** the plaintiff (in the view of a reasonable listener or reader)? ***and***

- ***"published"*** (*i.e.,* has it been intentionally or negligently communicated to a third person)?

No → No liability for defamation

Yes ↓

Is the statement:

Libel or slander per se → Damages are presumed; defendant is liable for defamation

Slander not within per se categories → If plaintiff shows special (*i.e.,* pecuniary) damages, defendant is liable for defamation

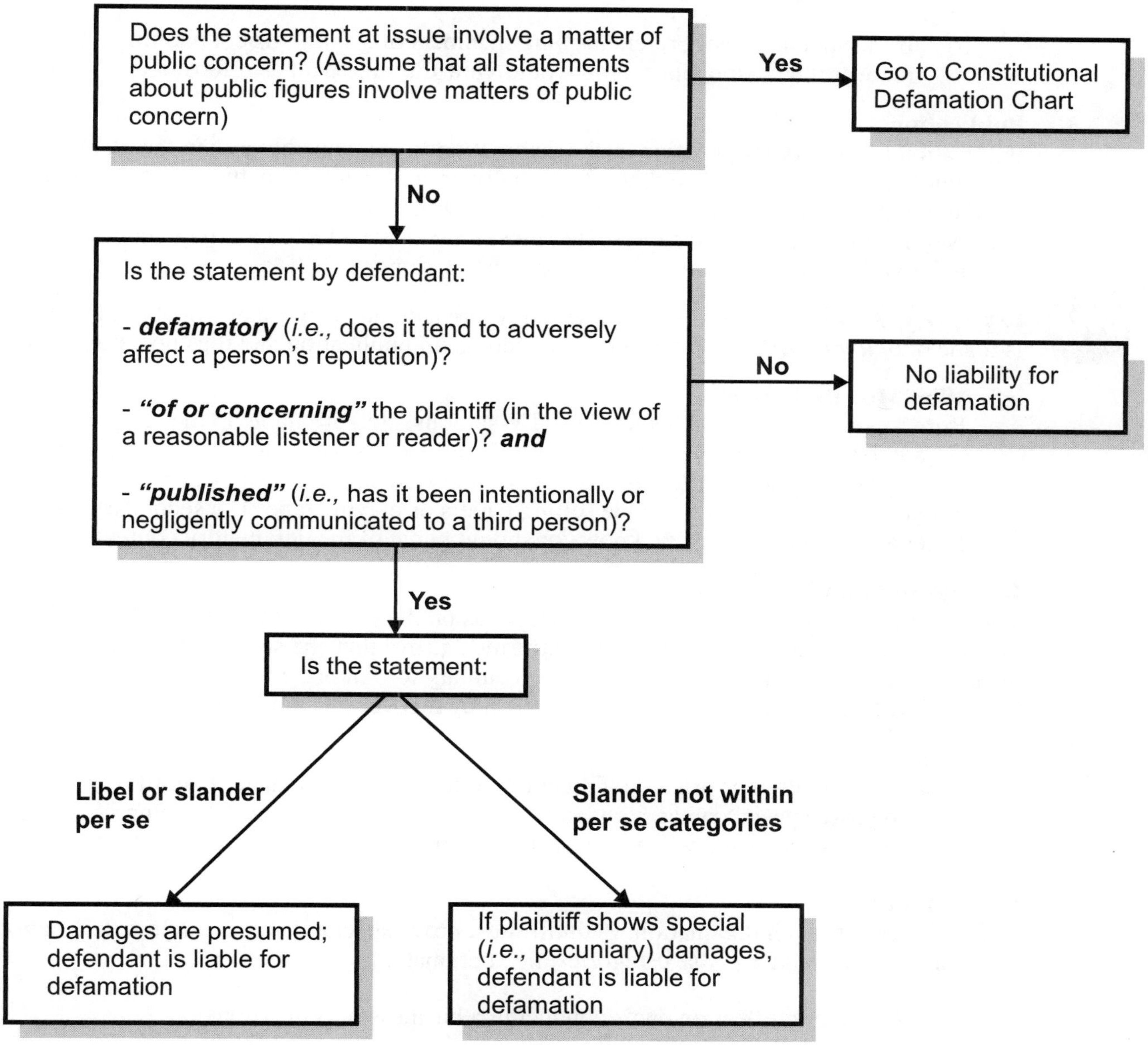

b. Group Defamation

1) If the defamatory statement refers to ***all*** members of a ***small*** group, each member may establish that the statement is "of and concerning" him by alleging that he is a group member (*i.e.,* everyone wins!).

2) If it is a ***large*** group, ***no*** member can prove that the statement is "of and concerning" him (*i.e.,* no one wins!).

3) If the statement only refers to ***some*** members of a ***small*** group, plaintiff can recover if a reasonable person would view the statement as referring to plaintiff.

3. Publication

Publication means communication of the defamation to someone other than the plaintiff. Such publication can be made either intentionally or negligently. It is the intent to publish, not the intent to defame, that is the requisite intent. Each repetition is a separate publication. However, for magazines, newspapers, etc., most states have adopted a "single publication" rule under which all copies are treated as one publication.

CMR Exam Tip An exam favorite is the situation where a defamatory statement about plaintiff is made only ***to plaintiff***. As a general rule, there is ***no*** publication and thus no defamation.

a. Who May Be Liable?

Primary publishers (*e.g.,* newspapers, TV stations, etc.) are liable to the same extent as the author or speaker. One who repeats a defamation is liable on the same general basis as the primary publisher (even if she states the source or makes it clear that she does not believe the defamation). One selling papers or playing tapes is a secondary publisher and is liable only if he knows or should know of the defamatory content.

4. Damage to Plaintiff's Reputation

The type of damages plaintiff must prove depends on the type of defamation (libel or slander) involved. In some slander cases, plaintiff must prove that she suffered special damages—that is, she must have suffered some pecuniary loss in order to recover anything. But once plaintiff has proved special damages, she may recover general damages as well.

a. Libel

Libel is the written or printed publication of defamatory language. Plaintiff does not need to prove special damages and general damages are presumed. The minority position distinguishes between libel per se and libel per quod (not defamatory on its face).

b. Slander

Slander is spoken defamation. Plaintiff must prove special damages, unless defamation falls within slander per se categories; *i.e.,* defamatory statements that:

1) Adversely reflect on one's conduct in a business or profession;

2) One has a loathsome disease;

3) One is or was guilty of a crime involving moral turpitude; or

4) A woman is unchaste.

c. **Slander vs. Libel**
Where it is difficult to determine whether something is slander or libel, look at the ***permanency***, the ***area of dissemination***, and the ***deliberate character*** of the publication. Where the original defamation is libel, any repetition, even if oral, is also libel. On the other hand, the written repetition of a slander will be characterized as libel. Radio and television programs are treated as libels if sufficiently permanent, premeditated, and broadly enough disseminated. The modern trend even treats "ad libbed" defamation on radio or television as libel.

5. **First Amendment Concerns**
When the defamation involves a ***matter of public concern***, plaintiff must prove, in addition to the common law elements:

(i) Falsity of the statement, and

(ii) Fault on the part of defendant.

a. **Falsity**
In cases where plaintiff is constitutionally required to prove some type of fault, plaintiff also has the burden of proving falsity.

CMR **Exam Tip** Where a statement of public interest is true, plaintiff has no cause of action for defamation. However, if you see this type of statement on the exam, consider whether plaintiff may have a cause of action for intentional infliction of emotional distress or invasion of right to privacy (unless plaintiff is a public figure).

b. **Fault on Defendant's Part**
The type of fault that a plaintiff must prove depends on the plaintiff's status.

1) **Public Official or Figure Must Prove Malice**
Under the *New York Times v. Sullivan* rule, malice must be proved in defamation cases brought by public officials and public figures.

a) **What Constitutes a Public Figure?**
A person becomes a "public figure" by achieving pervasive fame or notoriety or by voluntarily assuming a central role in a particular public controversy.

b) **Definition of Malice**
Malice (as defined by *New York Times v. Sullivan*) is:

(i) ***Knowledge*** that the statement was false, or

(ii) ***Reckless disregard*** as to whether it was false.

This is a subjective test. Defendant's spite or ill will is not enough to constitute malice. Deliberately altering a quotation may constitute malice if the alteration causes a ***material change*** in the meaning conveyed by the quotation.

CONSTITUTIONAL DEFAMATION

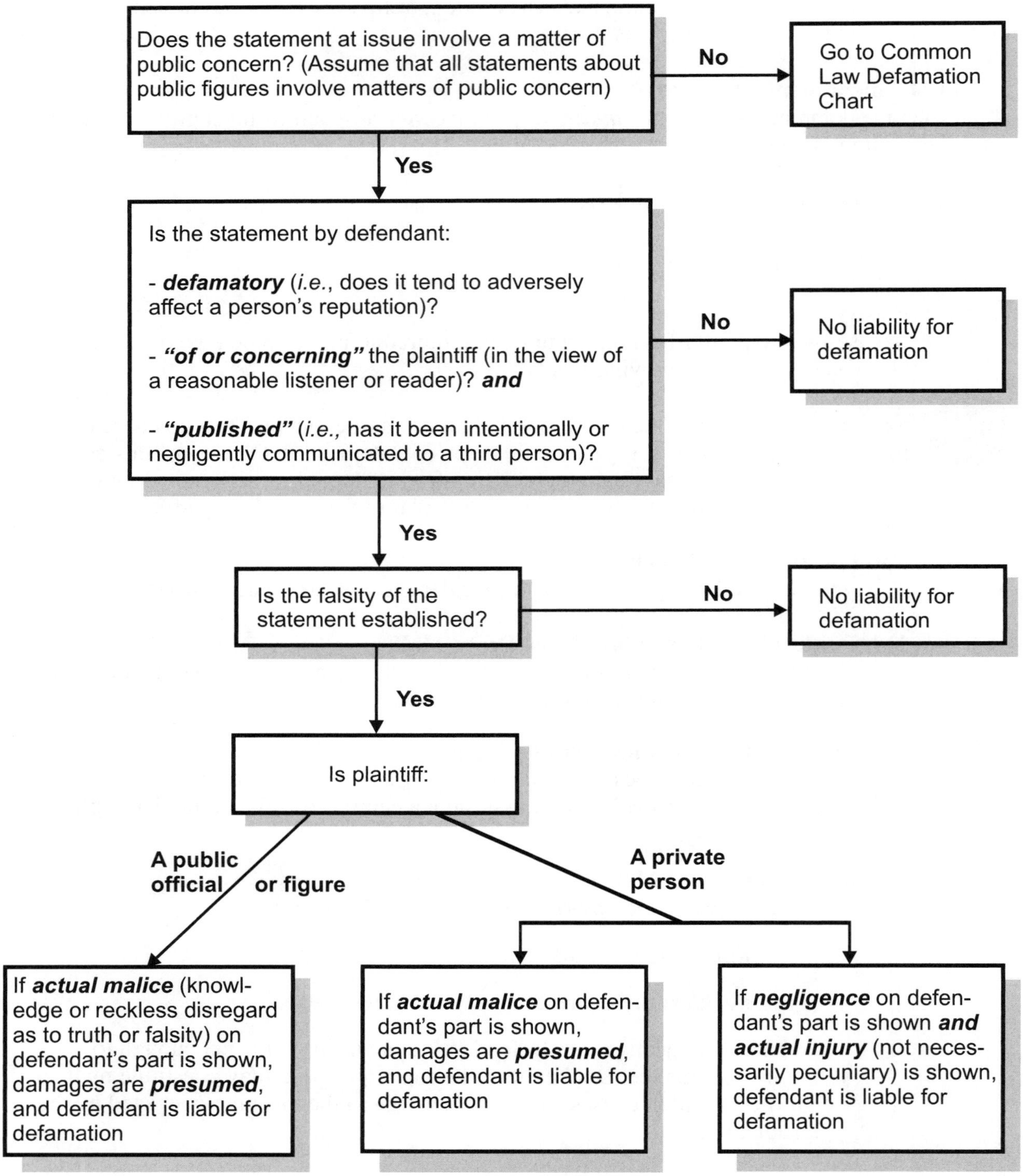

Does the statement at issue involve a matter of public concern? (Assume that all statements about public figures involve matters of public concern)

No → Go to Common Law Defamation Chart

Yes ↓

Is the statement by defendant:

- ***defamatory*** (*i.e.*, does it tend to adversely affect a person's reputation)?

- ***"of or concerning"*** the plaintiff (in the view of a reasonable listener or reader)? ***and***

- ***"published"*** (*i.e.,* has it been intentionally or negligently communicated to a third person)?

No → No liability for defamation

Yes ↓

Is the falsity of the statement established?

No → No liability for defamation

Yes ↓

Is plaintiff:

A public official or figure → If ***actual malice*** (knowledge or reckless disregard as to truth or falsity) on defendant's part is shown, damages are ***presumed***, and defendant is liable for defamation

A private person →

- If ***actual malice*** on defendant's part is shown, damages are ***presumed***, and defendant is liable for defamation
- If ***negligence*** on defendant's part is shown ***and actual injury*** (not necessarily pecuniary) is shown, defendant is liable for defamation

2) **Private Persons Need Not Prove Malice**
Under *Gertz v. Welch*, where a private person is the plaintiff, only ***negligence*** regarding the falsity must be proved if the statement involves a matter of "public concern." (If not a matter of public concern, constitutional restrictions do not apply.) Where the defendant is negligent, only "actual injury" damages are recoverable. However, where malice is found, damages may be presumed, and punitive damages allowed.

CMR **Exam Tip** Note that the status of the plaintiff (public figure or private person) is relevant ***only*** for the degree of fault required; the element of falsity must be proved regardless of the status of the plaintiff as long as a matter of public concern is involved (and you should assume that a matter of public concern is involved whenever the plaintiff is a public figure).

CMR SUMMARY CHART

FAULT AND DAMAGES RULES IN CONSTITUTIONAL DEFAMATION ACTIONS

Type of Plaintiff/Defamation	Fault Required	Damages Recoverable
Public official or public figure	Actual malice (knowledge of falsity or reckless disregard as to truth or falsity)	Presumed damages under common law rules (and punitive damages where appropriate)
Private person/matter of public concern	At least negligence as to statement's truth or falsity	Damages only for proved "actual injury" (If plaintiff proves actual malice, presumed and punitive damages may be available)
Private person/matter of private concern	No fault as to truth or falsity need be proved	Presumed damages under common law rules (and punitive damages where appropriate)

6. **Defenses to Defamation**

a. **Consent**
Consent is a complete defense. The rules relating to consent to intentional torts apply here.

b. **Truth**
Where plaintiff does not need to prove falsity (*i.e.,* the statement is about a purely private matter), defendant may prove truth as a complete defense.

CMR **Exam Tip** Remember that falsity and fault are prima facie case elements only in a ***constitutional*** defamation case. Plaintiff does not need to prove falsity in a ***common law*** defamation case because defamatory statements are presumed to be false; defendant has the burden to prove truth as a defense.

c. **Absolute Privilege—Can Never Be Lost**
Defendant may be protected by an absolute privilege for the following: remarks made during judicial proceedings, by legislators in debate, by federal executive officials, in "compelled" broadcasts, and between spouses.

d. **Qualified Privilege—Can Be Lost Through Abuse**
Sometimes the speaker may have a qualified privilege for the following: reports of official proceedings; statements in the interest of the publisher—defense of one's actions, property, or reputation; statements in the interest of the recipient; and statements in the common interest of the publisher and recipient.

The qualified privilege may be lost if (i) the statement is not within the scope of the privilege, or (ii) it is shown that the speaker acted with malice. Defendant bears the burden of proving that a privilege exists.

7. **Mitigating Factors**
Mitigating factors (*e.g.,* no malice, retraction, anger of the speaker provoked by plaintiff) may be considered by the jury on the damages issue; they are not defenses to liability.

B. INVASION OF RIGHT TO PRIVACY

1. **Four Branches**
This tort includes four kinds of wrongs:

a. **Appropriation of Plaintiff's Picture or Name**
It is necessary to show ***unauthorized use*** of plaintiff's picture or name for defendant's ***commercial advantage***. Liability is generally limited to advertisements or promotions of products or services. Mere economic benefit to defendant (not in connection with promoting a product or service) by itself is not sufficient.

b. **Intrusion upon Plaintiff's Affairs or Seclusion**
The act of ***prying or intruding*** must be ***objectionable to a reasonable person***. Furthermore, the thing into which there is an intrusion must be "***private***." Photographs taken in public places are not actionable.

c. **Publication of Facts Placing Plaintiff in False Light**
"False light" exists where one attributes to plaintiff views he does not hold or actions he did not take. The false light must be something ***objectionable to a reasonable*** person under the circumstances. For liability to attach, there must be publicity.

1) **First Amendment Limitation**
If the matter is in the public interest, ***malice*** on the defendant's part must be proved.

d. **Public Disclosure of Private Facts About Plaintiff**
This wrong involves public disclosure of ***private information*** about plaintiff (*e.g.*, matters of public record are not sufficient). The public disclosure must be ***objectionable to a reasonable person*** of ordinary sensibilities. Liability may attach even though the actual statement is true. First Amendment limitations probably apply if the matter is of legitimate public interest.

2. **Causation**
The invasion of plaintiff's interest in privacy (under any of the four kinds) must have been proximately caused by defendant's conduct.

3. **Proof of Special Damages Unnecessary**
Plaintiff need not plead and prove special damages. Emotional distress and mental anguish are sufficient damages.

4. **Defenses**
Some defenses to the right of privacy actions are consent and the defamation privilege defenses. Truth generally is ***not*** a good defense; nor is inadvertence, good faith, or lack of malice.

5. **Right of Privacy—Miscellaneous**
The right of privacy is a ***personal right*** and does not extend to members of a family, does not survive the death of the plaintiff, and is not assignable. The right of privacy is not applicable to corporations.

C. MISREPRESENTATION

1. **Intentional Misrepresentation (Fraud, Deceit)**
Prima facie case:

(i) ***Misrepresentation*** of a material fact (no duty to disclose and opinion not actionable unless rendered by someone with superior skill in the area). Silence is generally not enough; one must make affirmative misrepresentations;

(ii) ***Scienter,*** *i.e.,* when defendant made the statement, she ***knew*** or ***believed*** it was false or that there was no basis for the statement;

(iii) ***Intent*** to induce plaintiff to act or refrain from acting ***in reliance*** upon the misrepresentation;

(iv) ***Causation*** (actual reliance);

(v) ***Justifiable reliance*** (generally, reliance is justifiable only as to a statement of fact, not opinion); and

(vi) ***Damages*** (plaintiff must suffer ***actual pecuniary loss***).

There are no defenses to intentional misrepresentation.

2. Negligent Misrepresentation
Prima facie case:

(i) ***Misrepresentation*** by defendant in a ***business or professional capacity;***

(ii) ***Breach of duty*** toward a particular plaintiff;

(iii) ***Causation;***

(iv) ***Justifiable reliance;*** and

(v) ***Damages.***

Generally, this action is confined to misrepresentations made in a ***commercial setting***, and liability will attach only if reliance by the ***particular*** plaintiff could be contemplated.

D. WRONGFUL INSTITUTION OF LEGAL PROCEEDINGS

1. Malicious Prosecution
Prima facie case: (i) ***institution of criminal proceedings*** against plaintiff; (ii) ***termination in plaintiff's favor***; (iii) ***absence of probable cause*** for prior proceedings (insufficient facts for a reasonable person to believe that plaintiff was guilty, or defendant, in fact, did not actually believe plaintiff to be guilty); (iv) ***improper purpose*** (*i.e.,* something other than bringing a person to justice); and (v) ***damages***. Prosecutors are immune from liability.

a. Wrongful Civil Proceedings
Most jurisdictions have extended the malicious prosecution action to cover civil cases.

2. Abuse of Process
Prima facie case: (i) ***wrongful use*** of process for an ulterior purpose, and (ii) definite ***act or threat*** against plaintiff in order to accomplish an ulterior purpose.

E. INTERFERENCE WITH BUSINESS RELATIONS

Prima facie case: (i) existence of a ***valid contractual relationship*** between plaintiff and a third party ***or valid business expectancy*** of plaintiff; (ii) defendant's ***knowledge of the relationship or expectancy***; (iii) ***intentional interference*** by defendant inducing a breach or termination of the relationship or expectancy; and (iv) ***damages***.

1. Privileges
Defendant's conduct may be privileged where it is a proper attempt to obtain business for itself or protect its interests, particularly if defendant is interfering only with plaintiff's prospective business rather than with existing contracts.

III. NEGLIGENCE

A. PRIMA FACIE CASE

Elements of the prima facie case:

(i) A ***duty*** on the part of defendant ***to conform to a specific standard of conduct*** for protection of plaintiff against an unreasonable risk of injury;

(ii) A ***breach*** of that duty by defendant;

(iii) The breach is the ***actual and proximate cause*** of plaintiff's injury; and

(iv) ***Damage***.

B. DUTY OF CARE

A duty of care is owed to all foreseeable plaintiffs. The extent of the duty is determined by the applicable standard of care. Therefore, when confronted with a negligence question, always ask:

(i) Was the plaintiff foreseeable?

(ii) If so, what is the applicable standard of care?

1. Foreseeable/Unforeseeable Plaintiffs

A duty of care is owed only to foreseeable plaintiffs. However, a problem arises where defendant breaches a duty to one plaintiff ("P1") and also causes injury to another (possibly unforeseeable) plaintiff ("P2"). There are two possible outcomes:

a. Cardozo View (Majority)—Foreseeable Zone of Danger

P2 can recover only if she can establish that a reasonable person would have foreseen a risk of injury to her under the circumstances; *i.e.,* she was located in the foreseeable zone of danger.

b. Andrews View (Minority)—Everyone Is Foreseeable

P2 may establish the existence of a duty extending from defendant to her by a showing that defendant has breached a duty owed to P1.

2. Specific Situations

a. Rescuers

A rescuer is a foreseeable plaintiff where defendant negligently put himself or a third person in peril (*i.e.,* danger invites rescue).

b. Prenatal Injuries

A duty of care is owed to a viable fetus. In cases of failure to diagnose a congenital defect or properly perform a contraceptive procedure, the child may not recover for "wrongful life," but the parents may recover damages in a "wrongful birth" or "wrongful pregnancy" action for any additional medical expenses and for pain and suffering from labor; ordinary child rearing expenses, however, cannot be recovered.

c. Intended Beneficiaries of Economic Transactions

A third party for whose economic benefit a legal or business transaction was made (*e.g.*, a beneficiary of a will) may be a foreseeable plaintiff.

3. Standards of Care

a. Basic Standard—The Reasonable Person

The reasonable person standard is an ***objective*** standard, *i.e.*, one's conduct measured against what the average person would do. A defendant's ***mental*** deficiencies and inexperience are not taken into account (*i.e.*, stupidity is no excuse). However, the "reasonable person" is considered to have the same ***physical*** characteristics as defendant (but remember, one is expected to know one's physical handicaps and to exercise the care of a person with such knowledge—*e.g.*, a blind person should not fly a plane).

b. Particular Standards of Conduct

1) Professionals

A professional or someone with special occupational skills is required to possess the knowledge and skill of a member of the profession or occupation in good standing in similar communities. Specialists will be held to a still higher degree of care.

a) Duty to Disclose Risks of Treatment

A doctor has a duty to disclose the risks of treatment to enable a patient to make an informed consent.

2) Children

Children are held to the standard of a child of ***like age***, ***education***, ***intelligence***, ***and experience***. This is a ***subjective*** test. A child under four is usually without the capacity to be negligent. Children engaged in adult activities may be required to conform to an "adult" standard of care.

3) Common Carriers and Innkeepers

Common carriers and innkeepers are held to a very high degree of care; *i.e.*, they are liable for slight negligence.

CMR Exam Tip For the higher common carrier and innkeeper standards to apply, the plaintiff ***must*** be a passenger or guest.

4) Automobile Driver to Guest

A guest in an automobile is owed a duty of ordinary care. In the few guest statute states, one is liable to nonpaying passengers only for reckless tortious conduct.

5) Bailment Duties

a) Duties Owed by Bailor

For a ***gratuitous bailment***, the bailor must inform of known, dangerous defects in the chattel. For a ***bailment for hire***, the bailor must inform of chattel defects of which he is or should be aware.

b) Duties Owed by Bailee

The bailee's standard of care depends on who benefits from the bailment: (i) for a ***sole benefit of the bailor*** bailment, there is a low standard of care;

(ii) for a ***sole benefit of the bailee*** bailment, there is a high standard of care; and (iii) for a ***mutual benefit*** bailment, there is the ordinary care standard.

6) Emergency Situations
A defendant must act as a reasonable person would under the same emergency conditions. The emergency is not to be considered, however, if it is of defendant's own making.

c. Owners and/or Occupiers of Land
The extent of the liability of owners and/or occupiers of land (and those in privity with the owner/occupier) depends on where the injury occurred and on the status of the plaintiff.

1) Duty of Possessor to Those Off Premises
There is no duty to protect one off the premises from ***natural conditions*** on the premises; however, there is a duty for unreasonably dangerous ***artificial*** conditions or structures abutting adjacent land. Also, one must carry on activities on property so as to avoid unreasonable risk of harm to others outside the property.

CMR **Exam Tip** In urban areas, the owner/occupier is liable for damage caused off the premises by trees on the premises (*e.g.,* falling branches). This has been an exam favorite in recent years.

2) Duty of Possessor to Those On Premises
In most states the duty owed a plaintiff on the premises depends on the plaintiff's status as trespasser, licensee, or invitee.

a) Trespassers
No duty is owed to an ***undiscovered*** trespasser. As to ***discovered*** or ***anticipated*** trespassers, the landowner must: (i) warn of or make safe concealed, unsafe, ***artificial conditions known to the landowner*** involving risk of ***death or serious bodily harm,*** and (ii) use reasonable care in the exercise of "active operations" on the property. (No duty is owed for natural conditions or less dangerous artificial conditions.) Easement and license holders owe a duty of reasonable care to trespassers.

b) Infant Trespassers—Attractive Nuisance Doctrine
Most courts impose on a landowner the duty to exercise ordinary care to avoid a reasonably foreseeable risk of harm to children caused by ***artificial*** conditions on his property. To establish the doctrine's applicability, plaintiff must show: (i) a dangerous condition on the land that the owner is or should be aware of, (ii) the owner knows or should know children frequent the vicinity of the condition, (iii) the condition is likely to cause injury, *i.e.,* dangerous because of child's inability to appreciate the risk, and (iv) the expense of remedying the situation is slight compared with the magnitude of the risk.

CMR **Exam Tip** For liability to attach, the four requirements above must be shown. The child ***does not*** have to be attracted onto the land by the dangerous condition, nor is the attraction alone enough for liability.

c) **Duty Owed to Licensees**
A licensee is one who enters on the land with the possessor's permission for her ***own purpose or business***, rather than for the possessor's benefit. The possessor has a duty to (i) warn of dangerous conditions (natural or artificial) known to the owner that create an unreasonable risk of harm to the licensee and that licensee is unlikely to discover, and (ii) exercise reasonable care in the conduct of "active operations" on the property. The possessor has no duty to inspect or repair. (*Remember:* Social guests are considered licensees.)

d) **Duty Owed to Invitees**
Invitees enter land in response to an invitation by the landowner (*i.e.,* they enter for a purpose connected with the business of the landowner or enter as members of the public for a purpose for which the land is ***held open to the public***). The landowner or occupier owes the same duties owed to licensees ***plus*** a duty to make ***reasonable inspections*** to discover nonobvious dangerous conditions and, thereafter, make them safe. One will lose invitee status if she exceeds the scope of the invitation.

e) **Duty Owed to Users of Recreational Land**
A landowner who permits the general public to use his land for recreational purposes without charging a fee is not liable for injuries suffered by a recreational user, unless the landowner willfully and maliciously failed to guard against or warn of a dangerous condition or activity.

f) **Modern Trend Rejects Status Rules**
A strong minority of states reject the distinction between licensees and invitees (and, in a few states, trespassers as well), and simply apply a reasonable person standard to dangerous conditions on the land.

3) **Duties of Lessor and Lessee of Realty**
The lessee has a general duty to maintain the premises. The lessor must warn of existing defects of which he is aware or has reason to know, and which he knows the lessee is not likely to discover on a reasonable inspection. If the lessor covenants to repair, he is liable for unreasonably dangerous conditions. If the lessor volunteers to repair and does so negligently, he is liable.

Exam Tip If the guest of a tenant is injured, the landlord may be liable as lessor of the premises. But don't stop there—remember that the tenant may also be liable to the guest because of the tenant's status as the owner/occupier of the premises.

4) **Duties of Vendor of Realty**
A vendor must ***disclose*** to the vendee concealed, unreasonably dangerous conditions of which the vendor knows or has reason to know, and which he knows the vendee is not likely to discover on a reasonable inspection.

d. **Statutory Standards of Care**
A statute's specific duty may replace the more general common law duty of due care if: (i) the statute provides for a ***criminal penalty***, (ii) the statute ***clearly defines the standard*** of conduct, (iii) plaintiff is ***within the protected class***, and (iv) the statute was ***designed to prevent the type of harm suffered*** by plaintiff.

1) **Excuse for Violation**
Violation of some statutes may be excused where compliance would cause more danger than violation or where compliance would be beyond defendant's control.

2) **Effect of Violation or Compliance**
Under the majority view, an unexcused statutory violation is negligence per se; *i.e.,* it establishes the first two requirements in the prima facie case—a ***conclusive*** presumption of duty and breach of duty. In contrast, even though violation of the applicable statute may be negligence, compliance with the statute will not necessarily establish due care.

CMR SUMMARY CHART

DUTY OF POSSESSOR OF LAND TO THOSE ON THE PREMISES

Status of Entrant	Duties Owed: *Artificial Conditions*	Duties Owed: *Natural Conditions*	Duties Owed: *Active Operations*
Undiscovered Trespasser	No duty	No duty	No duty
Discovered or Anticipated Trespasser	Duty to warn of or make safe known conditions if non-obvious and ***highly*** dangerous	No duty	Duty of reasonable care
Infant Trespasser (if presence on land foreseeable)	Duty to warn of or make safe if foreseeable risk to child outweighs expense of eliminating danger	No duty	No duty (unless child also qualifies as discovered or anticipated trespasser)
Licensee (including social guest)	Duty to warn of or make safe known conditions if nonobvious and dangerous	Duty to warn of or make safe known conditions if nonobvious and dangerous	Duty of reasonable care
Invitee (*e.g.,* member of public, business visitor)	Duty to make reasonable inspections to discover nonobvious dangerous conditions and warn of or make them safe	Duty to make reasonable inspections to discover nonobvious dangerous conditions and warn of or make them safe	Duty of reasonable care

4. Duty Regarding Negligent Infliction of Emotional Distress

The duty to avoid causing emotional distress to another is breached when defendant creates a foreseeable risk of physical injury to plaintiff, either by (i) causing a threat of physical impact that leads to emotional distress or (ii) directly causing severe emotional distress that by itself is likely to result in physical symptoms.

a. Injury Requirement

Plaintiff can recover damages only if defendant's conduct caused some ***physical injury***. While pure emotional distress may be insufficient, a severe shock to the nervous system that causes physical symptoms is sufficient. Two cases in which a physical injury is ***not*** required, however, are: (i) an erroneous report of a relative's death; and (ii) a mishandling of a relative's corpse.

b. Zone of Danger Requirement

If plaintiff's distress is caused by threat of physical impact, most courts require that the threat be directed at plaintiff or someone in her immediate presence. A bystander outside the "zone of danger" of physical injury who sees defendant negligently injuring another cannot recover damages for her own distress. A strong modern trend allows recovery based on foreseeability factors rather than zone of danger if (i) plaintiff and the person injured by defendant are closely related, (ii) plaintiff was present at the scene, and (iii) plaintiff observed or perceived the injury.

CMR COMPARISON CHART

INFLICTION OF EMOTIONAL DISTRESS

	Intentional	Negligent
Conduct Required	Extreme and outrageous conduct by defendant	Subjecting plaintiff to threat of physical impact or severe emotional distress likely to cause physical symptoms
Fault Required	Intent to cause severe emotional distress or recklessness as to the effect of conduct	Negligence in creating risk of physical injury to plaintiff
Causation and Damages	Defendant's conduct must cause severe emotional distress	Defendant's conduct generally must cause tangible physical injury (*e.g.,* miscarriage)
Bystander Recovery When Another Is Physically Injured	Plaintiff bystander must be present when injury occurs and be a close relative of the injured person, and defendant must know these facts when he intentionally injures the other person (or defendant must have intent to cause plaintiff distress)	Plaintiff bystander must be within the "zone of danger" created by defendant's negligent conduct (*i.e.,* must be subjected to threat of impact). Modern trend allows recovery based on foreseeability factors

Exam Tip Keep in mind that the torts for infliction of emotional distress are not the only means of recovering damages for emotional distress. If physical injury has been caused by commission of another tort, plaintiff can "tack on" damages for emotional distress as a "parasitic" element of his physical injury damages, without the need to consider the elements of the emotional distress torts.

5. **Affirmative Duties to Act**
Generally, one does not have a legal duty to act. Exceptions to this rule exist, however:

a. **Assumption of Duty by Acting**
One may assume a duty to act by acting (*e.g.,* once defendant undertakes to aid someone, he must do so with reasonable care).

Exception: Many states have enacted Good Samaritan statutes, which exempt doctors, nurses, etc., from liability for ordinary, but not gross, negligence.

b. **Peril Due to Defendant's Negligence**
One has a duty to assist someone he has negligently placed in peril.

c. **Special Relationship Between Parties**
A special relationship between the parties (*e.g.,* parent-child) may create a duty to act. Similarly, ***common carriers***, ***innkeepers***, ***shopkeepers***, and others that gather the public for profit owe duties of reasonable care to aid or assist their patrons. In addition, places of public accommodation have a duty to prevent injury to guests by third persons.

d. **Duty to Control Third Persons**
Generally, there is no duty to prevent a third person from injuring another. An affirmative duty may be imposed, however, if one has the actual ability and authority to control a person's actions, and knows or should know the person is likely to commit acts that would require exercise of this control.

C. BREACH OF DUTY

Where defendant's conduct falls short of that level required by the applicable standard of care owed to the plaintiff, she has breached her duty. Whether the duty of care is breached in an individual case is a question for the trier of fact. The main problem relates to proof of the breach. Plaintiff may use one of the following theories:

1. **Custom or Usage**
Custom or usage may be used to establish standard of care, but does not control the question of whether certain conduct amounted to negligence. For example, although certain behavior is custom in an industry, a court may find that the entire industry is acting negligently.

2. **Violation of Statute**
Existence of a duty owed to plaintiff and breach thereof may be established as a matter of law by proof that defendant violated an applicable statute ("negligence per se"). Causation and damages must still be established by plaintiff.

3. **Res Ipsa Loquitur**
In some cases, the very occurrence of an event may tend to establish a breach of duty. The

doctrine of res ipsa loquitur requires plaintiff to show that (i) the accident causing the injury is a type that would not normally occur unless someone was negligent, and (ii) the negligence is attributable to defendant (*i.e.,* this type of accident ordinarily happens because of the negligence of someone in defendant's position). This can often be shown by evidence that the instrumentality causing the injury was in the exclusive control of defendant. (Plaintiff must also establish freedom from fault on his part.)

a. **Effect of Res Ipsa Loquitur**
Where res ipsa loquitur is established, plaintiff has ***made a prima facie case*** and no directed verdict may be given for defendant. Plaintiff can still lose, however, if the inference of negligence is rejected by the trier of fact.

Exam Tip Questions testing on res ipsa loquitur often have the defendant making a ***motion for a directed verdict***. These questions don't require you to memorize rules of civil procedure—all you need to remember is the following:

(i) ***Deny*** defendant's motion for directed verdict if plaintiff has established res ipsa loquitur or presented some other evidence of breach of duty (such as defendant's violation of a statute);

(ii) ***Grant*** defendant's motion if plaintiff has failed to establish res ipsa loquitur and failed to present some other evidence of breach of duty.

Occasionally, plaintiff may also move for a directed verdict. Plaintiff's motion should always be ***denied*** except in the rare case where plaintiff has established negligence per se through violation of an applicable statute ***and*** there are no issues of proximate cause.

D. CAUSATION

Once negligent conduct is shown (a breach of the standard of care owed a foreseeable plaintiff), plaintiff must show that the conduct was the cause of his injury. For liability to attach, plaintiff must show ***both*** actual cause and proximate cause.

1. Actual Cause (Causation in Fact)

Before defendant's conduct can be considered a proximate cause of plaintiff's injury, it must first be a cause in fact of the injury. Several tests exist:

a. **"But For" Test**
Act or omission is the cause in fact of an injury when the injury would not have occurred but for the act. This test applies where several acts (each insufficient to cause the injury alone) combine to cause the injury.

b. **Joint Causes—Substantial Factor Test**
Where several causes bring about injury, and any one alone would have been sufficient to cause the injury, defendant's conduct is the cause in fact if it was a substantial factor in causing the injury.

c. **Alternative Causes Approach**
This test applies when there are two acts, only one of which causes injury, but it is not known which one. The burden of proof shifts to defendants, and each must show that his negligence is not the actual cause. [Summers v. Tice]

Exam Tip Distinguish these last two tests: Under the joint causes approach, both parties caused the harm. Under the alternative causes approach, although both parties acted negligently, only one caused the harm.

2. **Proximate Cause (Legal Causation)**

In addition to being a cause in fact, the defendant's conduct must also be the proximate cause of the injury. Even though the conduct actually caused plaintiff's injury, it might not be deemed to be the proximate cause. Thus, the doctrine of proximate causation is a ***limitation of liability*** and deals with liability or nonliability for unforeseeable or unusual consequences of one's acts.

a. **General Rule—Scope of Foreseeable Risk**

A defendant generally is liable for all harmful results that are the normal incidents of and within the increased risk caused by his acts. This is a ***foreseeability*** test.

Exam Tip Questions raising proximate cause issues will not require you to make a judgment call on foreseeability in a close case. If the answer turns on the proximate cause issue, the correct choice will almost always be phrased in "if" or "unless" terms (*e.g.,* "plaintiff will prevail if it was reasonably foreseeable that . . ." or "defendant will not be liable unless he should have foreseen that . . ."). Otherwise, the facts in the question will be so clear-cut that common sense will tell you immediately whether the harm that occurred was foreseeable.

b. **Liability in Direct Cause Cases**

In a direct cause case, where there is an uninterrupted chain of events from the negligent act to plaintiff's injury, defendant is liable for all ***foreseeable harmful results***, regardless of unusual manner or timing. Defendant is not liable for ***unforeseeable harmful results*** not within the risk created by defendant's negligence. Most harmful results will be deemed foreseeable in direct cause cases.

c. **Liability in Indirect Cause Cases**

In an indirect cause case, an affirmative intervening force (*e.g.,* an act by a third person, an act of God) comes into motion after defendant's negligent act and combines with it to cause plaintiff's injury.

1) **Foreseeable Results Caused by Foreseeable Intervening Forces—Defendant Liable**

Defendant is liable where his negligence caused a foreseeable harmful response or reaction from a dependent intervening force or created a foreseeable risk that an independent intervening force would harm plaintiff.

a) **Common Dependent Intervening Forces**

The following dependent intervening forces are ***almost always foreseeable:*** (i) subsequent medical malpractice, (ii) negligence of rescuers, (iii) efforts to protect the person or property of oneself or another, (iv) injuries caused by another "reacting" to defendant's actions, (v) subsequent diseases caused by a weakened condition, and (vi) subsequent accident substantially caused by the original injury.

b) **Independent Intervening Forces**

Independent intervening forces that are not a natural response or reaction to the situation created by the defendant's conduct may be foreseeable if defendant's negligence increased the risk of harm from these forces. Independent intervening forces include (i) negligent acts of third persons, (ii) crimes and intentional torts of third persons, and (iii) acts of God.

2) Foreseeable Results Caused by Unforeseeable Intervening Forces—Defendant Usually Liable

Defendant is liable where his negligence increased the risk of a foreseeable harmful result and that result is ultimately produced by an unforeseeable intervening force. This rule does not apply where the unforeseeable intervening force was a crime or intentional tort of a third person.

3) Unforeseeable Results Caused by Foreseeable Intervening Forces—Defendant Not Liable

In the rare case where a totally unforeseeable result was caused by a foreseeable intervening force, most courts hold defendant not liable.

4) Unforeseeable Results Caused by Unforeseeable Intervening Forces—Defendant Not Liable

Intervening forces that produce unforeseeable results (results not within the increased risk created by defendant's negligence) are generally deemed unforeseeable and ***superseding***. Superseding forces break the causal connection between defendant's initial negligent act and plaintiff's ultimate injury, thus relieving defendant of liability.

d. Unforeseeable Extent or Severity of Harm—Defendant Liable

In all cases, defendant takes his plaintiff as he finds him; *i.e.,* defendant is liable for all damages, including aggravation of an existing condition, even if the extent or severity of the damages was unforeseeable. This is also known as the "eggshell-skull plaintiff" rule.

CMR SUMMARY CHART

PROXIMATE CAUSE RULES

	Direct Cause Cases	Indirect Cause Cases: *Foreseeable Intervening Force*	Indirect Cause Cases: *Unforeseeable Intervening Force*
Foreseeable Harmful Result	Defendant liable	Defendant liable	Defendant liable unless intervening force is crime or intentional tort
Unforeseeable Harmful Result	Defendant not liable	Defendant not liable	Defendant not liable; intervening force is ***superseding***

E. DAMAGES

Damage is an essential element of negligence; thus, damage will not be presumed (and nominal damages are not available).

1. Personal Injury

Plaintiff is to be compensated for all his damages (past, present, and prospective), both special and general. Foreseeability of the extent of harm is generally irrelevant; *i.e.*, one takes one's plaintiff as one finds him.

2. Property Damage

The measure of damage is the reasonable cost of repair or, if the property is nearly destroyed, the fair market value at the time of the accident.

3. Punitive Damages

Plaintiff may recover punitive damages if defendant's conduct is "wanton and willful," reckless, or malicious.

4. Nonrecoverable Items

Nonrecoverable items include: (i) interest from the date of damage in a personal injury action, and (ii) attorneys' fees.

5. Duty to Mitigate

As in all cases, plaintiff has a duty to take reasonable steps to mitigate damages (*e.g.*, seek appropriate treatment).

6. Collateral Source Rule

Damages are not reduced just because plaintiff received benefits from other sources, *e.g.*, health insurance.

F. DEFENSES TO NEGLIGENCE

1. Contributory Negligence

Contributory negligence is negligence on the part of the plaintiff that contributes to her injuries. The standard of care for contributory negligence is the same as for ordinary negligence.

a. No Defense to Intentional Torts

Contributory negligence is not a defense to wanton and willful misconduct or intentional tortious conduct.

b. Effect of Contributory Negligence

Contributory negligence completely barred plaintiff's right to recovery at common law. Most jurisdictions now favor a comparative negligence system (*see infra*).

c. Last Clear Chance—An Exception to Contributory Negligence

Last clear chance permits plaintiff to recover despite her contributory negligence. Under this rule, the person with the last clear chance to avoid an accident who fails to do so is liable for negligence. (Last clear chance is essentially plaintiff's rebuttal to the defense of contributory negligence.)

1) **Helpless Peril**
In many states, where the plaintiff is in "helpless peril," defendant will be liable if he knew or should have known of plaintiff's predicament.

2) **Inattentive Peril**
In "inattentive peril" situations (*i.e.,* plaintiff could have extricated herself if attentive), defendant must actually have known of plaintiff's predicament.

3) **Prior Negligence Cases**
For the last clear chance doctrine to apply, defendant must have been able, but failed, to avoid harming plaintiff at the time of the accident. If defendant's only negligence occurred earlier, the doctrine will not apply.

d. **Imputed Contributory Negligence**
As a general rule, the contributory negligence of a third party will be imputed to a plaintiff (and bar her claim) only when the relationship between the third party and the plaintiff is such that a court could find the plaintiff vicariously liable for the third party's negligence. Negligence is imputed in master-servant, partner, and joint venturer relationships. Negligence is not imputed between husband and wife, parent and child, and automobile owner and driver.

2. **Assumption of Risk**
Plaintiff may be denied recovery if she assumed the risk of any damage caused by defendant's act. Plaintiff must have (i) known of the risk and (ii) voluntarily proceeded in the face of the risk.

a. **Implied Assumption of Risk**
Knowledge may be implied where the risk is one that an average person would clearly appreciate. Plaintiff may ***not*** be said to have assumed the risk where there is no available alternative to proceeding in the face of the risk or in situations involving fraud, force, or an emergency. Also, common carriers and public utilities may not limit their liability by disclaimer, and members of a class protected by statute will not be deemed to have assumed any risk.

b. **Express Assumption of Risk**
The risk may be assumed by an express agreement.

c. **No Defense to Intentional Torts**
Assumption of risk is not a defense to intentional torts, but it is a defense to wanton and willful misconduct.

3. **Comparative Negligence**
In comparative negligence states, plaintiff's contributory negligence is not a complete bar to recovery. Rather, the trier of fact weighs plaintiff's negligence and reduces damages accordingly (*e.g.,* if plaintiff is 10% at fault, her damages are reduced by 10%). A majority of states allow plaintiff to recover only if her negligence was less serious or no more serious than that of defendant (partial comparative negligence). "Pure" comparative negligence states, however, allow recovery no matter how great plaintiff's negligence.

Exam Tip On the MBE, you will be told to assume that pure comparative negligence applies unless the question states otherwise.

a. **Effect on Other Doctrines**
Last clear chance is not used in comparative negligence jurisdictions. Most comparative negligence jurisdictions have abolished the defense of implied assumption of risk but have retained the defense of express assumption of risk. In most states, plaintiff's negligence will be taken into account even though defendant's conduct was "wanton and willful" or "reckless," but not if it was intentional.

CMR COMPARISON CHART

NEGLIGENCE DEFENSES

	Contributory Negligence	Implied Assumption of Risk	Pure Comparative Negligence	Partial Comparative Negligence
Defined	Plaintiff's own negligence contributes to her injury	Plaintiff knew of a risk of injury and voluntarily assumed it	Plaintiff's own negligence contributes to her injury	Plaintiff's own negligence contributes to her injury
Effect	Plaintiff's claim completely barred	Plaintiff's claim completely barred	Plaintiff's damage award reduced by percentage of fault attributable to her	Plaintiff's damage award reduced if her fault is below the threshold level; otherwise, plaintiff's claim is barred
Defense Negated by Defendant's "Last Clear Chance"?	Yes	Not applicable	Not applicable	Not applicable
Defense Applies to Wanton or Reckless Tortious Conduct?	No	Yes	Yes	Yes

IV. LIABILITY WITHOUT FAULT (STRICT LIABILITY)

A. PRIMA FACIE CASE

For strict liability, the following elements must be shown: (i) existence of an ***absolute duty*** on the part of the defendant ***to make safe;*** (ii) ***breach*** of that duty; (iii) the breach of the duty was the ***actual*** and ***proximate cause*** of the plaintiff's injury; and (iv) ***damage*** to the plaintiff's person or property.

B. LIABILITY FOR ANIMALS

1. Trespassing Animals

An owner is strictly liable for reasonably foreseeable damage done by a trespass of his animals.

2. Personal Injuries

a. Strict Liability for Wild Animals

An owner is strictly liable to licensees and invitees for injuries caused by wild animals as long as the injured person did nothing to bring about the injury.

b. No Strict Liability for Domestic Animals

An owner is not strictly liable for injuries caused by domestic animals unless he has knowledge of that particular animal's dangerous propensities that are not common to the species.

c. Strict Liability Not Available to Trespassers

Strict liability will generally not be imposed in favor of trespassers in the absence of the owner's negligence. However, a landowner may be liable on intentional tort grounds for injuries inflicted by vicious watchdogs.

C. ULTRAHAZARDOUS OR ABNORMALLY DANGEROUS ACTIVITIES

There are three requirements for the application of strict liability to ultrahazardous activities: (i) the activity must involve ***risk of serious harm*** to persons or property; (ii) the activity must be one that ***cannot be performed without risk of serious harm*** no matter how much care is taken; and (iii) the activity ***is not commonly engaged in*** in the particular community (blasting, manufacturing explosives, etc.). Some courts also consider the value of the activity and its appropriateness to the location.

CMR **Exam Tip** Exam questions testing on strict liability often include a statement in the facts or in an answer choice that the defendant exercised reasonable care. Remember that no amount of due care on the part of the defendant will relieve him of liability in a strict liability situation.

D. EXTENT OF LIABILITY

1. Scope of Duty Owed

The duty owed is the absolute duty to make safe the normally dangerous characteristic of the animal or activity. It is owed to all foreseeable plaintiffs.

2. Defenses

In ***contributory negligence*** states, contributory negligence is no defense if plaintiff has failed to realize the danger or guard against it. It is a defense if plaintiff knew of the danger and his unreasonable conduct was the very cause of the ultrahazardous activity miscarrying. Assumption of the risk is a good defense to strict liability. Most ***comparative negligence*** states apply their comparative negligence rules to strict liability cases.

V. PRODUCTS LIABILITY

A. BASIC PRINCIPLES

Products liability refers to the liability of a supplier of a defective product to someone injured by the product.

1. Theories of Liability

There are five theories of liability that plaintiff may use: (i) intent, (ii) negligence, (iii) strict liability, (iv) implied warranties of merchantability and fitness for a particular purpose, and (v) representation theories (express warranty and misrepresentation).

Exam Tip If the question does not indicate what theory of liability plaintiff is using, apply a strict liability theory.

2. Common Elements

To find liability under any products liability theory, plaintiff must show: (i) a ***defect*** and (ii) existence of the defect ***when the product left defendant's control***.

a. Types of Defects

1) Manufacturing Defects

If a product emerges from manufacturing different and more dangerous than the products made properly, it has a manufacturing defect.

2) Design Defects

When all products of a line are the same but have dangerous propensities, they may be found to have a design defect.

3) Inadequate Warnings

A product may be defective as a result of the manufacturer's failure to give adequate warnings as to the risks involved in using the product. For liability to attach, the danger must not be apparent to users.

b. Proving a Defect

1) Manufacturing Defects

For a manufacturing defect, defendant will be liable if plaintiff can show that the product failed to perform as safely as an ordinary consumer would expect (defendant must anticipate reasonable misuse). This test also applies to defective food products.

2) Design Defects

For a design defect, plaintiff usually must show that the defendant could have made the product safer, without serious impact on the product's price or utility.

3) Government Safety Standards

A product's ***noncompliance*** with government safety standards establishes that it is defective, while ***compliance*** with safety standards is evidence—but not conclusive—that the product is ***not*** defective.

4) **Scientifically Unknowable Risks**
Defendant will not be held liable for dangers not foreseeable at the time of marketing.

5) **Unavoidably Unsafe Products**
Manufacturers will not be held liable for some dangerous products (*e.g.,* knives) if the danger is apparent and there is no safer way to make the product.

c. **Existence of Defect When Product Left Defendant's Control**
The defect must have existed when the product left defendant's control. This will be inferred if the product moved through normal channels of distribution.

CMR Exam Tip In virtually all products liability actions, the fact that there was no contractual ***privity*** between the plaintiff and defendant will not prevent plaintiff from recovering. Nevertheless, it is still a favorite ***wrong choice*** in products liability exam questions based on negligence or strict liability theories. Remember that any foreseeable plaintiff, including a bystander, can sue any commercial supplier in the chain of distribution regardless of the absence of a contractual relationship between them.

B. LIABILITY BASED ON INTENT

Defendant will be liable to anyone injured by an unsafe product if defendant intended the consequences or knew that they were substantially certain to occur. If intent is present, the most likely tort is battery.

1. **Who Can Sue?**
Privity is not required, so any injured plaintiff can sue.

2. **Damages**
In addition to compensatory damages, punitive damages are available.

3. **Defenses**
The defenses are those available in other intentional torts cases.

C. LIABILITY BASED ON NEGLIGENCE

The prima facie case is the same as in any negligence case. Plaintiff must show (i) duty, (ii) breach, (iii) actual and proximate cause, and (iv) damages.

1. **Duty of Care**
A duty of care is owed to any foreseeable plaintiff.

a. **Who Can Sue?**
Privity with the defendant is no longer required, so any foreseeable plaintiff can sue. This includes:

1) Users;

2) Consumers; and

3) Bystanders.

b. **Who Can Be Held Liable?**
Commercial suppliers such as manufacturers, wholesalers, and retailers can be held liable.

2. **Breach of Duty**
Breach of duty is shown by (i) ***negligent conduct*** of defendant leading to (ii) the supplying of a ***defective product*** (as defined above).

a. **Proof of Negligence**
Negligence is proved the same as in a "standard" negligence case. The plaintiff may invoke res ipsa loquitur.

b. **Liability of Retailers and Wholesalers**
It is very difficult to hold retailers and wholesalers liable for negligence since they can usually satisfy their duty through a cursory inspection.

3. **Causation**
An intermediary's (*e.g.,* wholesaler's) negligent failure to discover a defect does not supersede the original manufacturer's negligence unless the intermediary's conduct exceeds ordinary foreseeable negligence.

4. **Nature of Damages Recoverable**
Physical injury or property damage must be shown. (Recovery will be denied if the sole claim is for economic loss.)

5. **Defenses**
The defenses are the same as in a general negligence action.

D. **LIABILITY BASED ON STRICT TORT LIABILITY**
The prima facie case: (i) a strict duty owed by a ***commercial supplier*** of a product; (ii) breach of that duty; (iii) actual and proximate cause; and (iv) damage.

1. **Duty**
Defendant has a duty to supply safe products.

a. **Who Can Sue?**
Privity is not required—users, consumers, and bystanders can sue.

1) **No Substantial Alteration**
For liability to attach, the product must reach plaintiff without substantial alteration.

2) **Does Not Extend to Services**
Strict products liability applies only to products. Even where a product is provided incident to a service (*e.g.,* blood during an operation), there is no strict liability. Plaintiff may, however, sue in negligence.

b. **Who Can Be Held Liable?**
Any commercial supplier can be held liable. Casual sellers will not be held strictly liable.

2. Breach of Duty

For breach of duty, plaintiff must show that the product is defective (as defined above). The defect must make the product unreasonably dangerous. Retailers may be liable even if they have no opportunity to inspect the product.

3. Causation

For actual cause, plaintiff must show that the defect existed when the product left defendant's control. Proximate cause is the same as in negligence cases.

4. Nature of Damages Recoverable

Physical injury or property damage must be shown. Recovery will be denied if the sole claim is for economic loss.

5. Defenses

In ***contributory negligence*** states, ordinary contributory negligence is no defense where plaintiff merely failed to discover the defect or guard against its existence, or where plaintiff's misuse was reasonably foreseeable. Assumption of the risk is a defense. In most ***comparative negligence*** states, courts will apply their comparative negligence rules.

6. Disclaimers Ineffective

Disclaimers are ***irrelevant*** in negligence or strict liability cases if personal injury or property damages occur.

E. IMPLIED WARRANTIES OF MERCHANTABILITY AND FITNESS

There are two warranties implied in every sale of goods that can serve as the basis for a suit by a buyer against a seller:

(i) ***Merchantability***, which refers to whether the goods are of average acceptable quality and are generally fit for the ordinary purpose for which the goods are used; and

(ii) ***Fitness for a particular purpose***, which arises when the seller knows or has reason to know the particular purpose for which the goods are required and that the buyer is relying on the seller's skill and judgment in selecting the goods.

1. Who Can Sue?

Most courts no longer require vertical privity. Most states adopted a narrow version of the horizontal privity requirement. This means the buyer, family, household, and guests can sue for personal injuries.

a. Bailee and Lessee

These warranties extend to bailments and leases as well as sales.

2. What Constitutes Breach?

If the product fails to live up to either of the above standards, the warranty is breached and the defendant will be liable.

a. Proof of Fault Unnecessary

Plaintiff does not have to prove any fault on the part of defendant.

3. Causation
Actual cause and proximate cause are handled as in ordinary negligence cases.

4. Damages
Personal injury and property damages, ***and purely economic*** loss, are recoverable.

5. Defenses
Defenses include assumption of risk (using a product while knowing of breach of warranty) and contributory negligence to the same extent as in strict liability cases. Failure to give notice of breach is a defense under the U.C.C. (even in personal injury cases).

6. Effect of Disclaimers
Disclaimers are generally rejected in personal injury cases but upheld for economic loss.

F. REPRESENTATION THEORIES
In addition to the theory of implied warranties, a defendant may be liable when a product does not live up to some affirmative representation. The two representation theories are:

1. Express Warranty
Any affirmation of fact or promise concerning goods that becomes part of the basis of the bargain creates an express warranty.

a. Who Can Sue?
Any consumer, user, or bystander can sue. If a buyer sues, the warranty must have been "part of the basis of the bargain." If plaintiff is not in privity (*e.g.,* bystander), she need not have relied on the representation as long as someone did.

1) Bailee and Lessee
This warranty extends to bailments and leases as well as sales.

b. Breach
Fault need not be shown to establish breach. Plaintiff need only show that the product did not live up to its warranty.

c. Causation, Damages, and Defenses
Causation, damages, and defenses are treated just as under implied warranties.

d. Disclaimers
A disclaimer will be effective only in the unlikely event that it is consistent with the warranty.

2. Misrepresentation of Fact
A seller will be liable for misrepresentations of facts concerning a product where:

(i) The statement was of a material fact concerning quality or uses of goods (mere puffery insufficient), and

(ii) The seller intended to induce reliance by the buyer in a particular transaction.

Liability is usually based on strict liability but may also arise for intentional or negligent misrepresentations.

PRODUCTS LIABILITY THEORIES

	Negligence	Strict Liability	Implied Warranties
Who Can Sue?	Any foreseeable plaintiff	Any foreseeable plaintiff	Purchaser and her family, household, and guests
Who Can Be Sued?	Any commercial supplier (*e.g.,* manufacturer, wholesaler, retailer)	Any commercial supplier	*Merchantability:* A merchant dealing in the kind of goods sold *Fitness for a Particular Purpose:* Any seller of the goods
What Constitutes Breach?	Negligent conduct that results in the supplying of a defective product	The supplying of a defective product	*Merchantability:* Sale of goods not generally acceptable or fit for ordinary purposes *Fitness for a Particular Purpose:* Sale of goods not fit for purpose that seller knows or has reason to know of (and knows that buyer is relying on seller's judgment)
What Damages Can Be Recovered?	Personal injury and property damage (no recovery for economic loss standing alone)	Personal injury and property damage (no recovery for economic loss standing alone)	Personal injury and property damage (recovery solely for economic loss also permitted)
What Defenses Are Available?	Assumption of the risk and any type of contributory negligence	*Contributory Negligence States:* Assumption of the risk and unreasonable misuse (failure to discover or guard against defect ***not*** a defense) *Comparative Negligence States:* Any type of fault (under state's comparative negligence rules)	*Contributory Negligence States:* Assumption of the risk, unreasonable misuse, and failure to give reasonable notice of breach *Comparative Negligence States:* Any type of fault (under state's comparative negligence rules)

a. **Justifiable Reliance**
Justifiable reliance is required (*i.e.,* the representation was a substantial factor in inducing the purchase). Reliance need not be the victim's (it may be a prior purchaser's). Privity is irrelevant.

b. **Causation and Damages**
Actual cause is shown by reliance. Proximate cause and damages are the same as for strict liability.

c. **Defenses**
Assumption of risk is not a defense if plaintiff is entitled to rely on the representation. Contributory negligence is the same as in strict liability, unless defendant committed intentional misrepresentation.

VI. NUISANCE

Nuisance is not a separate tort in itself. Rather, nuisances are a type of harm—the invasion of either private property rights or public rights by conduct that is tortious because it falls into the usual categories of tort liability (*i.e.,* intentional, negligent, strict liability). There are two types of nuisance: private and public.

A. PRIVATE NUISANCE

Private nuisance is a ***substantial***, ***unreasonable interference*** with another private individual's ***use or enjoyment*** of property that he actually possesses or to which he has a right of immediate possession.

CMR **Exam Tip** Nuisance questions on the MBE will often flag the correct choice with a key term from the definition of nuisance—*e.g.,* defendant is liable because the activity created a "substantial" (or "unreasonable") interference with plaintiff's use of her land.

1. **Substantial Interference**
Substantial interference is interference that is offensive, inconvenient, or annoying to the average person in the community. It is not substantial if it is merely the result of plaintiff's hypersensitivity or specialized use of his own property.

2. **Unreasonable Interference**
To establish unreasonable interference, required for nuisances based on intent or negligence, the severity of the inflicted injury must outweigh the utility of defendant's conduct. In balancing these respective interests, courts take into account that every person is entitled to use his own land in a reasonable way, considering the neighborhood, land values, and existence of any alternative courses of conduct open to defendant.

3. **Trespass to Land Distinguished**
In a trespass, there is an interference with the landowner's ***exclusive possession*** by a physical invasion; in a private nuisance, there is an interference with ***use or enjoyment***.

B. PUBLIC NUISANCE

Public nuisance is an act that unreasonably interferes with the ***health***, ***safety***, ***or property rights of***

the community, *e.g.,* using a building for criminal activities such as prostitution. Recovery by a private party is available for a public nuisance only if the private party suffered unique damage not suffered by the public at large.

C. REMEDIES

1. Damages

Plaintiff will usually be awarded damages.

2. Injunctive Relief

If the legal remedy of damages is unavailable or inadequate (*e.g.,* the nuisance will cause irreparable injury), injunctive relief will be awarded. In this case, the court will consider the relative hardships. However, hardships will not be balanced where defendant's conduct was either willful or against an assertion of right by plaintiff.

3. Abatement by Self-Help

In the case of a private nuisance, self-help abatement is available after notice to defendant and his refusal to act. Only necessary force may be used. In public nuisance cases, only a public authority or a private party who has suffered some unique damage can seek an injunction or abatement.

D. DEFENSES

1. Legislative Authority

Legislative authority for "nuisance activity" (*e.g.,* zoning ordinance) is not an absolute defense but is persuasive.

2. Conduct of Others

No one actor is liable for all damage caused by concurrence of his acts and others.

Example: Ten steel mills are polluting a stream. Each steel mill is responsible only for the pollution it causes.

3. Contributory Negligence

Contributory negligence generally is no defense to nuisance unless plaintiff's case rests on a negligence theory.

4. Coming to the Nuisance

One may "come to a nuisance" (purchasing land next to an already existing nuisance) and, thereafter, pursue an action. It is generally not a bar to plaintiff's action unless she "came to the nuisance" for the sole purpose of bringing a harassing lawsuit.

VII. GENERAL CONSIDERATIONS FOR ALL TORT CASES

A. VICARIOUS LIABILITY

Vicarious liability is liability that is derivatively imposed. In short, this means that one person commits a tortious act against a third party and another person will be liable to the third party for this act. The basic situations that you should note for bar examination purposes are set out below.

1. **Doctrine of Respondeat Superior**
A master/employer will be vicariously liable for tortious acts committed by her servant/ employee if the tortious acts occur within the ***scope of the employment*** relationship.

   a. **Frolic and Detour**
   An employee making a ***minor*** deviation from his employer's business for his own purposes is still acting within the scope of his employment. If the deviation in time or geographic area is substantial, the employer is not liable.

   b. **Intentional Torts**
   It is usually held that intentional tortious conduct by servants is not within the scope of employment. ***Exceptions:***

      1) Force is authorized in the employment, *e.g.,* bouncer.

      2) Friction is generated by employment, *e.g.,* bill collector.

      3) The servant is furthering the business of the master, *e.g.,* removing customers from the premises because they are rowdy.

2. **Independent Contractor Situations**
In general, a principal will not be liable for tortious acts of her agent if the agent is an independent contractor. Two ***broad exceptions*** exist, however:

   (i) The independent contractor is engaged in inherently dangerous activities, *e.g.,* blasting.

   (ii) The duty, because of public policy considerations, is simply nondelegable, *e.g.,* the duty to use due care in building a fence around an excavation site.

   a. **Liability for Negligent Selection**
   Both in respondeat superior and independent contractor cases, the employer may be liable for her ***own*** negligence in selecting the servant or independent contractor (*e.g.,* hospital liable for contracting with physician who negligently treats hospital's patient). (This is not vicarious liability.)

3. **Partners and Joint Venturers**
Each member of a partnership or joint venture is vicariously liable for the tortious conduct of another member committed in the ***scope and course*** of the affairs of the partnership or joint venture.

4. **Automobile Owner for Driver**
The general rule is that an automobile owner is not vicariously liable for the tortious conduct of another person driving his automobile. In some jurisdictions, courts employ theories other than vicarious liability to hold an automobile driver liable.

   a. **Family Car Doctrine**
   In many states, the owner is liable for tortious conduct of immediate family or household members who are driving with the owner's express or implied permission.

b. **Permissive Use**
A number of states have now gone further by imposing liability on the owner for damage caused by anyone driving with the owner's consent.

c. **Negligent Entrustment**
An owner may be liable for her ***own*** negligence in entrusting the car to a driver. Some states have also imposed liability on the owner if she was present in the car at the time of the accident, on the theory that she could have prevented the negligent driving, and hence was negligent herself in not doing so. (This is not vicarious liability.)

5. **Bailor for Bailee**
Under the general rule, the bailor is not vicariously liable for the tortious conduct of his bailee.

a. **Negligent Entrustment**
As above, the bailor may be liable for her ***own*** negligence in entrusting the bailed object. (This is not vicarious liability.)

6. **Parent for Child**
A parent is not vicariously liable for the tortious conduct of the child at common law. Note, however, that most states, by statute, make parents liable for the willful and intentional torts of their minor children up to a certain dollar amount (*e.g.,* $10,000).

a. **Child Acting as Agent for Parents**
Courts may impose vicarious liability if the child committed a tort while acting as the agent for the parents.

b. **Parent Liable for Own Negligence**
The parent may be held liable for her own negligence in allowing the child to do something, *e.g.,* use a dangerous object without proper instruction. Further, if the parent is apprised of the child's conduct on past occasions showing a tendency to injure another's person or property, she may be liable for not using due care in exercising control to mitigate such conduct, *e.g.,* by allowing the child to play with other children he has a history of attacking.

7. **Tavernkeepers**

a. **Common Law**
No liability was imposed on vendors of intoxicating beverages for injuries resulting from the vendee's intoxication, whether the injuries were sustained by the vendee or by a third person as a result of the vendee's conduct.

b. **Modern Law**
Many states, in order to avoid this common law rule, have enacted Dramshop Acts. Such acts usually create a cause of action in favor of any third person injured by the intoxicated vendee. Several courts have imposed liability on tavernkeepers even in the absence of a Dramshop Act. This liability is based on ordinary negligence principles (the foreseeable risk of serving a minor or obviously intoxicated adult) rather than vicarious liability.

Exam Tip When you see an MBE question on vicarious liability, recognizing whether the doctrine applies is only the first step in your analysis. Even where defendant is not vicariously liable, plaintiff may prevail if defendant personally was negligent in supervising the person causing the injury. Always look for this option among your answer choices.

CMR SUMMARY CHART

VICARIOUS LIABILITY

Party Committing Tortious Act	Vicarious Liability of Related Party
Employee/Servant	Employer/master vicariously liable if tortious act within scope of employment relationship
Independent Contractor	Employer of independent contractor ***not*** vicariously liable unless activity is inherently dangerous or duty is nondelegable on public policy grounds
Partner or Joint Venturer	Other partners or joint venturers vicariously liable if tortious act within scope and course of partnership or joint venture
Driver of Automobile	Owner of automobile ***not*** vicariously liable unless jurisdiction has family car doctrine or permissive use statute
Bailee of Chattel	Bailor ***not*** vicariously liable
Child	Parent ***not*** vicariously liable (except for limited statutory liability for willful and intentional torts)
Patron of Tavern	Tavernkeeper ***not*** vicariously liable in absence of Dramshop Act

Note: Even if the related party is not vicariously liable, she may be liable for her ***own negligence*** (*e.g.,* negligent selection of independent contractor, negligent entrustment of automobile, negligent supervision of child).

B. PARTIES—MULTIPLE DEFENDANT ISSUES

1. Joint and Several Liability

Where two or more negligent acts combine to proximately cause an indivisible injury, each negligent actor will be jointly and severally liable (*i.e.,* liable to plaintiff for the entire damage incurred). If the injury is divisible, each defendant is liable only for the identifiable portion.

a. **Defendants Acting in Concert**
Where two or more defendants act in concert and injure plaintiff, each is jointly and severally liable for the entire injury. This is so even if the injury is divisible.

b. **Statutory Limitations**
Many states have abolished joint liability either (i) for those defendants judged to be less at fault than plaintiff, or (ii) for all defendants regarding noneconomic damages. In these cases, liability will be proportional to defendant's fault.

2. **Satisfaction and Release**

a. **Satisfaction**
Recovery of full payment is a "satisfaction." Only one satisfaction is allowed. Until there is satisfaction, however, one may proceed against all jointly liable parties.

b. **Release**
At common law, a release of one joint tortfeasor was a release of all joint tortfeasors. A majority of states now provide that a release of one tortfeasor does not discharge other tortfeasors unless expressly provided in the release agreement.

3. **Contribution and Indemnity**
Contribution and indemnity are doctrines that determine how joint tortfeasors allocate between them the damages they must pay to a successful plaintiff.

Exam Tip To keep these two doctrines separate in your mind, recall that generally, for ***contribution*** to apply, both defendants must have a ***measurable degree*** of culpability for the tort, but ***indemnity*** usually applies when one of the parties is ***much more responsible*** than the other. It is important to note that neither of these doctrines affects how much the ***plaintiff*** receives. Rather, they deal with how much of the total award ***each defendant*** ultimately must pay.

a. **Contribution**
The contribution allows a defendant who pays more than his share of damages to have a claim against other jointly liable parties for the excess; *i.e.,* it ***apportions responsibility*** among those at fault.

1) **Limitations**
Contribution defendant must be originally liable to plaintiff. Also, contribution is not applicable to intentional torts.

2) **Methods of Apportionment**

a) **Comparative Contribution**
Most states have a comparative contribution system, whereby contribution is imposed in proportion to the ***relative fault*** of the various defendants.

b) **Equal Shares**
In a minority of states, apportionment is in ***equal shares*** regardless of degrees of fault.

b. **Indemnity**

Indemnity involves ***shifting the entire loss*** between or among tortfeasors. Indemnity is available in the following circumstances: (i) by contract, (ii) in vicarious liability situations, (iii) under strict products liability, and (iv) in some jurisdictions, where there has been an identifiable difference in degree of fault (*e.g.,* retailers who negligently rely on a product's condition may receive indemnification from the manufacturer who negligently manufactured it; one whose liability is based on a secondary duty may recover indemnification from a person who had a primary duty; one who is passively negligent may recover indemnification from a joint tortfeasor who is actively negligent).

c. **Comparative Contribution**

As noted above, most comparative negligence states have adopted a comparative contribution system where contribution is in proportion to the relative fault of the various defendants. This approach ***also*** supplants indemnification rules based on identifiable differences in degree of fault.

C. SURVIVAL AND WRONGFUL DEATH

1. Survival of Tort Actions

Survival acts allow one's cause of action to survive the death of one or more of the parties. The acts apply to actions involving torts to property and torts resulting in personal injury. However, torts invading intangible personal interest (*e.g.,* defamation, invasion of right of privacy, malicious prosecution) expire upon victim's death.

2. Wrongful Death

Wrongful death acts grant recovery for pecuniary injury resulting to the spouse and next of kin. A decedent's creditors have no claim against the amount awarded. Recovery is allowed only to the extent that the deceased could have recovered in action if he had lived (*e.g.,* deceased's contributory negligence reduces recovery in comparative negligence states).

D. TORTIOUS INTERFERENCES WITH FAMILY RELATIONSHIPS

1. Husband-Wife

Either spouse may bring an action for indirect interference with consortium and services caused by defendant's intentional or negligent tortious conduct against the other spouse.

2. Parent-Child

A parent may maintain an action for loss of a child's services as a result of defendant's tortious conduct, whether intentional or negligent. A child, however, has no action in most states against one who tortiously injures the parent.

3. Nature of Action

Actions for interference with family relationships are derivative. Hence, any defense that would prevent recovery by the injured family member also prevents recovery for interference with the family relationship.

E. TORT IMMUNITIES

1. Intra-Family Tort Immunities

Under the traditional view, one member of a family unit could not sue another in tort for personal injury. Most states have ***abolished husband-wife immunity***. A slight majority have also abolished parent-child immunity (but generally do not allow children to sue merely for negligent supervision). Those that retain it do not apply it (i) for intentional tortious conduct, and (ii) in automobile accident cases to the extent of insurance coverage.

2. Governmental Tort Immunity

In varying degrees, federal, state, and municipal tort immunity has been eliminated. Where it survives, immunity attaches to ***governmental***, not proprietary, functions.

a. Federal Government

Under the Federal Tort Claims Act, the United States has ***waived immunity*** for tortious acts. However, immunity will still attach for (i) assault, (ii) battery, (iii) false imprisonment, (iv) false arrest, (v) malicious prosecution, (vi) abuse of process, (vii) libel and slander, (viii) misrepresentation and deceit, and (ix) interference with contract rights. Immunity is not waived for acts that are characterized as "discretionary," as distinguished from those acts termed "ministerial."

b. State and Local Governments

Most states have substantially waived their immunity to the same extent as the federal government; about half have also abolished municipal immunity to the same extent. Where municipal immunity has been abolished, the "public duty" rule provides that a duty owed to the public at large is not owed to any particular citizen absent a special relationship between the governmental body and the citizen. Where municipal immunity still exists, contrast "governmental" functions (*i.e.,* functions that could only be performed adequately by the government) and "proprietary" functions (functions that might as well have been provided by a private corporation). Courts limit application of sovereign immunity by ***not*** granting it for proprietary functions.

c. Immunity of Public Officials

Public officials carrying out official duties are immune from tort liability for discretionary acts done without malice or improper purpose. Liability attaches, however, for ministerial acts.

3. Charitable Immunity

The majority of jurisdictions have eliminated charitable immunity.

USING INFORMATION Technology

USING INFORMATION Technology

Eleventh Edition

A Practical Introduction to Computers & Communications

BRIAN K. WILLIAMS | STACEY C. SAWYER

USING INFORMATION TECHNOLOGY, ELEVENTH EDITION
Published by McGraw-Hill Education, 2 Penn Plaza, New York, NY 10121.
This book is printed on acid-free paper.

5 6 7 8 9 10 QVS/QVS 20 19 18 17 16

ISBN 978-0-07-351688-2
MHID 0-07-351688-0

Senior Vice President, Products & Markets: *Kurt L. Strand*
Vice President, Content Production & Technology Services: *Kimberly Meriwether David*
Director: *Scott Davidson*
Senior Brand Manager: *Wyatt Morris*
Executive Director of Development: *Ann Torbert*
Development Editor II: *Alan Palmer*
Digital Development Editor II: *Kevin White*
Senior Marketing Manager: *Tiffany Russell*
Director, Content Production: *Terri Schiesl*
Content Project Manager: *Jean R. Starr*
Buyer: *Susan K. Culbertson*
Design: *Jana Singer*
Photo researcher: *Judy Mason*
Cover Image: *Image Source/Getty Images*
Senior Content Licensing Specialist: *Jeremy Cheshareck*
Typeface: *10/12 Times*
Compositor: *Laserwords Private Limited*
Printer: Quad Graphics

All credits appearing on page or at the end of the book are considered to be an extension of the copyright page.

Library of Congress Cataloging-in-Publication Data

Williams, Brian K., 1938
Using information technology / Brian K. Williams, Stacey C. Sawyer.—Eleventh edition.
pages cm
Includes bibliographical references and index.
ISBN 978-0-07-351688-2 (alk. paper)—ISBN 0-07-351688-0 (alk. paper)
1. Telecommunication systems. 2. Information technology. I. Sawyer, Stacey C. II. Title.
QA76.5.W5332 2015
004—dc23

2013046637

The Internet addresses listed in the text were accurate at the time of publication. The inclusion of a website does not indicate an endorsement by the authors or McGraw-Hill Education, and McGraw-Hill Education does not guarantee the accuracy of the information presented at these sites.

www.mhhe.com

Brief Contents

TO THE INSTRUCTOR xv

1 INTRODUCTION TO INFORMATION TECHNOLOGY: The Future Now 1

2 THE INTERNET & THE WORLD WIDE WEB: Exploring Cyberspace 49

3 SOFTWARE: Tools for Productivity & Creativity 113

4 HARDWARE: THE CPU & STORAGE—The Source of Computing Power 191

5 HARDWARE: INPUT & OUTPUT—Taking Charge of Computing & Communications 247

6 COMMUNICATIONS, NETWORKS, & CYBERTHREATS: The Wired & Wireless World 303

7 PERSONAL TECHNOLOGY: The Future Is You 367

8 THE ERA OF BIG DATA: Databases, Information Systems, & Artificial Intelligence 407

9 THE CHALLENGES OF THE DIGITAL AGE: Society & Information Technology Today 459

10 BUILDING SYSTEMS & APPLICATIONS: Software Development, Programming, & Languages 503

NOTES 551

CREDITS 569

INDEX 571

Contents

To the Instructor xv

1 INTRODUCTION TO INFORMATION TECHNOLOGY: THE FUTURE NOW 1

UNIT 1A: *The Mobile World, Information Technology, & Your Life* 2

1.1 Information Technology & Your Life: The Future Now 4

Two Parts of IT: Computers & Communications 4
Education: The Promise of More Interactive & Individualized Learning 4
Health: High Tech for Wellness 6
Money & Business: Toward the Cashless Society 10
Government & Electronic Democracy: Participating in the Civic Realm 10
Jobs & Careers 12
Your Personal Life 14

1.2 Information Technology Is Pervasive: Cellphones, Email, the Internet, & the E-World 15

The Phone Grows Up 15
"You've Got Mail!" Email's Mass Impact 16
The Internet, the World Wide Web, & the "Plumbing of Cyberspace" 17

UNIT 1B: *The Basics of Information Technology* 20

1.3 The Practical User: How Becoming Tech Smart Benefits You 20

1.4 The "All-Purpose Machine": The Varieties of Computers 22

All Computers, Great & Small: The Categories of Machines 22
Supercomputers 23
Mainframe Computers 24
Workstations 24
Microcomputers 24
Microcontrollers 26
Servers 26

1.5 Understanding Your Computer 27

How Computers Work: Three Key Concepts 27
Customizing a Desktop Computer: Basic Knowledge of How a Computer Works 28
Input Hardware: Keyboard & Mouse 28
Processing & Memory Hardware: Inside the System Cabinet 30
Storage Hardware: Hard Drive & CD/DVD Drive 30
Output Hardware: Video & Sound Cards, Monitor, Speakers, & Printer 32
Communications Hardware: Modem 33
Software 33

1.6 Where Is Information Technology Headed? 34

Computers: Miniaturization, Speed, & Affordability 34
Communications: Connectivity, Interactivity, & Multimedia 35
When Computers & Communications Converge: Portability, Personalization, Collaboration, Cloud Computing, & Artificial Intelligence 36
"E" Also Stands for Ethics 38

2 THE INTERNET & THE WORLD WIDE WEB: EXPLORING CYBERSPACE 49

UNIT 2A: *The Internet & the Web* 50

2.1 Connecting to the Internet: Narrowband, Broadband, & Access Providers 52

Narrowband (Dial-Up Modem): Low Speed but Inexpensive 53
High-Speed Phone Lines: More Expensive but Available in Cities & Most Towns 53
Problem for Telephone Internet Connections: The Last Mile 56
Cable Modem: Close Competitor to DSL 56
Satellite Wireless Connections 57
Other Wireless Connections: Wi-Fi, 3G, & 4G 58
Internet Access Providers 58

2.2 How Does the Internet Work? 59

Internet Connections: POPs, IXPs, Backbone, & Internet2 59

Internet Communications: Protocols, Packets, & IP Addresses 60

Who Runs the Internet? 62

2.3 The World Wide Web 62

The Face of the Web: Browsers, Websites, & Web Pages 62

How the Browser Finds Things: URLs 63

The Nuts & Bolts of the Web: HTML & Hyperlinks 65

Using Your Browser to Get around the Web 66

Web Portals: Starting Points for Finding Information 70

Search Services & Search Engines & How They Work 70

Four Web Search Tools: Individual Search Engines, Subject Directories, Metasearch Engines, & Specialized Search Engines 71

Smart Searching: Three General Strategies 73

Multimedia Search Tools: Image, Audio, & Video Searching 74

Tagging: Saving Links for Easier Retrieval Later 74

UNIT 2B: *The Riches & Risks of Internet Use* 76

2.4 Email, Instant Messaging, & Other Ways of Communicating over the Net 77

Two Ways to Send & Receive Email 78

How to Use Email 78

Instant Messaging 81

Discussion Groups: Mailing Lists, Newsgroups, & Message Boards 83

FTP: For Transferring Large Files 83

2.5 The Online Gold Mine: Telephony, Multimedia, Webcasting, Blogs, E-Commerce, & Social Networking 84

Telephony: The Internet Telephone 84

Multimedia on the Web 85

The Web Automatically Comes to You: Webcasting, Blogging, & Podcasting 88

E-Commerce: B2C, B2C, & C2C 90

Web 2.0, the Social Web: Social Networking, Media Sharing, & Social-Network Aggregation 92

Web 3.0: Computer-Generated Information with Less Human Interaction 93

2.6 The Intrusive Internet: Snooping, Spamming, Spoofing, Phishing, Pharming, Cookies, Spyware, & Malware 96

Snooping on Your Email & Texts: Your Messages Are Open to Anyone 96

Spam: Electronic Junk Mail 97

Spoofing, Phishing, & Pharming: Phony Email Senders & Websites 97

Cookies: Convenience or Hindrance? 98

Spyware—Adware, Browser & Search Hijackers, & Key Loggers: Intruders to Track Your Habits & Steal Your Data 98

Malware: The Viciousness of Viruses 100

Passwords 101

3 SOFTWARE: TOOLS FOR PRODUCTIVITY & CREATIVITY 113

UNIT 3A: *System Software: The Power behind the Power* 114

3.1 The Operating System: What It Does 115

Booting 116

CPU Management 118

File Management 118

Task Management 119

Security Management 120

3.2 Other System Software: Device Drivers & Utility Programs 121

Device Drivers: Running Peripheral Hardware 121

Utilities: Service Programs 121

3.3 Common Features of the User Interface 124

The GUI: The Graphical User Interface 126

The Help Command 133

3.4 Common Operating Systems 133

Stand-Alone Operating Systems: Macintosh & Windows 134

Network Operating Systems: OES, Windows Server, Unix, & Linux 140

Embedded Operating Systems 142

UNIT 3B: *Application Software: Getting Started* 144

3.5 Application Software: Where to Get It, How to Use It 144

Sources of Software: For Sale, For Free, or For Rent? 145

Tutorials & Documentation 148

Types of Application Software 149

3.6 Data Files & Program Files 150
Data Files 150
Program Files 152
Exchanging Data Files: Exporting & Importing 152
Data Compression: Putting More Data in Less Space 152

3.7 Word Processing Software 153

3.8 Spreadsheet Programs 158
The Basics: How Spreadsheet Programs Work 158
Analytical Graphics: Creating Charts 160

3.9 Database Software 161
The Benefits of Database Software 161
The Basics: How Databases Work 162

3.10 Software Suites & Integrated Packages 164
Software Suites 164
Integrated Packages 164
Personal Information Managers 164

3.11 Specialty Application Software 165
Presentation Graphics Software 166
Financial Software 168
Desktop Publishing 169
Drawing & Painting Programs 172
Video/Audio Editing Software 172
Animation Software 173
Multimedia Authoring Software 174
Web Page Design/Authoring Software 174
Project Management Software 176
Portable Document Format (PDF) 177
Computer-Aided Design (CAD) 178

4 HARDWARE: THE CPU & STORAGE—THE SOURCE OF COMPUTING POWER 191

UNIT 4A: *Processing: The System Unit, Microprocessors, & Main Memory* 192

4.1 Microchips, Miniaturization, & Mobility 193
Miniaturization Miracles: Microchips & Microprocessors 193
Miniaturization Leads to Mobility 195
The System Unit 196

4.2 Representing Data Electronically 197
The Binary System: Using On/Off Electrical States to Represent Data & Instructions 197
Machine Language 200

4.3 Inside the System Unit: Power Supply, Motherboard, & Microprocessors 200
Bays, Buttons, & Boards 201
Power Supply 201
The Motherboard & the Microprocessor Chip 203
The System Clock & Processing Speeds 208

4.4 The Central Processing Unit & the Machine Cycle 209
The Control Unit & the Machine Cycle 210
The Arithmetic/Logic Unit 211
Registers 211
Buses & Word Size 211

4.5 Memory 212
RAM 212
Cache Memory 213
ROM 214
Flash Memory 214
CMOS 214

4.6 Expansion Cards, Bus Lines, & Ports 215
Expansion Slots & Adapter Cards 215
Expansion Bus Lines 216
Ports 217

UNIT 4B: *Secondary Storage* 221

4.7 Secondary Storage 221
Hard Disks 221
Optical Disks: CDs, DVDs, & Blu-ray Disks 225
Flash & Solid-State Memory 228
Smart Cards 228
Cloud Storage 231

4.8 Future Developments in Processing & Storage 232
Future Developments in Processing 232
Future Developments in Secondary Storage 235

5 HARDWARE: INPUT & OUTPUT—TAKING CHARGE OF COMPUTING & COMMUNICATIONS 247

UNIT 5A: *Input Hardware* 249

5.1 Keyboards 249
The Different Types of Keyboards 250
Terminals 252

5.2 Pointing Devices 252

The Mouse 253
Variations on the Mouse: Trackball, Touchpad, & Pointing Stick 254
Touch Screen 256
Multitouch Screen 256
Pen Input 258

5.3 Source Data-Entry Devices 260

Scanning & Reading Devices 260
Image-Capture Devices 265
Audio-Input Devices 268
Sensors 270
Biometric-Input Devices 271

5.4 The Future of Input 271

Toward More Input from Remote Locations 272
Toward More Source Data Automation 273
Designs That Imitate the Physical World: Will They Be Abandoned? 275

UNIT 5B: *Output Hardware* 275

5.5 Softcopy Output: Display Screens 276

Features of Display Screens 276
Types of Display Devices 278

5.6 Hardcopy Output: Printers 280

Impact Printers 280
Nonimpact Printers 281
Multifunction Printers: Printers That Do More Than Print 284
Plotters 284
Specialty Printers 285

5.7 Mixed Output: Sound, Voice, & Video 286

Sound Output 287
Voice Output 287
Video Output 287

5.8 The Future of Output 288

More Unusual Forms of Output 288
More Data Used in Output 288
More Realistic Output 288

5.9 Quality of Life: Health & Ergonomics 290

Health Matters 290
Ergonomics: Design with People in Mind 292

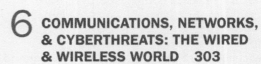

6 COMMUNICATIONS, NETWORKS, & CYBERTHREATS: THE WIRED & WIRELESS WORLD 303

UNIT 6A: *Networks & Wired & Wireless Media* 304

6.1 From the Analog to the Digital Age 305

Analog versus Digital Electrical Signals: Continuous Waves versus Discontinuous Bursts 305
Purpose of the Modem: Converting Digital Signals to Analog Signals & Back 306

6.2 Networks 308

The Benefits of Networks 308
Types of Networks: WANs, MANs, & Others 310
Network Architectures: How Networks Are Structured—Client-Server & Peer to Peer 312
Intranets, Extranets, VPNs, & Firewalls 313
Components of a Network 315
Network Topologies 318
Ethernet 321

6.3 Wired Communications Media 324

Wired Communications Media: Wires & Cables 324
Wired Communications Media for Homes 325

6.4 Wireless Communications Media 327

The Electromagnetic Spectrum, the Radio-Frequency (RF) Spectrum, & Bandwidth 327
Five Types of Wireless Communications Media 329
Long-Distance Wireless: One-Way Communication 332
Long-Distance Wireless: Two-Way Communication 335
Short-Range Wireless: Two-Way Communication 338

UNIT 6B: *Cyberthreats, Security, & Privacy Issues* 343

6.5 Cyberintruders: Trolls, Spies, Hackers, & Thieves 343

Trolls 343
Spies 344
Hackers 344
Thieves 345

6.6 Cyberattacks & Malware 347

Online Safety 350

6.7 Concerns about Privacy & Identity Theft 352

The Threat to Privacy 353
Identity Theft 354

7 PERSONAL TECHNOLOGY: THE FUTURE IS YOU 367

UNIT 7A: *Personal Devices for Improving Productivity at School & Work* 368

7.1 Convergence, Portability, & Personalization 369

Convergence 369
Portability 370
Personalization 371
Popular Personal Technologies 371

7.2 Smartphones: More Than Talk 371

How Do Cellphones & Smartphones Differ? 373
How a Mobile Phone Works 373
Text Messaging 375
Using Mobile Phones in College 376
The Societal Effects of Mobile Phones 376

7.3 Tablets & E-Readers 377

The Tablet: What It Is, What It Does 378
The E-Reader: The Reading Machine 380
The Benefits of E-Readers 380
How an E-Reader Works 381
The Drawbacks of E-Readers 382

7.4 Portable Media Players 382

Principal Features of MP3 Players 383
The Societal Effects of MP3 Players 384
Using MP3 Players in College 385

UNIT 7B: *Personal Devices for Enriching Leisure & Life* 386

7.5 Digital Cameras: Changing Photography 386

How Digital Cameras Work 387
The Societal Effects of Digital Cameras 392

7.6 High-Tech Radio: Satellite, Hybrid Digital, & Internet 393

Satellite Radio 393
HD Radio 394
Internet Radio 394

7.7 Digital Television 396

Interactive, Internet, & Internet-Ready TV: What's the Difference? 396
Three Kinds of Television: DTV, HDTV, SDTV 397
The Societal Effects of the New TV 398

7.8 Videogame Systems: The Ultimate Convergence Machine? 399

8 THE ERA OF BIG DATA: DATABASES, INFORMATION SYSTEMS, & ARTIFICIAL INTELLIGENCE 407

UNIT 8A: *Files & Databases* 408

8.1 Managing Files: Basic Concepts 409

How Data Is Organized: The Data Storage Hierarchy 409
The Key Field 411

8.2 Database Management Systems 412

The Benefits of Database Management Systems 412
Three Database Components 414
The Database Administrator 416

8.3 Database Models 416

Hierarchical Database 416
Network Database 418
Relational Database 419
Object-Oriented Database 422
Multidimensional Database 423

8.4 Data Mining 425

The Process of Data Mining 426

UNIT 8B: *Big Data, Information Systems, & Artificial Intelligence* 428

8.5 The Evolving World of Big Data 428

Three Implications of Big Data 428
The Uses of Big Data 429

8.6 Information Systems in Organizations: Using Databases to Help Make Decisions 430

The Qualities of Good Information 430
Information Flows within an Organization 430
Computer-Based Information Systems 432
Office Information Systems 433
Transaction Processing Systems 434
Management Information Systems 435
Decision Support Systems 435
Executive Support Systems 437
Expert Systems 437

8.7 Artificial Intelligence 438

Conventional AI versus Computational Intelligence: "Neats" versus "Scruffies" 438
Weak AI versus Strong AI 438
Expert Systems 439
Natural Language Processing 442
Intelligent Agents 442
Pattern Recognition 442
Virtual Reality & Simulation Devices 442
Robotics 444
Fuzzy Logic 446
Neural Networks 447

8.8. Artificial Life, the Turing Test, & the Singularity 447

How Can We Know a Machine Is Truly Intelligent? 448
"The Singularity": The Concept of Smarter-Than-Human Computers 450
Ethics in AI 451
Databases: Concerns about Privacy & Identity Theft 451

9 THE CHALLENGES OF THE DIGITAL AGE: SOCIETY & INFORMATION TECHNOLOGY TODAY 459

UNIT 9A: *Security, Privacy, & Surveillance Concerns* 460

9.1 Security Issues: Threats to Computers & Communications Systems 461

Errors, Accidents, & Natural Hazards 461
Computer Crimes 464

9.2 Security Safeguards: Protecting Computers & Communications 470

Deterrents to Computer Crime 470
Identification & Access 472
Encryption 474
Protection of Software & Data 474
Disaster-Recovery Plans 475

9.3 Privacy & Surveillance: Data Collectors & Spies 475

Business & Cyberspying 476
Government & Cyberspying 477
Spying, Hacking, & Cyberwarfare by Foreign Governments & Groups 482

UNIT 9B: *Other Social, Economic, & Political Issues* 484

9.4 Truth Issues: Manipulating Digital Data 484

Manipulation of Sound 485
Manipulation of Photos 485
Manipulation of Video & Television 487

9.5 Quality-of-Life Issues: The Environment, Mental Health, Child Protection, & the Workplace 487

Environmental Problems 487
Mental Health Problems 490
Protecting Children: Pornography, Sexual Predators, & Online Bullies 492
Workplace Problems: Impediments to Productivity 494

9.6 Economic & Political Issues: Employment & the Haves/Have-Nots 496

Technology, the Job Killer? 496
Digital Divide between Rich & Poor 497
Whom Does the Internet Serve? 497
In a World of Breakneck Change, Can You Still Thrive? 498

10 BUILDING SYSTEMS & APPLICATIONS: SOFTWARE DEVELOPMENT, PROGRAMMING, & LANGUAGES 503

UNIT 10A: *Systems Development & Programming* 504

10.1 Systems Development & the Life Cycle of a Software Project 505

The Purpose of Systems Analysis & Design 505
Getting the Project Going: How It Starts, Who's Involved 506
The Six Phases of Systems Analysis & Design 507
The First Phase: Preliminary Investigation 507
The Second Phase: Systems Analysis 509
The Third Phase: Systems Design 511
The Fourth Phase: Systems Development 512
The Fifth Phase: Systems Implementation 513
The Sixth Phase: Systems Maintenance 514

10.2 Programming: Traditionally a Five-Step Procedure 515

The First Step: Clarify the Programming Needs 516
The Second Step: Design the Program 517

The Third Step: Code the Program 523
The Fourth Step: Test the Program 523
The Fifth Step: Document & Maintain the Program 525

UNIT 10B: *Programming Languages* 526

10.3 Five Generations of Programming Languages 526

First Generation: Machine Language 528
Second Generation: Assembly Language 528
Third Generation: High-Level or Procedural Languages 529
Fourth Generation: Very-High-Level or Problem-Oriented Languages 531
Fifth Generation: Natural Languages 531

10.4 Programming Languages Used Today 532

FORTRAN 532
COBOL 532
BASIC 534
Pascal 534
C 534
C++ 534
LISP 534

10.5 Object-Oriented & Visual Programming 535

Object-Oriented Programming (OOP) 535
Visual Programming: The Example of Visual BASIC 537

10.6 Markup & Scripting Languages 537

HTML 540
VRML 540
XML 540
JavaScript 541
Flash 541
ActiveX 541
CGI (Common Gateway Interface) 542
Perl 542
PHP (Personal Home Page, or PHP Hypertext Preprocessor) 542

Notes 551
Credits 569
Index 571

Practical Action Box

How to Be a Successful Online Student 7
Managing Email 18
Evaluating & Sourcing Information Found on the Web 75
Serious Web Search Techniques 76
Social Networking: The Downside 94
Tips for Avoiding Spyware 100
Utility Programs: Specialized Programs to Make Computing Easier 122
Help in Building Your Web Page 177
Power Issues: Problems with Electric Power to Your Computer 205
Starting Over with Your Hard Drive: Erasing, Reformatting, & Reloading 224
Storing Your Stuff: How Long Will Digitized Data Last? 230
Buying a Printer 286
Telecommuting & Telework: The Virtual Workplace 323
Virtual Meetings: Linking Up Electronically 342
The Consequences of Choice Overload 372
Multitasking—Good for Productivity? 381
Online Viewing & Sharing of Digital Photos 391
Accuracy & Completeness 415
Is the Boss Watching You? Trust in the Workplace 478

Experience Box

Better Organization & Time Management: Dealing with the Information Deluge in College—& in Life 39
Web Research, Term Papers, & Plagiarism 102
Getting Help from Tech Support 180
How to Buy a Laptop 237
Good Habits: Protecting Your Computer System, Your Data, & Your Health 293
Guarding Your Privacy & Preventing Your Identity from Getting Stolen 357
The "Always On" Generation 402
How the Rise of the Robots Will Affect Future Employment 452
Student Use of Computers: Some Controversies 499
Critical Thinking Tools 543

Tech Tales

The Rise of Mobile Computing: The Getting-Smarter Smartphone 2
Technology in Education: Adjusting Instructor Presentations to the Students 5

New Telemedicine: The Doctor Will See You Now—Right Now 8

What Apps Do You Really Need? 20

Artificial Intelligence: The Use of Algorithms to Create a Hit Song 38

How a World-Shaking Technology Came About: Tim Berners-Lee Invents the World Wide Web 63

The Continuing Development of Browsers: The War for Smartphones & Tablets 66

Web Imaging & Aerial Mapping: Google Earth 86

Animation: The Making of "Fetch," a Mobile Game 87

The Rise of the Blogosphere: "Writing Out Loud" 89

Changing Retail Practices: The Fight against "Showrooming" 91

How Difficult It Is to Keep Your Emails & Texts Private 96

The War for Dominance in Mobile Operating Systems 116

New Technology to Replace the Mouse: The Gesture Interface 125

China Adopts Linux as Its National Standard 142

Software Evolution: 40 Years of Blasting Space Aliens—the Incredible Growth in Videogames 144

Free Software for Cash-Strapped Students 148

Vacuum Tubes Still Beat People Power 192

The Fabulous Fab—What Does It Take to Support a Chip Manufacturing Plant? 194

Where Are Data Centers Located? 207

The World's DVD Zones 227

Nanotechnology, the Movie 233

Loren Brichter, Popularizer of "Pull to Refresh" & the "Cell Swipe" 257

RFID Tags for Security 263

"Know What I'm Sayin'?": The Uses of Speech-Recognition Systems 268

Sensors Get Data We Never Had Before 270

Input & Output Together: Paving the Way for the Self-Driving Car 275

Dreams of 3-D Printing 290

Painful Technology for College Students 290

Can Cellphones Cause Cancer? 292

Recording Music: From Analog Life to Digital Life 308

"Gotcha, Thief!" & Other Uses of GPS 334

Microsoft Pays "Bug Bounties" to White-Hat Hackers 345

Too-Good-to-Be-True Deals Online 346

The Love Bug & Other Viruses 348

Famous Worms: Klez, Conficker, & Stuxnet 348

The Weird Experience of Identity Theft 354

The Ruggedized Tablet for Splashes & Spills 379

The Rise of the Selfie: What Does It Mean? 392

Pandora's Music Genome Project 395

Using Your Xbox to Order Pizza 400

Databases Everywhere 409

How Amazon.com Used Databases to Become the World's Largest Online Bookstore 413

The Uses of Data Mining 427

The Brute Force of Weak AI 439

Some Interestingly Named Expert Systems 439

Using Virtual Reality & Simulation for Training, Treatment, & Research 444

All Types of Robots 446

Applying Fuzzy Logic to Elevators 446

A Scene from the Turing Test 449

How Slow Perceptions Lead to Errors: Texting While Driving 461

Glitches in the System: How Electrical & Mechanical Problems Can Make Computers Fail 462

The Risks of Natural Hazards: How Bad Can It Get? 464

Stealing Music & Movies 466

The Nigerian Letter, a Classic Internet Scam 469

Police Use of License Plate Scanners 479

Cyberattacks That Challenge Governments & Corporations 483

Is It Fraudulent to Manipulate Sound? 485

Is It Fraudulent to Manipulate Photos? 485

Gambling in the New IT World 492

"Bring Your Own Device" to Work: Applying Systems Analysis & Design to the BYOD Trend 507

Stumbles on the Road to Progress: When Big Systems Fail 514

Who Decides When Programs Are Okay to Go? The Release Engineer 524

Student Entrepreneurs Create a New App in Five Days with "Premade Programming Lego Blocks" 536

To the Instructor

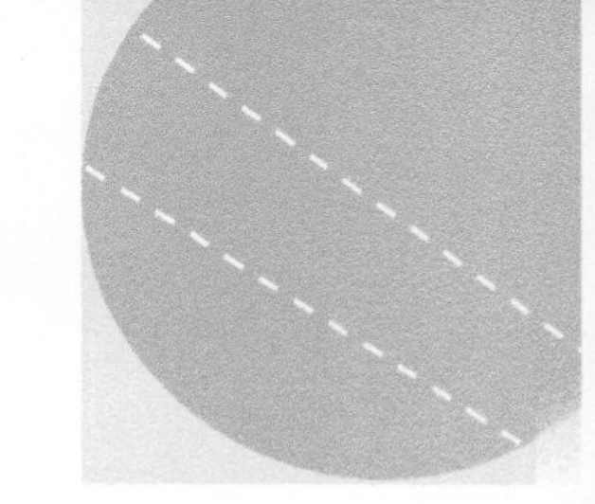

INTRODUCTION: Not Just a Revision, a Reimagining

The tumultuous changes in the landscape of information technology over the last two years have led us to make extensive modifications in this edition of *Using Information Technology*—to do **not just a revision but a remaking and reimagining** of this introductory computer concepts book.

In addition, because of the rise in distractions, stresses, and information overload on students, we have made every effort **to increase the readability, teachability, and memorability** of our material—using more storytelling, more headings, more mnemonic aids.

CONTENT CHANGES IN THIS EDITION: Addressing New Paradigms

Throughout its 18-year history, *Using Information Technology* has been written and substantially **revised around historic paradigm changes**—in the *First Edition* the impact of digital convergence, or the fusion of computers and communications; in the *Fourth Edition* the new priorities of cyberspace imposed by the Internet and World Wide Web; in the *Seventh Edition* the ascendancy of the "Always On" generation of students, who are at ease with but not always knowledgeable about digital technology.

In this *Eleventh Edition,* **we address the following history-altering developments:**

- **The explosion of mobile computing:** In the United States there are now more smartphones, tablets, laptops, and other such portable devices than there are people.
- **The rise of "the cloud":** Moving data storage and processing from desktops and laptops to online servers is changing the economics and availability of computing power.
- **The boom in Big Data:** The growth in servers, software sophistication, and data collection methods results in 2.5 quintillion bytes of data being created every day.
- **The evolution of artificial intelligence:** Supercomputers, mammoth databases, and powerhouse software make AI a force that's sure to alter nearly every field of human endeavor.
- **The acceleration in computer threats:** Every day the efforts of black-hat hackers, virus writers, and cyberwar makers threaten to sabotage our major institutions.
- **The shrinking of privacy:** Search companies, mobile carriers, and retailers track our Internet patterns, cellphone usage, and shopping habits to learn more and more about us.
- **The increase in government surveillance:** Cyberspying by U.S. agencies, as well as by foreign governments, challenges individual and institutional freedom and security.

The extensive content changes for this edition are described beginning on p. xx.

PRESENTATION CHANGES IN THIS EDITION: Making the Material Easier to Learn

To help students realize the valuable education they have paid for, we have done our best to make this text **practical, readable, and current** by presenting information in ways that *motivate, entertain, and get quickly to the point* by using **the following new features:**

- **We teach concepts by referring to what students already know:** Most students come to this book **already knowledgeable about mobile technology.** In this edition, then, we introduce new concepts by building on the student's existing knowledge.
- **We present compelling examples through storytelling:** Most people seem to learn more from stories than from having facts thrown at them. This edition offers **a new feature called TECH TALES, which provide "*mini-cases,*" business related and otherwise, to illustrate concepts.**
- **We expand the use of headings:** Our approach is to have frequent headings as organizers. In this edition, **each chapter is divided into two units, UNIT A and UNIT B, to help students get a better grasp of the material.** We've also added more subheadings throughout.
- **We open each chapter with an overview—a CHAPTER FORECAST:** Every chapter opens with a short summary, to give the student a clear vision of the road ahead.

MOTIVATING THE UNMOTIVATED & TEACHING TO A DISPARITY OF BACKGROUNDS

As authors, we find information technology tremendously exciting, but we recognize that many students take the course reluctantly. And we also recognize that many students come to the subject with attitudes ranging from complete apathy and unfamiliarity to a high degree of experience and technical understanding.

To address the problem of **motivating the unmotivated and teaching to a disparity of backgrounds,** *Using Information Technology* offers unequaled treatment of the following:

1. **Practicality**
2. **Readability**
3. **Currentness**
4. **Three-level critical thinking system**

We explain these features on the following pages.

FEATURE 1: Emphasis on Practicality

This popular feature received overwhelming acceptance by both students and instructors in past editions. **Practical advice,** of the sort found in computer magazines, newspaper technology sections, and general-interest computer books, is expressed not only in the text but also in the following features:

- Experience Box
- Practical Action Box
- Survival Tips

Experience Box

Appearing at the end of each chapter, the Experience Box has optional material that may be assigned at the instructor's discretion. However, students will find the subjects covered are of immediate value.

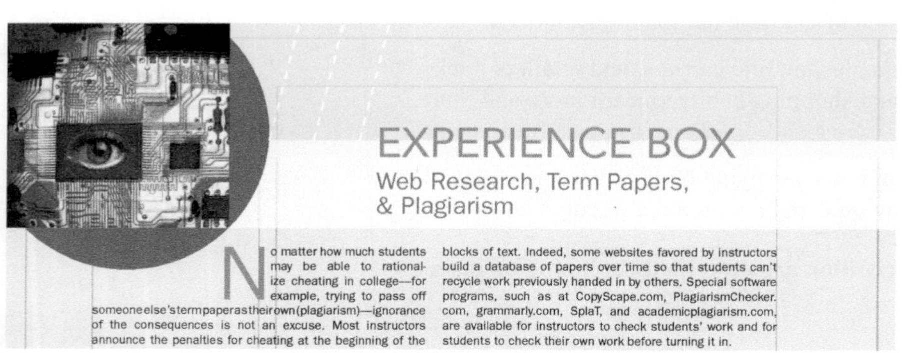

EXPERIENCE BOX

Web Research, Term Papers, & Plagiarism

No matter how much students may be able to rationalize cheating in college—for example, trying to pass off someone else's term paper as their own (plagiarism)—ignorance of the consequences is not an excuse. Most instructors announce the penalties for cheating at the beginning of the blocks of text. Indeed, some websites favored by instructors build a database of papers over time so that students can't recycle work previously handed in by others. Special software programs, such as at CopyScape.com, PlagiarismChecker.com, grammarly.com, SplaT, and academicplagiarism.com, are available for instructors to check students' work and for students to check their own work before turning it in.

Examples: "Web Research, Term Papers, & Plagiarism," "Getting Help from Tech Support," "How to Buy a Laptop," and "How the Rise of the Robots Will Affect Future Employment."

Practical Action Box

This box consists of optional material on practical matters.

Examples: "How to Be a Successful Online Student," "Evaluating & Sourcing Information Found on the Web," "Tips for Avoiding Spyware," "Utility Programs: Specialized Programs to Make Computing Easier," "Social Networking: The Downside," "Help in Building Your Web Page," "Storing Your Stuff: How Long Will Digitized Data Last?," "Starting Over with Your Hard Drive: Erasing, Reformatting, & Reloading," "Telecommuting & Telework: The Virtual Workplace," "The Consequences of Choice Overload," "Online Viewing & Sharing of Digital Photos," and "Is the Boss Watching You? Trust in the Workplace."

PRACTICAL ACTION

How to Be a Successful Online Student

1. **Familiarize yourself with the computer and software.** Be comfortable with the computer, Internet, email, web browser, and search engine software. Use tutorials to become familiar with the software used by your online school.

    Take advantage of technology. Learn the various ways of communicating on the web. Blogging, podcasting, video conferencing, and chatting (discussed later

time. You may feel that taking an online course will free up your time for other tasks. If you are feeling overwhelmed by other responsibilities, such as work or family obligations, then perhaps you had better postpone your involvement. Online courses require as much and often more personal preparation time than on-campus courses. Remember everything that you would nor-

Survival Tips

In the margins throughout we present utilitarian **Survival Tips** to aid students' explorations of the infotech world.

Examples: "Broadband: Riskier for Security," "Connection Speeds," "Finding Things on a Web Page or in a Web Document," "Urban Legends & Lies on the Internet," "Social-Networking Privacy," "Control Those Cookies!" "New Software & Compatibility," "What RAM for Your PC?," "ATMs & Fraud/Safety," "Firewalls," "E-Book Cautions," "Alleviating Info-Mania," "Fraud Baiters," and "What Happens to Your Smartphone Data?"

Survival Tip

New Software & Compatibility

Pay attention to compatibility requirements when you obtain new software. The system requirements for running the software will be listed on the box or included with the downloaded information. When it is time to update the software, you can usually do that by paying a small upgrade fee to the software manufacturer and then downloading the new version and/or obtaining a new CD/DVD.

FEATURE 2: Emphasis on Readability & Reinforcement for Learning

We offer the following features for reinforcing student learning:

Interesting Writing—Based on Good Scholarship

Where is it written that textbooks have to be boring? Can't a text have personality?

Actually, studies have found that textbooks **written in an imaginative style** significantly improve students' ability to retain information. Both instructors and students have commented on the distinctiveness of the writing in this book. In this edition, we have added **Tech Tales, stories or mini-cases, to illustrate concepts.** We also employ a number of journalistic devices—colorful anecdotes, short biographical sketches, and interesting observations—to make the material as engaging as possible. In addition we use real anecdotes and examples rather than fictionalized ones.

Finally, **unlike most computer concepts books, we provide references for our sources—see the endnotes in the back of the book. Many of these are from the year preceding publication.** We see no reason why introductory computer books shouldn't practice good scholarship by revealing their information sources. And we see no reason why good scholarship can't go along with good writing—scholarship need not mean stuffiness.

Key Terms AND Definitions Emphasized

To help readers avoid confusion about important terms and what they actually mean, we print each key term in **red bold** and its definition in **black boldface.** ***Example:*** "**Data consists of raw facts and figures that are processed into information.**"

Material in Easily Manageable Portions

Major ideas are presented in **bite-size form,** with generous use of advance organizers, bulleted lists, and new paragraphing when a new idea is introduced. Most **sentences have been kept short,** the majority not exceeding 22–25 words in length.

"Terms & Explanations" Displayed in Easily Reviewable Form

To help students review the technical terms and vocabulary used in computing, we have created at the end of every chapter a section titled "Terms & Explanations," which not only gives the meaning of every key term introduced in the chapter but also explains why it is important. See, for example, pages 239, 296, and 359.

Emphasis throughout on Ethics

See Ethics examples on pages 38, 81, 96,146, 236, 264, 344, and 353.

Many texts discuss ethics in isolation, usually in one of the final chapters. We believe this topic is too important to be treated last or lightly, and users have agreed. Thus, **we cover ethical matters throughout the book,** as indicated by the special icon shown at left. ***Example:*** We discuss such all-important questions as online plagiarism, privacy, computer crime, and netiquette.

ethics

Emphasis throughout on Security

See Security icons on pages 38, 96, 120, 229, 230, 263, 271, 275, 315, 334, 343, 347, 353, and 357.

In the post 9-11 era, security concerns are of gravest importance. Although we devote several pages (in Chapters 2, 6, and 9) to security matters, we also reinforce student awareness by **highlighting with page-margin Security icons instances of security-related material throughout the book. *Example:*** In one case, we use the special icon shown at left to highlight the advice that one should pretend that every email message one sends "is a postcard that can be read by anyone."

SECURITY

"More Info!" Icons Help Students Find Their Own Answers to Questions

In addition, our **"More Info!" feature encourages students to get actively involved in the material.**

Examples: "Finding Wi-Fi Hot Spots," "Do You Need to Know HTML to Build a Website?," "Blog Search Engines," "Some Online Communities," "Links to Security Software," and "Where to Learn More about Freeware & Shareware."

more info!

GPS & Cellphone Tracking

Cellphone companies may be tracking your every move and compiling information about you . . .

www.bloomberg.com/news/2013-06-06/carriers-sell-users-tracking-data-in-5-5-billion-market.html

Eight Timelines to Provide Historical Perspective

See timelines beginning on pages 16, 50, 164, 194, 254, 304, 416, and 532.

Some instructors like to see coverage of the history of computing. Not wishing to add greatly to the length of the book, we decided on **a student-friendly approach: the presentation of eight pictorial timelines showing the most significant historical IT events.** These timelines, which occur in most chapters, appear along the bottom page area. (See the example at the bottom of this page.) Each timeline repeats certain "benchmark"

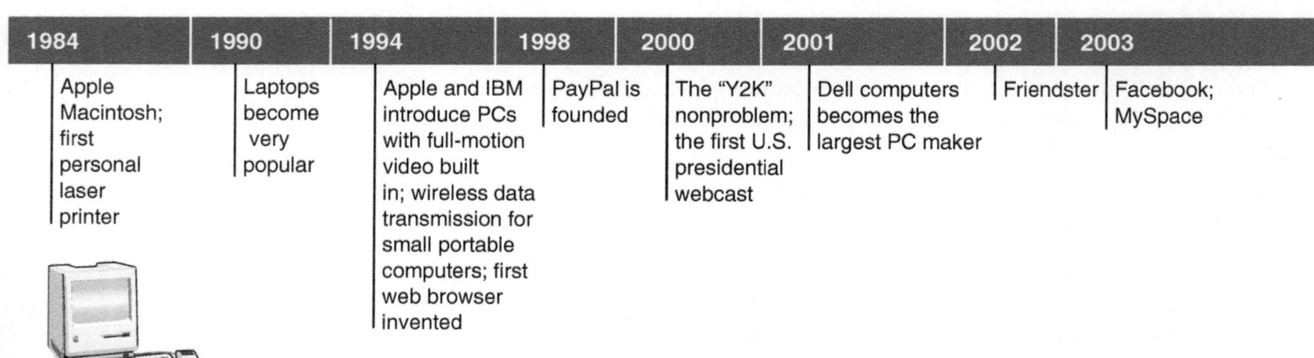
1984
Apple Macintosh; first personal laser printer
1990
Laptops become very popular
1994
Apple and IBM introduce PCs with full-motion video built in; wireless data transmission for small portable computers; first web browser invented
1998
PayPal is founded
2000
The "Y2K" nonproblem; the first U.S. presidential webcast
2001
Dell computers becomes the largest PC maker
2002
Friendster
2003
Facebook; MySpace

events to keep students oriented, but **each one is modified to feature the landmark discoveries and inventions appropriate to the different chapter material.** ***Examples:*** In Chapter 3 on software, the timeline features innovations in operating systems. In Chapter 6 on communications, the timeline highlights innovations in data transmission.

FEATURE 3: Currentness

Reviewers have applauded previous editions of *UIT* for being **more up to date than other texts.** For example, we have traditionally ended many chapters with a forward-looking section that offers a preview of technologies to come—some of which are realized even as students are using the book.

Among the new topics and terms covered in this edition are: *Accelerated Graphics Port (ACP) bus, air mouse, AMOS, Apple iCloud, apps, Big Data, Bootcamp, booting from the cloud, Bring Your Own Device (BYOD) policy, bug bounty, business-to-consumer (B2C) commerce, Chrome, Chrome OS, Chromebook, cloud-based apps, computational AI, condensed keyboards, consumer-to-consumer (C2C) commerce, conventional AI, convertible tablets, cyberattacks, Dashboard, data centers, Detrx keyboard, distributed denial of service, drones, email bombs, embedded Linux OS, EMV cards, eSATA ports, ethical hackers, ExpressCards, FireWire bus, FISA court, Google Apps, Google Glass, heuristics, hybrid tablets/PCs, Instagram, iPhone 5, iPhone iOS, KALC keyboard, Kinect, Leap Motion, LTE telecommunication standards, machine learning, massive open online courses (MOOCs), mesh networks, metadata, Microsoft Xbox One, Mountain Lion, Mozilla Firefox OS, multitouch screens, National Security Agency (NSA), Nintendo Wii U, octa-core processors, online dating, passphrases, personal browser, Pinterest, Pokki, power-line network, predictive search apps, robots grouped by application, robots grouped by locomotion, Privacy and Civil Liberties Oversight Board, self-driving cars, selfies, semantic markup, showrooming, slate tablets, Snapkeys Si, Sony PlayStation 4, Spotlight, Surface tablet, T3 lines, T4 lines, T5 lines, texting, threaded discussion, tree networks, trolls, wearable technology, Web 1.0, Web 3.0, Web app, WiMax, Windows 7, Windows 8, Windows Phone 8, Windows RT, Windows Server 2012,* and *wireless Internet service provider (WISP).*

Material has also been updated on the following: *Android, artificial intelligence (AI), cellphone malware, cloud computing, cyberwarfare, data collection on consumers by business, e-readers, gesture interface, government spying, image-capture devices, image-compression technology, improved digital cameras, Internet usage, Mac OS X, malware, metadata mining, mobile-payment services, nanotechnology, online (distance) learning, passwords, privacy, 3-D printers,* and *tablets.*

A complete update of the chapter-by-chapter changes from the previous edition begins on p. xx.

FEATURE 4: Three-Level System to Help Students Think Critically about Information Technology

This feature has been well received. More instructors are familiar with **Benjamin Bloom's *Taxonomy of Educational Objectives,*** describing a hierarchy of six critical-thinking skills: (a) two lower-order skills—*memorization* and *comprehension*—and (b) four higher-order skills—*application, analysis, synthesis,* and *evaluation.* Drawing on our experience in writing books to guide students to college success, we have implemented Bloom's ideas in a three-stage pedagogical system, using the following hierarchical approach in the Chapter Review at the end of every chapter:

Stage 1 Learning—Memorization: "I Can Recognize and Recall Information"

Using self-test questions, multiple-choice questions, and true-false questions, we enable students to test how well they recall basic terms and concepts.

Stage 2 Learning—Comprehension: "I Can Recall Information in My Own Terms and Explain It to a Friend"

Using open-ended, short-answer questions, we enable students to re-express terms and concepts in their own words.

Stage 3 Learning—Applying, Analyzing, Synthesizing, Evaluating: "I Can Apply What I've Learned, Relate These Ideas to Other Concepts, Build on Other Knowledge, and Use All These Thinking Skills to Form a Judgment"

In this part of the Chapter Review, we ask students to put the ideas into effect using the activities described. The purpose is to help students take possession of the ideas, make them their own, and apply them realistically to their own ideas. **Our web exercises are also intended to spur discussion in classroom and other contexts.**

Examples: "Using Text Messaging in Emergencies," "What's Wrong with Using Supermarket Loyalty Cards?," and "Are You in the Homeland Security Database?"

RESOURCES FOR INSTRUCTORS

Online Learning Center

The Online Learning Center *(www.mhhe.com/uit11e)* is designed to provide students with additional learning opportunities and instructors with additional teaching tools. For instructors, the website includes PowerPoint presentations for each chapter. For the convenience of instructors, all the following resources are available for download.

To help maintain high quality in the supplements, the textbook authors have personally updated the Instructor's Manual, Testbank, and PowerPoint presentation.

Instructor's Manual

The electronic Instructor's Manual, which is available as part of the Instructor's Resource Kit, helps instructors create effective lectures. The Instructor's Manual is easy to navigate and simple to understand. Each chapter contains a chapter overview, lecture outline, teaching tips, additional information, and answers to end-of-chapter questions and exercises.

Testbank

The format of the Testbank allows instructors to effectively pinpoint areas of content within each chapter on which to test students. The test questions include learning difficulty level, answers, and text page numbers, as well as the learning objective head under which the question content falls and the level of Bloom's Taxonomy that applies to the question.

EZ Test

McGraw-Hill's EZ Test is a flexible and easy-to-use electronic testing program. The program allows instructors to create tests from book-specific items. It accommodates a wide range of question types, and instructors may add their own questions. Multiple versions of the test can be created and any test can be exported for use with course management systems such as WebCT, BlackBoard, or PageOut. EZ Test Online is a new service and gives you a place to easily administer your EZ Test–created exams and quizzes online. The program is available for Windows and Macintosh environments.

PowerPoint Presentation

The PowerPoint presentation includes material that expands on main topics from the text, allowing instructors to create engaging classroom sessions. Each chapter's presentation includes helpful illustrations that emphasize important concepts.

CHAPTER-BY-CHAPTER CHANGES FROM THE PREVIOUS EDITION

1. Introduction to Information Technology: The Future Now

UNIT 1A: THE MOBILE WORLD, INFORMATION TECHNOLOGY, & YOUR LIFE. **Chapter introduction and Section 1.1 repurposed to stress importance of mobile computing. Smartphones, tablet computers, and social networks introduced. Concept of database introduced.** Material updated on high-paying salaries and attractiveness of IT careers. New **material added: "Starting Up Your Own Venture," social media in job hunting, and technology in your personal life, including online dating sites.** Obsolete chart deleted on technology areas that people devote their time to. Subsections deleted on leisure and on college students and the e-world.

UNIT 1B: THE BASICS OF INFORMATION TECHNOLOGY. Former Section 1.1, "The Practical User," now Section 1.3. Material updated on fastest supercomputers. **New material added on mobile devices, Big Data, machine learning, algorithms, and overview of artificial intelligence.**

Tech Tales added: "The Rise of Mobile Computing: The Getting-Smarter Smartphone," "Technology in Education: Adjusting Instructor Presentations to the Students," "New Telemedicine: The Doctor Will See You Now—Right Now," "What Apps Do You Really Need?," and "Artificial Intelligence: The Use of Algorithms to Create a Hit Song."

2. The Internet & the World Wide Web: Exploring Cyberspace

UNIT 2A: THE INTERNET & THE WEB. **New material on T4, T5 lines, username and password, desktop browsers.** Chrome added to bookmarks discussion. **New material on wikis and Wikipedia added under smart web searching.** Obsolete material deleted about desktop search engines.

UNIT 2B: THE RICHES & RISKS OF INTERNET USE. Reorganization of material and **new material added** on email, instant messaging, and other ways of communicating over the Internet and on discussion groups and FTP. Obsolete material deleted on listservs. **New material added to e-commerce discussion, B2C, C2C, showrooming.** Under Web 2.0, **new material on Web 1.0 and other data.** Practical Action box, "Social Networking: The Downside," repurposed and **new material added. New section added: "Malware: The Viciousness of Viruses," with introduction of antivirus software. New section added, "Passwords," with practical suggestions.**

Tech Tales added: "How a World-Shaking Technology Came About: Tim Berners-Lee Invents the World Wide Web," "The Continuing Development of Browsers: The War for Smartphones & Tablets," "Web Imaging & Aerial Mapping: Google Earth," "Animation: Making of 'Fetch,' a Mobile Game," "The Rise of the Blogosphere: 'Writing Out Loud,'" "Changing Retail Practices: The Fight against 'Showrooming,'" and "How Difficult It Is to Keep Your Emails & Texts Private."

3. Software: Tools for Productivity & Creativity

UNIT 3A: SYSTEM SOFTWARE: THE POWER BEHIND THE POWER. Obsolete introductory material replaced with discussion of cloud computing and Google Apps. Immediate distinction made between application and system software. **Subsection added, "Booting from the Cloud."** Under Mac OS, **material added about OS X Lion.** Under Microsoft Windows, **material added on different types of Windows 8, as well as 8.1.** Excess material on Linux deleted. **Embedded operating systems discussion expanded on smartphone OSs.** Panel 3.19 added on market share of top smartphone OSs.

UNIT 3B: APPLICATION SOFTWARE: GETTING STARTED. Discussion of sources of software reorganized for clarity. **New material and subhead added, "Web Application" software.** Discussion of types of files moved from end of chapter to here under "3.6 Data Files & Program Files." Section on importing and exporting moved to later in this section. Section on compression moved here from end of chapter. New Section 3.10, "Software Suites & Integrated Packages," with material moved from later in chapter on software suites and integrated suites and **new material added on productivity suites.**

Tech Tales added: "The War for Dominance in Mobile Operating Systems," "New Technology to Replace the Mouse: The Gesture Interface," "China Adopts Linux as Its National Standard," "Software Evolution: 40 Years of Blasting Space Aliens—The Incredible Growth in Videogames," and "Free Software for Cash-Strapped Students."

4. Hardware: The CPU & Storage—The Source of Computing Power

UNIT 4A: PROCESSING: THE SYSTEM UNIT, MICROPROCESSORS, & MAIN MEMORY. Obsolete introduction replaced with material about sales plummeting on PCs compared to mobile devices. Obsolete illustration material deleted on making of a chip. Material reorganized under "Miniaturization Leads to Mobility." **New section "The System Unit," with new material about desktop PC, laptop, notebook, tablet, and handheld system units.** Obsolete material on advertisement for a PC deleted. Material reorganized for better comprehension under heading, "4.3 Inside the System Unit: Power Supply, Motherboard, & Microprocessors." Under multicore processors, **material added** on **octa-core processors. Material added on processors for data centers.** Recast material on processing speed into section, "The System Clock & Processing Speeds." Old material on MIPS, flops, and milliseconds deleted. Old head about more on the system unit retitled "The Central Processing Unit & the Machine Cycle," and material resequenced so word size discussed later. New section created, "4.5 Memory," and material reorganized and added to. **Material added on MRAM;** material deleted on SDRAM and DDR-SDRAM. Material deleted on interleaving, bursting, pipelining, superscalar architecture, and hyperthreading. Old head about ports and cables retitled "4.6 Expansion Cards, Bus Lines, & Ports," with **new material added.**

UNIT 4B: SECONDARY STORAGE. Obsolete coverage of magnetic tape deleted. **New material added on perpendicular recording technology.** Material on flash memory and solid-state memory moved ahead of smart cards, and term flash memory drive replaced by USB flash drive. **LaserCard added** under discussion of smartcards. Obsolete material on optical memory cards deleted. Section on online secondary storage recast as **"Cloud Storage" and new material added.** Under "4.8 Future Developments in Processing & Storage," obsolete introductory material deleted, and **new material added** throughout. Obsolete material deleted on higher-density disks, and **new material added on image-compression technology.**

Tech Tales added: "Vacuum Tubes Still Beat People Power," "The Fabulous Fab—What Does It Take to Support a Chip Manufacturing Plant?," "Where Are Data Centers Located?," "The World's DVD Zones," and "Nanotechnology, the Movie."

5. Hardware: Input & Output—Taking Charge of Computing & Communications

UNIT 5A: INPUT HARDWARE. Obsolete material on ATMs and kiosks deleted. **New material added on wearable technology,** including Google's Glass. Under "5.1 Keyboards," **new terms introduced—enhanced keyboards, Ketrix, Snapkey Si, CALC. Tactile keyboards distinguished from touch screen, wired from wireless** (infrared, radio frequency). In discussion of terminals, Internet terminals deleted and ATMs, POS terminals, and **mobile data terminals added.** Under "5.2 Pointing Devices," **wireless mouse and air mouse added.** Under variations of the mouse, touch screen deleted and pointing stick added; touch screen made a separate category. New heading created, "5.3 Source Data-Entry Devices," including scanners, bar-code readers, RFID tags, mark recognition and character recognition devices, audio-input devices, speech-recognition systems, webcams and video-input cards, digital cameras, sensors, and biometric input devices. Discussion of RFID moved to follow bar-code discussion. Obsolete material on fax machines deleted. **New section added, "Image-Capture Devices,"** with discussion of digital cameras and webcams. Audio-input devices now follows image-capture discussion. Heading on human-biology input devices now reads "Biometric-Input Devices." Futuristic material moved from end of chapter to new section, "5.4 The Future of Input," and **new material added under input from remote locations, on source data automation, speech recognition, touch and gesture recognition, pattern-recognition and biometric devices, and brain-wave devices; material added on designs that imitate the physical world.**

UNIT 5B: OUTPUT HARDWARE. Obsolete introductory material deleted. Under "5.5 Softcopy Output: Display Screens," features of screens are described first, including size and aspect ratio, screen clarity with refresh rate, then types of screens, including flat-panel displays (both passive and active matrix), **new material on plasma display,** and CRT; **new material on multiple screens.** New section heading, "5.6 Hardcopy Output: Printers." New section heading, "5.8 The Future of Output," which includes the principal heads "More Unusual Forms of Output," **with added material;** "More Data Used in Output," including **coverage of Big Data;** and "More Realistic Output," **with new coverage on microreplication, printers using reduced ink, more realistic animation, and latest on**

three-dimensional printing. New material added on health and ergonomics. Some obsolete material deleted and **new material added to Experience Box,** "Good Habits: Protecting Your Computer System, Your Data, & Your Health."

Tech Tales added: "Loren Brichter, Popularizer of 'Pull to Refresh' & the 'Cell Swipe,'" "RFID Tags for Security," "'Know What I'm Sayin'?,' The Uses of Speech-Recognition Systems," "Sensors Get Data We Never Had Before," "Input & Output Together: Paving the Way for the Self-Driving Car," "Dreams of 3-D Printing," "Painful Technology for College Students," and "Can Cellphones Cause Cancer?"

6. Communications, Networks, & Cyberthreats: The Wired & Wireless World

UNIT 6A: NETWORKS & WIRED & WIRELESS MEDIA. Obsolete introductory material deleted. Four ways of accessing the Internet identified: telephone modem, high-speed phone lines, cable modem, and wireless modem. Disadvantages of networks deleted for space reasons. Under LANS, **wireless LAN (WLAN) added as one type of LAN.** Discussion reduced of home area network, home automation network, garden area network, and personal area networks, now made examples of LANs. Material reorganized to contrast client-server and peer to peer. Material reorganized as "Intranets, Extranets, VPNs, & Firewalls"; material on firewalls moved here from late in chapter. Under "Switches," definition modified and material reduced. Under "Network Topologies," material on **tree network and mesh network topologies added.** Ethernet redefined and description edited for clarity. Under "6.3 Wired Communications Media," subheads added on "Phone Line Network" (instead of HomePNA) and "Power Line Network" (instead of HomePlug). Under discussion of 4G, **material added on LTE.** Technical discussion of Wi-Fi reduced for readability and Wi-Fi standards summarized in a table (Panel 6.16); **WiMax added.** Practical Action box moved from end of section, "Virtual Meetings: Linking Up Electronically."

UNIT 6B: CYBERTHREATS, SECURITY, & PRIVACY ISSUES. **Unit considerably expanded to cover new issues.** Material added on BYOD (bring your own device) policy. Practical Action box deleted, "WikiLeaks & DDoS." Section 6.5 retitled and **new material added, "6.5 Cyberintruders: Trolls, Spies, Hackers, & Thieves." Cyberattacks introduced and defined.** Discussion of hackers moved here from later in the chapter, with new subheads, "Malicious Hackers," "Benign Hackers," and "Benevolent Hackers." Material on "Thieves" moved here from Chapter 9. Section formerly on cyberthreats reorganized and now titled "Section 6.6 Cyberattacks & Malware," with subheads "Denial-of-Service Attacks," "Viruses," "Worms," "Trojan Horses," "Rootkits & Backdoors," "Blended Threats," "Zombies," "Ransomware," "Time, Logic, & Email Bombs," and "Phone Malware." Former section on how malware is spread and Practical Action box "Ways to Minimize Virus Attacks" material relocated to Chapter 2. Practical Action box "How to Deal with Passwords" deleted and material relocated to Chapter 2. New section created with material from Chapter 8, "6.7 Concerns about Theft," with principal headings "The Threat to Privacy" and "Identity Theft." **Definition of privacy added** and subheads "Name Migration," "Résumé Rustling & Online Snooping," "Government Prying & Spying." Under identity theft appears material from Chapter 8. Experience Box added, "Guarding Your Privacy & Preventing Your Identity from Getting Stolen," using old material from Chapter 8.

Tech Tales added: "Recording Music: From Analog Life to Digital Life," "'Gotcha, Thief!' & Other Uses of GPS," "Microsoft Pays 'Bug Bounties' to White-Hat Hackers," "Too-Good-to-Be-True Deals Online," "The Love Bug & Other Viruses," "Famous Worms: Klez, Conficker, & Stuxnet," and "The Weird Experience of Identity Theft."

7. Personal Technology: The Future Is You

UNIT 7A: PERSONAL DEVICES FOR IMPROVING PRODUCTIVITY AT SCHOOL & WORK. Chapter sections resequenced: "7.1 Convergence, Portability, & Personalization," "7.2 Smartphones," "7.3 Tablets & E-Readers," "7.4 Portable Media Players." Obsolete introductory material deleted and replaced. In-text material converted to Practical Action box, "The Consequences of Choice Overload." Material on multitasking moved to Section 7.3. Under "7.2 Smartphones: More Than Talk," principal headings are "How Do

Cellphones & Smartphones Differ?" with **new material;** "How a Mobile Phone Works," and "Using Mobile Phones in College." **New material on mobile phone OSs, apps, display areas, keyboards and voice commands, output, and GPS technology.** Obsolete material deleted on email, Internet access, QR codes, radio, and music. **New material on benefits and drawbacks of mobile phones in college.** Under "7.3 Tablets & E-Readers," two technologies discussed in one section, with **new material on tablet types and OSs.** Earlier material on multitasking from first section made into Practical Action box, "Multitasking—Good for Productivity?" **New material added to** discussion of how an e-reader works and drawbacks of e-readers. Under "7.4 Portable Media Players," **new material distinguishing among uses of music players, media players, and smartphones.** Under portable media players, subheads reorganized: "Storage Methods" (flash memory drive and hard-disk drive), "Sampling Rate," "Transferring Files," "Battery Life," "Display Screens," "Other Features," and "MP3 in Your Car."

UNIT 7B: PERSONAL DEVICES FOR ENRICHING LEISURE & LIFE. Chapter sections resequenced: "7.5 Digital Cameras," "7.6 High-Tech Radio," "7.7 Digital Television," "7.8 Videogame Systems." Under digital cameras, discussion of storage expanded. **Material added** to Practical Action box, "Online Viewing & Sharing of Digital Photos." Under societal effects of digital cameras, subheads and **new material added** about photos no longer just of special events and whether photo gazing gives skewed impressions of others. Under "7.8 Videogame Systems," **new material added.** Some **new material added** to Experience Box, "The 'Always On' Generation."

Tech Tales added: "The Ruggedized Tablet for Splashes & Spills," "The Rise of the Selfie: What Does It Mean?," "Pandora's Music Genome Project," and "Using Your Xbox to Order Pizza."

8. The Era of Big Data: Databases, Information Systems, & Artificial Intelligence

UNIT 8A: FILES & DATABASES. Obsolete introductory material deleted. **New material added about Big Data.** Under discussion of data dictionary, **metadata added and defined.** Under discussion of data mining, some obsolete in-text examples deleted.

UNIT 8B: BIG DATA, INFORMATION SYSTEMS, & ARTIFICIAL INTELLIGENCE. **Unit considerably expanded to cover new issues. New introductory material to distinguish between data mining and Big Data.** Old section, "8.5 Databases & the Digital Economy," repurposed as "8.5 The Evolving World of Big Data," with **new material added.** Old material on e-commerce either moved to Chapter 2 or deleted. **New principal head added, "Three Implications of Big Data," with new material. New principal head added, "The Uses of Big Data," with new material** and subsection heads, "Big Data in Medicine: Using Varieties of Old & New Data," "Smarter Junk Mail: Refining Measurement," "Netflix's Original TV Programming: Making Better Management Decisions." **Artificial intelligence redefined and new material and principal head added, "Conventional AI versus Computational Intelligence,"** with subheads, "Conventional AI: Based on Machine Learning" and "Computational Intelligence: Based on Heuristics," with **machine learning and heuristics defined and discussed.** Discussion of material from later in the chapter moved here under principal head "Weak AI versus Strong AI." Main areas of AI reorganized and discussed in following order: expert systems, natural language processing, intelligent agents, pattern recognition, virtual reality and simulation devices, robotics, fuzzy logic, and neural networks, followed by discussion of artificial life. Under discussion of robotics, **new material and subheads added, "Robots Grouped by Locomotion System" and "Robots Grouped by Application." New principal section added, "Neural Networks,"** using material formerly part of Panel 8.18, which now contains only genetic algorithms and cyborgs as examples of two other types of AI. Existing text material put beneath new section head, "8.8 Artificial Life, the Turing Test, & the Singularity." Old section "8.8 Databases: Concerns about Privacy & Identity Theft" deleted, and its material redistributed to Chapters 6 and 9. Old Experience Box, "Preventing Your Identity from Getting Stolen," deleted, and its contents moved to Chapter 6. **New Experience Box added, "How the Rise of Robotics Will Affect Future Employment," with new material.**

Tech Tales added: "Databases Everywhere," "How Amazon.com Used Databases to Become the World's Largest Online Bookstore," "The Uses of Data Mining," "The Brute Force of Weak AI," "Some Interestingly Named Expert Systems," "Using Virtual Reality & Simulation for Training, Treatment, & Research," "All Types of Robots," "Applying Fuzzy Logic to Elevators," and "A Scene from the Turing Test."

9. The Challenges of the Digital Age: Society & Information Technology Today

UNIT 9A: SECURITY, PRIVACY, & SURVEILLANCE CONCERNS. **Unit considerably expanded to cover new issues.** Old section "9.1 Truth Issues" now section "9.4 Truth Issues" in Unit 9B. In new "9.1 Security Issues," obsolete introductory material deleted; **new material added on predictive apps in relation to privacy issues,** and principal headings reorganized to combine two sections, on errors and accidents and on natural hazards, as "Errors, Accidents, & Natural Hazards." Under discussion of theft of hardware, in-text bulleted list converted to Panel 9.2, "Keeping your mobile devices safe." **New material added to discussion of theft of software.** Material on theft of online music and movies converted to a subsection, "Theft of Intellectual Property," with **extra material added.** Material in old section on "Taking Over Your PC: Zombies, Botnets, & Blackmail" moved to Chapter 6. Under discussion of crimes of malice, **new material on attacks on infrastructure** added to attacks on power-control systems. Under discussion of attacks on the Internet, old material on border gateway protocol replaced with new material. Material in old section "Computer Criminals" deleted here and moved to Chapter 6. Old section "9.3 Security Safeguards" now Section 9.2. Under discussion of passwords, **new material added on saving passwords in software with encrypted file and in using fingerprint readers for master passwords.** Under discussion of physical traits, material on biometric devices moved here from Chapter 6. Under discussion of encryption, lots of text discussion moved to considerations of surveillance later in the chapter. **New section added, "9.3 Privacy & Surveillance: Data Collectors & Spies,"** beginning with discussion of federal privacy laws, moved here from Chapter 8. Main threats to privacy listed under principal heads "Business & Cyberspying," "Government & Cyberspying," and "Spying, Hacking, & Cyberwarfare by Foreign Governments & Groups." Under "Business & Cyberspying," **new material under new subheads, "How Businesses Obtain & Use Data about Us" and "Who Owns Your Data & What Are Your Rights?"** Under "Government & Cyberspying," some old material from Chapter 8 and **new material appears under subheads "Local Police Data Collection," "A National Identity Card?," "The National Security Agency: The Rise of the Surveillance State?" (covering NSA, FBI, FISA court, secret mining of metadata), and "Drones: Snooping from the Skies."** Under "Spying, Hacking, & Cyberwarfare by Foreign Governments & Groups," **mostly new material under subheads "Cyberspying by Foreign—& the U.S.—Governments" and "Cyberattacks & Cyberwarfare."**

UNIT 9B: OTHER SOCIAL, ECONOMIC, & POLITICAL ISSUES. **New introductory material on technology as disrupter of nearly everything.** New section "9.4 Truth Issues: Manipulating Digital Data" was formerly Section 9.1. New Section "9.5 Quality-of-Life Issues: The Environment, Mental Health, Child Protection, & the Workplace" was formerly Section 9.4. Under discussion of stress, **new material added about effect of mobile devices.** Discussion of online sexual predators reduced and replaced with **new material under new subhead, "Sexting."**

Tech Tales added: "How Slow Perceptions Lead to Errors: Texting While Driving," "Glitches in the System: How Electrical & Mechanical Problems Can Make Computers Fail," "The Risks of Natural Hazards: How Bad Can It Get?," "Stealing Music & Movies," "The Nigerian Letter, a Classic Internet Scam," "Police Use of License Plate Scanners," "Cyberattacks That Challenge Governments & Corporations," "Is It Fraudulent to Manipulate Sound?," "Is It Fraudulent to Manipulate Photos?," and "Gambling in the New IT World."

10. Building Systems & Applications: Software Development, Programming, & Languages

UNIT 10A: SYSTEMS DEVELOPMENT & PROGRAMMING. Introductory material replaced by **new material on how learning systems development and programming can be a great career booster.** Under "10.1 Systems Development & the Life Cycle of a Software Project," **introductory material added on creation of apps. New material:** Developing a businesswide plan to utilize mobile devices is applied to the six phases of systems development.

UNIT 10B: PROGRAMMING LANGUAGES. **New introductory material on software developers being in explosive demand.**

Tech Tales added: "'Bring Your Own Device' to Work: Applying Systems Analysis & Design to the BYOD Trend," "Stumbles on the Road to Progress: When Big Systems Fail," "Who Decides When Programs Are Okay to Go? The Release Engineer," and "Student Entrepreneurs Create a New App in Five Days with 'Premade Programming Lego Blocks.'"

ACKNOWLEDGMENTS

This book has only two names on its title page, but we are extraordinarily grateful for the many others who have been important contributors to its development. First, we wish to thank our brand manager, Wyatt Morris, and our development editor, Alan Palmer, for their help in rolling out this edition. Thanks also go to our marketing champion, Tiffany Russell, and to Jean Starr, our content project manager. We also thank Kevin White and Thuan Vinh for their media and digital support.

Outside McGraw-Hill we want to state our appreciation for the contributions of Judy Mason, our San Francisco Bay Area photo researcher, whose history with us goes back many, many years. We also thank Chet Gottfried, copyeditor; Mary Carole Hollingsworth, Georgia Perimeter College, and Beverly Swisshelm, Cumberland University, technical readers of the revised manuscript; Sharon O'Donnell, our excellent proofreader; and James Minkin, our stalwart and sensitive indexer.

Finally, we are grateful to the following reviewers for helping to make this the most market-driven book possible.

Olga Blinova
Hudson County Community College

Anthony Cameron
Fayetteville Technical Community College

Paulette Comet
Community College of Baltimore County

Bernice Eng
Brookdale Community College

John Enomoto
East Los Angeles College

Rachelle Hall
Glendale Community College

Mary Carole Hollingsworth
Georgia Perimeter College

Mark Jackson
Columbus State Community College

Donna Lohn
Lakeland Community College

Robert Myers
Florida State University

Brenda Nickel
Moraine Park Technical College

Joanne Patti
Community College of Philadelphia

Greg Pauley
Moberly Area Community College

Barbara Purvis
Centura College

Candice Spangler
Columbus State Community College

Beverly Swisshelm
Cumberland University

Perry Tonni
Lakeland Community College

David Trimble
Park University

Charles Whealton
Delaware Technical Community College

Sophia Wilberscheid
Indian River State College

Mary Williams
University of Akron

Reviewers & Other Participants in Previous Editions

We are grateful for the magnificent help over the past 18 years from all the instructors who have given us the benefit of their opinion, as follows:

Nancy Alderdice
Murray State University

Margaret Allison
University of Texas–Pan American

Angela Amin
Great Lakes Junior College

Leon Amstutz
Taylor University

Sharon Anderson
Western Iowa Tech

Valerie Anderson
Marymount College

Hashem Anwari
Northern Virginia Community College–Loudoun Campus

Connie Aragon
Seattle Central Community College

Tahir Azia
Long Beach City College

Bonnie Bailey
Morehead State University

Don Bailey
Plymouth State University

David Brent Bandy
University of Wisconsin–Oshkosh

Robert L. Barber
Lane Community College

Vic Barbow
Purdue University

Robert Barrett
Indiana University and Purdue University at Fort Wayne

Anthony Baxter
University of Kentucky

Gigi Beaton
Tyler Junior College

Virginia Bender
William Rainey Harper College

Hossein Bidgoli
California State University–Bakersfield

Warren Boe
University of Iowa

Beverly Bohn
Park University

Randall Bower
Iowa State University

Russell Breslauer
Chabot College

Bob Bretz
Western Kentucky University

William C. Brough
University of Texas–Pan American

Phyllis Broughton
Pitt Community College

Charles Brown
Plymouth State College

Bidi Bruno
Portland Community College

David Burris
Sam Houston State University

Jeff Butterfield
University of Idaho

J. Wesley Cain
City University, Bellevue

Patrick Callan
Concordia University

Anthony Cameron
Fayetteville Technical Community College

Judy Cameron
Spokane Community College

Ralph Caputo
Manhattan College

Robert Caruso
Santa Rosa Junior College

Joe Chambers
Triton College

Kris Chandler
Pikes Peak Community College

William Chandler
University of Southern Colorado

John Chenoweth
East Tennessee State University

Ashraful Chowdhury
Dekalb College

Erline Cocke
Northwest Mississippi Community College

Jennifer Cohen
Southwest Florida College

Robert Coleman
Pima County Community College

Paulette Comet
Community College of Baltimore

Ronald E. Conway
Bowling Green State University

Helen Corrigan-McFadyen
Massachusetts Bay Community College

Jami Cotler
Siena College

Glen Coulthard
Okanagan University

Dale Craig
Fullerton College

Robert Crandall
Denver Business School

Hiram Crawford
Olive Harvey College

Thad Crews
Western Kentucky University

Martin Cronlund
Anne Arundel Community College

Rebecca Cunningham
Arkansas Technical University

Jim Dartt
San Diego Mesa College

Joseph DeLibro
Arizona State University

Edouard Desautels
University of Wisconsin–Madison

William Dorin
Indiana University–Northwest

Maryan Dorn
Southern Illinois University

Patti Dreven
Community College of Southern Nevada

John Durham
Fort Hays State University

Laura A. Eakins
East Carolina University

Bonita Ellis
Wright City College

John Enomoto
East Los Angeles College

Nancy Jo Evans
Indiana University–Purdue University

Ray Fanselau
American River College

Pat Fenton
West Valley College

Eleanor Flanigan
Montclair State University

Ken Frizane
Oakton Community College

James Frost
Idaho State University

Susan Fry
Boise State University

Bob Fulkerth
Golden Gate University

Susan Fuschetto
Cerritos College

Janos Fustos
Metropolitan State College

Yaping Gao
College of Mount St. Joseph

Enrique Garcia
Laredo Community College

JoAnn Garver
University of Akron

Jill Gebelt
Salt Lake Community College

Charles Geigner
Illinois State University

David German
Cerro Coso Community College

Candace Gerrod
Red Rocks Community College

Bish Ghosh
Metropolitan State College, Denver

Julie Giles
DeVry Institute of Technology

Frank Gillespie
University of Georgia

Mindy Glander
North Metro Technical College

Myron Goldberg
Pace University

Dwight Graham
Prairie State College

Bob Grill
College of Alameda

Fillmore Guinn
Odessa College

Norman P. Hahn
Thomas Nelson Community College

Sallyann Hanson
Mercer County Community College

Dorothy G. Harman
Tarrant County College, Northeast Campus

Debra Harper
Montgomery County Community College–North Harris

Albert Harris
Appalachian State University

Jan Harris
Lewis & Clark Community College

Michael Hasset
Fort Hays State University

Carson Haury
Central Oregon Community College

Richard Hauser
East Carolina University

Cheryl R. Heemstra
Anne Arundel Community College

Julie Heine
Southern Oregon State College

Richard Hewer
Ferris State University

Marilyn Hibbert
Salt Lake Community College

Ron Higgins
Grand Rapids Community College

Martin Hochhauser
Dutchess Community College

Don Hoggan
Solano Community College

James D. Holland
Okaloosa-Waltoon Community College

Marie Carole Hollingsworth
Georgia Perimeter College

Stan Honacki
Moraine Valley Community College

Wayne Horn
Pensacola Junior College

Tom Hrubec
Waubonsee Community College

Jerry Humphrey
Tulsa Junior College

Christopher Hundhausen
University of Oregon

Alan Iliff
North Park College

Washington James
Collin County Community College–Plano

John Jansma
Palo Alto College

Jim Johnson
Valencia Community College

Linda Johnsonius
Murray State University

Julie Jordahl
Rock Valley College

Laleh Kalantari
Western Illinois University

Jan Karasz
Cameron University

Linda Kavanaugh Varga
Robert Morris University

Hak Joon Kim
Southern Connecticut State University

Jorene Kirkland
Amarillo College

Linda Kliston
Broward College–North

Paul Koester
Tarrant County College

Kurt W. Kominek
Northeast State Community College

Shawn Krest
Genesee Community College

Victor Lafrenz
Mohawk Valley Community College

Jackie Althea Lamoureux
Central New Mexico Community College

Sheila Lancaster
Gadsden State Community College

David Lee Largent
Ball State University

Dana Lasher
North Carolina State University

Dawn D. Laux
Purdue University–West Lafayette

Stephen Leach
Florida State University

Paul Leidig
Grand Valley State University

Mary Levesque
University of Nebraska

Andrew Levin
Delaware Valley College

Chang-Yang Lin
Eastern Kentucky University

Janet D. Lindner
Midlands Technical College

Nicholas Lindquist
Arizona State University

Donna Lohn
Lakeland Community College

Gina Long
Southwestern Community College

John Longstreet
Harold Washington College

Paul Lou
Diablo Valley College

Beata Lovelace
Pulaski Technical College

Pamela Luckett
Barry University

Deborah Ludford
Glendale Community College

Evelyn Lulis
DePaul University

Peter MacGregor
Estrella Mountain Community College

Warren Mack
Northwest Vista College, San Antonio

Donna Madsen
Kirkwood Community College

Ed Mannion
California State University–Chico

Alan Maples
Cedar Valley College

Kenneth E. Martin
University of North Florida

Thomas Martin
Shasta College

Roberta Mae Marvel
Casper College

Jerry Matejka
Adelphi University

Diane Mayne-Stafford
Grossmont College

Elizabeth McCarthy
Kirkwood Community College

Sue A. McCrory
Missouri State University

Jacob McGinnis
Park University

Veronica F. McGowan
Delaware Valley College

Todd McLeod
Fresno City College

Curtis Meadow
University of Maine

Jennifer Merritt
Park University

Timothy Meyer
Edinboro University

Michael Michaelson
Palomar College

Cindy Minor
John A. Logan College

Alanah Mitchell
Appalachian State University

Norman Muller
Greenfield Community College

Rebecca Mundy
University of California, Los Angeles, and University of Southern California

Paul Murphy
Massachusetts Bay Community College

Kathleen Murray
Drexel University

Marry Murray
Portland Community College

Sonia Nayle
Los Angeles City College

Charles Nelson
Rock Valley College

Bruce Neubauer
Pittsburgh State University

Philip H. Nielson
Salt Lake Community College

Wanda Nolden
Delgado Community College

E. Gladys Norman
Linn-Benton Community College

George Novotny
Ferris State University

Janet Olpert
Cameron University

Pat Ormond
Utah Valley State College

John Panzica
Community College of Rhode Island

Rajesh Parekh
Iowa State University

Bettye Jewel Parham
Daytona Beach Community College

Merrill Parker
Chattanooga State Technical Community College

Michelle Parker
Indiana Purdue University

James Gordon Patterson
Paradise Valley Community College

David E. Pence
Moberly Area Community College

Teresa Marie Peterman
Grand Valley State University

Marie Planchard
Massachusetts Bay Community College

Jim Potter
California State University–Hayward

Tammy Potter
West Kentucky Community & Technical College

Leonard Presby
William Patterson State College

William Pritchard
Wayne State University

Delores Pusins
Hillsborough Community College

Janak Rajani
Howard Community College

Eugene Rathswohl
University of San Diego

Alan Rea
Western Michigan University

Carol B. Reed
Mount Wachusett Community College

Jerry Reed
Valencia Community College

John Rezac
Johnson County Community College

Pattie Riden
Western Illinois University

Jane Ritter
University of Oregon

Fernando Rivera
University of Puerto Rico–Mayaguez Campus

Donald Robertson
Florida Community College–Jacksonville

Stan Ross
Newbury College

Russell Sabadosa
Manchester Community College

Glen Sagers
Illinois State University

Behrooz Saghafi
Chicago State University

Greg Saxon
New Jersey Institute of Technology

Barbara Scantlebury
Mohawk Valley Community College

Judy Scheeren
Westmoreland County Community College

Al Schroeder
Richland College

Dick Schwartz
Macomb County Community College

Earl Schweppe
University of Kansas

Susan Sells
Wichita State University

Tom Seymour
Minot State University

Naj Shaik
Heartland Community College

Harry D. Shea
Missouri State University

Morgan Shepherd
University of Colorado–Colorado Springs

Elaine Shillito
Clark State Community College

Jack Shorter
Texas A&M University

James Sidbury
University of Scranton

Bonnie Sue Specht Smith
Fresno City College

Maureen Smith
Saddleback College

Stephanie Spike
Tallahassee Community College

Diane Mayne-Stafford
Grossmont College

Esther Steiner
New Mexico State University

Randy Stolze
Marist College

Kathleen Tamerlano
Cuyahoga Community College

Kasia Taylor
Anne Arundel Community College

Susan Taylor
Mount Wachusett Community College

Charlotte Thunen
Foothill College

Denis Tichenell
Los Angeles City College

Angela Tilaro
Butte College

Martha Tillman
College of San Mateo

DeLyse Totten
Portland Community College

David Trimble
Park University

Jack VanDeventer
Washington State University

Sue VanBoven
Paradise Valley Community College

James Van Tassel
Mission College

Michelle Vlaich-Lee
Greenville Technical College

Jim Vogel
Sanford Brown College

Dale Walikainen
Christopher Newport University

Reneva Walker
Valencia Community College

Ron Wallace
Blue Mountain Community College

Nancy Webb
City College of San Francisco

Steve Wedwick
Heartland Community College

Sandra M. (Sandy) Week
University of Nevada–Reno

Patricia Lynn Wermers
North Shore Community College

Cora Lee Whitcomb
Bentley College

Doug White
Western Michigan University

Melinda White
Seminole State College of Florida

Pauline White
Siena College

Anita Whitehill
Foothill College

Edward Winter
Salem State College

Floyd Winters
Manatee Community College

Nancy Ann Woolridge
Fullerton College

Israel Yost
University of New Hampshire

Alfred Zimermann
Hawai'i Pacific University

Eileen Zisk
Community College of Rhode Island

Mary Ann Zlotow
College of DuPage

1 INTRODUCTION to INFORMATION TECHNOLOGY: The Future Now

Chapter Topics & Key Questions

UNIT 1A: *The Mobile World, Information Technology, & Your Life*

1.1 **Information Technology & Your Life: The Future Now** What is information technology, and how does it affect education, health, money, leisure, government, and careers?

1.2 **Information Technology Is Pervasive: Cellphones, Email, the Internet, & the E-World** How does information technology facilitate email, networks, and the use of the Internet and the web; what is the meaning of the term *cyberspace*?

UNIT 1B: *The Basics of Information Technology*

1.3 **The Practical User: How Becoming Tech Smart Benefits You** What does being *tech smart* mean, and what are its practical payoffs?

1.4 **The "All-Purpose Machine": The Varieties of Computers** What are the different sizes of computers, and what are clients and servers?

1.5 **Understanding Your Computer** What four basic operations do all computers use, and what are some of the devices associated with each operation? How does communications affect these operations?

1.6 **Where Is Information Technology Headed?** What are three directions of computer development and three directions of communications development?

Download the free UIT 11e App for key term flash cards quizzes and a game, *Over the Edge*

CHAPTER FORECAST In this chapter we begin by discussing how computing and the Internet affect your life. We then discuss smartphones, the Internet, the World Wide Web, and other aspects of the electronic world (e-world). Next we describe how being smart about information technology can benefit you, and then we cover the varieties of computers. We then explain three key concepts behind how a computer works and what goes into a personal computer, both hardware and software. We conclude by describing three directions of computer development and three directions of communications development. All these concepts are discussed in greater detail in subsequent chapters.

UNIT 1A: *The Mobile World, Information Technology, & Your Life*

"Mobile computing . . . will be the catalyst that brings society the most dramatic changes of the Information Revolution."

So writes Michael Saylor, author of *The Mobile Wave.*[1] The information revolution that began with writing on clay tablets, then continued through the invention of the printing press, radio and TV, and room-size and desktop computers, is now at a "tipping point," he asserts. Now mobile devices such as **smartphones—cellphones with built-in applications, multimedia capability, and Internet access**—and **tablet computers—wireless portable computers primarily operated by a touch screen**—are changing nearly everything we do.

Consider the example below, the first in a number of *"mini-cases,"* business related and otherwise, that we present in this book:

TECH TALES The Rise of Mobile Computing: The Getting-Smarter Smartphone

While growing up, Nick Bilton noticed that as his father aged, his wallet expanded as he added new credit cards, membership cards, family photos, stamps, tickets, and other things—until it became so large that he would pull it out of his back pocket when he sat down, "dropping it on the table like a brick," Bilton says.[2]

However, for Bilton, a *New York Times* technology columnist, it's been the reverse experience: Each year his wallet has become slimmer. "Things that once belonged there have been [taken over] by my smartphone," he reports, to the point where "I realized I didn't need to carry a wallet anymore. My smartphone had replaced almost everything in it."

Today Bilton's address books, calendars, maps, music players, and photos have all been absorbed into his smartphone. So have most identification cards—customer cards, gym membership ID, insurance cards, and so on—which now exist as photos carried in the phone. Movie tickets, coupons, and airline boarding passes also can be stored as replicas.

The only two non–mobile phone items Bilton carries are his driver's license and a bank debit card (instead of cash). "But I'm confident," he says, "that those, too, will disappear someday" and become part of the smartphone. ■

It would be simplistic, however, to predict that we'll be doing *all* our computing on just smartphones and tablets anytime soon. As one writer points out, "Heavier productivity tasks—like, you know, typing—are still much easier to pull off on standard laptops and desktops."[3] Moreover, the uses of smartphones and other portable devices cannot be truly mastered without understanding their huge supporting infrastructure of computing and communications technologies—the subjects of the rest of this book.

Even so, people ages 16 to 39, members of the "Millennial Generation," who generally spend eight hours a day or more looking at various screens—on cellphones, on computers, on TVs—generally have a head start on computer technology.[4] They are, as one anthropologist called them, "digital natives" or computer-technology natives, constantly busy with text messaging, email, and the *Internet,* the global "network of networks," and its most well-known feature, the multimedia *World Wide Web*—the "Web" or "web," with its massive collection of *websites,* or related collections of files.[5] Indeed, among college students, 98% are Internet users and 92% are wireless (laptop or cellphone) users.[6] While their parents continue to shop in retail stores (often using clipped-out paper coupons), Millennials are more likely than older shoppers (by 50% vs. 21%[7]) to check out brands on **social networks—sites on the World Wide Web such as Facebook and Twitter that (as we'll describe) allow users to interact and develop communities around similar interests**—and use mobile devices to research products and compare prices.

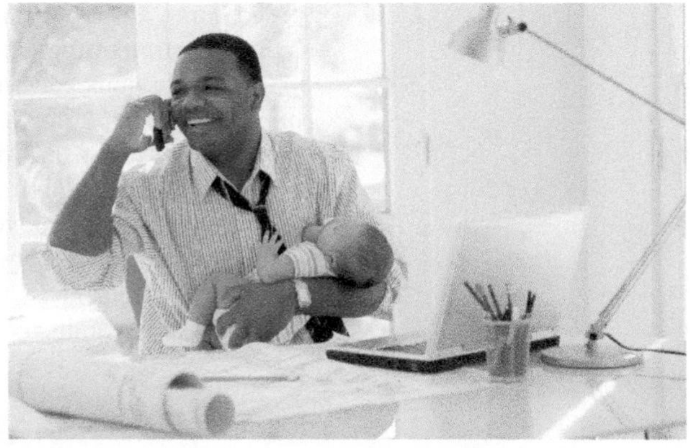

"Well, I keep busy." Multiple electronic devices allow people to multitask, or do multiple tasks simultaneously—sometimes too many tasks.

In addition, Millennials are 2½ times more likely than older generations to be early adopters of technology.[8] This is a good thing, because we live in what Tom Peters, author of *In Search of Excellence,* calls *discontinuous times,* or "a brawl with no rules," where dealing with change is an ongoing challenge.[9] Others speak of the "disruptive" effect of computers and their software that "is going to eat not just the technology industry but every industry systematically."[10]

What are the developments that have led to these turbulent times? The answer is *information technology.* **Information technology (IT) is a general term that describes any technology that helps produce, manipulate, store, communicate, and/or disseminate information.** Of the top 30 innovations from 1969 to 2009, according to a panel of professionals at the University of Pennsylvania's Wharton School, *most were related to information technology.*[11] *(• See Panel 1.1.)* Among the first items on their list, for example, are (1) the Internet, broadband, and the World Wide Web; (2) PC and laptop computers; (3) mobile phones (cellphones); and (4) email. Indeed, the Internet, along with semiconductors

1. Internet, broadband, World Wide Web
2. PC and laptop computers
3. Mobile phones
4. Email
5. DNA testing and sequencing
6. Magnetic resonance imaging
7. Microprocessors
8. Fiber optics
9. Office software
10. Laser/robotic surgery
11. Open-source software
12. Light-emitting diodes
13. Liquid crystal display
14. GPS devices
15. E-commerce and auctions
16. Media file compression
17. Microfinance
18. Photovoltaic solar energy
19. Large-scale wind turbines
20. Internet social networking
21. Graphic user interface
22. Digital photography
23. RFID and applications
24. Genetically modified plants
25. Biofuels
26. Barcodes and scanners
27. ATMs
28. Stents
29. SRAM flash memory
30. Antiretroviral treatment for AIDS

To be more than just a new invention, an event was defined as an innovation if it created more opportunities for growth and development and if it had problem-solving value.
Source: Adapted from "A World Transformed: What Are the Top 30 Innovations of the Last 30 Years?" *Knowledge@Wharton,* February 18, 2009, *http://knowledge.wharton.upenn.edu/article.cfm?articleid=2163* (accessed May 10, 2013).

panel 1.1

Top innovations in recent years

The majority (23 of the 30) are in the field of information technology.

(processors), is said to rank among the 15 greatest innovations in all history, as important as the invention of the number zero, money, printing, and participatory democracy.[12]

Unlike previous generations, you live in a world of *pervasive computing* or *ubiquitous computing*—computing is everywhere. The basis for this phenomenon is the Internet, the "Net" or "net," that sprawling global connection of smaller computer networks that enable data transmission at high speeds. Everything that presently exists on a personal computer, experts suggest, will move onto the Internet, giving us greater mobility and involving the Internet even more closely in our lives.[13] Already, in fact, the United States has more devices connecting to the Internet than it has people—425 million smartphones, tablets, personal computers, and gaming consoles divided among the USA's 311.5 million residents.[14]

1.1 INFORMATION TECHNOLOGY & YOUR LIFE: The Future Now

Information technology affects almost all aspects of our lives, including education, health, finance, recreation and entertainment, government, jobs and careers, and your personal life.

This book is about computers, of course. But not just about computers. It is also about the way computers communicate with one another. When computer and communications technologies are combined, the result is *information technology,* or "infotech." *Information technology (IT),* we said, is a general term that describes any technology that helps produce, manipulate, store, communicate, and/or disseminate information. IT merges computing with high-speed communications links carrying data, sound, and video. Examples of information technology include personal computers but also various forms of handheld devices, televisions, appliances, and other machines.

Two Parts of IT: Computers & Communications

Information technology comprises both computer technology and communications technology.

Note that there are two important parts to information technology—computers and communications.

COMPUTER TECHNOLOGY You likely know what a computer is, but to get to a formal definition: **a computer is a programmable, multiuse machine that accepts data—raw facts and figures—and processes, or manipulates, it into information we can use,** such as summaries, totals, or reports. Its main purpose is to speed up problem solving and increase productivity.

COMMUNICATIONS TECHNOLOGY **Communications technology, also called *telecommunications technology*, consists of electromagnetic devices and systems for communicating over any distance.** The principal examples are telephone, radio, satellite, broadcast television, and cable TV. We also have communication among computers—which is what happens when people "go online" on the Internet. **Online means using a computer or some other information device, connected through a network, to access information and services from another computer or information device. A network is a communications system connecting two or more computers; the Internet is the largest such network.**

Information technology is already affecting your life in multiple ways, of course, and will do so even more in the future. Let's consider how.

Education: The Promise of More Interactive & Individualized Learning

Education has become heavily involved in information technology.

Education pays, with recent college graduates having lower rates of unemployment, higher earnings, and better career prospects than their lesser educated peers.[15] At every level, the education system benefits from information technology, whether it's online systems allowing families to track their elementary students' grades, high schools enabling use of smartphones for students to get help on assignments, or colleges offering free online education.[16]

TECH TALES Technology in Education: Adjusting Instructor Presentations to the Students

In her physics classes at the Massachusetts Institute of Technology, Professor Gabriella Sciolla's high-tech classroom has whiteboards and huge display screens instead of blackboards. The professor can make brief presentations of general principles and then throw out multiple-choice questions that students "vote" on, using wireless "personal response clickers."

These devices transmit the answers to a computer monitored by the professor, helping her gauge the level of understanding in the room. "You know where they are," she says. She can then adjust, slow down, or engage students in guided discussions of their answers.[17]

In her mathematics classes at Hillcrest High School in Greenville, South Carolina, teacher Jennifer Southers has flipped education upside-down. Instead of coming to school and listening to a lecture in class and then going home to try out what they learned, her students first listen to an online video lecture at home before class and then come to class where they can apply their knowledge with their teacher there to help them.

"The level of frustration has almost disappeared completely on those lessons when we do that," says Southers.[18] ■

Survival Tip

Online Colleges and Accreditation

For-profit institutions are not accredited by the same standards as traditional not-for-profit universities. Often the course work in these proprietary schools is not eligible for transfer into traditional schools. For more information on how schools are accredited:

www2.ed.gov/admins/finaid/accred/index.html

http://ope.ed.gov/accreditation/

www.guidetoonlineschools.com/online-schools

http://chronicle.com/article/Online-Programs-Face-New/129608/

www.prweb.com/releases/2012/non-profit/prweb9090071.htm

http://distancelearn.about.com/od/onlinecourses/a/Are-For-Profit-Online-Colleges-A-Rip-Off.htm

THE USES OF INFORMATION TECHNOLOGY IN COLLEGE When properly integrated into the curriculum and the classroom, information technology can (1) allow students to personalize their education, (2) automate many tedious and rote tasks of teaching and managing classes, and (3) reduce the teacher's workload per student, so that the teacher can spend more time on reaching individual students.[19] For instance, **email, or *"electronic mail,"* messages transmitted over a computer network, most often the Internet,** are used by students to set up appointments with professors (62%), discuss grades (58%), or get clarification of an assignment (75%).[20]

From now on, whenever you see the **more info!** icon in the margin, you'll find information about Internet sites to visit and how to search for terms related to the topic just discussed.

Besides using the Internet to help in teaching, today's college instructors also use *presentation graphics software* such as PowerPoint to show their lecture outlines and other materials on classroom screens (as we discuss in Chapter 3). In addition, they use Blackboard, It's Learning, Inc., and other *course-management software (CMS)* (or learning management systems) for administering online assignments, individual learning plans, schedules, examinations, and grades.

ONLINE LEARNING One of the most significant developments in education at all levels is the rise of **distance learning, or online learning, or e-learning, the names given to online education programs,** which at the college level counted over 6.7 million students taking at least one online course in 2012.[21] A relatively recent development was the appearance of free online courses called *massive open online courses,* or *MOOCs.*[22] Examples are courses offered by companies such as Coursera, edX, Udacity, and Udemy, which feature offerings from Princeton, Stanford, Brown, Duke, Columbia, and other universities.

E-learning has also propelled the rise of for-profit institutions, such as Colorado Technical

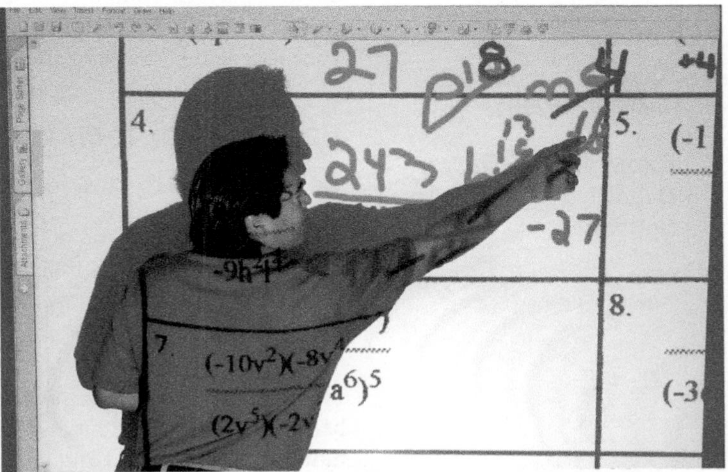

Interactive education. Interactive whiteboard math class. A whiteboard is a white surface with multitouch, multiuser, and pen/stylus functionalities that also displays the contents of a computer screen. A projector projects the computer's desktop onto the board's surface. The board is typically mounted to a wall or floor stand.

Avatar. The simulated depictions of humans are a staple not only of videogames but also of computerized training programs. (What culture does "avatar" come from? See *www.answers.com/topic/avatar?cat=technology*.)

Institute, Kaplan University, Strayer University, and the University of Phoenix. More than a third of institutions of higher education—and 97% of public universities—offer online courses, and many have attracted on-campus students, who say they like the flexibility of not having to attend their classes at a set time.[23]

E-learning has been put to such varied uses as bringing career and technical courses to high school students in remote prairie towns, pairing gifted science students with master teachers in other parts of the country, and helping busy professionals obtain further credentials outside business hours.

Online Colleges

The following websites provide detailed information about getting college degrees online:

- www.onlinecollegedegrees.net/
- www.earnmydegree.com/index.html
- www.classesusa.com/indexall/?campusType=online
- www.guidetoonlineschools.com/
- www.usdla.org/
- http://distancelearn.about.com/ (includes information about bad programs, called *diploma mills*)
- www.distancelearning.com/
- www.elearners.com/resources/

TUTORING, SIMULATION, & AVATARS But the reach of information technology into education has only begun. "Intelligent tutoring systems" software is now available that gives students individualized instruction when personal attention is scarce—such as the software Cognitive Tutor, which not only helps high school students to improve their performance in math but also sparks them to enjoy a subject they might have once disliked.

In colleges, more students may use interactive simulation games, such as McGraw-Hill's Business Strategy Game, to apply their knowledge to real-world kinds of problems. And employees in company training programs may find themselves engaged in mock conversations with avatars—**computer depictions of humans,** as are often found in online videogames—that represent imaginary customers and coworkers, combining the best parts of computer-based learning with face-to-face interaction. An avatar is also part of your online representation of yourself; it gives other users a "face" to go with your username ("online name").

Carnegie Learning's Cognitive Tutor Software

www.carnegielearning.com/specs/cognitive-tutor-overview/

Health: High Tech for Wellness

Computers are now often used in the fields of health and medicine.

"Digital technology—on phones and tablets, in electronic record keeping, and in a host of clinical innovations—is transforming medicine in virtually every way," says one account. "Not the least of the changes is the shifting relationship between doctors and patients."[24] (For now we use the word *digital* to mean "computer-based.")

TELEMEDICINE *Telemedicine*—medical care delivered via telecommunications—has been around for some time. For example, physicians in rural areas lacking local access to radiologists have used "teleradiology" to exchange computerized images such as X-rays via telephone-linked networks with expert physicians in metropolitan areas. Now telemedicine is moving to an exciting new level, as the use of digital cameras and sound, in effect, moves patients to doctors rather than the reverse.

PRACTICAL ACTION

How to Be a Successful Online Student

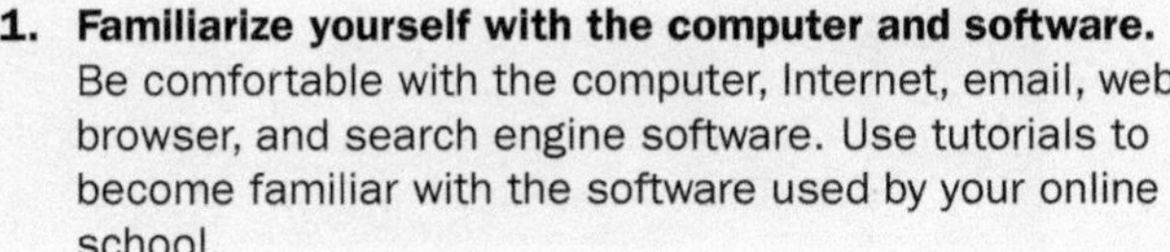

1. **Familiarize yourself with the computer and software.** Be comfortable with the computer, Internet, email, web browser, and search engine software. Use tutorials to become familiar with the software used by your online school.

   Take advantage of technology. Learn the various ways of communicating on the web. Blogging, podcasting, videoconferencing, and chatting (discussed later in the book) are tools that will help you with online studying.

2. **Do you have regular access to the Internet?** Do you have your own email account? It is necessary to maintain regular communication with the instructor with whom you are taking the course. *You must be able to answer your email quickly* during the school week, which means within 24 hours after receipt. And you should be able to successfully send and receive email with attachments. Students must have a reliable Internet service provider (ISP) and email account before the start of class. (Students are often required to use a school email account.)

3. **Read every document within your syllabus within the first five days of your online course.** This is usually the time to begin introducing yourself to your classmates and instructor and to start asking questions concerning the expectations described in the syllabus. You need to know what is expected of you.

   Know how to find assignments and course material, as well as be able to participate in and post to discussions and send emails with attachments.

4. **Are you comfortable working on your own? Are you self-motivated?** You will have flexible use of the time to spend on course work. Due dates are set by the instructor. Flexibility and independence are agreeable to some, but for others it is difficult to self-start. Be honest with yourself about your capabilities.

   It is the student's responsibility to take the course seriously and to be able to budget time to receive a successful grade. Make a schedule and stick to it.

5. **Can you make deadlines?** Your instructor is counting on you to finish your work on time. Your communication may be virtual (online), but your tasks and assigned deadlines are not.

   Be consistent in the amount of time you take to read and study. Every week you will be expected to read sections in your textbook.

   Try not to get behind in your class work; try to stay on course or ahead. Some online learning programs move at an advanced rate; missing one week is like missing two in a traditional classroom.

6. **Is this the right time for you to take an online class?** You should be confident that you can set aside enough time for your online course assignments and study time. You may feel that taking an online course will free up your time for other tasks. If you are feeling overwhelmed by other responsibilities, such as work or family obligations, then perhaps you had better postpone your involvement. Online courses require as much and often more personal preparation time than on-campus courses. Everything that you would normally communicate by speech in class must be typed in an online course.

7. **You will need good written communication skills.** Remember, your primary means of communication is through writing. Being able to send well-structured messages and essays will help with the communication process.

8. **Pay attention to detail, particularly when following written directions.** Assignments, projects, and so on are posted in written form. Grades are drawn from work accomplished as directed. When grading assignments, the instructor will look for competence in the work submitted. This means that all the required steps were followed and presented in a professional manner.

9. **Create a private study area.** This will help you to focus on your studies without distractions and ensure that others do not to disturb you while you are in your study area. Keep all your study materials here, so you know where to look for them.

10. **Interact with your peers.** Contribute and exchange your ideas, perspective, and comments with your online classmates. Join online student communities and blogs.

11. **Interact with your faculty.** Constantly stay in touch with your professors. Consult them if you have technical difficulties or problems in understanding something related to the course. Since your professors cannot see you, you must be absolutely clear in expressing your ideas and needs.

12. **Evaluate and test yourself.** Take tests after thorough preparation. Don't hurry to take the tests; time them carefully. Have your work evaluated by fellow classmates.

13. **Netiquette: Remember the dos and don'ts.** When you are online, be careful of netiquette (online etiquette). Both the real world and the virtual world are inhabited by people, so the same rules apply. Never be rude or disrespectful. Respect the privacy of other people.

Source: Adapted from *www.olhcc.edu/Documents/academics/1%20Online%20Courses%20Are%20You%20Ready.pdf*; *www.brighthub.com/education/online-learning/articles/26877.aspx*; and *www.onlinedegreedirect.com/onlinedegreedirect-articles/10-Easy-Ways-to-Become-a-Good-Online-Student.htm*.

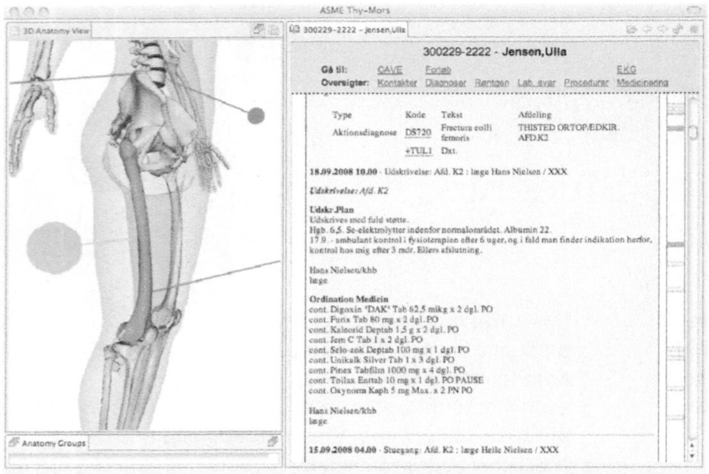

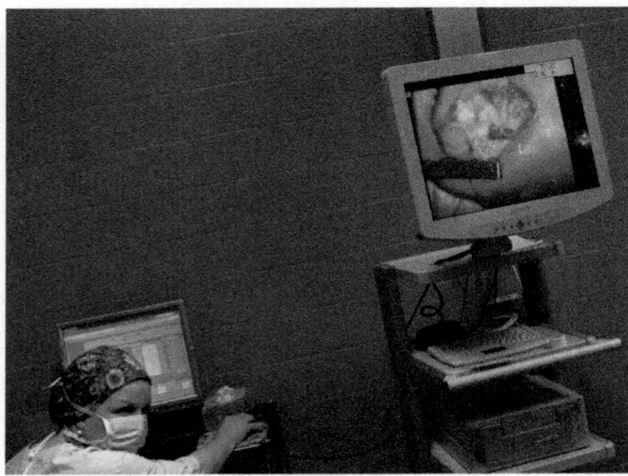

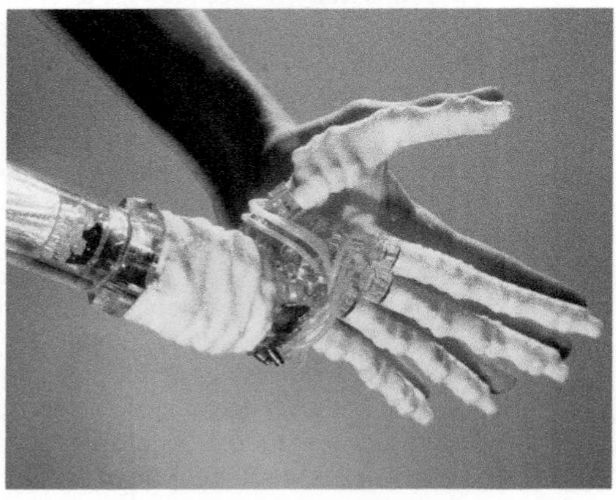

High-tech medicine. (*left*) Screenshot of the visual patient record software pioneered at Thy-Mors hospital. This patient has had a fracture of the femur in the right leg. This computer-based image shows a close-up view of the treated area. A click on the arrow on the highlighted femur would show the pertinent medical information from the record on the right panel. The tool allows doctors to easily zoom in and out on a particular body region or part and choose between many different views. (*top right*) Open heart surgery is seen on a computer monitor as an Israeli medical team repairs a congenital defect in a boy's heart at the Wolfson Medical Center in Tel Aviv. (*bottom* right) Ultralight Anthropomorphic Hand compared with a human hand. This artificial hand is for use as a prosthetic or as an attachment on a humanoid robot. Unlike conventional alternatives, it performs human-like movements and can grasp a wide range of objects. The hand uses hydraulic fluid actuators, positioned in the fingers and wrist. These allow flexibility of movement and are also self-adapting, ensuring that the hand's grasp is never too hard or soft. The actuators also ensure that the hand is lightweight and inexpensive to produce. The surface of the hand is soft to the touch, making it feel more natural. It was developed at Forschungszentrum Karlsruhe, Germany.

Health Websites

Some reliable sources:

www.medlineplus.gov
www.nimh.nih.gov
www.womenshealth.gov/
www.mayoclinic.com
www.nationalhealthcouncil.org
www.yourdiseaserisk.wustl.edu/

TECH TALES New Telemedicine: The Doctor Will See You Now—Right Now

New York technology writer Michael Wolff had a rotten cold and his regular doctor was on vacation. So he used a program called ZocDoc. "I entered my particulars: my ZIP code, my malady, my insurance," he wrote. "And bingo, I had my choice of doctors in the vicinity and available appointments that day. I chose an ear-nose-and-throat man a 10-minute walk from my house."[25]

Similarly, Anna Keyes, an employee of a Houston-based Caterpillar dealer, who couldn't shake chest congestion, walked down the office hallway and, with the help of a clinical paramedic, connected to a physician 20 minutes away, who examined her with an Internet-linked stethoscope and a handheld video camera. In 20 minutes, she was back at her desk with the diagnosis of an allergy and a prescription to cope with it.[26] ■

Image transfer technology allows radiologic images such as CT scans and MRIs to be immediately transmitted to electronic charts and physicians' offices.[27] Patients in intensive care, who are usually monitored by nurses during off-times, can also be watched over by doctors in remote "control towers" miles away. Recent telemedicine innovations include use of smartphones to enable doctors to take an electrocardiogram almost anywhere and to help patients track for signs of skin cancer.[28]

Electronic medical records and other computerized tools enable heart attack patients to get follow-up drug treatment and diabetics to have their blood sugar measured. Software can compute a woman's breast cancer risk.

ROBOT MEDICINE Various **robots—automatic devices that perform functions ordinarily performed by human beings,** with names such as ROBO DOC, RoboCart,

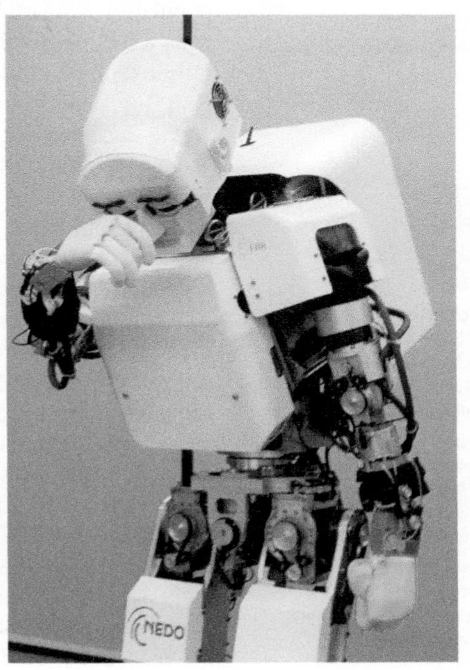

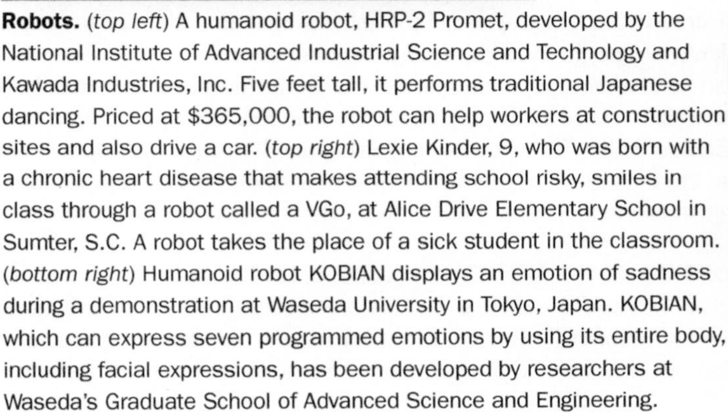

Robots. (*top left*) A humanoid robot, HRP-2 Promet, developed by the National Institute of Advanced Industrial Science and Technology and Kawada Industries, Inc. Five feet tall, it performs traditional Japanese dancing. Priced at $365,000, the robot can help workers at construction sites and also drive a car. (*top right*) Lexie Kinder, 9, who was born with a chronic heart disease that makes attending school risky, smiles in class through a robot called a VGo, at Alice Drive Elementary School in Sumter, S.C. A robot takes the place of a sick student in the classroom. (*bottom right*) Humanoid robot KOBIAN displays an emotion of sadness during a demonstration at Waseda University in Tokyo, Japan. KOBIAN, which can express seven programmed emotions by using its entire body, including facial expressions, has been developed by researchers at Waseda's Graduate School of Advanced Science and Engineering.

TUG, and HelpMate—help free medical workers for more critical tasks. The four-armed da Vinci Si surgical robot, for instance, can do the smallest incisions and stitches for complex surgery deep inside the body, so that surgery is less traumatic and recovery time faster.[29] Hydraulics and computers are being used to help artificial limbs get "smarter,"[30] and pressure-sensitive artificial skin made of tiny circuits is expected to improve limbs' effectiveness.[31] An international team of researchers at of Tel Aviv University is working on a biomimetic computer chip for brain stimulation that is programmable, responsive to neural activity, and capable of bridging broken connections in the brain. This device could be used to replace diseased or damaged brain tissue, restore brain functions lost to aging, and even treat epilepsy, chronic pain, and Parkinson's disease.[32]

HEALTH SELF-HELP Want to calculate the odds on how long you will live? Go to *www.livingto100.com*, an online calculator developed by longevity researchers at Harvard Medical School and Boston Medical Center. Want to gather your family health history to see if you're at risk for particular inherited diseases? Go to *www.hhs.gov/familyhistory* to find out how.

One in three Americans has also gone online to figure out a medical condition, and 59% of adults say they have looked online for health information in the past year.[33] (However, some online health information can be misleading and even dangerous.) Some cancer patients have created fund-raising sites on the web to raise money to pay for their out-of-pocket costs, an activity known as *crowdfunding.*[34]

Crowdfunding

Some information on successful crowdfunding:

www.cfpa.org/

http://mashable.com/category/crowdfunding/

www.startupexemption.com/crowdfunding-101#axzz2NR6m7NJa/

Financial Information

The Internet contains lots of financial information. Some of the better sources:

http://financialsoft.about.com/od/morefinancialsoftware/tp/Online_Software_List.htm

www.financialcalculators.com/

www.finance.yahoo.com

www.fool.com

www.ragingbull.com

www.usatoday.com/money/default.htm

Showrooming Articles

http://bits.blogs.nytimes.com/2013/02/27/more-retailers-at-risk-of-amazon-showrooming/

http://blogs.seattletimes.com/monica-guzman/2013/05/04/smart-shopping-or-petty-theft-caught-in-the-act-of-showrooming/

www.forbes.com/sites/abrambrown/2013/04/04/a-new-move-by-best-buy-to-eliminate-showrooming-trap/

Money & Business: Toward the Cashless Society

Information technology is reducing the use of traditional money.

"The future of money is increasingly digital, likely virtual, and possibly universal," says one writer.[35] **Virtual means that something is created, simulated, or carried on by means of a computer or a computer network but also that it seems almost real.** We certainly have come a long way toward becoming a cashless—and virtual money—society. Besides currency, paper checks, and credit and debit cards, the things that serve as "money" include cash-value cards (such as subway fare cards), automatic transfers (such as direct-deposit paychecks), and digital money ("electronic wallet" accounts such as PayPal).

SMARTPHONES & SHOPPING Consumers have long been able to do online buying and selling via computers, ordering products and having them delivered by UPS or FedEx, but the popularity of smartphones is altering the shopping experience even more. For instance, as you enter a shopping mall, your phone might start buzzing with alerts for coupons at nearby stores, information on traffic patterns, or advice on gifts.[36] Or as you check the price on a camera at Best Buy, your phone might tell you that Target is responding by aggressively cutting the price on the same product, and as other retailers scan their competition on the Internet, prices might change several times even within the space of a day.[37] Some retailers, you may discover, may vary the price of the same product depending on the ZIP code you live in and how close you are to a rival's store.[38] Many of these efforts are traditional retailers' response to the phenomenon known as *showrooming*—the practice of customers examining merchandise in traditional brick-and-mortar retail store without buying it and then shopping online to find a lower price, which 75% of respondents to one survey acknowledged having done.[39]

Your phone may also be used as a payment system, so that, for instance, at Starbucks you can pay for your coffee at the register by displaying a code (bar code) on your mobile device, using a feature called Square Wallet.[40] Or you can pay using the Starbucks Card app. Companies such as Square and PayPal also offer mobile credit-card swiping devices that cab drivers and small merchants can attach to their smartphones to accept credit cards from customers.[41]

USING DIGITAL TOOLS TO EARN MONEY "As communication and information technologies advance," says a Census Bureau analyst, "we are seeing that workers are increasingly able to perform work at home."[42] Indeed, the share of *telecommuters,* or people who work from home at least one day a week, jumped from 7.8% to 9.5% of all workers during the years 2005–2010.[43]

Among the home-based or "micro-jobs" that people hoping to pick up extra cash can do are these:[44]

- Selling art, crafts, or collectibles online—those you've created, such as jewelry or pottery, or those you found at garage sales. (See Artbreak, Etsy.com, or Redbubble.)
- Licensing your photos to microstock photo agencies. (See iStockphoto, Shutterstock, or Dreamstime.)
- Taking on quick tasks, such as doing odd jobs or quick fieldwork assignments. (See Gigwalk, EasyShift, or TaskRabbit.)
- Putting your experience to work as a tutor. (See Smartthinking or Tutor.)

Government & Electronic Democracy: Participating in the Civic Realm

Information technology is helping governments to deliver services and affecting political activism.

The Internet and other information technology have helped government deliver better services and have paved the way for making governmental operations more transparent to the public. They have also changed the nature of politics.

IMPROVING GOVERNMENT SERVICES In Boston, the next time your car hits a pothole, you can use a feature (called Street Bump) to report it to someone in city

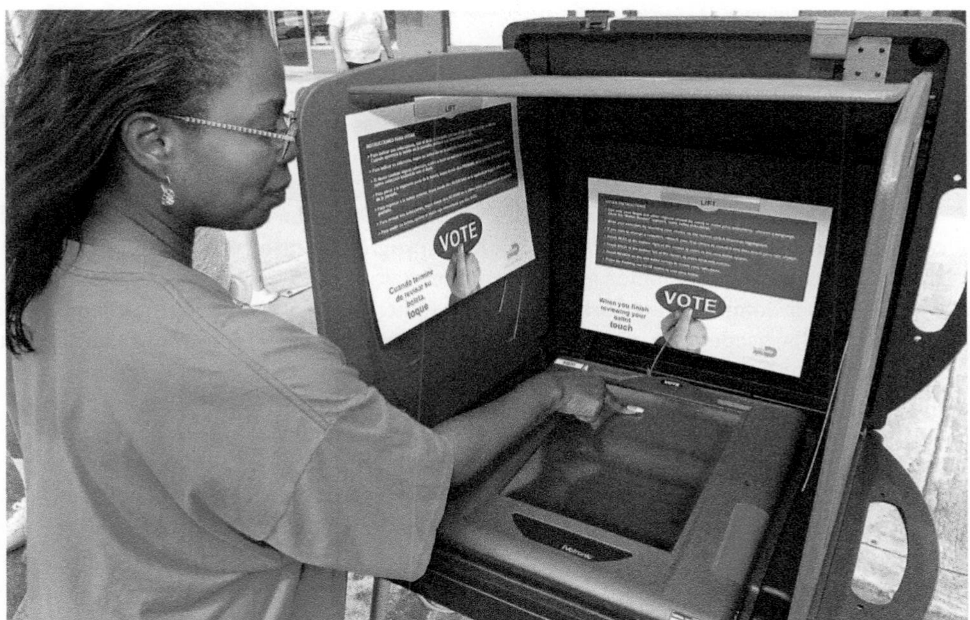

Electronic voting. Voting using computer technology and a touch screen

government who can do something about it. Boston also has a smartphone feature with which you can adopt a fire hydrant, keeping it snowfree and making sure there's access.[45] In 2012, Redwood City, California, became the first city in the nation to allow residents to chat with a police officer online via voice, text, or video.[46] In Seattle, San Diego, and Oakland, police departments use social media such as Twitter and Facebook to provide residents with moment-to-moment crime reports.[47] In Chicago, police are fighting back against shootings and murders by building a **database, a computer system with a collection of interrelated files,** to track the social connections of the city's dozens of street gangs and their myriad factions.[48] Some city officials, such as former Newark, New Jersey, mayor Cory Booker, use social media such as Twitter to make major announcements and to communicate more quickly with constituents than traditional channels, such as radio and TV, allow.[49]

The federal government, as you might expect, is also a big user of information technology. The U.S. State Department has a "DipNote" blog read by more than 2 million readers, and it holds press conferences on YouTube. Congress has a publicly searchable site on the web for all federal contracts and grants over $25,000, and a growing number of states are putting everything from budgets to contracts to travel expenses online for the public to look at. The White House also has its own site (*www.whitehouse.gov*), with its Open Government Dialogue blog.

CHANGING POLITICS Online voting is on the rise, with voters in the tiny East European nation of Estonia, for instance, being able to vote in the comfort of their homes via the Internet. Security is preserved with the help of a special electronic ID card.[50] In the United States, however, where voting is regulated at the state level and secure IDs are problematic, only overseas and military personnel can cast ballots via email, and only under certain conditions.[51] Still, in 12 states, systems have been launched that allow citizens to register online to vote, which has the effect of increasing voter registration.[52]

The Internet is also changing the nature of politics, enabling political candidates and political interest groups to connect with voters in new ways, to raise money from multiple small donors instead of just wealthy groups, and (using cellphones and text messaging) to organize protests.[53] Yet information technology also has its downside, as computers have helped incumbent legislators to design (gerrymander) voting districts that make it nearly impossible for them to be dislodged.[54] Electronic tools have also made it easier for political parties to skirt campaign laws, and computerized voting machines still don't always count votes as they are supposed to.[55] Still, many users of the web have become important watchdogs on government. The site E-Democracy (*http://forums.e-democracy.org/*), for instance, can help citizens dig up government conflicts of interest, and sites such as Project Vote Smart (*www.votesmart.org/*) outline candidates' positions.

Online Government Help

You can gain access to U.S. government (federal, state, and local) agencies through the following websites:

www.usa.gov

www.govspot.com

www.info.gov

www.statelocalgov.net/

www.globalcomputing.com/states.html

Foreign governments' websites:

http://libguides.northwestern.edu/ForeignGovernmentList

2013 Best Computer Careers Comparisons & Reviews (Tech Media network)

http://computer-careers-review.toptenreviews.com/

Jobs & Careers

People now use computers to post résumés and find jobs.

Whether ordinary jobs in which computers are used as ordinary tools or specialized jobs involving advanced computer and professional training, almost every occupation today requires computer skills of some sort.

Among the top 12 occupations with a promising future and requiring at least a bachelor's degree are five in information technology: programmer, software developer, systems analyst, network and computer systems administrator, and information security analyst/ web developer/computer network architect.[56] Other top-paying jobs also require good computer skills: accounting, market research, human resources, specialized sales, mechanical engineering, industrial engineering, and financial analysis.[57] The average starting salaries for jobs most college graduates are apt to consider are shown below. (• *See Panel 1.2.)*

"Most jobs today require a working knowledge of certain computer skills," says one analyst. "Employers seek and reward employees with the skills and knowledge to send messages across the country via email; use a spreadsheet to create a graph and paste it into a report; add and edit data in a database; understand the implications of file sizes, memory limitations, and network arrangements; and recognize the function and features of modern computer components. Any job candidate who already possesses these skills will stand above those who do not" (University of Central Florida Continuing Education; *www.ce.ucf.edu/Program/3121/Computer-Skills-For-The-Workplace/*).

STARTING UP YOUR OWN VENTURE So pervasive have computers and the Internet become that now is a fantastic time to "find new [career] routes into the uncharted wilderness of the 21st-century economy," writes Bard College professor Walter Russell Mead.[58] Start-up costs for new ventures are incredibly low. "A decent computer and an Internet connection gives a business startup the kind of information and access that only large

panel 1.2

The job market

Average 2012 salaries

Source: Data from National Association of Colleges and Employers; TheProfessionalEngineer.com; SalaryExpert.com; MySalary.com; www.cnn.com.

Discipline (bachelor's degree)	Current Average Starting Salary
Family practice physician	$176,183
Management information (IT) systems	$115,780
Chemical engineer	$109,195
Computer science professor	$99,102
Lead video game designer	$90,000
Database manager	$90,000
Website developer	$87,946
Entry-level attorney	$86,068
English professor	$81,099
Software development engineer	$80,000
Marketing manager	$80,000
Financial analyst	$74,389
Computer programmer	$74,354
Registered nurse	$71,692
Assoc. professor of biology	$67,131
Mechanical engineer	$60,721
Graphic designer	$58,370
Crime lab analyst	$55,660
Computer technician (III)	$55,241
High school teacher	$54,902
Accountant	$45,339
Special education teacher	$43,500
Bookkeeper	$37,369
Preschool (daycare) teacher	$27,000

Discipline (bachelor's degree)	Average Starting Salaries for Selected Majors
Marketing	$59–61,000
Computer science	$47–49,000
Chemistry	$44,500
Political science	$40,400
Biology	$40,100
Criminal justice	$38–40,000
English	$38,900
Psychology	$35,200
Physics	$33,600
Communications (not IT)	$31–33,000
Elementary education	$29–31,000

corporations used to be able to afford," he says. "You don't need nearly as much money to start up a business as you used to—and there are many businesses that a recent college grad can launch with little more equipment than that old college computer."

Among the possibilities are photography, home design, travel, food preparation and delivery, fashion, financial planning, tutoring, educational counseling services, fitness training, child care, or any number of other activities. The best method is to consider the needs and problems of your friends and neighbors and build a small business around satisfying those needs. In particular, look toward solving the problem of bottling the "hose of the Internet," filtering, organizing, and customizing the torrent of information so people can benefit from it. The life you build that way will probably be more satisfying, says Mead, "and may well be substantially more remunerative than anything a traditional, off-the-shelf career has to offer."

> **Survival Tip**
>
> **Some Basic Computer Skills Needed for Office Jobs**
>
> **Keyboarding (typing)**
> **Microsoft Word**
> **Microsoft Excel**
> **Internet browser and email (communications both on the Internet and within a business environment)**
> **File sharing**

WAYS FOR YOU TO FIND EMPLOYERS To have a chance of succeeding in today's job market, you need to combine a traditional education with training in computer skills. You also need to be smart about job searching, résumé writing, interviewing, and postings of employment opportunities. Advice about careers and job hunting is available at CareerBuilder.com, Career Advice Blogs, Working World, National Careers Service, and other sites on the web.

As you might expect, the first to use cyberspace as a job bazaar were companies seeking people with technical backgrounds, such as computer programmers. Now, however, online job exchanges have broadened to include openings for forest rangers in Idaho, physical

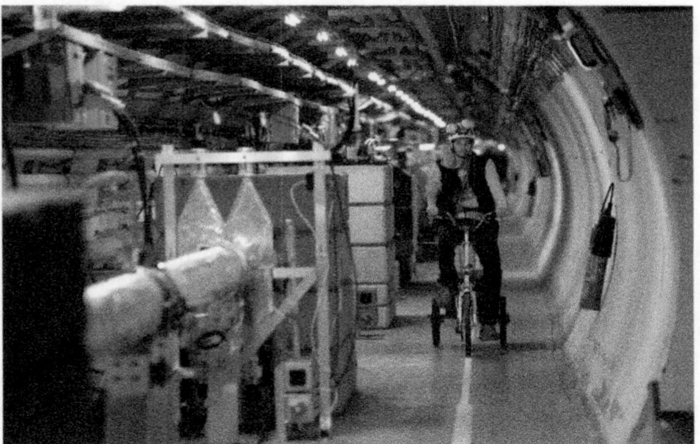

Careers. (*left*) Front-desk workers at many hotels use computers to check in guests. (*right*) A technician cycles in the Large Hadron Collider (LHC) at the European Organization for Nuclear Research (CERN) in the French village of Cessy near Geneva in Switzerland. As hundreds of engineers and workers start two years of work to fit out the giant LHC particle collider to reach deep into unknown realms of nature, CERN physicists look to the vast machine to unveil by the end of the decade the nature of the mysterious dark matter that makes up a quarter of the universe and perhaps find new dimensions of space.

Police work. Syracuse, New York: An Onondaga County sheriff's deputy enters information into a laptop in his squad car as he issues a ticket for an uninspected vehicle.

Beyond.com: *www.beyond.com*	Indeed.com: *www.indeed.com*
CareerBuilder: *www.careeronestop.org*	Yahoo! Careers: *http://us.careers.yahoo.com*
CareerOneStop: *www.careeronestop.org*	Jobs.com: *www.jobs.com*
CollegeGrad: Job Hunter: *www.collegegrad.com*	JobsOnline: *www.jobsonline.com*
Dice: *www. dice.com*	MonsterCollege: *http://college.monster.com/?wt.mc_n=monstertrak*
FedWorld (U.S. government jobs): *www.fedworld.gov*	Monster: *www.monster.com*
FindTheRightJob: *www.findtherightjob.com*	Simply Hired: *www.simplyhired.com*
NationJob Network: *www.nationjob.com*	U.S. Dept. of Labor: *www.bls.gov/oco/*

panel 1.3

Some websites that post job listings

therapists in Atlanta, models in Florida, and English teachers in China. Most online job boards—Monster, Craigslist, CareerBuilder, and others—are free to job seekers, although many require that you fill out an online registration form. *(• See Panel 1.3.)* More companies are also turning to social media, such as Twitter, Facebook, and the professional site LinkedIn as a way to broadcast job openings.[59] Facebook, for instance, offers a featured called the Social Jobs App for a central hub for members to find postings to about 1.7 million open jobs in the United States.[60]

Computer Basic Skills Test

A computer basic skills test is usually a prerequisite for a job or for placement companies:

www.cvtips.com/interview/computer-basic-skills-test-job-interview-tips.html

WAYS FOR EMPLOYERS TO FIND YOU Posting your résumé online for prospective employers to see has to be done with some care. Besides featuring a succinct summary of your top achievements and related skills, it should also include links or web addresses to social-media profiles and online portfolios (as of projects you have done). If you're applying for a specific job, your résumé should include applicable keywords from the employer's job description.[61] Indeed, some companies now use tracking programs to scan résumés for keywords, former employers, years of experience, and schools attended to identify candidates of likely interest.[62]

Some companies are even ditching résumés and the conventional job interview process for "Twitterviews"—interviews on Twitter.[63] Indeed, says one account, some "recruiters are filling openings faster by relying on new tools that scour social networks and target workers who aren't necessarily looking for jobs," one example being Recruiter by LinkedIn.[64] Obviously, if you want to be found, you need to make yourself visible. Thus, some experts suggest you need to set up a Facebook page that allows you to interact with others on a professional level, to participate in Twitter, and to write comments (posts) on other people's online journals—their **blogs (weblogs), frequently updated sites on the World Wide Web intended for public consumption that contain a writer's observations, opinions, images, and links to other websites.**[65] Also, your personal Facebook page should be professional, because companies now do searches to examine a job candidate's web presence (*http://online.wsj.com/article/SB10000872396390443759504577631410093879278.html*).

Your Personal Life

Computers are playing important roles in our personal lives.

Celebrating Thanksgiving away from home? No matter. You may join the festivities through a laptop set on the family table in your usual spot, connected by high-definition TV camera and a communication service such as Skype or Google Hangout.[66] Or you might post photos of the dinner you're enjoying to show to your family and close friends on Facebook, send a general Thanksgiving cheer to your Twitter followers, and post images of the most interesting dishes on an online photo-sharing service such as Instagram.[67]

Technology has affected our personal lives in ways that were almost unimaginable 15 years ago. Two examples:

ONLINE RELATIONSHIP SITES Online relationship sites, or *online dating sites*, provide electronic forums that people may join in the hope of meeting compatible companions or mates. There are over 1,000 such sites, the biggest and best-known being the mainstream sites Match.com, PlentyOfFish, Zoosk, eHarmony, and Singles.net. Then there are niche sites, such as those for people of the same ethnicity (LatinAmerican Cupid, Black People Meet, Asian People Meet), religion (ChristianMingle, JDate for Jewish daters), occupations (FarmersOnly.com), and over 50 (Senior Friend Finder).[68] There are also niche sites for smokers, vegetarians, dog lovers, and so on. One website, Find Your

FaceMate, uses facial recognition to match couples who look alike.[69] Of course, other websites help people to find new friends, not potential mates, such as, for women, SocialJane.com and GirlFriendCircles.

Social-networking websites are not specifically designed for finding dates, but that is how they are being used. Facebook, Twitter, and others let users build personal sites to express their interests and display their personality. Facebook's Graph Search extends searches for singles on the network to friends of friends.[70] Many online matchmakers are, of course, accessible on smartphones.

OTHER AREAS OF PERSONAL LIFE "As we sit here," says the head of consulting firm Creative Strategies, "digital is embedded into the fiber of every aspect of our culture and our personal lives."[71] Worried about walking across campus at night? Armed Safety Button is a smartphone feature that, once activated, will track your location, set off an alarm, take a series of photos of an assailant, project a blinding light, and place a call to 911.[72] Need more exercise or want to lose weight? There's a Nike Training Club iPad feature that you can use in your living room. There's also an electronic fork, the HAPIfork, that monitors eating speed and, through use of vibrations, encourages the user to slow down.[73] New baby in the family? A subscription to Diapers.com might be just the ticket.[74] There seems to be technology for every phase of life—and even beyond it, including memorial websites that celebrate the lives of those who have departed.[75]

1.2 INFORMATION TECHNOLOGY IS PERVASIVE: Cellphones, Email, the Internet, & the E-World

Email, network, Internet, web, smartphone, text, tweet, *and* cyberspace *are now common terms in many languages.*

One of the first computers, the outcome of military-related research, was delivered to the U.S. Army in 1946. ENIAC (short for *E*lectronic *N*umerical *I*ntegrator *A*nd *C*alculator) weighed 30 tons, and was 80 feet long, and 2 stories high, but it could multiply a pair of numbers in the then-remarkable time of three-thousandths of a second. (• *See Panel 1.4.*) This was the first general-purpose, programmable electronic computer, the grandparent of today's lightweight handheld machines—including the smartphone. Some of the principal historical developments are shown in the timeline on the next page. (• *See Panel 1.5.*)

The Phone Grows Up

The telephone is not what it used to be.

Cellphone mania has swept the world. All across the globe, people have acquired the portable gift of gab, with some users making over 45 calls and writing more than 90 texts a day. By the end of 2013, overall mobile penetration rates will probably have reached 96% globally; and the International Telecommunication Union (ITU) said

panel 1.4
Grandparent and offspring: ENIAC (*left*) is the grandparent of today's iPad (*right*).

Smartphones. (*left*) Apple 5G iPhone; (*middle*) Android Samsung Galaxy III smartphone; (*right*) Nexus smartphone

mobile subscriber numbers may top 7 billion in 2014 (about the total population of the planet).[76] About 88% of Americans 18 and older owned a cellphone in 2012.[77] It has taken more than 100 years for the telephone to get to this point—getting smaller, acquiring push buttons, and losing its cord connection. In 1964, the * and # keys were added to the keypad. In 1973, the first cellphone call was processed.

In its most basic form the telephone is still so simply designed that even a young child can use it. However, as a smartphone, it is now becoming more versatile and complex—a way of connecting to the Internet and the World Wide Web and allowing you not only to make voice calls but also to send and receive email and text messages, take and send photos and videos, get map directions, and obtain news, research, music, photos, movies, and TV programs.

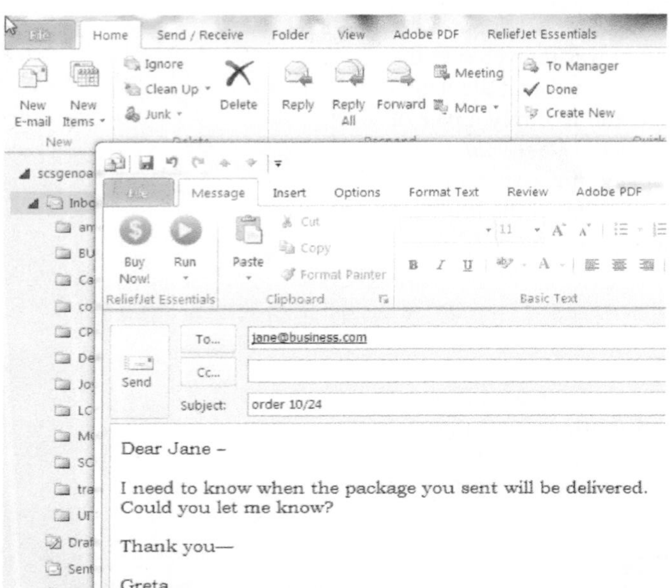

"You've Got Mail!" Email's Mass Impact

Email revolutionized communication, and has many benefits, but in many areas it is being supplanted by texting.

It took the telephone 40 years to reach 10 million customers, and fax machines 20 years. Personal computers made it into that many American homes 5 years after they were introduced. Email, which appeared in 1981, became popular far more quickly, reaching 10 million users in little more than a year.[78] No technology has ever become so universal so fast.

Until 1998 hand-delivered mail was still the main means of correspondence. But in that year the volume of email in the United States surpassed the volume of

4000–1200 BCE	3500 BCE–2900 BCE	3000 BCE	1270 BCE	900 BCE	530 BCE	100 CE
Inhabitants of the first known civilization in Sumer keep records of commercial transactions on clay tablets	Phoenicians develop an alphabet; Sumerians develop cuneiform writing; Egyptians develop hieroglyphic writing	Abacus is invented in Babylonia	First encyclopedia (Syria)	First postal service (China)	Greeks start the first library	First bound books

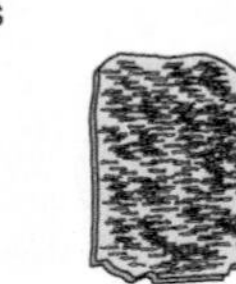

hand-delivered mail. In 2013 there were reportedly 2.2 billion email users worldwide, and global email traffic reached 144 billion messages a day.[79]

Using electronic mail clearly is different from calling on a telephone or writing a conventional letter. As one writer puts it, email "occupies a psychological space all its own. It's almost as immediate as a phone call, but if you need to, you can think about what you're going to say for days and reply when it's convenient."[80] Email has been popular, points out another writer, not because it gives us more immediacy but because it gives us *less*. "The new appeal of email is the old appeal of print," he says. "It isn't instant; it isn't immediate; it isn't in your face." Email has succeeded for the same reason that the videophone—which allows callers to see each other while talking—has been so slow to catch on: because "what we actually want from our exchanges is the minimum human contact commensurate with the need to connect with other people."[81]

Always on. Most of today's students have never experienced life without cyberspace.

Young people are more apt to send instant messages and to do **texting, or text messaging—sending and receiving short written messages between mobile phones or other portable or fixed devices.**[82]

What is interesting, though, is that in these times, when images often seem to overwhelm words, email is actually *reactionary.* "The Internet is the first new medium to move decisively backward," points out one writer, because it essentially involves writing. Twenty years ago, "even the most literate of us wrote maybe a half a dozen letters a year; the rest of our lives took place on the telephone."[83] Email has changed all that—and has put pressure on businesspeople in particular to sharpen their writing skills. (A countertrend, unfortunately, is that the informal style of electronic messages, especially texting, is showing up in schoolwork.)[84]

The Internet, the World Wide Web, & the "Plumbing of Cyberspace"

The net, the web, and cyberspace are not the same things.

As the success of the smartphone shows, communications has extended into every nook and cranny of civilization (with poorer nations actually the leaders in cellphone growth), a development called the "plumbing of cyberspace." The term *cyberspace* was coined by William Gibson in his novel *Neuromancer* (1984) to describe a futuristic computer network into which users plug their brains. (*Cyber* comes from "cybernetics," a term coined in 1948 to apply to the comparative study of automatic control systems, such as the brain and the nervous system and mechanical-electrical communication systems.) In everyday use, this term has a rather different meaning.

Today many people equate cyberspace with the Internet. But it is much more than that. Cyberspace includes not only the web, chat rooms, online diaries and articles (blogs), and social networking—all features we explain in this book—but also such things as conference calls and automated teller machines (ATMs). We may say, then, that **cyberspace encompasses not only the online world and the Internet in particular but also the whole wired and wireless**

panel 1.5

Timeline

Overview of some of the historical developments in information technology. In upcoming chapters we modify the timelines to show you more about the people and advances contributing to developments in information technology.

700–800	1049	1450	1455	1621	1642	1666
Arabic numbers introduced to Europe	First movable type (clay) invented in China	Newspapers appear in Europe	Printing press (J. Gutenberg, Germany)	Slide rule invented (Edmund Gunther)	First mechanical adding machine (Blaise Pascal)	First mechanical calculator that can add and subtract (Samuel Morland)

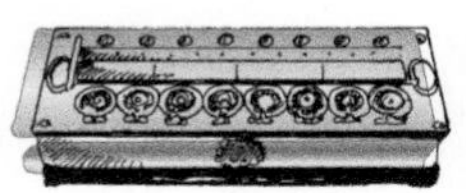

PRACTICAL ACTION

Managing Email

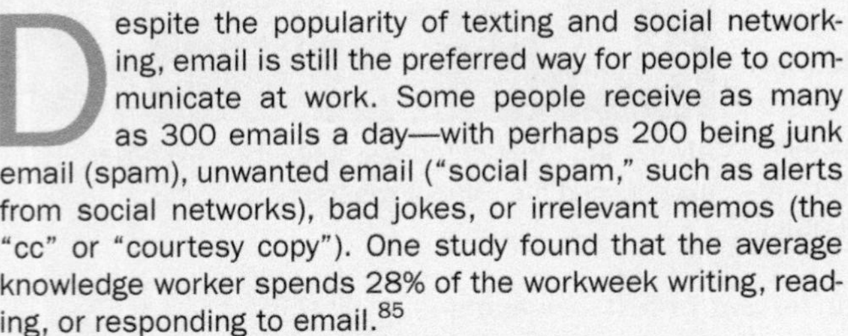

Despite the popularity of texting and social networking, email is still the preferred way for people to communicate at work. Some people receive as many as 300 emails a day—with perhaps 200 being junk email (spam), unwanted email ("social spam," such as alerts from social networks), bad jokes, or irrelevant memos (the "cc" or "courtesy copy"). One study found that the average knowledge worker spends 28% of the workweek writing, reading, or responding to email.[85]

Shayne Hughes, CEO at Learning for Leadership, mandated the unthinkable—forcing his workers to communicate for one week the old-fashioned way, face to face, which actually boosted productivity. Hughes believes dealing with email distracts employees from strategic thinking and discussions. He also argues that "there's a feeling senders get when emailing someone with a problem or issue—a misplaced feeling of relief." He adds, "It's as if that person is simply detailing the problem, clicking send, and all of sudden that problem is now someone else's."[86]

Some tips:[87]

- **Send less email, and send better email:** The more email you send, the more you'll get. Put short messages in the subject line so that recipients don't have to open the email to read the note. Make one point per email. Don't reply to every email message you get. Don't "cc" (copy to) people unless absolutely necessary. Don't send chain letters or lists of jokes. Don't overuse the high-priority flag.
- **Don't waste time constantly checking email:** Process email for 5 to 10 minutes each hour rather than as messages come in or at times when you can't really send a reply. Incidentally, research has shown that students who engage in very high email usage also often show depressive symptoms.[88] Conversely, other research finds that people who do not look at email frequently at work were less stressed and more productive than others.[89]
- **Avoid using "Reply All":** People hate getting all those "thanks" and "appreciated" emails, as well as the deluge of "reply alls" with messages of only minimal interest to them. Avoid using this feature unless your message is really important.[90]
- **Don't send long attachments:** Attachments—computer files of long documents or images attached to an email—are supposed to be a convenience, but large files often just clog the mail system.
- **Don't open attachments you don't recognize:** Some dangerous computer viruses—renegade programs that can damage your computer—have been spread by email attachments that automatically activate the virus when they are opened.
- **Be aware that anyone might read the emails you send:** Don't send a message electronically you would be ashamed of if a third party read it. Email messages are not written with disappearing ink; they remain in a computer system long after they have been sent. "Delete" removes the email from the visible list, but the messages remain on your hard disk and some servers and can be retrieved by experts. (Special software,

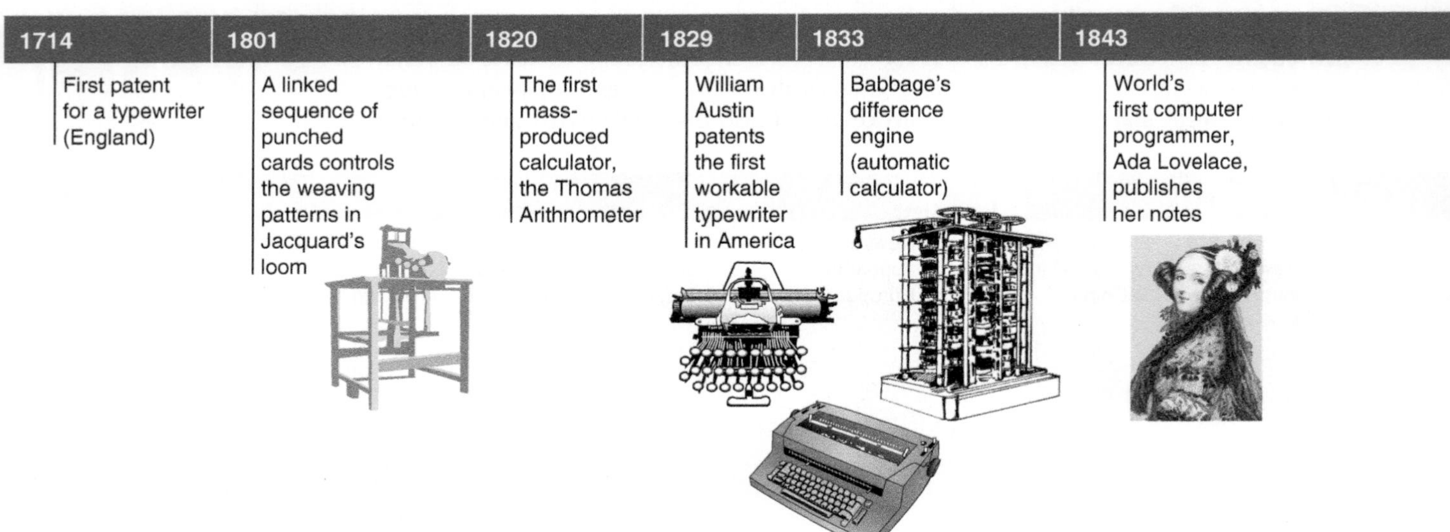
1714
First patent for a typewriter (England)
1801
A linked sequence of punched cards controls the weaving patterns in Jacquard's loom
1820
The first mass-produced calculator, the Thomas Arithnometer
1829
William Austin patents the first workable typewriter in America
1833
Babbage's difference engine (automatic calculator)
1843
World's first computer programmer, Ada Lovelace, publishes her notes

such as Spytech Eradicator and Revo, can completely erase email from the hard disk, as we discuss later.)

- **Make sure emails to bosses, coworkers, and customers are literate:** It's okay to be informal when emailing friends, but employers and customers expect a higher standard. Pay attention to spelling and grammar.
- **Don't use email to express criticism and sarcasm:** Because email carries no tone or inflection, it's hard to convey emotional nuances. Avoid criticism and sarcasm in electronic messaging. Nevertheless, you can use email to provide quick praise, even though doing it in person will take on greater significance.
- **Be aware that email you receive at work is the property of your employer:** Be careful of what you save, send, and back up.

world of communications in general—the nonphysical terrain created by computer and communications systems. Cyberspace is where you go when you go online with your computer.

Apple Cloze

Cloze, a free Apple iPhone app, functions as an inbox-analyzing expert. Cloze studies emails and other social-network interactions, sorts messages according to who sent them, and prioritizes those from people it thinks matter most to you.

http://online.wsj.com/article/SB10001424127887324338604578328190148068924.html

THE NET & WEB DEFINED The two most important aspects of cyberspace are the Internet and that part of the Internet known as the World Wide Web. To give them formal definition:

- **The Internet—the heart of the Information Age:** Called "the mother of all networks," the **Internet (the "Net" or "net") is a worldwide computer network that connects hundreds of thousands of smaller networks**. These networks link educational, commercial, nonprofit, and military entities, as well as individuals.
- **The World Wide Web—the multimedia part of the Internet:** The Internet has been around for more than 40 years. But what made it popular, apart from email, was the development in the early 1990s of the **World Wide Web, often called simply the "Web" or the "web"—an interconnected system of Internet computers (called *servers*) that support specially formatted documents in multimedia form.** The word *multimedia,* from "multiple media," refers to technology that presents information in more than one medium, such as text, still images, moving images, and sound. In other words, the web provides information in more than one way.

THE INTERNET'S INFLUENCE: LIKE A "SECOND SKIN" There is no doubt that the influence of the net and the web is tremendous. At present, about 82% of U.S. adults (94% of ages 19–29) use the Internet, according to Pew Internet.[91] But just how revolutionary is the Internet? Is it equivalent to the invention of television, as some technologists say? Or is it even more important—equivalent to the invention of the printing press? "Television turned out to be a powerful force that changed a lot about society," says technology writer

1844	1854	1876	1890	1895	1907	1920–1921
Samuel Morse sends a telegraph message from Washington to Baltimore	George Boole publishes "An Investigation on the Laws of Thought," a system for symbolic and logical reasoning that will become the basis for computer design	Alexander Graham Bell patents the telephone	Electricity used for first time in a data-processing project—Hollerith's automatic census-tabulating machine (used punched cards)	First radio signal transmitted	First regular radio broadcasts, from New York	The word *robot,* derived from the Czech word for compulsory labor, is first used to mean a humanlike machine

Brief History of the Internet

We cover the Internet in more detail in the next chapter, but if you would like a brief history of the Internet now, go to:

www.isoc.org/internet/history/brief.shtml

Kevin Maney. "But the printing press changed everything—religion, government, science, global distribution of wealth, and much more. If the Internet equals the printing press, no amount of hype could possibly overdo it."[92]

Unquestionably, however, for most of us the Internet and information technology have become like a second skin—an extension of our intellects and even emotions, creating almost a parallel universe of "digital selves."

UNIT 1B: *The Basics of Information Technology*

Perhaps you have been using computers a long time and in a multitude of ways. Or perhaps not. In either case, this book aims to deliver important practical rewards by helping you become "computer streetwise"—that is, tech smart.

1.3 THE PRACTICAL USER: How Becoming Tech Smart Benefits You

Being informed about information technology has practical payoffs.

Being *tech smart* means knowing what information technology can do and what it can't, knowing how it can benefit you and how it can harm you, and knowing when you can solve computer problems and when you have to call for help.

Among the practical payoffs are these: You will know how to . . .

MAKE BETTER BUYING DECISIONS No matter how much prices on computers and portable devices come down, you will always have to make judgments about quality and usefulness when buying services, equipment, and software, including *apps*—short for "applications," small, specialized programs downloaded onto mobile devices.

Incidentally, **downloading is defined as transferring data from a remote computer to one's own computer or mobile device. Uploading is the reverse—transferring data from your own device to a remote computer.**

TECH TALES What Apps Do You Really Need?

When you acquire a new smartphone, you may find that it comes with many apps already preinstalled, with millions of others available on the Internet for free or very reasonable prices. The challenge: Deciding which apps are really useful, since having too many apps can drain the power from the battery on your phone, use too much memory, and possibly introduce security risks (which we discuss in a later chapter).

A frequent traveler, for instance, may find an app such as HotelTonight (showing last-minute hotel rooms available in a particular city) or Airbnb (which lets people rent their homes to travelers) practical, but a college

1924	1927	1941	1942	1944	1945
T.J. Watson renames Hollerith's machine company, founded in 1896, to International Business Machines (IBM)	First demonstration of television in USA	Konrad Zuse (Germany) produces the first fully functional programmable digital computer, the Z3 (ran by perforated celluloid strips)	First electronic digital computer (but non-programmable) developed by John Atanasoff and Clifford Berry	First programmable electromechanical computer (Mark I) (owned by the U.S. government)	John von Neumann introduces the concept of a stored program

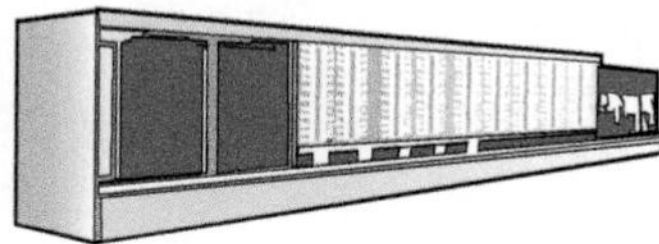

student may have no use for them. Students will, however, probably benefit from adding the following free or low-cost apps to their smartphones or tablets:[93]

- Swype, SwiftKey 3, Path Input Pro: Make typing on a smartphone or touch-screen tablet faster and more accurate; some of these even make corrections as you type.
- Skype, FaceTime: Allow you to video chat for free with others throughout the world, using your device's front- or rear-facing cameras.
- Evernote: Write, type, or speak your ideas to Evernote, which helps you to stay organized.
- Google Earth: Lets you explore the world through satellite and ground-level photos.
- Pocket: Lets you save content you like, so you can read it later.
- Snapguide: Provides user-created how-to guides. ■

FIX ORDINARY COMPUTER PROBLEMS Whether it's replacing a printer cartridge, obtaining a software improvement ("patch" or "upgrade"), or pulling photos from your digital camera or smartphone's camera, we hope this book gives you the confidence to deal with the continual challenges that arise with computers—and know when and how to call for help.

UPGRADE YOUR EQUIPMENT & INTEGRATE NEW TECHNOLOGY New gadgetry and software are constantly being developed. A knowledgeable user learns under what conditions to upgrade, how to do so, and when to start over by buying a new machine or mobile device.

USE THE INTERNET EFFECTIVELY The sea of data that exists on the Internet and other online sources is so great that finding what's best or what's really needed can be a hugely time-consuming activity. We hope to show you the most workable ways to approach this problem.

PROTECT YOURSELF AGAINST ONLINE DANGERS The online world poses real risks to your time, your privacy, your finances, and your peace of mind—spammers, hackers, virus developers, identity thieves, and companies and agencies constructing giant databases of personal profiles—as we will explain. This book aims to make you streetwise about these threats.

KNOW WHAT KINDS OF TECHNOLOGICAL USES CAN ADVANCE YOUR CAREER Top executives use technological devices, as do people in careers ranging from police work to politics, from medicine to music,

Tech smart. To be able to choose a computer system or the components to build one, you need to be tech smart.

1946	1947	1951	1952	1958	1962	1969
First programmable electronic computer in United States (ENIAC)	Invention of the transistor (enabled miniaturization of electronic devices)	Computers are first sold commercially	UNIVAC computer correctly predicts election of Eisenhower as U.S. president	Integrated circuit; first modem	The first computer game is invented (Spacewar)	ARPANET established by U.S. Advanced Research Projects Agency; leads to Internet

from retail to recreation. We hope you will come away from this book with ideas about how the technology can benefit you in whatever work you choose.

Along the way—in the Experience Boxes, Practical Action boxes, Survival Tips, and More Info! features—we offer many kinds of practical advice that we hope will help you to become truly computer smart in a variety of ways, large and small.

1.4 THE "ALL-PURPOSE MACHINE": The Varieties of Computers

Computers come in different sizes; they also function as clients and/or servers.

When the ★alarm blasts you awake, you leap out of bed and head for the kitchen, where you check the ★coffee maker. You probably also check your ★smartphone. After using your ★electronic toothbrush and showering and dressing, you stick a bagel in the ★microwave, and then pick up the ★TV remote and click on the ★TV to catch the weather forecast. Later, after putting dishes in the ★dishwasher, you may go out and start up the ★car and head toward campus or work. Pausing en route at a ★traffic light, you turn on your ★iPod to listen to some music.

You haven't yet touched a PC, a personal computer, but you've already dealt with at least 11 computers—as you probably guessed from the ★s. All these familiar appliances rely on tiny "computers on chips" called *microprocessors.* Maybe, then, the name "computer" is inadequate. As computer pioneer John von Neumann has said, the device should not be called the computer but rather the "all-purpose machine." It is not, after all, just a machine for doing calculations. The most striking thing about it is that it can be put to *any number of uses.*

What are the various types of computers? Let's take a look.

All Computers, Great & Small: The Categories of Machines

There are five basic computer sizes.

At one time, the idea of having your own computer was almost like having your own personal nuclear reactor. In those days, in the 1950s and 1960s, computers were enormous machines affordable only by large institutions. Now they come in a variety of shapes and sizes, which

1970	1972	1975	1976	1978	1981	1982
Microprocessor chips come into use; floppy disk introduced for storing data; first dynamic RAM chip	First videogame (Pong)	First microcomputer (MIT's Altair 8800)	Apple I computer (first personal computer sold in assembled form)	5¼" floppy disk; Atari home videogame; first spam email sent	IBM introduces personal computer; mouse becomes regular part of a computer	Portable computers

panel 1.6

Top five supercomputers

1. Titan	17.6–20 petaflops	U.S.A.
2. Sequoia	16.32 petaflops	U.S.A.
3. K-Computer	10.51 petaflops	Japan
4. Mira	10.1 petaflops	U.S.A.
5. Juqueen	5 petaflops	Germany

Source: From *CNN Money,* "The 5 Fastest Supercomputers," *http://money.cnn.com/gallery/technology/enterprise/2012/11/12/fastest-supercomputer/index.html,* July 21, 2013.

can be generally classified according to their processing power: *supercomputers, mainframe computers, workstations, microcomputers,* and *microcontrollers.* We also consider *servers.*

Supercomputers

Supercomputers are used in very special situations.

Typically priced from $1 million to more than $350 million, **supercomputers are high-capacity machines with thousands of processors that can perform more than several quadrillion calculations per second. These are the most expensive and fastest computers available.** "Supers," as they are called, have been used for tasks requiring the processing of enormous volumes of data, such as doing the U.S. census count, forecasting weather, designing aircraft, modeling molecules, and breaking encryption codes. More recently they have been employed for business purposes—for instance, sifting demographic marketing information—and for film animation. The fastest computer in the world, costing $100 million to build and with roughly the computing power of .5 million of today's most powerful laptops, is the Titan supercomputer, capable of 17.6–20 petaflops (17.6–20 quadrillion calculations per second), located at the Oak Ridge National Laboratory in the Tennessee Valley. *(• See Panel 1.6.)* This almost unimaginable computational capability is about equal to 7 billion people solving 3 million math problems per second. It would take 60,000 years for 1,000 people working at a rate of one calculation per second to complete the number of calculations that Titan can process in a single second.[94]

The cost of electricity for the Titan is more than was $9 million a year. "The sound of 20 quadrillion calculations happening every second is dangerously loud"; "anyone spending more than 15 minutes in the same room with the Titan supercomputer must wear earplugs or risk permanent hearing damage. The din in the room [does] not come from the computer's 40,000 whirring processors, but from the fans and water pipes cooling them."[95]

Supercomputers are still the most powerful computers, but a new generation may be coming that relies on **nanotechnology, in which molecule-size nanostructures are used to create tiny machines for holding data or performing tasks.** (*Nano* means "one-billionth.") Computers the size of a pencil eraser could become available that work 10 times faster than today's fastest supercomputer. Eventually nanotech could show up in every device and appliance in your life.

The Titan. This is the world's fastest supercomputer.

more info!

Flops

In computing, FLOPS is an abbreviation of *Fl*oating-point *O*perations *P*er *S*econd. Flops is used as a measure of a computer's performance, especially in fields of scientific calculations. With floating-point encoding, extremely long numbers can be handled relatively easily. Computers operate in the trillions of flops; for comparison, any response time below 0.1 second is experienced as instantaneous by a human operator, so a simple pocket calculator could be said to operate at about 10 flops. Humans are even worse floating-point processors. If it takes a person a quarter of an hour to carry out a pencil-and-paper long division with 10 significant digits, that person would be calculating in the milliflops range.

1984	1990	1994	1998	2000	2001	2002	2003
Apple Macintosh; first personal laser printer	Laptops become very popular	Apple and IBM introduce PCs with full-motion video built in; wireless data transmission for small portable computers; first web browser invented	PayPal is founded	The "Y2K" nonproblem; the first U.S. presidential webcast	Dell computers becomes the largest PC maker	Friendster	Facebook; MySpace

IBM zEnterprise mainframe computer

Mainframe Computers

Mainframe computers are used in many large businesses.

The only type of computer available until the late 1960s, **mainframes are water- or air-cooled computers that cost \$5,000–\$5 million and vary in size from small, to medium, to large, depending on their use.** Small mainframes (\$5,000–\$200,000) are often called *midsize computers;* they used to be called *minicomputers,* although today the term is seldom used. Mainframes are used by large organizations—such as banks, airlines, insurance companies, and colleges—for processing millions of transactions. Often users access a mainframe by means of a **terminal, which has a display screen and a keyboard and can input and output data but cannot by itself process data.** Mainframes process billions of instructions per second.

Workstations

Workstations are used for graphics, special effects, and certain professional applications.

Workstation

Introduced in the early 1980s, **workstations are expensive, powerful personal computers usually used for complex scientific, mathematical, and engineering calculations and for computer-aided design and computer-aided manufacturing;** they are usually connected to a network. Providing many capabilities comparable to those of midsize mainframes, workstations are used for such tasks as designing airplane fuselages, developing prescription drugs, and creating movie special effects. Workstations have caught the eye of the public mainly for their graphics capabilities, which are used to breathe three-dimensional life into movies such as *Avatar, Harry Potter, Iron Man,* and *Lord of the Rings.* The capabilities of low-end workstations overlap those of high-end desktop microcomputers.

Microcomputers

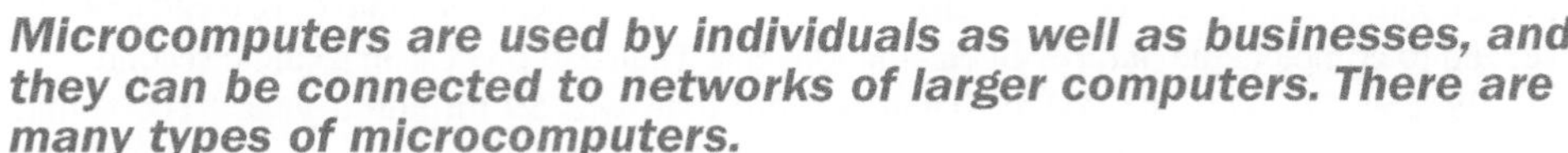

Microcomputers are used by individuals as well as businesses, and they can be connected to networks of larger computers. There are many types of microcomputers.

Desktop PC

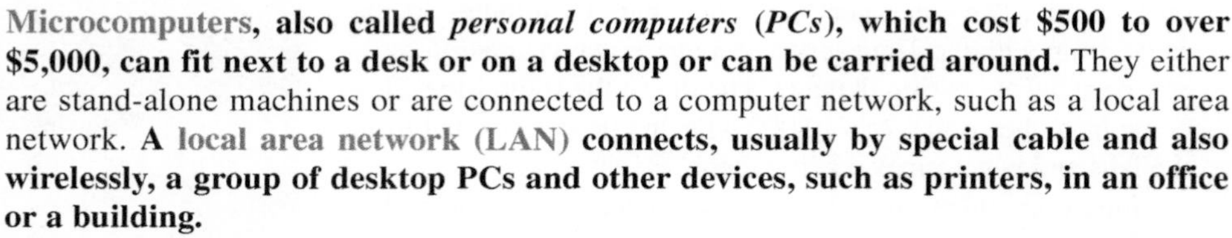

Microcomputers, also called *personal computers (PCs)*, which cost \$500 to over \$5,000, can fit next to a desk or on a desktop or can be carried around. They either are stand-alone machines or are connected to a computer network, such as a local area network. **A local area network (LAN) connects, usually by special cable and also wirelessly, a group of desktop PCs and other devices, such as printers, in an office or a building.**

Microcomputers are of several types: desktop PCs, tower PCs, notebooks (laptops) and netbooks, tablets, mobile devices, and personal digital assistants—handheld computers or palmtops. Also, some microcomputers are powerful enough be used as workstations.

DESKTOP PCS Desktop PCs are the original style of microcomputers whose case or main housing sits on a desk, with keyboard in front and monitor (screen) often on top.

Tower PC (with speakers, keyboard, and mouse)

TOWER PCS Tower PCs are microcomputers whose case sits as a "tower," often on the floor beside a desk, thus freeing up desk space. Some desktop computers, such as Apple's iMac, no longer have a boxy housing; most of the computer components are built into the back of the flat-panel display screen.

2004	2005	2006	2007	2008	2010	2015	2017	2030–2045
IBM PC sold to Lenovo Group; Flickr	You Tube; Wii	Twitter	Skype; Apple introduces iPhone	Netbooks become popular	Apple releases iPad	Foldable computers	Teleportation?; self-aware machine intelligence	The Singularity

Small! The Mac Mini has the smallest desktop microcomputer case, just 6.5 inches square and 1.25 inches tall.

NOTEBOOKS AND NETBOOKS **Notebook computers, also called *laptop computers*, are lightweight portable computers with built-in monitor, keyboard, hard-disk drive, CD/DVD drive, battery, and AC adapter that can be plugged into an electric outlet; they weigh anywhere from 1.8 to 12 pounds.**

Netbooks are mini-notebooks—low-cost, lightweight, small computers with functions designed for basic tasks, such as web searching, email, and word processing. They weigh anywhere from 2.25 to 3.2 pounds, cost generally between $200 and $400, have less processing power than notebooks, and have screens between 7 and 10 inches wide diagonally. Netbooks are being used less now in favor of tablets and smaller laptops, such as Chromebooks.

Laptop computers: MacBook Air and Chromebook

TABLET COMPUTERS Computers such as those in Apple's iPad line, Google's Nexus, the Kindle Fire, and Samsung's Galaxy Tab are examples of a **tablet computer, a wireless portable computer that uses a touch screen (or a kind of pen called a stylus) to access information.** The *touch screen* is a 7- to 10-inch screen on which you can manipulate words, images, and commands directly with your finger. Tablets are rapidly eroding sales of notebook and netbook computers.[96] Tablets might soon be replaced by *phablets*—tablets that are also smartphones.[97]

Tablets. Hewlett-Packard Touchsmart touch screen and Apple iPad tablet

Mobile devices

MOBILE DEVICES & PERSONAL DIGITAL ASSISTANTS **Smaller than notebook and netbook computers and tablets, mobile devices are small, handheld multimedia devices for consumers and business professionals.** Fully Internet integrated, they are highly compatible with desktop microcomputers and notebooks.

Personal digital assistants (PDAs) are handheld computers that combine personal organization tools—schedule planners, address books, to-do lists—with the ability in some cases to send email and faxes. Some PDAs have touch-sensitive screens. Some also connect to desktop computers for sending or receiving information.

E-READERS Produced by Amazon (the Kindle) and by Barnes & Noble (the Nook), **e-readers, or *e-book readers*, are electronic devices that can download e-books—digital versions of regular books, articles, and magazines from various suppliers.** E-readers are generally book-size and can easily be put in a purse or a pocket.

The range of handheld wireless devices, such as smartphones, has surged in recent years, and we consider these later in the book (Chapters 6 and 7).

Kindle Paperwhite 2 and Nook Simple Touch

Microcontroller. *(left)* Various microcontrollers in a car. *(right)* Injection of a VeriChip, which, when implanted in a person's forearm or shoulder, can provide medical and identity information when scanned.

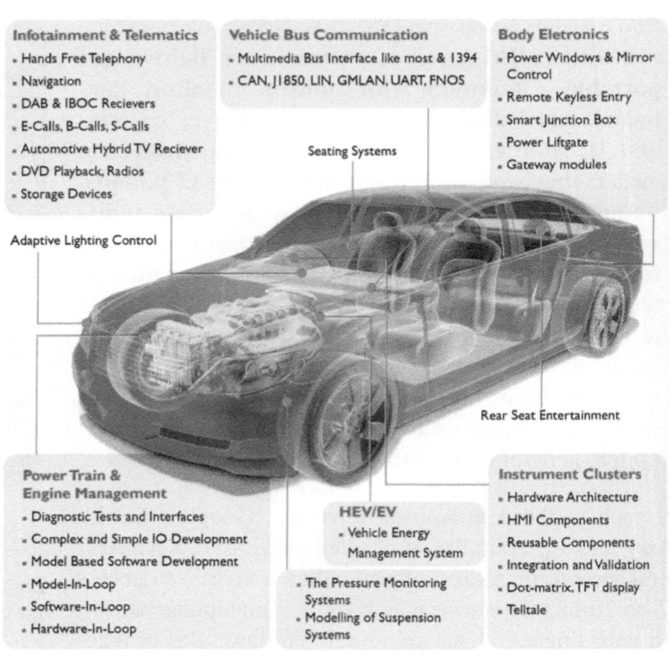

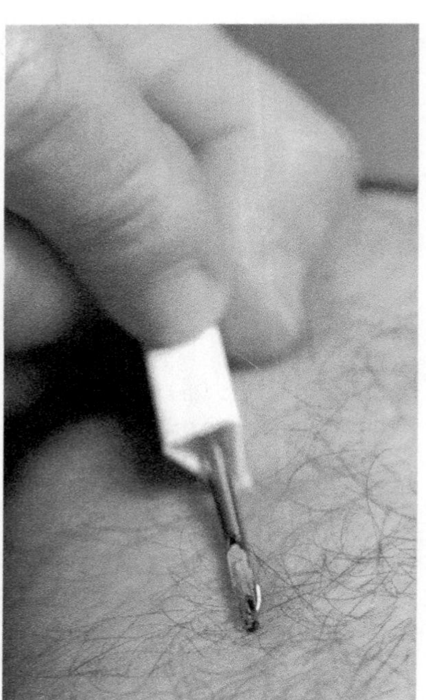

Servers. *(top)* Lead technician services different companies' Internet servers at Switch and Data PAIX in Palo Alto, California. Switch and Data PAIX is one of the primary Internet exchange points in North America, serving hundreds of businesses servers. *(bottom)* A group of networked servers that are housed in one location is called a *server farm* or a *server cluster.*

Microcontrollers

Many personal and household gadgets contain microcontrollers.

Microcontrollers, also called *embedded computers*, are the tiny, specialized microprocessors installed in "smart" appliances and automobiles. These microcontrollers enable microwave ovens, for example, to store data about how long to cook your potatoes and at what power setting. Microcontrollers have been used to develop a new universe of experimental electronic appliances—e-pliances. For example, they are behind single-function products such as digital cameras and digital music players, which have been developed into hybrid forms such as gadgets that store photos and videos as well as music. They also help run tiny machines embedded in clothing, jewelry, and such household appliances as refrigerators. In addition, microcontrollers are used in blood-pressure monitors, air bag sensors, gas and chemical sensors for water and air, and vibration sensors.

Servers

Servers are computers having special software dedicated to providing services to other computers.

The word *server* describes not a size of computer but rather a particular way in which a computer is used. Nevertheless, because servers have become so important to telecommunications, especially with the rise of the Internet and the web, they deserve mention here.

A server, or *network server*, is a central computer that holds collections of data (databases) and programs for connecting or supplying services to PCs, workstations, and other devices, which are called clients. These clients are linked by a wired or wireless network. The entire network is called a *client-server network.* In small organizations, servers can store files, provide printing stations, and transmit email. In large organizations, servers may also house enormous libraries of financial, sales, and product information.

You may never lay eyes on a supercomputer or mainframe or even a tiny microcontroller. But most readers of this book already have seen and used a personal computer. We consider this machine next.

1.5 UNDERSTANDING YOUR COMPUTER

All computers use four basic operations and can be connected to various types of devices.

Perhaps you know how to drive a car. But do you know what to do when it runs badly? And you've probably been using a personal computer. But do you know what to do when it doesn't act right—when, for example, it suddenly crashes (shuts down)?

Cars are now so complicated that professional mechanics are often required for even the smallest problems. With personal computers, however, there are still many things you can do yourself—and should learn to do, so that, as we've suggested, you can be effective, efficient, and employable. To do so, you first need to know how computers work.

How Computers Work: Three Key Concepts

All computer users must understand three basic principles: (1) Data is turned into information; (2) hardware and software have their own specific functions; and (3) all computers involve input, processing, storage, and output, plus communications.

Do you always have to buy an off-the-shelf computer? No. Could you customize your own personal computer? Yes. Many ordinary users order their own customized PCs. Let's consider how you might do this.

We're not going to ask you to actually order a PC—just to pretend to do so. The purpose of this exercise is to give you a basic overview of how a computer works. This information will help you when you go shopping for a new system. It will also help you understand how your existing system works, if you have one.

Before you begin, you need to understand three key concepts.

1. PURPOSE OF A COMPUTER: TURNING DATA INTO INFORMATION. Very simply, the purpose of a computer is to process data into information.

- Data: Data **consists of the raw facts and figures that are processed into information**—for example, the votes for different candidates being elected to student-government office.
- Information: Information **is data that has been summarized or otherwise transformed for use in decision making**—for example, the total votes for each candidate, which are used to decide who won.

2. DIFFERENCE BETWEEN HARDWARE & SOFTWARE. What is the difference between hardware and software?

- Hardware: Hardware **consists of all the machinery and equipment in a computer system.** The hardware includes, among other devices, the keyboard, the screen, the printer, and the "box"—the computer or processing device itself. Hardware is useless without software.
- Software: Software**, or *programs*, consists of all the electronic instructions that tell the computer how to perform a task.** These instructions come from a software developer in a form (such as a CD, or compact disk, or an Internet download) that will be accepted by the computer. Examples are Microsoft Windows 7 and Windows 8, Microsoft Office 2013, and Apple Mac OS X Mountain Lion and Mavericks.

3. THE BASIC OPERATIONS OF A COMPUTER. Regardless of type and size, all computers use the same four basic operations: (1) input, (2) processing, (3) storage, and (4) output. To this we add (5) communications.

- Input operation: Input **is whatever is put in ("input") to a computer system.** Input can be nearly any kind of data—letters, numbers, symbols, shapes, colors, temperatures, sounds, pressure, light beams, or whatever raw material needs processing. When you type some words or numbers on a keyboard, those words are considered input data.

Survival Tip

Input is covered in detail in Chapter 5.

Survival Tip

Processing is covered in detail in Chapter 4.

Survival Tip

Storage is covered in detail in Chapter 4.

Survival Tip

Output is covered in detail in Chapter 5.

Survival Tip

Communications are covered in detail in Chapters 2, 6, and 7.

- Processing operation: **Processing is the manipulation a computer does to transform data into information.** When the computer adds 2 + 2 to get 4, that is the act of processing. The processing is done by the *central processing unit*—frequently called the *CPU*—a chip device consisting of electronic circuitry that executes instructions to process data.
- Storage operation: Storage is of two types—temporary (primary) storage and permanent (secondary) storage. **Primary storage, or *memory*, is the internal computer circuitry (chips) that temporarily holds data waiting to be processed. Secondary storage, simply called *storage*, refers to the devices and media that store data or information permanently.** A hard disk or CD/DVD is an example of this kind of storage. (Storage also holds the software—the computer programs.)
- Output operation: **Output is whatever is output from ("put out of") the computer system—the results of processing, usually information.** Examples of output are numbers or pictures displayed on a screen, words printed on paper by a printer, digital files stored on a CD, and music piped over loudspeakers.
- Communications operation: These days, most (though not all) computers have communications ability, which offers an extension capability—in other words, it extends the power of the computer. With wired or wireless communications connections, data may be input from afar, processed in a remote area, stored in several different locations, and output in yet other places. However, you don't need communications ability to write letters, do calculations, or perform many other computer tasks.

These five operations are summarized in the illustration at right. *(• See Panel 1.7.)*

Customizing a Desktop Computer: Basic Knowledge of How a Computer Works

Customizing a computer is not as hard as you might think.

Survival Tip

Hardware Info

For a listing of most types of hardware, their descriptions, ratings, and prices, and the names of sellers, go to:

http://reviews.cnet.com/

www.juggle.com/computers/hardware-and-software/

www.pcmag.com/

Now let's see how you would order a custom-built desktop PC. Remember, the purpose of this is to help you to understand the internal workings of a computer so that you'll be knowledgeable about buying one and using it.

Note: All the system components you or anyone else chooses *must be compatible*—in other words, each brand must work with other brands. If you work with one company—such as Dell or Hewlett-Packard (HP) or Apple or Asus—to customize your system, you won't have to worry about compatibility. If you choose all the components yourself—for example, by going to a computer-parts seller such as ComputerGeeks.com (*www.geeks.com*)—you will have to check on compatibility as you choose each component. And you'll have to make sure each component comes with any necessary cables, instructions, and component-specific software (called a *driver*) that allows the component to run (the software "drives" the device).

This section of the chapter gives you a brief overview of the components, which are all covered in detail in Chapters 2–6. We describe them in the following order: (1) input hardware (keyboard and mouse); (2) processing and memory hardware; (3) storage hardware (disk drives); (4) output hardware (video and sound cards, monitor, speakers, and printer); (5) communications hardware (the modem); and (6) software (system and application).

Input Hardware: Keyboard & Mouse

The two principal input devices are the keyboard and the mouse.

Keyboard

Input hardware consists of devices that allow people to put data into the computer in a form that the computer can use. For most computers used at school and in offices, at a minimum you will need two things: a *keyboard* and a *mouse.*

KEYBOARD On a microcomputer, a keyboard is the primary input device. **A keyboard is an input device that converts**

2 **Processing:** Once in the computer, data can be processed—numbers compared or sorted, text formatted, images or sounds edited.

1 **Input:** You input **data** into the computer, using a keyboard, mouse, or other device (such as a scanner, microphone, still camera, or video camera). The input data may be text, numbers, images, and/or sounds.

3 **Storage:** Data and programs not currently being used are held in storage. Primary storage is computer circuitry. Secondary storage is usually some kind of disk (such as hard disk or CD/DVD) or tape.

5 **Communications:** Often data or information can be transmitted by modem to or from other computers, as via email or posting to a website.

4 **Output:** Processed **information** is output on a monitor, speakers, printer, or other device.

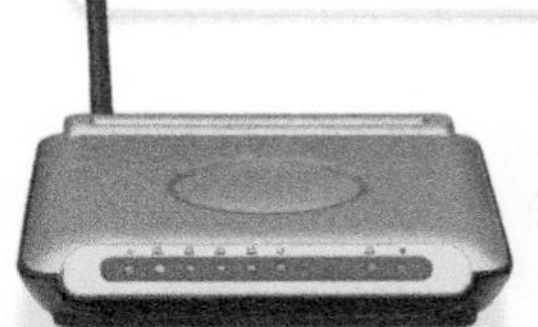

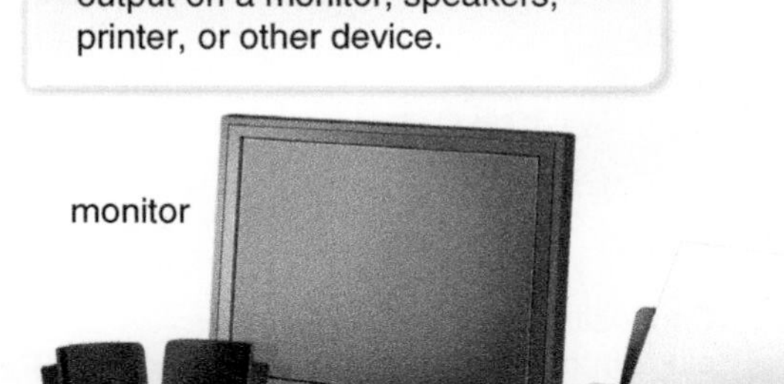

panel 1.7

Basic operations of a computer. (Many more components can be added; these operations are illustrated in more detail in Chapters 4, 5, and 6.)

letters, numbers, and other characters into electrical signals readable by the processor. A microcomputer keyboard looks like a typewriter keyboard, but besides having keys for letters and numbers, it has several keys (such as *F* keys and *Ctrl, Alt,* and *Del* keys) intended for computer-specific tasks. After other components are assembled, the keyboard will be plugged into the back of the computer in a socket intended for that purpose. (Cordless keyboards work differently, as, of course, do smartphone keypads.)

MOUSE **A mouse is a nonkeyboard input device ("pointing device") that is used to manipulate objects viewed on the computer display screen.** The mouse cord is plugged into the back of the computer or into the back of the keyboard after the other components are assembled. Cordless mice are also available.

In the next few years, it's possible the mouse will be made obsolete by the *touch-screen interface,* as with the Asus VivoBook laptop and Lenovo's ThinkPad Twist, and even the *gesture interface,* with our hands, moving through the air, sending commands to the computer.[98] (We discuss this further in Chapter 5.)

Mouse

Case

Processing & Memory Hardware: Inside the System Cabinet

A computer's processing and memory devices are inside the computer case on the main circuit board, called the motherboard.

The brains of the computer are the *processing* and *memory* devices, which are installed in the case, also called the system cabinet or system unit.

CASE & POWER SUPPLY **Also known as the system unit, the case or *system cabinet* is the box that houses the processor chip (CPU), the memory chips, the motherboard (main circuit board), the power supply, and some secondary-storage devices**—hard-disk drive and CD or DVD drive, as we will explain. The case generally comes in desktop or tower models. It includes a power supply unit and a fan to keep the circuitry from overheating.

Processor chip

PROCESSOR CHIP It may be small and not look like much, but it could be the most expensive hardware component of a build-it-yourself PC—and doubtless the most important. **A processor chip (CPU, for central processing unit) is a tiny piece of silicon that contains millions of miniature electronic circuits.** The speed at which a chip processes information is expressed in *megahertz (MHz),* millions of processing cycles per second, or *gigahertz (GHz),* billions of processing cycles per second. The faster the processor, the more expensive it is.

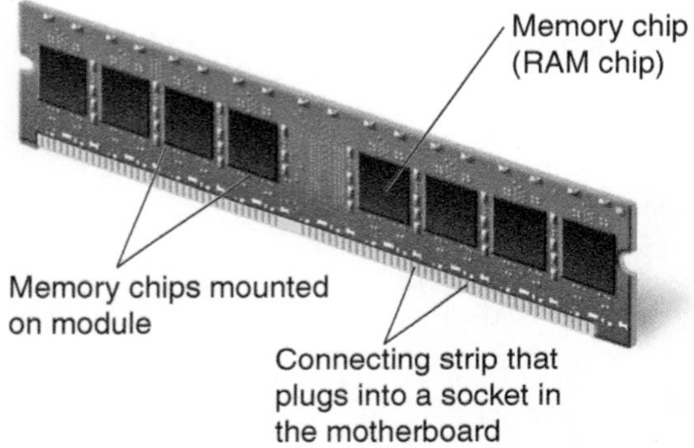

Memory chip

MEMORY CHIPS These chips are also small. **Memory chips, also known as *RAM (random access memory) chips*, represent *primary* storage, or temporary, storage; they hold data before processing and information after processing, before it is sent along to an output or storage device.** You'll want enough memory chips to hold at least 2–5 gigabytes, or roughly 2–5 billion characters, of data, which is adequate for most student purposes. Students into heavy graphics use and game playing will need more memory. (We will explain the numbers used to measure storage capacities in a moment.)

MOTHERBOARD **Also called the *system board*, the motherboard is the main circuit board in the computer.** This is the big (usually) green circuit board to which everything else—such as the keyboard, mouse, and printer—attaches through connections (called *ports*) in the back of the computer. The processor chip and memory chips are also installed on the motherboard.

The motherboard has **expansion slots—for expanding the PC's capabilities—which give you places to plug in additional or upgraded circuit boards,** such as those for video, sound, and communications (modem). *(• See Panel 1.8.)*

PUTTING THE COMPONENTS TOGETHER Now the components can be put together. As the illustration at right shows, ❶ the memory chips are plugged into the motherboard. Then ❷ the processor chip is plugged into the motherboard. Now ❸ the motherboard is attached to the system cabinet. Then ❹ the power supply unit is connected to the system cabinet. Finally, ❺ the wire for the power switch, which turns the computer on and off, is connected to the motherboard.

Storage Hardware: Hard Drive & CD/DVD Drive

Computers can have several types of storage devices.

With the motherboard in the system cabinet, the next step is installation of the storage hardware. Whereas memory chips deal only with temporary storage, *secondary storage,* or *permanent storage,* stores your data for as long as you want.

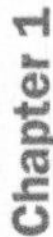

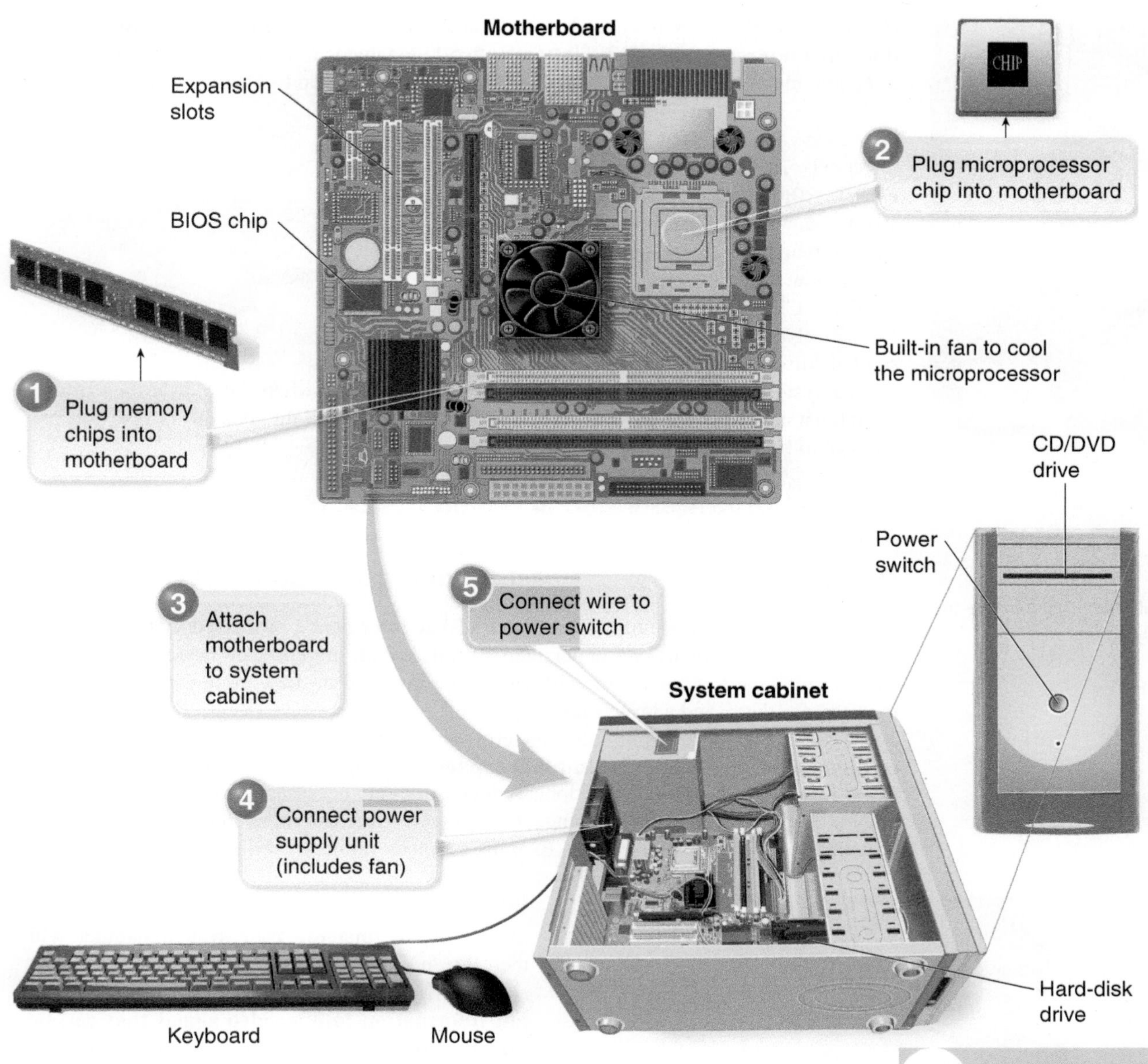

panel 1.8

Putting the components together

For today's student purposes, you'll need a hard drive and a CD/DVD drive. These storage devices slide into the system cabinet from the front and are secured with screws. Each drive is attached to the motherboard by a cable. Also, each drive must be hooked up to a plug extending from the power supply.

A computer system's data/information storage capacity is represented by bytes, kilobytes, megabytes, gigabytes, terabytes, petabytes, exabytes, and zettabytes, as follows:

1 byte = *1 character of data (A character can be alphabetic—A, B, or C—or numeric—1, 2, or 3—or a special character—!, ?, *, $, %.)*

1 kilobyte = *1,024 characters (about ½ page of text)*

1 megabyte = *1,048,576 characters (about 500 pages of text)*

1 gigabyte = *more than 1 billion characters (about 500,000 pages of text)*

1 terabyte = *more than 1 trillion characters (about 1 million thick books)*

1 petabye = *about 1 quadrillion characters (about 180 Libraries of Congress)*

1 exabyte = *about 1 quintillion characters (about 180,000 Libraries of Congress)*

1 zettabyte = *about 1 sextillion characters (180 million Libraries of Congress* Source: *www.wisegeek.org/how-much-text-is-in-a-kilobyte-or-megabyte.htm).*

Hard-disk drive (goes inside the computer case)

HARD-DISK DRIVE A **hard-disk drive is a device that stores billions of characters of data on a nonremovable disk platter.** With 500 gigabytes of storage, you should be able to handle most student needs. (Many hard-disk drives store up to 4 terabytes of data.)

CD/DVD DRIVE **A CD (compact disk) drive, or its more recent variant, a DVD (digital video disk) drive, is a storage device that uses laser technology to read data from optical disks.** Today new software is generally supplied on CDs or downloaded via the Internet. (Note that "disk" is sometimes spelled "disc.")

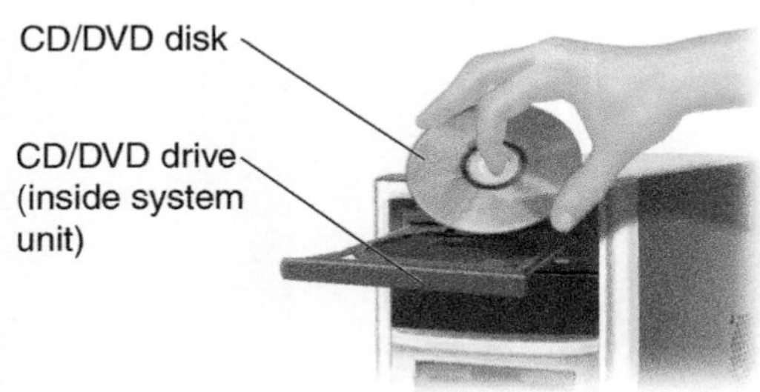

The system cabinet has lights on the front that indicate when these drives are in use. (You must not remove a disk from the optical drive until its light goes off, or else you risk damage to both disk and drive.)

Output Hardware: Video & Sound Cards, Monitor, Speakers, & Printer

Output hardware provides users with the information they need.

Output hardware consists of devices that translate information processed by the computer into a form that humans can understand—print, sound, graphics, or video, for example. Now a video card and a sound card need to be installed in the system cabinet. Next the monitor, speakers, and a printer are plugged in.

This is a good place to introduce the term *peripheral device.* **A peripheral device is any component or piece of equipment that expands a computer's input, storage, or output capabilities.** In other words, a peripheral device does not necessarily contribute to the computer's primary function (computing). Peripheral devices can be inside the computer case or connected to it from the outside. Examples include printers, monitors, and disk drives.

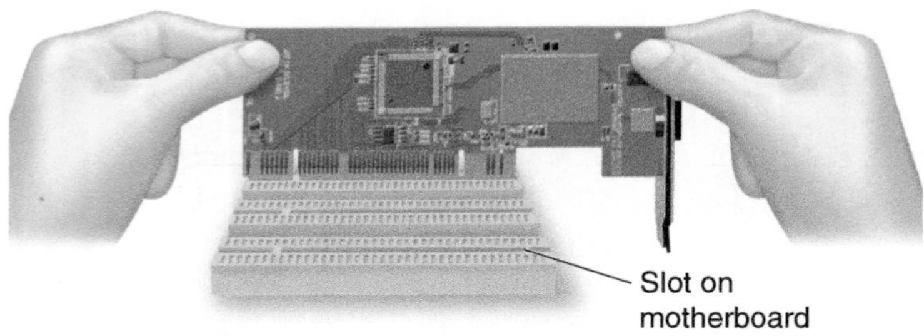

VIDEO CARD You will certainly want your monitor to display images. Your system cabinet will therefore need to have a device to make this possible. **A video card converts the processor's output information into a video signal that can be sent through a cable to the monitor.** Remember the expansion slots we mentioned? The video card is plugged into one of these on the motherboard.

SOUND CARD To listen to music and sound effects on your PC, you'll need a **sound card, which enhances the computer's sound-generating capabilities by allowing sound to be output through speakers,** either built into the computer or connected externally. This card, too, would be plugged into an expansion slot on the motherboard. With the CD drive connected to the card, you can listen to music CDs.

Monitor

MONITOR As with television sets, the inch dimension on monitors is measured diagonally corner to corner. **The monitor is the display device that takes the electrical signals from the video card and forms an image using points of colored light on the screen.** Later, after the system cabinet has been closed up, the monitor will be connected by means of a cable to the back of the computer, using the clearly marked connector. The power cord for the monitor will be plugged into a wall plug

External speakers

SPEAKERS **Speakers are the devices that play sounds transmitted as electrical signals from the sound card.** They may not be very sophisticated, but unless you're into high-fidelity recordings they're probably good enough. The speakers are either built into the computer or connected to a single wire that is plugged into the back of the computer.

PRINTER Especially for student work, you certainly need a **printer, an output device that produces text and graphics on paper.** There are various types of printers, as we discuss later. The printer has two connections. One, which relays signals from the computer, goes to the back of the PC, where it connects with the motherboard. (Wireless printers are also available.) The other is a power cord that goes to a wall plug. Color printers are more expensive than black-and-white printers, and fast printers cost more than slow ones.

Printer

Communications Hardware: Modem

Computers often need some kind of modem in order to communicate and become part of a network.

Computers can be stand-alone machines, unconnected to anything else. If all you're doing is word processing to write term papers, you can do it with a stand-alone system. As we have seen, however, the communications component of the computer system vastly extends the range of a PC. Thus, while the system cabinet is still open, there is one more piece of hardware to install.

MODEM **A standard modem is a device that sends and receives data over telephone lines, or wirelessly via a network, to and from computers.** The modem is sometimes mounted on an expansion card, which is fitted into an expansion slot on the motherboard; sometimes the modem is wired directly into the motherboard. (Other types of computer communications connections are discussed in Chapters 2 and 6.)

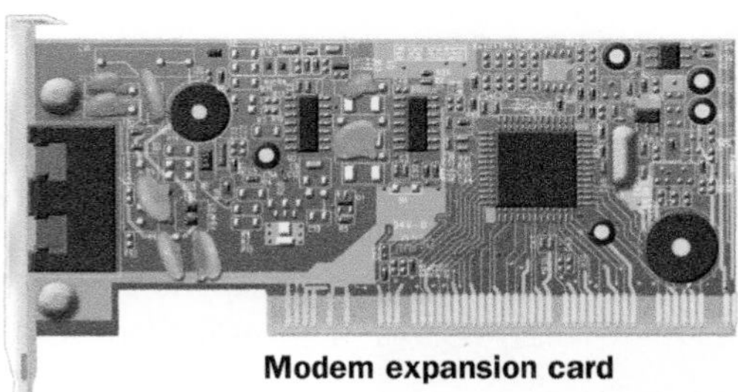

Modem expansion card

Now the system cabinet is closed up. The person building or customizing the system will plug in all the input and output devices and turn on the power "on" button. Your microcomputer system will look similar to the one shown below. *(• See Panel 1.9.)* Are you now ready to roll? Not quite.

Software

Computers use two basic types of software: system software and application software.

After the computer has been assembled, it will be tested. But first the software, the electronically encoded instructions that tell the computer hardware what to do, must be installed. (*Installation* is the process of copying software programs from a main secondary-storage

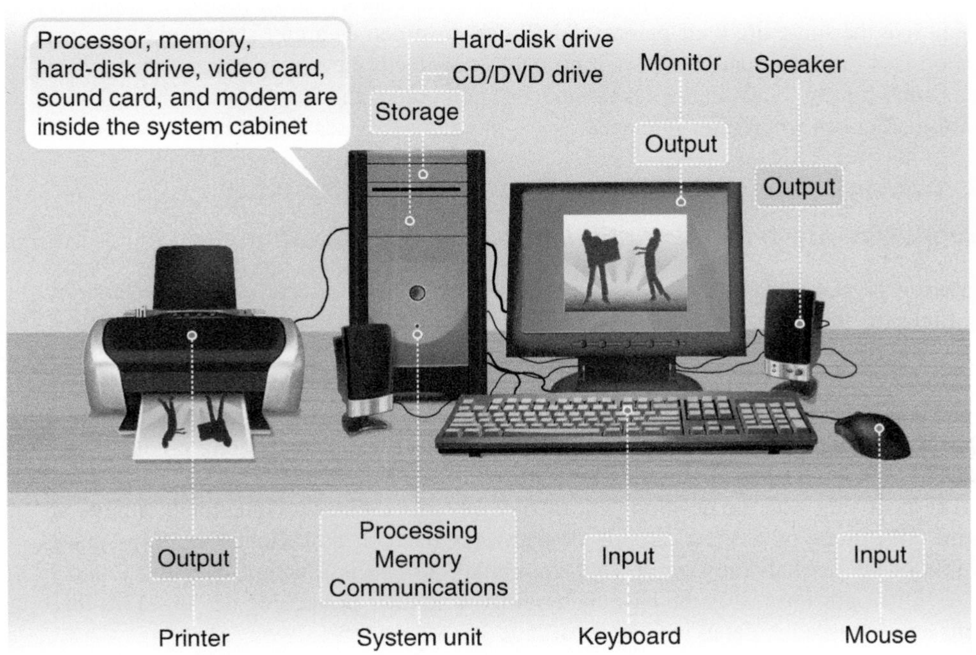

panel 1.9

Completely assembled basic PC hardware system (Some of the components will be without wires—that is, will be connected wirelessly.)

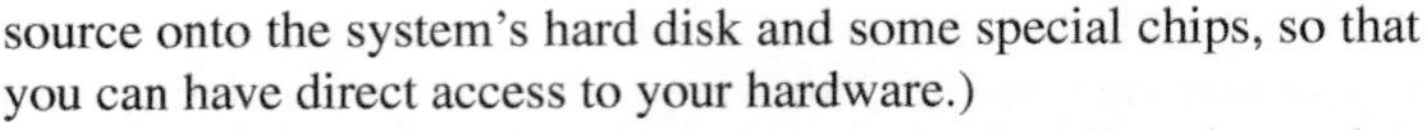

source onto the system's hard disk and some special chips, so that you can have direct access to your hardware.)

Software is what makes the computer worthwhile, what makes it functional for the user. There are two types—*system software* and *application software.*

System software. A version of Apple's OS X system software

SYSTEM SOFTWARE **System software enables the computer to perform essential operating tasks and makes it possible for application software to run.** System software consists of several electronically coded programs. The most important is the *operating system,* the master control program that runs the computer. Examples of operating system (OS) software for the PC are various Microsoft programs (such as Windows XP, Vista, 7, and 8), Unix, and Linux. The Apple Macintosh microcomputer has its own software, as we explain in Chapter 3.

After the system software is installed, setup software for the hard drive, the video and sound cards, and the modem must be installed. These setup programs (*drivers,* discussed in Chapter 3) often come on CDs and can also be downloaded from the Internet.

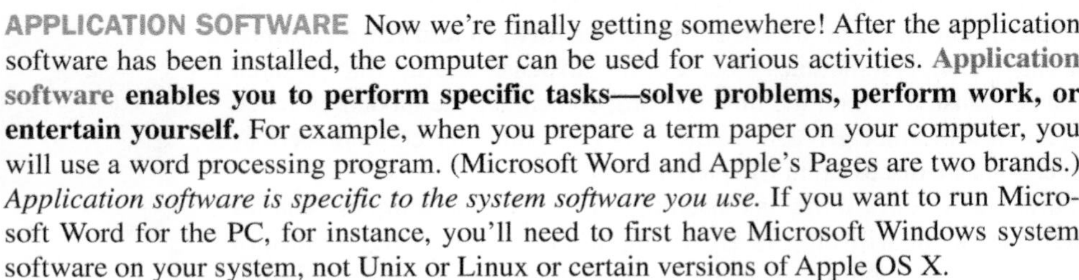

System software for the PC. A version of Microsoft Windows 7

APPLICATION SOFTWARE Now we're finally getting somewhere! After the application software has been installed, the computer can be used for various activities. **Application software enables you to perform specific tasks—solve problems, perform work, or entertain yourself.** For example, when you prepare a term paper on your computer, you will use a word processing program. (Microsoft Word and Apple's Pages are two brands.) *Application software is specific to the system software you use.* If you want to run Microsoft Word for the PC, for instance, you'll need to first have Microsoft Windows system software on your system, not Unix or Linux or certain versions of Apple OS X.

Application software comes on CDs packaged in boxes that include instructions, or it can be downloaded from manufacturers' websites on the Internet.

We discuss software in more detail in Chapter 3.

1.6 WHERE IS INFORMATION TECHNOLOGY HEADED?

Computers are headed in three basic directions—miniaturization, faster speeds, and greater affordability—and communications are improving connectivity, interactivity, and support of multimedia.

How far we have come. At the beginning of the 20th century, most people thought they would live the same life their parents did. Today most people aren't surprised by the prediction that the Information Age will probably transform their lives beyond recognition. Let's consider the trends in the development of computers and communications and, most exciting, the area where they intersect.

Application software. Adobe Creative Suite, which, among other things, is used to create art, manipulate photos, and build websites

Computers: Miniaturization, Speed, & Affordability

Computers are becoming smaller, faster, and cheaper.

Since the days of ENIAC, computers have developed in three directions—and are continuing to do so.

MINIATURIZATION Everything has become smaller. ENIAC's old-fashioned radio-style vacuum tubes gave way after 1947 to the smaller, faster, more reliable transistor. A *transistor* is a small device used as a gateway to transfer electrical signals along predetermined paths (circuits).

The next step was the development of tiny *integrated circuits.* Integrated circuits are entire collections of electric circuits or pathways that are now etched on tiny squares (chips) of silicon half the size of your thumbnail. *Silicon* is a natural element found in sand. In its pure form, it is the base material for computer processing devices. (All these items are discussed in detail in Chapter 4.)

Miniaturization. (*left*) Worker wearing Golden-i headset. The Golden-i unit is operated by voice commands and head movements and allows the wearer to access vital information without using his or her hands. The device also offers the ability to see through walls, thanks to infrared technology. (*right*) M2A Imaging Capsule, a miniature camera and transmitter that can be swallowed by a patient to give physicians a wireless real-time view of the patient's digestive tract. The capsule transmits the images to a device, worn on the patient's belt, which can be downloaded into a specially configured computer.

The miniaturized processor, or microprocessor, in a personal desktop computer today can perform calculations that once required a computer filling an entire room. And with nanotechnology, the trend can only continue.[99]

SPEED Thanks to miniaturization and new material used in making processors, computer makers can cram more hardware components into their machines, providing faster processing speeds and more data storage capacity.

AFFORDABILITY Processor costs today are only a fraction of what they were 15 years ago. A state-of-the-art processor costing less than $1,000 provides the same processing power as a huge 1980s computer costing more than $1 million.

These are the three major trends in computers. What about communications?

Communications: Connectivity, Interactivity, & Multimedia

Information technology systems are becoming more connected and interactive, and they support more and more kinds of multimedia.

Once upon a time, we had the voice telephone system—a one-to-one medium. You could talk to your Uncle Joe, he could talk to you, and with special arrangements (conference calls) more than two people could talk with one another. We also had radio and television systems—one-to-many media (or mass media). News announcers could talk to you on a single medium such as television, but you couldn't talk to them.

Three recent developments in communications include:

CONNECTIVITY **Connectivity refers to the connection of computers to one another by a communications line in order to provide online information access and/or the sharing of peripheral devices.** The connectivity resulting from the expansion of computer networks has made possible email and online shopping, for example.

INTERACTIVITY **Interactivity refers to two-way communication; the user can respond to information he or she receives and modify what a computer is doing.** That is, there is an exchange or dialogue between the user and the computer, and the computer responds to user requests. A noninteractive program, once started, continues without requiring human contact, or interaction. The ability to interact means users can be active rather than passive participants in the technological process. On the television networks MSNBC or CNN, for example, you can immediately go on the Internet and respond to news from broadcast anchors. Today, most application software is interactive. We already have cars that have computers built into the dashboard that can respond to voice commands.

Interactivity. A dashboard touch-screen computer allows drivers to request information about the car's operation, their location, and any nearby services.

MULTIMEDIA Radio is a single-dimensional medium (sound), as is most email (mainly text). As mentioned earlier, **multimedia**

refers to technology that presents information in more than one medium—such as text, pictures, video, sound, and animation—in a single integrated communication. The development of the World Wide Web expanded the Internet to include pictures, sound, music, and so on, as well as text.

Exciting as these developments are, truly mind-boggling possibilities have emerged as computers and communications have cross-pollinated.

When Computers & Communications Converge: Portability, Personalization, Collaboration, Cloud Computing, & Artificial Intelligence

Information technology systems have moved away from stand-alone personal hardware to more extensive networks and smaller devices, as well as use of massive online storage.

Sometime in the 1990s computers and communications started to converge, beginning a new era within the Information Age. *Convergence* describes the combining of several industries through various devices that exchange data in the format used by computers. The industries are computers, communications, consumer electronics, entertainment, and mass media. Convergence has led to electronic products that perform multiple functions, such as TVs with Internet access, cellphones that are also digital cameras, and a refrigerator that allows you to send email.

Convergence has led to five additional developments:

PORTABILITY In the 1980s portability, or mobility, meant trading off computing power and convenience in return for smaller size and weight. Today, however, we are at the point where we don't have to give up anything. As a result, experts have predicted that small, powerful, wireless personal electronic devices will transform our lives far more than the personal computer has done so far. "The new generation of machines will be truly personal computers, designed for our mobile lives," wrote one journalist two decades ago. "We will read office memos between strokes on the golf course and answer messages from our children in the middle of business meetings."[100] Today, of course, smartphones and tablets make such activities commonplace.

PERSONALIZATION Personalization is the creation of information tailored to your preferences—for instance, programs that will automatically cull recent news and information from the Internet on just those topics you have designated. Companies can send you messages about forthcoming products based on your pattern of purchases, usage, and other criteria. Or they will build products (cars, computers, clothing) customized to suit your tastes.

COLLABORATION A more recent trend is mass collaboration. Says technology writer John Markoff, "A remarkable array of software systems makes it simple to share anything instantly, and sometimes enhance it along the way."[101] Another writer observed that the huge numbers of people "online worldwide—along with their shared knowledge, social contacts, online reputations, computing power, and more—are rapidly becoming a collective force of unprecedented power."[102] Examples are file-sharing, photo-sharing websites, calendar-sharing services, group-edited informational (encyclopedic) sites called *wikis,* social-networking services, and so-called citizen-journalism sites, in which average people write their own news items on the Internet and comment on what other people post—an interactive, democratic form of mass media.[103] Pooled ratings, for instance, enable people to create personalized Internet music radio stations or Amazon.com's millions of customer-generated product reviews.

CLOUD COMPUTING: THE GLOBAL COMPUTER Previously called *on-demand computing, grid computing,* or *software as a service,* **cloud computing basically means that instead of storing your software and/or data on your own PC or your own company's computers, you store it on servers on the Internet.**[104] You don't

Cloud computing involves delivering services over the Internet. The name *cloud computing* was inspired by the cloud symbol that's often used to represent the Internet in professional diagrams. Cloud services are usually sold on demand, typically by the minute or the hour; users can have as much or as little of a service as they want at any given time; and the service is fully managed by the provider (the consumer/user needs nothing but a personal computer/mobile device and Internet access). A "cloud" (the server business connected to the Internet) can be private or public.

More on Cloud Computing

www.20thingsilearned.com/cloud-computing/1/
http://searchcloudcomputing.techtarget.com/definition/cloud-computing/
www.wikinvest.com/concept/Cloud_Computing/
www.youtube.com/watch?v=uYGQcmZUTaw

care where the servers are located; they're out there somewhere—"in the cloud"—run by special cloud-service businesses, such as Amazon Web Services, Rackspace, Google, and Microsoft. The idea here is that companies can tap into computers/servers as they are needed, just as they do now with the electric power grid, splitting their computing workload among data centers in different parts of the world. The expectation of technology experts is that companies will find cloud computing cheaper and easier than managing their own microcomputers, servers, and software (although security is a worry).[105] Google, says one technology writer, is betting that its touch-screen Chromebook laptop will "propel the shift toward a computing model where most of our applications and data live online" in the cloud.[106]

"BIG DATA" & ARTIFICIAL INTELLIGENCE Ninety percent of the data in the world today was created in just the last two years, according to an IBM source. "This data comes from everywhere: sensors used to gather climate information, posts to social media sites, digital pictures and videos, purchase transaction records, and cellphone . . . signals, to name a few. This data is *Big Data.*"[107]

More formally, **Big Data is data that is so large and complex that it cannot be processed using conventional methods,** such as ordinary database management software. The data may consist of not only traditional sources for the study of words, such as books, news articles, and academic journals, but also websites, Twitter messages, and blog posts.[108] With companies doing computing "in the cloud" and providing tools for mobile users, the economics of processing huge amounts of data or providing access for millions of users has become considerably cheaper.[109]

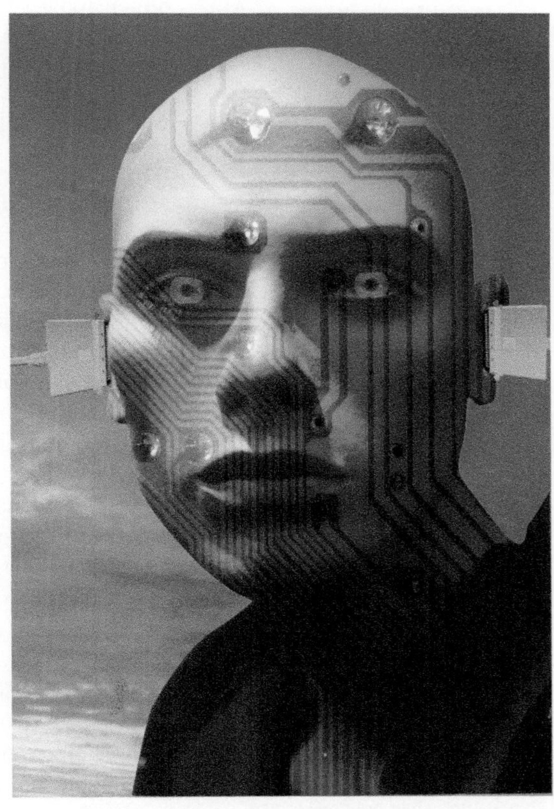

According to inventor and futurist Raymond Kurzweil, technological change will become so rapid and so profound that human bodies and brains will merge with machines.

The combination of cloud-computing storage of Big Data, along with the tremendous processing power of supercomputers, takes us into a world of *machine learning,* in which computers can derive meaning and make predictions from things like language, intentions, and behavior—something that Microsoft, for instance, is doing with a cloud-computing system called Azure.[110] Machine learning is a branch of **artificial intelligence (AI), a group of related technologies used for developing machines to emulate human qualities, such as learning, reasoning, communicating, seeing, and hearing.** Much of AI is based on the use of **algorithms, formulas or sets of steps for solving particular problems.**

Survival Tip

Be Ethical about Disposing of Old Computer Equipment

Just got a new computer? Where to donate or recycle your old one? Check with schools, after-school programs, churches, and the following websites:

www.crc.org/

http://ngm.nationalgeographic.com/geopedia/E-Waste

http://earth911.com/recycling/electronics/computers/

www.epa.gov/epawaste/conserve/materials/ecycling/

www.recycles.org/

http://ww1.pcdisposal.com/

www.computerhope.com/disposal.htm

The 10 Commandments of Computer Ethics

The Computer Ethics Institute says:

1. Thou shalt not use a computer to harm other people.
2. Thou shalt not interfere with other people's computer work.
3. Thou shalt not snoop around in other people's computer files.
4. Thou shalt not use a computer to steal.
5. Thou shalt not use a computer to bear false witness.
6. Thou shalt not copy or use proprietary software for which you have not paid.
7. Thou shalt not use other people's computer resources without authorization or proper compensation.
8. Thou shalt not appropriate other people's intellectual output.
9. Thou shalt think about the social consequences of the program you are writing or the system you are designing.
10. Thou shalt always use a computer in ways that ensure consideration and respect for your fellow humans.

Source: *http://computerethics-institute.org/images/ The Ten Commandments Of Computer Ethics.pdf.*

TECH TALES Artificial Intelligence: The Use of Algorithms to Create a Hit Song

In 2004, guitarist-songwriter New Zealander Ben Novak, hoping to land a record deal, came across a website that claimed, for $50, to provide an algorithm that would find hit songs. The algorithm, which compared the structure of his song with those of the past, gave his song, "Turn Your Car Around," a high rating for hit potential—on a level with such standards as the Eagles' "Take It Easy" and Steppenwolf's "Born to Be Wild." The algorithm's owner, Mike McCready, connected Novak with a record label, and the song eventually ended up near the top of the European popular music charts.

The same algorithm, incidentally, predicted the success of the band Maroon 5 and the artist Norah Jones before they became stars.[111] ■

There are several fields of AI, among them the following. *Pattern recognition* identifies recurring patterns and recognizes the connections between the patterns and similar patterns stored in a database, as was the case with the McReady algorithm. *Virtual reality* is computer-generated artificial reality that projects a person into a sensation of three-dimensional space. *Robotics* is the development and study of machines that can perform work that is normally done by people. *Natural language processing* is the study of ways for computers to recognize and understand human language.

"E" Also Stands for Ethics

Many important ethical issues are involved in the use of information technology.

Every computer user will have to wrestle with ethical issues related to the use of information technology. **Ethics is defined as a set of moral values or principles that govern the conduct of an individual or a group.** Because ethical questions arise so often in connection with information technology, we will note them, wherever they appear in this book, with the symbol shown at left. Below, for example, are some important ethical concerns pointed out by Tom Forester and Perry Morrison in their book *Computer Ethics.*[112] These considerations are only a few of many; we'll discuss others in subsequent chapters.

SPEED & SCALE Great amounts of information can be stored, retrieved, and transmitted at a speed and on a scale not possible before, especially now in the era of cloud computing and Big Data. Despite the benefits, this has serious implications "for data security and personal privacy," as well as employment, Forester and Morrison say, because information technology can never be considered totally secure against unauthorized access.

UNPREDICTABILITY Computers and communications are pervasive, touching nearly every aspect of our lives. However, at this point, compared to other pervasive technologies—such as electricity, television, and automobiles—information technology seems a lot less predictable and reliable.

COMPLEXITY Computer systems are often incredibly complex—some so complex that they are not always understood even by their creators. "This," say Forester and Morrison, "often makes them completely unmanageable," producing massive foul-ups or spectacularly out-of-control costs.

Ethics and security can often be talked about in the same breath, since secure computer systems obviously go a long way toward keeping people ethical and honest. When we discuss security, you will see the icon below.

EXPERIENCE BOX

Better Organization & Time Management: Dealing with the Information Deluge in College—& in Life

An Experience Box appears at the end of each chapter. Each box offers you the opportunity to acquire useful experience that directly applies to the Digital Age. This first box illustrates skills that will benefit you in college, in this course and others. (Students reading the first 10 editions of our book have told us they received substantial benefit from these suggestions.)

"How on earth am I going to be able to keep up with what's required of me?" you may ask yourself. "How am I going to handle the information glut?" The answer is *by learning how to learn.* By building your skills as a learner, you certainly help yourself do better in college, and you also train yourself to be an information manager in the future.

Using Your "Prime Study Time"

Each of us has a different energy cycle. The trick is to use it effectively. That way, your hours of best performance will coincide with your heaviest academic demands. For example, if your energy level is high during the evenings, you should plan to do your studying then.

To capitalize on your prime study time, take the following steps: (1) Make a study schedule for the entire term, and indicate the times each day during which you plan to study. (2) Find some good places to study—places where you can avoid distractions. (3) Avoid time wasters, but give yourself frequent rewards for studying, such as a TV show, a favorite piece of music, or a conversation with a friend.

Learning to Focus

Multitasking is shifting focus from one task to another in rapid succession. When you read this textbook while listening to music and watching TV, you may think you're simultaneously doing three separate tasks, but you're really not. "It's like playing tennis with three balls," says one expert.[113] Today multitasking is easy and focus is hard because of all the things demanding our attention—phone calls, email, text messages, music, radio, TV, Twitter, MySpace, Facebook, various blogs and websites. "You can drive yourself crazy trying to multitask and answer every email message instantly," says one writer. "Or you can recognize your brain's finite capacity for processing information."[114]

Here are some tips on learning to concentrate:[115]

Choose What to Focus On. "People don't realize that attention is a finite resource, like money," one expert says. "Do you want to invest your cognitive cash on endless Twittering or Net surfing or couch potatoing [watching TV]?" She adds, "Where did the idea come from that anyone who wants to contact you can do so at any time? You need to take charge of what you pay attention to instead of responding to the latest stimuli."[116] For example, to block out noise, you can wear earplugs while reading.

Devote the First 1½ Hours of Your Day to Your Most Important Task. Writing a paper? Studying a hard subject? Make it your first task of the day, and concentrate on it for 90 minutes. After that, your brain will probably need a rest, and you can answer email, return phone calls, and so on. But until that first break, don't do anything else, because it can take the brain 20 minutes to refocus.

Improving Your Memory Ability

Memorizing is, of course, one of the principal requirements for succeeding in college. And it's a great help for success in life afterward. Some suggestions:

Space Your Studying, Rather Than Cramming. Cramming—making a frantic, last-minute attempt to memorize massive amounts of material—is probably the least effective means of absorbing information. Research shows that it's best to space out your studying of a subject over successive days. A series of study sessions over several days is preferable to trying to do it all during the same number of hours on one day. It is repetition that helps to move information into your long-term memory bank.

Review Information Repeatedly—Even "Overlearn" It. By repeatedly reviewing information—known as "rehearsing"—you can improve both your retention and your understanding of it. Overlearning is continuing to review material even after you appear to have absorbed it. Also, recent research studies show that taking a test after reading a block of material improves recall of the material, even a week later. This method seems to work better than simple reading, reading the block in segments, and concept mapping (creating a diagram of the concepts after one has finished reading the block of material).[117]

Use Memorizing Tricks. There are several ways to organize information so that you can retain it better. For example, you can make drawings or diagrams (as of the parts of a computer system). Some methods of establishing associations between items you want to remember are given on the next page. *(• See Panel 1.10.)*

Improving Your Reading Ability: The SQ3R Method

SQ3R stands for "survey, question, read, recite, and review."[118] The strategy behind the method is to break down a reading assignment into small segments and master each before moving on. The five steps of the SQ3R method are as follows:

1. *Survey the chapter before you read it:* Get an overview of the chapter before you begin reading it. If you have a sense of what the material is about before you begin reading it, you can predict where it is going. In this text, we

- **Mental and physical imagery:** Use your visual and other senses to construct a personal image of what you want to remember. Indeed, it helps to make the image humorous, action-filled, or outrageous in order to establish a personal connection. Example: To remember the name of the 21st president of the United States, Chester Arthur, you might visualize an author writing the number "21" on a wooden chest. This mental image helps you associate chest (Chester), author (Arthur), and 21 (21st president).
- **Acronyms and acrostics:** An acronym is a word created from the first letters of items in a list. For instance, *Roy G. Biv* helps you remember the colors of the rainbow in order: red, orange, yellow, green, blue, indigo, violet. An acrostic is a phrase or sentence created from the first letters of items on a list. For example, *Every Good Boy Does Fine* helps you remember that the order of musical notes on the treble staff is *E-G-B-D-F.*
- **Location:** Location memory occurs when you associate a concept with a place or imaginary place. For example, you could learn the parts of a computer system by imagining a walk across campus. Each building you pass could be associated with a part of the computer system.
- **Word games:** Jingles and rhymes are devices frequently used by advertisers to get people to remember their products. You may recall the spelling rule "I before E except after C or when sounded like A as in *neighbor* or *weigh.*" You can also use narrative methods, such as making up a story.

panel 1.10

Some memorizing tricks

offer on the first page of every chapter a list of the main headings and accompanying key questions. At the end of each chapter we offer a review of terms and explanations.

2. *Question the segment in the chapter before you read it:* This step is easy to do, and the point, again, is to get you involved in the material. After surveying the entire chapter, go to the first segment—whether a whole section, a subsection, or even just a paragraph, depending on the level of difficulty and density of information. Look at the topic heading of that segment (or first sentence of a very difficult paragraph). In your mind, restate the heading as a question.

   After you have formulated the question, go to steps 3 and 4 (read and recite). Then proceed to the next segment of the chapter, and restate the heading there as a question, and so on.
3. *Read the segment about which you asked the question:* When you read the segment you asked the question about, read with purpose, to answer the question you formulated. Underline or color-mark sentences that you think are important, if they help you to answer the question. Read this portion of the text more than once, if necessary, until you can answer the question. In addition, determine whether the segment covers any other significant questions, and formulate answers to these too. After you have read the segment, proceed to step 4. (Perhaps you can see where this is all leading. If you read in terms of questions and answers, you will be better prepared when you see exam questions about the material later.)
4. *Recite the main points of the segment:* Recite means "say aloud." Thus, you should speak out loud (or softly) the answer to the principal question or questions about the segment and any other main points.
5. *Review the entire chapter by repeating questions:* After you have read the chapter, go back through it and review the main points. Then, without looking at the book, test your memory by repeating the questions and answers you formulated.

Clearly the SQ3R method takes longer than simply reading with a rapidly moving color marker or underlining pencil. However, *the technique is far more effective because it requires your involvement and understanding*. These are the keys to all effective learning.

Learning from Lectures

Does attending lectures really make a difference? Research concludes that students with grades of B or above were more apt to have better class attendance than students with grades of C– or below.[119]

Some tips for getting the most out of lectures:

Take Effective Notes by Listening Actively. Research shows that good test performance is related to good note taking.[120] And good note taking requires that you listen actively—that is, participate in the lecture process. Here are some ways to take good lecture notes:

- *Read ahead and anticipate the lecturer:* Try to anticipate what the instructor is going to say, based on your previous reading. Having background knowledge makes learning more efficient.
- *Listen for signal words:* Instructors use key phrases such as, "The most important point is . . . ," "There are four reasons for . . . ," "The chief reason . . . ," "Of special importance . . . ," "Consequently. . . ." When you hear such signal phrases, mark your notes with a ! or *.
- *Take notes in your own words:* Instead of just being a stenographer, try to restate the lecturer's thoughts in your own words, which will make you pay attention more.
- *Ask questions:* By asking questions during the lecture, you necessarily participate in it and increase your understanding.

Review Your Notes Regularly. Make it a point to review your notes regularly—perhaps on the afternoon after the lecture, or once or twice a week. We cannot emphasize enough the importance of this kind of reviewing.

TERMS & EXPLANATIONS

algorithm (p. 37) Formula, procedure, or set of steps for solving a particular problem. Why it's important: *Algorithms are essentially the foundation, the building blocks, of computer science. Much of AI is based on the use of algorithms, as is software code.*

application software (p. 34) Software that enables you to perform specific tasks—solve problems, perform work, or entertain yourself. Why it's important: *Application software such as word processing, spreadsheet, database management, graphics, and communications packages are commonly used tools for increasing people's productivity.* (Apps *is short for "applications.")*

artificial intelligence (AI) (p. 37) Group of related technologies used for developing machines to emulate human qualities, such as learning, reasoning, communicating, seeing, and hearing. Why it's important: *Given the potential of artificial intelligence, it will likely have far-reaching effects on human life in the years to come; the studies of the creation of intelligence involve a continual process to eventually solve many problems.*

avatar (p. 6) Computer depiction of a human, often found in online videogames. Why it's important: *Avatars can be helpful in training, such as by representing imaginary customers.*

Big Data (p. 37) Data that is so large and complex that it cannot be processed using conventional methods. Why it's important: The amount of data in our world has been exploding, and analyzing large data sets—Big Data—has become a key basis of business competition, productivity growth, and innovation. Managing Big Data has also become critical to the functioning of government.

blogs (weblogs) (p. 14) Frequently updated sites on the World Wide Web intended for public consumption that contain a writer's observations, opinions, images, and links to other websites. Why it's important: *Blogs are used, for example, for low-cost marketing, improving writing skills, trying out new ideas with people, getting experience in certain areas before looking for a job, satisfying one's need for creativity, and for putting something interesting out into the world.*

case (p. 30) Also known as the *system unit* or *system cabinet;* the box that houses the processor chip (CPU), the memory chips, the motherboard, the power supply, and storage devices—hard-disk drive and CD or DVD drive. Why it's important: *The case protects many important processing and storage components.*

CD (compact disk) drive (p. 32) Storage device that uses laser technology to read data from optical disk. Why it's important: *New software is often supplied on CDs, in addition to being downloaded from websites. The newest version is called DVD (digital video disk). The DVD format stores more data than the CD format.*

central processing unit (CPU) *See* **processor chip.**

chip *See* **processor chip.**

clients (p. 26) Computers and other devices connected to a server, a central computer. Why it's important: *Client-server networks are used in many organizations for sharing databases, devices, and programs.*

cloud computing (p. 36) Method of storing your software and/or data not on your own PC or company's computers but rather on servers on the Internet. Why it's important: *Users could tap into computers as they are needed, distributing computing workload among data centers in different parts of the world, perhaps making computing cheaper and more reliable.*

communications technology (p. 4) Also called *telecommunications technology;* consists of electromagnetic devices and systems for communicating over any distance. Why it's important: *Communications systems using electronic connections have helped expand human communication beyond face-to-face meetings.*

computer (p. 4) Programmable, multiuse machine that accepts data—raw facts and figures—and processes (manipulates) it into useful information, such as summaries and totals. Why it's important: *Computers greatly speed up problem solving and other tasks, increasing users' productivity.*

connectivity (p. 35) Ability to connect computers to one another by communications lines to provide online information access and/or the sharing of peripheral devices. Why it's important: *Connectivity is the foundation of the advances in the Information Age. It provides online access to countless types of information and services. The connectivity resulting from the expansion of computer networks has made possible email and online shopping, for example.*

cyberspace (p. 17) Area that includes not only the online world and the Internet in particular but also the whole wired and wireless world of communications in general. Why it's important: *More and more human activities take place in cyberspace.*

data (p. 27) Raw facts and figures that are processed into information. Why it's important: *Users need data to create useful information.*

database (p. 11) Computer system with a collection of interrelated files that is designed and built for a specific purpose; technology for pulling together facts that allows the slicing and dicing and mixing and matching of data. Why it's important: *Businesses and organizations build databases to help them to track and manage their affairs. In addition, online database services put enormous research resources at the user's disposal.*

desktop PC (p. 24) Microcomputer unit that sits on a desk, with the keyboard in front and the monitor often on top. Why it's important: *Desktop PCs and tower PCs are the most commonly used types of microcomputer.*

distance learning (p. 5) Also known as *e-learning* and *online learning;* name given to online education programs. Why it's important: *Provides students increased flexibility because they do not have to be in an actual classroom. Online classes are becoming increasingly popular.*

downloading (p. 20) Transferring data from a remote computer to one's own computer. Why it's important: *Allows text, music, and images to be transferred quickly by telecommunications.*

DVD (digital video disk) drive See **CD (compact disk) drive.**

e-learning See **distance learning.**

email (electronic mail) (p. 5) Messages transmitted over a computer network, most often the Internet. Why it's important: *Email has become universal and is heavily used in business and professional work.*

e-readers (e-book readers) (p. 25) Electronic devices that can download e-books—digital versions of regular books, articles, and magazines from various suppliers. Why it's important: *E-books are cheaper than print books, and e-readers can easily be put in a purse or a pocket. They can download books via a wireless network almost anywhere or from a computer and are relatively inexpensive.*

ethics (p. 38) Set of moral values or principles that govern the conduct of an individual or a group. Why it's important: *Ethical questions arise often in connection with information technology.*

expansion slots (p. 30) Internal "plugs" used to expand the PC's capabilities. Why it's important: *Expansion slots give you places to plug in additional circuit boards, such as those for video, sound, and communications (modem).*

hard-disk drive (p. 32) Device that stores billions of characters of data on a nonremovable disk platter usually inside the computer case. Why it's important: *Hard disks have a very large storage capacity. Nearly all microcomputers use hard disks as their principal secondary-storage medium.*

hardware (p. 27) All the machinery and equipment in a computer system. Why it's important: *Hardware runs under the control of software and is useless without it. However, hardware contains the circuitry that allows processing.*

information (p. 27) Data that has been summarized or otherwise transformed for use in decision making. Why it's important: *The whole purpose of a computer (and communications) system is to produce (and transmit) usable information.*

information technology (IT) (p. 3) Technology that helps produce, manipulate, store, communicate, and/or disseminate information. Why it's important: *Information technology is bringing about the fusion of several important industries dealing with computers, telephones, televisions, and various handheld devices.*

input (p. 27) Whatever is put in ("input") to a computer system. Input devices include the keyboard, the touch screen, and the mouse. Why it's important: *Useful information cannot be produced without input data.*

interactivity (p. 35) Two-way communication; a user can respond to information he or she receives and modify the process. Why it's important: *Interactive devices allow the user to actively participate in a technological process instead of just reacting to it.*

Internet (the "Net" or "net") (p. 19) Worldwide computer network that connects hundreds of thousands of smaller networks linking computers at academic, scientific, and commercial institutions, as well as individuals. Why it's important: *Thanks to the Internet, millions of people around the world can share all types of information and services.*

keyboard (p. 28) Input device that uses keys to convert letters, numbers, and other characters into electrical signals readable by the processor. Why it's important: *Keyboards are the most common kind of input device.*

local area network (LAN) (p. 24) Network that connects, usually by special cable and also wirelessly, a group of desktop PCs and other devices, such as printers, in an office or a building. Why it's important: *LANs have replaced mainframes for many functions and are considerably less expensive.*

mainframe (p. 24) Second-largest computer available, after the supercomputer; capable of great processing speeds and data storage. Small mainframes are often called *midsize computers.* Why it's important: *Mainframes are used by large organizations (banks, airlines, insurance companies, universities) that need to process millions of transactions.*

memory chip (p. 30) Also known as *RAM* (for "random access memory") *chip;* primary (temporary) storage. Why it's important: *Holds data before processing and information after processing, before it is sent along to an output or storage device.*

microcomputer (p. 24) Also called *personal computer (PC);* small computer that fits on or next to a desk or can be carried around. Why it's important: *The microcomputer reduced the reliance on mainframes and has provided more ordinary users with access to computers. It can be used as a stand-alone machine or connected to a network and is essential in many businesses and professions.*

microcontroller (p. 26) Also called an *embedded computer;* the smallest category of computer. Why it's important: *Microcontrollers are the tiny, specialized microprocessors built into "smart" electronic devices, such as appliances and automobiles.*

mobile device (p. 25) Fully Internet-integrated, handheld multimedia computer highly compatible with desktop microcomputers and laptops. Why it's important: *Some mobile devices are too small to adequately view images on screen, but viewers still want more pocket-size portability than is possible with a laptop.*

modem (p. 33) Device that sends and receives data over telephone lines or cable lines, or wirelessly over a network, to and from computers. Why it's important: *A modem enables users to transmit data from one computer to another.*

monitor (p. 32) Display device that takes the electrical signals from the video card and forms an image using points of colored light on the screen. Why it's important: *Monitors enable users to view output without printing it out.*

motherboard (p. 30) Also called the *system board;* main circuit board in the computer. Why it's important: *This is the big green circuit board to which everything else—such as the keyboard, mouse, and printer—is attached. The processor chip and memory chips are also installed on the motherboard.*

mouse (p. 29) Nonkeyboard input device, called a "pointing device," used to manipulate objects viewed on the computer display screen. Why it's important: *For many purposes, a mouse is easier to use than a keyboard for inputting commands. Also, the mouse is used extensively in many graphics programs.*

multimedia (p. 35) From "multiple media"; technology that presents information in more than one medium—including text, graphics, animation, video, and sound—in a single integrated communication. Why it's important: *Multimedia is used increasingly in business, the professions, and education to improve the way information is communicated.*

nanotechnology (p. 23) Technology whereby molecule-size nanostructures are used to create tiny machines for holding data or performing tasks. Why it's important: *Could result in tremendous computer power in molecular-size devices.* (Nano *means "one-billionth."*)

netbook (p. 25) Low-cost, lightweight computer with tiny dimensions and with functions designed for basic tasks, such as web searching, email, and word processing; weighs 2.25–3.2 pounds. Why it's important: *These cheaper computers fill a technological category between notebooks and handheld devices.*

network (p. 4) Communications system connecting two or more computers. Why it's important: *Networks allow users to share applications and data and to use email. The Internet is the largest network.*

notebook computer (p. 25) Also called *laptop computer;* lightweight portable computer with a built-in monitor, keyboard, hard-disk drive, battery, and adapter; weighs 1.8–12 pounds. Why it's important: *Notebooks and other small computers have provided users with computing capabilities in the field and on the road; however, they are now being displaced by tablets.*

online (p. 4) Use of a computer or some other information device, connected through a network, to access information and services from another computer or information device. Why it's important: *Online communication is widely used by businesses, services, individuals, and educational institutions.*

online learning *See* **distance learning.**

online relationship site (p. 14) Electronic forum that people may join in the hope of meeting compatible companions or mates. Why it's important: This is an example of how information technology is changing people's personal lives.

output (p. 28) Whatever is output from ("put out of") the computer system; the results of processing. Why it's important: *People use output to help them make decisions. Without output devices, computer users would not be able to view or use the results of processing.*

peripheral device (p. 32) Any component or piece of equipment that expands a computer's input, storage, or output capabilities. Examples include printers and disk drives. Why it's important: *Most computer input and output functions are performed by peripheral devices.*

personal digital assistant (PDA) (p. 25) Also known as *handheld computer;* used as a schedule planner and address book and to prepare to-do lists and send email and faxes. Why it's important: *PDAs make it easier for people to do business and communicate while traveling.*

primary storage (p. 28) Also called *memory;* internal computer circuitry that temporarily holds data waiting to be processed. Why it's important: *By holding data, primary storage enables the processor to process.*

printer (p. 33) Output device that produces text and graphics on paper. Why it's important: *Printers provide one of the principal forms of computer output.*

processing (p. 28) The manipulation a computer does to transform data into information. Why it's important: *Processing is the essence of the computer, and the processor is the computer's "brain."*

processor chip (p. 30) Also called the *processor,* the *CPU (central processing unit),* or simply *chip;* tiny piece of silicon that contains millions of miniature electronic circuits used to process data. Why it's important: *Chips have made possible the development of small computers.*

robot (p. 8) Automatic device that performs functions ordinarily performed by human beings. Why it's important: *Robots help perform tasks that humans find difficult or impossible to do.*

secondary storage (p. 28) Also called *storage;* devices and media that store data and programs permanently—such as disks and disk drives, tape and tape drives, CDs and CD drives. Why it's important: *Without secondary storage, users would not be able to save their work. Storage also holds the computer's software.*

server (p. 26) Also called *network server;* central computer in a network that holds collections of data (databases) and programs for connecting PCs, workstations, and other devices, which are called *clients.* Why it's important: *Servers enable many users to share equipment, programs, and data (linked together in a client-server network).*

smartphone (p. 2) Cellphone with built-in applications, multimedia capability, and Internet access. Why it's important: *The smartphone has made almost everything we do more portable and immediate.*

social network (p. 3) Site on the World Wide Web (such as Facebook and Twitter) that allows users to interact and develop communities around similar interests—and use mobile devices to research products and compare prices. Why it's important: *Social networks—for good or ill—are affecting almost every way people interact and how all their personal information is used.*

software (p. 27) Also called *programs;* step-by-step electronically encoded instructions that tell the computer hardware how to perform a task. Why it's important: *Without software, hardware is useless.*

sound card (p. 32) Special circuit board that enhances the computer's sound-generating capabilities by allowing sound to be output through speakers. Why it's important: *Sound is used in multimedia applications. Also, many users like to listen to music CDs on their computers.*

speakers (p. 32) Devices that play sounds transmitted as electrical signals from the sound card. Speakers are connected to a single wire plugged into the back of the computer, or they are built into the computer. Why it's important: See **sound card.**

supercomputer (p. 23) High-capacity computer with thousands of processors; the fastest calculating device ever invented. Costs up to $350 million or more. Why it's important: *Supercomputers are used primarily for research purposes, airplane design, oil exploration, weather forecasting, and other activities that cannot be handled by mainframes and other less powerful machines.*

system software (p. 34) Software that enables the computer to perform essential operating tasks. Why it's important: *Application software cannot run without system software. System software consists of several programs. The most important is the operating system, the master control program that runs the computer. Examples of operating system software for the PC are various Microsoft programs (Windows), Unix, Linux, and the Macintosh operating system.*

system unit See **case.**

tablet computer (pp. 2, 25) Wireless portable computer, such as Apple's iPad, primarily operated via a touch screen. Why it's important: *Tablet computers are easy to use and easy to carry around, and they don't require a keyboard. The screen is a 7- to 10-inch touch screen (one can manipulate the screen contents directly with one's hand or a stylus.) Tablet computers support multimedia.*

terminal (p. 24) Input and output device that uses a keyboard for input and a monitor for output; it cannot process data. Why it's important: *Terminals are generally used to input data to and receive data from a mainframe computer system.*

texting (text messaging) (p. 17) Sending and receiving short written messages between mobile phones or other portable or fixed devices. Why it's important: *Text messaging is the most widely used data application.*

tower PC (p. 24) Microcomputer unit that sits as a "tower," often on the floor, freeing up desk space. Why it's important: *Tower PCs and desktop PCs are the most commonly used types of microcomputer.*

uploading (p. 20) Transferring data from one's own computer to a remote computer. Why it's important: *Allows text, music, and images to be transferred quickly by telecommunications.*

video card (p. 32) Circuit board that converts the processor's output information into a video signal for transmission through a cable to the monitor. Why it's important: *Virtually all computer users need to be able to view video output on the monitor.*

virtual (p. 10) Something that is created, simulated, or carried on by means of a computer or a computer network. Why it's important: *Allows actual objects to be represented in computer-based form.*

workstation (p. 24) Smaller than a mainframe; expensive, powerful computer generally used for complex scientific, mathematical, and engineering calculations and for computer-aided design and computer-aided manufacturing. Why it's important: *The power of workstations is needed for specialized applications too large and complex to be handled by PCs.*

World Wide Web (the "Web" or the "web") (p. 19) The interconnected system of Internet servers that support specially formatted documents in multimedia form—sounds, photos, and video as well as text. Why it's important: *The web is the most widely known part of the Internet.*

CHAPTER REVIEW

More and more educators are favoring an approach to learning (presented by Benjamin Bloom and his colleagues in *Taxonomy of Educational Objectives*) that follows a hierarchy of six critical-thinking skills: (a) two lower-order skills—memorization and comprehension—and (b) four higher-order skills—application, analysis, synthesis, and evaluation. While you may be able to get through many introductory college courses by simply memorizing facts and comprehending the basic ideas, to advance further you will probably need to employ the four higher-order thinking skills.

In the Chapter Review at the end of each chapter, we have implemented this hierarchy in a three-stage approach, as follows:

- *Stage 1 learning—memorization:* "I can recognize and recall information." Self-test questions, multiple-choice questions, and true-false questions enable you to test how well you recall basic terms and concepts.
- *Stage 2 learning—comprehension:* "I can recall information in my own terms and explain it to a friend." Using open-ended, short-answer questions, we ask you to reexpress terms and concepts in your own words.
- *Stage 3 learning—applying, analyzing, synthesizing, evaluating:* "I can apply what I've learned, relate these ideas to other concepts, build on other knowledge, and use all these thinking skills to form a judgment." In this part of the Chapter Review, we ask you to put the ideas into effect using the activities described, some of which include Internet activities. The purpose is to help you take possession of the ideas, make them your own, and apply them realistically to your life.

"I can recognize and recall information."

Self-Test Questions

1. The ________ ________ ________ refers to the part of the Internet that presents information in multimedia form.
2. "________ technology" merges computing with high-speed communications.
3. A(n) ________ is an electronic machine that accepts data and processes it into information.
4. The ________ is a worldwide network that connects hundreds of thousands of smaller networks.
5. ________ refers to information presented in nontextual forms such as video, sound, and graphics.
6. ________ are high-capacity computers with thousands of processors.
7. Embedded computers, or ________, are installed in "smart" appliances and automobiles.
8. The kind of software that enables users to perform specific tasks is called ________ software.
9. RAM is an example of ________ storage, and a hard drive is an example of ________ storage.
10. ________ is data that is so large and complex that it cannot be processed using conventional methods.
11. A(n) ________ is a communications system connecting two or more computers.
12. The four basic operations of all computers are ________, ________, ________, and ________.
13. The first programmable computer in the United States, which appeared in 1946, was called ________.
14. The ________ is the display device that takes the electrical signals from the video card and forms an image using points of colored light on the screen.
15. The base material for computer processing devices is ________, a natural element found in sand.
16. The general term for all the machinery and equipment in a computer system is ________.
17. The ________ and the ________ are the two most common input devices.
18. The processor chip, commonly called the ________ or a(n) ________, is a tiny piece of silicon that contains millions of miniature electronic circuits.
19. One gigabyte is approximately ________ characters.
20. ________ refers to two-way communication; the user can respond to information received via the computer and modify what the computer is doing.

Multiple-Choice Questions

1. Which of the following devices converts computer output into displayed images?
   a. printer
   b. monitor
   c. modem
   d. processor
   e. hard-disk drive
2. Which of the following computer types is the smallest?
   a. mainframe
   b. microcomputer
   c. microcontroller
   d. supercomputer
   e. workstation
3. Which of the following is a secondary-storage device?
   a. processor
   b. main memory chip
   c. hard-disk drive
   d. printer
   e. modem
4. Since the days when computers were first made available, computers have developed in three directions. What are they?
   a. increased expense
   b. miniaturization
   c. increased size
   d. affordability
   e. increased speed
5. Which of the following operations constitute the four basic operations followed by all computers?
   a. input
   b. storage
   c. programming
   d. output
   e. processing
6. Supercomputers are used for
   a. breaking codes.
   b. simulations for explosions of nuclear bombs.
   c. forecasting weather.
   d. keeping planets in orbit.
   e. all of these
   f. only *a, b,* and *c.*
7. What is the leading use of computers?
   a. web surfing
   b. email, texting, and social networking
   c. e-shopping
   d. word processing
8. Which is the main circuit board in the computer?
   a. RAM chip (random access memory)
   b. CPU processor chip (central processing unit)
   c. motherboard (system board)
   d. hard drive

9. A terabyte is approximately
    a. one million characters.
    b. one billion characters.
    c. one trillion characters.
    d. one quadrillion characters.
10. Speakers are an example of
    a. an input device.
    b. an output device.
    c. a processor.
    d. a storage device.

True-False Questions

T F 1. Microcontrollers process faster than supercomputers.

T F 2. Main memory is a software component.

T F 3. The operating system is part of the system software.

T F 4. Processing is the manipulation by which a computer transforms data into information.

T F 5. Primary storage is the area in the computer where data or information is held permanently.

T F 6. The keyboard and the mouse are examples of input devices.

T F 7. Movies are a form of multimedia.

T F 8. Computers are becoming larger, slower, and more expensive.

T F 9. Modems store information.

T F 10. A hard disk is an example of software.

T F 11. Computers continue to get smaller and smaller.

T F 12. A modem is a programmable, multiuse machine that accepts data—raw facts and figures—and processes, or manipulates, it into information we can use.

T F 13. Online education programs are called *computer learning*.

T F 14. PDAs are devices that can download books in digital form.

LEARNING COMPREHENSION

"I can recall information in my own terms and explain it to a friend."

Short-Answer Questions

1. What does *online* mean?
2. What is the difference between system software and application software?
3. Briefly define *cyberspace*.
4. What is the difference between software and hardware?
5. What is a local area network?
6. What is multimedia?
7. What is the difference between microcomputers and supercomputers?
8. What is the function of RAM?
9. What does *downloading* mean?
10. What is meant by *connectivity?*
11. Describe some ways that information technology can be used to help people find jobs and to help jobs find people.
12. Compare the use of email to the use of the telephone and of conventional letters sent via the postal system. Which kinds of communications are best suited for which medium?
13. What is the basic meaning of *cloud computing?*

LEARNING APPLYING, ANALYZING, SYNTHESIZING, EVALUATING

"I can apply what I've learned, relate these ideas to other concepts, build on other knowledge, and use all these thinking skills to form a judgment."

Knowledge in Action

1. Do you wish there was an invention to make your life easier or better? Describe it. What would it do for you? Come up with ideas on how that device may be constructed.
2. Determine what types of computers are being used where you work or go to school. In which departments are the different types of computer used? Make a list of the input devices, output devices, and storage devices. What are they used for? How are they connected to other computers? Are any offices or departments using cloud services? If yes, do any users have complaints about using the cloud?
3. Imagine a business you could start or run at home. What type of business is it? What type(s) of computer(s) and mobile devices do you think you'll need? Describe the computer system in as much detail as possible, including hardware components in the areas we have discussed so far. Keep your notes, and then refine your answers as you complete the course.
4. Has reality become science fiction? Or has science fiction become science fact? First, watch an old futuristic movie, such as *2001—A Space Odyssey,* and take note of the then-futuristic technology displayed. Classify what you see according to input, output, processing, storage, and communications. Then watch a recent science fiction movie, and also list all the futuristic

technology used according to the given categories. What was futuristic in the old movie that is now reality? What in the new movie is not yet reality but seems already feasible?

5. From what you've read and what you have experienced and/or observed in your life, do you have a positive, negative, or impartial view of our rapidly converging technological society? Why? Reevaluate your answers as you work through the course.

6. Computer prices are constantly falling. Whatever you pay for a computer today, you can be certain that you will be able to buy a more powerful computer for less money a year from now and, quite possibly, even just a month from now. So how can you decide when it's a good time to upgrade to a better computer? Paradoxically, it seems that no matter how you time it, you'll always lose, because prices will go down again soon, and yet you will also always gain, because, since you were going to upgrade sooner or later anyway, you will reap the benefits of having the more powerful equipment that much longer.

   Discuss the benefits and costs, both material and psychological, of "waiting until prices drop." Gather more information on this topic by asking friends and colleagues which choices they have made about upgrading equipment over the years and whether they feel satisfaction or regret about the timing when they finally did upgrade.

7. Computers are almost everywhere, and they affect most walks of life—business, education, government, military, hobbies, shopping, socializing, research, and so on. What aspects of your life can you think of that still seem relatively unaffected by computers and technology? Is this a good thing or a bad thing, and is it likely to last? What aspects of your life have been the most conspicuously affected by technology? Has anything been made worse or harder in your life by the advance of computers? What about things that have been made better or easier?

8. Have you become extremely dependent on some technologies? Some people no longer write down telephone numbers anywhere; instead, they simply program them into their cellphones. Some people feel helpless in a foreign country unless they have a calculator in hand to compute currency conversions. Many people rely on their email archive or cellphone to hold essential information, such as addresses and appointments. When any of these technologies fails us, we can feel lost.

   Make a list of technologies that have become indispensable to your life. Imagine the consequences if any of these technologies should fail you. What can you do to protect yourself against such failure?

   Write down what you think are the advantages and disadvantages of social networking (for example, Facebook). Keep this list, and revise it after you have finished the course. What has changed on your list?

9. It has been said that the computer is a "meta medium" because it can simulate (behave as) any other medium. Thus a computer can present text that can be read from virtual "pages" as if it were a book; it can let you compose and print text as if it were a typewriter; it can play music like an MP3 player; it can display video as if it were a television set; it can make telephone calls as if it were a telephone; it can let you "draw" and "paint"; it can be programmed to serve as an answering machine; and so forth.

   Imagine a future in which digital electronic devices have replaced all the things they can emulate. What benefits to your life can you see in such a future? What things might be worse? What dangers can you see? Do you think this kind of radical convergence is likely? If so, how long do you think it will take?

Web Exercises

If you are not yet familiar with web surfing, wait until you have finished Chapter 2 to do the following web exercises.

1. Are computers, cellphones, and other electronic devices bad for our health? You may have heard the term *electromagnetic radiation* and dismissed it as an obscure scientific term not worth understanding. Visit the links below to become educated on a topic that will be discussed more seriously and frequently as our society becomes completely wireless.

   www.cancer.gov/cancertopics/factsheet/Risk/cellphones/

   http://www.huffingtonpost.com/devra-davis-phd/cell-phone-radiation-_b_828330.html

   www.howstuffworks.com/cell-phone-radiation.htm

   www.fda.gov/Radiation-EmittingProducts/Radiation EmittingProductsandProcedures/HomeBusiness andEntertainment/CellPhones/ucm116282.htm

   www.ewg.org/cellphone-radiation/

2. List some pros and cons of a "paperless" environment. Do you believe that a paperless environment is something worth striving for in the workplace? In the home? In the classroom? In banking? Run a web search to see what others are doing to implement this idea. What might be the downsides of using less paper?

3. Computer pioneer John von Neumann was one of a group of individuals who conceived the idea of the "stored program." He could also divide two 8-digit numbers in his head. Spend some time researching this remarkable man; at online bookstores, look up some of the books he wrote and read the reviews.

4. Looking for legally free programs? Some places to start:

   www.download.com/

   www.freewarefiles.com/

   www.freedownloadscenter.com/

5. Visit the following websites to become aware of some topics of interest in the computing world. Full comprehension of these topics isn't necessary at this time; this is only to familiarize you with subject matter you may come in contact with.

   www.sciencedaily.com/news/computers_math/computer_science/

   www.computeruser.com/

   www.infoworld.com/

   http://slashdot.org/

   www.slideshare.net/dheerajmehrotra/basic-concepts-of-information-technology-it-presentation/

6. "Moore's Law" predicts the rate at which computers will continue to get smaller (and hence faster). The "law" has proved to be astonishingly accurate over many years. Do a web search for Moore's Law, and see if you can find answers to the following questions:
   a. Who is Moore, and when did he make the prediction we know as Moore's Law?
   b. What is the simplest statement of the law's prediction?
   c. How has the law changed over time?
   d. Is the law still valid? If yes, how much longer is the law expected to hold true?
   e. How does the law affect business projections?
7. A wiki is a website on which authoring and editing can be done very easily by anyone, anywhere, anytime using a web browser such as Internet Explorer or Mozilla Firefox, with no need for special software or other special requirements. (*Wiki* is Hawaiian for "quick.") Most web pages are less than perfect. If it is a wiki page and you are annoyed by something, you can just hit the Edit button and change it! Over time, the site gets better (people hope)!

   Here are some examples of wikis that deal with general knowledge:

   http://en.wikipedia.org/

   www.wikimedia.org/

   http://wiki.ehow.com/Main-Page/

   And here are some specialized wikis:

   http://recipes.wikia.com/wiki/Recipes_Wiki/

   http://webtrends.about.com/od/wikilists/tp/list_of_wiki_sites.htm

   www.wikispaces.com/

   www.wikia.com/Wikia/

   http://wikisineducation.wetpaint.com/

   Historical note: The first wiki site was created for the Portland Pattern Repository in 1995. That site now hosts tens of thousands of pages.

   - *http://c2.com/cgi/wiki?WelcomeVisitors*
   - *http://c2.com/cgi/wiki?WikiHistory*
   - *http://c2.com/cgi/wiki?WikiDesignPrinciples*

   a. Make a small change on a page on one of the listed sites or on some other wiki site you have identified. Submit your change, and note the results. Anyone navigating to that site will now see your change. Did you know that website authoring could be that easy? Are you surprised that someone would unconditionally open up his or her website for anyone to edit?
   b. Since you can make any change you wish, even something totally nonsensical or simply wrong, it's obviously possible for incorrect or misleading content to appear on a wiki. Given that, why do you think that wikis have become so popular and so widespread?
   c. How significant a problem do you think vandalism and other acts of poor citizenship might be on "open" wikis? How can you find out?
   d. Some wikis contend with the threat of vandalism by requiring that a password be provided before a user is allowed to make changes. What advantages can you see to this approach? What disadvantages? Do you think the advantages of password protection outweigh the disadvantages? What do the wikis you browse through have to say about this issue?
   e. What measures do you think an online shared space can take to limit the potential damage from vandalism, while not being overly restrictive?
   f. If you knew that a particular person was defacing a wiki, what would you do about it? Report the person? Wait for the vandal to get bored and turn his or her mischief elsewhere? Or try to reform the person? Are the basic ethical considerations here the same as those regarding other forms of vandalism in our society?
   g. Do you think that open-access systems such as unrestricted wikis will become more common over time, or do you think that abuse of such systems will destroy their usefulness and that wikis will eventually disappear?

2

THE INTERNET & THE WORLD WIDE WEB

Exploring Cyberspace

Chapter Topics & Key Questions

UNIT 2A: *The Internet & the Web*

2.1 **Connecting to the Internet: Narrowband, Broadband, & Access Providers** What are the means of connecting to the Internet, and how fast are they? Who provides Internet access?

2.2 **How Does the Internet Work?** What is the basic structure of the Internet, and who controls it?

2.3 **The World Wide Web** How do the following work: websites, web pages, browsers, URLs, web portals, search tools, and search engines? What are HTML and hyperlinks?

UNIT 2B: *The Riches & Risks of Internet Use*

2.4 **Email, Instant Messaging, & Other Ways of Communicating over the Net** What are email and webmail, attachments, netiquette, instant messaging, FTP, newsgroups, and mailing lists?

2.5 **The Online Gold Mine: Telephony, Multimedia, Webcasting, Blogs, E-Commerce, & Social Networking** What are the various types of telephony, multimedia, different web feeds, e-commerce, and social networking?

2.6 **The Intrusive Internet: Snooping, Spamming, Spoofing, Phishing, Pharming, Cookies, Spyware, & Malware** How can I protect myself against the various kinds of Internet dangers, such as snoopers, spam, spoofing, phishing, pharming, cookies, spyware, and malware such as viruses?

Download the free UIT 11e App for key term flash cards quizzes and a game, *Over the Edge*

CHAPTER FORECAST

The first half of this chapter describes the Internet and the World Wide Web. We discuss the ways of connecting to the Internet, both narrowband and broadband, and the types of Internet access providers. We cover the basic structure of the Internet and who controls it. We also consider the parts of the World Wide Web—websites, web pages, browsers, URLs, web portals, search tools, and search engines. We probe the mysteries of HTML and hyperlinks. In the second half of the chapter, we consider the riches of Internet use, and then we look at the risks. Among the riches are email, instant messaging, FTP, newsgroups, and mailing lists. We also have telephone, multimedia, webcasting, blogs, e-commerce, and social networking. Among the risks: snoopers, spam, spoofing, phishing, pharming, cookies, spyware, and malware such as viruses.

UNIT 2A: *The Internet & the Web*

"The immensity of the changes wrought—and still to come—cannot be underestimated," says futurist Graham Molitor. "This miraculous information channel—the Internet—will touch and alter virtually every facet of humanity, business, and all the rest of civilization's trappings."[1]

Molitor said that over a decade ago, and nothing has changed to disprove him, with the Internet now touching and altering nearly every sphere of life. *(• See Panel 2.1, next page.)* Indeed, pervasive computing, ubiquitous computing, is already an established fact, with "everything connected to everything," from smartphones to cameras to car navigation systems. Because of its standard interfaces and generally low rates, the Internet has been the great leveler for communications—just as the personal computer was for computing.

The basis for the Internet began in 1969 as ARPANET (for ARPA, the Advanced Research Projects Agency of the U.S. Department of Defense), with four linked-together computers at different universities and defense contractors. From there the network expanded to 62 computers in 1974, 500 computers in 1983, and 28,000 in 1987. However, it still remained the domain of researchers and academics, and it was still all text—no graphics, video, or sound.

Not until the development of the World Wide Web in the early 1990s, which made multimedia available on the Internet, and the first browser (for locating web pages), which opened the web to commercial uses, did the global network really take off. *(• See Panel 2.2 for a brief history of telecommunications.)* In 2012, 2.4 billion people were using the Internet, with people in North America making up 11.4% of the world's total users. China had the highest numbers of users, followed by the United States, Japan, India, and Brazil.[2] By 2015, 5 billion people may be connected to the Internet.[3]

panel 2.2

Timeline: Brief graphical history of telecommunications and the Internet

1621	1642	1843	1844	1876	1895	1907
Slide rule invented (Edmund Gunther)	First mechanical adding machine (Blaise Pascal)	World's first computer programmer, Ada Lovelace, publishes her notes	Samuel Morse sends a telegraph message from Washington to Baltimore	Alexander Graham Bell patents the telephone	First radio signal transmitted	First regular radio broadcast from New York

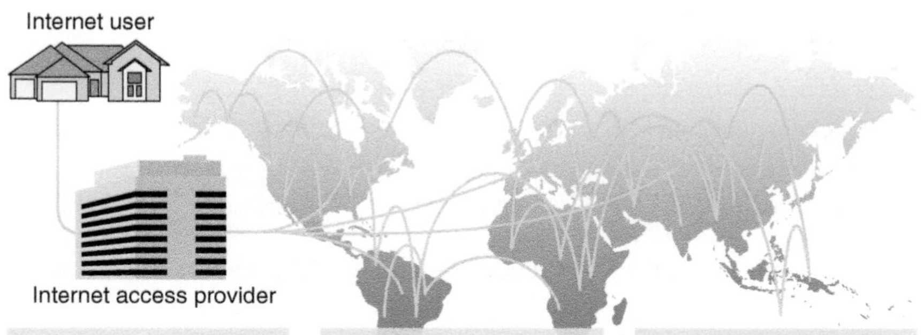

panel 2.1

Some areas in the world of the Internet

Email & discussion groups
Stay in touch worldwide and do business via email.

Research & information
Find information on any subject, using browsers and search tools.

News
Stay current on politics, weather, entertainment, sports, and financial news.

Entertainment
Amuse yourself with internet games, music, videos, and movies.

File downloading
Get software, music, videos, and documents such as e-books.

E-shopping
Price anything from plane tickets to cars; order anything from books to sofas.

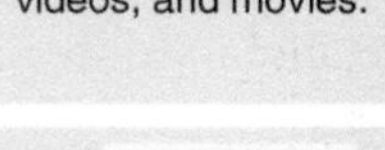

Financial matters
Do investing, banking, and bill paying online.

Auctions
Sell old stuff, acquire more stuff, with online auctions.

Telephony & conferencing
Make inexpensive phone calls; have online meetings.

Career advancement
Search job listings, post résumés, interview online.

Distance learning
Attend online lectures, have discussions, write research papers, earn degrees.

E-business
Connect with coworkers, buy supplies, support customers, conduct negotiations, do marketing.

Social networking
Facebook,Twitter, LinkedIn, Myspace, Flickr, blogging.

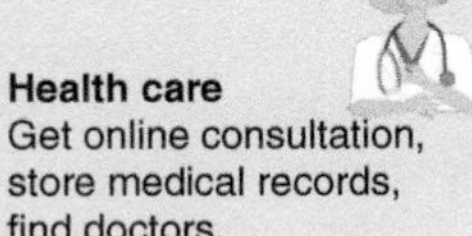

Health care
Get online consultation, store medical records, find doctors.

Law enforcement
Checking car plates and registration, tracking criminals, finding Internet criminals, fighting fraud.

more info!

Hobbes's Internet Timeline & Others

For more detailed Internet timelines, go to:

www.zakon.org/robert/internet/timeline

www.computerhistory.org/internet_history

www.webopedia.com/quick_ref/timeline.asp

www.internetsociety.org/internet/what-internet/history-internet/brief-history-internet

www.historyofthings.com/history-of-the-internet

1927 First demonstration of television in USA

1944 First electro-mechanical computer (Mark I)

1946 First programmable electronic computer in United States (ENIAC)

1947 Vannevar Bush proposes hypertext; mobile phones first invented (cellphones not sold commercially until 1983)

1958 Eisenhower administration creates the Advanced Research Projects Agency (ARPA) as part of the U.S. Department of Defense

1962 First commercially available modem (developed in the 1950s)

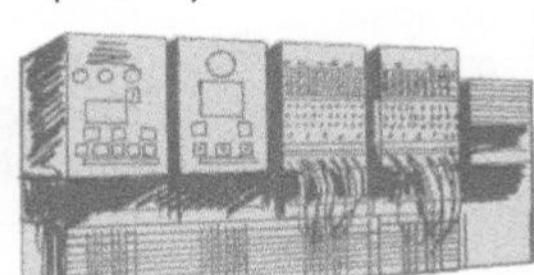

How do you connect to this network of networks? You need three things:

- An *access device,* such as a personal computer with a modem;
- A *means of connection,* such as a telephone line, cable hookup, or wireless capability;
- An *Internet access provider,* such as an Internet service provider (ISP), a commercial online service provider, or a wireless Internet service provider.

We cover these subjects in the next section. We then describe how the Internet works.

2.1 CONNECTING TO THE INTERNET: Narrowband, Broadband, & Access Providers

However you connect to the Internet, the bandwidth will determine the speed of your connection.

In general terms, **bandwidth, or *channel capacity*, is an expression of how much data—text, voice, video, and so on—can be sent through a communications channel in a given amount of time.** The type of data transmission that allows only one signal at a time is called *baseband transmission.* When several signals can be transmitted at once, it's called *broadband transmission.* **Broadband—high-speed—connections** include various kinds of high-speed wired connections, such as coaxial and fiber-optic cable (described in Chapter 6), as well as DSL and wireless connections, such as satellite, discussed shortly.

THE PHYSICAL CONNECTION: WIRED OR WIRELESS? What are your choices of a *physical connection*—the wired or wireless means of connecting to the Internet? A lot depends on where you access the Internet. As you might expect, urban and many suburban areas offer more broadband connections than rural areas do. Among the principal means of connection are (1) telephone (dial-up) modem (used mostly in rural areas); (2) high-speed phone lines, including DSL modem and T1 and T3 lines; (3) cable modem; and (4) wireless modem, including satellite and other through-the-air links.

We elaborate on these connections, along with types of networks and their details, in Chapter 6, "Communications, Networks, & Safeguards." Here we simply give you the basic background you need to know to understand the Internet and the World Wide Web.

DATA TRANSMISSION SPEEDS Data is transmitted in characters or collections of bits. A *bit,* as we discuss in detail in Chapter 4, is the smallest unit of information used by computers. Today's data transmission speeds are measured in *bits, kilobits, megabits,* and *gigabits* per second:

- **bps:** A computer with an old modem might have a speed of 56,000 bps, which is considered the minimum speed for visiting websites with graphics. The **bps stands for bits per second** (8 bits equals 1 character [a byte, p. 31], such as *A, 3,* or *#.*)
- **Kbps: Kilobits per second, or Kbps, are 1 thousand bits per second.** The speed of a modem that is 56,000 bps may be expressed as 56 Kbps.

1969	1970	1971	1973	1974	1975	1976
ARPANET established at 4 U.S. universities (4 computers linked by leased lines); leads to Internet (4 hosts)	Microprocessor chips come into use; 15 ARPANET sites established (universities/research), each with own address; 13 hosts on network	Email invented by computer engineer Ray Tomlinson; 23 hosts on network	ARPANET becomes international; 35 hosts on network	TCP (Transmission Control Protocol) specification developed by U.S. Dept. of Defense; 62 hosts on network; first use of the word *Internet*	First microcomputer (MITS Altair 8800)	Queen Elizabeth sends the first royal email

- **Mbps:** Faster means of connection are measured in **megabits per second, or Mbps—1 million bits per second.**
- **Gbps:** At the extreme are **gigabits per second, or Gbps—1 billion bits per second.**

UPLOADING & DOWNLOADING Why is it important to know these terms? Because the number of bits affects how fast you can upload and download information from a remote computer. As we've said (Chapter 1, p. 20), *downloading* is the transmission of data from a remote computer to a local computer, as from a website to your own PC—for example, downloading a movie. *Uploading* is the transmission of data from a local computer to a remote computer, as from your PC to a website you are constructing or putting one of your videos on YouTube.

Narrowband (Dial-Up Modem): Low Speed but Inexpensive

Dial-up modems are used primarily in rural areas, where broadband connections are not always available.

The landline telephone line that many people use for voice calls is still the cheapest means of online connection and is available everywhere. Although the majority of U.S. adults favor broadband Internet connections, many rural home users still use **narrowband, or low-bandwidth,** connections. To date, this has mainly consisted of **dial-up connections—use of landline telephone modems to connect computers to the Internet.**

CONNECTING THE MODEM As we mentioned in Chapter 1, a *modem* is a device that sends and receives data over telephone lines to and from computers. A dial-up modem is attached to the telephone wall outlet. *(• See Panel 2.3, page 55.)* (We discuss modems in a bit more detail in Chapter 6.)

Most dial-up modems today have a maximum speed of 56 Kbps. That doesn't mean, however, that dial-up users will be sending and receiving data at that rate. The modem in the computer must negotiate with the modems used by the *Internet access provider,* the regional, national, or wireless organization or business that connects you to the Internet. Downloading a 16 megabyte (MB) movie via a 56 Kbps dial-up connection would take about 31 minutes and 45 seconds.

High-Speed Phone Lines: More Expensive but Available in Cities & Most Towns

Dial-up connections are becoming obsolete, in favor of high-speed connections.

Waiting while your computer's modem takes 25 minutes to transmit a 1-minute low-quality video from a website may have you pummeling the desk in frustration. To get some relief, you could enhance your **POTS—"plain old telephone system"**—connection with a high-speed adaptation. The choices are DSL and T1/T3, available in most major cities, though not in many rural areas.

Survival Tip

Megabits vs. Megabytes

People often say megabytes when they mean megaBITS. And vice versa. But there is a difference.

Mbps = megabits per second
MBps = megabytes (Chapter 1, p. 31) per second

To determine mega*bytes* per second from mega*bits* per second just *divide by 8*. For example, if we have a transmission speed of 11 Mbps per second, that equals 1.37 MBps (11/8 = 1.37). So, if your photo is 12 MB, then it will download in 12/1.37 = 8.75 seconds.

- 8 bits = 1 byte
- 1,000 bytes = 8 kilobits (kb) = 1 kilobyte (KB)
- 1,000 kilobytes (KB) = 8 megabits (Mb) = 1 megabyte (MB)

(See the bandwidth conversion calculator: *http://web.forret.com/tools/bandwidth.asp?speed=11&unit=Mbps.*)

1976	1978	1979	1981	1983	1984	1986	1987
Apple I computer (first personal computer sold in assembled form)	TCP/IP developed (released in 1983) as standard Internet transmission protocol; 111 hosts on Internet; first spam email	First Usenet newsgroups; 188 hosts on Internet	IBM introduces personal computer; 213 hosts on Internet	TCP/IP use required	Apple Macintosh; first personal laser printer; William Gibson coins term *cyberspace*; Domain Name System (DNS) introduced	NSFNET (National Science Foundation Network) backbone established	Digital cellular phones invented; first email message sent from China

To check your Internet connection speed in Windows 7, go to Control Panel, click on Internet and Network, then Network and Sharing Center, and then click on Local Area Connection.

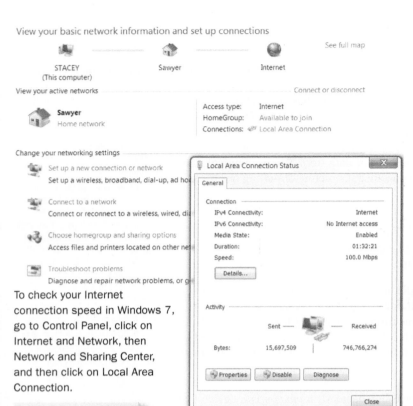

Broadband: Riskier for Security

Unlike dial-up services, broadband and DSL services, because they are always switched on, make your computer vulnerable to over-the-Internet security breaches. Solution: Install firewall software, which prevents unauthorized users from accessing a private network that is connected to a public network, such as the Internet.

DSL LINE **DSL (digital subscriber line) uses regular phone lines, a DSL modem, and special technology to transmit data in megabits per second.** Incoming data is significantly faster than outgoing data. That is, your computer can *receive* data at the rate of 7–15 Mbps, but it can *send* data at only 384 Kbps–1 Mbps. This arrangement may be fine, however, if you're principally interested in obtaining very large amounts of data (video, music) rather than in sending such data to others. A big advantage of DSL is that it is always on (so you don't have to make a dial-up connection), and, unlike cable (discussed shortly), its transmission rate is relatively consistent. Also, you can talk on the phone and send data at the same time.

There is one big drawback to DSL: You have to live within 4.5 miles of a phone company central switching office, because the access speed and reliability degrade with distance. However, DSL phone companies are building thousands of remote switching facilities to enhance service throughout their regions. Another drawback is that you have to choose from a list of Internet service providers that are under contract to the phone company you use, although other DSL providers exist. (DSL service costs users about $50 to $250 per month.) Still, the real problem for DSL—or any other kind of broadband—is that it is not available to many rural Americans, who thus lack the sort of high-speed services and opportunities, such as distance learning and web-based commerce, that urban dwellers take for granted. (About 94–98% of Americans now have access to broadband—DSL, cable, fiber-optic cables—but not necessarily at home. Where does that leave people living in rural counties and one-third of the people living on tribal lands who don't have it?)[4]

T LINES Is high speed worth $550–$1,200 a month to you? If yes, then consider getting a **T1 line, essentially a traditional trunk line, a fiber-optic or copper line separate from the phone line, that carries 24 normal telephone circuits and has a transmission rate of 1.5–6 Mbps.** Generally, T1 lines are leased by corporate, government, and academic sites. Another high-speed line, the T3 line, transmits at 6–47 Mbps and costs about $3,000–$15,000

1989	1990	1984	1989–1991	1992	1993	1994
World Wide Web established by Tim Berners-Lee while working at the European Particle Physics Laboratory in Geneva, Switzerland; first home trials of fiber communications network; number of Internet hosts breaks 100,000; first commercial dial-up Internet availability	ARPANET decommissioned; first ISP comes online (dial-up access); Berners-Lee develops first web browser, WorldWideWeb; 313,000 hosts on Internet (9,300 domains)	9.6 K modem	14.4 K modem	"Surfing the Internet" coined by Jean Armour Polly; 1,136,000 hosts on Internet (18,100 domains)	Multimedia desktop computers; IXPs replace NSFNET; first graphical web browser, Mosaic, developed by Marc Andreessen; the U.S. White House goes online; Internet talk radio begins broadcasting; 2,056,000 hosts on Internet (28,000 domains)	Apple and IBM introduce PCs with full-motion video built in; wireless data transmission for small portable computers; Netscape Navigator released; 28.8 K modem; the Japanese prime minister goes online; 3,864,000 hosts on Internet (56,000 domains)

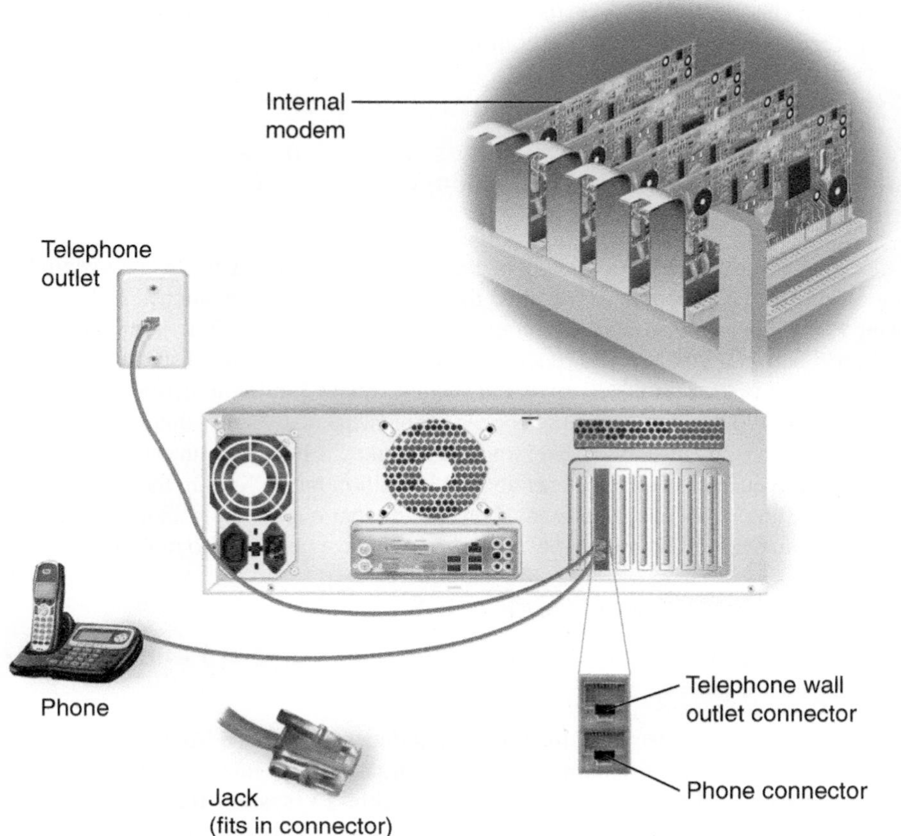

panel 2.3

Telephone dial-up modem connection

You connect the modem inside your desktop computer from a port (socket) in the back of your computer to a line that is then connected to a wall jack. Your landline telephone is also connected to your computer so that you can make voice calls. (Note that this kind of connection, if using only one telephone number, cannot be used to make voice calls and connect to the Internet at the same time.)

a month, depending on location and T3 provider availability. (There are some T2 lines, which are somewhat faster than T1, but they are not popular.)

Transmitting 100 MB of data on a standard 56 K modem would take 4 hours, 9 minutes, and 39 seconds, whereas a T1 line could transmit it in 8 minutes, 33 seconds, and a T3 line could be finished in about 17 seconds.

T3 lines are commonly used by businesses connecting to the Internet, by Internet access providers, and in the Internet high-speed transmission lines.

A T4 line can carry the equivalent of six T3 lines and transmit 274,176 million bits per second. This type of line is used only by major corporations.

T5 lines are over 250 times faster than a full T1 line, with a maximum transmission speed of 400,352 megabits per second. (Even though the technology behind T5 lines

1995	1996	1998	1999	2000	2001	2002	2003
NSFNET reverts to research project; Internet now in commercial hands; the Vatican goes online	Microsoft releases Internet Explorer; 56 K modem invented; cable modem introduced; 12,881,000 hosts on Internet (488,000 domains); Internet2	Google is funded	Wi-Fi is standardized	Web surpasses 1 billion indexable pages; 93,047,785 hosts on Internet	AOL membership surpasses 28 million; Wikipedia is launched	Blogs become popular; Friendster	First official Swiss online election; flash mobs start in New York City; Facebook; MySpace; iTunes

existed in the 1980s, most of its features are still in various stages of development. Therefore, it is rare to find a telecommunications company providing T5 lines.)

Problem for Telephone Internet Connections: The Last Mile

The medium that connects homes and business to the central switching office is usually old copper wire, which slows data movement.

The length of the connections from all homes and businesses to the telephone's central switching office, the local loop, is often called the "last mile." As we mentioned earlier, if you are using POTS for your initial Internet connection—even if you use DSL—data must pass back and forth between you and your telephone switching station. (This distance is usually more than a mile; it is shorter than 20 miles and averages about 3 miles in metropolitan areas.) This "last mile" of old, often poor-quality copper wire is what really slows things down. This problem can be solved by installing newer transmission media, but communications companies are reluctant to incur this cost. There are about 130 million phone lines in the United States that use 650 million miles of copper wire. Considering that our planet is about 93 million miles from the sun, 650 million miles of wire represents a huge challenge to replace!

Cable Modem: Close Competitor to DSL

Cable connections can be faster than DSL and are more popular in the United States.

Cable modems can transmit (upload) outgoing data at about 2–8 Mbps and incoming data at up to 100 Mbps. (The common residential transmission rate is 6–30 Mbps.) **A cable modem connects a personal computer to a cable-TV system that offers an Internet connection.** The cable runs underground from a street cable-box connection to the house or business; it is separate from the phone line.

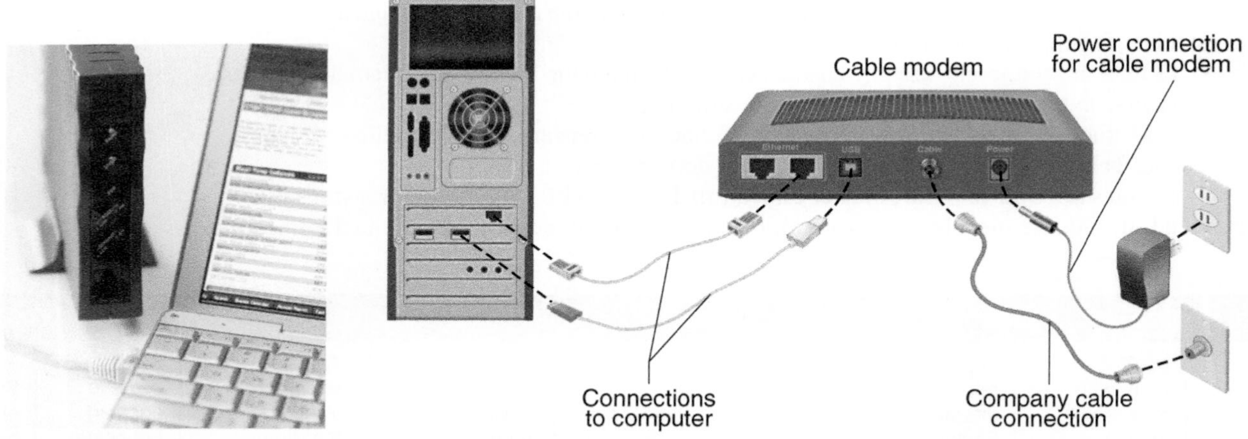

Cable modem. Cable modems connect similarly to a dial-up modem—but you have an external cable modem connected to your computer and also connected to company cable that comes into your house or office from the outside; the cable modem also connects to a power wall socket.

2004	2005	2006	2007	2012	2013	2020	2030–2045
More than 285,000,000 hosts on Internet; Facebook launched	YouTube; Wii	Twitter	Skype	More than 634 million hosts on the Internet—top 10 Internet users (countries) are China, USA, India, Japan, Brazil, Russia, Germany, UK, Indonesia, France	5G phones	3D processing chip	The singularity

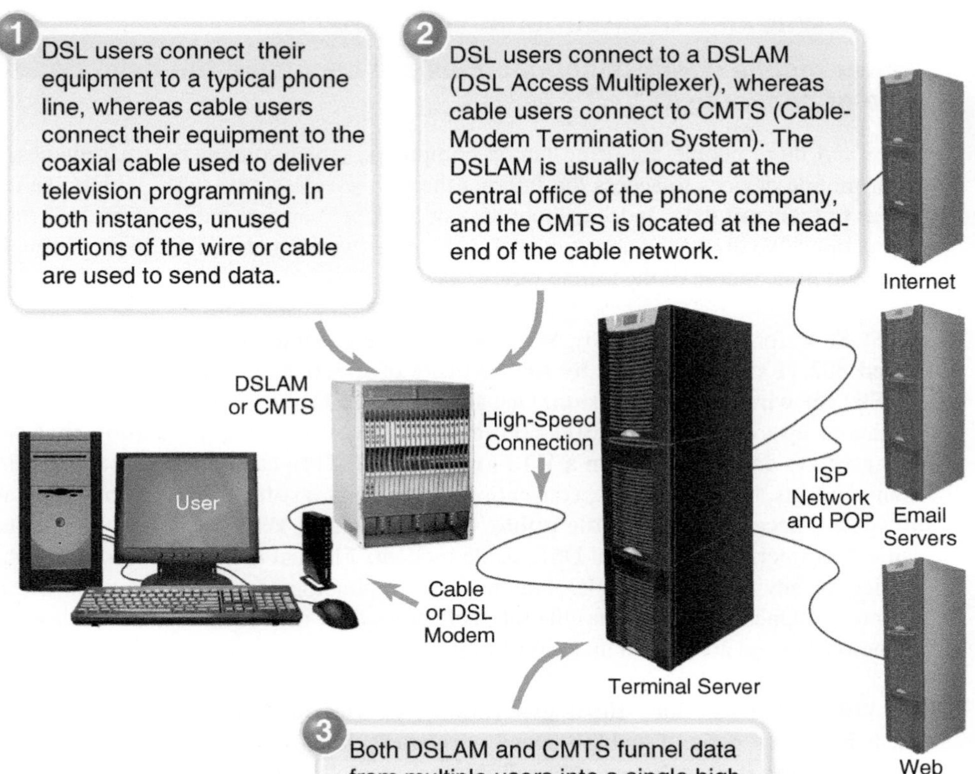
1
DSL users connect their equipment to a typical phone line, whereas cable users connect their equipment to the coaxial cable used to deliver television programming. In both instances, unused portions of the wire or cable are used to send data.
2
DSL users connect to a DSLAM (DSL Access Multiplexer), whereas cable users connect to CMTS (Cable-Modem Termination System). The DSLAM is usually located at the central office of the phone company, and the CMTS is located at the head-end of the cable network.
Internet
DSLAM or CMTS
High-Speed Connection
User
ISP Network and POP
Email Servers
Cable or DSL Modem
Terminal Server
3
Both DSLAM and CMTS funnel data from multiple users into a single high-bandwidth connection to the Internet.
Web Server

panel 2.4

Basic DSL/cable-PC system

The advantage of a cable modem is that, like a DSL connection, it is always on. However, unlike DSL, you don't need to live near a telephone switching station. (• *See Panel 2.4.)* A disadvantage, however, is that you and your cable-TV-viewing-Internet-surfing neighbors are sharing the system, and consequently, during peak-load times (in many places, from 7 P.M. to 2 A.M.), your service may be slowed down significantly. Also, using an Internet connection that is always on—and that, in the case of cable, you share with other people—invites outside interference with your computer, a risk that we discuss later in the book.

Cable companies may contract you to use their own Internet access provider, but more commonly you may choose your own. (Some cable companies also supply voice phone service.)

Survival Tip

Connection Speeds

To test the speed of your Internet connection, go to:

www.speedtest.net

http://reviews.cnet.com/internet-speed-test

www.testmyspeed.com

www.computerhope.com/issues/ch000539.htm

Satellite Wireless Connections

Satellite connections provide Internet access without telephone lines or cables; however, satellite connection involves signal delay.

If you live in a rural area and are tired of the molasses-like speed of your cranky local phone system, but you have no DSL or cable access, you might—if you have an unobstructed view of the southern sky—consider taking to the air. With a pizza-size satellite dish on your roof or on the side of your house, you can send data at the rate of about 200–512 Kbps and receive data at speeds up to about 1–5 Mbps from a **communications satellite, a space station that transmits radio waves called *microwaves* from earth-based stations.**

Satellite Internet connections, which cost about $25–$100 per month, are always on. To surf the Internet using this kind of connection, you need an Internet access provider that supports two-way satellite transmission. You will also have to lease or purchase satellite-access hardware, such as a dish and satellite modem, and have the dish connected by cable to at least one computer inside your house or office, along with the modem. Note that satellite connectivity providers often impose use quotas on their customers. If you exceed your usage quota for the month, the service provider may slow you down significantly. (We cover satellites in more detail in Chapter 6.)

Sky connection. Setting up a home satellite dish

Other Wireless Connections: Wi-Fi, 3G, & 4G

Newer mobile wireless connections are becoming the most popular type of connectivity.

More and more people are using laptop computers, tablet computers, smartphones, and other mobile devices to access the Internet through **wireless networks, which use radio waves to transmit data.** Indeed, about 85% of all Americans are part of a wireless, mobile population.[5] We discuss various types of wireless networks in detail in Chapter 6, but here we mention just three of the technologies.

WI-FI Short for *Wireless Fidelity,* **Wi-Fi is the name given to any of several standards—called 802.11 standards—set by the Institute of Electrical and Electronic Engineers (IEEE) for wireless transmission.** One standard, 802.11b, permits wireless transmission of data at up to 54 Mbps for 300–500 feet from an **access point, a station that sends and receives data to and from a Wi-Fi network;** 802.11n can transmit up to 140 Mpbs. Many airports, hotels, libraries, convention centers, and fast-food facilities offer so-called **hotspots—access points for the public to use to access Wi-Fi networks.** The hotspot can get its Internet access from DSL, cable modem, T1 local area network, dial-up phone service, or any other method. (Communications technology is covered in more detail in Chapter 6.) Once the hotspot has the Internet connection, it can broadcast it wirelessly. All the newer laptops are able to make Wi-Fi Internet connections.

3G WIRELESS 3G, for "third generation," carries both voice and Internet traffic; it is loosely defined as high-speed wireless technology that does not need access points because it uses the existing cellphone system. This technology, which is found in many mobile devices such as smartphones and tablets, can transfer data at rates as high as 3.8 Mbps (or even more); it is being provided by AT&T, Sprint, Verizon, T-Mobile, and others. About 98% of Americans have access to 3G wireless service today.[6]

HTC 4G LTE Android smartphone

4G WIRELESS 4G, for "fourth generation," is specifically built for Internet traffic; it is a successor to 3G and 2G standards, aiming to provide data rates up to 100 Mbps or more, although most providers now deliver in the range of 6–11 Mbps. Whereas 3G networks carry voice and Internet traffic, 4G networks are built specifically for Internet content, which means they don't require equipment to route voice phone calls, thus creating energy efficiencies. But, says one account, carriers can claim whatever they want, because the International Telecommunications Union, the wireless industry standards body, hasn't given 4G a firm definition.[7] Regardless, there are as many 4G subscribers in the United States as in the rest of the world combined.[8] (We cover 4G, and its successor, 5G, in more detail in Chapter 6.)

4G smartphones have been released by Motorola, Apple, Samsung, HTC Evo, Sprint, T-Mobile, Verizon, Google, and a few other companies.

Internet Access Providers

Users need to know how to choose an Internet access provider that is right for them.

Finding Wi-Fi Hotspots

www.openwifispots.com/
www.wififreespot.com/
http://reviews.cnet.com/4520-6659_7-726628-1.html
http://compnetworking.about.com/od/wireless/tp/wifihotspotfind.htm

As we mentioned, in addition to having an access device and a means of connection, to get on the Internet, you need to go through an *Internet access provider,* or an **Internet service provider (ISP)—a local, regional, or national organization that provides access to the Internet for a fee.** The ISP may own the facilities that it uses to deliver services, or it may lease the facilities of another provider. Examples of national providers are Comcast, CenturyLink, Charter, Cox Cable, AT&T, Frontier, and Verizon; there are many others. There are also still some free ISPs (search *www.all-free-isp.com/*).

A wireless Internet service provider (WISP) enables users with computers containing wireless modems—mostly laptops, tablets, and smartphones—to gain access to the Internet. A WISP offers public wireless network services and Internet access. WISPs typically install Wi-Fi wireless hotspots in airports, hotels, cafés, and other public business places.

To use a WISP, you may have to subscribe to its wireless service. Some WISPs offer free Internet service, but many others charge fees and/or require service contracts. When choosing a WISP, you should ensure that the provider's equipment and software are compatible with your own system. WISPs also vary in the speed and security features they offer.

Examples of WISPs are AT&T, Sprint, T-Mobile, Credo, and Verizon Wireless.

Finding ISPs

For ISP comparison shopping, go to:

www.theispguide.com/
http://isp-review.toptenreviews.com/
www.e-wisdom.com/internet/

2.2 HOW DOES THE INTERNET WORK?

The Internet is basically a huge network that connects hundreds of thousands of smaller networks.

The *inter*national *net*work known as the *Internet* consists of hundreds of thousands of smaller networks linking educational, commercial, nonprofit, and military organizations, as well as individuals. Central to this arrangement is the client-server network (Chapter 1, p. 22). **A client computer is a computer requesting data or services. A server, or *host computer*, is a central computer supplying data or services requested of it.** When the client computer's request—for example, for information on various airline flights and prices—gets to a server computer, that computer sends the information back to the client computer.

Internet Connections: POPs, IXPs, Backbone, & Internet2

The foundation of the Internet is the backbone, the fastest part, which links to slower types of connections, such as those of ISPs.

Your journey onto the Internet starts with connecting the modem in your client computer or mobile device to your Internet access provider, such as an Internet service provider (ISP). (• *See Panel 2.5.*) This is the slowest part of the entire Internet connection. An ISP's headquarters and network servers may be located almost anywhere.

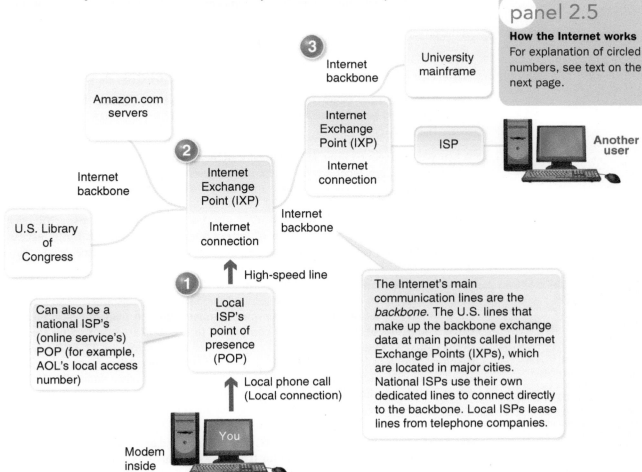

panel 2.5

How the Internet works

For explanation of circled numbers, see text on the next page.

Where Are the IXPs?

For a map of IXP locations, go to:

www.datacentermap.com/ixps.html

POINT OF PRESENCE ISPs provide each customer with a ❶ **point of presence (POP)—a local access point to the Internet—a collection of modems and other equipment in a local area.** The POP acts as a local gateway to the ISP's network.

INTERNET EXCHANGE POINT (IXP) The ISP in turn connects to an ❷ **Internet Exchange Point (IXP), a routing computer at a point on the Internet where several connections come together.** IXPs are run by private companies that control physical infrastructures that allow different ISPs to exchange Internet traffic.

INTERNET BACKBONE Each IXP has at least one computer whose task is simply to direct Internet traffic from one IXP to the next. IXPs are connected by the equivalent of interstate highways known collectively as the ❸ **Internet backbone, high-speed, high-capacity transmission lines, usually fiber-optic lines, that use the newest communications technology to transmit data across the Internet.** Backbone connections are supplied by Internet backbone providers such as AT&T, British Telecom, Sprint, VSNL, Verizon, CenturyLink, and Deutsche Telekom. Usually data travels over many different networks before it reaches your computer.

INTERNET2 Internet2 is a not-for-profit cooperative university/business education and research project that enables high-end users to quickly and reliably move huge amounts of data over high-speed networks. In effect, Internet2 adds "toll lanes" to the older Internet to speed things up. The purpose is to advance videoconferencing, research, and academic collaboration—to enable a kind of "virtual university." By bringing research and academia together with technology leaders from industry, government, and the international community, Internet2 promotes collaboration and innovation that have a fundamental impact on the future of the Internet. Beyond just providing network capacity, Internet2 actively engages in the development of important new technology including security, network research, and performance measurement capabilities, which are critical to the progress of the Internet.[9]

Internet Communications: Protocols, Packets, & IP Addresses

The data transmitted over the Internet must be set up to follow certain rules so that all the computers on the network can understand it.

When you connect to your ISP's POP location, the two entities go through a process called *handshaking,* whereby the fastest-available transmission speed is established. Then *authentication* occurs: your ISP needs to know you are who you say you are, so you need to provide a username and a password. **A username, or *user ID,* is a unique combination of characters, such as letters and/or numbers, that identifies a specific user. A password is a special combination of letters and/or numbers that limits access to information.** You establish your username and password when you open your account with your ISP.

The Internet Traffic Report

The Internet Traffic Report monitors the flow of data around the world. It displays values between 0 and 100 for many networks. Higher values indicate faster and more reliable connections. Check out your area at:

www.internettrafficreport.com/

PROTOCOLS How do computers understand the data being transmitted? The key lies in the **protocol, or set of rules, that computers must follow to transmit data electronically. The protocol that enables all computers to use data transmitted on the Internet is called Transmission Control Protocol/Internet Protocol, or *TCP/IP,*** which was developed in 1978 by ARPA. TCP/IP is used for all Internet transactions, from sending email to downloading pictures off a friend's website. Among other things, TCP/IP determines how the sending device indicates that it has finished sending a message and how the receiving device indicates that it has received the message.[10]

PACKETS Most important, perhaps, TCP/IP breaks the data in a message into separate **packets, fixed-length blocks of data for transmission.** This allows a message to be split up and its parts sent by separate routes, yet still all wind up in the same place. IP is used to send the packets across the Internet to their final destination, and TCP is used to reassemble the

packets in the correct order. The packets do not have to follow the same network routes to reach their destination because all the packets have the same *IP address,* as we explain next.

IP ADDRESSES The most popular website in 2013 was Google, whose Internet address is *www.google.com*. When you type that address, your computer converts *www.google.com* to a set of numbers, called an *Internet Protocol (IP) address,* by checking your Internet service provider's online database (called a Domain Name System—we explain domain names on p. 64) of Internet addresses. **An Internet Protocol (IP) address uniquely identifies each computer and device connected to the Internet.** An IP address consists of four sets of numbers between 0 and 255 separated by decimals (called a *dotted quad*)—for example, 1.160.10.240.

There are two types of IP addresses, dynamic and static.

- **Dynamic IP addresses—used for most websites:** Street addresses rarely change, but IP addresses often do. Each time you connect to your ISP, it assigns your computer a new IP address, called a *dynamic IP address,* for your online session. When you request data from the Internet, it is transmitted to your computer's IP address. When you disconnect, your provider frees up the IP address you were using and reassigns it to another user. If you are using a computer that gets connected to the Internet only intermittently, you're most likely picking up a dynamic IP address each time from a pool of possible IP addresses at your Internet access provider.
- **Static IP addresses—used for established organizational websites:** Whereas a dynamic IP address changes each time you connect to the Internet, a *static IP address* is the same every time you connect. Established organizational websites have their own static IP addresses, which they pay for. If your computer is constantly connected to the Internet through a local network at work or school, most likely you have a static IP address.

  Why can't every computer that connects to the Internet have its own static IP number? The answer is that the Internet's original architects didn't foresee the need for an unlimited number of IP addresses. Later they realized there are not enough such numbers to go around, and so many Internet access providers now limit the number of static IP addresses they give out and economize by temporarily assigning dynamic IP addresses to various users.
- **To avoid running out of addresses—the new approach:** This dynamic/static approach to determining IP addresses, created in the early 1980s, is called *Internet Protocol Version 4 (IPv4)*. After Internet use exploded in the 1990s, it was clear that even with this dual approach the world would soon run out of IP addresses. The result was a new scheme, devised by the Internet Engineering Task Force, called *Internet Protocol Version 6 (IPv6),* in which an IP address would take the following format:

  0000:0000:0000:0000:0000:0000:0000:0000

  This approach, which uses both numbers and characters, provides a nearly unlimited number of IP addresses and allows the connection of non-microcomputer devices, such as smartphones and home electronic equipment. Whereas IPv4 had about 4.3 billion addresses, IPv6 will allow 340 trillion, trillion, trillion unique IP addresses.[11]

Your IP Address

Want to find out what your IP address is while you're online? Go to:

http://whatismyipaddress.com/

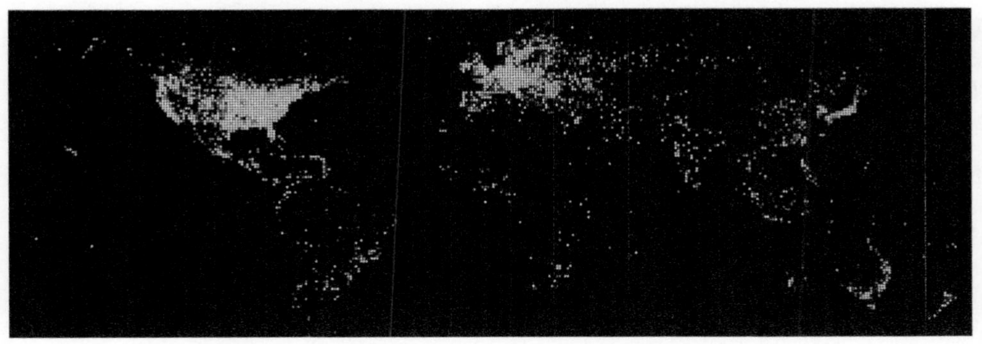

Relative densities of Internet connectivity across the globe

Who Runs the Internet?

Although no one really "owns" the Internet, several global and U.S. organizations establish standards for it.

Although no one owns the Internet, everyone connected with it adheres to standards overseen by the Internet Society and follows naming rules set by the Internet Corporation for Assigned Names and Numbers.

THE INTERNET SOCIETY The Internet Society (*www.internetsociety.org*) is a worldwide professional, nonprofit society counting more than 90 chapters enrolling 145 organizational members (companies, governments, foundations) and 65,000 individual members. The society provides leadership in addressing issues that confront the future of the Internet and is the organizational home for groups responsible for Internet infrastructure standards, including the Internet Engineering Task Force, the Internet Architecture Board (IAB), and the World Wide Web Consortium.

THE INTERNET CORPORATION FOR ASSIGNED NAMES & NUMBERS In June 1998 the U.S. government proposed the creation of a series of nonprofit corporations to manage such complex issues as fraud prevention, privacy, and intellectual-property protection. The first such group, the **Internet Corporation for Assigned Names and Numbers (ICANN), was established to regulate human-friendly Internet domain names—those addresses ending with *.com, .org, .net,* and so on, that overlie IP addresses and identify the website type.** (These domain names are discussed in more detail shortly.)

ICANN (*www.icann.org*) is a global, private-sector, nonprofit corporation that has no statutory authority and imposes policies through contracts with its world members. In 2003 it outlined what it called ICANN 2.0, intended to make itself more responsive to the world Internet community about the adoption of standards. One of its improvements is the ICANN Whois Database, which returns the name and address of any domain name entered (entering *microsoft.com,* for instance, returns the name and address of Microsoft Corp.).

ICANN doesn't control content or deal with access to the Internet. But by coordinating the naming system, it has an important influence on the Internet's evolution.[12]

2.3 THE WORLD WIDE WEB

The World Wide Web brought multimedia to the Internet.

The Internet and the World Wide Web, as we have said, are not the same. The Internet is a massive network of networks, connecting millions of computers via protocols, hardware, and communications channels. It is the infrastructure that supports not only the web but also other communications systems such as email, instant messaging, and other activities that we discuss. The part of the Internet called the *web* is a *multimedia-based* technology that enables you to access more than just text. That is, you can also download art, audio, video, and animation and engage in interactive games.

Why the Word *Web*?

Why did people perceive the need for a "web," and how did Berners-Lee develop what they needed? Go to:

www.ibiblio.org/pioneers/lee.html

www.ideafinder.com/history/inventors/berners-lee.htm

The Face of the Web: Browsers, Websites, & Web Pages

A browser is software that gets you to websites and their individual web pages and displays the content in such a way that the content appears mostly the same regardless of the computer, operating system, and display monitor.

If the storybook character Rip Van Winkle had fallen asleep, instead of in the mid-1700s, in 1989—the year computer scientist Tim Berners-Lee developed the web software—and awoke today, he would be completely baffled by much of the vocabulary that we now encounter on a daily basis: *browser, website, web page, www.* Let's see how we would explain to him what these and similar web terms mean.

TECH TALES How a World-Shaking Technology Came About: Tim Berners-Lee Invents the World Wide Web

The son of British mathematicians employed on the team that built the early computer Manchester Mark I, Tim Berners-Lee was born in London and graduated from Oxford University's Queen's College, where he built a computer with a soldering iron.

In 1980, while an independent contractor at the Switzerland-based European Organization for Nuclear Research (CERN), Berners-Lee proposed a project based on the concept of hypertext (text with links, or references to other text), to facilitate sharing and updating information among researchers. With other researchers, he built a prototype system named Enquire.

After leaving CERN he took ideas similar to those used in Enquire to create what he then called the WorldWideWeb, for which he designed and built the first browser. The first website, which appeared as *http://info.cern.ch/* (still in operation under that name) and went online August 6, 1991, provided an explanation about what we now call the World Wide Web and how one could own a browser, set up a web server, and so on.

In 1994 Berners-Lee founded the World Wide Web Consortium (W3C) at the Massachusetts Institute of Technology. It comprised various companies willing to create standards and recommendations to improve the quality of the Internet. It was not until 2000 and 2001 that popular browsers began to support this standard.

For his pioneering work, Berners-Lee was knighted by Queen Elizabeth II in 2004. In 2009 he was elected to the United States National Academy of Sciences in Washington, D.C. ■

Sir Tim Berners-Lee. The British engineer and computer scientist devised the World Wide Web.

BROWSERS: SOFTWARE FOR SURFING THE WEB **A web browser, or *browser,* is software that enables you to find and access the various parts of the web.** As of early 2013, the most popular desktop browsers were Google's *Chrome* (36.5% global market share), Microsoft's *Internet Explorer* (30.1%), and Mozilla's *Firefox* (21.4%).[13] They are followed by Apple's *Safari* (8.29%) and Opera Software's *Opera* (1.19%). Technology observers were shocked when, in spring 2012, Google's Chrome suddenly toppled Internet Explorer as the most popular browser in the world, even though it does not come to consumers already loaded on computers, as Explorer and Safari do.[14] Like riding a wave on a surfboard, browsers allow you to **surf the web—to explore the World Wide Web by using your mouse to move via a series of connected paths, or *links,* from one location, or website, to another.**

Chrome

Firefox

Explorer

WEBSITE: THE LOCATION ON THE COMPUTER **A website, or simply *site,* is a location on a particular computer on the web that has a unique address** (called a *URL,* for Uniform Resource Locator, as we'll explain). If you decided to buy books online from bookseller Barnes & Noble, you would visit its website, *www.barnesandnoble.com*; the website is the location of a computer or group of computers somewhere on the Internet. The computers might be located in Barnes & Noble's offices, but they might be located somewhere else entirely.

WEB PAGES: THE DOCUMENTS ON A WEBSITE A website is composed of a web page or collection of related web pages. **A web page is a document on the World Wide Web that can include text, pictures, sound, and video.** The first page you see at a website is like the title page of a book. This is the **home page, the starting point, or the main page, of a website that contains links to other pages at the site.** *(• See Panel 2.6, next page.)* This page usually has some sort of table of contents on it and often describes the purpose of the site. If you have your own personal website, it might consist of just one page—the home page. Large websites have scores or even hundreds of pages.

Survival Tip

Do Home Pages Endure?

The contents of home pages often change. Or they may disappear, and so the connecting links to them in other web pages become links to nowhere. To find out how to view "dead" pages, go to:

http://web.ticino.com/multilingual/Search.htm

www.searchengineshowdown.com/others/archive.shtml

How the Browser Finds Things: URLs

URLs are Uniform Resource Locators, or web addresses.

Now let's look at the details of how the browser finds a particular web page.

panel 2.6

Home page

This is a website's first page, or welcome page.

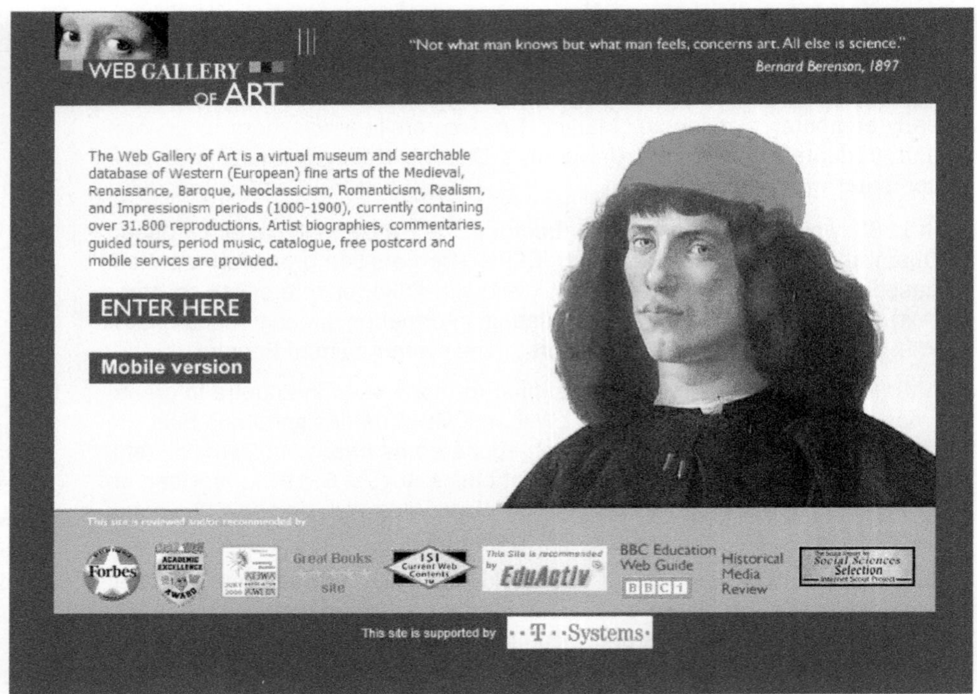

What Are the Best Web Pages?

StumbleUpon.com is a giant collection of the best pages on the Internet.

You tell the site your interests; it recommends websites, photos, and videos.

www.StumbleUpon.com/

URLS: ADDRESSES FOR WEB PAGES Before your browser can interpret a website and get you there, it needs to know the site's address, the URL. **The URL (Uniform Resource Locator) is a string of characters that points to a specific piece of information anywhere on the web.** In other words, the URL is the website's unique address.

A URL consists of (1) the web *protocol,* (2) the *domain name* or web server name, (3) the *directory name* (or folder) on that server, and (4) the *file* within that directory (perhaps with an extension, such as *html* or *htm*). Consider the following example of a URL for a website offered by the National Park Service for Yosemite National Park:

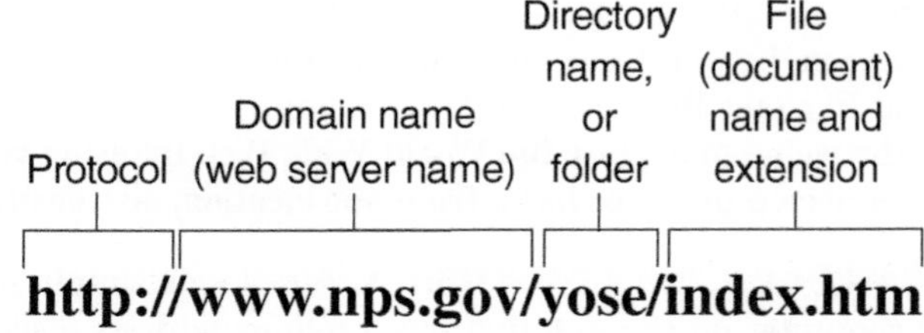

Let's look at these elements.

- **The protocol: http://** As mentioned, a protocol is a set of communication rules for exchanging information. The web protocol, HTTP, was developed by Tim Berners-Lee, and it appears at the beginning of some web addresses (as in *http://www.mcgraw-hill.com*). It stands for **Hypertext Transfer Protocol (HTTP), the communications rules that allow browsers to connect with web servers.** (Note: Most browsers assume that all web addresses begin with *http://*, and so you don't need to type this part; just start with whatever follows, such as *www.*)

  Often you will see *https://*, which refers to a secure, encrypted form of information transfer on the Internet. (Encryption is discussed in Chapter 6.)

- **The domain name (web server name): www.nps.gov/** **A domain is simply a location on the Internet, the particular web server.** Domain names tell the location and the type of address. Domain-name components are separated by periods (called "dots"). The last part of the domain, called the *top-level domain,* is usually a three-letter extension that describes the domain type: *.gov, .com, .net, .edu, .org, .mil, .int*—government, commercial, network, educational, nonprofit, military, or international organization. (Some extensions are longer.) In our example, the *www*

Domain Name	Authorized Users	Example
.aero	air-transport industry	*director@bigwings.aero*
.biz	businesses	*ceo@company.biz*
.com	originally commercial; now anyone can use	*editor@mcgraw-hill.com*
.coop	cooperative associations	*buyer@greatgroceries.coop*
.edu	postsecondary accredited educational and research institutions	*professor@harvard.edu*
.gov	U.S. government agencies and bureaus	*president@whitehouse.gov*
.info	generic information service providers	*contact@research.info*
.int	organizations established by international treaties between governments	*sectretary_general@unitednations.int*
.jobs	human resources managers	*AnnChu@Personnel.jobs*
.mil	U.S. military organizations	*chief_of_staff@pentagon.mil*
.mobi	providers of mobile products and services	*user@phonecompany.mobi*
.museum	museums	*curator@modernart.museum*
.name	individuals	*joe@smith.name*
.net	generic networking organizations	*contact@earthlink.net*
.org	generic organizations, often nonprofit and professional (noncommercial)	*director@redcross.org*
.post	Universal Postal Union*	*manager@UPS.post*
.pro	credentialed professionals & related entities	*auditor@accountant.pro*
tel.	For businesses and individuals to publish their contact data	*OurCorporationInfo@MyInc.tel*
.travel	travel industry	*JoeAgent@flyright.travel*
.xxx	adults-only websites	*proprietor@badtaste.xxx*

Note: The number of domain names is expanding; for a list of current domain names, go to *www.domainsherpa.com/top-level-domains/*.

Some groups pay $45,000 or more to ICANN for a particular domain name.

panel 2.7

Internet top-level domain abbreviations and users

stands for "World Wide Web," of course; the *.nps* stands for "National Park Service," and *.gov* is the top-level domain name indicating that this is a government website.

The meanings of other Internet top-level domain abbreviations appear in the box above *(• See Panel 2.7.)* Some top-level domain names also include a two-letter code extension for the country—for example, *.us* for United States, *.ca* for Canada, *.mx* for Mexico, *.uk* for United Kingdom, *.jp* for Japan, *.in* for India, *.cn* for China. These country codes are optional.

- **The directory name: yose/** The *directory* name is the name on the server for the directory, or folder, from which your browser needs to pull the file. Here it is *yose* for "Yosemite." For Yellowstone National Park, it is *yell.*
- **The file name and extension: index.htm** The *file* is the particular page or document that you are seeking. Here it is *index.htm,* because you have gone to the index page—the home page or welcome page—for Yosemite National Park. The *.htm* is an extension to the file name, and this extension informs the browser that the file is an HTML file. Let us consider what HTML means.

The Nuts & Bolts of the Web: HTML & Hyperlinks

HTML is the Internet's formatting language, and links allows users to jump easily around web pages.

The basic communications *protocol* that makes the Internet work, as we described, is *TCP/IP.* The communications protocol used to access that part of the Internet called the World Wide Web, we pointed out, is called *Hypertext Transfer Protocol (HTTP).* A hypertext document

Do You Need to Know HTML to Build a Website?

Most general web users do not need to know HTML. If you want to convert a word-processed document to HTML so that someone can post it on a website, applications such as Microsoft Word will convert it for you (for example, using the options "Save as, Web page"). Also, many website builders offer their services on the web; you can hire them to build a website for you. Many Internet access providers supply help with building websites and offer website storage on their servers to their subscribers.

If you want to learn more about HTML formatting, try these websites:

www.htmlcodetutorial.com/

www.w3schools.com/html/default.asp

uses *hypertext markup language (HTML),* which uses *hypertext links,* to connect with other documents. The foundations of the World Wide Web, then, are HTML and its hypertext links.

HYPERTEXT MARKUP LANGUAGE (HTML) Hypertext markup language (HTML) is the set of special instructions (called "tags" or "markups") that are used to specify document structure, formatting, and links to other multimedia documents on the web. Extensible hypertext markup language (XHTML) is the new and current version of HTML, a stricter version required by the fact that web content now needs to be delivered to smartphones and other devices that have fewer resources than traditional computers have.

HYPERTEXT LINKS Hypertext links—also called *hyperlinks, hotlinks,* or just links—are HTML connections to other documents or web pages that contain related information; a word or phrase in one document becomes a connection to a document in a different place. Hyperlinks usually appear as underlined or colored words and phrases. On a home page, for instance, the hyperlinks serve to connect the main page with other pages throughout the website. Other hyperlinks will connect to pages on other websites, whether located on a computer next door or one on the other side of the world.

An example of an HTML document with hyperlinks is shown below. (• *See Panel 2.8.)*

Using Your Browser to Get around the Web

A browser is software that interprets HTML and thus allows you to move around the web and to access, retrieve, and post information, including multimedia.

You can find almost anything you want on the approximately 13.34 billion indexed web pages available around the world.[15] Among the droplets of what amounts to a Niagara Falls of information: Weather maps and forecasts. Guitar chords. Recipe archives. Sports schedules. Daily newspapers in all languages. Nielsen television ratings. The Alcoholism Research Data Base. U.S. government phone numbers. The Central Intelligence Agency world map. The daily White House press releases. Radio stations. And on and on. But it takes a browser and various kinds of search tools to find and make any kind of sense of this enormous amount of data.

TECH TALES The Continuing Development of Browsers: The War for Smartphones & Tablets

In the 1990s, browser companies struggled for dominance of the personal computer, with Chrome, Internet Explorer, and Firefox coming out on top in 2013. Today it's all about which browsers will control the mobile world of small screens—of smartphones and tablets—which all rely on cloud computing, storing data and programs not in the devices themselves but on servers in massive data centers throughout the world.

"Browsers give Web companies more control over how people use their products and data about how people use the Web," says one technology writer. "Faster browsing leads to more Web activity, which in turn leads to more revenue for Web companies—whether searching on Google or shopping on Amazon.com."[16]

Google's Chrome, with 36% of the world's browser market, has the inside track for mobile browsing, although smaller companies, such as Rockmelt and Opera, are competing for market share. (Amazon also has a browser,

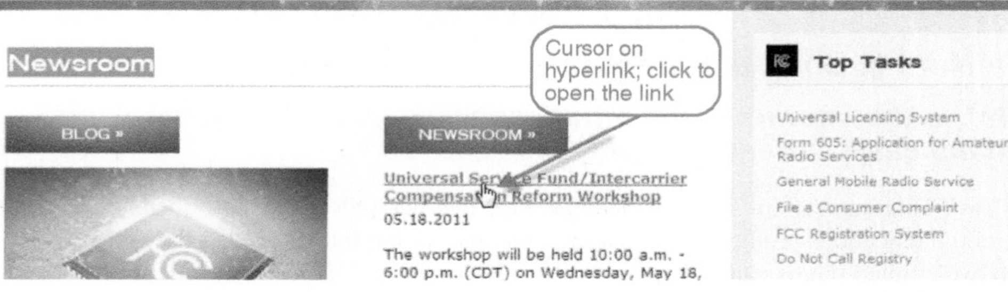

panel 2.8

An HTML document and hyperlinks

Using the mouse to click on the hyperlinked (underlined) text connects to another location in the same website or at a different site.

Silk, for its e-book, the Kindle.) What makes Chrome a particular threat is that it makes it easier to browse the web, makes searches faster and simpler, and offers popular apps like Gmail, as well as Drive for file storage and Docs for word processing. As mobile browsers become of better quality and more important, Google hopes that users will be able to do more complex things, such as shopping or playing games, on the mobile web. ■

BASIC ELEMENTS OF THE BROWSER If you buy a new computer, it will come with a browser already installed. Most browsers have a similar look and feel and similar navigational tools. Note that many web browser screens have a few basic elements: *menu bar, toolbar, address bar, workspace,* and *status bar.* To execute menu-bar and toolbar commands, you use the mouse to move the pointer over the word, known as a *menu selection,* and click the left button of the mouse. This will result in a pull-down menu of other commands for other options. (• *See Panel 2.9.*)

STARTING OUT FROM HOME: THE HOME PAGE The first page you see when you start up your browser is the *home page* or *start page.* (You can also start up from just a blank page, if you don't want to wait for the time it takes to connect with a home page.) You can choose any page on the web as your start page, but a good start page offers links to sites you want to visit frequently. Often you may find that the Internet access provider with which you arrange your Internet connection will provide its own start page. However, you can customize it to make it your own personal home page—just follow your browser's instructions for personalizing.

GETTING AROUND: BACK, FORWARD, HOME, & SEARCH FEATURES Driving in a foreign city (or even Boston or San Francisco) can be an interesting experience in which street names change, turns lead into unknown neighborhoods, and signs aren't always evident, so that soon you have no idea where you are. That's what the Internet is like, although on a far more massive scale. Fortunately, your browser toolbar provides navigational aids. (• *See Panel 2.10, next page.*) *Back* takes you back to the previous page. *Forward* lets you look again at a page you returned from. If you really get lost, you can start over by clicking on *Home,* which returns you to your home page. *Search* lists various other search tools, as we will describe. Other navigational aids are *history lists* and *favorites* or *bookmarks.*

HISTORY LISTS If you are browsing through many web pages, it can be difficult to keep track of the locations of the pages you've already visited. The *history list* allows you to quickly return to the pages you have recently visited. (• *See Panel 2.11, next page.*)

BOOKMARKS OR FAVORITES One great helper for finding your way is the Bookmarks or Favorites feature, which lets you store the URLs of web pages you frequently visit so that you don't have to remember and retype your favorite addresses. (• *See Panel 2.12, page 69.*)

panel 2.9

Common browser tools and functions

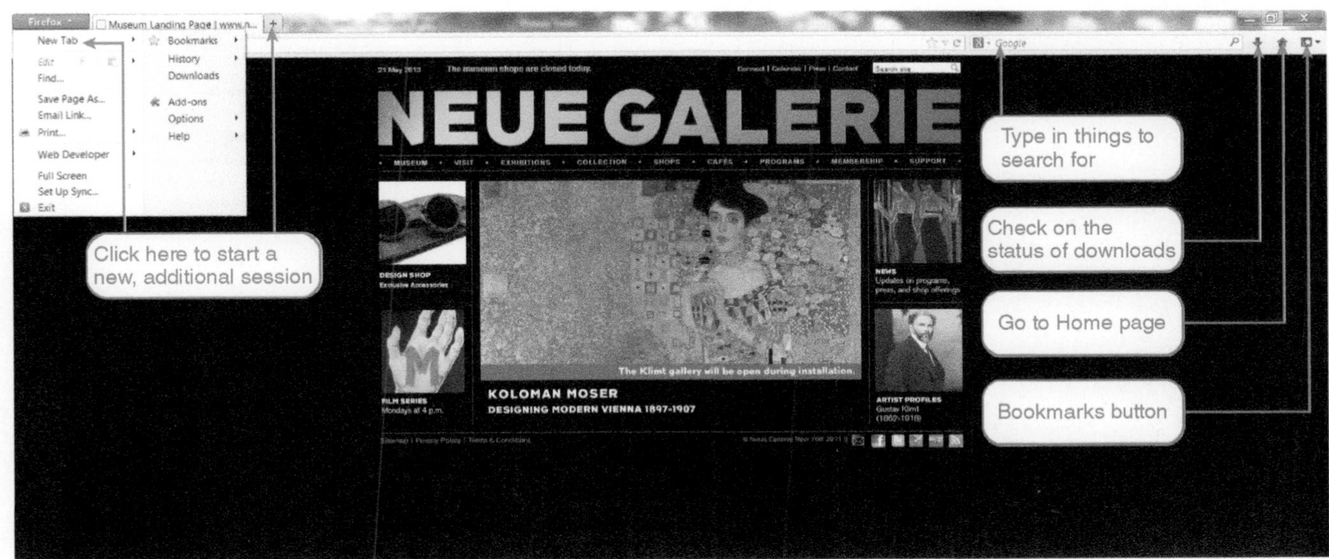

panel 2.10

More information on common browser functions (icons vary according to the browser)

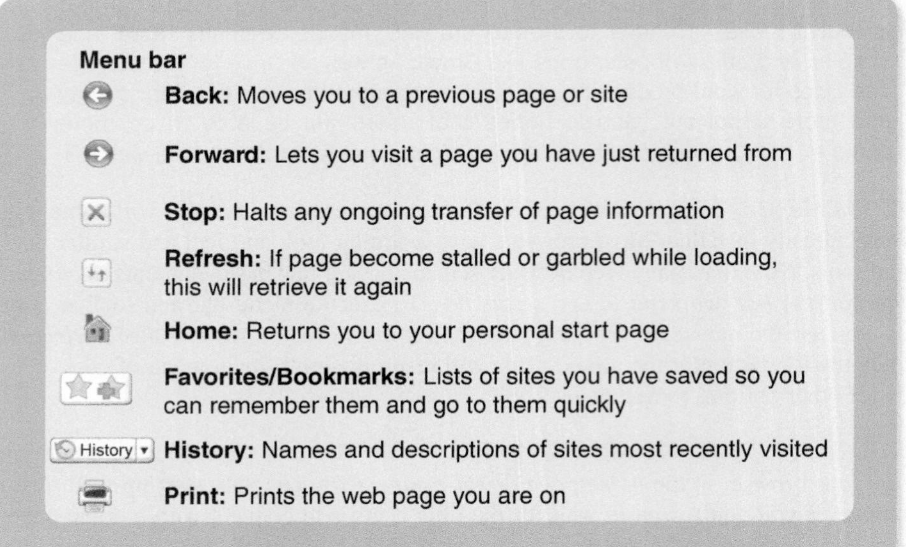

Menu bar

Back: Moves you to a previous page or site

Forward: Lets you visit a page you have just returned from

Stop: Halts any ongoing transfer of page information

Refresh: If page become stalled or garbled while loading, this will retrieve it again

Home: Returns you to your personal start page

Favorites/Bookmarks: Lists of sites you have saved so you can remember them and go to them quickly

History: Names and descriptions of sites most recently visited

Print: Prints the web page you are on

---

panel 2.11

History list

Returning to a previously viewed site in Firefox or Chrome

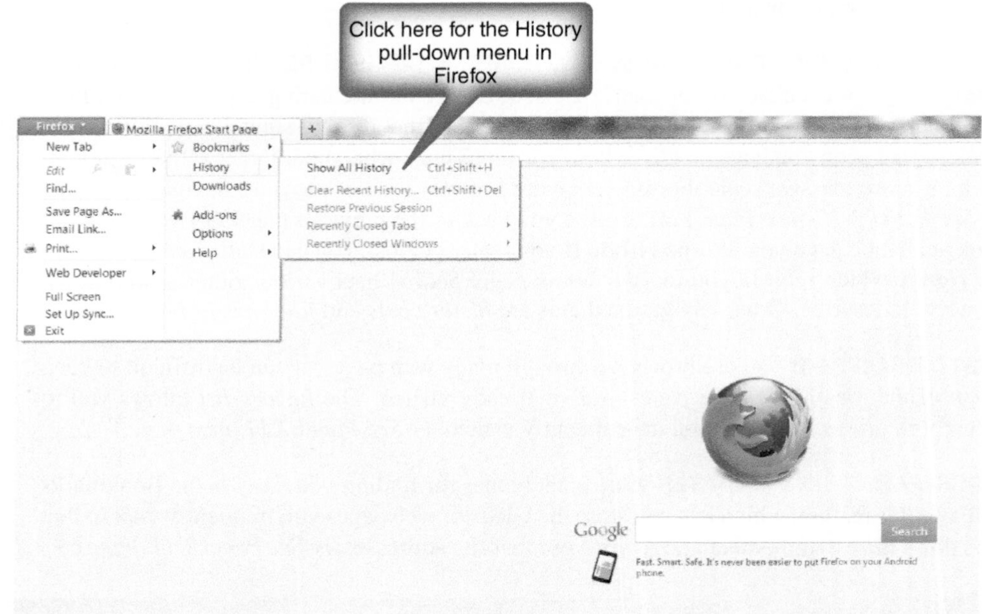

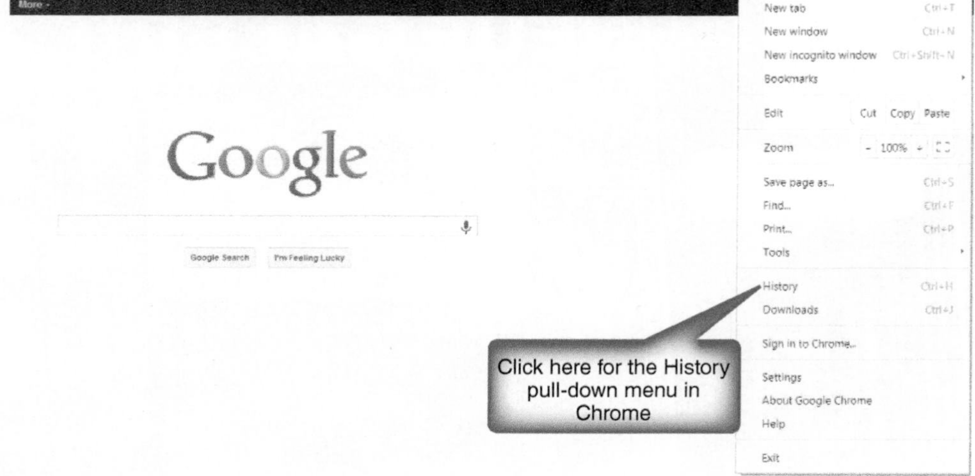

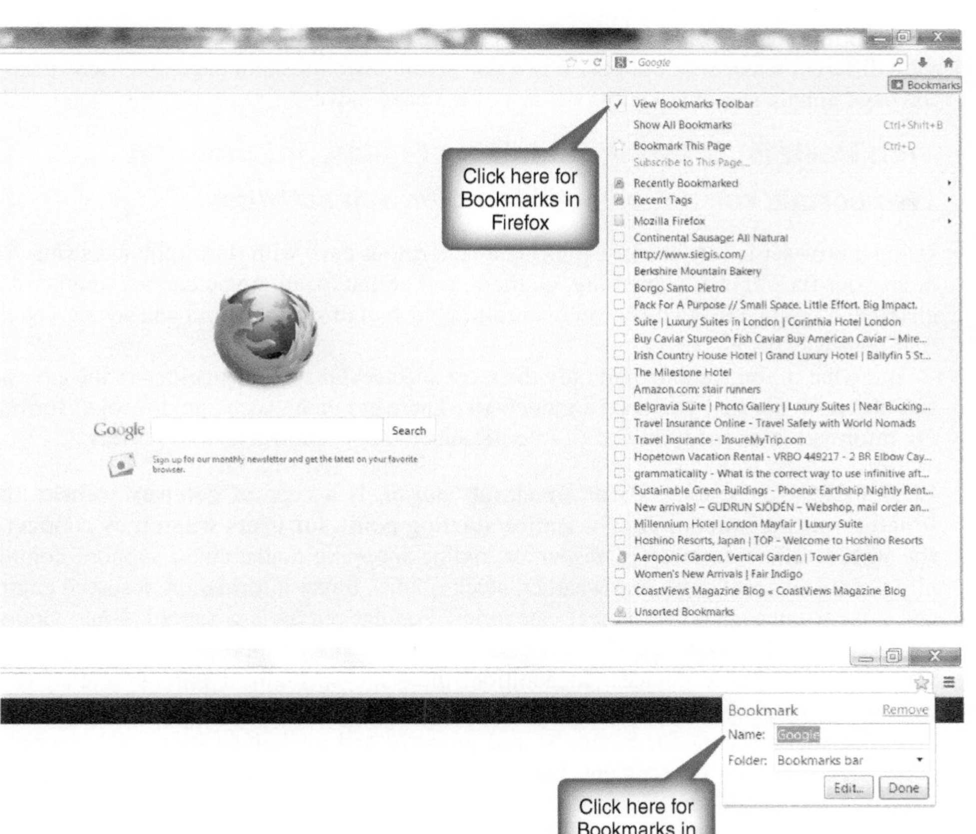

panel 2.12

Favorites

If you are at a website you may want to visit again, click on *Bookmarks* (in Firefox) and choose *Add to Bookmarks.* Later, to revisit the site, go to the Favorites menu, and the site's URL will reappear. In Google Chrome, click on the bookmark star.

In Chrome, for example, you can click on the *Bookmarks* symbol (a star) while visiting a site you might want to come back to, which automatically stores the address. In Internet Explorer you click on *Favorites* (*Bookmarks* in Firefox), which displays the URL on your screen, and then click on *Add.* Later you can locate the site name on your *Bookmarks/Favorites* menu and click on it, and the site will reappear.

INTERACTIVITY: HYPERLINKS, RADIO BUTTONS, & TEXT BOXES For any given web page that you happen to find yourself on, there may be several ways to interact with it. (• *See Panel 2.13.*) Here are three common ways:

1. By using your mouse to click on the hyperlinks, which will transfer you to another web page.
2. By using your mouse to click on a *radio button* and then clicking on a *Submit* command or pressing the *Enter* key. **Radio buttons are little circles located in front of various options; selecting an option with the mouse places a dot in the corresponding circle.**
3. By typing text in a **text box** and then hitting the *Enter* key, or clicking on a *Go* or *Continue* command, which will transfer you to another web page.

SCROLLING & FRAMES To the bottom and side of your screen display you will note **scroll arrows, small up/down and left/right arrows. Clicking on scroll arrows with your mouse pointer moves the screen so that you can see the rest of the web page, a movement known as scrolling.** You can also use the arrow keys on your keyboard for scrolling.

Some web pages are divided into different rectangles known as *frames,* each with its own scroll arrows. **A frame is an independently**

panel 2.13

Radio buttons and text box

Radio buttons

Act like station selector buttons on a car radio

Page range
All
Current page
Selection
Pages:
Enter page numbers and/or page ranges separated by commas. For example, 1,3,5–12

Search (text) boxes

Require you to type in information

Pages: 17-33

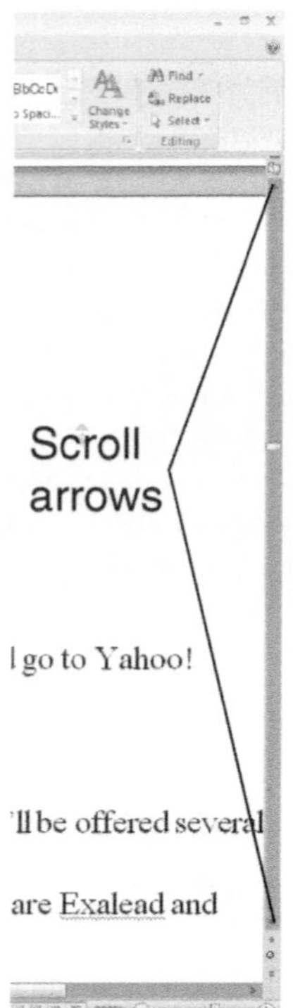

controllable section of a web page. A web page can be divided into separate frames, each with different features or options. When you scroll down the main page, the frame parts of the page remain stationary while the rest of the page moves.

Web Portals: Starting Points for Finding Information

Web portals can act as organizers for web activities.

Using a browser is sort of like exploring an enormous cave with flashlight and string. You point your flashlight at something, go there, and at that location you can see another cave chamber to go to; meanwhile, you're unrolling the ball of string behind you so that you can find your way back.

But what if you want to visit only the most spectacular rock formations in the cave and skip the rest? For that you need a guidebook. There are many such "guidebooks" for finding information on the web, sort of Internet superstations known as *web portals.*

WEB PORTALS **A web portal, or simply *portal,* is a type of gateway website that functions as an "anchor site," a major starting point, for users when they connect to the web.** It offers an array of resources, online shopping malls, email support, community forums, current news and weather, stock quotes, travel information, a search engine, and links to other popular subject categories. Popular portals are Yahoo!, Bing, Google, Lycos, and AOL. There are also *wireless portals,* such as Yahoo! Mobile, designed for web-enabled portable devices. In addition, there are specialized portals—called *vertical portals,* or *vortals,* which focus on specific narrow audiences or communities—such as PoliceAuctions.com for buying seized property and unclaimed property from police departments and the government, Fool.com for investors, and Searchnetworking.techtarget.com for network administrators.

WHAT TO DO ON A PORTAL In general, when you access a portal, you can do three things: (1) check the home page for general information, such as news and weather; (2) use the directory to find a topic you want, or (3) type a **keyword—the subject word or words of the topic you wish to find**—into a search text box to search for a topic. (● *See Panel 2.14.)*

Search Services & Search Engines & How They Work

Search engines collect and organize information from all over the web.

Search services are organizations that maintain databases accessible through websites to help you find information on the Internet. Examples are not only parts of portals

Survival Tip

Finding Things on a Web Page or in a Web Document

When you are on a web page or in a document, type Ctrl + F to bring up a text box on your screen. Type in a word or words that relate to what you are looking for, and hit Enter. You will be taken to the first occurrence of the words. Keep hitting Enter, and you will be taken to subsequent appearances of the words.

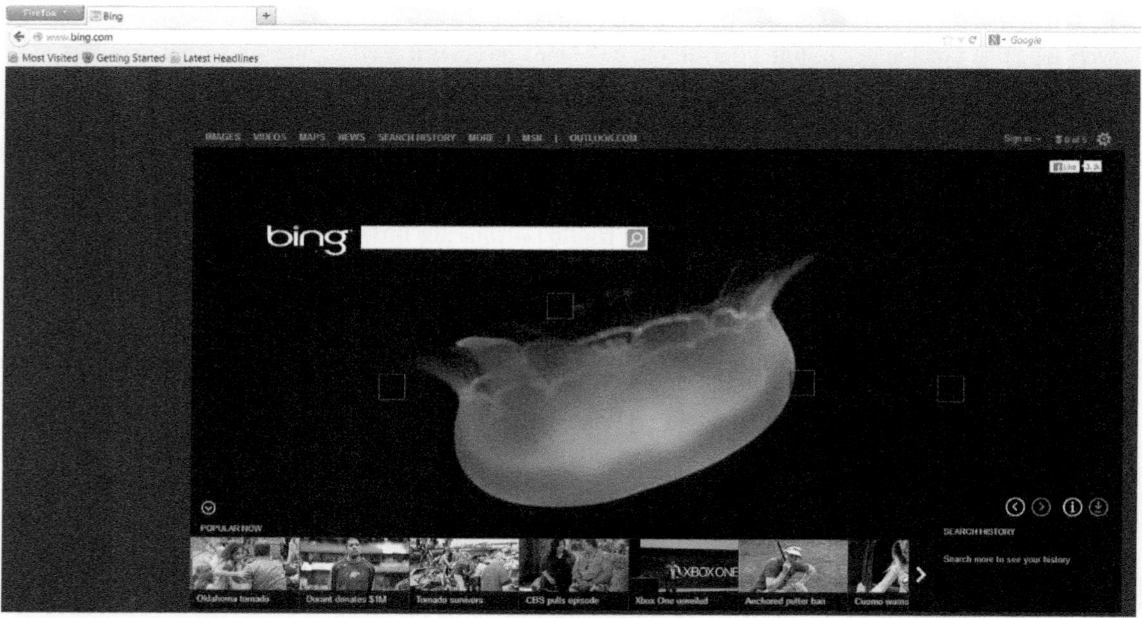

Bing is a popular web portal.

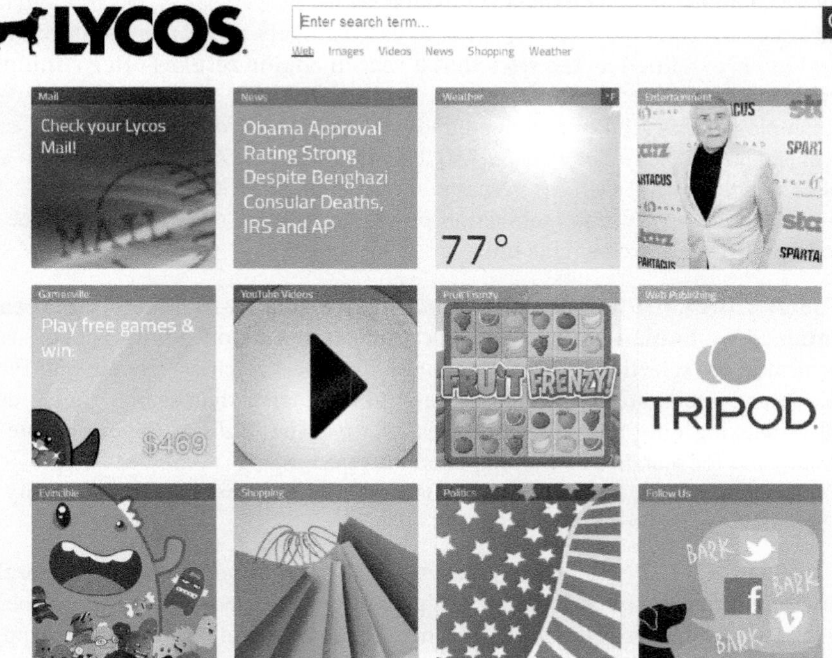

panel 2.14

Lycos home page
You can read headlines for news and weather, use the directory to find a topic, or use keywords in the Search text box to research specific topics.

Survival Tip

Urban Legends & Lies on the Internet

To check the veracity of material on the Internet, go to www.snopes.com, which lists, according to category, information circulated on the Internet that isn't true. Each category includes a key to color-coded bullets that precede each entry; the color lets you know how much truth there is to each item: Green = true; red = false; yellow = undetermined; white = unclassifiable.

such as Yahoo! and Bing but also Google, Ask.com, and Gigablast, to name just a few. Search services also maintain **search engines, programs that enable you to ask questions or use keywords to help locate information on the web.**

Search services compile their databases by using special programs called **spiders—also known as *crawlers, bots* (for "robots"), or *agents*—that crawl through the World Wide Web, following links from one web page to another and indexing the words on that site.** Spiders feed pages to search engines.

This method of gathering information has two important implications.

A SEARCH NEVER COVERS THE ENTIRE WEB Whenever you are doing a search with a search engine, you are never searching the entire web. As one writer points out: "You are actually searching a portion of the Web, captured in a fixed index created at an earlier date."[17] (An exception: Some news databases, such as Yahoo! News and Google Breaking News, offer up-to-the-minute reports on a number of subjects.) In addition, you should realize that there are a lot of databases whose material is not publicly available. Finally, a lot of published material from the 1970s and earlier has never been scanned into databases and made available.

SEARCH ENGINES DIFFER IN WHAT THEY COVER Search engines list their results according to some kind of relevance ranking, and different search engines use different ranking schemes. Some search engines, for instance, rank web pages according to popularity (frequency of visits by people looking for a particular keyword), but others don't.

Four Web Search Tools: Individual Search Engines, Subject Directories, Metasearch Engines, & Specialized Search Engines

Web users should learn how to use the main types of search tools.

There are many types of search tools, but the most popular versions can be categorized as (1) *individual search engines,* (2) *subject directories,* (3) *metasearch engines,* and (4) *specialized search engines.* The most popular search sites, measured in share of visitors, are Google, Yahoo!, Bing, and Ask.

INDIVIDUAL SEARCH ENGINES An individual search engine compiles its own searchable database on the web. You search for information by typing one or more

Who's Killing Organic Search?

In a search, results that pop up naturally are called "organic," because they are directly relevant to the search keyword(s). However, more and more search results are taken up by ads ("sponsored" and "featured" results) and product listings:

http://wiki.answers.com/Q/What_are_organic_search_results_and_inorganic_search_results

http://searchenginewatch.com/article/2282508/Organic-vs.-Paid-Listings-Do-Users-Know-the-Difference

keywords, and the search engine then displays a list of web pages, or "hits," that contain those keywords, ordered from most likely to least likely to contain the information you want. **Hits are defined as the sites that a search engine returns after running a keyword search.**

Examples of this kind of search engine are Ask, Bing, Google, and Yahoo!, as well as Gigablast and Lycos. *(• See Panel 2.15.)* The search engine Ask allows users to ask questions in a natural way, such as, "What is the population of the United States?" Answers.com is a site-and-software combination providing instant "one-click" reference answers rather than lists of search engine links.

SUBJECT DIRECTORIES Unlike a search engine, **a subject directory is created and maintained by human editors, not electronic spiders, and allows you to search for information by selecting lists of categories or topics,** such as "Health and Fitness" or "Science and Technology." Directories tend to be smaller than search engine databases, usually indexing only the top-level pages of a website. Subject directories are best for browsing and for searches of a more general nature.

Examples of subject directories are Beaucoup!, LookSmart, Open Directory Project, and Yahoo! Directory. *(• See Panel 2.16.)*

METASEARCH ENGINES A metasearch engine allows you to search several search engines simultaneously. Metasearch engines are very fast and can give you a good picture of what's available across the web and where it can be found. Examples are Yippy!, Dogpile, Mamma, MetaCrawler, and Webcrawler. *(• See Panel 2.17.)*

SPECIALIZED SEARCH ENGINES There are also *specialized search engines,* which help locate specialized subject matter, such as material about movies, health, and jobs. These overlap with the specialized portals, or vortals, that we discussed above. *(• See Panel 2.18.)*

panel 2.15

Some individual search engines (see also *www.searchengineguide.com/*)

Search Tool	Site
Answers.com	*www.answers.com*
Ask	*www.ask.com*
Bing	*www.bing.com*
Gigablast	*www.gigablast.com*
Lycos	*www.lycos.com*
Yahoo!	*www.yahoo.com*

panel 2.16

Some subject directories

Search Tool	Site
Beaucoup!	*www.beaucoup.com*
Google Directory	*http://directory.google.com*
Open Directory Project	*www.dmoz.org*
Yahoo! Directory	*http://dir.yahoo.com*

panel 2.17

Some metasearch engines

Search Tool	Site
Clusty	*http://clusty.com*
Dogpile	*www.dogpile.com*
Grokker	*www.grokker.com*
Kartoo	*www.kartoo.com*
Mamma	*www.mamma.com*
MetaCrawler	*www.metacrawler.com*
Webcrawler	*www.webcrawler.com*
Zuula	*www.zuula.com*

Search Tool	Site
Career.com (jobs)	*www.career.com*
Expedia (travel)	*www.expedia.com*
Internet Movie Database (movies)	*www.imdb.com*
Monster Board (jobs)	*www.monster.com*
Motley Fool (personal investments)	*www.fool.com*
U.S. Census Bureau (statistics)	*www.census.gov*
WebMD (health)	*www.webmd.com*

panel 2.18

Some specialized search engines

Smart Searching: Three General Strategies

Learn a few searching basics to help speed up your searches.

The phrase "trying to find a needle in a haystack" will come annoyingly to mind the first time you type a word into a search engine and back comes a response on the order of "63,173 listings found." Clearly, it becomes mandatory that you have a strategy for narrowing your search. The following are some tips.

Generalized Lists of Search Engines

www.thesearchenginelist.com/

http://searchenginewatch.com/2156241

www.20search.com/

IF YOU'RE JUST BROWSING—TWO STEPS If you're just trying to figure out what's available in your subject area, do as follows:

- **Try a subject directory:** First try using a subject directory, such as Yahoo! Directory or Open Directory Project.
- **Try a metasearch engine:** Next enter your search keywords into a metasearch engine, such as Dogpile or Mamma—just to see what else is out there.

  Example: You could type "*search engine tutorial.*"

IF YOU'RE LOOKING FOR SPECIFIC INFORMATION If you're looking for specific information, you can try Answers.com "one-click" search (*www.answers.com*). Or you can go to a major search engine such as Google or Yahoo! and then go to a specialized search engine.

Example: You could type *"Life expectancy in U.S."* first into Google and then into the Centers for Disease Control and Prevention's search engine (*www.cdc.gov*).

IF YOU'RE LOOKING FOR EVERYTHING YOU CAN FIND ON A SUBJECT If you want to gather up everything you can find on a certain subject, try the same search on several search engines.

Example: You could type *"pogonip"* (a type of dense winter fog) into more than one search tool. (Of course, you will probably get some irrelevant responses, so it helps to know how to narrow your search, as explained in the box on page 75.)

Wikipedia Problems

http://wikipediocracy.com/press-release/

http://isites.harvard.edu/icb/icb.do?keyword=k70847&pageid=icb.page346376

www.npr.org/2012/02/22/147261659/gauging-the-reliability-of-facts-on-wikipedia/

http://edudemic.com/2012/10/teachers-guide-to-wikipedia/

WHAT ABOUT WIKIS & WIKIPEDIA? *Wiki* is a word that founding programmer Ward Cunningham got from the Hawaiian term for "quick" ("wiki wiki") when he created the WikiWiki Web in 1995. **A wiki is a simple piece of software that can be downloaded for free and used to make a website** (also called a wiki) **that can be corrected or added to by anyone.** Thus, for example, some corporations use business wikis for cross-company collaboration, such as a Word document memo that is worked on by several coworkers simultaneously. That use of wikis is valuable.

Want to begin research on a topic you know nothing about? You could try the immensely popular Wikipedia (*http://en.wikipedia.org*). *Wikipedia* is a free online encyclopedia that anyone around the world can contribute to or edit. It has more than 25 million articles in more than 285 languages; over 4.1 million articles appear in the English Wikipedia alone.

Unfortunately, *Wikipedia is not considered reliable or authoritative by academics and librarians.* As Ohio State University lecturer Larry Sanger, former Wikipedia editor in chief, says, "The wide-open nature of the Internet encourages people to disregard the importance of expertise." As a result, Sanger does not allow his students to use Wikipedia for their papers.[18]

One of the primary concerns about Wikipedia is that it is openly edited—anyone can change or update entries. Although many "Wikipedians" spend hours of volunteer time

panel 2.19

Some multimedia search engines

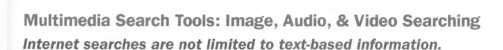

Search Tool	Site
Blinkx	*www.blinkx.com*
Digital Library System	*www.fws.gov/dls*
Find Sounds	*www.findsounds.com/types.html*
Google Video	*www.google.com/videohp*
Internet Archive for Audio	*www.archive.org/details/audio*
Internet Archive for Moving Images	*www.archive.org/details/movies*
Picsearch	*www.picsearch.com*
The University of Delaware Library	*www.lib.udel.edu/filmandvideo/*
Yahoo! Video	*http://video.yahoo.com*

Citing Web Sources in College Papers

The four principal kinds of styles for citing sources—books, articles, and so on—are (1) the Modern Language Association (MLA) style (for humanities), (2) the American Psychological Association (APA) style (for social science subjects), (3) the University of Chicago's *Chicago Manual of Style (CMS),* and (4) the Turabian style. Your instructor/professor will tell you which style guide to use. To learn the format of these styles—including those for Internet sources—go to:

www.apastyle.org/apa-style-help.aspx

http://owl.english.purdue.edu/owl/resource/747/01/

http://citationmachine.net/

www.easybib.com/

www.libraries.psu.edu/psul/researchguides/citationstyles.html

Collaborative Categorization

Some "social bookmarking" or photo-sharing web services with tagging features:

BlinkList www.blinklist.com

Delicious www.delicious.com

eBiz www.ebizmba.com/articles/social-bookmarking-websites

squidoo www.squidoo.com

Flickr www.flickr.com

maintaining the site, even Jimmy Wales, the site's cofounder, says that neither Wikipedia nor any other encyclopedia should be used as an academic source.[19] In general, Wikipedia should be regarded only as a starting point for additional specialized research.

Multimedia Search Tools: Image, Audio, & Video Searching

Internet searches are not limited to text-based information.

Most web searches involve text, but there are many nontext kinds of resources as well, including videos and still images. (• *See Panel 2.19.*)

STILL IMAGES Interested in particular photos? You could go to Yahoo! Search–Image Search (*images.search.yahoo.com*), Google Image Search (*http://images.google.com*), or Bing Images (*www.bing.com/images*), where you'll be offered several million choices of photos and other images. Other good image search engines are listed on Fagan Finder (*www.faganfinder.com/img/*).

AUDIO & VIDEO Other multimedia search engines offer audio as well as image and video searching. ShadowTV, for instance, can provide continuous access to live and archived television content via the web. Yahoo! allows users to search for closed captioning associated with a broadcast and then to click for full-motion video of the words being spoken.

Among the audio search engines available are Yahoo! Music, Lycos MP3 Search, AltaVista Audio Search, BlogDigger, FindSounds, and Blinkx. Among video search engines you can select from are AOL.video, AlltheWeb, the Open Video Project, AltaVista Video, Yahoo! Video Search, Google Video Search, and Blinkx Video Search.

SCHOLARLY Google offers Google Scholar (*http://scholar.google.com/advanced_scholar_search*), described as "a one-stop shop of scholarly abstracts, books, peer-reviewed papers, and technical papers intended for academics and scientists."[20]

Google has also launched an ambitious project, the Google Books Library Project (*www.google.com/googlebooks/library.html*), in which it is scanning page by page more than 50 million books (at a cost of about $10 for each book scanned) from many libraries—for example, at Harvard, Stanford, Oxford, Columbia University, the Austrian National Library, the University of Michigan, Keio University Library (Japan), and the New York Public Library. Because of copyright issues, most scanned books are those that are out of copyright; however, Google Books is known to scan books still protected under copyright unless the publisher specifically excludes them. Thus the Google Project is being studied by the U.S. Justice Department to see if massive book scanning violates antitrust laws, since authors, campus researchers, and library groups have expressed serious concerns over the move.[21]

Tagging: Saving Links for Easier Retrieval Later

Tags help you find your favorite websites again.

Once you've found favorite websites, how do you keep them found so that you can get back to them easily? You can always use the bookmarking or favorites feature, but there

PRACTICAL ACTION

Evaluating & Sourcing Information Found on the Web

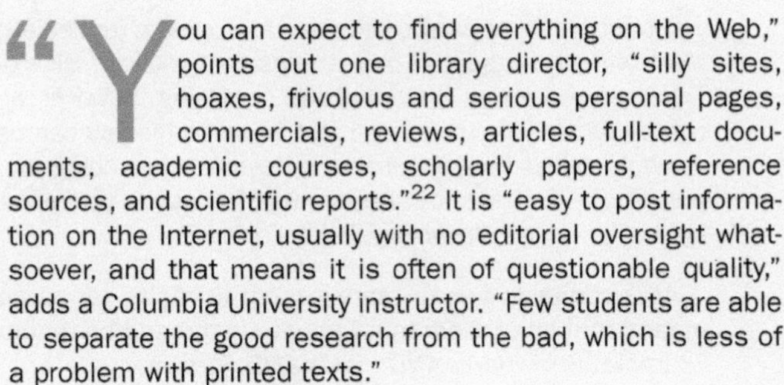

"You can expect to find everything on the Web," points out one library director, "silly sites, hoaxes, frivolous and serious personal pages, commercials, reviews, articles, full-text documents, academic courses, scholarly papers, reference sources, and scientific reports."[22] It is "easy to post information on the Internet, usually with no editorial oversight whatsoever, and that means it is often of questionable quality," adds a Columbia University instructor. "Few students are able to separate the good research from the bad, which is less of a problem with printed texts."

Guidelines for Evaluating Web Resources

If you're relying on web sources for research for a term paper, how do you determine what's useful and what's not? Here are some ways to assess credibility of the information you find there:[23]

- **On what kind of website does the information appear?** Websites may be *professional sites,* maintained by recognized organizations and institutions. They may be *news and journalistic sites,* which may be anything from *The New York Times* to e-zines (electronic magazines, or small web-based publications) such as *Network Audio Bits.* They may be *commercial sites,* sponsored by companies ranging from the Disney Company to The Happy House Painter. They may be *special-interest sites,* maintained by activists ranging from those of the major political parties to proponents of legalization of marijuana. They may be *blogs* or *personal home pages,* maintained by individuals of all sorts, from professors to children to struggling musicians.
- **Does the website author appear to be a legitimate authority?** What kind of qualifications and credentials does the author have, and what kind of organization is he or she associated with? Does a web search show that the author published in other scholarly and professional publications?
- **Is the website objective, complete, and current?** Is the website trying to sell you on a product, service, or point of view? Is the language balanced and objective, or is it one-sided and argumentative? Does the author cite sources, and do they seem to come from responsible publications?

A variant on these guidelines has been framed by Butler University librarian Brad Matthies as CRITIC. (• See Panel 2.20.)

- *C—Claim:* Is the source's claim clear and reasonable, timely and relevant? Or is there evidence of motivationally based language?
- *R—Role of the claimant:* Is the author of the information clearly identifiable? Are there reasons to suspect political, religious, philosophical, cultural, or financial biases?
- *I—Information backing the claim*: Is evidence for the claim presented? Can it be verified, or is the evidence anecdotal or based on testimony? Does the author cite credible references?
- *T—Testing:* Can you test the claim, as by conducting your own quantitative research?
- *I—Independent verification:* Have reputable experts evaluated and verified the claim?
- *C—Conclusion:* After taking the preceding five steps, can you reach a conclusion about the claim?

Source: Adapted from Brad Matthies, "The Psychologist, the Philosopher, and the Librarian: The Information-Literacy Version of CRITIC, "*Skeptical Inquirer*, May/June 2005, pp. 49–52.

panel 2.20

CRITIC

These guidelines will help you think critically about the reliability of online information.

is also another way called *tagging.* **Tags are do-it-yourself labels that people can put on anything found on the Internet, from articles to photos to videos.** Using so-called social-bookmarking websites such as delicious.com or BlinkList or photo-sharing services such as Flickr, users can tag anything for easy retrieval later. Unlike bookmarks or favorites, these tags can be shared easily with other people, which allows people to share similar interests and ideas.

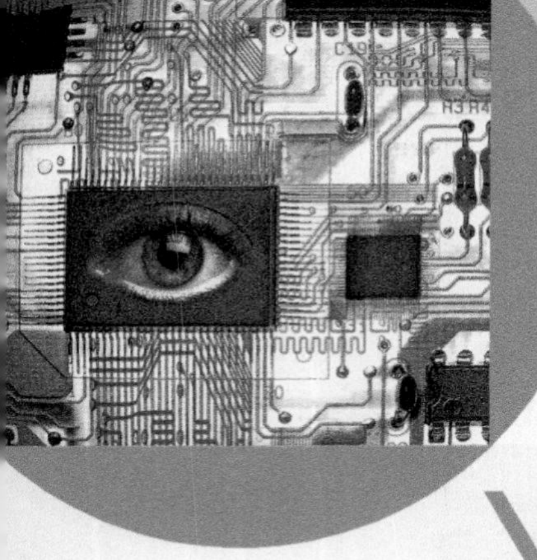

PRACTICAL ACTION

Serious Web Search Techniques

You type *Steve Jobs* into Google on a particular day and get more than 1 million hits; in Yahoo!, 85,900,000. How useful is that? Following are some tips for efficient searching:

- **Choose your search terms well, and watch your spelling:** Use the most precise words possible. If you're looking for information about novelist Thomas Wolfe (author of *Look Homeward Angel,* published 1929) rather than novelist-journalist Tom Wolfe (author of *Back to Blood,* 2012), details are important: *Thomas,* not *Tom; Wolfe,* not *Wolf.*

  Use *poodle* rather than *dog, Maui* rather than *Hawaii, Martin guitar* rather than *guitar,* or you'll get thousands of responses that have little or nothing to do with what you're looking for. You may need to use alternative words and spellings to explore the topic you're investigating: *e-mail, email, electronic mail.* And remember that searching is repetitive (iterative)—that is, you may have to do many searches to narrow down your search terms efficiently in order to get the kind of results you want.
- **Type words in lowercase:** When it's appropriate, typing words in lowercase will help you to find both lowercase and capitalized variations.
- **Use phrases with quotation marks rather than separate words, and add a keyword:** If you type *land of the free,* you could be referred to (1) a State Department report on individual rights, (2) the national anthem of Belize, (3) an album by a German power metal band, and (4) a foundation that supports military veterans—*before* you get to the lyrics to the "Star Spangled Banner." Sometimes it's better, therefore, to put your phrase in quotation marks and add a keyword or phrase—*"land of the free" U.S. anthem*—to narrow your search.
- **Put unique words first in a phrase:** Better to have *"Tom Wolfe novels"* rather than *"Novels Tom Wolfe."* Or if you're looking for the Hoagy Carmichael song rather than the southern U.S. state, indicate *"Georgia on My Mind."*
- **Use Boolean operators—AND, OR, and NOT:** Most new search tools eliminate the need for operators, because when you start typing keywords the search programs immediately start offering suggested possibilities that you can click on. This feature can be annoying and confusing, however, and can be turned off. Thus with most search sites you can use symbols called *Boolean operators* to make searching more precise. To illustrate how they are used, suppose you're looking for the song "Strawberry Fields Forever."

  AND connects two or more search words or terms and means that all of them must appear in the search results. Example: *Strawberry AND Fields AND Forever.*

  OR connects two or more search terms but indicates that either of the two may appear in the results. Example: *Strawberry Fields OR Strawberry OR Fields.*

  NOT, when inserted before a word, excludes that word from the results. Example: *Strawberry Fields NOT W.C.* (to distinguish from the long-ago comedian W.C. Fields).
- **Use wildcards—asterisks (*) and question marks (?):** If you want as many results as possible on a keyword, use an asterisk (*) or question mark (?) to mean "anything/everything."

  Example: Type *dance** and you will get hits for *dance, dances, dancers, dancing, dancewear,* and so on.

  If you can't remember how to spell something, use the question mark (?). Example: If you type *Solzhe?* you will get page matches for the Russian author *Solzhenitsyn.*
- **Read the Help or Search Tips section:** All search sites provide a Help section and tips. This could save you time later.
- **Try an alternative general search site or a specific search site:** As we indicated in the text, if you're looking for very specific information, a general type of search site such as Yahoo! may not be the best way to go. Instead, you should turn to a specific search site. Examples: For news stories, try Google News (*http://news.google.com*), Yahoo! News (*http://news.yahoo.com*), or CNN (*www.cnn.com*). For pay-per-view information from all sorts of articles, journals, and reports, try LexisNexis (*www.lexisnexis.com*) and Factiva (Dow Jones at *www.factiva.com*).

UNIT 2B: *The Riches & Risks of Internet Use*

New apps, websites, and other Internet uses appear almost daily, adding richness and variety to our experience—and many dangers as well. Let us consider both these sides of cyberspace technology, starting with email and instant messages.

2.4 EMAIL, INSTANT MESSAGING, & OTHER WAYS OF COMMUNICATING OVER THE NET

Email still has many uses, in many different contexts; other ways of communicating on the Internet include FTP, newsgroups, listservs, and chat.

From his rural home in northern California, Jake sends (via telephone modem) Maria in New York an email message ("Received the package. What a fantastic gift! Thank you!") that arrives instantly—or maybe, unaccountably, a day later. (We expect email to be immediate, but it can get hung up in transit for all kinds of technical reasons.) On its way to Maria, Jake's outgoing email went first to his Internet access provider's local point of presence (POP), then to a *Simple Mail Transfer Protocol (SMTP) server,* which broke down the message into multiple packets and sent each packet by a separate route to the destination, where they were regrouped into a coherent message for Maria. (• *See Panel 2.21.)*

Jake's ISP
(SMTP server)
Internet Exchange
Point (IXP)
Cable
company
Maria's
ISP
Regional
network
Routers
Routers
POP3
POP
Telephone
company
Internet Exchange Point
(IXP)
Jake
Maria
1 Jake on the West Coast logs into his dial-up ISP and sends an email message to Maria on the East Coast.
2 In this case, the message travels from Jake's computer over a standard telephone line to his ISP's local POP (point of presence). From there, the message is sent to an SMTP (Simple Mail Transfer Protocol) server used to send outgoing mail.
3 The SMTP server breaks down the message into multiple packets that take different routes to their eventual destination. The packets are forwarded by routers and may travel over faster regional networks before eventually ending up on one of several high-speed Internet backbones.
4 The packets are eventually routed off the backbone and delivered to the proper email server at Maria's ISP. The packets are reassembled to re-create the message.
5 Maria uses her cable modem to connect to the Internet. When she checks her email, she is sending a request from her PC to the CMTS (Cable-Modem Termination System), which connects her to her ISP's network.
6 Maria's ISP routes the "check email" request to its POP3 (Post Office Protocol 3) email server where messages are temporarily stored. The POP3 server sends Jake's email message to Maria's PC, along with other waiting messages.
Key to Connection types
Regular phone lines
DSL
Cable
Satellite
T1, T2, T3 Lines
Fiber-optic cable

When Maria went on her computer to retrieve her email messages, her "check email" request went to her Internet access provider's *mail server* storing her incoming emails. Jake's message, stored on the mail server, was sent to Maria's computer using Post Office Protocol version 3 (POP3—not the same as "point of presence," p. 60). (Some mail servers use an improvement on POP3 called IMAP, for Internet Message Access Protocol, which allows users to have a preview look at their email messages on the mail server and

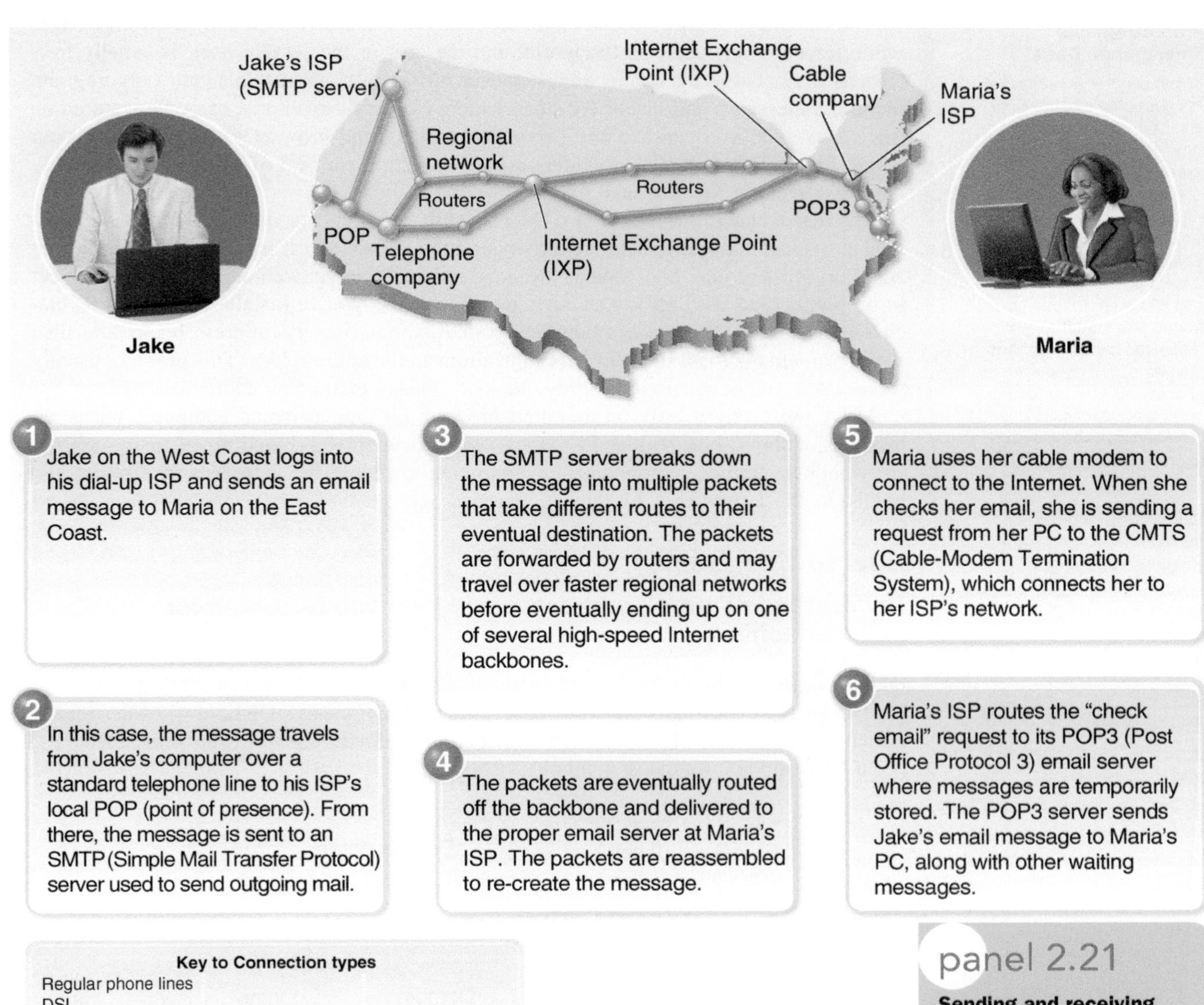

panel 2.21

Sending and receiving emails

then decide which ones they want to download—a way of protecting one's computer from being disrupted by possibly harmful, virus-containing emails from unfamiliar senders.)

Two Ways to Send & Receive Email

You can use email via software on your own computer or via web-based services, with a browser.

There are two ways to send and receive email—via an *email program* or via *web-based email.*

EMAIL PROGRAM **An email program enables you to send email from your computer, which interacts with an email server at your Internet access provider to send and receive email.** Your incoming mail is stored on the server in an electronic mailbox. When you access the email server, your incoming messages are sent to your software's *inbox,* where they are ready to be opened and read. Examples of such programs are Microsoft's Outlook Express and Apple's Mail.

The advantage of standard email programs is that you can easily integrate your email with other applications, such as calendar, task list, and contact list.

WEB-BASED EMAIL **With web-based email, or *webmail,* you send and receive messages by interacting via a browser with a website.** The big four email carriers are Yahoo! Mail, Microsoft Outlook.com, Gmail (Google), and AIM Mail (AOL.com).

The advantages of web-based email are that you can easily send and receive messages while traveling anywhere in the world, and the cost of the service itself is usually free. (Hotels may charge for connecting, however.) Moreover, because all your outgoing and incoming messages and means for storing them (folders—explained below) are stored on the mail server, you can use any personal computer and browser to keep up with your email. Finally, big webmail providers usually offer a great deal of storage, so you rarely have to delete messages to save space.

The disadvantages, however, are that, because you aren't paying for the service, webmail providers support it with advertising, which means you'll have to deal with lots of ads. Purveyors of junk mail (spam) also tend to heavily target webmail services, so expect to be bombarded with unwanted sales pitches (unless you've installed spam filters, discussed later). Finally, hackers commonly steal webmail users' address books and then send scam emails to all the people/organizations in the address lists. This problem usually forces users and people in the address books to change their email addresses often.

Many users rely mostly on an email program on their personal computer, but when traveling without their regular PCs, they switch over to web-based email (using tablets, smartphones, friends' computers, or computers available for a fee (as in airports and hotels) to check messages. Or they do text messaging.

Survival Tip

Protecting Your Smartphone Data

"If you don't at least have a PIN (Personal Identification Number) that you have to enter to access your phone, you really need to do that right now. You can do it with either a PIN, pass phrase, swipe pattern, or even face and voice recognition. **Any** of these is better than **none** of these. You may also want to take any lock screen widgets off as well. These can reveal what town you live in, or maybe even what stocks you are following" (*www.makeuseof.com/tag/how-to-encrypt-data-on-your-smartphone/*).

How to Use Email

Understanding email addresses will help you to use email more effectively.

Of course, to use email, you'll need an email address, a sort of electronic mailbox used to send and receive messages. An email address is not the same as a URL, or website address. All email addresses follow the same approach: *username@domain;* the @ is called "at." (Web URLs do not use the @ symbol.)

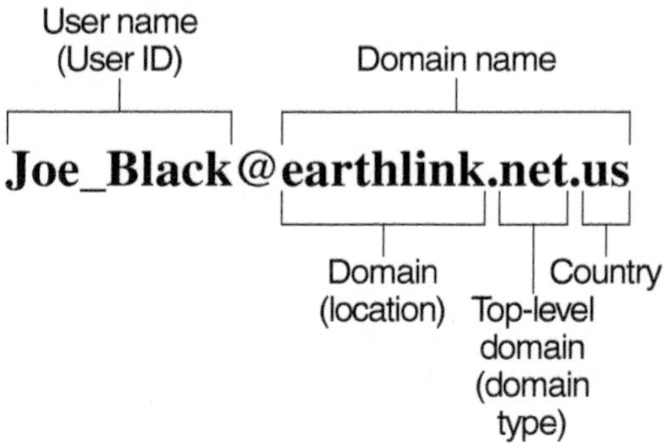

User name (User ID)
Domain name

Joe_Black@earthlink.net.us

Domain (location)
Top-level domain (domain type)
Country

- **The username: Joe_Black** The *username,* or *user ID,* identifies who is at the address—in this case, *Joe_Black* (note the underscore). There are many ways that Joe Black's username might be designated, with and without capital letters: *Joe_Black, joe_black, joe.black, joeblack, jblack, joeb,* and so on. If someone else has not already chosen the username you want, you are free to use it.
- **Domain name: @earthlink** The *domain name,* which follows the @ symbol, tells the location and type of address. Domain-name components are separated by periods (called "dots"). The domain portion of the address (such as *Earthlink,* an Internet access provider) provides specific information about the location—where the message should be delivered.
- **Top-level domain: .net** The *top-level domain,* or *domain code,* is usually a three-letter extension that describes the domain type: *.net, .com, .gov, .edu, .org, .mil, .int*—network, commercial, government, educational, nonprofit, military, or international organization (p. 62). In 2012, with more websites being built and domain names becoming scarce, ICANN launched a program to allow companies, organizations, and even cities to turn their own brands into generic top-level domain (gTLD) name extensions, such as *.nike, .google, .hotel, .ymca, .chicago, .cafe, .forsale,* and the like.
- **Country: .us** Some domain names also include a two-letter extension for the country—for example, *.us* for United States, *.ca* for Canada, *.mx* for Mexico.

The illustration on the next page shows some generic basics about sending, receiving, and replying to email. *(• See Panel 2.22, next page.)*

Some tips for managing and using your email are as follows.

USE THE ADDRESS-BOOK FEATURE The *address book* allows you to organize your correspondents' email addresses by real names (such as *Joe Black*) instead of nicknames or usernames *(bugsme2),* which you might not remember, and to organize addresses into groups (friends, club members) so you can send them all the same message with a single command.

Country Abbreviations

What do you think the country abbreviations are for Micronesia? Botswana? Saint Lucia? Go to:

www.eubank-web.com/William/Webmaster/c-codes.htm
www.thrall.org/domains.htm

History of the @ Sign

In 1972, Ray Tomlinson sent the first electronic message using the @ symbol to indicate the location or institution of the recipient. Tomlinson knew that he had to use a symbol that would not appear in anyone's name. Before the @ sign became a character on the keyboard, where was it used? Some linguists believe that the symbol dates back to the 6th or 7th centuries, when Latin scribes adapted the Latin word *ad,* meaning "at," "to," or "toward." Other linguists say that @ dates to its use in the 18th century as a symbol in commerce to indicate price per unit, as in 4 CDs @ $5 (each). In 2000, a professor of history in Italy discovered some original 14th-century documents clearly marked with the @ sign to indicate a measure of quantity, based on the word *amphora,* meaning "jar." The amphora was a standard-size earthenware jar used by merchants for wine and grain. In Florence, the capital "A" was written with a flourish and later became @ ("at the price of").

Other countries have different names for this symbol. For example:

South Africa—*aapstet*, or "monkey's tail"
Czech Republic—*zavinac*, or "pickled herring"
Denmark—*snable-a*, or "elephant's trunk"
France—*petit escargot*, "little snail"
Greece—*papaki*, "little duck"
Hungary—*kukac*, "worm"
Taiwan—*xiao lao-shu*, "mouse sign"
Norway—*grisehale*, "pig's tail"
Russia—*sobachka*, "little dog"
Turkey—*kulak*, "ear"

Source: www.pcwebopedia.com, January 28, 2003; and *www.webopedia.com*, August 2005.

Sending email

Address Book: Lists email addresses you use most; can be attached automatically to messages

Send: Command for sending messages

cc: For copying ("carbon/ courtesy copy") message to others

bcc: For copying others ("blind carbon copy") without the primary recipient knowing it

Message area

You can conclude every message with a custom "signature"

Subject line: Preview incoming email by reviewing the subject lines to see if you really need to read the messages

Receiving email

Reply, Reply All, Forward, Delete: For helping you handle incoming email

Inbox lists messages waiting in email box. (Unopened envelope icon shows unread mail.)

Selected message displayed here

Replying to email

Use the **Reply** command icon, and the email program automatically fills in the To, From, and Subject lines in your reply.

panel 2.22

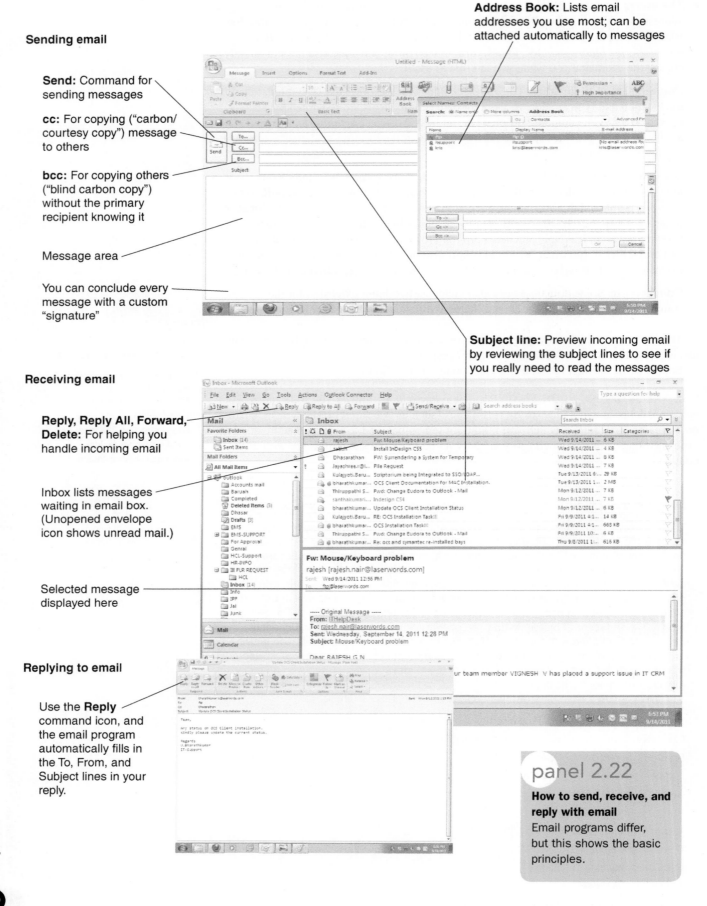

How to send, receive, and reply with email

Email programs differ, but this shows the basic principles.

KEEP YOUR EMAIL ORGANIZED IN FOLDERS Putting your email into *folders* (also called *filters* or *rules*) enables you to stay organized by sorting messages according to names of senders or mailing list. Then you can read emails sent to this folder later when you have time, freeing up your inbox for mail that needs your more immediate attention. Instructions on how to set up such organizers are in your email program's Help section.

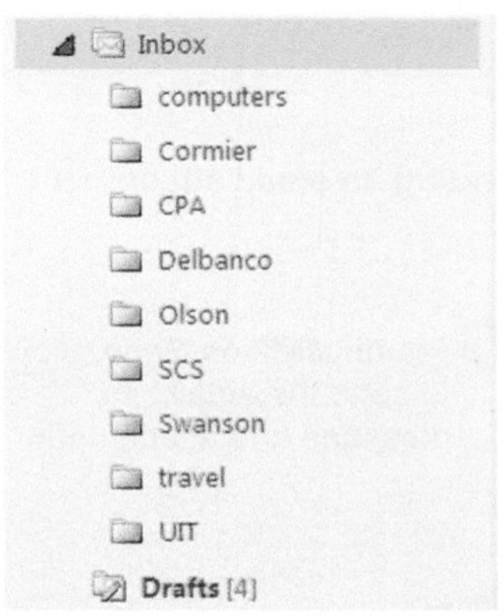

BEING CAREFUL WITH ATTACHMENTS If you've written a paper and saved it as a file in the computer you use to send email, you can write an email message and use the Attach File command to attach the document. (• *See Panel 2.23, next page.*) (Sending yourself an email with an attached file is a good way to back up that file when you have no other backup methods available—or even when you do.)

While you could also copy your document into the main email message and send it that way, some email software loses formatting options such as special symbols or the end-of-line breaks for song lyrics or poetry; using the attachment feature preserves all such formatting. You can also attach pictures, sounds, videos, and other files to your email message.

NETIQUETTE: APPROPRIATE ONLINE BEHAVIOR You would hate it if you accidentally offended your new boss or a coworker or customer in an email message simply because you were unaware of **netiquette, or "network etiquette"—appropriate online behavior.** In general, netiquette has two basic rules: (1) Don't waste people's time, and (2) don't say anything to a person online that you wouldn't say to his or her face.

Some more specific rules to maintain professionalism, which apply to both email and texting, are as follows:[24]

- **Include helpful subject and signature lines:** To help your recipients organize their email messages, write a subject line that is clear and meaningful. Also, make sure your signature line includes your contact information.
- **Be clear and concise:** Except among friends, avoid shorthand such as LOL ("laugh out loud"), u r ("you are"), and OMG ("oh my god"). Avoid buzzwords (especially if you're working for a company doing international business). Also, don't ramble; get right to the point.
- **Avoid spelling and grammatical errors:** Use the spelling checker and grammar checker, if necessary, and proofread your message before sending it. *(Remember: Emails are not the same as texts. Make sure your email is clear and properly presented.)*
- **Avoid SHOUTING and flaming:** Avoid using all-capital letters, considered the equivalent of SHOUTING in email communication. Also, avoid **flaming—using derogatory, obscene, or inappropriate language**—with people with whom you wildly disagree (or think are idiots). Something that smoothes communication online is the use of *emoticons,* keyboard-produced pictorial representations of expressions, such as :-) (smile), ;-) (wink), :-((frown). In texting, people use *emoji,* images of cute animals, food items, and expressive smiley faces to express what words cannot. (These images and emoticons are not approriate in professional communications.)

Good Websites on Netiquette, including a Quiz

http://netforbeginners.about.com/od/netiquetteonlineculture/l/bl_netiquette_quiz.htm

www.albion.com/netiquette/

http://email.about.com/od/email-netiquette/tp/core_netiquette.htm

www.networketiquette.net/

Survival Tip

Access Email from Many Places

Set your email program settings to allow you to keep messages on your email service's server when you download them to your computer/device. This allows you to access your messages from multiple places before you finally delete them.

Instant Messaging

Instant messaging enables you to communicate by email with specified other users ("buddies") in real time.

Allowing communication that is far speedier than conventional email, **instant messaging (IM) lets users communicate instantly—that is, in real time—over an email system with one or more persons who are logged onto that system at the same time.**

When you log on to your IM account, you see a *buddy* list, a list you created of other IM users you want to communicate with. If all parties agree, they can initiate online typed conversations in real time (in a "chat room"). The messages appear on the display screen in a small **window—a rectangular area containing a document or activity**—so that users can exchange messages almost instantaneously while operating other programs. Examples of proprietary instant-message systems are AIM, Google Chat, Windows Messenger, and Yahoo! Messenger; these allow you to IM or chat only with others sharing the same IM

Sending an email attachment

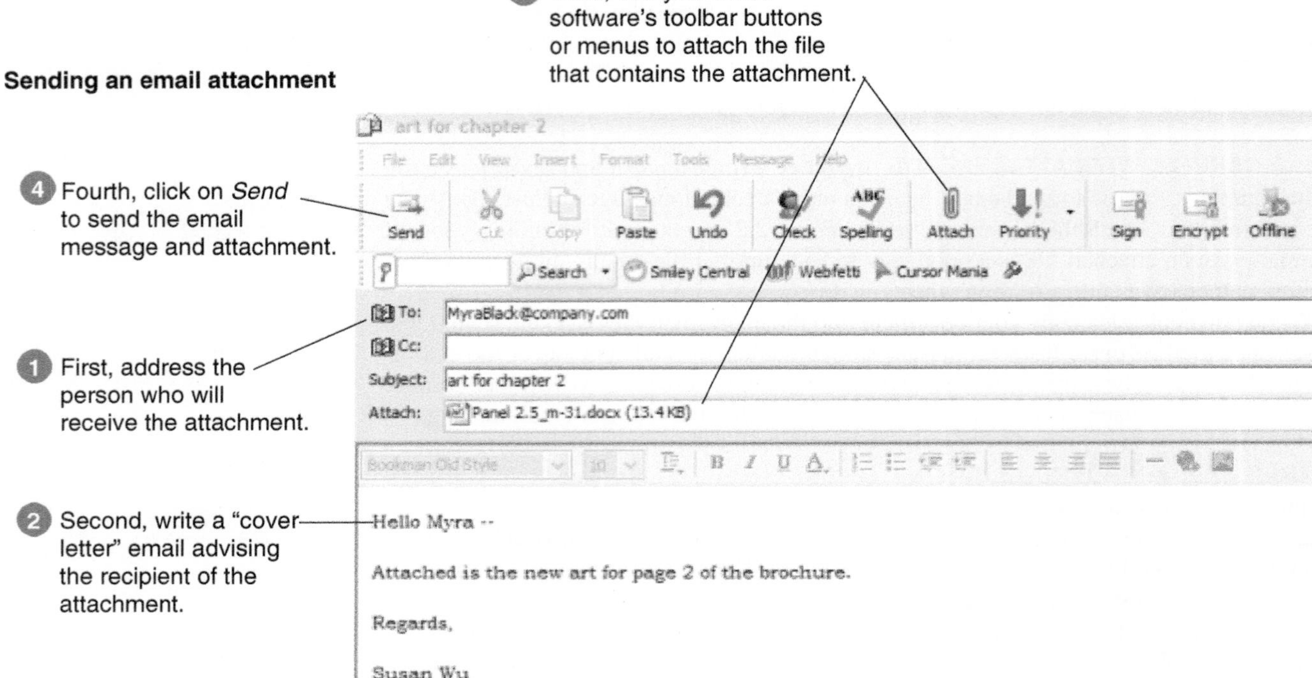

Receiving an email attachment

When you receive a file containing an attachment, you'll see an icon indicating the message contains more than just text. You can click on the icon to see the attachment. If you have the software the attached file was created in, you can open the attachment immediately to read or print, or you can save the attachment in a location of your choice (on your computer). You can also forward the attachment to another person.

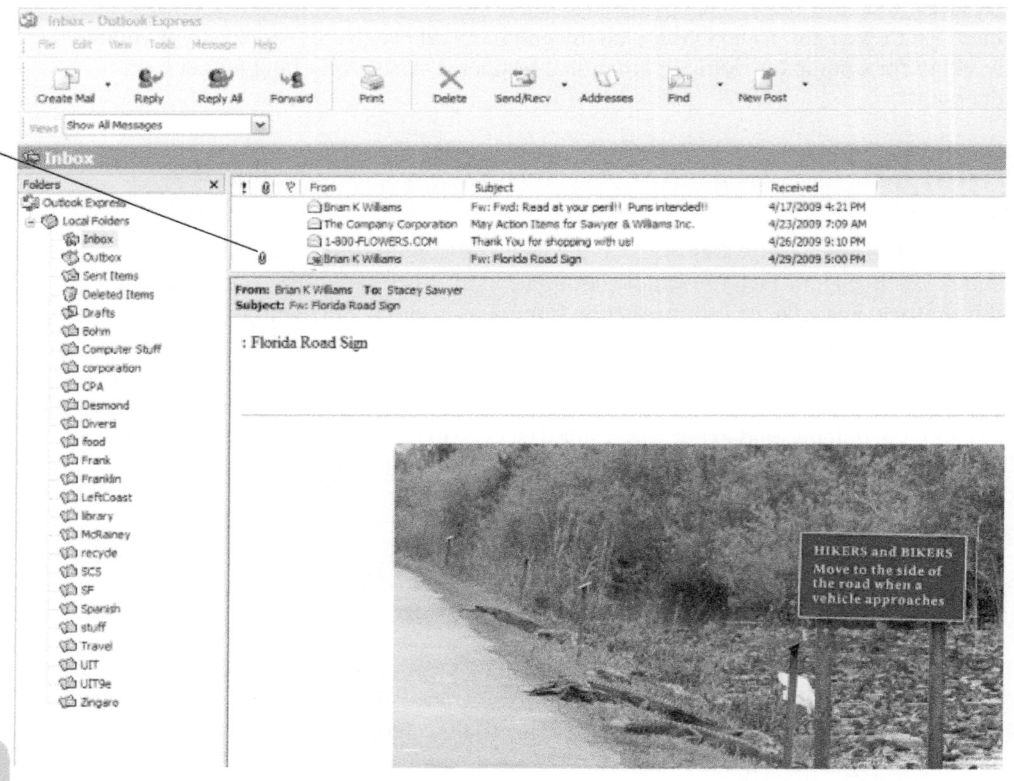

panel 2.23
Attach File function

service and on your buddy list. You can also chat with users, or "friends," on Facebook through the Facebook chat feature. Digsby and Trillian represent universal services that allow you to chat with users of all principal IMs. Instant messaging is done on a computer and is *not* the same as *text messaging* or *texting,* which is the exchange of messages between mobile phones. Nor is it the same as *tweeting,* the use of Twitter to send and receive short, 140-character messages to and from other Twitter users, using the small display area on a cellphone. (We discuss texting and tweeting elsewhere.) IM is especially useful in the workplace as a way of reducing long-distance telephone bills when you have to communicate with colleagues who are geographically remote but with whom you must work closely.

Discussion Groups: Mailing Lists, Newsgroups, & Message Boards

Discussion groups on special-interest topics may be found on three Internet-based technologies.

Want to have discussions or receive news from people locally or globally who share your interests? Three possibilities are electronic *mailing lists, newsgroups,* and *message boards.*

MAILING LISTS: ONE-WAY OR TWO-WAY EMAIL SUBSCRIPTION LISTS You can *subscribe to* (sign up for) an email mailing list just as you would for a free newsletter. **A mailing list is an email discussion group on a special-interest topic, in which all subscribers receive email messages sent to the group's email address.** Some mailing lists are one-way; they simply make announcements, such as those from the Democratic and Republican parties about upcoming events. Others are two-way; they are discussion lists (on subjects such as politics, jokes, or science) in which a subscriber sends a message to all the other subscribers, who may respond in similar fashion.

NEWSGROUPS: ELECTRONIC BULLETIN BOARDS WITH NEWSREADERS A **newsgroup is a giant electronic bulletin board on which users conduct written discussions about a specific subject.** The newsgroup is traditionally distributed via *Usenet,* a worldwide public network of servers accessed through the Internet. Messages are posted on a bulletin board that anyone can read at any time.

To participate in a newsgroup, you need a program called a *newsreader.* Before it was ended in early 2013, the Google Reader was a popular newsreader.[25] (Alternative newsreaders are NewsBlur, Netvibes, and The Old Reader.)[26] There are thousands of Internet newsgroups—which charge no fee—and they cover an amazing array of topics. Students, for instance, may find a newsgroup for discussions about the topics in a particular course.

MESSAGE BOARDS: SPECIAL-INTEREST DISCUSSION GROUPS WITHOUT NEWSREADERS Easier to use than a newsgroup, a **message board is a web-based discussion group that does not require a newsreader.** Sometimes called a *web forum,* these special-interest discussions may be accessed through a web browser (not email) from Yahoo! Groups and Google Groups. Some groups are open to the public; others are members only.

With either a newsgroup or a message board, a user posts a particular message—which is called an *article*—to the bulletin board, which other users can read and write replies to. **A collection of messages on a particular subject is called a thread or threaded discussion.**

FTP: For Transferring Large Files

FTP makes it easy to send large files between computers.

FTP (File Transfer Protocol) is an Internet standard for uploading and downloading files between computers, including those with different operating systems. You can download FTP files using your web browser or using special software (called an *FTP client program*), such as Fetch or CuteFTP.

Some files on FTP sites are open to the public (*anonymous FTP sites*); some are not, such as, for instance, a university's private files of lectures. To download files, you connect to a remote computer called an *FTP site* and transfer files to your own microcomputer's hard disk over the Internet. Many such files are available for free: software, games,

FTP Clients & Servers

FTP software programs, called *FTP clients,* come with many operating systems. Web browsers also come with FTP clients. For lists of FTP clients and FTP servers, go to:

www.answers.com/topic/comparison-of-ftp-clients/

FileZilla The free FTP solution

Home

FileZilla
Features
Screenshots
Download
Documentation

FileZilla Server
Download

General
Contact
Forum
Project page
Wiki

Development
Source code
Nightly builds
Translations
Version history
Changelog
Issue tracker

Other projects
Octochess

PayPal DONATE

Sponsors:

Overview

Welcome to the homepage of FileZilla, the free FTP solution. Both a client and a server are available. FileZilla is open source software dis

Support is available through our forums, the wiki and the bug and feature request trackers.

In addition, you will find documentation on how to compile FileZilla and nightly builds for multiple platforms in the development section.

Quick download links

Pick the client if you want to transfer files. Get the server if you want to make files available for others.

News

2013-05-10 - FileZilla Client 3.7.0.1 released

Bugfixes and minor changes:

- Fixed a bug in bundled GnuTLS affecting FileZilla 3.7.0
- Updated translations

2013-05-09 - FileZilla Client 3.7.0 released

Bugfixes and minor changes:

- Fix typo

2013-04-29 - FileZilla Client 3.7.0-rc1 released

panel 2.24

FTP software

photos, maps, art, music, books, statistics. (• *See Panel 2.24.*) You can also set up your own private FTP site (for example, through ShareFile.com) to enable you and other people you allow to use your site to upload and download files that are too large to send as email attachments.

2.5 THE ONLINE GOLD MINE: Telephony, Multimedia, Webcasting, Blogs, E-Commerce, & Social Networking

The Internet and the web are offering new services every day. Social networking is currently one of the most popular activities.

The opportunities offered by the Internet and the web seem inexhaustible. Here we examine several resources available to you.

Telephony: The Internet Telephone

Internet telephony enables you to make international phone calls inexpensively or for free.

Whereas conventional telephone voice lines carry a conversation over a single path, the Internet breaks up conversations (or other transmitted data) into "information packets" that can be sent over separate lines and then regrouped at the destination. Thus, the Internet can move a lot more traffic over a network than the traditional telephone link can.

Internet telephony, or VoIP (Voice over Internet Protocol), uses the Internet to make phone calls, either one to one or for audioconferencing—that is, with many people talking. The benefit of VoIP (such as Skype) is that you can make long-distance phone calls that are surprisingly inexpensive or even free. (• *See Panel 2.25.*) Indeed, it's possible to do this with a standard telephone (as with MagicJack) on the public switched telephone network, simply by dialing a number that will "packetize" your conversation. However,

FCC Federal Communications Commission

Voice-Over-Internet Protocol

Search the FCC: Go

Help | Advanced

Headlines

FAQs

VoIP Forum - 12/1/03

VoIP Summit - 5/7/04

VoIP Fact Sheet

VoIP & 911 Advisory

Note

Aspects of these considerations may change with new developments in internet technology. You should always check with the VoIP service provider you choose to confirm any advantages and limitations to their service.

FCC > Voice-Over-Internet Protocol

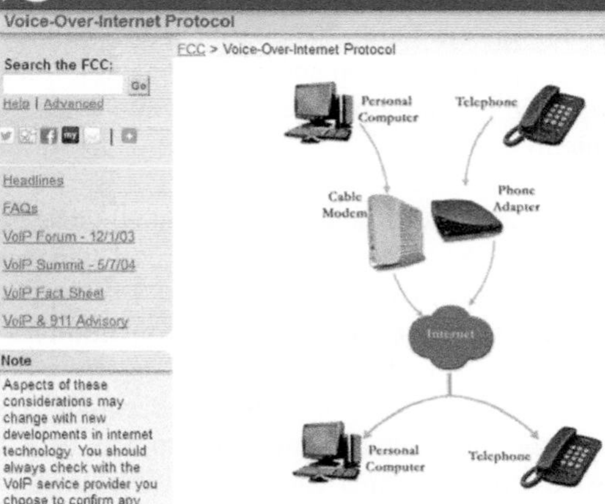

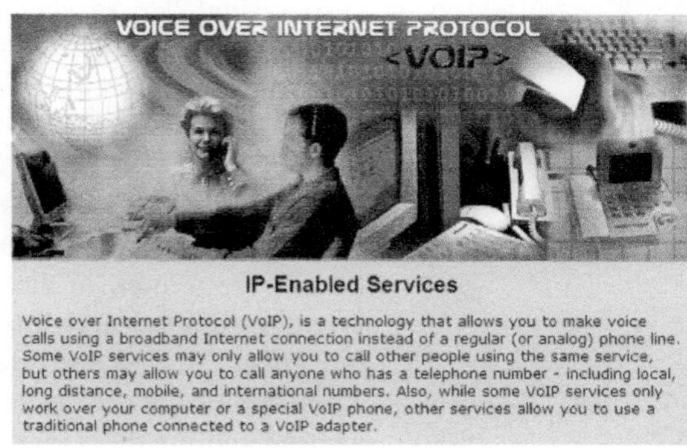

IP-Enabled Services

Voice over Internet Protocol (VoIP), is a technology that allows you to make voice calls using a broadband Internet connection instead of a regular (or analog) phone line. Some VoIP services may only allow you to call other people using the same service, but others may allow you to call anyone who has a telephone number - including local, long distance, mobile, and international numbers. Also, while some VoIP services only work over your computer or a special VoIP phone, other services allow you to use a traditional phone connected to a VoIP adapter.

Frequently Asked Questions

How VoIP / Internet Voice Works

VoIP services convert your voice into a digital signal that travels over the Internet. If you are calling a regular phone number, the signal is converted to a regular telephone signal before it reaches the destination. VoIP can allow you to make a call directly from a computer, a special VoIP phone, or a traditional phone connected to a special adapter. In addition, wireless "hot spots" in locations such as airports, parks, and cafes allow you to connect to the Internet and may enable you to use VoIP service wirelessly.

What Kind of Equipment Do I Need?

A broadband (high speed Internet) connection is required. This can be through a cable modem, or high speed services such as DSL or a local area network. **A computer, adaptor, or specialized phone is required.** Some VoIP services only work over your computer or a special VoIP phone, while other services allow you to use a traditional phone connected to a VoIP adapter. If you use your computer, you will need some software and an inexpensive microphone. Special VoIP phones plug directly into your broadband connection and operate largely like a traditional telephone. If you use a telephone with a VoIP adapter, you'll be able to dial just as you always have, and the service provider may also provide a dial tone.

Is there a difference between making a Local Call and a Long Distance Call?

Some VoIP providers offer their services for free, normally only for calls to other subscribers to the service. Your VoIP provider may permit you to select an area code different from the area in which you live. It also means that people who call you may incur long distance charges depending on their area code and service.

Some VoIP providers charge for a long distance call to a number outside your calling area, similar to existing, traditional wireline telephone service. Other VoIP providers permit you to call anywhere at a flat rate for a fixed number of minutes.

If I have VoIP service, who can I call?

Depending upon your service, you might be limited only to other subscribers to the service, or you may be able to call anyone who has a telephone number - including local, long distance, mobile, and international numbers. If you are calling someone who has a regular analog phone, that person does not need any special equipment to talk to you. Some VoIP services may allow you to speak with more than one person at a time.

What Are Some Advantages of VoIP?

Some VoIP services offer features and services that are not available with a traditional phone, or are available but only for an additional fee. You may also be able to avoid paying for both a broadband connection and a traditional telephone line.

What Are Some disadvantages of VoIP?

If you're considering replacing your traditional telephone service with VoIP, there are some possible differences:

- Some VoIP services don't work during power outages and the service provider may not offer backup power.
- Not all VoIP services connect directly to emergency services through 9-1-1. For additional information, see VoIP & 911 Advisory.
- VoIP providers may or may not offer directory assistance/white page listings.

Can I use my Computer While I talk on the Phone?

In most cases, yes.

panel 2.25

Internet telephony (*http://transition.fcc.gov/voip*)

people also can use a microcomputer with a sound card and a microphone and a high-speed Internet connection such as a DSL or cable modem. VoIP is also offered on many mobile devices that have wireless Internet service.

Sound quality used to be a problem with VoIP, but that has improved with the widespread availability of broadband. Be aware, however, that many VoIP companies cannot handle 911 emergency calls because they are not locally based (*www.fcc.gov/guides/voip-and-911-service*). Also, if your Internet access provider is having problems, then you may not be able to place calls until the problems are fixed. Local or distant power outages can also shut down VoIP service.

more info!

How VoIP Works

http://communication.howstuffworks.com/ip-telephony5.htm

http://pma101.com/101/howdoesvoipwork.html

Multimedia on the Web

Multimedia on the web is usually handled by plug-ins and small, special programs (software).

Many websites (especially those trying to sell you something) employ complicated multimedia effects, using a combination of text, images, sound, video, and animation. While most web browsers can handle basic multimedia elements on a web page, eventually you'll probably want more dramatic capabilities.

PLUG-INS In the 1990s, as the web was evolving from text to multimedia, browsers were unable to handle many kinds of graphic, sound, and video files. To do so, external

more info!

Plug-Ins List

www.fileinfo.com/filetypes/plugin/

application files called *plug-ins* had to be loaded into the system. **A plug-in (add-on) is a program that adds a specific feature or function to a browser, allowing it to play or view certain files.** Examples of plug-ins are Flash, QuickTime, and RealPlayer. (• *See Panel 2.26.*) Today many plug-ins come preinstalled on new computers; if a website requires a plug-in that you don't have, you will probably be directed to a site where you can download it—sometimes for free, sometimes not.

TOOLS FOR DEVELOPING MULTIMEDIA How do website developers get all those nifty special multimedia effects? Often web pages embed links to **applets, small programs that can be quickly downloaded and run by most browsers.** Applets ("little applications") are written in **Java, a programming language that enables programmers to create animated and interactive web pages.** Java applets enhance web pages by playing music, displaying graphics and animation, and providing interactive games. Java-compatible browsers such as Internet Explorer automatically download applets from the website and run them on your computer so that you can experience the multimedia effects. With Firefox and Chrome, Java is available via plug-ins.

TEXT & IMAGES Of course, you can call up all kinds of text documents on the web, such as newspapers, magazines, famous speeches, and works of literature. You can also view images, such as scenery, famous paintings, and photographs. Most web pages combine both text and images. An especially interesting kind of imaging consists of aerial maps.

TECH TALES Web Imaging & Aerial Mapping: Google Earth

Google Earth (*www.google.earth.com*) is a satellite imaging program that Google has described as "part flight simulator, part search tool."[27] You type in your ZIP code or street address, and it feels like you're looking down on a high-resolution aerial view of your house from a plane at 30,000 feet. "Google sightseers can zoom in close enough to see airplanes parked in the desert, the baseball diamond at Wrigley Field, and cars in the Mall of America parking lot," says one writer.[28] Using Google Local Search, you can search for a business or other attraction in some city, and you'll get an indicator on your satellite image; if you click again, the establishment's web page opens.

panel 2.26

QuickTime

This plug-in is *required* to view high-quality video and hear radio.

Store
Mac
iPod
iPhone
iPad
iTunes
Support
QuickTime
Extending QuickTime
Download Now
What is QuickTime 7?
A powerful multimedia technology with a built-in media player, QuickTime lets you view Internet video, HD movie trailers, and personal media in a wide range of file formats. And it lets you enjoy them in remarkably high quality.

It's a multimedia platform.

Video from your digital camera or mobile phone. A movie on your Mac or PC. A media clip on a website. No matter what you're watching or where you're watching it, QuickTime technology makes it all possible.

It's a sophisticated media player.

With its simple design and easy-to-use controls, QuickTime Player makes everything you watch even more enjoyable. Its clean, uncluttered interface never gets in the way of what you're watching. Want to speed through a movie or slow things down? A handy slider lets you set playback from 1/2x to 3x the normal speed. And you can search through individual movie frames quickly.

It's advanced video technology.

QuickTime features advanced video compression technology called H.264 to deliver brilliant, crisp HD video using less bandwidth and storage. So you'll experience pristine video quality wherever you watch your movies or videos.

H.264

It's a flexible file format.

QuickTime lets you do more with your digital media. With QuickTime 7 Pro, you can convert your files to different formats and record and edit your work. Third-party plug-ins extend QuickTime technology in many different directions. And QuickTime streaming solutions let you stream your media across the Internet.

AAC AIFF MP4

You can also use the feature to look at the moon and Mars and even under the sea. The company's 3-D mapping service "lets users explore the ocean as if they were dolphins, swimming past submerged volcanoes and through underwater canyons," according to one description.[29]

Google's camera-equipped cars roam the world's streets taking 360-degree photographs "for display to anyone who types in the correct address, or latitude and longitude, or any number of other ways to indicate a location that Google can figure out," says one writer.[30] This has led to various privacy concerns. The company's online map service, Street View, has been accused of taking pictures, and coming too close inside people's private homes or to people walking on the street not knowing they are being watched (and of hacking into people's private Wi-Fi networks). The German government was considering making it illegal for Street View to use camouflaged or hidden cameras in their videotaping of residential properties and to allow citizens to opt out of the privacy-invasive technology. ■

ANIMATION Another type of multimedia, **animation is the rapid sequencing of still images to create the appearance of motion,** as in cartoons and in most videogames and apps as well as in moving banners displaying sports scores or stock prices.

■ **TECH TALES** Animation: The Making of "Fetch," a Mobile Game

"What if a boy's dog was stolen by a hungry fire hydrant?" That was the premise that a nine-person team at Seattle's Big Fish Games wrestled with to create Fetch, an animated game for use mainly on mobile devices.

Artists began by sketching hundreds of drawings of the game's two main characters, the dog and the boy who rescues it, as well as the setting. "Illustrators converted the concept drawings into computer renderings," says a reporter's account. "3-D animators gave the characters a digital 'skeleton,' which they then used to 'rig' and 'weight' the [three-dimensional] models."[31] Artists, animators, and game developers then collaborated on a "production map" to detail different if-then scenarios that would respond to the different choices players would make. Later Fetch was passed along to a quality-control team, which tried to see if it could make the game not work.

The tested game was eventually sent to Apple for approval for its App Store. Total development time and cost for Big Fish: one year and $1 million. ■

VIDEO: DOWNLOAD BEFORE OR WHILE WATCHING? Video can be transmitted in two ways:

- **Download before watching:** It may be transmitted as a file to be completely downloaded before you can view it. This downloading may take several minutes with some movies or video clips.
- **Download while watching:** Video may be transmitted as a file to be displayed as streaming video and viewed while it is still being downloaded.

Streaming video is the process of transferring data in a continuous flow (in real time) so that you can begin viewing a file even before the end of the file is sent. For instance, RealPlayer offers live, television-style broadcasts over the Internet as streaming video for viewing on your computer or mobile device. You download and install this software and then point your browser to a site featuring RealVideo. That will produce a streaming-video television image in a window a few inches wide.

With more and more U.S. households having the broadband connections that permit streaming video, firms such as Netflix, whose main business formerly was renting movies by mail, have moved toward the near-instant delivery of movies streamed to subscribers' computers, mobile devices, Internet-enabled TV sets, and the like.

AUDIO Audio, such as sound or music files, may also be transmitted in two ways:

- **Download before playing:** Many online music services, such as Apple's iTunes Store, Google's Play Store, Yahoo! Music, and MusicMatch, offer music, some for free, but usually for a fee, either by subscription or by the song. Generally, music must be downloaded completely before the file can be played on a computer or portable music player.
- **Downloaded while playing—as streaming audio:** Music that is downloaded as **streaming audio allows you to listen to the file while the data is being downloaded to your computer.** Popular standards for transmitting audio are Pandora and RealAudio. Supported by most web browsers, they compress sound so that it can be played in real time, even if sent over telephone lines. You can, for instance, listen to 24-hour-a-day Internet radio of CNN radio news, 1950s vintage rock, or shortwave outlets from World Radio Network in London. Many large radio stations outside the United States have Net radio, allowing people around the world to listen in.

The Web Automatically Comes to You: Webcasting, Blogging, & Podcasting

You don't always have to search for what you want on the web; the web can also come to you.

PUSH TECHNOLOGY & WEBCASTING The trend of bringing web content to users without their having to do any searching began in the late 1990s with **push technology, software that automatically downloads information to personal computers** (as opposed to *pull technology,* in which you go to a website and request, or "pull down," the information you want). One result of push technology was **webcasting ("web broadcasting"), in which customized text, video, and audio are sent to you automatically on a regular basis or live on demand.**

The idea here is that webcasting companies, called subscription services, offer you choices of categories (called "channels" in Microsoft Internet Explorer) of websites that will automatically send you updated information, saving you from having to search it out.

A lot of push technology fell out of favor because it clogged networks with information that readers often didn't want. Then along came RSS.

RSS, XML, BLOGS, & THE BLOGOSPHERE RSS (said to be short for *really simple syndication* or *rich site summary*) was built to be simpler than push technology. **RSS newsreaders, or *RSS aggregators,* are programs that scour the web, sometimes hourly, sometimes more frequently, and pull together in one place "feeds" from several websites.** "RSS allows you to play news editor and zero in on the information you really need," says one account, "even as you expand the number of sites you sample."[32] This is because the information is so specifically targeted.

RSS is based on **XML, or *extensible markup language,* a web-document tagging and formatting language that is an advance over HTML** (p. 66) **and that two computers can use to exchange information.** XML, in the form of RSS, has allowed people to have access to a whole new universe of content. One of the earliest adopters, for instance, was the Mormon Church, which used the system to keep in touch with members.

Now RSS has morphed into the **blogosphere, the total universe of blogs.** As we mentioned in Chapter 1, *blogs* (weblogs) are frequently updated sites on the World Wide Web intended for public consumptions that contain a writer's observations, opinions, images, and links to other websites. *(• See Panel 2.27.)* Among the variations are *video blogs,* or *vblogs,* which are video versions of blogs, a kind of Internet TV, and *moblogs,* or *mobile blogs,* in which picture blogs are posted to websites directly from camera-enabled cellphones. *Microblogs,* or text messages sent from your cellphone or mobile device, consist of a few short sentences, which take little time to write compared with traditional blogs. The most popular microblogging service is *Twitter,* which allows you to send text messages—up 140 characters—from your browser or smartphone. *(• See Panel 2.28, page 90.)* Another microblogging platform is Tumblr, which lets you express yourself creatively using media. (What is the age of the average Twitter user? 37.3 years. Surprised? See *http://royal.pingdom.com/2013/01/16/internet-2012-in-numbers/*).

SimpleSite.com ▸ How it works ▸ Customer Service

Create your own blog with SimpleSite

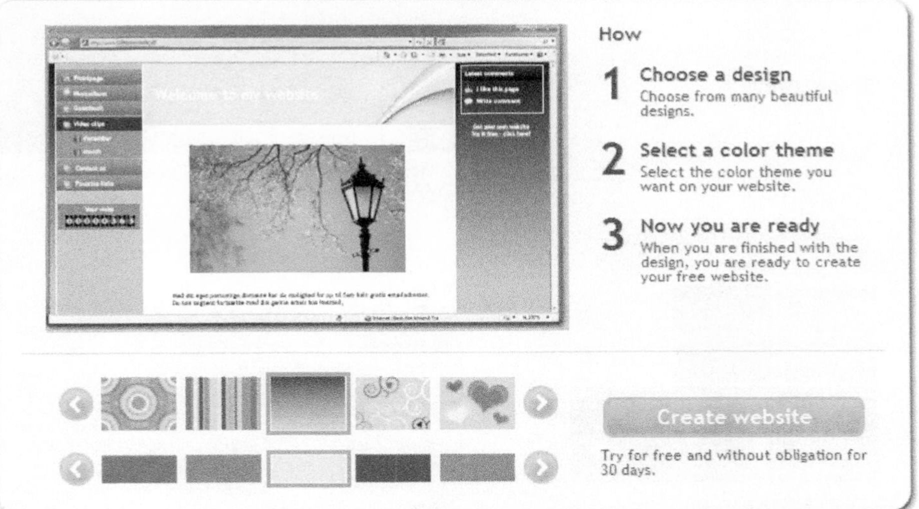

How
1 Choose a design
Choose from many beautiful designs.
2 Select a color theme
Select the color theme you want on your website.
3 Now you are ready
When you are finished with the design, you are ready to create your free website.
Create website
Try for free and without obligation for 30 days.

SimpleSite makes it easy to try creating a blog

With SimpleSite, you can easily, and entirely without obligation, try creating a website with a blog for free.
In just minutes you can start blogging, with picture galleries, videos, a guestbook, your dog's pedigree and much more. We have over 200 different creative templates to choose from. You will be able to blog completely free for the first 30 days, then it is entirely up to you whether you want to continue your blog or website, or whether the blog should lapse automatically.

You can easily start your own blog
When you decide to create a blog, start by selecting the colors and design of your website. Then click next to begin. The setup takes a maximum 2 to 3 minutes, and you'll have your very own blog on the net, with your own name, a personal picture on the homepage and a design that suits your style.

Your own personal email addresses.
Along with your own personal domain name, you receive the option of up to five free email addresses. You can of course continue using your old Hotmail, Gmail, etc. account; we will simply forward emails sent to your new email address to your old email account.

You can buy myself@YourBlog'sName.com or maybe dad@YourBlog'sName. com, mother@YourBlog'sName.com, etc. so that the whole family can have their own personal email addresses.

Personal, company or association
Regardless of whether a blog is used as a family area on the web, to showcase your hobby or pet or maybe as a site for your company or association, it is 100% free to try.

We have close to 100,000 active websites with blogs dealing with everything that matters to our many users, and what

panel 2.27

The blogosphere. One way to create your own blog

Blogs postings are arranged in order by time, with the latest item appearing first. Often readers of blog sites are allowed to post their own comments. Two widely used tools for creating blogs are Blogger and WordPress.

TECH TALES The Rise of the Blogosphere: "Writing Out Loud"

"Blogs can be anything their creators want them to be, from newsy to deeply personal, argumentative to poetic," says one writer. "Some are written by individuals. Some are group projects. Some have readerships in the thousands and influence world media. Others are read by a handful of people—or not read at all, because they're all pictures. Bloggers are a new breed of homegrown journal writers and diarists who chronicle life as it happens, with words, photos, sound, and art."[33]

Says another dedicated blogger, "Blogging is . . . to writing what extreme sports are to athletics: more free-form, more accident-prone, less formal, more alive. It is, in many ways, writing out loud."[34]

Some people have succeeded in turning blogging into successful businesses, with those who receive 100,000 or more unique visitors a month earning an average of $75,000 a year (aided by online ads).[35] But 95% of blogs are essentially abandoned, so the key to building a successful audience for a blog seems to be a nonstop, work-every-day work week.[36] ■

Blogging Products

Some popular blogging products are these:

e-Blogger www.blogger.com/

Movable Type's TypePad www.typepad.com/

quackit *www.quackit.com/create-a-blog/*

HowToMakeMyBlog.com www.howtomakemyblog.com/

Blog Search Engines

Some blog search engines:

Technorati www.technorati.com/blogs/directory/

Bloglines www.bloglines.com/

Blogdigger www.blogdigger.com/

Blog Search Engine www.blogsearchengine.com/

Google Blog Search http://blogsearch.google.com/

panel 2.28

Twitter

The person with the most followers—33.5 million—on Twitter is President Obama (*http://au.ibtimes.com/articles/495101/20130729/twitter-pope-francis-barack-obama-vatican-news.htm#.UfbZodgx18E*).

PODCASTING **Podcasting involves delivering Internet music, radio, or video from the Internet to a computer.** Unlike webcasting, podcasts do not use streaming technology; the music or media files must first be downloaded and saved to your computer or mobile device. That is, a podcast delivers a program in a compressed digital format via the Internet to a subscriber for playing back on computers or portable digital audio players. Podcasts can also be posted on a website for downloading. Some colleges offer lectures available via podcasting.

E-Commerce: B2C, B2C, & C2C

The Internet and the web are also important in the world of business.

E-commerce, or *electronic commerce,* is the buying and selling of goods and services over the Internet. Products may be *hard goods* that can be viewed and purchased online and delivered by mail or truck, such as computers, clothes, and furniture, or *soft goods* that can be purchased and downloaded directly from the retailer's site, such as music, software, tickets, and greeting cards.

The explosion in e-commerce is not only widening consumers' choice of products and services but also creating new businesses and compelling established businesses to develop Internet strategies. Many so-called brick-and-mortar retailers—those operating out of physical buildings—have lost business to such online "e-tailers" as Amazon, seller of books, CDs, and many other products. Indeed, traditional retailers such as Target and Best Buy have found themselves losing ground to **showrooming** (Chapter 1, p. 10), **the phenomenon in which shoppers browse for products in stores, only to buy them from an online rival, frequently at a lower price.**

TECH TALES Changing Retail Practices: The Fight against "Showrooming"

Target has made it clear it's fighting back. "What we aren't willing to do," its management says, "is let online-only retailers use our brick and mortar stores as a showroom for their products and undercut our prices without making investments, as we do, to proudly display our brands."[37]

Mobile phones are indispensable to showroomers for comparing prices. E-tailer Amazon even provides its users with a mobile app with "the ability to simplify price lookups on its site by letting them scan product bar codes using their smartphone cameras," according to one report.[38] Bed Bath & Beyond, PetSmart, and Toys "R" Us were found to be among the retailers visited most by Amazon showroomers.

What can traditional retailers do? One strategy, found to be successful at Target and Best Buy during the 2012 holiday shopping period, is for a retailer to announce that it will match an e-tailer's low prices. That practice is now a year-round policy. ■

Three forms of e-commerce are abbreviated as B2B, B2C, and C2C, as follows:

B2B COMMERCE: BUSINESS-TO-BUSINESS **Business-to-business commerce, or *B2B commerce,* is the electronic sale or exchange of goods or services directly between companies, cutting out traditional intermediaries.** This kind of commerce covers a broad range of activities, such as supplier-to-buyer display of inventories, provision of wholesale price lists, and sales of closed-out items and used materials—usually without agents, brokers, or other third parties.

B2C COMMERCE: BUSINESS-TO-CONSUMER **Business-to-consumer commerce, or *B2C commerce,* is the electronic sale or exchange of goods and services from the companies directly to the public, or end users.** Manufacturers, for instance, may use this kind of commerce to eliminate the wholesaler and sell directly to customers, as some bands do by avoiding the record companies and selling their musical recordings directly to the public. Some other B2C examples:

- **Online shopping:** Petco.com (pet food), 1800petmeds.com (pet medicines), Zappos (shoes), and iGourmet.com (food and drink items) all offer products for online shoppers. The biggest online retailer is Amazon.com, which started out selling books and now sells almost everything.
- **Online banking:** In addition to their walk-in banks, Bank of America, Wells Fargo, and JPMorgan Chase all offer online banking services—checking account access, funds transfers, bill payment, loan applications, and the like. Ally Bank offers services through such social media as Facebook, YouTube, and Twitter.
- **Online stock trading:** E*Trade, Scottrade.com, and TD Ameritrade are examples of B2C stock brokers that allow consumers to buy and sell stocks and bonds directly via the Internet, often at a lower cost compared to traditional brokers.

C2C COMMERCE: CONSUMER-TO-CONSUMER **Consumer-to-consumer commerce, or *C2C commerce,* is the electronic sale or exchange of goods and services between individuals.** Probably the most popular examples of C2C are *online classified ads,* such as Craigslist, and *web auctions,* such as eBay and etsy.com.

There are generally two types of auction sites:

- **Person-to-person auctions:** *Person-to-person auctions,* such as eBay, connect buyers and sellers for a listing fee and a commission on sold items. (• *See Panel 2.29, next page.*)
- **Vendor-based auctions:** *Vendor-based auctions,* such as OnSale and ebid.net/, buy merchandise and sell it at discount. Some auctions are specialized, such as Priceline, an auction site for airline tickets and other items.

Some Auction Websites

eBay www.ebay.com/

WeBidz www.webidz.com/

shopgoodwill www.shopgoodwill.com/

Listia www.listia.com/

panel 2.29

eBay auction

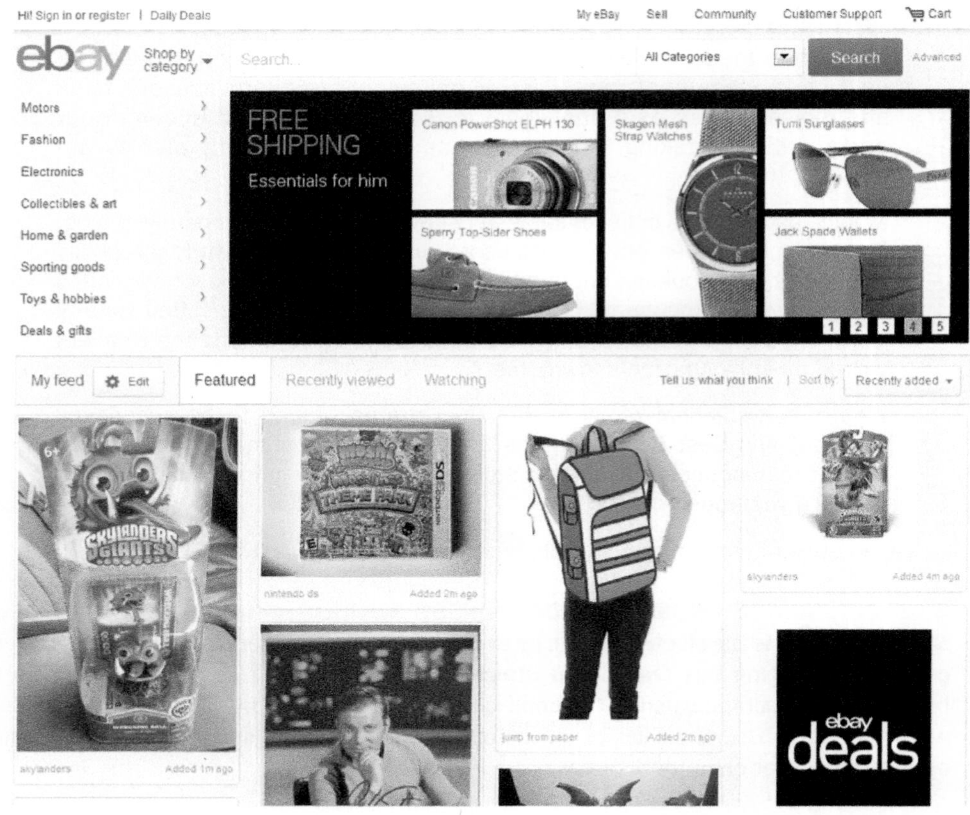

Web 2.0, the Social Web: Social Networking, Media Sharing, & Social-Network Aggregation

Web 2.0 refers to the web viewed as a medium in which interactive experience, in the form of blogs, wikis, forums, social networking, and so on, plays a more important role than simply accessing information.

Comparison of the Top 10 Social-Networking Sites

http://social-networking-websites-review.toptenreviews.com/

According to web inventor Tim Berners-Lee, the first generation of his creation could be called *Web 1.0* and could be considered the "read-only web," because it allowed users only to search for information and read it; there was little user interaction or content contribution.[39]

Since then it has become what is known as **Web 2.0, which can be defined as the move toward a more social, collaborative, interactive, and responsive web that puts information in the hands of the people.**[40] As websites have become easier to use, they allow users to better harness the collective power of people, which has led to a "social web" or "social media," involving not only blogs and wikis (for sharing information and providing content) but also social networks and media sharing. The common theme of all these is human interaction.

Let's consider some principal features of Web 2.0: social networking, media sharing, and social-network aggregators. (In the future, we may well see a *Web 3.0,* as we describe on p. 93.)

Survival Tip

Social-Networking Privacy

Check your social-networking and messaging privacy options carefully:

http://mashable.com/2011/09/28/new-facebook/

www.sophos.com/en-us/security-news-trends/best-practices/facebook.aspx

http://epic.org/privacy/socialnet/

www.huffingtonpost.com/2012/03/20/social-media-privacy-infographic_n_1367223.html

SOCIAL-NETWORKING WEBSITES: MYSPACE, FACEBOOK, & LINKEDIN A **social-networking website is an online community that allows members to keep track of their friends and share photos, videos, music, stories, and ideas with other registered members.** Social-networking websites are led by Facebook (1.11 billion users in May 2013) and MySpace (25 million users) but also include the business-contact site LinkedIn (225 million users).[41] (The average age of a Facebook user is 40.5 years [*http://royal.pingdom.com/2013/01/16/internet-2012-in-numbers/*].)

facebook

Connect with friends and the world around you on Facebook.

See photos and updates from friends in News Feed.

Share what's new in your life on your Timeline.

Find more of what you're looking for with Graph Search.

About Us

Welcome to LinkedIn, the world's largest professional network with 225 million members in over 200 countries and territories around the globe.

Mission

Our mission is simple: connect the world's professionals to make them more productive and successful. When you join LinkedIn, you get access to people, jobs, news, updates, and insights that help you be great at what you do.

Company Info

LinkedIn started out in the living room of co-founder Reid Hoffman in 2002, and it officially launched on May 5, 2003.

Jeff Weiner is the CEO, and the company's management team is made up of seasoned executives from companies like Yahoo!, Google, Microsoft, TiVo, PayPal, and Electronic Arts.

MEDIA-SHARING WEBSITES: YOUTUBE, FLICKR, & OTHER WAYS OF SHARING PHOTOS, VIDEOS, & MUSIC A **media-sharing website is a type of online social network in which members share media such as photos, videos, and music.** The most popular example is YouTube, but others are Hulu, Flickr, Shutterfly, and Yahoo! Video. Video-sharing sites include YouTube, Flickr, Photobucket, Imageshack, and Vimeo.

Protest in Tahir Square, Cairo, Egypt, February 2011. Smartphone cameras and Facebook were instrumental in spreading news about the uprising.

SOCIAL-NETWORK AGGREGATORS: FRIENDFEED, SPOKEO, & OTHER FRIEND-TRACKING TOOLS Cathy Brooks, 39, of San Francisco is described as a "typically unapologetic" web addict. In one week alone, it's reported, "she produced more than 40 pithy updates on the text messaging service Twitter, uploaded two dozen videos to various video-sharing sites, posted seven graphs on . . . Flickr and one item to the online community calendar Upcoming."[42] She and her friends follow one another's activities by funneling them into a single information broadcast, a content-aggregation system known as FriendFeed.

Social-network aggregators, or *social aggregators,* collect content from all of a user's various social network profiles into one place, then allow the user and others to track friends and share their other social network activities. Besides FriendFeed, other examples of "friend-tracking services" are Iminta, Plaxo, Readr, and Mugshot.

Does Being "Always On" Change Your Personality?

A Stanford study observed that "even at a subpathological level, time spent communicating electronically or plugged into web-based activities . . . pushes people toward developing a separate e-personality that then bleeds back into their real life."

www.stanfordalumni.org/news/magazine/2011/janfeb/features/digital.html

Web 3.0: Computer-Generated Information with Less Human Interaction

In Web 3.0, information will be computer-generated with less human interaction required to discover and integrate that information.

In the next generation of the web, you could type, "I want to see a funny movie, and then eat at a good Mexican restaurant. What are my options?"[43] The browser will analyze your response, search the Internet for all possible answers, and then organize the results for you.

With Web 2.0, you can't do this kind of search; it might require the use of keywords and multiple searches. With Web 3.0, it will be routine to find things by typing in a complex sentence or two, such as the one above. In *Web 3.0,* information will be computer-generated, and less human interaction will be required to discover and integrate that information.

Two ideas might form the basis for Web 3.0—*semantic markup* and a *personal browser.*[44]

SEMANTIC MARKUP Presently Web 2.0 can't really understand what is relevant and what is not; it can't provide context to data. Another name suggested for Web 3.0 is the

PRACTICAL ACTION

Social Networking: The Downside

Social networking was supposed to make us closer, and in many ways it has, allowing us to get back in touch with old friends; share photos, histories, and enthusiasms; and become better acquainted with people we otherwise might not meet. But the Internet can also be a nasty place. University of Chicago law professor Martha Nussbaum sees it, in one description, as "a cesspool, a porn store, a form of pinkeye, a raunchy fraternity, a graffiti-filled bathroom wall, a haven for sociopaths, and the breeder of online mobs who are no better than 'masked Klan members' in their determination to 'interfere with victims' basic rights."[45]

Some risks of this side of the Internet and of social networking are these:

- **Social communication skills are diminished:** Too much online interaction can hurt real-life relationships. Uploading photos, forwarding inane quizzes, posting dumb jokes, or tweeting unimportant information about our whereabouts are no substitute for face-to-face or phone communication. Body language and voice inflection can express nuances that typing cannot. Are we losing some of the best parts of human interaction?
- **Your supposedly private data is used to sell you stuff:** Even people who set their Facebook profiles to the strictest privacy settings aren't necessarily protected from having their personal information leaked all over the web.[46] A *Wall Street Journal* investigation found that some popular apps on social-networking sites have been transmitting identifying information, including users' passwords, home addresses, phone numbers, and email addresses, to dozens of advertising and Internet tracking companies and other third-party entities.[47] Indeed, you may already have discovered that your supposedly private data is being used to try to sell you things and sell people you don't even know things that you "like" *under your real name.* (See "Are You Safe on Facebook?" *http://tech.fortune.cnn.com/2011/01/28/are-you-safe-on-facebook/* and "Why I'm Quitting Facebook," *www.cnn.com/2013/02/25/opinion/rushkoff-why-im-quitting-facebook.*)
- **Your online data may exist forever and can be used against you:** Your supposedly "deleted" photos and messages may remain online for years. This gives potential employers the opportunity to turn up inappropriate photos you posted and criminals the chance to use them in fraudulent schemes, such as fake adoption scams.
- **Social networks may be used to attack others:** Social-networking sites can become platforms for anonymous bullying and other types of attacks. Anonymity, suggests Nussbaum, allows Internet bloggers and site users "to create for themselves a shame-free zone in which they can inflict shame on others." Their power "depends on their ability to insulate their Internet selves from responsibility in the real world, while ensuring real-world consequences" for the victims.[48] (For more on bullying on Facebook, see *www.consumerreports.org/cro/magazine-archive/2011/june/electronics-computers/state-of-the-net/facebook-concerns/index.htm*. For information on fake "friends," see *www.huffingtonpost.com/2011/02/10/facebook-friend-request-spam_n_821584.html.*)
- Also, the U.S. Congress is working on passing the Cyber Intelligence Sharing and Protection Act (CISPA), which would help individuals to protect their right to privacy and prohibit an employer from impersonating an employee online when other employees are interacting across social media platforms. Removed from this bill was a provision that would have banned employers from asking job candidates and employees for their social media passwords.[49]
- Employers don't often ask for this information right now, but be aware that, when you are looking for a job, what's on your Facebook page may hurt your chances.

"Every new technology will bite back," writes technical journalist Kevin Kelley. "The more powerful its gifts, the more powerfully it can be abused. Look for its costs."[50] This warning should certainly be taken to heart when it comes to social networking.

"semantic web" because it will use *semantic markup,* or data interchange formats, that will allow machines to understand the meaning—or "semantics"—of information on the web. With semantic markup, data could be put into a form that could be understood by the computer while also being accessible to humans.

PERSONAL BROWSER The Web 3.0 browser will probably act as a personal assistant because every user will have a unique Internet profile based on his or her browsing history. As you search the web and the browser learns more about you, the less specific you'll need

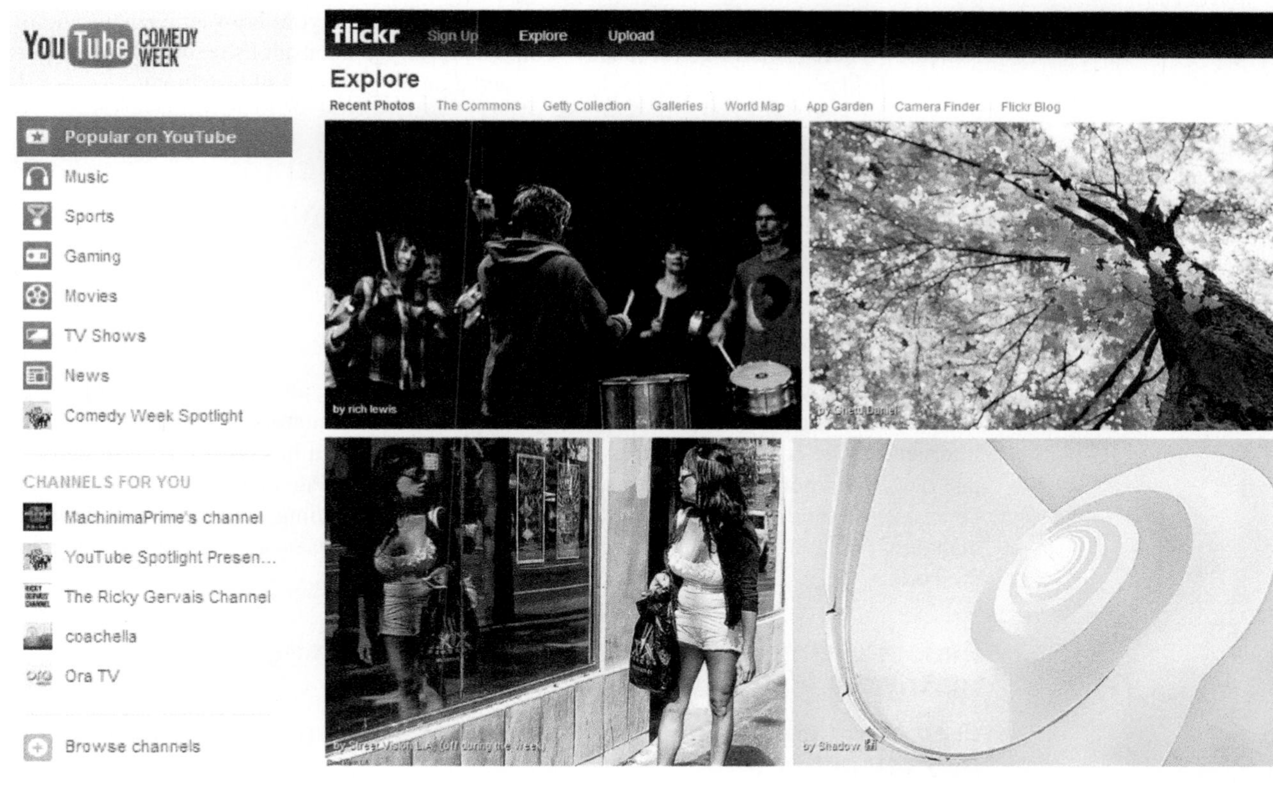

About FriendFeed

FriendFeed is a service that makes it easy to share with friends online. It offers a fun and interactive way to discover and discuss information among friends.

Sign up for FriendFeed, invite some friends, and get an instant, customized feed made up of the content that your friends shared — from photos to interesting links and videos to messages just for you. And your friends get their customized feeds, full of the cool stuff that you've shared.

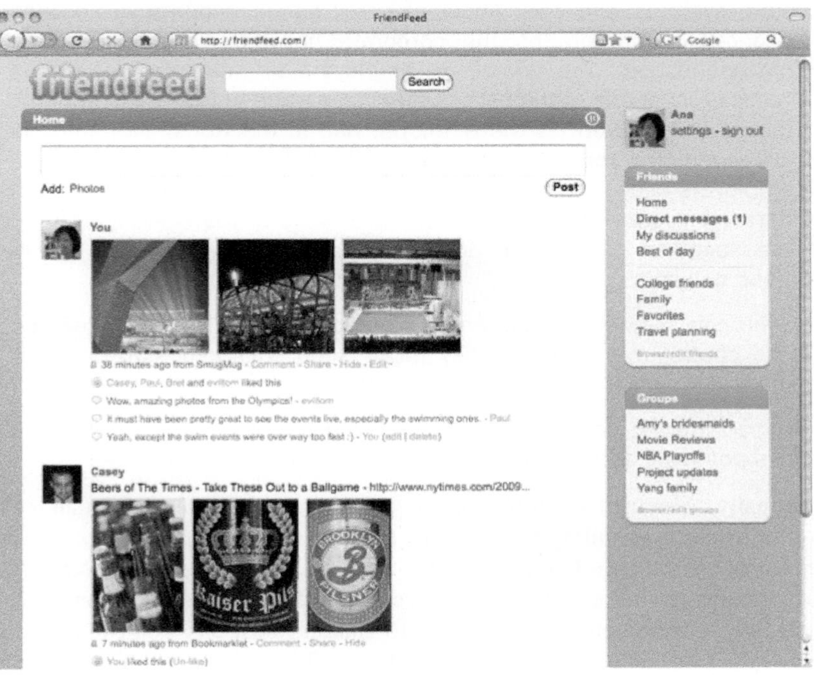

more info!

Top Media-Sharing Websites

- Flickr
- Hulu
- Photobucket
- Imageshack
- Shutterfly
- Twango
- Yahoo! Video
- YouTube

to be with your questions. Eventually you might be able to ask your browser open questions such as, "Where should I go for lunch?" Your browser would consult its records of what you like and dislike, check your current location, and then suggest a list of restaurants.

2.6 THE INTRUSIVE INTERNET: Snooping, Spamming, Spoofing, Phishing, Pharming, Cookies, Spyware, & Malware

Protect your identity, your financial information, and your privacy while online and while using your computer.

The Internet is wide open. "The Internet is just too accessible, and it's too easy for people to make anything they want out of it," say one pair of commentators.[51] Thus, although the Internet may be constrained somewhat by regulatory bodies, it has pitfalls and dangers—just like life in general. Here let us touch on a few of immediate concern that you should be aware of: snooping, spamming, spoofing, phishing, pharming, cookies, spyware, and malware. (This is not a complete list. We describe other nuisances and dangers later in the book.)

Snooping on Your Email & Texts: Your Messages Are Open to Anyone

Even if you delete your emails and texts, they are not "gone." And they are not private.

The single best piece of advice that can be given about sending email and texts is this: *Pretend every electronic message is a postcard that can be read by anyone.* Because the chances are high that it could be.

TECH TALES How Difficult It Is to Keep Your Emails & Texts Private

Think the boss can't snoop on your email at work? Well, you don't own your employee email account; your employer does. Thus, anything included in your employee email account is fair game for human resources or your employer's lawyers—you have no defensible expectation of privacy on corporate systems. But what about *personal* email accounts you access on corporate computers on the corporate network via the corporate Internet connection? The law allows employers to "intercept" employee communications if *one* of the parties involved agrees to the "interception"; and the party "involved" is the employer. And in the workplace, email is typically saved on a server, at least for a while. Indeed, federal laws require that employers keep some email messages for years. Mobile smartphone providers store data—from three months to several years—ranging from text messages to pictures, IP addresses, browsing history, cell towers used, and call logs.

Think you can keep your email and texts secret among your friends? You have no control over whether they might send your e-messages on to someone else—who might in turn forward them again.

Think your Internet access provider will protect your privacy? Often such services post your address publicly or even sell their customer lists. ■

SECURITY

If you're really concerned about preserving your privacy, you can try certain technical solutions—for instance, installing software that encodes and decodes messages (discussed in Chapter 6). But the simplest solution is the easiest: Don't put any sensitive or embarrassing information in your email and text messages. Even deleted email removed from the trash can still be traced on your hard disk. To guard against this, you can use software such as Spytech Eradicator and Revo to completely eliminate deleted files. (Be aware, however: Your email and texts may already have been backed up on the company—or campus—server.)

Spam: Electronic Junk Mail

Spam is unwanted junk mail.

Some years ago, Monty Python, the British comedy group, did a sketch in which restaurant customers were unable to converse because people in the background (a group of Vikings, actually) kept chanting "Spam, spam, eggs and spam. . . ." The term *spam* was picked up by the computer world to describe another kind of "noise" that interferes with communication. Now **spam refers to unsolicited email, or junk mail, in the form of advertising or chain letters.** But the problem of spam has spread well beyond the stage of annoyance.

Spam has become so pestiferous that *Smart Computing* magazine referred to it as a "cockroach infestation."[52] In 2012, the number of spam messages sent *daily* was 99 billion.[53] Spam plagues email users and social networks, such as Facebook. It has migrated from computers to cellphones, messages that the recipients have to pay for.

Usually, of course, you don't recognize the spam sender on your list of incoming mail, and often the subject line will give no hint, stating something such as "The status of your application" or "It's up to you now." The solicitations range from moneymaking schemes to online pornography. To better manage spam, some users get two email boxes. One is used for online shopping, business, research, and the like—which will continue to attract spam. The other is used (like an unlisted phone number) only for personal friends and family—and will probably not receive much spam. Also, never click on the "unsubscribe" link often shown at the bottom of spam emails. If you do, you are only confirming that you are a real person with a valid email address.

Survival Tip

Look for the Padlock Icon or the "s"

To avoid having people spying on you when you are sending information over the web, use a secure connection. This is indicated at the bottom of your browser window by an icon that looks like a padlock or key. Also, the "s" in "https://" indicates a secure site.

Tips for Fighting Spam

http://ezinearticles.com/?Tips-to-Fight-SPAM&id=2321867

http://email.about.com/od/spamfightingtips/Spam_Fighting_Tips_Tricks_and_Secrets.htm

www.uc.edu/infosec/info/fightspam.html

Spoofing, Phishing, & Pharming: Phony Email Senders & Websites

Don't be fooled by real-looking but phony emails and websites.

A message shows up in your email supposedly from someone named "Sonia Saunders." The subject line reads "Re: Hey cutie." It could have been from someone you know, but it's actually a pitch for porn. Or you receive what appears to be an "Urgent notice from eBay," the online auction company, stating that "failure to update billing information will result in cancellation of service" and asking you to go to the web address indicated and update your credit-card information. In the first instance you've been *spoofed;* in the second you've been *phished.*[54]

SPOOFING—USING FAKE EMAIL SENDER NAMES **Spoofing is the forgery of an email sender name so that the message appears to have originated from someone or somewhere other than the actual source.** Spoofing is one of the main tactics used by spammers (and virus writers) to induce or trick recipients into opening and perhaps responding to their solicitations. Spoofing is generally not illegal and might even serve a legitimate purpose under some circumstances—say, a whistle-blowing employee fearful of retaliation after reporting a company's illegalities to a government agency. Spoofing is illegal, however, if it involves a direct threat of violence or death.[55]

Deciphering Fake Email

For more about spoofing and how to identify origins of fake emails, go to:

www.mailsbroadcast.com/email.broadcast.faq/46.email.spoofing.htm

http://usgovinfo.about.com/cs/consumer/a/aaspoofing.htm

PHISHING—USING TRUSTED INSTITUTIONAL NAMES TO ELICIT CONFIDENTIAL INFORMATION **Phishing (pronounced "fishing" and short for *password harvesting fishing*) is (1) the sending of a forged email that (2) directs recipients to a replica of an existing web page, both of which pretend to belong to a legitimate company. The purpose of the fraudulent sender is to "phish" for, or entice people to share, their personal, financial, or password data.** The names may be trusted names such as Citibank, eBay, or Best Buy. A variant is *spear-phishing,* in which a message seems to originate within your company, as when a "security department assistant" asks you to update your name and password or risk suspension. Thus, you should be suspicious of *any* email that directs you to a website that requests confidential information, such as credit-card info or Social Security number.

Smishing, or *SMS phishing,* uses SMS services to send bogus text messages in an effort to obtain personal information (identity theft).

Verifying Valid Websites

For more on verifying if you're dealing with a legitimate company website, go to:

www.wikihow.com/Find-if-a-Website-Is-Legitimate/

http://howto.cnet.com/8301-11310_39-20098098-285/how-to-check-if-a-web-site-is-safe/

PHARMING—REDIRECTING YOU TO AN IMPOSTOR WEB PAGE Pharming is a newer kind of phishing that is harder to detect. **In pharming, thieves implant malicious software**

on a victim's computer that redirects the user to an impostor web page even when the individual types the correct address into his or her browser. One way to protect yourself is to make sure you go to special secure web pages, such as any financial website, which begin with *https* (p. 64) rather than the standard *http* and which use encryption to protect data transfer.

> **Survival Tip**
>
> **Control Those Cookies!**
>
> You can use your browser's Help function to accept or reject cookies. For instance, in Internet Explorer, go to the Tools menu and click *Internet Options;* on the General tab, click *Settings;* then click *View files,* select the cookie you want to delete, and on the File menu click *Delete.* Software such as Cookie Pal (*www.kburra.com*) will also help block and control cookies, as will Revo. Also go to *www.allabout-cookies.org/manage-cookies/stop-cookies-installed.html.*

Cookies: Convenience or Hindrance?

Cookies can make some Internet processes go faster, but they can also be used by companies to track your Internet use and your personal information.

Cookies **are little text files—such as your username, password, and preferences—left on your hard disk by websites you visit. The websites retrieve the data when you visit again.** A website that welcomes you by name uses cookies.

THE BENEFITS OF COOKIES Cookies can be a convenience. If you visit an online merchant—such as BarnesandNoble.com for a book—and enter all your address and other information, the merchant will assign you an identification number, store your information with that number on its server, and send the number to your browser as a cookie, which stores the ID number on your hard disk. The next time you go to that merchant, the number is sent to the server, which looks you up and sends you a customized web page welcoming you.

"Cookies actually perform valuable services," says technology writer and computer talk-radio-show host Kim Komando. "For instance, they can shoot you right into a site so you don't have to enter your password."[56] Says another writer: "They can also fill in a username on a site that requires logging in, or help a weather site remember a Zip code so that it can show a local forecast on return visits."[57]

THE DRAWBACKS OF COOKIES Cookies are not necessarily dangerous—they are not programs, and they can't transmit computer viruses, for example. However, some websites sell the information associated with your ID number on their servers to marketers, who might use it to target customers for their products. "Unsatisfactory cookies," in Microsoft's understated term, are those that might allow someone access to personally identifiable information that could be used without your consent for some secondary purpose. This can lead to *spyware,* as we describe next.

Deleting cookies in Windows 7

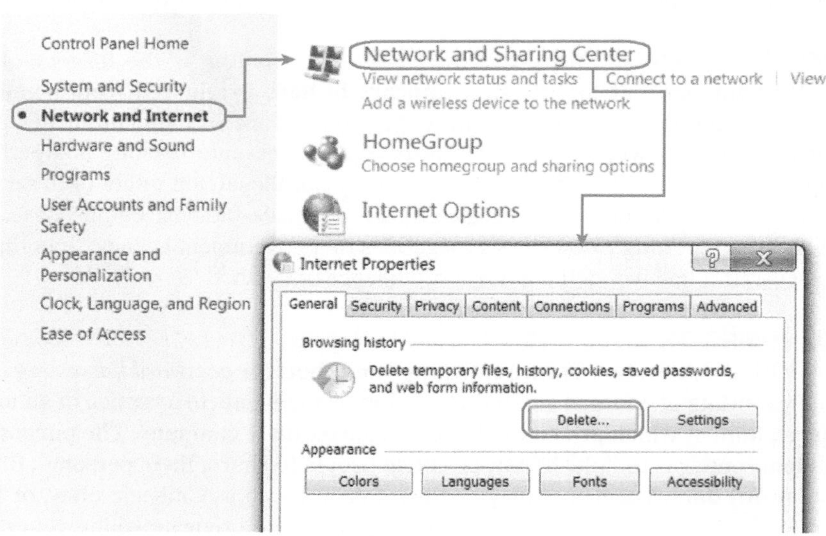

How to Shop Safely on the Internet

www.wikihow.com/Shop-Online-Safely/

www.microsoft.com/security/online-privacy/online-shopping.aspx

www.safeshopping.org/

http://usgovinfo.about.com/od/consumerawareness/l/blonline-shopsaf.htm

Spyware—Adware, Browser & Search Hijackers, & Key Loggers: Intruders to Track Your Habits & Steal Your Data

Learn how to protect your data against intruders.

You visit a search site such as Yahoo! or Google and click on a text ad that appears next to your search results. Or you download a free version of some software, such as Kazaa, the popular file-sharing program. Or you simply visit some web merchant to place an order.

The next thing you know, you are getting **pop-up ads, a form of online advertising in which, when you visit certain websites, a new window opens, or "pops up," to display advertisements.** You have just had an encounter with *spyware,* of which pop-up ads are only one form. **Spyware is deceptive software that is surreptitiously installed on a computer via the web; once installed on your hard disk, it allows outsiders to gather confidential information without your knowledge**—for example, keystrokes, passwords, your email address, your credit-card numbers and Social Security number, and your history of website visits. Ways to avoid getting spyware are shown in the more info! feature opposite.

The most common forms of spyware are these.

Fighting Spyware

More information about ways to combat spyware may be found at:

www.microsoft.com/security/pc-security/spyware-whatis.aspx

www.technicianplatoon.com/how-to-fight-spyware/

http://reviews.cnet.com/4520-10165_7-5601335-1.html

ADWARE OR POP-UP GENERATORS **Adware, or *pop-up generator,* is a kind of spyware that tracks web surfing or online buying so that marketers can send you targeted and unsolicited pop-up and other ads.** This is the most common, and benign, type of spyware. Adware can be developed by legitimate companies such as Verizon and Panasonic but also by all kinds of fly-by-night purveyors of pornography and gambling operating from computer servers in Russia, Spain, and the Virgin Islands.

BROWSER HIJACKERS & SEARCH HIJACKERS More damaging kinds of spyware are **browser hijackers, which change settings in your browser without your knowledge, often changing your browser's home page and replacing it with another web page, and search hijackers, which intercept your legitimate search requests made to real search engines and return results from phony search services designed to send you to sites they run.**

How do you know if your browser has been hijacked?

- The home page or other settings change on your computer. Links are added that point to websites that you'd usually avoid.
- You can't navigate to certain web pages, such as antispyware and other security software sites.
- A seemingly endless barrage of ads pops up on your screen.
- New toolbars or favorites are installed that give you icons and links to web pages that you don't want.
- Your computer runs sluggishly. Malicious software (malware) can slow down your computer.[58]

How to get Rid of a Browser Hijacker

http://askbobrankin.com/my_browser_got_hijacked.html

www.ehow.com/how_4886023_remove-browser-hijacking-programs.html

And for information on combatting malware ("badware"):

www.stopbadware.org/

KEY LOGGERS **Key loggers, or *keystroke loggers,* can record each character you type and transmit that information to someone else on the Internet, making it possible for strangers to learn your passwords and other information.** For instance, some may secretly record the keystrokes you use to log into online bank accounts and then send the information off to who knows where.

Some Internet access providers offer spyware scan-and-removal tools, but you can also employ specialized antispyware software. Some of the good ones appear below. (• *See Panel 2.30.*)

One big problem with spyware is that overburdened PCs begin to run more slowly as the hard drives cope with random and uncontrollable processes. If none of the antispyware works, you will need to wipe your hard drive clean of programs and data and start from scratch—a complicated matter that we discuss in Chapter 4.

Ad-Aware	*www.lavasoft.com/*
Malwarebytes	*www.malwarebytes.org/products/malwarebytes_pro/*
PC Tools	*www.pctools.com/simple/*
Spycatcher	*www.tenebril.com/products.html* .
Superantispyware	*www.superantispyware.com/*

panel 2.30

Some antispyware programs

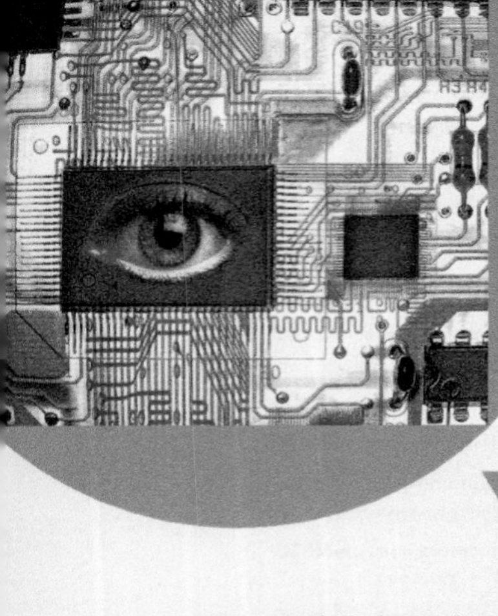

PRACTICAL ACTION

Tips for Avoiding Spyware

You may not be able to completely avoid spyware, but doing the following may help:

- **Be careful about free and illegal downloads:** Be choosy about free downloads or illegal downloads of songs, movies, or TV shows. Often they use a form of spyware. File-sharing programs, which are popular with students, often contain spyware. Pornographic websites also are common carriers of spyware.
- **Don't just say "I agree"; read the fine print:** Sites that offer games, music-sharing videos, screen savers, and weather data often are paid to distribute spyware. When you install their software, you might be asked to agree to certain conditions. If you simply click "I agree" without reading the fine print, you may be authorizing installation of spyware. "People have gotten in the habit of clicking next, next, next, without reading" when they install software, says a manager at McAfee Inc., which tracks spyware and viruses.[59]
- **Beware of unsolicited downloads:** If while you're surfing the net your browser warns you a file is being downloaded and you're asked if you choose to accept, keep clicking *no* until the messages stop.

Malware Types

How many types of malware are there actually? Lots!

www.givemebackmycredit.com/blog/2012/03/march-madness-2012-new-types-of-malware-scams.html

www.veracode.com/blog/2012/10/common-malware-types-cyber-security-101/

www.pandasecurity.com/homeusers/security-info/types-malware/

www.kaspersky.com/threats/what-is-malware/

www.ecommerce-web-hosting-guide.com/what-is-malware.html

Malware: The Viciousness of Viruses

There are many forms of malicious software—so-called malware—that can harm a computer system, a common danger being viruses.

Besides spyware, there are other kinds of deceptive software, known as **malware, for "malicious software"**—that can attack your computer systems and mobile devices. They include an army of plagues such as worms and Trojan horses, zombies and bots, ransomware and rootkits, as we discuss in detail in Chapter 6. Here, however, let us describe just one deadly form of malware, known as a virus, so that you'll know how to protect yourself during your Internet explorations.

VIRUSES: ROGUE PROGRAMS TO AVOID **A virus is a rogue program that migrates through the Internet or via operating systems and attaches itself to different programs that spread from one computer to another, leaving infections.** There are millions of viruses in circulation, but at one time they were mainly threats only to conventional computers. Now, however, viruses have targeted programs and websites popular with smartphone and tablet users, such as Facebook, Twitter, and YouTube, as well as website ads.

HOW TO REDUCE YOUR MALWARE RISKS Because a virus is spread by human action, people will unknowingly continue to spread it by sharing infected files or sending emails with infected attachments. What can you do to minimize your risks? The principal defense is to install **antivirus software, which scans a computer to detect viruses and, sometimes, to destroy them.** Following are suggestions for protecting yourself:

- Download virus protection software, such as McAfee VirusScan (*www.mcafee.com*) or Norton AntiVirus (*www.symantec.com/nav*); then follow instructions for installing it on your machine. (Don't use antivirus software from companies you know nothing about.) Scan your entire system with antivirus software the first time it's installed; then scan it regularly after that. Also scan any new CDs and drives before using them.
- Don't open, download, or execute any files, email messages, or email attachments if the source is unknown or if the subject line of an email is questionable or unexpected.
- Delete all spam and email messages from strangers. Don't open, forward, or reply to such messages.

- Use webmail sparingly, since viruses can hide in the HTML coding of the email. Even the simple act of previewing the message in your email program can activate the virus and infect your computer.
- Don't start your computer with a flash drive, USB thumb drive, or CD/DVD in place.
- Back up your data files regularly, and keep at least one backup device in a location separate from your computer or use an online (cloud) backup service.
- If you discover you have a virus, ask McAfee or Norton to scan your computer online; then follow its directions for cleaning or deleting the virus.

Passwords

When inventing a password, choose a combination of letters and/or numbers that is easy for you to remember but that no one else can guess.

Passwords won't necessarily protect you against being infected by malware, but they do make it more difficult for intruders to get into your computer system. A *password,* as we said, is a special combination of letters and/or numbers that limits access to information.

The best kind of password is one that is easy for you to remember but can't be guessed by anyone else. Some advice for formulating a password is as follows:[60]

- Never choose a real word or variations of your or your family's name, address, phone number, Social Security number, license plate, or birth date.
- Don't use passwords that can be easily guessed, such as "12345" or "password."
- Avoid any word that appears in a dictionary. Instead, mix letters, numbers, and punctuation marks in an oddball sequence of no fewer than eight characters, such as *2b/orNOT2b%* and *Alfred!E!Newman7.* Or choose a password that is memorable but shift the position of your fingers on the keyboard, so that, for instance, *TIMBERWOLVES* becomes *YO,NRTEP;BRD* when you move your fingers one position right. For sensitive sites, such as financial accounts, create long passwords, such as 15-character passwords.
- Don't use the same password for multiple sites, so that if someone obtains the password to one account, that person won't have access to your entire online life.
- Finally, don't write passwords on sticky notes or in a notebook or tape them under your keyboard. Don't carry the passwords in your wallet. If you have to write down all your passwords, find a safe place to put the paper, or use a software password manager, such as Kaspersky Password Manager, RoboForm Everywhere, or Last Pass Premium.

We discuss passwords and other security matters further in Chapter 6.

Survival Tip

Protect against Cellphone Viruses & Spyware

According to HowStuffWorks (*http://electronics.howstuffworks.com/cell-phone-virus4.htm*), the best way to protect yourself from cellphone viruses is the same way you protect yourself from computer viruses: Never open anything if you don't know what it is, haven't requested it, or have any suspicions whatsoever that it's not what it claims to be. See also:

www.pcworld.com/article/252235/protect_your_smartphone_from_mobile_malware.html

www.nospysoftware.com/spyware-articles/cell-phone-virus.php

http://anti-virus-software-review.toptenreviews.com/mobile-phones-are-under-malware-attack.html

http://securitywatch.pcmag.com/mobile-security/309980-five-signs-your-android-device-is-infected-with-malware/

http://edition.cnn.com/2013/04/16/business/world-most-mobile-infected-countries/

Survival Tip

Passwords That Are Easiest to Guess (& Steal)

Here is the list of the worst passwords of 2012. (For a short video on how to create strong online passwords, go to *http://techland.time.com/2011/06/29/two-minute-video-how-to-create-strong-online-passwords/*.)

1. password
2. 123456
3. 12345678
4. abc123
5. qwerty
6. monkey
7. letmein
8. dragon
9. 111111
10. baseball
11. iloveyou
12. trustno1
13. 1234567
14. sunshine
15. master
16. 123123
17. welcome
18. shadow
19. ashley
20. football
21. jesus
22. michael
23. ninja
24. mustang
25. password1

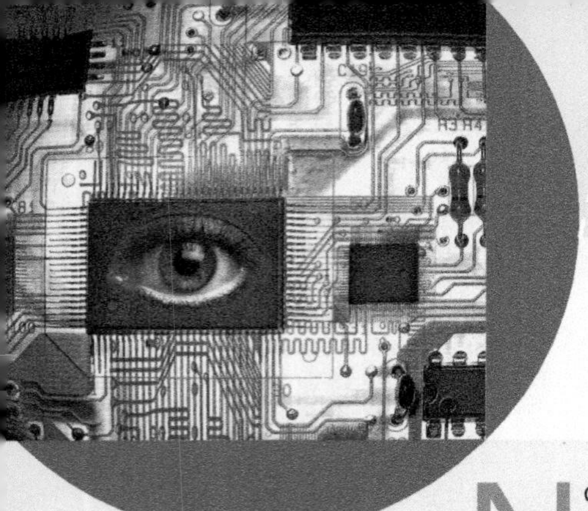

EXPERIENCE BOX

Web Research, Term Papers, & Plagiarism

No matter how much students may be able to rationalize cheating in college—for example, trying to pass off someone else's term paper as their own (plagiarism)—ignorance of the consequences is not an excuse. Most instructors announce the penalties for cheating at the beginning of the course—usually a failing grade in the course and possible suspension or expulsion from school.

Even so, probably every student becomes aware before long that the World Wide Web contains sites that offer term papers, either for free or for a price. Some dishonest students may download papers and change the author's name to their own. Others are more likely to use the papers for ideas.

How the Web Can Lead to Plagiarism

Two types of term-paper websites are as follows:

- **Sites offering papers for free:** Such a site requires that users fill out a membership form and then provides at least one free student term paper. (Good quality is not guaranteed, since free-paper mills often subsist on the submissions of poor students, whose contributions may be subliterate.)
- **Sites offering papers for sale:** Commercial sites may charge $6–$10 or more a page, which users may pay with a credit card. (Expense is no guarantee of quality. Moreover, the term-paper factory may turn around and make your $350 custom paper available to others—even fellow classmates working on the same assignment—for half the price.)

How Instructors Catch Cheaters

How do instructors detect student plagiarism? Professors are unlikely to be fooled if they tailor term-paper assignments to work done in class, monitor students' progress—from outline to completion—and are alert to papers that seem radically different from a student's past work.

Just as the Internet can be a source of cheating, it is also a tool for detecting cheaters. Search programs make it possible for instructors to locate texts containing identified strings of words from the millions of pages found on the web. Thus, a professor can input passages from a student's paper into a search program that scans the web for identical blocks of text. Indeed, some websites favored by instructors build a database of papers over time so that students can't recycle work previously handed in by others. Special software programs, such as at CopyScape.com, PlagiarismChecker.com, grammarly.com, SplaT, and academicplagiarism.com, are available for instructors to check students' work and for students to check their own work before turning it in.

How the Web Can Lead to Low-Quality Papers

Philosophy professor David Rothenberg, of New Jersey Institute of Technology, reported that as a result of students' doing more of their research on the web, he saw "a disturbing decline in both the quality of the writing and the originality of the thoughts expressed."[61] How can an instructor spot a term paper based primarily on web research? Rothenberg offers four clues:

- **No books cited:** The student's bibliography cites no books, just articles or references to websites. Sadly, says Rothenberg, "one finds few references to careful, in-depth commentaries on the subject of the paper, the kind of analysis that requires a book, rather than an article, for its full development."
- **Outdated material:** A lot of the material in the bibliography is strangely out of date, says Rothenberg. "A lot of stuff on the web that is advertised as timely is actually at least a few years old."
- **Unrelated pictures and graphs:** Students may intersperse the text with a lot of impressive-looking pictures and graphs that actually bear little relation to the precise subject of the paper. "Cut and pasted from the vast realm of what's out there for the taking, they masquerade as original work."
- **Superficial references:** "Too much of what passes for information online these days is simply advertising for information," points out Rothenberg. "Screen after screen shows you where you can find out more, how you can connect to this place or that." Other kinds of information are detailed but often superficial: "pages and pages of federal documents, corporate propaganda, snippets of commentary by people whose credibility is difficult to assess."

Remember one main point: *citing sources adds to the credibility of a paper.*

access point (p. 58) Station that sends and receives data to and from a Wi-Fi network. Why it's important: *Many public areas, such as airports and hotels, offer hotspots, or access points, that enable Wi-Fi-equipped users to go online wirelessly.*

adware (p. 99) Also called *pop-up generators;* kind of spyware that tracks web surfing or online buying. Why it's important: *Adware enables marketers to send you targeted and unsolicited pop-up and other ads.*

animation (p. 87) The rapid sequencing of still images to create the appearance of motion, as in a cartoon. Why it's important: *Animation is a component of multimedia; it is used in online videogames as well as in moving banners displaying sports scores or stock prices.*

antivirus software (p. 100) A program that scans a computer to detect viruses and, sometimes, to destroy them. Why it's important: *Antivirus software can protect your computer from disaster and from spreading viruses over networks.*

applets (p. 86) Small programs that can be quickly downloaded and run by most browsers. Why it's important: *Web pages embed links to applets, which add multimedia capabilities.*

backbones *See* **Internet backbone.**

bandwidth (p. 52) Also known as *channel capacity;* expression of how much data—text, voice, video, and so on—can be sent through a communications channel in a given amount of time. Why it's important: *Different communications systems use different bandwidths for different purposes. The wider the bandwidth, the faster the data can be transmitted.*

bits per second (bps) (p. 52) 8 bits make up a character. Why it's important: *Data transfer speeds are measured in bits per second.*

blogosphere (p. 88) The total universe of blogs. Why it's important: *The blogosphere has allowed the rise of a new breed of homegrown journal writers and diarists to chronicle life as it happens.*

broadband (p. 52) High-speed connection. Why it's important: *Access to information is much faster than access with traditional phone lines, and multimedia such as movies and online games will not work well without broadband connectivity.*

browser *See* **web browser.**

browser hijacker (p. 99) A damaging kind of spyware that changes settings in your browser without your knowledge. Why it's important: *Spyware can reset your home page to a porn site or obscure search engine or change your home page and replace it with another web page.*

business-to-business (B2B) commerce (p. 91) Electronic sale or exchange of goods and services directly between companies, cutting out traditional intermediaries. Why it's important: *Expected to grow even more rapidly than other forms of e-commerce, B2B commerce covers an extremely broad range of activities, such as supplier-to-buyer display of inventories, provision of wholesale price lists, and sales of closed-out items and used materials—usually without agents, brokers, or other third parties.*

business-to-consumer (B2C) commerce (p. 91) Electronic sale or exchange of goods and services directly between companies and the public, or end users. Why it's important: *Manufacturers may use this kind of commerce to eliminate the wholesaler and sell directly to customers, as some bands do by avoiding the record companies and selling their musical recordings directly to the public.*

cable modem (p. 56) Device connecting a personal computer to a cable-TV system that offers an Internet connection. Why it's important: *Cable modems transmit data faster than do standard modems.*

client (p. 59) Computer requesting data or services. Why it's important: *Part of the client-server network, in which the server is a central computer supplying data or services requested of it to the client computer.*

communications satellite (p. 57) Space station that transmits radio waves called *microwaves* from earth-based stations. Why it's important: *An orbiting satellite contains many communications channels and receives signals from ground microwave stations anywhere on earth.*

consumer-to-consumer (C2C) commerce (p. 91) Electronic sale or exchange of goods and services between individuals (consumers). Why it's important: *C2C occurs via online classified ads, such as Craigslist, and web auctions, such as eBay.*

cookies (p. 98) Little text files, such as your username, password, and preferences, that are left on your hard disk by websites you visit; the websites retrieve the data when you visit again. Why it's important: *Cookies can be beneficial in that they put you right into a website without having to enter your password. However, some websites sell the information associated with your ID number on their servers to marketers, who might use it to target you as a customer for their products.*

dial-up connection (p. 53) Use of a telephone modem to connect a computer to the Internet. Why it's important: *Cheapest means of online connection and available everywhere.*

domain (p. 64) A location on the Internet; the particular web server. Why it's important: *A domain name is necessary for sending and receiving email and for many other Internet activities.*

DSL (digital subscriber line) (p. 54) A hardware and software technology that uses regular phone lines to transmit data in megabits per second. Why it's important: *DSL connections are much faster than dial-up modem connections. It's often used in areas where cable and satellite are not available.*

e-commerce (electronic commerce) (p. 90) Conducting business activities online. Why it's important: *E-commerce not only is widening consumers' choice of products and services but is also creating new businesses and compelling established businesses to develop Internet strategies. E-commerce includes B2C, B2B, and C2C.*

email program (p. 78) Software that enables you to send email from your computer, which interacts with an email server at your Internet access provider to send and receive email. Why it's important: *With standard email software, unlike web-based email, you can easily integrate your email with other applications, such as calendar, task list, and contact list.*

flaming (p. 81) Writing an online message that uses derogatory, obscene, or inappropriate language. Why it's important: *Flaming should be avoided. It is a form of public humiliation inflicted on people who have failed to read FAQs or have otherwise not observed netiquette (although it can happen just because the sender has poor impulse control and needs a course in anger management).*

4G (fourth generation) (p. 58) Successor to 3G and 2G cellphone standards, with the aim to provide a wide range of data rates up to ultrabroadband (gigabit-speed) Internet access to mobile as well as stationary users. Why it's important: *4G devices have better access to multimedia.*

frame (p. 69) An independently controllable section of a web page. Why it's important: *A web page designer can divide a page into separate frames, each with different features or options.*

FTP (File Transfer Protocol) (p. 83) Method whereby you can connect to a remote computer called an *FTP site* and copy publicly available files to your own microcomputer's hard disk via TCP/IP over the Internet. Why it's important: *The free files offered cover nearly anything that can be stored on a computer: software, games, photos, maps, art, music, books, statistics.*

gigabits per second (Gbps) (p. 53) 1 billion bits per second. Why it's important: *Gbps is a common measure of data transmission speed.*

hit (p. 72) Site that a search engine returns after running a keyword search. Why it's important: *The web pages, or hits, that a search engine returns after you type in a keyword are the beginning of the types of information you are looking for.*

home page (p. 63) The starting point, or the main page, of a website that contains links to other pages at the site. This page usually has some sort of table of contents on it and often describes the purpose of the site. Why it's important: *The first page you see at a website is the home page.*

hotspot (p. 58) Public access to Wi-Fi networks. Why it's important: *Hotspots in airports, hotels, and the like enable wireless-equipped users to go online without a physical connection.*

hypertext links (p. 66) Also called *hyperlinks, hotlinks,* or just *links;* HTML connections to other documents or web pages that contain related information. Why it's important: *Hypertext links allow a word or phrase in one document to become a connection to a document in a different place.*

hypertext markup language (HTML) (p. 66) Set of special instructions (called "tags" or "markups") used to specify web document structure, formatting, and links to other documents. Why it's important: *HTML enables the creation of web pages.*

Hypertext Transfer Protocol (HTTP) (p. 64) Communications rules that allow browsers to connect with web servers. Why it's important: *Without HTTP, files could not be transferred over the web.*

individual search engine (p. 71) Type of Internet search tool that compiles its own searchable database on the web. You search for information by typing one or more keywords, and the search engine then displays a list of web pages, or "hits," that contain those keywords, ordered from most likely to least likely to contain the information you want. Why it's important: *Examples of this kind of search engine are Ask, Bing, Google, and Yahoo!, as well as AllTheWeb, Gigablast, and Lycos. These are the search engines most commonly used by individual users.*

instant messaging (IM) (p. 81) Service that enables any user on a given email system to send a message and have it pop up instantly on the screen of anyone else logged onto that system. Why it's important: *People can initiate online typed conversations in real time. As they are typed, the messages appear on the display screen in a small window.*

Internet backbone (p. 60) High-speed, high-capacity transmission lines that use the newest communications technology. Why it's important: *The Internet backbone transmits data across the Internet.*

Internet Corporation for Assigned Names and Numbers (ICANN) (p. 62) Global, private-sector, nonprofit corporation that was established to regulate human-friendly Internet domain names, those addresses ending with *.com, .org, .net,* and so on, that overlie IP addresses and identify the website type. Why it's important: *This organization helps humans organize and understand websites.*

Internet Exchange Point (IXP) (p. 60) A routing computer at a point on the Internet where several connections come together. Why it's important: *IXPs connect Internet service providers to the Internet backbone.*

Internet Protocol (IP) address (p. 61) Uniquely identifies every computer and device connected to the Internet; consists of four sets of numbers between 0 and 255 separated by decimals—for example, 1.160.10.240. This address is similar to a street address. However, street addresses rarely change, but IP addresses often do. Why it's important: *Each time you connect to your ISP, the ISP will assign your computer a new IP address, called a* dynamic IP address, *for your online session. When you request data from the Internet, it is transmitted to your computer's IP address. When you disconnect, your ISP frees up the IP address you were using and reassigns it to another user. Established organizational websites have their own* static IP addresses.

Internet service provider (ISP) (p. 58) Local, regional, or national organization that provides access to the Internet for a fee. Why it's important: *Unless subscribing to an online information service (such as AOL) or having a direct network connection* *(such as a T1 line), microcomputer users need an ISP to connect to the Internet.*

Internet telephony (p. 84) Also known as *VoIP,* short for *Voice over Internet Protocol;* method of making phone calls via the Internet, either one-to-one or for audioconferencing. Why it's important: *Long-distance phone calls by this means are surprisingly inexpensive.*

Internet2 (p. 60) A cooperative university/business education and research project that enables high-end users to quickly and reliably move huge amounts of data over high-speed networks. Why it's important: *Internet2 creates a kind of "virtual university" by advancing videoconferencing, research, and academic collaboration.*

IP address See **Internet Protocol address**

Java (p. 86) Complex programming language that enables programmers to create animated and interactive web pages using applets. Why it's important: *Java applets enhance web pages by playing music, displaying graphics and animation, and providing interactive games.*

key logger (p. 99) Also known as *keystroke logger;* spyware that can record each character you type and transmit that information to someone else on the Internet. Why it's important: *A key logger can make it possible for strangers to learn your passwords and other information.*

keyword (p. 70) A keyword is the subject word or words that refer to the topic you wish to find. Why it's important: *You must use keywords to research topics on the Internet.*

kilobits per second (Kbps) (p. 52) One thousand bits per second. Why it's important: *Kbps is a common measure of data transfer speed. The speed of a modem that is 56,000 bps may be expressed as 56 Kbps.*

links See **hypertext links.**

mailing list (p. 83) Email discussion group on a special-interest topic, in which all subscribers receive email messages sent to the group's email address. Why it's important: *Some mailing lists are one-way; they simply make announcements, such as those from the Democratic and Republican parties about upcoming events. Others are two-way; they are discussion lists (on subjects such as politics, jokes, or science) in which a subscriber sends a message to all the other subscribers, who may respond in similar fashion.*

malware ("malicious software") (p. 100) "Bad" programs that can attack your computer systems and mobile devices. They include viruses, worms and Trojan horses, zombies and bots, ransomware and rootkits. Malware can crash your computer/device, steal personal information, and track and control your digital activity.

media-sharing website (p. 93) Online social network, such as YouTube, Flickr, and Shutterfly, that allows members to share media. Why it's important: *Members can share their photos, videos, and music with others with great ease and convenience.*

megabits per second (Mbps) (p. 53) One million bits per second. Why it's important: *Mbps is a common measure of data transmission speed.*

message board (p. 83) Web-based discussion group that does not require a newsreader. Why it's important: *Sometimes called a web forum, these special-interest discussions may be accessed through a web browser (not email) from such sites as Yahoo! Groups and Google Groups. Some groups are open to the public; others are members-only. With either a newsgroup or a message board, a user posts a particular message—which is called an article—to the bulletin board, which other users can read and write replies to.*

metasearch engine (p. 72) Type of Internet search tool that allows you to search several search engines simultaneously. Why it's important: *A metasearch engine enables you to expand the range of your search.*

modem (p. 56) Device that sends and receives data over telephone lines, cables, or satellite to and from computers. Why it's important: *The modem was developed as a means for computers to communicate with one another using the standard copper-wire telephone network, an analog system that was built to transmit the human voice but not computer signals.*

narrowband (p. 53) Low-bandwidth connection, such as dial-up (telephone). Why it's important: *Narrowband connecting technology is inexpensive and widely available.*

netiquette (p. 81) "Network etiquette," or appropriate online behavior. Why it's important: *In general, netiquette has two basic rules: (1) Don't waste people's time, and (2) don't say anything to a person online that you wouldn't say to his or her face.*

newsgroup (p. 83) Also called *forum;* giant electronic bulletin board on which users conduct written discussions about a specific subject. Why it's important: *There are thousands of newsgroup forums—which charge no fee—and they cover an amazing array of topics.*

packet (p. 60) Fixed-length block of data for transmission. Why it's important: *TCP/IP breaks data in a message into separate packets, which allows the message to be split up and its parts sent by separate routes yet still all wind up in the same place.*

password (p. 60) A special combination of letters and/or numbers that limits access to information. Why it's important: *You establish your username and password when you open your account with your ISP, so that only you have access to it.*

pharming (p. 97) A type of phishing in which malicious software is implanted on a victim's computer that redirects the user to an impostor web page even when the individual types the correct address into his or her browser. Why it's important: *The purpose is to trick people into sharing their personal, financial, or password data.*

phishing (p. 97) Short for *password harvesting fishing;* (1) the sending of a forged email that (2) directs recipients to a replica of an existing web page, both of which pretend to belong to a legitimate company. Why it's important: *The purpose of the* *fraudulent sender is to "phish" for, or entice people to share, their personal, financial, or password data.*

plug-in (add-on) (p. 86) Program that adds a specific feature or function to a browser, allowing it to play or view certain files. Why it's important: *To fully experience the contents of many web pages, you need plug-ins.*

podcasting (p. 90) Recording of Internet audio or video that can be downloaded. Why it's important: *Podcasting is another expression of personalized media.*

point of presence (POP) (p. 60) Collection of modems and other equipment in a local area. Why it's important: *To avoid making their subscribers pay long-distance phone charges, ISPs provide POPs across the country. The POP acts as a local gateway to the ISP's network.*

pop-up ads (p. 99) Form of online advertising in which, when you visit certain websites, a new window opens, or "pops up," to display advertisements. Why it's important: *Pop-up ads are one form of the nuisance known as* spyware.

portal *See* **web portal.**

POTS (plain old telephone system) (p. 53) Basic connection to the Internet. Why it's important: *Slowest method of connecting to the Internet.*

protocol (p. 60) Set of communication rules for exchanging information. Why it's important: *Transmission Control Protocol/Internet Protocol (TCP/IP) enables all computers to use data transmitted on the Internet. HyperText Transfer Protocol (HTTP) provides the communication rules that allow browsers to connect with web servers.*

push technology (p. 88) Software that automatically downloads information to your computer, as opposed to *pull technology,* in which you go to a website and pull down the information you want. Why it's important: *With little effort, users can obtain information that is important to them.*

radio button (p. 69). Interactive tool displayed as little circles in front of options; selecting an option with the mouse places a dot in the corresponding circle. Why it's important: *Radio buttons are one way of interacting with a web page.*

RSS newsreaders (p. 88) Also called *RSS aggregators;* programs that scour the web, sometimes hourly or more frequently, and pull together in one place web "feeds" from several websites. Why it's important: *RSS newsreaders give people access to a whole new universe of content and have led to the creation of the blogosphere.*

scroll arrows (p. 69) Small up/down and left/right arrows located to the bottom and side of your screen display. Why it's important: *Clicking on scroll arrows with your mouse pointer moves the screen so that you can see the rest of the web page, or the content displayed on the screen.*

scrolling (p. 69) Moving quickly upward or downward through text or some other screen display, using the mouse and scroll arrows (or the arrow keys on the keyboard). Why it's important: *Normally a computer screen displays only part of, for example, a web page. Scrolling enables users to view an entire document, no matter how long.*

search engine (p. 71) Search tool that allows you to find specific documents through keyword searches and menu choices, in contrast to directories, which are lists of websites classified by topic. Why it's important: *Search engines enable users to find websites of specific interest or use to them.*

search hijacker (p. 99) A damaging kind of spyware that can intercept your legitimate search requests made to real search engines and return results from phony search services. Why it's important: *Phony search services may send you to sites they run.*

search service (p. 70) Organization that maintains databases accessible through websites. Why it's important: *A search service helps you find information on the Internet.*

server (p. 59) Central computer supplying data or services. Why it's important: *Part of the client-server network, in which the central computer supplies data or services requested of it to the client computer.*

showrooming (p. 90) Phenomenon in which shoppers browse for products in stores, only to buy them from an online rival, frequently at a lower price. Why it's important: *Showrooming is an increasing problem for chains ranging from Best Buy to Barnes & Noble Inc. at the same time that it's a boon for* Amazon.com *and other online retailers.*

site *See* **website.**

social-network aggregator (p. 93) Also called *social aggregator;* technology that collects content from all of a user's various social network profiles into one place. Why it's important: *Aggregators such as FriendFeed and Spokeo are "friend-tracking services" that allow members to track friends and share their other social network activities.*

social-networking website (p. 92) An online community that allows members to keep track of their friends and share ideas and media. Why it's important: *Social-networking websites, such as Facebook and LinkedIn, allow members to expand their circle of acquaintances and to exchange photos, videos, music, stories, and ideas with one another.*

spam (p. 97) Unsolicited email in the form of advertising or chain letters. Why it's important: *Spam filters are available that can spare users the annoyance of receiving junk mail, ads, and other unwanted email.*

spider (p. 71) Also known as *crawler, bot,* or *agent;* special program that crawls through the World Wide Web, following links from one web page to another. Why it's important: *A spider indexes the words on each site it encounters and is used to compile the databases of a search service.*

spoofing (p. 97) The forgery of an email sender name so that the message appears to have originated from someone or somewhere other than the actual source. Why it's important: *Spoofing is one of the main tactics used by spammers to induce or trick recipients into responding to their solicitations.*

spyware (p. 99) Deceptive software that is surreptitiously installed on a computer via the web. Why it's important: *Once spyware is installed on your hard disk, it allows an outsider to harvest confidential information, such as keystrokes, passwords, or your email address.*

streaming audio (p. 88) Process of downloading audio in which you can listen to the file while the data is being downloaded to your computer. Why it's important: *Users don't have to wait until the entire audio is downloaded before listening to it.*

streaming video (p. 87) Process of downloading video in which the data are transferred in a continuous flow so that you can begin viewing a file before the end of the file is sent. Why it's important: *Users don't have to wait until the entire video is downloaded before watching it.*

subject directory (p. 72) Type of search engine that allows you to search for information by selecting lists of categories or subjects. Why it's important: *Subject directories allow you to look for information by categories such as "Business and Commerce" or "Arts and Humanities."*

surf (p. 63) To explore the web by using your mouse to move via a series of connected paths, or links, from one location, or website, to another. Surfing requires a browser. Why it's important: *Surfing enables you to easily find information on the web that's of interest to you.*

T1 line (p. 54) Traditional trunk line that carries 24 normal telephone circuits and has a transmission rate of 1.5–6 Mbps. Why it's important: *High-capacity T1 lines are used at many corporate, government, and academic sites; these lines provide greater data transmission speeds than do regular modem connections.*

tags (p. 75) Do-it-yourself labels that people can put on anything found on the Internet, from articles to photos to videos. Why it's important: *A tag is more powerful than a bookmark, because tags can be shared easily with other people.*

text box (p. 69) Fill-in text box. Why it's important: *Text boxes are often used on the Internet for pages that require input from a user; allows interaction with a web page.*

3G (third generation) (p. 58) High-speed wireless technology that does not need access points because it uses the existing cellphone system. Why it's important: *The technology is found in many new smartphones and PDAs that are capable of delivering downloadable video clips and high-resolution games.*

thread (p. 83) Also known as *threaded discussion;* a collection of messages on a particular subject posted in an online discussion. Why it's important: *Web-based bulletin boards are made up of many topics, or threads. The replies posted in response to the original posting are all part of the same thread. In email, a thread can refer to a series of replies back and forth pertaining to a certain message.*

Transmission Control Protocol/Internet Protocol (TCP/IP) (p. 60) Protocol that enables all computers to use data transmitted on the Internet by determining (1) the type of error checking to be used, (2) the data compression method, if any, (3) how the sending device will indicate that it has finished sending a message, and (4) how the receiving device will indicate that it has received a message. TCP/IP breaks data into *packets,* which are the largest blocks of data that can be sent across the Internet (less than 1,500 characters, or 128 kilobytes). IP is used to send the packets across the Internet to their final destination, and TCP is used to reassemble the packets in the correct order. Why it's important: *Internet computers use TCP/IP for all Internet transactions, from sending email to downloading stock quotes or pictures off a friend's website.*

URL (Uniform Resource Locator) (p. 64) String of characters that points to a specific piece of information anywhere on the web. A URL consists of (1) the web protocol, (2) the name of the web server, (3) the directory (or folder) on that server, and (4) the file within that directory (perhaps with an extension such as *html* or *htm*). Why it's important: *URLs are necessary to distinguish among websites.*

username (user ID) (p. 60) A unique combination of characters, such as letters and/or numbers, that identifies a specific user of an account. Why it's important: *You establish your username and password when you open your account with your ISP; your unique ID and password are supposed to keep your account accessible to only you.*

virus (p. 100) Malware program that migrates through the Internet or via operating systems and attaches itself to different programs that spread from one computer to another, leaving infections. Why it's important: *There are millions of viruses in circulation that are threats not only to conventional computers but also to programs and websites popular with smartphone and tablet users, such as Facebook, Twitter, and YouTube, as well as website ads.*

VoIP (Voice over Internet Protocol) See **Internet telephony.**

Web 2.0 (p. 92) The move toward a more social, collaborative, interactive, and responsive World Wide Web. Why it's important: *As websites have become easier to use, they allow users to better harness the collective power of people, which has led to a "social web" or "social media," involving blogs, wikis, social networks, and media sharing. The common theme of all these is human interaction.*

web-based email (p. 78) Email messages that you send and receive by interacting via a browser with a website. Why it's important: *Unlike standard email, web-based email allows you to easily send and receive messages while traveling anywhere in the world and to use any personal computer and browser to access your email.*

web browser (browser) (p. 63) Software that enables users to locate and view web pages and to jump from one page to another and displays the content in such a way that the content appears mostly the same regardless of the computer, operating system, and display monitor. Why it's important: *Users can't surf the web without a browser. Examples of browsers are Microsoft Internet Explorer, Safari, Mozilla Firefox, and Chrome.*

webcasting (p. 88) Service based on push technology whereby customized text, video, and audio are sent to the user automatically on a regular basis or live on demand. Why it's important: *Users choose the categories, or the channels, of websites that will automatically send updated information. Thus, webcasting* *saves time because users don't have to go out searching for the information.*

web page (p. 63) Document on the World Wide Web that can include text, pictures, sound, and video. Why it's important: *A website's content is provided on web pages. The starting page is the home page.*

web portal (p. 70) Type of gateway website that functions as an "anchor site," a major starting point, for users when they connect to the web. Portals are also called *links pages* or *gateways*. The most popular portals are America Online, Yahoo!, Google, Bing, and Lycos. Why it's important: *Web portals provide an easy way to access the web. They generally offer a broad array of resources and services, online shopping malls, email support, community forums, current news and weather, stock quotes, travel information, a search engine, and links to other popular subject categories.*

website (site) (p. 63) Location of a web domain name in a computer somewhere on the Internet. Why it's important: *Websites provide multimedia content to users.*

Wi-Fi (p. 58) Short for "wireless fidelity." The name given to any of several standards—so-called 802.11 standards—set by the Institute of Electrical and Electronic Engineers for wireless transmission. Why it's important: *Wi-Fi enables people to use their Wi-Fi-equipped laptops to go online wirelessly in certain areas such as airports that have public access to Wi-Fi networks.*

wiki (p. 73) Simple piece of software that can be downloaded for free and used to make a website that can be corrected or added to by anyone. Why it's important: *Some corporations use business wikis for cross-company collaboration. They can also help you start research on various topics.*

window (p. 81) A rectangular area on a computer display screen that contains a document or activity. Why it's important: *In instant messaging, a window allows a user to exchange IM messages with others almost simultaneously while operating other programs.*

wireless Internet service provider (WISP) (p. 58) Organization that enables users with computers containing wireless modems—mostly laptops, tablets, and smartphones—to gain access to the Internet. Why it's important: *A WISP offers public wireless network services and Internet access. WISPs typically install Wi-Fi wireless hotspots in airports, hotels, cafés, and other public business places.*

wireless network (p. 58) Network that uses radio waves to transmit data, such as Wi-Fi. Why it's important: *Wireless networks enable people—with laptops and other devices—to access the Internet without having a cabled or wired connection.*

XML (extensible markup language) (p. 88) A web-document tagging and formatting language that two computers can use to exchange information. Why it's important: *XML is an improvement over HTML and enables the creation of RSS newsreaders.*

CHAPTER REVIEW

LEARNING MEMORIZATION

"I can recognize and recall information."

Self-Test Questions

1. Today's data transmission speeds are measured in _____, Kbps, _____, and _____.
2. A(n) _____ _____ connects a personal computer to a cable-TV system that offers an Internet connection.
3. A space station that transmits data as microwaves is a(n) _____.
4. A company that connects you through your communications connection to its server, which connects you to the Internet, is a(n) _____.
5. A rectangular area on the computer screen that contains a document or displays an activity is called a(n) _____.
6. _____ is writing an online message that uses derogatory, obscene, or inappropriate language.
7. Browsing for products in stores but buying them from an online rival and frequently at a lower price is called _____.
8. A(n) _____ is software that enables users to view web pages and to jump from one page to another.
9. A computer with a domain name is called a(n) _____.
10. A(n) _____ comprises the communications rules that allow browsers to connect with web servers.
11. "Bad" programs of types that can attack your computer systems and mobile devices are called _____.
12. A(n) _____ is a program that adds a specific feature to a browser, allowing it to play or view certain files.
13. Unsolicited email in the form of advertising or chain letters is known as _____.
14. The expression of how much data—text, voice, video, and so on—can be sent through a communications channel in a given amount of time is known as _____.
15. A(n) _____ is a string of characters that points to a specific piece of information somewhere on the web.
16. Websites may leave files on your hard disk that contain information such as your name, password, and preferences; they are called _____.

17. Using trusted institutional names to elicit confidential information is called _____.
18. The kind of spyware that can record each character you type and transmit that information to someone else on the Internet, making it possible for strangers to learn your passwords and other information, is called a(n) _____.

Multiple-Choice Questions

1. *Kbps* means how many bits per second?
   a. 1 billion
   b. 1 thousand
   c. 1 million
   d. 1 hundred
   e. 1 trillion
2. A location on the Internet is called a
   a. network.
   b. user ID.
   c. domain.
   d. browser.
   e. web.
3. In the email address *Kim_Lee@earthlink.net.us,* Kim_Lee is the
   a. domain.
   b. URL.
   c. site.
   d. user ID.
   e. location.
4. Which of the following is *not* one of the four components of a URL?
   a. web protocol
   b. name of the web server
   c. name of the browser
   d. name of the directory on the web server
   e. name of the file within the directory
5. Which of the following is the fastest method of data transmission?
   a. ISDN
   b. DSL
   c. modem
   d. T1 line
   e. cable modem
6. Which of the following is *not* a netiquette rule?
   a. Consult FAQs.
   b. Flame only when necessary.
   c. Don't shout.
   d. Avoid huge file attachments.
   e. Avoid sloppiness and errors.
7. Which protocol is used to retrieve email messages from the server to your computer?
   a. HTTP (Hypertext Transfer Protocol)
   b. SMTP (Simple Mail Transfer Protocol)
   c. POP3 (Post Office Protocol version 3)
   d. POP (point of presence)
8. Who owns the Internet?
   a. Microsoft.
   b. IBM.
   c. Apple.
   d. U.S. government.
   e. No one owns the Internet; the components that make up the Internet are owned and shared by thousands of public and private entities.
9. Each time you connect to your ISP, it will assign your computer a new address called a(n)
   a. domain.
   b. IP address.
   c. plug-in.
   d. POP.
   e. URL (Universal Resource Locator).
10. ISPs that don't run their own backbones connect to an Internet backbone through a(n)
    a. Internet Exchange Point.
    b. web portal.
    c. web browser.
    d. URL.
    e. TCP/IP.
11. Which of the following is *not* a protocol?
    a. TCP/IP
    b. IE
    c. HTTP
    d. SMTP
12. The sending of phony email that pretends to be from a credit-card company or bank, luring you to a website that attempts to obtain confidential information from you, is called
    a. spoofing.
    b. phishing.
    c. spamming.
    d. key logging.
    e. cookies.

True-False Questions

T F 1. POP3 is used for sending email, and SMTP is used for retrieving email.

T F 2. A dial-up modem is an ISP (Internet service provider).

T F 3. The Internet Corporation for Assigned Names and Numbers (ICANN) was established to assign IP addresses.

T F 4. Replying to spam email messages with the statement "unsubscribe" will always get spammers to stop sending you unsolicited email.

T F 5. All computer communications use the same bandwidth.

T F 6. A T1 line is the slowest but cheapest form of Internet connection.

T F 7. A dynamic IP address gives you faster Internet access than a static IP address does.

T F 8. A bookmark lets you return to a favorite website quickly.

T F 9. A server is also called a host computer.

T F 10. Radio buttons are used for listening to radio stations on the Internet.

T F 11. Spoofing means using fake email sender names.

T F 12. Hypertext refers to text presented with very large letters.

LEARNING COMPREHENSION

"I can recall information in my own terms and explain it to a friend."

Short-Answer Questions

1. Name three methods of data transmission that are faster than a dial-up connection.
2. What is netiquette, and why is it important?
3. Briefly define *bandwidth.*
4. Many web documents are "linked." What does that mean?
5. Compare and contrast a cable modem service to a DSL service.
6. Explain the basics of how the Internet works.
7. What expanded functions does IMAP (Internet Message Access Protocol) have?
8. Briefly explain what TCP/IP does.
9. Why was ICANN established?
10. What's the difference between a dynamic IP address and a static IP address?
11. Explain what a blog is.
12. State your answer to a person who asks you the question, "Who owns the Internet?"
13. What is B2B commerce?
14. List and briefly describe three kinds of spyware.

LEARNING APPLYING, ANALYZING, SYNTHESIZING, EVALUATING

"I can apply what I've learned, relate these ideas to other concepts, build on other knowledge, and use all these thinking skills to form a judgment."

Knowledge in Action

1. Distance learning uses electronic links to extend college campuses to people who otherwise would not be able to take college courses. Are you, or is someone you know, involved in distance learning? If so, research the system's components and uses. What hardware and software do students need in order to communicate with the instructor and classmates? What courses are offered? Discuss the pros and cons of distance learning compared to classroom-based learning.
2. It's difficult to conceive how much information is available on the Internet and the web. One method you can use to find information among the millions of documents is to use a search engine, which helps you find web pages on the basis of typed keywords or phrases. Use your browser to go to the Google home page, and click in the Search box. Type the keywords *"personal computers";* then click on *Google Search,* or press the *Enter* key. How many results did you get?
3. As more and more homes get high-speed broadband Internet connections, the flow of data will become exponentially faster and will open up many new possibilities for sharing large files such as video. What types of interactive services can you envision for the future?
4. Draw a diagram of what happens when you log onto your ISP; include all the connections you think possible for your situation.
5. How do the latest smartphones incorporate the Internet into their functions? What functions could be improved? Have any of these extra functions affected your daily life?
6. How does the Internet affect your life? Start keeping a list.
7. Email, instant messaging (IM), and texting are ways of sending text messages back and forth to other people on the Internet. They seem very similar: In all, you compose a message, and when it's ready, you send it; and when someone else sends something to you, you receive it on your device and can read it.

   But in practice, email, IM, and texting can be surprisingly different; each has its own rhythm, its own strengths and weaknesses, its own sociology, and its own etiquette.

   As you use these messaging systems during the course of the term, watch for differences between them. Which medium is more appropriate for which kinds of relationships and communications? Which medium is more stressful to use? Which takes more time? Which is more convenient for you? Which one is more useful for getting real work done? Which one would you use if you knew that whatever you wrote was eventually going to be published in a book? If you were restricted to using only one of these communications methods, which would it be?
8. Internet service providers (ISPs) often place limits on upload speeds, thus making it take much longer to send (upload) a large file than it would take to receive (download) a file of the same size. Do a comparison between upload and download speeds on your Internet connection, perhaps by emailing yourself a file large enough to allow you to notice the difference. Why do you think there is a difference? (Consider both technological and economic factors.)

9. Imagine that a relative or friend wants to start using the Internet for the first time. You want to help this beginner get started, but you need to be careful not to get carried away and bombard him or her with more information than he or she can use. What three or four things would you tell and show this person first? What things do you think will be hardest for him or her to master? How do you think using the Internet is likely to change this person's life?

Web Exercises

1. Some websites go overboard with multimedia effects, while others don't include enough. Locate a website that you think makes effective use of multimedia. What is the purpose of the site? Why is the site's use of multimedia effective? Take notes, and repeat the exercise for a site with too much multimedia and one with too little.
2. If you have never done a search before, try this: find out how much car dealers pay for your favorite cars, what they charge consumers for them, and what you should know about buying a new car. Kelley Blue Book and Edmunds both publish magazines with all that information, but you can get the same information on their websites for free.

   Using the Google search engine (*www.google.com*), type *"automobile buyer's guide"* and *"Edmunds"* in the Search box, and hit the *Google Search* button. How many entries did you get? Click on a link to the Edmunds website. Explore the site, and answer the questions at the beginning of this exercise. Try the same exercise for "*Kelley Blue Book*"; are the results different?
3. Ever wanted your own dot-com in your name? Visit these sites to see if your name is still available:

   www.register.com/

   www.namezero.com/

   www.domainname.com/

   www.businessweek.com/smallbiz/content/jan2010/sb20100128_249641.htm
4. Interested in PC-to-phone calls through your Internet connection? Visit these sites and check out their services:

   www.iconnecthere.com/

   www.skype.com/

   www.voip.com/
5. HTTP (Hypertext Transfer Protocol) on the World Wide Web and cloud storage aren't the only methods of transferring data. FTP is the original method and is still a useful Internet function. To use FTP, you'll need an FTP client software program, just as you need a web browser to surf the web. Download one of these shareware clients, and visit its default FTP sites, which come preloaded:

CuteFtp	*www.globalscape.com/products/ftp_clients.aspx*
FileZilla	*http://filezilla-project.org/*
WS_FTP	*www.ipswitch.com/*
FTP Voyager	*www.ftpvoyager.com/*
SmartFTP	*www.smartftp.com/*

   You will need an FTP client program to upload files to a server if you ever decide to build a website. Some online website builders have browser uploaders, but the conventional method has always been FTP.
6. There are many ways to have a website created or to do it yourself without learning HTML; but if you want to learn more about creating websites with HTML:

   www.w3schools.com/html/default.asp

   www.make-a-web-site.com/

   www.htmlgoodies.com/primers/html/

   www.htmlcodetutorial.com/

   Or do an Internet search for *"html primer," "learn html,"* or *"html tutorial."*
7. To learn more about Internet emoticon/symbol/acronym conventions, go to:

   http://members.tripod.com/~paandaa/smiley.htm

   http://piology.org/smiley.txt

   www.cygwin.com/acronyms/

   For chat acronyms and texting shorthand:

   www.netlingo.com/acronyms.php

   www.webopedia.com/quick_ref/textmessageabbreviations.asp
8. Some hobbies have been dramatically changed by the advent of the World Wide Web. Particularly affected are the "collecting" hobbies, such as stamp collecting, coin collecting, antique collecting, memorabilia collecting, plate collecting, and so forth. Choose some such hobby that you know something about or have some interest in. Run a web search about the hobby, and see if you can find:
   a. A mailing list about the hobby.
   b. An auction site that lists rare items and allows you to bid on them.
   c. A chat room or other discussion forum allowing enthusiasts to gather and discuss the hobby.
   d. A site on which someone's formidable collection is effectively displayed.
   e. Social-networking sites that have tags for your hobby.
9. When the web first came into widespread use, the most popular search engine was AltaVista. For several years there were a variety of search engines available, but in recent years one search engine, Google, has become predominant, and the word *google* has entered the language as a verb that means "to use a search engine to find information."

   Visit *http://searchenginewatch.com/links/* for a list of many alternative search engines, as well as explanations about how they work and how to get your site listed on them.
10. E-commerce is booming. For any given product you may wish to buy on the web, there may be hundreds or thousands of possible suppliers, with different prices and terms—and not all of them will provide equally reputable and reliable service. The choices can be so numerous that it may seem difficult to know how to choose a vendor.

    Websites featuring comparison shopping can be a great help. Such a service communicates with many individual vendors' websites, gathering information as it proceeds; it then presents its findings to you in a convenient form. Often, ratings of the various vendors are provided as well, and sales tax and shipping charges are calculated for you.

Here are a few sites that can assist with comparison shopping:

www.epinions.com/

www.bizrate.com/

http://shopper.cnet.com/

Note that the reviews offered in such sites (for example, Amazon.com) are often self-reported reviews that may be biased, or may be reviews solicited by the company/publication in return for offers of free products. Most people reading the reviews probably assume that the reviewers are regular shoppers just like them—when, in fact, their relationship to the products they review can be complicated. The "customers" may not really be customers. And the rules for deciding whose reviews to accept and how to rank the reviewers may be biased.

Thus we should always regard reviews with some caution.

Practice "catch-and-release e-commerce" by researching the best deals you can find for:

A rare or at least out-of-print book that you'd like to have.

A high-end smartphone.

A replacement ink or toner cartridge for your laser or inkjet printer.

A pair of athletic shoes exactly like the shoes you currently have.

Pursue each transaction right up to the last step before you would have to enter your credit-card number and actually buy the item, and then quit. (Don't buy it. You can always do that another time.)

11. Webcams, or web cameras, are used by some websites to show pictures of their locations—either live video or stills. To run your own webcam site requires a suitable camera and a continuous Internet connection. But to look at other people's webcam sites requires only a web browser.

    For example, try searching for "webcam Antarctica." Or go to *www.webcam-index.com*.

    Find and bookmark at least one interesting webcam site in each of the following places: Tanzania, Japan, Chile, Scotland, Australia, Antarctica, and Hawaii.

12. A wiki is a website on which authoring and editing can be done very easily by anyone, anywhere, anytime using a web browser such as Chrome or Firefox, with no need for special software or other special requirements. (*Wiki* is Hawaiian for "quick.") Most web pages are less than perfect. If it is a wiki page and you are annoyed by something, you can just hit the Edit button and change it! Over time, the site gets better (people hope)!

    Here are some examples of wikis that deal with general knowledge:

    http://en.wikipedia.org/

    www.wikimedia.org/

    http://wiki.ehow.com/Main-Page/

    And here are some specialized wikis:

    http://recipes.wikia.com/wiki/Recipes_Wiki/

    http://webtrends.about.com/od/wikilists/tp/list_of_wiki_sites.htm

    www.wikispaces.com/

    www.wikia.com/Wikia/

    http://wikisineducation.wetpaint.com/

    Historical note: The first wiki site was created for the Portland Pattern Repository in 1995. That site now hosts tens of thousands of pages.

    - *http://c2.com/cgi/wiki?WelcomeVisitors*
    - *http://c2.com/cgi/wiki?WikiHistory*
    - *http://c2.com/cgi/wiki?WikiDesignPrinciples*

    a. Make a small change on a page on one of the listed sites or on some other wiki site you have identified. Submit your change, and note the results. Anyone navigating to that site will now see your change. Did you know that website authoring could be that easy? Are you surprised that someone would unconditionally open up his or her website for anyone to edit?

    b. Since you can make any change you wish, even something totally nonsensical or simply wrong, it's obviously possible for incorrect or misleading content to appear on a wiki. Given that, why do you think that wikis have become so popular and so widespread?

    c. How significant a problem do you think vandalism and other acts of poor citizenship might be on "open" wikis? How can you find out?

    d. Some wikis contend with the threat of vandalism by requiring that a password be provided before a user is allowed to make changes. What advantages can you see to this approach? What disadvantages? Do you think the advantages of password protection outweigh the disadvantages? What do the wikis you browse through have to say about this issue?

    e. What measures do you think an online shared space can take to limit the potential damage from vandalism while not being overly restrictive?

    f. If you knew that a particular person was defacing a wiki, what would you do about it? Report the person? Wait for the vandal to get bored and turn his or her mischief elsewhere? Or try to reform the person? Are the basic ethical considerations here the same as those regarding other forms of vandalism in our society?

    g. Do you think that open-access systems such as unrestricted wikis will become more common over time, or do you think that abuse of such systems will destroy their usefulness and that wikis will eventually disappear?

13. As we have discussed in this chapter, the Internet is both a gold mine and a minefield. There are vast riches of information, entertainment, education, and communication to be found, but there are also snoopers, spam, spoofing, phishing, spyware, adware, browser hijackers, and key loggers. What should you do to avoid these threats? Research what new types of malware may be on the horizon.

3

SOFTWARE

Tools for Productivity & Creativity

Chapter Topics & Key Questions

UNIT 3A: *System Software: The Power behind the Power*

3.1 **The Operating System: What It Does** What are the principal functions of the operating system?

3.2 **Other System Software: Device Drivers & Utility Programs** What are the characteristics of device drivers and utility programs?

3.3 **Common Features of the User Interface** What are some common features of the graphical software environment (GUI), and how do they relate to the keyboard and the mouse?

3.4 **Common Operating Systems** What are some common desktop, network, and portable (embedded) OSs?

UNIT 3B: *Application Software: Getting Started*

3.5 **Application Software: Where to Get It, How to Use It** What are seven ways of obtaining application software, and what are tools to help me learn to use it?

3.6 **Data Files & Program Files** What are data files, program files, and file name extensions, and what purposes are served by export/import and data compression?

3.7 **Word Processing Software** What can I do with word processing software that makes creating, formatting, and illustrating documents easy?

3.8 **Spreadsheet Programs** What can I do with electronic spreadsheet worksheets that I can't do with pencil and paper and a standard calculator?

3.9 **Database Software** What is database software, and what is personal information management software?

3.10 **Office Suites & Integrated Packages** What is the difference between software suites and integrated packages?

3.11 **Specialty Application Software** What are some principal kinds of specialty software?

Download the free UIT 11e App for key term flash cards quizzes and a game, *Over the Edge*

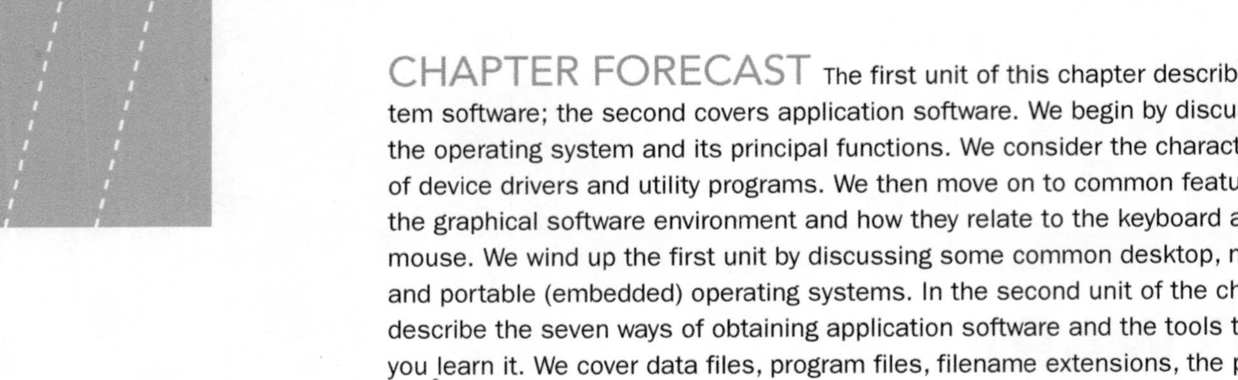

CHAPTER FORECAST The first unit of this chapter describes system software; the second covers application software. We begin by discussing the operating system and its principal functions. We consider the characteristics of device drivers and utility programs. We then move on to common features of the graphical software environment and how they relate to the keyboard and the mouse. We wind up the first unit by discussing some common desktop, network, and portable (embedded) operating systems. In the second unit of the chapter, we describe the seven ways of obtaining application software and the tools to help you learn it. We cover data files, program files, filename extensions, the purposes served by export/import, and data compression. We then discuss several kinds of application software: word processing, spreadsheet, database, office suites, integrated packages, and specialty application software.

UNIT 3A: *System Software: The Power behind the Power*

"Massive digital disruption," says James McQuivey, is occurring "at a scale and pace most are simply not prepared for."[1]

McQuivey, an executive with Forrester Research, a global business advisory firm, believes that technology—new software, wireless phones, home Internet connections, and so on—allows almost anyone with a new powerful idea to assemble the tools to make that idea a reality.[2] And such disruptor innovators can vastly and quickly alter the landscape for existing businesses and industries.

Microsoft, for instance, for years provided the most popular software for businesses, through its suite, or collection, of programs called Office, which is installed on a desktop PC or laptop. Now Microsoft's dominance is being undermined by the arrival of cloud computing, which is cheaper because software need not be on an office worker's computer. Instead, a company might opt for Google Apps, Google's software for businesses, which consists of cloud-based, lower-priced, and faster-operating applications not only for document writing and data analysis but also for collaboration and video communications.[3] And cloud-based apps constitute another disruptive force in that they move the use of business software from desktop-bound machines to smartphones, tablets, and other mobile devices.

Install Definition

In computer terminology, *install* refers to copying software files to a computer and setting them up to run properly or adding hardware components to a computer system.

Whether you are using a desk-bound, stand-alone computer installed with conventional business programs or the latest high-tech portable wireless gadget drawing on applications through the air, you are dealing with two kinds of *software,* or *programs,* the electronic instructions that tell a computer how to perform a task:

- **Application software: Application software is software that has been developed to solve a particular problem for users—to perform useful work on specific tasks or to provide entertainment.**
- **System software: System software runs at the most basic level of your computer and enables the application software to interact with the computer and helps the computer to manage its internal and external resources, as well as manage the hardware.**

Who Was John Tukey?

The term *software* was coined by John Tukey. Who was he? Did he coin any other important computer terms? Do a keyword search on his name, and see what you can find out.

We humans, of course, interact mainly with the application software. Application software interacts with the system software, which controls the hardware, and so we cover systems software first.

There are three basic components of system software that you need to know about. (• *See Panel 3.1.*)

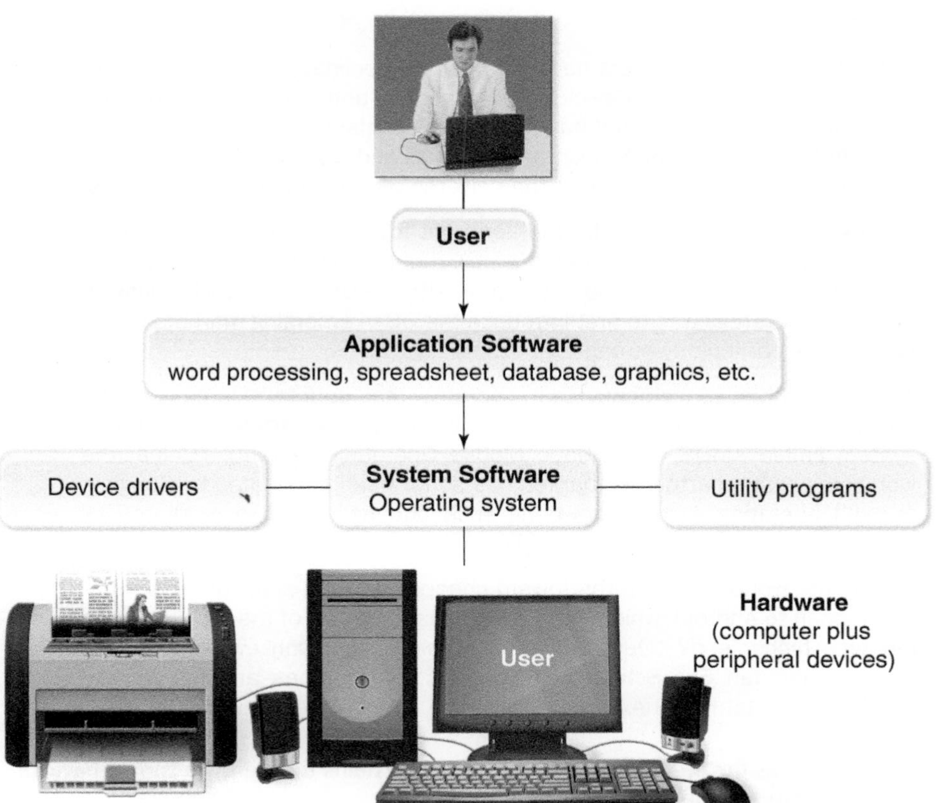

panel 3.1

Three components of system software

In general, system software is the interface between the user and the application software and the computer hardware.

- **Operating systems:** An operating system is the principal component of system software in any computing system.
- **Device drivers:** Device drivers help the computer control peripheral devices.
- **Utility programs:** Utility programs are generally used to support, enhance, or expand existing programs in a computer system.

A fourth type of system software, *language translators,* convert the instructions written by programmers in a programming language into a language (machine language) that computers can understand and process.

3.1 THE OPERATING SYSTEM: What It Does

The operating system manages the entire computer system.

The operating system (OS) consists of the low-level, master system of programs that manage the basic operations of the computer. These programs provide resource management services of many kinds. In particular, they handle the control and use of hardware resources, including disk space, memory (Chapter 1, p. 30), CPU (processor) time allocation, and peripheral devices. Every general-purpose computer must have an operating system to run other programs. The operating system, through its interface, allows you to concentrate on your own tasks or applications rather than on the complexities of managing the computer. Each application program is written to run on top of a particular operating system.

Different sizes and makes of computers have their own operating systems. For example, Cray supercomputers use UNICOS and COS; IBM mainframes use MVS and VM; PCs run Windows or Linux; Apple Macintoshes run the Macintosh OS; Chromebooks and Chromeboxes run Chrome OS (from the cloud). Smartphones and other mobile devices have their own operating systems—such as the Apple iPhone iOS, the Windows Phone 8, the BlackBerryOS, and Android (used in several smartphones)—which we discuss later in this chapter. With a few exceptions, an operating system written for one kind of hardware will not be able to run on another kind of machine.

TECH TALES The War for Dominance in Mobile Operating Systems

Sales of personal computers have been rapidly declining, a sign that buyers are turning toward mobile devices—smartphones and tablets—to fulfill their computing needs.[4] The trend has put great financial pressure on makers of PC software and hardware, such as Microsoft and Dell.[5] Simultaneously, it has spurred great competition in the universe of mobile operating systems.

For instance, in 2013, Mozilla, the nonprofit foundation behind the Firefox browser, announced it would debut a new mobile operating system, Firefox OS, in 16 countries by the end of the year, with the United States to follow in 2014. The strategy was to first introduce the OS in emerging markets where Firefox was particularly strong.[6]

Alibaba, a Chinese company that operates that country's largest online shopping sites, announced it would release its own smartphone operating system called AMOS (for Alibaba Mobile Operating System).[7] China, the world's biggest smartphone market, has so far been dominated by Google's Android operating system, powering such phones as those marketed by Samsung, the leader, and Lenovo. (The Apple smartphone is third.)

And as the world market turns toward cheaper, low-end smartphones, what will happen to Android, which owns a significant portion of the mobile phone market's higher end? "Our goal with Android is to reach everyone," says Google chairman Eric Schmidt. "If low-end smartphones are inexpensive now, imagine just how inexpensive they'll be a few years from now."[8] ■

Survival Tip

New Software & Compatibility

Pay attention to compatibility requirements when you obtain new software. The system requirements for running the software will be listed on the box or included with the downloaded information. When it is time to update the software, you can usually do that by paying a small upgrade fee to the software manufacturer and then downloading the new version and/or obtaining a new CD/DVD.

Before we discuss the different kinds of operating systems in detail, we should have an idea of what operating systems do. We consider:

- Booting
- CPU management
- File management
- Task management
- Security management

Safe Mode

If Windows doesn't boot properly, it may go into Safe Mode. You can also get into Safe Mode by pressing the F8 key during the boot process. Safe Mode is used for diagnosing problems and fixing them. When the system is in Safe Mode, only the essential parts of the system work—monitor, mouse, keyboard—and there are no fancy interface graphics on the screen.

www.computerhope.com/issues/chsafe.htm

http://pcsupport.about.com/od/windows-8/ss/windows-8-safe-mode.htm

www.bleepingcomputer.com/tutorials/how-to-start-windows-in-safe-mode/

Once you are in Safe Mode, you use the Device Manager to help you fix problems:

https://kb.wisc.edu/helpdesk/page.php?id=502

www.igennie.net/en/tip-of-the-day/computer-tips-uninstall-graphics-driver-in-safe-mode-using-device-manager/

Booting

When you turn on a computer, you boot it, meaning that the operating system starts to load.

The work of the operating system begins as soon as you turn on, or "boot," the computer. **Booting** (from "bootstrapping") **is the process of loading an operating system into a computer's main memory.** This loading is accomplished automatically by programs stored permanently in the computer's electronic circuitry (called *read-only memory,* or *ROM,* described in Chapter 4). When you turn on the machine, programs called *diagnostic routines* test the main memory, the central processing unit, and other parts of the system to make sure they are running properly. Next, BIOS (for "basic input/output system") programs are copied to main memory and help the computer interpret keyboard characters or transmit characters to the display screen or to a disk. Then the boot program obtains the operating system, usually from the hard disk, and loads it into the computer's main memory, where it remains until you turn the computer off. *(• See Panel 3.2.)*

COLD BOOTS & WARM BOOTS When you power up a computer by turning on the power "on" switch, this is called a *cold boot.* If your computer is already on and you restart it, this is called a *warm boot* or a *warm start.*

After installing new software on your computer, you will usually see a "Restart" button displayed; by clicking on this button, you authorize a warm boot and restart the computer, which allows the new software to be recognized by the computer.

THE BOOT DISK Normally, your computer would boot from the hard drive, but if that drive is damaged, you can use a disk called a *boot disk* (or a *restore disk*) to start up your

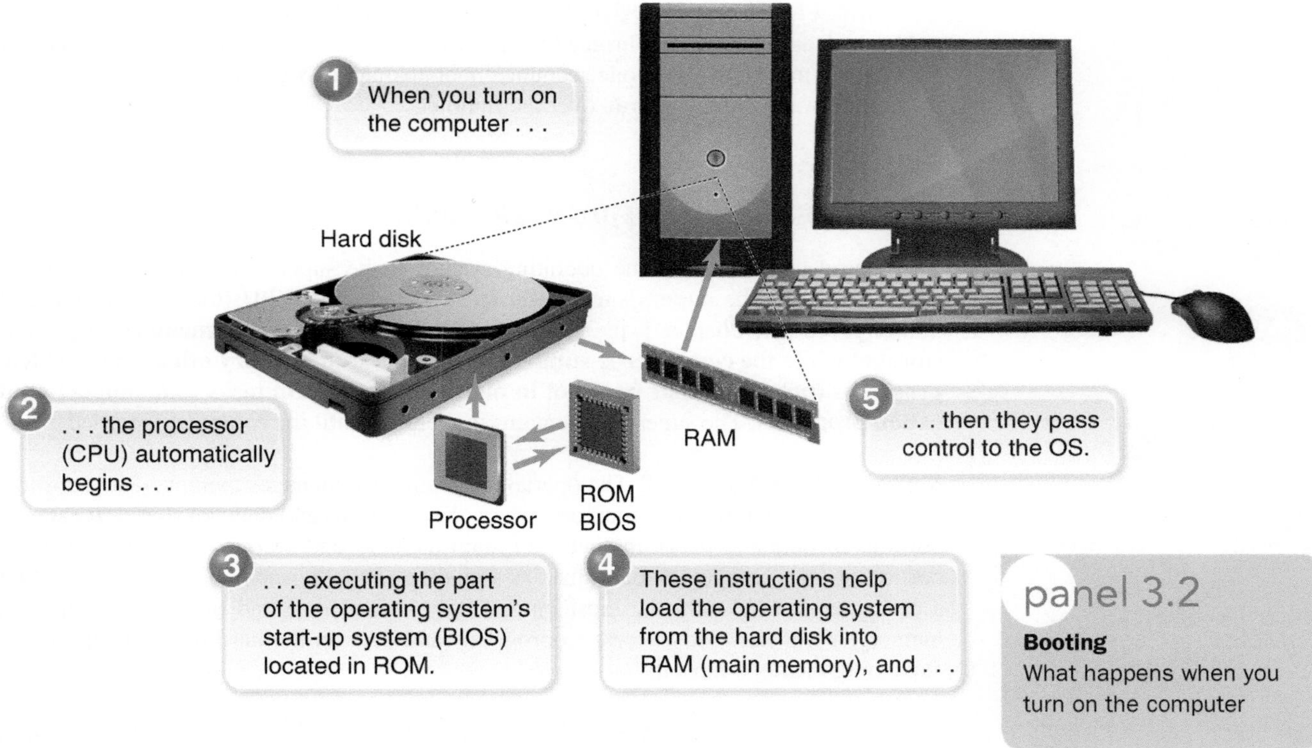

panel 3.2

When you turn on the computer . . .
Hard disk
. . . the processor (CPU) automatically begins . . .
Processor
ROM BIOS
RAM
. . . then they pass control to the OS.
. . . executing the part of the operating system's start-up system (BIOS) located in ROM.
These instructions help load the operating system from the hard disk into RAM (main memory), and . . .

Booting

What happens when you turn on the computer

computer. A boot disk is usually a CD or a flash drive (Chapter 4) that contains all the files needed to launch the OS. When you insert the boot disk into your computer's CD drive, you answer the displayed queries to feed the OS files to the BIOS, thereby enabling it to launch the OS and complete the start-up routine. After the OS loads completely, you then can access the contents of the hard drive, run basic drive maintenance utilities, and perform troubleshooting tasks that will help you resolve the problem with the drive.

If a boot disk did not come with your computer system, then make your own by following the instructions in the online user's manual on your system manufacturer's website (which you can also download to your computer).

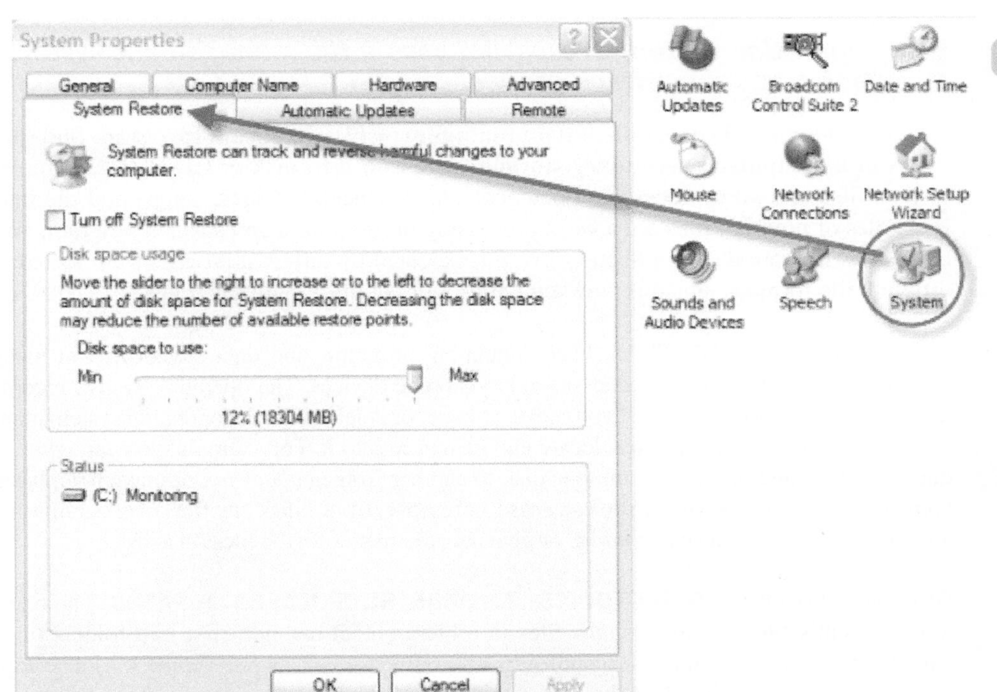

more info!

Going Backward

One way to get out of a system problem in Windows is to use System Restore, found by clicking on the System icon via Start, Control Panel. Restore System restores the system files to a previous date and/or time. Your data files (for example, documents) are not affected, and you can customize your System Restore points (dates and times) via the System Restore icon. The Mac operating system's restore program is called Time Machine. (Note that if you restore your system to a previous date, you may uninstall applications that were installed after that date; however, you can always reinstall those applications.)

BOOTING FROM THE CLOUD With a computer that boots from the cloud (Chapter 1, p. 66), such as one running Chrome OS, the start-up is much the same—except faster. "The Chrome OS machines," says one account, "boot up quickly because they don't have to load a lot of software—all that is run over the Internet."[9]

CPU Management

The CPU is the central processing unit.

The central component of the operating system is the supervisor. Like a police officer directing traffic, the **supervisor, or *kernel,* manages the CPU** (the central processing unit or processor, Chapter 1, p. 30). **It remains in memory (main memory or primary storage) while the computer is running and copies into memory other "nonresident" programs (programs that were not in memory) to perform tasks that support application programs.** The supervisor remains in memory until the computer is turned off.

MEMORY MANAGEMENT The operating system also manages memory—it keeps track of the locations within main memory, where the programs and data are stored. It can swap portions of data and programs between main memory and secondary storage, such as a portion of your computer's hard disk, as so-called *virtual memory.* This capability allows a computer to hold only the most immediately needed data and programs within main memory. Yet it has ready access to programs and data on the hard disk, thereby greatly expanding memory capacity.

GETTING IN LINE: QUEUES, BUFFERS, & SPOOLING Programs and data that are to be executed or processed wait on disk in *queues* (pronounced "Qs"). A queue is a first-in, first-out sequence of data and/or programs that "wait in line" in a temporary holding place to be processed. The disk area where the programs or documents wait is called a *buffer.* Print jobs are usually *spooled*—that is, placed—into a buffer, where they wait in a queue to be printed. This happens because the computer can send print jobs to the printer faster than the printer can print them, so the jobs must be stored and then passed to the printer at a rate it can handle. Once the CPU has passed a print job to the buffer, it can take on the next processing task. (The term *spooling* dates back to the days when print jobs were reeled, or copied, onto spools of magnetic tape, on which they went to the printer.)

File Management

Every operating system or program uses a file management system to organize and keep track of files.

A file is (1) a named collection of data (data file) or (2) a program (program file) that exists in a computer's secondary storage, such as a hard disk or CD/DVD. Examples of data files are word processing documents, spreadsheets, images, songs, and the like. Examples of program files are a word processing program or a spreadsheet program. (We cover files in more detail in Section 3.6. Files created by different programs are stored in different file formats, which is why some files will not open in all programs.)

FINDING & HANDLING FILES Files containing programs and data are located in many places on your hard disk and other secondary-storage devices. The operating system records the storage location of all files. If you move, rename, or delete a file, the operating system manages such changes and helps you locate and gain access to it. For example, you can *copy,* or duplicate, files and programs from one disk to another. You can *back up,* or make a duplicate copy of, the contents of a disk. You can *erase,* or remove, from a disk any files or programs that are no longer useful. You can *rename,* or give new file names to, the files on a disk.

ORGANIZING FILES: DIRECTORIES/FOLDERS, SUBFOLDERS, & PATHS The operating system's file system arranges files in a hierarchical manner, first into folders (also called *directories*) and then into subfolders (subdirectories). *(• See Panel 3.3.)* The topmost folder/directory is called the *root directory;* a folder below another folder is called a *subfolder* (*subdirectory*); any folder above a subfolder is called its *parent folder* (*parent directory*).

To find a particular file in an operating system's file system, you type in the file's *pathname*. The *path* is the route through the file system. A simple example of a pathname in Windows is

C:\mydocuments\termpaper\section1.doc

"C" refers to the hard disk (the root directory); "mydocuments" is the main (or primary) folder, the parent folder to "termpaper," which is a subfolder; "section 1" is the name of the file (file name); and "doc" is a file extension that indicates what type of file it is (.doc = document). (In Unix-based operating systems and the Mac OS X operating system, the pathnames use a forward slash [/] instead of a backward slash [\ ].)

Root Directory
C:
Folders
My Music
My Documents
My Pictures
Subfolders
Files
Term Paper
Letters
Section 1 . . .

panel 3.3

Directories/folders, subfolders, and files

Task Management

The operating system is the manager of the tasks that the computer performs.

A computer is required to perform many different tasks at once (multitasking). In word processing, for example, it accepts input data, stores the data on a disk, and prints out a document—seemingly simultaneously. Most desktop and laptop operating systems are single-user systems that can handle more than one program at the same time—word processing, spreadsheet, database searcher. Each program is displayed in a separate window on the screen. Other operating systems (multiuser systems) can accommodate the needs of several different users at the same time. All these examples illustrate *task management*. A *task* is an operation such as storing, printing, or calculating.

MULTITASKING: HANDLING MORE THAN ONE PROGRAM CONCURRENTLY **Multitasking is the execution of two or more programs by one user almost at the same time on the same computer with one or two central processors;** that is, the programs are sharing the same processing resources. You may be writing a report on your computer with one program while another program plays a music CD. How does the computer handle both programs at once? The answer is that the operating system directs the processor(s) to spend a predetermined amount of time executing the instructions for each program, one at a time. Thus, a small part of the first program is processed, and then a processor moves to the remaining programs, one at a time, processing small parts of each. The cycle is repeated

Windows Task Manager

File Options View Help

Applications | Processes | Services | Performance | Networking | Users

Image Name	User Name	CPU	Memory (P...	Description
acrotray.exe	Stacey C Sawyer	00	904 K	AcroTray
BcmDeviceAndT...	Stacey C Sawyer	00	13,536 K	Dell Securit..
ccsvchst.exe		00	2,240 K	Symantec ...
csrss.exe		00	1,408 K	
dwm.exe	Stacey C Sawyer	00	11,744 K	Desktop Wi..
explorer.exe	Stacey C Sawyer	02	22,800 K	Windows E...
ipoint.exe	Stacey C Sawyer	00	3,504 K	IPoint.exe
KHALMNPR.exe	Stacey C Sawyer	00	3,688 K	Logitech KH..
mbamgui.exe	Stacey C Sawyer	00	2,188 K	Malwarebyt..
nvvsvc.exe		00	2,488 K	
PDVD9Serv.exe	Stacey C Sawyer	00	1,004 K	PowerDVD ..
RoxioBurnLaunc...	Stacey C Sawyer	00	3,672 K	Roxio Burn ..
RtDCpl.exe	Stacey C Sawyer	00	1,652 K	HD Audio C..
SetPoint.exe	Stacey C Sawyer	00	5,848 K	Logitech Se..
Snagit32.exe	Stacey C Sawyer	00	39,368 K	Snagit
SnagitEditor.exe	Stacey C Sawyer	00	23,812 K	Snagit Editor
SnagPriv.exe	Stacey C Sawyer	00	1,056 K	Snagit RPC ..
taskhost.exe	Stacey C Sawyer	00	1,540 K	Host Proces..
taskmgr.exe	Stacey C Sawyer	00	1,924 K	Windows T..
TdmNotify.exe	Stacey C Sawyer	00	1,220 K	TdmNotify ...
TscHelp.exe	Stacey C Sawyer	00	836 K	TechSmith ..
WavXDocMgr.exe	Stacey C Sawyer	00	1,916 K	WavX Docu..
winlogon.exe		00	1,844 K	
WINWORD.EXE	Stacey C Sawyer	00	45,452 K	Microsoft ...

more info!

Task Manager

Task Manager shows you the programs, processes, and services that are currently running on your computer. You can use Task Manager to monitor your computer's performance or to close a program that is not responding.

If you are connected to a network, you can also use Task Manager to view network status and see how your network is functioning. If more than one user is connected to your computer, you can see who is connected, what they are working on, and you can send them a message. Open the Task Manager (*shown at left*) in Windows by holding down the Ctrl, Alt, and Del keys.

until processing is complete. Because the processors are usually very fast, it may appear that all the programs are being executed at the same time. However, the processors are still executing only one instruction at a time.

> **Survival Tip**
>
> **Use a Passphrase, Not a Password**
>
> Don't choose a password that can be easily guessed, as we advised in Chapter 2. One security technique: Use multi-word passwords called *passphrases.* "Using several words instead of one," suggests one article, "means an attacker has to guess more letters, which creates more security—but only if the phrase chosen is not one likely to turn up, through familiar usage, in a dictionary of phrases."[10] A phrase of four or five randomly chosen words is best (such as *skysail dactyl gimcrack golem*). The problem, of course, is remembering it, which is why most people use short passwords. But, points out the article, it is "the need for memorability [that] is a boon to attackers."

Security Management

Operating systems also take care of some security management.

Operating systems allow users to control access to their computers—an especially important matter when several people share a computer or the same computer network.

Users gain access in the same manner as accessing their email—via a username (user ID) and a password. As we stated in Chapter 2, a *password* is a special word, code, or symbol required to access a computer system. If you are using a computer at work, you may give yourself a password. When you first boot up a new personal computer, the OS will prompt you to choose a username and a password. Then, every time after that, when you boot up your computer, you will be prompted to type in your username and password. Some OSs even allow you to protect individual files with separate access passwords. (The Help feature explains how to change or turn off your password.)

The password is usually displayed as asterisks or dots, so that anyone looking over your shoulder—a "shoulder surfer"—cannot read it.

SECURITY

Computer systems and security issues have become complicated and critically important. We discuss this subject in more detail later in the book.

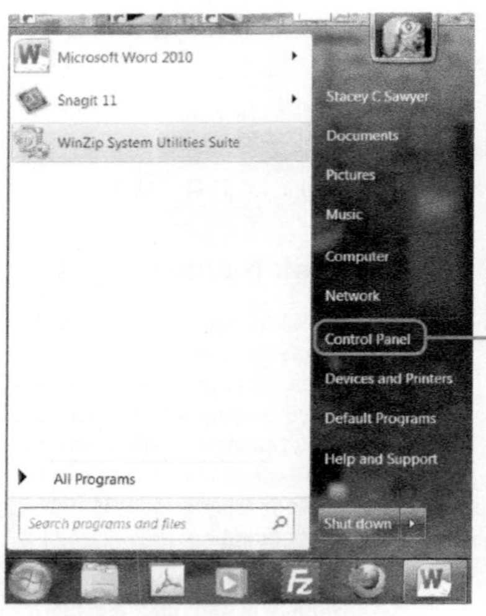

In Windows, you can access the Security Center (*middle*) via the Control Panel (*left*) to control additional security features (*right*).

3.2 OTHER SYSTEM SOFTWARE: Device Drivers & Utility Programs

Drivers and utility programs add functionality to your computer and help it perform better.

We said that the three principal parts of system software are the operating system, device drivers, and utility programs. Let's now consider the last two.

Device Drivers: Running Peripheral Hardware

Device drivers communicate with peripherals (usually input/output devices).

Device drivers **are specialized software programs that allow input and output devices to communicate with the rest of the computer system.** Each device's brand and model are supported by a different driver that works with only one operating system. Many basic device drivers come with (are preinstalled in) the system software when you buy a computer, and the system software will guide you through choosing and installing the necessary drivers. If, however, you buy a new peripheral device, such as a mouse, a scanner, or a printer, the package will include a device driver for the device (probably on a CD or DVD, or downloaded from the Internet).

Most new operating systems recognize many new hardware devices on their own and automatically install them. If your OS does not recognize your new hardware, it will display a message and ask you to install the driver from the CD that came with your hardware. (• *See Panel 3.4.)*

Utilities: Service Programs

Utilities are small programs that play supporting roles.

Utility programs, **also known as *service programs,* perform tasks related to the control, allocation, and maintenance of computer resources.** They enhance existing functions or provide services not supplied by other system software programs. Most computers come with built-in utilities as part of the system software. However, they may also be bought separately as external utility programs (such as Norton SystemWorks and McAfee Utilities).

Among the tasks performed by utilities are backing up data, compressing files, recovering lost data, and identifying hardware problems. *(See the Practical Action box on page 122.)*

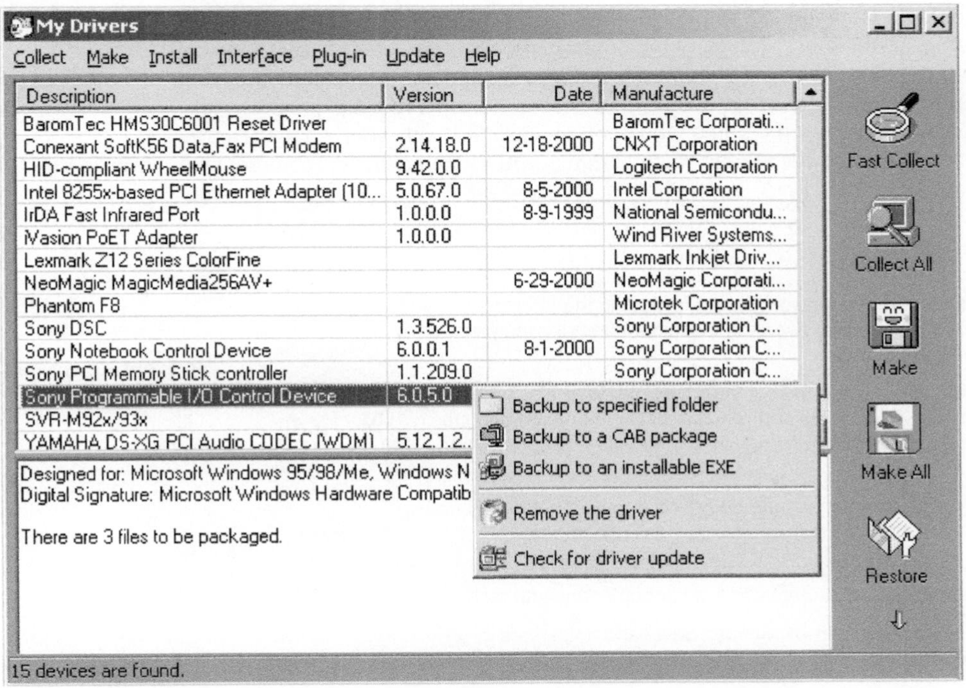

Survival Tip

Update Your Drivers

You should regularly (once a year, say) update your drivers. To do so, visit the websites of your peripheral devices' manufacturers and download any updates. You can also buy utilities for backing up and restoring drivers, such as 3D2F.com Software Directory (*http://3d2f.com/programs/54-281-my-drivers-download.shtml*), Driver Guide (*www.driverguide.com/*), or cnet's Download.com (*http://download.cnet.com/windows/drivers/*).

Survival Tip

What to Set Up First?

When setting up a new microcomputer system, install your peripherals first—first your printer, any external storage drives, scanner, and so on. Test each one separately by restarting the computer. Then install the next peripheral. After this, install your application software, again testing each program separately.

My Drivers

Collect Make Install Interface Plug-in Update Help

Description	Version	Date	Manufacture
BaromTec HMS30C6001 Reset Driver			BaromTec Corporati...
Conexant SoftK56 Data,Fax PCI Modem	2.14.18.0	12-18-2000	CNXT Corporation
HID-compliant WheelMouse	9.42.0.0		Logitech Corporation
Intel 8255x-based PCI Ethernet Adapter (10...	5.0.67.0	8-5-2000	Intel Corporation
IrDA Fast Infrared Port	1.0.0.0	8-9-1999	National Semicondu...
iVasion PoET Adapter	1.0.0.0		Wind River Systems...
Lexmark Z12 Series ColorFine			Lexmark Inkjet Driv...
NeoMagic MagicMedia256AV+		6-29-2000	NeoMagic Corporati...
Phantom F8			Microtek Corporation
Sony DSC	1.3.526.0		Sony Corporation C...
Sony Notebook Control Device	6.0.0.1	8-1-2000	Sony Corporation C...
Sony PCI Memory Stick controller	1.1.209.0		Sony Corporation C...
Sony Programmable I/O Control Device	6.0.5.0		
SVR-M92x/93x			
YAMAHA DS-XG PCI Audio CODEC (WDM)	5.12.1.2..		

Backup to specified folder
Backup to a CAB package
Backup to an installable EXE
Remove the driver
Check for driver update

Designed for: Microsoft Windows 95/98/Me, Windows N
Digital Signature: Microsoft Windows Hardware Compatib

There are 3 files to be packaged.

Fast Collect
Collect All
Make
Make All
Restore

15 devices are found.

panel 3.4

Windows 8 device drivers

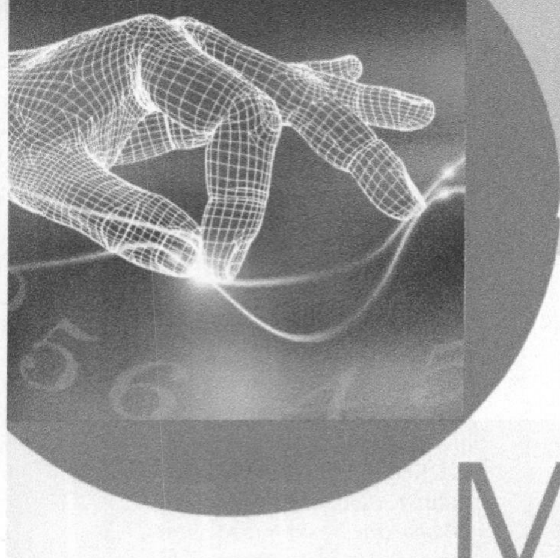

PRACTICAL ACTION

Utility Programs: Specialized Programs to Make Computing Easier

Many utility programs are incorporated into the operating system; others, such as some antivirus programs, are sold as stand-alone versions. Some of the important such programs are as follows:

Backup

Suddenly your hard-disk drive fails, and you have no more programs or files. Fortunately, we hope, you have used a *backup utility* to make a backup, or duplicate copy, of the information on your hard disk. The backup can be made to an external hard drive, an off-site networked (online, or "cloud") site, or other choices discussed later in the book. Examples of free-standing backup utilities are Norton Ghost (from Symantec) and DT Utilities PC Backup.

Data Recovery

A *data-recovery utility* is used to restore data that has been physically damaged, deleted, or corrupted. Data can be damaged by viruses (explained next), bad software, hardware failure, and power fluctuations that occur while data is being written/recorded.

Virus Protection

If there's anything that can make your heart sink faster than the sudden failure of your hard disk, it may be the realization that your computer system has been invaded by a virus. As we explained in Chapter 2 (p. 100), a *virus* consists of hidden programming instructions that are buried within an application or system program. Sometimes viruses copy themselves to other programs, causing havoc. Sometimes the virus is merely a simple prank that pops up in a message. Other times, however, it can destroy programs and data and wipe your hard disk clean. Viruses are spread when people exchange CDs and flash drives, download information from the Internet and other computer networks, or open files attached to email. (• *See Panel 3.5.*)

You should, therefore, install antivirus software. *Antivirus software* is a utility program that scans your computer and notifies you of possible viral behavior or destroys the virus on the spot. Because new viruses are constantly being created, you need the type of antivirus software that can constantly update itself (preferably at no additional cost to you) against newly discovered viruses. Examples of antivirus software are Symantec's Norton AntiVirus, Webroot Antivirus, and McAfee AntiVirus.

We discuss viruses again in more detail in Chapter 6.

> **Survival Tip**
>
> **Free Antivirus Software**
>
> For a list of free antivirus software, see:
>
> www.thefreecountry.com/security/antivirus.shtml
>
> www.pcmag.com/article2/0,2817,2388652,00.asp

Data Compression

With the increasing use of large graphic, sound, and video files, data compression is necessary both to reduce the storage space required on your hard-disk drive and to reduce the time required to transmit such large files over a network. *Data compression utilities* remove redundant elements, gaps, and unnecessary data from computer files so that less storage space is needed. Examples of such utilities are PK Zip, ZipIt, WinZip, and StuffIt. (Inspired by the name "Zip," people now refer to compressing a file as "zipping" and decompressing a file as "unzipping." Zip programs are often included with your computer system's OS.) Increasingly, compression

WinZip icon

panel 3.5

Preventing viruses

- If you download or install software from a network server (including the Internet), or an online service, always run virus scanning software on the folder/directory you place the new files in before you run/execute them.
- Make sure that you have a disk (e.g., CD) with your virus program so that you can reinstall the software if necessary. Or print out your purchase ID information and the link to the manufacturer's website so that you can re-download your software if you need to.
- Do not open any email from unknown sources, and do not open any attachments from unknown sources. (Also, set your antivirus software to check all attachments.)
- If your Internet connection is always on (e.g., cable), purchase firewall software or make sure that your OS is set properly to protect you from unauthorized intrusion.
- Never start your computer from an unknown CD or flash drive, and make sure secondary-storage drives are empty before you boot your computer.

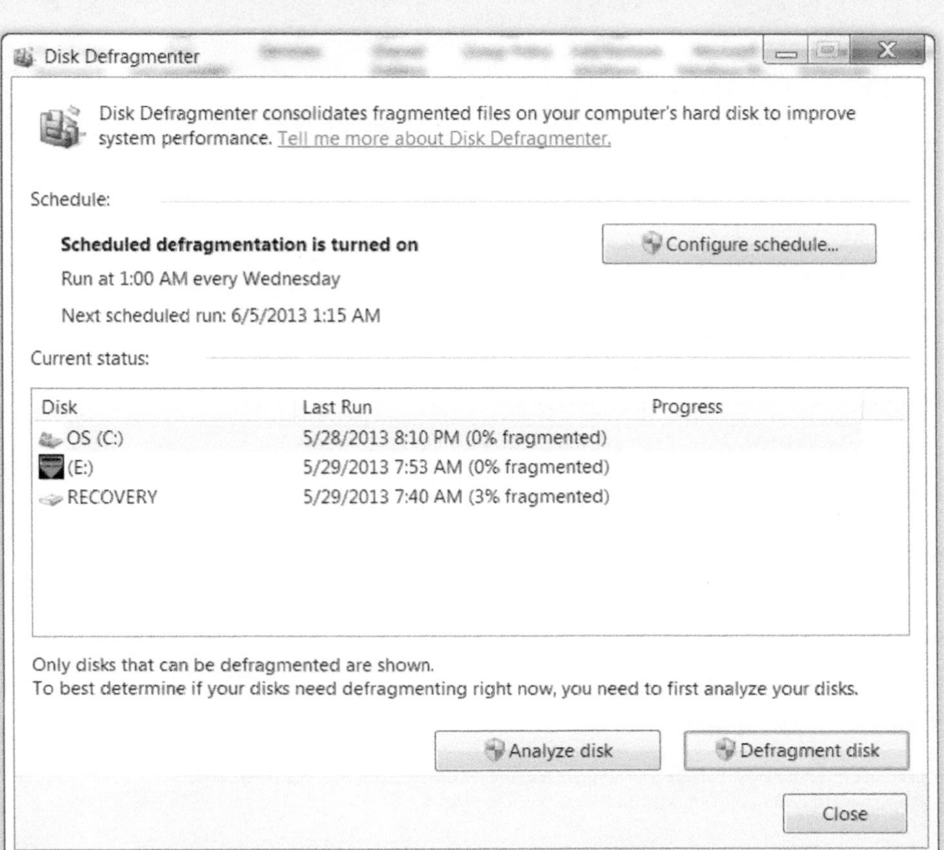

Windows 7 defragmenter screen

More on Utilities

For some different utilities, go to:

Piriform	**www.piriform.com/defraggler/**
Fences	**www.stardock.com/products/fences/**
PCWorld	**www.pcworld.com/downloads/file/fid,114526-order,4/description.html**
DoubleKiller	**www.bigbangenterprises.de/en/doublekiller/**
Top Ten Reviews	**http://pc-system-utilities-software-review.toptenreviews.com/**

PC Tune-Up: Stop at the Pitstop

To find out what problems your PC has and to learn which utilities might improve its performance, go to:

www.pcpitstop.com/default.asp

And try their free computer scans.

and decompression are being taken over by built-in hardware boards, and compression/decompression software utilities are therefore becoming obsolete.

File Defragmentation

If you notice your computer slowing down, it might be a good idea to "defrag" the hard-disk drive. When a hard disk is new, the operating system puts files on the disk contiguously (next to one another). However, as you update a file over time, new data for that file is distributed to unused spaces; the files become *fragmented.* Because these spaces may not be contiguous to the older data in that file, takes the operating system longer to read these fragmented files, slowing down the system.

A *defragmenter* utility program, or "defragger," will find all the scattered files on your hard disk and reorganize them as contiguous files, which will speed up the drive's operation. Computer users who use their machines for hours every day might want to defrag every few days.

Disk Cleanup

Operating systems such as Windows include a *disk cleanup* utility, which is used to remove unnecessary files. This utility removes unnecessary files, such as temporary Internet files ("temp files"; .tmp files), deleted files, and unused program files.

Survival Tip

Temp File Removal

In Windows 7, to remove temporary and unnecessary files from your hard drive, Click *Start, All Programs, Accessories, System Tools,* and *Disk Cleanup.* Put checks in the boxes next to the types of file you want to delete, and click *OK.* In Windows 8, press the Windows key + r on the keyboard; type %temp; then click on "ok." This opens up the Temp folder. Select the files you want to delete, and press the Del key (*www.youtube.com/watch?v=Gr-m71hR-_U*).

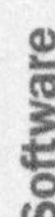

View temporary Internet files

This information applies to Windows Internet Explorer 7 and Windows Internet Explorer 8.

Webpages are stored in a temporary Internet files folder the first time you view them in your web browser. This speeds up the display of pages you frequently visit or have already seen, because Internet Explorer can open them from your hard disk instead of from the Internet.

To view temporary Internet files

1. Open Internet Explorer by clicking the **Start** button, and then clicking **Internet Explorer**.
2. Click the **Tools** button, and then click **Internet Options**.
3. Click the **General** tab, and then, under **Browsing history**, click **Settings**.
4. In the **Settings** dialog box, click **View files**.

To delete temporary Internet files

It's a good idea to delete temporary Internet files periodically to free hard disk space.

1. Open Internet Explorer by clicking the **Start** button, and then clicking **Internet Explorer**.
2. Click the **Tools** button, and then click **Internet Options**.
3. Click the **General** tab, and then, under **Browsing history**, click **Delete**.
4. In the **Delete Browsing History** dialog box, do one of the following:
   - In Internet Explorer 8, select the check boxes for the information you want to delete, click **Delete**, and then click **OK**.
   - In Internet Explorer 7, click the individual type of information you want to delete. You can also click **Delete all** to remove all temporary files. When you're finished, click **Close**, and then click **OK**.

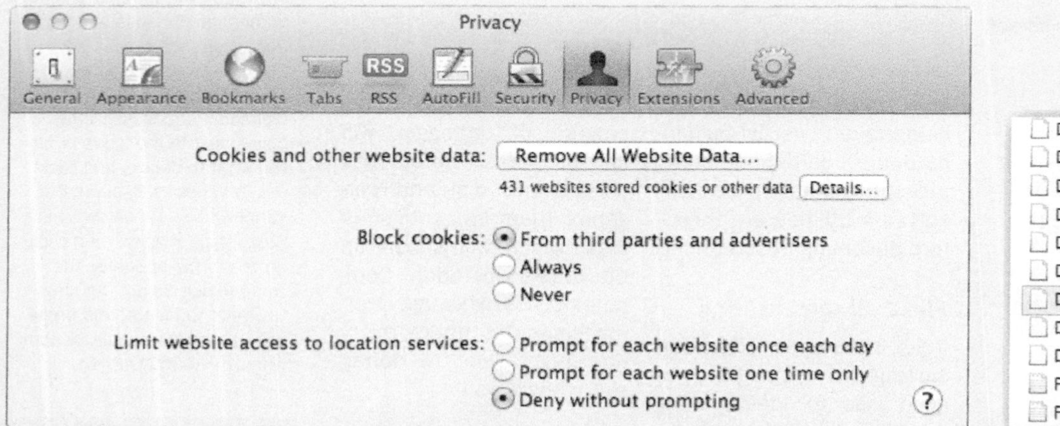

DMI45B9.tmp
DMI45E9.tmp
DMI58BE.tmp
DMI58BF.tmp
DMI445F.tmp
DMI450B.tmp
DMI455A.tmp
DMIB32F.tmp
DMIB330.tmp
FireFly(20130417183739ED4).log
FireFly(20130531153042A40).log

Temp files. (*top*) Deleting temp files in Windows 7; (*bottom*) in Mac Safari, go to the Preferences tab, then the Privacy tab, and remove all website data.

3.3 COMMON FEATURES OF THE USER INTERFACE

User-interface features use graphics to facilitate a person's interaction with the computer.

The first thing you look at when you call up any system software on the screen is the **user interface—the user-controllable graphic display screen that allows you to**

communicate, or interact, with the computer. Like the dashboard on a car, the user interface has gauges that show you what's going on and switches and buttons for controlling what you want to do. From this screen, you choose the application programs you want to run or the files of data you want to open.

You can interact with the display screen using the keys on your keyboard. Besides having letter, number, and punctuation keys and often a calculator-style numeric keypad, computer keyboards have special-purpose and function keys. (• *See Panel 3.6, next page.*)

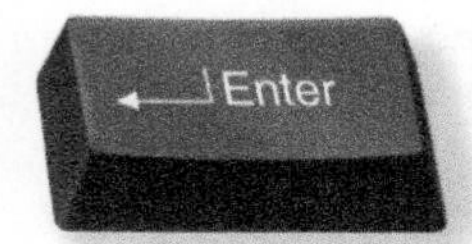

SPECIAL-PURPOSE KEYS **Special-purpose keys are used to enter, delete, and edit data and to execute commands.** An example is the Esc (for "Escape") key, which tells the computer to cancel an operation or leave ("escape from") the current mode of operation. The Enter, or Return, key, which you will use often, tells the computer to execute certain commands and to start new paragraphs in a document. *Commands* are instructions that cause the software to perform specific actions.

Special-purpose keys are generally used the same way regardless of the application software package being used. Most keyboards include the following special-purpose keys: *Esc, Ctrl, Alt, Del, Ins, Home, End, PgUp, PgDn, Num Lock,* and a few others. (For example, *Ctrl* means "Control," *Del* means "Delete," *Ins* means "Insert.")

FUNCTION KEYS **Function keys, labeled "F1," "F2," and so on, are usually positioned along the top of the keyboard. They are used to execute commands specific to the software being used.** For example, one application software package may use F6 to exit a file, whereas another may use F6 to underline a word.

MACROS: KEYBOARD SHORTCUTS Sometimes you may wish to reduce the number of keystrokes required to execute a command. To do this, you use a macro. **A macro, also called a *keyboard shortcut,* is a single keystroke or command—or a series of keystrokes or commands—used to automatically issue a longer, predetermined series of keystrokes or commands.** Thus, you can consolidate several activities into only one or two keystrokes. The user names the macro and stores the corresponding command sequence; once this is done, the macro can be used repeatedly. (To learn how to set up a macro in your software, access the Help menu and type in *macro.*)

Although many people have no need for macros, individuals who find themselves continually repeating complicated patterns of keystrokes say they are quite useful.

Common Shortcuts (Macros)

Instead of using the mouse and menus to select options and perform functions—for example, to save, to print, to boldface a word, to copy text—you can often use two-key shortcuts:

Windows:

www.microsoft.com/enable/products/KeyboardSearch_xp.aspx

http://support.microsoft.com/kb/126449/

http://windows.microsoft.com/en-US/windows7/Keyboard-shortcuts/

Mac:

http://support.apple.com/kb/ht1343/

www.danrodney.com/mac/

THE MOUSE & POINTER You will also frequently use your mouse to interact with the user interface. The mouse allows you to direct an on-screen pointer to perform any number of activities. **The pointer usually appears as an arrow, although it changes shape depending on the application. The mouse is used to move the pointer to a particular place on the display screen or to point to little symbols, or icons.** You can activate the function corresponding to the symbol by pressing ("clicking") buttons on the mouse. Using the mouse, you can pick up and slide ("drag") an image from one side of the screen to the other or change its size. (• *See Panel 3.7, page 127.*)

TECH TALES New Technology to Replace the Mouse: The Gesture Interface

"Gesture," says scientist John Underkoffler, "is the richest possible digital input that we, as humans, can deliver."[11] Underkoffler's work in gesture recognition was used in the 2002 sci-fi film *Minority Report,* in which Tom Cruise used a hand wave to move between screens.

Whereas the movements to guide a mouse take place on a two-dimensional plane, a gesture interface involves three dimensions. Microsoft was early to capitalize on gesture control when in 2010 it announced Kinect as a $150 in-the-air motion-sensing controller for the Xbox 360 videogame console. Kinect was "way ahead of its time," reports *Computerworld,* "and broke the Guinness World Record for the fastest-selling consumer electronics gadget ever."[12]

Despite the successful beginning, Microsoft may have missed its chance. The Leap Motion sensor, released in May 2013, is tinier than the Kinect gadget,

Escape Key
You can press Esc to quit a task you are performing.
Function Keys
These keys let you quickly perform specific tasks. For example, in many programs you can press F1 to display help information.
Caps Lock and Shift Keys
These keys let you enter text in uppercase (ABC) and lowercase (abc) letters.
Press Caps Lock to change the case of all letters you type. Press the key again to return to the original case.
Press Shift in combination with another key to type an uppercase letter.
Esc
F1
F2
F3
F4
F5
F6
F7
F8
Tab
Caps Lock
Shift
Ctrl
Alt
Ctrl and Alt Keys
You can use the Ctrl or Alt key in combination with another key to perform a specific task. For example, in some programs, you can press Ctrl and S to save a document.
Windows Key
You can press the Windows key to quickly display the Start menu when using many Windows operating systems.
Spacebar
You can press the Spacebar to insert a blank space.

100 times more accurate, available at half the price—and, unlike the Microsoft product, able to respond to much finer, more demanding gestures than Kinect's arm movements.[13] "The Leap can detect all 10 fingers at once," says one report. "It can accurately sense when your hand swipes, pokes, reaches, and grabs, allowing you to operate compatible software without the use of a mouse."[14]

Because the makers of Leap Motion provided detailed information about their product to outside developers (as Microsoft did not), it opens up the possibility of a wide variety of applications becoming available. "The idea we envision in the near future," says one developer, "is that a Leap Motion–like device will be integrated into a smartphone. Instead of just interacting on the touch screen, the space around the phone will be available too."[15]

"Soon," says one commentator, "the mouse will no longer feel like a throwback—it will simply be obsolete."[16] ■

The GUI: The Graphical User Interface

The GUI's use of graphics makes it easy for computer users to interact with their machine.

In the beginning, personal computers had *command-driven interfaces*, which required that you type in complicated-looking instructions (such as *copy a:\filename c:* to copy a file from an old floppy disk to a hard disk). In the next version, they also had *menu-driven interfaces,* in which you could use the arrow keys on your keyboard (or a mouse) to choose a command from a menu, or a list of activities.

Today the computer's "dashboard" is usually a **graphical user interface (GUI)** (pronounced "gooey"), **which allows you to use a mouse or keystrokes to select icons (little graphic symbols) and commands from menus or menu bars (lists of activities).** The GUIs on the PC and on the Apple Macintosh (which was the first easy-to-use personal computer available on a wide scale) are somewhat similar. Once you learn one

Backspace Key
You can press **Backspace** to remove the character to the left of the cursor.

Status Lights
These lights indicate whether the **Num Lock** or **Caps Lock** features are on or off.

Delete Key
You can press **Delete** to remove the character to the right of the cursor.

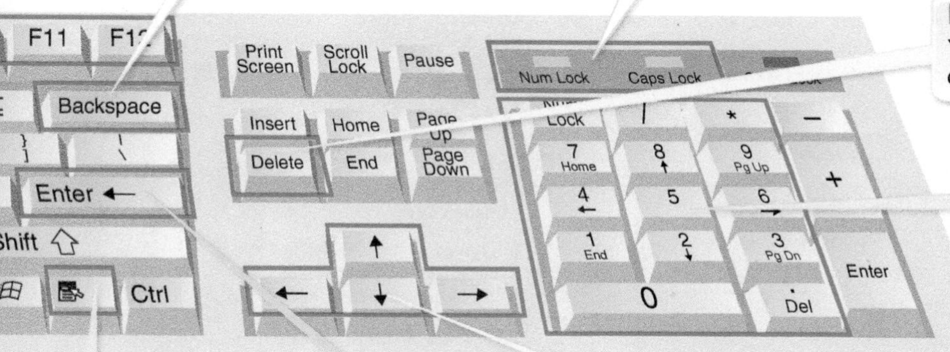

Numeric Keypad
When the **Num Lock** light is on, you can use the number keys (0 through 9) to enter numbers. When the **Num Lock** light is off, you can use these keys to move the cursor around the screen. To turn the light on or off, press **Num Lock.**

Arrow Keys
These keys let you move the cursor around the screen.

Application Key
You can press the **Application** key to quickly display the shortcut menu for an item on your screen. Shortcut menus display a list of commands commonly used to complete a task related to the current activity.

Enter Key
You can press **Enter** to tell the computer to carry out a task. In a word processing program, press this key to start a new paragraph.

panel 3.6

Keyboard functions

Point 	Move mouse across desk to guide pointer to desired spot on screen. The pointer assumes different shapes, such as arrow, hand, or I-beam, depending on the task you're performing.	To execute commands, move objects, insert data, or perform similar actions on screen.
Click 	Press and quickly release left mouse button.	To select an item on the screen.
Double-click 	Quickly press and release left mouse button twice.	To open a document or start a program.
Drag and drop 	Position pointer over item on screen, press and hold down left mouse button while moving pointer to location in which you want to place item, then release.	To move an item on the screen.
Right-click 	Press and release right mouse button.	To display a shortcut list of commands, such as a pop-up menu of options.

panel 3.7

Mouse language

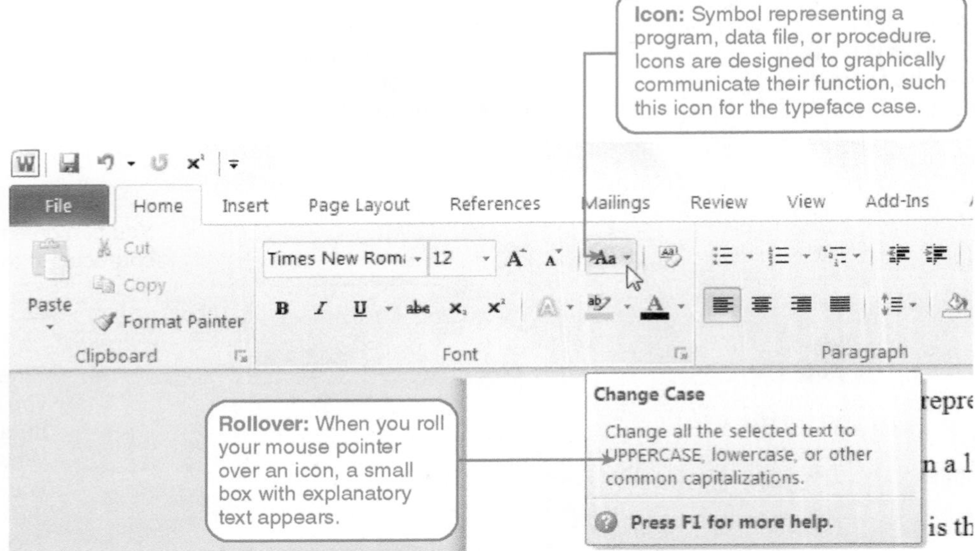

version, it's fairly easy to learn the other. However, the best-known GUI is that of Microsoft Windows system software. *(• See Panel 3.8.)*

DESKTOP, ICONS, & MENUS Three features of a GUI are the desktop, icons, and menus.

- **Desktop:** After you turn on the computer, the first screen you will encounter is the *desktop (Panel 3.8),* a term that embodies the idea of folders of work (memos, schedules, to-do lists) on a businessperson's desk. **The desktop, which is the system's main interface screen, displays pictures (icons) that provide quick access to programs and information.**
- **Icons and rollovers:** We've already mentioned icons, but to give a formal definition: **Icons are small pictorial figures that represent programs, data files, or procedures.** For example, a trash can represents a place to dispose of a file you no longer want. If you click your mouse pointer on a little picture of a printer, you can print out a document. One of the most important icons is the *folder,* a representation of a manila folder; folders hold the files in which you store your documents and other data.

  Of course, you can't always be expected to know what an icon or graphic means. **A rollover feature (also called a *tooltip*), a small text box explaining the icon's function, appears when you roll the mouse pointer over the icon. A rollover may also produce an animated graphic.**
- **Menus:** Like a restaurant menu, a **menu offers you a list of options to choose from**— in this case, a list of commands for manipulating data, such as Print or Edit. Menus are of several types. Resembling a pull-down window shade, a *pull-down menu,* also called a *drop-down menu,* is a list of options that pulls down from the menu bar at the top of the screen. For example, if you use the mouse to "click on" (activate) a command (for example, File) on the menu bar, you will see a pull-down menu offering further commands.

Survival Tip

Don't Trash Those Icons

In Windows, don't delete unwanted software programs on the desktop by using the mouse to drag their icons to the recycle bin. This might leave behind system files that could cause problems. Instead, use an "uninstall" utility. In Windows, go to *Start, Settings, Control Panel;* double-click *Add/Remove Programs.* Find the program you want to delete, and click the *Add/Remove* button. (In the Mac OS, one can often—but not always—uninstall programs by dragging icons into the trash; see the Mac user's manual.)

When you click the mouse on the menu bar, a list of options appears or pulls down like a shade.

panel 3.8

PC graphical user interfaces (desktop)
(*top*) Windows 8; (*middle*) Windows 7; (*bottom*) Mac (icons may differ on your PC)

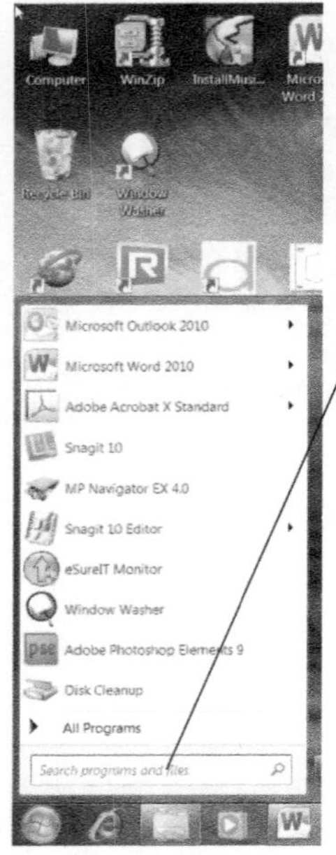

Pull-up menu—When you click the mouse pointer on the Start button at the bottom-left corner of the screen, it produces a pull-up menu offering access to programs and documents.

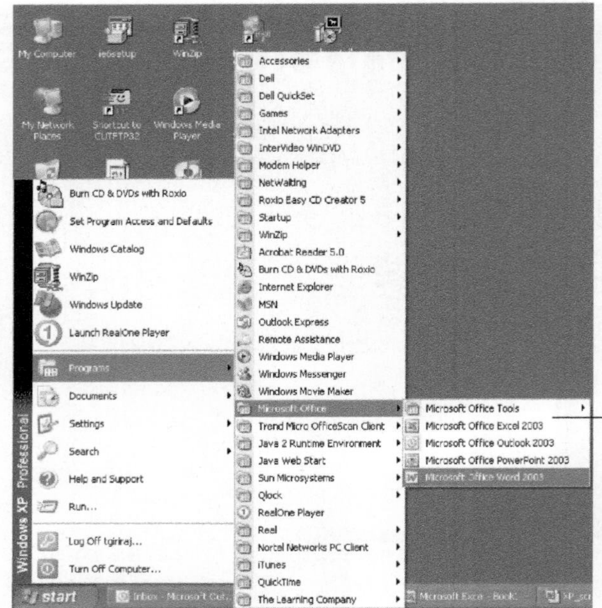

Cascading menu—Moving the mouse pointer to an option on the pull-up menu in some versions of Windows produces flyout (cascading) menus with more options.

DOCUMENTS, TITLE BARS, MENU BARS, TOOLBARS, TASKBARS, & (SMALL "W") WINDOWS If you're working in Microsoft Windows 7 and you want to go to a document file, the easiest way is to click on the *Start* button at the lower left corner and then make a selection from *Documents* on the pull-up menu that appears. (• *See Panel 3.9.*)

panel 3.9

Ways to go to a document file in Windows 7

FROM MY DOCUMENTS ICON

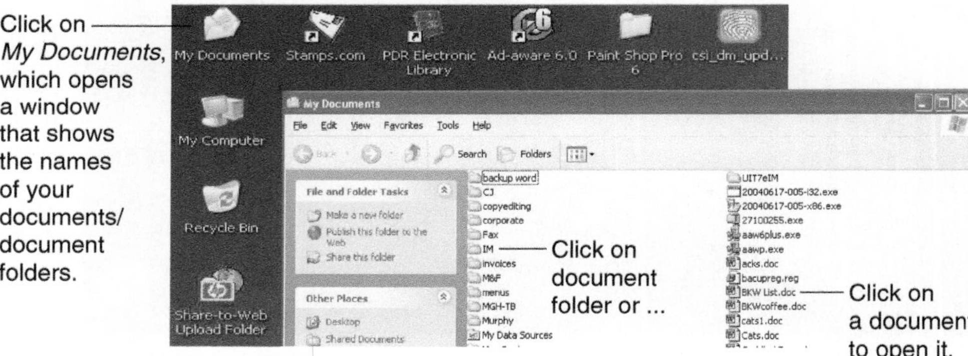

Click on *My Documents*, which opens a window that shows the names of your documents/document folders.

Click on document folder or ...

Click on a document to open it.

IN WINDOWS 7

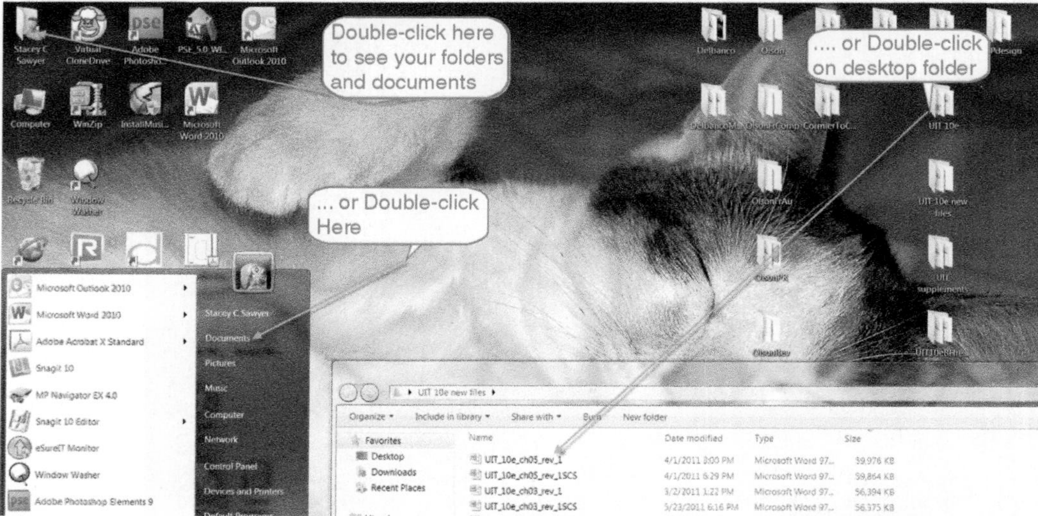
Double-click here to see your folders and documents
.... or Double-click on desktop folder
... or Double-click Here

panel 3.10

Opening a file in Windows 8: double-click on a tile, such as Microsoft Word, and you will see files and folders. Double-click on any of them to open them.

In you're working in Microsoft Windows 8, click the word File on the program's menu bar, along the program's top. (If your program hides its menu bar, pressing the Alt key reveals it.) When the File menu drops down, choose Open. If you are in Tile view, just click on a tile and choose the files that you want. *(• See Panel 3.10.)*

Once past the desktop—which is the GUI's opening screen—you will encounter various "bars" and window functions. *(• See Panel 3.11, next page.)*

- **Title bar: The title bar runs across the very top of the display window and shows the name of the folder you are in**—for example, "My Computer."
- **Menu bar:** Below the title bar is the **menu bar, which shows the names of the various pull-down menus available.** Examples of menus are File, Edit, View, Favorites, Tools, and Help.
- **Toolbar: The toolbar, below the menu bar, displays menus and icons representing frequently used options or commands.** An example of an icon is the picture of two pages in an open folder with a superimposed arrow, which issues a *Copy to* command.
- **Taskbar:** In Windows, the **taskbar is the bar across the bottom of the desktop screen that contains the Start button and that appears by default.** Small boxes appear here that show the names of open files. You can switch among the files by clicking on the boxes.

The taskbar in Windows 7 uses large icons that can be "pinned" to the taskbar even when they are not running.

The taskbar in Windows 8 is almost the same as in Windows 7—except for the removal of the Start button.

The taskbar in Windows 8.1 is almost the same as in Windows 7; however, the Start button is a shortcut to the Start screen.

- **Windows:** When spelled with a capital "W," Windows is the name of Microsoft's system software (Windows XP, Vista, 7, 8, and so on). When spelled with a lowercase "w," a **window is a rectangular portion of the display on a computer screen. Through this rectangle you can view a file of data—such as a document, spreadsheet, or database—or an application program.**

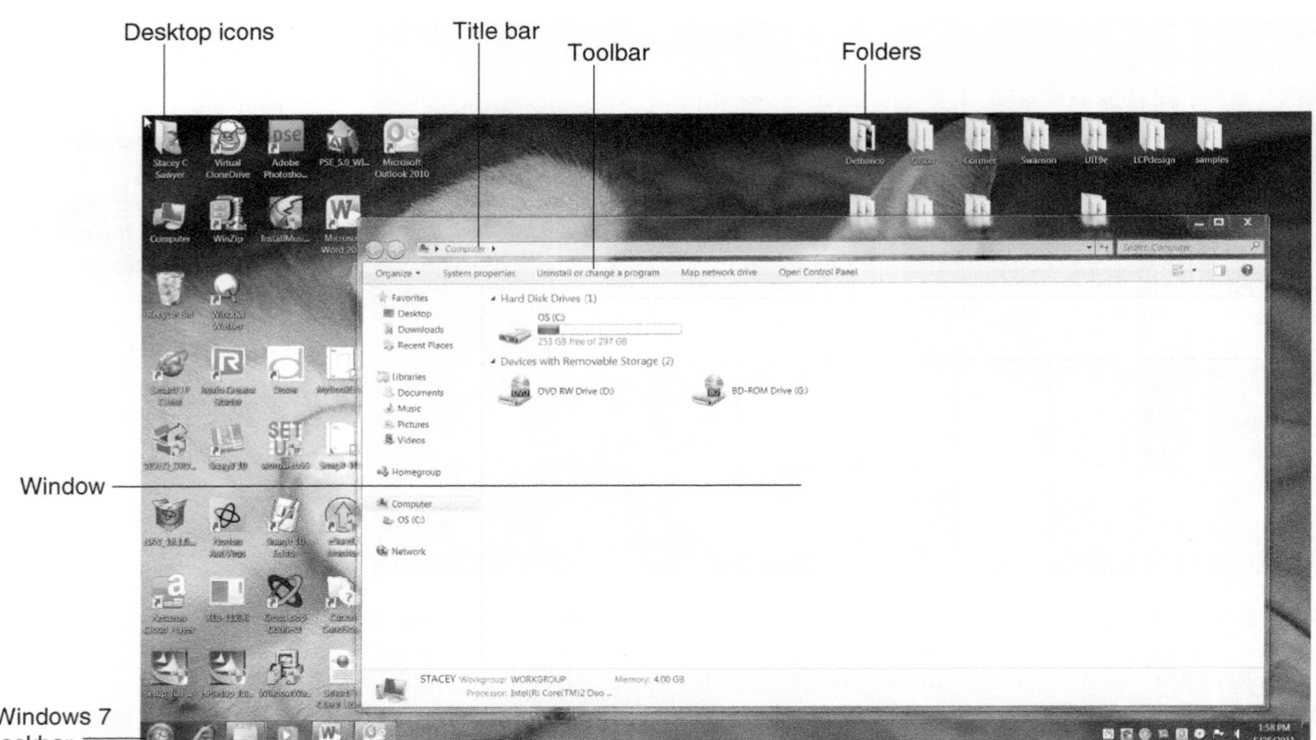

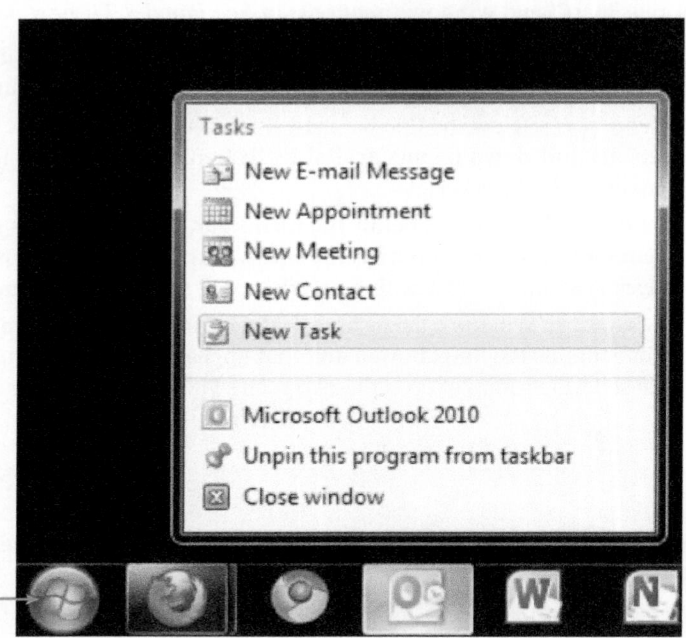

panel 3.11

(*top*) Bars and windows functions in Windows 7 (This desktop view is also available in Windows 8.) (*bottom*) Jumplists offer a quick way to open and work with programs and files pinned to the taskbar.

In the upper right-hand corner of the Windows title bar are some window controls—three icons that represent *Minimize, Maximize and Restore Down,* and *Close.* By clicking on these icons, you can *minimize* the window (shrink it down to an icon at the bottom of the screen), *make the application window fill the entire desktop window* (*maximize*) *or restore the application window to its original size* (*restore down*), or *close* it (exit the file and make the window disappear). You can also use the mouse to move the window around the desktop, by clicking on and dragging the title bar.

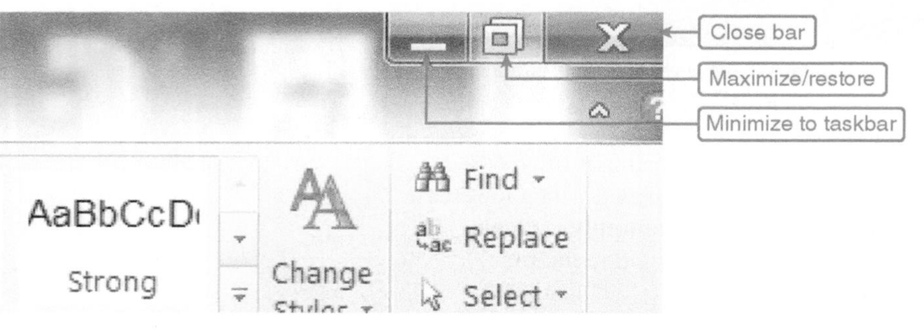

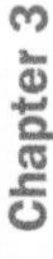

Finally, you can create *multiple windows* to show programs running concurrently, as illustrated below. For example, one window might show the text of a paper you're working on, another might show the reference section for the paper, and a third might show something you're downloading from the Internet. If you have more than one window open, click on the Maximize button of the window you want to be the main window to *restore* it (have it fill the screen).

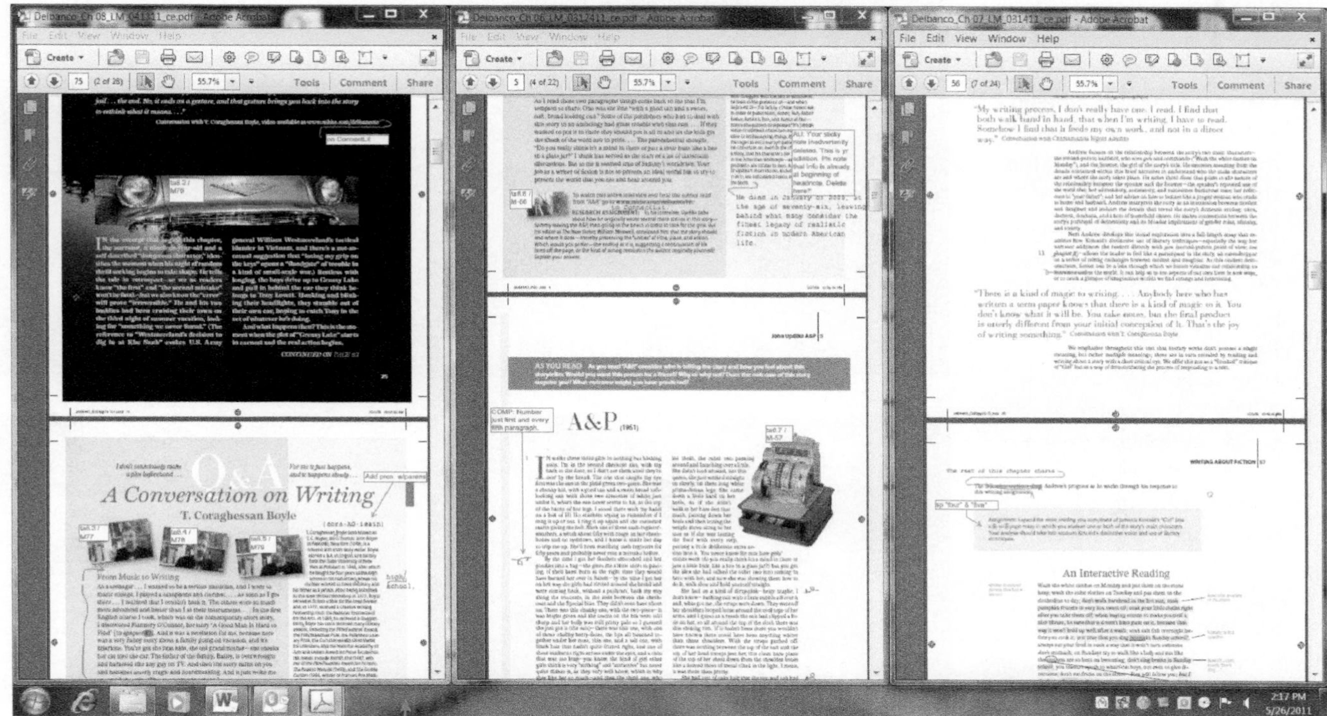

Multiple windows

The Help Command

The Help function solves problems for you when you've forgotten how to do something on the computer.

Don't understand how to do something? Forgotten a command? Accidentally pressed some keys that messed up your screen layout and you want to undo it? Most toolbars contain a **Help command—a command generating a table of contents, an index, and a search feature that can help you locate answers,** often on the web. In addition, many applications have *context-sensitive help,* which leads you to information about the task you're performing. *(• See Panel 3.12, next page.)*

3.4 COMMON OPERATING SYSTEMS

The main operating systems for general computer users are Windows, Mac OS, and Unix/Linux.

The platform is the particular processor model and operating system on which a computer system is based. Apple Macintosh computers are "Mac platforms"; personal computers (Dell, Hewlett-Packard, Lenovo) running Microsoft Windows are "Windows platforms" or "PC platforms." Large computer systems are often "Unix/Linux platforms."

In addition, there are older computers running *legacy systems,* outdated yet still functional technology, such as *DOS* (rhymes with "boss"), for *Disk Operating System.* DOS was the original operating system produced in the 1980s by Microsoft and had a hard-to-use command-line interface. In a *command-line interface,* a computer user types commands or presses special keys on the keyboard to enter instructions and data. *(• See Panel 3.13, page 135.)* This kind of interface requires more accuracy and is more difficult to use than a graphical user interface.

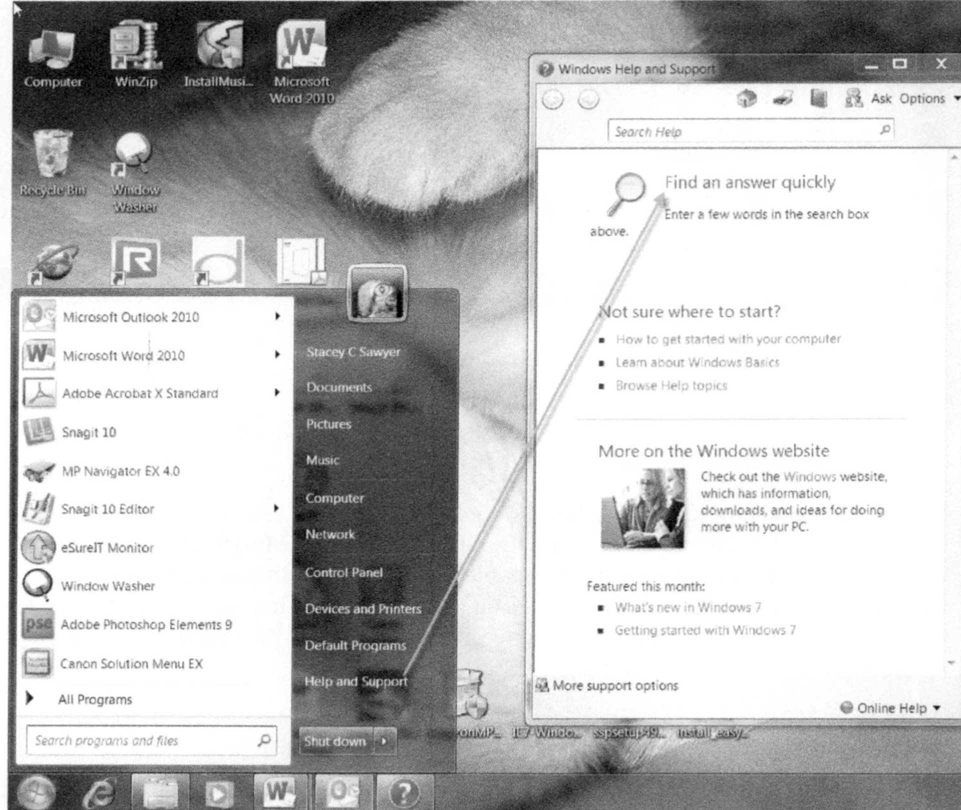

panel 3.12

Help features

(*top*) In the Mac OS X Dock, click the Finder icon or the Help option at the top of the screen. A search field appears. You can type words or questions into the search field. You can also search for menu commands, and the Help menu will highlight them. (To view Help for any other application in OS X, simply open that application and click the Help menu.) (*bottom*) Help screen for Windows 7, reached from the Start button at the bottom left corner of the screen or press the F1 key; in Windows 8, press the Windows key and the F1 key at the same time. In the Mac OS, you use the Finder (*above*).

Here we briefly describe the three principal categories of operating systems:

- Stand-alone
- Network
- Embedded

Stand-Alone Operating Systems: Macintosh & Windows

A stand-alone operating system, often called a *desktop operating system,* is an operating system that works on a single desktop or notebook (laptop) computer. Some stand-alone operating systems also work in conjunction with network (or server) operating systems, and so are called *client operating systems.*

```
C:\WINDOWS\System32\cmd.exe
(C) Copyright 1985-2001 Microsoft Corp.

C:\Documents and Settings\Stacey C. Sawyer>
C:\Documents and Settings\Stacey C. Sawyer>DIR
 Volume in drive C has no label.
 Volume Serial Number is B0EB-7091

 Directory of C:\Documents and Settings\Stacey C. Sawyer

04/25/2003  07:14 PM    <DIR>          .
04/25/2003  07:14 PM    <DIR>          ..
03/01/2003  12:58 PM    <DIR>          .java
03/01/2003  12:58 PM    <DIR>          .jpi_cache
04/25/2003  07:17 PM             1,106 .plugin140_01.trace
08/23/2003  03:31 PM    <DIR>          Desktop
02/11/2003  11:35 AM               831 Eudora.lnk
08/23/2003  03:29 PM    <DIR>          Favorites
08/25/2003  11:48 AM    <DIR>          My Documents
08/25/2003  10:45 AM         3,145,728 ntuser.dat
07/17/2003  10:24 AM    <DIR>          Start Menu
02/28/2002  09:31 PM    <DIR>          WINDOWS
               3 File(s)      3,147,665 bytes
               9 Dir(s)  29,842,452,480 bytes free

C:\Documents and Settings\Stacey C. Sawyer>_
```

panel 3.13

Legacy system: DOS, with command-line interface

With 90% of the market, Microsoft Windows is the most popular stand-alone operating system in use today, especially in offices. However, among college students, the Apple Macintosh OS seems to be the most popular. Because the Macintosh was the first to launch a graphical user interface (GUI), we will describe it first.

MACINTOSH OPERATING SYSTEM The Macintosh operating system (Mac OS), which runs on Apple Macintosh computers, set the standard for icon-oriented, easy-to-use GUIs. Apple based its new interface on work done at Xerox, which in turn had based its work on early research at Stanford Research Institute (now SRI International). (For a brief history of software, see the timeline starting on p. 164.) The software generated a strong legion of fans shortly after its launch in 1984 and inspired rival Microsoft to upgrade DOS to the more user-friendly Windows operating systems. The system's ease of use has made the Mac popular with home users and students, as well as desktop publishers and graphic designers.

MAC OS X The Mac OS X ("ex" or "10") is the most widely used of the Macintosh operating systems and is available only on computers made by Apple. *(• See Panel 3.14, next page.)* Mac OS X offers free universal email services, improved graphics and printing, improved security, easier ways to find files, and support for building and storing web pages.

Special features include:

- *Bootcamp:* This is a built-in ("native") utility that lets users boot up a Macintosh computer so that it can run both the Mac OS and the Windows operating system. (You can also purchase "nonnative" Parallels Desktop or VMware Fusion software to run Windows software.)
- *Spotlight:* This advanced desktop search technology can quickly locate files, email messages, addresses, and other things.
- *Dashboard:* Dashboard is a desktop area that displays specialized programs called Widgets that constantly update and display information.

The current version, *Mac OS 10.8,* known as *Mountain Lion,* offers 200 new features, some of which bring OS X closer to the iOS operating system at the heart of Apple's tablet and smartphone, which we discuss later.[17] This version of the OS syncs new information wirelessly and automatically with your other Apple gadgets, such as

panel 3.14

Mac OS X screen. The dashboard showing widgets is at the bottom of this iPad's screen.

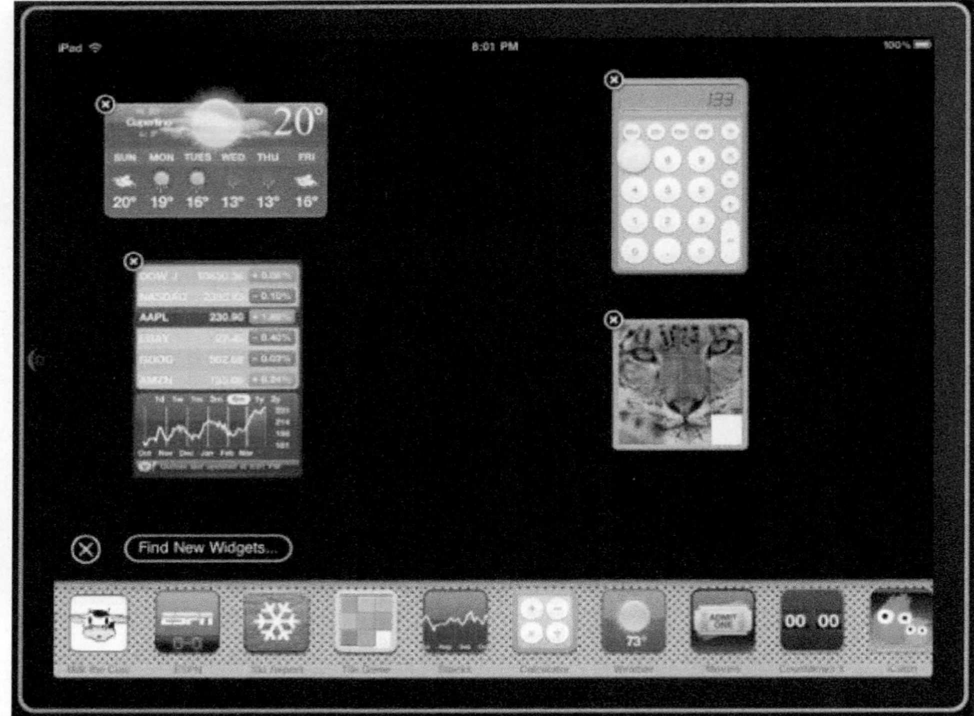

the iPhone, iPad, and iPod, courtesy of Apple's iCloud service. Mountain Lion (which evolved out of the earlier Mac OS 10.7, called Lion) also offers some of the following new features:

- *Power Nap:* This feature enables the laptop to update Internet data even while it's asleep.
- *Dictation:* This allows you to use your own voice to dictate instead of typing.
- *Messaging:* This brings Internet-borne text messages on the iPhone and iPad to the Mac.
- *Airplay Mirroring:* If you have an Apple TV, you can wirelessly display the screen contents of your Mac on an HDTV.

Mac Apps

To see the wide variety of applications available to download for the Mac, go to:

www.apple.com/downloads/

As of early 2013, Mac OS X 10.8 is the fourth most popular desktop operating system in use (2.44%), after Microsoft Windows 7, Windows XP (which is no longer being supported by Microsoft), and Windows Vista (totaling about 89%).[18] (• *See Panel 3.15.)*

MICROSOFT WINDOWS Microsoft Windows **is the most common operating system for desktop and portable PCs.** Early attempts did not catch on, but in 1992 Windows 3.*x* emerged as the preferred system among PC users. Windows 3.*x* was succeeded by a series of other Windows systems—Windows 95, 98, 2000, ME, XP, and Vista among them. Vista, introduced in 2007, required so much computing power and had so many hardware

panel 3.15

Desktop operating systems market shares, October 2013 (adapted from *www.netmarketshare.com/operating-system-market-share.aspx?qprid510&qpcustomd=0*)

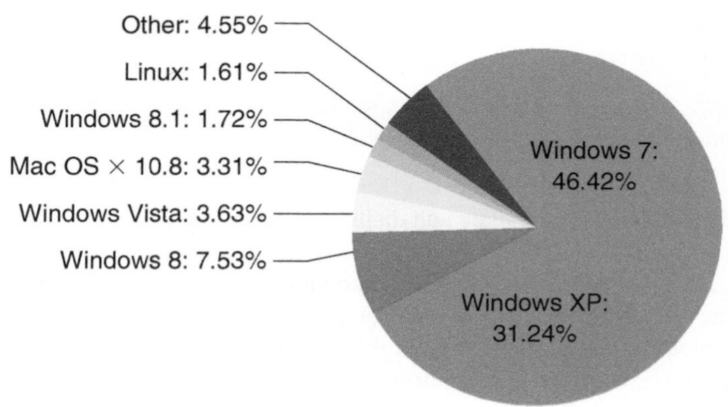

panel 3.16

Windows 7 desktop screen

You can pin a program directly to the taskbar so you can open it quickly and conveniently, rather than looking for the program in the Start menu.

incompatibility issues that many businesses declined to upgrade to it. The operating system did not sell well, and Microsoft moved on to Windows 7 and, more recently, Windows 8.

WINDOWS 7 Released in 2009, Microsoft Windows 7 **at the time was the fastest, most efficient version of the Windows operating systems to date,** and it is still the most widely used OS. (• *See Panel 3.16, above.*) Besides being less power hungry than Vista, Windows 7 offers faster start-up, easy-to-use interface, improved networking and security features, enhanced searching capabilities for finding data on your computer, and improved handwriting recognition for tablet computers.

Windows 7 is available in several versions, including the following:

- Home Premium: Intended for general PC users, this version includes basic multimedia functions.
- Ultimate: Intended for advanced PC users, gamers, and multimedia professionals, this version adds additional security features and allows users to switch among 35 languages.
- Professional: This version is mainly for small businesses, but it is appropriate for the advanced home user.
- Enterprise: This version is designed for multiuser businesses.

WINDOWS 8 Microsoft Windows 8, says one reviewer, "is the company's effort to reshape the computer industry it built for a new future, one in which tablets and smartphones are the dominant way we get online and computers are almost an afterthought."[19]

Released in October 2012, the Microsoft Windows 8 **operating system has two user interfaces—one for the traditional desktop, with overlapping, resizable windows just like earlier Windows, the other a radical redesign resembling the Windows Phone interface, with "tile-based," tablet-style features geared for touch screens (but also working with regular screens).**[20]

One writer says Windows 8 "looks and feels like a tablet operating system slapped overtop Windows 7."[21]

Users can switch back and forth between the two interfaces, which might be called "Desktop Windows" ("classic view") and "Tile-Based Windows."[22] (These are not the names Microsoft gives them.)

- "Desktop Windows"—designed for mouse and keyboard: This version is basically the Windows 7 conventional desktop interface, with the taskbar across the bottom and

Survival Tip

OEM

If you buy a computer with Windows (or any other operating system) already installed, the OS is called an *OEM (original equipment manufacturer) version.* If you buy your OS off the shelf, it is called a *retail version.* These two versions are almost identical, except an OEM version will install only on the *specific* machine for which it was intended. A retail version will install on any compatible machine. If you have an OEM version, you have to call the computer manufacturer, not the OS producer, for technical support. Because a retail version is not specifically tailored for your particular computer, Microsoft recommends that, before you buy a retail version of an OS, you run a compatibility check at its website (*http://support.microsoft.com*).

Windows 7

To explore Windows 7 on videos, go to:

http://windows.microsoft.com/en-us/windows7/products/videos#1TC=compare

Survival Tip

New Installation

Every time you install or reinstall Windows, you will have to get Microsoft's permission to activate it. You can do this over the Internet or via phone.

Microsoft's headquarters. Aerial view of Microsoft's Redmond, Washington, main corporate campus, which spreads over several square miles of the Seattle suburb

all the overlapping windows and menus. However, it lacks the traditional Start menu icon of past Windows programs; instead, you have to go to "Tile-Based Windows" to start it up. (• *See Panel 3.17.)* (A free program called Pokki restores the Start menu to the desktop.) This is the version you can use to run all the 4 million old traditional Windows applications (what Microsoft calls desktop apps), such as Photoshop, Quicken, tax software, and others we discuss later in this chapter. The "Desktop Windows" is clearly designed for the mouse, since most of the menus and buttons are too small for touch operation.

- **"Tile-Based Windows"—designed primarily for touch screens:** This second part, which Microsoft used to call Metro but now (confusingly) calls simply Windows 8, is clearly designed for touch screens, although there are mouse and keyboard equivalents. Modeled on Microsoft's Windows Phone software, the opening screen is filled with colorful large square and rectangular tiles, each one representing an application. You can move the tiles around with a swipe of your finger, "pin" frequently used tiles (such as your contacts list) to the Start screen, and otherwise rearrange, resize, and cluster the tiles. A single tile can represent an app with multiple possibilities. "A People app offers an entry to your social media world," says one report, "aggregating info from Facebook, LinkedIn, and other social networks and letting you post and share information back to them. The tile flips over every few seconds, with photos of your friends and college roommates, begging you to click on them."[23]

Screen Views

How to make Windows 8 look like Windows 7:

http://reviews.cnet.co.uk/software-and-web-apps/how-to-make-windows-8-look-like-windows-7-50009546/

- **Windows 8 Start screen:** The two parts of Windows 8 are not completely separate; that is, you cannot live exclusively in one environment or the other. For instance, you have to use "Desktop Windows" to work with files or disks. You have to use "Tile-Based Windows" for searching and address-book lookups. There are also different designs for the same thing—for instance, the address bar is at the top in "Desktop Windows" and at the bottom in "Tile-Based Windows."

Another potential for confusion is that Windows 8 comes in three versions:

Survival Tip

Shortcuts

Keyboard shortcuts for Windows 8 and Windows RT are shown at *http://windows.microsoft.com/en-us/windows-8/new-keyboard-shortcuts#1TC=t1.*

- **Standard Windows 8:** Called simply Windows 8, this version will run on standard PCs (those running Intel chips, as we discuss in Chapter 4). With this version, you can run both your old Windows apps and the new tablet-type apps.
- **Windows RT:** Made for cheaper tablets and laptops, this version is far less capable than the standard Windows 8. It is intended to be used as a mobile operating system, to run on the same type of processor that powers competing smartphones and tablets

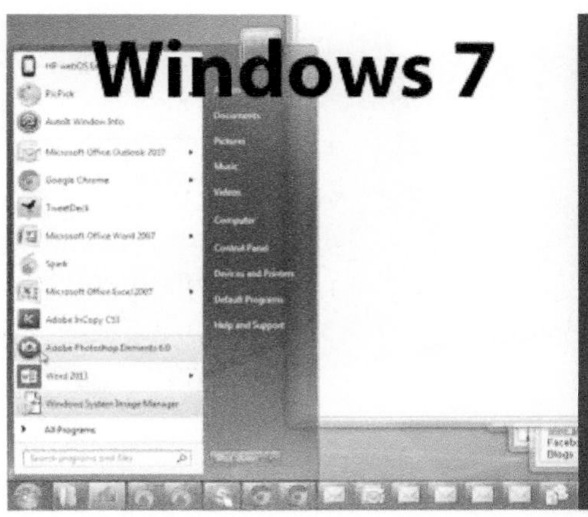

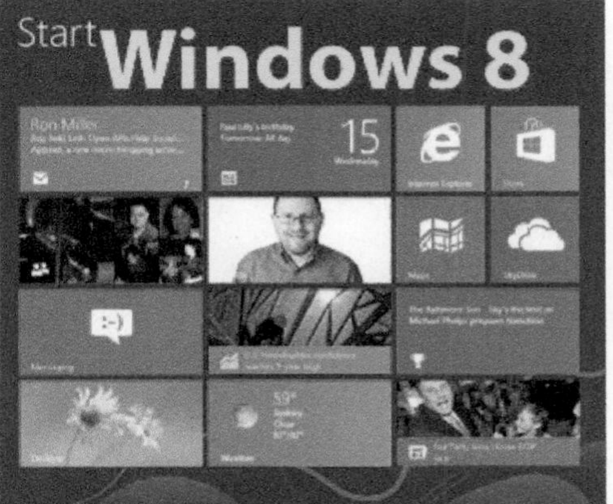

panel 3.17

Windows 8 screen views

(*top right*) Windows 8 tile view, compared to Windows 7 (*top left*); (*middle*) Start screen, tile view; (*bottom*) desktop view

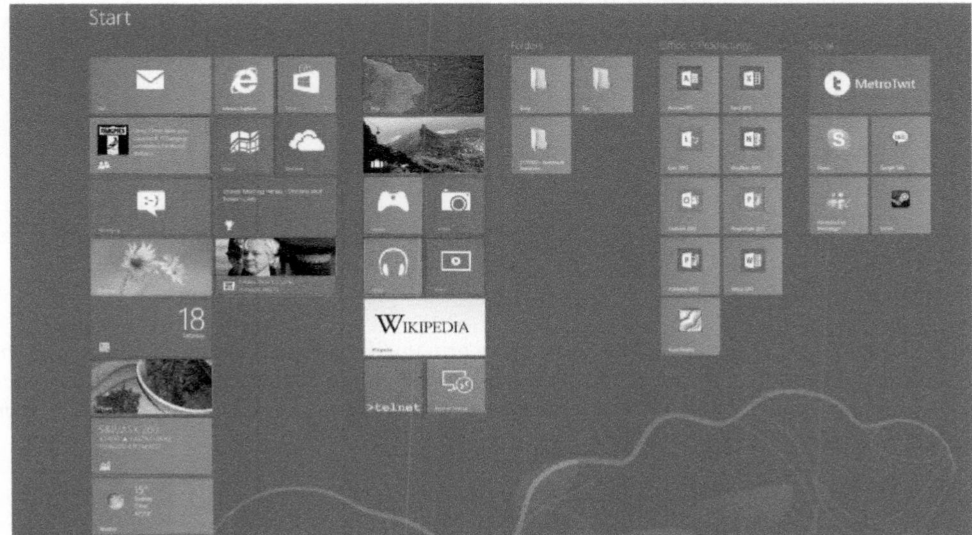

RT will also run on the Surface tablet, the first personal computer made and sold by Microsoft in its history. (• *See Panel 3.18, next page.*)

- **Windows 8 Pro:** This version adds some corporate features to Windows 8.

To address Windows 8 drawbacks, Microsoft launched Windows 8.1, or Windows Blue, as a free update through the Windows Store, improving its Start screen interface and

Windows vs. Mac

To compare Windows to the Mac, go to:

www.diffen.com/difference/Mac_vs_PC/

http://usatoday30.usatoday.com/tech/story/2012/09/23/pcs-vs-macs-how-they-stack-up/57818700/1/

www.howstuffworks.com/macs/10-differences-between-macs-and-pcs.htm

http://lifehacker.com/mac-vs-windows-your-best-arguments-486125257/

Or do keyword searches for "Mac vs. Windows" and "Mac vs. PC."

panel 3.18

Surface tablets

The first personal computer made by Microsoft, this tablet runs either Windows 8 or Windows RT.

supporting additional screen sizes. Windows Blue put back the Start button and allows the use of smaller tiles on the Start screen, several new apps, new navigation gestures, a new Snap View that lets you easily place two Windows 8 apps side by side on the screen, and a new version of Internet Explorer 11. The update also added the option to boot directly to the desktop, bypassing the Start screen completely. (Aspects of the Windows Blue code hint that Microsoft's plans for Windows 9 may eliminate the desktop.)

Network Operating Systems: OES, Windows Server, Unix, & Linux

Abbreviated NOS, a network operating system includes special functions for connecting computers and devices to a local area network (LAN).

The operating systems described so far were principally designed for use with stand-alone desktop and laptop machines. Now let's consider the important operating systems designed to work with sizable networks—*Open Enterprise Server* (OES, formerly NetWare), *Windows Server, Unix/Solaris,* and *Linux.*

NOVELL'S OPEN ENTERPRISE SERVER *NetWare,* now called *Open Enterprise Server (OES*), has long been a popular network operating system for coordinating microcomputer-based local area networks (LANs) throughout a company or a campus. LANs allow PCs to share programs, data files, and printers and other devices. A network OS is usually located on a main server (see Chapter 1, p. 4), which controls the connectivity of smaller networks and individual computers. Novell, the maker of OES, thrived as corporate data managers realized that networks of PCs could exchange information more cheaply than the previous generation of mainframes and midrange computers.

WINDOWS SERVER Windows desktop operating systems can be used to link PCs in small networks in homes and offices. However, something more powerful was needed to run the huge networks linking a variety of computers—PCs, workstations, mainframes—used by many companies, universities, and other organizations, which previously were served principally by Unix and NetWare operating systems. The server version of Windows 8, *Microsoft Windows Server 2012,* is the company's family of multitasking operating systems designed to run on network servers in businesses of all sizes. Of the four versions or "editions," most are intended for businesses—small to medium-size (Windows Server 2012 Essential), medium- to large-size (Windows Server 2012 Standard), and huge-size with gigantic databases (Windows Server 2012 Datacenter). It allows multiple users to share resources such as data, programs, and printers and to build web applications and connect to the Internet.

UNIX, SOLARIS, & BSD Unix (pronounced "*you*-nicks") was developed at AT&T's Bell Laboratories in 1969 as an operating system for minicomputers. By the 1980s AT&T entered into partnership with Sun Microsystems to develop a standardized version of Unix for sale to industry. Today **Unix is a proprietary multitasking operating system for multiple users that has built-in networking capability and versions that can run on all kinds of computers.**

Unix uses a command-line interface (but the commands are different for each system). (• *See Panel 3.19.*) Some companies market Unix systems with graphical interface shells that make Unix easier to use.

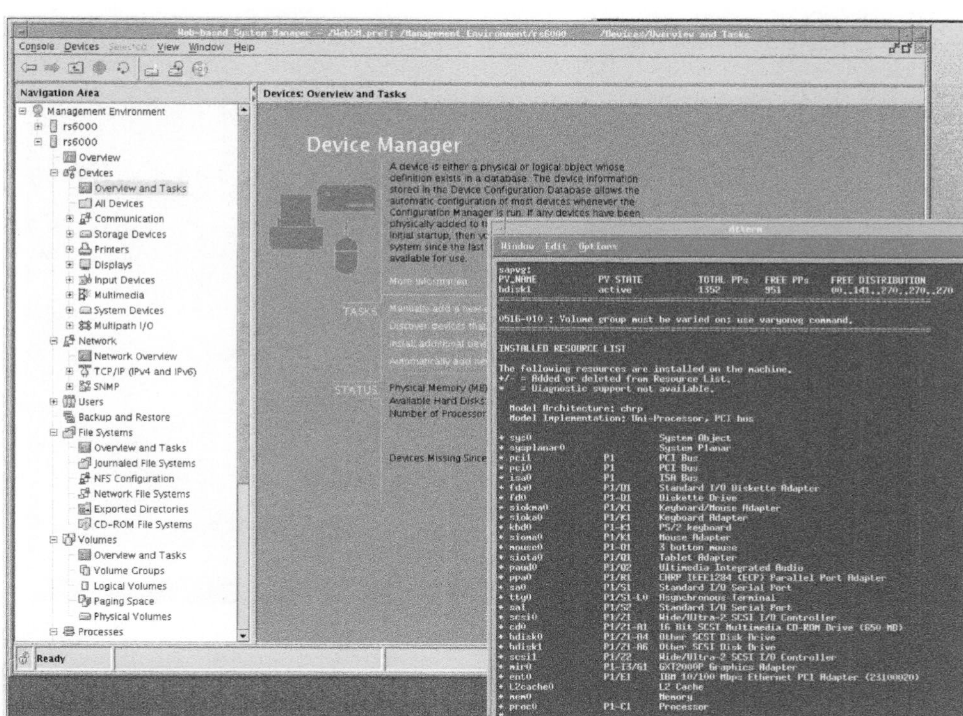

panel 3.19

Device manager in Unix

Unix is considered a multipurpose operating system because it can be both a stand-alone and server operating system. However, it is used mostly on mainframes, workstations, and servers rather than on microcomputers. Government agencies, universities, research institutions, large corporations, and banks commonly use Unix for everything from designing airplane parts to currency trading. Because it is particularly stable and reliable, Unix is also used for website management and runs the backbone of the Internet. The developers of the Internet built their communications system around Unix because it has the ability to keep large systems (with hundreds of processors) churning out transactions day in and day out for years without fail.

- **Solaris:** Developed by Sun Microsystems, *Solaris* is a version of Unix that is popular for handling large e-commerce servers and large websites.
- **BSD:** A free software derived from Unix, *BSD* began in the 1970s in the computer science department of the University of California, Berkeley, when students and staff began to develop their own derivative of Unix, known as the Berkeley Software Distribution, or BSD.

LINUX It began in 1991 when programmer Linus Torvalds, a graduate student in Finland, posted his free Linux operating system on the Internet. Linux (pronounced "*linn*-uks") is the rising star of network software. **Linux is a free (nonproprietary) version of Unix, and its continual improvements result from the efforts of tens of thousands of volunteer programmers.**

Whereas Windows Server is Microsoft's proprietary product, Linux is **open-source software—meaning any programmer can download it from the Internet for free and modify it with suggested improvements.** The only qualification is that changes can't be copyrighted; they must be made available to all and remain in the public domain. (Note: It is a common misconception that Unix is open-source software; only a few versions of Unix-like OSs are open source.)

Linux is available with a command-line interface or a GUI. It is used on a wide range of computers and devices, including mobile phones. It is a leading server operating system and runs some of the fastest supercomputers in the world. Linux has become the basis of other operating systems, one of them being Google's *Chrome OS,* which is targeted at netbooks and other mobile devices that utilize cloud computing.

Open-Source Software

Advantages and disadvantages:

www.hrsa.gov/healthit/toolbox/HealthITAdoptiontoolbox/OpenSource/softwareadvantage.html

www.cioinsight.com/it-strategy/linux-open-source/slideshows/five-pros-and-five-cons-of-open-source-software/

Linux screen (Linux Mint)

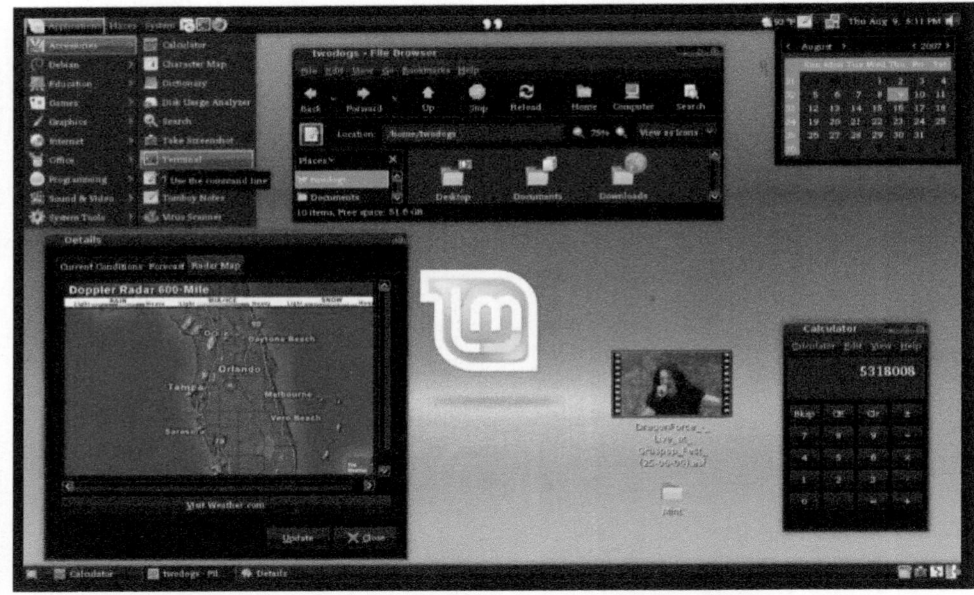

more info!

OS Comparisons

For more details on OS comparisons, go to:

www.operating-system.org/

www.pcmag.com/category2/0,2806,2362,00.asp-www.pcmag.com/category2/0,2806,2362,00.asp

TECH TALES China Adopts Linux as Its National Standard

In 2000, the People's Republic of China announced that it was adopting Linux as a national standard for operating systems because it feared being dominated by the OS of a company of a foreign power—namely, Microsoft. Five years later, China's leading Linux software developer, Red Flag Software Company, Ltd., joined the Open Source Development Labs (OSDL), a global consortium dedicated to accelerating the adoption of Linux in the business world. In 2007, OSDL and the Free Standards Group merged to form The Linux Foundation (*http://osdl.org/en/Main_Page*), narrowing their respective focuses to that of promoting Linux in competition with Microsoft Windows.

Because it was originally built for use on the Internet, Linux is more reliable than Windows for online applications. Hence, it is better suited to run websites and e-commerce software. Its real growth, however, may come as it reaches outward to other applications and, possibly, replaces Windows in many situations, especially embedded systems, as we discuss next. ■

Rules for Upgrading Your Operating System

http://blog.macsales.com/1411-the-golden-rules-of-upgrading-tips-from-the-owc-technical-support-team/

www.ehow.com/how_2157557_upgrade-computers-operating-system.html

Embedded Operating Systems

In general, embedded operating systems are used in small or specialized devices, such has mobile phones.

An embedded operating system **resides on a CPU chip called a ROM** (read-only memory; see Chapter 4) **chip and is the operating system used on consumer electronic devices, including smartphones and tablets.** Embedded operating systems used in portable devices are also called *mobile operating systems.* Some of the best known of these operating systems are Google Android, iOS, BlackBerry, and Windows Phone, among others. In mid-2013, Android led with a 79.3% market share, followed by iOS with 13.2%—combining for 92.5% of the market.[24] (• *See Panel 3.20.*)

panel 3.20

Top smartphone operating systems: shipments and market share for quarter 3, 2013 (units in millions)

Source: www.firstpost.com/tech/79-percent-of-smartphones-shipped-in-q2-of-2013-were-androids-idc-1021261.html.

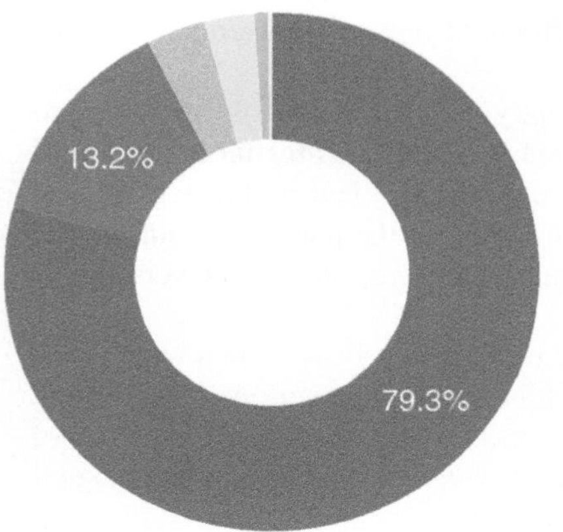

Android
iOS
Windows Phone
BlackBerry OS
Linux
Symbian

GOOGLE ANDROID Introduced in 2007 and based on Linux, *Google Android* is a mobile operating system used on more than 20 different devices, including smartphones produced by Samsung, HTC, and Motorola, as well as tablets and e-book readers. *(• See Panel 3.21.)* Users can choose from a great many apps or program their own.

panel 3.21

Google Android runs on Samsung smartphones, such as the Samsung Galaxy4.

IOS Developed in 2007 and formerly called the iPhone OS, *iOS is an operating system developed by Apple for the iPhone as well as Apple's iPod Touch and iPad tablet.* *(• See Panel 3.22.)* It was the first mobile OS to allow gesture inputs, such as tapping, sliding, squeezing, and pinching and unpinching.

panel 3.22

Apple's iPod Touch and iPad tablet, which run on iOS

The Windows Phone

WINDOWS PHONE 8 A successor to Windows Mobile and Windows Phone 7 (which had a combined mobile OS market share of 3.7%), *Windows Phone 8* was designed by Microsoft to support a variety of mobile devices, including smartphones marketed by Nokia and HTC. Like Windows 8 for computers, the Phone 8 interface is based on dynamic live tiles, representing apps, favorite websites, and the like, which can be manipulated and moved about. One limitation has been that fewer apps are available compared to those of rivals—120,000 in the Windows Store in late 2012 compared to 700,000-plus apps for the Android and iOS.[25]

BLACKBERRY OS Fourth in popularity among mobile operating systems, with 2.9% market share in 2013, the *BlackBerry OS* was introduced in 1999 by Canadian company Research In Motion (RIM) for its BlackBerry keyboard-equipped handheld computer. Most of today's smartphones have touch-screen keyboards, but for lovers of physical keyboards RIM has offered a new operating system, BlackBerry 10, to power the BlackBerry Q10, which has both a classic physical keyboard and a touch screen.[26] *(• See Panel 3.23.)*

panel 3.23

The BlackBerry Q10, which has both a physical keyboard and a touch-screen keyboard, runs on the BlackBerry 10 operating system.

EMBEDDED LINUX With a market share of 0.8% in 2013, *embedded Linux* is a scaled-down Linux operating system found on K-Touch and Haier phones, with new smartphones

Embedded Systems

For updates on smartphone OSs try:

www.pcmag.com/article2/0,2817,2417059,00.asp

www.android.com/

www.apple.com/ios/

www.techhive.com/article/2039240/jolla-announces-first-sailfishbased-smartphone.html

www.businesswire.com/news/home/20130516005342/en/Android-iOS-Combine-92.3-Smartphone-Operating-System/

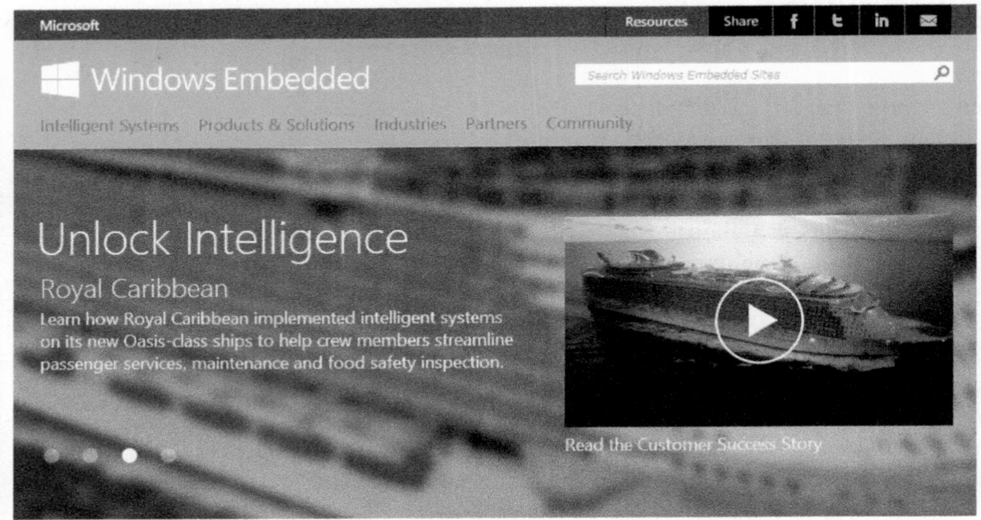

Intelligent systems powered by Microsoft

Microsoft provides one trusted platform to gather, store and process your organization's data—from devices on the edge of your network, to developer tools, backend systems and services. The Windows Embedded solution portfolio allows your enterprise to drive a new level of business intelligence and identify opportunities that would be otherwise out of reach. Together with the power and resources of the cloud, intelligent systems with edge devices running on Windows Embedded span companies, communities and countries within the Internet of Things.

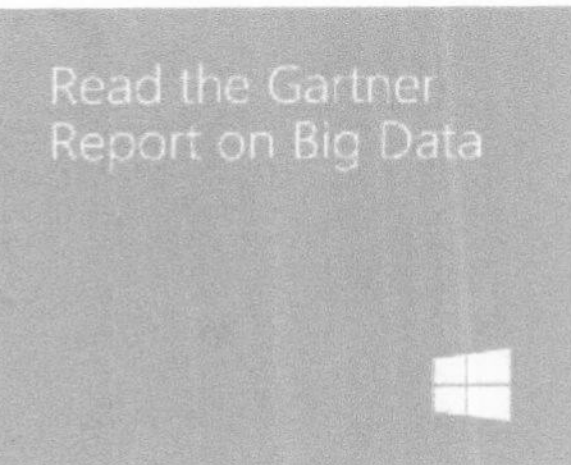

from SailFish, Tizen, and Ubuntu scheduled to launch in 2013. Embedded Linux is also found on other computers and mobile devices, including portable media players and Internet phones.

Other mobile operating systems, including Symbian OS and WebOS (formerly Palm OS), made up only 1.3% of the 2012 market share for embedded OSs.

UNIT 3B: *Application Software: Getting Started*

Application software, as we said at the beginning of this chapter, is software that has been developed to solve a particular problem for users—to perform useful work on specific tasks or to provide entertainment. People interact mainly with the application software, which interacts with the system software, which interacts with the computer.

3.5 APPLICATION SOFTWARE: Where to Get It, How to Use It

Application software comprises the programs that do the work that users are directly interested in.

No doubt you're already using application software every day—on a smartphone, a tablet, a laptop, a desktop, or all of these. This kind of software has a variety of uses—for business purposes; for home, personal, and educational uses; for communications; and for graphics and multimedia, such as for videogames.

TECH TALES Software Evolution: 40 Years of Blasting Space Aliens—the Incredible Growth in Videogames

"Today, videogames are more popular than either music or film," says technology writer Marshall Honorof. In this particular kind of applications software, titles like *Halo* or *Mass Effect* "are triumphs of visual, aural, and narrative ingenuity," he says.[27] Their development requires an army of artists to do the "nearly photorealistic visuals and silky animation" plus designers, producers, writers, and musicians.

How far we've come from the days when a single programmer could take a few months to work on a videogame, writing all the software code and creating all the graphics and sound effects. In 1975 only 24 videogames were available, nearly all of them played on arcade machines, such as *Pac-Man* (1980). Ten years later, the market was flooded with 1,225 new titles; a popular one launched in 1989 was *SimCity.* Personal computers running such games were the Apple II and Commodore 64, along with "platforms," or computer systems, running Microsoft DOS.

In 1998, 37% of videogames were developed for Microsoft Windows, "the highest-ever proportion of titles for one platform," according to *Bloomberg Businessweek* writer Jennifer Daniel.[28] Today videogames are still being developed for Windows, the oldest platform in use.

In the first decade of the 21st century, videogame software was being written not only for Windows but also for such systems as Nintendo, Xbox and Xbox 360, and PlayStations 1 and 2. At this point, programmers began creating products for web browsers as well. Costs for developing software for a multiplatform AAA-rated games skyrocketed—to an average of $28 million.[29] The *Call of Duty* series, for instance, was said to be in the $50 million range for development, far more than the $5 million to $10 million software budgets of a decade earlier.

Now the industry has moved onto a different phase—games for smartphones and tablets. "In 2011 at least 737 iPhone games were released," says Daniel, "more than for any other platform. Just four years earlier there were only 26." ■

Sources of Software: For Sale, For Free, or For Rent?

The availability of software depends on how it is licensed or copyrighted by its creators or owners.

Application software can be obtained in a variety of ways: *custom, packaged, web application, shareware, freeware,* and *public domain.* It can also be *rented.*

CUSTOM SOFTWARE Occasionally companies or individuals need software written specifically for them, to meet unique needs. **Custom software is tailor-made software crafted by an individual or team of programmers for a particular function or business purpose** that cannot be served by buying readily available off-the-shelf or packaged software, as discussed next.

PACKAGED SOFTWARE Also called *proprietary software* or *commercial software,* **packaged software is copyrighted, mass-produced software that's offered for sale in stores or on the web to a variety of users** (not created for just one client, as custom software is). Examples are Microsoft Office or Adobe Reader, which often come to customers preinstalled on their new computers.

Packaged software is protected by *copyright*—the exclusive legal right that prohibits copying intellectual property without the permission of the copyright holder.

Software manufacturers don't sell you their software; rather, they sell you a license to become an authorized user of it. The difference? In paying for a **software license, you sign a contract in which you agree not to make copies of the software to give away or resell.** That is, you have bought only the company's permission to use the software and not the software itself. This legal nicety allows the company to retain its rights to the program and limits the way its customers can use it. The small print in the licensing agreement usually allows you to make one copy *(backup copy* or *archival copy)* for your own use and to run the program on only one to three machines.

Several types of software licenses exist, as shown on the next page. (• *See Panel 3.24.)*

panel 3.24

Types of software licenses

Type	Definition
Site license	Allows the software to be used on all computers at a specific location
Concurrent-use license	Allows a certain number of copies of the software to be used at the same time
Multiple-user license	Specifies the number of people who may use the software
Single-user license	Limits software use to one user at a time

Part of a Windows 8 software license

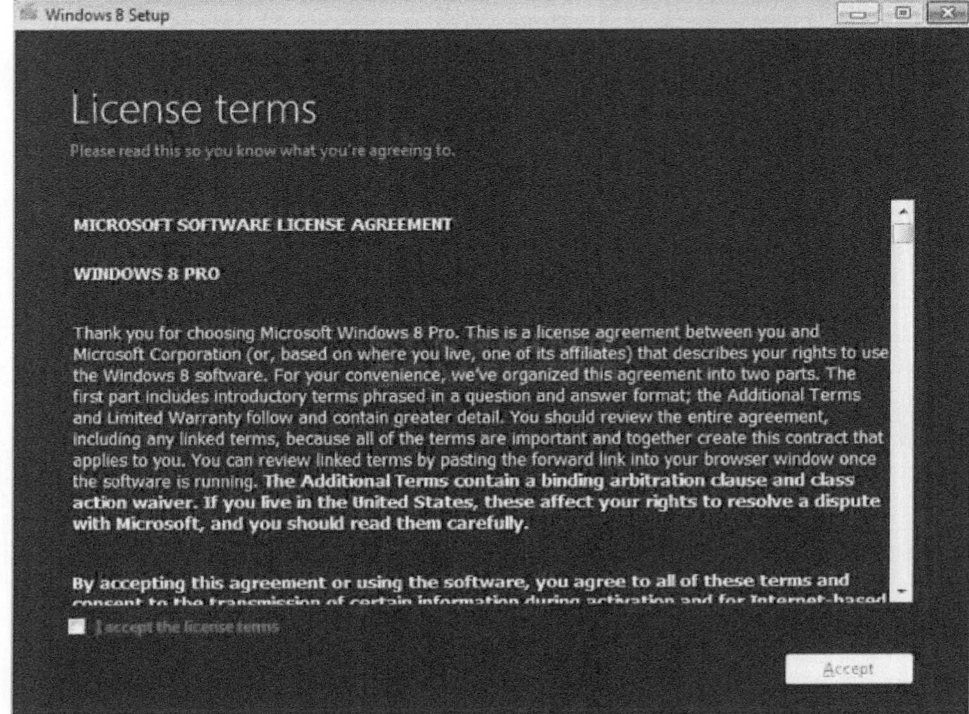

In trying to observe the legalities, there are two pitfalls to avoid:

- **Abandonware:** Sometimes a software publisher will abandon selling or supporting a software program, so that it is considered "abandonware." Still, U.S. copyrights continue to be valid for up to 95 years from the date the software was first published, so you shouldn't think it's legal to copy abandoned software.
- **Pirated software: Pirated software is software obtained illegally, such as downloaded off the Internet, transmitted via an illicit CD/DVD copy made by a friend, or bought in a market in a foreign country.** With pirated software, not only do the copyright owners not get paid for their creative work, but you risk getting inferior goods and, worse, picking up a virus.

  U.S. laws prohibiting pirated software are stricter now than they ever have been. Simply possessing pirated software could land you in serious legal trouble. The fine for every incident of title infringement is up to $100,000 and possible jail time. Ignorance of the law is no excuse; neither is unknowingly purchasing pirated software.

  To discourage software piracy, many software manufacturers require that users register their software when they install it on their computers. If the software is not registered, it will not work properly.

How to Spot Pirated Software

www.howtolearn.com/2012/06/how-to-identify-and-avoid-pirated-software/

www.adobe.com/antipiracy/identify-and-avoid-piracy.html

www.dpmag.com/blog/identifying-pirated-software.html

PUBLIC-DOMAIN SOFTWARE Public-domain software is not protected by copyright and thus may be duplicated by anyone at will, with no fear of legal prosecution. Such

THE FBI FEDERAL BUREAU OF INVESTIGATION

CONTACT US | ABOUT US | MOST WANTED | NEWS | STATS

Intellectual Property Theft

Home • About Us • What We Investigate • White-Collar Crime • Intellectual Property Theft • FBI Anti-Piracy Warning Seal

FBI Anti-Piracy Warning Seal

Download the FBI Anti-Piracy Warning Seal

A new federal regulation regarding the FBI's Anti-Piracy Warning (APW) Seal took effect on August 13, 2012. The new 41 CFR Section 128-1.5009 authorizes use of the APW Seal by all U.S. copyright holders, subject to specific conditions of use. Copyrighted works can include, but are not limited to, films, audio recordings, electronic media, software, books, photographs, etc.

The purpose of the APW Seal is to remind media users of the serious consequences of pirating copyrighted works. Use of this seal does not indicate that the FBI has reviewed or validated copyright interests in the particular work and does not provide greater legal protection to the work. It simply serves as a widely recognizable reminder of the FBI's authority and mission with respect to the protection of intellectual property rights.

programs—sometimes developed by government agencies or universities and often downloadable from the web—have been donated to the public by their creators.

FREEWARE Also usually distributed over the Internet, **freeware is copyrighted software that is distributed free of charge** because the developers want to test user response, further some scholarly or humanitarian purpose, or expect to make money by attracting users to their advertising. The web browsers Internet Explorer and Mozilla Firefox are both freeware.

SHAREWARE Distributed primarily through the Internet, **shareware is copyrighted software that is distributed free for a trial period, but users must then pay the software developer to continue using it.** In other words, you can try it before you buy it. Once you pay the fee, you usually get supporting documentation, access to updated versions, and perhaps some technical support. "In general," says one expert, "shareware from established companies that offer trial versions of their programs is O.K."[30] Other kinds of shareware (and freeware) may deliver spyware or malware.

RENTALWARE Rentalware is online software that users lease for a fee and download whenever they want it. Microsoft, for instance, makes Office 2013, a bundle of personal computer applications, available in a subscription version known as Office 365. This can be rented for a monthly fee, just as people now can subscribe to cable TV. Office 365 Home Premium can be rented for $99.99 a year for up to five computers, PC and/or Mac. With subscriber benefits come updates and added features on a regular basis. Rentalware is the basis of ASP (application service provider), software. An ASP is a company that provides remote software that you access through a web browser. Instead of installing software on your local drive, you rent the use of ASP software that exists elsewhere on the Internet. You don't own ASP software; you borrow it for a fee.

This brings us to web apps, discussed next.

WEB APPLICATION A web application, or *web app,* is software that runs on a remote Internet server rather than on a person's own personal computer. A web app is typically, but not always, accessed using a web browser. Here, for instance, you can find word processing, spreadsheet, and email programs, often free, although some websites (such as Office 365) charge for access. Web apps are booming in popularity as cloud computing becomes more established.

Public Domain Software

For information on public domain software and where to obtain it, go to:

www.webcrawler.com/webcrawler301/ws/results/web/public+domain+software/1/417/topnavigation/relevance/iq=true/zoom=off/_iceurl-flag=7?_iceurl=true&gclid=ckik1ifjspscfrwdagodtafvpa

http://voices.yahoo.com/guide-explaining-public-domain-software-7861208.html

Shareware & Freeware

What kinds of shareware and freeware are available? To find out, go to:

www.searchalot.com/?p=&q=shareware

www.passtheshareware.com/

www.techsupportalert.com/content/best-freeware-download-sites.htm

www.pcworld.com/article/2038736/best-free-stuff-2013-edition-alphabetical-list-by-category.html

TECH TALES Free Software for Cash-Strapped Students

Keeping down college expenses is not always easy, but here's one place to do it: Help yourself to freeware and cloud-based web app software.[31]

Need a free set of word processing, spreadsheet, and presentation programs—programs available in multiple languages and supporting files created by other software, including Microsoft Office? Try Apache's no-cost OpenOffice, developed by volunteers, which can be downloaded and installed on as many computers as you like.[32] Another freeware suite, or all-in-one package of word processing, spreadsheet, and other programs, is LibreOffice, which is available for computers running Windows, Mac, and Linux operating systems.[33]

Students may also avail themselves of suites of web apps, such as the Zoho applications, which are free to individuals and which you sign up for and access from the Zoho website. Programs offered include Zoho Writer (word processing), Zoho Sheet (spreadsheet), and Zoho Show (presentation software). ■

Tutorials & Documentation

Application software documentation is the same as a user's manual; tutorials, often on video, take you through practice learning sessions.

How are you going to learn a given software program? Most commercial packages come with tutorials and documentation. YouTube also has tutorials.

TUTORIALS A *tutorial* is an instruction book or program that helps you learn to use the product by taking you through a prescribed series of steps. For instance, our publisher offers several how-to books that enable you to learn different kinds of software. Tutorials may also be included in the software package.

DOCUMENTATION *Documentation* is all information that describes a product to users, including a user guide or reference manual that provides a narrative and graphical description of a program. Although documentation may be print-based, today it is usually available

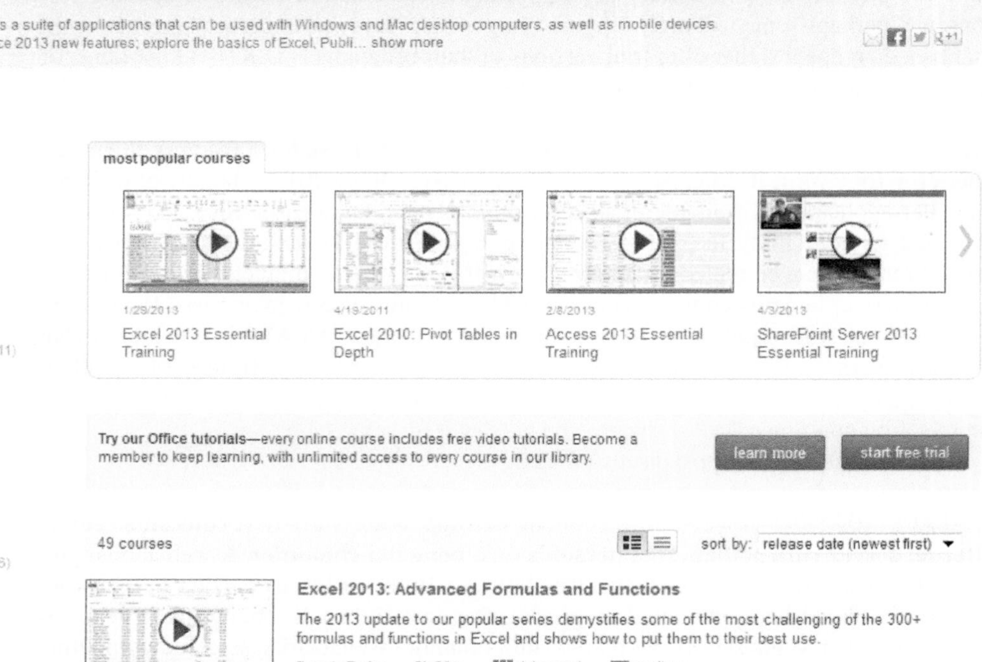

Tutorials: How to use Microsoft Office 2013 in Windows and on the Mac (*www.lynda.com*)

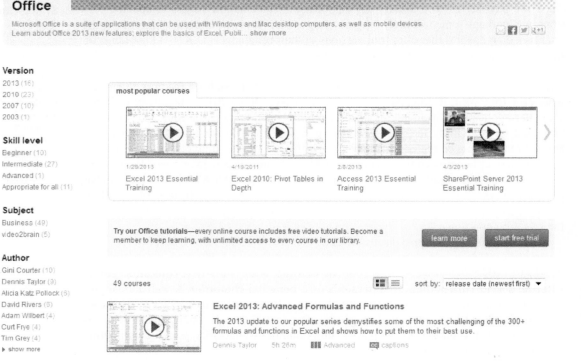

in downloaded form from the Internet or as a CD. Documentation may be instructional, but features and functions are usually grouped by category for reference purposes. For example, in word processing documentation, all features related to printing are grouped together so that you can easily look them up.

Unusual Software

For information on new and unusual software applications and where to obtain them, go to:

www.appscout.com/about_appscout/

Types of Application Software

There are many types of application software; productivity software is the type used in business and in many educational situations.

Application software can be classified in many ways—for entertainment, personal, education/reference, productivity, and specialized uses. *(• See Panel 3.25.)*

In the rest of this chapter we discuss types of **productivity software—such as word processing programs, spreadsheets, and database managers—whose purpose is to make users more productive at particular tasks.** Some productivity software comes in the form of an *office suite,* which bundles several applications together into a single large package. Microsoft Office 2013, for example, includes (among other things) Word, Excel, PowerPoint, and Access—word processing, spreadsheet, presentation, and database programs, respectively. (Office is available for both the PC and the Mac platforms.) Corel Corporation offers similar programs, such as the WordPerfect word processing program. Other productivity software, such as Lotus Notes, is sold as *groupware*—online software that allows several people to collaborate on the same project and share some resources. Google offers a free suite of applications called Google Apps (from *www.google.com/apps*).

Most of these types of programs must be *installed* on your computer before you can use them. For example, if you buy Microsoft Office, you need to install it on your computer before you can run any of the included programs such as Word or Excel. You can install software by downloading it from the Internet or a networked computer or taking it from a CD, DVD, or an external hard drive.

panel 3.25

Some types of application software

APPLICATION SOFTWARE

Entertainment software	Personal software	Education/ reference software	Productivity software	Specialty software
• Games, etc. • MP3 • Videoplayer	• Cookbooks • Medical • Home decoration • Gardening • Home repair • Tax preparation, etc.	• Encyclopedias • Phone books • Almanacs • Library searches, etc. • Children's learning programs • Course management • Computer-aided instruction	• Word processing • Spreadsheets • Database managers • Personal information managers • Web browser } Ch. 2 • Email, } Ch. 2 etc.	• Presentation graphics • Financial • Desktop publishing • Drawing & painting (image editing) • Video/audio editing • Animation • Multimedia authoring • Web page design • Project management • Computer-aided design PDF, etc.

Software Installation Basics

http://windows.microsoft.com/en-US/windows-vista/Install-a-program
www.installsoftware.com/
http://support.apple.com/kb/HT1148/
http://lifehacker.com/5833817/how-to-install-a-new-program-on-your-computer/

Installing a software program writes the necessary data instructions for running the program on your hard drive. Often the installer program will decompress the data included with the installer immediately before writing the information to your hard drive. Software updates, which are typically downloaded from the Internet, work the same way. When you run the update, the installer file decompresses the data and then updates the correct program.

Installing software is usually a simple process. It involves double-clicking an installer icon and then clicking "I Agree" when the license agreement displays. You may have to choose what directory on your hard disk you would like to install the software in, but often the installer will choose that for you. A *clean install* is a software installation in which any previous version is erased. The alternative to a clean install is an *upgrade,* in which elements of the previous version remain and new elements are added. An upgrade is typically less expensive, but because some elements of the earlier version remain, any existing problems may remain as well, and new compatibility-related issues may arise. A clean install should make the computer's software run like new. (Often you must uninstall the old version of a program before installing the new one; check the instructions.)

3.6 DATA FILES & PROGRAM FILES

Data files contain data; program files contain executable software instructions.

There is only one reason for having application software: to take raw data and manipulate it into useful files of information. Before discussing the most useful kinds of application software, let us consider the most important kinds of files. A *file,* we said, is (1) a named collection of data or (2) a program that exists in a computer's secondary storage, such as a hard disk. That is, a *file* can be (1) a *data file* or (2) a *program file.*

Data Files

Data files, which contain data, such as document, spreadsheet, or database data, are processed by program files.

Data files are files that contain data, such as words, numbers, pictures, or sounds. Data files don't instruct the computer to do anything; they are there to be acted on by program files.

Data files are given names—file names. If you're using a word processing program such as Microsoft Word to write a psychology term paper, for instance, you might name it "Psychreport." In a database, a file name might be "AccountingPersonnel."

File names also have *extensions,* or *extension names,* usually three or four letters added after a period following the file name. For example, the *.doc* in *Psychreport.doc* is recognized by Microsoft Word as a "document," as is *.docx,* which refers to a Word 2007, 2010, or 2013 document. Extensions are usually inserted automatically by the application software.

Survival Tip

Some Records Have to Be Hardcopy

You could scan your birth certificate, will, or car ownership title into your computer to make a digital record. But such records printed off a hard drive aren't always legally acceptable. Original documents are often required by government agencies and the court system.

Some well-known types of data files are the following:

- **Document files:** Created by word processing programs, these data files consist of documents: reports, letters, memos, and the like. The file names often end with *.doc* or *.docx.*
- **Workbook files:** Created by electronic spreadsheets, these data files usually consist of collections of numerical data such as budgets, sales forecasts, and schedules. The file names for Microsoft Excel spreadsheet files end with *.xls or .xlsx.*
- **Database files:** Created by database management programs, these data files consist of organized data that can be analyzed and displayed in various useful ways, such as student names, addresses, grade-point averages, and so on. File names for the database program Microsoft Access end in *.mdb, .accdb,* or *mdbx.*
- **Graphics files:** Some important ones have extension names *.bmp, .tiff (tif.), .gif, .jpeg,* and *.png.*
- **Audio files:** The extension names you're most apt to encounter are *.mp3, .wav,* and *.mid.*
- **Animation/video files:** Common file extensions are *.qt, .mpg, .wmv, .avi,* and *.rm.*

The box on the next page describes these and other common types of files, such as .pdf. (• *See Panel 3.26, next page.*)

Graphic files

- *.bmp (BitMap):* Bitmapped graphic format native to Microsoft Windows. Some Macintosh programs can also read .bmp files.
- *.gif (Graphic Interchange Format):* Pronounced "Jiff." Format used on web pages and downloadable images.
- *.jpeg or .jpg (Joint Photographic Experts Group):* Pronounced "*Jay-peg.*" Used for web images and for digital photography, especially for high-resolution images.
- *.pcx:* Format introduced for PC Paintbrush. Used for other graphics packages as well.
- *.pict (PICTure):* Format used by Apple for use on Macintosh computers.
- *.png (Portable Network Graphic):* Pronounced "ping." Patent-free alternative to *.gif.*
- *.tiff or .tif (Tagged Image File Format):* High-resolution bitmapped graphics file widely used on both Macintosh and PC computers. Used in exchanging bitmapped files that will be printed.

Audio files

- *.au:* Low-fidelity monaural format now often used to distribute sample sounds online.
- *.mid (MIDI, Musical Instrument Digital Interface):* Format meant to drive music synthesizers.
- *.mp3 (MPEG-3):* File format used to compress CD-quality music while preserving much of the original sound quality.
- *.wav (WAVe):* Waveform file format that contains all the digital information needed to play speaker-quality music.

Video files

- *.avi (Audio Video Interleaved):* Video file format recognized by Windows Media Player. Not good for broadcast-quality video.
- *.mov or .qt (QuickTime):* Video file formats developed by Apple for QuickTime video player. Can play broadcast-quality video.
- *.mpg or .mpeg (Motion Picture Experts Group):* Video formats for full-motion video. MPEG-2 format used by DVD-ROM disks. MPEG-4 recognized by most video player software.
- *.rm (RealMedia):* Popular file format for streaming video.
- *.wmv (Windows Media Video):* Video format recognized by Windows Media Player.

Other files

- *ASCII files:* Text-only files containing no graphics and no formatting such as boldface or italic. ASCII format is used to transfer documents between computers, such as PC and Macintosh. Such files may use the *.txt* (for text) extension.
- *Web files:* Files carried over World Wide Web. Extensions include *.html, .htm, .xml, and .asp* (active server page).
- *Desktop publishing files:* Include commands, which instruct a PostScript printer how to print a file and use *.eps* (encapsulated PostScript).
- *Drivers:* Software drivers often have the extension *.drv.*
- *Windows operating system files:* Files such as *Autoexec.bat* and *Config.sys* relate to OS setup.
- *PDF (Portable Document Format) files:* Files that use Adobe Acrobat's format for all types of document exchange as well as for publishing documents on the web that are downloaded and read independently of the HTML pages. These files use the extension *.pdf.* Editable PDF files are created with Adobe's Acrobat software. Acrobat can convert a wide variety of document types on Windows, Mac, and Unix to PDF format.

panel 3.26

Common types of files

File Formats

For a complete list of file formats, go to:

http://en.wikipedia.org/wiki/List_of_file_formats/

Program Files

Program files are composed of executable software instructions.

Program files **are files containing software instructions that execute, or run, when the program is opened.** Examples are word processing or spreadsheet programs, which are made up of several different program files.

SOURCE PROGRAM FILES & EXECUTABLE FILES The two most important program files are *source program files* and *executable files.*

- Source program files: *Source program files* contain high-level computer instructions in the original form written by the computer programmer. Some source program file names end in an extension of the language in which they are written, such as *.bas* for BASIC or *.java* for Java.
- Executable files: To be made useful to the computer for processing, a source program file must be translated into an executable file**, which contains the instructions that tell the computer how to perform a particular task.** You use an executable file by running it, as when you select the spreadsheet program Microsoft Excel from your on-screen menu and open it. Executable files can often be identified by an extension to the file name of *.exe* (Microsoft computers) or *.app (*Apple computers). (There are some executable files, called *runtime libraries,* that you cannot run—other programs cause them to execute. These are identified by such extensions as *.dll* [dynamic link library], *.drv* [*driver file*], *.ocx* [*object control extension*], and *.sys* [*system file*].)

Exchanging Data Files: Exporting & Importing

Exporting is taking data out of one data file and importing is putting that data into another data file.

Often data files can be exchanged between programs—exported from (sent from) one program or imported to (accepted by) another. The difference between the two is that *exporting* implies that the sending application reformats the data for the receiving application; *importing* implies that the receiving application does the reformatting.

EXPORTING Exporting **is defined as transforming data into a format that can be used in another program and then transmitting it.** For example, you might work up a list of names and addresses in your database program and then send it—export it—to a document you wrote in your word processing program.

IMPORTING Importing **is defined as getting data from another source and then converting it into a format compatible with the program in which you are currently working.** For example, you might write a letter in your word processing program and include in it—that is, import—a column of numbers from your spreadsheet program. The ability to import data is very important in software applications because it means that one application can complement another.

Data Compression: Putting More Data in Less Space

Data compression methods enable devices to transmit or store the same amount of data in fewer bits.

The vast streams of text, audio, and visual information threaten to overwhelm us. To fit large multimedia files into less space and increase the speed of data transmission, a technique called compression/decompression, or *codec,* is used. Compression **is a method of removing repetitive elements from a data file so that it requires less storage space and therefore less time to transmit.** Later the data is decompressed—the repeated patterns are restored.

The two principal methods of compressing data are *lossless* and *lossy,* the technique being chosen depending on whether data quality is more important (in which case lossless is used) or storage space (lossy) is more critical.

LOSSLESS COMPRESSION *Lossless compression* uses mathematical techniques to replace repetitive patterns of bits with a kind of coded summary. During decompression, the coded summaries are replaced with the original patterns of bits. In this method, the data that comes out is exactly the same as what went in; it has merely been repackaged for purposes of storage or transmission.

Lossless techniques are used when it's important that nothing be lost—for instance, for computer data, database records, spreadsheets, and word processing files.

LOSSY COMPRESSION *Lossy compression* techniques permanently discard some data during compression. Lossy data compression involves a certain loss of accuracy in exchange for a high degree of compression (to as little as 5% of the original file size). Examples of two lossy compression file formats are *.jpeg* and *.mpeg.*

This method of compression is often used for graphics files and sound files. Thus, a lossy codec might discard subtle shades of color or omit sounds outside the range of human hearing. Most users wouldn't notice the absence of these details.

In the rest of this chapter we consider the most important types of application software you will encounter.

3.7 WORD PROCESSING SOFTWARE

Word processing involves the creation and editing of documents.

Word processing software **allows you to use computers to create, edit, format, print, and store text material,** among other things. Word processing is the most common software application. The best-known word processing program is Microsoft Word, but there are others, such as Corel WordPerfect, Apple iWork Pages, Google Apps (a free download from *www.google.com/apps*), and Zoho Writer (a free download from *www.zoho.com*). There is even a full-fledged office suite for word processing, known as Quickoffice, that can be used on Android phones, Apple iPhones, BlackBerrys, and Symbian OS devices. Word processing software allows users to work through a document and *delete, insert,* and *replace* text, the principal edit/correction activities. It also offers such additional features as *creating, formatting, importing illustrations, printing,* and *saving.*

Of course, creating a document means entering text using the keyboard or the dictation function associated with speech-recognition software. Word processing software has three features that affect this process—the *cursor, scrolling,* and *word wrap.*

CURSOR **The cursor is the movable symbol on the display screen that shows you where you may next enter data or commands.** The symbol is often a blinking rectangle or an I-beam. You can move the cursor on the screen using the keyboard's directional arrow keys or a mouse. The point where the cursor is located is called the *insertion point.*

SCROLLING Scrolling **means moving quickly upward, downward, or sideways through the text or other screen display.** A standard computer screen displays only 20–22 lines of standard-size text. Of course, most documents are longer than that. Using the directional arrow keys, or the mouse and a scroll bar located at the side of the screen, you can move ("scroll") through the display screen and into the text above and below it.

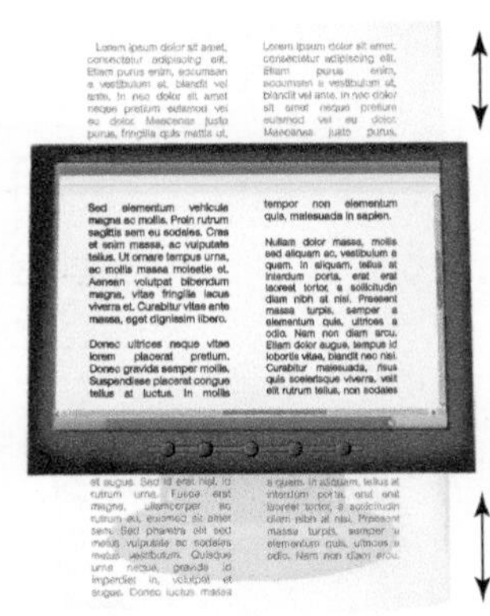
Scrolling

WORD WRAP Word wrap **automatically continues text to the next line when you reach the right margin.** That is, the text "wraps around" to the next line. You don't have to hit a "carriage-return" key or Enter key, as was necessary with a typewriter.

ORGANIZING & EDITING FEATURES To help you organize term papers and reports, the *Outline View* feature puts tags on various headings to show the hierarchy of heads—for example, main head, subhead, and sub-subhead. Word processing software also allows you to insert footnotes that are automatically numbered and renumbered when changes are made. Some word processing functions are shown below. (• *See Panel 3.27.*)

- **Editing:** *Editing* is the act of making alterations in the content of your document. Some features of editing, as we will discuss briefly, are *insert* and *delete, undelete, find and replace,* and *cut/copy and paste.*

  Inserting is the act of adding to the document. Simply place the cursor wherever you want to add text and start typing; the existing characters will be pushed along. If you want to write over (replace) text as you write, press the *Insert* key before typing. When you're finished typing, press the *Insert* key again to exit Insert mode.

  Deleting is the act of removing text, usually using the *Delete* key or the *Backspace* key.

  The *Undo command* allows you to change your mind and undo your last action (or several previous actions) and restore text that you have deleted.

  The *Find,* or *Search, command* allows you to find any word, phrase, or number that exists in your document. The *Replace command* allows you to automatically replace it with something else.

  Typewriter users who wanted to move a paragraph or block of text from one place to another in a manuscript used scissors and glue to "cut and paste." With word processing, moving text takes only a few keystrokes. You select (highlight with the mouse) the portion of text you want to copy or move. Then you use the *Copy* or *Cut command* to move it to the *clipboard,* a special holding area in the computer's memory. From there, you use *Paste* to transfer the material to any point (indicated with the cursor) in the existing document or in a new document. The clipboard retains its material, so repeated pastes of the same item will work without your having to recopy each time.

panel 3.27

Some word processing functions in Word 2013

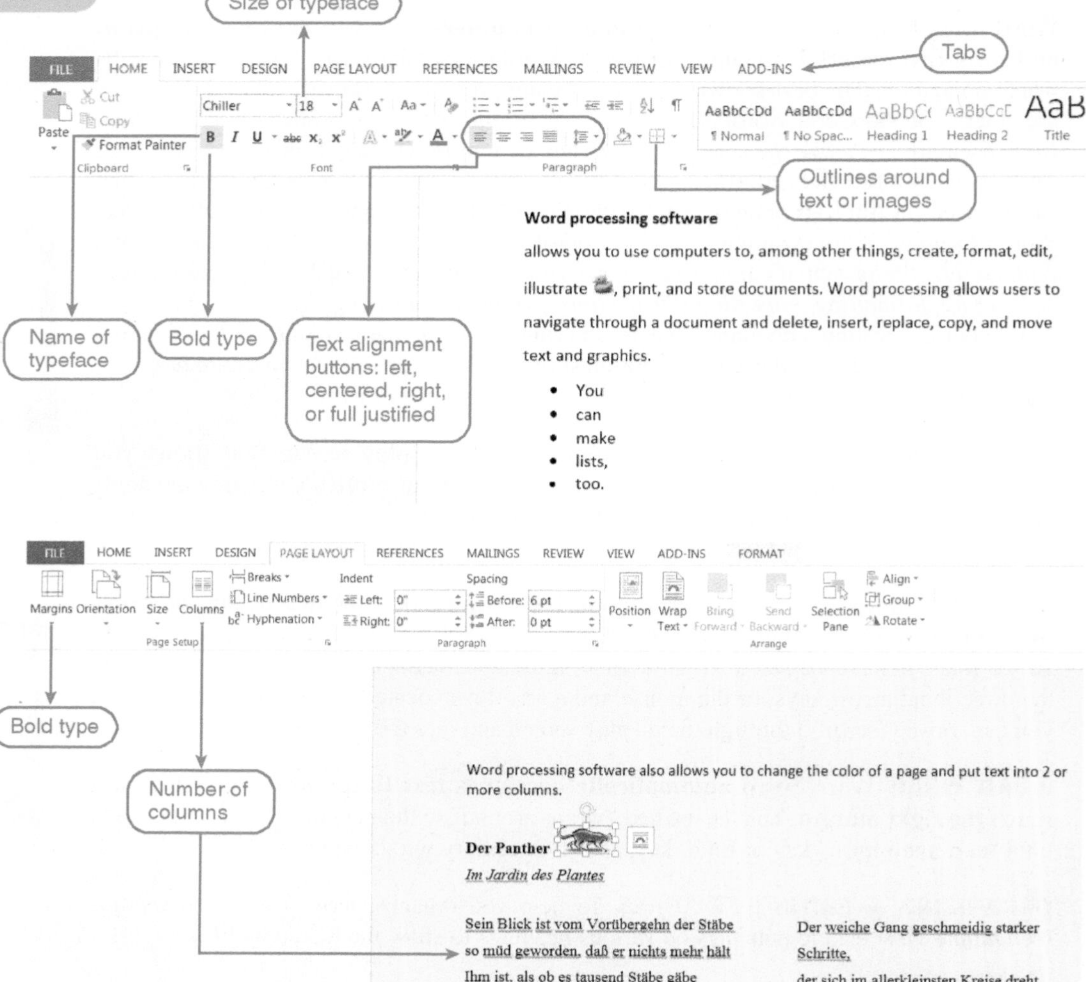

- **Editing aids:** Additional tools to help you get your words just right are *AutoCorrect, spelling checker, grammar checker,* and *thesaurus.*

  Word processing programs such as Microsoft Word have an *AutoCorrect* function that automatically fixes such common mistakes as transposed letters—replacing "teh" with "the," for instance. (However, the system frequently guesses wrong, filling in the wrong word—replacing "you're" with "your," for example. You can switch off Auto-Correct if you find it a hindrance.)

  Most word processors have a *spelling checker,* which tests for incorrectly spelled words. As you type, the spelling checker indicates (perhaps with a squiggly line) words that aren't in its dictionary and thus may be misspelled. *(• See Panel 3.28.)* Special add-on dictionaries are available for medical, engineering, and legal terms.

  A *grammar checker* highlights poor grammar, wordiness, incomplete sentences, and awkward phrases. The grammar checker won't fix things automatically, but it will flag (perhaps with a different-color squiggly line) possible incorrect word usage and sentence structure. *(• See Panel 3.29.)*

panel 3.28

Spelling checker Word 2013

How a word processing program checks for misspelled words and offers alternatives (Microsoft Word 2013)

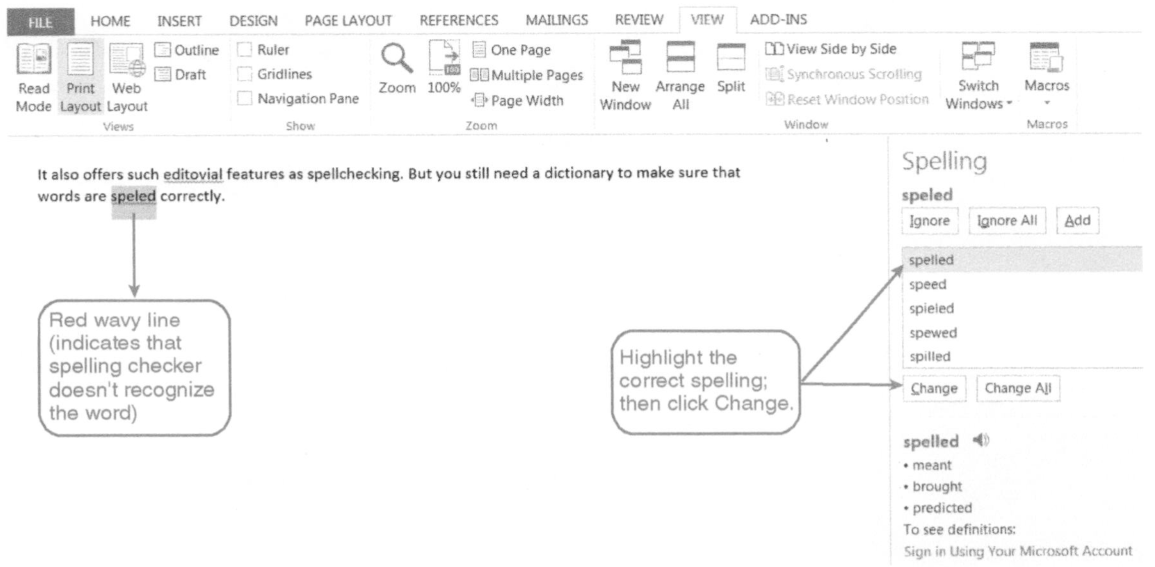

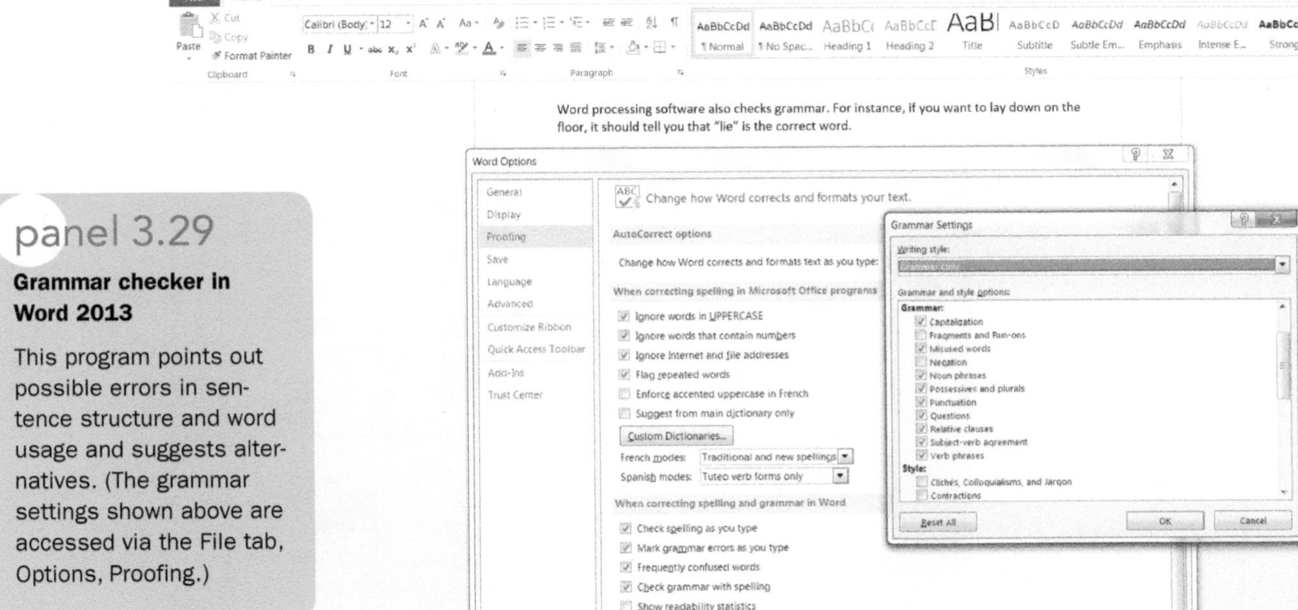

panel 3.29

Grammar checker in Word 2013

This program points out possible errors in sentence structure and word usage and suggests alternatives. (The grammar settings shown above are accessed via the File tab, Options, Proofing.)

If you find yourself stuck for the right word while you're writing, you can call up an on-screen *thesaurus,* which will present you with the appropriate word or alternative words. You can also purchase more comprehensive thesaurus add-on programs, such as WordWeb55.

TRACKING FEATURES Word processing programs also have *tracking* features. What if you have written an important document and have asked other people to edit it? Word processing software allows editing changes to be tracked by highlighting them, underlining additions, and crossing out deletions. Each person working on the document can choose a different color so that you can tell who's done what and when. And anyone can insert hidden questions or comments that become visible when you pass the mouse pointer over yellow-highlighted words or punctuation. An edited document can be printed out showing all the changes, as well as a list of comments keyed to the text by numbers. Or it can be printed out "clean," showing the edited text in its new form, without the changes.

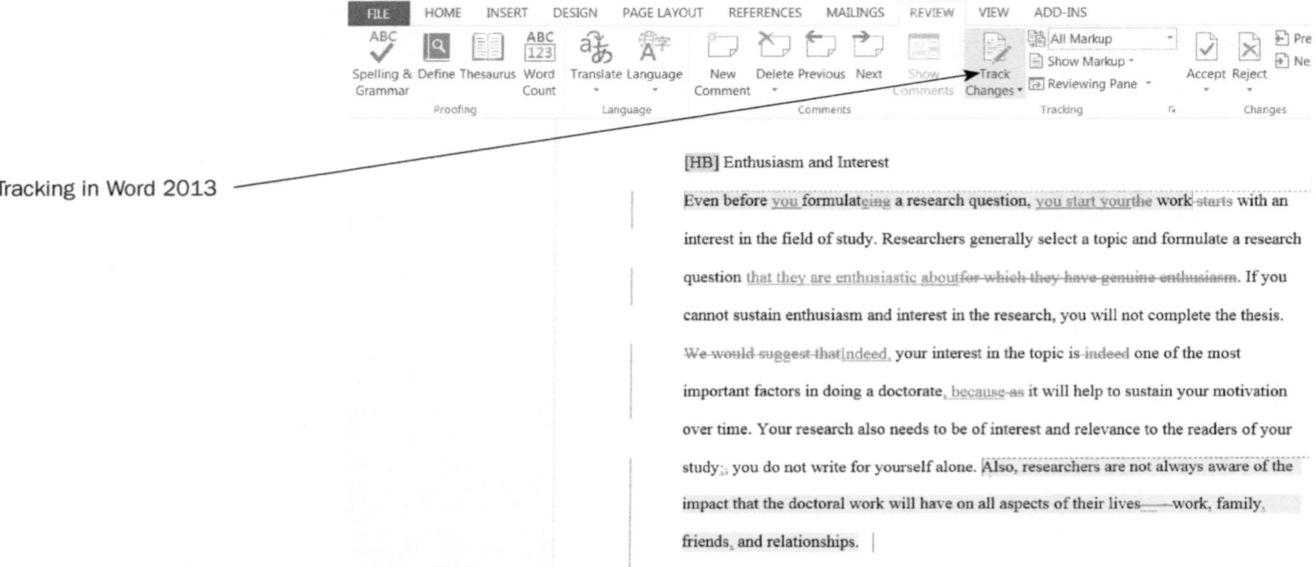

Tracking in Word 2013

FORMATTING FEATURES In the context of word processing, *formatting* means determining the appearance of a document. You can always format your documents manually, but word processing programs provide a helpful device to speed the process up and make it more sophisticated. **A template is a preformatted document that provides basic tools for shaping a final document**—the text, layout, and style for a letter, for example. Simply put, it is a style guide for documents. Because most documents are fairly standard in format, every word processing program comes with at least a few standard templates. When

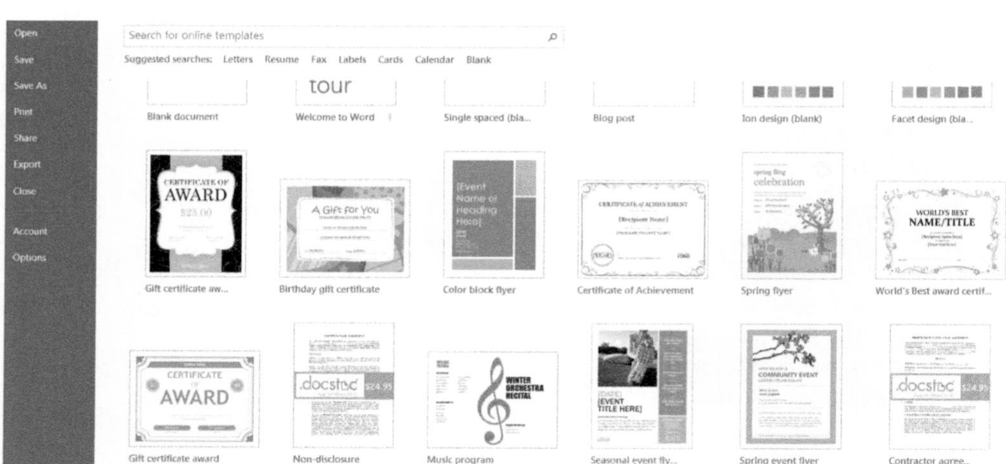

Word can help you choose templates.

you use a template, you're actually opening a copy of the template. In this way you'll always have a fresh copy of the original template when you need it. After you open a copy of the template and add your text, you save this version of the template under the file name of your choice. In this way, for example, in a letterhead template, your project's name, address, phone number, and web address are included every time you open your letterhead template file.

Among the many aspects of formatting are these:

- **Fonts:** You can decide what *font*—typeface and type size—you wish to use. For instance, you can specify whether it should be Arial, Courier, or Freestyle Script. You can indicate whether the text should be, say, 10 points or 12 points in size and the headings should be 14 points or 16 points. (There are 72 points—6 picas—in an inch.) You can specify what parts should be underlined, *italic,* or **boldface.**
- **Spacing and columns:** You can choose whether you want the lines to be *single-spaced* or *double-spaced* (or something else). You can specify whether you want text to be *one column* (like this page), *two columns* (like many magazines and books), or *several columns* (like newspapers).
- **Margins and justification:** You can indicate the dimensions of the margins—left, right, top, and bottom—around the text. You can specify the text *justification*—how the letters and words are spaced in each line. To *justify* means to align text evenly between left and right margins, as in most newspaper columns. To *left-justify* means to align text evenly on the left. (Left-justified text has a "ragged-right" margin, as do many business letters and this paragraph.) *Centering* centers each text line in the available white space between the left and right margins. To *right-justify* means to align text evenly on the right. (Right-justified text has a "ragged-left" margin.)
- **Headers and footers:** You can indicate headers or footers and include page numbers. A *header* is common text (such as a date or document name) printed at the top of every page. A *footer* is the same thing printed at the bottom of every page. If you want page numbers, you can determine what number to start with, among other things.
- **Other formatting:** You can specify *borders* or other decorative lines, *shading, tables,* and *footnotes.* You can even import *graphics* or drawings from files in other software programs, including *clip art*—collections of ready-made pictures and illustrations available online or on CDs/DVDs.

Fonts

10 point
Times Roman

14 point
Arial Black

16 point
Courier

60

(60 point Arial)

Justification

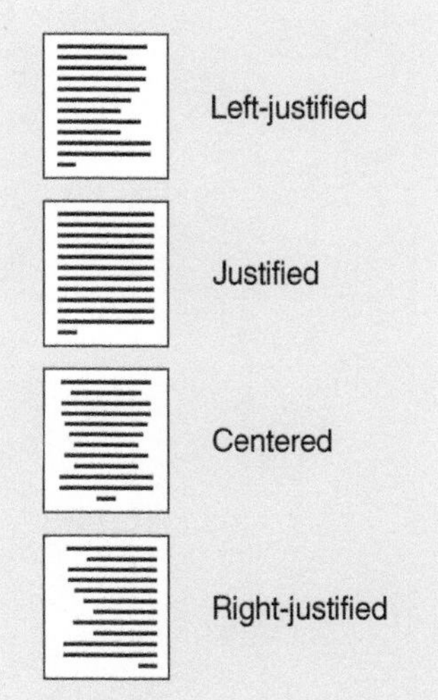

DEFAULT SETTINGS Like most forms of application software, word processing programs come from the manufacturer with default settings. **Default settings are the settings automatically used by a program unless the user specifies otherwise, thereby overriding them.** Thus, for example, a word processing program may automatically prepare a document single-spaced, left-justified, with 1-inch right and left margins, unless you alter these default settings.

PRINTING OPTIONS Most word processing software gives you several options for printing. For example, you can print *several copies* of a document. You can print *individual pages* or a *range of pages.* You can even preview a document before printing it out. *Previewing (print previewing)* means viewing a document on-screen to see what it will look like in printed form before it's printed. Whole pages are displayed in reduced size.

You can also send your document off to someone else by fax or email attachment if your computer has the appropriate communications link.

SAVING YOUR WORK Of course, you must also be able to save your work. **Saving means storing, or preserving, a document as an electronic file permanently**—on your hard disk, a CD, or online. You need only retrieve the document from storage and make the changes you want. Then you can print it out or save it again—or email it. (*Always save your documents often while you are working; don't wait!*)

Most word processing programs allow you to automatically format your documents into HTML (p. 65) so that they can be used on the web. To do this in Microsoft Word, open *File, Save As, Save As Type: Web page (*.htm, *.html; see illustration, p. 158).*

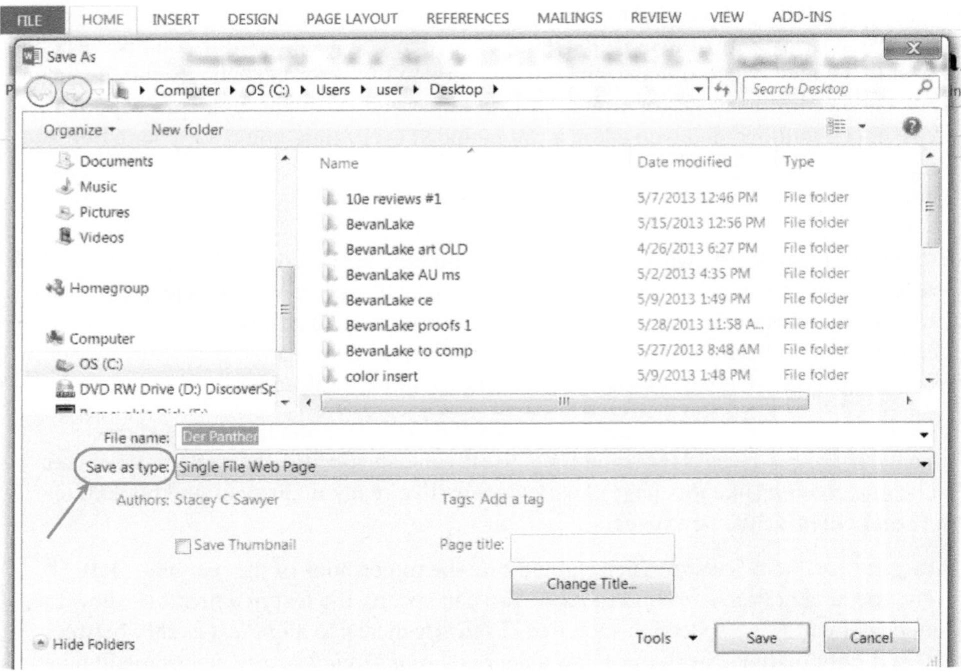

Saving a document as a web page in Word 2013

3.8 SPREADSHEET PROGRAMS

A spreadsheet program uses rectangular grids for laying out linked, usually financial, data in a very organized fashion.

What is a spreadsheet? Back in the paper-and-pencil days, it was simply a grid of rows and columns, printed on special light-green paper, that was used to produce financial projections and reports. A person making up a spreadsheet spent long days and weekends at the office penciling tiny numbers into countless tiny rectangles. When one figure changed, all other numbers on the spreadsheet had to be erased and recomputed. Ultimately, there might be wastebaskets full of jettisoned worksheets.

In 1978 Daniel Bricklin was a student at the Harvard Business School. One day he was staring at columns of numbers on a blackboard when he got the idea for computerizing the spreadsheet. He created the first electronic spreadsheet, now called simply a worksheet. **A spreadsheet program, or *worksheet,* allows users to create tables and financial schedules by entering data and formulas into rows and columns arranged as a grid on a display screen.** Before long the electronic spreadsheet was the most popular small business program. Unfortunately for Bricklin, his version (called VisiCalc) was quickly surpassed by others. Today the principal spreadsheet programs are Microsoft Excel, Corel Quattro Pro, Apple iWork Numbers, and IBM's Lotus 1-2-3. These programs are used for maintaining student grade books, tracking investments, creating and tracking budgets, calculating loan payments, estimating project costs, and creating other types of financial reports.

The Basics: How Spreadsheet Programs Work

Spreadsheet programs provide tools for collecting and calculating data of all types. Beyond working with numerical data, worksheets can be formatted to create clear, concise reports and can be easily sorted and updated.

A worksheet is arranged as follows. *(• See Panel 3.30.)*

HOW A SPREADSHEET FILE IS ORGANIZED The word *spreadsheet* usually refers to the type of application program. A spreadsheet file is called a *workbook.* A workbook's grid arrangement of columns, rows, and labels is called a *worksheet.* So, for example, when you open the Excel spreadsheet program, it loads an empty workbook file consisting of three blank worksheets for you to use. The worksheets have columns, rows, and labels:

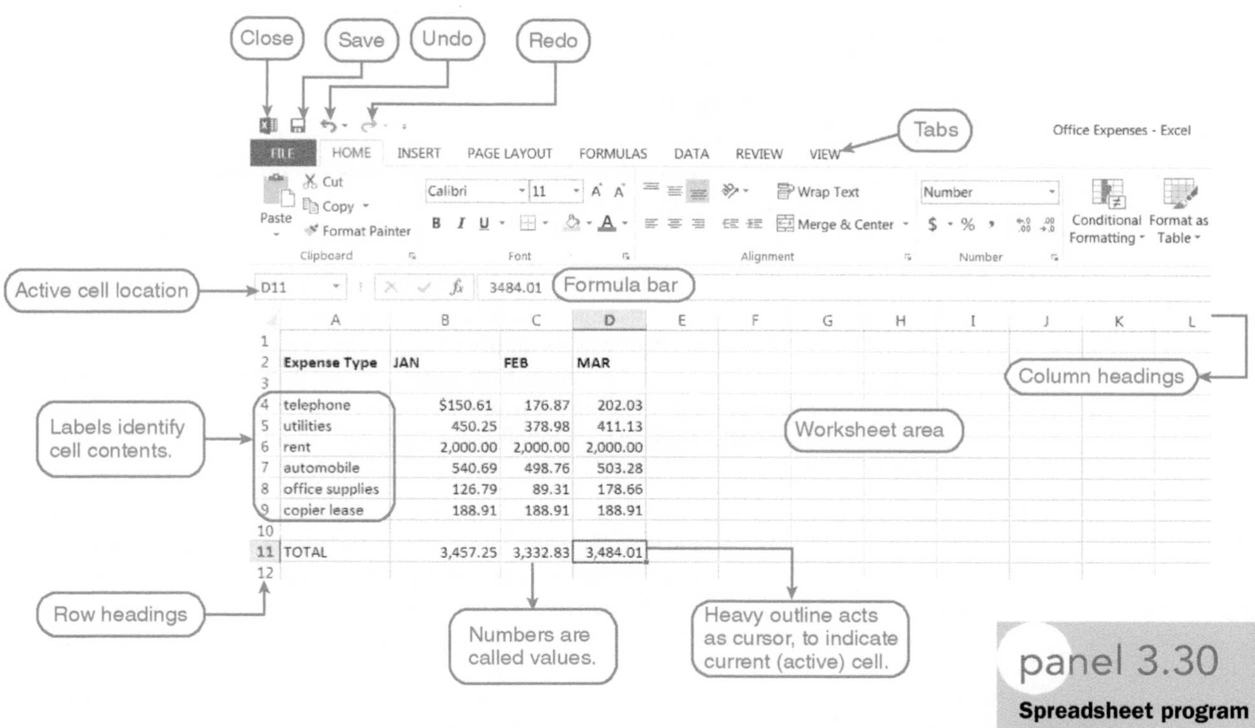

panel 3.30

Spreadsheet program worksheet

This program is Microsoft Excel 2013.

- **Column headings:** In the worksheet's frame area (work area), lettered *column headings* appear across the top ("A" is the name of the first column, "B" the second, and so on).
- **Row headings:** Numbered *row headings* appear down the left side ("1" is the name of the first row, "2" the second, and so forth).
- **Labels:** *Labels* are any descriptive text that identifies categories, such as APRIL, RENT, or GROSS SALES.

Use your keyboard to type in the various headings and labels. Each Microsoft Office Excel worksheet has 16,384 columns and 1,048,576 rows, and each spreadsheet file (workbook) can technically hold up to 650 related worksheets—but the computer's memory will not likely hold more than about 200.

CELLS: WHERE COLUMNS & ROWS MEET Each worksheet has more than 17 million cells.

- **Cells and cell addresses:** **A cell is the place where a row and a column intersect; its position is called a *cell reference* or *cell address.*** For example, "A1" is the cell address for the top left cell, where column A and row 1 intersect. (The column letter is always listed first.)
- **Ranges:** **A range is a rectangular group of adjacent cells**—for example, B5 to D10. Ranges are identified by the cell references of the cells in the upper left and lower right corners of the range. The two cell references used for a range are separated by a colon (:), which tells Excel to include all the cells between these start and end points—B5:D10.
- **Values:** **A number or date entered in a cell is called a value.** The values are the actual numbers used in the spreadsheet—dollars, percentages, grade points, temperatures, or whatever. Headings, labels, and formulas also go into cells.
- **Cell pointer:** A *cell pointer,* or *spreadsheet cursor,* indicates where data is to be entered. The cell pointer can be moved around like a cursor in a word processing program.

How to Plan Worksheets

For a start on how to set up a worksheet, try:

http://spreadsheets.about.com/od/excel101/ss/enter_data.htm

FORMULAS, FUNCTIONS, RECALCULATION, & WHAT-IF ANALYSIS Why has the spreadsheet program become so popular? The reasons lie in the features known as formulas, functions, recalculation, and what-if analysis.

- **Formulas: Formulas are instructions for calculations; they define how one cell relates to other cells.** For example, a formula might be =SUM(A5:A15) or @ SUM(A5:A15), meaning "Sum (that is, add) all the numbers in the cells with cell addresses A5 through A15."
- **Functions: Functions are built-in formulas that perform common calculations.** For instance, a function might average a range of numbers or round off a number to two decimal places.
- **Recalculation:** After the values have been entered into the worksheet, the formulas and functions can be used to calculate outcomes. However, what was revolutionary about the electronic spreadsheet was its ability to easily do recalculation. **Recalculation is the process of recomputing values,** either as an ongoing process as data is entered or afterward, with the press of a key. With this simple feature, the hours of mind-numbing work required to manually rework paper spreadsheets have become a thing of the past.
- **What-if analysis:** The recalculation feature has opened up whole new possibilities for decision making. In particular, **what-if analysis allows the user to see how changing one or more numbers changes the outcome of the calculation.** That is, you can create a worksheet, putting in formulas and numbers, and then ask, "What would happen if we change that detail?"—and immediately see the effect on the bottom line.

WORKSHEET TEMPLATES You may find that your spreadsheet software makes worksheet templates available for specific tasks. *Worksheet templates* are forms containing formats and formulas custom-designed for particular kinds of work. Examples are templates for calculating loan payments, tracking travel expenses, monitoring personal budgets, and keeping track of time worked on projects. Templates are also available for a variety of business needs—providing sales quotations, invoicing customers, creating purchase orders, and writing a business plan.

Analytical Graphics: Creating Charts

Worksheet and workbook data can be displayed in graphic form.

You can use spreadsheet packages to create analytical graphics, or charts. **Analytical graphics, or *business graphics,* are graphical forms that make numeric data easier to analyze than it is when organized as rows and columns of numbers.** Whether viewed on a monitor or printed out, analytical graphics help make sales figures, economic trends, and

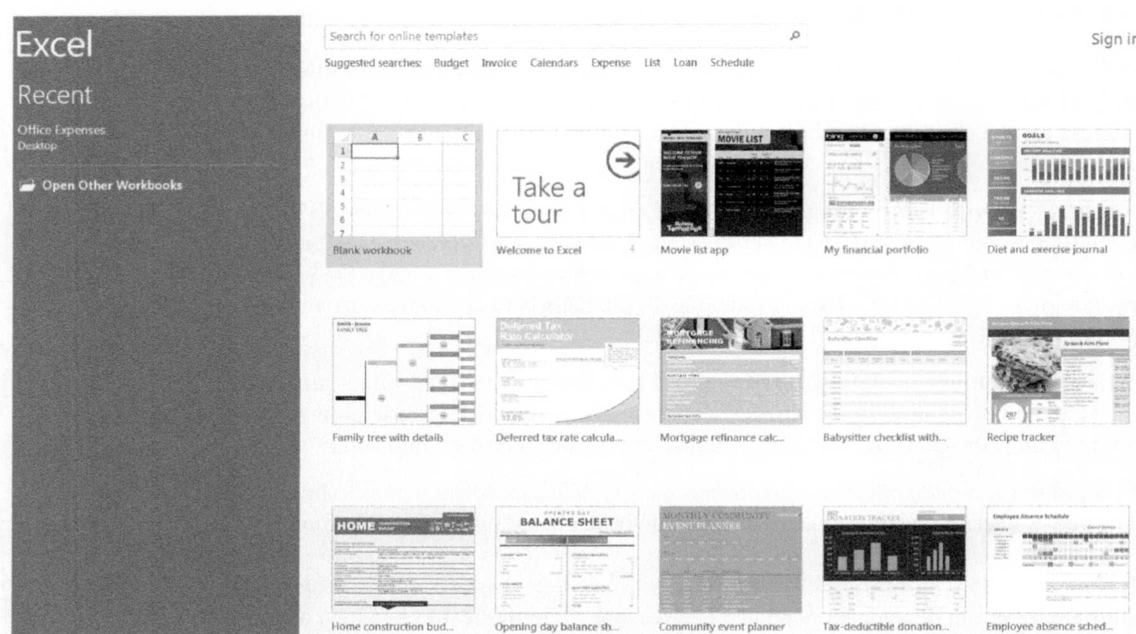

Microsoft Excel 2013 worksheet templates

the like easier to comprehend and visualize. In Excel, you enter your data to the worksheet, select the data, and use the chart-formatting tools to step through the process of choosing the chart type and various options.

Examples of analytical graphics are *column charts, bar charts, line graphs, pie charts,* and *scatter charts.* (• *See Panel 3.31.*) If you have a color printer, these charts can appear in color. In addition, they can be displayed or printed out so that they look three-dimensional.

Most spreadsheet applications are *multidimensional,* meaning that you can link one spreadsheet file to another. A three-dimensional spreadsheet model is like a stack of worksheets all connected by formulas. A change made in one worksheet automatically affects the others. Looking at data in several dimensions could include, for example, sales by region, sales by sales representative, sales by product category, sales by month, and so on. A spreadsheet program's multidimensional view might take on a 3-D graphics form.

panel 3.31

Analytical graphics

Various types of charts are used to display numbers in graphical form: (*top*) 3-D bar chart; (*bottom*) line chart (with other chart options shown).

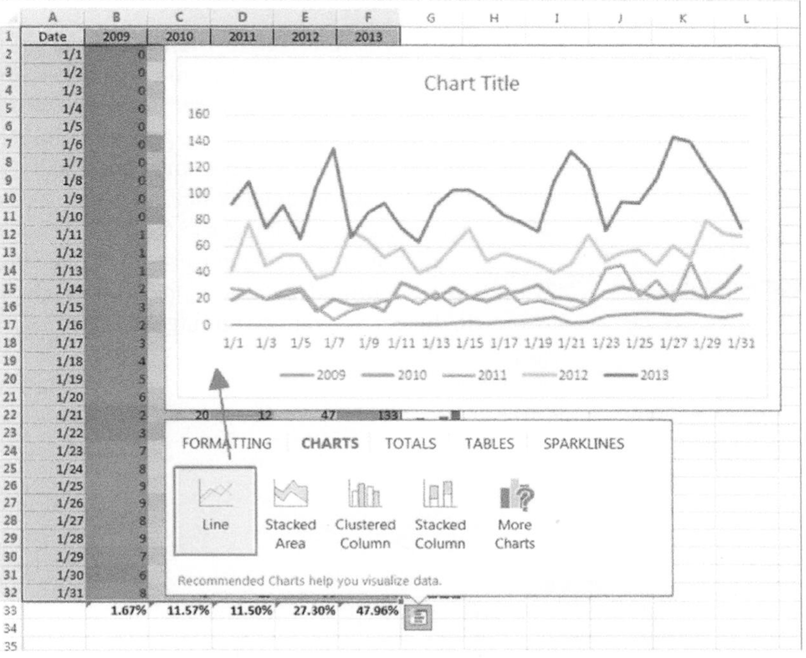

3.9 DATABASE SOFTWARE

A database is a collection of data that is organized so that its contents can easily be accessed, managed, and updated.

In its most general sense, a database is any electronically stored collection of data in a computer system. In its more specific sense, a **database is a collection of interrelated files in a computer system.** These computer-based files are organized according to their common elements, so that they can be retrieved easily. (Databases are covered in Chapter 8.) Sometimes called a *database manager* or *database management system (DBMS),* **database software is a program that sets up and controls the structure of a database and access to the data.**

The Benefits of Database Software

The correct setup and use of databases can improve the reliability of data.

When data is stored in separate files, the same data will be repeated in many files. In the old days, each college administrative office—registrar, financial aid, housing, and so on—might have a separate file on you. Thus, there was *redundancy*—your address, for example, was repeated over and over. This means that when you changed addresses, all the college's files on you had to be updated separately. Thus, database software has two advantages.

INTEGRATION With database software, the data is not in separate files. Rather, it is *integrated.* Thus, your address need only be listed once, and all the separate administrative offices will have access to the same information.

INTEGRITY For that reason, information in databases is considered to have more *integrity.* That is, the information is more likely to be accurate and up to date.

Databases are a lot more interesting than they used to be. Once they included only text. Now they can also include pictures, sound, animation, and video. It's likely, for instance, that your personnel record in a company database will include a picture of you and even a clip of your voice. If you go looking for a house to buy, you can view a real estate agent's database of video clips of homes and properties without leaving the realtor's office or your own computer.

Today the principal microcomputer database programs are Microsoft Access and FileMaker Pro. (In larger systems, Oracle, Advantage Database Server, and SQL Anywhere are major players.)

The Basics: How Databases Work

The main type of microcomputer database program is the relational database.

Let's consider some basic features of databases.

HOW A RELATIONAL DATABASE IS ORGANIZED: TABLES, RECORDS, & FIELDS

The most widely used form of database, especially on PCs, is the **relational database, in which data is organized into related tables.** Each table contains rows and columns; the rows are called *records,* and the columns are called *fields.* An example of a record is a person's address—name, street address, city, and so on. An example of a field is that person's last name; another field would be that person's first name; a third field would be that person's street address; and so on. (• *See Panel 3.32.)*

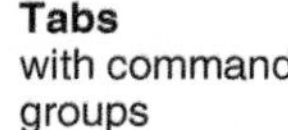

panel 3.32

Some database functions

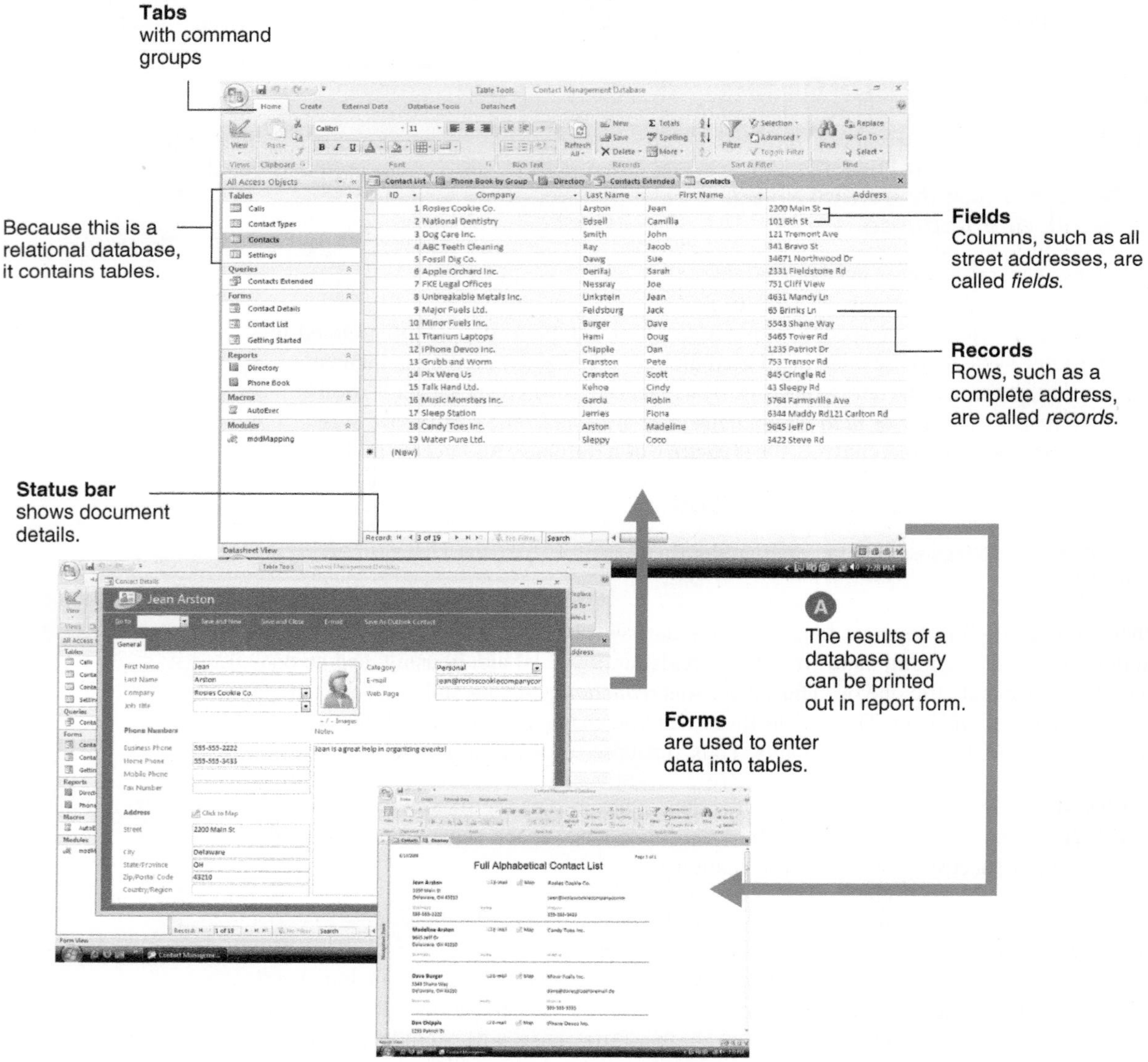

Just as a spreadsheet program may include a workbook with several worksheets, so a relational database program might include a database with several tables. For instance, if you're running a small company, you might have one database headed

Tabs with command groups

Because this is a relational database, it contains tables.

Fields Columns, such as all street addresses, are called *fields.*

Records Rows, such as a complete address, are called *records.*

Status bar shows document details.

A The results of a database query can be printed out in report form.

Forms are used to enter data into tables.

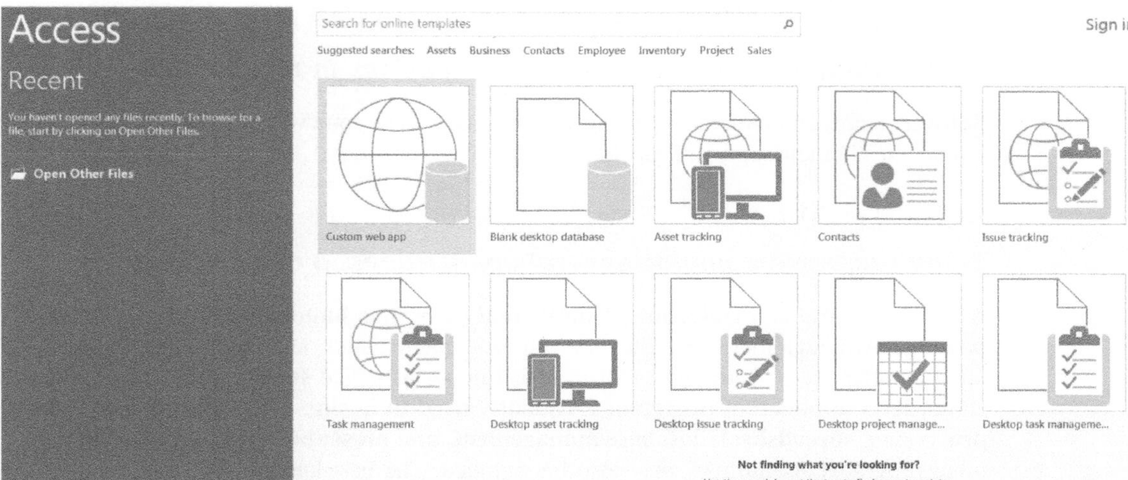

Access 2013 database templates

Employees, containing three tables—*Addresses, Payroll,* and *Benefits.* You might have another database headed *Customers,* with *Addresses, Orders,* and *Invoices* tables.

LINKING RECORDS, USING A KEY In relational databases a **key—also called *key field, sort key, index,* or *keyword*—is a field used to sort data.** For example, if you sort records by age, then the age field is a key. The most frequent key field used in the United States is the Social Security number, but any unique identifier, such as employee number or student number, can be used. Most database management systems allow you to have more than one key so that you can sort records in different ways. One of the keys is designated the *primary key* and must hold a unique value for each record. A key field that identifies records in different tables is called a *foreign key.* A foreign key is a field in a relational table that matches the primary key of another table. Foreign keys are used to cross-reference data among relational tables.

FINDING WHAT YOU WANT: QUERYING & DISPLAYING RECORDS The beauty of database software is that you can locate records quickly. For example, several offices at your college may need access to your records but for different reasons: registrar, financial aid, student housing, and so on. Any of these offices can *query records*—locate and display records—by calling them up on a computer screen for viewing and updating. Thus, if you move, your address field will need to be corrected for all relevant offices of the college. A person making a search might make the query, *"Display the address of [your name]."* Once a record is displayed, the address field can be changed. Thereafter, any office calling up your file will see the new address.

SORTING & ANALYZING RECORDS & APPLYING FORMULAS With database software you can easily find and change the order of records in a table—in other words, they can be *sorted* in different ways—arranged alphabetically, numerically, geographically, or in some other order. For example, they can be rearranged by state, by age, or by Social Security number.

In addition, database programs contain built-in mathematical *formulas* so that you can analyze data. This feature can be used, for example, to find the grade-point averages for students in different majors or in different classes.

PUTTING SEARCH RESULTS TO USE: SAVING, FORMATTING, PRINTING, COPYING, OR TRANSMITTING Once you've queried, sorted, and analyzed the records and fields, you can simply save them to your hard disk, CD, or other secondary-storage medium. You can format them in different ways, altering headings and typestyles. You can print them out on paper as reports, such as an employee list with up-to-date addresses and phone numbers. A common use is to print out the results as names and addresses on *mailing labels*—adhesive-backed stickers that can be run through your printer and then stuck on envelopes. You can use the Copy command to copy your search results and then paste them into a paper produced on your word processor. You can also cut and paste data into an email message or make the data an attachment file to an email, so that it can be transmitted to someone else.

3.10 SOFTWARE SUITES & INTEGRATED PACKAGES

Some programs combine several applications in one package.

Software suites and integrated packages would seem to be somewhat the same, but the difference lies in their degree of capabilities.

Software Suites

Some programs combine several applications in one package.

A software suite is a collection of individual programs bundled together in a single package. Although there are suites for graphics, mathematics, and other applications, the most popular are **productivity suites, also known as *office suites,* which are professional-level application programs frequently used in business—at a minimum word processing, spreadsheet, database management, and presentation programs,** although other programs and utilities may also be included. The best-known productivity suite is Microsoft Office. Others are Apple iWork, Corel WordPerfect Office, Lotus SmartSuite, and StarOffice. *Cloud suites,* or *online office suites,* include Microsoft Web Apps, Google Docs, and Zoho. So far Windows tablets are the only tablets to run a full version of Microsoft Office; no version is available for iPad and Android tablets.[34]

Integrated Packages

Integrated packages combine the functionality of word processing, spreadsheet, and database management in a program that's simpler than a suite.

An integrated package is a single program for personal computers that combines the functionality of word processing, spreadsheet, and database management. Presentation graphics, page layout, paint, calendar, address book, email, and other applications may also be included.

A principal advantage of integrated packages, such as Microsoft Works and AppleWorks, is their low cost. Another is their simplicity; integrated software eliminates the need to open a separate software application for reference purposes or to perform a few quick tasks. Integrated packages may be useful for some people for home use, but because they do not offer all the features and functions of each program, software suites are generally superior.

Personal Information Managers

A personal information manager is software that serves as a planner, notebook, and address book all in one.

Many people find ready uses for specialized types of database software known as personal information managers. **A personal information manager (PIM) is software that helps you keep track of and manage information you use on a daily basis, such as addresses,**

Timeline.
Developments in software

3000 BCE	1621 CE	1642	1801	1820	1833
Abacus is invented in Babylonia	Slide rule invented (Edmund Gunther)	First mechanical adding machine (Blaise Pascal)	A linked sequence of punched cards controls the weaving patterns in Jacquard's loom	The first mass-produced calculator, the Thomas Arithnometer	Babbage's difference engine (automatic calculator)

iWork

Pages Numbers Keynote Tutorials Resources Buy Now

Make your documents, spreadsheets, and presentations even more brilliant.

Everything you create in Pages, Numbers, and Keynote is bound to impress. And with iCloud, it's even easier to work everywhere — whether it's on your Mac, iPhone, iPad, or iPod touch.

Keynote Pages Numbers

Apple's productivity suite.

telephone numbers, appointments, to-do lists, and miscellaneous notes. Some programs feature phone dialers, outliners (for roughing out ideas in outline form), and ticklers (or reminders). With a PIM, you can key in notes any way you like and then retrieve them later based on any of the words you typed.

Popular PIMs are Microsoft Outlook, Lotus Notes, Contactizer Pro, and Yojimbo. Microsoft Outlook, for example, has sections such as Inbox, Calendar, Contacts, Tasks (to-do list), Journal (to record interactions with people), Notes (scratchpad), and Files. *(• See Panel 3.33, next page.)*

3.11 SPECIALTY APPLICATION SOFTWARE

There's an app for that!

After learning some of the productivity software just described, you may wish to become familiar with more specialized programs. For example, you might first learn word processing and then move on to desktop publishing, or first learn spreadsheets and then learn personal-finance software. We will consider the following kinds of software, although they

1843	1854	1890	1924	1930	1944
World's first computer programmer, Ada Lovelace, publishes her notes	George Boole publishes "An Investigation on the Laws of Thought," a system for symbolic and logical reasoning that will become the basis for computer design	Electricity used for first time in a data-processing project — Hollerith's automatic census-tabulating machine (used punched cards)	T.J. Watson renames Hollerith's machine company, founded in 1896, to International Business Machines (IBM)	General theory of computers (MIT)	First electro-mechanical computer (Mark I)

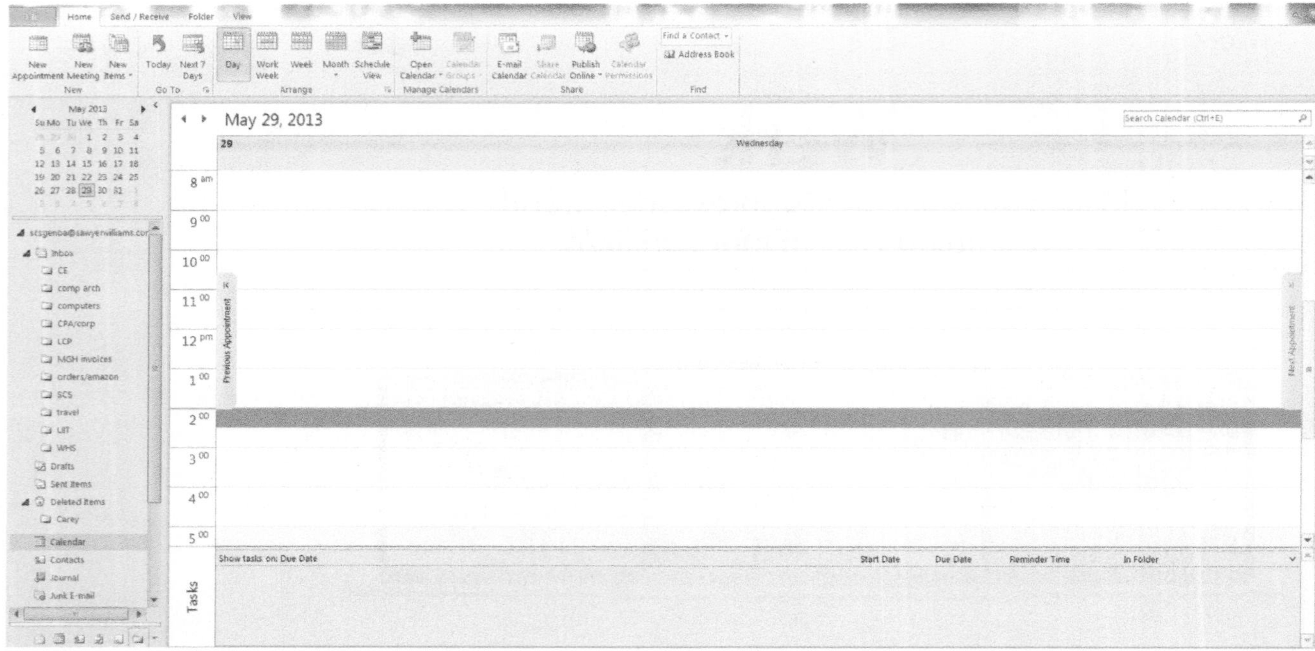

panel 3.33

Personal information manager

Microsoft Outlook 2013

are but a handful of the thousands of specialized programs available: *presentation graphics, financial, desktop-publishing, drawing and painting, project management, computer-aided design, video/audio editing, animation,* and *web page design software.*

Presentation Graphics Software

Presentation graphics make information more accessible.

Presentation graphics software is intended primarily for creating slide-show presentations, reports, portfolios, and training materials. **Presentation graphics software uses graphics, animation, sound, and data or information to make visual presentations.** Presentation graphics are much fancier and more complicated than are analytical graphics. Pages in presentation software are often referred to as *slides,* and visual presentations are commonly called *slide shows.* They can consist, however, not only of slides but also of video, animation, and sound. Completed presentations are frequently published in multiple formats, which may include print, the web, and electronic files.

Most often, presentation projects are used in live sessions and commonly projected onto large screens or printed as handouts to accompany the live presentation. Slides are generally intended to be followed in an ordered sequence, although some presentations may utilize interactive forms of navigation. This software also has the ability to export to HTML for posting presentations on the web.

You may already be accustomed to seeing presentation graphics, because many college instructors now use such software to accompany their lectures. Well-known presentation graphics packages include Microsoft PowerPoint, Corel Presentations, Harvard Graphics, and Presentation Graphics SDK. (• *See Panel 3.34.*) Companies such as Presentation Load (*www.presentationload.com/*) specialize in professional templates for sophisticated business presentations.

1946

First programmable electronic computer in United States (ENIAC)

1967

A graphical user interface (GUI) is a main theme of Jeff Raskin, who later became an Apple Macintosh team leader; handheld calculator

1969–1971

Unix is developed and released by Bell Laboratories

1970

Microprocessor chips come into use; floppy disk introduced for storing data

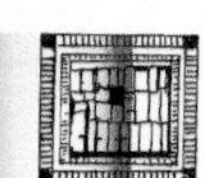

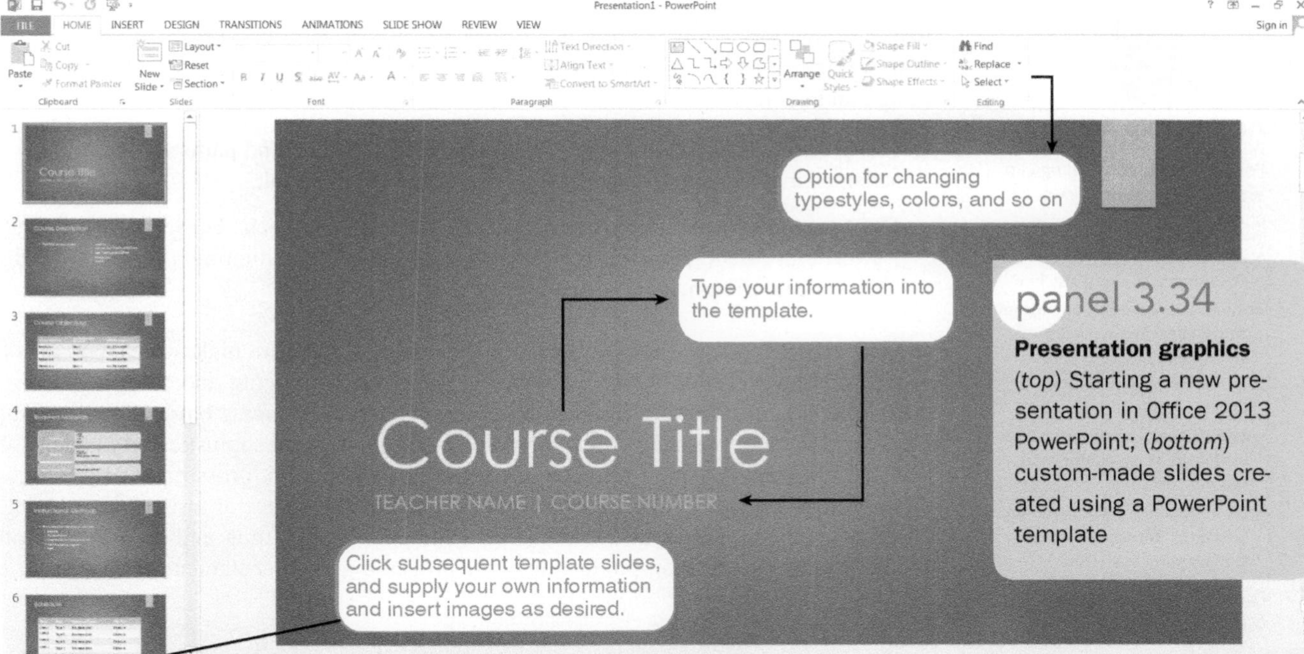

panel 3.34

Presentation graphics

(*top*) Starting a new presentation in Office 2013 PowerPoint; (*bottom*) custom-made slides created using a PowerPoint template

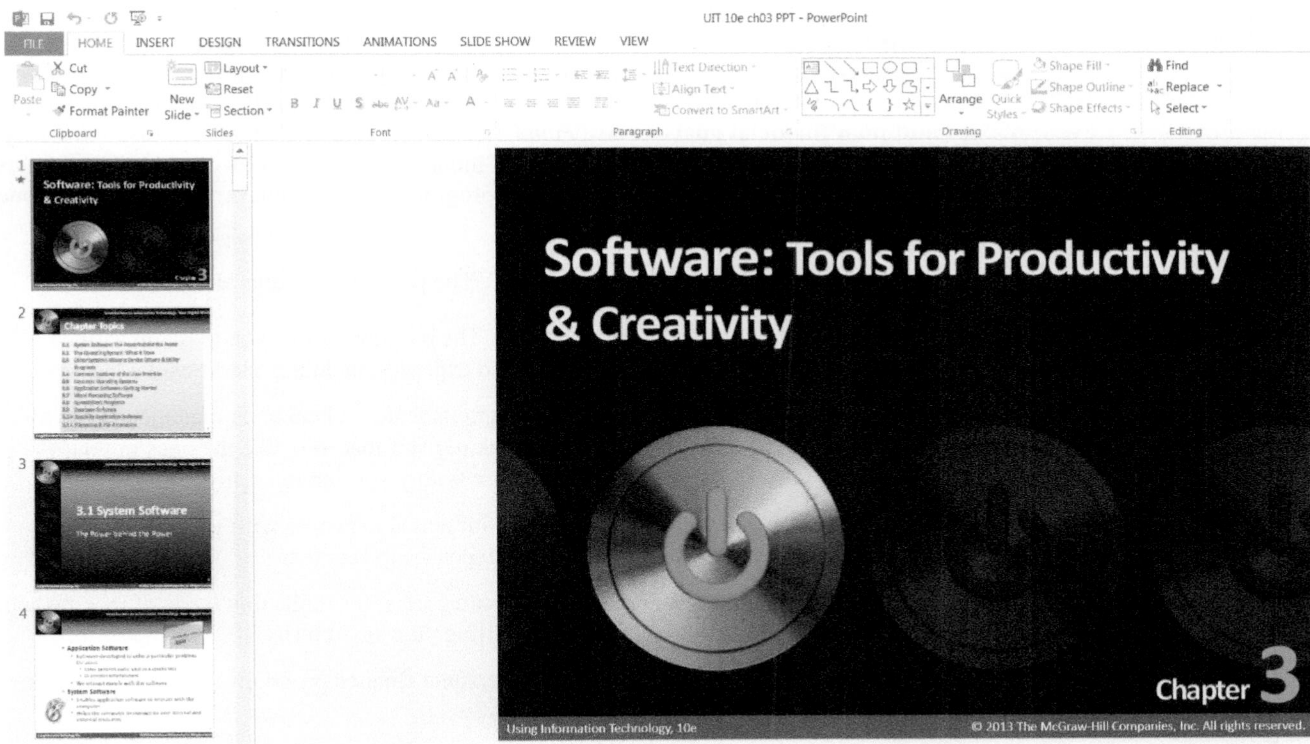

1973

Xerox PARC develops an experimental PC that uses a mouse and a GUI

1975

Bill Gates and Paul Allen start Microsoft in Albuquerque, NM (move to Seattle in 1979); first microcomputer (MITS Altair 8800)

1976

Apple I computer (first personal computer sold in assembled form)

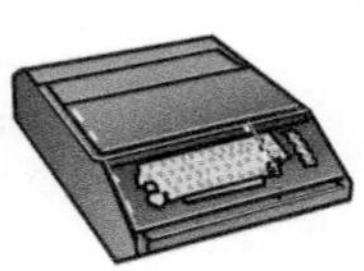

1977

Apple II's floppy disk drive leads to writing of many software programs

Adding Clip Art

For information on adding clip art to presentation slides, check out:

www.thinkoutsidetheslide.com/articles/using_clip_art_photo.htm

http://presentationsoft.about.com/od/nextstepsinpowerpoint/ss/add_pics.htm

http://webclipart.about.com/library/weekly/bluse.htm

www.ideabook.com/tutorials/illustrations/how_to_choose_and_use_clip_art.html

http://office.microsoft.com/en-us/help/5-tips-for-using-clip-art-and-graphics-HA001083323.aspx

For information on obtaining clip art, go to:

www.clipartinc.com/

http://dir.yahoo.com/Computers_and_Internet/Graphics/Clip_art/

http://office.microsoft.com/en-us/images/

Just as word processing programs offer templates for faxes, business letters, and the like, presentation graphics programs offer templates to help you organize your presentation, whether it's for a roomful of people or over the Internet. Templates are of two types: design and content.

- **Design templates:** These offer formats, layouts, background patterns, and color schemes that can apply to general forms of content material.
- **Content templates:** These offer formats for specific subjects. For instance, PowerPoint offers templates for "Selling Your Ideas," "Facilitating a Meeting," and "Motivating a Team."

DRESSING UP YOUR PRESENTATION Presentation software makes it easy to dress up each visual page ("slide") with artwork by pulling in ("dragging and dropping") clip art from other sources. Although presentations may make use of some basic analytical graphics—bar, line, and pie charts—they generally use much more sophisticated elements. For instance, they may display different textures (speckled, solid, cross-hatched), color, and three-dimensionality. In addition, you can add sound clips, special visual effects (such as blinking text), animation, and video clips. (You can, in fact, drag and drop art and other enhancements into desktop-publishing, word processing or other standard PC applications.)

Financial Software

Financial software can help you with regular budgets and bill paying, as well as taxes and financial planning.

Financial software is a growing category that ranges from personal-finance managers to entry-level accounting programs to business financial-management packages.

Consider the first of these, which you may find particularly useful. **Personal-finance managers let you keep track of income and expenses, write checks, do online banking, and plan financial goals.** *(• See Panel 3.35.)* Such programs don't promise to make you rich, but they can help you manage your money. They may even get you out of trouble. Popular microcomputer personal finance programs include Quicken, Ace Money, Moneydance, and YNAB (You Need A Budget).

FEATURES OF FINANCIAL SOFTWARE The principal features are these:

1. **Tracking of income and expenses:** The programs allow you to set up various account categories for recording income and expenses, including credit-card expenses.
2. **Checkbook management:** All programs feature checkbook management, with an on-screen check-writing form and check register that look like the ones in your checkbook. Checks can be purchased to use with your computer printer.
3. **Reporting:** All programs compare your actual expenses with your budgeted expenses. Some will compare this year's expenses to last year's.
4. **Income tax:** All programs offer tax categories, for indicating types of income and expenses that are important when you're filing your tax return.
5. **Other:** Some of the more versatile personal-finance programs also offer financial-planning and portfolio-management features.

1978	1980	1981	1982	1983	1984
The first electronic spreadsheet, VisiCalc, is introduced; WordStar, the first commercial word processor for consumers, is introduced	Microsoft obtains DOS version that becomes PC-DOS for IBM PC	Xerox introduces mouse-operated icons, buttons, and menus on the Star computer; IBM introduces personal computer (IBM PC)	Portable computers	Bill Gates announces the first version of the Windows operating system (and releases it two years later)	Apple Macintosh; first personal laser printer; the Apple Macintosh introduces the first widely used GUI; Mac System 1.0 is introduced

Features

Online Banking

Home Page

Graphing

Account Register

Reminders

Mobile

Investments

Account Registers

The account register is used to enter, edit, and delete transactions in an account. It is visually similar to a paper checkbook register, but the calculation of balances and sorting of transactions is all done automatically. The payee auto-complete feature makes it easier to enter and categorize your transactions.

panel 3.35

Financial software
Moneydance personal finance software for Mac, Windows, and other platforms can be used for all sorts of money-related management. It includes guidance tips for setting up your accounts (*moneydance.com*).

GOING BEYOND PERSONAL FINANCE Besides personal-finance managers, financial software includes small business accounting and tax software programs, which provide virtually all the forms you need for filing income taxes. Tax programs such as TaxCut and TurboTax make complex calculations, check for mistakes, and even unearth deductions you didn't know existed. Tax programs can be linked to personal-finance software to form an integrated tool.

Many financial software programs may be used in all kinds of enterprises. For instance, accounting software such as Intuit Quickbooks and Sage Software's Peachtree automates bookkeeping tasks, while payroll software keeps records of employee hours and produces reports for tax purposes.

Some programs go beyond financial management and tax and accounting management. For example, Business Plan Pro and Small Business Management Pro can help you set up your own business from scratch.

Finally, there are investment software packages, such as StreetSmart Pro from Charles Schwab, as well as various retirement-planning programs.

Desktop Publishing

Desktop-publishing software can make all types of documents look professional.

Adobe Systems was founded in 1982, when John Warnock and Charles Geschke began to work on solving some of the long-standing problems that plagued the relationship

1985	1986	1987	1988	1990	1991
Aldus PageMaker becomes the first integrated desktop publishing program; Microsoft Windows 1.0 is released; Mac System 2.0	Mac System 3.0	Microsoft's Excel program introduced; Mac System 4.0, then 5.0	Mac System 6.0	Microsoft introduces Windows 3.0 in May, intensifying its legal dispute with Apple over the software's "look and feel" resemblance to the Macintosh operating system	Linus Torvalds introduces Linux; Mac System 7.0

between microcomputers and printers. Collaboration with Apple Computers produced the first desktop-publishing package, using Adobe PostScript, a printer language that can handle many fonts and graphics, in 1984. By 1987, Adobe had agreements with IBM, Digital, AST Research, Hewlett-Packard, and Texas Instruments for them to use PostScript in their printers.

Desktop publishing (DTP) involves mixing text and graphics to produce high-quality output for commercial printing, using a microcomputer and mouse, scanner, digital cameras, laser or ink-jet printer, and DTP software. Often the printer is used primarily to get an advance look before the completed job is sent to a typesetter service bureau or a professional printer for even higher-quality output. Service bureaus and printers have special machines that convert the DTP files to film, which can then be used to make plates for offset printing or be used to go straight to digital printing. Offset printing produces higher-quality documents, especially if color is used, but is generally more expensive than digital printing.

FEATURES OF DESKTOP PUBLISHING Desktop publishing has these characteristics:

- **Mix of text with graphics:** Desktop-publishing software allows you to precisely manage and merge text with graphics. As you lay out a page on-screen, you can make the text "flow," liquidlike, around graphics such as photographs. You can resize art, silhouette it, change the colors, change the texture, flip it upside down, and make it look like a photo negative.

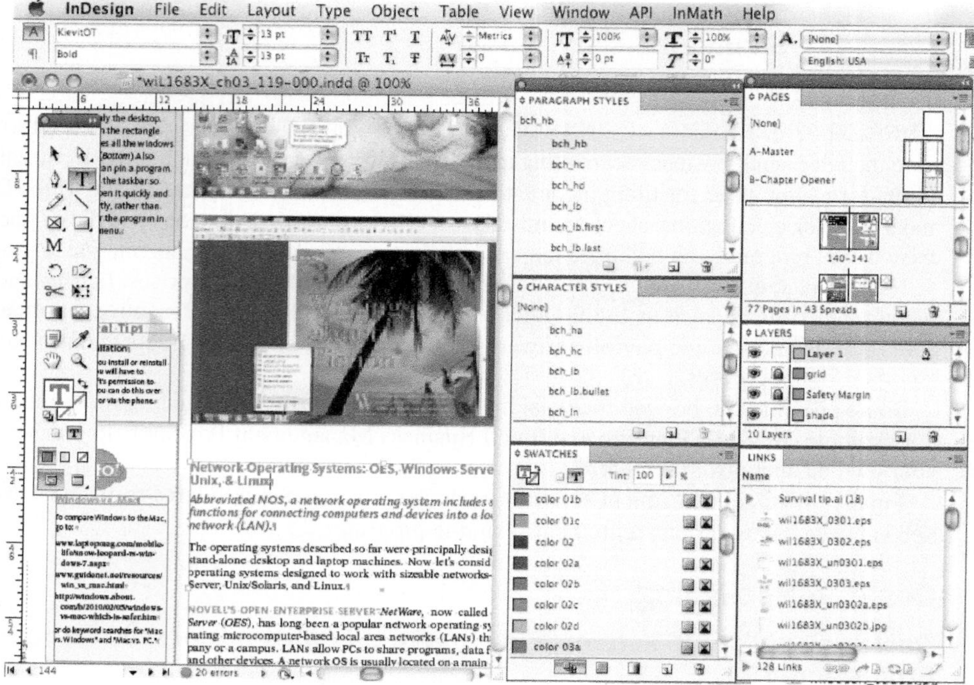

Desktop-publishing software. Adobe InDesign allows users to create interactive documents with sound, video, graphics, colors, text, and photos, all ready to go to a professional printer. (For InDesign videos, go to *http://blogs.adobe.com/indesigndocs/2010/04/a_complete_list_of_indesign_cs_1.html.*)

1992	1993	1994	1995	1997	1998	1999	2000
Microsoft's Access database program released	Multimedia desktop computers PDF software	Apple and IBM introduce PCs with full-motion video built in; wireless data transmission for small portable computers; Netscape's first web browser is introduced (based on Mosaic, introduced in 1993)	Windows 95 is released	Mac OS 8 sells 1.25 million copies in its first two weeks	Windows 98 is released	Adobe InDesign	Windows 2000 (ME) is released; Mac System 9.0

- **Varied type and layout styles:** As do word processing programs, DTP programs support a variety of fonts, or typestyles, from readable Times Roman to staid Tribune to wild Jester and Scribble. Additional fonts can be purchased on disk or downloaded online. You can also create all kinds of rules, borders, columns, and page-numbering styles.
- **Use of files from other programs:** It's usually not efficient to do word processing, drawing, and painting with the DTP software. As a rule, text is composed on a word processor, artwork is created with drawing and painting software, and photographs are input using a scanner and then modified and stored using image-editing software. Prefabricated art to illustrate DTP documents may be obtained from clip-art sources. The DTP program is used to integrate all these files. You can look at your work on the display screen as one page, as two facing pages (in reduced size), or as "thumbnails." Then you can see it again after it has been printed out. (• *See Panel 3.36.*)

BECOMING A DTP PROFESSIONAL Not everyone can be successful at desktop publishing, because many complex layouts require experience, skill, and knowledge of graphic design. Indeed, use of these programs by nonprofessional users can lead to rather unprofessional-looking results. Nevertheless, the availability of microcomputers and reasonably inexpensive software has opened up a career area formerly reserved for professional typographers and printers.

panel 3.36

How desktop publishing uses other files

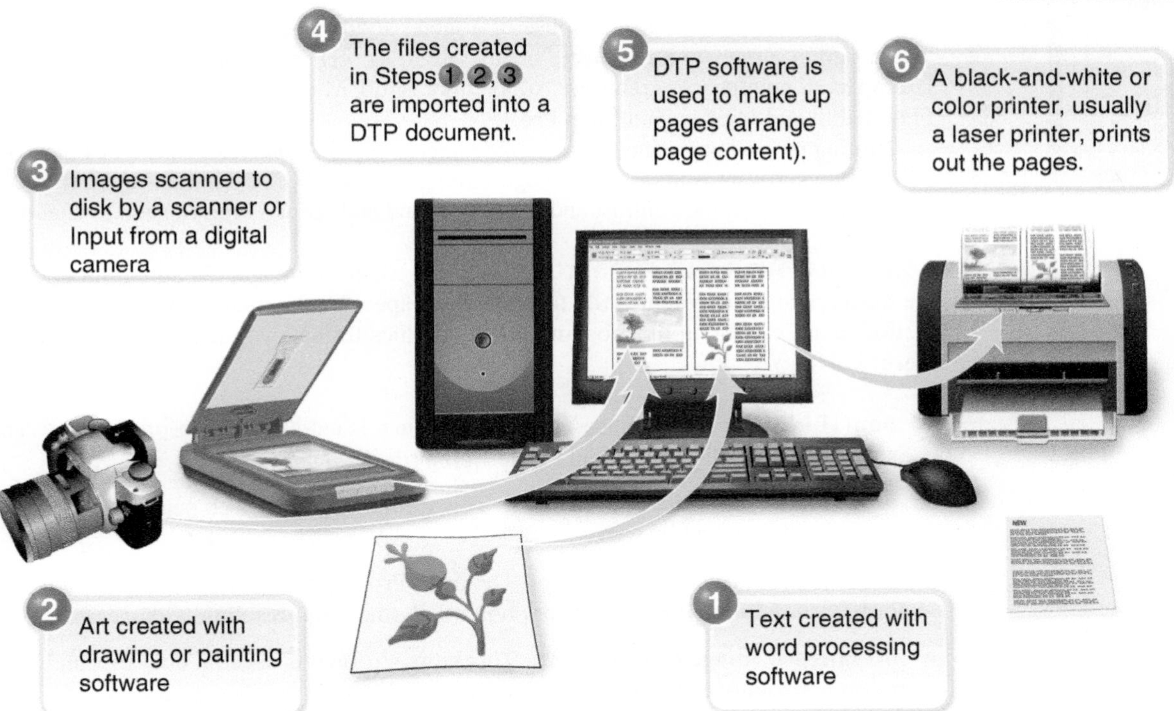

1 Text created with word processing software
2 Art created with drawing or painting software
3 Images scanned to disk by a scanner or Input from a digital camera
4 The files created in Steps 1, 2, 3 are imported into a DTP document.
5 DTP software is used to make up pages (arrange page content).
6 A black-and-white or color printer, usually a laser printer, prints out the pages.

2001	2003	2007	2008	2009	2012	2013	2015?
Windows XP becomes available; Mac OS X ships	Microsoft Vista OS (Pre-Beta) first introduced; Windows Mobile released	Windows Vista commercially available; Mac OS X.5 (Leopard) available	Cloud computing starts to take off	Windows 7	Web has a greater reach than TV	Windows 8 released	Most software will be open-source; 3-D user interface

Adobe InDesign is a "high-end" professional DTP program. Microsoft Publisher 2013 is a "low-end," consumer-oriented DTP package. Some word processing programs, such as Word and WordPerfect, also have many DTP features, although still not at the sophisticated level of the specialized DTP software. DTP packages, for example, give you more control over typographical characteristics and provide more support for full-color output.

Drawing & Painting Programs

There are several types of software for illustrators.

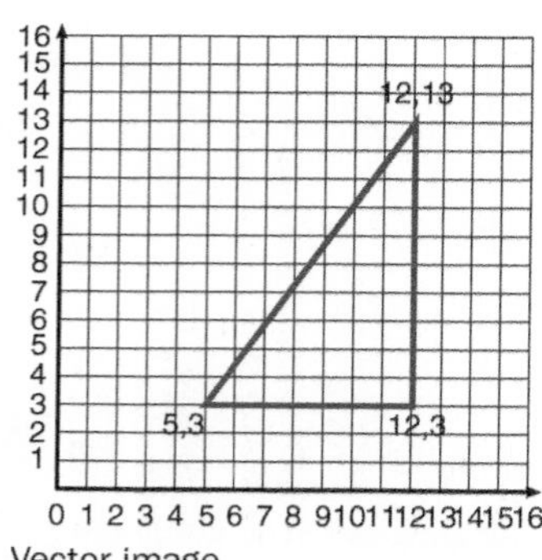

Vector image

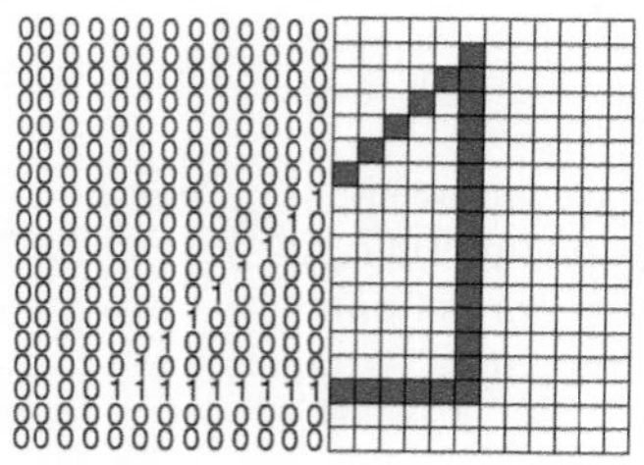
Bit-mapped image

Commercial artists and fine artists have largely abandoned the paintbox and pen-and-ink for software versions of palettes, brushes, and pens. However, even nonartists can produce good-looking work with these programs.

There are two types of computer art programs, also called *illustration software*—drawing and painting.

DRAWING PROGRAMS A *drawing program* is graphics software that allows users to design and illustrate objects and products. Some drawing programs are CorelDRAW, Adobe Illustrator, and SmartDraw.

Drawing programs create *vector images*—images created from geometrical formulas. Almost all sophisticated graphics programs use vector graphics.

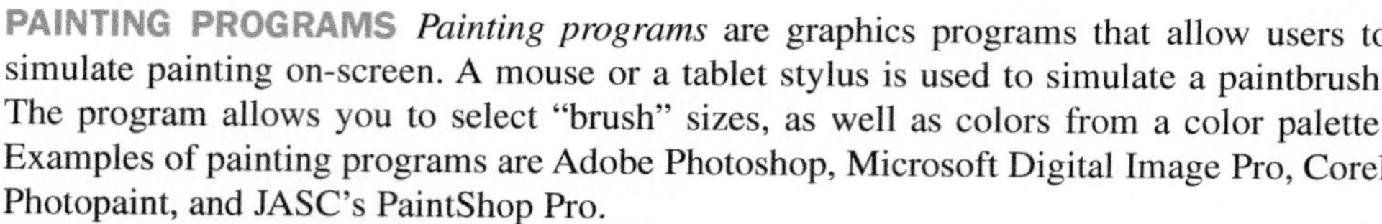

PAINTING PROGRAMS *Painting programs* are graphics programs that allow users to simulate painting on-screen. A mouse or a tablet stylus is used to simulate a paintbrush. The program allows you to select "brush" sizes, as well as colors from a color palette. Examples of painting programs are Adobe Photoshop, Microsoft Digital Image Pro, Corel Photopaint, and JASC's PaintShop Pro.

Painting programs produce *bit-mapped images,* or *raster images,* made up of little dots.

Painting software is also called *image-editing software* because it allows you to retouch photographs, adjust the contrast and the colors, and add special effects, such as shadows.

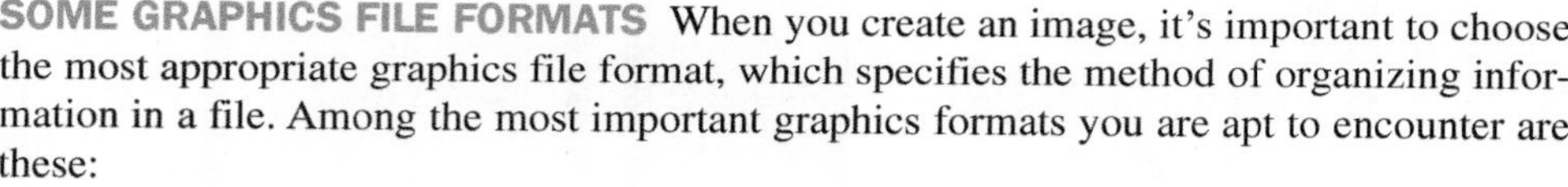

SOME GRAPHICS FILE FORMATS When you create an image, it's important to choose the most appropriate graphics file format, which specifies the method of organizing information in a file. Among the most important graphics formats you are apt to encounter are these:

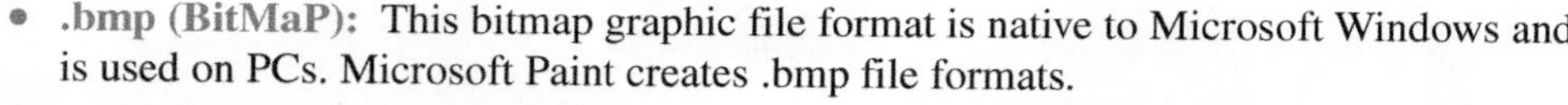

- **.bmp (BitMaP):** This bitmap graphic file format is native to Microsoft Windows and is used on PCs. Microsoft Paint creates .bmp file formats.
- **.gif (Graphic Interchange Format):** This format is used in web pages and for downloadable online images.
- **.jpeg (Joint Photographic Experts Group):** Pronounced "*jay-peg,*" this bitmap format is used for websites and for photos and other high-resolution images.
- **.tiff (Tagged Image File Format):** This bitmap format is used on both PCs and Macs for high-resolution files that will be printed.
- **.png (Portable Network Graphics):** This file format was specifically created for web page images and can be used as a public domain alternative to .gif for compression.

Video/Audio Editing Software

Video and audio editing has become easier to do on microcomputer systems.

The popularity of digital camcorders ("camera recorders") has caused an increase in sales of video-editing software. This software allows you to import video footage to your PC and edit it, for example, deleting parts you don't want, reordering sequences, and adding special effects. Popular video-editing software packages include Adobe Premiere Elements, Corel Video Studio, Sony Pictures Digital Vegas, Magix Movie Edit Pro, Roxio Creator, Apple Final Cut Express, Pinnacle Studio DV, CyberLink Power Director, and Ulead VideoStudio.

Audio-editing software provides similar capabilities for working with sound tracks, and you can also clean up background noise (called *artifacts*) and emphasize certain sound qualities. Sound-editing software includes Windows Sound Recorder, Sony Pictures Sound Forge, Audacity (freeware), Felt Tip Software's Sound Studio (shareware), GoldWave, and WavePad.

Video and audio are covered in more detail in Chapter 5.

Survival Tip

Compressing Web & Audio Files

Video and audio files tend to be very large, so they need to be edited down and compressed to be as short as possible, especially if they are to be used on web pages. Your software documentation will explain how to do this.

Animation Software

Animation is usually a part of multimedia presentations.

Animation is the simulation (illusion) of movement created by displaying a series of still pictures, or frames, very quickly in sequence. *Computer animation* refers to the creation of moving images by means of a computer. Whereas video devices record continuous motion and break it up into discrete frames, animation starts with independent pictures and puts them together to form the illusion of continuous motion. Animation is one of the chief ingredients

Sophisticated application software. Animation artist at work at the Studio Ghibli, Mitaka, Japan

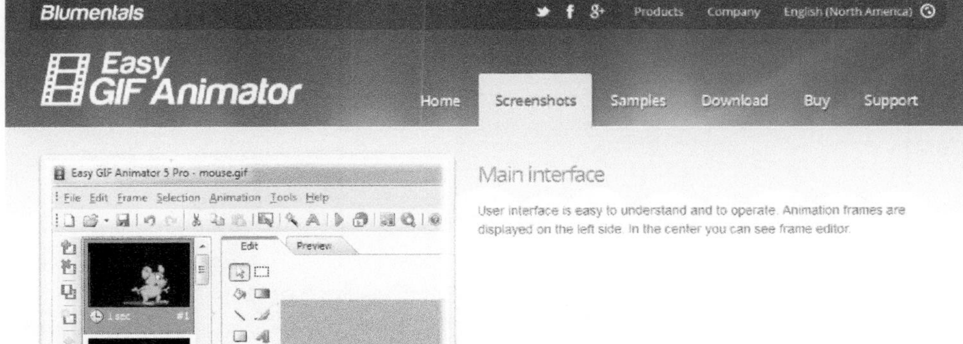
Blumentals
Products
Company
English (North America)
Easy GIF Animator
Home
Screenshots
Samples
Download
Buy
Support
Easy GIF Animator 5 Pro - mouse.gif
File Edit Frame Selection Animation Tools Help
Edit
Preview
Main interface
User interface is easy to understand and to operate. Animation frames are displayed on the left side. In the center you can see frame editor.

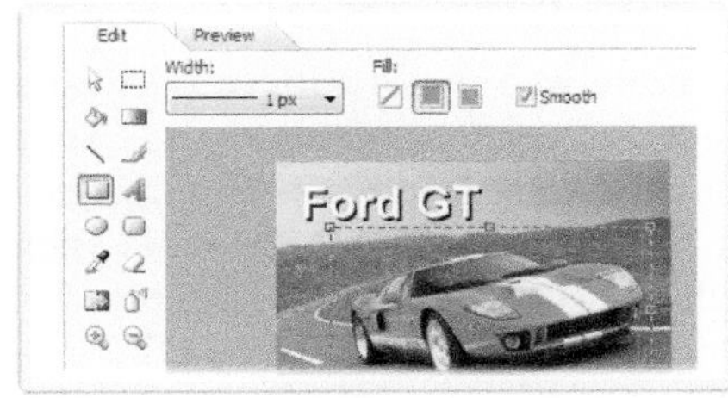
Edit
Preview
Width:
Fill:
1 px
Smooth
Ford GT
Image editor and drawing tools
Create, edit and modify your GIF animation images directly from Easy GIF Animator. You can draw lines and shapes, paint image areas and even add text with a shadow.

Learn-as-you-go animation software from *www.blumentals.net/egifan/highlights.php*

About Animation

For sources about animation, go to:

http://animation.about.com/od/referencematerials/a/freesoftware.htm

www.sciencedaily.com/articles/c/computer_animation.htm

http://entertainment.howstuffworks.com/computer-animation.htm

www.edb.utexas.edu/minliu/multimedia/Computer%20Animation.pdf

For schools offering training in computer-based graphics, including animation, check out:

www.collegexpress.com/lists/list/colleges-with-fine-programs-in-computer-animation/134/

of multimedia presentations and is commonly used on web pages. There are many software applications that enable you to create animations that you can display on a computer monitor.

The first type of animation to catch on for web use was called *GIF* (for Graphics Interchange Format) animation, and it is still very popular today. GIF files contain a group of images that display very quickly to simulate movement when a web page viewer clicks on the file icon. Animated GIF Construction Professional enables users to easily create animation via the use of a wizard. It allows the creation of many special effects and supports compression, as well as offering tutorials. Among the many other GIF animation software packages are Ulead Gif Animator and Easy Gif Animator.

Multimedia Authoring Software

Multimedia software brings together many components.

Multimedia authoring software combines text, graphics, video, animation, and sound in an integrated way to create stand-alone multimedia applications. Content can be copied to CDs/DVDs or delivered via the web. Until the mid-1990s, multimedia applications were relatively uncommon, owing to the expensive hardware required. With increases in performance and decreases in price, however, multimedia is now commonplace. Nearly all microcomputers are capable of displaying video, though the resolution available depends on the power of the computer's video adapter and CPU. Adobe Director and Adobe Macromedia Authorware are two popular multimedia authoring packages.

Many websites, as well as business training centers and educational institutions, use multimedia to develop interactive applications.

Multimedia authoring software: Adobe Director

Web Authoring

This site offers a lot of information on web-authoring tools:

http://webdesign.about.com/od/htmleditors/HTML_Editors_Web_Page_Authoring_Tools.htm

Web Page Design/Authoring Software

Software that allows you to create your own websites.

Web page design/authoring software is used to create web pages with sophisticated multimedia features. A few of these packages are easy enough for beginners to use. Some of the best known are Adobe Dreamweaver, Seamonkey, Coffee Cup Visual Site Designer, RealMac Rapid Weaver, Microsoft Expression Web 4, and Dynamic HTML Editor. These tools generate the necessary HTML coding (and other, newer language coding) based on the user's design and content and present everything to the design in a WYSIWYG ("what you see is what you get") form. (• *See Panel 3.37.*)

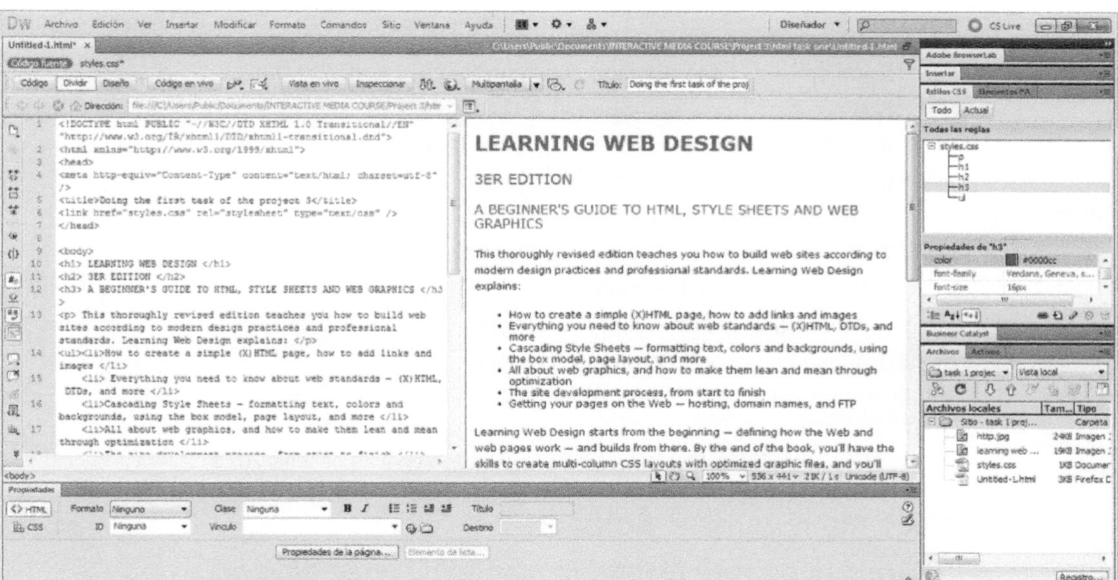

panel 3.37

HTML code (*left*) translated into WYSIWYG text (*right*)

Internet access providers also offer some free, easy-to-use web-authoring tools for building simple websites. They help you create web pages, using icons and menus to automate the process; you don't need to know hypertext markup language (HTML, Chapter 2, p. 66) to get the job done. These automated tools let you select a prepared, template web page design, type a few words, add a picture or two—and you're done. To save the pages and make them accessible on the Internet, the provider grants you a certain amount of space on its web servers.

Website design can include much more than text: for example, animation, video, sound, interactivity, search-engine functions. But before creating a website, the designer must first plan exactly what is needed in the website—define the audience, as well as the purpose and the content. Once a website is completed, it must be uploaded ("published") in order to be available to Internet users via a browser. Some people with powerful personal computers and an always-on Internet connection, such as cable, leave their websites on their own computers; the website is accessed by users typing in the site's URL (web address; Chapter 2, p. 64) in their browsers. Most people, however, use ftp software (covered shortly) to upload their website files to a server host, where, for a fee, the website is stored for access.

Complicated business websites are created and maintained by professional website developers.

Web Page Design

For some basic steps of web design, go to:

www.chromaticsites.com/blog/12-steps-to-creating-a-professional-web-design/

www.rcaguilar.com/html-design.htm

http://uxdesign.smashingmagazine.com/2008/01/31/10-principles-of-effective-web-design/

http://webstyleguide.com/

For information on becoming a professional website designer, try:

www.wikihow.com/Become-a-Professional-Web-Designer-and-Programmer

http://websitetips.com/business/education/

http://webdesign.about.com/od/jobs/p/aa031703a.htm

http://jobsearchtech.about.com/od/careerplanning/l/aa070201.htm

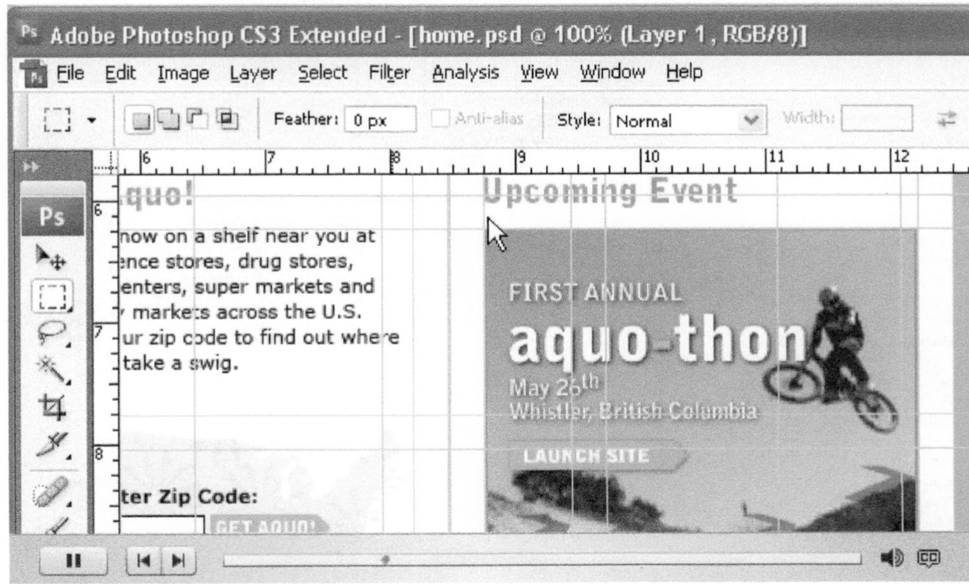

Inserting an Adobe Photoshop photo file into a Dreamweaver web page that is being designed

1. Norton 360 2013 (Symantec)
2. Windows 7 Home Premium (Microsoft)
3. Office Mac Home and Student 2011 (Microsoft)
4. Norton Internet Security 2013 (Symantec)
5. Quicken Deluxe 2013 (download) (Intuit)
6. Kaspersky Internet Security (Kaspersky Lab)
7. Adobe Photoshop Elements 11 (Adobe)
8. Norton 360 2013 (Symantec)
9. Windows 8 System Builder (Microsoft)
10. Adobe Photoshop Lightroom 5 (Adobe)

Source: www.dailycamera.com/topbusinessstories/ci_23555299/biz-bits-best-sellingsoftware-july-1-2013.

Top 10 best-selling software programs on Amazon.com as of June 2013

Social Media Management Software

There is also software for managing your social-networking and media activities:

www.sysomos.com/?campaigntype=ppc&gclid=CI7BldOIt7cCFaU5QgodHU0ACA

www.vivalogo.com/vl-resources/open-source-social-networking-software.ht

http://blog.crowdcontrolhq.com/crowdcontrolhq-is-the-first-social-media-management-software-to-incorporate-g-into-buzz-monitor-feature/

Project Management Software

Software can be very helpful in managing large projects.

As we have seen, a personal information manager (PIM) can help you schedule your appointments and do some planning. That is, it can help you manage your own life. But what if you need to manage the lives of others in order to accomplish a full-blown project, such as steering a political campaign or handling a nationwide road tour for a band? Strictly defined, a *project* is a one-time operation involving several tasks and multiple resources that must be organized toward completing a specific goal within a given period of time. The project can be small, such as an advertising campaign for an in-house advertising department, or large, such as construction of an office tower or a jetliner.

Project management software is a program used to plan and schedule the people, costs, and resources required to complete a project on time. (• *See Panel 3.38.*) For instance, the associate producer on a feature film might use such software to keep track

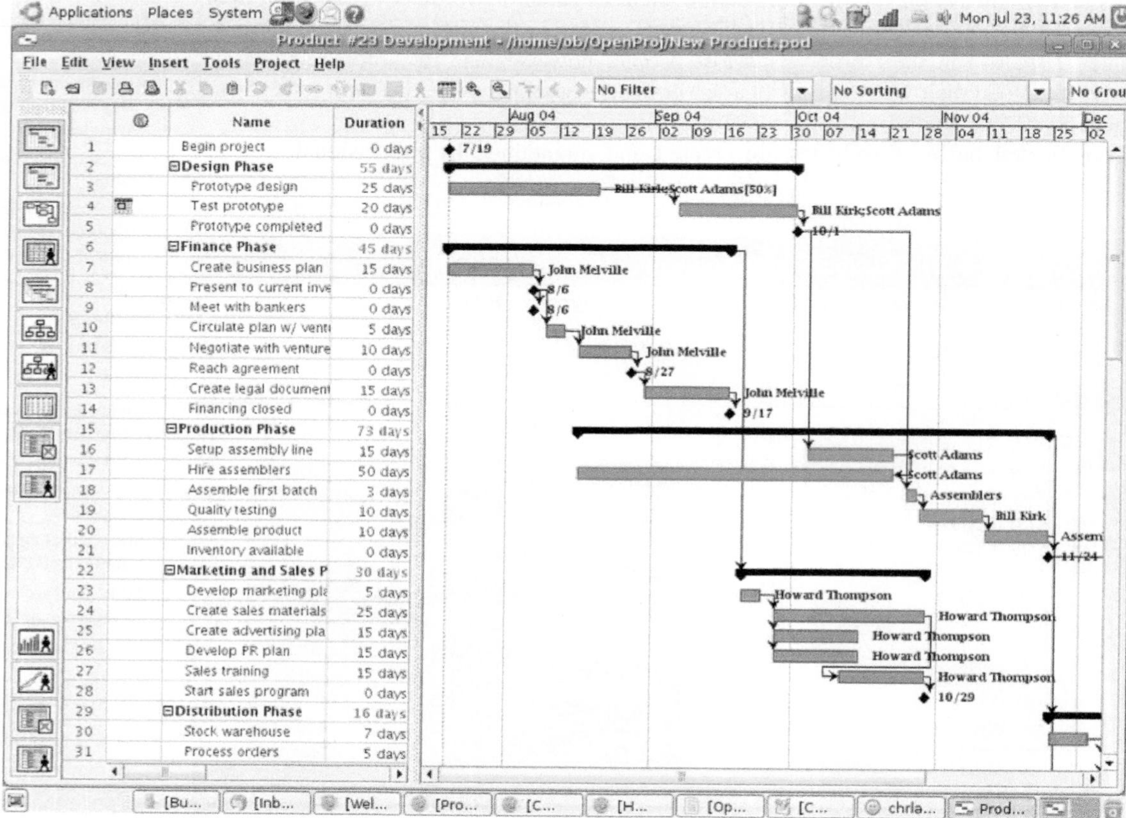

panel 3.38

Project management software example (*www.enterprisescreenshots.com/project_screenshots/*)

PRACTICAL ACTION

Help in Building Your Web Page

Local and national Internet access providers often offer web-page-building tools, as well as space on their servers for storing your web page. Other sources of information for designing and building web pages are these.

For Novices

- **Yahoo!:** Yahoo! offers web-page-building tools and templates under the name SiteBuilder (*http://webhosting.yahoo.com/ps/sb/index.php*), which enables you to add music and other special effects to your web pages and have components that track how many people visit your site. For a fee, Yahoo! offers unlimited storage for your website and will help you determine your URL (website address).
- **Lycos:** Lycos offers templates and tools, and it also offers tutorials to help you get started if you want to build your own pages from scratch. Lycos also offers free space in its Tripod area (*www.tripod.lycos.com*). As with Yahoo!, you will have advertisements on your pages unless you pay a small fee to get rid of them.
- **Google Sites:** Google offers this free online tool that makes it easy for anyone to create and publish web pages in just minutes. You can see what your pages will look like, and you can edit your pages right in your browser. Google will host your web pages on your own site at *www.google.com/sites/help/intl/en/overview.html*.

Once you've created your website, you'll need to "publish" it—upload it to a web server for viewing on the Internet. You can get upload instructions from your online service or Internet access provider, which may also provide space (for free or for a fee) on its servers. (Or, as we mentioned earlier, if you have a powerful, large-storage-capacity microcomputer that has an always-on Internet connection, you can use it to host your own website.)

For much more information about building and storing your own web pages, just do a keyword search using "build web page" or "website design" in any good search engine.

of the locations, cast and crew, materials, dollars, and schedules needed to complete the picture on time and within budget. The software would show the scheduled beginning and ending dates for a particular task—such as shooting all scenes on a certain set—and then the date that task was actually completed. Examples of project management software are Mindjet MindManager, MatchWare MindView, Microsoft Project, AEC FastTrackSchedule, and Project KickStart.

Survival Tip

Try before You Buy

Free trial versions of software are often offered as downloads from company sites.

Portable Document Format (PDF)

PDF is a multiplatform file format that allows documents to be used with any operating system.

Short for **Portable Document Format, PDF is a file format developed by Adobe Systems that preserves most attributes (including text, color, formatting, graphics, layout, and more) of a source document no matter which application, platform, and hardware type was originally used to create it.** PDF captures information from a variety of applications on different platforms, making it possible to send documents and have them appear on the recipient's monitor (or printer) as they were intended to be viewed. *(• See Panel 3.39, next page.)*

Originally PDF was mostly used by graphic artists, designers, and publishers for producing color page proofs. Today, however, PDF is used for virtually any data that needs to be exchanged among applications and users. Individuals, businesses, and government agencies around the world trust and rely on PDF to communicate. PDF files are widely used on websites and are also used to distribute electronic documents over networks and via email.

A PDF file can be shared, viewed, and printed by anyone using the free downloadable Adobe Reader software regardless of the operating system and original application used. PDF can also be used on mobile devices. In addition, many applications, such as

Search
Log In or Sign Up

Learning Center Get Expert Advice Exchange Resources Members Area

Home > Get Started > Acrobat XI

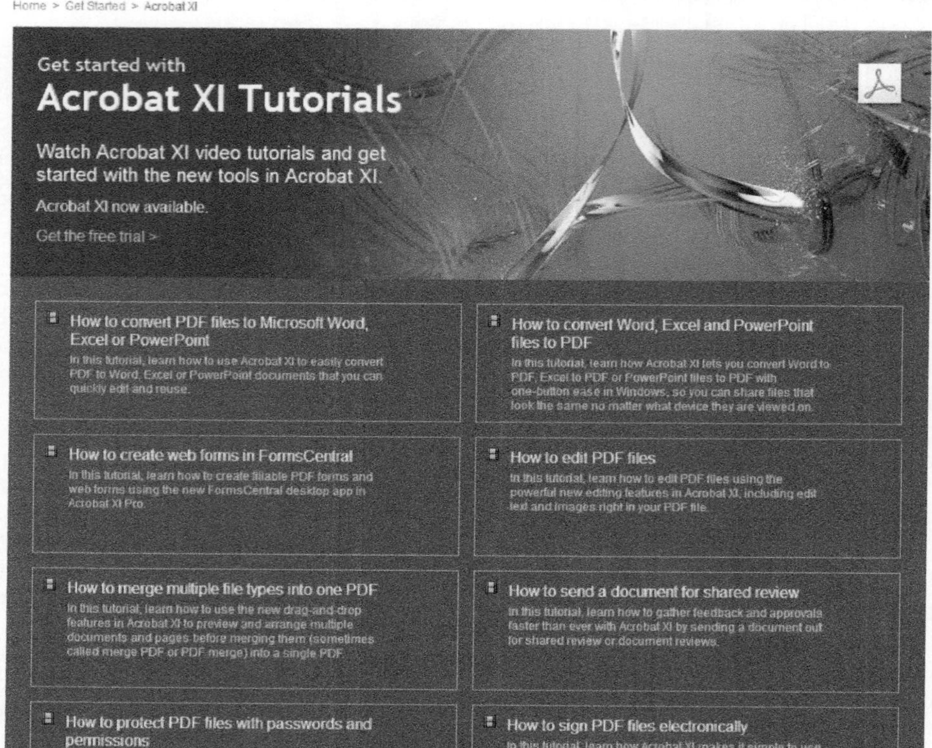

panel 3.39

Adobe Acrobat PDF tutorial screen

(*upper right corner*) Adobe PDF file icon. Any file in the PDF format will have this icon next to the file name.

Microsoft Word, enable users to save their files in a PDF version. To be able to create and work with all of Adobe's PDF features, you need to purchase the complete Adobe Acrobat Suite.

Computer-Aided Design (CAD)

CAD uses computer programs to design two- and three-dimensional models.

The Ultimate CAD Directory

This directory has information about all sorts of CAD products to suit every type of need:

www.tenlinks.com/CAD/

Computers have long been used in engineering design. **Computer-aided design (CAD) programs are intended for the design of products, structures, civil engineering drawings, and maps.** CAD programs, which are available for microcomputers, help architects design buildings and workspaces and help engineers design cars, planes, electronic devices, roadways, bridges, and subdivisions. CAD and drawing programs are similar. However, CAD programs provide precise dimensioning and positioning of the elements being drawn, so they can be transferred later to computer-aided manufacturing (CAM) programs. Also, CAD programs lack some of the special effects for illustrations that come with drawing programs. One advantage of CAD software is that the product can be drawn in three dimensions and then rotated on the screen, so the designer can see all sides. (• *See Panel 3.40.*) Examples of popular CAD programs are Autodesk, AutoCAD, TurboCAD, Alibre Design, and PowerCADD.

Computer-aided design/computer-aided manufacturing (CAD/CAM) software allows products designed with CAD to be input into an automated manufacturing system that makes the products. For example, CAD/CAM systems brought a whirlwind of enhanced creativity and efficiency to the fashion industry. The designs and specifications are then input into CAM systems that enable robot pattern-cutters to automatically cut thousands of patterns from fabric with only minimal waste. Whereas previously the fashion industry worked about a year in advance of delivery, CAD/CAM has cut that time to only a few months—a competitive edge for a field that feeds on fads.

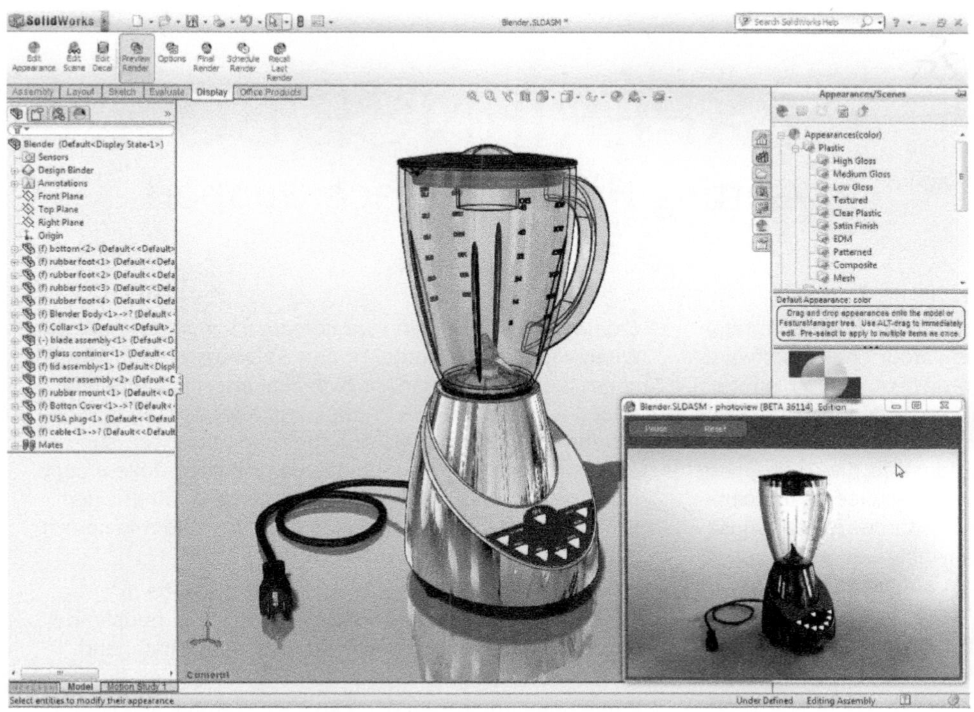

panel 3.40

CAD

CAD software is used for nearly all three-dimensional designing. (*CAD software by SolidWorks*)

A Few More Types of Application Software

Gaming software examples:

Unity 3D http://unity3d.com/

XNA Games Studio www.microsoft.com/en-us/download/details.aspx?id=23714

Pygame www.pygame.org/news.html

Blitz Max www.blitzbasic.com/

Unreal Development Kit www.unrealengine.com/udk/

Educational software examples (multilevel):

Literary skills: Kurzweil Firefly (Cambium Learning)

Math fluency: ExploreLearning Reflex

Special education: PresenceLearning

Language arts: Read & Write Gold with Web Apps (TextHelp)

Math & science online simulations: ExploreLearning Gizmos

Remediation: GradPoint (Connections Education)

Digital literacy: Digital Literacy (Rosen Digital)

Financial literacy: Financial Literacy (Rosen Digital)

SAT preparation

GMAT preparation

LSAT preparation

MCAT preparation

Brain training: lumosity.com

Simulation program examples:

Flight Simulator X

Physion (physics simulation software)

CCENT 640-822 Network Simulator

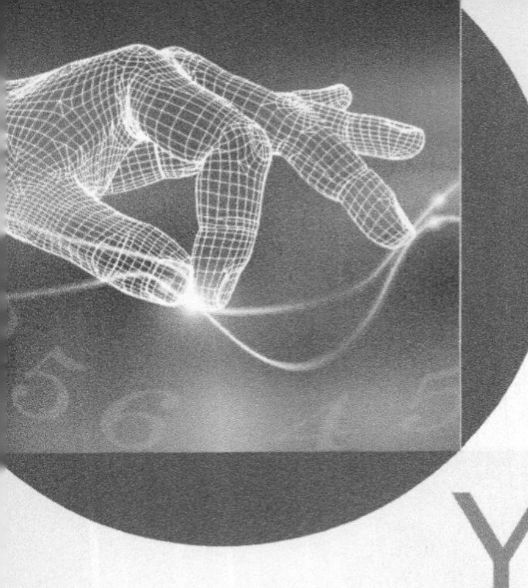

EXPERIENCE BOX

Getting Help from Tech Support

Your screen flashes "Fatal Error." Your new software upgrade disrupts your printer. You can't connect to your Internet access provider. No wonder one online survey found that nearly 20% of the respondents admitted they'd dropped a computer on the floor out of anger.[35] Because of the complicated mesh of elements—software, hardware, communications, people—Murphy's law ("If anything can go wrong, it will") seems to apply in computing as almost nowhere else. Information technology is becoming more complex. The more personal computers and other infotech devices are expected to do—music, video, photos, DVDs, home networking, email, and so on—the more complex the interaction between the components and the harder it is to figure out what's wrong. Also, the proliferation of viruses, worms, spyware, and other types of malware makes the support task more daunting. Thus, one of the most valuable tasks you can learn is how to deal with tech support—getting technical help on the phone or online (via email or websites) when things don't work. *(• See Panel 3.41.)*

Improving Your Chances with Tech Support

Here are three things that you can do in advance to improve your chances of success:

- *Use the web to research a manufacturer's tech support before you buy:* If you decide to purchase or upgrade, go to the manufacturer's website and look at tech support resources to see how coherent and easily accessible they are. This will also give you some feel for the kinds of problems customers are having. Also check out some online comment forums on the item you are planning to buy/upgrade (for example, *www.techsupportforum.com/forums*). Another good idea is to print out some articles on tech help, such as *PC Magazine*'s "Top Tips for Tech Support Success" (*www.pcmag.com/article2/0,2817,2192075,00.asp*), and keep them on hand when you can't get online for help.
- *Call tech support before you buy:* Calling tech support in advance of purchasing may cost you something in long-distance charges, but you'll also find out how confusing the voice menu is and how long it takes to reach a live human.
- *Create a fact sheet with your computer's important specs:* When you get a computer or new software, create a fact sheet listing the important technical specifications and attach it to the outside of the computer case. This will provide you with the kind of information that tech support personnel will ask should you call them. Take a copy along with you whenever you buy a game or other video- and sound-intensive application to make sure it is compatible with the rest of your system.
- *If you have a communication problem, ask to be referred to another person:* Many companies now hire people in offshore call centers as tech support specialists, and sometimes you may have trouble with unfamiliar accents. If this happens to you, don't give up your place in line; ask to be connected to another service representative.

Other Sources of Help

Although usually less specific in solving your problem, other sources of help are available:

- *Help programs: instruction manuals, software, and online:* User guides or instruction manuals printed on paper have traditionally accompanied software. Now most software publishers rely more on Help programs on a CD/DVD or in downloadable PDF manuals. Help programs are also available through the Internet. The problem with this approach, of course, is, How do you go online to solve the problem of your computer not working if your computer isn't working? (It helps to have two computers.)
- *Commercial how-to books:* How-to books are the kind of books found both in computer stores and in general bookstores such as Barnes & Noble and on Amazon.com. Examples are the "For Dummies" or "Complete Idiot's" books (such as *PCs for Dummies* and *The Complete Idiot's Guide to Microsoft Office*).
- *Knowledgeable friends:* Nothing beats having a knowledgeable friend: your instructor, a student more advanced than you, or someone with a technical interest in computers. We can't stress enough how important it is to get to know people—from your classes, from computer user groups (including online Internet groups), from family friends, or whatever—who can lend aid and expertise when your computer software or hardware gives you trouble.

AAATechSupport.com B00-392-5938 *www.aaatechsupport.com*	iYogi 866-242-4609 *www.iyogi.net/tollfree1/tech.support*	Itoknet *www.itok.net/services.aspx*
Geeks to go! Toll free: 888-433-5435 *www.geekstogo.com/*	Mac Help *954-725-9525* *www.lookatmymac.com*	Rescuecom *www.rescue.com*
Geek Squad 1-800-433-5778 *www.geeksquad.com*	JustAnswer.mac *www.justanswer.com/mac-computers/*	Support.com *www.support.com/pcsupport/services/subscriptionplans*
Geeks on Call 1-800-905-GEEK *www.geeksoncall.com*	GoToAssist *www.gotoassist.com/*	

panel 3.41

Some individual technical support services

The 800 and 888 numbers are toll-free. Most services are available 24 hours a day, 7 days a week. Note that not all operations serve Macintosh users, and not all have a phone option—which can be a handicap when you're not able to go online.

TERMS & EXPLANATIONS

analytical graphics (p. 160) Also called *business graphics;* graphical forms that make numeric data easier to analyze than it is when organized as rows and columns of numbers. The principal examples of analytical graphics are bar charts, line graphs, and pie charts. Why it's important: *Whether viewed on a monitor or printed out, analytical graphics help make sales figures, economic trends, and the like easier to comprehend and analyze.*

animation (p. 173) The simulation (illusion) of movement created by displaying a series of still pictures, or frames, very quickly in sequence. Why it's important: *Animation is used in videogames, movies, special-effects presentations, and even in email, to make it more interesting.*

application software (p. 114) Software that has been developed to solve a particular problem for users—to perform useful work on specific tasks or to provide entertainment. Why it's important: *Application software consists of most of the software you are familiar with and use on a daily basis.* (Compare **system software.**)

booting (p. 116) Loading an operating system into a computer's main memory. Why it's important: *Without booting, computers could not operate. The programs responsible for booting are stored permanently in the computer's electronic circuitry. When you turn on the machine, programs called* diagnostic routines *test the main memory, the central processing unit, and other parts of the system to make sure they are running properly. Next, BIOS (basic input/output system) programs are copied to main memory and help the computer interpret keyboard characters or transmit characters to the display screen or to a disk. Then the boot program obtains the operating system, usually from the hard disk, and loads it into the computer's main memory, where it remains until you turn off the computer.*

cell (p. 159) Place where a row and a column intersect in a spreadsheet worksheet; its position is called a *cell reference or a cell address.* Why it's important: *The cell is the smallest working unit in a spreadsheet. Data and formulas are entered into cells. Cell addresses provide location references for worksheet users.*

compression (p. 152) Method of removing repetitive elements from a file so that the file requires less storage space and then later decompressing the removed data, or restoring the repeated patterns. Why it's important: *Compression/decompression makes storage and transmission of large files, such as multimedia files, more feasible.*

computer-aided design (CAD) (p. 178) Programs intended for the design of products, structures, civil engineering drawings, and maps. Why it's important: *CAD programs, which are available for microcomputers, help architects design buildings and workspaces and help engineers design cars, planes, electronic devices, roadways, bridges, and subdivisions. While similar to drawing programs, CAD programs provide precise dimensioning and positioning of the elements being drawn, so they can be transferred later to computer-aided manufacturing programs; however, they lack special effects for illustrations. One advantage of CAD software is that three-dimensional drawings can be rotated on-screen, so the designer can see all sides of the product.*

cursor (p. 153) Movable symbol on the display screen that shows where the user may next enter data or commands. The symbol is often a blinking rectangle or an I-beam. You can move the cursor on the screen using the keyboard's directional arrow keys or a mouse. The point where the cursor is located is called the *insertion point.* Why it's important: *All application software packages use cursors to show the current work location on the screen.*

custom software (p. 145) Tailor-made software crafted by an individual or team of programmers for a particular function or business purpose. Why it's important: *Custom software fills needs that cannot be served by buying readily available off-the-shelf or packaged software.*

data files (p. 150) Files that contain data—words, numbers, pictures, sounds, and so on. Why it's important: *Unlike program files, data files don't instruct the computer to do anything. Rather, data files are there to be acted on by program files. Examples of common extensions in data files are* .txt, .doc/.docx *(text), and* .xls *(spreadsheets). Certain proprietary software programs have their own extensions, such as .html for Hypertext Markup Language,* .ppt *for PowerPoint, and* .mdb *for Access.*

database (p. 161) Collection of interrelated files in a computer system. These computer-based files are organized according to their common elements, so that they can be retrieved easily. Why it's important: *Businesses and organizations build databases to help them keep track of and manage their affairs. In addition, online database services put enormous resources at the user's disposal.*

database software (p. 161) Also called *database manager* or *database management system (DBMS);* application software that sets up and controls the structure of a database and access to the data. Why it's important: *Database software allows users to organize and manage huge amounts of data.*

default settings (p. 157) Settings automatically used by a program unless the user specifies otherwise, thereby overriding them. Why it's important: *Users need to know how to change default settings in order to customize documents and/or applications.*

desktop (p. 128) The operating system's main interface screen. Why it's important: *The desktop displays pictures (icons) that provide quick access to programs and information.*

desktop publishing (DTP) (p. 170) Application software and hardware system that involves mixing text and graphics to produce high-quality output for commercial printing, using a microcomputer and mouse, scanner, digital cameras, laser or ink-jet printer, and DTP software (such as InDesign or, at a more consumer-oriented level, Microsoft Publisher). Often the printer is used primarily to get an advance look before the completed job is sent to a typesetter for even higher-quality output. Some word processing programs, such as Word and WordPerfect, have rudimentary DTP features. Why it's important: *Desktop publishing has reduced the number of steps, the time, and the money required to produce professional-looking printed projects.*

device drivers (p. 121) Specialized software programs—usually components of system software—that allow input and output devices to communicate with the rest of the computer system. Why it's important: *Drivers are needed so that the computer's operating system can recognize and run peripheral hardware.*

embedded operating system (p. 142) Operating system for any electronic system that uses a CPU chip but that is not a general-purpose workstation, desktop, or laptop computer. It is a specialized computer system that is part of a larger system or a machine. Why it's important: *Embedded operating systems are used, for example, in smartphones, tablets, automobiles, planes, trains, bar-code scanners, fuel pumps, space vehicles, machine tools, watches, appliances, cellphones, and robots. Such operating systems include Android, Symbian, iOS, Windows Phone, BlackBerry OS, Embedded Linux, and many others.*

executable file (p. 152) File containing the instructions that tell the computer how to perform a particular task. Why it's important: *Programs won't run without executable files.*

exporting (p. 152) Transforming data into a format that can be used in another program and then transmitting it. Why it's important: *Users need to know how to export many types of files.*

file (p. 118) A named collection of data (data file) or a program (program file) that exists in a computer's secondary storage, such as on a hard disk or CD. Why it's important: *Dealing with files is an inescapable part of working with computers. Users need to be familiar with the different types of files.*

file name (p. 150) The name given to a file. Why it's important: *Files are given names so that they can be differentiated. File names also have extension names of three or four letters added after a period following the file name.*

financial software (p. 168) Application software that ranges from personal-finance managers to entry-level accounting programs to business financial-management packages. Why it's important: *Financial software provides users with powerful management tools (personal-finance managers) as well as small business programs. Tax programs provide virtually all the forms needed for filing income taxes, make complex calculations, check for mistakes, and even unearth deductions you didn't know existed. Accounting software automates bookkeeping tasks, while payroll software keeps records of employee hours and produces reports for tax purposes. Some programs allow users to set up a business from scratch. Financial software often includes investment software packages and various retirement planning programs.*

formulas (p. 160) In a spreadsheet, instructions for calculations entered into designated cells. Why it's important: *When spreadsheet users change data in one cell, all the cells linked to it by formulas automatically recalculate their values.*

freeware (p. 147) Copyrighted software that is distributed free of charge, today most often over the Internet. Why it's important: *Freeware saves users money.*

function keys (p. 125) Keys labeled "F1," "F2," and so on, positioned along the top of the keyboard. Why it's important: *They are used to execute commands specific to the software being used.*

functions (p. 160) In a spreadsheet, built-in formulas that perform common calculations. Why it's important: *After the values have been entered into the worksheet, formulas and functions can be used to calculate outcomes.*

graphical user interface (GUI) (p. 126) User interface in which icons and commands from menus may be selected by means of a mouse or keystrokes. Why it's important: *GUIs are easier to use than command-driven interfaces.*

Help command (p. 133) Command generating a table of contents, an index, and a search feature that can help users locate answers to questions about the software. Why it's important: *Help features provide a built-in electronic instruction manual and/or an online connection to one.*

icons (p. 128) Small pictorial figures that represent programs, data files, or procedures. Why it's important: *Icons have simplified the use of software. The feature represented by the icon can be activated by clicking on the icon.*

importing (p. 152) Getting data from another source and then converting it into a format compatible with the program in which the user is currently working. Why it's important: *Users will often have to import files.*

integrated package (p. 164) Program for personal computers that combines the functionality of word processing, spreadsheet, and database management. Presentation graphics, page layout, paint, calendar, address book, email, and other applications may also be included. Why it's important: *A principal advantage of integrated packages is their low cost. Another is their simplicity; integrated software eliminates the need to open a separate software application for reference purposes or to perform a few quick tasks.*

key (p. 163) Also called *key field, primary key, sort key, index,* or *keyword;* field used to sort data in a database. For example, if users sort records by age, then the age field is a key. Why it's important: *Key fields are needed to identify and retrieve specific items in a database. Most database management systems allow you to have more than one key so that you can sort records in different ways. The most frequent key field used in the United States is the Social Security number, but any unique identifier, such as employee number or student number, can be used.*

Linux (p. 141) Free (open-source) version of the Unix OS, supported by the efforts of thousands of volunteer programmers. Why it's important: *Linux is useful for online applications and for PC users who have to maintain a web server or a network server.*

Macintosh operating system (Mac OS) (p. 135) System software that runs only on Apple Macintosh computers.

Why it's important: *Although Macs are not as common as PCs, many people believe they are easier to use. Macs are often used for graphics and desktop publishing.*

macro (p. 125) Also called *keyboard shortcut;* a single keystroke or command—or a series of keystrokes or commands—used to automatically issue a longer, predetermined series of keystrokes or commands. Why it's important: *Users can consolidate several activities into only one or two keystrokes. The user names the macro and stores the corresponding command sequence; once this is done, the macro can be used repeatedly.*

menu (p. 128) Displayed list of options—such as commands—to choose from. Why it's important: *Menus are a feature of GUIs that make software easier to use.*

menu bar (p. 131) Bar across the top of the display window, below the title bar. Why it's important: *It shows the names of the various pull-down menus available.*

Microsoft Windows (p. 136) Most common operating system for desktop and portable microcomputers. Windows 95 was succeeded by Windows 98, Windows 2000, Windows ME, Windows XP, Vista, Windows 7, and Windows 8. Why it's important: *Windows supports the most applications written for microcomputers.*

Microsoft Windows 7 (p. 137) Currently the most commonly used operating system developed by Microsoft. Why it's important: *Windows 7 is less power hungry than the previous Windows version, boots up more quickly, and has improved networking and security features. The Windows platform is still the major OS platform used today.*

Microsoft Windows 8 (p. 137) Newest Windows operating system; it has two user interfaces—one for the traditional desktop, with overlapping, resizable windows just like earlier Windows, the other a radical redesign resembling the Windows Phone interface, with tile-based, tablet-style features geared for touch screens (but also working with regular screens). Why it's important: *Windows 8 will likely replace Windows 7 as the major OS platform.*

multimedia authoring software (p. 174) Application software that combines text, graphics, video, animation, and sound in an integrated way to create stand-alone multimedia applications. Why it's important: *Multimedia is now commonplace and an important feature of the web and many software applications, including those for mobile devices.*

multitasking (p. 119) Feature of OS software that allows the execution of two or more programs concurrently by one user almost at the same time on the same computer with one or two CPUs. For instance, you might write a report on your computer with one program while another plays a music CD. Why it's important: *Multitasking allows the computer to switch rapidly back and forth among different tasks. The user is generally unaware of the switching process and thus can work in more than one application at a time.*

open-source software (p. 141) Software that any programmer can download from the Internet free and modify with suggested improvements. The only qualification is that changes can't be copyrighted; they must be made available to all and remain in the public domain. Why it's important: *Because this software is not proprietary, any programmer can make improvements, which can result in better-quality software.*

operating system (OS) (p. 115) Low-level master system of programs that manage the basic operations of the computer. Why it's important: *These programs provide resource management services of many kinds. In particular, they handle the control and use of hardware resources, including disk space, memory, CPU time allocation, and peripheral devices. The operating system allows users to concentrate on their own tasks or applications rather than on the complexities of managing the computer.*

packaged software (p. 145) Copyrighted, mass-produced software that's offered for sale in stores or on the web to a variety of users (not created for just one client, as custom software is). Why it's important: *Packaged software is the most common type used by general consumers and computer users. (Software manufacturers don't sell you their software; rather, they sell you a license to become an authorized user of it.)*

PDF *See* **Portable Document Format.**

personal-finance manager (p. 168) Application software that lets users keep track of income and expenses, write checks, do online banking, and plan financial goals. Why it's important: *Personal-finance software can help people manage their money more effectively.*

personal information manager (PIM) (p. 164) Software that helps users keep track of and manage information they use on a daily basis, such as addresses, telephone numbers, appointments, to-do lists, and miscellaneous notes. Some programs feature phone dialers, outliners (for roughing out ideas in outline form), and ticklers (or reminders). Why it's important: *PIMs can help users better organize and manage daily business activities.*

pirated software (p. 146) Software that is obtained illegally. Why it's important: *If you buy such software, not only do the original copyright owners not get paid for their creative work but you risk getting inferior goods and, worse, picking up a virus, and you could be fined. To discourage software piracy, many software manufacturers require that users register their software when they install it on their computers. If the software is not registered, it will not work properly.*

platform (p. 133) Particular processor model and operating system on which a computer system is based. Why it's important: *Software written for one platform may not run on any other. Users should be aware that there are Mac platforms (Apple Macintosh) and Windows platforms, or "PC platforms" (for personal computers such as Dell, Asus, Lenovo, Toshiba, Samsung, Hewlett-Packard, and others that run Microsoft Windows).*

pointer (p. 125) Indicator that usually appears as an arrow, although it changes shape depending on the application. The mouse is used to move the pointer to a particular place on the display screen or to point to little symbols, or icons. Why it's important: *Manipulating the pointer on the screen by means of the mouse is often easier than typing commands on a keyboard.*

Portable Document Format (PDF) (p. 177) File format developed by Adobe Systems. PDF captures text, graphic, and formatting information from a variety of applications on different platforms making it possible to send documents and have them appear on the recipient's monitor (or printer) as they were intended to be viewed. Why it's important: *A properly prepared PDF file maintains the original fonts (type styles and type sizes), images, colors, and graphics, as well as the exact layout of the file. A PDF file can be shared, viewed, and printed by anyone using the free downloadable Adobe Reader software. PDF can also be used on mobile devices. With the complete Adobe Acrobat suite, users can also edit PDF files.*

presentation graphics software (p. 166) Software that uses graphics, animation, sound, and data or information to make visual presentations. Why it's important: *Presentation graphics software provides a means of producing sophisticated graphics.*

productivity software (p. 149) Application software such as word processing programs, spreadsheets, and database managers. Why it's important: *Productivity software makes users more productive at particular tasks.*

productivity suite (p. 164) Also known as *office suite;* professional-level application program groups frequently used in business—at a minimum word processing, spreadsheet, database management, and presentation programs. Why it's important: *Many people use productivity suites. The best known productivity suite is Microsoft Office.*

program files (p. 152) Files containing software instructions that execute, or run, when opened. Why it's important: *Contrast* **data files.**

project management software (p. 176) Program used to plan and schedule the people, costs, and resources required to complete a project on time. Why it's important: *Project management software increases the ease and speed of planning and managing complex projects.*

public-domain software (p. 146) Software, often available on the Internet, that is not protected by copyright and thus may be duplicated by anyone at will. Why it's important: *Public-domain software offers lots of software options to users who may not be able to afford much commercial software. Users may download such software from the Internet for free and make as many copies as they wish.*

range (p. 159) A group of adjacent cells in a spreadsheet—for example, A1 to A5. Why it's important: *Ranges help sort data for calculation or reports.*

recalculation (p. 160) The process of recomputing values in a spreadsheet, either as an ongoing process as data is entered or afterward, with the press of a key. Why it's important: *With this simple feature, the hours of mind-numbing work required to manually rework paper spreadsheets have become a thing of the past.*

relational database (p. 162) Database in which data is organized into related tables. Each table contains rows and columns; the rows are called *records,* and the columns are called *fields.* An example of a record is a person's address—name, street address, city, and so on. An example of a field is that person's last name; another field would be that person's first name; a third field would be that person's street address; and so on. Why it's important: *The relational database is the most common type of database.*

rentalware (p. 147) Software that users lease for a fee and download whenever they want it. Why it's important: *This is the concept behind application service providers (ASPs).*

rollover (p. 128) Icon feature, also called a *tooltip,* in which a small text box explaining the icon's function appears when you roll the mouse pointer over the icon. A rollover may also produce an animated graphic. Why it's important: *The rollover gives the user an immediate explanation of an icon's meaning.*

saving (p. 157) Storing, or preserving, a document as an electronic file permanently—on hard disk, flash drive, CD, or online (in the cloud) for example. Why it's important: *Saving is a feature of nearly all application software. Having the document stored in electronic form spares users the tiresome chore of retyping it from scratch whenever they want to make changes. Users need only retrieve it from the storage medium and make the changes, then resave it and print it out again.*

scrolling (p. 153) Moving quickly upward, downward, or sideways through the text or other screen display. Why it's important: *A standard computer screen displays only 20–22 lines of standard-size text; however, most documents are longer than that. Using the directional arrow keys, or the mouse and a scroll bar located at the side of the screen, users can move ("scroll") through the display screen and into the text above and below it.*

shareware (p. 147) Copyrighted software that is distributed free of charge for a trial period but requires that users make a monetary contribution in order to continue using it. Shareware is distributed primarily through the Internet. Because it is copyrighted, you cannot use it to develop your own program that would compete with the original product. Why it's important: *Like public-domain software and freeware, shareware offers an inexpensive way to obtain new software.*

software license (p. 145) Contract by which users agree not to make copies of software to give away or resell. Why it's important: *Software manufacturers don't sell people software; they sell them licenses to become authorized users of the software.*

software suite (p. 164) Collection of individual programs bundled together in a single package. Why it's important: *Although there are suites for graphics, mathematics, and other applications, the most popular are* productivity suites, *also known as office suites, which are professional-level application programs frequently used in business—at a minimum word processing, spreadsheet, database management, and presentation programs. The best known productivity suite is Microsoft Office.*

special-purpose keys (p. 125) Keys used to enter, delete, and edit data and to execute commands. For example, the *Esc* (for "Escape") key tells the computer to cancel an operation or leave ("escape from") the current mode of operation. The Enter, or Return, key tells the computer to execute certain commands and to start new paragraphs in a document. Why it's important: *Special-purpose keys are essential to the use of software.*

spreadsheet program (p. 158) Application software that allows users to create tables and financial schedules by entering data and formulas into rows and columns arranged as a grid on a worksheet display screen. A spreadsheet file is called a workbook. Why it's important: *When data is changed in one cell, values in other cells in the linked worksheets are automatically recalculated.*

stand-alone operating system (p. 134) Often called a *desktop operating system;* operating system that works on a single desktop or notebook (laptop) computer. Why it's important: *Microsoft Windows is the most popular stand-alone operating system in use today, especially in offices. Among college students, the Apple Macintosh OS seems to be the most popular.*

supervisor (p. 118) Also called *kernel;* the central component of the operating system that manages the CPU. Why it's important: *The supervisor remains in main memory while the computer is running. As well as managing the CPU, it copies other nonresident programs into memory to perform tasks that support application programs.*

system software (p. 114) The software that runs at the most basic level of your computer and helps the computer to perform essential operating tasks and enables the application software to run. The most important component of system software is the *operating system,* the master control program that runs the computer. Examples of operating system software for the PC are various Microsoft programs (such as Windows 7 and 8), Apple Macintosh OS X, Unix, and Linux. Why it's important: *Computers cannot run application software without having system software.*

taskbar (p. 131) Graphic toolbar that appears at the bottom of the Windows screen. Why it's important: *The taskbar presents the applications that are running.*

template (p. 156) In word processing, a preformatted document that provides basic tools for shaping a final document—the text, layout, and style for a letter, for example. Why it's important: *Templates make it very easy for users to prepare professional-looking documents, because most of the preparatory formatting is done.*

title bar (p. 131) Bar across the very top of the display window. Why it's important: *It shows the name of the folder the user is in.*

toolbar (p. 131) Bar across the top of the display window, below the menu bar. It displays menus and icons representing frequently used options or commands. Why it's important: *Toolbars make it easier to identify and execute commands.*

Unix (p. 140) Proprietary multitasking operating system for multiple users that has built-in networking capability and versions that can run on all kinds of computers. Why it's important: *Government agencies, universities, research institutions, large corporations, and banks all use Unix for everything from designing airplane parts to currency trading. Unix is also used for website management. The developers of the Internet built their communication system around Unix because it has the ability to keep large systems (with hundreds of processors) churning out transactions day in and day out for years without fail.*

user interface (p. 124) User-controllable graphic display screen that allows the user to communicate, or interact, with his or her computer. Why it's important: *The interface determines the ease of use of hardware and software. The three types of user interface are command-driven, menu-driven, and graphical (GUI), which is now the most common. Without user interfaces, no one could operate a computer system.*

utility programs (p. 121) Also known as *service programs;* system software components that perform tasks related to the control, allocation, and maintenance of computer resources. Why it's important: *Utility programs enhance existing functions or provide services not supplied by other system software programs. Most computers come with built-in utilities as part of the system software; they usually include backup, data recovery, virus protection, data compression, and file defragmentation, along with disk cleanup.*

value (p. 159) A number or date entered in a spreadsheet cell. Why it's important: *Values are the actual numbers used in the spreadsheet—dollars, percentages, grade points, temperatures, or whatever.*

web application (app) (p. 147) Software that runs on a remote Internet server rather than on a person's own personal computer. Why it's important: *A web app is typically, but not always, accessed using a web browser. Here you can find word processing, spreadsheet, and email programs, often free, although some websites charge for access. Web apps are booming in popularity as cloud computing becomes more established.*

web page design/authoring software (p. 174) Software used to create web pages with sophisticated multimedia features. Why it's important: *Allows beginners as well as professional web designers to create web pages, which have become extremely important communications tools on the Internet, for all sorts of purposes.*

what-if analysis (p. 160) Spreadsheet feature that employs the recalculation feature to investigate how changing one or more numbers changes the outcome of the calculation. Why it's important: *Users can create a worksheet, putting in formulas and numbers, and then ask, "What would happen if we change that detail?"—and immediately see the effect.*

window (p. 131) Rectangular portion of the display on a computer screen. Through this rectangle users can view a file of data—such as a document, spreadsheet, or database—or an application program. Why it's important: *Using windows, users can display at the same time portions of several documents and/or programs on the screen.*

word processing software (p. 153) Application software that allows users to use computers to format, create, edit, print, and store text material, among other things. Why it's important: *Word processing software allows users to maneuver through a document and delete, insert, and replace text, the principal correction activities. It also offers such additional features as creating, editing, formatting, printing, and saving.*

word wrap (p. 153) Special feature that automatically continues text to the next line by "wrapping around" when the user reaches the right margin. Why it's important: *You don't have to hit a "carriage-return" key or Enter key to move to the next line.*

worksheet *See* **spreadsheet program.**

CHAPTER REVIEW

stage 1 LEARNING MEMORIZATION

"I can recognize and recall information."

Self-Test Questions

1. _____ software enables the computer to perform essential operating tasks.
2. _____ _____ is the term for programs designed to perform specific tasks for the user.
3. _____ is the activity in which a computer works on more than one process at a time.
4. _____ is the scattering of portions of files about the disk in nonadjacent areas, thus greatly slowing access to the files.
5. A(n) _____ is software that runs on a remote Internet server rather than on a person's own personal computer.
6. Windows and Mac OS are generally used on _____ computers.
7. _____ is the process of loading an operating system into a computer's main memory.
8. A(n) _____ is a utility that will find all the scattered files on your hard disk and reorganize them as contiguous files.
9. The _____ is the component of system software that comprises the master system of programs that manage the basic operations of the computer.
10. The _____ is the user-controllable display screen that allows you to communicate, or interact, with your computer.
11. Disk scanner and disk cleanup utilities detect and correct certain types of common problems on hard disks, such as removing unnecessary files called _____ files that are created by Windows only for short tasks and system restore after system problems.
12. OSs allow users to control access to their computers via use of a(n) _____ and a(n) _____.
13. Software or hardware that is _____ means that it is privately owned and controlled by a company.
14. Linux is _____ _____ software—meaning any programmer can download it from the Internet for free and modify it with suggested improvements.
15. When you power up a computer by turning on the power "on" switch, this is called a(n) _____ boot. If your computer is already on and you restart it, this is called a(n) _____ boot.
16. _____ software allows you to create and edit documents.
17. _____ is the activity of moving upward or downward through the text or other screen display.
18. Name four editing features offered by word processing programs:_____, _____, _____, _____.
19. In a spreadsheet, the place where a row and a column intersect is called a(n) _____.
20. The _____ is the movable symbol on the display screen that shows you where you may next enter data or commands.
21. When you buy software, you pay for a(n) _____, a contract by which you agree not to make copies of the software to give away or resell.
22. Records in a database are sorted according to a(n) _____.
23. _____ involves mixing text and graphics to produce high-quality output for commercial printing.
24. A(n) _____ allows users to create tables and do "what-if" financial analyses by entering data and formulas into rows and columns arranged as a grid on a display screen.
25. _____ automatically continues text to the next line when you reach the right margin.
26. Settings that are automatically used by a program unless the user specifies otherwise are called _____ _____.
27. _____ _____ software is not protected by copyright and may be copied by anyone.
28. _____ _____ are specialized software programs that allow input and output devices to communicate with the rest of the computer system.
29. The _____ format allows documents to be sent to almost any platform and be opened without losing any of their characteristics (text, colors, graphics, formatting).
30. _____ files contain software instructions; _____ files contain words, numbers, pictures, sounds, and so on.

Multiple-Choice Questions

1. Which of the following are functions of the operating system?
   a. file management
   b. CPU management
   c. task management
   d. booting
   e. all of these
2. Which of the following was the first major microcomputer OS?
   a. Mac OS
   b. Windows
   c. DOS
   d. Unix
   e. Linux
3. Which of the following is a prominent network operating system?
   a. Linux
   b. Microsoft Server

c. OES
d. DOS
e. Mac OS

4. Which of the following is the newest Microsoft Windows operating system?
   a. Windows Vista
   b. Windows 8
   c. Windows Server
   d. Windows OS
   e. Windows CE
5. Which of the following refers to the execution of two or more programs by one user almost at the same time on the same computer with one central processor?
   a. multitasking
   b. multiprocessing
   c. time-sharing
   d. multiprogramming
   e. coprocessing
6. Which of the following are specialized software programs that allow input and output devices to communicate with the rest of the computer system?
   a. multitasking
   b. boot disks
   c. utility programs
   d. device drivers
   e. service packs
7. Which of the following is *not* an advantage of using database software?
   a. integrated data
   b. improved data integrity
   c. lack of structure
   d. elimination of data redundancy
8. Which of the following is *not* a feature of word processing software?
   a. spelling checker
   b. cell address
   c. formatting
   d. cut and paste
   e. find and replace
9. What is the common consumer computer interface used today?
   a. command-driven interface
   b. graphical user interface
   c. menu-driven interface
   d. electronic user interface
   e. biometric user interface
10. _____ remove redundant elements, gaps, and unnecessary data from computer files so that less storage space is needed.
   a. maintenance utilities
   b. data compression utilities
   c. backup utilities
   d. data-recovery utilities
   e. multitasking utility
11. Which type of software can you download and duplicate without any restrictions whatsoever and without fear of legal prosecution?
   a. packaged software
   b. shareware
   c. public-domain software
   d. pirated software
   e. rentalware
12. Which of these is *not* a common file extension?
   a. .doc
   b. .nos
   c. .docx
   d. .xls
   e. .jpeg

True-False Questions

T F 1. The supervisor manages the CPU.

T F 2. The first graphical user interface was provided by Microsoft Windows.

T F 3. All operating systems are mutually compatible.

T F 4. *Font* refers to a preformatted document that provides basic tools for shaping the final document.

T F 5. Unix crashes often and thus is not normally used for running important large systems.

T F 6. Windows 7 is the most recent Microsoft OS.

T F 7. Spreadsheet software enables you to perform what-if calculations.

T F 8. Public-domain software is protected by copyright and so is offered for sale by license only.

T F 9. The records within the various tables in a database are linked by a key field.

T F 10. Adobe InDesign is a professional desktop-publishing program.

T F 11. The best-known graphical user interface is the command-driven one.

T F 12. Microsoft PowerPoint is an example of financial software.

T F 13. Drawing programs create vector images, and painting programs produce bit-mapped images.

T F 14. Data files are identified by file names.

T F 15. A software license is a contract by which users agree not to make copies of software to give away or resell.

Stage 2 LEARNING COMPREHENSION

"I can recall information in my own terms and explain it to a friend."

Short-Answer Questions

1. Briefly define *booting.*
2. What is the difference between a command-driven interface and a graphical user interface (GUI)?
3. Why can't you run your computer without system software?
4. Why is multitasking useful?
5. What is a device driver?
6. What is a utility program?
7. What is a platform?
8. What are the three components of system software? What is the basic function of each?
9. What is open-source software?
10. What does defragmenting do?
11. What is an embedded operating system?
12. What are the following types of application software used for?
    a. project management software
    b. desktop-publishing software
    c. database software
    d. spreadsheet software
    e. word processing software
13. Which program is more sophisticated, analytical graphics or presentation graphics? Why?
14. How are the following different from one another? Pop-up menu; pull-down menu; cascading menu.
15. What is importing? Exporting?
16. Briefly compare drawing programs and painting programs.
17. Explain what computer-aided design (CAD) programs do.

Stage 3 LEARNING APPLYING, ANALYZING, SYNTHESIZING, EVALUATING

"I can apply what I've learned, relate these ideas to other concepts, build on other knowledge, and use all these thinking skills to form a judgment."

Knowledge in Action

1. Here's a Windows 7 exercise in defragmenting your hard-disk drive. Defragmenting is a housekeeping procedure that will speed up your system and often free up hard-disk space.

   Click on the Start button at the bottom left corner of your screen. Click on All Programs, then Accessories, then System Tools, Disk Defragmenter. Click on the Analyze Disk button to find out how much of your hard disk is fragmented, and click on Defragment Disk to run the defragmentation utility.

   Many times when your PC isn't performing well, such as when it's sluggish, running both ScanDisk and Defragment will solve the problem.
2. Ray Kurzweil is, among other things, the author of *The Age of Intelligent Machines; The Age of Spiritual Machines: When Computers Exceed Human Intelligence;* and *The Singularity Is Near: When Humans Transcend Biology.* He has said: "We are entering a new era. I call it 'the Singularity.' It's a merger between human intelligence and machine intelligence that is going to create something bigger than itself. It's the cutting edge of evolution on our planet" (*www.edge.org/3rd_culture/kurzweil_singularity/kurzweil_singularity_index.html*). He envisions a future in which information technologies have advanced so far that they enable humans to transcend their biological limitations (*www.singularity.com*).

   What is "singularity"? Will it hurt? Will we hate it? Will we be able to notice it? Search the terms "Kurzweil" and "Singularity" on *www.singularity.com, www.kurzweilai.net*, and other sites, and see if you can explain the concept to friends within 5 minutes or so.
3. What do you think is the future of Linux? Experts currently disagree about whether Linux will become a serious competitor to Windows. Research Linux on the web. Which companies are creating application software to run on Linux? Which businesses are adopting Linux as an OS? What are the predictions about Linux use?
4. How do you think you will obtain software for your computer in the future? Explain your answer.
5. Design your own handheld. Draw what your ideal handheld would look like, and draw screens of what your user interface would look like. Describe the key features of your handheld.
6. What sorts of tasks do operating systems *not* do that you would like them to do?
7. If you were in the market for a new microcomputer today, what application software would you want to use on it? Why? What are some "dream" applications that you would like that have not yet been developed?
8. Several websites include libraries of shareware programs. Visit the *www.5star-shareware.com* site, and identify three shareware programs that interest you. State the name of each program, the operating system it runs on, and its capabilities. Also, describe the contribution you must make to receive technical support. What about freeware? Check out *www.freewarehome.com*.

9. What is your opinion of downloading free music from the web to play on your own computer and/or CDs? Much attention has been given lately to music downloading and copyright infringement. Research this topic in library magazines and newspapers or on the Internet, and take a position in a short report.
10. How do you think you could use desktop publishing at home? For personal items? Family occasions? Holidays? What else? What hardware and software would you have to buy?
11. Think of three new ways that software companies could prevent people from pirating their software.
12. What is your favorite application software program of all? Why?
13. Did your computer come with a Windows Startup disk, and have you misplaced it? If your computer crashes, you'll need this disk to reinstall the operating system.

    To learn the benefits of having a Startup disk, visit *www.microsoft.com*. Type *startup* in the "search for" box; then click on the links that interest you.

Web Exercises

1. Go to *http://list.driverguide.com/list/company243/* and identify the drivers that correspond to equipment you use. How does this website let you know which devices the drivers are for and which operating systems are compatible with them? If you own your own computer, go to the manufacturer's website and locate its resource for updating drivers. Does the manufacturer recommend any driver updates that you could use?
2. Use a web search tool such as Google or Yahoo! to find some online antivirus sites—sites where users can regularly download updates for their antivirus software. Do you know what kind of antivirus software is installed on your computer?
3. Microsoft offers "patches," or updates, for its Windows OS. Go to *www.microsoft.com* and search for the list of updates. What kinds of problems do these updates fix? Do you need any?
4. The History of Operating Systems: Visit the following websites to get an overview of the evolution and history of the theory and function of operating systems:

    www.microsoft.com/windows/winhistoryintro.mspx

    www.computinghistorymuseum.org/teaching/papers/research/history_of_operating_system_Moumina.pdf

    www.osdata.com/kind/history.htm

    www.answers.com/topic/history-of-operating-systems/
5. Some people are fascinated by the error message commonly referred to as the "Blue Screen of Death" (BSOD) or "Doom." Run a search on the Internet and find websites that sell T-shirts with the BSOD image on it, photo galleries of public terminals displaying the BSOD, fictional stories of BSOD attacks, and various other forms of entertainment based on the infamous error message.

    Do a search on the web to find users' hypotheses of why the BSOD occurs, and find methods to avoid it. Here are a few sites:

    www.maximumpc.com/article/features/blue_screen_survival_guide/

    http://bluescreenofdeathfixer.com/

    http://bsod.org/

    http://bbspot.com/News/2000/9/bsod_death.html

    http://technet.microsoft.com/en-us/library/cc750081.aspx
6. Using Microsoft Excel or another spreadsheet program, make a food shopping list incorporating the estimated price for each item, and then have Excel calculate the overall cost. Then go buy your groceries, and compare Excel's price with the supermarket's price. What else could Excel help you with?
7. The Windows operating system comes with a basic word processing program called *Wordpad*. Go to the Microsoft home page and to *http://en.wikipedia.org/wiki/WordPad/* and find out how Wordpad differs from Microsoft Word. Then use a keyword search in a search engine to get more information about these programs. Which one is right for you?
8. Curriculum Data Wales (CDW) is a public-private partnership that has been charged by the Welsh Assembly Government with the task of designing, building, and maintaining the National Grid for Learning Cymru as a bilingual service to schools and colleges in Wales. CDW's website includes some short tutorials on desktop-publishing (DTP), spreadsheet, word processing, and database management software:

    www.ngfl-cymru.org.uk/vtc-home/vtc-ks4-home/vtc-ks4-ict/vtc-ks4-ict-application_software.htm

    Work through the tutorials. Did they expand your knowledge of these applications?

    Do a search for *"application software & tutorials."* What other useful tutorials did you find?

4

HARDWARE: THE CPU & STORAGE

The Source of Computing Power

Chapter Topics & Key Questions

UNIT 4A: *Processing: The System Unit, Microprocessors, & Main Memory*

4.1 **Microchips, Miniaturization, & Mobility** What are the differences between transistors, integrated circuits, chips, and microprocessors?

4.2 **Representing Data Electronically** How is data represented in a computer, and what is machine language?

4.3 **Inside the System Unit: Power Supply, Motherboard, & Microprocessors** What are the important components of the system unit?

4.4 **The Central Processing Unit & the Machine Cycle** What are the parts of the CPU, and how do they work in the machine cycle?

4.5 **Memory** How do RAM, ROM, CMOS, and flash differ?

4.6 **Expansion Cards, Bus Lines, & Ports** How do expansion cards, bus lines, and ports give computers more versatility?

UNIT 4B: *Secondary Storage*

4.7 **Secondary Storage** What are the features of hard disks, optical disks, flash memory, smart cards, and cloud storage?

4.8 **Future Developments in Processing & Storage** What are some forthcoming developments that could affect processing power and storage capacity?

Download the free UIT 11e App for key term flash cards quizzes and a game, *Over the Edge*

CHAPTER FORECAST The first half of this chapter describes how a computer operates in processing data. We discuss transistors and microchips, show how data is represented electronically in the computer, explore the inside of the system unit—including the power supply, the motherboard, and microprocessors—and outline the operations of the central processing unit and the machine cycle. We then discuss the different kinds of main memory and conclude this unit by showing how expansion cards, bus lines, and ports give a computer more versatility.

In the second half of the chapter we describe the various devices used to store data before and after it is processed—hard disks, optical disks (CD, DVD, Blu-ray), flash and solid-state memory, smart cards, and cloud-based (online) storage.

UNIT 4A: *Processing: The System Unit, Microprocessors, & Main Memory*

Hybrids. Sliders. Convertibles. These are among the new milestones of the "post-PC era."

A slogan coined by the late Apple CEO Steve Jobs, the "post-PC era" embodied his prediction that personal computers (PCs) would endure but that people would tend to use smartphones and tablets for most of their computing needs.[1] Today, as sales of PCs have plummeted, computer manufacturers have scrambled to replace them with all kinds of other, more mobile devices—hybrids, sliders, and convertibles, as we explain.[2] (*See p. 196.*) Inside, however, the electronic circuitry is much the same. In this chapter we describe the two principal parts—*processing* and *storage.*

A *circuit* is a closed path followed or capable of being followed by an electric current. Without circuits, electricity would not be controllable, and so we would not have electric or electronic appliances. Old-time radios and computers used vacuum tubes—small lightbulb-size electronic tubes with glowing filaments, or wire circuits, inside them—to facilitate the flow of electrons. Eventually vacuum tubes were succeeded by transistors.

TECH TALES Vacuum Tubes Still Beat People Power

One computer with vacuum tubes, the ENIAC (Electronic Numerical Integrator And Computer; see Chapter 1, p. 15), was switched on in 1946 at the University of Pennsylvania and employed almost 18,000 of them. Unfortunately, a tube failure occurred on average once every 7 minutes. Since it took more than 15 minutes to find and replace the faulty tube, it was difficult to get any useful computing work done—during a typical week, ENIAC was down for about one-third of the time. Moreover, the ENIAC was enormous, occupying 1,800 square feet and weighing more than 50 tons.

ENIAC could perform about 5,000 calculations per second—more than 10,000 times *slower* than modern PCs. Yet even at that relatively slow speed, ENIAC took about 20 seconds to complete a problem that had taken experts 1 or 2 days to complete manually. (The 6 people who did most of the programming of ENIAC were women.)

ENIAC is now being displayed at the Smithsonian Institution in Washington, D.C. ■

4.1 MICROCHIPS, MINIATURIZATION, & MOBILITY

Since the early 1970s, microchips have gotten smaller and smaller yet more and more powerful and faster.

A transistor is essentially a tiny electrically operated switch, or gate, that can alternate between "on" and "off" many millions of times per second. The transistor was developed by Bell Labs in 1947. The first transistors were one-hundredth the size of a vacuum tube, needed no warm-up time, consumed less energy, and were faster and more reliable. (*• See Panel 4.1.*) Moreover, they marked the beginning of a process of miniaturization that has not ended yet. In 1960 one transistor fit into an area about a half-centimeter square. This was sufficient to permit Zenith, for instance, to market a transistor portable radio weighing about 1 pound (convenient, the company advertised, for "pocket or purse"). Since then, the number of transistors per unit area has been doubling every 1½ years, and today up to 3 billion transistors can be squeezed onto one computer chip. Still, scientists are working on new technologies that could make chips 1,000 times faster than those currently available.

Miniaturization Miracles: Microchips & Microprocessors

There are different kinds of microchips; the microprocessor is one.

In the old days, transistors were made individually and then formed into an electronic circuit with the use of wires and solder. Today transistors are part of an **integrated circuit—an entire electronic circuit, including wires, formed on a single "chip," or piece, of special material, usually silicon,** as part of a single manufacturing process. Integrated circuits were developed by Jack Kilby at Texas Instruments, who demonstrated the first one in 1958. (*• See the timeline, Panel 4.2, next page.*)

An integrated circuit embodies what is called solid-state technology. **In a solid-state device, the electrons travel through solid material with no moving parts**—in this case, silicon. They do not travel through a vacuum, as was the case with the old radio vacuum tubes.

panel 4.1

Shrinking circuit components

(*left*) The lightbulb-size 1940s vacuum tube was replaced in the 1950s by a transistor one-hundredth its size. Many of today's transistors are much smaller, being microscopic in size. (*right and bottom*) Typical transistors for a computer circuit board

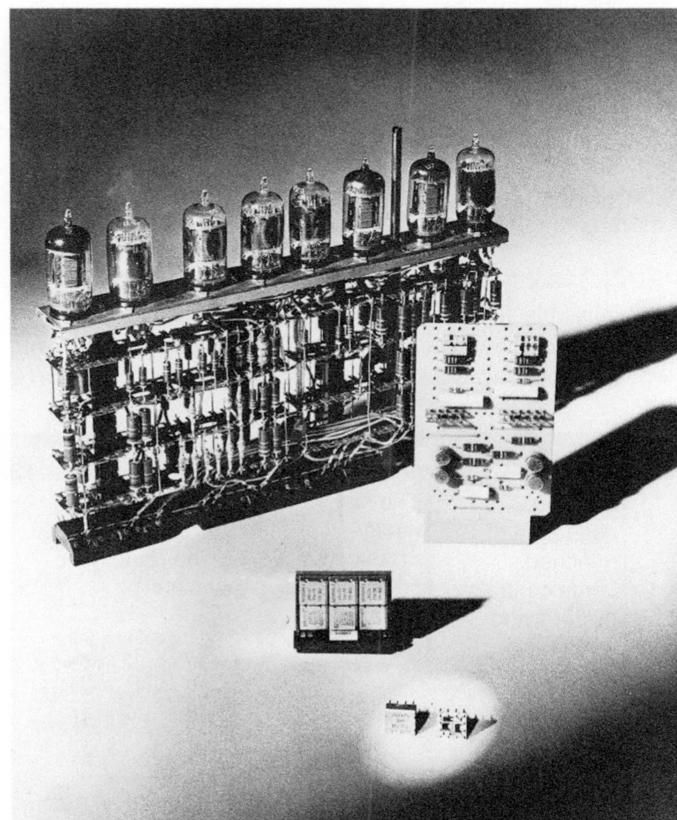

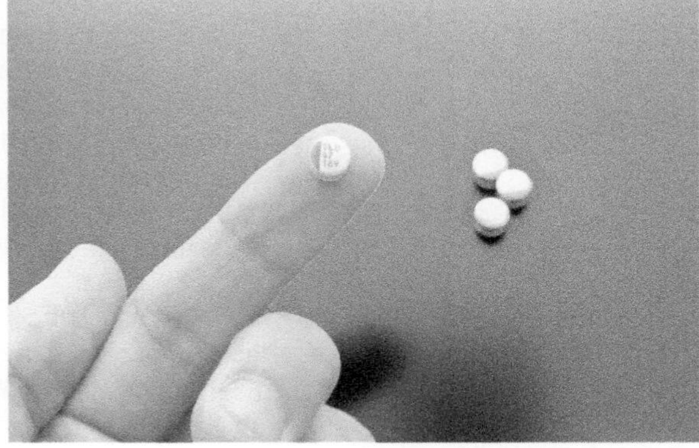

SILICON & SEMICONDUCTORS What is silicon, and why use it? **Silicon is an element that is widely found in clay and sand. It is used not only because its abundance makes it cheap but also because it is a semiconductor.**

A semiconductor is a material whose electrical properties are intermediate between a good conductor of electricity and a nonconductor of electricity. (An example of a good conductor of electricity is the copper in household wiring; an example of a nonconductor is the plastic sheath around that wiring.) Because it is only a semiconductor, silicon has partial resistance to electricity. As a result, highly conducting materials can be overlaid on the silicon to create the electronic circuitry of the integrated circuit.

Silicon alone has no processing power. **A chip, or *microchip,* is a tiny piece of silicon that contains millions of microminiature etched integrated electronic circuits.** Chip manufacturing requires very clean environments, which is why chip-manufacturing workers dress almost as though they are getting ready for a surgical operation. Such workers must also be highly skilled, which is why chip makers are not found everywhere in the world.

TECH TALES The Fabulous Fab—What Does It Take to Support a Chip Manufacturing Plant?

A chip manufacturing plant, known in the industry as a *fab* (for "fabricator"), can cost anywhere from $2 billion to $5 billion. Technology changes can be difficult, with the switch to smaller, more powerful chips for smartphones bringing with it costly problems.[3] Nevertheless, for a computer maker, having just one fab may not be enough. "To be a serious, profitable player in this business," says reporter Ashlee Vance, "you need several fabs and the orders to keep those factories humming all the time."[4]

If, however, you have your chip fabrication done by someone else, as Apple does, using Samsung to make chips for its iPhones and iPads, this can lead to some awkward arrangements. South Korea–based Samsung Electronics began making low-power chips for the iPhone, and after sales of the phone exploded, it invested in more and more factories to make the Apple chips. At the same time, it decided to compete *against* Apple by making and marketing its own smartphones and tablets.

Samsung's chip-making group has shown that it does not seem to talk to other parts of Samsung about customers' plans, as demonstrated by the fact that Samsung phones lag Apple's in key chip advances and component features. Nevertheless, we might expect Apple to shift to other chip suppliers in the near future. At that point, we will see whether Samsung has become so popular from sales of its own smartphones, tablets, and other devices that it can keep its fabs running all by itself. ■

THE MICROPROCESSOR: "PROCESSOR ON A CHIP" Microchips—"industrial rice," as the Japanese call them—are responsible for the miniaturization that has revolutionized consumer electronics, computers, and communications. They store and process data in all the electronic gadgetry we've become accustomed to—from microwave ovens to

panel 4.2

Timeline: Developments in processing and storage

3000 BCE	1621 CE	1642	1666	1801	1820	1833
Abacus is invented in Babylonia	Slide rule invented (Edmund Gunther)	First mechanical adding machine (Blaise Pascal)	First mechanical calculator that can add and subtract (Samuel Morland)	A linked sequence of punched cards controls the weaving patterns in Jacquard's loom	The first mass-produced calculator, the Thomas Arithnometer	Babbage's difference engine (automatic calculator)

smartphones, to music synthesizers, to cameras, to automobile fuel-injection systems, and to satellites.

There are different kinds of microchips—for example, microprocessor, memory, logic, communications, graphics, and math coprocessor chips. We discuss some of these later in this chapter. Perhaps the most important is the microprocessor chip. **A microprocessor ("microscopic processor" or "processor on a chip") is the miniaturized circuitry of a computer processor**—the CPU (central processing unit), the part that processes, or manipulates, data into information. When modified for use in machines other than computers, microprocessors are called *microcontrollers,* or *embedded computers.*

Computer chip design and manufacturing lab

Miniaturization Leads to Mobility

Microprocessors and microcontrollers have enabled mobility of electronic devices.

In the 1980s, portability, or mobility, meant trading off computing power and convenience in return for smaller size and less weight. Today, however, we are almost at the point where we don't have to give up anything. The result is that small, powerful, wireless personal electronic devices will probably transform our lives far more than the personal computer has done so far.

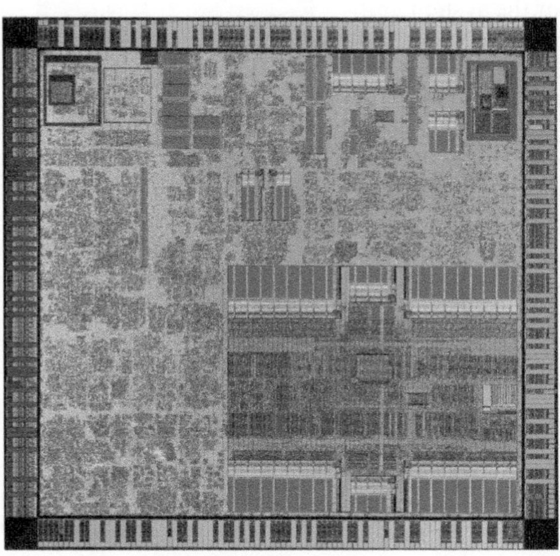

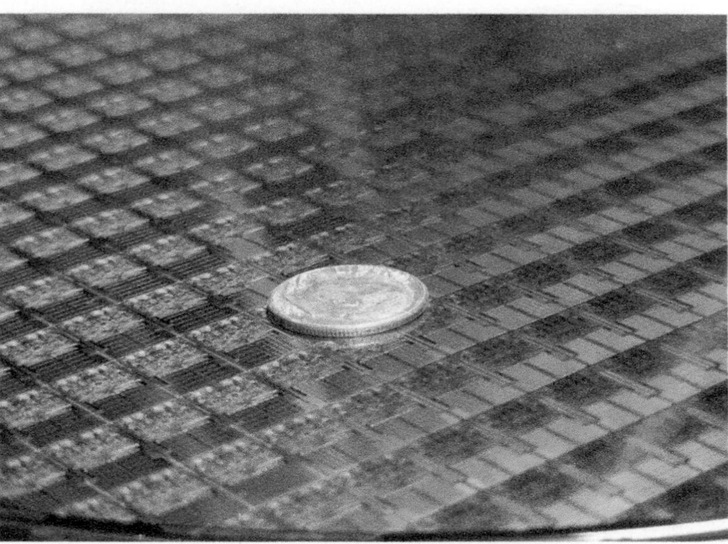

Chip with etched transistors. (*left*) This chip (magnified view) would be about ½ inch by ½ inch and be several layers deep, with transistors etched on each level. Chips are placed in sockets on a circuit board. (*right*) Chip's size relative to a dime

1843 World's first computer programmer, Ada Lovelace, publishes her notes

1854 George Boole publishes "An Investigation on the Laws of Thought," a system for symbolic and logical reasoning that will become the basis for computer design

1877 Thomas Edison invents the phonograph

1890 Electricity used for first time in a data-processing project – Hollerith's automatic census-tabulating machine (used punched cards)

1915 78 rpm record platters are introduced

more info!

Learning More about Computer Technology

Try the magazine *Smart Computing in Plain English* (*www.smartcomputing.com/DigitalReader/Default.aspx ? IssueName = SC_____ 2406 _____#1*). A more technical publication is *PC Magazine* (*www.pcmag.com*). See also:

www.gcflearnfree.org/computerbasics

www.webopedia.com

http://computer.howstuffworks.com

www.homeandlearn.co.uk

At *www.pcpitstop.com* you can get all sorts of information about testing your system's performance and improving it.

MacPro tower system

The System Unit

The system unit is a case that contains the computer's electronic components used to process data.

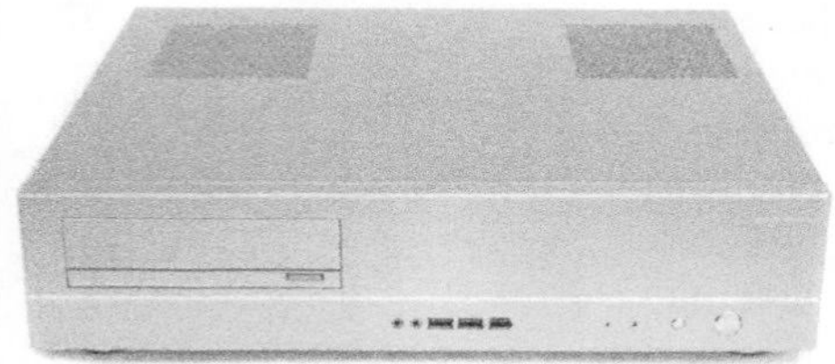

Desktop system unit

The system unit, also called the *chassis,* is the metal or plastic case housing a computer's electronic components used to process data. Among the types of system units are the following.

DESKTOP PC SYSTEM UNITS On a traditional desktop personal computer or a tower PC (one that sits on the floor), the processor and some secondary-storage devices appear inside the system unit. Such input and output devices as the keyboard, mouse, monitor, speakers, and microphone normally appear outside the system unit.

Tower system unit

LAPTOP & NETBOOK SYSTEM UNIT On laptop (notebook) computers, the monitor is attached by a hinge to the system unit, so it appears outside of it. However, other input devices, such as the keyboard and mouselike pointing device, are considered to be part of the system unit. The same is true of these components for netbook computers, which are smaller and less powerful than notebooks. Notebooks and netbooks with hinged screens are called *clamshells.* The term *ultrabook,* trademarked by Intel, is a particularly light kind of laptop.Notebook system unit, with keyboard and display screen

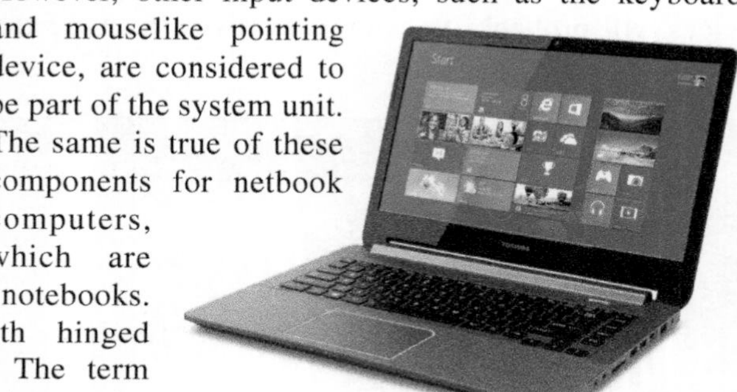

Laptop system unit, with keyboard and display screen

TABLET SYSTEM UNITS Most notebooks and netbooks started out with hardware keyboards, or traditional keyboards, but many are now made with *touch-screen* keyboards. A **tablet computer is a wireless, portable personal computer with a touch-screen interface.** Tablets, which are typically smaller than notebooks but larger than smartphones, are of three types:[5]

- **Slate tablets:** *Slate tablets* lack a hardware keyboard, and the display screen overlays the system unit. Examples of the slate style are Apple's iPad and Microsoft's Surface.
- **Convertible tablets:** Designed to be both a laptop and a tablet, a *convertible tablet* has a display that rotates 180 degrees and can be folded to close screen up over a hardware

1924	1930	1936	1944	1945	1946	1947
T.J. Watson renames Hollerith's machine company, founded in 1896, to International Business Machines (IBM)	General theory of computers (MIT)	Konrad Zuse develops the concept of a computer memory to hold binary information	First electro-mechanical computer (Mark I)	John von Neumann introduces the concept of a stored program	First programmable electronic computer in United States (ENIAC)	Magnetic tape enters the U.S. market; the first transistor is developed

keyboard on the outside of the system unit. Users may enter input not only through the hardware keyboard but via natural handwriting with a stylus or digital pen. An example of a convertible tablet is the Fujitsu LifeBook T580.

- **Hybrid tablets/PCs:** A *hybrid tablet* or *hybrid PC,* also known as a *detachable PC,* is like a regular notebook with a touchpad on the outside of the system unit, but it has a detachable display that functions independently as a slate. An example of a detachable is the Hewlett-Packard Envy x2. A variant on this arrangement is the *slider PC,* which has a screen that slides over the hardware keyboard on the outside of the system; this act turns the machine from a laptop to a tablet. An example of a slider is the Toshiba Satellite U925t.

Slate tablet

HANDHELD SYSTEM UNITS With handheld devices, such as smartphones, personal digital assistants, and e-books, all the electronic components are contained within the device, including display, secondary storage, and keyboard.

Regardless of the size and design of the system unit, all such devices have the same basic components. First, however, we need to look at how the system represents data electronically and processes it. We then consider the main parts of the computer: the computer case, the power supply, the motherboard and processor chip, and main memory. In the second half of this chapter, we consider *secondary-storage devices.* In Chapter 5, we look at *input devices* and *output devices.*

Sony Vaio hybrid tablet with a detachable display

4.2 REPRESENTING DATA ELECTRONICALLY

Data is represented in a computer by binary code.

Computers run on electricity. What is the most fundamental thing you can say about electricity? It is either *on* or *off.* This two-state situation allows computers to use the binary system to represent data and programs.

The Binary System: Using On/Off Electrical States to Represent Data & Instructions

The binary numeral system uses two numbers: 0 and 1.

The decimal system that we are accustomed to has 10 digits (0, 1, 2, 3, 4, 5, 6, 7, 8, 9). By contrast, the **binary system has only two digits: 0 and 1.** Thus, in the computer, the 0 can be represented by the electric current being off and the 1 by the current being on. Although the use of binary systems is not restricted to computers, *all data and program instructions that go into the computer are represented in terms of binary numbers.* *(• See Panel 4.3, next page.)*

For example, the letter "G" is a translation of the electronic signal 01000111, or off-on-off-off-off-on-on-on. When you press the key for "G" on the computer keyboard, the character is automatically converted into the series of electronic impulses that the computer

1947–1948	1949	1952	1954	1956	1958	1962	1963
Magnetic drum memory is introduced as a data storage device for computers	45 rpm record platters are introduced	UNIVAC computer correctly predicts election of Eisenhower as U.S. president	Texas Instruments introduces the silicon transistor	First computer hard disk is used	Stereo records are produced	Integrated circuit is nicknamed the "chip"; timesharing becomes common	The American National Standards Institute accepts ASCII-7 code for information exchange

panel 4.3

Binary data representation

How the letters "G-R-O-W" are represented in one type of on/off, 1/0 binary code

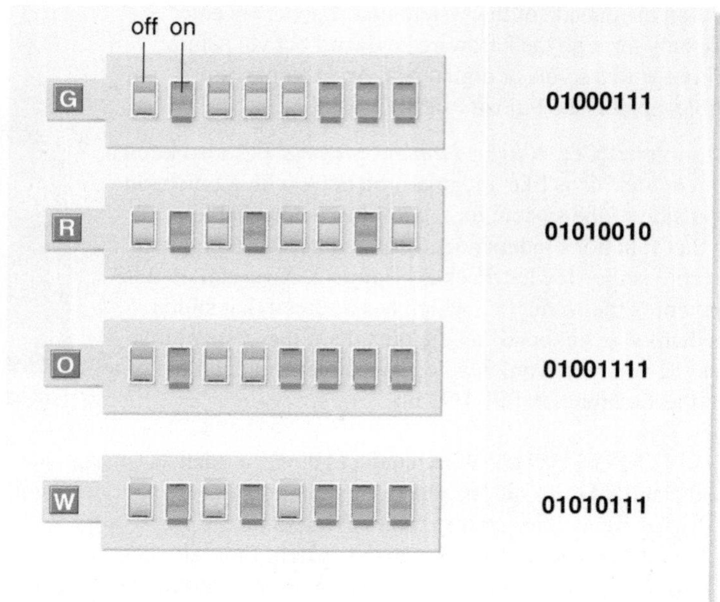

can recognize. Inside the computer, the character "G" is represented by a combination of eight transistors. Some are off, or closed (representing the 0s), and some are on, or open (representing the 1s).

MEASURING CAPACITY How many representations of 0s and 1s can be held in a computer or a storage device such as a hard disk? As we mentioned in Chapter 1 (p. 31), capacity is denoted by *bits* and *bytes* and multiples thereof—kilobytes, megabytes, gigabytes, and so on:

- **Bit:** In the binary system, **each 0 or 1 is called a bit, which is short for "binary digit."**
- **Byte:** To represent letters, numbers, or special characters (such as ! or *), bits are combined into groups. **A group of 8 bits is called a byte, and a byte represents one character, digit, or other value.** (As we mentioned, in one scheme, 01000111 represents the letter "G.")
- **Kilobyte: A kilobyte (K, KB) is about 1,000 bytes.** (Actually, it's precisely 1,024 bytes.) 1 KB = about one-half page of text; 10 KB = about 1 encyclopedia page. The kilobyte was a common unit of measure for memory or secondary-storage capacity on older computers.
- **Megabyte: A megabyte ("meg"; M, MB) is about 1 million bytes** (1,048,576 bytes). 1 MB = about 768 pages of text; 100 MB = about 2 encyclopedia volumes. Measures of some secondary-storage devices are expressed in megabytes.
- **Gigabyte: A gigabyte ("gig"; G, GB) is about 1 billion bytes** (1,073,741,824 bytes). 1 GB = about 786,432 pages of text; 20 GB = an audio collection of the

1964	1965	1968	1969	1970
IBM introduces 360 line of computers; IBM's seven-year-long Sabre project, allowing travel agents anywhere to make airline reservations via terminals, is fully implemented; Control Data Corp.'s CDC 6600, designed by Seymour Cray, becomes the first commercially successful supercomputer	Audio cassette tape introduced; Gordon Moore pronounces "Moore's Law"	Robert Noyce, Andy Grove, and Gordon Moore establish Intel, Inc.	Klass Compaan conceives idea for CD	Microprocessor chips come into use; floppy disk introduced for storing data; a chip 1/10 inches square contains 1,000 transistors; the first and only patent on the smart card is filed

Inside a Google data center

complete works of Beethoven. Formerly used mainly with mainframe computers, this measure is typical of the secondary-storage (hard-disk, flash disk) capacity and main memory (RAM) of today's microcomputers.

- **Terabyte: A terabyte (T, TB) represents about 1 trillion bytes** (1,009,511,627,776 bytes). 1 TB = about 500,000,000 pages of text; 2 TB = the contents of 1 academic research library. As of May 2013, the U.S. Library of Congress has collected about 422 TB of web archive data. The web archives grow at a rate of about 5 TB per month (*www.loc.gov/webarchiving/faq.html*).
- **Petabyte: A petabyte (P, PB) represents about 1 quadrillion bytes** (1,048,576 gigabytes). 2 PB = about the contents of all U.S. academic research libraries. The huge storage capacities of modern databases are expressed in petabytes; Google data centers process more than 24 PB per day.
- **Exabyte: An exabyte (EB) represents about 1 quintillion bytes**—that's *1 billion billion* bytes (1,024 petabytes—or 1,152,921,504,606,846,976 bytes). Google's servers contain about 1 EB of data.
- **And:** yottabye, xenottabyte, shilentnobyte, domegemegrottebyte, icosebyte, monoicosebyte.

What Is the Memory Capacity of the Human Brain?

www.scientificamerican.com/article.cfm?id=what-is-the-memory-capacity

www.slate.com/articles/health_and_science/explainer/2012/04/north_korea_s_2_mb_of_knowledge_taunt_how_many_megabytes_does_the_human_brain_hold_.html

BINARY CODING SCHEMES Letters, numbers, and special characters are represented within a computer system by means of binary coding schemes. *(• See Panel 4.4, next page.)* That is, the off/on 0s and 1s are arranged in such a way that they can be made to represent characters, digits, or other values.

1971	1972	1973	1974	1975	1976	1978
First pocket calculator; the Intel 4004 micro-processor is developed—a "computer on a chip"	Intel 8008 8-bit micro-processor	Large-scale integration: 10,000 components are placed on a 1-sq.-cm. chip	A DRAM chip becomes available	First micro-computer (MITS Altair 8800)	Apple I computer (first personal computer sold in assembled form); has 512 KB RAM	5¼" floppy disk; Atari home videogame; Intel's first 16-bit microprocessor, the 8086, debuts

Character	ASCII	Character	ASCII
A	0100 0001	N	0100 1110
B	0100 0010	O	0100 1111
C	0100 0011	P	0101 0000
D	0100 0100	Q	0101 0001
E	0100 0101	R	0101 0010
F	0100 0110	S	0101 0011
G	0100 0111	T	0101 0100
H	0100 1000	U	0101 0101
I	0100 1001	V	0101 0110
J	0100 1010	W	0101 0111
K	0100 1011	X	0101 1000
L	0100 1100	Y	0101 1001
M	0100 1101	Z	0101 1010
0	0011 0000	5	0011 0101
1	0011 0001	6	0011 0110
2	0011 0010	7	0011 0111
3	0011 0011	8	0011 1000
4	0011 0100	9	0011 1001
!	0010 0001	;	0011 1011

panel 4.4

Binary coding scheme: ASCII. This chart shows uppercase (capital) letters; lowercase letters have different codes.

- **ASCII:** Pronounced "*ask*-ee," **ASCII (American Standard Code for Information Interchange) is the binary code most widely used on microcomputers in English and Western European languages.** In the principal version, ASCII uses 8 bits (1 byte) for each character. Besides having the more conventional characters, the version known as Extended ASCII includes such characters as math symbols and Greek letters. ASCII's 256 characters, however, are not enough to handle such languages as Chinese and Japanese, with their thousands of characters.
- **Unicode:** Developed in the early 1990s, **Unicode uses 2 bytes for each character, rather than 1 byte.** Instead of having the 256 character combinations of Extended ASCII, Unicode can handle 65,536 character combinations. Thus, it allows almost all the written languages of the world to be represented using a single character set.
- **EBCDIC:** Pronounced "*eb*-see-dick," **EBCDIC (Extended Binary Coded Decimal Interchange Code) is a binary code used with large IBM and IBM-compatible computers, such as mainframes.** It was developed in 1963–1964 by IBM and uses 1 byte for each character.

Machine Language

Machine code is the computer's "native language."

Every brand of microprocessor has its own binary language, called *machine language.* **Machine language is a binary-type programming language built into the processor (CPU) that the computer can run directly.** The machine language is specific to the particular processor model; this is why, for example, most software written for a Macintosh will not run on a PC. To most people, an instruction written in machine language, consisting only of 0s and 1s, is incomprehensible. To the computer, however, the 0s and 1s represent precise storage locations and operations.

How do people-comprehensible program instructions become computer-comprehensible machine language? Special system programs called *language translators* rapidly convert the instructions into machine language. This translating occurs virtually instantaneously, so you are not aware it is happening.

Want to Learn How to Count in Binary?

Try playing the Cisco Binary game at:

http://forums.cisco.com/CertCom/game/binary_game_page.htm

4.3 INSIDE THE SYSTEM UNIT: Power Supply, Motherboard, & Microprocessors

The system unit is the main part of a computer system.

Whatever the type of computer you favor, the components can be best understood by looking at the inside of a microcomputer.

1979	1981	1982	1983	1984	1985
Motorola introduces the 68000 chip, which later will support the Mac	IBM introduces personal computer (with 8088 CPU and 16 KB RAM)	Portable computers	The capacity of floppy disks is expanded to 360 KB; CDs are introduced to U.S. market	Apple Macintosh; first personal laser printer; Sony and Philips introduce the CD-ROM; Intel's 80286 chip is released	Intel's 80386 32-bit micro-processor is introduced

Bays, Buttons, & Boards

The system unit houses the essential parts of the computer.

The *system unit* houses the power supply; the motherboard, with its microprocessor chip and memory chips; and storage devices. (• *See Panel 4.5, next page.*) In computer ads, the part of the system unit that is the empty box with just the power supply is called the *case* or *system cabinet.* For today's desktop PC, the system unit may be advertised as something like a "2-bay mini-tower case." A *bay* is a shelf or an opening used for the installation of electronic equipment, generally storage devices such as a hard drive or DVD drive. Empty bays are covered by a panel.

A *tower* is a cabinet that is tall, narrow, and deep, so that it can sit on the floor beside or under a table, rather than short, wide, and deep. Originally a full tower was considered to be 24 inches high. Mini- (micro) and mid-towers are smaller. At 6.5 inches square and 2 inches high, the Mac mini is the smallest desktop microcomputer.

The number of buttons on the outside of the computer case will vary, but the on/off power switch will appear somewhere, probably on the front. Inside the case—not visible unless you remove the cabinet—are various electric circuit boards, chief of which is the motherboard, as we discuss.

Front and back of a Mac Pro Mini, the smallest desktop system unit

Power Supply

The power supply unit provides power for the motherboard and other main components of the computer.

The electricity available from a standard wall outlet is alternating current (AC), but a microcomputer runs on direct current (DC). **The power supply is a device that converts AC to DC to run the computer.** The on/off switch in your computer turns on or shuts off the electricity to the power supply. Because electricity can generate a lot of heat, a fan inside the computer keeps the power supply and other components from becoming too hot.

Electric power drawn from a standard AC outlet can be quite uneven. For example, a sudden surge, or "spike," in AC voltage can burn out the low-voltage DC circuitry in your computer ("fry the motherboard"). Instead of plugging your computer directly into a wall electric outlet, it's a good idea to plug it into a power protection device. The three principal types are surge protectors, voltage regulators, and UPS units.

SURGE PROTECTOR A *surge protector,* or *surge suppressor,* is a device that protects a computer from being damaged by surges (spikes) of high voltage. The computer is plugged into the surge protector, which in turn is plugged into a standard electric outlet. (*See the Practical Action box on page 205.*)

iGo Surge protector

UPS A *UPS (uninterruptible power supply)* is a battery-operated device that provides a computer with electricity if there is a power failure. The UPS will keep a computer going for 5–30 minutes or more. It goes into operation as soon as the power to your computer fails. UPSs usually also operate *voltage regulators,* which protect a computer from being damaged by insufficient power—"brownouts" or "sags" in voltage. Brownouts can occur when a large machine such as a power tool starts up and causes the lights in your house to dim. They also may occur on very hot summer days

1986
The 3½" diskette is introduced for the Mac and becomes popular for the PC as well

1988
Motorola's 32-bit 88000 series of RISC microprocessors is introduced

1989
Double-sided, double-density floppy disks come on the market, increasing the 5¼" diskette to 1.2 MB and the 3½" diskette to 1.4 MB; Intel's 80486 chip with 1.2 million transistors is introduced; first portable Mac

1990
Motorola's 68040 and Intel's 1486 chips are released

panel 4.5

The system unit for a tower PC

Interior view of the box, or case. It includes the power supply, motherboard, and storage devices. (The arrangement of the components varies among models.)

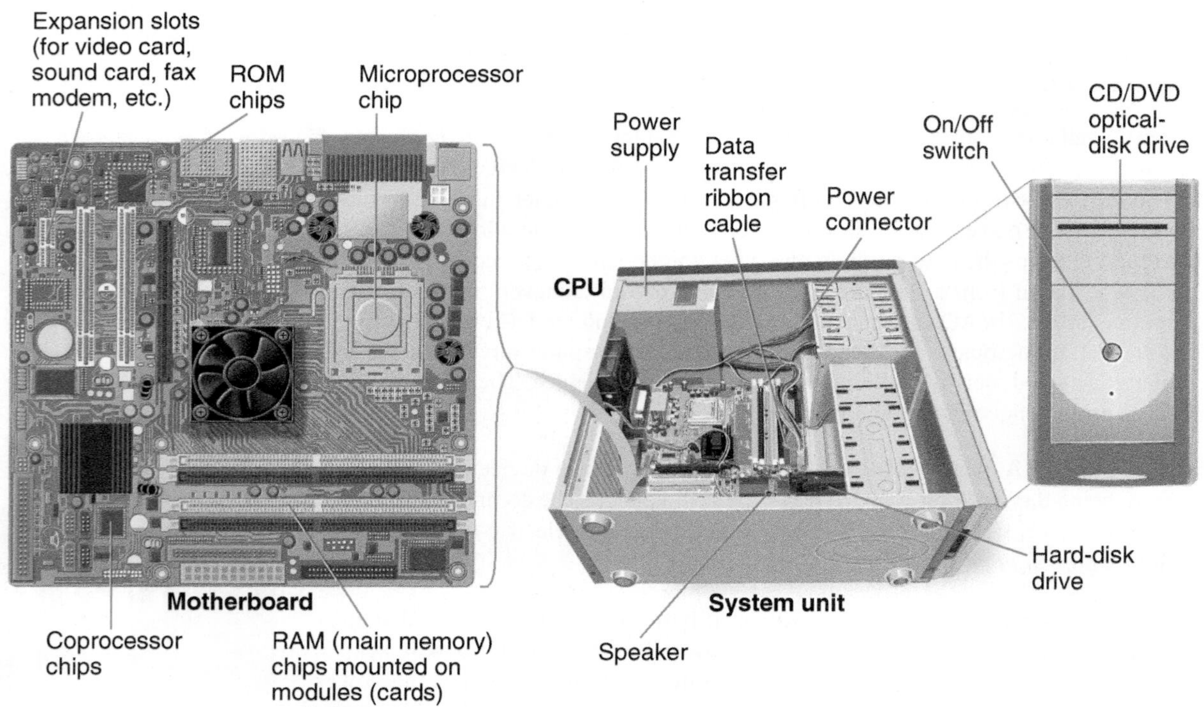

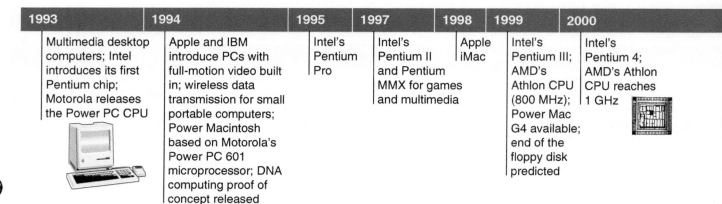

1993	1994	1995	1997	1998	1999	2000
Multimedia desktop computers; Intel introduces its first Pentium chip; Motorola releases the Power PC CPU	Apple and IBM introduce PCs with full-motion video built in; wireless data transmission for small portable computers; Power Macintosh based on Motorola's Power PC 601 microprocessor; DNA computing proof of concept released	Intel's Pentium Pro	Intel's Pentium II and Pentium MMX for games and multimedia	Apple iMac	Intel's Pentium III; AMD's Athlon CPU (800 MHz); Power Mac G4 available; end of the floppy disk predicted	Intel's Pentium 4; AMD's Athlon CPU reaches 1 GHz

when the power company has to lower the voltage in an area because too many people are running their air conditioners all at once. UPSs also act as surge protectors.

Power supply units are often rated in *joules,* named after a 19th-century English physicist. The higher the number of joules, the better the power protection. (One hundred joules of energy keep a 100-watt light going for 1 second.)

UPS

The Motherboard & the Microprocessor Chip

The motherboard is the computer's central printed circuit board.

As we mentioned in Chapter 1, the *motherboard,* or *system board,* is the main circuit board in the system unit. The motherboard consists of a flat board that fills one side of the case. It contains both soldered, nonremovable components and sockets or slots for components that can be removed—microprocessor chip, RAM chips, and various expansion cards, as we explain later. (• *See Panel 4.6, next page.*)

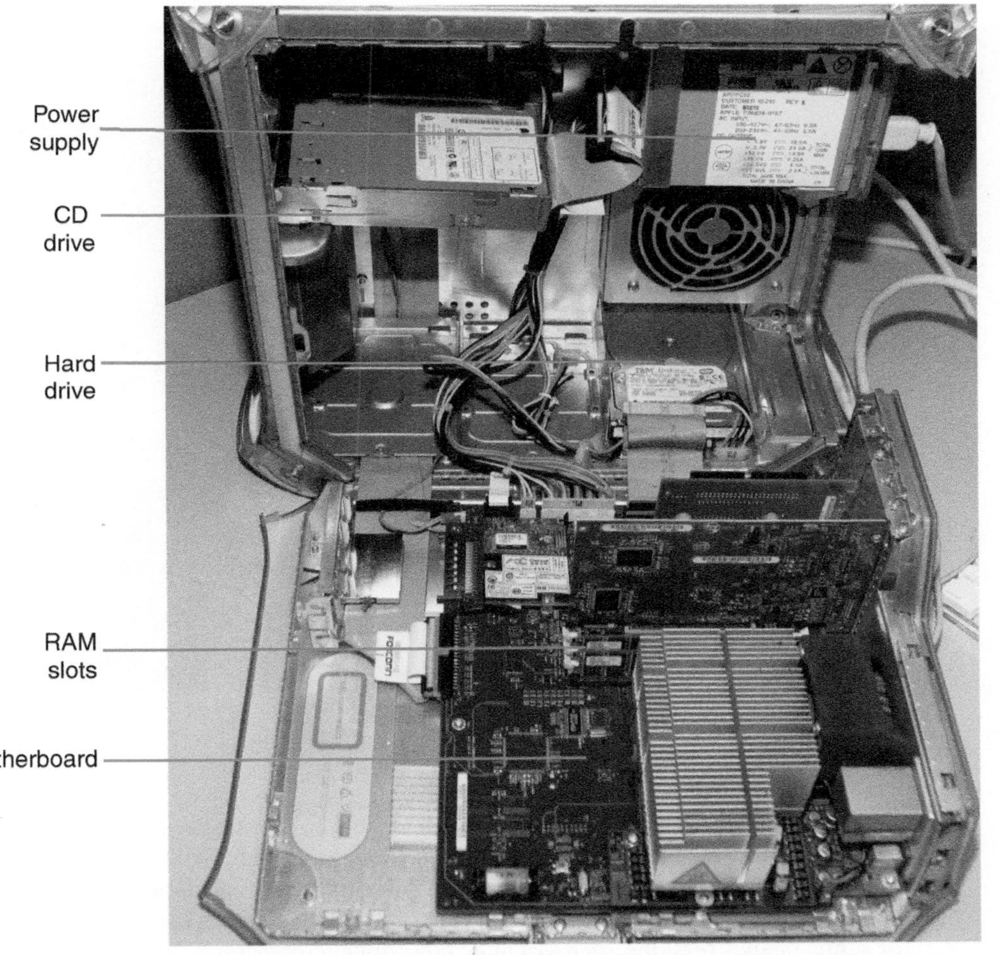

Mac motherboard (*Mark Dierker*)

2001	2002	2003	2004	2005	2006	2009
Pentium 4 reaches 2 GHz; USB 2.0 is introduced	Pentium 4 reaches 3.06 GHz; Power Mac has 2 1-GHz Power PC CPUs; about 1 billion PCs have been shipped worldwide since the mid-70s	Intel's Pentium M/Centrino for mobile computing; 64-bit processors	Intel Express chipsets for built-in sound and video capabilities (no cards needed); IBM sells its PC computing division to Lenovo Group	Perpendicular recording for disk drives	Intel and AMD introduce dual-core processors; 64-bit processors enter the market	Multicore processors

panel 4.6

The motherboard and an expansion card

This example of a motherboard (*top*) offers slots or sockets for removable components: microprocessor chip, RAM chips, and various expansion cards, such as that shown below.

Making some components removable allows you to expand or upgrade your system. **Expansion is a way of increasing a computer's capabilities by adding hardware to perform tasks that are beyond the scope of the basic system.** For example, you might want to add video and sound cards. **Upgrading means changing to newer, usually more powerful or sophisticated versions,** such as a more powerful microprocessor or more memory chips.

2010	2013	2015?	2017?	2025?	2030	2030–2045
$1,000 buys a computer working at 10 quadrillion calculations per second; USB 3.0 available	Speech-to-speech translation available in cellphones	Microcomputer storage in zettabytes; batteries that charge in seconds	Use of bacteria for processing and storage DNA computer; desktop computer as fast as human brain	Computers are able to simulate the entire human brain	$1,000 buys a computer more powerful than the human brain	The point of "singularity" is reached, when technical progress is so fast that unenhanced human intelligence can't follow it

PRACTICAL ACTION

Power Issues: Problems with Electric Power to Your Computer

Ben Veligdan, a Brooklyn, New York, music teacher, wondered why his monthly electricity bill exceeded $100 a month when his household consisted only of him, his wife, and his cat. Then he looked around his modest one-bedroom apartment and thought, Could it be the computer? When he decided to unplug it while he was sleeping or not working, his electricity bill fell almost immediately.[6]

You need power to run your computer, of course, but electricity can be very problematic: Leaving a computer turned on all the time is expensive, even in standby mode—because of "vampire power," the electric power consumed by electronic appliances while they are switched off or in a standby mode. Sudden power surges can devastate your hardware. Sudden power drops can wipe out your data.

Here are a few things you can do to deal with these problems:

- ***To reduce your electricity bill, disconnect your computer when you're not using it for a significant length of time:*** It's not just your computer. Many electronic gadgets—cellphone chargers, microwave ovens, and so on—drain electricity when they're not being used. Indeed, it amounts to 5%–10% every year in American homes.[7] Leaving PCs on overnight costs U.S. companies $2.8 billion a year.[8] Devices are coming to market that can detect when an appliance is in standby mode (not working). But you can plug your computer into a UPS (uninterruptible power supply) unit, so that you can turn off the on/off switch when your PC is not in use.
- ***If a laptop's heat on your thighs is uncomfortable, put it on a "cool tray" ("chill pad"):*** A computer on your lap can generate heat that can quickly make you uncomfortable. Some companies now offer pads and so-called cool trays ($30–$50) with fans or pads made from special materials that you can slide under your laptop and can cool off both the machine and your lap.
- ***Back up data regularly:*** You should faithfully make backup (duplicate) copies of your data every few minutes as you're working. Then, if your computer has power problems, you'll be able to get back in business fairly quickly once the machine is running again.
- ***Use a surge protector to protect against too much electricity:*** Plug all your hardware into a surge protector/voltage regulator, which will prevent damage to your equipment if there is a power surge. (You'll know you've experienced a power surge when the lights in the room suddenly get very bright.) Surge protectors cost $10–$35. (Note that surge protectors will not help you in case of a close-by lightning strike; in severe storms, unplug everything.)
- ***Use a UPS to protect against brownouts and power failures***: Consider plugging your computer into a UPS, (available at electronics stores for $35–$200). It will keep your computer running long enough (5–30 minutes) for you to save your data before you turn off the machine. It also acts as a surge protector.
- ***Turn ON highest-power-consuming hardware first:*** When you turn on your computer system, you should turn on the devices that use the most power first. This will avoid causing a power drain on smaller devices. The most common advice is to turn on (1) printer, (2) other external peripherals, (3) system unit, (4) monitor—in that order.
- ***Turn OFF lowest-power-consuming hardware first:*** When you turn off your system, follow the reverse order. This avoids a power surge to the smaller devices.
- ***Unplug your computer system during lightning storms:*** Unplug all your system's components—including phone lines—during electrical (thunder/lightning) storms. If lightning strikes your house or the power lines, it can ruin your equipment.

THE MICROPROCESSOR CHIP Once upon a time, the processor in a computer was measured in feet. A processing unit in the 1946 ENIAC (which had 20 such processors) was about 2 feet wide and 8 feet high. Today, as we have said, computers are based on *micro*processors, less than 1 centimeter square.

The motherboard may be thought of as your computer's central nervous system. The brain of your computer is the microprocessor chip. As we described in Chapter 1, a *microprocessor* is the miniaturized circuitry of a computer processor, contained on a small silicon chip. It stores program instructions that process, or manipulate, data into information.

- **Transistors—key parts of a chip:** The key parts of the microprocessor are transistors. *Transistors,* we said, are tiny electronic devices that act as on/off switches, which

(*left*) AMD 690G chipset;
(*right*) schematic of a chipset

process the on/off (1/0) bits used to represent data. According to *Moore's law,* named for legendary Intel cofounder Gordon Moore, the number of transistors that can be packed onto a silicon chip doubles about every two years, while the price stays the same, which has enabled the industry to shrink the size and cost of things such as computers and cellphones while improving their performance.[9]

- **The chipset—chips for controlling information among system components: The chipset consists of groups of interconnected chips on the motherboard that are designed to work together to control the flow of information between the microprocessor and other system components connected to the motherboard.** The chipset determines what types of processors (along with memory and video card ports, as we describe) will work on the same motherboard. It also establishes the types of multimedia, storage, network, and other hardware the motherboard supports.

TRADITIONAL MICROCOMPUTER MICROPROCESSORS The leading microprocessor makers today are Intel, AMD, IBM, Nvidia, and Motorola.

- **Intel-type processors for microcomputers—Intel and AMD chips:** Most PCs use microprocessors manufactured by Intel Corporation or Advanced Micro Devices (AMD). Indeed, the Microsoft Windows operating system was designed to run on Intel chips. **Intel-type chips have a similar internal design and are made to run microcomputers.** They are used by manufacturers such as Dell, Lenovo, Toshiba, and Hewlett-Packard in their PC microcomputers. They are also now used in Macs, so that they can run both Microsoft- and Apple-based programs by supporting both Mac OS X and Windows.

- **Multicore processors for PCs—dual (2), quad (4), hexa (6), and octa (8) core:** "You'll be typing along on an email when suddenly the PC stops responding to your keystrokes, then catches up a few seconds later," wrote *BusinessWeek*'s Stephen Wildstrom. "Or a program that used to load in a few seconds inexplicably takes three times as long. Processors are faster than ever, but the demands of even routine computing are overwhelming them."[10]

  The reason computers bog down is that, as Wildstrom explained, "no matter how fast a processor runs, it can do only one thing at a time." Adding more transistors doesn't help, because they generate too much heat. Enter **the multicore processor,**

designed to let the operating system divide the work over more than one processor, with two or more processor "cores" on a single piece of silicon.

The concept is not new; large computer systems, such as Japan's K supercomputer, feature many more than 80,000 multicore processors working in unison. The beauty of having two or more cores is that chips can take on several tasks at once, eliminating the annoying pauses that Wildstrom mentioned. For multicore processors to operate effectively, computers must employ *parallel processing,* using special software that divides problems into portions for each processor to work on and that brings the results back together again.

Common multicore processors for microcomputers today are *dual-core processors* (two cores—for example, AMD Phenom II X2, Intel Core Duo), *quad-core processors* (four cores—for instance, AMD Phenom II X4 and the Intel "Bay Trail" Atom processor), *hexa-core processors* (six cores—for example, AMD Phenom II X6, Intel Core i7 Extreme Edition 980X), and *octa-core processors* (for example, AMD Opteron 6100 series 6128, Intel Xeon E5-2450). The Intel Tri-Gate (3D) transistor, used in Intel's Atom line of microprocessors, has doubled the transistor count in the same area space, thus making Tri-Gate chips even faster than multicore transistors.[11]

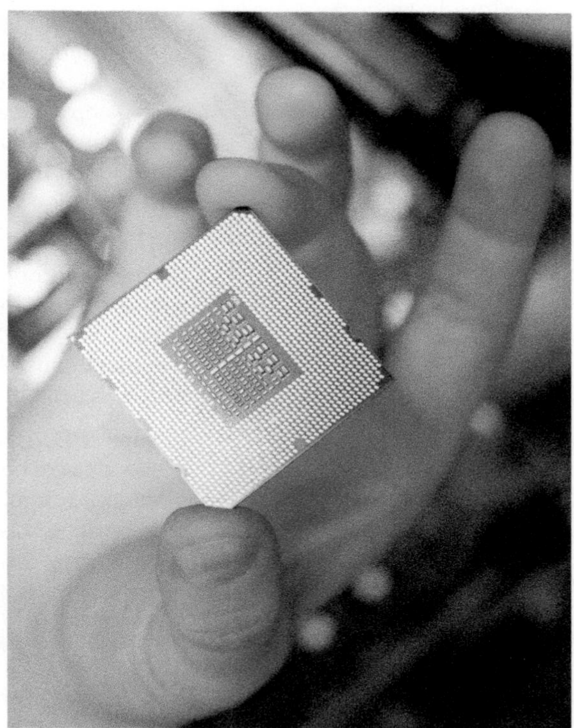

Intel i7 quadcore microprocessor

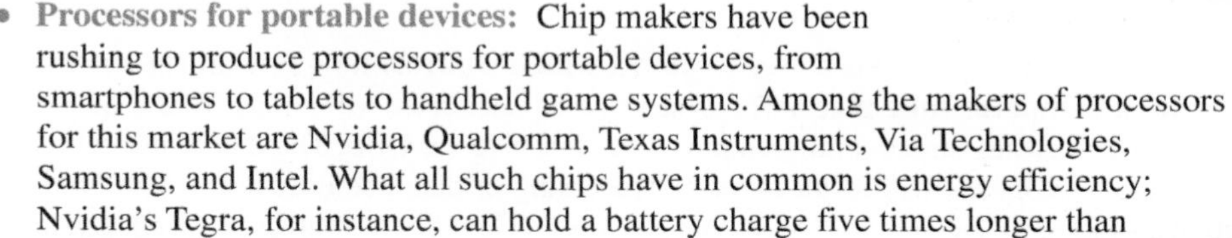

- **Processors for portable devices:** Chip makers have been rushing to produce processors for portable devices, from smartphones to tablets to handheld game systems. Among the makers of processors for this market are Nvidia, Qualcomm, Texas Instruments, Via Technologies, Samsung, and Intel. What all such chips have in common is energy efficiency; Nvidia's Tegra, for instance, can hold a battery charge five times longer than Intel's Atom.

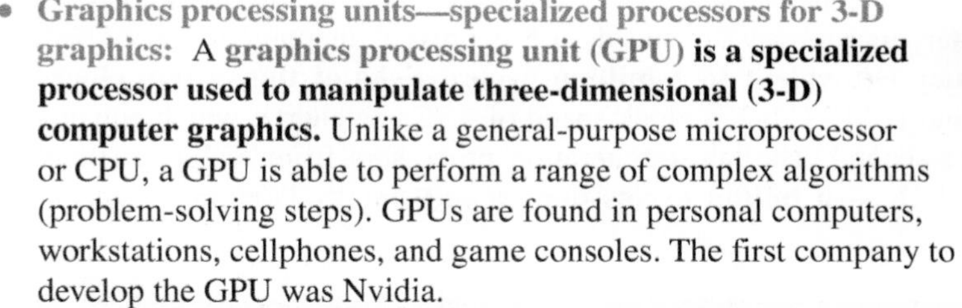

- **Graphics processing units—specialized processors for 3-D graphics:** A **graphics processing unit (GPU) is a specialized processor used to manipulate three-dimensional (3-D) computer graphics.** Unlike a general-purpose microprocessor or CPU, a GPU is able to perform a range of complex algorithms (problem-solving steps). GPUs are found in personal computers, workstations, cellphones, and game consoles. The first company to develop the GPU was Nvidia.

  Some GPUs are integrated into the motherboard; high-powered GPUs are on the video cards and have their own RAM.

Graphics processing unit

- **Processors for data centers:** "With more than 33 million servers in the world," says a spokesperson for IBM, "cooling the computers is an acute problem. Most data centers use 25% of their total energy to simply cool their machines."[12] A **data center, or *datacenter,* sometimes called a *server farm,* is a facility that holds servers and related network equipment.** Such facilities, which may be employed by search engines or cloud computing providers, may hold anywhere from dozens to thousands of rack-mounted servers, and their biggest problem is that they give off a phenomenal amount of heat. "A single location can slurp as much power as a medium-size town, or about 10.5 million watts," says one researcher.[13] As a result, energy-efficient chips once used exclusively in cellphones are now making their way into data centers.

TECH TALES Where Are Data Centers Located?

Some data centers are located close to their power source, such as secluded sites in Oregon near the power generators on the Columbia River, where Google, Yahoo!, Facebook, and Amazon have built enormous server farms.[14] Others may be right near your neighborhood.

Green Server Farms?

"If the Internet were a country, it would be in fifth place for using energy and producing greenhouse gas" (*www.mnn.com*). What is being done to conserve server-farm energy use and reduce pollution, such as waste heat?

www.mnn.com/green-tech/computers/blogs/running-big-draw-server-farms-on-fuel-cells-solar-and-wind

www.kplu.org/post/greenpeace-how-clean-and-green-your-server-farm

www.gizmag.com/fjord-cooled-data-center/20938/

http://2ndgreenrevolution.com/2012/04/20/fff-green-peace-study-on-server-farms/

Bankers and high-frequency stock traders in New York City insist that the servers they use be as close to them as possible. "Shorter distances make for quicker trades," explains a *New York Times* account, "and microseconds can mean millions of dollars made or lost."[15] As a result, companies are paying top dollar to lease server space in buildings across the Hudson River in New Jersey, in places such as Weehawken, Secaucus, and Mahwah.

Says the *Times:* "When the [data] centers opened in the 1990s as quaintly termed 'Internet hotels,' the tenants paid for space to plug in their servers with a proviso that electricity would be available. As computing power has soared, so has the need for power, turning that relationship on its head: electrical capacity is often the central element of lease agreements, and space is secondary."

In June 2012 the online auction company eBay announced it would build a new data center in South Jordan, Utah, that would rely less on coal-fired electricity to run. Instead, it would use energy fuel cells.[16] ■

The System Clock & Processing Speeds

A computer's main CPU is its fastest piece of processing hardware.

Often a PC ad will say something like "Intel i5 processor 3.30 GHz." *GHz* stands for "gigahertz," a measure of how fast the microprocessor can process data and execute program instructions.

Every microprocessor contains a **system clock, which controls how fast all the operations within a computer take place.** The system clock uses fixed vibrations from a quartz crystal to deliver a steady stream of digital pulses or "ticks" to the CPU. These ticks are called *cycles.* Faster *clock speeds* will result in faster processing of data and execution of program instructions, as long as the computer's internal circuits can handle the increased speed. Cycle times can be measured in fractions of a second. A microcomputer operates in microseconds—millionths of a second. A supercomputer operates in nanoseconds—billionths of a second.

Older microcomputer microprocessor speeds are expressed in **megahertz (MHz), a measure of frequency equivalent to 1 million cycles (ticks of the system clock) per second.** The original IBM PC had a clock speed of 4.77 megahertz, which equaled 4.77 million cycles per second. The latest-generation processors from AMD and Intel operate in **gigahertz (GHz)—a billion cycles per second.** Intel's Pentium i5 and i7

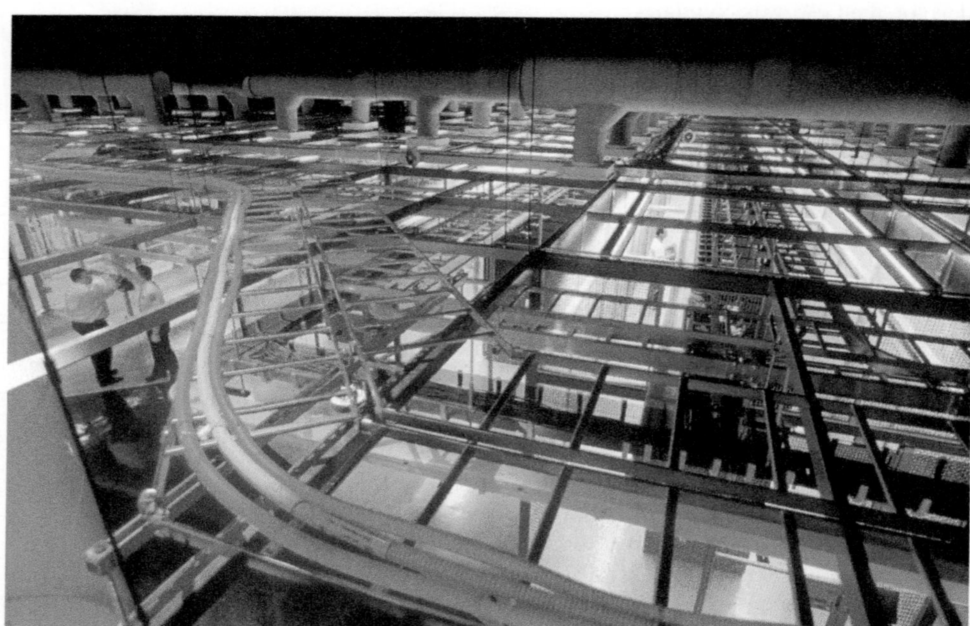

An Internet highway of cables links servers at Equinix Internet Business Exchange, a data center.

Comparison of Some Popular Recent Microcomputer Processors

Year	Processor Name	Clock Speed	Transistors
2013	Intel 6-Core i7-3970X	3.6–3.9 GHz	2.27 billion
	AMD 8-Core FX-8350	4–4.2 GHz	1.2 billion (each core)
2011	Intel Xeon	3.47 GHz	2.3 billion (each core)
2010	Intel Core i7 995X	3.60 GHz	731 million (each core)
	AMD Phenom II X6		
2009	AMD Phenom II	3.2 GHz	1.17 billion (each core)
	Athlon 2	3.0 GHz	
2008	Intel Core i7	3.1 GHz	153–221 million
	Intel Tukwila Quad Core	3.0 GHz	410 million (each core)
		2.66 GHz	2 billion (each core)
		2 GHz	2 billion
2007	Intel Core Quad	2.4–2.7 HZ	582 million
2006	Intel Pentium EE 840 dual core	3.2 GHZ	230 million
2005	Intel Pentium 4 660	3.6–3.7 GHz	169 million
2005	AMD Athlon 64 X2 dual core	2 GHz	105.9 million
2005	Intel Itanium 2 Montecito dual core	2 GHz	1.7 billion
2004	IBM PowerPC 970FX (G5)	2.2 GHz	58 million
2003	AMD Opteron	2–2.4 GHz	37.5 million
2002	Intel Itanium 2	1 GHz and up	221 million
2002	AMD Athlon MP	1.53–1.6 GHz	37.5 million
2001	Intel Xeon	1.4–2.8 GHz	140 million
2001	Intel Mobile Pentium 4	1.4–3.06 GHz	55 million
2001	AMD Athlon XP	1.33–1.73 GHz	37.5 million
2001	Intel Itanium	733–800 MHz	25.4–60 million
2000	Intel Pentium 4	1.4–3.06 GHz	42–55 million
1999	Motorola PowerPC 7400 (G4)	400–500 MHz	10.5 million

operate at up to 3.80 gigahertz, or 3.80 billion cycles per second. However, unfortunately, the faster a CPU runs, the more power it consumes and the more waste heat it produces. Thus, rather than increasing clock speeds, which requires smaller transistors and creates tricky engineering problems, chip makers such as Intel and AMD are now employing additional CPU cores and running them in parallel—dual-core or multicore technology, as we've described.

As for you, since a new high-speed processor can cost many hundreds of dollars more than a previous-generation chip, experts often recommend that buyers fret less about the speed of the processor, since the work most people do on their PCs doesn't even tax the limits of the current hardware, and more about spending money on extra memory. However, game playing *does* tax the system. Thus, if you're an avid computer game player, you may want to purchase the fastest processor.

4.4 THE CENTRAL PROCESSING UNIT & THE MACHINE CYCLE

Each time the central processing unit executes an instruction, it takes a series of steps. The complete series of steps is called a machine cycle.

A processor, we said, is also called the *CPU,* and it works hand in hand with other circuits known as *main memory,* or simply *memory,* to carry out processing. **The CPU, for central processing unit, is the "brain" of the computer; it follows the instructions of the software (program) to manipulate data into information. The CPU consists of two parts—(1) the control unit and (2) the arithmetic/logic unit (ALU), both of which contain registers, or high-speed storage areas** (as we discuss shortly). All are linked by a kind of electronic "roadway" called a *bus.* (• *See Panel 4.7, next page.)*

panel 4.7

The CPU and main memory

The two main CPU components on a microprocessor are the control unit and the ALU, which contain working storage areas called *registers* and are linked by a kind of electronic roadway called a *bus*.

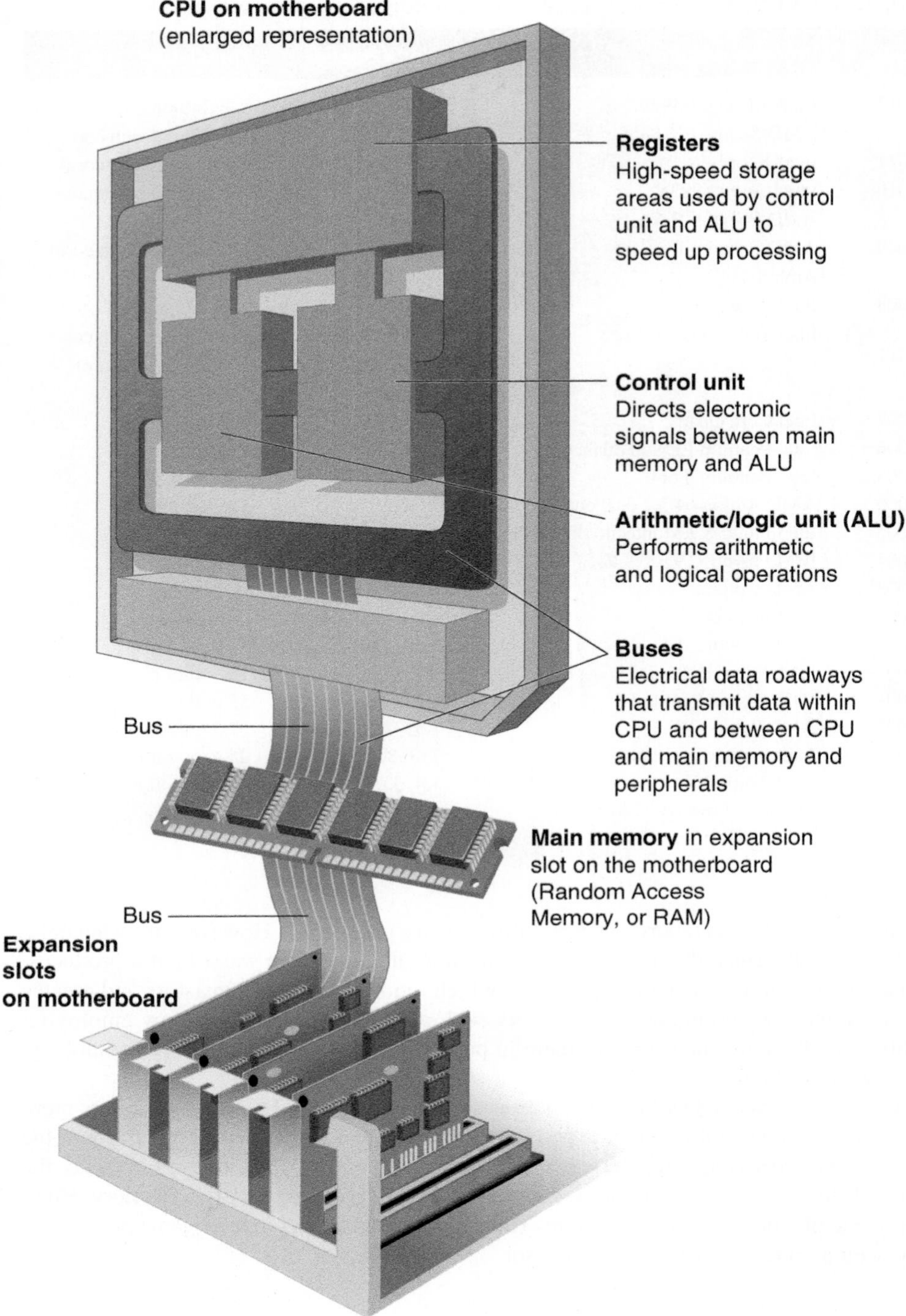

CPU on motherboard
(enlarged representation)
Registers
High-speed storage areas used by control unit and ALU to speed up processing
Control unit
Directs electronic signals between main memory and ALU
Arithmetic/logic unit (ALU)
Performs arithmetic and logical operations
Buses
Electrical data roadways that transmit data within CPU and between CPU and main memory and peripherals
Bus
Main memory in expansion slot on the motherboard (Random Access Memory, or RAM)
Bus
Expansion slots on motherboard

The Control Unit & the Machine Cycle

The control unit carries out instructions stored in the CPU, following the four operations of the machine cycle.

The control unit deciphers each instruction stored in the CPU and then carries out the instruction. It directs the movement of electronic signals between main memory and the arithmetic/logic unit. It also directs these electronic signals between main memory and the input and output devices.

For every instruction, the control unit carries out four basic operations, known as the *machine cycle.* In the **machine cycle, the CPU (1) fetches an instruction, (2) decodes the instruction, (3) executes the instruction, and (4) stores the result.** *(• See Panel 4.8.)*

Some computers carry out these four operations one instruction at a time, waiting until one instruction is processed before another is started. However, most modern personal

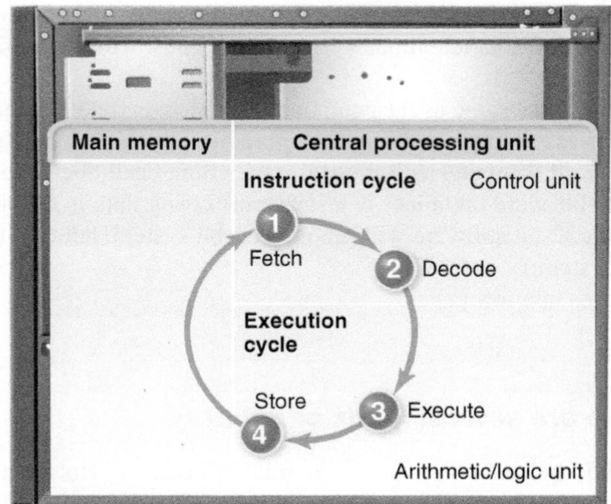

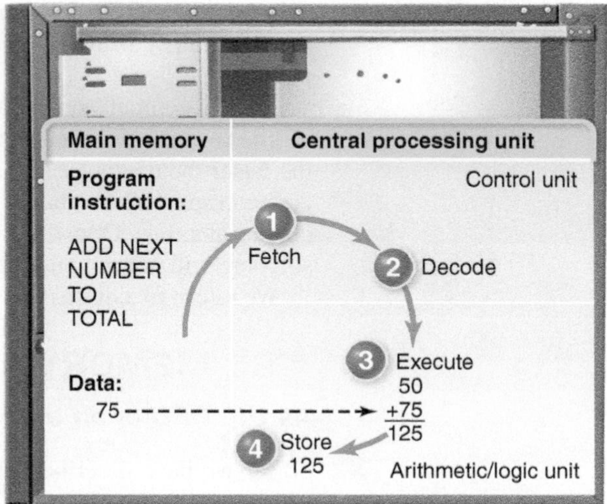

panel 4.8

The machine cycle

(*left*) The machine cycle executes instructions one at a time during the instruction cycle and the execution cycle. (*right*) Example of how the addition of two numbers, 50 and 75, is processed and stored in a single cycle.

computers are faster than this because they follow a concept called *pipelining*. In pipelining, the CPU does not wait for one instruction to complete the machine cycle before fetching the next one. Most PC processors can pipeline up to four instructions.

The Arithmetic/Logic Unit

The arithmetic/logic unit performs arithmetic operations and logical operations.

The arithmetic/logic unit (ALU) performs arithmetic operations and logical operations and controls the speed of those operations.

As you might guess, *arithmetic operations* are the fundamental math operations: addition, subtraction, multiplication, and division.

Logical operations are comparisons. That is, the ALU compares two pieces of data to see whether one is equal to (=), greater than (>), greater than or equal to (>=), less than (<), less than or equal to (<=), or not equal to (≠) the other.

Registers

Registers are high-speed storage areas for temporarily storing data during processing.

The control unit and the ALU also use registers, special CPU areas that enhance the computer's performance. **Registers are high-speed storage areas that temporarily store data during processing.** They may store a program instruction while it is being decoded, store data while it is being processed by the ALU, or store the results of a calculation.

All data must be represented in a register before it can be processed. For example, if two numbers are to be multiplied, both numbers must be in registers, and the result is also placed in a register. (The register can contain the address of a memory location where data is stored rather than the actual data itself.)

The number of registers that a CPU has and the size of each (number of bits) help determine the power and speed of a CPU. For example, a 32-bit CPU is one in which each register is 32 bits wide. Therefore, each CPU instruction can manipulate 32 bits of data. (There are several types of registers, including *instruction register, address register, storage register, general register,* and *accumulator register.*)

Buses & Word Size

Buses are data roadways for transferring data within the CPU and to the motherboard.

Buses, or *bus lines*, are electrical data roadways through which bits are transmitted within the CPU and between the CPU and other components of the motherboard. A bus resembles a multilane highway: The more lanes it has, the faster the bits can be transferred. The old-fashioned 8-bit bus of early microprocessors had only eight pathways. Data is transmitted four times faster in a computer with a 32-bit bus, which has 32 pathways.

In most computers, the bus width is the same as the computer's **word size, the number of bits that the processor can process at any one time.** The more bits in a word, usually the faster the computer. A 32-bit-word computer will transfer data within each microprocessor chip in 32-bit chunks. A 64-bit-word computer is faster, transferring data in 64-bit chunks at a time. (Most, but not all, 32-bit software will run on a 64-bit system, but 64-bit software will not run on a 32-bit system.)

We return to a discussion of buses in a few pages.

4.5 MEMORY

As the CPU is on a chip, so are several kinds of memory.

So far we have described only the kinds of chips known as microprocessors. But other silicon chips called *memory chips* are also attached to the motherboard. The four principal types of memory chips are *RAM, ROM, CMOS,* and *flash.*

RAM

RAM is used to temporarily store program instructions and data.

Recall from Chapter 1 that there are two types of storage: primary and secondary (p. 28). Primary storage is temporary or working storage and is often called *memory* or *main memory.* Secondary storage, usually called just *storage,* is relatively permanent storage. *Memory* refers to storage media in the form of chips, and *storage* refers to media such as disks and tape.

RAM (random access memory) chips temporarily hold (1) software instructions and (2) data before and after it is processed by the CPU. Think of RAM as the primary workspace inside your computer. When you open a file, a copy of the file transfers from the hard disk to RAM, and this copy in RAM is the one that changes as you work with the file. When you activate the Save command, the changed copy transfers from RAM back to permanent storage on the hard drive.

Because its contents are temporary, most RAM is said to be **volatile—the contents are lost when the power goes off or is turned off.** This is why you should *frequently*—every 5–10 minutes, say—transfer (save) your work to a secondary-storage medium such as your hard disk, in case the electricity goes off while you're working. (However, *MRAM* and *flash RAM* are not temporary, as we'll discuss shortly.)

TYPES OF RAM Three types of RAM exist—*DRAM, SRAM,* and *MRAM:*

- **DRAM:** The first type (pronounced "dee-ram"), *DRAM (dynamic RAM),* must be constantly refreshed by the CPU or it will lose its contents. Faster variations on the basic DRAM include *SDRAM (synchronous dynamic RAM),* which is synchronized by

> **Survival Tip**
>
> **What RAM for Your PC?**
>
> Before adding more RAM to improve your computer's performance, check the manufacturer's website as to the type of RAM modules required for the motherboard. RAM slots and chipsets vary, and different computer models cannot work with all kinds of RAM chips.

> **Survival Tip**
>
> **Need More RAM?**
>
> If your system is giving you low-system-resources messages, you may need more memory. For detailed information on your system, use the Windows Task Manager, or go to:
>
> **www.crucial.com**
>
> **www.kingston.com**
>
> **http://pcsupport.about.com/od/toolsofthetrade/tp/memorytest.htm**
>
> **http://pcsupport.about.com/b/2008/03/27/free-computer-memory-test-programs-software.htm**

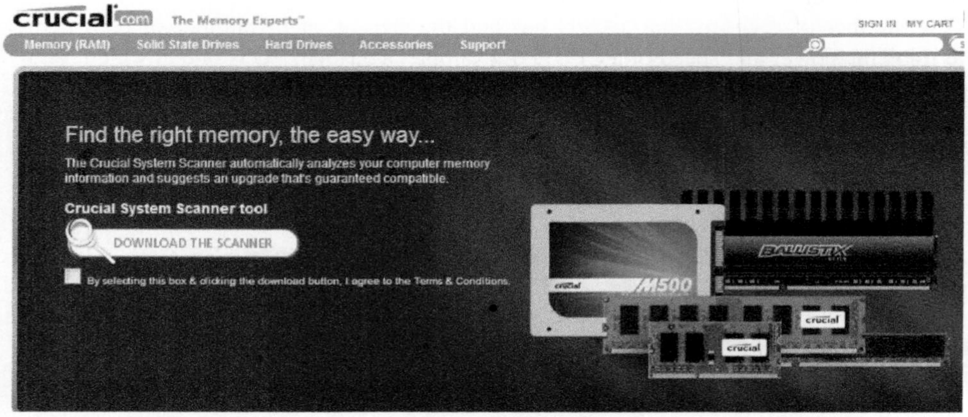

the system clock; *DDR-SDRAM (double-data rate synchronous dynamic RAM),* and its later variations DDR2 and DDR3; and *RDRAM (Rambus DRAM),* which is much faster than SDRAM.

- **SRAM:** The second type, *static RAM,* or *SRAM* (pronounced "ess-ram"), is faster than DRAM and retains its contents without having to be refreshed by the CPU.
- **MRAM:** The third and newer type is *MRAM* (pronounced "em-ram" and short for *magnetoresistive RAM),* which stores data using magnetic charges rather than electric charges and is faster and stores more data than electronic RAM. MRAM retains its contents when the power is shut off.

Magnetic RAM

MRAM is the focus of the website at:

www.mram-info.com

HOW MUCH RAM IS ENOUGH? Microcomputers come with different amounts of RAM, which is usually measured in megabytes or gigabytes. An ad might list "2 GB SDRAM," but you will probably need more. The Mac Pro, for instance, can provide up to 128 gigabytes (GB) of RAM. The more RAM you have, the more efficiently the computer operates and the better your software performs. *Having enough RAM is a critical matter.* Before you buy a software package, look at the outside of the box or check the manufacturer's website to see how much RAM is required. To run Microsoft Office 2013, for instance, you need a *minimum* of 1 gigabyte of RAM.

ADDING MORE RAM CHIPS If you're short on memory capacity, you can usually add more RAM chips by plugging a RAM *memory module* into the motherboard. A memory module is a small fiberglass circuit board that can be plugged into a RAM slot on the motherboard. Most memory modules used in microcomputers are DIMMs. A *DIMM (dual inline memory module)* has RAM chips on both sides.

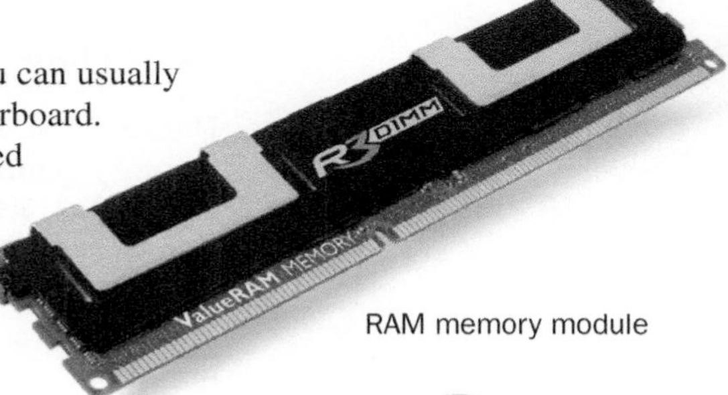

RAM memory module

Cache Memory

Cache is special memory to speed up processing.

Because the CPU runs so much faster than the main system RAM does, it ends up waiting for information, which is inefficient. To allow faster receipt and delivery of data, computers use cache (pronounced "cash"), extremely fast memory that is built into the CPU or located next to it on a separate chip. **Cache memory speeds up processing by temporarily storing instructions and data that the processor is likely to use frequently,** such as instructions repeatedly required to run programs. The computer determines what information in RAM is being used frequently and copies that information into cache, to be quickly accessed as needed.

RAM-ifications

To find out more about how RAM works, go to:

http://computer.howstuffworks.com/ram.htm

http://pcsupport.about.com/od/componentprofiles/p/p_ram.htm

www.ehow.com/how-does_4564791_ram-work.html

www.life123.com/technology/computer-hardware/ram/how-does-ram-work.shtml

THREE KINDS OF CACHE There are three kinds of cache, as follows:

- **Level 1 (L1) cache—part of the microprocessor chip:** *Level 1 (L1) cache,* also called *internal cache,* is built into the processor chip. Ranging from 8 to 128 kilobytes, its capacity is less than that of Level 2 cache, although it operates faster.
- **Level 2 (L2) cache—not part of the microprocessor chip:** This is the kind of cache usually referred to in computer ads. *Level 2 (L2) cache,* also called *external cache,* resides on a chip outside the processor chip. Capacities range from 64 kilobytes to 16 megabytes. L2 cache is generally quite a bit larger than L1 cache (most new systems have at least 1–6 megabytes of L2 cache) and is the most commonly cited type of cache for measuring PC performance.
- **Level 3 (L3) cache—on the motherboard:** *Level 3 (L3) cache* is also a cache chip separate from the processor chip on the motherboard. On personal computers, it holds 2–8 megabytes.

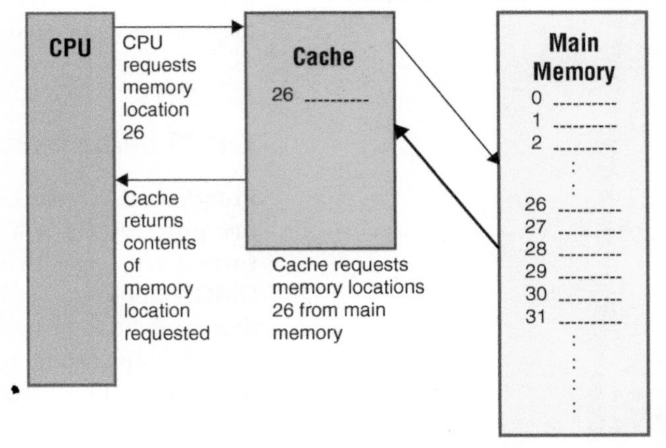

Without the cache memory, every time the CPU requested data it would have to send a request to main memory that would then be sent back across the memory bus to the CPU. This is a slow process in computing terms. When the microprocessor accesses main memory (RAM), it does it in about 60 nanoseconds (60 billionths of a second). That's pretty fast, but it is much slower than the typical microprocessor. Microprocessors can have cycle times as short as 2 nanoseconds, so to a microprocessor 60 nanoseconds seems like an eternity.

Cache is not upgradable; it is set by the type of processor purchased with the system.

VIRTUAL MEMORY In addition to including cache, most current computer operating systems allow the use of **virtual memory—that is, some free hard-disk space is used to extend the capacity of RAM.** The processor searches for data or program instructions in the following order: first L1, then L2, then RAM, then hard disk (or CD). In this progression, each kind of memory or storage is slower than its predecessor.

Memory Management

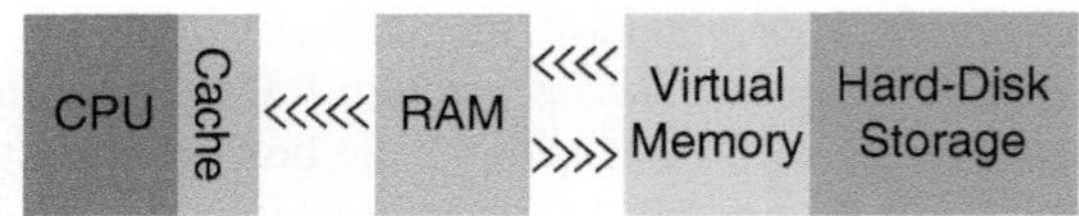

ROM

ROM chips store fixed start-up instructions.

Unlike RAM, to which data is constantly being added and removed, **ROM (read-only memory) cannot be written on or erased by the computer user without special equipment. ROM chips contain fixed start-up instructions.** That is, ROM chips are loaded, at the factory, with programs containing special instructions for basic computer operations, such as those that start the computer (BIOS) or put characters on the screen. These chips are nonvolatile; their contents are not lost when power to the computer is turned off.

In computer terminology, **read means to transfer data from an input source into the computer's memory or CPU. The opposite is write—to transfer data from the computer's CPU or memory to an output device.** Thus, with a ROM chip, *read-only* means that the CPU can retrieve programs from the ROM chip but cannot modify or add to those programs. A variation is *PROM (programmable read-only memory),* which is a ROM chip that allows you, the user, to load read-only programs and data. However, this can be done only once.

Flash Memory

Flash memory chips store flexible programs.

A nonvolatile form of memory, **flash memory chips can be erased and reprogrammed more than once** (unlike PROM chips, which can be programmed only once). Flash memory, which doesn't require a battery and which can range from 2 gigabytes to 256 gigabytes in capacity, is used to store programs not only in personal computers but also in pagers, cellphones, MP3 players, printers, and digital cameras. Flash memory is also used in newer PCs for BIOS instructions; they can be updated electronically on flash memory—the chip does not need to be replaced, as a ROM chip would.

CMOS

CMOS chips store flexible start-up instructions.

Pronounced "*see*-moss," **CMOS (complementary metal-oxide semiconductor) chips are powered by a battery and thus don't lose their contents when the power is turned off.** Used for some RAM chips, flash memory chips, and other memory chips, CMOS chips contain flexible start-up instructions—such as time, date, and calendar—that must be kept current even when the computer is turned off. Unlike ROM chips, CMOS chips can be reprogrammed, as when you need to change the time for daylight saving time. (Your system software used to prompt you to do this; newer systems do it automatically.)

4.6 EXPANSION CARDS, BUS LINES, & PORTS

Expansion cards plug into slots on the motherboard that are connected by buses to ports that the user can access.

Many computers, particularly desktop personal computers, are marvelously versatile machines, capable of being modified for many different purposes.

Expansion Slots & Adapter Cards

There are several ways to make a computer faster and more powerful.

As mentioned earlier, *expansion* is a way of increasing a computer's capabilities by adding hardware to perform tasks that are not part of the basic system. *Upgrading* means changing to a newer, usually more powerful or sophisticated version. (Computer ads often make no distinction between expansion and upgrading. Their main interest is simply to sell you more hardware or software.)

CLOSED & OPEN ARCHITECTURE Whether a computer can be expanded depends on its "architecture"—closed or open. *Closed architecture* means a computer has no expansion slots; *open architecture* means it does have expansion slots. Alternatively, closed architecture means a computer's design specifications are not made freely available by the manufacturer, so that other companies cannot create ancillary devices to work with it. With open architecture, the manufacturer shares specifications with outsiders. A number of desktop PC computers offer open architecture, but most Apple computers, whether desktop or portable, are closed architecture.

EXPANSION SLOTS & CARDS Expansion slots **are sockets on the motherboard into which you can plug expansion cards.** Expansion cards**—also known as *expansion boards, adapter cards, interface cards, plug-in boards, controller cards, add-ins,* or *add-ons*—are circuit boards that provide more memory or that control peripheral devices.** (• *See Panel 4.9.*)

Most desktop computers have four to eight expansion slots, some of which may already contain expansion cards included in your initial PC purchase. New computers support Plug and Play**, a set of hardware and software standards that allow the computer to automatically configure expansion cards and other peripherals while they are being installed.** This avoids the hassle of setting switches and creating special files, as was required of early users.

Among the types of expansion cards are the following:

- Graphics cards—for monitors: **Also called a *video card, video RAM (VRAM),* or *video adapter,* a** graphics card **converts signals from the computer into video signals that are displayed as images on a monitor.** Each graphics card has its own memory chips, a graphics BIOS ROM chip, and a dedicated processor, the graphics processing unit (GPU), discussed earlier. The GPU works in tandem with the computer's CPU to ease the load, resulting in faster overall speed.
- Sound cards—for speakers and audio output: **A** sound card **is used to convert and transmit digital sounds through analog speakers, microphones, and headsets.** Sound cards come installed on most new PCs. Cards such as PCI wavetable sound cards are used to add music and sound effects

panel 4.9

Expandability

How an expansion card fits into an expansion slot

to computer videogames. *Wavetable synthesis* is a method of creating music based on a wave table, which is a collection of digitized sound samples taken from recordings of actual instruments. The sound samples are then stored on a sound card and are edited and mixed together to produce music. Wavetable synthesis produces higher-quality audio output than other sound techniques.

- **Network interface cards—for remote communication via cable: A network interface card (NIC), or *network adapter card,* allows the transmission of data over a cabled (wired) network,** which connects various computers and other devices such as printers. (Various types of networks are covered in Chapter 6.)
- **Wireless network cards—for through-the-air connections: A wireless network card, which often has an antenna, enables wireless data transmission.**
- **PC Cards or ExpressCards—primarily for wireless Internet access: PC Cards or, more recently, the smaller *ExpressCards,* are thin, credit-card-size reusable (flash) memory devices used on traditional and notebook computers and tablets to expand capabilities, such as to access the Internet wirelessly** (when the capability is not already built in to the motherboard). *(• See Panel 4.10.)*

panel 4.10

ExpressCard

Example of a PC Card used in a laptop

Expansion Bus Lines

Expansion bus lines connect the CPU with expansion slots and peripheral devices.

As we mentioned, *buses* or *bus lines* are electric data roadways through which bits are transmitted, and every bus deals with a particular kind of traffic. Buses are of two types:

- **Frontside bus:** The bus that connects the CPU within itself and to main memory is the *frontside bus,* also called the *system bus* or *memory.*
- **Expansion bus:** The buses that connect the CPU with expansion slots on the motherboard and thus with peripheral devices are *expansion buses. (• See Panel 4.11.)*

Common expansion buses found in personal computers are as follows:

PCI BUS: FOR HIGH-SPEED CONNECTIONS At 32 or 64 bits wide, the *peripheral component interconnect (PCI) bus* is a high-speed bus that has been widely used to connect PC graphics cards, sound cards, modems, and high-speed network cards.

panel 4.11

Bus lines on the motherboard

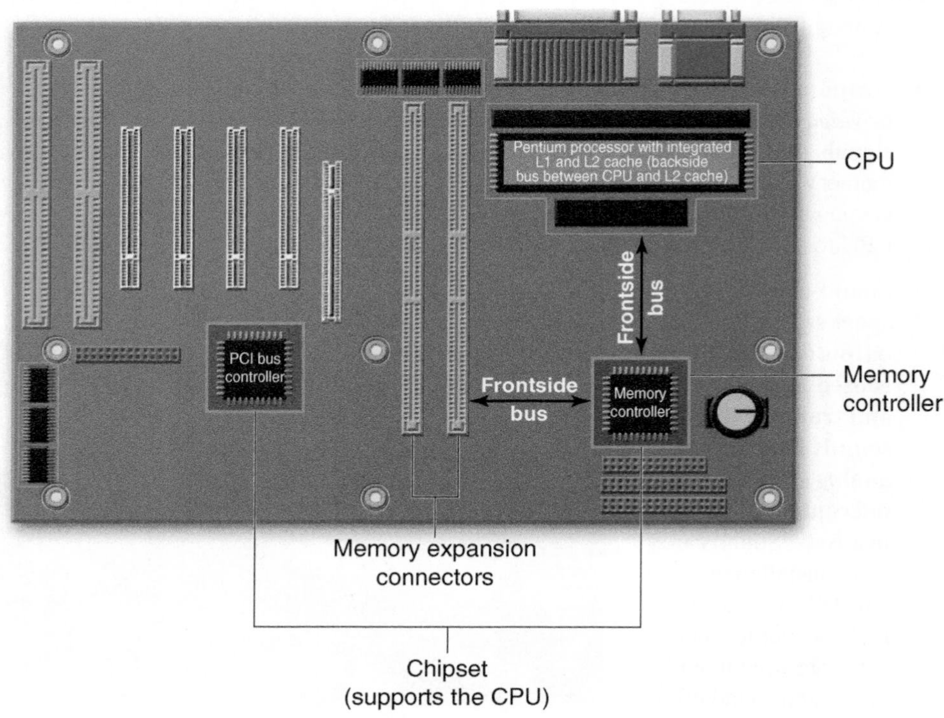

PCI EXPRESS BUS: FOR DOUBLING THE SPEED Developed in 2004, the *PCI Express (PCIe) bus* doubles the speed of the original PCI bus. PCIe is the latest standard for expansion cards available on mainstream personal computers. This electrical interface is also used in a variety of formats, including ExpressCard.

THE ACCELERATED GRAPHICS PORT BUS: FOR 3-D GRAPHICS Because the PCI bus couldn't handle all the information passing between the main processor and the graphics processor needed for three-dimensional games, the *Accelerated Graphics Port (AGP) bus* was developed, which transmits data at twice the speed of a PCI bus and is designed to support video and 3-D graphics.

THE UNIVERSAL SERIAL BUS: FOR ELIMINATING THE NEED FOR EXPANSION CARDS IN SLOTS The *Universal Serial Bus (USB)* does away with the need to install cards in expansion slots. USB devices can connect one to another outside the system unit, and then the USB bus connects to the PCI bus on the motherboard.

FIREWIRE BUS: FOR CONNECTING AUDIO & VIDEO DEVICES The *FireWire bus* resembles the USB bus, but is used for more specialized purposes, such as to connect audio and video equipment to the motherboard.

Ports

A port is a socket for some kind of plug, of which there are many types.

A port is a connecting socket or jack on the outside of system unit into which are plugged different kinds of cables. (• *See Panel 4.12, next page.*) A port allows you to plug in a cable to connect a peripheral device, such as a monitor, printer, scanner, or microphone, so that it can communicate with the motherboard or with cards inserted into slots of the motherboard.

Ports are of several types, as follows.

DEDICATED PORTS—FOR KEYBOARD, MOUSE, MONITOR, AUDIO, & MODEM/NETWORK CONNECTION *Dedicated ports* are ports for special purposes, such as the ports for connecting the keyboard and the mouse, the monitor port, the audio ports (green for speakers or headphones, pink for microphone, yellow for home stereo connection), the modem port to connect your computer to a phone line, and a network port for a high-speed Internet connection. There is also one connector that is not a port at all—the power plug socket, into which you insert the power cord that brings electricity from a wall plug.

STANDARD PORTS—FOR USB, FIREWIRE, ETHERNET, & GRAPHICS Most of the standard ports other than the dedicated ones just described are as follows:

- **USB ports—the most widely used connection for peripherals: A USB (Universal Serial Bus) port is a high-speed hardware standard for interfacing peripheral devices, such as scanners and printers, to computers without a need for special expansion cards or other hardware modifications to the computer.** USB ports are multipurpose, useful for all kinds of peripherals, and are included on all of today's microcomputers.

  Up to 127 different peripheral devices (if they are all USB devices) can be connected to a single USB port. You can also hook up a *USB hub* to a USB port: You plug the hub into your computer, and then plug your devices—or other hubs—into that. By chaining hubs together, you can build up dozens of available USB ports on a single computer (although using a hub weakens data signals).

  Just about every peripheral made now comes in a USB version, today's most common standards being *USB 2.0 and USB 3.0.* USB 3.0 is about 10 times faster than USB 2.0 and can handle higher levels of power. You can hook up a 3.0 USB device to a 2.0 port, but it will run at the slower 2.0 speed.

Survival Tip

Powered versus Unpowered USB Hubs

USB peripheral devices can draw their power from their USB connection. Printers and scanners have their own power supply. Mice and digital cameras draw power from the PC. If you have lots of self-powered devices (like printers and scanners), your hub need not be powered. If you have lots of unpowered devices (like mice and cameras), you probably need a powered hub (*www.howstuffworks.com/usb2.htm*).

(*top*) USB ports; (*bottom*) the USB symbol on a USB connector

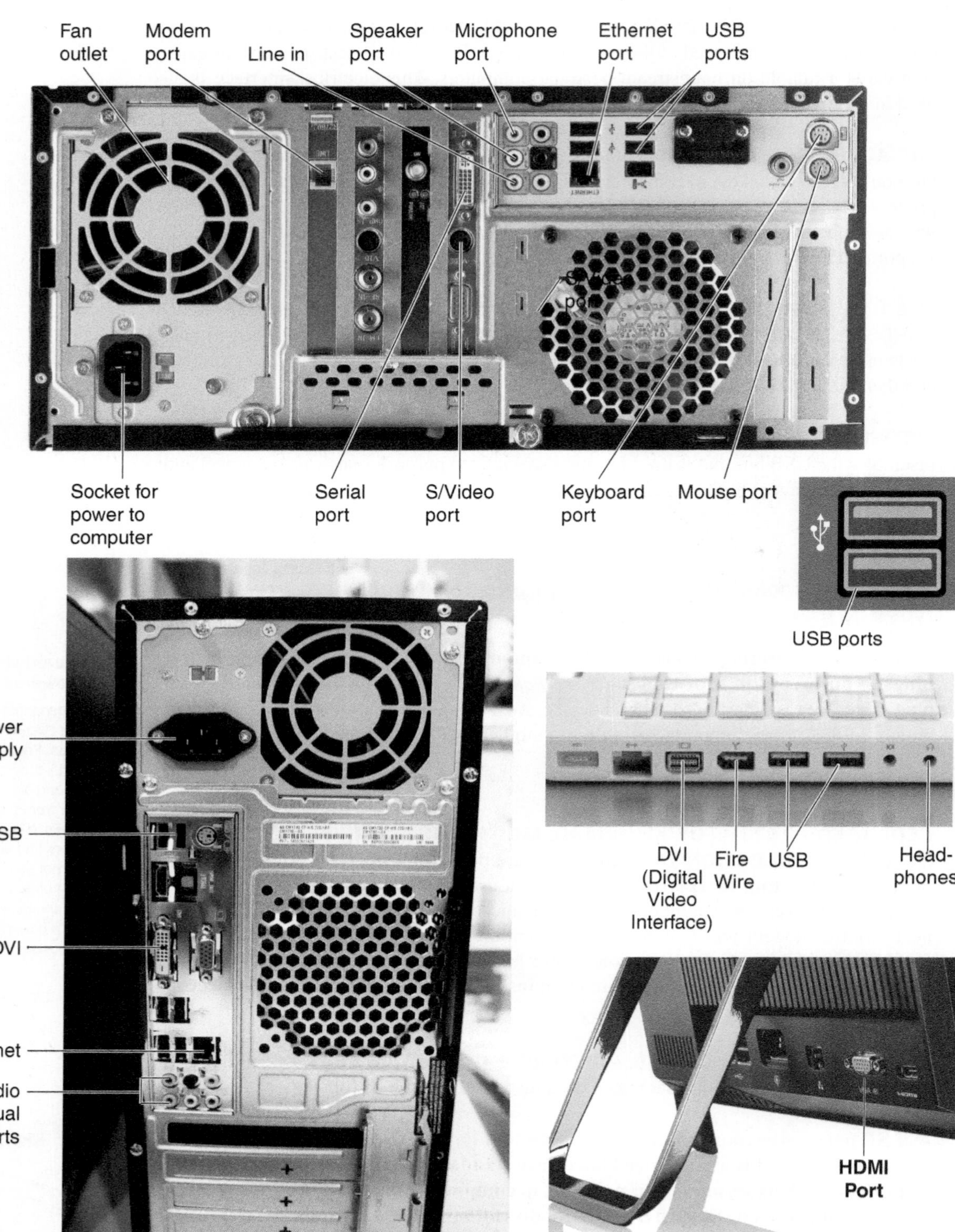

panel 4.12

Ports

The backs of a PC (*top*) and a Macintosh (*bottom*). Additional USB ports may be on the front or side of some system units.

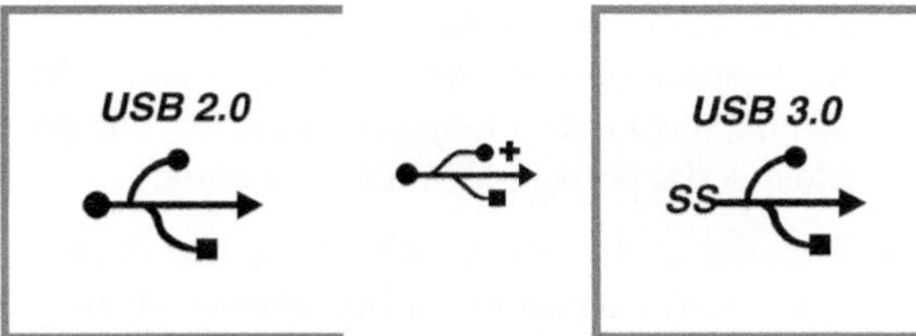

USB 2.0 may or may not use a plus sign; USB 3.0 has "SS."

> **Survival Tip**
>
> **Types of USB Connectors**
>
> Different USB devices use different types of USB connectors. For a pictorial chart of all the connectors and descriptions of what devices they are used for, go to:
>
> **www.cablestogo.com/support/connector-guides/usb**

- **FireWire ports—for connecting devices with lots of data:** Previously called an *IEEE-1394 port,* the FireWire port actually preceded the USB port and had similar goals. The **FireWire port is intended for multiple devices working with lots of data and requiring fast transmission speeds,** such as DVD drives, digital video cameras, and gaming consoles. You can connect up to 63 peripheral FireWire devices to a single FireWire port, and, as with USB, the devices can be plugged or unplugged at any time (they are "hot pluggable").

FireWire port and symbol

- **Ethernet ports—for wired network connection:** An **Ethernet port supports a network standard for linking a wired local area network** (p. 24) **and connecting it to a DSL or a cable modem for high-speed Internet access.** To use Ethernet, computers must have an Ethernet network interface card, and special Ethernet cables are required.

  An Ethernet port looks much like a regular phone jack, but it is slightly wider.

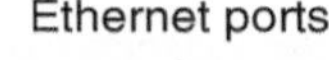
Ethernet ports

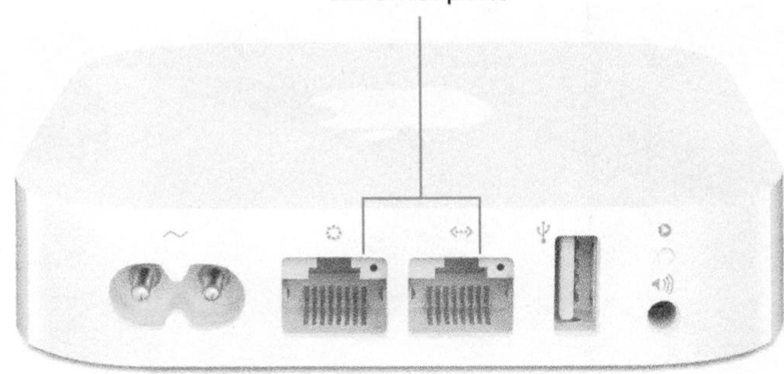

Ethernet plug

- **Graphics ports—for connecting monitors and multimedia devices:** *Graphics ports* include *DVI (Digital Video Interface) ports* for connecting digital monitors and multimedia digital devices, such as TVs and DVD players. They also include the older *VGA (Video Graphics Adapter) ports* for connecting analog monitors.

DVI port

DVI plug

OTHER PORTS—SERIAL, PARALLEL, eSATA, BLUETOOTH, IrDA, HDMI, & MIDI Some other less common ports that you may encounter are these:

- **Serial ports—for transmitting slow data over long distances: A line connected to a serial port will send bits one at a time, one after another,** like cars on a one-lane highway. Because individual bits must follow each other, a serial port is usually used to

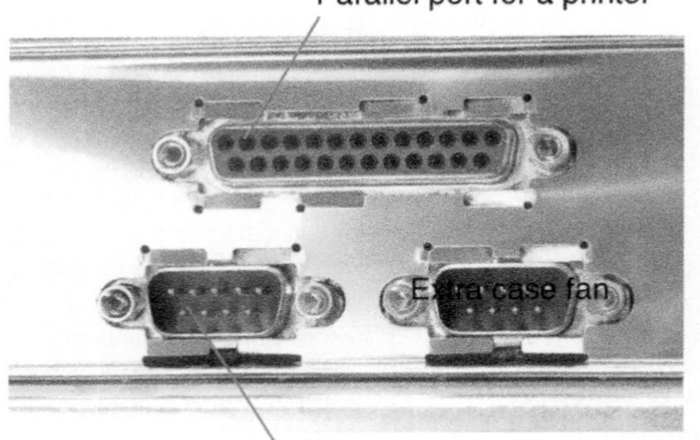

connect devices that do not require fast transmission of data, such as keyboard, mouse, monitors, and dial-up modems. It is also useful for sending data over a long distance. New computers have eliminated older serial ports in favor of USB ports.

- **Parallel ports—for transmitting fast data over short distances:** **A line connected to a parallel port allows 8 bits (1 byte) to be transmitted simultaneously,** like cars on an eight-lane highway. Parallel lines move information faster than serial lines do, but they can transmit information efficiently only up to 15 feet. Thus, parallel ports are used principally for connecting older printers or external disk or magnetic-tape backup storage devices (although these peripheral devices now generally use USB connections).

- **eSATA ports—for connecting fast external hard disks:** *SATA* stands for Serial Advanced Technology Attachment. An **eSATA port, or *external SATA port,* allows the attachment of an eSATA hard disk, which has fast data transmission speeds.**
- **Bluetooth ports—for wireless connections up to 30 feet:** **Bluetooth ports allow you to connect technology that uses short-range radio waves that transmit up to 30 feet.** Bluetooth is used to connect Bluetooth-enabled cellphones to computers but also to

Using a Bluetooth headset; Bluetooth logo

Bluetooth-enabled car dashboard

connect computers to enabled printers, keyboards, headsets, and other appliances (including refrigerators). Bluetooth transmitters may use different ports, depending on the device being used; or the device may be Bluetooth-enabled, meaning that the transmitter is built in.

- **IrDA ports—for transmitting data via infrared light waves:** *IrDA* stands for *Infrared Data Association.* IrDA ports **transfer data via infrared light wavevs between directly aligned devices,** as between a smartphone and a desktop computer. IrDA is still used in certain business and professional contexts, but wireless technology has basically superseded it.

The USB2IR3 USB to IR Adapter turns a USB port into an IrDA-compliant infrared port for communication with a wide variety of IrDA-compliant devices, such as test equipment and medical instruments.

- **HDMI ports—for high-definition video and audio:** *HDMI* stands for *High-Definition Multimedia Interface.* HDMI ports **can carry both video and audio signals** and are used for connecting HDTVs, DVD players, and game consoles to computers, laptops, and other devices.

- **MIDI ports—for connecting electronic musical instruments:** Short for *Musical Instrument Digital Interface,* MIDI ports **are used to connect electronic musical instruments to a sound card that converts the signals to digital instructions that can be saved or manipulated.** We discuss MIDI technology further in Chapter 5 (p. 268).

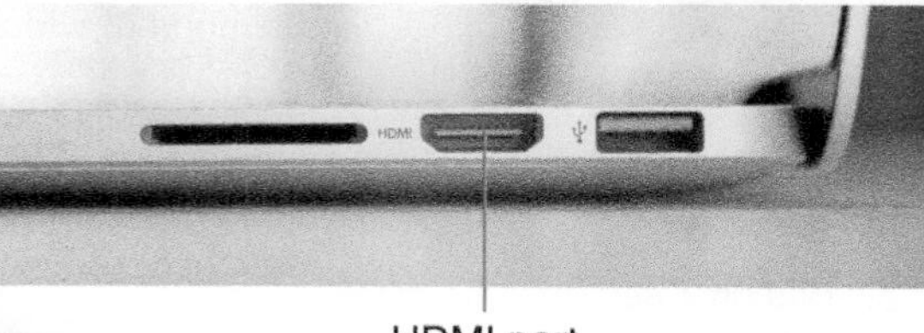

UNIT 4B: *Secondary Storage*

You're on a trip with your notebook, tablet, or smartphone and find you need a crucial phone number or file of data not currently in your possession. Fortunately, you have stored essential data online "in the cloud" and can access it wirelessly.

This is another, by now commonplace example of the alternatives the World Wide Web offers to traditional computer functions that once resided within stand-alone machines. Still, we are not fully into the all-online era. Let us therefore consider more traditional forms of secondary-storage hardware, **devices that permanently hold data and information as well as programs.**

4.7 SECONDARY STORAGE

Secondary storage is all data storage that is not currently in a computer's primary storage (main memory, or RAM).

We look at the following types of secondary storage:

- Hard disks
- Optical disks: CD, DVD, and Blu-ray
- Flash and solid-state memory: solid-state drives, flash memory cards, and USB flash drives
- Smart cards
- Cloud storage

Hard Disks

Hard disks are still the major secondary-storage device for desktop computers.

Relative size of a hard-disk drive

Hard disks **are thin but rigid metal, glass, or ceramic platters covered with a substance that allows data to be held in the form of magnetized spots.** Most hard-disk drives have at least two platters;

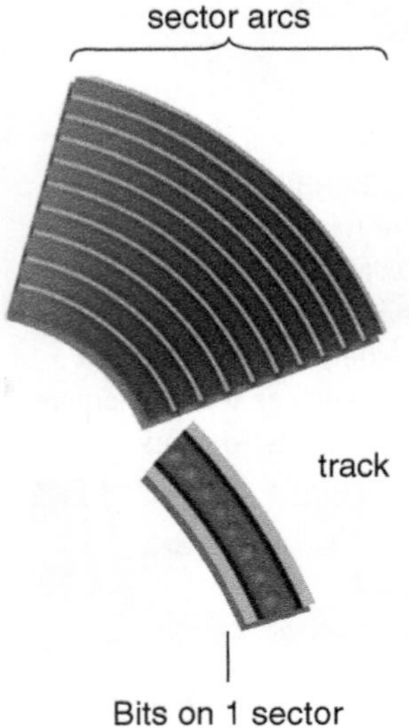

the greater the number of platters, the larger the capacity of the drive. The platters in the drive are separated by spaces and are clamped to a rotating spindle that turns all the platters in unison. Hard disks are tightly sealed within an enclosed hard-disk-drive unit to prevent any foreign matter from getting inside. Data may be recorded on both sides of the disk platters. (• *See Panel 4.13.)*

Hard disks store data in *tracks, sectors,* and *clusters.* Computer operating systems keep track of hard-disk sectors according to clusters.

- **Tracks, sectors, and clusters:** On the disk, **data is recorded in concentric recording bands called tracks.** Unlike on a vinyl phonograph record, these tracks are neither visible grooves nor a single spiral. Rather, they are closed concentric rings; each track forms a full circle on the disk. **When a disk is formatted, the disk's storage locations are divided into wedge-shaped sections, which break the tracks into small arcs called sectors.** When you save data from your computer to a disk, the data is distributed by tracks and sectors on the disk. That is, the system software uses the point at which a sector intersects a track to reference the data location.
- **The read/write head:** Each disk is fixed in place over the spindle of the drive mechanism. **The read/write head is used to transfer data between the computer and the disk.** When the disk spins, the read/write head moves back and forth over the *data access area* on the disk.

The smallest unit of disk space that can be written/read from is called a cluster. A *cluster* is a group of sectors on a storage device. The Windows operating system assigns a unique number to each cluster and then keeps track of files on a disk by using a kind of table, a *Virtual File Allocation Table (VFAT),* as a method for storing and keeping track of files according to which clusters they use. (The VFAT was called a FAT in earlier operating systems.) That is, the VFAT includes an entry for each cluster that describes where on the disk the cluster is located.

Occasionally, the operating system numbers a cluster as being used even though it is not assigned to any file. This is called a *lost cluster.* You can free up lost clusters and thus increase disk space in Windows by using the ScanDisk utility.

HEAD CRASHES Hard disks are sensitive devices. The read/write head does not actually touch the disk but rather rides on a cushion of air about 0.000001 inch thick. (• *See Panel 4.14.)* The disk is sealed from impurities within a container, and the whole apparatus is manufactured

panel 4.13

(*left*) Maxtor desktop computer hard drive; (*right*) hard-disk schematic

In a microcomputer, the hard disk is enclosed within the system unit.

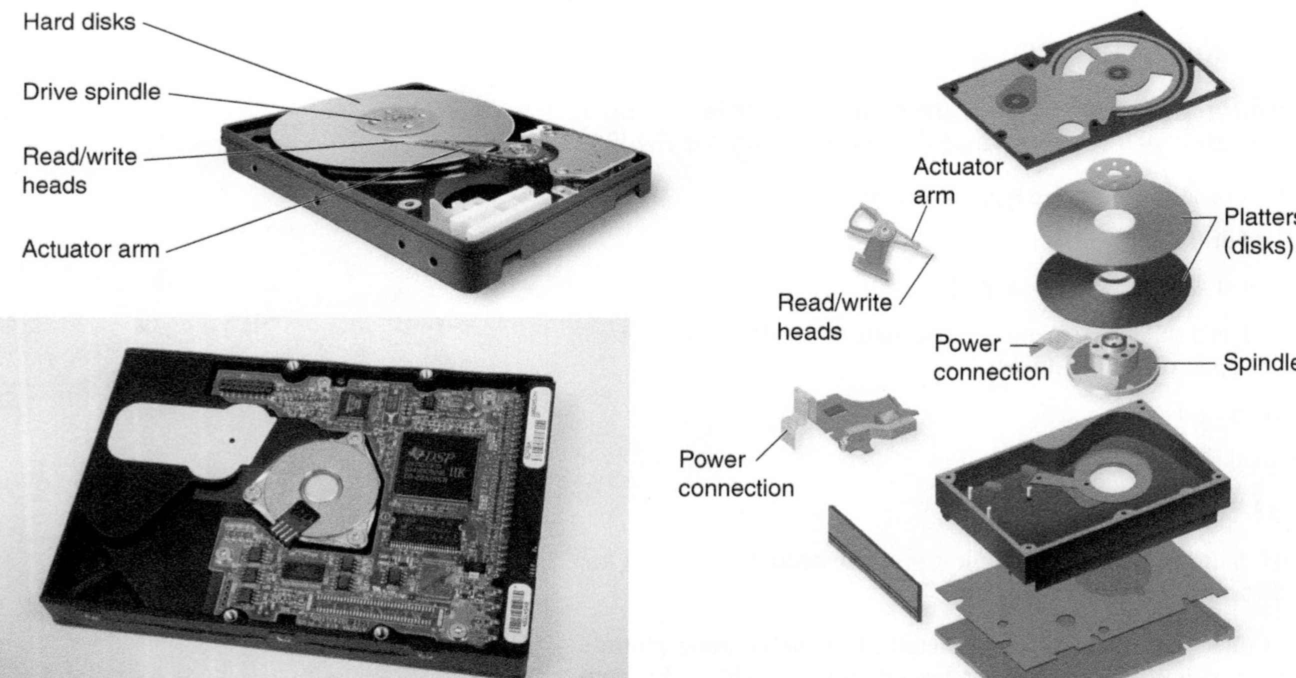

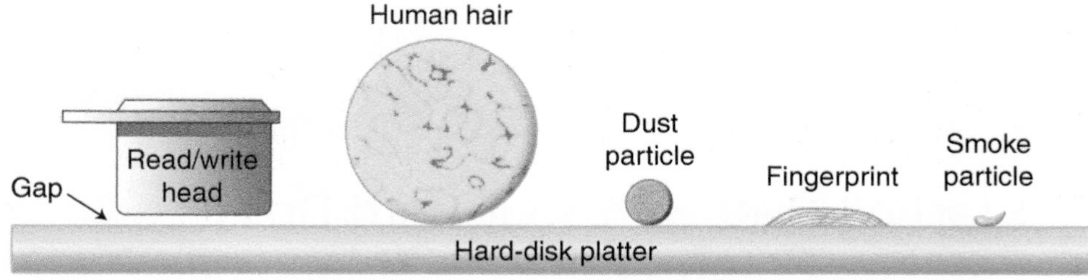

panel 4.14

Gap between hard-disk read/write head and platter

Were the apparatus not sealed, all it would take is a human hair, dust particle, fingerprint, or smoke particle to cause a head crash.

under sterile conditions. Otherwise, all it would take is a human hair, a dust particle, a fingerprint smudge, or a smoke particle to cause what is called a head crash. A *head crash* happens when the surface of the read/write head or particles on its surface come into contact with the surface of the hard-disk platter, causing the loss of some or all of the data on the disk. A head crash can also happen when you bump a computer too hard or drop something heavy on the system cabinet. An incident of this sort could, of course, be a disaster if the data has not been backed up. There are firms that specialize in trying to retrieve data from crashed hard disks (for a hefty price), though this cannot always be done.

Survival Tip

Data Recovery

Crashed your hard disk? Try these:

http://hard-drive-recovery-services-review.toptenreviews.com/

www.apple.com/osx/recovery/

NONREMOVABLE HARD DISKS An internal *nonremovable hard disk,* also known as a *fixed disk,* is housed in the microcomputer system unit and is used to store nearly all programs and most data files. Usually it consists of several metallic or glass platters, from 1 to 5.25 inches (most commonly 3.5 inches) in diameter, stacked on a spindle, with data stored on both sides. Read/write heads, one for each side of each platter, are mounted on an access arm that moves back and forth to the right location on the platter. The entire apparatus is sealed within an airtight case to protect it from contaminants such as dust. The storage capacities of nonremovable hard drives for microcomputers range from 120 gigabytes to 4 terabytes.

Bits on disk. Magnetic bits on a disk surface, caught by a magnetic force microscope. The dark stripes are 0 bits; the bright stripes are 1 bits.

PORTABLE HARD-DRIVE SYSTEMS: EXTERNAL HARD DISKS A *portable hard disk,* or *hard-disk cartridge,* consists of one or two platters enclosed along with read/write heads in a hard plastic case Portable drives, which have storage capacities of 80 gigabytes–1 terabyte and more, are frequently used to back up and transport huge files of data, such as those for large spreadsheets or desktop-publishing files. These external hard drives are usually connected to the computer via USB.

more info!

Storage in the Old Days

In 1978, a pioneering drive for home computers, the external Shugart SA4000, weighed 35 pounds, wholesaled for $2,550, and stored only 14.5 megabytes. Hard drives began to become popular with PC users in 1983, when Seagate made one that fit into the PC case. For more history, go to:

www.computerhistory.org/

www.crn.com/slide-shows/storage/240142353/the-history-of-the-hard-drive-and-its-future.htm

HARD-DISK TECHNOLOGY FOR LARGE COMPUTER SYSTEMS: RAID Large databases, such as those maintained by insurance companies or Google, require far bigger storage systems than the fixed-disk drives we've been describing, which send data to a computer along a single path. A *RAID (redundant array of independent disks) storage system,* which links any number of disk drives within a single cabinet or multiple cabinets, sends data to the computer along several parallel paths simultaneously. Response time is thereby significantly improved. RAID systems also store the same data in different places (thus, redundantly) on multiple hard disks; storing data redundantly also increases fault tolerance, meaning that the system can keep working in spite of a failure.

LaCie 4big Quadra Enterprise Class 4-bay RAID, which connects to a computer system (6.8 × 8.6 × 7.7 in.)

History of Storage

For a short pictorial history of computer storage, go to:

http://royal.pingdom.com/?p=274

HIGHER-DENSITY HARD DISKS When IBM introduced the world's first disk drive in 1956, it was capable of storing 2,000 bits per square inch. Today the company is shipping hard disks with densities of 14.3 billion bits or more per square inch. But that, too, is changing. Hard-drive makers are now employing a technology known as *perpendicular recording technology,* which involves stacking magnetic bits vertically on the surface of a platter (instead of horizontally, as is usual; • *See Panel 4.15).* Based on this innovation,

PRACTICAL ACTION

Starting Over with Your Hard Drive: Erasing, Reformatting, & Reloading

There may come a time when your hard drive is so compromised by spyware and other parasites and slows down your computer so much it's as though you had lost two cylinders on your car engine. (This situation might have been avoided had you been running antispyware software, such as, for example, Ad-Aware, AntiSpyware, CounterSpy, PestPatrol, Spybot Search & Destroy, SpyCatcher, or Spy Sweeper. But many people don't do this, which is why one study found that more than 96% of the respondents felt protected from outside threats using traditional antivirus and firewall solutions, yet nearly 82% reported their desktop computers to be infected with spyware.)[17]

Or perhaps you've installed a new application, such as a speech-recognition program or new piece of hardware, whose drivers have the effect of causing such chaos in your system that you wish you'd never acquired the new item.

What should you do now? Give up your computer, buy a new one (if you can afford it), and transfer all your old data to it? (Some people actually do this.) Or erase everything on your hard drive and reinstall your software and data files? Here's what to do.[18]

Make a List of Everything in Your System & Tech Support Phone Numbers

The first thing you need to do is take paper and pencil and make a list of all (1) hardware components, (2) software registration codes and product keys, and (3) technical support phone numbers for your computer maker and your Internet access provider, in case you run into problems while rebuilding your system.

Make Sure You Have Disks with Copies of Your Software

See if you have the original disks for all your software (your program files), including the operating system installation ("recovery" or "restore") disks that came with your computer. If you don't, create CD/DVD copies. Or contact your computer maker for new ones (for which the company will probably charge you). You can also get online instructions for redownloading software after you have reset your system.

Make Backup Copies of Your Data Files

There are several different ways to back up your data files—for example, those listed under My Documents, My Pictures, My Scans, and My Music:

- ***Copy to a server:*** If you're on a network, you can save all your data files to a networked folder.
- ***Copy to CDs or DVDs:*** Using a CD/DVD recorder (called a burner), you can back up your data files onto writable CDs or DVDs.
- ***Copy to a keychain (flash) drive or an MP3 player:*** You can save all your data files to a keychain (flash) drive, an MP3 player, or another external hard drive and then transfer them to another computer to burn them onto CD/DVD disks.

You might wish to make two copies of your backed-up files—just in case.

Reformat Your Hard Drive & Reinstall Your Operating System

Insert your operating system CD-ROM installation disks into the CD drive. When your computer asks you if you want to reformat your hard drive, answer yes. When it advises that if you continue, all files will be deleted, respond that this is okay. It will take perhaps 60 minutes to reformat the hard disk and reinstall your OS. You will then be asked to fill in your name, time zone, country, and type of Internet connection. Probably at this point you should also download any operating system updates (patches) from the manufacturer's website. Reboot your computer.

Reinstall Your Programs & Drivers

Reinstall all your applications, such as Microsoft Office, and all the drivers for your printer, camera, CD burner, and other peripherals. (Drivers may not be needed, because new OSs can recognize almost anything and find the driver online.)

Install Security Software & Firewall

To be sure you're starting over with a secure system, now you should install updated security software (such as McAfee Virus Protection, Kaspersky, Norton AntiVirus, or ZoneAlarm Antivirus), which contains antivirus software and a firewall that prevents unauthorized users from gaining access to your network. Reboot your computer.

Reinstall All Your Data Files

Copy your saved data files from the backup source. Run virus and spyware scans on everything, using the security software. Reboot. By now, it's hoped, you will have gotten rid of all your spyware and other nuisances.

Longitudinal magnetic recording Perpendicular magnetic recording

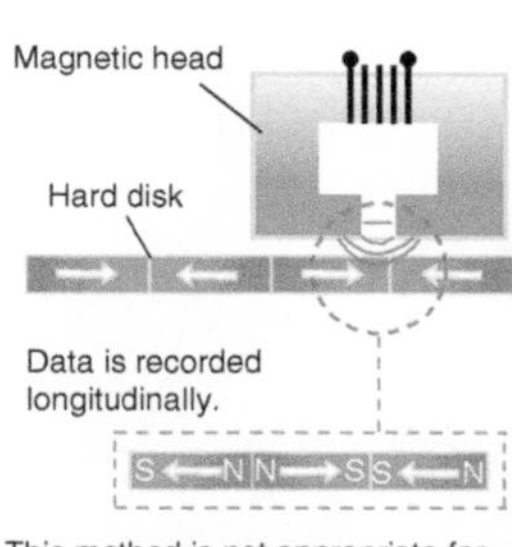
Magnetic head
Hard disk
Data is recorded longitudinally.
S←N N→S S←N
This method is not appropriate for high-density recording because the magnetization directions face each other. weakening their magnetism.

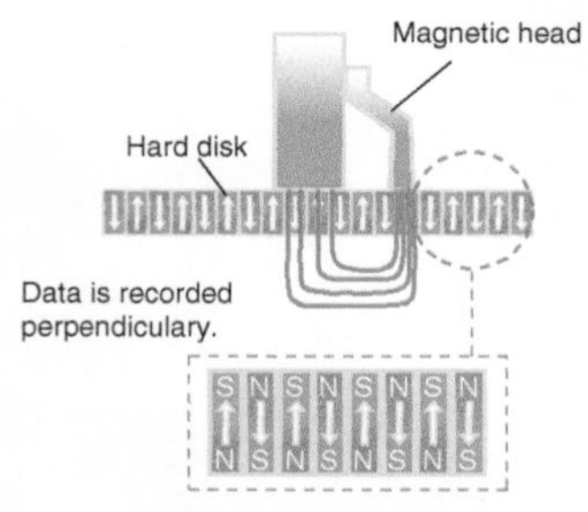
Magnetic head
Hard disk
Data is recorded perpendiculary.
S N S N S N S N
N S N S N S N S
The interaction of neighboring magnetic field is weak, realizing high-density recording with high data storing capacity.

panel 4.15

Conventional (longitudinal) versus perpendicular optical recording technologies

Seagate Technology makes a 4-terabyte (TB) hard drive, the Barracuda, for desktop PCs, servers, and external storage. Also using perpendicular recording, Hitachi Ltd's Ultrastar can store up to 4 terabytes.

Optical disk and disk drive in a laptop

Optical Disks: CDs, DVDs, & Blu-ray Disks

The optical disk is the preferred medium for music, movies, and software programs because of its advantages: compact, lightweight, durable, and digital.

Everyone who has ever played an audio CD is familiar with optical disks. **An optical disk** (also spelled *disc*) **is a removable disk, usually 4.75 inches in diameter and about .05 inch thick, on which data is written and read through the use of laser beams.** An audio CD holds up to 74 minutes (2 billion bits' worth) of high-fidelity stereo sound. Some optical disks are used strictly for digital data storage, but many are used to distribute multimedia programs that combine text, visuals, and sound.

Survival Tip

CD Read, Write, & Rewrite Speeds

PC ads present CD speeds in different ways—for example, *44X/24X/24X* for "read/write/rewrite" or *48X/24X/48X* for "write/rewrite/read." To clarify, do a web search for the CD drive manufacturer, brand, and model. Click on *product details* or *specs.*

HOW OPTICAL-DISK STORAGE WORKS With an optical disk, there is no mechanical read/write arm, as with hard disks. Instead, a high-power laser beam is used to write data by burning tiny pits or indentations into the surface of a hard plastic disk. To read the data, a low-power laser light scans the disk surface: pitted areas are not reflected and are interpreted as 0 bits; smooth areas are reflected and are interpreted as 1 bits. (• *See Panel 4.16, next page.*) Because the pits are so tiny, a great deal more data can be represented than is possible in the same amount of space on many hard disks. An optical disk can hold over 100 gigabytes of data.

Many PCs marketed today contain a CD/DVD drive, which can also read audio CDs. These, along with their recordable and rewritable variations, are the two principal types of optical-disk technology used with computers.

CD-ROM—FOR READING ONLY The first kind of optical disk for microcomputers was the CD-ROM. **CD-ROM (compact disk read-only memory) is an optical-disk format that is used to hold prerecorded text, graphics, and sound.** Like music CDs, a CD-ROM is a read-only disk. *Read-only* means the disk's content is recorded at the time of manufacture and cannot be written on or erased by the user. As the user, you have access only to the data imprinted by the disk's manufacturer. A CD-ROM disk can hold from 650 megabytes to 1 gigabyte of data on one side.

A CD-ROM drive's speed is important because, with slower drives, images and sounds may appear choppy. In computer ads, drive speeds are indicated by the symbol "X," as in "56X," which is a high speed. The *X* denotes the original data-transfer rate of 150 kilobytes per second. Today's drives have speeds of 48X to 75X or higher, the faster ones being more expensive.

Lens on a CD/DVD drive inside an Acer Aspire laptop

panel 4.16

How a laser reads data on an optical disk

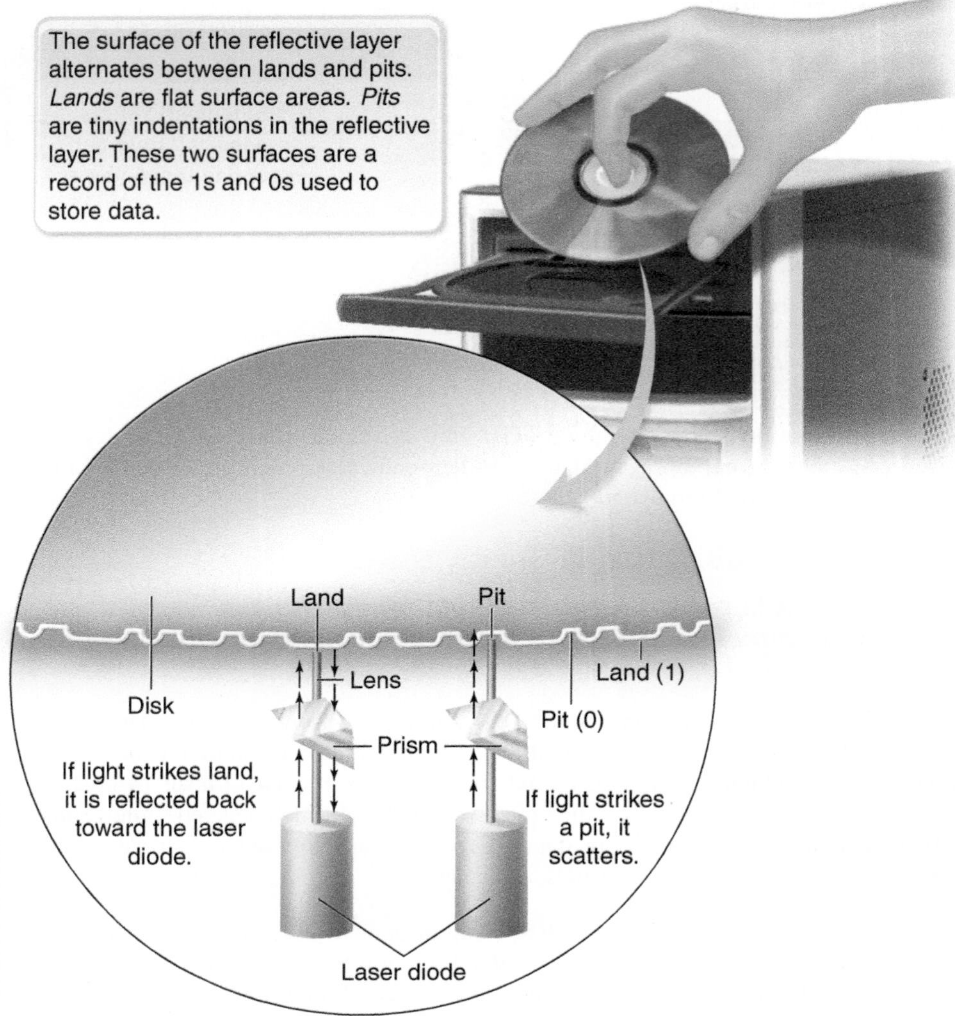
The surface of the reflective layer alternates between lands and pits. *Lands* are flat surface areas. *Pits* are tiny indentations in the reflective layer. These two surfaces are a record of the 1s and 0s used to store data.
Land
Pit
Lens
Land (1)
Disk
Pit (0)
Prism
If light strikes land, it is reflected back toward the laser diode.
If light strikes a pit, it scatters.
Laser diode

Survival Tip

Did You Back Up Your Files?

One recent survey found that most computer users, over 52%, ignore backup maintenance, failing to perform regular backups of their data (*http://agbeat.com/tech-news/most-people-unprepared-for-data-loss-ignore-backup-matinenance/*). Generally, consumers don't know how to back up their data, and if they do, they're failing to back up data because they claim it takes too much time. The average American adult has 1,800 digital files.[19] A more recent study showed that although significantly more people back up their data, 90% of computer users continue to not do *regular* backups. Photos, music, financial data, work documents, and more are lost every single day as the result of computers not being backed up.[20]
How about you? Will you be able to get your files back if something goes wrong with your computer system? For common mistakes people make regarding computer backup and other info, see:

www.pcmag.com/article2/0,2817,2363057,00.asp

www.datadoctors.com/help/columns/21736-The-most-common-backup-mistakes/

CD-R—FOR RECORDING ONLY ONCE **CD-R (compact disk–recordable) disks can be written to only once but can be read many times.** This allows users to make their own CD disks. Once recorded, the information cannot be erased.

CD-RW—FOR REWRITING MANY TIMES **A CD-RW (compact disk–rewritable) disk, also known as an *erasable optical disk,* allows users to record and erase data, so the disk can be used over and over again.** CD-RW disks are useful for archiving and backing up large amounts of data or work in multimedia production or desktop publishing. Currently, 185 megabytes (21 minutes of audio), 650 megabytes (74 minutes of audio), and 700 megabytes (80 minutes of audio) are the market standards.

DVD-ROM—THE VERSATILE VIDEO DISK (DISC) **A DVD-ROM (digital versatile disk or *digital video disk, with read-only memory)* is a CD-style disk with extremely high capacity, able to store 4.7–17 gigabytes.** How is this done? Like a CD or CD-ROM, the surface of a DVD contains microscopic pits, which represent the 0s and 1s of digital code that can be read by a laser. The pits on the DVD, however, are much smaller and grouped more closely together than those on a CD, allowing far more information to be represented. Also, the laser beam used focuses on pits roughly half the size of those on current audio CDs. In addition, the DVD format allows for two layers of data-defining pits, not just one. Finally, engineers have succeeded in squeezing more data into fewer pits, principally through data compression.

Most computer systems come with a DVD drive as standard equipment. These drives can also take standard CD-ROM disks, so you can watch DVD movies and play CD-ROMs using just one drive. DVDs are replacing CDs for archival storage, mass distribution of software, and entertainment. They not only store far more data but are different in quality from CDs, because they can handle multiple dialogue tracks and screen formats, and high-quality sound and video.

Like CDs, DVDs have their write-once and rewritable variants:

How to hold a DVD/CD while inserting it

- **DVD + R and DVD-R—write-once recordable DVDs:** *DVD + R* and *DVD-R (DVD-recordable) disks* are competing formats that allow one-time recording by the user. That is, they cannot be reused—written on more than once.
- **DVD-RW, DVD-RAM, DVD + RW—reusable DVDs:** Three types of reusable disks are *DVD-RW (DVD-rewritable), DVD-RAM (DVD–random access memory),* and *DVD + RW (DVD + rewritable)*, all of which can be recorded on and erased (except for video) many times. These disks are replacing CD rewritable drives. New DVD players can read any of these formats.

BLU-RAY DISK: THE NEXT-GENERATION OPTICAL DISK *Blu-ray,* also known as *Blu-ray disk (BD),* is the name of a next-generation optical-disk format. The name comes from the blue laser used to read the disk. **The Blu-ray optical format was developed to enable recording, rewriting, and playback of high-definition video, as well as storing large amounts of data.** The format offers more than five times the storage capacity of traditional DVDs and can hold up to 128 gigabytes, with future disks expected to hold 200 gigabytes or more. Blu-ray products are backward-compatible and allow use of CDs and DVDs.

Audiovisual receiver with a Blu-ray disk player

TECH TALES The World's DVD Zones

As a way to maximize movie revenues, in the 1990s the film industry decided to split the world into six DVD zones. Theoretically this was to prevent the DVD version of a movie made in one country from being distributed in another country in which the theater version has not yet opened.

DVDs with a particular region code will play only on DVD players, including in some computers and other devices, with that region code. For example, the United States is in region 1. (*See map below.*) Thus all DVD players sold in the United States are made to region 1 specifications. As a result,

Six DVD regions. The DVD world is divided into six regions. This means that many DVD players and DVDs are encoded for operation in a specific geographic region. The region number can be found on the back of each DVD package.

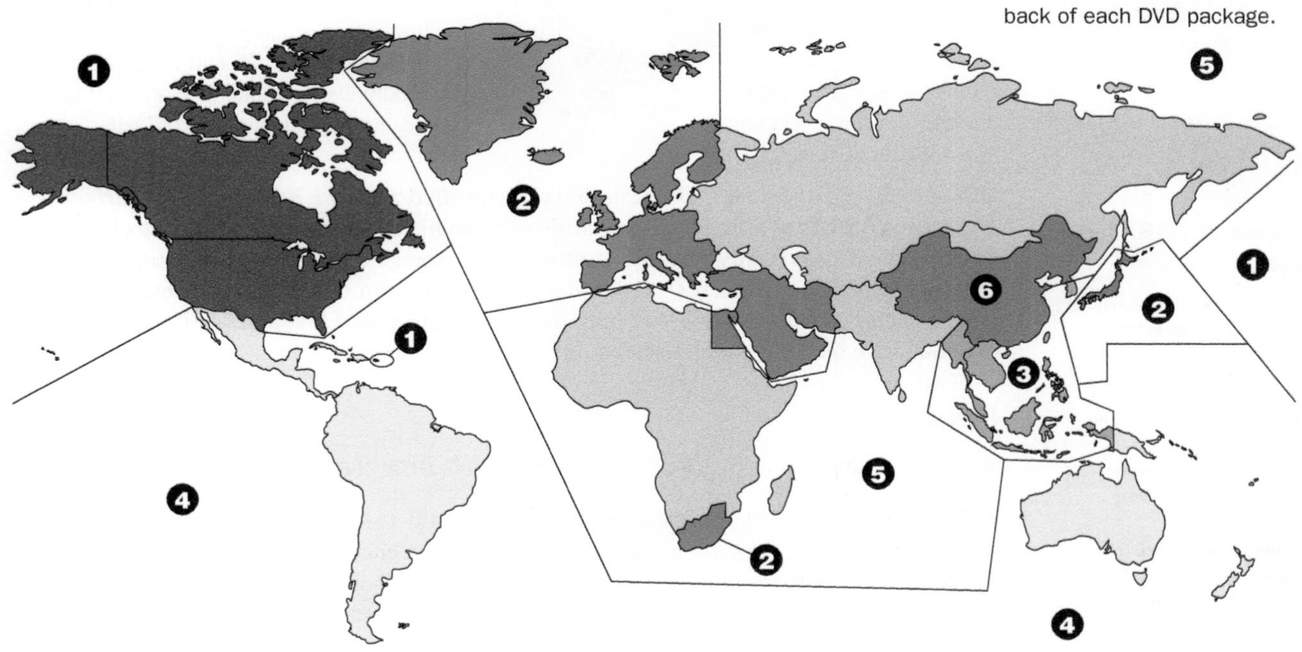

region 1 players can play only region 1 DVDs. Region 2 encompasses most of Europe, the Middle East, and Japan. The regions concept also allows manufacturers to charge differing prices to consumers, taking advantage of the fact that buyers in one region may be willing to pay more than consumers in another.

However, some of the newest DVDs are "region-free"—they can be played anywhere in the world. And some region-free DVD players are capable of handling disks from anywhere.[21] ■

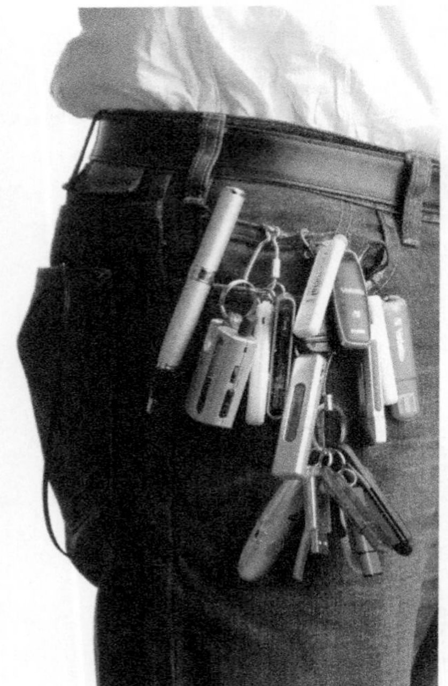

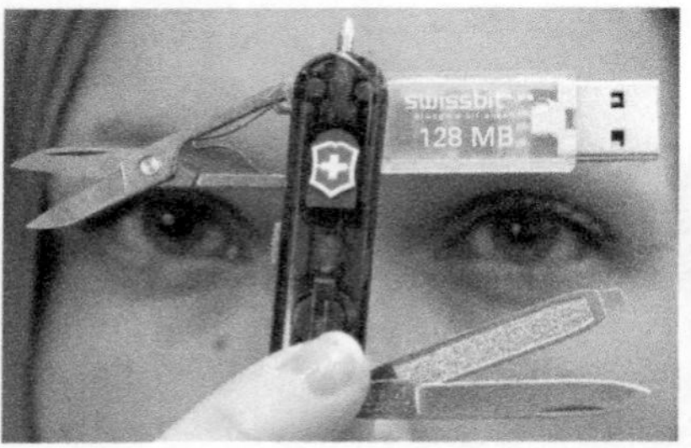

(*top*) A collection of USB flash drives; (*bottom*) Swiss Army knife with a flash drive that folds out

Flash & Solid-State Memory

Flash memory and solid-state memory have become the most important form of mobile secondary storage.

Disk drives, whether for hard disks or CDs/DVDs, all involve some moving parts—and moving parts can break. By contrast, *flash memory,* which is a variation on conventional computer memory chips (p. 214), has no moving parts; it is "solid state." Flash memory is also nonvolatile—it retains data even when the power is turned off. A drawback, however, is that flash memory circuits wear out after repeated use, limiting their life span.

Flash memory media are available in three forms: *solid-state drives, flash memory cards,* and *USB flash drives.*

SOLID-STATE DRIVES Instead of hard-disk drives, some tablets, laptops, desktops, and servers feature a solid-state drive (SSD), **which uses flash memory to store data, instructions, and information.** SSDs have a capacity of 16–256 gigabytes and have no moving parts to break down, as disk drives do. Some solid-state drives use SDRAM instead of flash memory, but in either case such drives are lighter, faster, and use less power than conventional disk drives and can better withstand bumps and bangs. Solid-state drives are currently much more expensive than hard-disk drives, but this is changing as they become more popular.

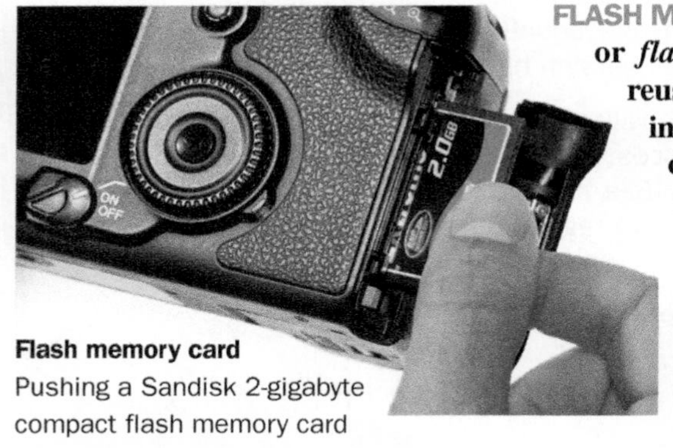

Flash memory card
Pushing a Sandisk 2-gigabyte compact flash memory card into a digital camera

FLASH MEMORY CARDS **Flash memory cards, or *flash RAM cards,* are removable and reusable storage media that are inserted into a flash memory slot in a digital camera, notebook, smartphone, or other mobile device.** Flash memory cards have no processor; they are useful only for storage, which can range up to 128 gigabytes (the most commonly used are 16 and 32 gigabytes). Examples are Sandisk, CompactFlash, Secure Digital, and microSDHC.

USB FLASH DRIVES **A USB flash drive, also called a *thumb drive, keychain drive,* or *key drive,* consists of a finger-size module of reusable flash memory that plugs into the USB ports of nearly any microcomputer.** It has storage capacities up to 256 gigabytes, making the device extremely useful if you're traveling from home to office, say, and don't want to carry a laptop. When you plug the device into your USB port, it shows up as an external drive on the computer screen.

Dangers of USB Flash Drives

Cyber criminals create malware that specifically target flash drives:

www.ehow.com/facts_6934868_flash-drive-dangerous_.html

www.hyphenet.com/blog/2012/07/11/dangers-of-plugging-a-lost-usb-flash-drive-into-your-pc/

http://blog.premiumusb.com/2011/02/usb-flash-drive-risks-how-to-combat-them/

Smart Cards

A smart card is a pocket-size card with integrated circuits.

Today in the United States, most credit cards are still the old-fashioned magnetic-stripe cards. A *magnetic-stripe card* has a band of magnetically encoded data on its back and holds about 0.2–0.9 kilobytes of data. The encoded data might include your name, account number, and PIN (personal identification number). The stripe contains information needed to use the card, but the stripe also has drawbacks. First, it can degrade over time, making the data

Smart card (*left*) with a chip, compared to a regular credit card, which has only a magnetic stripe on the back (*right*)

unreadable. Second, the magnetic band doesn't hold much information. Third, such data as the magnetic stripe does contain is easy to access and duplicate, raising the risk of fraud.

Popular in Europe and Canada, **smart cards are plastic cards the size of a credit card with an integrated circuit—a microprocessor and memory chips—built into it.** Most smart cards have been designed with the look and feel of a credit or debit card but can function on at least three levels: credit, debit, and personal information. Smart cards include data storage capacity of around 10 megabytes. Owing to the portability and the size of smart cards, they are seen as the next generation of data exchange.

Commercial smart cards are also called EMV cards, for Europay, Visa, MasterCard. In the United States, MasterCard and Visa have plans in place to change over from the old magnetic-stripe cards to smart cards by 2015. This will make all financial transactions with credit cards more secure, especially those made using mobile devices such as smartphones. Until then U.S. visitors to Europe will have some trouble using their credit cards at non-attended kiosks and services such as gas pumps and ticket-selling machines.

One form of smart card is the LaserCard, which is used by the U.S. Immigration and Naturalization Service as the Permanent Resident Card (PRC) or Border Crossing Card (BCC) because of its highly secure, counterfeit-resistant features. In addition, LaserCards containing shipping manifest data are attached to shipping containers and sea vans, speeding up receipt processing considerably.

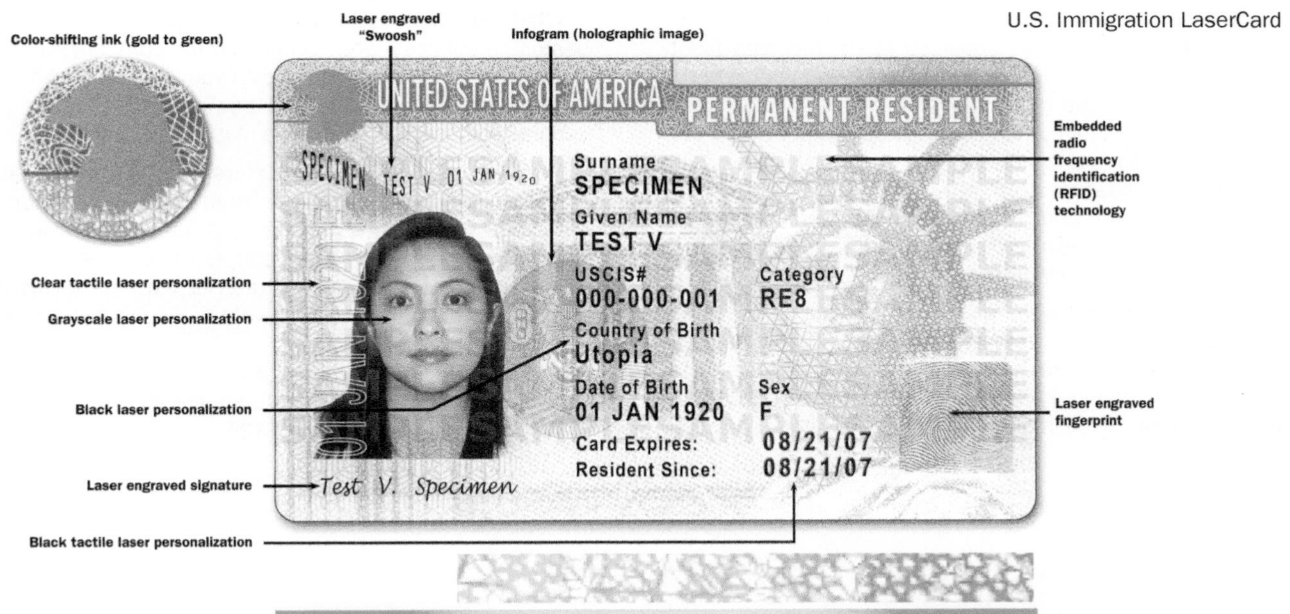

U.S. Immigration LaserCard

PRACTICAL ACTION

Storing Your Stuff: How Long Will Digitized Data Last?

How long are those CDs or flash drives on which you're storing your important documents going to last? Will you, or anyone else, be able to make use of them 15 or 25 or 50 years from now?

In 1982 software pioneer Jaron Lanier created a video game called *Moondust* for the then-popular Commodore 64 personal computer. Fifteen years later, when asked by a museum to display the game, he couldn't find a way to do it—until he tracked down an old microcomputer of exactly that brand, type, and age, along with a joystick and video interface that would work with it.

Would this have been a problem if Lanier had originally published a game in a *book?* Probably not. Books have been around since about 1453, when Johannes Gutenberg developed the printing press and used it to print 150 copies of the Bible in Latin. Some of these Gutenberg Bibles still exist—and are still readable (if you can read Latin).

Digital storage has a serious problem: It isn't as long-lived as older forms of data storage. Today's books printed on "permanent" (low-acid, buffered) paper may last up to 500 years. Even books printed on cheap paper that crumbles may still be readable.

By contrast, data stored on disks, magnetic tape, optical disks, and flash drives is subject to two hazards:

- ***Short life span of storage media:*** The storage media themselves have varying life expectancies, and often the degradation is not apparent until it's too late. Most consumer-grade hard drives last 5–10 years; CDs/DVDs and their drives last about 2–5 years. The maximum life of a CD-RW seems to be about 10 years. Very high-quality CD-Rs and DVD-Rs might last up to 100 years, but light (UV rays) can "kill" the disks way before that. (Optical disks commonly used for burning, such as CD-R and CD-RW, have a recording surface consisting of a layer of dye that can be modified by heat to store data. The degradation process can result in the data "shifting" on the surface and thus becoming unreadable to the laser beam.) USB drives last about 10 years, flash drives also about 10 years.
- ***Hardware and software obsolescence:*** As Jaron Lanier found out, even when disks and drives remain intact, the hardware and software needed to read them may no longer be available. Without the programs and computers used to encode data, digital information may no longer be readable.

Eight-inch floppy disks and drives, popular 25 years ago, are now extinct, as are their 5¼-inch and 3½-inch successors. Optical disks and magnetic disks will be increasingly useless one day because of the lack of working equipment to read them.

What about the personal records you store on your own PC, such as financial records, inventories, genealogies, and photographs? Here are a few suggestions for preserving your data:

1. Choose your storage media carefully and research their longevity.
2. Store files in a standard format, such as simple text (.txt) files and uncompressed bitmapped files. (Compression schemes can change, as well as the software and hardware able to deal with them.)
3. Keep copies of the software that created the data that you are saving.
4. Keep two copies, stored in separate places, preferably cool, dry environments.
5. Use high-quality media, not off-brands.
6. When you upgrade to a new hardware or software product, have a strategy for migrating and/or resaving the old data. (However, keep in mind that migrating data can degrade the data; keeping electronic data pristine over many years is becoming an increasingly important problem.)
7. If you use cloud storage, check out the company's arrangements for preserving data for a long time. What happens to your data if you stop paying for the storage service? What happens if the company closes down? If you want to retrieve all your data from the company, in what format will it be delivered? What bandwidth will be required to migrate the data?

Remember that although the storage media might last some years, the devices used to read them may become obsolete during that time; so it's a good idea to transfer stored data to new media every couple of years. And don't store media in extreme temperatures or extreme levels of humidity. Keep disks in plastic jewel boxes and store them upright.

And remember that there are always printouts (paper!!); books from the 15th and 16th centuries are still around, as is the first photograph, dating from 1826.

Different forms of smart-card technology are available:

- **Contact smart cards:** These kinds of cards, which must be swiped through card readers or inserted in mobile phones, are less prone to misalignment and being misread than magnetic-stripe cards, but they tend to wear out from the contact.
- **Contactless smart cards:** These cards, which are read when held in front of a low-powered laser or a radio-frequency reader, can be used in mobile applications, as by automated toll-collecting devices reading cards as drivers pass through toll booths without stopping. (Radio-frequency card use is discussed in more detail in Chapter 5.)

Cloud Storage

Cloud storage is online storage.

Cloud storage, or *online storage,* is use of an Internet service to store data. Among the top cloud storage providers are Amazon, AT&T, Google, HP, IBM, and Microsoft.[22] *(• See Panel 4.17.)* Cloud storage services are offered for individual users, home users, small business users, and large organizations needing archival services.[23] When you sign up for cloud storage, you obtain software that lets you upload files to the cloud company's server. For security, you are given a password, and the files are supposedly encrypted to guard against unwanted access.

Note that cloud storage is not necessarily the same thing as cloud backup; there is disagreement about terms and definitions, but, in general, online backup, or cloud backup, is primarily designed to back up your files and restore them to your computer in case of hard-drive failure or other problems. Cloud storage is designed to make it easy to back up and also regularly access, share, and sync your files across multiple devices. ("Sync" is short for synchronization, which ensures the same set of files are updated on all the user's devices.)

DropBox, Microsoft's SkyDrive, Amazon's CloudDrive, Apple's iCloud, and Google's Drive are examples of cloud storage options that provide cheap or free storage for easy sharing of documents, photos, audio files, and videos. However, there is not necessarily any tech support or guarantee of security, and if one or more of the company's servers goes down, you may lose some or all of your files.

Examples of cloud backup services are Carbonite and Mozy. When you choose a cloud service, be sure you understand what options are available: Back up data files only? Back up applications also? Back up email files? Synching across devices? Tech support? Good security? Automatic updating of files when you make changes on your computer hard disk or mobile device? Easy access to files? Which file formats are supported? Is the service free, and for how much storage space?

An interesting variant on cloud computing is *application virtualization,* the practice of running software from a remote server rather than on the user's computer (cloud computing, Chapter 1, p. 36).

Application Virtualization

For more information about this kind of cloud computing, go to:

http://searchenterprisedesktop.techtarget.com/definition/application-virtualization

www.microsoft.com/systemcenter/appv/default.mspx

www.citrix.com/products/xenapp/how-it-works/application-virtualization.html

http://searchvirtualdesktop.techtarget.com/definition/app-virtualization

panel 4.17

Top cloud storage providers

According to Gartner, an information technology research firm, the top 10 cloud storage providers as of January 2013 are these:

- Amazon Web Services
- AT&T Synaptic Cloud Storage
- Google Cloud Storage
- HP Cloud Object Storage
- IBM SmartCloud Storage
- Internap AgileFiles
- Microsoft Windows Azure Blob Storage
- Nirvanix
- Rackspace
- Softlayer Cloudlayer

Moore's Law

In 1965, an article in *Electronics* magazine by Gordon Moore, the future founder of Intel, predicted that computer processing power would double roughly every 18 months; he later increased that to 24 months (*http://slashdot.org/story/11/01/04/1922239/45-years-later-does-moores-law-still-hold-true*).

Is Moore's "law" still believed to be true?

http://dujs.dartmouth.edu/spring-2013-15th-anniversary-edition/keeping-up-with-moores-law#.UbDVZ9hwu8A

www.tomshardware.com/news/intel-tri-gate-3d-transistor-CPU-moores-law,12710.html

www.pcworld.com/article/2030005/why-moores-law-not-mobility-is-killing-the-pc.html

http://news.cnet.com/8301-11386_3-57526581-76/moores-law-the-rule-that-really-matters-in-tech/

www.howstuffworks.com/moores-law.htm

More about Nanotechnology

How far has nanotechnology progressed? To begin to find out, check out nanotechnology's leading forum, the Foresight Institute (*www.foresight.org*), and leading critic, ETC (*www.etcgroup.org*). Then check out some of the current uses for nanotechnology:

www.advanceteclle.com/nanotechnology_microelectronics.html

www.which.co.uk/campaigns/technology/what-you-need-to-know-about-nanotechnology/where-is-nanotechnology-used/

www.understandingnano.com/nanotech-applications.html

www.howstuffworks.com/nanotechnology3.htm

Also, what effects might nanoparticles have on the body's systems? Go to:

www.epa.gov/nanoscience/quickfinder/hh_effects.htm

4.8 FUTURE DEVELOPMENTS IN PROCESSING & STORAGE

What are some forthcoming developments that could affect processing power and storage capacity?

How small do computer chips, both processing and storage, need to be? Already electronic components have been shrunk to the point that a dime-size circuit board, along with a microphone, a radio, and a battery, can be attached to a 2-inch-long cockroach. The purpose: "to use the insects to communicate with people trapped in collapsed buildings, mines, and other areas rescuers can't easily reach," says one article. "The insects might also conduct surveillance."[24]

However, future electronics may be even smaller, operating at the molecular level, as we consider next.

Future Developments in Processing

Nanotechnology, optical computing, and DNA computing are already becoming realities.

Eventually transistors will become so tiny that their components will approach the size of molecules, and the laws of physics will no longer allow the kind of doubling in computing power predicted by Moore's Law. The reason: Scientists assume that silicon chips can't be made infinitely smaller because of leakage of electrons across boundaries that are supposed to serve as insulators. What, then, comes next?

NANOTECHNOLOGY Nanotechnology, nanoelectronics, nanostructures, nanofabrication—all start with a measurement known as a *nanometer,* a billionth of a meter, which means we are operating at the level of atoms and molecules. (• *See Panel 4.18.*) A human hair is between 100,000 and 200,000 nanometers thick, while a typical virus can be just 100 nanometers wide. Atoms are typically between one-tenth and one-half of a nanometer wide. Line up 5 million carbon atoms, and the line would be as long as a grain of sand.

In *nanotechnology,* molecules are used to create tiny machines for holding data or performing tasks. Experts attempt to do nanofabrication by building tiny nanostructures one atom or molecule at a time. When applied to chips and other electronic devices, the field is called *nanoelectronics.*

Nanotechnology is seen as a truly viable alternative when silicon chips hit their limit.[25]

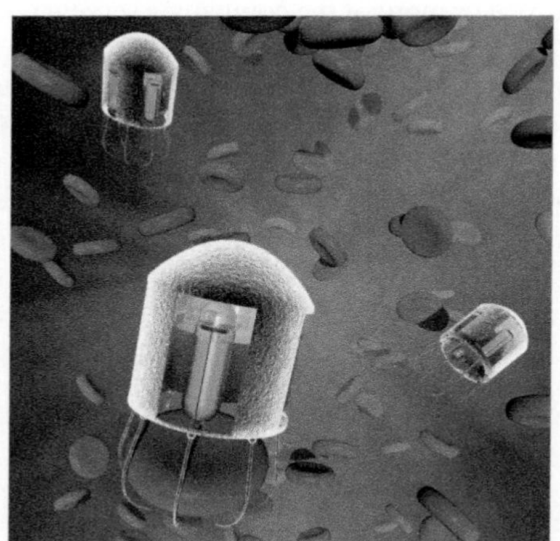

Medical nanorobots. Computer artwork of nanorobots in a human body targeting red blood cells. One of the aims of nanotechnology is to develop microscopically small probes that could be used to target cancer cells or deliver specific treatments to certain types of cell. Here, one of the nanorobots has used clamps to attach itself to a red blood cell and is using a syringe to inject drugs or genetic material. Other nanorobots and red blood cells are seen in the background.

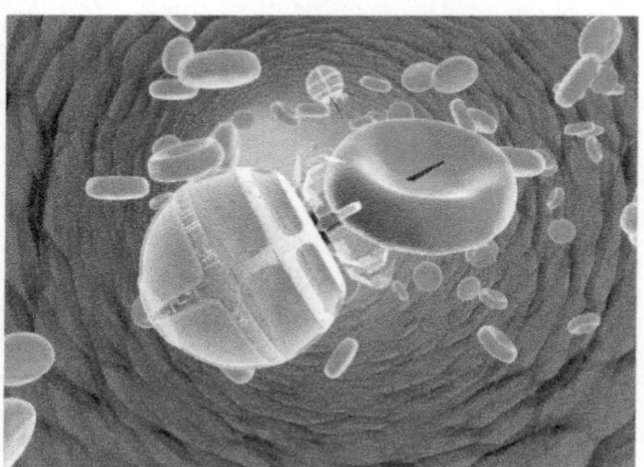

This nanorobot is also a drug injector; it is clinging to the cell with legs, like those of a spider.

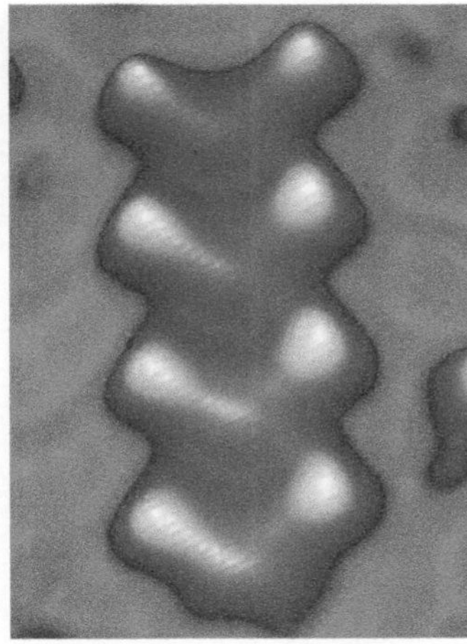

The smallest superconductor, measuring just .87 nanometer wide

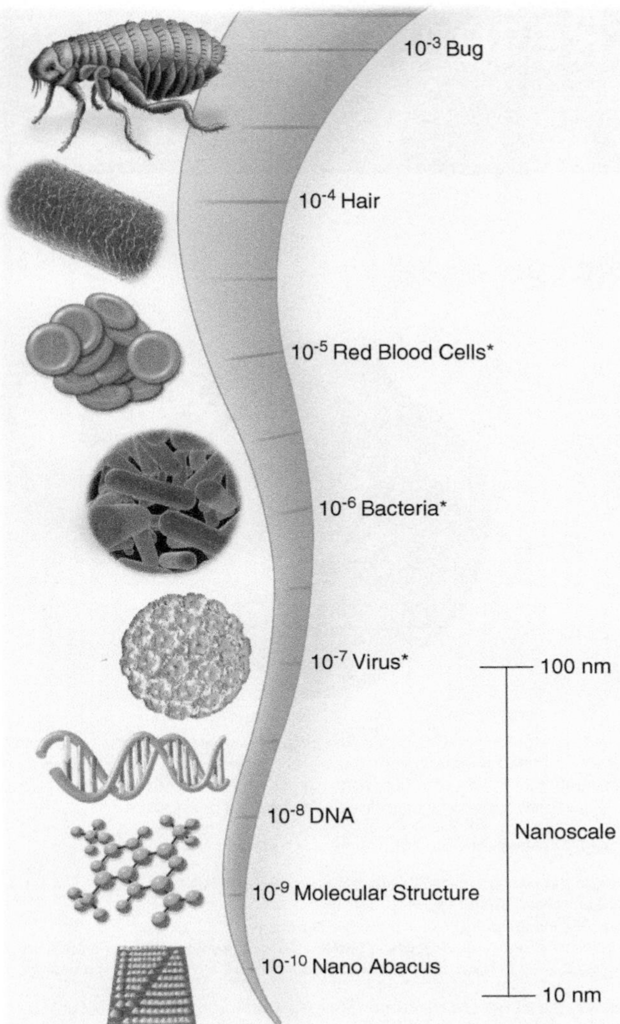

panel 4.18

Nanotechnology: A matter of scale

The world of nanotechnology is so small it defies imagination (adapted from *www.discovernano.northwestern.edu/whatis/index_html/images/* and *www.mindfully.org/Technology/2004/Buckyball-Football1jul04.htm*).

TECH TALES Nanotechnology, the Movie

Seen the flick *A Boy and His Atom?* It was released by IBM in May 2013 and shows the image of a boy "as almost a stick-figure character made up of single lines of atoms for his arms, legs, even mouth," according to one description.[26] IBM's engineers were able "to manipulate those atoms so that the boy looks like he's moving his legs and playing with a single atom like it was a ball, all set to a musical background."

The movie, which can be seen at *www.research.ibm.com/articles/madewithatoms.shtml*, is the smallest stop-motion film ever made, according to the *Guinness World Records* organization.

The purpose of the film is to demonstrate advances in nanotechnology. The oxygen atoms seen in the movie are 2.36 millionths of an inch across in size. All the action takes place using 10,000 molecules made of oxygen and carbon atoms, arranged to tell the tale of a boy and his tiny toy atom. "We have learned a lot about moving atoms around," said one IBM researcher, "and we wanted to show that to the public." ■

OPTICAL COMPUTING Today's computers are electronic; tomorrow's might be optical, or optoelectronic—using light, not electricity. With optical technology, a machine using lasers, lenses, and mirrors would represent the on/off codes of data with pulses of light.

Light is much faster than electricity. Indeed, fiber-optic networks, which consist of hair-thin glass fibers instead of copper wire, can move information at speeds 3,000 times faster than conventional networks. However, the signals get bogged down when they have to be

Nokia Research Center

Research | Open Innovation | Locations | People | News & Events | Videos | Publications | About NRC | Search

Home > Research > Nokia Morph Concept

The Morph Concept

Launched alongside The Museum of Modern Art "Design and The Elastic Mind" exhibition, the Morph concept device is a bridge between highly advanced technologies and their potential benefits to end-users. This device concept showcases some revolutionary leaps being explored by Nokia Research Center (NRC) in collaboration with the Cambridge Nanoscience Centre (United Kingdom) – nanoscale technologies that will potentially create a world of radically different devices that open up an entirely new spectrum of possibilities.

Morph concept technologies might create fantastic opportunities for mobile devices:

- Newly-enabled flexible and transparent materials blend more seamlessly with the way we live
- Devices become self-cleaning and self-preserving
- Transparent electronics offering an entirely new aesthetic dimension
- Built-in solar absorption might charge a device, whilst batteries become smaller, longer lasting and faster to charge
- Integrated sensors might allow us to learn more about the environment around us, empowering us to make better choices

In addition to the advances above, the integrated electronics shown in the Morph concept could cost less and include more functionality in a much smaller space, even as interfaces are simplified and usability is enhanced. All of these new capabilities will unleash new applications and services that will allow us to communicate and interact in unprecedented ways.

Nokia's nanotech Morph telephone. The phone's theoretical feature list would include the ability to bend into numerous shapes, so it can be worn around the wrist or held up to the face; transparent electronics would allow the device to be see-through yet functional; self-cleaning surfaces could absorb solar energy to recharge the phone's battery.

processed by silicon chips. Optical chips would remove that bottleneck. It's suggested that mass-produced versions of optical chips could not only slash costs of voice and data networks but also become a new type of technology for delivering high-bandwidth movies, music, and games.

DNA COMPUTING Potentially, biotechnology could be used to grow cultures of bacteria that, when exposed to light, emit a small electric charge, for example. The properties of this "biochip" could be used to represent the on/off digital signals used in computing. Or a strand of synthetic DNA might represent information as a pattern of molecules, and the information might be manipulated by subjecting it to precisely designed chemical reactions that could mark or lengthen the strand. For instance, instead of using binary, it could manipulate the four nucleic acids (represented by *A, T, C, G*), which holds the promise of processing big numbers. This is an entirely *nondigital* way of thinking about computing.[27] "Can you instruct a biomolecule to move and function in a certain way—researchers at the interface of computer science, chemistry, biology, and engineering are attempting to do just that," says Mitra Basu, a program director at the National Science Foundation responsible for the agency's support to this research.[28]

Recent molecular robotics work has produced so-called DNA walkers, or strings of reprogrammed DNA with "legs" that enabled them to briefly walk. Now this research team has shown these molecular robotic spiders can in fact move autonomously through a specially

Living Computers

www.livescience.com/28273-biological-computers-possible-using-dna.html

created, two-dimensional landscape. The walkers acted in rudimentary robotic ways, showing they are capable of starting motion, walking for a while, turning, and stopping.

Quantum Computing

For more information about quantum computing, go to:

www.usatoday.com/story/tech/sciencefair/2013/05/19/d-wave-sale-speed/2216255/

http://bits.blogs.nytimes.com/2013/05/16/google-buys-a-quantum-computer/

www.economist.com/news/science-and-technology/21578027-first-real-world-contests-between-quantum-computers-and-standard-ones-faster

QUANTUM COMPUTING Sometimes called the "ultimate computer," the *quantum computer* is based on quantum mechanics, the theory of physics that explains the erratic world of the atom. Whereas an ordinary computer stores information as 0s and 1s represented by electric currents or voltages that are either high or low, a quantum computer stores information by using states of elementary particles called *qubits.* Scientists envision using the energized and relaxed states of individual atoms to represent data. For example, hydrogen atoms could be made to switch off and on like a conventional computer's transistors by moving from low-energy states (off) to high-energy states (on).[29] A U.S. company called D-Wave Systems claims to have made a quantum computer, which an independent researcher found was 3,600 times as fast as a conventional high-performance computer.[30]

EXTENDING BATTERY & RECHARGING TECHNOLOGY Where is the weak link in our high-tech world? Says one writer, "Computer chips double in speed every two years—your current BlackBerry is as powerful as your desktop computer once was—but the batteries powering these devices are improving only about 8% per year."[31] Notebook, tablet, and smartphone users are tired of having their devices run out of electric charge after only a few hours. And claims that a laptop will get up to 5 hours and 40 minutes of battery life are often not accurate, says one expert, although new tablets are getting much better.[32]

Among the areas under development: Various companies are marketing wireless chargers, freeing gadgets from their recharging cords.[33] Companies are also experimenting with developing new lithium-ion batteries, which may extend battery life. Other companies are exploring metallic alternatives to lithium, such as magnesium.[34] Silver-zinc batteries may provide up to 30% higher capacity compared to existing lithium-ion batteries.[35] Vanadium, extracted from shale, can be used to make powerful, long-lasting batteries.[36] Tiny fuel-cell batteries, powered by combustible liquids or gases, could potentially power a laptop for days between refills. Marvell Technology Group, which makes chips, is promoting "plug computers," computing devices that plug into electric sockets and that are about the same size yet would have enough power to manage people's digital media.[37] Direct methanol fuel cells (DMFCs) are another new technology planned for green, low-cost, and long-running batteries.

Nanotechnology & NBIC

For more information, go to:

www.nanotech.upenn.edu/

ETHICAL MATTERS Of these future developments, nanotechnology has probably received the most attention, and indeed the U.S. government has launched the National Nanotechnology Initiative. In fact, however, nanotechnology and other important fields have been melding into a new field of science vital to U.S. security and economic development. This field is known by the acronym *NBIC* (pronounced either "*en*-bick" or "*nib*-bick"), which represents the convergence of nanotechnology, biotechnology, information technology, and cognitive (brain) science.

But is there a possibility of "Gray Goo"? This is a scenario hypothesized in *Wired* magazine in which self-replicating molecule-size robots run amok and transform all earthly matter into nanobots.[38]

Future Developments in Secondary Storage

New memory technology could sidestep all current RAM technologies.

One promising technology is the *microholographic* disk developed by General Electric Co. that stores 540 gigabytes, or the content of 100 standard DVDs, on a single DVD (equivalent to 20 single-layer Blu-ray disks). Holographic technology can store data beneath the surface of a disk, whereas CDs, DVDs, and Blu-ray disks store data only on the surface. A team of Australian researchers is going beyond this to develop "five-dimensional" storage, which would permit a 10-terabyte disk, the equivalent of storing 10,000 standard-definition movies on one disk.[39]

MOLECULAR ELECTRONICS—STORAGE AT THE SUBATOMIC LEVEL An emerging field, molecular electronics, may push secondary storage into another dimension entirely. Some possibilities include polymer memory, holograms, molecular magnets, subatomic lines, and bacteria.

Metamaterials

Is the army testing an invisible tank?

http://science.howstuffworks.com/invisible-tank1.htm

Also:

http://phys.org/news/2013-05-tackle-collapsing-bridges-technology.html

http://phys.org/news/2013-01-ultrathin-invisibility-cloak-wide-applications.html

www.scienceworldreport.com/articles/7364/20130606/replacing-bulky-optics-micrometer-thin-metamaterial-sheets.htm

Polymer memory involves developing an alternative to silicon to create chips that store data on polymers, or plastics, which are cheaper than silicon devices. A bonus with polymers is that, unlike conventional RAM memory, it is nonvolatile—it retains information even after the machine is shut off. Polymer memory involves storing data based on the polymer's electric resistance. IBM is also developing so-called *probe storage* that uses tiny probes to burn pits in a Plexiglas-like polymer, in which each hole is about 10 nanometers wide, resulting in an experimental storage device of 200 gigabits per square inch. IBM has said that someday it expects as many as 25 million pages of text will be stored in an area no larger than a postage stamp.

NEW IMAGE-COMPRESSION TECHNOLOGY Scientists at Duke University have designed a new technology that compresses images far more efficiently than present methods, such as .jpeg. The technology uses a sensor that uses special materials (called *metamaterials*) that can bend light and radio waves in unusual ways to compress both still and video images.[40]

System Crashes

What can you do if your system crashes? For information, go to:

http://windows.microsoft.com/en-us/windows-vista/picking-up-the-pieces-after-a-computer-crash

www.networkworld.com/supp/2011/041811-windows-7-crashes.html

www.slideshare.net/StenaWhite/windows-8-crash-best-solution-to-repair-windows-8

www.ehow.com/how_2181871_fix-mac-os-crash.html

www.macworld.com/article/2027920/mac-troubleshooting-how-to-handle-freezes-and-crashes.html

www.infohq.com/Computer/Recover_From_Windows_System_Crashes.html

Laptop Buying Guides

www.laptopmag.com/laptops/default.aspx

http://reviews.cnet.com/laptops/

www.pcmag.com/article2/0,2817,2356818,00.asp

http://online.wsj.com/article/SB10001424127887324482504578454854284679888.html

EXPERIENCE BOX

How to Buy a Laptop

"*Choosing a laptop computer is trickier than buying a desktop PC,*" says Wall Street Journal technology writer Walter Mossberg.[41] *The reason: laptops are more diverse and more personal and include "a mind-boggling array of computers, from featherweight models that are great for travel to bulky multimedia machines that double as TV sets." In addition, desktop "generic boxes" tend to be similar, at least within a price class. Trying to choose among the many Windows-based laptops is a particularly brow-wrinkling experience. Windows laptops cost less than Apple laptops, and they offer more variety; Macintosh laptops used to tend to be more straightforward and safer from malware attacks, but that seems to be no longer true.*[42]

Choosing a tablet can be a bit easier because the screen size does not fundamentally change the nature of the machine—all tablets can browse the web, check email, and run apps.[43]

Nevertheless, here are some suggestions:

Purpose

What are you going to use your laptop for? You can get one that's essentially a desktop replacement and won't be moved much. If you expect to use the machine a lot in class, in libraries, or on airplanes, however, weight and battery life are important.

Whatever kind of laptop you get, be sure it works with your school's system. Some departments within a college may require a specific computer configuration or software, so check beforehand. Certainly it should be up to date and able to get Internet access through Ethernet and wireless connections.

If you choose a tablet, you can probably be comfortable with a smaller or midsize version, which is easier to hold. The exception is if you have to do a lot of note taking, write a lot of emails, or do a lot of writing in general—laptops are better for that.

Basics

For laptops, most technology writers advise getting a 64-bit machine with 4 GB RAM for best performance, and a 500-gigabytes hard drive. And make sure that you install antivirus and firewall software right away. (Macs can run well with only 2 gigabytes, unless you are working with complex graphics.) Aim for newer processors, but don't feel you have to have the fastest one around; for most people, all processors are fine. A few USB 2.0 ports are necessary (not all peripheral devices can use USB 3.0), an HDMI port, an Ethernet port, and a CD/DVD slot and burner software. Of course, a Wi-Fi connection is necessary, and Bluetooth can be useful.

Budget & Weight

Laptops range from $300 (with rebates) to $3,000, with high-end brands aimed mainly at businesspeople, hard-core videogamers, and people doing video production. You can get a perfectly fine laptop for $500. Weight can range from about 3 pounds to over 10 pounds. The general rule is not to buy more laptop than you need.

Batteries: The Life–Weight Trade-Off

Since laptops are designed to be used as a source of portable computing, one of their major features is the length of time the computer can be used away from an external power source. The battery is the only thing keeping the laptop running when it isn't plugged in with the AC adapter. As laptops have become more common and used in more situations, the battery technology used in laptops has become more sophisticated. You should find a laptop that will run for at least 3 hours on its battery.

A rechargeable lithium-ion battery lasts longer than a nickel-metal hydride battery. Even so, a battery in the less expensive machines will usually run continuously for only about 2¼ hours. (DVD players are particularly voracious consumers of battery power, so it's the rare laptop that will allow you to finish watching a 2-hour movie; a laptop with a bigger screen, faster processor, and better graphics will require more power from the battery.)

Heavier machines usually have longer battery life. The lightweight machines tend to get less than 2 hours, and toting extra batteries offsets the weight savings—a battery can weigh a pound or so. (When shopping for a laptop you will often see manufacturers list the amount of cells contained within a laptop battery such as 6-cells and 9-cells. A 9-cell battery has 50% more capacity than a 6-cell, and a 12-cell battery more than a 6-cell battery, but more cells also increase the weight.)

For more information on laptop batteries, try *www.geek.com/laptop-battery/*.

Software

Laptops might come with less software than you would get with a typical desktop, though what you get will probably be adequate for most student purposes. You will have to purchase most of your software separately.

Keyboards & Pointing Devices

The keys on a laptop keyboard are usually the same size as those on a desktop machine, although they can be smaller. However, the up-and-down action feels different, and the keys may feel wobbly. In addition, some keys may be omitted altogether, or keys may do double duty or appear in unaccustomed arrangements. So check out the keyboard on the laptop you are interested in.

Most laptops have a small touch-sensitive pad in lieu of a mouse—you drag your finger across the touchpad to move the cursor. (But be sure to carry a regular USB wireless mouse with your laptop, so when you are working on a large flat surface, you can just plug the USB mouse connector into a USB port on the laptop and use it as you would on a desktop computer.)

Screens

If you're not going to carry the laptop around much, go for a big, bright screen. Most people find they are comfortable with a 13- to 15-inch display, measured diagonally, though screens can be as small as 8 inches and as large as 17 or 20 inches (which is better for viewing movies).

Memory, Speed, & Storage Capacity

If you're buying a laptop to complement your desktop, you may be able to get along with reduced memory, slow processor, small hard disk, and no CD/DVD drive. Otherwise, all these matters become important.

Memory (RAM) is the most important factor in computer performance, even though processor speed is more heavily hyped. Most laptops have at least 1 gigabyte of memory, but 4 gigabytes of high-speed DDR SDRAM is best. A microprocessor running 2.0 gigahertz should be adequate. (But if you plan to work with a lot of graphics and/or video, get more RAM and a higher-speed processor, as well as a laptop with a separate video card inside with its own additional memory.)

A hard drive of 320 gigabytes or more is sufficient for most people, and make sure that you have an internal CD/DVD drive, for backing up your files and to play movies and the like.

Wireless

Laptops come with Wi-Fi for wireless networking; 802.11 technology is fine for ordinary use, but try to buy a laptop with the faster 802.11n version.

For more information about buying a laptop, go to:

http://allthingsd.com/video/mossbergs-annual-holiday-laptop-buyers-guide/

http://reviews.cnet.com/laptop-buying-guide/

www.laptopmag.com/laptops/default.aspx?tab=buying%20advice

www.pcmag.com/article2/0,2817,2356818,00.asp

Also, go green: look for manufacturers that sell Energy Star systems and provide instructions for recycling old computer equipment.

TERMS & EXPLANATIONS

arithmetic/logic unit (ALU) (p. 211) Part of the CPU that performs arithmetic operations and logical operations and controls the speed of those operations. Why it's important: *Arithmetic operations are the fundamental math operations: addition, subtraction, multiplication, and division. Logical operations are comparisons such as "equal to," "greater than," or "less than."*

ASCII (American Standard Code for Information Interchange) (p. 200) Binary code used on microcomputers. Besides having more conventional characters, the Extended ASCII version includes such characters as math symbols and Greek letters. Why it's important: *ASCII is the binary code most widely used in microcomputers.*

binary system (p. 197) A two-state system used for data representation in computers; has only two digits—0 and 1. Why it's important: *In the computer, 0 can be represented by electric current being off and 1 by the current being on. All data and program instructions that go into the computer are represented in terms of binary numbers.*

bit (p. 198) Short for "binary digit," which is either a 0 or a 1 in the binary system of data representation in computer systems. Why it's important: *The bit is the fundamental element of all data and information processed and stored in a computer system.*

Bluetooth port (p. 220) Wireless technology that consists of short-range radio waves that transmit up to 30 feet. Why it's important: *It is used not only to connect cellphones to computers and to headsets but also to connect computers to printers, keyboards, and other appliances.*

Blu-ray (p. 227) Optical format developed to enable recording, rewriting, and playback of high-definition video, as well as storing large amounts of data. Why it's important: *It's possible to fit more data on a Blu-ray disk even though it's the same size as a CD/DVD.*

bus (p. 211) Also called *bus line;* electrical data roadway through which bits are transmitted within the CPU and between the CPU and other components of the motherboard. Why it's important: *A bus resembles a multilane highway: The more lanes it has, the faster the bits can be transferred.*

byte (p. 198) Group of 8 bits. Why it's important: *A byte represents one character, digit, or other value. It is the basic unit used to measure the storage capacity of main memory and secondary-storage devices (kilobytes and megabytes).*

cache memory (p. 213) Special high-speed memory area on a chip that the CPU can access quickly. It temporarily stores instructions and data that the processor is likely to use frequently. Why it's important: *Cache speeds up processing.*

CD-R (compact disk–recordable) disk (p. 226) Optical-disk form of secondary storage that can be written to only once but can be read many times. Why it's important: *This format allows consumers to make their own CDs. Once recorded, the information cannot be erased. CD-R is often used by companies for archiving.*

CD-ROM (compact disk read-only memory) (p. 225) Optical-disk form of secondary storage that is used to hold prerecorded text, graphics, and sound. Why it's important: *Like music CDs, a CD-ROM is a read-only disk.* Read-only *means the disk's content is recorded at the time of manufacture and cannot be written on or erased by the user.*

CD-RW (compact disk–rewritable) disk (p. 226) Also known as *erasable optical disk;* optical-disk form of secondary storage that allows users to record and erase data, so the disk can be used over and over again. Special CD-RW drives and software are required. Why it's important: *CD-RW disks are useful for archiving and backing up large amounts of data.*

chip (p. 194) Also called a *microchip;* consists of millions of microminiature integrated electronic circuits printed on a tiny piece of silicon. Silicon is an element widely found in sand that has desirable electrical (or "semiconducting") properties. Why it's important: *Chips have made possible the development of small computers. There are different kinds of chips; one is the CPU, the "brain" of the computer.*

chipset (p. 206) Groups of interconnected chips on the motherboard that control the flow of information between the microprocessor and other system components connected to the motherboard. Why it's important: *The chipset determines what types of processors, memory, and video card ports will work on the same motherboard. It also establishes the types of multimedia, storage, network, and other hardware the motherboard supports.*

cloud storage (p. 231) Online storage; the use of an Internet service to store data. Why it's important: *Cloud storage allows you to access all your files from anywhere and from different devices.*

CMOS (complementary metal-oxide semiconductor) chips (p. 214) Battery-powered chips that don't lose their contents when the power is turned off. Why it's important: *CMOS chips contain flexible start-up instructions—such as time, date, and calendar—that must be kept current even when the computer is turned off. Unlike ROM chips, CMOS chips can be reprogrammed, as when you need to change the time for daylight saving time.*

control unit (p. 210) Part of the CPU that deciphers each instruction stored in it and then carries out the instruction. Why it's important: *The control unit directs the movement of electronic signals between main memory and the arithmetic/logic unit. It also directs these electronic signals between main memory and the input and output devices.*

CPU (central processing unit) (p. 210) The processor; it follows the instructions of the software (program) to manipulate data into information. The CPU consists of two parts—(1) the control unit and (2) the arithmetic/logic unit (ALU), both of which contain registers, or high-speed storage areas. All are linked by a kind of electronic "roadway" called a *bus*. Why it's important: *The CPU is the "brain" of the computer.*

data center (p. 207) Sometimes called a *server farm;* a facility that holds servers and related network equipment. Why it's important: *Many Internet activities—such as social networking, Google searches, electronic financial transactions, and so on—would not be possible without data centers.*

DVD-ROM (digital versatile disk or digital video disk, with read-only memory) (p. 226) CD-type disk with extremely high capacity, able to store 4.7–17 or more gigabytes. Why it's important: *It is a powerful and versatile secondary-storage medium.*

EBCDIC (Extended Binary Coded Decimal Interchange Code) (p. 200) Binary code used with large computers. Why it's important: *EBCDIC is commonly used in mainframes.*

eSATA port (p. 220) *SATA* stands for Serial Advanced Technology Attachment. An eSATA port, or external SATA port, allows the attachment of an eSATA hard disk. Why it's important: *SATA disks support fast data transmission speeds.*

Ethernet port (p. 219) Network standard for linking all devices in a local area network (LAN). Why it's important: *It's commonly used to connect microcomputers, cable modems, and printers. (To use Ethernet, the computer must have an Ethernet network interface card, and special Ethernet cables are required.)*

exabyte (EB) (p. 199) Approximately 1 quintillion bytes—1 billion billion bytes (1,024 petabytes—or 1,152,921, 504,606,846,976 bytes). Why it's important: *Although this number is seldom used, it is estimated that all the printed material in the world represents about 5 exabytes.*

expansion (p. 204) Way of increasing a computer's capabilities by adding hardware to perform tasks that are beyond the scope of the basic system. Why it's important: *Expansion allows users to customize and/or upgrade their computer systems.*

expansion card (p. 215) Also known as *expansion board, adapter card, interface card, plug-in board, controller card, add-in,* or *add-on;* circuit board that provides more memory or that controls peripheral devices. Why it's important: *Common expansion cards connect to the monitor (graphics card), speakers and microphones (sound card), and network (network card). Most computers have four to eight expansion slots, some of which may already contain expansion cards included in your initial PC purchase.*

expansion slot (p. 215) Socket on the motherboard into which the user can plug an expansion card. Why it's important: *See also* ***expansion card.***

FireWire port (p. 219) A specialized port intended to connect devices working with lots of data. Why it's important: *FireWire is used for DVD drives, digital video cameras, and gaming consoles.*

flash drive *See* **USB flash drive.**

flash memory card (p. 228) Also known as *flash RAM cards;* form of secondary storage consisting of circuitry on credit-card-size cards that can be inserted into slots connecting to the motherboard on notebook computers. Why it's important: *Flash memory is nonvolatile, so it retains data even when the power is turned off. Flash memory is used in digital cameras, smartphones, and other mobile devices.*

flash memory chip (p. 214) Chip that can be erased and reprogrammed more than once (unlike PROM chips, which can be programmed only once). Why it's important: *Flash memory, which can range from 2 to 256 gigabytes in capacity, is used to store programs not only in personal computers but also in pagers, cellphones, printers, and digital cameras. Unlike standard RAM chips, flash memory is nonvolatile—data is retained when the power is turned off.*

flash memory stick (p. 228) Smaller than a stick of chewing gum, a form of flash memory media that plugs into a memory stick port in a digital camera, camcorder, notebook PC, photo printer, and other devices. Why it's important: *It holds from 2 gigabytes to 2 terabytes of data and is very convenient to transport and use.*

gigabyte (G, GB) (p. 198) Approximately 1 billion bytes (1,073,741,824 bytes); a measure of storage capacity. Why it's important: *This measure was formerly used mainly with "big iron" (mainframe) computers but is typical of the secondary-storage (hard-disk) capacity of today's microcomputers.*

gigahertz (GHz) (p. 208) Measure of speed used for the latest generation of microprocessors: 1 billion cycles per second. Why it's important: *People need units of measurement to help them choose equipment that matches their needs.*

graphics card (p. 215) Also called a *video card, video RAM (VRAM),* or *video adapter;* expansion card that converts signals from the computer into video signals that are displayed as images on a monitor. Why it's important: *The power of a graphics card determines the clarity of the images on the monitor.*

graphics processing unit (GPU) (p. 207) Specialized processor used to manipulate three-dimensional (3-D) computer graphics. Why it's important: *Unlike a general-purpose CPU, a GPU is able to perform a range of complex algorithms (problem-solving steps). GPUs are found in personal computers, workstations, tablets, smartphones, and game consoles.*

hard disk (p. 221) Secondary-storage medium; thin but rigid metal, glass, or ceramic platter covered with a substance that allows data to be stored in the form of magnetized spots. Hard disks are tightly sealed within an enclosed hard-disk-drive unit to prevent any foreign matter from getting inside. Data may be recorded on both sides of the disk platters. Why it's important: *Most microcomputers use hard disks as their principal storage medium. (Networked computers may have no internal storage.)*

HDMI (High-Definition Multimedia Interface) port (p. 221) Multimedia connection that can carry both video and audio signals. Why it's important: *HDMI is used for HDTVs, DVD players, and game consoles.*

integrated circuit (p. 193) A set of electronic circuits, including wires, formed (etched) on a single "chip," or piece, of special material, usually silicon. An integrated circuit is formed as part of a single manufacturing process. Why it's important: *Today* *integrated circuits are important parts of daily life and can be found in most electrical devices, from kitchen appliances to the circuitry that controls life support machines in hospitals. Without integrated circuits, many of the modern tools, devices, and conveniences that we have gotten used to would not be possible.*

Intel-type chip (p. 206) Processor chip originally made for microcomputers; made principally by Intel Corp. and Advanced Micro Devices (AMD), but also by Cyrix, DEC, and others. Why it's important: *These chips are used by many computer and device manufacturers, such as Dell, Hewlett-Packard, Asus, Apple, Toshiba, Samsung, and Lenovo.*

IrDA port (p. 221) Short for Infrared Data Association. Why it's important: *IrDA ports transfer data via infrared light waves between directly aligned devices, as between a smartphone and a desktop computer.*

kilobyte (K, KB) (p. 198) Approximately 1,000 bytes (1,024 bytes); a measure of storage capacity. Why it's important: *The kilobyte was a common unit of measure for memory or secondary-storage capacity on older computers.*

machine cycle (p. 210) Series of operations performed by the control unit to execute a single program instruction. It (1) fetches an instruction, (2) decodes the instruction, (3) executes the instruction, and (4) stores the result. Why it's important: *The machine cycle is the essence of computer-based processing.*

machine language (p. 200) Binary code (language) that the computer uses directly. The 0s and 1s represent precise storage locations and operations. Why it's important: *For a program to run, it must be in the machine language of the computer that is executing it.*

megabyte (M, MB) (p. 198) Approximately 1 million bytes (1,048,576 bytes); measure of storage capacity. Why it's important: *Some microcomputer secondary-storage capacity is expressed in megabytes.*

megahertz (MHz) (p. 208) Measure of microcomputer processing speed, controlled by the system clock; 1 million cycles per second. Why it's important: *People need units of measurement to help them choose equipment that matches their needs.*

microprocessor (p. 195) Miniaturized circuitry of a computer processor. It stores program instructions that process, or manipulate, data into information. The key parts of the microprocessor are transistors. Why it's important: *Microprocessors enabled the development of microcomputers.*

MIDI port (p. 221) Short for Musical Instrument Digital Interface. Why it's important: *MIDI ports are used to connect electronic musical instruments to a sound card that converts the signals to digital instructions that can be saved or manipulated.*

multicore processor (p. 206) Microcomputer chip such as Intel's dual-core, quad-core, hex-core, and octo-core processors, with two or more processor "cores" on a single piece of silicon. Why it's important: *Chips can take on several tasks at once because the operating system can divide its work over more than one processor. Thus multicore processors increase speed over single processors.*

network interface card (NIC) (p. 216) Expansion card that allows the transmission of data over a cabled (wired) network. Why it's important: *Installation of a network interface card in the computer enables the user to connect with various computers and other devices such as printers.*

optical disk (p. 225) Removable disk, usually 4.75 inches in diameter and about .05 inch thick, on which data is written and read through the use of laser beams. Why it's important: *An audio CD holds up to 74 minutes (2 billion bits' worth) of high-fidelity stereo sound. Some optical disks are used strictly for digital data storage, but many are used to distribute multimedia programs that combine text, visuals, and sound.*

parallel port (p. 220) A connector for a line that allows 8 bits (1 byte) to be transmitted simultaneously, like cars on an eight-lane highway. Why it's important: *Parallel lines move information faster than serial lines do. However, because they can transmit information efficiently only up to 15 feet, they are used principally for connecting printers or external disk or magnetic-tape backup storage devices. (Parallel ports are being replaced by USB ports.)*

PC card (p. 216) Thin, credit-card-size flash memory device. Why it's important: *PC cards are used principally on laptop computers and tablets to expand capabilities.*

petabyte (P, PB) (p. 199) Approximately 1 quadrillion bytes (1,048,576 gigabytes); measure of storage capacity. Why it's important: *The huge storage capacities of modern databases are expressed in petabytes.*

Plug and Play (p. 215) Peripheral connection standard—such as USB and FireWire—that allows peripheral devices and expansion cards to be automatically configured while they are being installed. Why it's important: *Plug and Play avoids the hassle of setting switches and creating special files, which plagued earlier users.*

port (p. 217) A connecting socket or jack on the outside of the system unit into which are plugged different kinds of cables. Why it's important: *A port allows the user to plug in a cable to connect a peripheral device, such as a monitor, printer, or modem, so that it can communicate with the computer system.*

power supply (p. 201) Device that converts AC to DC to run the computer. Why it's important: *The electricity available from a standard wall outlet is alternating current (AC), but a microcomputer runs on direct current (DC).*

RAM (random access memory) chips (p. 212) Also called *primary storage* and *main memory;* chips that temporarily hold software instructions and data before and after it is processed by the CPU. RAM is a volatile form of storage. Why it's important: *RAM is the working memory of the computer. Having enough RAM is critical to users' ability to run many software programs.*

read (p. 214) To transfer data from an input source into the computer's memory or CPU. Why it's important: *Reading, along with writing, is an essential computer activity.*

read/write head (p. 222) Mechanism used to transfer data between the computer and the hard disk. When the disk spins inside its case, the read/write head moves back and forth over the data access area on the disk. Why it's important: *The read/write head enables the essential activities of reading and writing data.*

registers (p. 211) High-speed storage areas that temporarily store data during processing. Why it's important: *Registers may store a program instruction while it is being decoded, store data while it is being processed by the ALU, or store the results of a calculation.*

ROM (read-only memory) (p. 214) Memory chip that cannot be written on or erased by the computer user without special equipment. Why it's important: *ROM chips contain fixed start-up instructions. They are loaded, at the factory, with programs containing special instructions for basic computer operations, such as starting the computer or putting characters on the screen. These chips are nonvolatile; their contents are not lost when power to the computer is turned off.*

secondary-storage hardware (p. 221) Devices that permanently hold data and information as well as programs. Why it's important: *Secondary storage—as opposed to primary storage—is nonvolatile; that is, saved data and programs are permanent, or remain intact, when the power is turned off.*

sectors (p. 222) The small arcs created in tracks when a disk's storage locations are divided into wedge-shaped sections. Why it's important: *The system software uses the point at which a sector intersects a track to reference the data location.*

semiconductor (p. 194) Material, such as silicon (in combination with other elements), whose electrical properties are intermediate between a good conductor and a nonconductor of electricity. When highly conducting materials are laid on the semiconducting material, an electronic circuit can be created. Why it's important: *Semiconductors are the materials from which integrated circuits (chips) are made.*

serial port (p. 219) A connector for a line that sends bits one after another, like cars on a one-lane highway. Why it's important: *Because individual bits must follow each other, a serial port is still used to connect devices that do not require fast transmission of data, such as wired keyboards, mice, monitors, and modems. It is also useful for sending data over a long distance.*

silicon (p. 194) Element that is widely found in clay and sand and is used in the making of solid-state integrated circuits. Why it's important: *It is used not only because its abundance makes it cheap but also because it is a good semiconductor. As a result, highly conducting materials can be overlaid on the silicon to create the electronic circuitry of the integrated circuit.*

smart card (p. 229) Plastic card that looks like a credit card but has a microprocessor and memory chips embedded in it. When inserted into a reader, it transfers data to and from a central computer. Why it's important: *Unlike conventional credit cards, smart cards can hold a fair amount of data and can store some basic financial records. Thus, they are used as telephone debit cards, health cards, and student cards. They are more secure than traditional magnetic-stripe cards.*

solid-state device (p. 193) Electronic component, such as an integrated circuit, made of solid materials with no moving parts. Why it's important: *Solid-state integrated circuits are far more reliable, smaller, and less expensive than electronic circuits made from several components.*

solid-state drive (SSD) (p. 228) Storage technology that uses flash memory to store data, instructions, and information. SSDs have a capacity of 16–256 gigabytes and have no moving parts to break down, as disk drives do. Why it's important: *Some solid-state drives use SDRAM instead of flash memory, but in either case such drives are lighter, faster, and use less power than conventional disk drives and can better withstand bumps and bangs. Solid-state drives are currently much more expensive than hard-disk drives, but this is changing as they become more popular.*

sound card (p. 215) Expansion card used to convert and transmit digital sounds through analog speakers, microphones, and headsets. Why it's important: *Cards such as PCI wavetable sound cards are used to add music and sound effects to computer videogames.*

system clock (p. 208) Internal timing device that uses fixed vibrations from a quartz crystal to deliver a steady stream of digital pulses or "ticks" to the CPU. These ticks are called *cycles.* Why it's important: *Faster clock speeds will result in faster processing of data and execution of program instructions, as long as the computer's internal circuits can handle the increased speed.*

system unit (p. 196) The metal or plastic case that houses a computer's electronic components used to process data. Why it's important: *The system unit is the main part of a computer. It includes the motherboard, CPU, RAM, and other components. The term* system unit *is often used to differentiate between the computer and peripheral devices, such as the monitor, keyboard, and mouse.*

tablet computer (p. 196) Wireless, portable personal computer with a touch-screen interface. Tablets are typically smaller than notebooks but larger than smartphones. Why it's important: *Tablets have become very popular.*

terabyte (T, TB) (p. 199) Approximately 1 trillion bytes (1,009,511,627,776 bytes); measure of storage capacity. Why it's important: *High-capacity disk storage is expressed in terabytes.*

tracks (p. 222) The rings on a hard disk along which data is recorded. Why it's important: *See also* ***sectors.***

transistor (p. 193) Tiny electronic device that acts as an on/off switch, switching between "on" and "off" millions of times per second. Why it's important: *Transistors are part of a microprocessor.*

Unicode (p. 200) Binary coding scheme that uses 2 bytes (16 bits) for each character, rather than 1 byte (8 bits). Why it's important: *Instead of the 256-character combinations of Extended ASCII, Unicode can handle 65,536 character combinations. Thus, it allows almost all the written languages of the world to be represented using a single character set.*

upgrading (p. 204) Changing to newer, usually more powerful or sophisticated versions, such as a more powerful microprocessor or more memory chips. Why it's important: *Through upgrading,* users can improve their computer systems without buying completely new ones.*

USB flash drive (p. 228) Also called a *thumb drive, keychain drive, flash drive,* or *key drive;* a finger-size module of flash memory that plugs into the USB ports of nearly any PC or Macintosh, as well as many electronic devices. Why it's important: *They generally have storage capacities up to 256 gigabytes and are very useful for carrying files from place to place. When you plug the device into your USB port, it shows up as an external drive on the computer.*

USB (Universal Serial Bus) port (p. 217) High-speed hardware standard for interfacing peripheral devices, such as scanners and printers, to computers without a need for special expansion cards or other hardware modifications to the computer. Why it's important: *USB has replaced many varieties of serial and parallel ports. USB ports are useful for peripherals such as digital cameras, digital speakers, scanners, high-speed modems, and joysticks. Being "hot pluggable" or "hot swappable" means that USB allows such devices to be connected or disconnected while the computer is running.*

virtual memory (p. 214) Type of hard-disk space that is used to extend RAM capacity. Why it's important: *When RAM space is limited, virtual memory allows users to run more software at once, provided the computer's CPU and operating system are equipped to use it. The system allocates some free disk space as an extension of RAM; that is, the computer swaps parts of the software program between the hard disk and RAM as needed.*

volatile (p. 212) Temporary; the contents of volatile storage media, such as RAM, are lost when the power is turned off. Why it's important: *To avoid data loss, save your work to a secondary-storage medium, such as a hard disk, in case the electricity goes off while you're working.*

wireless network card (p. 216) An expansion card that supports networking. Why it's important: *It enables wireless data transmission.*

word size (p. 212) Number of bits that the processor may process at any one time. Why it's important: *The more bits in a word, the faster the computer. A 32-bit computer—that is, one with a 32-bit-word processor—will transfer data within each microprocessor chip in 32-bit chunks, or 4 bytes at a time. A 64-bit computer transfers data in 64-bit chunks, or 8 bytes at a time.*

write (p. 214) To transfer data from the computer's CPU or memory to an output device. Why it's important: *See also* **read.**

CHAPTER REVIEW

LEARNING MEMORIZATION

"I can recognize and recall information."

Self-Test Questions

1. A(n) _____ is about 1,000 bytes; a(n) _____ is about 1 million bytes; a(n) _____ is about 1 billion bytes.
2. The _____ is the part of the microprocessor that tells the rest of the computer how to carry out a program's instructions.
3. The process of retrieving data from a storage device is referred to as _____; the process of copying data to a storage device is called _____.
4. To avoid losing data, users should always _____ their files.
5. Formatted hard disks have _____ and _____ that the system software uses to reference data locations.
6. The _____ is often referred to as the "brain" of a computer.
7. The electrical data roadways through which bits are transmitted are called _____.
8. A(n) _____ is an expansion card plugged into a slot on the motherboard that allows the transmission of data over a cabled (wired) network.
9. Part of the disk-drive mechanism, the _____ transfers data between the computer and the disk.
10. _____chips, also called *main memory,* are critical to computer performance.
11. _____ operations are the fundamental math operations: addition, subtraction, multiplication, and division; _____operations are comparisons such as "equal to," "greater than," or "less than."
12. A group of 8 bits is a(n) _____.
13. In _____, molecules are used to create tiny machines for holding data or performing tasks.
14. A tiny electronic device that acts as an on/off switch, switching between "on" and "off" millions of times per second, is called a(n) _____.
15. _____is an element that is widely found in clay and sand. It is used not only because its abundance makes it cheap but also because it is a semiconductor.
16. The _____ system has only two digits: 0 and 1.
17. The specialized processor used to manipulate 3-D graphics is the _____.
18. The most widely used hardware interface for attaching peripherals to a computer is _____.
19. _____ is an optical-disk format used to hold prerecorded text, graphics, and sound.
20. _____ is a binary-type programming language built into the processor (CPU) that the computer can run directly; it is specific to the particular processor model.

Multiple-Choice Questions

1. Which of the following is another term for primary storage?
   a. ROM
   b. ALU
   c. CPU
   d. RAM
   e. CD-R
2. Which of the following is *not* included on a computer's motherboard?
   a. RAM chips
   b. ROM chips
   c. keyboard
   d. microprocessor
   e. expansion slots
3. Which of the following is used to hold data and instructions that will be used shortly by the CPU?
   a. ROM chips
   b. peripheral devices
   c. RAM chips
   d. CD-R
   e. hard disk
4. Which of the following coding schemes is widely used on microcomputers?
   a. ALU
   b. Unicode
   c. ASCII
   d. Microcode
   e. Unix
5. Which of the following is used to measure processing speed in microcomputers?
   a. MIPS
   b. flops
   c. picoseconds
   d. gigahertz
   e. millihertz
6. Which expansion bus specializes in graphics processing?
   a. PCI
   b. ROM
   c. CMOS
   d. AGP
   e. USB
7. Which element is commonly used in the making of solid-state integrated circuits?
   a. pentium
   b. lithium
   c. copper
   d. iron
   e. silicon
8. What are the high-speed areas called that *temporarily* store data during processing?
   a. control units
   b. registers
   c. machine cycles
   d. buses
   e. word banks
9. A(n) _____, also called a USB drive or a keychain drive, plugs into the USB port of nearly any microcomputer or other digital device and can store up to 256 gigabytes.
   a. CD
   b. DVD
   c. optical memory card
   d. flash drive
   e. smart card
10. Cloud storage is also called _____ storage.
   a. USB
   b. live
   c. online
   d. flash
   e. exabyte

True-False Questions

T F 1. A bus connects a computer's control unit and ALU.

T F 2. The machine cycle comprises the instruction cycle and the execution cycle.

T F 3. Virtual memory is hard-disk space used to expand RAM capacity.

T F 4. Main memory is nonvolatile.

T F 5. The multicore processor is designed to let the operating system divide the work over more than one processor, with two or more processor cores on a single piece of silicon.

T F 6. Pipelining is a method of speeding up processing.

T F 7. USB can theoretically connect up to 127 peripheral devices.

T F 8. A petabyte is approximately 1 quadrillion bytes.

T F 9. Online secondary-storage services test your computer's RAM capacity.

T F 10. HDMI connections support both video and audio signals.

T F 11. A megabyte is bigger than a terabyte.

T F 12. ASCII is the binary code most widely used on microcomputers.

stage 2 LEARNING COMPREHENSION

"I can recall information in my own terms and explain it to a friend."

Short-Answer Questions

1. What is ASCII, and what do the letters stand for?
2. Why should measures of capacity matter to computer users?
3. What's the difference between RAM and ROM?
4. What is the significance of the term *gigahertz?*
5. What is a motherboard? Name at least four components of a motherboard.
6. What are the most convenient forms of backup storage? Why?
7. Why is it important for your computer to be expandable?
8. What are three uses of a smart card?
9. What is nanotechnology?
10. What are the uses of a surge protector, voltage regulator, and UPS, and why are these devices important?
11. Explain the binary system.
12. What is Unicode?
13. Why is silicon used in the manufacture of microprocessors?
14. What is Blu-ray used for?

stage 3 LEARNING APPLYING, ANALYZING, SYNTHESIZING, EVALUATING

"I can apply what I've learned, relate these ideas to other concepts, build on other knowledge, and use all these thinking skills to form a judgment."

Knowledge in Action

1. f you're using Windows 7, you can easily determine what microprocessor is in your computer and how much RAM it has. To begin, click the *Start* button in the Windows desktop pull-up menu bar and then choose *Control Panel.* Then locate the System icon in the Control Panel window and double-click on the icon.

   On an Apple computer, click on the Apple icon and on *About This Mac.* The System Properties screen will appear, listing your system's specifications.

   Once you have determined your system's specifications, visit an online computer store and note the system requirements listed for five software packages. What are the processor requirements? RAM? Operating system? 32 bit or 64 bit? Minimum hard-disk space? CD/DVD speed? Are there any output hardware requirements (audio/video cards)?

   Did you find any software that you would like to use that you would not be able to install and run?
2. Develop a binary system of your own. Use any two objects, states, or conditions, and encode the following statement: "I am a rocket scientist, and you're not."
3. Storing humans: If the human genome is 800 million bytes (according to Raymond Kurzweil), how many humans could you fit on a 120-GB hard drive?
4. What are the predictions about how long Moore's Law will continue to apply? Do a web search for four opinions; list the website sources and their predictions, and state how reliable you believe the sites are, and why.

Web Exercises

1. The objective of this project is to introduce you to an online encyclopedia that's dedicated to computer technology. The *www.webopedia.com* website is a good resource for deciphering computer ads and clearing up difficult concepts. For practice, visit the site, type *processor* into the Search text box, and then press the *Enter* key or click on the *Go!* button. Click on some of the links that are displayed. Search for information on other topics of interest to you.
2. You can customize your own PC through a brand-name company such as Dell or Hewlett-Packard, or you can create your own personal model by choosing each component on your own. Decide which method is best for you.

   Go to the following sites and customize your ideal PCs:

   www.dell.com

   http://shop.lenovo.com/us/products/

   www.hpshopping.com

   www.apple.com/mac/

   www.cyberpowerpc.com/system/CyberPower_B75_Configurator/

   Write down the prices for your ideal customized PCs. Then go to—

   www.tigerdirect.com/sectors/category/computer-parts.asp

   www.microcenter.com/storefronts/byopc/index.html

   www.pricewatch.com

   http://store.sysbuilder.com/desktop.html

   —and see if you could save money by putting your own PC together piece by piece. (This includes purchasing each component separately and verifying compatibility of all components.)

   For a tutorial on building your own computer, go to *www.howstuffworks.com/how-to-tech/build-a-computer.htm* and *www.pcworld.com/article/203950/how_to_build_your_own_pc_part_1.html* (this includes a video) or *http://lifehacker.com/5828747/how-to-build-a-computer-from-scratch-the-complete-guide.* (YouTube has some good videos on building your own computer; however, the comments are often inappropriate.)

3. DVD formats: DVD + R, DVD-R, DVD + RW, DVD-RW, so many formats! Are they all the same? Visit these websites to get current information on the issues surrounding recordable DVD media:

   www.webopedia.com/DidYouKnow/Hardware_Software/2003/DVDFormatsExplained.asp

   www.videohelp.com/dvd

4. What is a qubit? You've learned about binary digits in this chapter; now learn about the qubit, the basic unit of information in a quantum computer. Beware: When you step into the realm of quantum theory, things become bizarre.

   www.qubit.org/

   www.answers.com/topic/qubit?method=6

   www.worldwidewords.org/turnsofphrase/tp-qub1.htm

   www.technologyreview.com/view/426586/worlds-largest-quantum-computation-uses-84-qubits/

5. DNA computing: Visit the following websites to learn more about DNA software and computing:

   www.livescience.com/28273-biological-computers-possible-using-dna.html

   www.economist.com/node/21548488

   www.arstechnica.com/reviews/2q00/dna/dna-1.html

   www.bbc.co.uk/news/science-environment-13626583

   http://computer.howstuffworks.com/dna-computer.htm

   www.britannica.com/EBchecked/topic/941575/DNA-computing

6. Security issue—credit-card fraud: When buying parts or making any kind of purchase over the Internet, always make sure that the web address says HTTPS to let you know it is an encrypted SSL (Secured Socket Layer) website. Visit these sites for safety tips when using your credit card online.

   http://credit.about.com/od/privacyconcerns/tp/safe-online-credit-card-shopping-tips.htm

   http://techtalk.pcpitstop.com/2012/03/23/daves-computer-tips-online-credit-card-security-part-1/

   http://money.howstuffworks.com/personal-finance/debt-management/credit-card4.htm

   www.microsoft.com/security/online-privacy/online-shopping.aspx

   http://usa.visa.com/personal/security/learn-the-facts/online-shopping.html

   http://idtheft.about.com/od/preventionpractices/a/OnlineShopping.htm

   www.money-rates.com/advancedstrategies/creditcards/10-tips-for-safe-online-credit-card-use.htm

7. This is a motherboard showing the mounted ports at the lower left of the board. Try to identify all the port types. Where are the expansion slots? Where is the CPU? Identify some transistors.

5

HARDWARE: INPUT & OUTPUT Taking Charge of Computing & Communications

Chapter Topics & Key Questions

UNIT 5A: *Input Hardware*

5.1 **Keyboards** What are the different kinds of keyboards and terminals?

5.2 **Pointing Devices** Besides the mouse, what do pointing devices include?

5.3 **Source Data-Entry Devices** What is meant by source data-entry devices, and what do they include?

5.4 **The Future of Input** What are some trends of future input technology?

UNIT 5B: *Output Hardware*

5.5 **Softcopy Output: Display Screens** What kinds of display devices produce softcopy input?

5.6 **Hardcopy Output: Printers** What are the different kinds of printers, and what are they used for?

5.7 **Mixed Output: Sound, Voice, & Video** What devices produce output that differs from softcopy and hardcopy output?

5.8 **The Future of Output** What are some trends of future output technology?

5.9 **Quality of Life: Health & Ergonomics** What are the principal health and ergonomic issues relating to computer use?

Download the free UIT 11e App for key term flash cards quizzes and a game, *Over the Edge*

CHAPTER FORECAST The first half of this chapter describes input, the second half output. We begin by considering the three categories of input hardware: *keyboards,* including terminals; *pointing devices,* including mice, touch screens, and pen-based devices; and *source data-entry devices,* ranging from scanners to bar-code readers, audio-input devices, image recognition, speech recognition, and sensors. We then describe various kinds of output hardware—*softcopy output,* including varieties of display screens; *hardcopy output,* covering all kinds of printers; and *mixed output,* describing sound, voice, and video output devices. We conclude with a discussion of the importance of ergonomics—what to do to avoid the negative health effects of computers.

"Wearables," says Apple CEO Tim Cook, are "an area ripe for exploitation, ripe for all of us getting excited about. I think there will be tons of companies [working on] this."[1]

Wearables, or *wearable technology,* consist of clothing and accessories worn close to the body that incorporate computer and advanced electronic technologies. "Wearable gizmos are the next frontier in the world of technology," some observers think, although most take a wait-and-see attitude.[2]

Wearables include wristband fitness trackers, such as Nike + FuelBand, and so-called smart watches, such as Pebble, but the device that has stirred the most excitement is computerized eyeglasses, Google's Glass. This kind of wearable computing "promises to marry the worlds of fashion and technology, ushering in accessories capable of meeting 24/7 digital needs," raves one writer.[3]

Wearables

"Can devices like Google Glass augment our activities without distracting us from the physical world?"

www.technologyreview.com/news/517346/the-paradox-of-wearable-technologies/

First revealed in summer 2012, Glass puts computing processing power plus a tiny screen, a camera, a microphone, and real-time wireless communications into a pair of cool-looking lightweight glasses. The all-in-one "smart" glasses can display images and video and have a button that can take pictures.[4] Wearers can also give vocal commands, as by saying "OK Glass"—which lets the eyewear know to listen for a command—followed by "Record video" or "Take a picture" or the Mandarin translation of "Two beers, please." You can check out weather reports, get GPS directions, and perform web searches, the results of which appear in the small display area in the upper right corner of the frame.[5] "This could be a whole new way of appreciating the world," said one investor. "It's amplified reality."[6]

Google Glass

Whether or not Glass is successful—you may know by the time you read this—the device represents an extraordinary all-in-one collection of the two faces of computing that are important to humans: the *input of data* and the *output of information.*[7]

This chapter focuses on the common input and output devices used with a computer. *(• See Panel 5.1.)* **Input hardware consists of devices that translate data into a form the computer can process.** The people-readable form of the data may be words like those on this page, but the computer-readable form consists of binary 0s and 1s, or off and on electrical signals.

Output hardware consists of devices that translate information processed by the computer into a form that humans can understand. The computer-processed information consists of 0s and 1s, which need to be translated into words, numbers, sounds, and pictures.

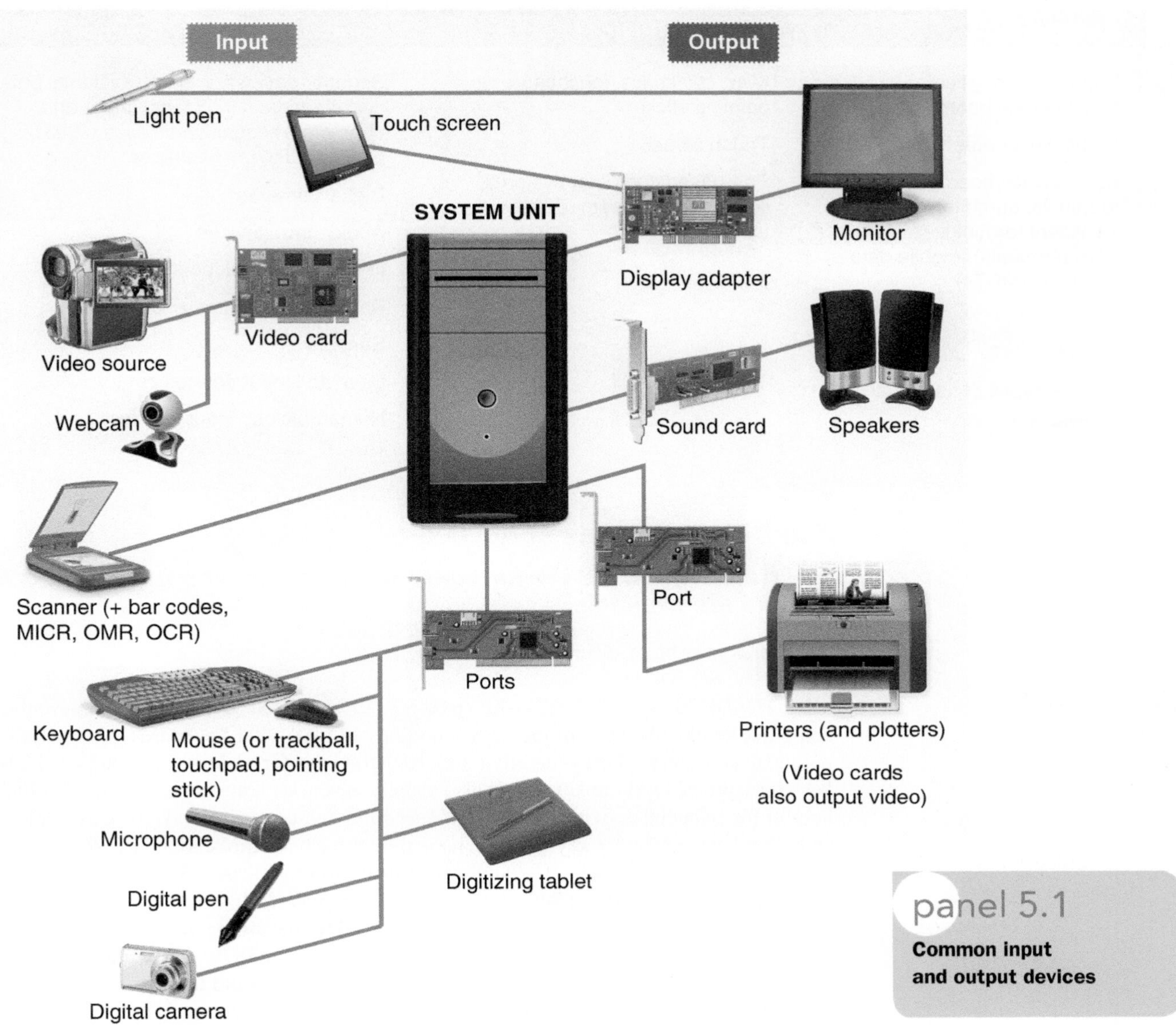

panel 5.1

Common input and output devices

UNIT 5A: *Input Hardware*

Recall from Chapter 1 that *input* refers to data entered into a computer for processing—for example, from a keyboard or from a file stored on disk. Input includes program instructions that the CPU receives after commands are issued by the user. Commands can be issued by typing keywords, defined by the application program, or pressing certain keyboard keys. Commands can also be issued by choosing menu options or clicking on icons. Finally, input includes user responses—for example, when you reply to a question posed by the application or the operating system, such as "Are you sure you want to put this file in the Recycle Bin?"

The three major types of input hardware devices are *keyboards, pointing devices,* and *source data-entry devices.* *(• See Panel 5.2, next page.)* Quite often a computer system uses all three.

5.1 KEYBOARDS

The keyboard is still one of the most important main computer input devices.

A keyboard is a device that converts letters, numbers, and other characters into electrical signals that can be read by the computer's processor. The keyboard does this with its own processor and a grid of circuits underneath the keys.

Keyboards	Pointing Devices	Source Data-Entry Devices
Traditional (physical) computer keyboards	Mice, trackballs, touchpads, pointing sticks	Scanner devices: imaging systems, bar-code readers, RFID tags, mark- and character-recognition devices (MICR, OMR, OCR), fax machines
Virtual keyboards	Touch screens	Digital cameras
Specialty keyboards and terminals: dumb terminals, intelligent terminals (ATMs, POS terminals), mobile data terminals (MDTs)	Pen-based computer systems, light pens, digitizers (digitizing tablets)	Audio-input devices
		Webcams and video-input cards
		Speech-recognition systems
		Sensors
		Biometric input devices
		Human-biology input devices

panel 5.2

Three types of input devices

The Different Types of Keyboards

The traditional QWERTY keyboard is still the most popular, but other layouts are available.

Keyboards may be of several types.

THE TRADITIONAL QWERTY KEYBOARD LAYOUT & VARIATIONS Conventional computer keyboards have all the keys found on old typewriter keyboards, plus other keys unique to computers. This generally totals 104–108 keys for desktop computers and 80–85 keys for laptops. Desktop keyboards also usually have a separate numeric *keypad,* which is helpful for financial activities. *Enhanced keyboards* include function keys; Ctrl, Shift, Alt, and other keys; and extra keys for special activities such as Application key, Windows key, and instant web access key. The keyboard illustration in Chapter 3 shows keyboard and numeric keypad functions. *(Refer back to Panel 3.6, page 127.)*

Most keyboards are QWERTY keyboards, named for the arrangement of letters that start the top row of keys, which was invented for typewriters in 1878. Many alternatives have been proposed, but, observes one technology writer, "none could improve on QWERTY's ability to let touch-typers use both hands in harmony for fast typing."[8]

Inside a computer keyboard. In most keyboards, each key sits over a small, flexible rubber dome with a hard carbon center (*right*). When the key is pressed, a plunger on the bottom of the key pushes down against the dome. This pushes the carbon center down, which presses against the keyboard circuitry to complete an electric circuit and send a signal to the computer.

However, some variants are being tried to accommodate users of the small-screen keyboards on smartphones, since touch-typing can't be done on a 4-inch screen. (Most people use their thumbs.) Among the challengers:

Dvorak keyboard layout

- **Dvorak keyboard:** This layout, designed for speed and efficiency by August Dvorak in the 1930s, places all the vowels in the left hand of the home row and the most commonly used consonants in the right hand of the home row. Because the frequently used letters are right there underneath your fingertips and the next most common are directly above, typing involves much less reaching (*www.theworldofstuff.com/dvorak/*). Some people claim that Dvorak is faster and more comfortable to use than QWERTY, but this opinion seems to be subjective. Both Windows and Mac OS X support Dvorak keyboards.
- **Dextr keyboard:** The *Dextr keyboard,* available as an app for Android phones, features five rows of keys in alphabetical order.
- **Snapkeys Si:** The *Snapkeys Si* is an app that abandons the QWERTY layout altogether, forcing users to type on just four squares that hold 12 letters, with other letters being produced by tapping in the blank space between these four squares.[9]
- **KALQ keyboard:** Another non-QWERTY keyboard designed for thumb typing on Android phones, the *KALQ keyboard* rearranges the letters for optimal speed, dividing the alphabet into halves for easier thumb access.[10]

KALQ. Developed by the Max Plank Institute for Informatics, KALQ has a split layout with 16 keys on the left and 12 keys on the right. All vowels, with the exception of the Y, which can sometimes be considered a vowel, are located on the right along with G, K, L, Q, and J. The KALQ design relies on users moving both thumbs simultaneously, with one thumb moving toward its next target as the other is typing. These improvements allowed users to reach 37 words per minute, which is better than the roughly 20 words per minute users achieve on a split QWERTY keyboard.

TACTILE VERSUS TOUCH-SCREEN KEYBOARDS Keyboards are of two types:

- **Tactile keyboards:** Most desktop computers, some laptops, and the BlackBerry 10D smartphone use **tactile keyboards, or *physical keyboards*, which are perceptible to the sense of touch.** For instance, when using her BlackBerry, says one writer, "my thumbs can speed along on its tactile keys without forcing me to look down as I walk."[11]
- **Touch-screen keyboards: Touch-screen keyboards, also called *on-screen* or *virtual keyboards,* are those in which the image of a keyboard is displayed on a touch screen.** Touch-screen keyboards are standard on tablets, smartphones, and other mobile devices (although in some cases tactile keyboards are available as well). A variation is the kind of technology that, like the virtual keyboard, uses light (laser) to project a full-size computer keyboard onto almost any surface.

Seeing the light. The virtual keyboard uses light to project a full-size computer keyboard onto almost any surface. This technology provides a way for one to do email, word processing, and other basic tasks without having to carry a laptop.

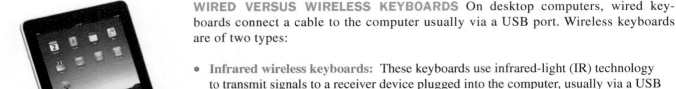

Wireless keyboard

WIRED VERSUS WIRELESS KEYBOARDS On desktop computers, wired keyboards connect a cable to the computer usually via a USB port. Wireless keyboards are of two types:

- **Infrared wireless keyboards:** These keyboards use infrared-light (IR) technology to transmit signals to a receiver device plugged into the computer, usually via a USB port. Such keyboards have a transmission range of 6–10 feet and cannot have any obstacles in the transmission path (called the *line of sight).*
- **Radio-frequency wireless keyboards:** Radio-based keyboards, which also transmit signals to a receiver plugged into the computer, have a range of up to 100 feet and have no line-of-sight problems.

Terminals

Terminals may just input data to and output data from a central computer, but most can process some data as well.

A *terminal* has a display screen and a keyboard and can input and output data but has limited or no ability to process data. The purpose of a terminal is to send data to and/or receive information from a central computer. We distinguish between dumb terminals and intelligent terminals.

DUMB TERMINALS **A dumb terminal, also called a *video display terminal (VDT),* has a display screen and a keyboard and can input and output but cannot process data.** Usually the output is text only. For instance, airline reservations clerks use these terminals to access a mainframe computer containing flight information. Dumb terminals cannot perform functions independent of the mainframe to which they are linked.

INTELLIGENT TERMINALS **An intelligent terminal has its own memory and processor, as well as a display screen and a keyboard.** Such a terminal can perform some functions independent of any mainframe or other system to which it is linked. Some examples of intelligent terminals are as follows:

- **Automated teller machine:** An *automated teller machine (ATM)* is a self-service banking machine that is connected through a network to a central computer.
- **Point-of-sale terminal:** A *point-of-sale (POS) terminal* is used at many store checkout counters to record purchases, process debit and credit cards, and update inventory.
- **Mobile data terminal:** A *mobile data terminal (MDT)* is a computerized device used in emergency vehicles, public transit vehicles, trucking fleets, and the like to communicate with a central dispatch office. MDTs in police cars, for instance, let officers access databases to track dispatch information, search for local and national warrants, verify license plate and vehicle registration, check criminal records, and more. Some systems let officers complete reports online to avoid time-consuming in-office paperwork.

5.2 POINTING DEVICES

Pointing devices include the mouse and its variants, the touch screen, and various forms of pen input.

One of the most natural of all human gestures, the act of pointing is incorporated in several kinds of input devices. **Pointing devices control the position of the cursor or pointer on the screen and allow the user to select options displayed on the screen.** Pointing devices include the *mouse* and its variants, the *touch screen,* and various forms of *pen input.* We also describe innovations in *handwriting input* and *gesture input.*

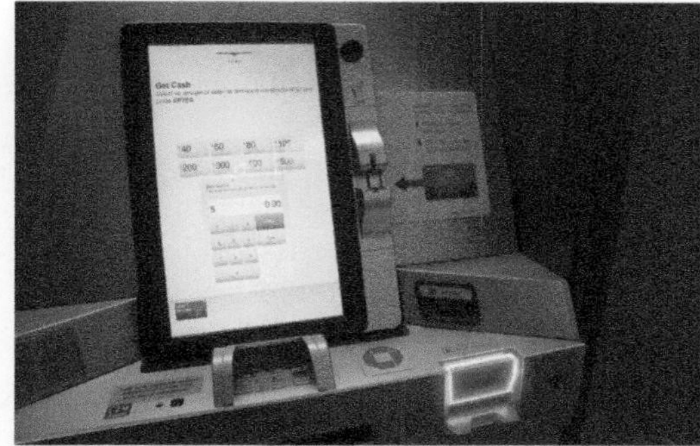

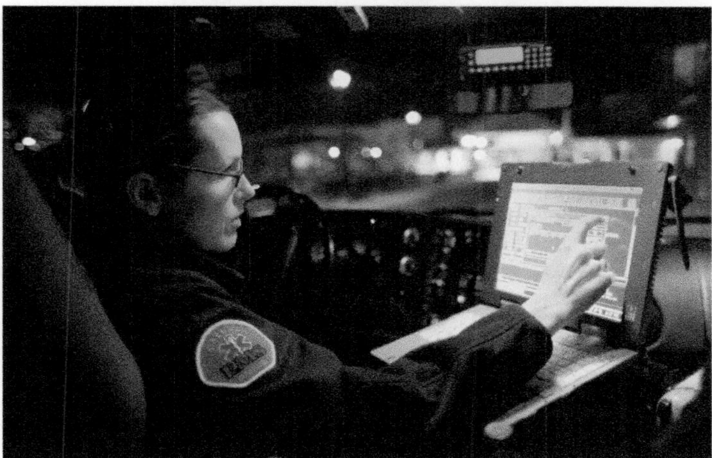

Terminals. (*top left*) Dumb terminals at an airline check-in counter. Intelligent terminals: (*top right*) ATM. (*bottom left*) A point-of-sale (POS) terminal at a retail store that records purchases and processes the buyer's credit card. (*bottom right*) MDT in an ambulance.

The Mouse

One of the most popular devices for giving on-screen commands, the mouse may be mechanical or optical, wired or wireless.

The principal pointing tool used with microcomputers is the **mouse, a device that is moved about on a surface and directs a pointer on the computer's display screen.** Making its first appearance at a demonstration in San Francisco in 1968, the mouse's name is derived from the device's shape, which is a bit like a mouse, with the cord to the computer being the tail. The mouse went public in 1984 with the introduction of the Apple Macintosh. (• *See the timeline, Panel 5.3, next page.*) Once Microsoft Windows 3.1 made the GUI (p. 126) PC standard, the mouse also became a standard input device.

The *mouse pointer*—an arrow, a rectangle, a pointing finger, depending on where the pointer is positioned—is the symbol that indicates the position of the mouse on the display screen or that activates commands. When the mouse pointer changes to the shape of an I-beam, it shows the place where text may be inserted or selected for special treatment.

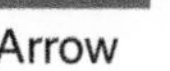

Arrow

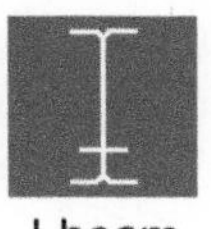

I-beam

The mouse is available in different designs: mechanical or optical, wired or wireless, as we describe. There is also one called an air mouse.

MECHANICAL MOUSE A mouse pad—a rectangular rubber/foam pad—provides traction for the old traditional mouse, often called a *mechanical mouse* or a *wheeled mouse.* This type of mouse has a ball on the bottom that rotates and controls the pointer on the screen as the mouse is rolled across the pad. The mechanical mouse, which is mainly used with desktop computers, is attached with a cord to the computer's system unit.

Mechanical mice generally have one to five buttons on the top, the first being used for clicking, dragging, and other common functions, the other buttons' functions determined by the software you're using. Most mice also have a *scroll wheel* or *wheel button* on top to make it easier for you to scroll up and down the screen.

Mouse mechanics. (*top*) Basic parts of a mouse. (*bottom left*) Inside an optical mouse. (*right*) The light sensor (LED, or light-emitting diode) shines through the bottom of the optical mouse.

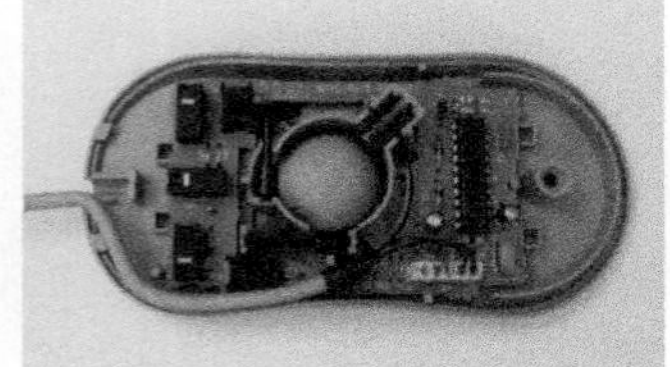

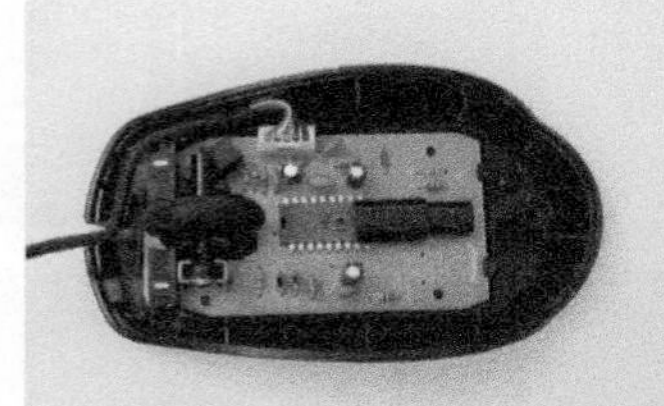

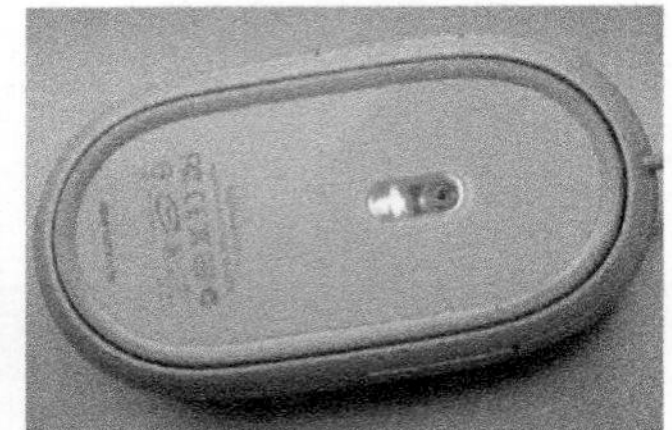

OPTICAL MOUSE Most mice now are *optical;* that is, they use light beams and special chips to encode data for the computer. Optical mice have a smoother response and don't require a mouse pad (unless you are working on a transparent glass surface). The optical mouse works by using LED (light-emitting diode), optical sensors, or laser to detect the mouse's movement.

Air mouse

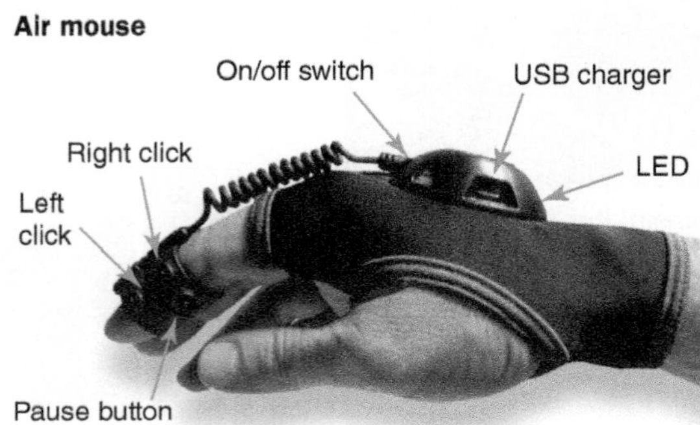

WIRELESS MOUSE The *wireless mouse,* also called *cordless mouse,* is a battery-operated mouse that uses radio waves or infrared-light waves to transmit data. Cordless mice free up desk space.

AIR MOUSE Designed for users making slide-show presentations, the *air mouse* is a wireless motion-sensing mouse that does not need to be in contact with any surface. It works by responding to hand motions that move the mouse in predetermined directions.

Variations on the Mouse: Trackball, Touchpad, & Pointing Stick

There are three alternatives to the mouse.

There are three main variations on the mouse, as follows:

TRACKBALL **The trackball is a movable ball, mounted on top or side of a stationary device, that can be rotated using your fingers or palm.** Instead of moving the mouse around on the desktop, you move the trackball with the tips of your fingers. A trackball is

panel 5.3

Timeline: Developments in input/output

3000 BCE	1621 CE	1642	Late 1700s	1814	1820
Abacus is invented in Babylonia	Slide rule invented (Edmund Gunther)	First mechanical adding machine (Blaise Pascal)	First attempts to produce human speech by machine made by C. G. Kratzenstein, professor of physiology in Copenhagen—he produced vowel sounds using resonance tubes connected to organ pipes; Wolfgang von Kempelen produces the first mechanical speaking machine in Vienna	First photographic image	The first mass-produced calculator, the Thomas Arithnometer

Trackball

not as accurate as a mouse, and it requires more frequent cleaning, but it's a good alternative when desktop space is limited. Trackballs come in wired and wireless versions, and the newest trackballs use laser technology.

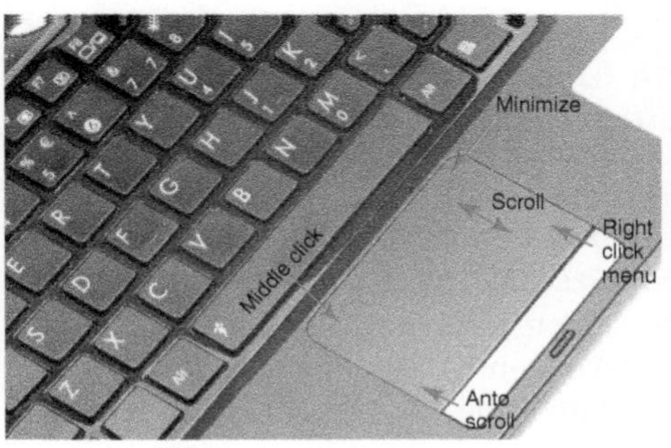

Touchpad

Pointing stick

TOUCHPAD **A touchpad is a small, flat surface over which you slide your finger, using the same movements as you would with a mouse.** The cursor follows the movement of your finger. You "click" by tapping your finger on the pad's surface or by pressing buttons positioned close by the pad. Touchpads are most often found on laptop computers, but freestanding touchpads are available for use with PCs.

POINTING STICK **Located between the keys on a laptop keyboard, a pointing stick is a pressure-sensitive device that allows the user to control the pointer by directing the stick with one finger.**

1821	1829	1843	1844	1876	1877
First microphone	William Austin patents the first workable typewriter in America	World's first computer programmer, Ada Lovelace, publishes her notes; facsimile transmission (faxing) over wires invented by Alexander Bain, Scottish mechanic (via telegraph wires)	Samuel Morse sends a telegraph message from Washington to Baltimore	A. G. Bell patents the electric telephone	Thomas Edison patents the phonograph

Interactive touch wall: Bluescape. Bluescape, made by Haworth/Obscura Digital, displays a unified image across 15 linked 55-inch flat-screen monitors, each equipped with 32 specialized sensors to read users' hand movements. The wall can be manipulated with the same finger-sliding techniques used to operate smartphones and tablets, as well as by a few extra tricks to manage its size.

Touch Screen

Touch-screen input uses a touch-sensitive display device.

We mentioned that some keyboards, such as those on smartphones and tablets, are touch screen. So are a number of other devices. **A touch screen is a display screen that has been sensitized to receive input from the touch of a finger.** *(• See Panel 5.4.)* This widely used form of input technology is seen on devices ranging from gas pumps to self-service DVD rental kiosks to interactive computer screens on some restaurant tables.[12] You can input requests for information by pressing on-screen buttons or menus, and the answers are then output as displayed words or pictures on the screen or even as sound.

Multitouch Screen

Multitouch screen input allows interactions with more than one finger or with sliding, rotating, and other gestures.

A multitouch screen is a display screen that allows two or more fingers or other gestures such as pinching motions to be recognized as input at any one time. It allows pinching and stretching gestures on the screen to control zooming—that is, pinch the screen to zoom in (make an image smaller) or spread the thumb and forefinger on the screen to zoom out, or spread images apart. With some software you can exercise a right-to-left swipe across the keyboard to delete the last word, a left-to-right swipe from the period button to insert a question mark, or a right-side diagonal swipe down to create a period. Some examples of gestures used on the Apple iPhone are shown on the top of the next page. *(• See Panel 5.5.)*

panel 5.4

Touch screens

(left) Young woman browsing YouTube videos on an Apple iPad tablet computer using free coffee shop Wi-Fi, London, England; *(right)* Children playing with a touch-screen computer during the opening of the new butterfly and insect section at the Bioparco in Rome, Italy.

1897	1898	1912	1924	1927
Karl Ferdinand Braun, German physicist, invents the first cathode-ray tube (CRT), the basis of all early TV and computer monitors	First telephone answering machine	Motorized movie camera replaces hand-cranked movie camera	T. J. Watson renames Hollerith's machine company, founded in 1896, to International Business Machines (IBM); first political convention photos faxed via AT&T telephone fax technology	The first electronic TV picture is transmitted

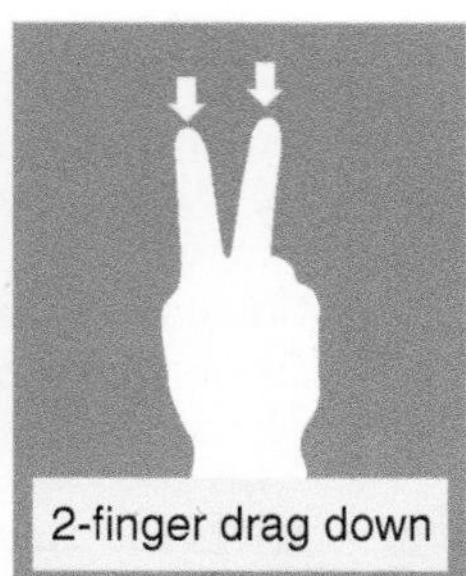

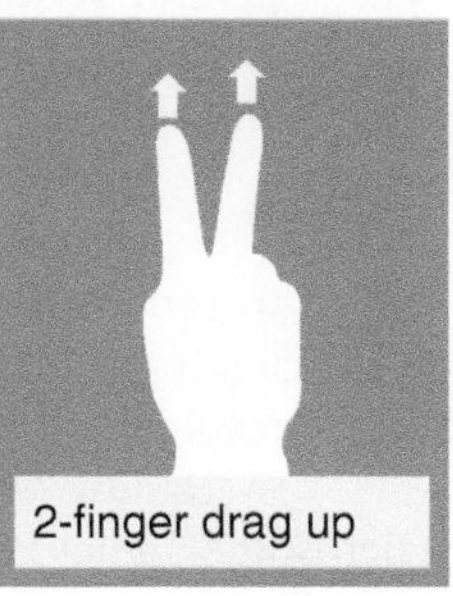

panel 5.5

Some gestures used on the Apple iPhone

Survival Tip

Games & Wireless Input

If you're a serious game fan, you're advised to stick with wired input devices. Wireless devices tend to lag during data transmission, which will slow down your game response. (The lag time is called *latency.*)

TECH TALES Loren Brichter, Popularizer of "Pull to Refresh" & the "Cell Swipe"

Who developed or helped popularize such touch-screen interactions as "pull to refresh" (dragging and releasing your finger on a screen to display the latest updated version of the page), the "cell swipe" (swiping a screen to uncover a list of hidden buttons), and sliding panels (pressing tabs that activate panels that slide out from the side of a screen)?

That would be a 28-year-old Philadelphia developer named Loren Brichter, a 2006 electrical engineering graduate of Tufts University, who operates from a small home office with a dog bed under his desk. The various apps just described are used by millions of people engaged with such familiar software as Facebook, LinkedIn, and Pinterest.

Inspired by information theorists like Edward Tufte, who believes graphic designs should have minimal extraneous information, Brichter "says he thinks up new features for apps based on how people move objects in the real world," according to one account.[13] He got his start working for Apple in a group making the iPhone's graphics hardware and software communicate and then left to go out on his own. His innovations have been picked up not only by Twitter but also by the makers of the new BlackBerry operating system, among others. "It's hard to understate the impact his ideas have had," says another developer. ■

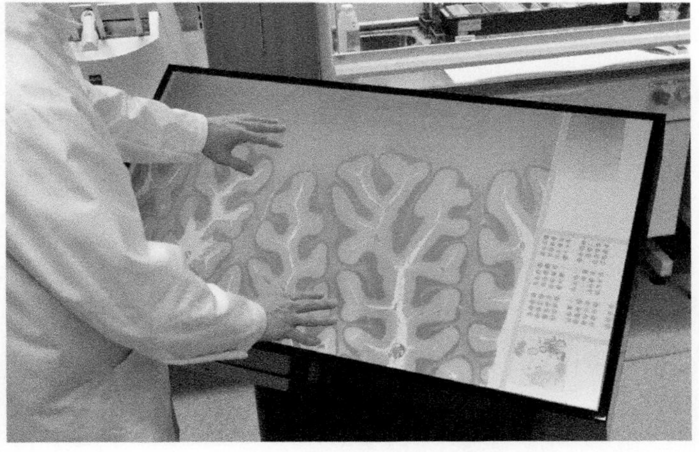

Multitouch screen at the Institute for Molecular Medicine, University of Helsinki, Finland

1931 Reynold B. Johnson, a Michigan high school science teacher, invents a test-scoring machine that senses conductive pencil marks on answer sheets

1936 Bell Labs invents the voice-recognition machine

1939 First electrical speech-producing machine—New York World's Fair; computer technology takes over speech synthesis in about 1970

1944 First electro-mechanical computer (Mark I)

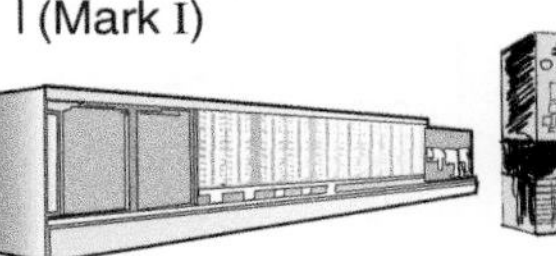

1946 First programmable electronic computer in United States (ENIAC)

1959 General Electric produces the first system to process checks in a banking application via magnetic-ink character recognition (MICR)

Pen Input

Pen input can be performed with pen-based computer systems, light pens, digitizers, and digital pens.

Some input devices use variations on an electronic pen. Examples are *pen-based systems, light pens, digitizers,* and *digital pens:*

PEN-BASED COMPUTER SYSTEMS **Pen-based computer systems allow users to enter handwriting and marks onto a computer screen by means of a penlike stylus rather than by typing on a keyboard.** A *stylus* is a penlike device that is used to write text or draw lines on a touch-sensitive surface as input to a computer.[14] Pen computers use *handwriting-recognition* software that translates handwritten characters made by the stylus into data that is usable by the computer. **Handwriting recognition refers to the ability of a computer to receive intelligible written input.** The system requires special software that interprets the movements of the stylus across the writing surface and translates the resulting cursive writing into digital information.

Handwriting recognition is commonly used as an input method for tablets, such as Microsoft's Tablet PC, a special notebook computer outfitted with a digitizer tablet and a stylus that allows a user to handwrite text on the unit's screen. *(• See Panel 5.6.)* A Mac version is the Modbook from Axiotron. A stylus can take the place of a keyboard when users use an on-screen input panel or tap letters and numbers directly on an on-screen keyboard.

panel 5.6

Pen-based computer systems

LIGHT PEN **The light pen is a light-sensitive penlike device that uses a wired connection to a computer terminal.** The user brings the pen to a desired point on the display screen and presses the pen button, which identifies that screen location to the computer. Light pens are used by engineers, graphic designers, and illustrators. They also are used in the health, food service, and chemical fields in situations in which users' hands need to be covered. *(• See Panel 5.7.)*

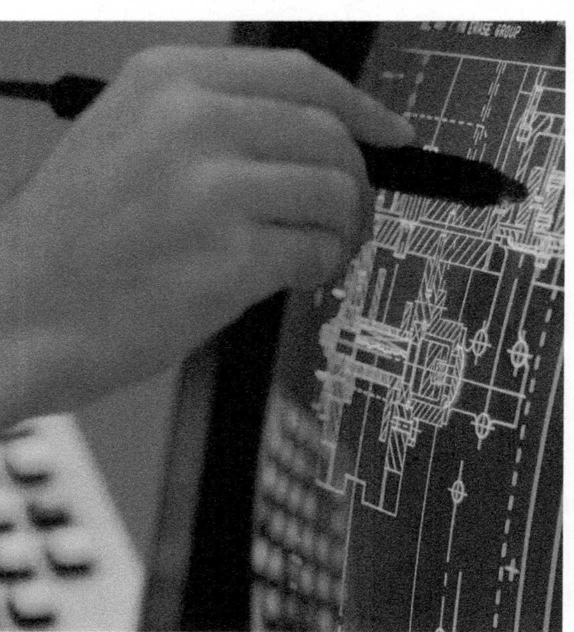

panel 5.7

Light pen

This person is using a light pen to design circuitry.

DIGITIZER **A digitizer uses an electronic pen or a mouselike copying device called a *puck* that can convert drawings and photos to digital data.** One form of digitizer is **the digitizing tablet, used in engineering and architecture applications, in which a specific location on an electronic plastic board corresponds to a location on the screen.** *(• See Panel 5.8.)*

1960	1962	1963	1967	1968	1970
DEC introduces the PDP-1, the first commercial computer with a monitor for output and a keyboard for input	Bell Laboratories develops software to design, store, and edit synthesized music	Ivan Sutherland uses the first interactive computer graphics in his Ph.D. thesis, which used a light pen to create engineering graphics	Hand-held calculator 	World debut of the computer mouse, in development since 1965 by Doug Engelbart at Stanford Research Institute (SRI)	Microprocessor chips come into use; floppy disk introduced for storing data; bar codes come into use; the daisy wheel printer makes its debut 

DIGITAL PEN **A digital pen is a writing instrument that allows users to write on paper and send the writing as an image file to the computer.** (• *See Panel 5.9.*) Basically, there are two kinds of digital pens. The first frog's FLY Fusion pen, requires you to write on special paper that's been printed with millions of nearly invisible microdots. A tiny camera in the pen tip learns its position, and a microchip in the pen converts the pen to digital ink, which can be transmitted to a PC. Pens such as the LiveScribe Sky Wi-Fi smartpen and the Nokia Digital Pen SU-27W also require special paper. The second version, such as the Mobile Digital Scribe, captures natural handwriting from any surface and stores it in the receiver for future use. No special digital notepad or ink is required. When the Mobile Digital Scribe is connected to a computer, handwritten text and drawings are displayed directly on the computer screen.

panel 5.8

Digitizing tablet
Such tablets are often used in engineering and architectural applications.

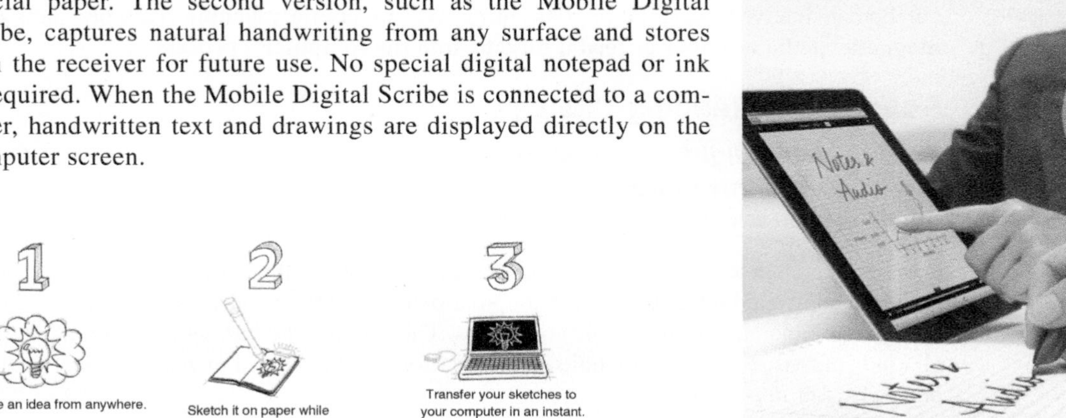

1
Capture an idea from anywhere.

2
Sketch it on paper while Inkling records it digitally.

3
Transfer your sketches to your computer in an instant.

Inkling. While you sketch on paper with a ballpoint pen, Inkling captures your sketches digitally, stroke by stroke (*www.wacom.com/gb/en/creative/inkling*).

panel 5.9

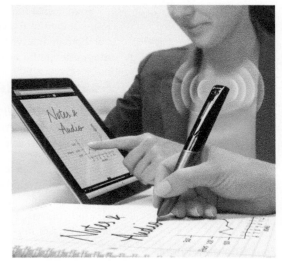

Handwritten notes via electronic pen (*above*)

1973	1974	1976	1984	1990
The Alto, an experimental PC that uses a mouse and a GUI, is developed at Xerox PARC	Simple version of optical character recognition (OCR) developed	IBM develops the inkjet printer	Apple Macintosh; first personal laser printer	Dragon speech-recognition program recognizes 30,000 words; SVGA video standard

What Is TWAIN?

Maybe "Technology Without An Interesting Name"? It's a driver that's a go-between for a scanner and the applications on the computer. Borrowing from a Rudyard Kipling poem ("and never the twain [that is, two] shall meet," about Eastern and Western cultures), someone used the word *TWAIN* to express the difficulty, at the time, of connecting scanners and personal computers, although this is no longer the case.

Do a web search for *TWAIN.* When was it developed, and how does it work?

Four Scanner Types

Differences between flatbed, sheet-fed, handheld, and drum scanners:

www.ehow.com/how-does_4569790_a-scanner-work.html

www.howstuffworks.com/scanner.htm

http://printscan.about.com/od/printerscannertypes/a/scannertypes.htm

5.3 SOURCE DATA-ENTRY DEVICES

Source data-entry devices include scanners, bar-code readers, radio-frequency identification (RFID) tags, mark-recognition and character-recognition devices, audio-input devices, speech-recognition systems, webcams and video-input cards, digital cameras, sensors, and biometric input devices.

In old-fashioned stores, checkout clerks read the price on every can and box and then enter those prices on the keyboard—a wasteful, duplicated effort. In most stores, of course, the clerks merely wave each product over a scanner, which automatically enters the item's inventory number and price (from the bar code) in digital form. This is the difference between keyboard entry and source data entry.

Source data-input devices do not require keystrokes (or require only a few keystrokes) to input data to the computer. In most cases, data is entered directly from the source, without human intervention. **Source data-entry devices create machine-readable data on magnetic media or paper or feed it directly into the computer's processor.**

Scanning & Reading Devices

Scanners use light to translate images into digital form, and reading devices read bar codes, radio-frequency identification (RFID) tags, or magnetic ink or optical mark characters.

Scanners and readers have led to a whole new industry called *electronic imaging,* the software-controlled integration and manipulation of separate images, using scanners, digital cameras, and advanced graphic computers. This technology has become invaluable for all kinds of reasons, such as to digitize and preserve old books and manuscripts that would otherwise fall into decay.

SCANNERS Scanners, or *optical scanners,* use light-sensing (optical) equipment to translate images of text, drawings, photos, and objects into digital form. *(• See Panel 5.10.)* The images can then be processed by a computer, displayed on a monitor, stored on a storage device, printed out, or transmitted to another computer.

One of the most popular types of scanners is the **flatbed scanner, or *desktop scanner,* which works much like a photocopier—the image to be scanned is placed on a glass surface, where it remains stationary, and the scanning beam moves across it.**

Three other types of scanners are *sheet-fed, handheld,* and *drum.* Other single-purpose scanners are available, such as business-card, slide, and photo scanners. There are even scanner pens, such as the DocuPen, that can scan text from books and articles. Personal computer users can get a decent scanner with good software for less than $100 or a fantastic one for about $1,000. A personal scanner, the HoverCam Mini 5, weighing only a third of a pound, is available for under $300.[15]

Scanners vary in image quality:

- **Dots and bitmaps:** Scanners are similar to photocopy machines except they create electronic files of scanned items instead of paper copies. The system scans each

1994	2005	2010	2011	2013	2016?	2019?
Apple and IBM introduce PCs with full-motion video built in; wireless data transmission for small portable computers; web browser invented	Wireless desktop printers commercially available	Multitouch screens	Apple's Magic (multitouch) Mouse	Air mouse; full voice interaction with PCs; 3-D technologies become widespread; real-time speech translation; human memory implants	Thought recognition as everyday input means; active wallpaper responds to people's moods	Bionic eyes are commercially available

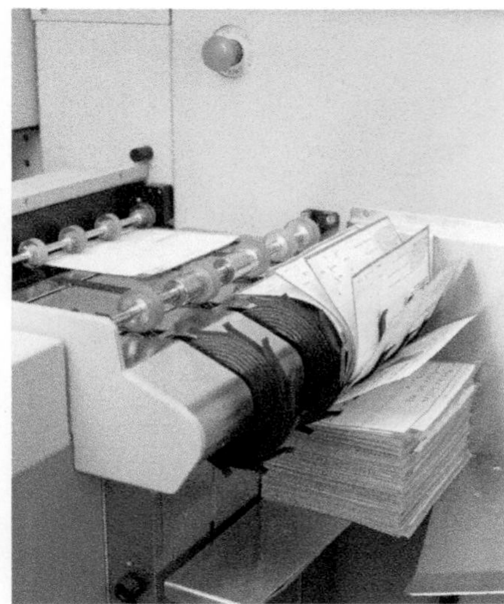

panel 5.10

Some image scanners
(*top left*) Sheet-fed scanner; (*top middle*) Air Copy scanner, a portable Wi-Fi scanner that can scan any photo, business card, or document directly into a tablet, smartphone, or computer; (*top right*) desktop scanner; (*bottom left*) technician operating a laser drum scanner in a commercial printing plant; (*bottom right*) 3-D scanner scanning an apple.

image—color or black and white—with light and breaks the image into rows and columns of color dots or black and white dots. Dots are stored in computer memory as digital code called a *bitmap,* a grid of dots. A *dot* is the smallest identifiable part of an image, and each dot is represented by one or more bits. The more bits in each dot, the more shades of gray and the more colors that can be represented. The amount of information stored in a dot is referred to as *color depth,* or *bit depth.* Scanners with higher bit depths tend to produce better color images. Today, most color scanners are at least 24 bit and are fine for normal use. For those wanting better image quality, 30- and 36-bit scanners are available. Really good scanners have a 48-bit color depth.

- **Resolution:** Scanners vary in resolution. In general, **resolution refers to the clarity and sharpness of an image and is measured in dots per inch (dpi)—the number of columns and rows of dots (pixels) per inch.** The higher the number of dots, the clearer and sharper the image—that is, in general, the higher the resolution. Popular color desktop scanners currently vary in dpi from 300 × 200 up to 2,400 × 2,400; some commercial scanners operate at 4,800 × 9,600 dpi. The quality of the scanner's optical equipment (*optical density,* or *dynamic range*) also affects the quality of the scanned images. Optical density is usually measured on a scale from white at 0.0 to black at 4.0, with the higher end of that scale important for scanning film. A scanner with an optical density of 2.0 to 3.0 will lose details in highlights and shadows. A scanner with a higher optical density of 3.2 to 4.0 will show a greater range of detail in highlights and shadows.

BAR-CODE READERS On June 26, 1974, a customer at Marsh's Supermarket in Troy, Ohio, made the first purchase of a product with a bar code—a pack of Wrigley's Juicy Fruit chewing gum (which pack is now in the Smithsonian National Museum in Washington, D.C.). **Bar codes are the vertical, zebra-striped marks you see on most manufactured retail products**—everything from candy to cosmetics to comic books. (• *See Panel 5.11, next page.*) In North America, supermarkets, food manufacturers, and

panel 5.11

Bar code and bar-code reader

This bar-code reader is being used to update inventory by scanning the information on the stickers put on the boxes coming into the warehouse.

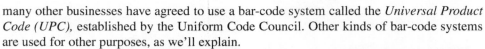

panel 5.12

Self-scanning system

A self-service scanning system allows consumers to check themselves out of the supermarket. The shopper begins the process by touching the computer's welcome screen. Then the computer's voice output provides the shopper with instructions about how to scan the items and where to place them once they've been scanned. When the shopper scans an item, the item's bar code provides the computer with the information it needs to determine the item being scanned, its weight, and its price. The system also deactivates any security tags on the items. The shopper places the items in shopping bags sitting on security scales, so the system can check that heavy items were not substituted for light ones.

many other businesses have agreed to use a bar-code system called the *Universal Product Code (UPC),* established by the Uniform Code Council. Other kinds of bar-code systems are used for other purposes, as we'll explain.

Bar-code readers **are photoelectric (optical) scanners that translate the symbols in the bar code into digital code.** In this system, the price of a particular item is set within the store's computer. Once the bar code has been scanned, the corresponding price appears on the salesclerk's point-of-sale terminal and on your receipt. Records of sales from the bar-code readers are input to the store's computer and used for accounting, restocking store inventory, and weeding out products that don't sell well.

Do-it-yourself checkout is an automated scanning process that enables shoppers to scan, bag, and pay for their purchases without human assistance. The self-scanning checkout lane looks like a traditional checkout lane except that the shopper interacts with a computer's user interface instead of a store employee. (• *See Panel 5.12.*) Self-scanning has become popular in many name-brand stores.

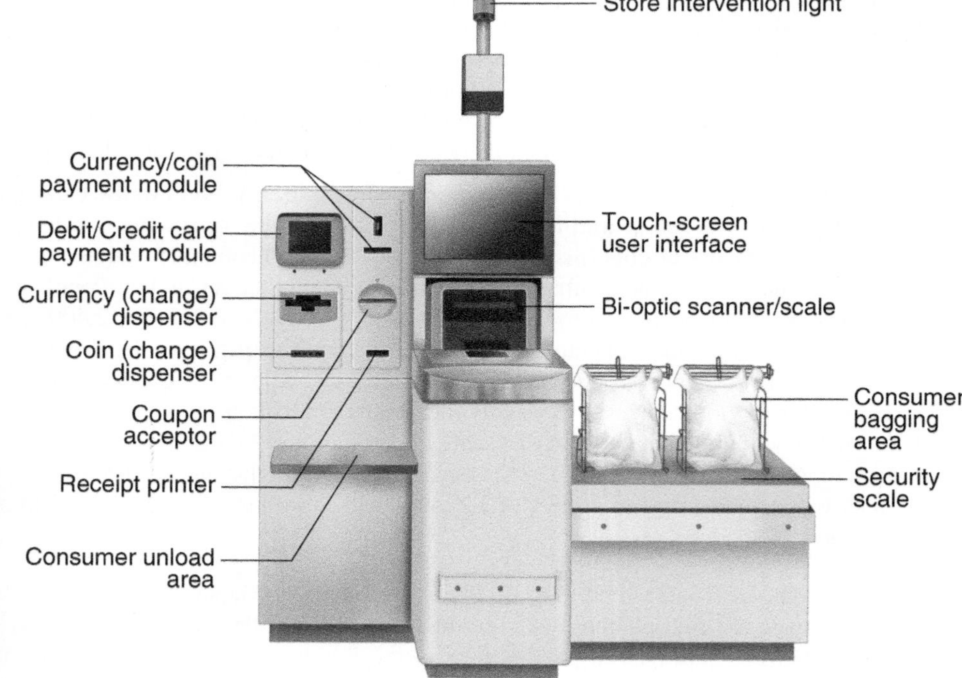

TYPES OF BAR CODES Bar codes may be 1-D, 2-D, or 3-D.

1-D bar code

- **1-D bar codes:** These are today's ordinary vertical bar codes, which can hold up to 16 ASCII characters. These are the bar codes commonly used by supermarkets.

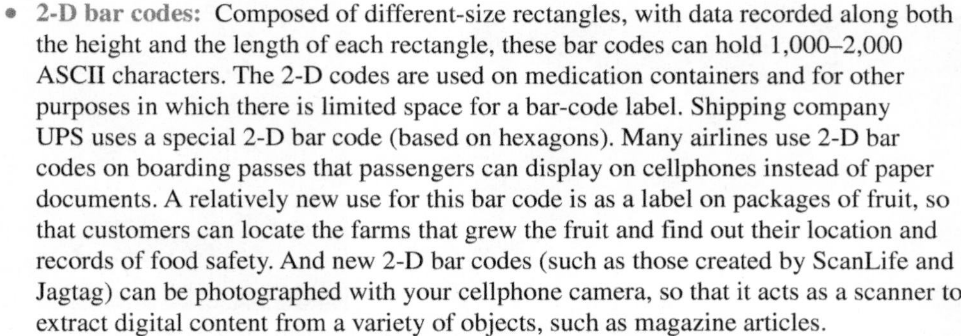

- **2-D bar codes:** Composed of different-size rectangles, with data recorded along both the height and the length of each rectangle, these bar codes can hold 1,000–2,000 ASCII characters. The 2-D codes are used on medication containers and for other purposes in which there is limited space for a bar-code label. Shipping company UPS uses a special 2-D bar code (based on hexagons). Many airlines use 2-D bar codes on boarding passes that passengers can display on cellphones instead of paper documents. A relatively new use for this bar code is as a label on packages of fruit, so that customers can locate the farms that grew the fruit and find out their location and records of food safety. And new 2-D bar codes (such as those created by ScanLife and Jagtag) can be photographed with your cellphone camera, so that it acts as a scanner to extract digital content from a variety of objects, such as magazine articles.

2-D bar code

Maxicode is a 2-D bar code used by UPS.

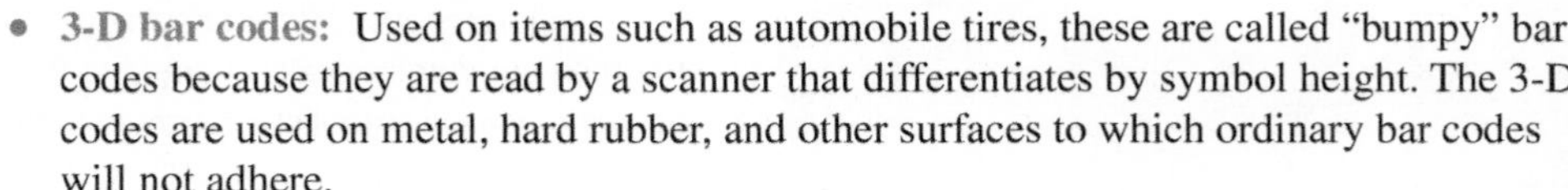

- **3-D bar codes:** Used on items such as automobile tires, these are called "bumpy" bar codes because they are read by a scanner that differentiates by symbol height. The 3-D codes are used on metal, hard rubber, and other surfaces to which ordinary bar codes will not adhere.

Another common type of code is the QR code, or tag, which is a type of matrix barcode designed to be read (scanned) by smartphones; in other words, it is a mobile barcode. QR, a registered trademark of Denso Wave, a subsidiary of Toyota, is short for Quick Response. QRs are used to take a piece of information from the web and put it into your phone. Once the code is in your phone, it can give you, for example, details about a website's business or details about a particular person, show you an URL that you click to see a movie trailer, or give you a coupon to use in a local business.

QR code

QR codes store more data than a regular 2-D barcode can hold; they include URLs, links, geo-coordinates, and text.

RADIO-FREQUENCY IDENTIFICATION (RFID) TAGS **Radio-frequency identification (RFID) tags are based on an identifying tag bearing a microchip that contains specific code numbers. These code numbers are read by the radio waves of a scanner linked to a database.** *Active RFID tags* have their own power source and can transmit signals over a distance to a reader device. *Passive RFID tags* have no battery power of their own and must be read by some sort of scanner.

RFID tags of both types are used for a wide range of purposes and are starting to replace bar codes in many situations. Drivers with RFID tags breeze through tollbooths without having to even roll down their windows; the toll is automatically charged to their accounts. Radio-wave-readable ID tags are used by the Postal Service to monitor the flow of mail, in the railroad industry to keep track of rail cars, and by Walmart and other stores for inventory control and warehousing. Visa and MasterCard "no-swipe" or "wave-and-pay" credit cards have been developed with embedded RFID technology that means cards don't have to be swiped across a magnetic-stripe reader but can just be waved near a scanner, which could help speed up lines in stores.

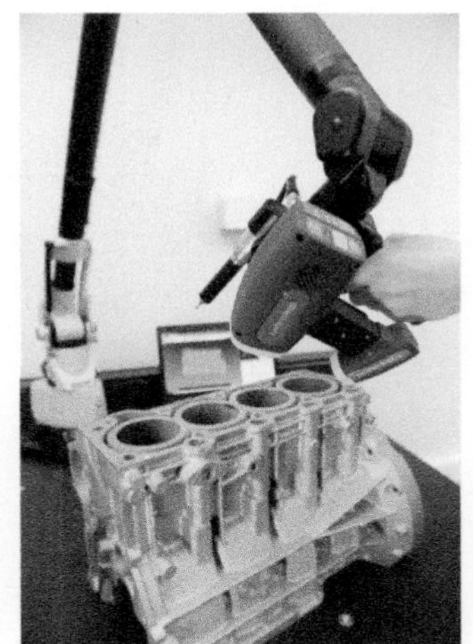

The 3-D scanning system can scan all types of surfaces in all sorts of lighting. It is used, among other things, to scan cars and motorcycles, or specific components, into a CAD/CAM system so that new models can be created.

TECH TALES RFID Tags for Security

A great many RFID uses have to do with security. All U.S. passports, for instance, must now have RFID tags embedded in them, which can help customs and immigration officials determine if the passports are authentic. The technology is also used to make supposedly "thiefproof" keys for millions of automobiles. In addition, tiny transmitters have been installed in things ranging from cars to gambling chips to National Park Service cactuses to help track thefts.

But the use of RFID technology goes beyond this. Years ago, pet owners began having RFID tags surgically implanted in their dogs and cats to allow veterinarians with the right scanning equipment to identify the animals if they became separated from their owners. Then in Mexico an epidemic of

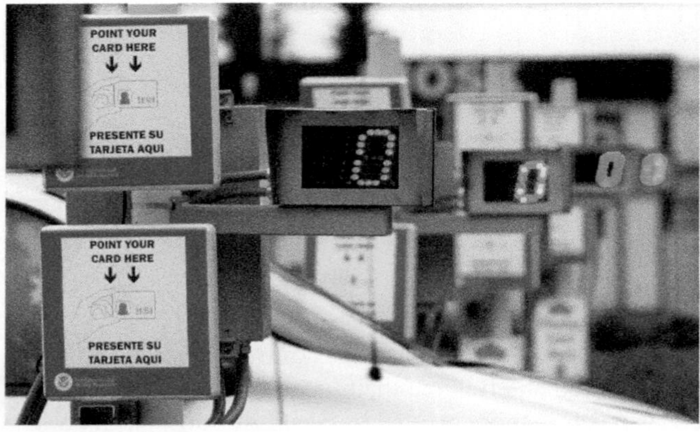

RFID. (*top left*) Drivers can buy RFID tags to drive past tollbooths without having to stop; the tolls are automatically charged to their account, usually established with a credit card. FastTrack is a common tollbooth RFID program in the United States. (*above*) RFID tags are replacing bar codes on passports. (*bottom left*) Sheep with RFID tags being counted via RFID ear tags and a scanner.

kidnappings led wealthy and some middle-class Mexicans to start implanting geolocator tags in their bodies, which could help satellites pinpoint a kidnap victim's location.

In the United States, the Food and Drug Administration has approved use of an implantable chip, the VeriChip, for medical purposes, on the premise that patient-specific data stored in the chip could provide speedy information about a person's medical history. About twice the length of a dime, the device is typically implanted between the shoulder and elbow area of an individual's right arm.

ethics

Many of these uses, however, stir concerns among privacy advocates, who fear that the technology could be used to track people's movements and put sensitive personal information at risk to hackers. ■

MARK-RECOGNITION & CHARACTER-RECOGNITION DEVICES There are three types of scanning devices that sense marks or characters. They are usually referred to by their abbreviations—MICR, OMR, and OCR:

- **Magnetic-ink character recognition: Magnetic-ink character recognition (MICR) is a character-recognition system that uses magnetizable ink and special characters.** When a MICR (pronounced "*mick*-er") document needs to be read, it passes through a special scanner that magnetizes the special ink and then translates the magnetic information into characters. MICR technology is used by banks. Numbers and characters found on the bottom of checks (usually containing the bank code number, check number, sort number, and account number) are printed with a laser printer that accepts MICR toner. MICR provides a secure, high-speed method of scanning and processing information.

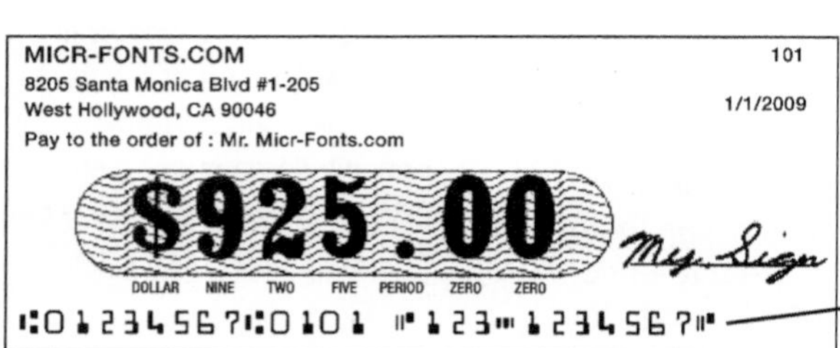

- **Optical mark recognition: Optical mark recognition (OMR) uses a special scanner that reads "bubble" marks and converts them into computer-usable form.** The best-known example is the OMR technology used to read students' answers to the College Board Scholastic Aptitude Test (SAT) and the Graduate Record Examination (GRE). In these cases, the scanner reads pencil marks that fill in circles, or bubbles, on specially designed documents. OMR is also used in forms and surveys.

- **Optical character recognition:** These days almost all scanners come with OCR software. **Optical character recognition (OCR) software converts scanned text from images (pictures of the text) to an editable text format (usually ASCII) that can be imported into a word processing application and manipulated.** Special OCR characters appear on utility bills and price tags on department-store merchandise. The wand reader is a common OCR scanning device. (• *See Panel 5.13.*)

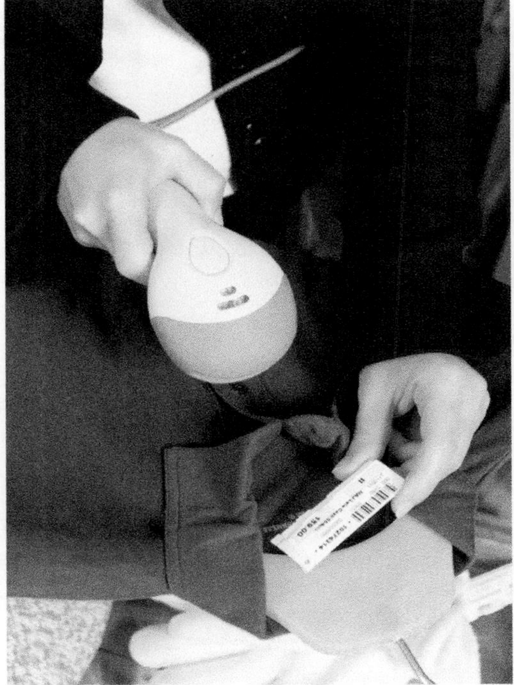

panel 5.13

Optical character recognition

OCR is often used in stores to encode and read price tags. A handheld wand is used as a reading device.

OCR-A	
NUMERIC	0123456789
ALPHA	ABCDEFGHIJ
SYMBOLS	KLMNOPQRST
	UVWXYZ
	>$/-+-#"

OCR-B	
NUMERIC	00123456789
ALPHA	ACENPSTVX
SYMBOLS	<+>-¥

OCR software can deal with nearly all printed characters, but script fonts and handwriting still present problems. In addition, OCR accuracy varies with the quality of the scanner—a text with 1,200 dpi will take longer to scan than one with 72 dpi, but the accuracy will be higher. Some OCR programs are better than others, with weaker versions unable to convert tables, boxes, or other extensive formatting; high-quality OCR software can read such complex material without difficulty. Users wanting to scan text with foreign-language (diacritical) marks, such as French accents, should check the OCR package to see if the program can handle this.

Image-Capture Devices

Image-capture devices include digital cameras, which record images in digital form, and webcams, which download images to a computer for transmission over a network.

As with scanners and readers, image-capture devices such as digital cameras and webcams have contributed to the rise of the *electronic imaging* industry, the integration and manipulation of different images.

DIGITAL CAMERAS Digital cameras, which have essentially replaced film cameras, have changed the entire industry of photography. Eliminating the environmentally undesirable stage of chemical development required of conventional film, **a digital camera uses a light-sensitive processor chip to capture photographic images in digital form and store them on a small disk inserted into the camera or on flash memory cards.** (• *See Panel 5.14, next page.*) The bits of digital information can then be copied right into a computer's hard disk for manipulation, emailing, posting on websites, and printing out.

Most digital cameras store picture data on flash memory cards, memory sticks, or keychains (Chapter 4), from which later you can transmit photo data to your computer through a USB cable. Popular software applications for sophisticated digital photo manipulation include Adobe Photoshop, Corel Paint Shop Photo Pro, Xara Photo & Graphic designer, Serif PhotoPlus, and Photo Explosion.

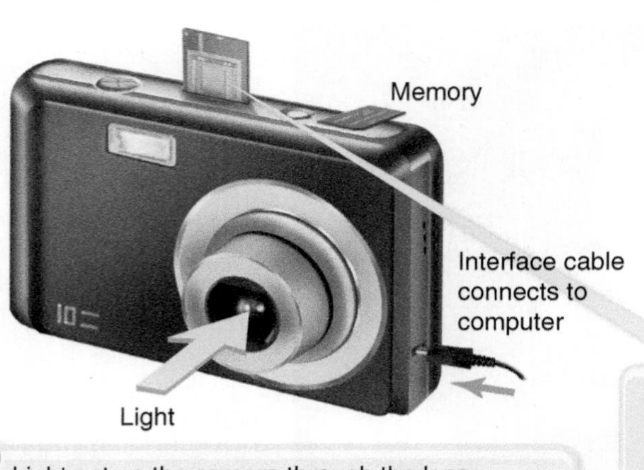

1. Light enters the camera through the lens.

2. The light is focused on the charge-coupled device (CCD), a solid-state chip made up of tiny, light-sensitive photosites. When light hits the CCD, it records the image electronically, just like film records images in a standard camera. The photosites convert light into electrons, which are then converted into digital information.

3. The digital information is stored in the camera's electronic memory, either built-in or removable.

4. Using an interface cable, the digital photo can be downloaded onto a computer, where it can be manipulated, printed, placed on a web page, or emailed.

A look at CCDs
The smallest CCDs are 1/8 the size of a frame of 35-mm film. The largest are the same size as a 35-mm frame.

- Lower-end cameras start with 180,000 photosites.
- Professional cameras can have up to 6 million photosites.

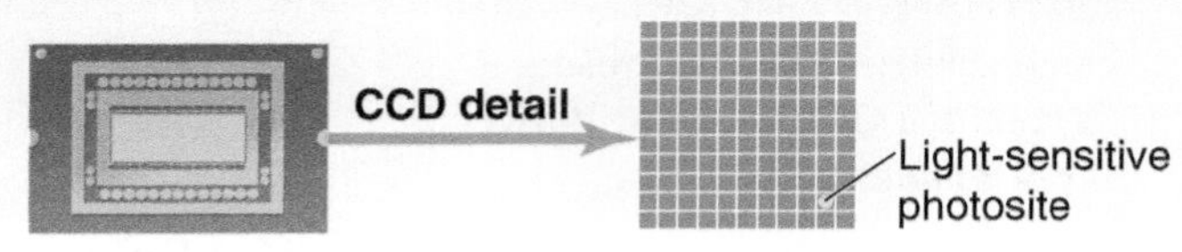

panel 5.14
Digital cameras and how they work

Digital-camera technology has, of course, migrated to cellphones, enabling you to share your photographic experiences in real time. We discuss camera phones further in Chapter 7.

WEBCAMS A **webcam is a video camera attached to a computer to record live moving images that can then be posted on a website in real time.** *(• See Panel 5.15.)* Webcam connections require special software, usually included with the camera, and a USB or video cable or a wireless radio-frequency connection.

Having fun with photo effects software

Laptops also come with webcams built in.

Initially intended for personal videoconferencing, the webcam has become popular with web users. You can join thousands of other webcam users hosting such riveting material as a live 24-hour view of the aquarium of a turtle named Pixel. Or you might show your living quarters or messy desk for all to see. Twenty20's VholdR Helmet Camera Camcorder is a digital video camera with a lens that straps onto your helmet—perfect for capturing your moves as you ski down a black-diamond trail.

panel 5.15
Webcam in use
(*left*) Externally mounted, solar-powered webcam; (*right*) webcam on front of laptop display screen

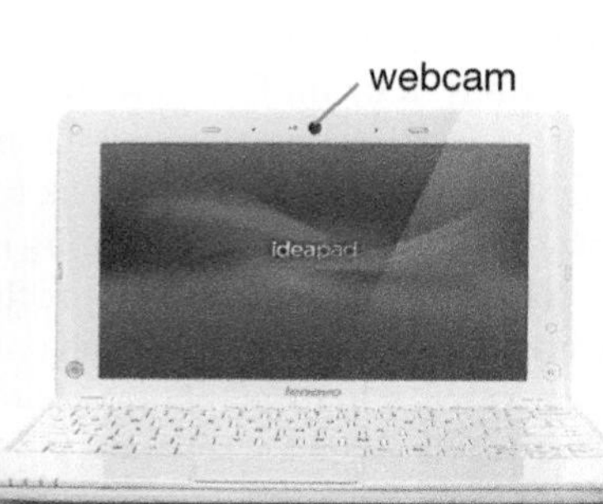

Mobiola
WebCamera
Use Your iPhone as a Webcam!
Turn your iPhone, BlackBerry, Windows Mobile or Symbian (Nokia only) smartphone into a high-quality wireless webcam. Connect it to a Mac (iPhone version only) or PC using a Wi-Fi connection, and share bright moments of your life that cannot be caught with a built-in webcam or USB camera!
New! Now works with iPhone 5 and iPad mini and supports portrait and landscape orientation!
Mobiola WebCamera is a great way to share what cannot be recorded with a built-in laptop camera, as it is wireless and can be easily moved around. Imagine talking to your mother on Skype and showing her her grandson taking his first steps. Or sitting in a WiFi hotspot near the Eiffel Tower, and sharing this moment with your friend while giving him a virtual tour of this famous attraction. With Mobiola WebCamera, anything can be shared wirelessly in a simple and fun way.
New! Now with video and audio recording on Mac OS and Windows, and flashlight in iPhone version!
WebCamera works with Skype, Google+, Yahoo!, Windows Live Messenger, AIM, ICQ and many other messaging applications, just as you can with a standard USB webcam. It also works with video production software such as Boinx TV, CamTwist, and Camtasia.
Mobiola WebCamera captures video in different resolutions: 192x144, 480x360, 1280x720, and 1920x1080 on iPhone 4S and iPhone 5. You may capture either individual frames or the whole video stream.

Full-motion video software

Smartphones can also now be used as webcams, with special downloaded applications, such as WebCamera Plus and Mobiola Webcamera, that are installed on both the phone and on a computer. The video feeds into the phone are transmitted by wired or wireless transmission to the computer.

Two types of video cards are available for webcams—frame-grabber and full-motion.

- **Frame-grabber video card:** The *frame-grabber video card* captures and digitizes only a single frame at a time. This type of video card is used less today than is the full-motion video card. It is still used by video enthusiasts and in certain professions, such as remote medical diagnosis and astronomy.
- **Full-motion video card:** The *full-motion video (FMV) card* converts analog to digital signals at rates up to 30 frames per second, giving the effect of a continuously flowing motion picture. Motion pictures are run at 24 fps, which is the minimum

Coffee Pot Cam

The first webcam was the "Trojan room coffee pot cam." What was this? Search the web to find out.

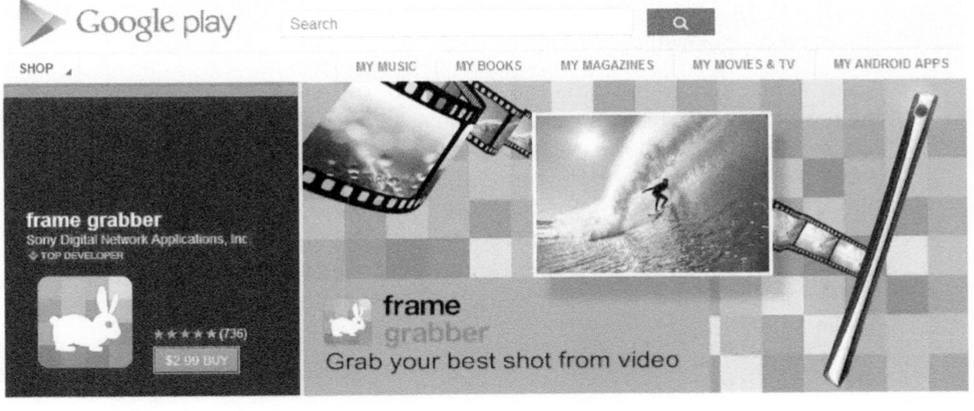

Frame-grabber video software

frequency required to eliminate the perception of moving frames and make the images appear visually fluid to the eye. Popular platforms for FMV include QuickTime, MPEG, and Smacker.

Note that both types of video cards need the appropriate software to be able to function.

Audio-Input Devices

Audio-input devices, which include speech recognition, allow users to send audio signals to a computer for processing, storing, recording, or carrying out commands.

An audio-input device **records analog sound and translates it for digital storage and processing.** An analog sound signal is a continuously variable wave within a certain frequency range. For the computer to process them, these variable waves must be converted to digital 0s and 1s. The principal use of audio-input devices is to produce digital input for multimedia computers.

TWO WAYS OF DIGITIZING AUDIO An audio signal can be digitized in two ways—by a *sound board* or a *MIDI board:*

- **Sound board:** Analog sound—the kind of sound that exists in nature, for example, human voices, sounds from a musical instrument—from a cassette player or a microphone goes through a special circuit board called a *sound board.* **A** sound board **is an add-on circuit board in a computer that converts analog sound to digital sound** (binary computer language, 0s and 1s) **and stores it for further processing and/or plays it back, providing output directly to speakers or an external amplifier.** (Chapter 6 discusses analog and digital sound in more detail.)
- **MIDI board:** **A** MIDI board**—*MIDI,* pronounced "middie," stands for "Musical Instrument Digital Interface"—uses a standard for the interchange of musical information between musical instruments, synthesizers, and computers.**

MICROPHONES Also supporting audio input are *microphones,* devices that take varying air pressure waves created by voice or other sound sources and convert them into varying electrical signals. Most new microcomputers and notebooks come with built-in microphones; stand-alone microphones can be connected via USB or some other connection.

SPEECH-RECOGNITION SYSTEMS Can your computer tell whether you want it to "recognize speech" or "wreck a nice beach"? A subset of audio input, **a** speech-recognition system**, or *voice input,* using a microphone as an input device, converts a person's speech into digital signals by comparing the electrical patterns produced by the speaker's voice with a set of prerecorded patterns stored in the computer.** *(• See Panel 5.16.)* Most of today's speech-recognition packages have a database of about 200,000 words from which they try to match the words you say. These programs let you accomplish two tasks: turn spoken dictation into typed text and issue oral commands (such as "Print file" or "Change font") to control your computer.

How to Set Up Your Computer for Speech Recognition in Windows 7, Windows 8, and Mac OS X

Go to:

http://windows.microsoft.com/en-US/windows7/Set-up-Speech-Recognition/

http://windows.microsoft.com/en-us/windows-8/using-speech-recognition/

www.dummies.com/how-to/content/setting-up-speech-recognition-in-mac-os-x-lion.html

TECH TALES "Know What I'm Sayin'?": The Uses of Speech-Recognition Systems

Speech-recognition systems have had to overcome many difficulties, such as different voices, pronunciations, and accents. Recently, however, the systems have measurably improved, at least up to a point. Major recognition systems are Dragon Naturally Speaking for the PC and for the Mac, Dragon Dictate for the Mac, and speech-recognition software built into the Windows OS and the Mac OS.[16] Other systems are Talking Desktop, Fonix Speech, Aculab, and Verbio. Special speech-recognition software is available for specific professions, such as law, medicine, and public safety.

Speech
A person who's going to use speech-recognition software usually must first go through an *enrollment*. This consists of the person dictating text that is already known to the software for 10 minutes to an hour. From this sampling, the software creates a table of *vocal references*, which are the ways in which the speaker's pronunciation of phonemes varies from models of speech based on a sampling of hundreds to thousands of people. *Phonemes* are the smallest sound units that combine into words, such as "duh," "aw," and "guh" in "dog." There are 48 phonemes in English. After enrollment, the speaker dictates the text he wants the software to transcribe into a microphone, preferably one that uses *noise-cancellation* to eliminate background sounds. The quality of the microphone and the computer's processing power are the most important hardware factors in speech recognition. The speaker can use continuous speech, which is normal speech without pauses between words.

Signal Processing
The sound wave is transformed into a sequence of codes that represent speech sounds.

1. Phonetic Models
Describe what codes may occur for a given speech sound.
In the word *how*, what is the probability of the "ow" sound appearing between an H and a D?

2. Dictionary
Defines the phonetic pronunciation (sequence of sounds) of each word.
How does it work
haw daz it werk

3. Grammar
Defines what words may follow each other, using parts of speech.

How does <it> [work]
adv vt pron v

Recognition Search
Using the data from 1, 2, and 3, the computer tries to find the best matching sequence of words as learned from a variety of examples.

Output
Computer recognizes word string and prints it on the screen.

panel 5.16

How a speech-recognition system works

Speech-recognition systems are used by warehouse workers to speed inventory taking by recording inventory counts verbally, traders on stock exchanges to communicate their trades by speaking to computers, and radiologists to dictate their interpretations of X-rays directly into transcription machines. Nurses can fill out patient charts by talking to a computer. Users can do online voice searches on their cellphones, using programs such as Google Mobile App, Yahoo! Search, Vlingo, and ChaCha. Speakers of Chinese can speak to machines that will print out Chinese characters. And for many individuals with disabilities, a voice-recognition system means a computer isn't so much a luxury as a necessity, providing freedom of expression, independence, and empowerment. ■

Microsoft Windows speech recognition software

Windows

MEET WINDOWS DOWNLOAD & SHOP HOW-TO SUPPORT

Installation Touch & search Personalization Security & accounts Apps & Windows Store Web & networking Email & comm

What can I do with Speech Recognition?

You can use your voice to control your computer. You can say commands that the computer will respond to, and you can dictate text to the computer.

Before you get started using Windows Speech Recognition, you'll need to connect a microphone to your computer. Once you've got the microphone set up, you can train your computer to better understand you by creating a voice profile that your computer uses to recognize your voice and spoken commands. For information about setting up your microphone, see **Set up your microphone for Speech Recognition**.

After you've got your microphone and voice profile set up, you can use Speech Recognition to do the following:

- **Control your computer.** Speech Recognition listens and responds to your spoken commands. You can use Speech Recognition to run programs and interact with Windows. For more information about the commands you can use with Speech Recognition, see **Common commands in Speech Recognition**.
- **Dictate and edit text.** You can use Speech Recognition to dictate words into word-processing programs or to fill out online forms in a web browser. You can also use Speech Recognition to edit text on your computer. For more information about dictating text, see **Dictate text using Speech Recognition**.

Sensors

A sensor is basically a device that receives and responds to a signal or a stimulus.

A sensor is an input device that collects specific data directly from the environment and transmits it to a computer. (• *See Panel 5.17.*) Although you are unlikely to see such input devices connected to a microcomputer in an office, they exist all around us, often in nearly invisible form and as part of some larger electronic system. Sensors can be used to detect all kinds of things: speed, movement, weight, pressure, temperature, humidity, wind, current, fog, gas, smoke, light, shapes, images, and so on. An electronic device is used to measure a physical quantity such as temperature or pressure and convert it into an electronic signal of some kind (for instance, a voltage).

TECH TALES Sensors Get Data We Never Had Before

The rapid spread of low-cost sensors, notes Harvard technology expert David B. Yoffie, makes it possible to monitor all kinds of physical objects—"from fruit shipments (sniffing for signs of spoilage) to jet engines (tracking wear

panel 5.17

Sensors

(*left*) On October 9, 2003, the 2,080-pound Liberty Bell made a 963-foot journey to a new home on Independence Mall in Philadelphia. High-tech sensors monitored the famous crack, to make sure it did not get larger. (*middle*) Mount Vesuvius, Italy. Perimeter of volcanic crater with seismic apparatus. (*right*) In 2010 a solar-powered airborne car-emissions monitor was installed at the St. Joe State Park by the Missouri Department of Natural Resources.

to predict when maintenance is needed." The prevalence of sensors is new, says Yoffie. "The sensors make it possible to get data we never had before."[17]

Your plant needs water? Your child opens the cookie jar one too many times? You want to reset your home thermostat as electricity prices rise and fall during the day? All such information can be determined with sensors.[18]

Sensors also help keep society's infrastructure going. In Los Angeles, magnetic sensors in the road measure the flow of traffic and help in synchronizing every red light throughout the city.[19] In San Diego, researchers have developed portable sensors that send air-pollution data to smartphones.[20] In wintertime Iowa, sensors are used on highways to tell workers when to roll out snowplows. In aviation, sensors are used to detect ice buildup on airplane wings or to alert pilots to sudden changes in wind direction.

Sensors are also a great aid to research. At Stanford University, scientists have put sensors in football helmets to help gauge what forces cause concussions on the field.[21] Sensors on the small unmanned aerial systems known as drones are used to make more accurate counts of bird populations. In California, sensors have been planted along major earthquake fault lines in an experiment to see whether scientists can predict major earth movements.[22] Indeed, ocean- and land-based sensors in and near Japan were shown to have provided a crucial alert to officials prior to the 2011 earthquake and tsunami, allowing them 10 minutes to activate a public warning system, probably saving hundreds of lives.[23] ■

Science Sensors

Want to see how biologists study nature with sensors? Go to:

www.jamesreserve.edu/webcams/meadow_cams.html

www.usgs.gov/blogs/features/usgs_science_pick/usgs-storm-surge-sensors/

Biometric-Input Devices

In information technology, biometrics refers to technologies that measure and analyze human body characteristics.

Security concerns following the terrorist attacks of September 11, 2001, on the New York World Trade Center and the Pentagon made more people aware of biometrics. Today there is a biometrics boom.[24]

Biometrics is the science of analyzing and measuring specific biological characteristics of an individual to create a unique digital identifier that can be electronically stored and subsequently matched against to verify or determine a person's identity. Biometric security devices identify a person through a fingerprint; hand, eye, or facial characteristics; vein patterns; voice intonation; or some other biological trait. *(• See Panel 5.18, next page.)* Many laptop, notebook, tablet, and smartphone manufacturers equip their devices with biometric sensors that read fingerprints, instead of passwords, before allowing access. At many U.S. airports, preapproved members of the Global Entry system present their machine-readable passport or U.S. permanent resident card, place their fingertips on a special scanner for fingerprint verification, and make a customs declaration. The Global Entry kiosk issues the traveler a transaction receipt and directs the traveler to baggage claim and the exit. Other entry programs use eye scanners.

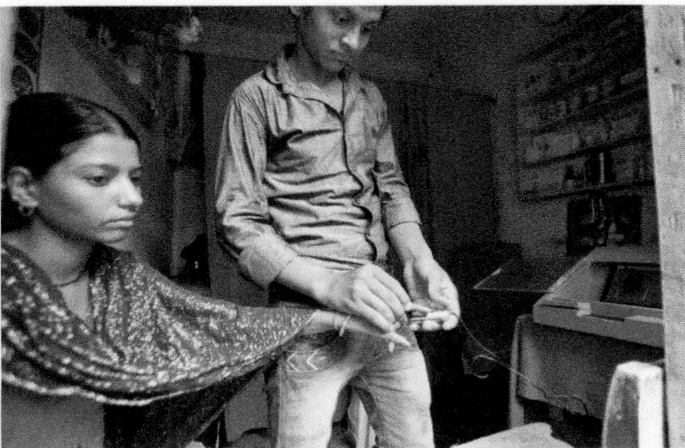

A counselor uses a biometric patient-record computer system to register a new tuberculosis patient by scanning her fingerprint in a health clinic in Delhi, India. They are using eDOTs, a low-cost biometric system that requires only a basic laptop and mobile phone. Internet access is not required.

5.4 THE FUTURE OF INPUT

We describe some trends of future input technology.

"Today," says a *Bloomberg Businessweek* report, "there's an explosion of innovation in interface design, driven by huge strides in processing power, memory, and bandwidth."[25] It started with the iPhone's touch-screen and swipe controls, and picked up speed with Microsoft's Kinect, the camera and sensor system that lets Xbox players control their videogame systems with gestures. What are some of the new directions being explored in input devices?

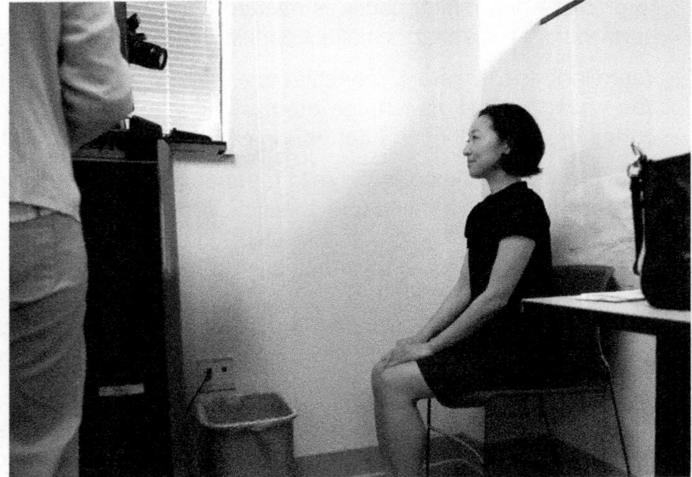

panel 5.18

Some types of biometric devices

(*top left*) Global Entry kiosk, Miami International Airport. Participants present their machine-readable passport or U.S. permanent resident card, place their fingertips on the scanner for fingerprint verification, and make a customs declaration. The kiosk issues the traveler a transaction receipt and directs the traveler to baggage claim and the exit. Travelers must be preapproved for the Global Entry program. All applicants undergo a rigorous background check and interview before enrollment. (*top right*) A Chinese immigrant is photographed during her biometrics appointment during her green card application process at the U.S. Citizenship and Immigration Service. (*bottom left*) Fingerprint recognition. (*bottom right*) A U.S. soldier scans the iris of a member of a neighborhood patrol in Baghdad.

Software That Can Identify People from Any Photograph Anywhere on the Internet?

How does this affect your privacy?

www.dailymail.co.uk/sciencetech/article-1305191/Facial-recognition-software-allow-ability-identify-people-photographs-internet.html

www.abine.com/blog/2011/the-top-6-facial-recognition-faqs/

www.cbsnews.com/8301-501465_162-20088678-501465.html

www.nbcnews.com/technology/facial-recognition-system-nets-2-500-identity-fraud-arrests-1C8692739

How does Facebook use facial recognition to tag users' photos? Do a keyword search and find out.

Toward More Input from Remote Locations

Data can be input from more and more remote locations.

The linkage of computers and telecommunications means that data may be input from nearly anywhere. For example, more U.S. businesses, small as well as large, are going to mobile payment services, where merchants can run credit or debit cards through their smartphones or tablets wherever they are, using services such as GoPayment, Square, and PayPal Here.[26] "Suddenly," says one technology writer, "anyone can accept cards: babysitters, cabdrivers, farmer's market vendors, piano teachers, personal trainers, bake salers, carpenters, and lawn-mowing teenagers."[27]

On the medical front, X-ray machines are now going digital, which means that a medical technician in the jungles of South America can take an X-ray of a patient and then transmit a perfect copy of it by satellite uplink to a hospital in Boston. Cell-PREVEN was created to allow access to real-time data to members of the health care ecosystem in Peru. (A digital health care ecosystem is intended to give patients and health care providers the means to exchange digital information quickly.) This interactive voice response system enables health workers in the field to collect and transmit data via basic mobile phones. The data is aggregated in a centralized database and made available to medical professionals, and the system is designed to send text messages or email alerts if certain symptoms are recorded.

Toward More Source Data Automation

The increased use of source data entry will increase the reliability of data.

Increasingly, input technology is being designed to capture data at its source, which will reduce the costs and mistakes associated with copying or otherwise preparing data in a form suitable for processing. We mentioned some possible innovations in high-capacity bar codes, more sophisticated scanners, smarter smart cards, and widespread use of sensors. Some reports from elsewhere on the input-technology front follow.

INPUT HELP FOR PEOPLE WITH DISABILITIES Some devices now available for people with physical disabilities, such as paraplegics, may portend new ways of entering and manipulating data input. For example, in one system a camera and special software enable users to operate the on-screen pointer with their eye movements instead of their hands. In another hands-free system, a camera tracks the user's body movements and the system converts them into mouse-pointer movements on the screen.[28]

In yet another system, the user's breathing controls the screen pointer. In still another, the nose is used to direct the cursor on a computer screen. There is also a system that can be attached to a baseball cap, enabling head movements to control the pointer. A web-based application called Web Anywhere provides verbal feedback and enables blind people to use any Internet-connected computer, allowing them to type up a quick email at an Internet café or check a flight time on a public computer at the airport. Finally, there are ideas about implanting video cameras behind the fake eyeball of those who have lost an eye.

In another field of research, computer engineers have designed an input device (called the Tongueduino) that allows blind people to "see" with the tongue, perhaps our most versatile sense organ. A small, square array of electrodes is placed on the tongue, where, "like a lollipop, it turns the feed from a video camera into a pointillist pattern of tactile stimulation," says one report. "After time and practice, blind users report the paradoxical sensation of seeing with their tongues."[29]

Mouse-Pointer Systems for People with Disabilities

To learn more about this subject, use these keywords to search the web: *Eye Gaze, CameraMouse, Quadjoy;* also try *www.laesieworks.com/spinal/spinal-comp.html.* A laptop with eye-tracking input technology is already available:

www.techspot.com/news/47693-eye-tracking-interface-promises-hands-free-gaming-glasses-free-3d.html

www.informationweek.com/hardware/peripherals/windows-8-meets-eye-tracking-at-ces-2012/232301531/

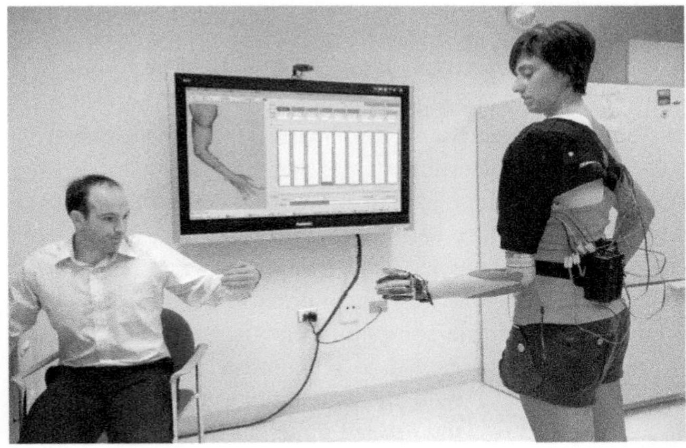

(*left*) A patient is training her new prosthetic arm with the Proto1 arm computer system. (*top right*) Zac Vawter, a 31-year-old software engineer from Seattle, Washington, pauses after climbing 103 floors to the top of the Willis Tower in Chicago using the world's first neural-controlled bionic leg. According to the Rehabilitation Institute of Chicago, its Center for Bionic Medicine has worked to develop technology that allow amputees to better control prosthetics with their own thoughts. (*bottom right*) Foot-operated keyboard

BETTER SPEECH RECOGNITION It's possible that speech recognition may someday fulfill world travelers' fondest dream: You'll be able to speak in English, and a speech-recognition device will instantly translate your remarks into another language, whether French, Swahili, or Japanese. At the moment, translation programs such as Easy Translator can translate text on web pages (English to Spanish, French, and German and the reverse), although they do so imperfectly.

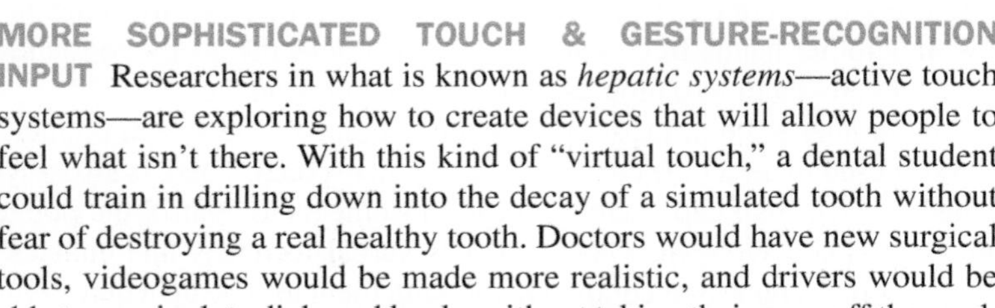

Research is also going forward on speech-recognition software that can decode slight differences in pitch, timing, and amplitude, so that computers can recognize anger and pain, for example. Researchers are working on a voice-enabled future, says one report, "where human speech brings responses from not only smartphones and televisions, cars and computers, but also coffee makers, refrigerators, thermostats, alarm systems, and other smart devices and appliances."[30]

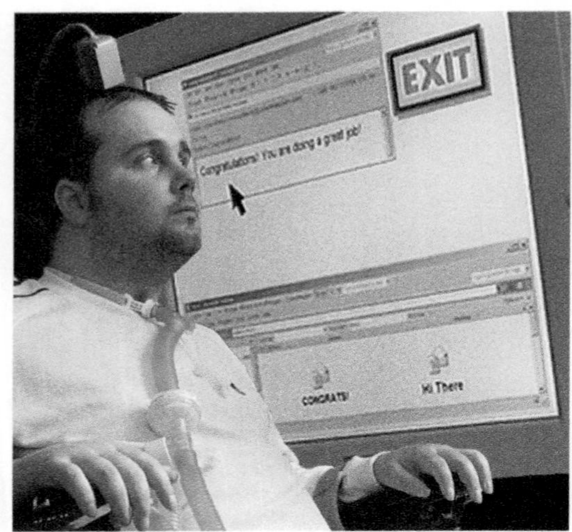

Matt Nagle, a quadriplegic, was the first person to use brain-computer interface called BrainGate—connected to a computer by a cable screwed into his head. The 4-millimeter square chip, placed on the surface of the motor cortex area of the brain, contained 100 electrodes, each thinner than a hair, that detected neural electrical activity. The sensor was connected to a computer via a small wire attached to a pedestal mounted on the skull. Nagle was able to check email and play computer games simply by using thoughts. He could also turn lights on and off and control a television, all while talking and moving his head.

MORE SOPHISTICATED TOUCH & GESTURE-RECOGNITION INPUT Researchers in what is known as *hepatic systems*—active touch systems—are exploring how to create devices that will allow people to feel what isn't there. With this kind of "virtual touch," a dental student could train in drilling down into the decay of a simulated tooth without fear of destroying a real healthy tooth. Doctors would have new surgical tools, videogames would be made more realistic, and drivers would be able to manipulate dials and knobs without taking their eyes off the road.

Researchers have been trying to apply gesturing to computing input devices for decades, and we have already seen the development of the *accelerometer,* a motion sensor that allows machines to respond to movement without waiting for humans to push a button. The Apple iPhone and Nintendo's Wii game console, for instance, currently feature similar technology, and many smartphones, computers, and other gadgets are being produced that are sensitive to motion. For example, with the Samsung Galaxy S4, you can wave your hand at the screen to accept calls and read content by tilting your head or phone. Pause any video that's playing by looking away from your phone; when you look back at the screen, the video resumes playing right where you left off (*www.samsung.com/us/guide-to-galaxy-smart-devices/galaxy-s-4-smartphone.html?cid=ppc-*). Now automakers are getting in on the act, devising gestures to let drivers control car functions—"whether it's an approaching hand to activate a dashboard infotainment system or the kick of a leg to open a . . . tailgate," says one article.[31]

Gesture recognition also is a key component in the idea of *pervasive computing,* which refers to having access to computing tools any place at any time. For example, a display could appear on a wall or wherever you want. To make pervasive computing work, however, users need to have an input device available wherever they are, a process often referred to as *human-centric computing.* Through human-centric computing, the user is always connected to computing tools. Gesture-recognition technology could provide the needed input capabilities for both types of computing.

panel 5.19

Computer-based analysis of emotions

Computer analysis of a smile on a baby girl's face to be used in lie detection testing. Each point making up the computerized grid overlaid on the baby's face shows whether that area of face has become lighter or darker owing to the expression. Unlike adults, babies make only genuine expressions, and so they can be used to work out the slight differences between sincere and false expressions in humans.

PATTERN RECOGNITION & BIOMETRIC DEVICES Would you believe a computer could read people's emotions from changes in their facial patterns, like surprise and sadness? Such devices are being worked on at Georgia Institute of Technology and elsewhere. *(• See Panel 5.19.)* Indeed, you can buy a face-recognition program so that you can have your computer respond only to your smile.

"Palm-scanning technology is popping up nationwide as a bona fide biometric tracker of identities," says one report.[32] Already used in some schools, where students may pay for lunch not with cash or a card but with a wave of their hand over a palm scanner, the technology seems poised to jump to retail and ATM usage. It has already been adopted in many hospitals for more efficient patient registration and to prevent sharing of information by patients that could lead to insurance fraud. Palm scanning works because the veins in the palm of your hand are as unique as a fingerprint and can be photographed under infrared light.

Gesture Recognition

For an update on the progress in gesture-recognition technology, go to:

www.washington.edu/news/2013/06/04/wi-fi-signals-enable-gesture-recognition-throughout-entire-home/

www.gesturecentral.com/

www.gesturetek.com/

www.extremetech.com/mobile/157432-a-standard-router-can-turn-your-entire-home-into-a-gesture-recognition-device/

BRAINWAVE DEVICES Perhaps the ultimate input device analyzes the electrical signals of the brain and translates them into computer commands. In one experiment, 100 tiny sensors were implanted in the brain of a 25-year-old quadriplegic who, using just his thoughts, was able to control a computer well enough to operate a TV, open email, and play Pong with 70% accuracy. At the University of Pittsburgh, macaque monkeys with electrical sensors in their brains have learned to feed themselves with robotic arms, an experiment billed as the first successful use of a "brain-machine interface" (or "brain-computer interface") to control a robotic limb for a practical function. NeuroSky of San Jose, California, sells an inexpensive MindWave Mobile headset with a forehead sensor that reads the electrical signals emitted by the brain, which can be used to control toys and videogames.[33]

Designs That Imitate the Physical World: Will They Be Abandoned?

Some icons and interfaces use images that are out of date.

When you turn a page in an Apple e-book, does the "paper" have to curl as you flip it over? Does the Apple Contacts app have to look like a physical address book—"complete with fake 'staples' in the 'binding' between 'pages,'" in one description?[34] These are examples of *skeuomorph* (pronounced "*skyoo*-uh-morph"), defined as "an element in an object's design that's no longer functionally necessary but has been retained anyway for ornamental purposes."[35]

In the digital age, design doesn't have to imitate the physical world, and some icons—such as reel-to-reel tape, no longer much used—are clearly obsolete. Thus, some design interfaces—Microsoft's Windows Phone, for example—are abandoning these depictions. Still, we should expect to see skeuomorphism continue for a while. When used well, says one commentator, "it can put you at ease with a new program in a flash and convey functions with simple visual metaphors."[36]

UNIT 5B: *Output Hardware*

Output refers to the results of processing—that is, information sent to the screen or the printer or to be stored on disk or sent to another computer in a network. Some devices combine input and output functions, examples being ATMs and kiosks—and the changing modern automobile.

TECH TALES Input & Output Together: Paving the Way for the Self-Driving Car

On the input side, automakers are starting to let drivers use gestures to control car functions, as in waving a hand to turn on the radio or make a phone call. There are also cameras mounted on the steering column that "read" drivers' faces to see if they're falling asleep.[37] Some experimental cars have wireless sensors in the headrest to measure the brain's electrical activity or electrodes embedded in the seat to measure the driver's heartbeat, helping to manage a car's safety systems.[38]

On the output side, automakers such as General Motors and Daimler are developing windshields that can display digital information, which companies hope will highlight hazards, such as pedestrians or erratic drivers.[39] The government has been testing vehicle-to-vehicle (V2V) communication, with cars that continuously communicate over wireless networks, "exchanging information on location, direction, and speed 10 times a second with other similarly equipped cars within about 1,000 feet," in one description. "A computer analyzes the information and issues danger warnings to drivers, often before they can see the other vehicle."[40]

These and other "active safety" systems are forerunners of what many automotive experts think will become driverless cars that will pilot themselves in stop-and-go traffic. Fully autonomous vehicles could be on the streets by 2025, some predict.[41]

There is a good deal of work to be done. Already as today's cars become heavy with proliferating dashboard electronics, carmakers have had to staff up call centers to help baffled owners sort through their problems.[42] In Mountain View, California, Google found that its experimental robot vehicles adorned with "Self-Driving Car" stickers followed the rules of the road perfectly—but they made drivers around them worse, as they took their eyes off the road to analyze what exactly was next to them. "The humans swerve," says one writer. "They drift."[43]

There seems little doubt, however, that input and output functions will in time be fully integrated in a self-driving car. The resulting autonomous vehicle technology could improve people's lives by making driving safer and more efficient.[44] ■

In this section, we discuss monitors and other output hardware, devices that convert machine-readable information, obtained as the result of processing, into people-readable form. The principal kinds of output are softcopy and hardcopy.

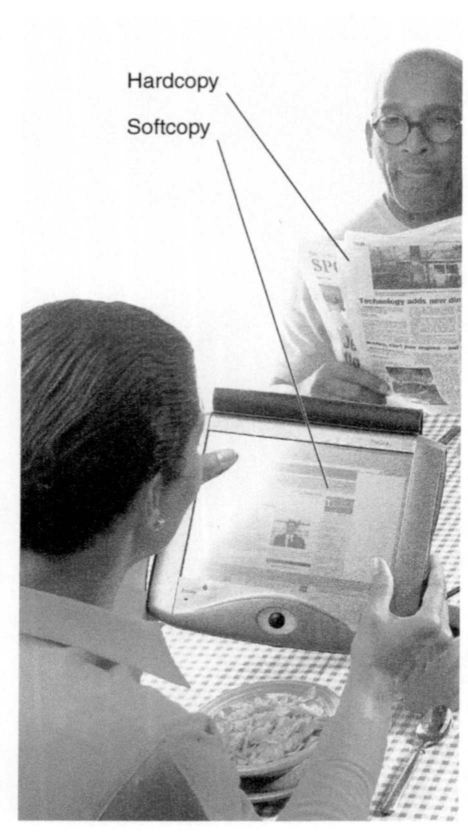

- **Softcopy: Softcopy is data that is shown on a display screen or is in audio or voice form; it exists only electronically.** This kind of output is not tangible; it cannot be touched. You can touch disks on which programs are stored, but the software itself is intangible. *Soft* is also used to describe things that are easily changed or impermanent. In contrast, *hard* is used to describe things that are relatively permanent.
- **Hardcopy: Hardcopy is tangible output, usually printed.** The principal examples are printouts, whether text or graphics, from printers. Film, including microfilm and microfiche, is also considered hardcopy output.

There are several types of softcopy and hardcopy output devices. In the following three sections, we discuss, first, *softcopy* output—*display screens;* second, *hardcopy* output—*printers;* and, third, *mixed* output—including *sound, voice,* and *video.*

5.5 SOFTCOPY OUTPUT: Display Screens

Screens, or monitors, display visual processing output in electronic form.

Display screens—also called *monitors* or simply *screens*—are output devices that show programming instructions and data as they are being input and information after it is processed. The monitor is the component that displays the visual output from your computer as generated by the video card. It is responsible not for doing any real computing but rather for showing the results of computing.

Features of Display Screens

Features of display screens to consider include screen dimension, screen clarity, and color and resolution standards.

In deciding which display screen to buy, you will need to consider issues of screen size, screen clarity (dot pitch, resolution, color depth, and refresh rate), and color and resolution standards.

SCREEN SIZE & ASPECT RATIO As with TV screens, the *active display area* is the size of a computer screen measured diagonally from corner to corner in inches. Desktop computers are commonly 15–30 inches (laptops 12–18 inches, tablets 8.4–14.1 inches, and smartphones 2.5–4.1 inches). The *aspect ratio* is the proportional relationship of a display screen's width and height. Standard displays have a 4:3 aspect ratio (4 units wide to 3 units high); wide-screen displays have 16:9 or 16:10.

Why does aspect ratio matter? Most television programming is formatted for standard 4:3 TVs. But many movies—on both DVD and cable TV—as well as a small but steadily increasing number of TV shows are broadcast in wide-screen format. If the content to be displayed is not formatted for the aspect ratio of the screen, viewing problems may result. For example, while viewing a new movie from Netflix on a 4:3 screen, you may see black "letterboxes" (black bands on the tops and the bottom of the screen); however, you will be seeing all the content. If you use zoom control to enlarge the image to fill the screen, you will then make it somewhat fuzzy and cut off some of the content at the edges of the image.

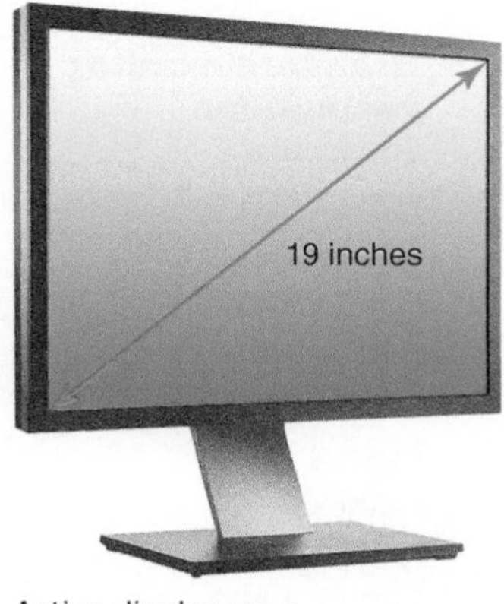

Active display area

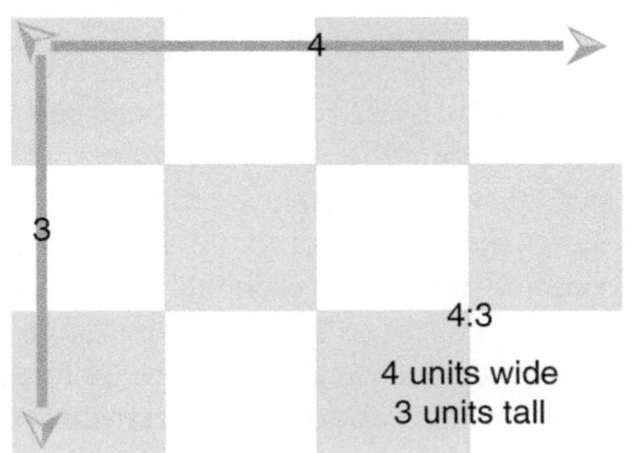

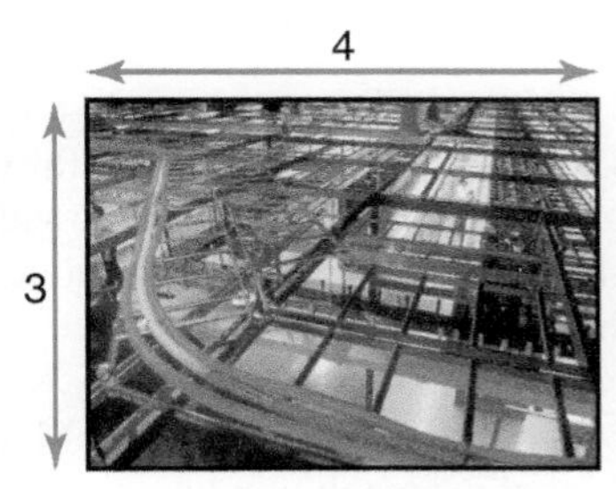

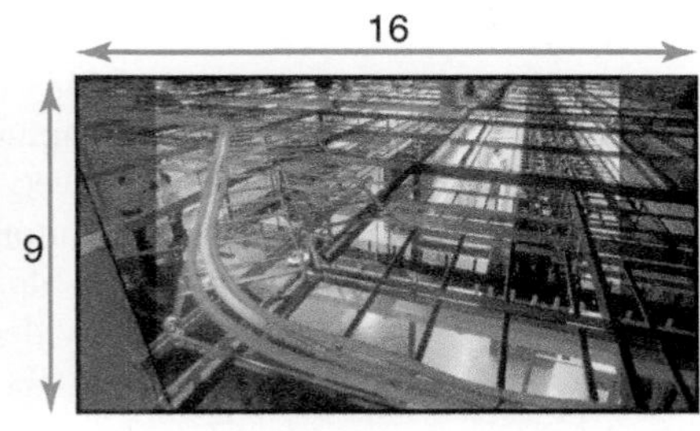

Examples of display screen aspect ratio

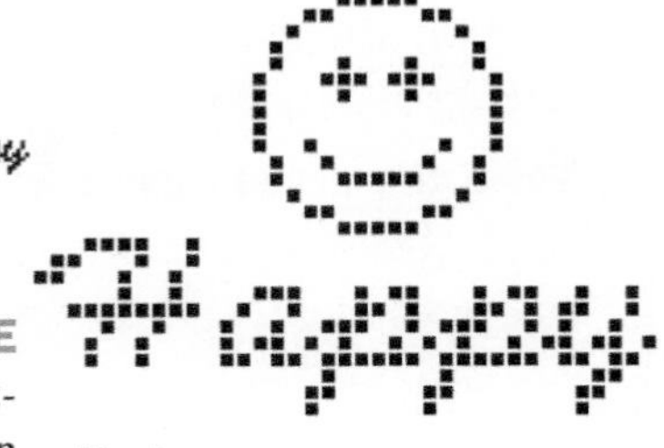

Pixels

SCREEN CLARITY: DOT PITCH, RESOLUTION, COLOR DEPTH, & REFRESH RATE Among the factors affecting screen clarity (often mentioned in ads) are *dot pitch, resolution, color depth,* and *refresh rate.* These relate to the individual dots on the screen known as *pixels,* which represent the images on the screen. **A pixel, for "*pic*ture *el*ement," is the smallest unit on the screen that can be turned on and off or made different shades.** Pixels are tiny squares, not circles.

- **Dot pitch: Dot pitch (dp) (also called pixel pitch) is the amount of space between the centers of adjacent pixels; the closer the pixels, the crisper the image.** For a 0.25-dp monitor, for instance, the dots (pixels) are 25/100ths of a millimeter apart. Generally, a dot pitch of 0.25–0.28 will provide clear images.
- **Resolution:** Here **resolution refers to the image sharpness of the display screen; the more pixels, or dots, there are per square inch, the finer the level of detail.** As with scanners, resolution is expressed in *dots per inch (dpi),* the number of columns and rows of dots (pixels) per inch. Generally, the higher the number of dots, the clearer and sharper the image. Resolution clarity is measured by the formula *horizontal-row pixels* × *vertical-row pixels.* For example, a 1,024 × 768 screen displays 1,024 pixels on each of 768 lines, for a total of 786,432 pixels. On color monitors, each pixel is assigned to be red, green, blue, or a particular shade of gray.

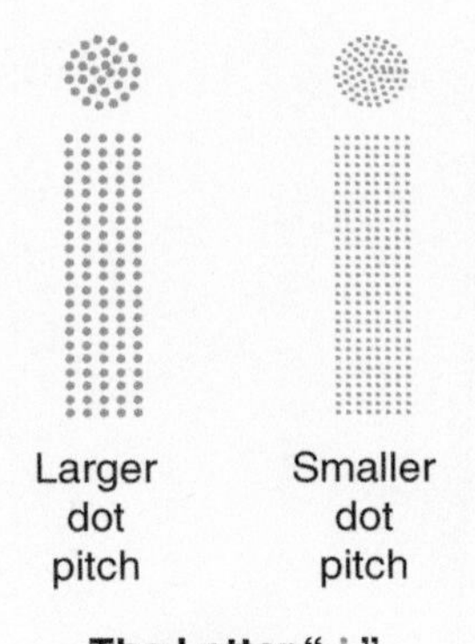

The Letter " i "

Standard monitor resolutions, in pixels

1,024 x 768 — These are becoming obsolete
1,152 x 864 — These are becoming obsolete
1,280 x 960
1,400 x 1,050
1,600 x 1,200
2,048 x 1,536
3,200 x 2,400
4,000 x 3,000
6,400 x 4,800 >

- Color depth: **Color depth, or *bit depth,* is the amount of information, expressed in bits, that is stored in a dot.** The more bits in a dot or pixel, the more shades of gray and colors can be represented. With 24-bit color depth, for example, 8 bits are dedicated to each primary color—red, green, and blue ($3 \times 8 = 24$). If you're not doing anything professionally with graphic art, photography, or videos, then you'll most likely be content with a monitor color depth of 24 bits, which is standard for most of computing; *30- to 64-bit color (called deep color: over 1 billion colors),* requires more resources, such as a special video card, supporting operating system, and a lot of video memory.
- Refresh rate: **Refresh rate is the number of times per second that the pixels are recharged so that their glow remains bright.** That is, refresh rate refers to the number of times that the image on the screen is redrawn each second. The higher the refresh rate, the more solid the image looks on the screen and the smoother the video (older monitors will flicker at a low refresh rate). In general, displays are refreshed 60–600 times per second, or *hertz (Hz).* A flat-screen monitor usually has a refresh rate (also called *response time*) of 60 Hz—the screen is redrawn 60 times per second.

Standard bit depths for color

8-bit—256 colors

16-bit—65,536 colors

24-bit—16,777,216 colors

COLOR & RESOLUTION STANDARDS FOR DISPLAY SCREENS As mentioned earlier, computers come with *graphics cards* (also known as *video cards* or *video adapters*) that convert signals from the computer into video signals that can be displayed as images on a monitor. The display screen then separates the video signal into three colors: red, green, and blue. Inside the monitor, these three colors combine to make up each individual pixel.

Video cards have their own memory, video RAM, or VRAM, which stores the information about each pixel. The more VRAM you have, which can range from 2 to 64 megabytes, the higher the resolution you can use. Videogamers and desktop publishers will want a video card with lots of VRAM.

The common resolution standards for monitors are *XGA, SXGA, UXGA, QXGA, WXGA, WSXGA+, and WUXGA.* *(• See Panel 5.20.)*

Types of Display Devices

Display devices include flat-panel displays, plasma monitors, and others.

Display devices can vary in size and quality, but their purpose is pretty much the same: to output text, graphics, and video images in color. The principal kinds of display devices are as follows.

panel 5.20
Video graphics standards

Common Display Standards and Resolutions

Standard	Resolution	Typical Use
XGA (Extended Graphics Array)	1,024 × 768	15-inch monitors
SXGA (Super XGA)	1,280 × 1,024	17- and 19-inch monitors
UXGA (Ultra XGA)	1,600 × 1,200	20-inch monitors
QXGA (Quad XGA)	2,048 × 1,536	20-inch and larger monitors
WXGA (Wide XGA)	1,280 × 800	Wide-screen 15.4-inch laptop displays
WSXGA+ (Wide SXGA plus)	1,680 × 1,050	Wide-screen 20-inch monitors
WUXGA (Wide Ultra XGA)	1,920 × 1,200	Wide-screen 22-inch and larger monitors

New flat-panel displays: (*left*) LCD; (*right*) plasma

FLAT-PANEL DISPLAYS The most common type of display screens, **flat-panel displays are made up of two plates of glass separated by a layer of a substance in which light is manipulated.** One type of flat-panel display is the **liquid crystal display (LCD), in which molecules of liquid crystal line up in a way that alters their optical properties, creating images on the screen by transmitting or blocking light.** (*• See Panel 5.21.*) LCDs are used in a wide range of applications, including computer monitors, televisions, instrument panels, signage, gaming devices, calculators, and phones.

There are two types of LCD:

- **Passive matrix:** Also called *dual-scan monitors, passive matrix* displays create images by scanning the entire screen. Thus, it requires little power, but the color is not as bright nor the images as sharp as in active matrix.
- **Active matrix:** Also called *thin-film transistor (TFT) display, active matrix* displays do not scan the entire screen but activate each liquid crystal cell (pixel) independently. Thus, this technology offers more colors and more clarity, although it is more expensive.

A newer alternative to TFT displays is *OLED* (for organic *light-emitting diode),* which is less expensive but brighter and easier to read.

panel 5.21

How a flat-panel display works

LCD monitors are composed of two flat pieces of polarized glass. Inside the two pieces is liquid crystal that is back-lit. When electric currents are added to the crystal molecules, they allow certain colors and light to pass through them. They do this by aligning in specific patterns of either on or off, depending on the command.

Microprocessor on the motherboard sends digital video data to the video card.

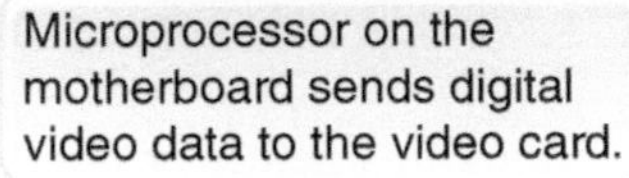

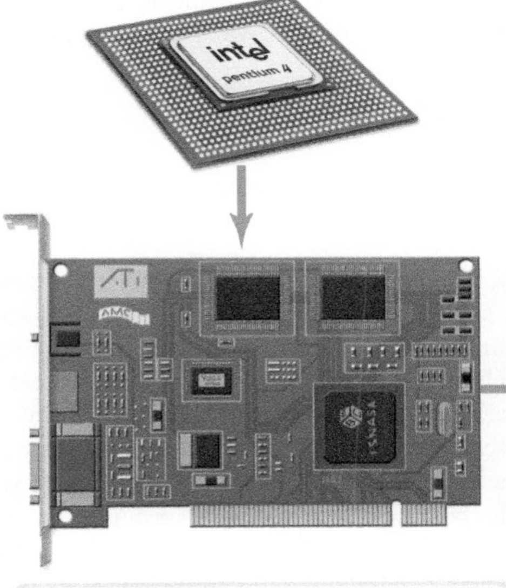

Video card on the motherboard converts digital signals to analog signals and sends them via a cable to the monitor.

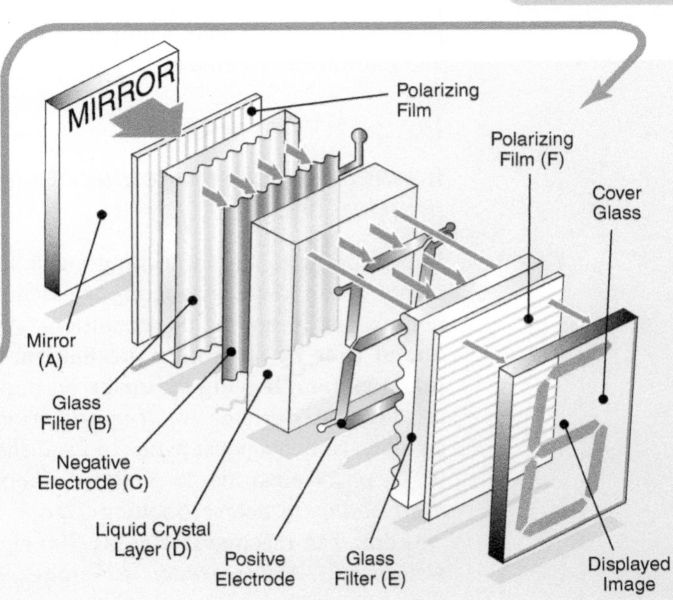

CRT display

PLASMA DISPLAYS In a plasma display, **a layer of gas is sandwiched between two glass plates, and when voltage is applied, the gas releases ultraviolet light, which activates the pixels on the screen and forms an image.** Although expensive, plasma monitors offer brighter colors and screen sizes up to 150 inches wide; however, they usually do not last as long as other display types.

CATHODE-RAY TUBE & OTHER DEVICES Rapidly falling out of use, *cathode-ray tube (CRT) displays* (*left*) resemble old desktop televisions, with an electron beam activating dots of phosphor material on the inside of the sealed glass cathode-ray tube to create an image. Other kinds of displays range from high-definition television sets to e-book readers to digital whiteboards.

MULTIPLE SCREENS Ready to move up from one screen to two when you're working at your computer? With only a single display screen, you find yourself switching back and forth between, say, a word processing document, email, and web searches. Multiple monitors reduce distractions. Indeed, a study showed that people who use *two* display screens, rather than one, are 44% more productive at certain text-editing operations.[45] "The study revealed that multiscreen users get on task quicker, work faster, and get more work done with fewer errors editing documents, spreadsheets, and graphic files in comparison with single screen users," said one of the study authors.[46] A cost-effective arrangement is to get two 22-inch monitors, one placed vertically, the other horizontally.[47]

Survival Tip

Buying a New Monitor?

Be sure that it can work with your computer and that your video card has enough video RAM to support what you want to do. Also, screens come with a "native" resolution: its normal default setting. You often can change your resolution setting by going to your computer's control panel, display setting icon. However, if you increase your resolution, the items on your computer's desktop, and the text type, will become smaller. You can fit more content on your screen that way, but the text may be difficult to read.

5.6 HARDCOPY OUTPUT: Printers

Hardcopy output hardware consists of impact printers but mostly nonimpact printers, such as laser, inkjet, thermal, thermal wax-transfer, and photo printers. There are also multifunction printers and plotters.

The prices in ads for computer systems often do not include a printer. Thus, if you are buying a new system, you may need to budget an additional $100–$5,000 or more for a printer. **A printer is an output device that prints characters, symbols, and graphics on paper or another hardcopy medium.** As with scanners, the resolution, or quality of sharpness, of the printed image is indicated by *dots per inch (dpi),* a measure of the number of rows and columns of dots that are printed in a square inch. For microcomputer printers, the resolution is in the range of 600 × 600 to 5,760 × 1,440, with 1,200 × 1,200 being most common.

Printers can be separated into two categories, according to whether or not the image produced is formed by physical contact of the print mechanism with the paper. *Impact printers* do have contact with paper; *nonimpact printers* do not. We also consider plotters and multifunction printers.

Impact Printers

Impact printers make direct contact with the medium that they are printing on.

Impact printers, an old printing technology, are most functional in specialized environments where low-cost printing is essential, such as for label printing, in shipping warehouses, and in hot factory conditions. **An impact printer forms characters or images one at time by striking a mechanism such as a print hammer or wheel against an inked ribbon, leaving an image on paper.** The most common form of impact printer is the dot-matrix printer. A *dot-matrix printer* contains a print head of small pins that strike an inked ribbon against paper, to form characters or images. Print heads are available with 9, 18, or 24 pins; the 24-pin head offers the best quality. Dot-matrix printers can print *draft quality,* a coarser-looking 72 dpi; or *near-letter-quality (NLQ),* a crisper-looking 240 dpi. The machines print 40–300 characters per second and can handle graphics as well as text. A *line printer* is a high-speed impact printer that prints an entire line at a time; this type of printer is used in the automotive, logistic, and banking worlds for high-speed and bar-code printing.

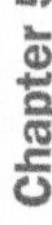

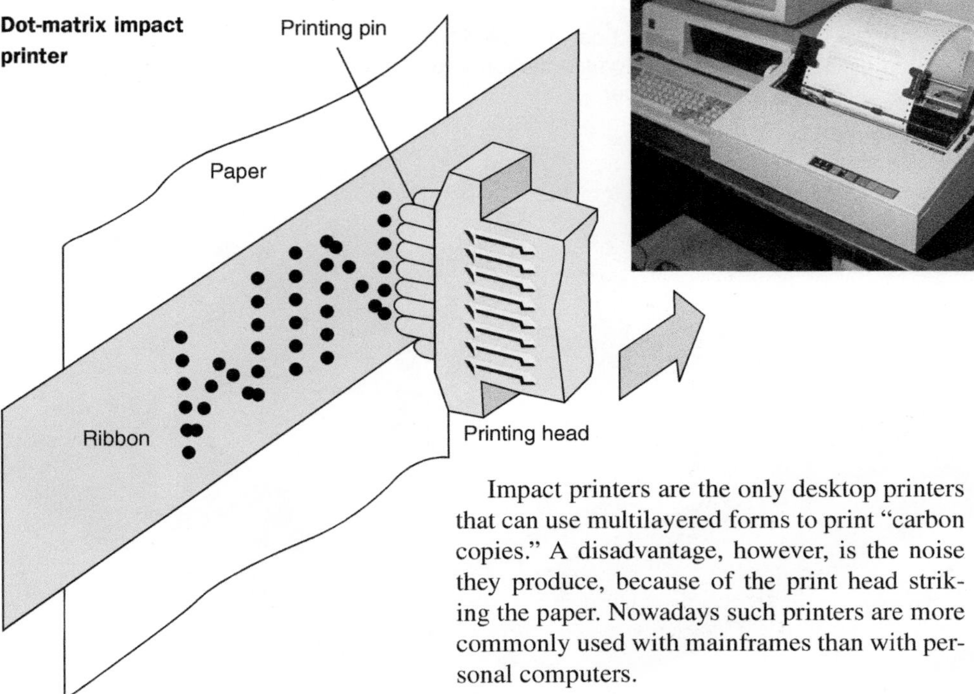

Impact printers are the only desktop printers that can use multilayered forms to print "carbon copies." A disadvantage, however, is the noise they produce, because of the print head striking the paper. Nowadays such printers are more commonly used with mainframes than with personal computers.

Nonimpact Printers

Nonimpact printers do not use print heads to make direct contact with the output medium.

Nonimpact printers are usually faster and quieter than impact printers because no print head strikes paper. **Nonimpact printers form characters and images without direct physical contact between the printing mechanism and paper.** Two types of nonimpact printers often used with microcomputers are *laser printers* and *inkjet printers.* A third kind, the *thermal printer,* is seen less frequently.

- **Laser printers:** Like a dot-matrix printer, a **laser printer creates images with dots. However, as in a photocopying machine, these images are produced on a drum, treated with an electrically charged inklike toner (powder), and then transferred from drum to paper.** *(• See Panel 5.22, next page.)*
- **Laser printers run with software called a page description language (PDL). This software tells the printer how to lay out the printed page, and it supports various fonts.** A laser printer comes with one or both types of PDL: PostScript (developed by Adobe) or PCL (Printer Control Language, developed by Hewlett-Packard). In desktop publishing, PostScript is the preferred PDL. Laser printers have their own CPU, ROM, and memory (RAM), usually 16 megabytes (expandable generally up to 512 megabytes for higher-cost printers). When you need to print out graphics-heavy color documents, your printer will need more memory.

  There are good reasons that laser printers are among the most common types of nonimpact printer. They produce sharp, crisp images of both text and graphics. They are quiet and fast—able to print 11–33 pages per minute (ppm) in color and 10.5–37 black-and-white pages per minute for individual microcomputers and up to 200 pages per minute for mainframes. They can print in different *fonts*—that is, sets of typestyles and type sizes. The more expensive models can print in different colors. Laser printers usually have a dpi of 1,200 × 1,200.
- **Inkjet printers: Inkjet printers spray onto paper small, electrically charged droplets of ink from four or more nozzles through holes in a matrix at high speed.** *(• See Panel 5.23, page 283.)* Like laser and dot-matrix printers, inkjet printers form images with little dots. Inkjet printers commonly have a dpi of 4,800 × 1,200 (but can be as high as 9,600 × 2,400); they spray ink onto the page a line at a time, in both high-quality black-and-white text and high-quality color graphics. (To achieve impressive color images, you should use high-quality, high-gloss paper, which prevents

Survival Tip

How Do I Use the Print Scrn key?

This PC key is a holdover from DOS days, before Windows. Then it sent the contents of the display screen to the printer. It still can, but in a roundabout way. The sole function of this key is to take a snapshot or picture of your computer screen and copy it to the clipboard (the clipboard is an invisible holding area for content that is copied). So, when you press the key, an image of the screen is placed on the Windows clipboard. Open a blank document in any program that accepts graphics, and choose *Edit, Paste.* The image is inserted, and you can print it. (Some new keyboards have eliminated this key.)

Survival Tip

Is Your Printer Telling the Truth?

Inkjet printers and laser printers display a message or a light when your ink/toner cartridges need to be replaced. But are they telling the truth? In general, no. Cartridge sales are profitable to the manufacturers. Your cartridges may have a much longer life than your printer is telling you. You can ignore the warning and wait until the toner really does run out; but you might be in the middle of a print job when that happens. Or you can locate the sensor and put a piece of black tape over it, and you may get much more printing out of your cartridges. But then you would not ever get any warning message at all. Before replacing a toner cartridge, try taking it out of the printer and shaking it a few times to redistribute the remaining toner inside the cartridge.

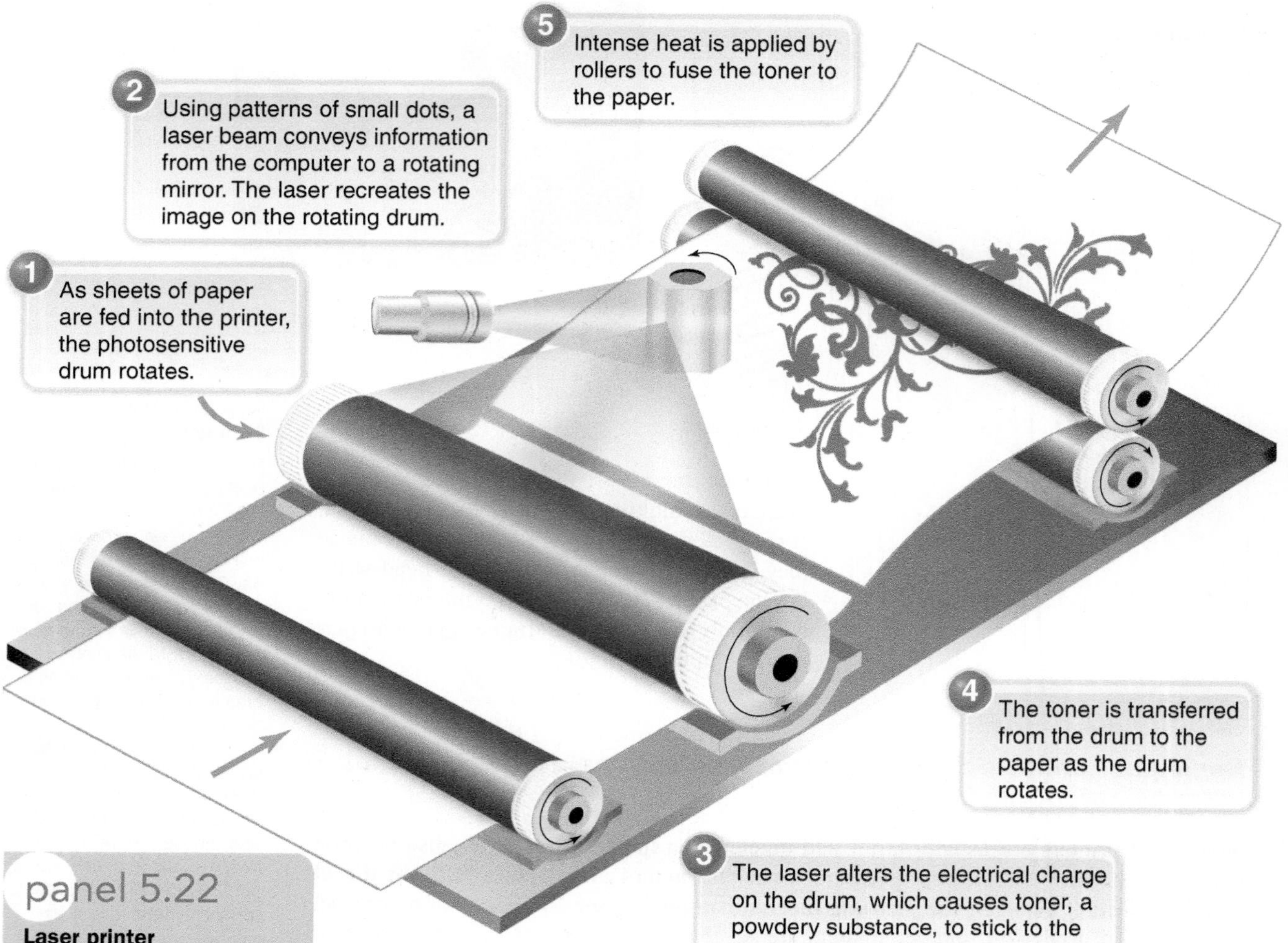

1 As sheets of paper are fed into the printer, the photosensitive drum rotates.

2 Using patterns of small dots, a laser beam conveys information from the computer to a rotating mirror. The laser recreates the image on the rotating drum.

3 The laser alters the electrical charge on the drum, which causes toner, a powdery substance, to stick to the drum.

4 The toner is transferred from the drum to the paper as the drum rotates.

5 Intense heat is applied by rollers to fuse the toner to the paper.

panel 5.22

Laser printer

How a laser printer works

inkjet-sprayed dots from *feathering,* or spreading.) Inkjet cartridges come in various combinations: a single cartridge for black and all color inks, two separate black and color cartridges, or separate cartridges for black and each color. Some cartridges also include the print head, which is apt to wear out before the rest of the machine.

The advantages of inkjet printers are that they can print in color, are quiet, and are generally less expensive than color laser printers. The disadvantages have been that they print a bit less precisely than laser printers do and traditionally they have been slower.

Another disadvantage is that inkjet cartridges have to be replaced more often than laser-toner cartridges do and so may cost more in the long run. Moreover, a freshly inkjet-printed page is apt to smear unless handled carefully. For users who print infrequently, laser printers (which use toner, a dry powder) have the advantage of not drying out. Laser owners don't have to deal with dried-out cartridges clogging nozzles and wasting expensive ink and time—common problems for inkjet users.

Still, experts maintain that users who want the best-quality photo output should get a photo inkjet printer. Laser printers in general are known for their mediocre photo output, with cheap personal laser printers often doing an especially poor job.

Laser printers are known for handling a much higher volume of printouts than inkjet printers. Buyers who do a lot of printing should pay close attention to a printer's monthly duty cycle, which determines how many printouts a printer can comfortably handle in a month. Going over this can shorten the life of a printer. In general, cheaper printers have much lower duty cycles than the higher-end printers.

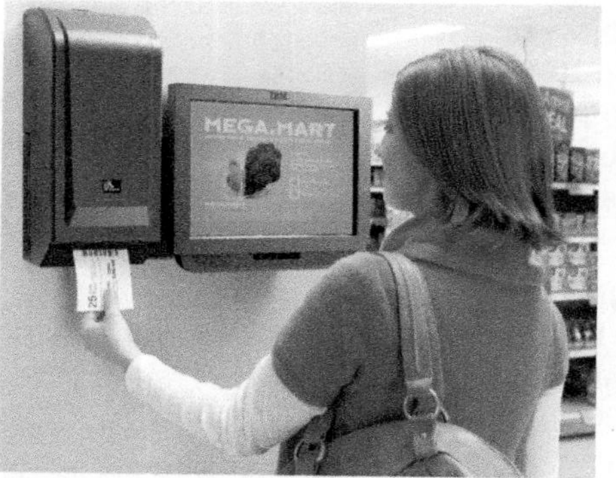

Thermal-printed cash-register receipt

- **Thermal printers: Thermal printers are low- to medium-resolution printers that use a type of coated paper that darkens when heat is**

❶ Four removable ink cartridges are attached to print heads with 64 firing chambers and nozzles apiece.

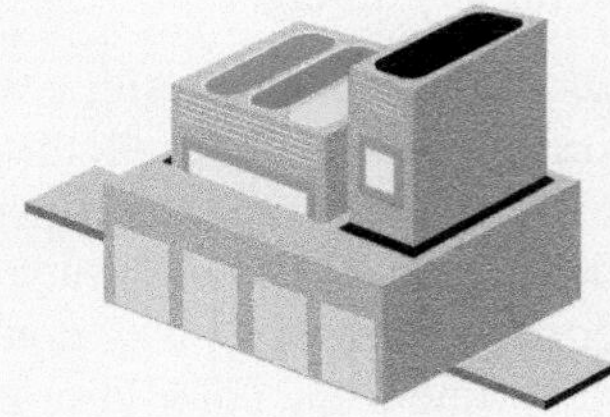

❷ As the print heads move back and forth across the page, software instructs them where to apply dots of ink, what colors to use, and in what quantity.

❸ To follow those instructions, the printer sends electrical pulses to thin resistors at the base of the firing chambers behind each nozzle.

❹ The resistor heats a thin layer of ink, which in turn forms a vapor bubble. That expansion forces ink through the nozzle and onto the paper at a rate of about 6,000 dots per second.

❺ A matrix of dots forms characters and pictures. Colors are created by layering multiple color dots in varying densities.

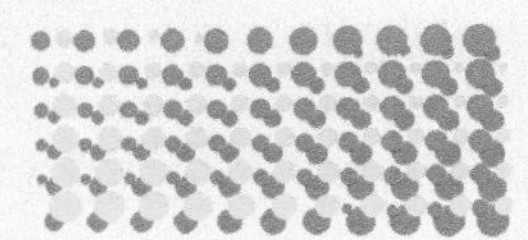

panel 5.23

Inkjet printer

How an inkjet printer works; (*below*) magnified inkjet dots

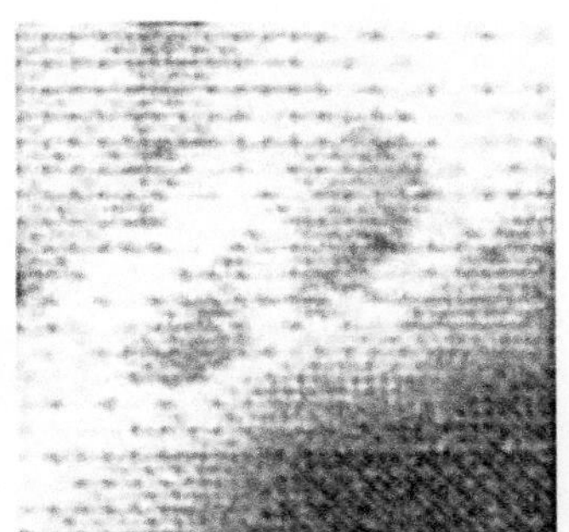

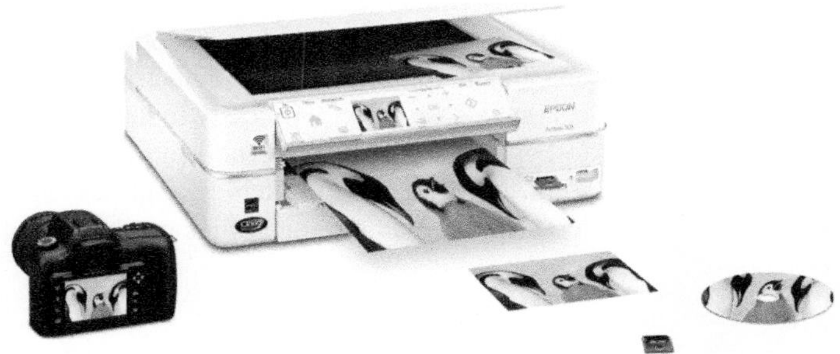

Homaro Cantu, chef at Chicago's Moto Restaurant, prints sushi on a Canon inkjet printer using edible paper made of soybeans and cornstarch and food-based inks of his own concoction. He then flavors the back of the paper with powdered soy sauce and seaweed. Even Cantu's menu is edible; diners crunch it up into soups.

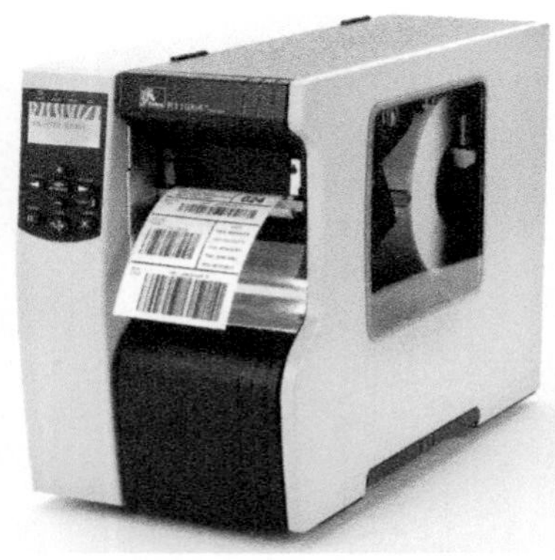

Wax-transfer thermal printed label

Portable dye-sublimation photo printer printing out a photo stored on an iPhone

applied to it. The paper is moved past a line of heating elements that burn dots onto the paper. This technology is typically used in business for bar-code label applications and for printing cash register receipts. Until about 2000, most fax machines used direct thermal printing, though now only the cheapest models use it, the rest having switched to thermal wax-transfer, laser, or inkjet printing.

- **Thermal wax-transfer printers:** *Thermal wax-transfer printers* print a wax-based ink onto paper. As the paper and ribbon travel in unison beneath the thermal print head, the wax-based ink from the transfer ribbon melts onto the paper. After it becomes cool, the wax adheres permanently to the paper. Although such printers are highly reliable, because of the small number of moving parts, they don't compare with the output quality of modern inkjet printers and color laser printers. However, because of their waterfastness, they find uses in industrial label printing.
- **Photo printers:** *Photo printers,* also called *dye-sublimation printers,* are specialized machines for printing continuous-tone photo prints (typically 3 × 5 or 4 × 6 inches), using special dye-receptive paper and ribbons with special transparent color dyes. Paper and ribbon pass together over the print head, which contains thousands of heating elements producing varying amounts of heat. The hotter the element, the more dye is released, and as the temperature is varied, shades of each color can be overlaid on top of one another. The dyes are transparent and blend (sublimate) into continuous-tone color. Some inexpensive ($70–$200) photo printers are designed to be unplugged and taken on the go; in fact, they connect directly to a digital camera. These printers connect to the computer or digital camera via USB cable or wireless infrared.

Multifunction Printers: Printers That Do More Than Print

Multifunction printers do more than just print.

Multifunction printers **combine several capabilities, such as printing, scanning, copying, and faxing.** *(• See Panel 5.24.)* Brother, Canon, Epson, and Hewlett-Packard make machines in a price range of $100–$500 that combine a photocopier, fax machine, scanner, and inkjet printer. Several manufacturers offer all-in-one printers that also connect wirelessly to the Internet, allowing users to bypass their computer and print out web content in paper form. Multifunction printers take up less space and can cost less than the four separate office machines that they replace.

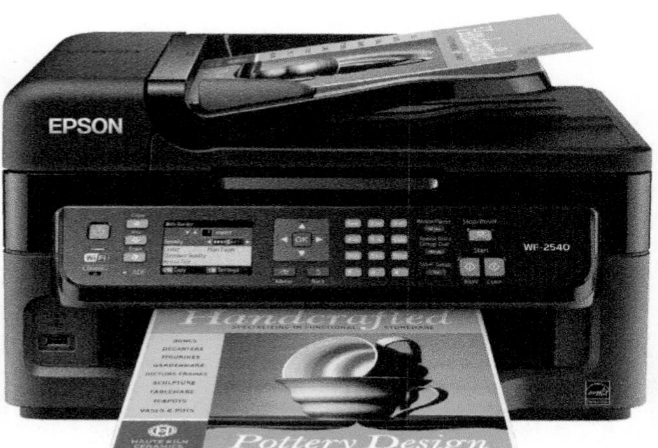

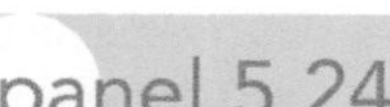

panel 5.24

Multifunction device

This machine combines four functions in one—printer, copier, fax machine, and scanner.

Plotters

Plotters are designed for large-format printing.

A plotter **is a specialized output device designed to produce large, high-quality graphics in a variety of colors.** *(• See Panel 5.25.)* Plotter lines are not made up of dots; they are actually drawn.

The plotter was the first computer output device that could not only print graphics but also accommodate full-size engineering, three-dimensional, and architectural drawings, as well as maps. Using different colored pens, it was also able to print in color long before inkjet printers became an alternative. Plotters are still the most affordable printing device for computer-aided design (CAD) and offer much higher resolutions than desktop printers do. Plotters are controlled by PCL and HPCL (Hewlett-Packard Control Language).

The three principal kinds of plotters are pen, electrostatic, and large-format:

- **Pen:** A *pen plotter* uses one or more colored pens to draw on paper or transparencies.
- **Electrostatic:** In an *electrostatic plotter,* paper lies partially flat on a tablelike surface, and toner is used in a photocopier-like manner.
- **Large-format:** *Large-format plotters* operate somewhat like an inkjet printer but on a much larger scale. This type of plotter is often used by graphic artists.

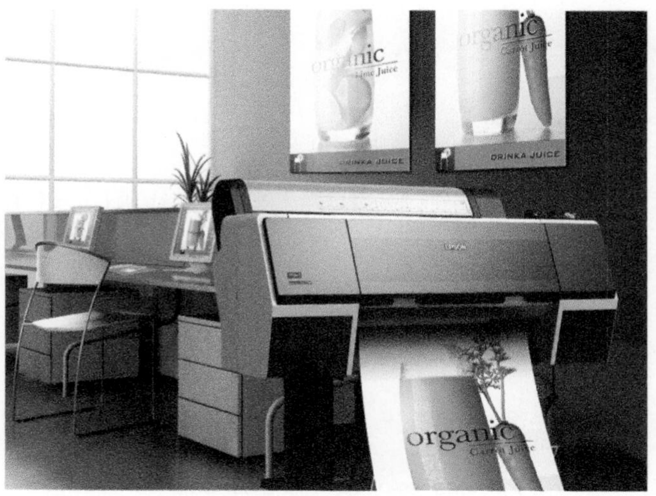

panel 5.25

Large-format plotters

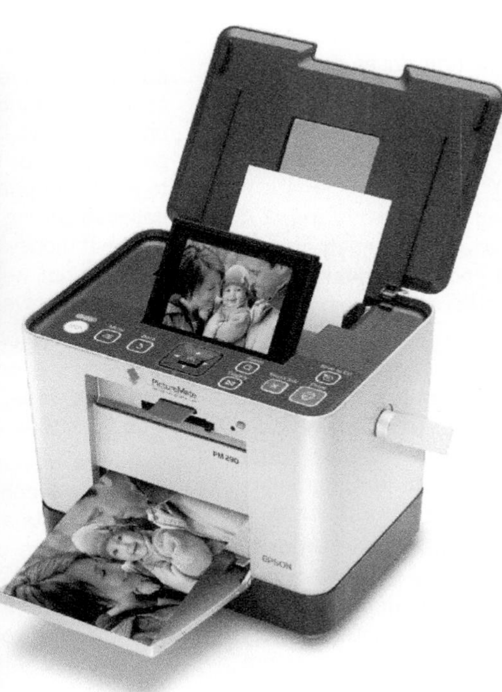

Specialty printers.
(*left*) Proofreader Ed Kochanowski proofreads a Braille edition of *Beowulf* printed at the National Braille Press in Boston. (*right*) Portable document printer, which can be connected to a laptop, smartphone, table, or other device.

Specialty Printers

Many printers have been developed to serve particular needs.

Specialty printers exist for such purposes as printing certain types of labels, tickets, and text in Braille, as well as for many industrial purposes.

PRACTICAL ACTION

Buying a Printer

Some questions to consider when you're buying a printer:

- *Do I need color, or will black-only do?* Are you mainly printing text, or will you need to produce color charts and illustrations (and, if so, how often)? If you print lots of black text, consider getting a laser printer. If you might occasionally print color, get an inkjet that will accept cartridges for both black and color. If you need to print lots of black *and* color materials, get a color laser printer.
- *Do I have other special output requirements?* Do you need to print envelopes or labels? Special fonts (type styles)? Multiple copies? Transparencies or on heavy paper? Unusual paper size? Find out if the printer comes with envelope feeders, sheet feeders holding at least 100 sheets, or whatever will meet your requirements
- *Is the printer easy to set up?* Can you easily plug in the hardware, and adjust the software (the driver programs) to make the printer work with your computer?
- *Is the printer easy to operate?* Can you add paper, replace ink/toner cartridges or ribbons, and otherwise operate the printer without much difficulty?
- *Does the printer provide the speed and quality I want?* A laser printer prints about 11–37 pages per minute (ppm); a color inkjet prints about 17–34 ppm. Colors and graphics take longer to print. Are the blacks dark enough and the colors vivid enough?
- *Will I get a reasonable cost per page?* Special paper, ink or toner cartridges (especially color), and ribbons are all ongoing costs. Inkjet color cartridges, for example, may last 100–500 pages and cost $2–$30 new. Laser toner cartridges can cost up to $100 each but last much longer. Ask the seller what the cost per page works out to.
- *Is printer memory an issue?* Printers have their own dedicated memory, and you can install more printer memory (in laser printers) to avoid problems and print larger files. All printers come with a certain amount of printer memory installed—usually 2, 4, or 16 megabytes—but most are upgradeable to handle more or larger print jobs. Printer memory is directly linked to two print characteristics: speed and print quality. More memory allows you to print faster and print larger, high-quality graphics at higher resolutions. (When you send a print job at a higher resolution than your printer can handle, it automatically reduces the print job's resolution to one it can handle.)

  Printer memory is used to store (buffer) print jobs after they are received from the computer. If it is overloaded, an error message saying "network printer is busy" will display. However, you shouldn't have to worry about memory unless you work in a crowded office with lots of print jobs.
- *What resolution do I need?* For general-purpose printing, 300 dpi should be sufficient; if you work in graphics, 600 (600 × 600) dpi is better; if you want high-quality photos, 1,200 dpi is preferred. Professionals in desktop publishing and graphics will probably want an even higher resolution.
- *Should I get a multifunction printer?* If you are short on space and have multiple tasks, then you should consider an all-in-one wireless printer: printer, scanner, fax machine, copier. Multifunction machines are good for people limited on space and money. Figuring out whether you need to go all-in-one or not is a matter of necessity. If you need to scan and print, then you need a multifunction machine because getting a separate scanner and printer would be a waste of money and space. If all you do is print documents and random web articles and never scan pictures, then you should save money and get a single-function printer.
- *Do I need wireless printing?* Wireless printing (or Wi-Fi) is one of the best innovations applied to printers. If you don't like wires, if you have a laptop, or you are just short on space, then you might want Wi-Fi.
- *Does the manufacturer offer a good warranty and good telephone technical support?* Find out if the warranty for a printer lasts at least 2 years. See if the printer's manufacturer offers telephone support in case you have technical problems. The best support systems offer toll-free numbers and operate evenings and weekends as well as weekdays. (If you can, try calling tech support before you buy and see what happens.)

5.7 MIXED OUTPUT: Sound, Voice, & Video

Multimedia output requires several peripherals.

Most PCs are multimedia computers, capable of displaying and producing not only traditional softcopy and hardcopy text and graphics but also sound, voice, and video, as we consider next.

Sound Output

Sound output requires a sound card.

Sound-output devices produce digitized sounds, ranging from beeps and chirps to music. To use sound output, you need appropriate software and a sound expansion card (p. 204). The sound card could be Sound Blaster or, since that brand has become a de facto standard, one that is "Sound Blaster–compatible." Well-known brands include Creative Labs, Diamond, and Turtle Beach. The sound card plugs into an expansion slot in your computer; on newer computers, it is integrated with the motherboard.

At one time, the audio emerging from a computer had the crackly sound of an old vacuum-tube radio. Then, in 1997, audio in personal computers began to shift to three-dimensional sound. Now, a PC with two speakers can sound more like a "surround sound" movie house. Unlike conventional stereo sound, 3-D audio describes an expanded field of sound—a broad arc starting at the right ear and curving around to the left. Thus, in a videogame, you might hear a rocket approach, go by, and explode off your right shoulder. The effect is achieved by boosting certain frequencies that provide clues to a sound's location in the room or by varying the timing of sounds from different speakers.

Laptop integrated speakers are usually good; desktop computers do require external speakers for good sound (or speakers integrated into the monitor).

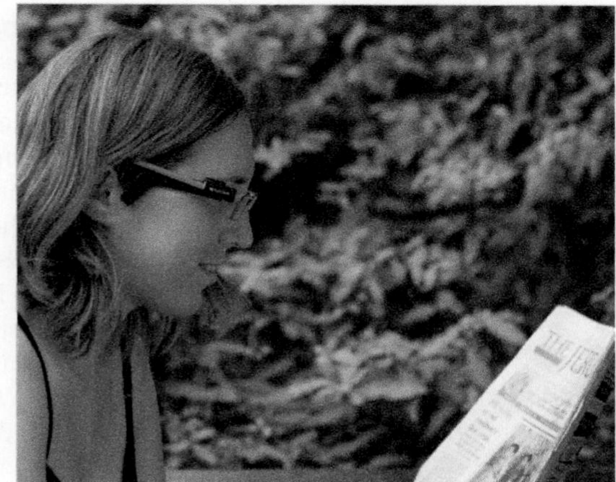

Woman in Israel wearing OrCam glasses, which compensate for lost visual abilities. Users can read newspapers and books, signs, and labels on any product, including medication and text on a computer, phone, or television screen. If the wearer points to a specific article or paragraph, OrCam will start reading from the beginning of that part. The device comprises a minicamera and a bone-conduction earpiece (for communicating the reading), which are strapped to the user's eyeglasses.

Voice Output

Voice output also requires a sound card.

Liat Negrin, an Israeli who has been visually impaired since childhood, can now use an OrCam, a device consisting of a camera and small computer attached to her glasses, to "read" the label on a can of vegetables. The OrCam then tells her what the label says by using voice output.[48]

Voice-output devices convert digital data into speechlike sounds. You hear such forms of voice output on telephones ("Please hang up and dial your call again"), in soft-drink machines, in cars, in toys and games, and in mapping software for vehicle-navigation devices. Voice portals read news and other information to users on the go.

One form of voice output that is becoming popular is *text-to-speech (TTS) systems,* which convert computer text into audible speech. TTS benefits not only those who are visually impaired but also anyone with a computer system sound card and speakers who wants to reduce reading chores (and eyestrain) and do other tasks at the same time. Windows offers a TTS program called Narrator; others are CoolSpeech, Balabolka, Natural Reader, NeoSpeech, and Digalo. AOL, Yahoo!, and MapQuest have licensed a high-quality TTS program developed by the AT&T Natural Voices Lab to read email, give driving directions, provide stock quotes, and more.

Video Output

Video output requires a video card.

Video consists of photographic images, which are played at 15–30 frames per second to give the appearance of full motion. Video is input into a multimedia system usually using a video camera and, after editing, is output on a computer's display screen. Because video files can require a great deal of storage—a 3-minute video may require 1 gigabyte of storage—video is often compressed. Good video output requires a powerful processor as well as a video card.

Another form of video output is **videoconferencing, in which people in different geographic locations can have a meeting—can see and hear one another—using computers and communications.** Videoconferencing systems range from videophones to group conference rooms with cameras and multimedia equipment to desktop systems with small video cameras, microphones, and speakers. (We discuss videoconferencing in more detail in Chapter 6, p. 342.)

5.8 THE FUTURE OF OUTPUT

We discuss some trends of output technology.

What will output look like in the future? Perhaps your smartphone could become the ultimate output device, telling you far more about the world than you ever thought possible. For example, it is already possible to buy a "personal environment monitor," the Russian-made Lapka, which plugs into an iPhone's headphone jack and will tell you about your surrounding humidity, radiation, electromagnetic fields, pollution level in your drinking water, and even the level of nitrates in your food.[49]

The three directions that output seems to be taking is that it is taking more and more unusual forms, uses more and more data, and is becoming more and more realistic.

Using the Smithsonian

What kind of technology does the Smithsonian Museum in Washington, D.C., have on display? Find the museum's website and enter keywords of computer terms.

More Unusual Forms of Output

Output technology will be available in forms that we don't have today.

We already mentioned output derived from the tongue that helps blind people "see." What about output you can smell? Entrepreneurs are now working on devices that produce odors, such as perfume samples that can be produced by TVs during Chanel commercials. For instance, in some movie theaters "technicians can deploy any of about 1,000 scents that correspond to the action on the screen—like the odor of burning rubber for car-chase scenes," says one report.[50]

Another unusual form of output is the bathroom mirror, which follows a trend toward making everyday objects smarter through digital technology and Internet connectivity. The Medical Mirror, for instance, uses a camera to measure a person's pulse rate and then uses a two-way mirror to create a reflection "while keeping visible the pulse reading on a computer monitor behind the mirror's surface."[51]

More Data Used in Output

Big data is affecting the quantity and quality of output.

A digital camera with 200 lenses that mimics the compound eyes of ants, dragonflies, bees, and other insects has been built for the purpose of helping doctors explore the insides of patients. Imagine the huge amount of data this and similar input devices could generate—and how it will affect the quantity and quality of output.[52]

Massive amounts of data, steadily increasing for decades, has sharply accelerated in the Internet age, leading toward what is being called *Big Data* (Chapter 1, p. 37). Big Data is the name used to describe a massive volume of both structured and unstructured data that is so large that it's difficult to process using traditional database and software techniques. In particular, machine-generated sensor data is becoming a larger portion of the Big Data world. According to a report by research organization IDC, machine-generated data will increase to 42% of all data by 2020, up from 11% in 2005.[53] This change will surely affect the look and feel of output.

More Realistic Output

Output technology is getting more and more refined.

People who have lost limbs, as in war or terrorist bombings, face a long road to recovery, but the prognosis for amputees is much better than it was a generation ago. "Thanks to advances in prosthetics," says one report, "even patients who have lost both legs can walk, run, and live generally normal lives."[54] This is only one example of how output is becoming more realistic and useful. Large, holographic 3-D images from smartphones and tablets; and retinal displays—via eye surgery—have been suggested.

DISPLAY SCREENS: BETTER & CHEAPER New gas-plasma technology is being employed to build flat-panel hang-on-the-wall screens as large as 50 inches from corner to corner. Using a technique known as *microreplication,* researchers have constructed a thin transparent sheet of plastic prisms that allows builders of portable computer screens to halve the amount of battery power required.

PRINTERS: REDUCING PRINTER INK Xerox is hoping to help companies survive with fewer printers and copiers and less paper through a new technology it calls *erasable paper.* The idea here is that you would print out a document you need only temporarily, then feed it through a machine with a heating element, which would make the document images disappear—so that you could reuse the paper for something else. Another company, called Zink (short for "zero ink"; *www.zink.com/how-ZINK-works*), is getting rid of ink entirely. Its approach is to encode paper with billions of dye crystals. To produce an image, a print head emits heat pulses that melt the dye crystals, turning them into the desired colors.

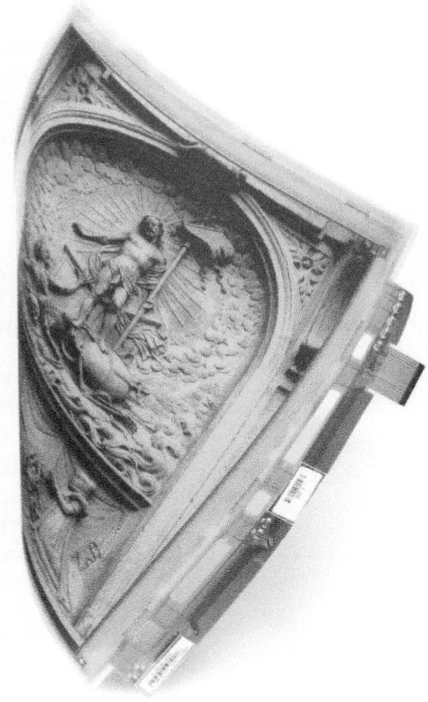

E Ink's flexible display screen (*above*) on 0.3-millimeter-thick electronic "paper" with millions of tiny capsules with black and white pigment chips and transmitting electrodes

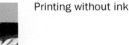

VIDEO: MOVIE QUALITY FOR PCS New technology based on digital wavelet theory, a complicated mathematical theory, has led to software that can compress digitized pictures into fewer bytes and do it more quickly than current standards. Indeed, the technology can display 30–38 frames a second—"real-time video."

In addition, advanced graphics chips from firms such as Nvidia and NTI have increased the realism of animation, making possible lifelike imagery through the use of geometric building blocks called *polygons.*

THREE-DIMENSIONAL OUTPUT—INCLUDING 3-D PRINTERS In the 1930s, radiologists tried to create three-dimensional images by holding up two slightly offset X-rays of the same object and crossing their eyes. Now the same effects can be achieved by computers. With 3-D technology, flat, cartoonlike images give way to rounded objects with shadows and textures. Artists can add "radiosity," so that a dog standing next to a red car, for instance, will pick up a red glow. As a result, movie theaters feature highly realistic 3-D films, and there are even "3-D ready" television sets being marketed. What will make home TV viewing take off in popularity, however, is the development of 3-D sets that don't require wearing special 3-D glasses—a technology that will take a while to deliver.[55]

However, the more remarkable advances in 3-D technology are in three-dimensional printers, in which inkjet-style printer heads are able to output layer after layer of images printed on starch, plaster, plastic, or even metal, producing 3-D objects.

How it works.
ZINK® stands for Zero Ink® - an amazing new way to print in full color without the need for ink cartridges or ribbons. ZINK Technology encompasses both the ZINK Paper® and the intelligence embedded in every ZINK-enabled device. ZINK enables a new category of color printing devices and paper that work as a system to print in a whole new way.

Printing without ink

TECH TALES Dreams of 3-D Printing

What is there that cannot be done with a three-dimensional printer? The appearance of 3-D printing holds out the promise of revitalizing industry, making many small businesses possible, and putting a factory in any home that wants one.[56]

The possibilities seem endless. New products output from these devices have ranged from plastic guitars to Barbie dolls, airplane parts, custom prostheses, and computer "chiplets" no larger than a grain of sand.[57] A 25-year-old law student has printed out, and then successfully fired, a 3-D plastic gun (something that worries law-enforcement officials).[58] Even clothing is being printed out.

Surgeons use 3-D-printed replicas of patients' organs to practice on before operations, and researchers are using the technology to produce living tissues, hoping someday to be able to print personalized body parts.[59] Doctors have even used a 3-D printer to custom-design a special windpipe implant to save a dying baby.[60] Scottish researchers have used human embryonic stem cells—which can transform into any cell type in the body—in a 3-D printer, printing them out in precise shapes while keeping the cells alive.[61]

One mechanical engineer envisions the end of food waste when every kitchen has a 3-D printer that would synthesize nutritionally appropriate meals one layer at a time from cartridges of powder and oils consumers buy at the grocery store.[62]

Where else will 3-D printing lead? ■

5.9 QUALITY OF LIFE: Health & Ergonomics

Computer use raises a host of health and ergonomic issues.

Danielle Weatherbee, 29, of Seattle, a medical supplies saleswoman who's on the road constantly, spends much of her time hunched over the keyboard of her notebook computer on planes, in coffee shops, in bed, and even in taxicabs. Her neck and wrists constantly ache. Her doctor has said she has the skeletal health of a 50-year-old. "But what can I do?" Weatherbee says. "My laptop is the only way to go for my work. I couldn't live without it."[63]

The technology tools that provide us with such marvelous benefits can also be the source of great ills, as we discuss.

Health Matters

Information technology can affect the health of human beings.

"It's true what they say," says one article. "Your keyboard is crawling with bacteria."[64] So are phones, says tech talk show host Kim Komando, which "are like petri dishes for germs and bacteria." With your phone, keyboard, and mouse, "it's a good idea to wipe them down daily during flu and cold season." To flu-proof your tech gadgets, she advises shutting them down, unplugging them, removing any batteries, and then using bleach-free disinfecting wipes.[65]

Transmitting colds and flu aren't the worst adverse health effects of computers. Others are repetitive strain injuries, eyestrain and headache, and back and neck pains, as we consider next.

TECH TALES Painful Technology for College Students

Technology clearly has negative health consequences for some people. College students, for example, may be susceptible to back, shoulder, wrist, and neck aches because they often use laptops and tablets, which—unlike desktop computers—have keyboard and screen too close to each other.

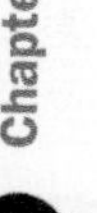

"When you use a laptop, you can make your head and neck comfortable, or you can make your hands and arms comfortable, but it's impossible to do both," says Tom Albin of the Human Factors and Ergonomics Society, an organization that issues standards on the use of computers.[66]

Observes another expert about students, "They sit in lecture halls with built-in tables, hunched over their laptops eight hours a day, and you can see it's very uncomfortable with them. Even if they could move their chairs, that would be a help.[67]

Frequent phone texting and browsing can lead to the frequent joint inflammation problems known as repetitive stress injury, as we'll describe. ■

REPETITIVE STRESS INJURIES **Repetitive stress (or strain) injuries (RSIs) are wrist, hand, arm, and neck injuries resulting when muscle groups are forced through fast, repetitive motions.** The two most common RSIs are tendinitis, the inflammation of a tendon, and bursitis, the inflammation of bursa sac.[68]

People who use computer keyboards—some superstar data-entry operators reportedly regularly average 15,000 keystrokes an hour—account for some RSI cases that result in lost work time. Before computers came along, typists would stop to make corrections or change paper. These motions had the effect of providing many small rest breaks. Today keyboard users must devise their own mini-breaks to prevent excessive use of hands and wrists (or install a computer program that uses animated characters to remind users to take breaks and provide suggestions for exercises). People who use a mouse for more than a few hours a day—graphic designers, desktop-publishing professionals, and the like—are also showing up with increased RSI injuries. The best advice is to find a mouse large enough so that your hand fits comfortably over it, and don't leave your hand on the mouse when you are not using it. You might also try using function keys instead of the mouse whenever possible.

RSIs

The United Food and Commercial Workers International Union provides detailed information about RSIs at:

http://my.clevelandclinic.org/orthopaedics-rheumatology/diseases-conditions/repetitive-stress-injury.aspx

www.nea.org/home/29829.htm

One type of RSI, carpal tunnel syndrome, is disabling and often requires surgery. **Carpal tunnel syndrome (CTS) is a debilitating condition caused by pressure on the median nerve in the wrist, producing damage and pain to nerves and tendons in the hands.** It is caused by short repetitive movements, such as typing, knitting, and using vibrating tools for hours on end. The lack of rest in between these motions irritates and inflames the flexor tendons that travel with the median nerve to the hand through an area in the wrist called the "carpal tunnel," which is surrounded by bones and a transverse ligament. The inflamed tendons squeeze the nerve against the ligament.[69]

EYESTRAIN & HEADACHES Vision problems are actually more common than RSI problems among computer users. Computers compel people to use their eyes at close range for a long time. However, our eyes were made to see most efficiently at a distance. It's not surprising, then, that people develop what's called *computer vision syndrome.*

Computer vision syndrome (CVS) consists of eyestrain, headaches, double vision, and other problems caused by improper use of computer display screens. By "improper use," we mean not only staring at the screen for too long but also failing to correct faulty lighting and screen glare and using screens with poor resolution.

More on CVSs

Do you have CVS? What are computer eyeglasses? Find out at:

www.allaboutvision.com/cvs/faqs.htm

www.aoa.org/x5253.xml

www.webmd.com/eye-health/computer-vision-syndrome/

www.allaboutvision.com/cvs/

BACK & NECK PAINS Improper chairs or improper positioning of keyboards and display screens can lead to back and neck pains. All kinds of adjustable, special-purpose furniture and equipment are available to avoid or diminish such maladies.

ELECTROMAGNETIC FIELDS Like kitchen appliances, hairdryers, and television sets, many devices related to computers and communications generate low-level electromagnetic field emissions. **Electromagnetic fields (EMFs) are waves of electric energy and magnetic energy.**

In recent years, stories have appeared in the mass media reflecting concerns that high-voltage power lines, cellphones, wireless mice, and old computer monitors might be harmful. There have been worries that old monitors might be linked to miscarriages and birth defects and that cellphones and power lines might lead to some types of cancers. Is there anything to this? The answer, so far, is that no one is sure.

TECH TALES Can Cellphones Cause Cancer?

The evolution of wireless phones and their effect on people's brains, says Swedish scientist Lief Salford, is "the largest biological experiment in the history of the world."[70] Salford's research found that cellphone radiation damaged neurons in the brains of young rats.

Although subsequent evidence seems scant that weak electromagnetic fields, such as those used for cellphones, cause cancer, the handheld phones do put the radio transmitter next to the user's head, which causes some health professionals concern about the effects of radio waves entering the brain. Thus, in the United Kingdom, the Independent Expert Study Group on Mobile Phones recommended that children should use cellphones only when necessary, and Norway's Ombudsman for Children has said that children under the age of 13 should not have their own mobile phones.

What does the research actually say? One study found that cellphone users face a 50% greater risk than non–cellphone users do of developing tumors of the parotid glands.[71] Another found cellphone radiation activated during a call makes nearby brain tissue use 7% more energy. "We have no idea what this means yet or how it works," says lead scientist Nora Volkow. "But this is the first reliable study showing the brain is activated by exposure to cellphone radio frequencies."[72] On the other hand, yet another study found no increased risk of brain tumors associated with using a cellphone for at least 10 years.[73]

The Federal Communications Commission (FCC) has created a measurement called Specific Absorption Rate (SAR) to give consumers data on the radiation levels their phones produce. See *http://reviews.cnet.com/cell-phone-radiation-levels*. ■

NOISE The chatter of impact printers or hum of fans in computer power units can be psychologically stressful to many people. Sound-muffling covers are available for impact printers. Some system units may be placed on the floor under the desk to minimize noise from fans.

Ergonomics: Design with People in Mind

People are any company's most important assets; if their work environment is poor, then their health and their work may be too.

Previously, workers had to fit themselves to the job environment. However, health and productivity issues have spurred the development of a relatively new field, called *ergonomics,* that is concerned with fitting the job environment to the worker.

The purpose of ergonomics is to make working conditions and equipment safer and more efficient. It is concerned with designing hardware and software that are less stressful and more comfortable to use and that blend more smoothly with a person's body or actions. Examples of ergonomic hardware are tilting display screens, detachable keyboards, and keyboards hinged in the middle to allow the users' wrists to rest in a more natural position. There are also height-adjustable desks, treadmill desks, and wearable feedback devices that send vibration signals to improve posture, and other technologies whose purpose is to overcome injuries stemming from just sitting.[74]

We address some other ergonomic issues in the Experience Box.

EXPERIENCE BOX

Good Habits: Protecting Your Computer System, Your Data, & Your Health

Whether you set up a desktop computer and never move it or carry a mobile device from place to place, you need to be concerned about protecting not only your computer but yourself. You don't want your computer to get stolen or zapped by a power surge. You don't want to lose your data. And you certainly don't want to lose your health for computer-related reasons. Here are some tips for taking care of these vital areas.

Guarding against Hardware Theft & Loss

Portable computers, tablets, and smartphones are easy targets for thieves, but they are also small enough that their owners sometimes forget where they are. Here are some suggestions for keep these devices close and safe:

- ***Don't make technology devices easily available to thieves:*** Never leave a mobile device unattended in a public place: Obviously, anything conveniently small enough to be slipped into your backpack or purse can be slipped into someone else's. When traveling, keep your laptop or tablet in the trunk of your car (unless it's too hot or cold) instead of in your car's back seat. Desktop computers are also easily stolen, but for under $25 you can buy a cable and lock, like those used for bicycles, and secure the computer, monitor, and printer to your work area.
- ***Keep an especially attentive eye on your equipment during plane travel:*** When flying, never check laptops or tablets as luggage; they can easily disappear en route. Also, be alert when putting your devices through the security X-ray scanner. A common two-person scam for stealing mobile devices is for one thief to pass through the scanner quickly while the second lingers and delays the passengers following, whose laptops or tablets have already been placed on the conveyor belt—easy targets for the first thief to walk off with. Thus, you should put your laptop or tablet on the conveyer belt only when you are about to walk through the X-ray scanner—and keep your eye on it as it comes off the conveyor belt. Alert security personnel right away if you think someone is attempting to steal your computer.
- ***Make the device easy to return if lost or stolen:*** It's possible to simply lose a mobile device—for example, forgetting it's in an airplane seatback pocket or overhead-luggage bin. To help in its return, use a wide piece of clear tape to tape a card with your name and address to the outside of the machine. For laptops, you should tape a similar card to the inside as well. In addition, scatter a few such cards in the pockets of the carrying case, if any.
- ***Use technological solutions to help:*** Install encryption software, which will (mostly) prevent thieves from accessing your data. Some software programs, such as Laptop Sentry, allow you to remotely delete files if your laptop is stolen and use geo-location technology to track where your laptop is. Consider purchasing a proximity device that attaches to your laptop or tablet; it sounds a loud alarm if the machine is moved more than a few feet from a device in your pocket. You can also purchase software programs that emit a signal when a thief uses your computer online, and a monitoring center will notify the local police of the laptop's location.
- ***Buy insurance:*** Finally, insurance to cover computer theft or damage is surprisingly cheap. Look for advertisements in technology magazines. (If you have standard tenants or homeowners insurance, it may not cover your computer. Ask your insurance agent.)
- ***Back up your data:*** Make frequent copies of your critical data and store the copies away from the computer.

Guarding against Damage to Hardware

Because desktop computers aren't moved around much, they are less susceptible to damage. Laptops, however, require more careful handling. According to a survey of 714 information technology managers, physical damage to laptops with data loss resulted from the following causes: 34% from spilled food or liquids on them, 28% from dropping them, 25% from not protecting them during travel, and 13% from worker anger.[75] Also, since such devices are sensitive to extreme temperatures, they should never be left in a very hot or very cold place. (Special "ruggedized" laptops exist, such as the Hewlett-Packard EliteBook and the Panasonic Toughbook, which are built to be shock resistant.)

Guarding against Damage to Software

Systems software and applications software generally come on DVDs or are downloaded. The rule is simply this: copy the original software either onto other disks and/or flash memory devices; or back everything up on a cloud server. If your computer gets stolen or your software destroyed, you can retrieve the originals and make additional copies as needed.

Protecting Your Data

Computer hardware and commercial software are nearly always replaceable, although perhaps with some expense and difficulty. Data, however, may be major trouble to replace or even be irreplaceable. If your hard-disk drive crashes, do you have the same data on a backup disk? Almost every microcomputer user sooner or later has the experience of accidentally wiping out or losing material and having no copy. This is what makes people true believers in backing up their data—making a duplicate in some form. If you're working on a research paper, for example, it's easy to copy your work onto a flash memory device, CD/DVD, external backup hard drive, or a cloud server during and at the end of your work session.

Flash drives are particularly useful because you can keep all important information on one of these drives and carry it in your pocket. (But be careful not to misplace it.) As an added protection measure, some flash drives now require your fingerprint to access the data.

Protecting Your Health

Could a computer put you in the emergency room? Actually, the number of injuries caused by computers in the home, resulting from people tripping over wires or getting hit by falling equipment, is significant. But injuries are also caused by not setting up computers correctly. Many people, for instance, set up their computers, particularly laptops, on a desk or table. This means "the keyboard is too high, which makes your arms reach up, your shoulders hunch, and your wrists bend down," says one report. "The monitor is too low, which pulls your head and neck forward and down and puts a strain on your neck."[76]

With a computer, it's important to sit with both feet on the floor, thighs at right angles to your body. The chair should be adjustable and support your lower back. Your forearms should be parallel to the floor. You should look down slightly at the screen. (• *See Panel 5.26.*) This setup is particularly important if you are going to be sitting at a computer for hours at a time.

To avoid wrist and forearm injuries, keep your wrists straight and hands relaxed as you type. Instead of putting the keyboard on top of a desk, put it on a low table or in a keyboard drawer under the desk. Otherwise the nerves in your wrists will rub against the sheaths surrounding them, possibly leading to RSI pains. Or try setting an hourly alarm on your watch or on an alarm clock; when the alarm goes off, take a short break and rotate your wrists and hands a bit.

Eyestrain and headaches usually arise because of improper lighting, screen glare, and long shifts staring at the screen. Make sure that your windows and lights don't throw a glare on the screen and that your computer is not framed by an uncovered window.

Back and neck pains occur because furniture is not adjusted correctly or because of heavy computer use, especially of laptops and tablets. Adjustable furniture and frequent breaks should provide relief.

Also remember that sitting for long periods of time is simply not good for the human body. Many computer users have switched to standing desks, height-adjustable desks, and even treadmill desks.

Protecting Your Computer Devices

Go to these sites for more information about computer and data security, including smartphones:

www.computersecurity.com/

http://computer.howstuffworks.com/security-channel.htm

www.consumer.ftc.gov/topics/computer-security

www.onguardonline.gov/articles/0009-computer-security

Special Mice

If your mouse is causing arm and wrist pain or other problems, you could try a special mouse model (including a vertical mouse):

www.fentek-ind.com/ergmouse.htm

www.thehumansolution.com/mice.html

www.evoluent.com/vm3.html

www.microsoft.com/hardware/en-us

www.consumersearch.com/computer-mice

http://store.ergoguys.com/quill-mouse.html?gclid=CMT4hunq4bcCFUZxQgodh2IA0w

Scanners & Airport Security

What kinds of scanners are used by the TSA (Transportation Security Administration), and are they a risk to our health?

www.propublica.org/special/scanning-the-scanners-a-side-by-side-comparison/

www.cnn.com/2013/05/29/travel/tsa-backscatter/

www.tsa.gov/traveler-information/advanced-imaging-technology-ait/

http://epic.org/privacy/airtravel/backscatter/epic_v_dhs_radiation.html

www.tsa.gov/traveler-information/advanced-imaging-technology-ait/

Head Directly over shoulders, without straining forward or backward, about an arm's length from screen.

Neck Elongated and relaxed.

Shoulders Kept down, with the chest open and wide.

Back Upright or inclined slightly forward from the hips. Maintain the slight natural curve of the lower back.

Elbows Relaxed, at about a right angle, try to keep forearms parallel to floor.

Wrists Relaxed, and in a neutral position, without flexing up or down.

Knees Slightly lower than the hips.

Light source Should come from behind the head.

Screen At eye level or slightly lower. Use an anti-glare screen.

Fingers Gently curved.

Keyboard Best when kept flat (for proper wrist positioning) and at or just below elbow level. Computer keys that are far away should be reached by moving the entire arm, starting from the shoulders, rather than by twisting the wrists or straining the fingers. Take frequent rest breaks.

Feet Firmly planted on the floor. Shorter people may need a footrest.

Chair Sloped slightly forward to facilitate proper knee position.

Keep wrists above the pad, and tilt the keyboard downward.

Yes

Use both hands to type combination key strokes.

Yes

Don't rest on the wrist pad.

No

Don't bend your hand in awkward angles to type key combinations.

No

Twisting your hands puts strain on them. Resting on a wrist rest, the table, or arm rests while typing forces you to twist your hand to reach some keys. Instead, keep your hands moving freely above the keyboard, letting the strong muscles of your arms move your hands.

It is also a bad idea to contort your hands in other ways. Your hand should be flat and parallel to the keyboard, without twisting. There should not be any pressure on your wrist or forearms while you type. You should NOT rest your wrists on a wrist rest except while taking a very short break from typing. A wrist rest of the proper height (level with the space bar) can serve as a reminder to keep your wrists straight. If you feel your wrist touching the rest, you know that your wrists are starting to dip.

panel 5.26

How to set up your computer work area

audio-input device (p. 268) Hardware that records analog sound and translates it for digital storage and processing. Why it's important: *Analog sound signals are continuous variable waves within a certain frequency range. For the computer to process them, these variable waves must be converted to digital 0s and 1s. The principal use of audio-input devices is to produce digital input for multimedia computers. An audio signal can be digitized in two ways—by an audio board or a MIDI board.*

bar-code reader (p. 262) Photoelectric (optical) scanner that translates bar codes into digital codes. Why it's important: *With bar-code readers and the appropriate software system, store clerks can total purchases and produce invoices with increased speed and accuracy, and stores and other businesses can monitor inventory and services with increased efficiency.*

bar codes (p. 261) Vertical, zebra-striped marks imprinted on most manufactured retail products. Why it's important: *Bar codes provide a convenient means of identifying and tracking items. In North America, supermarkets, food manufacturers, and others have agreed to use a bar-code system called the* Universal Product Code (UPC). *Other kinds of bar-code systems are used on everything from FedEx packages to railroad cars to the jerseys of long-distance runners.*

biometrics (p. 271) Science of measuring individual body characteristics. Why it's important: *Biometric security devices identify a person through a fingerprint, voice intonation, or some other biological characteristic. For example, retinal-identification devices use a ray of light to identify the distinctive network of blood vessels at the back of the eyeball.*

carpal tunnel syndrome (CTS) (p. 291) Debilitating condition caused by pressure on the median nerve in the wrist, producing damage and pain to nerves and tendons in the hands. Why it's important: *CTS can be caused by overuse or misuse of computer keyboards.*

color depth (p. 278) Also called *bit depth;* the amount of information, expressed in bits, that is stored in a dot. Why it's important: *The more bits in a dot or pixel, the more shades of gray and colors can be represented. With 24-bit color depth, for example, 8 bits are dedicated to each primary color—red, green, and blue; 24-bit color is standard for most computing.*

computer vision syndrome (CVS) (p. 291) Eyestrain, headaches, double vision, and other problems caused by improper use of computer display screens. Why it's important: *CVS can be prevented by not staring at the display screen for too long, by correcting faulty lighting, by avoiding screen glare, and by not using screens with poor resolution.*

digital camera (p. 265) Electronic camera that uses a light-sensitive processor chip to capture photographic images in digital form and store them on a small disk inserted into the camera or on flash memory chips (cards). Why it's important: *The bits of digital information—the snapshots you have taken, say—can be copied right onto a computer's hard disk for manipulation and printing. The environmentally undesirable stage of chemical development required for conventional film is completely eliminated.*

digital pen (p. 259) Writing instrument that allows users to write on paper and send the writing as an image file to the computer. Why it's important: *You can easily store your handwritten notes in digital form.*

digitizer (p. 258) Input unit based on an electronic pen or a mouselike copying device called a *puck* that converts drawings and photos to digital data. Why it's important: (See **digitizing tablet.**)

digitizing tablet (p. 258) One form of digitizer; an electronic plastic board on which each specific location corresponds to a location on the screen. When the user uses a puck, the tablet converts his or her movements into digital signals that are input to the computer. Why it's important: *Digitizing tablets are often used to make maps and engineering drawings, as well as to trace drawings.*

display screen (p. 276) Also called *monitor* or simply *screen;* output device that shows programming instructions and data as they are being input and information after it is processed. Why it's important: *Screens are needed to display softcopy output.*

dot pitch (dp) (p. 277) Amount of space between the centers of adjacent pixels; the closer the pixels (dots), the crisper the image. Why it's important: *Dot pitch is one of the measures of display-screen crispness. For a 0.25- to 0.28-dp monitor, for instance, the dots are 25/100ths of a millimeter apart. Generally, a dot pitch of 0.25 will provide clear images.*

dots per inch (dpi) (p. 261) Measure of the number of columns and rows of dots per inch. For microcomputer printers, resolution is usually in the range 1,200 × 1,200 dpi. Why it's important: *The higher the dpi, the better the resolution.* (See **resolution.**)

dumb terminal (p. 252) Also called *video display terminal (VDT);* display screen and a keyboard hooked up to a computer system. It can input and output but not process data. Why it's important: *Dumb terminals are used, for example, by airline reservations clerks to access a mainframe computer containing flight information.*

electromagnetic fields (EMFs) (p. 291) Waves of electric energy and magnetic energy. Why it's important: *Some people have worried that CRT monitors might be linked to miscarriages and birth defects and that cellphones and power lines might lead to some types of cancers. However, the evidence is unclear.*

ergonomics (p. 292) Study, or science, of working conditions and equipment with the goal of improving worker safety and efficiency. Why it's important: *On the basis of ergonomic principles, stress, illness, and injuries associated with computer use may be minimized.*

flat-panel display (p. 279) Display screen that is much thinner, weighs less, and consumes less power than a CRT. Flat-panel

(LCD) displays are made up of two plates of glass separated by a layer of a substance in which light is manipulated. Why it's important: *Flat-panel displays are essential to portable computers, desktop computers, TVs, instrument panels, phones, and so forth.*

flatbed scanner (p. 260) Also called *desktop scanner;* the image to be scanned is placed on a glass surface, where it remains stationary, and the scanning beam moves across it. Three other types of scanners are *sheet-fed, handheld,* and *drum.* Why it's important: *Flatbed scanners are one of the most popular types of scanner.*

handwriting recognition (p. 258) System in which a computer receives intelligible written input, using special software to interpret the movement of a stylus across a writing service and translating the resulting cursive writing into digital information. Why it's important: *Handwriting recognition is a commonly used input method for PDAs, some handheld videogames, and tablet PCs.*

hardcopy (p. 276) Tangible output, usually printed. The principal examples are printouts, whether text or graphics, from printers. Film, including microfilm and microfiche, is also considered hardcopy output. Why it's important: *Hardcopy is an essential form of computer output.*

impact printer (p. 280) Printer that forms characters or images by striking a mechanism such as a print hammer or wheel against an inked ribbon, leaving an image on paper. Why it's important: *Nonimpact printers are more commonly used than impact printers, but dot-matrix printers are still used in some businesses.*

inkjet printer (p. 281) Printer that sprays onto paper small, electrically charged droplets of ink from four or more nozzles through holes in a matrix at high speed. Like laser and dot-matrix printers, inkjet printers form images with little dots. Why it's important: *Because they produce high-quality images on special paper, inkjet printers are often used in graphic design and desktop publishing. However, traditionally inkjet printers have been slower than laser printers and they print at a lower resolution on regular paper.*

input hardware (p. 248) Devices that translate data into a form the computer can process. Why it's important: *Without input hardware, computers could not function. The computer-readable form consists of 0s and 1s, represented as off and on electrical signals. Input hardware devices are categorized as three types: keyboards, pointing devices, and source data-entry devices.*

intelligent terminal (p. 252) Hardware unit with its own memory and processor, as well as a display screen and keyboard, hooked up to a larger computer system. Why it's important: *Such a terminal can perform some functions independent of any mainframe to which it is linked. Examples include the automated teller machine (ATM), a self-service banking machine connected through a telephone network to a central computer, and the point-of-sale (POS) terminal, used to record purchases at a store's customer checkout counter. Recently, many intelligent terminals have been replaced by personal computers.*

keyboard (p. 249) Input device that converts letters, numbers, and other characters into electrical signals that can be read by the computer's processor. Why it's important: *Keyboards are the most popular kind of input device.*

laser printer (p. 281) Nonimpact printer that creates images with dots. As in a photocopying machine, images are produced on a drum, treated with an electrically charged inklike toner (powder), and then transferred from drum to paper. Why it's important: *Laser printers produce much better image quality than do dot-matrix printers and can print in many more colors; they are also quieter. Laser printers, along with page description languages, enabled the development of desktop publishing.*

light pen (p. 258) Light-sensitive penlike device connected by a wire to the computer terminal. The user brings the pen to a desired point on the display screen and presses the pen button, which identifies that screen location to the computer. Why it's important: *Light pens are used by engineers, graphic designers, and illustrators.*

liquid crystal display (LCD) (p. 279) Flat-panel monitor in which molecules of liquid crystal line up in a way that alters their optical properties, creating images on the screen by transmitting or blocking light. Why it's important: *LCD monitors take up less space and energy than older monitor types; they can be used at various sizes and weights appropriate for small electronic products, such as tablets and smartphones, as well as for desktop computers and TVs.*

magnetic-ink character recognition (MICR) (p. 264) Pronounced "*mick*-er"; scanning technology that reads magnetized-ink characters printed at the bottom of checks and converts them to digital form. Why it's important: *MICR technology is used by banks to sort checks.*

MIDI board (p. 268) *MIDI,* pronounced "middie," stands for "Musical Instrument Digital Interface." MIDI sound boards use this standard. Why it's important: *MIDI provides a standard for the interchange of musical information between musical instruments, synthesizers, and computers.*

mouse (p. 253) A pointing device that is moved about on a desktop (usually on a mousepad) and directs a pointer on the computer's display screen. Why it's important: *The mouse is the principal pointing tool used with microcomputers.*

multifunction printer (p. 284) Hardware device that combines several capabilities, such as printing, scanning, copying, and faxing. Why it's important: *Multifunction printers take up less space and cost less than the four separate office machines that they replace. The downside, however, is that if one component breaks, nothing works.*

multitouch screen (p. 256) Display screen that allows two or more fingers or other gestures such as pinching motions to be recognized as input at any one time. Why it's important: *It allows pinching and stretching gestures on the screen to control zooming—that is, pinch the screen to zoom in (make an image smaller) or spread the thumb and forefinger on the screen to zoom out, or spread images apart. It also support other gestures that have made touch screens easy and efficient to use.*

nonimpact printer (p. 281) Printer that forms characters and images without direct physical contact between the printing mechanism and paper. Two types of nonimpact printers often used with microcomputers are laser printers and inkjet printers. A third kind, the thermal printer, is seen less frequently. Why it's important: *Nonimpact printers are faster and quieter than impact printers.*

optical character recognition (OCR) (p. 265) Software technology that converts scanned text from images (pictures of the text) to an editable text format (usually ASCII) that can be imported into a word processing application and manipulated. Why it's important: *Special OCR characters appear on utility bills and price tags on department-store merchandise. The wand reader is a common OCR scanning device. These days almost all scanners come with OCR software.*

optical mark recognition (OMR) (p. 264) Scanning technology that reads "bubble" marks and converts them into computer-usable form. Why it's important: *OMR technology is used to read the College Board Scholastic Aptitude Test (SAT) and the Graduate Record Examination (GRE).*

output hardware (p. 248) Hardware devices that convert machine-readable information, obtained as the result of processing, into people-readable form. The principal kinds of output are softcopy and hardcopy. Why it's important: *Without output devices, people would have no access to processed data and information.*

page description language (PDL) (p. 281) Software that describes the shape and position of characters and graphics to the printer. PostScript and PCL are common page description languages. Why it's important: *Page description languages are essential to desktop publishing.*

pen-based computer system (p. 258) Input system that allows users to enter handwriting and marks onto a computer screen by means of a penlike stylus rather than by typing on a keyboard. Pen computers use handwriting-recognition software that translates handwritten characters made by the stylus into data that is usable by the computer. Why it's important: *Many handheld computers have pen input, as do digital notebooks and tablets.*

pixel (p. 277) Short for "picture element"; the smallest unit on the screen that can be turned on and off or made different shades. Why it's important: *Pixels are the building blocks that allow text and images to be displayed on a screen.*

plasma display (p. 280) A kind of flat-panel display that uses a layer of gas sandwiched between two glass plates; when voltage is applied, the gas releases ultraviolet light, which activates the pixels on the screen and forms an image. Why it's important: *Although expensive, plasma monitors offer bright colors and screen sizes up to 150 inches wide.*

plotter (p. 284) Specialized output device designed to produce high-quality graphics in a variety of colors. A *pen plotter* uses one or more colored pens to draw on paper or transparencies. The *inkjet plotter* employs the same principle as an inkjet printer; the paper is output over a drum, enabling continuous output. In an *electrostatic plotter,* paper lies partially flat on a tablelike surface, and toner is used in a photocopier-like manner. Why it's important: *Plotters are used to create hardcopy items such as maps, architectural drawings, and three-dimensional illustrations, which are usually too large for regular printers.*

pointing device (p. 252) Hardware that controls the position of the cursor or pointer on the screen. It includes the mouse and its variants, the touch screen, and various forms of pen input. Why it's important: *In many contexts, pointing devices permit quick and convenient data input.*

pointing stick (p. 255) Pointing device that looks like a pencil eraser protruding from the laptop keyboard between the G, H, and B keys. The user moves the pointing stick with a forefinger. Why it's important: *Pointing sticks are used principally in video-games, in computer-aided design systems, and in robots.*

printer (p. 280) Output device that prints characters, symbols, and perhaps graphics on paper or another hardcopy medium. Why it's important: *Printers provide one of the principal forms of computer output.*

radio-frequency identification (RFID) tags (p. 263) Source data-entry technology based on an identifying tag bearing a microchip that contains specific code numbers. These code numbers are read by the radio waves of a scanner linked to a database. Why it's important: *Drivers with RFID tags can breeze through tollbooths without having to even roll down their windows; the toll is automatically charged to their accounts. Radio-wave-readable ID tags are also used by the Postal Service to monitor the flow of mail, by stores for inventory control and warehousing, and in the railroad industry to keep track of rail cars.*

refresh rate (p. 278) Number of times per second that screen pixels are recharged so that their glow remains bright. Why it's important: *The higher the refresh rate, the more solid the image looks on the screen—that is, the less it flickers.*

repetitive stress (or strain) injuries (RSIs) (p. 291) Several wrist, hand, arm, and neck injuries resulting when muscle groups are forced through fast, repetitive motions. They include bursitis and tendinitis, which are painful but usually not crippling, and carpal tunnel syndrome, which is disabling and often requires surgery. Why it's important: *People who use computer keyboards or do repetitive scanning, for example, account for some of the RSI cases that result in lost work time, as well affect private time.*

resolution (pp. 261, 277) Clarity or sharpness of display-screen/scanned/printed images; the more pixels (dots) there are per square inch, generally the finer the level of detail attained. Resolution is expressed in terms of the formula: horizontal pixels × vertical pixels. Each pixel can be assigned a color or a particular shade of gray. Standard screen resolutions are 1,024 × 768, 1,280 × 1,024, and 1,600 × 1,200 pixels. Common scanner resolutions are 300 × 200, 600 × 600, 600 × 1,200, 1,200 × 1,200, and 2,400 × 2,400. Why it's important: *Users need to know what resolution is appropriate for their purposes.*

scanner (p. 260) Also called *optical scanner;* source data-input device that uses light-sensing (optical) equipment to translate images of text, drawings, photos, and the like into digital form. Why it's important: *Scanners simplify the input of complex data. The images can be processed by a computer, displayed on a monitor, stored on a storage device, or communicated to another computer.*

sensor (p. 270) Input device that collects specific data directly from the environment and transmits it to a computer. Why it's important: *Although you are unlikely to see such input devices connected to a PC in an office, they exist all around us, often in nearly invisible form. Sensors can be used to detect all kinds of things: speed, movement, weight, pressure, temperature, humidity, wind, water current, fog, gas, smoke, light, shapes, images, and* *so on. In aviation, for example, sensors are used to detect ice buildup on airplane wings and to alert pilots to sudden changes in wind direction.*

softcopy (p. 276) Data on a display screen or in audio or voice form. This kind of output is not tangible; it cannot be touched. Why it's important: *This term is used to distinguish nonprinted output from printed (hardcopy) output.*

sound board (p. 268) An add-on circuit board in a computer that converts analog sound to digital sound and stores it for further processing and/or plays it back, providing output directly to speakers or an external amplifier. Why it's important: *The sound board enables users to work with audible sound.*

sound-output device (p. 287) Hardware that produces digitized sounds, ranging from beeps and chirps to music. Why it's important: *To use sound output, the user needs appropriate software and a sound card.*

source data-entry devices (p. 260) Data-entry devices that create machine-readable data on magnetic media or paper or feed it directly into the computer's processor, without the use of a keyboard. Categories include scanning devices (imaging systems, bar-code readers, mark- and character-recognition devices, and fax machines), audio-input devices, video input, photographic input (digital cameras), voice-recognition systems, sensors, radio-frequency identification devices, and human-biology-input devices. Why it's important: *Source data-entry devices reduce reliance on keyboards for data entry and can make data entry more accurate.*

speech-recognition system (p. 268) Input system that uses a microphone (or a telephone) as an input device and converts a person's speech into digital signals by comparing the electrical patterns produced by the speaker's voice with a set of prerecorded patterns stored in the computer. Why it's important: *Voice-recognition technology is useful in situations where people are unable to use their hands to input data or need their hands free for other purposes.*

tactile keyboard (p. 251) A physical keyboard, perceptible to the sense of touch. Why it's important: *Tactile keyboards are still the most-used input device in business and professional situations. (Compare with* **touch screen.**)

thermal printer (p. 282) Printer that uses colored waxes and heat to produce images by burning dots onto special paper. The colored wax sheets are not required for black-and-white output. Thermal printers are expensive, and they require expensive paper. (*Thermal wax-transfer printers* print a wax-based ink onto paper.) Why it's important: *Their water-fastness makes them desirable for certain industrial purposes.*

touch screen (p. 256) Video display screen that has been sensitized to receive input from the touch of a finger. The screen is covered with a plastic layer, behind which are invisible beams of infrared light. Why it's important: *Users can input requests for information by pressing on buttons or menus displayed. The answers to requests are displayed as output in words or pictures on the screen. (There may also be sound.) Touch screens are found in ATMs, gas pumps, airport tourist directories, hotel TV screens (for guest checkout), and campus information kiosks making available everything from lists of coming events to (with proper ID and personal code) student financial-aid records and grades.*

touch-screen keyboard (p. 251) Also called *on-screen* or *virtual keyboard;* image of a keyboard displayed on a touch screen. Why it's important: *Touch-screen keyboards are standard on tablets, smartphones, and other mobile devices (although in some cases tactile keyboards are available as well).*

touchpad (p. 255) Input device; a small, flat surface over which the user slides a finger, using the same movements as those used with a mouse. The cursor follows the movement of the finger. The user "clicks" by tapping a finger on the pad's surface or by pressing buttons positioned close by the pad. Why it's important: *Touchpads let users control the cursor/pointer with a finger, and they require very little space to use. Most laptops have touchpads.*

trackball (p. 254) Movable ball, mounted on top or side of a stationary device, that can be rotated by the user's fingers or palm. Instead of moving the mouse around on the desktop, you move the trackball with the tips of your fingers. Why it's important: *A trackball requires less space to use than does a mouse.*

video (p. 287) Output consisting of photographic images played at 15–30 frames per second to give the appearance of full motion. Why it's important: *Video is input into a multimedia system generally using a video camera and, after editing, is output on a computer's display screen. Because video files can require a great deal of storage—a 3-minute video may require 1 gigabyte of storage—video is often compressed. Digital video has revolutionized the movie industry, as in the use of special effects.*

videoconferencing (p. 287) Form of video output in which people in different geographic locations can have a meeting—can see and hear one another—using computers and communications. Why it's important: *Many organizations use videoconferencing to take the place of face-to-face meetings. Videoconferencing systems range from videophones to group conference rooms with cameras and multimedia equipment to desktop systems with small video cameras, microphones, and speakers.*

voice-output device (p. 287) Hardware that converts digital data into speechlike sounds. Why it's important: *We hear such voice output on telephones ("Please hang up and dial your call again"), in soft-drink machines, in cars, in toys and games, and recently in mapping software for vehicle-navigation devices. Computers with voice output are very useful for people with physical challenges.*

webcam (p. 266) A video camera attached to a computer to record live moving images that can then be posted on a website in real time. Why it's important: *The webcam is an affordable tool that enables users to have videoconferencing capabilities and may change the future of communications.*

CHAPTER REVIEW

stage 1 LEARNING MEMORIZATION

"I can recognize and recall information."

Self-Test Questions

1. A(n) __________ terminal is entirely dependent for all its processing activities on the computer system to which it is connected.
2. The two main categories of printer are __________ and __________.
3. __________ is the study of the physical relationships between people and their work environment.
4. A(n) __________ is an input device that is rolled about on a desktop and directs a pointer on the computer's display screen.
5. __________ consists of devices that translate information processed by the computer into a form that humans can understand.
6. __________ is the science of measuring individual body characteristics.
7. A(n) __________ accepts input supplied with finger and hand gestures.
8. LCD is short for __________.
9. A(n) __________ is software that describes the shape and position of characters and graphics to the printer.
10. When people in different geographic locations can have a meeting using computers and communications, it is called __________.
11. An input device that collects specific data directly from the environment and transmits it to a computer is called a(n) __________.
12. A debilitating condition caused by pressure on the median nerve in the wrist, producing damage and pain to nerves and tendons in the hands, is called __________.
13. The measure of the number of dots that are printed in a linear inch is called __________ or __________.
14. A printer that forms characters or images by striking a mechanism such as a print hammer or wheel against an inked ribbon, leaving images on a paper, is called a(n) __________ printer.
15. __________ printers enabled the development of desktop publishing.
16. __________ is short for "picture element."

Multiple-Choice Questions

1. Which of the following is *not* a pointing device?
   a. mouse
   b. touchpad
   c. keyboard
   d. joystick
2. Which of the following is *not* a source data-entry device?
   a. bar-code reader
   b. sensor
   c. digital camera
   d. scanner
   e. mouse
3. Which of the following display standards has the highest screen resolution?
   a. XGA
   b. UXGA
   c. VGA
   d. SVGA
   e. QXGA
4. Which of the following *is not* considered hardcopy output?
   a. spreadsheet printout
   b. microfilm
   c. fax report
   d. Word document computer file
   e. printed invoice
5. Which of the following factors does *not* affect the quality of a screen display?
   a. refresh rate
   b. speed
   c. resolution
   d. pixels
   e. color depth
6. A device with a microchip that contains code numbers that can be read by a scanner's radio waves is a(n)
   a. optical character reader
   b. nanotube
   c. pointing device
   d. RFID tag
   e. multifunction mouse

True-False Questions

T F 1. On a computer screen, the more pixels that appear per square inch, the higher the resolution.

T F 2. Photos taken with a digital camera can be downloaded to a computer's hard disk.

T F 3. Resolution is the amount of space between the centers of adjacent pixels.

T F 4. The abbreviation *dpi* stands for "dense pixel intervals."

T F 5. Pointing devices control the position of the cursor on the screen.

T F 6. Output hardware consists of devices that translate information processed by the computer into a form that humans can understand.

T F 7. Optical character-recognition software reads "bubble" marks and converts them into computer-usable form.

T F 8. The lower the refresh rate, the more solid the image looks on the screen.

T F 9. Bar codes are input with pointing devices.

T F 10. Computer users have no need to be concerned about ergonomics.

T F 11. It has been proved that electromagnetic fields pose no danger to human beings.

T F 12. Plotters are used to print architectural drawings and in computer-aided design.

T F 13. Scanners use optical equipment to translate images of text, drawings, photos, and the like into digital form.

T F 14. A digital pen is a specialized output device designed to produce large, high-quality graphics in a variety of colors.

COMPREHENSION

"I can recall information in my own terms and explain it to a friend."

Short-Answer Questions

1. What is a common use of dumb terminals?
2. What characteristics determine the clarity of a computer screen?
3. Describe two situations in which scanning is useful.
4. What is source data entry?
5. What is *pixel* short for? What is a pixel?
6. Briefly describe RSI and CTS. Why are they problems?
7. What is a font?
8. Discuss the different types of printers and their features.
9. What is OCR used for?

LEARNING APPLYING, ANALYZING, SYNTHESIZING, EVALUATING

"I can apply what I've learned, relate these ideas to other concepts, build on other knowledge, and use all these thinking skills to form a judgment."

Knowledge in Action

1. Cut out several advertisements from newspapers or magazines that feature new microcomputer systems. Circle all the terms that are familiar to you now that you have read the first five chapters of this text. Define these terms on a separate sheet of paper. Is this computer expandable? How much does it cost? Is a monitor included in the price? A printer?

   What terms do you still not know? Save this exercise, and repeat after you have finished the rest of the book.
2. *Paperless office* is a term that has been around for some time. However, the paperless office has not yet been achieved. Do you think the paperless office is a good idea? Do you think it's possible? Why do you think it has not yet been achieved?

   Do a keyword search for various well-based opinions on this issue.
3. Compare and contrast the pros and cons of different types of monitors. Decide which one is best for you, and explain why. Do some research on how each monitor type creates displayed images.
4. Do you have access to a computer with (a) speech-recognition software and (b) word processing software that determines writing level (such as eighth grade, ninth grade, and so on)? Dictate a few sentences about your day into the microphone. After your speech is encoded into text, use the word processing software to determine the grade level of your everyday speech.
5. A pixel is the smallest unit on the screen that can be turned on and off. In most high-quality digital photos, you can't see the pixilation unless you zoom in real close. However, even when you don't zoom in, you know that the pixilation is there, a series of different pixels all plotted on a grid. How can you relate this to our experience of reality? Via high-tech microscopes we see that everything is made of smaller particles not visible to the naked eye, such as atoms, subatomic particles, and quarks. How are the basic building blocks of computer imaging and the basic building blocks of physical matter alike, and how are they different?
6. Biometrics: Which form of biometric technology do you prefer for identification purposes: fingerprints, voice intonation, facial characteristics, or retinal identification? Which do you think will become most commonly used in the future?

Web Exercises

1. Visit an online shopping site such as *www.yahoo.com.* Click on *Shopping;* then type *Printers* in the Shopping search box. Investigate five different types of printers by clicking on the printer names and then on *See Full Product Description*. Note (a) the type of printer, (b) its price, (c) its resolution, and (d) its speeds for black-and-white printing and for color printing, if applicable. Which operating system is each printer compatible with? Which printer would you choose? Why?

2. There is an abundance of information about electronic devices on the Internet. People write all kinds of reviews either raving about the device that made their lives better or *lamenting the device that became their evil* nemesis. Go to *www.consumerreports.org/cro/search.htm?query5reviews* and find out how people at ConsumerReports.org rate some of your favorite electronic devices.
3. Go to *www.touchscreens.com* and find a touch screen that appeals to you. Why do you like it? Is it practical?
4. Do you see any ethical problems involved with self-scanning checkout? Can people cheat the system? Are store jobs being lost to automation? Are people without credit cards and/or computer experience being excluded? Do a keyword search for *self-scanning* and *self-checkout* and other terms related to these issues. Do you think self-scanning is a good idea?
5. The human cyborg: Visit Professor Kevin Warwick's website to learn about the implant microchips he has been creating and surgically implanting in his body to allow it to communicate with a computer. Investigate the many applications he has been working on. After visiting his site, run a search on *"Kevin Warwick"* to read what others have to say about him and his ideas.

   www.kevinwarwick.com/

   www.kevinwarwick.com/Cyborg1.htm
6. PostScript is the most important page description language in desktop publishing. Read the information at Answer.com, *www.adobe.com/products/postscript/pdfs/psprintprime.pdf*, and *http://desktoppub.about.com/cs/printing/a/postscriptprint.htm* to find out why. You almost certainly will need some familiarity with PostScript.
7. What is the difference between a screen font and a printer font? Go to Answers.com and Wikipedia to find out. What does *WYSIWYG* mean?
8. How many images can digital-camera storage hold? Do a web search on new cameras and find out.

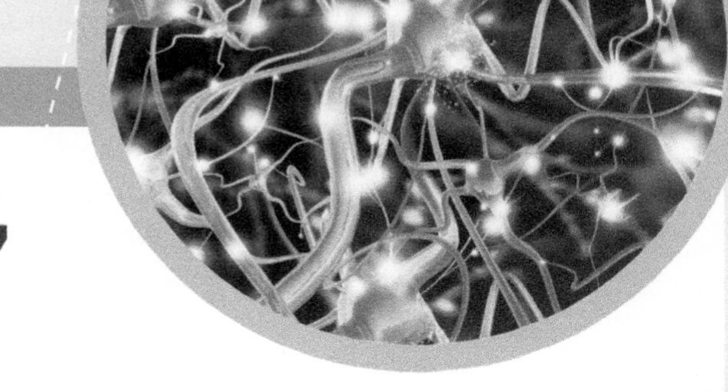

6 COMMUNICATIONS, NETWORKS, & CYBERTHREATS The Wired & Wireless World

Chapter Topics & Key Questions

UNIT 6A: *Networks & Wired & Wireless Media*

6.1 **From the Analog to the Digital Age**
How do digital data and analog data differ, and what does a modem do?

6.2 **Networks**
What are the benefits of networks, and what are their types, components, and variations?

6.3 **Wired Communications Media**
What are types of wired communications media?

6.4 **Wireless Communications Media**
What are types of wireless communications media, both long distance and short distance?

UNIT 6B: *Cyberthreats, Security, & Privacy Issues*

6.5 **Cyberintruders: Trolls, Spies, Hackers, & Thieves**
What kinds of people might do my system harm?

6.6 **Cyberattacks & Malware**
What are some key malware threats to networks and computers?

6.7 **Concerns about Privacy & Identity Theft**
How has communications technology facilitated loss of privacy and identity theft?

Download the free UIT 11e App for key term flash cards quizzes and a game, *Over the Edge*

CHAPTER FORECAST The first half of this chapter describes networks and wired and wireless media. We consider how analog and digital data differ and how a modem translates signals from one to the other. We also cover the benefits of networks and their types, components, and variations. We then discuss the various types of wired communications media. We conclude with a discussion of wireless communications media, both long distance and short distance. In the second half of this chapter, we consider cyberthreats, security, and privacy issues. We describe four types of cyberintruders: trolls, spies, hackers, and thieves. We discuss cyberattacks and malware threats to computers and networks. We end by considering issues of privacy and identity theft.

UNIT 6A: *Networks & Wired & Wireless Media*

"America now has more devices that connect to the Internet than it has people," says one report. "The nation's 311.5 million residents own more than 425 million personal computers, tablets, smartphones, and gaming consoles."[1]

How did we get to this point?

Before the 1950s, computing devices processed data into information, and communications devices communicated information over distances. The two streams of technology developed pretty much independently, like rails on a railroad track that never merge. Since then, we've had a revolution called **digital convergence, the gradual merger of computing and communications into a new information environment, in which the same information is exchanged among many kinds of equipment, using the language of computers.** *(• See Panel 6.1.)*

panel 6.1

Digital convergence—the fusion of computer and communications technologies

Today's new information environment came about gradually from the merger of two separate streams of technological development—computers and communications.

Computer Technology

1621 CE
Slide rule invented (Edmund Gunther)
1642
First mechanical adding machine (Blaise Pascal)
1833
Babbage's difference engine (automatic calculator)
1843
World's first computer programmer, Ada Lovelace, publishes her notes
1890
Electricity used for first time in a data-processing project (punched cards); Hollerith's automatic census-tabulating machine (used punched cards)

Communications Technology

1562	1594	1639	1827	1835	1846	1857	1876	1888	1894
First monthly newspaper (Italy)	First magazine (Germany)	First printing press in North America	Photographs on metal plates	Telegraph (first long-distance digital communication system)	High-speed printing	Trans-atlantic telegraph cable laid	Telephone invented	Radio waves identified	Edison makes a movie

At the same time, there has been a convergence of several important industries—computers, telecommunications, consumer electronics, entertainment, mass media—producing new electronic products that perform multiple functions. But this convergence still involves both analog and digital data transmission.

Why has the fusion of computers and of telecommunications been so long in coming?

6.1 FROM THE ANALOG TO THE DIGITAL AGE

Analog is the process of taking an audio or video signal and translating it into electronic pulses; digital is breaking the signal into a binary format whereby the audio or video data is represented by a series of 1s and 0s.

Humans experience most of the world in analog form—our vision, for instance, perceives shapes and colors as smooth gradations. But most analog events can be simulated digitally. A newspaper photograph, viewed through a magnifying glass, is made up of an array of dots—so small that most newspaper readers see the tones of the photograph as continuous. How does analog become digital?

Analog versus Digital Electrical Signals: Continuous Waves versus Discontinuous Bursts

"Analog" describes electrical signals in continuous electronic waves. "Digital" describes electrical signals in two states, on (1) and off (0).

"The shades of a sunset, the flight of a bird, or the voice of a singer would seem to defy the black or white simplicity of binary representation," points out one writer.[2] Indeed, these and most other phenomena of the world are **analog, continuously varying in strength and/or quality—fluctuating, evolving, or continually changing.** Sound, light, temperature, and pressure values, for instance, can be anywhere on a continuum or range.

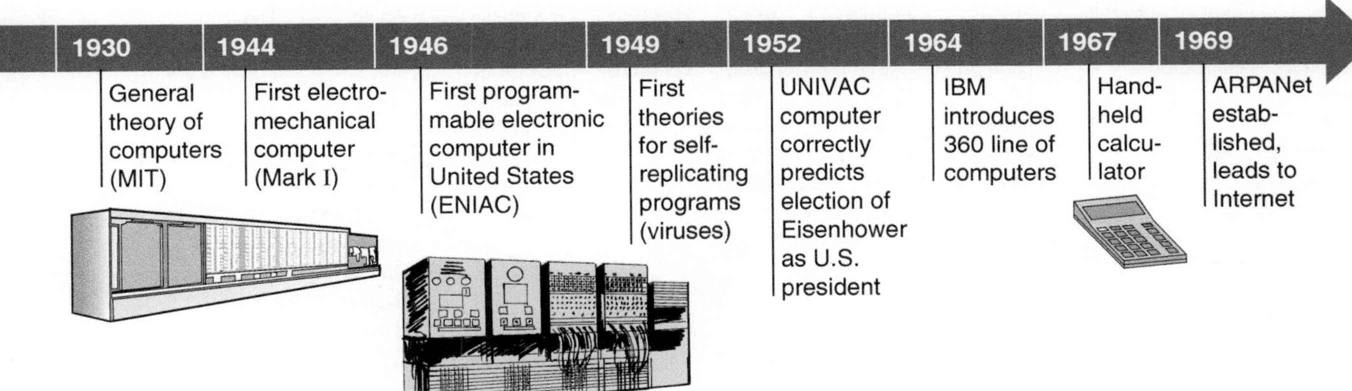

- **1895** Marconi develops radio; motion-picture camera invented
- **1907** First regular radio broadcast from New York
- **1912** Motion pictures become a big business
- **1915** AT&T long-distance service reaches San Francisco
- **1928** First TV demonstrated; first sound movie
- **1939** Commercial TV broadcasting
- **1946** Color TV demonstrated
- **1947** Transistor invented
- **1948** Reel-to-reel tape recorder
- **1950** Cable TV

HOLLYWOOD

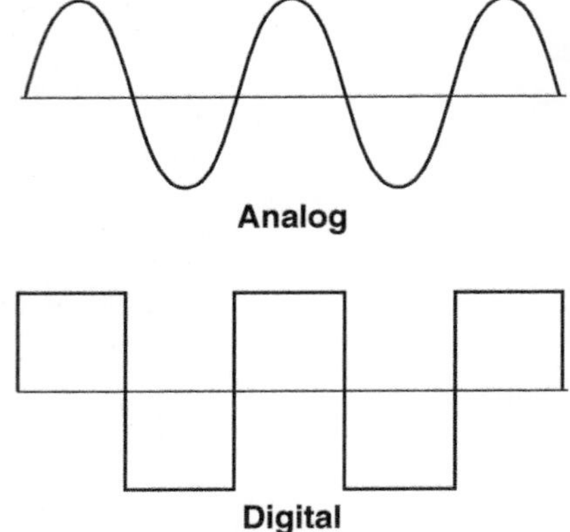
Analog
Digital

The highs, lows, and in-between states have historically been represented with analog devices rather than in digital form. Examples of analog devices are a speedometer, a thermometer, and a tire-pressure gauge, all of which can measure continuous fluctuations.

Digital describes any system based on discontinuous data or events; in the case of computers, it refers to communications signals or information represented in a two-state (binary) way using electronic or electromagnetic signals. Each 0 and 1 signal represents a *bit*. At their most basic level, computers can distinguish between just these two values, 0 and 1, or off and on (Chapter 4, p. 197).

Traditionally, electronic transmission of telephone, radio, television, and cable-TV signals has been analog. The electrical signals on a telephone line, for instance, have been analog data representations of the original voices, transmitted in the shape of a wave. Why bother to change analog signals into digital ones, especially since the digital representations are only *approximations* of analog events? The reason is that *digital signals are easier to store and manipulate electronically.*

Purpose of the Modem: Converting Digital Signals to Analog Signals & Back

Signals in the real world are analog—voice, light, sound—and must be converted into digital signals before they can be manipulated by digital equipment.

Because telephone lines have traditionally been analog, a *modem* (Chapter 2) is needed if a computer is to send communications signals over a telephone line. **Modem is short for "*mo*dulate/*dem*odulate." A sending modem modulates digital signals into analog signals for transmission over phone lines or other transmission media. A receiving modem demodulates the analog signals back into digital signals.** *(• See Panel 6.2.)*

- **1970** Microprocessor chips come into use; floppy disk introduced for storing data
- **1971** First pocket calculator
- **1973** FTP is developed
- **1975** First microcomputer (MITS Altair 8800)
- **1976** Apple I computer (first personal computer sold in assembled form); has 512 KB RAM
- **1978** 5¼" floppy disk; Atari home video game
- **1981** IBM introduces personal computer
- **1982** Portable computers; TCP/IP is established as an Internet standard; *Internet* is coined
- **1984** Apple Macintosh; first personal laser printer; desktop publishing takes hold; Domain Name System (DNS) is introduced
- **1993** Multimedia desktop computers; personal digital assistants (PDAs)

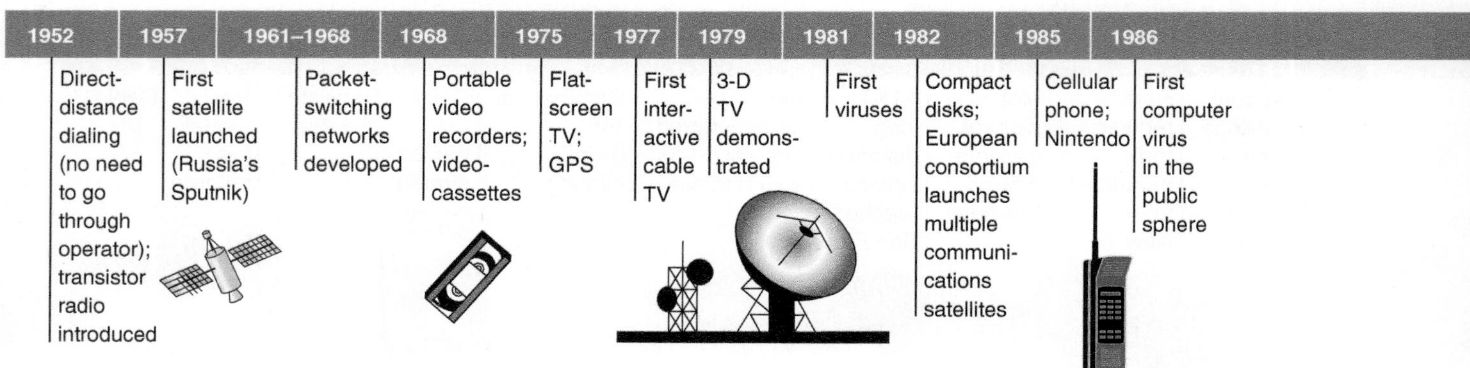
1952 Direct-distance dialing (no need to go through operator); transistor radio introduced
1957 First satellite launched (Russia's Sputnik)
1961–1968 Packet-switching networks developed
1968 Portable video recorders; video-cassettes
1975 Flat-screen TV; GPS
1977 First inter-active cable TV
1979 3-D TV demons-trated
1981 First viruses
1982 Compact disks; European consortium launches multiple communi-cations satellites
1985 Cellular phone; Nintendo
1986 First computer virus in the public sphere

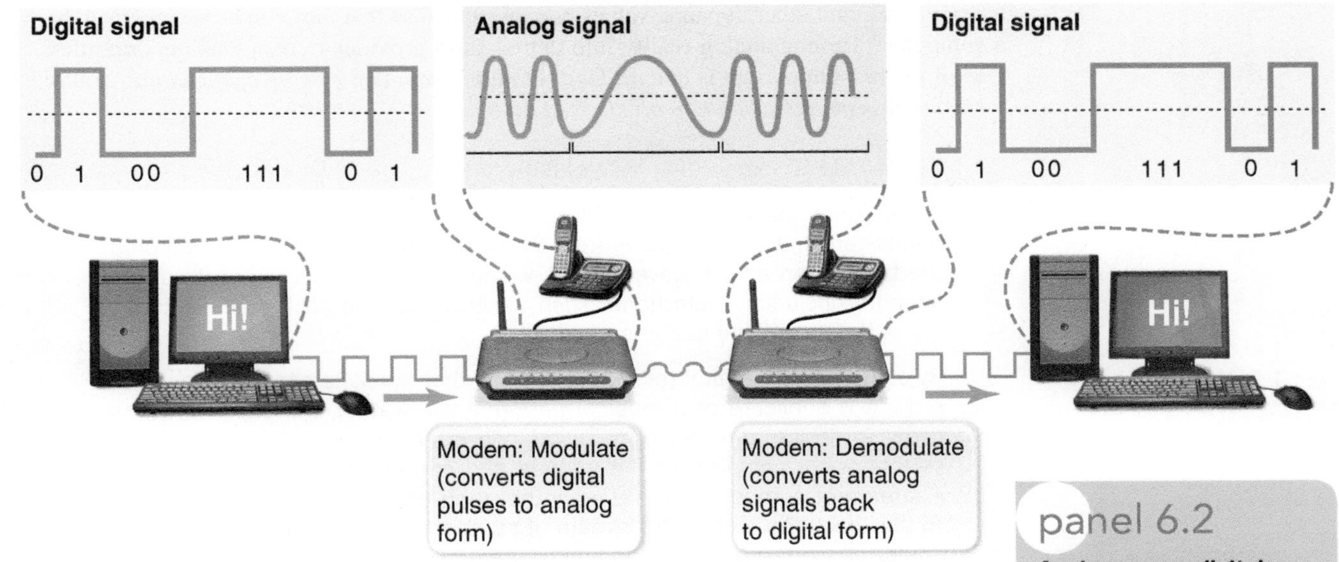

panel 6.2

Analog versus digital signals, and the modem
Note that an analog signal represents a continuous electrical signal in the form of a wave. A digital signal is discontinuous, expressed as discrete bursts of on/off electric pulses.

As we discussed in Chapter 2, the telephone modem is only one method of accessing the Internet. Other methods are:

- High-speed phone lines—DSL modem and T1 and T3 lines
- Cable modem
- Wireless modem—for satellite and other through-the-air links

Our concern, however, goes far beyond telephone transmission. How can the analog realities of the world be expressed in digital form? How can light, sounds, colors,

Computer Technology

1994	1997	2000	2001	2003	2005	2009	2010	2012	2047?
Apple and IBM introduce PCs with full-motion video built in; wireless data transmission for small portable computers; web browser Mosaic invented	Network computers; Pathfinder robot lands on Mars	Microsoft .NET announced; BlackBerry	Windows XP; Mac OS X; MP3	Mac G5; iPod 	Mac mini; Apple video iPod	Multicore processors	Windows 7	Windows 8	By this date, some experts predict, all electronically encodable information will be in cyberspace

Communications Technology

1991	1994	1997	2000	2001	2004	2005	2007	2010	2011	2014	2015–2020
CD-ROM games (Sega)	FCC selects HDTV standard	Internet telephone-to-telephone service	Napster popular; 3.8% of music sales online	2.5G wireless services; Wi-Fi and Bluetooth	Facebook launched; MySpace in operation	3G wireless services	112 million blogs are tracked	WikiLeaks controversy	4G	Google Glass sold to the public	5G; speech-to-speech translation for smartphones; power rationing due to grid shortage?

temperatures, and other dynamic values be represented so that they can be manipulated by a computer? Turning analog reality into digital form provides tremendous opportunities. One of the most important is that *all kinds of multimedia can now be changed into digital form and transmitted as data to all kinds of devices.*

TECH TALES Recording Music: From Analog Life to Digital Life

If you were using an analog tape recorder to record a singer during a performance, the analog wave from the microphone, which is recorded onto the tape as an analog wave as well, would produce a near duplicate of the sounds—including distortions, such as buzzings and clicks, or electronic hums if an amplified guitar is used.

By contrast, with digital recording, the way that music is captured does not provide a duplicate of a musical performance. Rather, the digital process uses a device (an *analog-to-digital converter*) to record *representative selections,* or *samples,* of the sounds and convert the analog waves into a stream of numbers that the computer then uses to express the sounds. To play back the music, the stream of numbers is converted (by a *digital-to-analog converter*) back into an analog wave.

The samples of sounds are taken at regular intervals—nearly 44,100 times a second—and the copy obtained is virtually exact and free from distortion and noise. The sampling rate of 44,100 times per second and the high precision fool our ears into hearing a smooth, continuous sound.

Digital photography also uses sampling: a computer takes samples of values such as brightness and color. The same is true of other aspects of real-life experience, such as pressure, temperature, and motion. ■

Sampling

For detailed information, go to:

www.informit.com/articles/article.aspx?p=372009

http://en.wikipedia.org/wiki/Digitizing

http://electronics.howstuffworks.com/analog-digital3.htm

http://audacity.sourceforge.net/manual-1.2/tutorial_basics_1.html

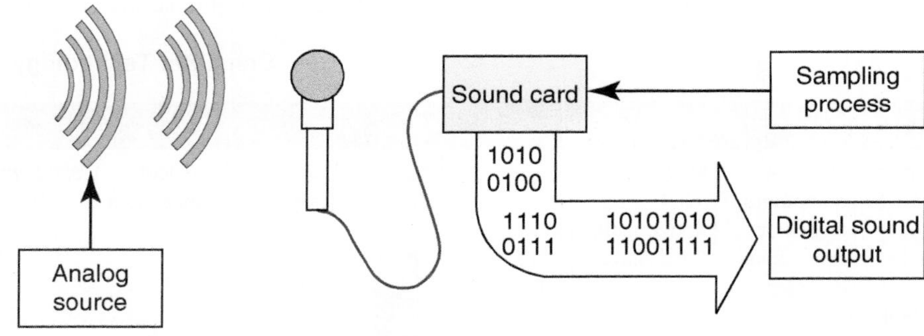

Now let us examine the digital world of telecommunications. We begin with the subject of networks and then discuss how networks are connected—first by wired means, then by wireless means.

6.2 NETWORKS

A network is a series of points interconnected by communications paths. Networks can interconnect with other networks and contain subnetworks.

Whether wired or wireless or both, **a network, or *communications network,* is a system of interconnected computers, telephones, or other communications devices that can communicate with one another and share applications and data.** The tying together of so many communications devices in so many ways is changing the world we live in.

The Benefits of Networks

Computer networks are now a vital part of almost all organizations.

People and organizations use networks for the following reasons.

SHARING HARDWARE Peripheral devices such as laser printers, disk drives, and scanners can be expensive. Consequently, to justify their purchase, management wants to maximize their use. Usually the best way to do this is to connect the peripheral to a network serving several computer users.

SHARING SOFTWARE In most organizations, people use the same software and need access to the same information. It is less expensive for a company to buy one word processing program licensed to serve many employees (site license; p. 146) than to buy a separate word processing program for each employee. Also, instead of using a disk or USB flash drive to carry files from one computer or office to another, you can share files directly using a network.

SHARING DATA & INFORMATION If all employees have access to the same data on a shared storage device, the organization can save money and avoid serious problems. Updating information on a shared server is much easier than updating every user's individual system. Network-linked employees can more easily work together online on shared projects or contribute to a document concurrently. Confidential data can be protected and shared with the users who have permission to access that data. Document tracking software can be used to prevent users from overwriting files, or changing files that others are accessing at the same time, and users can access their files from any workstation.

BETTER COMMUNICATIONS With email, everyone on a network can easily keep others posted about important information. And when connected to the Internet, network users can communicate with people around the world via their network. Networks provide several different collaboration tools in addition to email: forums and chats, voice and video, and instant messaging.

ACCESSING DATABASES Networks enable users to tap into numerous databases, whether private company databases or public databases available online through the Internet.

CENTRALIZED COMMUNICATIONS Centralized administration reduces the number of people needed to manage the devices and data on the network, reducing time and cost to the company. Individual network users do not need to manage their own data and devices. One administrator can control the data, devices, and permissions of users on the network. Backing up data is easier because the data is stored in a central location.

SECURITY OF INFORMATION Before networks became commonplace, an individual employee might have been the only one with a particular piece of information, which was stored in his or her desktop computer. If the employee was dismissed—or if a fire or flood

More on Network Advantages (& Disadvantages)

http://wiki.answers.com/Q/Advantages_and_disadvantages_of_topologies

www.buzzle.com/articles/advantages-and-disadvantages-of-computer-networks.html

http://homepages.uel.ac.uk/u0306091/Network.htm

www.bbc.co.uk/schools/gcsebitesize/ict/datacomm/2networksrev2.shtml

www.buzzle.com/articles/advantages-and-disadvantages-of-different-network-topologies.html

demolished the office—the company could have lost that information. Today such data would be backed up or duplicated on a networked storage device shared by others and backed up in the cloud (Chapter 1, p. 36; Chapter 4, p. 229). Specific directories can be password-protected to limit access to authorized users. Also, files and programs on a network can be designated as "copy inhibit," so the organization doesn't have to worry about the illegal copying of programs.

Types of Networks: WANs, MANs, & Others

Networks differ in size of coverage and degree of specialty of application.

Networks, which consist of various combinations of computers, storage devices, and communications devices, may be divided into several main categories, differing primarily in their geographic range and purposes.

WIDE AREA NETWORK **A wide area network (WAN) is a communications network that covers a wide geographic area, such as a country or the world.** Most long-distance and regional telephone companies are WANs. A WAN may use a combination of satellites, fiber-optic cable, microwave, and copper-wire connections and link a variety of computers, from mainframes to terminals. *(• See Panel 6.3.)*

WANs are used to connect local area networks (discussed shortly), so that users and computers in one location can communicate with users and computers in other locations. A wide area network may be privately owned or rented (or use both private and leased lines), but the term usually connotes the inclusion of public (shared-user) networks. The best example of a WAN is the Internet.

METROPOLITAN AREA NETWORK **A metropolitan area network (MAN) is a communications network covering a city or a suburb.** The purpose of a MAN is often to bypass local telephone companies when accessing long-distance services. Many cellphone systems are MANs, and some cities set up wireless MANs to connect local area networks to the Internet. Like WANs, MANs generally use a common carrier—a telecommunications company that hires itself out to the public to provide communications transmission services—for at least part of its connections.

panel 6.3
Wide area network (WAN)

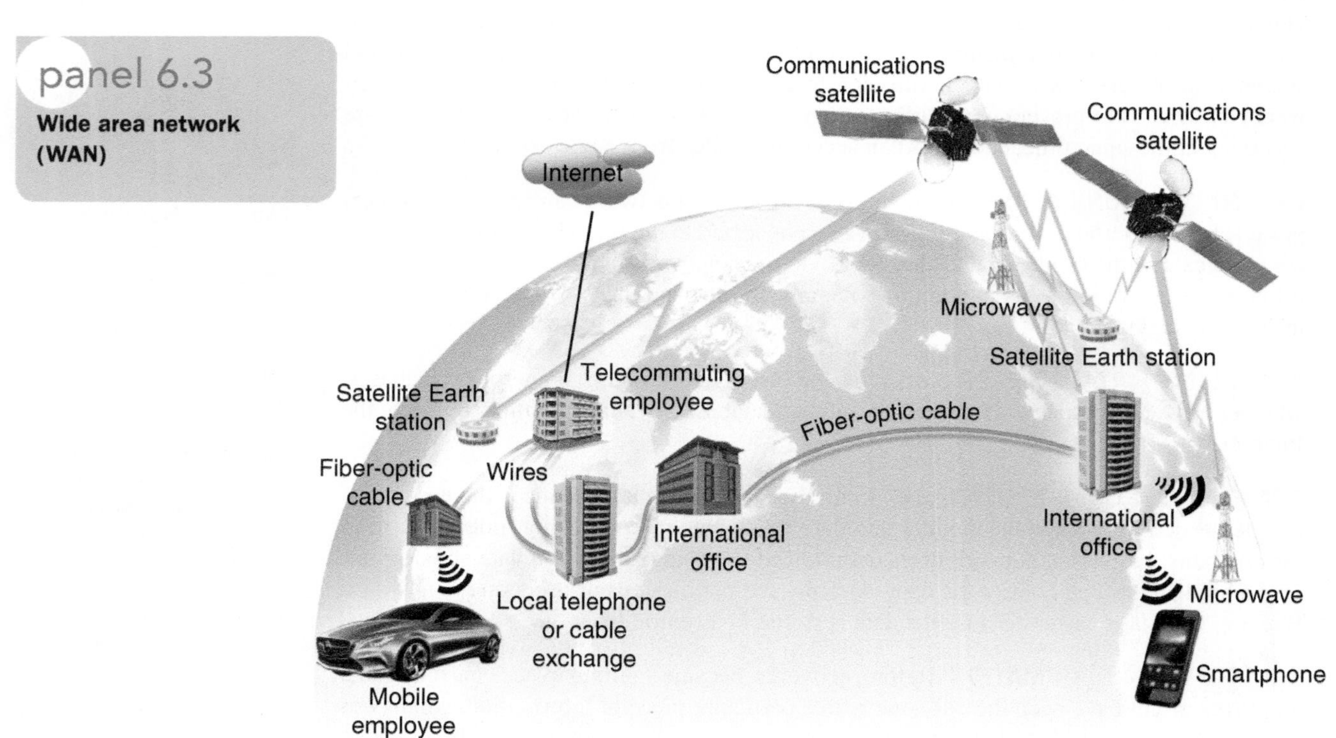

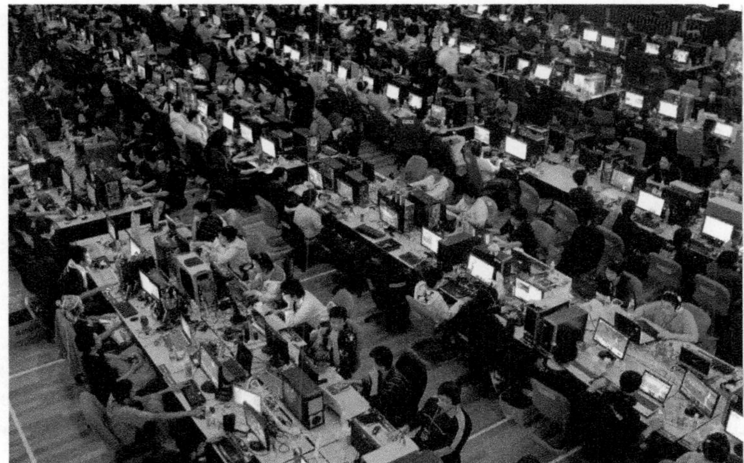

panel 6.4

A local area network by PlugLink (*www .asokatech.com/ home-area-net-page*)

LOCAL AREA NETWORK **A local area network (LAN), or *local net,* connects computers and devices in a limited geographic area, such as one office, one building, or a group of buildings close together.** (• *See Panel 6.4.*) LANs are the basis for most office networks and are usually proprietary—the organization that runs the LAN owns it. **A wireless LAN (WLAN) is a LAN that uses radio frequencies rather than physical wires to connect computers and other devices.**

A newer example of a LAN is **a home area network, which links a household's digital devices**—computers, printers, DVD players, television sets, and home security systems. Some variants are the *home automation network,* which relies on very inexpensive, very short-range, low-power wireless technology to link switches and sensors around the house, and the *garden area network,* which can be used to link watering systems, outdoor lights, and alarm systems. Another LAN is the *personal area network,* which uses short-range wireless technology (such as Bluetooth) to connect an individual's personal electronics, such as smartphone, laptop, tablet, and printer.

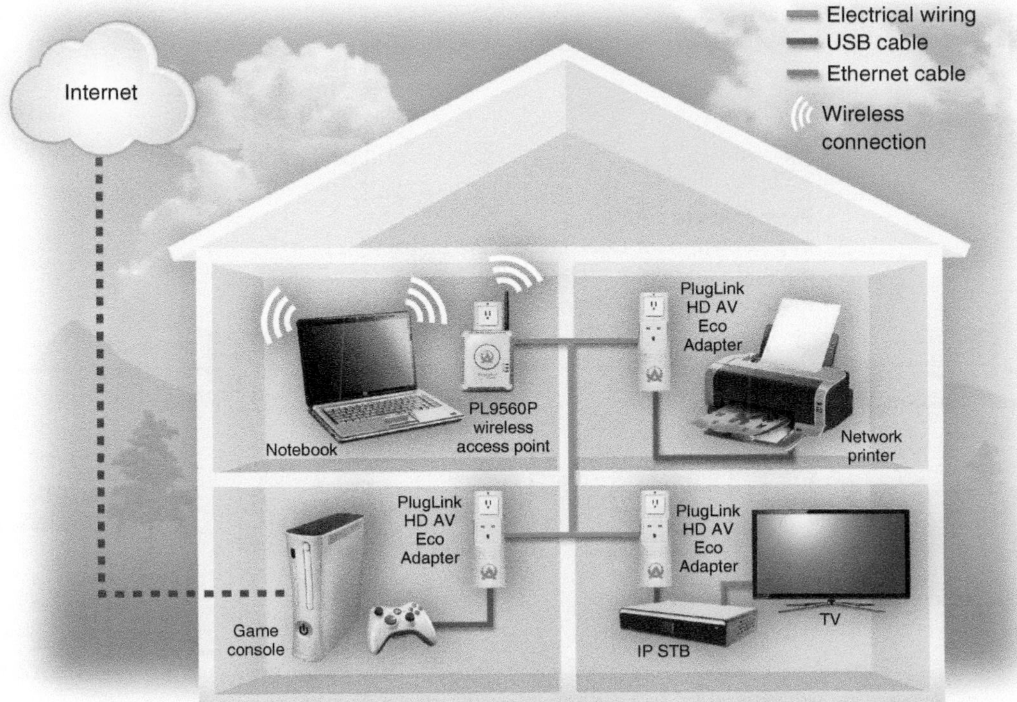

Home area network

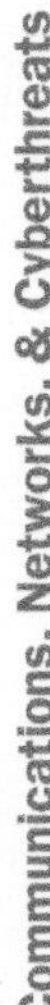

Network Architectures: How Networks Are Structured—Client-Server & Peer to Peer

Peer-to-peer networks are generally installed in homes or in very small businesses; client-server networks can be very large.

Network architecture **is the name given to how a network is structured and how it shares and coordinates resources.** Two principal network architectures are *client-server* and *peer to peer.* (• *See Panel 6.5.*) Client-server networks have a central computer that holds the data and manages the resources. Peer-to-peer networks connect computers so that each computer shares all or part of its resources.

CLIENT-SERVER NETWORKS **A client-server network consists of *clients,* which are microcomputers that request data, and *servers,* which are central computers used to supply data.** In the client-server scheme, central servers handle all security and file transactions; they are powerful microcomputers that also manage shared devices.

Different servers may be used to manage different tasks. A *file server* is a computer that acts like a disk drive, storing the programs and data files shared by users on a LAN. A *database server* is a computer in a LAN that stores data but doesn't store programs (except for the database program). A *print server* controls one or more printers and stores the

panel 6.5

Two network structures: client-server and peer to peer

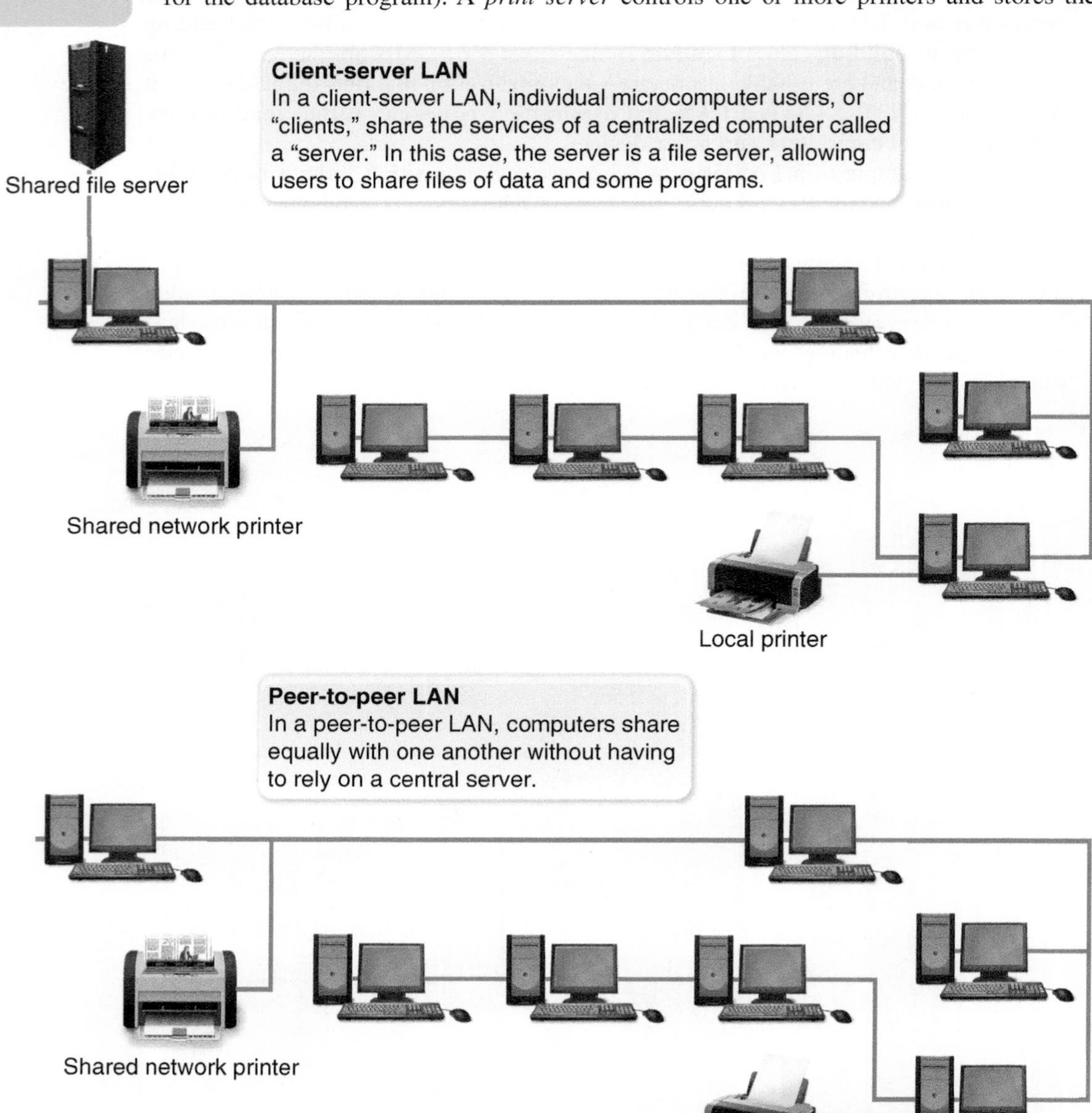
Shared file server
Client-server LAN
In a client-server LAN, individual microcomputer users, or "clients," share the services of a centralized computer called a "server." In this case, the server is a file server, allowing users to share files of data and some programs.
Shared network printer
Local printer
Peer-to-peer LAN
In a peer-to-peer LAN, computers share equally with one another without having to rely on a central server.
Shared network printer
Local printer

print-image output from all the microcomputers on the system. *Web servers* contain web pages that can be viewed using a browser. *Mail servers* manage email.

PEER-TO-PEER NETWORKS The word *peer* denotes one who is equal in standing with another (as in the phrases "peer pressure" and "jury of one's peers"). **In a peer-to-peer (P2P) network, all microcomputers on the network communicate directly with one another without relying on a server.** In these kinds of networks, there's no main server; each client functions both as a client and as a server simultaneously. Each computer can share files and peripherals with all other computers on the network, given that all are granted access privileges, and each machine handles its own security.

Peer-to-peer networks are easy to set up, less expensive than client-server networks, and work effectively for up to 25 computers, which makes them appropriate for small networks. Beyond that, they slow down under heavy use.

WHICH ARCHITECTURE IS BETTER? Client-server networks are more secure than peer-to-peer networks because users can't log on unless they supply valid usernames and passwords listed on the server, and the users may access only those resources the server allows them.

Peer-to-peer networks are less stable because certain shared resources reside on each user's machine. If users crash their computers, they can seriously affect their peer-to-peer network. Security can become a problem because users are free to create their own passwords for various resources available on their computers. The computer that contains the shared resources doesn't check on who's trying to access those resources. Any user can access them as long as he or she knows the password.

Network Tutorials

For more on how various types of networks operate:

www.networktutorials.info/

http://freevideolectures.com/Course/3162/Computer-Networking-Tutorial/

http://compnetworking.about.com/

Intranets, Extranets, VPNs, & Firewalls

Intranets, extranets, and VPNs are variations on the Internet used by organizations for inside and outside communications, protected by firewalls.

Early in the Online Age, businesses discovered the benefits of using the World Wide Web to get information to customers, suppliers, or investors. For example, in the mid-1990s,

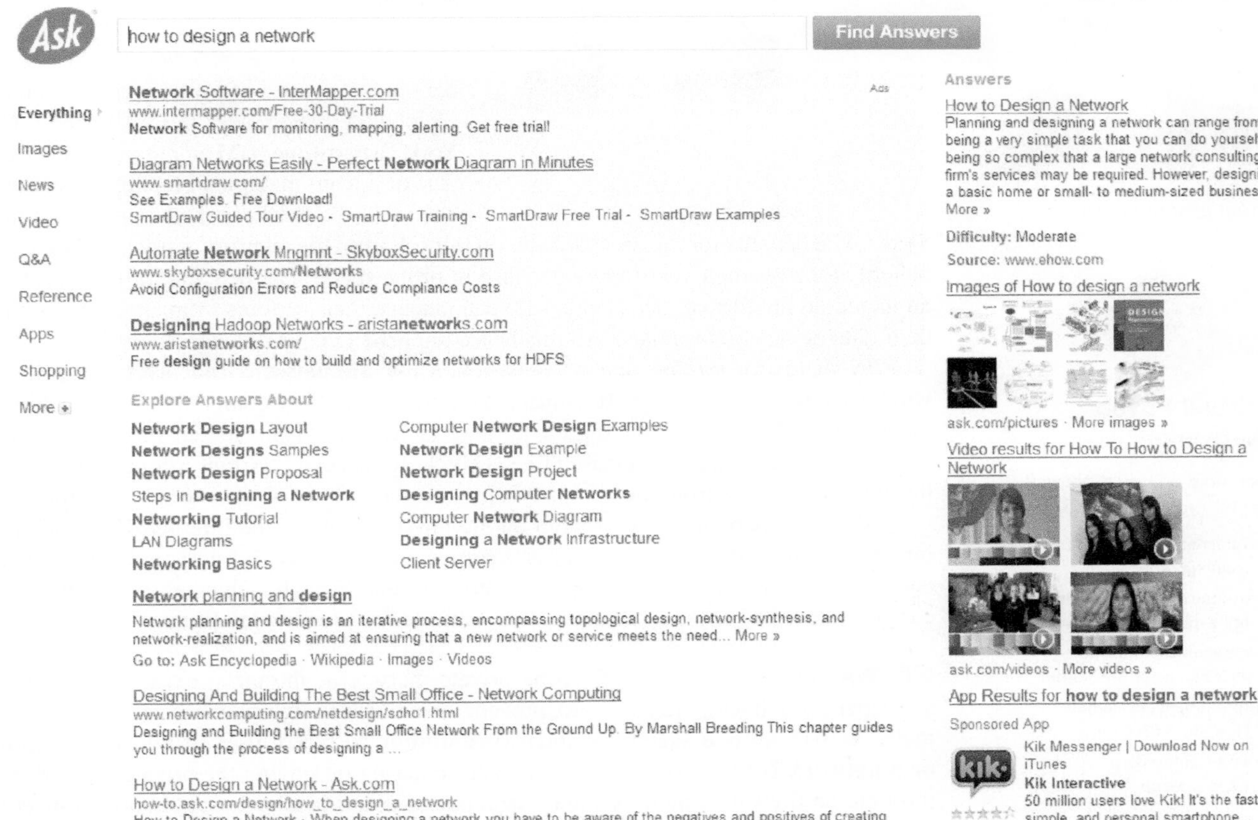

FedEx found it could save millions by allowing customers to click through web pages to trace their parcels, instead of having FedEx customer-service agents do it. From there, it was a short step to the application of the same technology inside companies—in internal Internet networks called *intranets.*

INTRANETS: FOR INTERNAL USE ONLY **An intranet is an organization's internal private network that uses the infrastructure and standards—technology, protocols, and hypertext links** (Chapter 2)—**of the public Internet and web.**

The intranet is an in-house website on the company's LAN that serves employees only. Although intranet pages may have links to websites on the Internet, the intranet is not exposed to, and is not accessed by, the general public. An intranet provides a standard in-company way to publish, for example, company policy, email addresses, news, schedules, medical and insurance forms, employee benefit information, jobs available within the company, and training manuals. Since a web browser is the primary interface, intranets offer cross-platform support for employees' Windows, Mac, and Linux desktops.

EXTRANETS: FOR CERTAIN OUTSIDERS Taking intranet technology a few steps further, extranets offer security and controlled access. Whereas intranets are internal systems designed to connect the members of a specific group, **extranets are private intranets that connect not only internal personnel but also selected suppliers and other strategic parties via the public communications systems.** Most extranets use the Internet as the entry point for outsiders, security restrictions (firewall) to limit access, and a secure protocol for authenticating users.

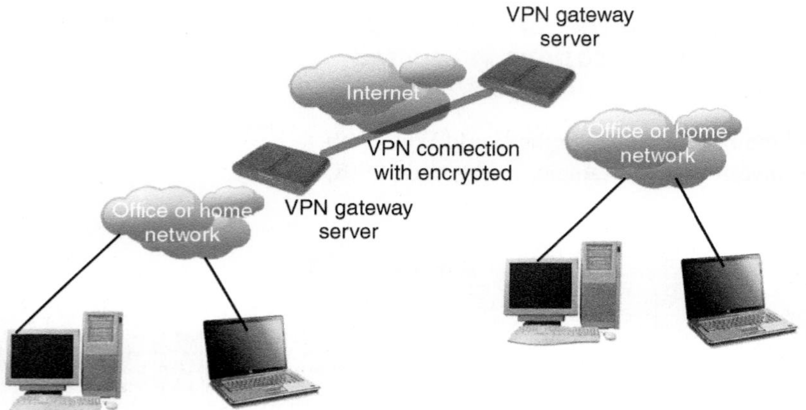

Virtual private network

Extranets have become popular for standard transactions such as purchasing, supporting a mobile sales force, communicating product plans, obtaining customer feedback, and servicing law-firm clients. One way for a small business to provide an extranet is through hosted applications, like WebEx's WebOffice, Trichys' Work Zone, and Microsoft SharePoint Services.

VIRTUAL PRIVATE NETWORKS "I'm living here in Delaware, but I work [remotely] out of a global delivery center in East Fishkill, New York," a part-time IBM employee writes. "I am part of a team that manages Unix systems for clients in the northeast and southwest United States. The benefits for me are that I can do this job from the comfort of my own home. The benefits for my employer are less expense in office space. The benefits for our clients are an increased number of consultants who can manage their systems from anywhere without their data being compromised. All this is accomplished via VPN technology."[3]

VPN stands for **virtual private network, a private network that uses a public network (usually the Internet) to connect remote sites.** Many companies have established their own VPNs because having an intranet or extranet using leased lines can become expensive. Instead of using a leased line, a VPN uses special ("virtual") connections routed through the Internet from the company's private network to the remote site or employee.

A VPN works by using the shared public infrastructure of the Internet while maintaining privacy through special security procedures. In effect, data is encrypted at the sending end and decrypted at the receiving end, and it is sent through a channel (or "tunnel") that can be entered only by data that has been subjected to proper encryption.

Virtual Private Networks

For more on how VPNs work, go to:

http://computer.howstuffworks.com/vpn.htm

www.howtogeek.com/133680/htg-explains-what-is-a-vpn/

www.ehow.com/how-does_4926227_a-vpn-work.html

http://hubpages.com/hub/How_do_VPNs_work

www.brightgreenvpn.com/what-is-a-vpn

FIREWALLS FOR SECURITY To be private, networks, intranets, extranets, and VPNs all depend on having firewalls to prevent unauthorized Internet users from accessing them. **A firewall is a system of hardware and/or software that protects a computer or a network from intruders.** All messages entering or leaving the private network pass through the firewall, which examines each message and blocks those that do not meet the specified security criteria.

There are two types of firewalls—software and hardware:

- **If you have one computer—software firewall:** Even if you're not on a private network—if you're just an individual with a single computer, tablet, or smartphone accessing the public Internet—you will want to have a firewall. Probably that would mean a software firewall, such as the one that is built into Windows and that can be activated quickly.
- **If you have more than one computer—hardware firewall:** If you have more than one computer and you are linked to the Internet by a cable modem or DSL, you probably need a hardware firewall (such as a router, as we'll explain).

Show all

> Browse A to Z

> Browse categories

Windows Firewall

A firewall is like locking the front door to your house—it helps keep intruders (in this case, hackers and malicious software) from getting in. Windows Firewall is on by default in Windows 7, so you don't need to set it up—plus we've made it more flexible and easier to use.

Now you can fine-tune the protection and notifications you want for each of your network profiles—Home, Work, and Public. When you're connected to a public network like a library or a coffee shop, you may want to block all incoming connections. At home or work, this might be overkill. Whatever level of protection you choose for your profiles, you'll be able to switch between them with ease.

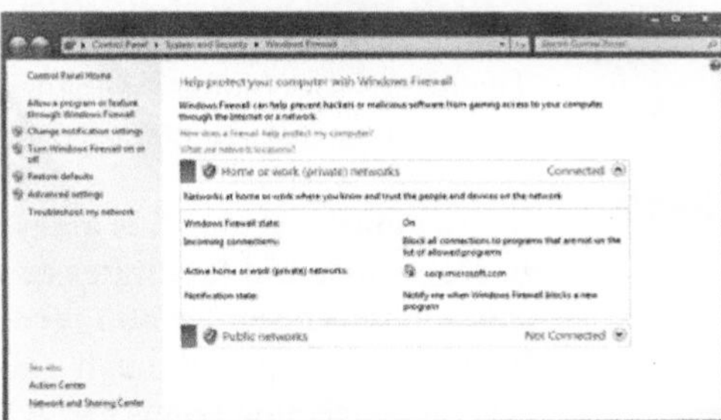

Windows Firewall can tailor protection for different network environments.

Learn how

- What is a firewall?
- Firewall: frequently asked questions
- Understanding Windows Firewall settings

Survival Tip

Firewalls

Windows 7 has a built-in firewall. Many companies sell their own firewall versions. If you buy separate firewall software, turn off the operating system's firewall.

The Use of Firewalls

Go to:

http://netforbeginners.about.com/od/f/g/def_firewall.htm

http://compnetworking.about.com/od/firewalls/g/bldef_firewall.htm

www.comodo.com/resources/home/how-firewalls-work.php

Components of a Network

Regardless of size, networks all have several components in common.

Networks use a wired or wireless connection system. Wired connections may be twisted-pair wiring, coaxial cable, or fiber-optic cable. Wireless connections may be infrared, microwave (such as Bluetooth), broadcast radio (such as Wi-Fi), or satellite, as we describe shortly.

HOSTS & NODES The client-server type of network has a **host computer, a central computer that controls the network.** The other devices on the network are called nodes. **A node is any device that is attached (wired or wireless) to a network—for example, a microcomputer, storage device, scanner, or printer.** A device called a *wireless access point (WAP)* when attached to a wired network essentially extends the range of the network by offering several wireless nodes, enabling you, say, to wirelessly connect a computer in a back bedroom to a network at the front of the house.

PACKETS Electronic messages are sent as packets. **A packet is a fixed-length block of data for transmission.** A sending computer breaks an electronic message apart into packets, each of which typically contains 1,000–1,500 bytes. The various packets are sent through a communications packet-switching network, such as the Internet—often using different (and the most expedient) routes, at different speeds, and sandwiched in between packets from other messages. Once the packets arrive at their destination, the receiving computer reassembles them into proper sequence to complete the message. The entire process is called *packet switching.*

PROTOCOLS **A protocol, or *communications protocol,* is a set of conventions governing the exchange of data between hardware and/or software components in a communications network.** Every device connected to a network has an Internet Protocol (IP) address (Chapter 2, p. 61) so that other computers on the network can properly route data to that address. Sending and receiving devices must follow the same set of protocols.

Protocols are built into the hardware or software you are using. The protocol in your communications software, for example, will specify how receiver devices will acknowledge sending devices, a matter called *handshaking.* Handshaking establishes the fact that the circuit is available and operational. It also establishes the level of device compatibility and the speed of transmission. In addition, protocols specify the type of electronic connections used, the timing of message exchanges, and error-detection techniques.

Each packet, or electronic message, carries four types of information that will help it get to its destination: (1) the sender's address (the IP), (2) the intended receiver's address, (3) how many packets the complete message has been broken into, and (4) the number of this particular packet. The packets carry the data in the protocols that the Internet uses—that is, TCP/IP.

Belkin switch

Sling Link Turbo bridges

NETWORK LINKING DEVICES: SWITCHES, BRIDGES, GATEWAYS, ROUTERS, & BACKBONES Networks are often linked together—LANs to MANs and MANs to WANs, for example. The means for connecting them are *switches, bridges, routers,* and *gateways.* (• *See Panel 6.6.*)

- **Switches:** **A switch is a device that connects computers to a network and facilitates communication by sending messages between sender and receiver nodes.** All data that passes between nodes goes through a switch. Switches, which have several connection points and which allow data to be transmitted back and forth at the same time, inspect data packets as they are received, determine the source and destination device of each packet, and forward them appropriately.

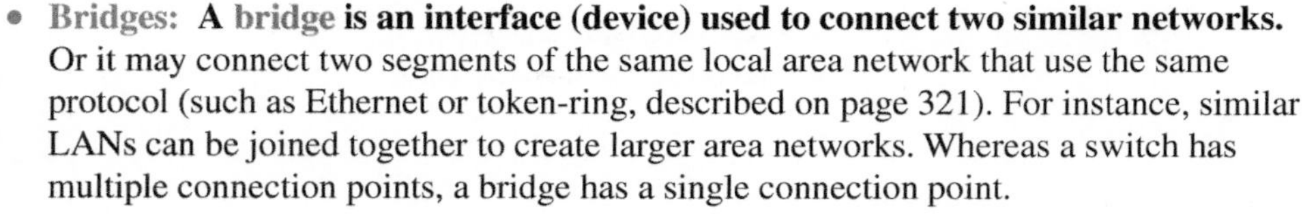

- **Bridges:** **A bridge is an interface (device) used to connect two similar networks.** Or it may connect two segments of the same local area network that use the same protocol (such as Ethernet or token-ring, described on page 321). For instance, similar LANs can be joined together to create larger area networks. Whereas a switch has multiple connection points, a bridge has a single connection point.

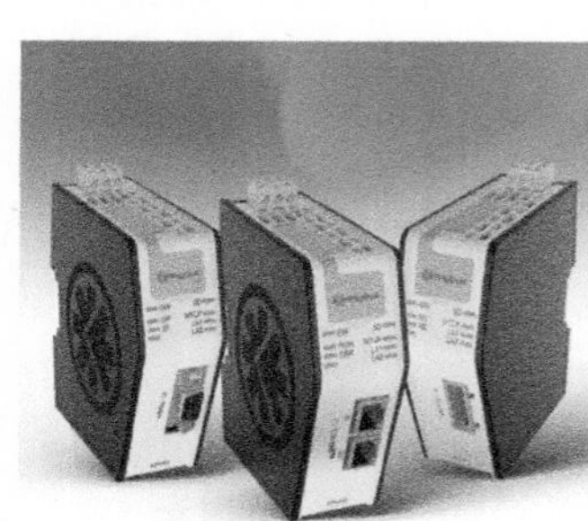
Anybus gateways

- **Gateways:** **A gateway is an interface permitting communication between dissimilar networks**—for instance, between a LAN and a WAN or between two LANs based on different network operating systems or different layouts. Gateways can be hardware, software, or a combination of the two.

- **Routers:** **Routers are specialized devices for transmitting data, physical devices that join multiple wired and/or wireless networks.** Routers have specific software and hardware designed for the routing and forwarding of information.

  Routers may be small, used as devices in offices and home offices to connect cable or DSL. They may be so-called enterprise routers, more powerful devices used by large companies, research facilities, and ISPs. Or they may be high-speed routers, which can serve as part of the main transmission path (backbone) of the Internet, handling the major data traffic and calculating the best possible transmission path of data packets between networks. In all cases, IP addresses are used to route the data.

Router

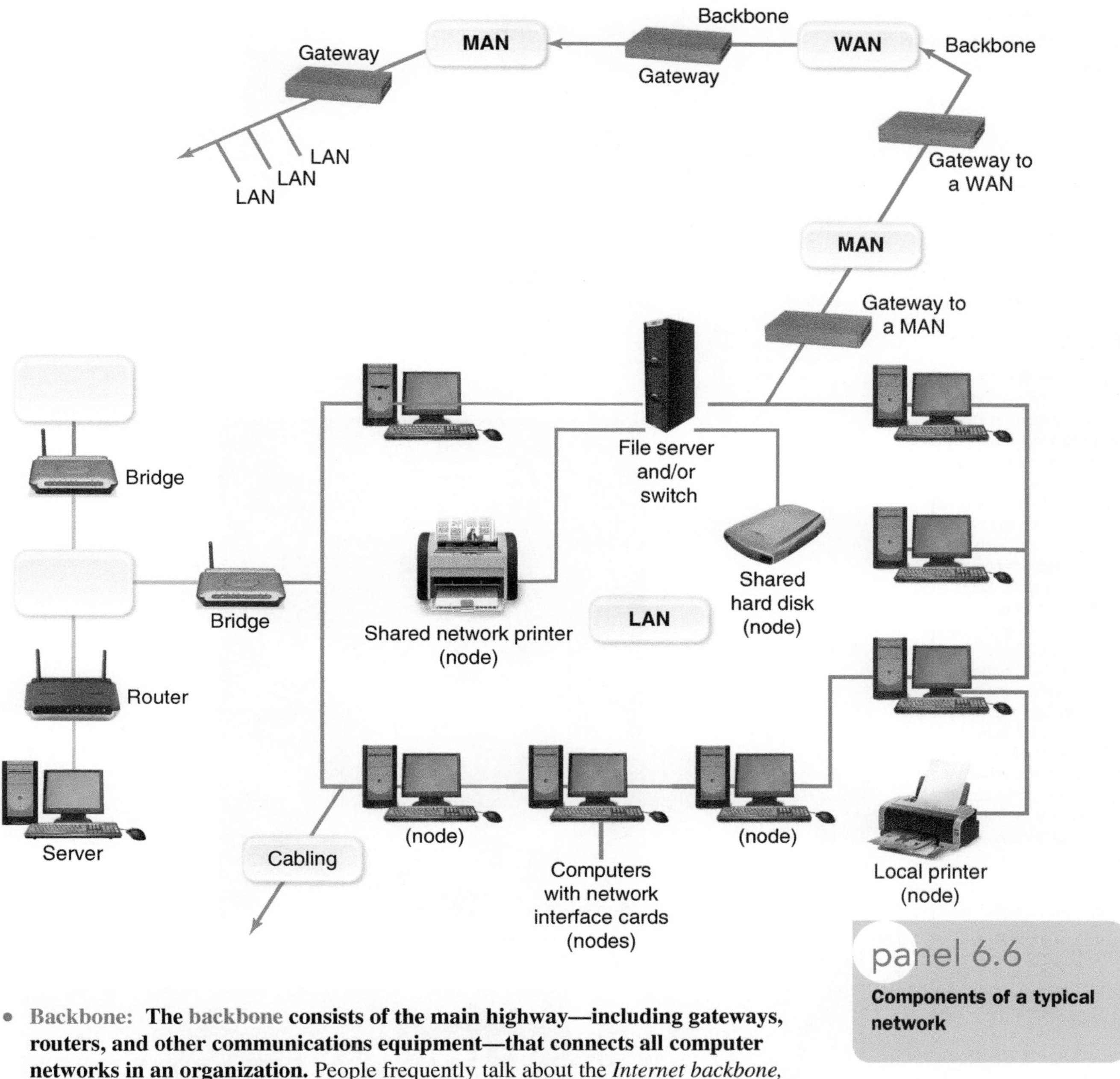

panel 6.6

Components of a typical network

- **Backbone: The backbone consists of the main highway—including gateways, routers, and other communications equipment—that connects all computer networks in an organization.** People frequently talk about the *Internet backbone,* the central structure that connects all other elements of the Internet. As we discussed in Chapter 2, several commercial companies provide these major high-speed links across the country; these backbones are connected at Internet Exchange Points (IXPs; Chapter 2, p. 60).

NETWORK INTERFACE CARDS As we stated in Chapter 4 (p. 216), a *network interface card (NIC),* or *network card,* enables the computer to send and receive messages over a cable network. The network card is built into the motherboard, as is usually the case with new computers, or can be inserted into an expansion slot. Alternatively, a network card in a stand-alone box may serve a number of devices. Each NIC has a unique identifier that allows the network to identify each computer as a unique location.

NETWORK OPERATING SYSTEM The *network operating system (NOS)* is the system software that manages the activity of a network. The NOS supports access by multiple users and provides for recognition of users based on passwords and terminal identifications. Depending on whether the LAN is client-server or peer to peer, the operating system may be stored on the main server, on each microcomputer on the network, or on a combination of both.

One communications company's recent backbone map (UUnet, which is now Verizon)

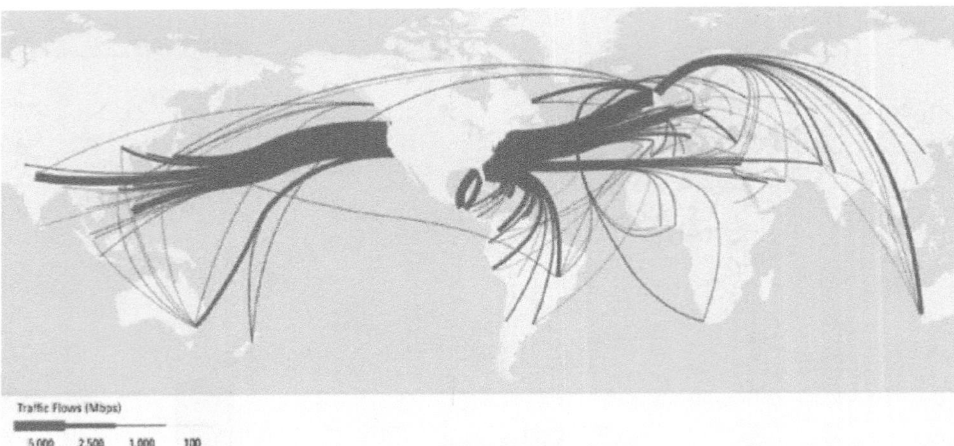

Backbones

The National Science Foundation (NSF) created the first high-speed backbone in 1987. Called NSFNET, it was a T1 line that connected 170 smaller networks together. A T3 line was developed the following year. Backbones are typically fiber-optic trunk lines, with multiple fiber-optic cables combined to increase capacity. Some large companies that provide backbone connectivity are UUnet, Verizon, AT&T, Qwest, Sprint, and IBM. Scientists in the United States invented the Internet, and the computers that oversee the network are still controlled by the U.S. Department of Commerce. Some people believe that the Internet should be put under international control through the United Nations. What do you think?

Undersea fiber-optic cable

A router and network computer switches

Network Topologies

Basic network topologies are star, ring, bus, tree, and mesh.

Networks can be laid out in different ways. **The layout, or shape, of a network is called a topology**, a schematic description that includes the network's nodes and connecting lines. The basic topologies are *star, ring, bus, tree,* and *mesh.* (• *See Panel 6.7.*)

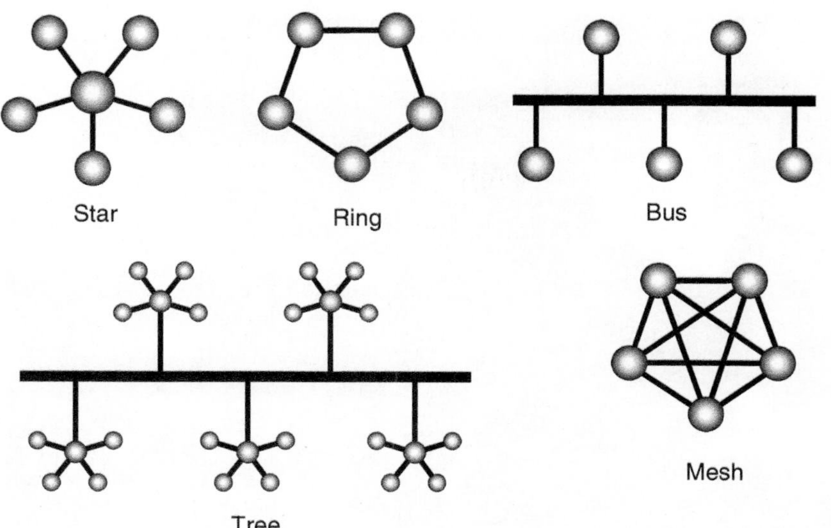

panel 6.7
The five basic network topologies

panel 6.8
Star network
This arrangement (*below*) connects all the network's devices to a central switch, through which all communications must pass.

STAR NETWORK One of the two most common topologies used in today's LANs (the other being tree), **a star network is one in which all microcomputers and other communications devices are directly connected to a central network switch.** *(• See Panel 6.8.)* Electronic messages are routed through the central switch to their destinations. The central switch monitors the flow of traffic. A PBX system—a "private branch exchange" telephone system, such as that found on some college campuses, which connects telephone extensions to one another—is an example of a star network. Traditional star networks are designed to be easily expandable, because switches can be connected to additional switches of other networks.

The advantage of a star network is that the switch prevents collisions between messages. Moreover, if a connection is broken between any communications device and the switch, the rest of the devices on the network will continue operating. However, if the switch goes down, the entire network stops.

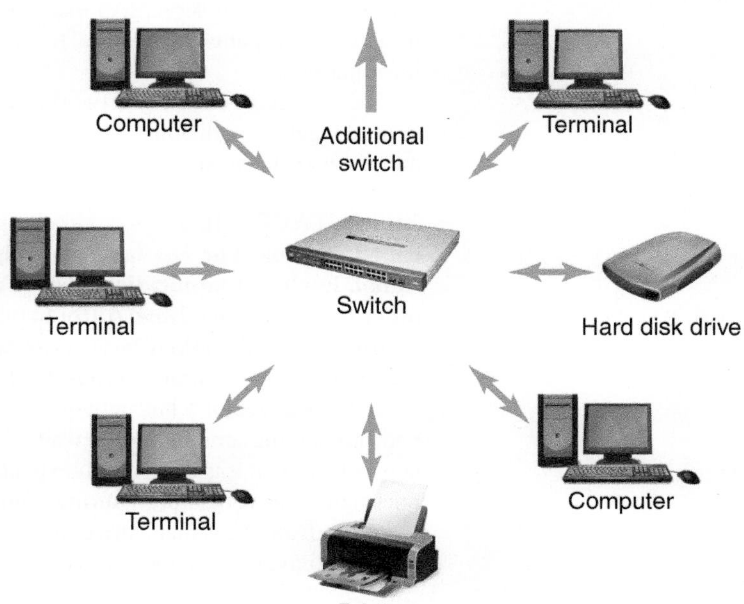

RING NETWORK **A ring network is one in which all microcomputers and other communications devices are connected in a continuous loop.** *(• See Panel 6.9.)*

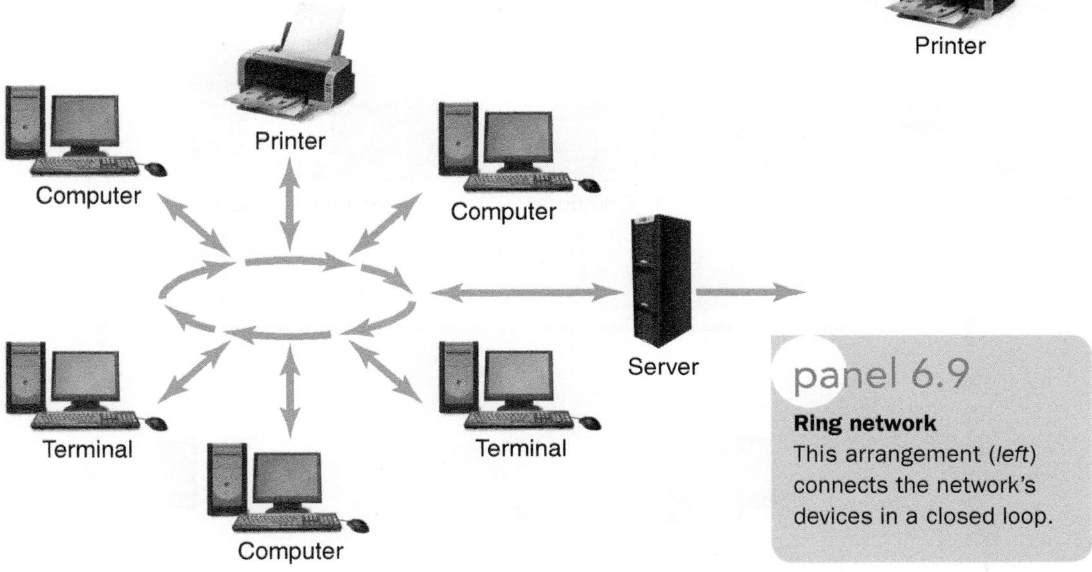

panel 6.9
Ring network
This arrangement (*left*) connects the network's devices in a closed loop.

Traders networking. Stock traders work on the heavily networked floor of the New York Stock Exchange in New York.

Electronic messages are passed around the ring until they reach the right destination. There is no central server. An example of a ring network is IBM's *Token Ring Network,* in which a bit pattern (called a "token") determines which user on the network can send information.

The advantage of a ring network is that messages flow in only one direction. Thus, there is no danger of collisions. The disadvantage is that if one workstation malfunctions, the entire network can stop working.

BUS NETWORK **In a bus network, all nodes are connected to a single wire or cable, called the bus. The *bus* has two endpoints, or terminators, which stop the network signal. Each communications device on the network transmits electronic messages to other devices.** *(• See Panel 6.10.)* In other words, the bus network works like a bus system at rush hour, with various buses pausing in different bus zones to pick up passengers. In a bus network, all communications devices are connected to a common, linear channel.

The advantage of a bus network is that if some of the messages being sent collide with one another, the sending device waits and tries to transmit again. Other advantages of a bus network are that it is relatively inexpensive, easy to use in peer-to-peer networks, and good for smaller networks not requiring high speeds.

A disadvantage is that extra circuitry and software are needed to develop access methods in order to avoid collisions between messages. A second disadvantage is that the network

panel 6.10

Bus network

A single channel connects all communications devices.

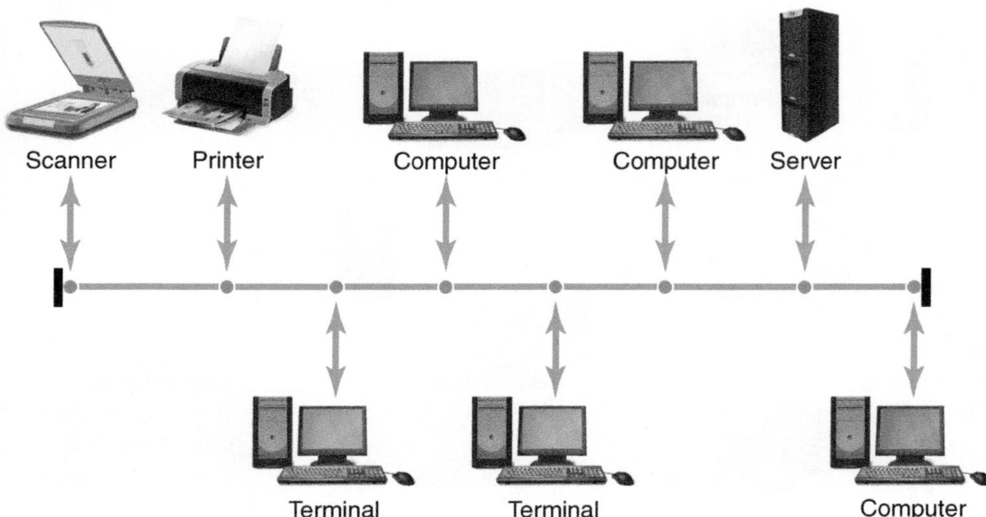

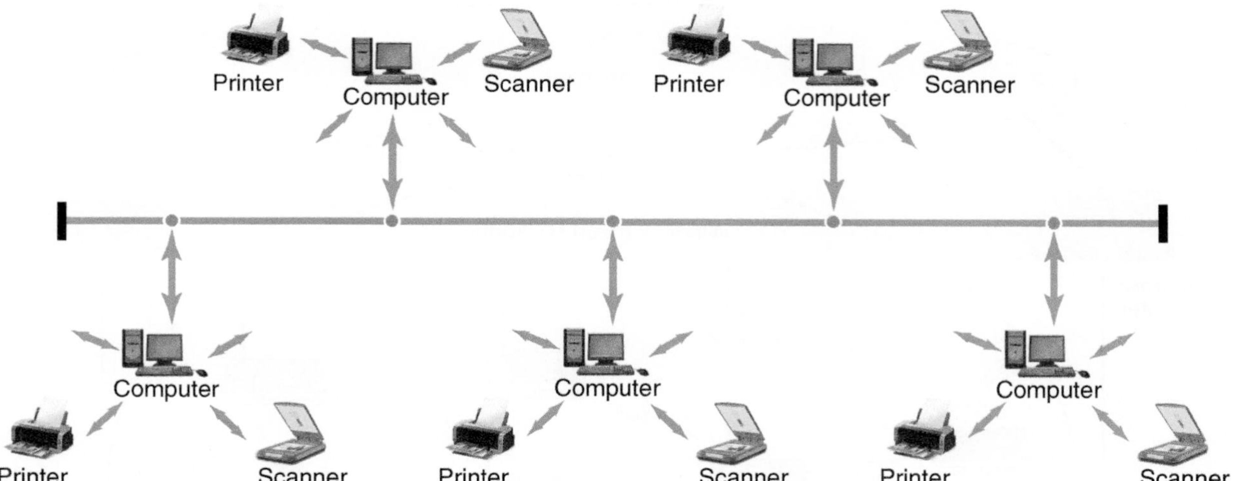

is limited to 20 devices on a network segment that cannot exceed 185 meters (606 feet) in length. A third drawback is that if a connection in the bus is broken—as when someone moves a desk and knocks out the connection—the entire network may stop working.

With the increased use of client-server networks and the decreased cost of Ethernet networks (discussed shortly), bus networks are being used less and less.

panel 6.11

Tree network

A succession of star networks connected to a main bus line

TREE NETWORK Often used by corporations to share organization-wide data, **a tree network is a bus network of star networks.** *(• See Panel 6.11.)* That is, a tree network is a combination of two or more connected star networks. Each star network is a LAN with a central computer with which microcomputers and other devices are directly connected. In turn the central computers of the star networks are connected to a main cable called the bus.[4] A tree network might be found on a university campus in which each department has its own star network with its own central computer. The various departments are then linked throughout the university by the main bus.

MESH NETWORK Unlike the four other networks, which follow a physical layout, a **mesh network is based on the principle that each node has more than one connection to the other nodes so that a message can take any possible shortest, easiest route to reach its destination.** *(• See Panel 6.12, next page.)* With this arrangement, if a path between two nodes is disrupted, data can be automatically rerouted along another path. Because of the alternative connections, the overall design resembles a mesh. The Internet employs the mesh network topology, which is why (most of the time) a message ultimately finds a route to its destination.

Ethernet

The Ethernet is a popular standard for linking devices in a LAN.

Ethernet is a network standard for linking all devices in a local area network that describes how data can be sent between computers and other networked devices usually in close proximity. Ethernet uses cables to connect devices; its wireless counterpart is Wi-Fi. Other network standards exist (two being TCP/IP, discussed in Chapter 2, p. 60, and IBM's Token Ring, mentioned above). But Ethernet is the most popular LAN standard in the world, particularly on star networks. This is because of the way it describes how data can be sent between nodes and enables it to be used with almost any kind of computer and network device. It is also inexpensive and easy to install and maintain. This popularity is the reason why most new microcomputers come equipped with an Ethernet card and an Ethernet port. Ethernet connections are available in the guest rooms of many hotel chains, such as Hilton and Hyatt.

The most common version of Ethernet (called *10Base-T*) handles about 10 megabits per second. A newer version, *Fast Ethernet* (or *100Base-T*), transfers data at 100 megabits per second. The newest version, *Gigabit Ethernet* (or *1000Base-T*), transmits data at the rate of 1 gigabit per second.

Internet

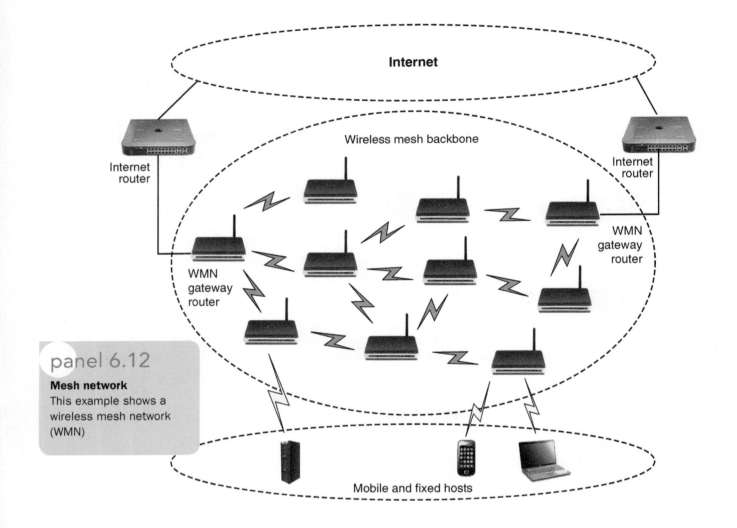

Wireless mesh backbone

Internet router

Internet router

WMN gateway router

WMN gateway router

Mobile and fixed hosts

panel 6.12

Mesh network
This example shows a wireless mesh network (WMN)

Inserting an Ethernet connector

PRACTICAL ACTION

Telecommuting & Telework: The Virtual Workplace

The rise of telecommunications, including both wired and wireless networks, has led to a concomitant rise in two kinds of virtual, or online, work arrangements: telecommuting and telework. *Telecommuting* is working away from the organization's standard workplace, often at home, and communicating with the office, using computer, telephone, and FedEx and UPS delivery services. *Telework* is working away from the office but encompasses working from anywhere, using mobile computers and smartphones.

Telecommuting: Working from Home

Telecommuting has surged in recent years. Some 9.4% of U.S. workers—13.4 million people—worked at home at least one day a week in 2010, up from 7% in 1997.[5] While about half the people who work at home are self-employed and others work from home only once a year, a great many others are *telecommuters,* people who are employed by others but who perform their main jobs at home, away from the standard office. (About 3.1 million employees consider "home" their primary workplace; this does not include the self-employed.)[6] This change has come about, of course, from the spread of telecommunications technology.[7]

The advantages of telecommuting to society are reduced traffic congestion, energy consumption, and air pollution. The advantages to employees are lower commuting and workplace-wardrobe costs and more flexibility in handling their work. The advantages to employers, it's argued, is increased productivity, reduced absenteeism, and reduced real estate costs.

Is Telecommuting Productive?

Most employees would rather work virtually (64%) rather than in an office (36%), according to one survey.[8] "Telecommuting," says one woman, "has allowed me to have a career as well as be a mother."[9] And despite some bosses' fears that at-home work is a cover for employees slacking off, telecommuting can actually *increase* a firm's productivity. One study found that businesses that allowed employees to work remotely at least three times a month were more likely to experience revenue growth of at least 10% within a year's time, compared with firms without such policies.[10] Aetna Inc., the insurance company, decided to let some of its 35,000 employees work from home, and today 47% do so, saving Aetna $80 million a year in real estate and related costs.[11]

Of course, it's possible for productivity to be hampered by distractions. Whereas in the office productivity may be masked by meetings, interruptions, and socializing, at home the distractions may range from email to crying babies and unwashed laundry—or to active dislike of the work itself.[12] Some managers use computer-monitoring programs that summarize what websites at-home employees are using and for how long, and others require "virtual face time" via email, instant messaging, or phone calls.[13] Of course, if top managers feel telecommuting is not working, they can order everyone to show up at the office—as Yahoo! CEO Marissa Mayer did in 2013 when she felt she needed "all hands on deck" to deal with the tech giant's slipping fortunes.[14]

Telework: Working from Anywhere

Telework is more than telecommuting because it connotes working from anywhere: "a client's office, a coffee shop, an airport lounge, a commuter train," in one description. "With cellphones, broadband at home, Wi-Fi, virtual private networks, and instant messaging becoming ubiquitous, telework has become easier than ever."[15] Thus, the workplace exists more in virtual than physical space, and the actual office may be little more than a laptop or tablet, a high-bandwidth connection, and a smartphone.

The "Always Working" Threat

However much telecommuting may raise productivity, telework threatens to kill it. "The skyrocketing use of mobile devices is upending much of what we know and experience in our work lives," says one commentator. "This constant access comes at a cost: Never clocking out has become so widespread that it has fueled a heated national debate on whether it is a benefit or detriment to society."[16]

Nearly two-thirds of full-time workers own smartphones, and one-third own a tablet, and 7 in 10 U.S. workers say that such technology has allowed work to move into their personal life.[17]

This has come about because employees feel that if some coworkers answer their boss's emails after hours, they feel compelled to as well. It is also fueled by the "Bring Your Own Device," or BYOD, workplace, in which employees put company applications on their personal gadgets. The result is that a new generation of workers is increasingly accustomed to using mobile devices for long hours while propped against pillows—as in bed. This can lead to all kinds of ergonomic problems (back and neck strain), disruption of the body clock and delays in sleep, and partner resentment and reduction in intimacy.[18]

More on Advantages & Disadvantages of Telecommuting

http://home.howstuffworks.com/telecommuting2.htm

http://altamsi.com/telecommuting-advantages-and-disadvantages/

www.pcworld.com/businesscenter/article/156195/17_telecommuting_disadvantages.html

www.referenceforbusiness.com/small/Sm-Z/Telecommuting.html

http://everydaylife.globalpost.com/advantages-disadvantages-telecommuting-3198.html

6.3 WIRED COMMUNICATIONS MEDIA

Communications media are the means of interchanging or transmitting and receiving information.

It used to be that two-way individual communications were accomplished mainly in two ways. They were carried by the medium of (1) a telephone wire or (2) a wireless method such as shortwave radio. Today there are many kinds of communications media, although they are still wired or wireless. **Communications media, or *communications channels,* carry signals over a *communications path,* the route between two or more communications media devices.** The speed, or data transfer rate, at which transmission occurs—and how much data can be carried by a signal—depends on the media and the type of signal.

Wired Communications Media: Wires & Cables

There are three basic types of wired communications media.

Three types of wired communications media are *twisted-pair wire* (conventional telephone lines), *coaxial cable,* and *fiber-optic cable.* The various kinds of wired Internet connections discussed in Chapter 2—dial-up modem, DSL, cable modem, T1 lines, as well as Internet backbones—are created by using these wired communications media.

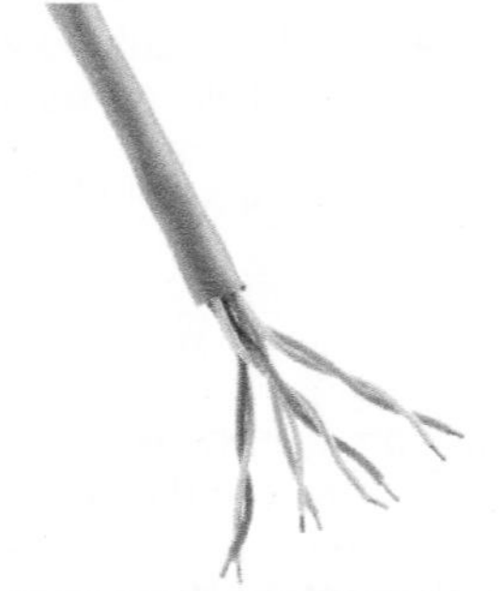

Twisted-pair wire and connector (telephone)

TWISTED-PAIR WIRE The telephone line that runs from your house to the pole outside, or underground, is probably twisted-pair wire. **Twisted-pair wire consists of two strands of insulated copper wire, twisted around each other. This twisted-pair configuration (compared to straight wire) somewhat reduces interference (called "crosstalk" or "noise") from electrical fields.** Twisted-pair is relatively slow, carrying data at the rate of 1–128 megabits per second (normally 56 Kbps). Moreover, it does not protect well against electrical interference. However, because so much of the world is already served by twisted-pair wire, it will no doubt be used for years to come, both for voice messages and for modem-transmitted computer data (dial-up connections).

The prevalence of twisted-pair wire gives rise to what experts call the "last-mile problem" (Chapter 2, p. 56). That is, it is relatively easy for telecommunications companies to upgrade the physical connections between cities and even between neighborhoods. But it is expensive for them to replace the "last mile" of twisted-pair wire that connects to individual houses. When replacements are made, however, a newer kind of high-speed twisted-wire cable called Cat7 (Category 7) may be used, a type of connector used for Ethernet networks but also excellent for carrying telephone and video signals.

COAXIAL CABLE **Coaxial cable, commonly called "co-ax," is a high-frequency transmission cable that consists of insulated copper wire wrapped in a solid or braided metal shield and then in an external plastic cover.** Co-ax is widely used for cable television and cable Internet connections. Thanks to the extra insulation, coaxial cable is much better than twisted-pair wiring at resisting noise. Moreover, it can carry voice and data at a faster rate (up to 200 megabits per second; residential cable, 4–10 megabits per second). Often many coaxial cables are bundled together.

Coaxial cable and connector

FIBER-OPTIC CABLE **A fiber-optic cable consists of dozens or hundreds of thin strands of glass or plastic that transmit pulsating beams of light rather than electricity.** These strands, each as thin as a human hair, can transmit up to about 2 billion pulses per second (2 gigabits); each "on" pulse represents 1 bit. When bundled together, fiber-optic strands in a cable 0.12 inch thick can support a quarter- to a half-million voice conversations at the same time. Moreover, unlike electrical signals, light pulses are not affected by random electromagnetic

More on the Last Mile: Why Is It Still an Issue?

http://searchnetworking.techtarget.com/definition/last-mile-technology

interference in the environment. Thus, fiber-optic cable has a much lower error rate than normal telephone wire and cable. In addition, fiber-optic cable is lighter and more flexible, and it requires less power to transmit signals than twisted-pair wire and co-ax cable. A final advantage is that it cannot easily be wiretapped, so transmissions are more secure.

(*left*) Fiber-optic strands; (*above*) fiber-optic cable being collected on a giant spool

Wired Communications Media for Homes

Ethernet, phone line network, and power line network are three ways to create a home network.

Many households now have more than one computer, and many have taken steps to link their equipment in a home network. Indeed, some new high-tech homes include network technology that links as many as 12 televisions positioned around the house plus computers, telephones, lights, audio, and alarm systems.

Traditionally, wired media have been used to connect equipment. Three wired network technologies are *Ethernet, phone line,* and *power line.*

ETHERNET Most personal PCs come with Ethernet capability. Homes wanting to network with this technology generally use the kind of cabling (Cat5) that permits either regular Ethernet data speeds (10 megabits per second) or Fast Ethernet speeds (100 megabits per second). Besides cabling, which will have to be installed throughout the house (by you or by a professional installer), a home Ethernet network may require a few routers.

PHONE LINE NETWORK: USING THE HOME'S EXISTING TELEPHONE WIRING Does your house have a phone jack in every room in which you have a computer? Then you might be interested in setting up a *phone line network,* using conventional phone lines to connect the nodes in a network. The means for doing this is HomePNA (HPNA) technology, an alliance of leading technology companies working to ensure the adoption of a single, unified existing wire (telephone and cable) home-networking standard that transmits data at about 320 megabits per second.

POWER LINE NETWORK: USING THE HOME'S EXISTING ELECTRIC POWER WIRING Alternatively, you might want to set up a *power line network,* using conventional power lines in a home to connect the nodes in a network, using HomePlug. HomePlug technology is a standard that allows users to send data over a home's existing electric (AC) power lines, which can be transmitted at up to 200 megabits per second. This kind of communications medium has an advantage, of course, in that there is at least one power outlet in every room.

Some households have a combination of wired and wireless networks, but more are going over to all wireless.

Do We Need More Fiber Optics?

Google has long been buying up data communications capacity, especially fiber optics. Its search engine works by making copies of nearly every page of the Internet in its own data centers. That requires Google to move a huge amount of data around the world on a regular basis. And its delivery of applications over the Internet uses even more bandwidth. So, it has already established home fiber-optic service in Kansas City, Austin, and Provo and is planning to expand.

www.technologyreview.com/news/514176/google-fibers-ripple-effect/

www.ibtimes.com/fiber-optic-innovation-could-hold-key-bandwidth-breakthrough-twist-data-transmission-1326511#

https://fiber.google.com/about/

http://en.wikipedia.org/wiki/Google_Fiber

HPNA adapter for house phone lines

Corinex AV192 Phoneline Ethernet Bridge Bundle, HPNA HomePNA V3.1

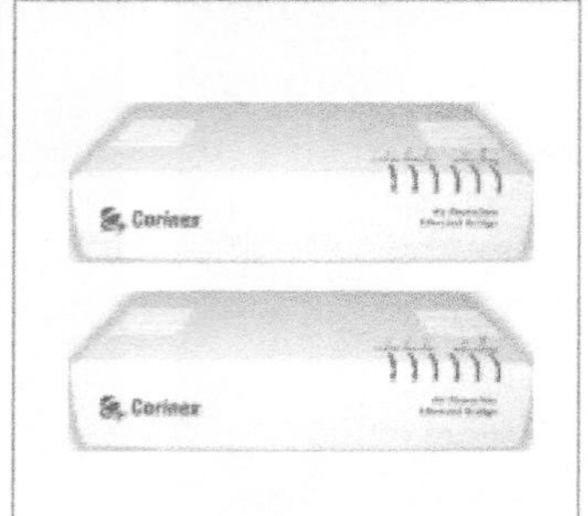

199,90 EUR

incl. 19 % Tax excl.Shipping costs

Shipping time: 1 Day (Available)**

1 add to Basket

Corinex AV192 PhoneLine Ethernet Adapter over Phone Line (2 Desktop Adapter)

Compatible with Corinex AV128 / Siemens HPN-3300 (Switzerland)

The Corinex AV192 Phoneline Desktop Adapter enables you to set up your private network at home with your existing telephone line. the Corinex adapter can quickly extend the existing lan environment. No additional network wiring is necessary when using the existing phoneline-ready connection in your wall, you can get up to 192Mbps in their home network for broadband internet or IPTV transmission. Corinex AV192 Phoneline Adapter can operate in parallel with any HPNA devices.

Home network web service site

Contact Us Site Map Password Help

HOME | ABOUT US | PRODUCTS | TECHNOLOGY | NEWS & EVENTS | JOIN | LOGIN

Latest News

nVoy Certification to Usher Hybrid Home Networking into the Mainstream more »

Consortium for Smart Energy Profile 2 Interoperability (CSEP) Applauds SEP Standard Ratification more »

Tech Tour Takes HomePlug Technology To Major U.S. TV Markets more »

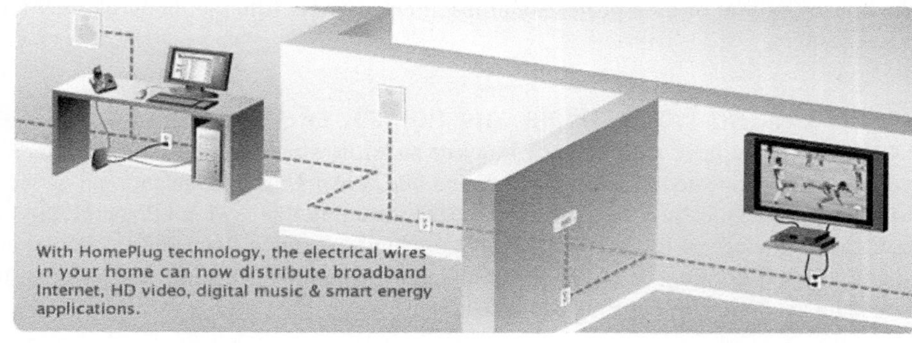

With HomePlug technology, the electrical wires in your home can now distribute broadband Internet, HD video, digital music & smart energy applications.

HomePlug Online Webinar
update on HomePlug activities

HomePlug 的信息

The HomePlug Alliance is a global industry organization with 60 member companies. more »

HOW HOMEPLUG TECHNOLOGIES ENABLE...

Smart Grid & Smart Energy

HDTV Networking

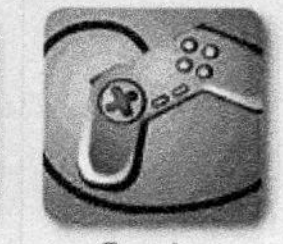

Whole Home Audio

Gaming

TECHNOLOGY STANDARDS

HOMEPLUG BROADBAND-SPEED TECHNOLOGIES

HOMEPLUG GP "GREEN PHY"

IEEE 1901 POWERLINE NETWORKING STANDARD

SMART ENERGY PROFILE 2

6.4 WIRELESS COMMUNICATIONS MEDIA

The term wireless describes telecommunications in which electromagnetic waves (rather than wire or cable) carry the signal over part or all of the communication path.

Wireless use has boomed in recent times. Today, 91% of American adults own some sort of cellphone, and 56% are smartphone owners.[19] A third also own a tablet.[20] Finally, 31% of current cell Internet users say that they mostly go online using their cellphone, and not using some other device such as a desktop or a laptop.[21]

Mobile devices are only one aspect of wireless communication. We consider (1) the electromagnetic spectrum, (2) the five types of long-distance wireless communications media, (3) long-distance wireless, and (4) short-distance wireless.

The Electromagnetic Spectrum, the Radio-Frequency (RF) Spectrum, & Bandwidth

The electromagnetic spectrum is the range of all possible frequencies of electromagnetic radiation that exist in the world and throughout the universe.

Often it's inefficient or impossible to use wired media for data transmission, and wireless transmission is better. To understand wireless communication, we need to understand transmission signals and the electromagnetic spectrum.

THE ELECTROMAGNETIC SPECTRUM Telephone signals, radar waves, microwaves, and the invisible commands from a garage-door opener all represent different waves on what is called the electromagnetic spectrum of radiation. The **electromagnetic spectrum of radiation is the basis for *all* telecommunications signals, carried by both wired and wireless media.** Part of the electromagnetic spectrum is the **radio-frequency (RF) spectrum, fields of electric energy and magnetic energy that carry most communications signals.** (• *See Panel 6.13, next page.*)

Internationally, the RF spectrum is allocated by the International Telecommunications Union (ITU) in Geneva, Switzerland. Within the United States, the RF spectrum is further allocated to nongovernment and government users. The Federal Communications Commission (FCC), acting under the authority of Congress, allocates and assigns frequencies to nongovernment users. The National Telecommunications and Information Administration (NTIA) is responsible for departments and agencies of the U.S. government.

HOW ELECTROMAGNETIC WAVES VARY Electromagnetic waves vary according to *frequency*—the number of times a wave repeats, or makes a cycle, in a second. As Panel 6.13 shows, the radio-frequency spectrum ranges from low-frequency waves, such as those used for garage-door openers (40 megahertz), through the medium frequencies for certain cellphones (824–849 megahertz) and air-traffic control monitors (1,000–1,600 megahertz), to deep-space radio communications (2,290–2,300 megahertz). Frequencies at the very ends of the spectrum take the forms of infrared rays, visible light, and (not shown in the illustration) ultraviolet light, X-rays, and gamma rays.

BANDWIDTH The bandwidth is the range, or *band,* of frequencies that a transmission medium can carry in a given period of time. For analog signals, bandwidth is expressed in *hertz (Hz),* or *cycles per second.* For example, certain cellphones operate in the range 824–849 megahertz—that is, their bandwidth is 26 megahertz. *The wider a medium's bandwidth, the more frequencies it can use to transmit data and thus the faster the transmission.*

There are two general classes of bandwidth—narrow and broad—which can be expressed in hertz but also in *bits per second (bps):*

- **Narrowband: Narrowband, also known as *voiceband,* is used for regular telephone communications**—that is, for speech, faxes, and data. Dial-up modems use this bandwidth.
- **Broadband:** In general, **broadband refers to telecommunications in which a wide band of frequencies is available to transmit information,** which means it can

Visible Light

name of wave: Radio waves, Microwaves, Infrared, Ultraviolet, X-rays, Gamma

wavelength (meters): 10^2, 1^1m, 1m, 10^{-1}, 10^{-2}, 10^{-3}, 10^{-4}, 10^{-5}, 10^{-6}m, 10^{-7}m, 10^{-8}, 10^{-9}, 10^{-10}, 10^{-11}, 10^{-12}

length of wavelength: football field, human, bee, pin head, cell, bacteria, virus, atom, nuclei

Varying wave size. Waves in the electromagnetic spectrum range in size from very long radio waves the size of buildings to very short gamma rays smaller than the size of the nucleus of an atom (*http://science.hq.nasa.gov/kids/imagers/ems/index.html*).

be sent on many different frequencies concurrently, so that more can be transmitted within a given amount of time (Chapter 2, p. 52). This resembles the situation in which more lanes on a highway allow more cars to travel on it at the same time.

Broadband is used to transmit high-speed data and high-quality audio and video. Transmission speeds are 1.5 megabits per second for regular broadband to 1 gigabit per second or more for super-broadband and ultra-broadband. Today in the United States *average* download broadband speed is 7.4 megabits per second, twice as fast as it was two years ago. This puts the United States in eighth place in the world, up from 22nd in 2009.[22]

The United States has had the reputation of lagging behind Europe and Asia in broadband networks, but by many measures it leads the world, and the networks are improving at a more rapid rate than those of other countries. Over the last three years, U.S. broadband systems have doubled in speed, while Europe's have not changed.[23] Today, 82% of U.S. homes have access to speeds in excess of 100 megabits per second, whereas in Europe, only 2% of the population does so.[24]

panel 6.13

The radio-frequency spectrum (below)
The radio-frequency spectrum, which carries most communications signals, appears as part of the electromagnetic spectrum.

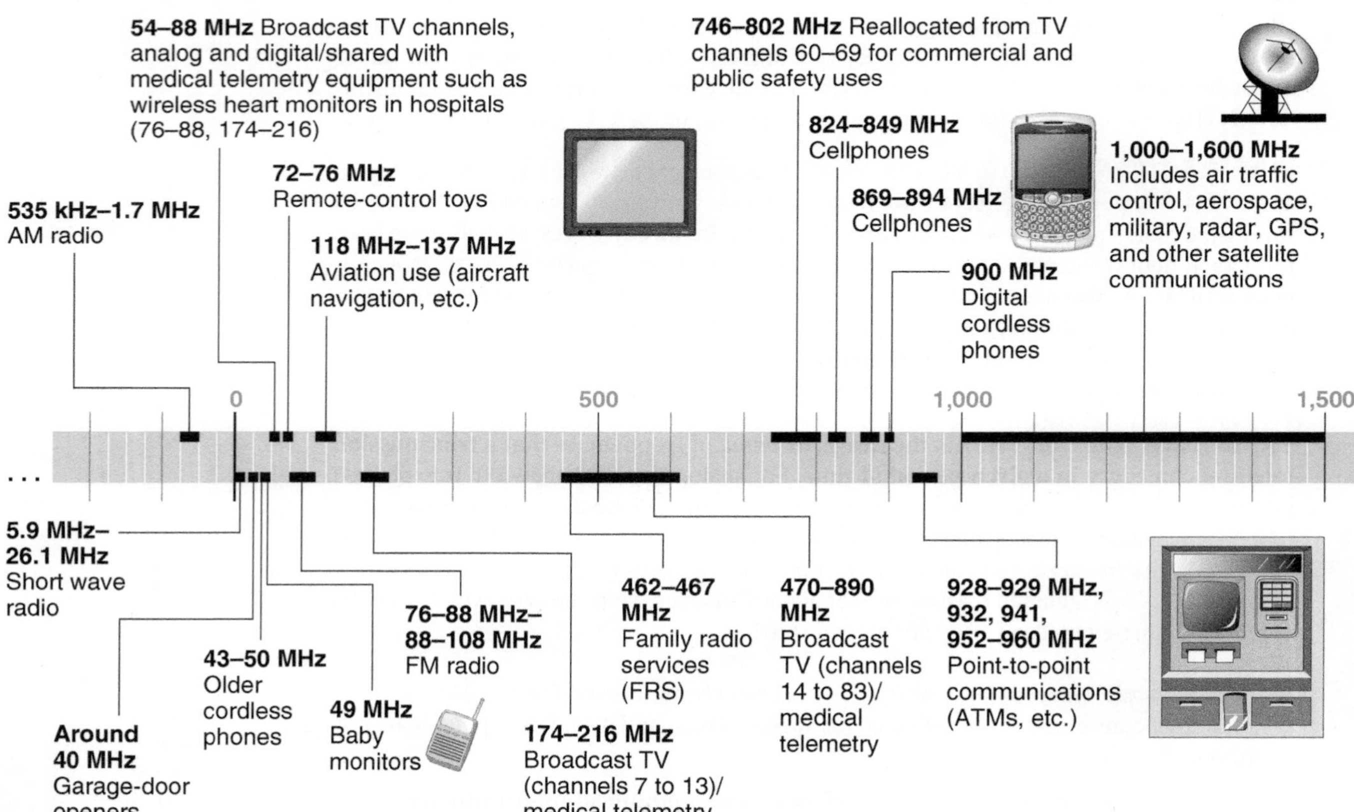

WAP: WIRELESS APPLICATION PROTOCOL Wireless handheld devices such as cellphones use the Wireless Application Protocol for connecting wireless users to the World Wide Web. Just as the protocol TCP/IP was designed to give you a wired connection to your Internet access provider, **the Wireless Application Protocol (WAP) is a standard designed to link nearly all mobile devices to your telecommunications carrier's wireless network and content providers.** WAP is supported by all operating systems, just as TCP/IP is. (Note that the acronym WAP is also used for wireless access point, p. 315.)

Five Types of Wireless Communications Media

The five types of wireless media are infrared transmission, broadcast radio, cellular radio, microwave radio, and communications satellite.

INFRARED TRANSMISSION **Infrared wireless transmission sends data signals using infrared-light waves at a frequency too low (1–16 megabits per second) for human eyes to receive and interpret.** Infrared ports (*IrDA,* for *Infrared Data Association,* discussed in Chapter 4, p. 221) can be found on some laptop computers, digital cameras, and printers, as well as wireless mice. TV remote-control units use infrared transmission. The drawbacks are that *line-of-sight* communication is required—there must be an unobstructed view between transmitter and receiver—and transmission is confined to short range.

BROADCAST RADIO When you tune in to an AM or FM radio station, you are using **broadcast radio, a wireless transmission medium that sends data over long distances at up to 2 megabits per second—between regions, states, or countries.** A transmitter is required to send messages and a receiver to receive them; sometimes both sending and receiving functions are combined in a *transceiver.*

In the lower frequencies of the radio spectrum, several broadcast radio bands are reserved not only for conventional AM/FM radio but also for broadcast television, CB (citizens band) radio, ham (amateur) radio, cellphones, and private radio-band mobile services (such as police, fire, and taxi dispatch). Some organizations use specific radio frequencies and networks to support wireless communications. For example, UPC (Universal Product Code) bar-code readers (p. 262) are used by grocery store clerks restocking store shelves to

AM & FM Radio: What's the Difference?

FM radio works the same way that AM radio works. The difference is in how the carrier wave is modulated, or altered. With AM radio, the amplitude, or overall strength, of the signal is varied to incorporate the sound information. With FM, the frequency (the number of times each second that the current changes direction) of the carrier signal is varied.

FM signals have a great advantage over AM signals. Both signals are susceptible to slight changes in amplitude. With an AM broadcast, these changes result in static. With an FM broadcast, slight changes in amplitude don't matter; since the audio signal is conveyed through changes in frequency, the FM receiver can just ignore changes in amplitude. The result: no static at all.

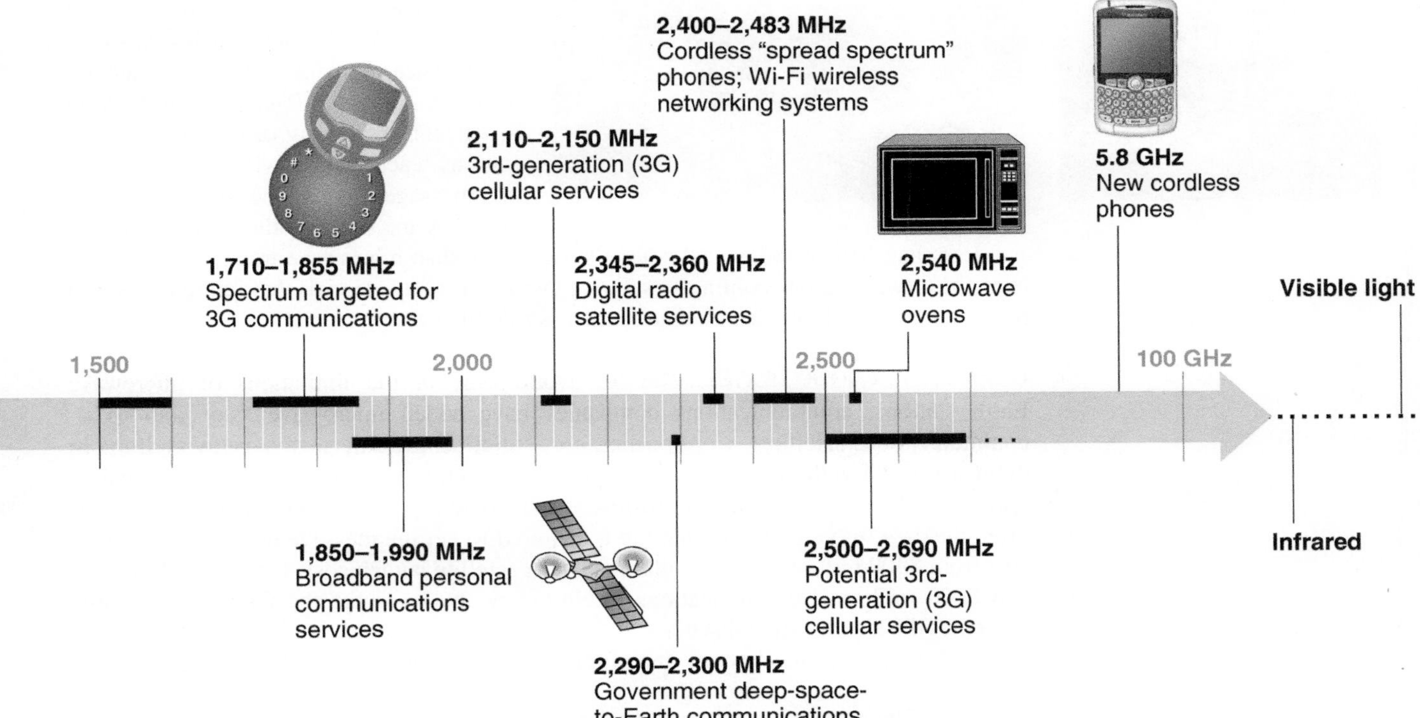

communicate with a main computer so that the store can control inventory levels. In addition, there are certain web-enabled devices that follow standards such as Wi-Fi (wireless fidelity), as we discuss in a few pages.

CELLULAR RADIO Actually a form of broadcast radio, **cellular radio is widely used for cellphones and wireless modems, using high-frequency radio waves to transmit voice and digital messages.** Unlike CB (citizens band) radio, used by truck drivers, which has a few radio channels that everyone must share, cellular radio channels are reused simultaneously in nearby geographic areas, yet customers do not interfere with one another's calls.

We discuss cellphones in more detail starting on page 335.

MICROWAVE RADIO Microwave radio transmits voice and data at 45 megabits per second through the atmosphere as superhigh-frequency radio waves called *microwaves,* which vibrate at 2.4 gigahertz (2.4 billion hertz) per second or higher. These frequencies are used not only to operate microwave ovens but also to transmit messages between ground-based stations and satellite communications systems. One short-range microwave standard used for communicating data is *Bluetooth,* as we shall discuss.

Nowadays horn-shaped microwave reflective dishes, which contain transceivers and antennas, are nearly everywhere—on towers, buildings, and hilltops. Why, you might wonder, do we have to interfere with nature by putting a microwave dish on top of a mountain? As with infrared waves, microwaves are line of sight; they cannot bend around corners or around Earth's curvature, so there must be an unobstructed view between transmitter and receiver. Thus, microwave stations need to be placed within 25–30 miles of each other, with no obstructions in between. The size of the dish varies with the distance (perhaps 2–4 feet in diameter for short distances, 10 feet or more for long distances). In a string of microwave relay stations, each station will receive incoming messages, boost the signal strength, and relay the signal to the next station.

More than half of today's telephone systems use dish microwave transmission. However, the airwaves are becoming so saturated with microwave signals that future needs will have to be satisfied by other channels, such as satellite systems.

COMMUNICATIONS SATELLITES To avoid some of the limitations of microwave Earth stations, communications companies have added microwave "sky stations"—communications satellites. **Communications satellites are microwave relay stations in orbit around Earth.** Transmitting a signal from a ground station to a satellite is called *uplinking;* the reverse is called *downlinking.* The delivery process will be slowed if, as is often the case, more than one satellite is required to get the message delivered. Satellites cost from $300 million to $700 million each. A satellite launch costs between $50 million and $400 million. Communications satellites are the basis for the Global Positioning System (GPS), as we shall discuss.

Satellite systems may occupy one of three zones in space: *GEO, MEO,* and *LEO.*

- **GEO:** The highest level, known as *geostationary Earth orbit (GEO),* is 22,300 miles and up and is always directly above the equator. Because satellites in this orbit travel at the same speed as Earth's rotation, they appear to an observer on the ground to be stationary in space—that is, they are geostationary. Consequently, microwave Earth stations are always able to beam signals to a fixed location above. The orbiting satellite has solar-powered transceivers to receive the signals, amplify them, and retransmit them to another Earth station. At this high orbit, fewer satellites are required for global coverage; however, their quarter-second delay (latency, or lag) makes two-way conversations and real-time online activities difficult.

Broadband satellite Internet has a high latency problem owing to the signal having to travel to an altitude of 22,300 miles above sea level (from the equator) out into space to a satellite in geostationary orbit and back to earth again. The signal delay can be as much as 500–900 milliseconds,

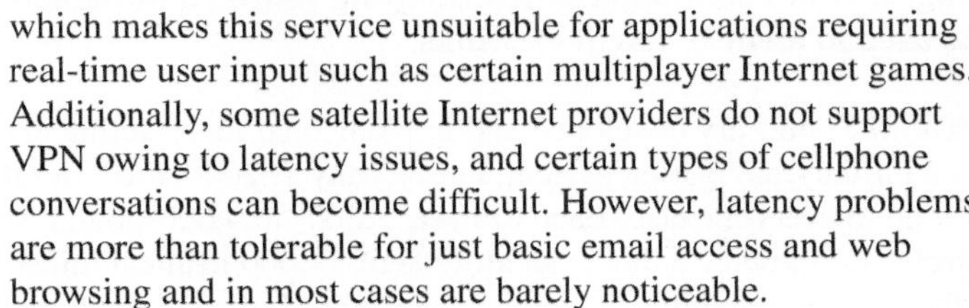

which makes this service unsuitable for applications requiring real-time user input such as certain multiplayer Internet games. Additionally, some satellite Internet providers do not support VPN owing to latency issues, and certain types of cellphone conversations can become difficult. However, latency problems are more than tolerable for just basic email access and web browsing and in most cases are barely noticeable.

- **MEO:** The *medium-Earth orbit (MEO)* is 5,000–10,000 miles up. It requires more satellites for global coverage than does GEO.
- **LEO:** The *low-Earth orbit (LEO)* is 200–1,000 miles up and has no signal delay. LEO satellites may be smaller and are much cheaper to launch.

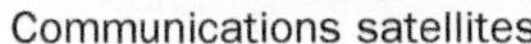

Communications satellites

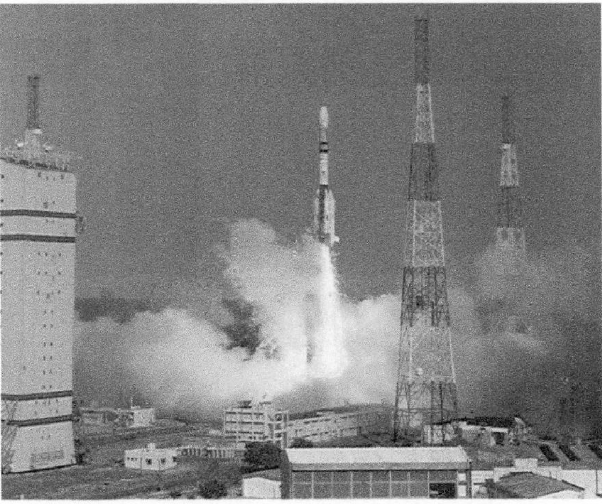

Satellite launch in India

GEO

MEO

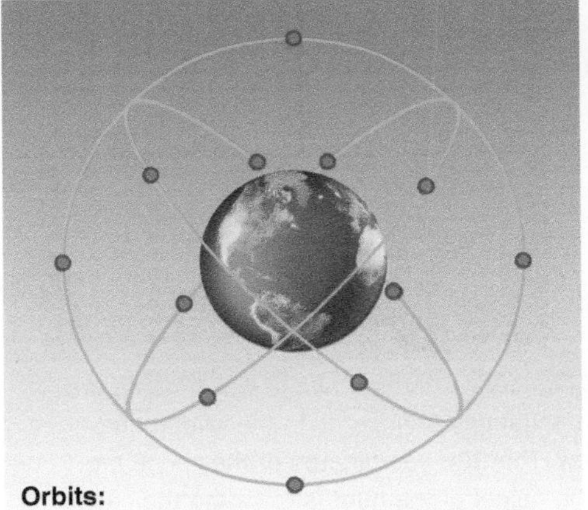

LEO

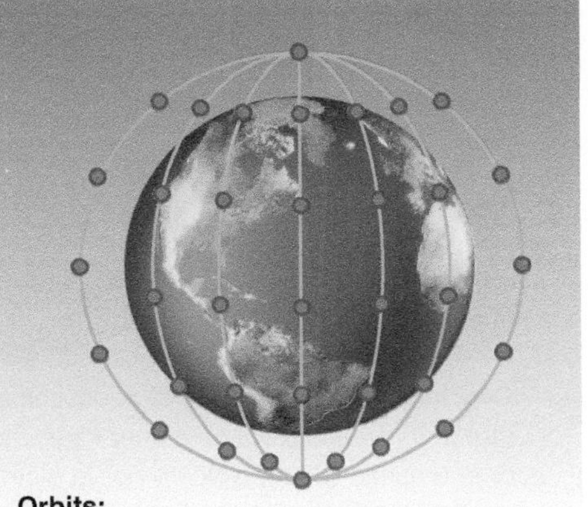

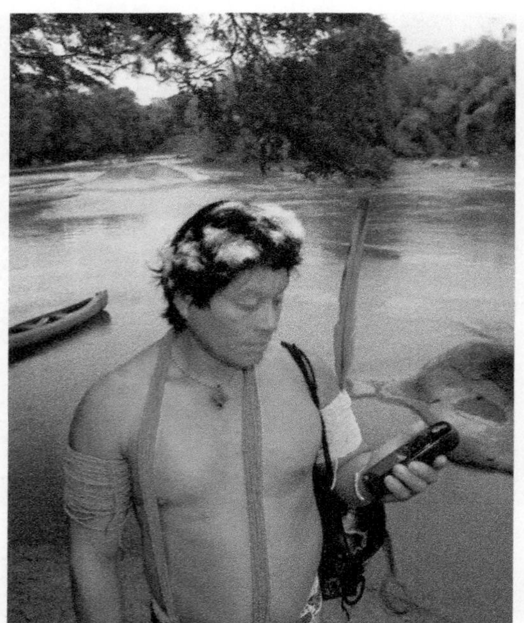

Trio Indian using GPS for mapping in Kwamalasamutu, Suriname

Long-Distance Wireless: One-Way Communication

GPS is an important one-way wireless communications technology.

Mobile wireless communications have been around for some time. The Detroit Police Department started using two-way car radios in 1921. Mobile telephones were introduced in 1946. Today, however, we are in the midst of an explosion in mobile wireless use that is making worldwide changes.

There are essentially two ways to move information through the air long distance on radio frequencies—one way and two way. *One-way communications,* discussed below, is typified by the satellite navigation system known as the Global Positioning System and by some pagers. *Two-way communication,* described on page 335, is exemplified by cellphones.

GPS SYSTEMS A $10 billion infrastructure developed by the military, the **Global Positioning System (GPS) consists of 24–32 MEO Earth-orbiting satellites continuously transmitting timed radio signals that can be used to identify Earth locations.**

- **How GPS works:** The U.S. military developed and implemented this satellite network in the 1970s as a military navigation system, but on May 1, 2000, the federal government opened it up to everyone else. Each of these 3,000- to 4,000-pound, solar-powered satellites circles Earth twice a day at an altitude of 11,000 nautical miles. A GPS receiver—handheld or mounted in a vehicle, plane, or boat—can pick up transmissions from any four satellites, interpret the information from each, and pinpoint the receiver's longitude, latitude, and altitude. (• *See Panel 6.14.)* The system is accurate within 3–50 feet, with 10 feet being the norm. Most smartphones include a GPS.
- **The limitations of GPS:** Not all services based on GPS technology are reliable, as any frequent user of online mapping systems knows by now. For those systems to generate accurate directions, they need to have the latest data about road characteristics—such as one-way streets, turns, and exits.

Geocaching

For more details on how to go geocaching and what equipment is needed, try:

www.geocaching.com/

http://adventure.howstuffworks.com/outdoor-activities/hiking/geocaching.htm

http://blog.geocaching.com/2013/01/a-geocaching-beginners-guide-geocache-container-pictures/

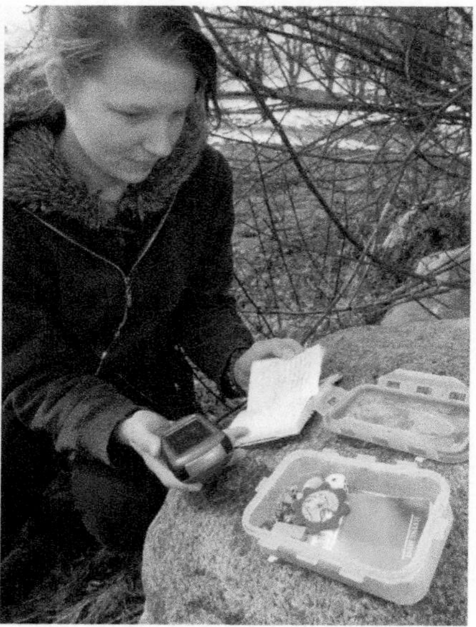

Geocaching. GPS is used for geocaching, a high-tech treasure hunt in which items are stored in a waterproof container ("geocache") that can be located in the wilderness or in a public venue, typically not in plain view. The GPS coordinates of the cache are published on the geocaching website, and the object of the hunt is to locate the cache and enter your name in the logbook as well as move objects from one cache to the next. In addition, geocachers may want to share their experiences online.

The ABCs of GPS

Developed by the U.S. military to aid ship and plane navigation, the Global Positioning System has evolved to serve a variety of purposes, with GPS receivers in everything from cars to handheld devices. The system has three main components—a satellite constellation, ground control, and receivers.

Space

There are about 24–32 satellites orbiting Earth at an altitude of 11,000 nautical miles. Each is equipped with an atomic clock that keeps time to three-billionths of a second. The satellites send time-stamped radio signals to Earth at the speed of light.The signals include information about each satellite's exact position.

Ground control

Five stations around the world monitor the satellites and send them information about their orbital position. The main control center is in Colorado Springs, Colorado.

The receiver

The receiver must pick up signals from at least four satellites. It calculates its distance from each satellite by comparing the time stamp of the signal to the time it reached the receiver. The receiver's clock isn't nearly as accurate as the atomic clocks in the satellites, but mathematical adjustments are made to account for inaccuracies.

Connect four

The basic premise of GPS is a concept called triangulation. Using this concept, the exact location of a golf ball on a two-dimensional course can be calculated by determining its distance from three pins.

The distance from pin 1 reveals possible locations anywhere along the edge of an imaginary circle.

The distances from pins 1 and 2 reveal two possible ball locations—the point where the circles intersect.

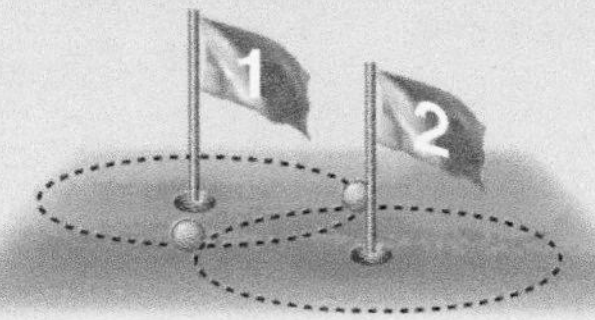

The distances from pins 1, 2, and 3 reveal one possible location—the point where all three circles intersect.

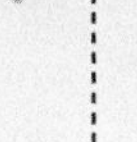

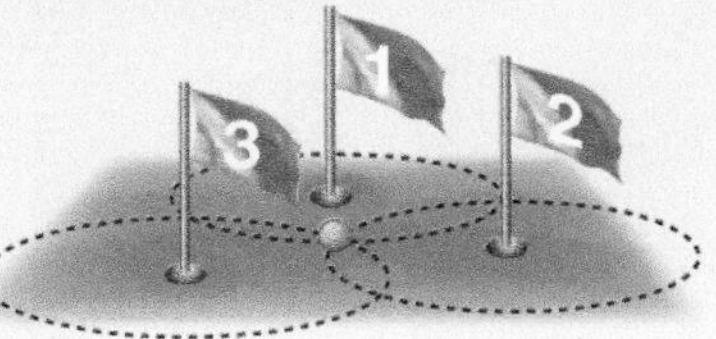

Triangulation works the same way in three-dimensional space, but with spheres instead of circles and a fourth reference point is needed.

panel 6.14

GPS

The Global Positioning System uses 24 satellites, developed for military use, to pinpoint a location on Earth's surface.

A location technology advanced by the Federal Communications Commission (FCC) is E911 (Enhanced 911), which enables mobile phones to process 911 emergency calls and enables emergency services to locate the geographic position of the caller. Most 911 systems automatically report the telephone number and location of 911 calls made from landline phones, and the FCC also requires wireless telephone carriers to provide 911 and E911 capability.[25] However, emergency operators answering E911 cellphone calls have also often found some unsettling results, in which the information giving the caller's location either didn't appear or was inaccurate.

GPS & Cellphone Tracking

Are cellphone companies tracking your every move and compiling information about you?

www.bloomberg.com/news/2013-06-06/carriers-sell-users-tracking-data-in-5-5-billion-market.html

www.nytimes.com/2012/07/15/sunday-review/thats-not-my-phone-its-my-tracker.html

www.stopcellphonetracking.com/are-cellphone-companies-profiting-from-tracking-you/

https://ssd.eff.org/wire/protect/cell-tracking

http://bits.blogs.nytimes.com/2013/04/25/for-congress-a-question-of-cellphone-tracking/?_r=0

TECH TALES "Gotcha, Thief!" & Other Uses of GPS

Hoping to deter addicts who steal painkillers, the New York Police Department is stocking pharmacy shelves with decoy pill bottles that appear to be oxycodone, a drug that is widely abused and susceptible to theft. Instead of the painkiller, however, each bottle will contain a GPS device that will allow detectives to track thieves in the period immediately after a robbery.[26] In Oklahoma and other parts of the West, where drought and grass fires have pushed the price of hay to record highs, sheriffs have bugged hay bales in theft-prone fields with GPS units, leading to some arrests.[27]

An aerial camera connected to a GPS receiver can automatically tag photos with GPS coordinates, showing where the photograph was taken, which can be useful to surveyors, search-and-rescue teams, and archaeologists. GPS has been used by scientists to tag great white sharks to track them in the water and to help foresters tally the size, number, and species of trees they oversee.[28] They have helped to keep a satellite watch over a Hawaiian volcano, Mauna Loa, and to capture infinitesimal movements that may be used to predict eruptions. And GPS has been used in Mexico to monitor manta rays, to save them from extinction.

Of course the principal use of GPS systems seems to be for online mapping systems such as Google Maps or Mapquest or as car navigation units, although $50 smartphone alternatives now exist to the $1,500 in-dash units.[29] You can even buy a gadget (called BackTrack) that you can carry on your key ring that will record your car's GPS location, so you can find it in a giant parking lot.[30]

Still, GPS systems such as Siri and their ilk are by no means infallible. One recent survey found that 63% of GPS-using U.S. drivers said the navigating device has given them erroneous directions.[31] Sometimes the fault is with the online mapmakers, as when the technology instructed a Yosemite tourist to take what turned out to be an old wagon road that had been closed since 1938.[32] More often, the research shows, driver error is involved—as when a San Diego man who had flown to the East Coast unthinkingly programmed his California address as the destination in his rental car's GPS system and found himself following a route back to San Diego, 3,000 miles away.[33] ■

Many cars come with GPS units to guide users to their destinations and tell them where needed services, such as gas stations, restaurants, and so on, are located.

PAGERS Known as *beepers,* for the sound they make when activated, pagers are also a form of one-way communication. **Pagers are simple radio receivers that receive data sent from a special radio transmitter.** The radio transmitter broadcasting to the pager sends signals over a specific frequency. All the pagers for that particular network have a built-in receiver that is tuned to the same frequency broadcast from the transmitter. The pagers listen to the signal from the transmitter constantly as long as the pager is turned on.

Although generally obsolete, because they are now built into smartphones, pagers are still used in areas where cellphones are unreliable or prohibited, such as large hospital complexes. They are also used to reach some emergency personnel and to control traffic signals and some irrigation systems.

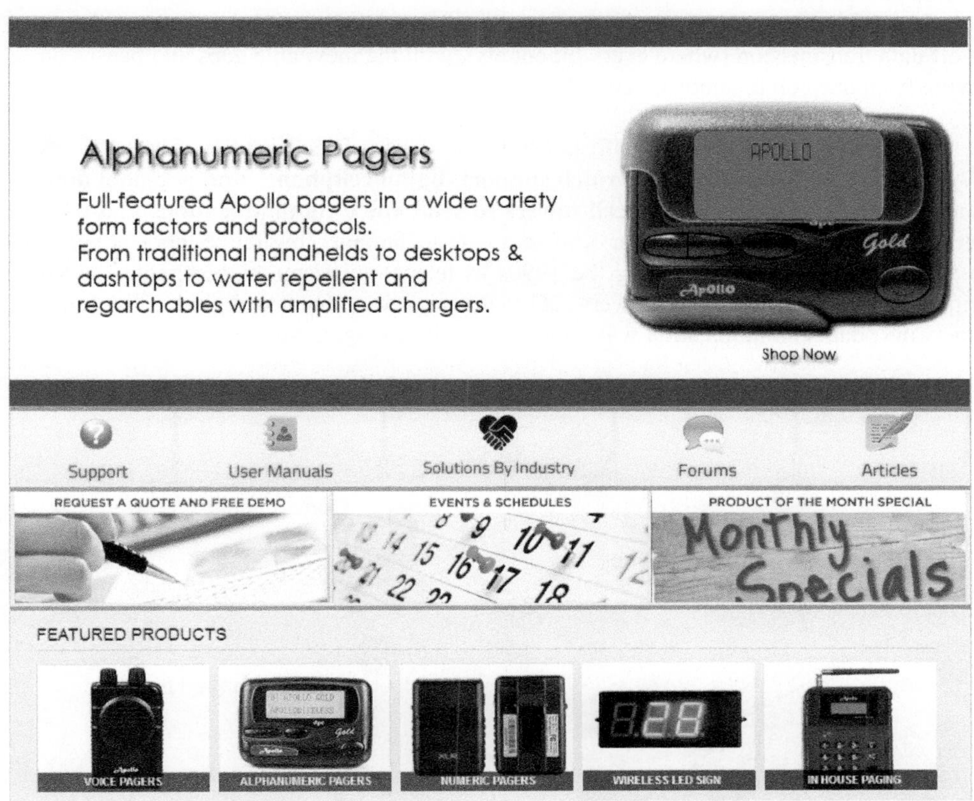

Long-Distance Wireless: Two-Way Communication

There are four generations of cellular radio, used for two-way, long-distance communication.

Two-way wireless communications devices have evolved over time from two-way pagers and wireless email devices such as the original BlackBerry, which has become an all-in-one wireless data and voice device. The categories of long-distance wireless devices we discuss here use the transmission medium known as cellular radio (p. 330), which has several levels, or generations: 1G, 2G, 3G, and 4G.

1G (FIRST-GENERATION) CELLULAR SERVICE: ANALOG CELLPHONES "In the fall of 1985," wrote *USA Today* technology reporter Kevin Maney, "I went to Los Angeles to research a story about a new phenomenon called a cellphone. I got to use one for a day. The phones then cost $1,000 and looked like field radios from *M*A*S*H.* Calls were 45 cents a minute, and total cellphone users in the world totaled 200,000."[34]

Digital cellphones are now ubiquitous. Mary Meeker, Morgan Stanley analyst, says that the world is currently in the midst of the fifth major technology cycle of the past half a century. The previous four were the mainframe era of the (1)1950s and the (2)1960s, the minicomputer era of the (3)1970s, and the desktop Internet era of the (4) 1980s. The current cycle is the era of the mobile Internet, she says—predicting that by 2014 "more users will connect to the Internet over mobile devices than desktop PCs."[35]

Cellphones are essentially two-way radios that operate using either analog or digital signals. *Analog cellphones* are designed primarily for communicating by voice through a system of ground-area cells. Each cell is hexagonal in shape, usually 8 miles or less in diameter, and is served by a transmitter-receiving tower. Communications are handled in the bandwidth of 824–849 megahertz. Calls are directed between cells by a mobile-telephone switching office (MTSO). Movement between cells requires that calls be "handed off" by this switching office. (• *See Panel 6.15.)* This technology is known as *1G,* for "first generation."

Handing off voice calls between cells poses only minimal problems. However, handing off data transmission (where every bit counts), with the inevitable gaps and pauses on moving from one cell to another, is much more difficult.

2G (SECOND-GENERATION) WIRELESS SERVICES: DIGITAL CELLPHONES & PDAS Digital wireless services—**which support digital cellphones and personal digital assistants—use a network of cell towers to send voice communications and data over the airwaves in digital form.** Known as *2G* technology, digital cellphones began replacing analog cellphones during the 1990s as telecommunications companies added digital transceivers to their cell towers. 2G technology was the first digital voice cellular network; data communication was added as an afterthought, with data speeds ranging

panel 6.15

Cellular connections

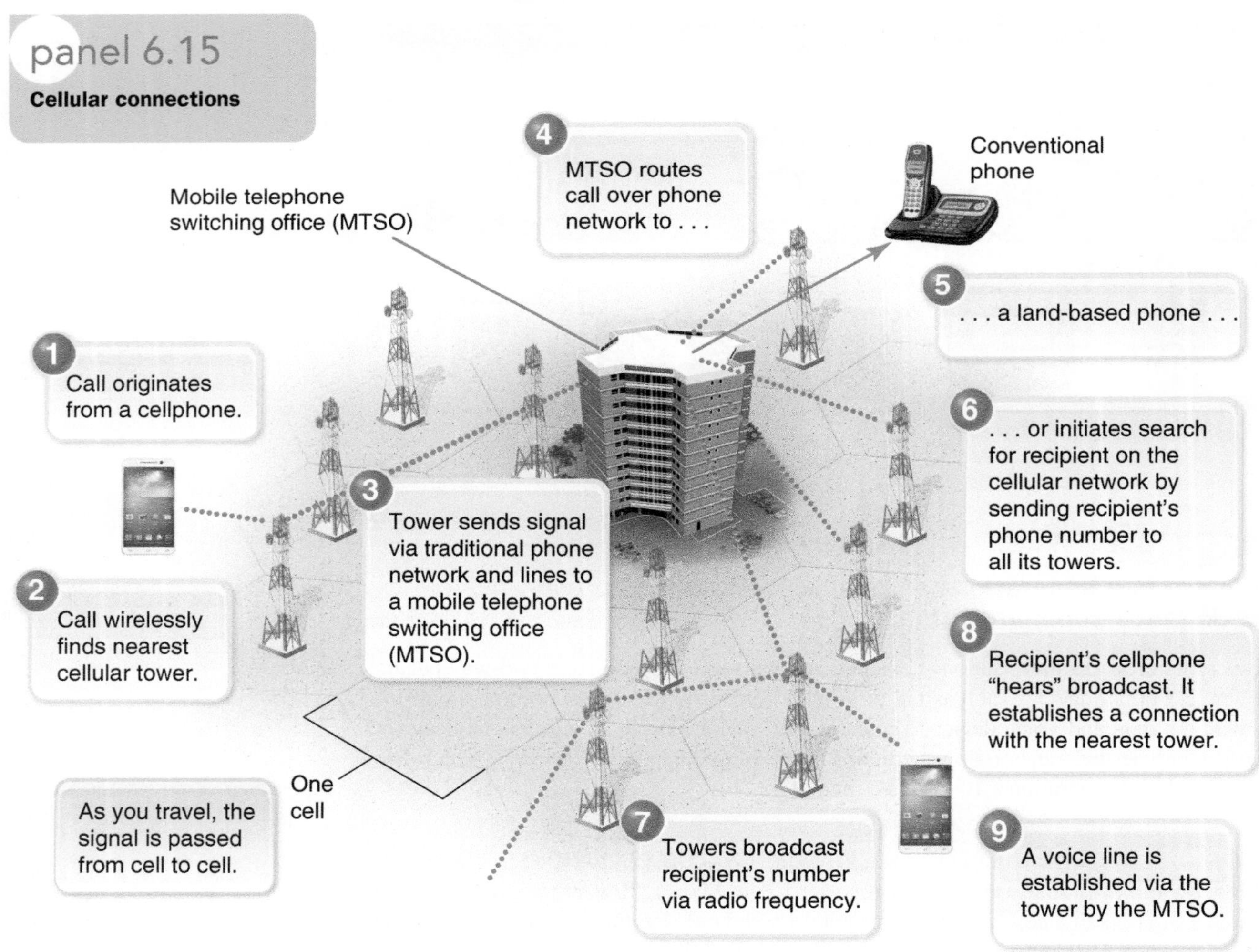
4 MTSO routes call over phone network to . . .
Conventional phone
Mobile telephone switching office (MTSO)
5 . . . a land-based phone . . .
1 Call originates from a cellphone.
6 . . . or initiates search for recipient on the cellular network by sending recipient's phone number to all its towers.
3 Tower sends signal via traditional phone network and lines to a mobile telephone switching office (MTSO).
2 Call wirelessly finds nearest cellular tower.
8 Recipient's cellphone "hears" broadcast. It establishes a connection with the nearest tower.
One cell
As you travel, the signal is passed from cell to cell.
7 Towers broadcast recipient's number via radio frequency.
9 A voice line is established via the tower by the MTSO.

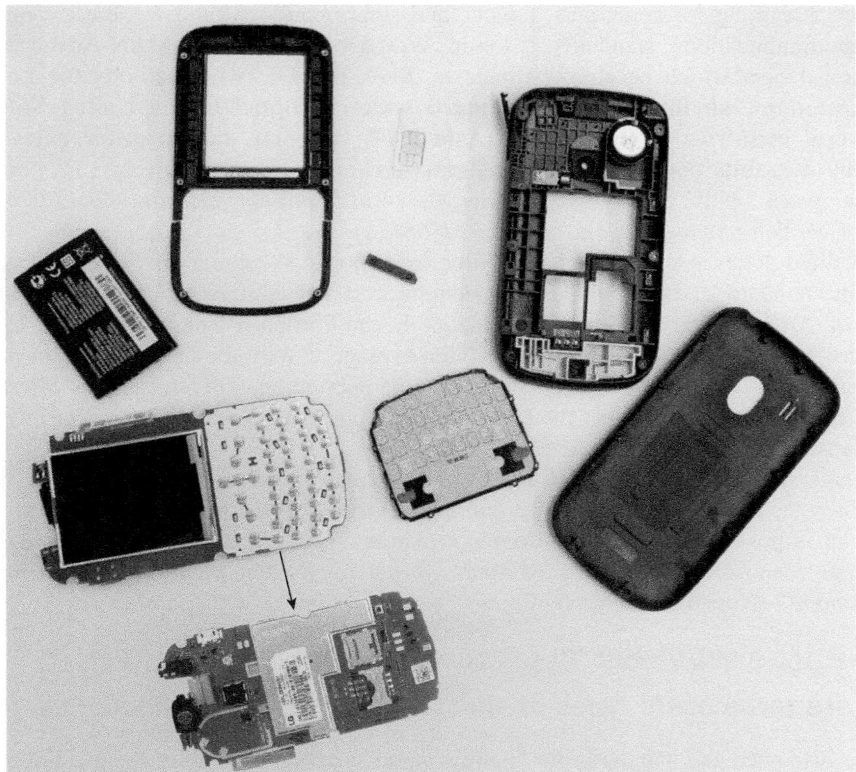

Inside a cellphone

Choosing CDMA or GSM

Many cellphones in the United States are CDMA; a few are GSM; some can work with both systems. Which one should you choose?

www.pcmag.com/article2/0,2817,2407896,00.asp

http://reviews.cnet.com/world-phone-guide/

https://en.wikipedia.org/wiki/Dual_mode_mobile

Ideal Cellphone & Service

What's the ideal cellphone and service for your area? To compare plans, go to:

http://cell-phone-providers-review.toptenreviews.com/

www.nytimes.com/2013/04/04/technology/personaltech/t-mobile-breaks-free-of-cellphone-contracts-and-penalties.html?pagewanted=all

www.cellreception.com/

www.cellphonebattles.com/

from 9.6 to 19.2 kilobits per second. 2G technology not only dramatically increased voice clarity; it also allowed the telecommunications companies to cram many more voice calls into the same slice of bandwidth.

3G (THIRD-GENERATION) WIRELESS SERVICES: SMARTPHONES 3G wireless digital services, often called *broadband technology,* are based either on the U.S. Code-Division Multiple Access (CDMA, currently the dominant network standard in North America) or Global System for Mobile Communications (GSM, used more widely in the rest of the world). They support devices that are "always on," carry data at high speeds (144 kilobits per second up to 3.1 megabits per second), accept emails with attachments, provide Internet and web access and videoconferencing capabilities, are able to display color video and still pictures, and play music.

CDMA was established earlier in North America and thus has a bit more coverage there than GSM. GSM is an international standard backed by an international organization, and the protocol is more mature and more robust. There is no clear winner in the CDMA versus GSM debate; what you use depends on your needs. Just make sure that the carrier you want to use supports the standard of the phone that you want to use.

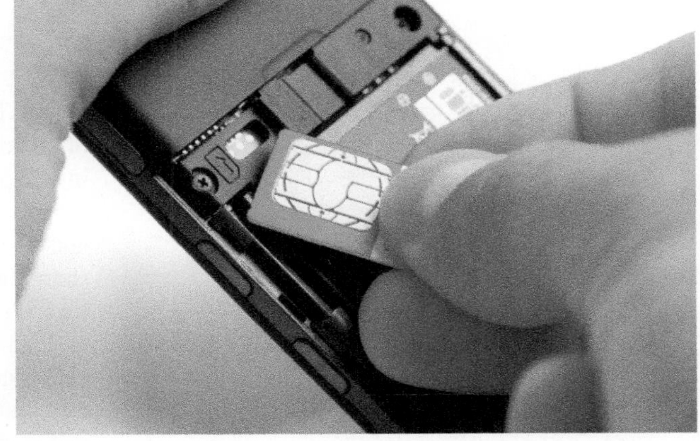

Inserting a Subscriber Identity Module (SIM) card in a smartphone; SIM cards, which allow the phone using the card to attach to a mobile network, are usually GSM; CDMA phones rely on different types of cards.

4G (FOURTH-GENERATION) WIRELESS DIGITAL SERVICES: SMARTER PHONES In 2008, the International Telecommunications Union specified the peak speed standards for 4G (fourth-generation) technology as 100 megabits per second for high-mobility communication, such as communications from cars and trains, and 1 gigabit per second for low-mobility communication (such as stationary users and pedestrians).[36] 4G does not introduce any innovative applications, but it does enable faster Internet surfing

Your Most Dangerous Possession?

Answer: Your smartphone.

http://finance.yahoo.com/news/10-dumbest-risks-people-smartphones-110029209.html

http://money.cnn.com/2011/01/11/pf/smartphone_dangers/index.htm

http://ajw.asahi.com/article/behind_news/social_affairs/AJ201306040069

and video streaming for computers, tablets, and smartphones. Although there are other 4G telecommunications standards (Mobile WiMAX and WirelessMAN-Advanced), the principal one, which became available in 2009, is **LTE (which stands for *Long Term Evolution*), an international standard widely adopted in the United States and several countries in Europe and Asia. LTE supports data transfer rates of up to 100 megabits per second over cellular networks.** (Note that every LTE phone will not work with every LTE carrier; *www.usatoday.com/story/tech/2013/07/07/sprint-att-verizon-phones-network-carriers/2486813/.*)

The United States is a leader in LTE, with most major U.S. cellular providers now supporting the standard, and 19% of U.S. connections are expected to be on LTE networks by the end of 2013, compared with fewer than 2% in the European Union. Moreover, U.S. speeds are 75% faster than the European Union average.[37] With the help of LTE, in four years nearly 286.7 million Americans, or 87% of the population, will have mobile Internet devices, and they will outnumber the U.S. home computers with broadband, according to one forecast.[38]

Although in 2013 many users still are not connected to 4G networks, Samsung has successfully tested a 5G network that promises data transmission rates hundreds of times faster than is possible today, but it does not plan to market it until 2020 (*www.new5gphone.net/; www.foxnews.com/tech/2013/05/13/forget-4g-samsung-claims-5g-smartphone-breakthrough/*). (Note that the Apple iPhone 5 is not the same as a 5G phone.)

Short-Range Wireless: Two-Way Communication

There are three basic types of short-range wireless technologies.

We have discussed the standards for high-powered wireless digital communications in the 800–1,900 megahertz part of the radio-frequency spectrum, which are considered long-range waves. Now let us consider low-powered wireless communications in the 2.4–7.5 gigahertz part of the radio spectrum, which are short range and effective only within about 30 and 250 feet of a wireless access point. This band is available globally for unlicensed, low-power uses and is set aside as an innovation zone where new devices can be tested without the need for a government license; it's also used for industrial, scientific, and medical devices.

There are three kinds of networks covered by this range:

- **Local area networks—range 100–228 feet:** These include the popular Wi-Fi standards.
- **Personal area networks—range 30–33 feet:** These use Bluetooth, ultra-wideband, and wireless USB.
- **Home automation networks—range 100–150 feet:** These use the Insteon, ZigBee, and Z-Wave standards.

SHORT-RANGE WIRELESS FOR LOCAL AREA NETWORKS: WI-FI B, A, G, & N Wi-Fi is known formally as an *802.11 network,* named for the wireless technical standard specified by the Institute of Electrical and Electronics Engineers (IEEE). As we mentioned in Chapter 2 (p. 58), *Wi-Fi*—short for *wi*reless *fi*delity—is a short-range wireless digital standard aimed at helping portable computers and handheld wireless devices to communicate at high speeds and share Internet connections at distances of 100–228 feet. You can find Wi-Fi connections, which operate at 450 megabits per second to 1.75 gigabits per second, inside offices, airports, and Internet cafés, and some enthusiasts have set up transmitters on rooftops, distributing wireless connections throughout their neighborhoods. (• *See Panel 6.16.*)

The first standard was 802.11b, which was followed by a second standard called 802.11a. Because of its higher cost, 802.11a is usually found on business networks, whereas 802.11b better serves the home market. Others that consumers use are 802.11g and 802.11n.

The Samsung Galaxy camera has Wi-Fi and 3G technology built in, allowing you to share shots in an instant without being dependent on a smart phone or tablet to make a connection to the internet.

One example of a Wi-Fi camera

Wi-Fi

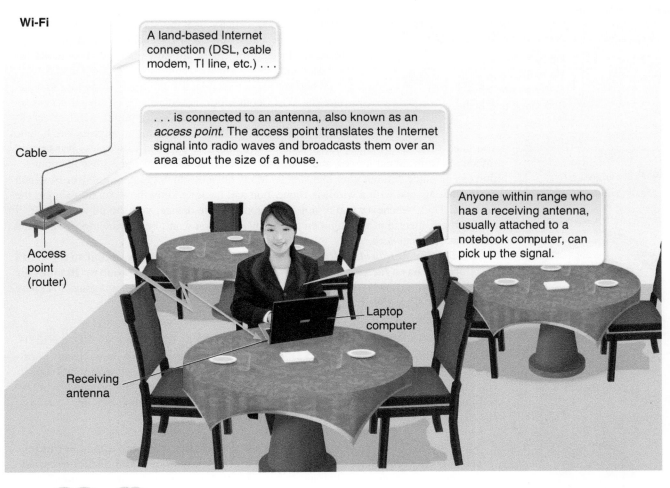

A land-based Internet connection (DSL, cable modem, TI line, etc.) . . .

. . . is connected to an antenna, also known as an *access point.* The access point translates the Internet signal into radio waves and broadcasts them over an area about the size of a house.

Anyone within range who has a receiving antenna, usually attached to a notebook computer, can pick up the signal.

Cable

Access point (router)

Laptop computer

Receiving antenna

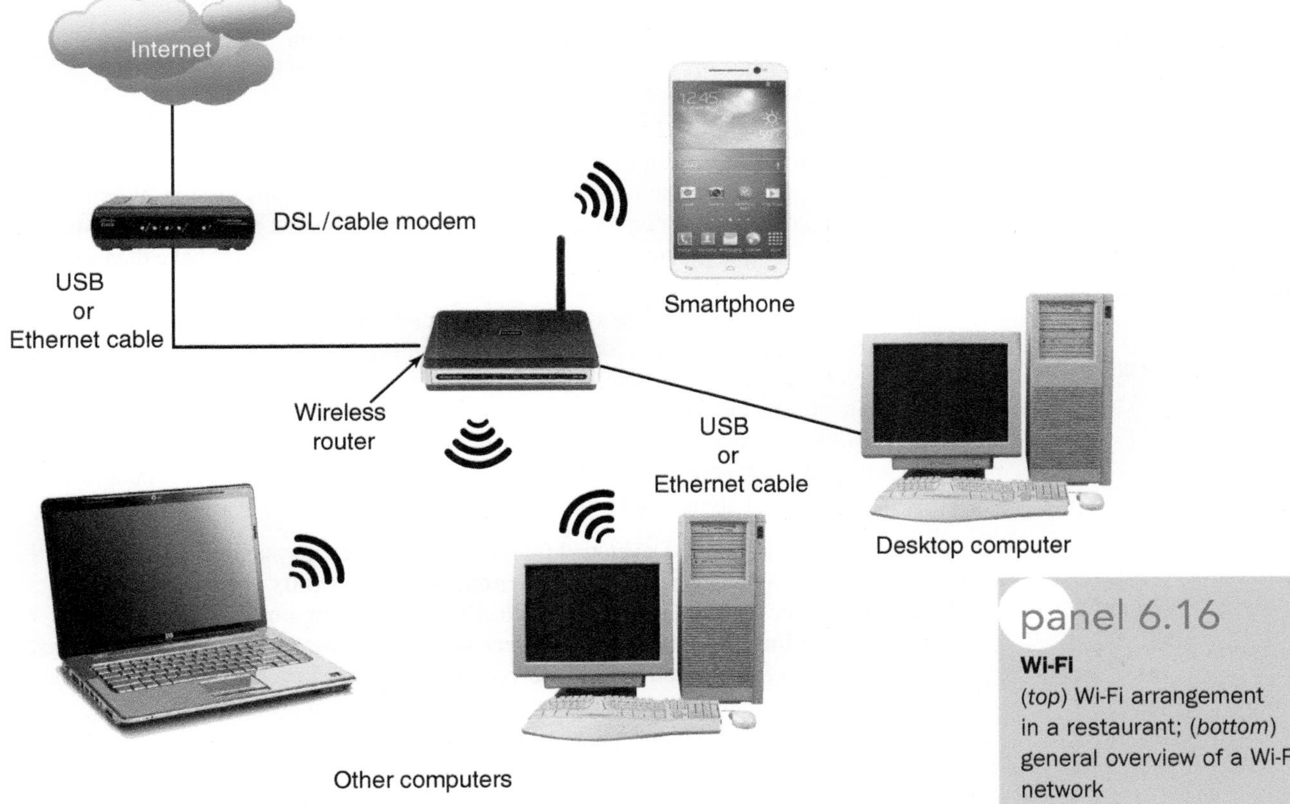

panel 6.16

Wi-Fi

(*top*) Wi-Fi arrangement in a restaurant; (*bottom*) general overview of a Wi-Fi network

Wi-Fi standards

Standard	Maximum Data Transfer Rate
802.11b	Up to 11 Mbps
802.11a	Up to 54 Mbps
802.11g	54 Mbps and higher
802.11n	600 Mbps and higher

panel 6.17

Wi-Fi standards

When you buy a router for your home Wi-Fi network, the product package usually lists the standards as "a," "b," "g," and "n." For each new Wi-Fi standard, speed and range increase. In addition, there are new encryption methods for security and other complex technology.[39] (• *See Panel 6.17.*)

Wherever the connection, it's extremely important to make sure the Wi-Fi connection is secure against illegal access by others. If you're a user of *hotspots,* or public wireless access points (Chapter 2, p. 58), such as those in airports and hotels, you need to be aware that your mobile device could be exposed to wireless transmitted infections from illegal users—and you may not even be aware of it, because the connection can be made without your knowledge. Many hotspots do not require passwords, which means that anyone with a wireless connection and hacking know-how can hop aboard the network. Thus, whenever you're not using your mobile device, you should disable Wi-Fi (in Settings), instead of leaving it on autoconnect, so you won't be unknowingly connected to a fraudulent network.

Wi-Fi symbol

WiMax (for *Worldwide Interoperability for Microwave Access*) is similar to the Wi-Fi standard but has a far greater range—up to 30 miles for a fixed station or 10 miles for a mobile station. WiMax is being employed by many users, such as universities, to extend the range of existing Wi-Fi networks.

SHORT-RANGE WIRELESS FOR PERSONAL AREA NETWORKS: BLUETOOTH, ULTRA-WIDEBAND, & WIRELESS USB As we stated, personal area networks use short-range wireless technology to connect personal electronics, such as cellphones, MP3 players, and printers in a range of 30–33 (sometimes up to 320) feet. The principal wireless technology used so far has been *Bluetooth,* which is now being joined by *ultra-wideband (UWB)* and *wireless USB.*

Bluetooth symbol

Latest Bluetooth Devices

What are the newest Bluetooth devices? See:

www.bluetooth.com

- **Bluetooth: Bluetooth is a short-range wireless digital standard aimed at linking cellphones, computers, and peripherals up to distances of about 33 feet** in casual networks called *piconets.* Piconets are established dynamically and automatically as Bluetooth-enabled devices enter and leave radio proximity, meaning that you can easily connect whenever and wherever it's convenient for you. (The name comes from Harald "Bluetooth" Gormsson, the 10th-century Danish king who unified Denmark and Norway.)

  Now transmitting up to 24 megabits per second, the original version of Bluetooth was designed to replace cables connecting PCs to printers and PDAs or wireless phones and to overcome line-of-sight problems with infrared transmission. When Bluetooth-capable devices come within range of one another, an automatic electronic "conversation" (called *pairing*) takes place to determine whether they have data to share, and then they form a mini-network to exchange that data. (• *See Panel 6.18.*)

  Bluetooth allows two devices to interact wirelessly in sometimes novel ways. A Bluetooth-equipped notebook, for example, can connect through a similarly enabled cellphone or Internet access point to send and receive email. Bluetooth is also used in automobiles for hands-free use of cellphones. In addition to the links shown, Bluetooth can be used to network similar devices—for example, to send data from PC to PC, as long as they are not more than 33 feet apart (up to about 300 feet with special added equipment). Line of sight is not required.

- **Ultra-wideband (UWB):** Developed for use in military radar systems, **ultra-wideband (UWB) is a technology operating in the range of 480 megabits per second up to 1.6 gigabytes per second up to about 30 feet that uses a low-power source to send out millions of bursts of radio energy every second over many different frequencies, which are then reassembled by a UWB receiver.** It operates over low frequencies not used by other technologies, making it a candidate to replace many of the cables that connect household and office devices. UWB systems tend to be short-range and indoor applications. High-data-rate UWB can enable wireless monitors, the efficient transfer of data from digital camcorders, wireless printing of digital pictures from a camera without the need for an intervening personal computer, and the transfer of files among cellphones

panel 6.18
Bluetooth

and other handheld devices. Uses for ultra-wideband technology in consumer networks include wireless USB, wireless high-definition video, medical imaging, next-generation Bluetooth, and peer-to-peer connections.

- **Wireless USB:** **Wireless USB (WUSB) has a typical range of 32 feet and a maximum data rate of 110–480 megabits per second.** Wireless USB is used in game controllers, printers, scanners, digital cameras, MP3 players, hard disks, and flash drives. With more than 2 billion legacy wired USB connections in the world today, USB is the de facto standard in the personal computing industry. Now these fast connections are available in the wireless world, with the introduction of wireless USB. Wireless USB combines the speed and security of wired technology with the ease of use of wireless technology. Wireless USB supports robust high-speed wireless connectivity by using a common UWB radio platform as developed by the WiMedia Alliance. The wireless standard will preserve the functionality of wired USB while also unwiring the cable connection and providing enhanced support for streaming media devices and peripherals.

Beginners Guide to Going Wireless

For some tutorials on using wireless technology, go to:

www.palowireless.com/wireless/tutorials.asp

http://compnetworking.about.com/cs/wirelessproducts/a/howtobuildwlan.htm

www.microsoft.com/athome/organization/wirelesssetup.aspx#fbid=fnnuEVQcM5r

SHORT-RANGE WIRELESS FOR HOME AUTOMATION NETWORKS: INSTEON, ZIGBEE, & Z-WAVE Home automation networks (smart homes)—those that link switches and sensors around the house and yard—use low-power, narrowband wireless technology, which operate in a range of 100–150 feet but at relatively slow data rates of 13.1–250 kilobits per second. The current standards are Insteon (*www.insteon.net/about-howitworks.html*), ZigBee (*www.zigbee.org*), and Z-Wave (*www.zwaveproducts.com*). All three are so-called mesh technologies—networked devices equipped with two-way radios that can communicate with each other rather than just with the controller, the device that serves as central command for the network.

- **Insteon:** *Insteon* combines electric power line and wireless technologies and is capable of sending data at 13.1 kilobits a second at a typical range of 150 feet. With this kind of technology, you might drive up to your house, and the garage-door device would recognize your car and open to let you in. The lights would come on, and your favorite radio station would start playing.

Meshing

The following websites provide more information about these mesh technologies:

www.insteon.net

www.zigbee.org

www.z-wavealliance.com

http://communication.howstuffworks.com/how-wireless-mesh-networks-work1.htm

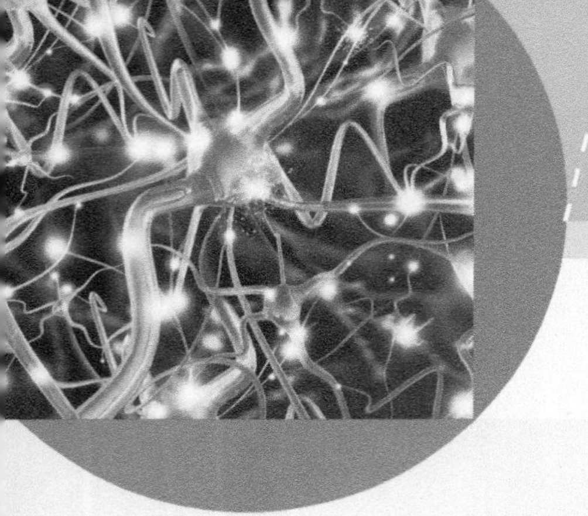

PRACTICAL ACTION

Virtual Meetings: Linking Up Electronically

There are several ways in which people can conduct "virtual meetings"—meetings that don't entail physical travel—as follows.

Audioconferencing. *Audioconferencing* (or *teleconferencing*) is simply telephone conferencing. A telephone conference-call operator can arrange this setup among any three or more users. Users don't need any special equipment beyond a standard telephone. Audioconferencing is an inexpensive way to hold a long-distance meeting and is often used in business.

Computer-based audio, involving microphones, headsets or speakers, and Internet-based telephony, is also used for audioconferencing. (See VoIP and Skype in Chapter 2.)

Videoconferencing Using Closed-Circuit TV. Some of the more sophisticated equipment is known as *telepresence technology,* high-definition videoconference systems that simulate face-to-face meetings between users (for example, *www.tandberg.com/telepresence/* and *www.telepresenceoptions.com*). Whereas traditional videoconferencing systems can be set up in a conventional conference room, telepresence systems require specially designed rooms with multiple cameras and high-definition video screens, simulating the sensation of two groups of people at identical tables facing each other through windows.

Videoconferencing Using a Webcam. A *webcam* is a tiny, often eyeball-shaped camera that sits atop a computer monitor or is built into the computer and that displays its output on a web page (Chapter 2, p. 266). Some cameras are able to automatically follow your face as you move. Headsets with built-in speakers and microphones are required. Yahoo! and MSN offer free video chatting through their instant-message programs. Webcams can also be used for VoIP and Skype conferences.

Videoconferencing Using Videophones. Videophones don't involve use of a PC, although the calls take place on the Internet. The Internet company 8 × 8 Inc., for example, makes a VoIP videophone.

Workgroup Computing or Web Conferencing. The use of groupware allows two or more people on a network to share information, collaborating on graphics, slides, and spreadsheets while linked by computer and telephone. Participants conduct meetings using tools such as "whiteboards," which can display drawings or text, along with group presentations (using PowerPoint, which displays slides on everyone's screen) and online chatting. Usually people do these things while talking to one another on the telephone. Users can collaborate by writing or editing word processing documents, spreadsheets, or presentations.

GoToMeeting offers online web conferencing support.

- **ZigBee:** *ZigBee* is an entirely wireless, very power-efficient technology that can send data at 128 kilobytes per second at a range of about 250 feet. It is primarily touted as sensor network technology and can be used in everything from automatic meter readers and medical sensing and monitoring devices to wireless smoke detectors and TV remote controls. One of the best features is that it can run for years on inexpensive batteries, eliminating the need to be plugged into an electric power line.
- **Z-Wave:** *Z-Wave* is also an entirely wireless, power-efficient technology, which can send data at 127 kilobits per second to a range of 100 feet. With a Z-Wave home, you could program the lights to go on when the garage door opens. You could program devices remotely, turning up the thermostat on the drive home from work.

Curious about Networked Homes?

For starters, try:

www.msichicago.org/whats-here/exhibits/smart-home/

www.wfs.org/futurist/july-august-2012-vol-46-no-4/smart-house-networked-home

http://arstechnica.com/business/2012/03/the-five-technologies-that-will-transform-homes-of-the-future/

www.futuretechnologyportal.com/future-home.htm

UNIT 6B: *Cyberthreats, Security, & Privacy Issues*

Do your employers allow you to use your personal smartphone, laptop, or tablet on the job—the so-called bring your own device (BYOD) policy? Then you—and they—should be aware of the security issues involved. If, for instance, the company doesn't insist cellphones should be password-protected, then what happens, asks one expert, "when the employee leaves it in a bar and anyone can look at whatever sensitive information is on it."[40]

The ongoing dilemma of the Digital Age is balancing convenience against security. **Security consists of safeguards for protecting information technology against unauthorized access, system failures, and disasters that can result in damage or loss.** Security matters are a never-ending problem, with attacks on computers and data becoming more powerful and more complex.[41]

We consider some global aspects of security and privacy in Chapter 9, but here let us discuss some of these matters that can relate to you personally:

- **Cyberintruders:** trolls, spies, hackers, and thieves
- **Cyberthreats:** denial-of-service attacks; viruses; worms; Trojan horses; rootkits and backdoors; blended threats; zombies; ransomware; and time, logic, and email bombs
- **Privacy and identity theft:** sources of these threats

6.5 CYBERINTRUDERS: Trolls, Spies, Hackers, & Thieves

Networks are susceptible to violations by unpleasant cyberintruders of all kinds.

"There isn't a corporation in the world that can't be penetrated, not one," says Mike McConnell, former U.S. Director of National Intelligence.[42] McConnell was talking about companies' openness to **cyberattacks, attempts to gain unauthorized access to or to disrupt or damage a computer system or electronic communications network.**

If no corporation is safe, what about you? And who are the penetrators or attackers? We describe the following violators, not all of whom are criminals: trolls, spies, hackers, ethical hackers, hacktivists, cyberterrorists, thieves—and employees.

Trolling

Why is trolling a meme ("meem")?

http://netforbeginners.about.com/od/weirdwebculture/f/What-Is-an-Internet-Meme.htm

Can you stop a troller?

http://keepingmumcommunications.com/stop-trolls-in-5-easy-steps/

www.osnews.com/story/25540

Trolls

Trolls aren't necessarily destructive, but they can be disruptive on online comment boards.

Not a scary fairytale creature who lives under a bridge, a **troll is a person who posts intentionally offensive, incendiary, or off-topic comments online,** to upset people. "In recent years, trolls have become a scourge," says one report. "Reasoned political discussion is often so overwhelmed by venomous, tit-for-tat name-calling that websites have to shut down their comment boards, as hundreds and even thousands of invective-filled

responses pour in."[43] The phenomenon occurs, it's suggested, because of an "online disinhibition effect" that "allows people who might never utter a hateful word in person to unleash withering vitriol on comment boards."

Spies

Many companies have extensive data-collection efforts that constantly track our personal activities.

In 2010, the average visit to one of the 50 most popular U.S. websites (such as Google, Facebook, or Yahoo!) yielded 10 instances of data collection. By March 2013, that figure had jumped to 42 instances.[44]

"The rise in data collection has been driven by the online-advertising business," says one report, "which uses information about web users to target ads. Over the past few years, hundreds of companies have been vying to place tracking technologies across the web to determine what users might want to see or buy."[45] For instance, Facebook, which has a billion-plus users, is using new ways to cull information from outside the social network to match it with data from its users, the purpose being to win over advertisers such as General Motors.[46] Advertisers are also moving beyond people's personal computers to better pinpoint mobile users' online activity on their smartphones and tablets, the better to track users across such devices.[47]

All such data collecting—spying, really—is perfectly legal, as is much of the gathering of personal facts about us by credit agencies, educational and health institutions, and agencies of the U.S. government (as we explore in more detail in Chapter 9). Data brokers can easily buy all our health records and financial records, so that our personal data ends up wandering to places you've never been.[48] Even your car can collect data about you, using car "black boxes" (electronic data recorders), infotainment systems and onboard computers, and FasTrak fare collection transponders.[49]

Hackers

Hackers break into computers or networks; some are malicious, some are benevolent or benign.

Although the term originally referred to a computer enthusiast or a clever or expert programmer, **a hacker is now considered to be a person who gains unauthorized access to computers or networks.** Hackers may be malicious, but they may also be benign or benevolent.

MALICIOUS HACKERS Malicious hackers known as **crackers are people who break into computers for destructive purposes**—to obtain information for financial gain, shut down hardware, pirate software, steal people's credit information, or alter or destroy data. Among types of malicious hackers are the following:

- **Script kiddies:** On the low end are *script kiddies,* mostly teenagers without much technical expertise who use downloadable software or other existing code to perform malicious break-ins.
- **Hacktivists:** *Hacktivists* are "hacker activists," people who break into a computer system for a politically or socially motivated purpose. For example, a famous international hacktivist group calling itself "Anonymous" published phone numbers and addresses for supporters of the English Defence League, a British far-right street protest movement.[50]
- **Black-hat hackers:** *Black-hat hackers,* often professional criminals, are those who break into computer systems—recently including smartphones and Twitter—to steal or destroy information or to use it for illegal profit.
- **Cyberterrorists:** Cyberterrorism, according to the FBI, is any "premeditated, politically motivated attack against information, computer systems, computer programs, and data which results in violence against noncombatant targets by sub-national

groups or clandestine agents."[51] Thus, *cyberterrorists* are politically motivated persons who attack computer systems to bring physical or financial harm to a lot of people or destroy a lot of information. We cover this subject in more detail in Chapter 9.

BENIGN HACKERS *Thrill-seeker hackers* are hackers who illegally access computer systems simply for the challenge of it, not to damage or steal anything; their reward is the achievement of breaking in. Thus, as cyberintruders they are considered reasonably benign, but when discovered, they are nevertheless very upsetting to those whose systems they have hacked into.

BENEVOLENT HACKERS *Ethical hackers,* also known as *white-hat hackers,* are usually computer professionals who break into computer systems and networks with the knowledge of their owners to expose security flaws that can then be fixed.[52]

TECH TALES Microsoft Pays "Bug Bounties" to White-Hat Hackers

In 2013, Microsoft initiated a new policy—a so-called bug bounty program to pay white-hat (and gray-hat) hackers for their efforts in discovering security flaws in Microsoft software. Bug bounty programs, which have been around since 2004, encourage hackers to work with vendors to fix problems instead of simply publicly disclosing software bugs (errors in a program that cause it not to work properly).

An early adopter of the policy, Mozilla, offered $500 to hackers submitting security flaws to them. Facebook followed suit, paying $500 and sometimes a lot more, as did Google, which pays up to $20,000 for submitting bugs affecting its products.

Microsoft, says a company security strategist, hopes to "encourage the security research community"—meaning ethical hackers—"to report vulnerabilities in the latest browser and exploitation techniques across the latest platform to Microsoft as early as possible."[53] Hackers can claim bounties of up to $100,000, depending on the type of bug discovered. ■

Thieves

Thieves may be a company's employees or suppliers or professionals.

There is a widespread belief that cybercrime "is large, rapidly growing, profitable, and highly evolved," write Microsoft researchers Dinei Florencio and Cormac Herley. Actually, it's not; the popular accounts and statistics are wildly inflated. Most cyberthieves make very little money. "[Falsified] credentials and stolen credit-card numbers are offered for sale as pennies on the dollar for the simple reason that they are hard to monetize," they assert. "Cybercrime billionaires are hard to locate because there aren't any."[54] Still, we should know what kind of people are out there trying. There are so many types of cyberthievery going on that we cannot cover all the kinds of perpetrators. Some examples follow.

EMPLOYEES Employees are the largest group of cyberthieves, simply because they have better access to their companies' computer systems. Workers may use information technology for personal profit or to steal hardware or information to sell. They may also use it to seek revenge for real or imagined wrongs, such as being passed over for promotion; indeed, the disgruntled employee is a principal source of computer crime.

The U.S. Court of Appeals for the Ninth Circuit held that an employee "exceeds authorized access" under the federal Computer Fraud and Abuse Act when the employee obtains information from an employer's computer system and uses that information for a purpose that violates the employer's restrictions on the use of that information. The violation can range from obtaining information to damaging a computer or computer data.[55] What this boils down to is that employees can be criminally prosecuted for violating their employers' computer policies.

OUTSIDE PARTNERS & SUPPLIERS Suppliers and clients may also gain access to a company's information technology and use it to commit crimes, especially since intranets and extranets have become more commonplace. Partners and vendors also may be the inadvertent source of hacker mischief because their systems may not be as well protected as the larger partner's networks and computers, and so a third party may penetrate their security.

HARDWARE THIEVES Hardware theft can range from shoplifting an accessory in a computer store to removing a laptop or tablet from someone's car. Professional criminals may steal shipments of microprocessor chips off a loading dock; steal desktop computers, laptops, and other devices for their parts; or even pry cash machines out of shopping-center walls.

People distracted by gadgets, such as public transit riders gazing into the screens of their mobile devices, have become easy targets for thieves.[56] Smartphones and tablets are particularly at risk since many consumers do not secure them with antivirus software or take simple precautions such as enabling password protection.[57] Recently the tremendous surge in theft of cellphones has resulted in users pleading for manufacturers to install a "kill switch" that could be activated to keep a stolen phone from operating.[58] (Kill switches are already features of iPhones and mobile devices running Android and Windows 8 software.) Various manufacturers also offer apps that report the location of a stolen phone and even take a picture of any thief attempting to unlock the device.[59]

CON ARTISTS, SCAMMERS, & COUNTERFEITERS Fraudulent behavior extends to almost every area of life on the World Wide Web, and because it sometimes seems no different from standard e-commerce, it may be hard to discern the criminality in it. The difference, of course, is usually that it involves a deal that is almost too good to be believed.

TECH TALES Too-Good-to-Be-True Deals Online

Want to buy an "original" piece of art by a well-known artist such as Picasso for only $450—rather than the $100 million it might command at an art auction house such as Sotheby's?[60] A lot of fakes are being offered online by con artists all over the world. Intrigued by promises by "financial advisers" on Internet chat boards of no-risk, above-market returns on investments?[61] Brazen financial scams proliferate on the web. What about a "bank-repossessed" $10,000 minivan available online for only $800?[62] Used-car scams are easier to pull off online than face to face.

Will cellphone "killswitches" stop phone theft?

Free Online Virus & Security Check

Go to Symantec.com at:

http://security.symantec.com/sscv6/home.asp?langid=ie&venid=sym&plfid=23&pkj=IHQYJABOKQYWTFVRHRM

Then run the check. What are your results? What do you plan to do next?

Also try:

www.staysafeonline.org/ncsam/free-security-check-ups/

www.testmypcsecurity.com/

VIRUSES As we said in Chapter 2 (p. 100), a *virus* is a rogue program that migrates through the Internet or via operating systems and attaches itself to different program files that spread from one computer to another, leaving infections. Almost all viruses are attached to an executable file, which means the virus may exist on your computer but cannot infect your computer unless you run or open the malicious program. Because a virus is spread by human action, people will unknowingly continue the spread of a computer virus by sharing infecting files or sending emails with viruses as attachments in the email.

TECH TALES The Love Bug & Other Viruses

There are millions of viruses circulating in the cyberworld. One famous email, Love Bug (its subject line was "I LOVE YOU"), which originated in the Philippines in May 2000 and did perhaps as much as $10 billion in damage worldwide, was both a worm and a virus, spreading faster and causing more damage than any other bug before it.

The Love Bug was followed almost immediately by a variant virus. This new Love Bug didn't reveal itself with an I LOVE YOU line but changed to a random word or words each time a new computer was infected.

More recent viruses have targeted Twitter, YouTube, website advertising, and digital photo-holding frames. A virus called Koobface attacked Facebook. Fast-spreading Clampi took aim at business financial accounts. A fired computer programmer embedded a malicious virus in servers run by financial institution Fannie Mae. ■

WORMS **A worm is a program, a subclass of a virus, that copies itself repeatedly into a computer's memory or onto a disk or flash drive or USB device.** But unlike a virus, it has the capability to travel without any human action. A worm takes advantage of file or information transport features on your system, which is what allows it to travel unaided. Sometimes it will copy itself so often it will cause a computer to crash.

TECH TALES Famous Worms: Klez, Conficker, & Stuxnet

Among some famous worms are Code Red, Nimda, Sasser, Bagle, Blaster, Sobig, and Melissa. Here let's look at Klez, Conflicker, and Stuxnet. Klez, for example, spread its damage through Microsoft products by being inside email attachments or part of email messages themselves, so that merely opening an infected message could infect a computer running Outlook or Outlook Express. (The problem has since been fixed.)

In 2008–2010, a worm known as Conficker spread through a Microsoft Windows vulnerability that allowed guessing of network passwords, by people hand-carrying such gadgets as USB drives and flash drives, and it infected millions of computers. The Conficker authors cleverly updated the worm through several versions, playing a cat-and-mouse game that kept them one step ahead of security experts. Some researchers feared that Conficker would launch a massive cyberattack on April 1, 2009, that would disrupt the Internet itself, but the day came and went without incident. In 2010, 170 Conficker-infected computers at German training institutes were chucked in the garbage heap—unnecessarily, probably, since most malware-infected computers can be cleaned up by antivirus software or the drives can be wiped clean and restored from a recent backup.[66]

Conficker works mostly by spreading across networks. When it finds a vulnerable computer, it turns off the automatic backup, disables many security services, blocks access to a number of security websites, and allows infected machines to receive additional malware.

Discovered in July 2010, Stuxnet is a worm that was actively targeting Windows PCs that managed large-scale industrial-control systems in manufacturing and utility firms. Iran was hardest hit by Stuxnet, according to Symantec researchers, who said that nearly 60% of all infected PCs were located in that country. ■

More on Famous Worms

www.eweek.com/c/a/Security/The-Most-Famous-or-Infamous-Viruses-and-Worms-of-All-Time/

www.zdnet.com/blog/btl/the-5-worst-computer-viruses/79014

http://abcnews.go.com/Technology/top-computer-viruses-worms-internet-history/story?id=8480794#.UdohJNgmgS4

TROJAN HORSES If, as a citizen of Troy around 1200–1500 B.C.E., you looked outside your fortified city and saw that the besieging army of Greeks was gone but a large wooden horse was left standing on the battlefield, what would you think? Maybe you would decide it was a gift from the gods, as the Trojans did, and haul it inside the city gates—and be unpleasantly surprised when late at night Greek soldiers climbed out of the horse and opened the gates for the invading army. This is the meaning behind the illegal program known as a Trojan horse, which, though not technically a virus, can act like one.

A Trojan horse is a program that pretends to be a useful program, usually free, such as a game or screen saver, but carries viruses, or destructive instructions, that perpetrate mischief without your knowledge. (Trojans do not inject themselves into other files as a computer virus does.) The Trojan horse at first appears to be useful software but will do damage once installed or run on your computer. Those on the receiving end of a Trojan horse are usually tricked into opening it, because they believe that they are receiving legitimate software or files from a reputable source. Once the Trojan horse is activated, the results may be merely annoying, or they may be severely damaging, as when files are deleted and information destroyed.

ROOTKITS & BACKDOORS **A rootkit is a secret software program installed in a computer's operating system that someone in another location can use to take control of the computer.** As the name suggests, the goal of the rootkit program is to gain "root" access to the computer and install a "kit" of software files to create mischief: change settings, access files, delete files, install rogue programs, and otherwise perpetrate unsavory and illegal activities. Rootkits may then change the operating system settings so that the malware program is not visible.

Rootkits may work by exploiting security weaknesses in operating systems and applications. They may also create a *backdoor,* a means of accessing a computer program that bypasses security mechanisms. A backdoor may be a legitimate device that a programmer puts into a program as an undocumented means of entry so that the program can be accessed for troubleshooting or other purposes. But the backdoor may also be discovered by, or installed by, hackers and used for nefarious purposes. Backdoors are frequently found in Trojan horses and other kinds of malware.

Although most operating systems and software programs are designed to prevent security breaches from rootkits and other malware, hackers are constantly modifying rootkits to try to gain unauthorized access. This is why installing antivirus and other security software on your computer system to monitor such illegal activity is so important.

BLENDED THREATS **Blended threats use multiple techniques to attack a computer systems.** That is, a blended threat bundles some of the worst aspects of viruses, worms, Trojan horses, and other malware and then uses server and Internet vulnerabilities to initiate and spread a cyberattack. The distinguishing feature of a blended threat is that it transports multiple attacks simultaneously—for example, not just a DoS attack but also installation of a backdoor plus damage to a local system. In addition, blended threats are designed to use multiple means of transport—email, flash drives, USB drives, networks, and so on.

ZOMBIES A New Jersey grandmother of three was flabbergasted when her Internet access provider curtailed her outbound email privileges. The reason: An intruder had taken over her PC without her knowledge and turned it into a device for disseminating as many as 70,000 emails a day.[67] Her computer had become a **zombie, a computer taken over covertly and programmed to respond to instructions sent remotely.**

The grandmother's PC, however, was only one of many computers in what is known as a *botnet.* A *bot* is a program that performs a repetitive task on a network. **A botnet, or *robot network,* is a network of computers in which each computer has been implanted with instructions to wait for commands from the person controlling the botnet.** The commands may send spam, launch phishing attacks, or institute denial-of-service attacks. A recent use of botnets has been by concert ticket scalpers, who use them to buy up tickets to hot shows being sold by brokers such as Ticketmaster—sometimes more than 60% of them—to resell on the secondary market.[68] Botnets are best detected by the Internet access provider, which can block the illicit network connections and help users disinfect their PCs.

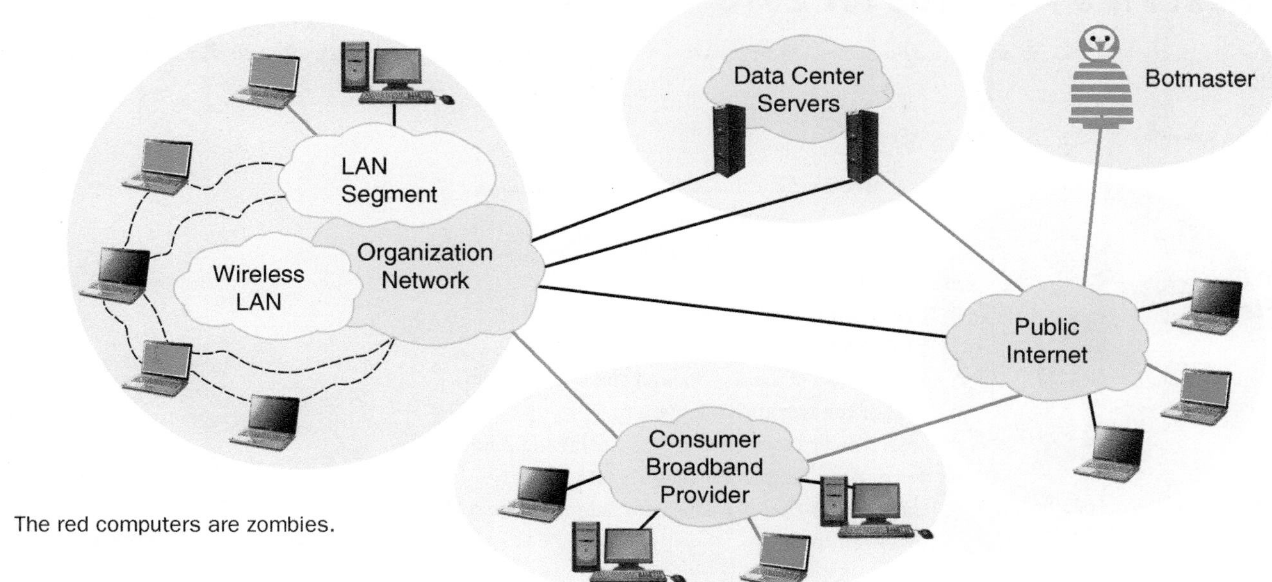

The red computers are zombies.

Survival Tip

Risky Behavior

What are the symptoms of an infected computer?

www.kaspersky.com/symptoms/

www.techsupportalert.com/content/how-know-if-your-computer-infected.htm

Cyber Security Tips

For more details about staying cybersafe, try:

www.staysafeonline.org/ncsam

www.rferl.org/content/how_to_stay_safe_online/3544056.html

www.google.com/goodtoknow/online-safety/

Survival Tip

Keep Antivirus Software Updated

The antivirus software that comes with your computer won't protect you forever. To guard against new worms and viruses, visit the antivirus software maker's website frequently and enable your software's automatic update feature.

RANSOMWARE A botnet may be used to install *ransomware,* malware that holds a computer, its data, or a particular function hostage until a ransom is paid. Ransomware encrypts the target's files, and the attacker tells the victim to make a payment of a specified amount to a special account to receive the decryption key.

TIME, LOGIC, & EMAIL BOMBS A *time bomb* is malware programmed to "go off" at a particular time or date. A *logic bomb* is "detonated" when a specific event occurs—for example, all personnel records are erased when an electronic notation is made that a particular person was fired. *Email bombs* overwhelm a person's email account by surreptitiously subscribing it to dozens or even hundreds of mailing lists.

PHONE MALWARE Worms and viruses and other malware are attacking smartphones. The most common type of cellphone infection occurs when a cellphone downloads an infected file from a PC or the Internet, but phone-to-phone viruses are also on the rise. Infected files usually show up disguised as applications such as games, security patches, add-on functionalities, and, of course, erotica and free stuff.

Future possibilities include cellphone spyware—so someone can see every number you call and listen to your conversations—and viruses that steal financial information, which will become more serious as smartphones are used as common payment devices. Ultimately, more connectivity means more exposure to viruses and faster spreading of infection.

Online Safety

Antivirus software, passwords, biometric authentication, and encryption help block intruders.

How do you keep your computer, tablet, or smartphone safe against unwanted intruders? We discussed two principal methods in Chapter 2—antivirus software and password protection—and we described firewalls earlier in this chapter. Two more technical methods are biometric authentication and encryption, discussed below.

ANTIVIRUS SOFTWARE As we said in Chapter 2, *antivirus software* scans a computer's hard disk, other designated storage devices, and main memory to detect viruses and, sometimes, to destroy them. Such virus watchdogs operate in two ways. First, they scan disk drives for "signatures," characteristic strings of 1s and 0s in the virus that uniquely identify it. Second, they look for suspicious viruslike behavior, such as attempts to erase or change areas on your disks.

For a list of free antivirus software, go to *www.pcmag.com/article2/0,2817,2388652,00.asp.*

The Best Free Antivirus for 2013

Even if your budget doesn't include any money for antivirus protection, you've got plenty of good choices for free antivirus.

By Neil J. Rubenking | May 8, 2013 | 20 Comments

VIEW ALL PHOTOS IN GALLERY

If you're reading this article and you don't have antivirus protection installed on all your PCs, stop reading right now and install some kind of free antivirus protection. I don't care which, for now. Done? I thank you, and the rest of the world thanks you as well. Fewer unprotected PCs worldwide means fewer easy targets for botnets and virus infestations that can affect far more than just the owner of the PC.

Contents

The Best Free Antivirus for 2013

Ad-Aware to Emsisoft

Malwarebytes to ZoneAlarm

Now that you've got an antivirus working to protect your PC (and the rest of us), you can take the time to consider what's the best free solution for your situation. That's the nice thing about free antivirus; you're not locked in by your choice. You won't be wasting 40 or 50 dollars if you decide to switch. Which is best for you can depend on your situation.

The Best Free Antivirus for 2013

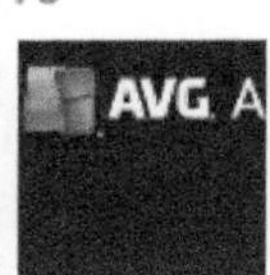

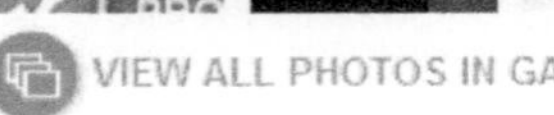

Root Out Entrenched Malware

Maybe you never worried about antivirus protection on the children's computer. All they ever do is play Minecraft and chat on Facebook, right? You'll find out how smart that was when the kids suddenly can't play their games or chat with friends because malware has taken over. They've got nothing else to do, so they'll hound you mercilessly until you solve the problem.

In a situation like this, the absolute most important task is to clear out the entrenched malware. The tool that's best for that purpose isn't necessarily the same tool you'll want to install for continuing protection. In fact, Malwarebytes Anti-Malware 1.70, PCMag's Editors' Choice for free cleanup-only antivirus, doesn't include ongoing protection at all. Its sole purpose is to wipe out viruses, Trojans, rootkits, and all types of malware, and it does a fine job.

Examples of antivirus programs, some of which we have already mentioned, are McAfee VirusScan, Norton AntiVirus, PC-cillin Internet Security, Avast!, and ZoneAlarm with Antivirus. Free programs include Grisoft AVG Free, Microsoft Security Essentials, Zone Alarm, and Comodo. Others worth considering are CA Internet Security Suite Plus, Panda Antivirus Platinum, and McAfee VirusScan for Macs.

PASSWORDS We discussed passwords in Chapter 2 (p. 60) and presented advice for creating effective passwords. To repeat, to foil a stranger from guessing your password, experts say, you should never choose a real word or variations of your name, your birth date, or those of your friends or family. Instead you should mix letters, numbers, and punctuation marks in an oddball sequence of no fewer than eight characters.

BIOMETRIC AUTHENTICATION A hacker or cracker can easily breach a computer system with a guessed or stolen password. But some forms of identification can't be easily faked—such as your physical traits. As we discussed in Chapter 5 (p. 271), security devices

Protect against Phone Viruses & Spyware

According to HowStuffWorks (*http://electronics.howstuffworks.com/cell-phone-virus4.htm*), the best way to protect yourself from smartphone viruses is the same way you protect yourself from computer viruses: never open anything if you don't know what it is, haven't requested it, or have any suspicions whatsoever that it's not what it claims to be. See also:

www.fbi.gov/sandiego/press-releases/2012/smartphone-users-should-be-aware-of-malware-targeting-mobile-devices-and-the-safety-measures-to-help-avoid-compromise

www.ic3.gov/media/2012/121012.aspx

http://us.norton.com/handheld-security/article

http://securitywatch.pcmag.com/mobile-security/309980-five-signs-your-android-device-is-infected-with-malware

More Password Tips

Get more password tips at:

www.itworld.com/security/272942/what-makes-good-password

www.us-cert.gov/cas/tips/ST04-002.html

www.microsoft.com/protect/yourself/password/create.mspx

www.wikihow.com/Choose-a-Secure-Password

panel 6.19

Biometric device

A U.S. soldier holds a HIIDE scanner. HIIDE stands for Handheld Interagency Identity Detection Equipment enrollment and recognition device. It is a biometric security camera, used to identify unknown military people; it incorporates an iris scanner, fingerprint scanner, face scanner, and passport reader.

can include *biometrics,* the science of measuring individual body characteristics. *Biometric authentication devices* authenticate a person's identity by comparing his or her physical or behavioral characteristics with digital code stored in a computer system.

Several kinds of devices use physical or behavioral characteristics to authenticate a person's identity. They include fingerprint scanners, full-hand palm scanners, iris-recognition systems, face-recognition systems, and voice-recognition systems. (• *See Panel 6.19.)*

ENCRYPTION **Encryption is the process of altering readable data into unreadable form to prevent unauthorized access.** Encryption uses powerful mathematical concepts to create coded messages that are difficult or even virtually impossible to break.

Suppose you wanted to send a message to a company colleague stating, "Our secret product will be revealed to the world on April 14." If you sent it in this undisguised, readable form, it would be known as *plain text.* To send it in disguised, unreadable form, you would *encrypt* that message into *cybertext,* and your colleague receiving it would then *decrypt* it, using an *encryption key*—a formula for encrypting and decrypting a coded message.

Basic encryption. Both the sender and the receiver have the appropriate encryption key.

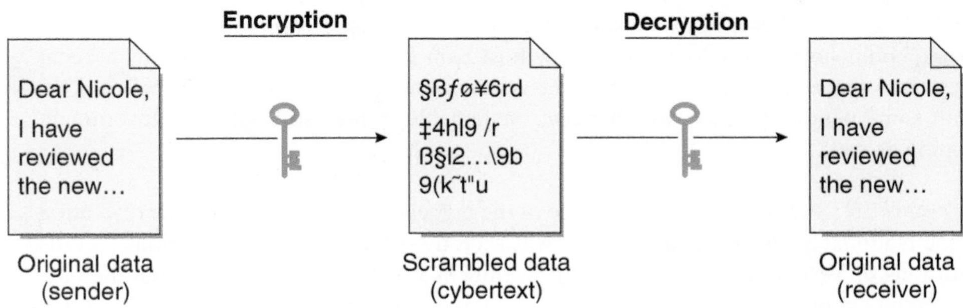

6.7 CONCERNS ABOUT PRIVACY & IDENTITY THEFT

Technology has facilitated loss of privacy and identity theft.

The good news, according to research, is that most U.S. teenagers, even as they post more and more personal information on social media sites, are taking measures to protect their online privacy and reputations. "Teenagers are not nearly as oblivious to the implications of sharing too much information as many adults think they are," says Internet safety expert Larry Magid.[69]

Still, a lot of people seem unworried that their movements are being tracked, as through the GPS locators in their phones and through E-ZPasses. Or that the phone companies are selling data about them to advertisers.[70] Or that much of their lives is recorded in government databases. Why aren't they more concerned?

"Despite how much we say we value our privacy—and we do, again and again—we tend to act inconsistently," points out Somini Sengupta.[71] We go for immediate rewards, such as giving up personal data in return for an offer of, say, a pair of cheap sandals, and ignore intangible risks downstream, such as compromising our privacy. "Privacy is delayed gratification," says one scholar.[72]

But there are plenty of threats out there to exploit our mistakes.

The Threat to Privacy

The proliferation of networks and databases have put privacy under great pressure.

Privacy is the right of people not to reveal information about themselves. However, the ease of pulling together information from databases and disseminating it over the Internet has put privacy under extreme pressure, as the following shows.

Ways to Guard Your Privacy

The following websites offer ways to guard your privacy:

www.internetsociety.org/protecting-your-privacy?gclid=CMqF84WHj7gCFapcMgodc2cAnw

www.theatlantic.com/magazine/archive/2013/06/youve-been-warned/309320/

www.epic.org

www.privacyfoundation.org

www.eff.org

www.ftc.gov/privacy/index.html

http://gpsmaestro.com/10-ways-to-guard-your-privacy-on-a-smartphone/

NAME MIGRATION "If iron ore was the raw material that enriched the steel baron Andrew Carnegie in the Industrial Age," says Sengupta, "personal data is what fuels the barons of the Internet age."[73] Once you're in a database, your name can easily migrate to other databases. Parents installing software (Sentry, FamilySafe) to monitor their children's online activities unwittingly may have allowed the software developer to gather marketing data from children as young as 7 and to sell that information.[74] Making certain purchases, such as flowers, through your smartphone may put your name on the mailing list of 1-800-FLOWERS.com and lead to targeted ads for flowers on your phone, a form of advertising known as behavioral targeting.[75] No wonder the Federal Trade Commission has expressed sharp words to Internet companies, saying they are not explaining to users clearly enough what information they collect about them and how they are using it.[76]

RÉSUMÉ RUSTLING & ONLINE SNOOPING When you post your résumé on an Internet job board, you assume that it's private, and indeed it is supposed to be restricted to recruiters and other employers. But job boards that are just starting up may poach résumés from other job websites as a way of building up their own databases.

You've probably been advised that you should never use a company computer or smartphone for personal business, because your moves are being watched. Yet "employees get fired and disciplined every day for questionable web surfing, downloading, and emailing at work," points out technology radio show host Kim Komando. "Your First Amendment right to free speech protects you against the government—not private employers."[77]

But some people question whether our "inalienable rights" still apply to government snooping as well.

Ways to Protect Your Online Résumé

http://jobsearch.about.com/od/jobsearchprivacy/a/privacy.htm

http://guides.wsj.com/careers/how-to-start-a-job-search/how-to-protect-your-privacy-when-job-hunting/

http://blog.gcflearnfree.org/2010/09/21/how-to-protect-yourself-while-job-hunting-online/

www.privacyrights.org/fs/fs25-JobSeekerPriv.htm

GOVERNMENT PRYING & SPYING One of the biggest stories of 2013 was the revelation that the National Security Agency (NSA) was secretly collecting communications records of millions of Verizon customers.[78] The government was quick to point out that the data being collected did not include the speech in a phone call or words in an email. Still, the so-called metadata being saved by the NSA included almost everything else—the model of the phone and the "to" and "from" lines in the emails, for example. "By tracing metadata," one report pointed out, "investigators can pinpoint a suspect's location to specific floors of buildings. They can electronically map a person's contacts, and their contacts' contacts."[79]

The government has justified its data collection effort as an important tool for tracing terrorists, but it may well cross a blurry line in the balance between security and liberty. We take up the issue of government surveillance in more detail, along with a discussion of privacy laws, in Chapter 9.

Identity Theft

Identity theft is a crime in which an imposter obtains key pieces of personal information in order to impersonate someone else.

Identity (ID) theft, or *theft of identity (TOI),* is a crime in which thieves hijack your name and identity and use your information and credit rating to get cash or buy things. Often this begins with someone getting hold of your full name and Social Security number. Using these, they tap into Internet databases and come up with other information—your address, phone number, employer, driver's license number, mother's maiden name, and so on. Then they're off to the races, applying for credit everywhere.

In 2012 there were about 12.6 million victims of identity theft in the United States—more than the total number of burglaries, attempted burglaries, petty thefts, purse snatchings, pickpocketings, arsons, shoplifting, check fraud, and auto thefts combined.[80]

The U.S. Federal Trade Commission (*www.ftc.gov/bcp/edu/microsites/idtheft/*) tracks identity theft statistics, helps victims, and coordinates responses by various government agencies. It estimates that recovering from identity theft takes an average of six months and 200 hours of work. One survey found that a third of victims of identity theft had still been unable to repair their tainted identities even a year after the information was stolen.[81]

TECH TALES The Weird Experience of Identity Theft

One day, a special-events planner in California learned that she had a new $35,000 sports utility vehicle listed in her name, along with five credit cards, a $3,000 loan, and even an apartment—none of which she'd asked for.

"I cannot imagine what would be weirder, or would make you angrier, than having someone pretend to be you, steal all this money, and then leave you to clean up all their mess later," she said.[82] Added to this was the eerie matter of constantly having to prove that she was, in fact, herself: "I was going around saying, 'I am who I am!' "[83]

In the event planner's case, someone had used information lifted from her employee-benefits form. The spending spree went on for months, unknown to her. The reason it took so long to discover the theft was that the victim never saw any bills. They went to the address listed by the impersonator, a woman, who made a few payments to keep creditors at bay while she ran up even more bills. For the victim, straightening out the mess required months of frustrating phone calls, time off from work, court appearances, and legal expenses. ■

Identity theft typically starts in one of several ways:

- *Wallet or purse theft:* There was a time when a thief would steal a wallet or purse, take the cash, and toss everything else. No more. Everything from keys to credit cards can be used for theft. (One famous victim of identity theft was then Federal Reserve chair Ben Bernanke, whose wife, Anna, had her purse stolen in a Starbucks coffee shop. The thief, it turned out, made as much as $50,000 a day on identity theft scams.)
- *Mail theft:* Thieves also consider mailboxes fair game. The mail will yield them bank statements, credit-card statements, new checks, tax forms, and other personal information. (So it's best to receive your "snailmail" in a locked box—and mail your outgoing letters at a postbox.)
- *Mining the trash:* You might think nothing of throwing away credit-card offers, portions of utility bills, or old canceled checks. But "dumpster diving" can produce gold for thieves. Credit-card offers, for instance, may have limits of $5,000 or more.
- *Telephone solicitation:* Prospective thieves may call you up and pretend to represent a bank, credit-card company, government agency, or the like in an attempt to pry loose essential data about you. Do not give out information over the phone unless predetermined passwords and identifying phrases are used; and never give your entire Social Security number under any circumstances.

- *Insider access to databases:* You never know who has, or could have, access to databases containing your personnel records, credit records, car loan applications, bank documents, and so on. This is one of the harder ID theft methods to guard against.
- *Outsider access to databases:* In recent years, data burglars and con artists have tapped into big databases at such companies as ChoicePoint, Reed Elsevier, DSW Shoe Warehouse, and Bank of America/Wachovia. Other institutions, such as CitiFinancial, the University of California at Berkeley, and Time Warner have exposed files of data through carelessness. These losses have put millions of people at risk.

  Also, public use of debit cards has become very risky. Experts recommend that you use them only inside banks and other such secure places and, if necessary, only at bank being careful about covering your card while using it and your hand while typing in your PIN number. Also consider buying a specially lined wallet to prevent in-wallet scanning of credit and debit cards by thieves with special portable scanning equipment.

WHAT TO DO ONCE THEFT HAPPENS If you're the victim of a physical theft (or even loss), as when your wallet is snatched, you should immediately contact—first by phone and then in writing—all your credit-card companies, other financial institutions, the Department of Motor Vehicles, and any other organizations whose cards you use that are now compromised. Be sure to call utility companies—telephone, cellphone, electricity, and gas; identity thieves can run up enormous phone bills. Also call the local police and your insurance company to report the loss. File a complaint with the Federal Trade Commission (1-877-ID-THEFT, or *www.consumer.ftc.gov/features/feature-0014-identity-theft*), which maintains an ID theft database.

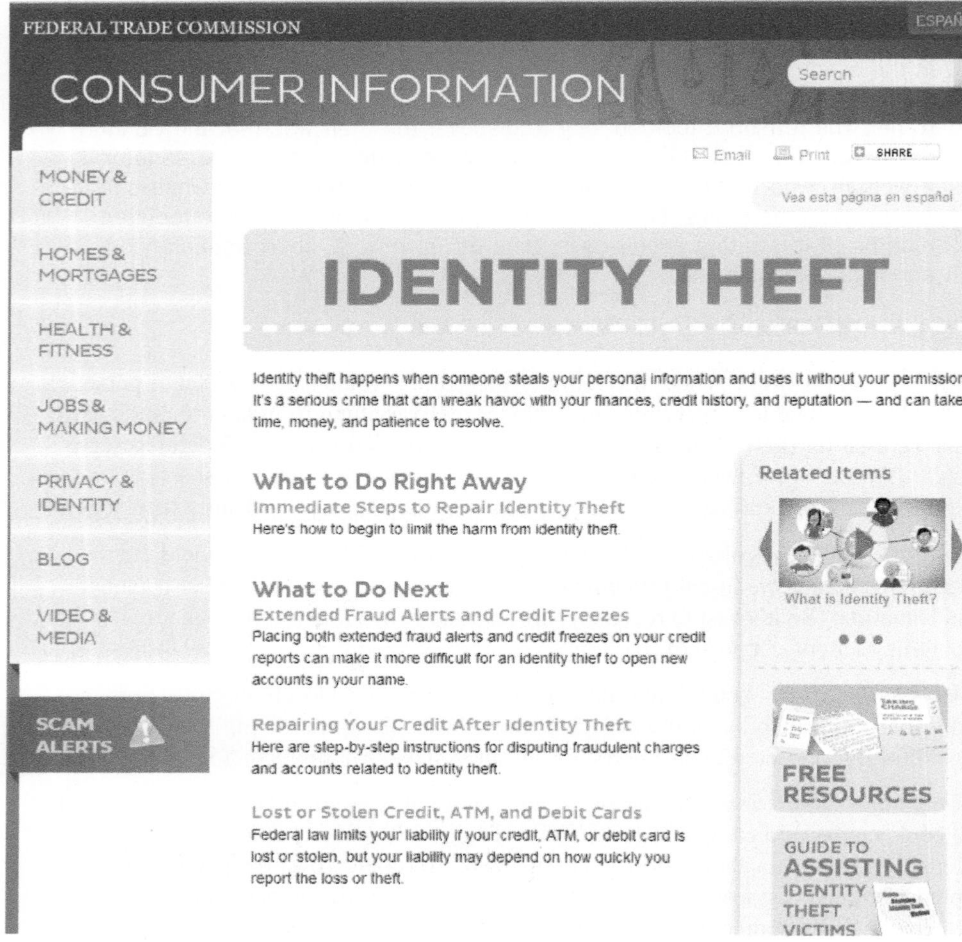

U.S. Federal Trade Commission's anti-ID theft site (*www.consumer.ftc.gov/features/feature-0014-identity-theft*)

panel 6.20

The three major credit bureaus

Equifax	Experian	TransUnion
To check your credit report 800-685-1111 *www.equifax.com*	To check your credit report 800-397-3742 *www.experian.com*	To check your credit report 877-322-8228 *www.transunion.com*

Notify financial institutions within two days of learning of your loss, because then you usually are legally responsible for only the first $50 of any theft. If you become aware of fraudulent transactions, immediately contact the fraud units of the three major credit bureaus: Equifax, Experian, and TransUnion. (• *See Panel 6.20.*) In some states, you can freeze your credit reports, preventing lenders and others from reviewing your credit history, which will prevent identity thieves from opening fraudulent accounts using your name. (The FTC identity theft website explains how to do this.)

If your Social Security number has been fraudulently used, alert the Social Security Administration (800-772-1213).

If you have a check guarantee card that was stolen, if your checks have been lost, or if a new checking account has been opened in your name, call your bank immediately.

If your mail has been used for fraudulent purposes or if an identity thief filed a change of address form, look in the phone directory under U.S. Postal Service for your local postal inspector's office and call it.

EXPERIENCE BOX

Guarding Your Privacy & Preventing Your Identity from Getting Stolen

"You can have privacy or you can have the Internet, but you can't have both," reads a newspaper.[84] *Is this true? Let's just say that if you're hoping to thwart the companies and government agencies collecting and collating your personal data, be prepared to do some serious work.*

Protecting Yourself from Internet Snoops

"The only real way to avoid data profiling," says one writer, "is to go off the grid. No Internet. No mobile phones. No credit cards. Basically, none of the conveniences and connectivity of modern life."[85] Let's begin with the Internet and your computer.[86]

- ***Use public computers:*** Sure, it's inconvenient, but if you really want to surf the Internet anonymously, use public computers, such as those in libraries. (To truly stay invisible, be sure you don't have to swipe a card to gain access to the machines and make sure you're not being watched by security cameras.)
- ***Use multiple browsers:*** One computer science professor uses three different browsers: Google Chrome, Apple Safari, and Mozilla Firefox. One is for email, another for social networking, and the third for general browsing—and no mingling is allowed. "To the extent that you as a consumer can frustrate the trackers," he says, "you may reduce the amount of tracking going on."[87]
- ***Adjust browser privacy settings:*** Because browsers are supposed to track the websites you visit, you can alter the privacy settings for Chrome, Safari, Firefox, and Internet Explorer to disallow tracking of your web activities.
- ***Adjust network privacy settings:*** Go into your account settings, and make sure your profile is private and can't be found by search engines.
- ***Get rid of cookies:*** You can install browser extensions such as Adblock Plus, which enables you to block ads and disable online tracking through cookies. You can also turn on private browsing mode, which prevents the browser from storing information from sites you're visiting during a particular online session.
- ***Create social network accounts without personal information:*** You might set up a Facebook or other social network account using fake personal information (although trackers may still cross-reference information with your computer and with other available data to figure out your identity and whereabouts).
- ***Use many email addresses, some fake:*** Because companies can share people's email addresses, allowing a user to be connected across many sites, consider registering for some services using bogus email addresses—temporary and dispensable email addresses set up through a special service, such as *www.guerrillamail.com/* and *http://mailinator.com/*.
- ***Use Tor to create an anonymous network:*** Many privacy experts endorse Tor, free software that is easy to download (see *www.torproject.org* for details), which can be used to create a decentralized network, which is more secure. (You should use an alternative email service with it, such as Hushmail, rather than established email clients like Hotmail, AOL, or Gmail.)

Reducing Phone Privacy Risks

The least risky mobile phone from a privacy standpoint is . . . no phone at all. The next best choice is a low-tech "dumb phone," the kind that only makes calls and sends text messages and that, unlike a smartphone, is not a tracking instrument.

Some alternative ways to avoid trackers snooping on your smartphone are as follows:[88]

- ***Use a prepaid phone:*** A so-called *burner phone* is one that comes with a calling plan that you pay for as you go. You pay cash for it, and it does not require you to submit personal information in order to purchase it.
- ***Turn off location tracking:*** On iPhones and Android phones you can turn off location services, or use them selectively, such as not using automatic "geotagging" when you take a picture with your phone.

Pay Cash

Even if you don't own a cellphone or have a Gmail account, "your bank account and any credit card data can also paint a pretty accurate picture of you to anyone who's interested and has access," points out one technology writer.[89] Indeed, credit cards, debit cards, and loyalty cards leave digital trails that are easy to track. The alternative, then, is to pay cash—or pay cash only for sensitive items (alcohol, health items) that other people might make certain inferences about.

How to Prevent Identity Theft

One of the best ways to keep your finger on the pulse of your financial life is, on a regular basis—once a year, say—to get a copy of your credit report from one or all three of the main credit bureaus. This will show you whether there is any unauthorized activity. Annual reports are free from the major credit bureaus (Equifax, Experian, and TransUnion). To learn more, go to *www.annualcreditreport.com* or call toll-free 877-322-8228.

In addition, there are some specific measures you can take to guard against personal information getting into the public realm.

- ***Check your credit-card billing statements:*** If you see some fraudulent charges, report them immediately. If you don't receive your statement, call the creditor first. Then call the post office to see if a change of address has been filed under your name.
- ***Treat credit cards and other important papers with respect:*** Make a list of your credit cards and other important documents and a list of numbers to call if you need to report them lost. (You can photocopy the cards front and back, but make sure the numbers are legible.)

  Carry only one or two credit cards at a time. Carry your Social Security card, passport, or birth certificate only when needed.

  Don't dispose of credit-card receipts in a public place.

  Don't give out your credit-card numbers or Social Security number over the phone or on the Internet unless you have some sort of trusted relationship with the party on the other end.

  Tear up credit-card offers before you throw them away. Even better, buy a shredder and shred these and other such documents.

  Keep a separate credit card for online transactions, so that if anything unusual happens you're more likely to notice it and you can more easily close the account.

  Keep tax records and other financial documents in a safe place.
- ***Treat checks with respect:*** Pick up new checks at the bank. Shred canceled checks before throwing them away. Don't let merchants write your credit-card number on the check.
- ***Watch out for "shoulder surfers" when using phones and ATMs:*** When using PINs and passwords at public telephones and automated teller machines, shield your hand so that anyone watching through binoculars or using a video camera—"shoulder surfers"—can't read them.
- ***Don't bother signing up for ID theft protection programs:*** Companies such as LifeLock and Invisus offer to keep watch on your credit reports and public records and to alert credit bureaus if they encounter fraud activity. Such companies have been sued for misleading advertising and misleading customers.

TERMS & EXPLANATIONS

analog (p. 305) Continuous and varying in strength and/or quality. An analog signal is a continuous electrical signal with such variation. Why it's important: *Sound, light, temperature, and pressure values, for instance, can fall anywhere on a continuum or range. The highs, lows, and in-between states have historically been represented with analog devices rather than in digital form. Examples of analog devices are a speedometer, a thermometer, and a tire-pressure gauge, all of which can measure continuous fluctuations. The electrical signals on a telephone line have traditionally been analog data representations of the original voices, as have been telephone, radio, television, and cable-TV technologies—most of which are now digital.*

backbone (p. 317) The main highway—including gateways, routers, and other communications equipment—that connects all computer networks in an organization. Why it's important: *A backbone is a main transmission path; for example, the Internet backbone is the central structure that connects all other elements of the Internet.*

bandwidth (p. 327) Also called *band;* range of frequencies that a transmission medium can carry in a given period of time and thus a measure of the amount of information that can be delivered. Why it's important: *In the United States, certain bands are assigned by the Federal Communications Commission (FCC) for certain purposes. The wider the bandwidth, the faster the data can be transmitted. The narrower the band, the greater the loss of transmission power. This loss of power must be overcome by using relays or repeaters that rebroadcast the original signal.*

blended threat (p. 349) Cyberattack that uses multiple techniques to attack a computer system; a blended threat bundles some of the worst aspects of viruses, worms, Trojan horses, and other malware and then uses server and Internet vulnerabilities to initiate and spread a cyberattack. Why it's important: *Blended threats transport multiple attacks simultaneously—for example, not just a DoS attack but also installation of a backdoor plus damage to a local system. In addition, blended threats are designed to use multiple means of transport—email, flash drives, USB drives, networks, and so on.*

Bluetooth (p. 340) Short-range wireless digital standard aimed at linking cellphones, PDAs, computers, and peripherals up to 33 feet apart. Why it's important: *Bluetooth technology can replace cables between PCs and printers and can connect PCs and wireless phones to hands-free headsets.*

botnet (p. 349) Short for *robot network;* a network of computers in which each computer has been implanted with instructions to wait for commands from the person controlling the botnet. Why it's important: *The commands may send spam, launch phishing attacks, or institute denial-of-service attacks. Once infected, a computer becomes part of a botnet—a zombie, part of a network of infected computers.*

bridge (p. 316) Interface (device) used to connect the same types of networks, such as two local area networks (LANs). Why it's important: *Similar networks can be joined together to create larger area networks.*

broadband (p. 327) Bandwidth characterized by very high speed; refers to telecommunications in which a wide band of frequencies is available to transmit information. Why it's important: *Because a wide band of frequencies is available, information can be sent on many different frequencies or channels within the band concurrently, allowing more information to be transmitted in a given amount of time. The wider a medium's bandwidth, the more frequencies it can use to transmit data and thus the faster the transmission. Broadband can transmit high-quality audio and video data. (Compare with* **narrowband.***)*

broadcast radio (p. 329) Wireless transmission medium that sends data over long distances—between regions, states, or countries. A transmitter is required to send messages and a receiver to receive them; sometimes both sending and receiving functions are combined in a transceiver. Why it's important: *In the lower frequencies of the radio spectrum, several broadcast radio bands are reserved not only for conventional AM/FM radio but also for broadcast television, CB (citizens band) radio, ham (amateur) radio, cellphones, and private radio-band mobile services (such as police, fire, and taxi dispatch). Some organizations use specific radio frequencies and networks to support wireless communications.*

bus network (p. 320) Type of network in which all nodes are connected to a single linear wire or cable (the bus) that has two endpoints (terminators). Each device transmits electronic messages to other devices. If some of those messages collide, the device waits and then tries to retransmit. Why it's important: *The bus network is relatively inexpensive, but it's limited to 20 devices on the network and 185 meters (606 feet) in length.*

cellular radio (p. 330) Type of radio widely used for cellphones and wireless modems, using high-frequency radio waves to transmit voice and digital messages. Why it's important: *Unlike CB (citizens band) radio, used by truck drivers, which has a few radio channels that everyone must share, cellular radio channels are reused simultaneously in nearby geographic areas, yet customers do not interfere with one another's calls.*

client-server network (p. 312) Local area network that consists of *clients,* which are microcomputers that request data, and *servers,* which are computers used to supply data. Why it's important: *In small organizations, servers can store files, provide printing stations, and transmit email. In large organizations, servers may also house enormous libraries of financial, sales, and product information. (Compare with* **peer-to-peer network.***)*

coaxial cable (p. 324) Also called *co-ax;* insulated copper wire wrapped in a solid or braided metal shield and then in an external plastic cover. Why it's important: *Co-ax is widely used for cable television. Because of the extra insulation, coaxial cable is much better than twisted-pair wiring at resisting noise. Moreover, it can carry voice and data at a faster rate.*

communications medium (p. 324) Any medium (or channel) that carries signals over a communications path, the route between two or more communications media devices. Why it's important: *Media may be wired or wireless. Three types of* *wired channels are twisted-pair wire (conventional telephone lines), coaxial cable, and fiber-optic cable. The speed, or data transfer rate, at which transmission occurs—and how much data can be carried by a signal—depends on the media and the type of signal.*

communications satellite (p. 330) Microwave relay station in orbit around Earth. Why it's important: *Transmitting a signal from a ground station to a satellite is called* uplinking; *the reverse is called* downlinking. *The delivery process will be slowed if, as is often the case, more than one satellite is required to get the message delivered.*

cracker (p. 344) Person who breaks into computers for malicious purposes—to obtain information for financial gain, shut down hardware, pirate software, steal people's credit information, or alter or destroy data. Why it's important: *Crackers can do major damage to computers and networks. (Compare with* **hacker.***)*

cyberattack (p. 343) An attempt to gain unauthorized access to or to disrupt or damage a computer system or electronic communications network. Why it's important: *Cyberattacks use malware to alter computer functions, resulting in harmful consequences that can compromise data and lead to cybercrimes, such as information and identity theft.*

denial-of-service (DoS) attack (p. 347) Also called *distributed denial of service (DDoS) attack;* form of technological assault that consists of making repeated fraudulent requests of a computer system or network, thereby overloading it. The assault may come from a single computer or from hundreds or thousands of computers that have been taken over by those intending harm. Why it's important: *A denial-of-service attack denies legitimate users access to the computer system.*

digital (p. 306) Communications signals or information represented in a discontinuous two-state (binary) way using electronic or electromagnetic signals. Why it's important: *Digital signals are the basis of computer-based communications.* Digital *is usually synonymous with* computer-based.

digital convergence (p. 304) The gradual merger of computing and communications into a new information environment, in which the same information is exchanged among many kinds of equipment, using the language of computers. Why it's important: *There has been a convergence of several important industries—computers, telecommunications, consumer electronics, entertainment, mass media—producing new electronic products that perform multiple functions.*

digital wireless services (p. 336) Two-way, second-generation (2G) wireless services that support digital cellphones and PDAs. They use a network of cell towers to send voice communications and data over the airwaves in digital form. Why it's important: *This technology was a dramatic improvement over analog cellphones. Voice clarity is better, and more calls can be squeezed into the same bandwidth. The 2G has been supplanted by 3G and 4G services, and 5G is already a prototype.*

electromagnetic spectrum of radiation (p. 327) All the fields of electric energy and magnetic energy, which travel in waves. This includes all radio signals, light rays, X-rays, and radioactivity. Why it's important: *The part of the electromagnetic spectrum of particular interest is the area in the middle, which is used for communications purposes. Various frequencies are assigned by the U.S. federal government for different purposes. (See* **radio-frequency [RF] spectrum.***)*

encryption (p. 352) The process of altering readable data into unreadable form to prevent unauthorized access; coded messages are difficult or impossible to read. To send a message in disguised, unreadable form, you would *encrypt* that message into *cybertext,* and your colleague receiving it would then *decrypt* it, using an *encryption key*—a formula for encrypting and decrypting a coded message. Why it's important: *Using encryption to alter readable data into unreadable form can prevent unauthorized access.*

Ethernet (p. 321) Wired LAN technology standard that can be used with almost any kind of computer and that describes how data can be sent between computers and other networked devices usually in close proximity. Why it's important: *Ethernet is a protocol that controls the way data is transmitted over a local area network. Ethernet has become the most popular and most widely deployed network technology in the world.*

extranet (p. 314) Private intranet that connects not only internal personnel but also selected suppliers and other strategic parties (outsiders). Why it's important: *Extranets have become popular for standard transactions such as purchasing.*

fiber-optic cable (p. 324) Cable that consists of dozens or hundreds of thin strands of glass or plastic that transmit pulsating beams of light rather than electricity. Why it's important: *These strands, each as thin as a human hair, can transmit up to 2 billion pulses per second (2 Gbps); each "on" pulse represents 1 bit. When bundled together, fiber-optic strands in a cable 0.12 inch thick can support a quarter- to a half-million voice conversations at the same time. Moreover, unlike electrical signals, light pulses are not affected by random electromagnetic interference in the environment. Thus, they have much lower error rates than normal telephone wire and cable. In addition, fiber-optic cable is lighter and more durable than twisted-pair wire and co-ax cable. A final advantage is that it cannot easily be wiretapped, so transmissions are more secure.*

firewall (p. 314) System of hardware and/or software that protects a computer or a network from intruders. Always-on Internet connections such as cable modem and DSL, as well as some wireless devices, are particularly susceptible to unauthorized intrusion and so need a firewall. Why it's important: *The firewall monitors all Internet and other network activity, looking for suspicious data and preventing unauthorized access.*

gateway (p. 316) Interface permitting communication between dissimilar networks. Why it's important: *Gateways permit communication between a LAN and a WAN or between two LANs based on different network operating systems or different layouts.*

Global Positioning System (GPS) (p. 332) A series of Earth-orbiting satellites continuously transmitting timed radio signals that can be used to identify Earth locations. Why it's important: *A GPS receiver—handheld or mounted in a vehicle, plane, boat, or smartphone—can pick up transmissions from any four satellites, interpret the information from each, and calculate to within a few hundred feet or less the receiver's longitude, latitude, and* *altitude. GPS receivers usually include map software for finding one's way around.*

hacker (p. 344) Person who gains unauthorized access to computers or networks. Hackers may be malicious, but they may also be benign or benevolent. Why it's important: *Unlike crackers who have malevolent purposes, a hacker may break into computers for more or less positive reasons, but they may sometimes cause problems.*

home area network (p. 311) Network that links a household's digital devices—computers, printers, DVD players, television sets, and home security systems. Why it's important: *A* home automation network *links switches and sensors around the house, and a* garden area network *links watering systems, outdoor lights, and alarm systems. A home area network can make a house "smart."*

host computer (p. 315) The central computer in a network that controls the network and the devices, called nodes, on it (such as a client-server network). Why it's important: *The host computer controls access to the hardware, software, and all other resources on the network.*

identity(ID) theft (p. 354) Also called *theft of identity (TOI);* crime in which thieves hijack your name and identity and use your information and credit rating to get cash or buy things. Often this begins with someone getting hold of your full name and Social Security number. Why it's important: *Identity thieves tap into Internet databases and come up with other information—your address, phone number, employer, driver's license number, mother's maiden name, and so on. Then they apply for credit everywhere and drain your accounts.*

infrared wireless transmission (p. 329) Transmission of data signals using infrared-light waves. Why it's important: *Infrared ports can be found on some laptop computers and printers, as well as wireless mice. TV remotes also use infrared wireless transmission. The advantage is that no physical connection is required among devices. The drawbacks are that line-of-sight communication is required—there must be an unobstructed view between transmitter and receiver—and transmission is confined to short range.*

intranet (p. 314) An organization's internal private network that uses the infrastructure and standards of the Internet and the web. Why it's important: *When an organization creates an intranet, it enables employees to have quicker access to internal information and to share knowledge so that they can do their jobs better. Information exchanged on intranets may include employee email addresses and telephone numbers, product information, sales data, employee benefit information, and lists of jobs available within the organization.*

local area network (LAN) (p. 311) Communications network that connects computers and devices in a limited geographic area, such as one office, one building, or a group of buildings close together (for instance, a college campus). Why it's important: *LANs have replaced large computers for many functions and are considerably less expensive. They are the basis for most office networks.*

LTE (p. 338) *Long Term Evolution;* a 4G telecommunications high-speed mobile-phone standard that became available in 2009. Why it's important: *LTE is faster than 3G; it supports data transfer rates of up to 100 megabits per second over cellular networks.*

mesh network (p. 321) Network in which messages take the shortest, easiest route to reach their destination. There must be at least two paths to any individual computer to create a mesh network. (Wireless networks are often implemented as a mesh.) Why it's important: *The Internet employs the mesh topology.*

metropolitan area network (MAN) (p. 310) Communications network covering a city or a suburb. Why it's important: *The purpose of a MAN is often to bypass local telephone companies when accessing long-distance services. Many cellphone systems are MANs.*

microwave radio (p. 330) Transmission of voice and data through the atmosphere as superhigh-frequency radio waves called *microwaves.* These frequencies are used to transmit messages between ground-based stations and satellite communications systems. Why it's important: *Microwaves are line-of-sight; they cannot bend around corners or around Earth's curvature, so there must be an unobstructed view between transmitter and receiver. Thus, microwave stations need to be placed within 25–30 miles of each other, with no obstructions in between. In a string of microwave relay stations, each station receives incoming messages, boosts the signal strength, and relays the signal to the next station.*

modem (p. 306) Short for "*modulate/demodulate*"; device that converts digital signals into a representation of analog form (modulation) to send over phone lines. A receiving modem then converts the analog signal back to a digital signal (demodulation). Why it's important: *The modem provides a means for computers to communicate with one another using the standard copper-wire telephone network, an analog system that was built to transmit the human voice but not computer signals.*

narrowband (p. 327) Also known as *voiceband;* bandwidth used generally for voice communication over short distances (a narrow band of frequencies). Why it's important: *Narrowband is used in telephone modems and for regular telephone communications—for speech, faxes, and data. (Compare with* ***broadband.****)*

network (p. 308) Also called *communications network;* system of interconnected computers, telephones, or other communications devices that can communicate with one another and share applications and data. Why it's important: *The tying together of so many communications devices enables the Internet and in many ways is changing the world we live in.*

network architecture (p. 312) The name given to how a network is structured and how it shares and coordinates resources. Why it's important: *Two principal network architectures are client-server and peer to peer. Client-server networks have a central computer that holds the data and manages the resources. Peer-to-peer networks connect computers so that each computer shares all or part of its resources.*

node (p. 315) Any device that is attached (wired or wireless) to a network. Why it's important: *A node may be a microcomputer, terminal, storage device, or peripheral device, any of which enhance the usefulness of the network.*

packet (p. 316) Fixed-length block of data for transmission. The packet also contains instructions about the destination of the packet. Why it's important: *By breaking electronic messages into packets, a transmission system can deliver the data more efficiently and economically. Each message's packets are reassembled when they reach their destination.*

pager (p. 335) Commonly known as *beeper;* simple radio receiver that receives data sent from a special radio transmitter. The pager number is dialed from a phone and travels via the transmitter to the pager. Why it's important: *Pagers are a way of receiving notification of phone calls so that the user can return the calls immediately; some pagers can also display messages of up to 80 characters and send preprogrammed messages. Pages are still used where cellphones are unreliable or prohibited, such as hospital complexes.*

peer-to-peer (P2P) network (p. 313) Type of network in which all computers on the network communicate directly with one another rather than relying on a server, as client-server networks do. Why it's important: *Every computer can share files and peripherals with all other computers on the network, given that all are granted access privileges. Peer-to-peer networks are less expensive than client-server networks and work effectively for up to 25 computers, making them appropriate for home networks. (Compare with* **client-server network.***)*

privacy (p. 353) Privacy is the right of people not to reveal information about themselves. Why it's important: *The ease of pulling together information from databases and disseminating it over the Internet has put privacy under extreme pressure. Ever-present monitoring of us can change our behaviors and self-perception; technologies are used to encroach on our lives.*

protocol (p. 316) Also called *communications protocol;* set of conventions governing the exchange of data between hardware and/or software components in a communications network. Why it's important: *Unless we have an agreement between communicating parties, information may get lost or miscommunicated. This agreement is the protocol. Protocols are built into hardware and software. Also, every device connected to a network must have an Internet protocol (IP) address so that other computers on the network can route data to that address.*

radio-frequency (RF) spectrum (p. 327) The part of the electromagnetic spectrum that carries most communications signals. Why it's important: *The radio spectrum ranges from low-frequency waves, such as those used for aeronautical and marine navigation equipment; through the medium frequencies for CB radios, cordless phones, and baby monitors; to ultrahigh-frequency bands for cellphones; and also microwave bands for communications satellites.*

ring network (p. 319) Type of network in which all communications devices are connected in a continuous loop and messages are passed around the ring until they reach the right destination. There is no central server. Why it's important: *The advantage of a ring network is that messages flow in only one direction, and so there is no danger of collisions. The disadvantage is that if a workstation malfunctions, the entire network can stop working.*

rootkit (p. 349) Secret software program installed in a computer's operating system that someone in another location can use to take control of the computer. Why it's important: *The goal of the rootkit program is to gain "root" access to the computer and install a "kit" of software files to create mischief: change settings, access files, delete files, install rogue programs, and otherwise perpetrate unsavory and illegal activities. Rootkits may then change the operating system settings so that malware program is not visible. Rootkits may work by exploiting security weaknesses in operating systems and applications. They may also create a backdoor, a means of accessing a computer program that bypasses security mechanisms.*

router (p. 316) Device that joins multiple wired and wireless networks. Routers have specific software and hardware designed for routing and forwarding information. Why it's important: *High-speed routers serve as part of the Internet backbone, or transmission path, handling the major data traffic. They also provide small network connectivity.*

security (p. 343) Safeguards for protecting information technology against unauthorized access, system failures, and disasters that can result in damage or loss. Why it's important: *Security matters are a never-ending problem, with attacks on computers and data becoming more powerful and more complex. The ongoing dilemma of the Digital Age is balancing convenience against security.*

star network (p. 319) Type of network in which all microcomputers and other communications devices are connected to a central switch. Electronic messages are routed through the central switch to their destinations. The central switch monitors the flow of traffic. Why it's important: *The star network is a very common computer network topology. One malfunctioning node doesn't affect the rest of the network, and it's easy to add and remove nodes.*

switch (p. 316) A device that connects computers to a network. Why it's important: *A switch facilitates the connection of multiple computers and other network devices.*

topology (p. 318) The logical layout, or shape, of a network. The five basic topologies are star, ring, bus, tree, and mesh. Why it's important: *Different topologies can be used to suit different office and equipment network configurations.*

tree network (p. 321) A bus network of star networks; that is, a tree network is a combination of two or more connected star networks. Each star network is a LAN with a central computer with which microcomputers and other devices are directly connected. In turn the central computers of the star networks are connected to a main cable called the bus. Why it's important: *Often used by corporations to share organization-wide data, a tree network might be found on a university campus in which each department has its own star network with its own central computer. The various departments are then linked throughout the university by the main bus.*

troll (p. 343) A person who posts intentionally offensive, incendiary, or off-topic comments online, to upset people. Why it's important: *Mean people have caused websites to shut down their comment boards. Trolling occurs, it's suggested, because of an "online disinhibition effect" that allows people who might not say hateful things in person to post poisonous comments on comment boards. The psychological effects of trolling can be devastating.*

Trojan horse (p. 349) A subclass of virus program that pretends to be a useful program, such as a game or screen saver, but that carries viruses, or destructive instructions. Why it's important: *A Trojan horse can cause trouble without your knowledge, such as allow installation of backdoor programs, illegal programs that allow illegitimate users to take control of your computer without your knowledge.*

twisted-pair wire (p. 324) Two strands of insulated copper wire, twisted around each other. Why it's important: *Twisted-pair wire has been the most common channel or medium used for telephone systems. However, it is relatively slow and does not protect well against electrical interference.*

ultra-wideband (UWB) (p. 340) Technology operating in the range of 480 megabits to 1.6 gigabytes per second up to about 30 feet that uses a low-power source to send out millions of bursts of radio energy every second over many different frequencies, which are then reassembled by a UWB receiver. Why it's important: *UWB operates over low frequencies not used by other technologies, making it a candidate to replace many of the cables that now currently connect household and office devices.*

virtual private network (VPN) (p. 314) Private network that uses a public network, usually the Internet, to connect remote sites. Why it's important: *Because wide area networks use leased lines, maintaining them can be expensive, especially as distances between offices increase. To decrease communications costs, some companies have established their own VPNs. Company intranets, extranets, and LANS can all be parts of a VPN.*

wide area network (WAN) (p. 310) Communications network that covers a wide geographic area, such as a country or the world. Why it's important: *Most long-distance and regional telephone companies are WANs. A WAN may use a combination of satellites, fiber-optic cable, microwave, and copper-wire connections and link a variety of computers, from mainframes to terminals.*

WiMax (p. 340) *Worldwide Interoperability for Microwave Access;* similar to the Wi-Fi standard but with a far greater range—up to 30 miles for a fixed station or 10 miles for a mobile station. Why it's important: *WiMax is being employed by many users, such as universities, to extend the range of existing Wi-Fi networks.*

Wireless Application Protocol (WAP) (p. 329) Communications protocol designed to link nearly all mobile devices to your telecommunications carrier's wireless network and content providers. Why it's important: *Wireless devices such as smartphones use the Wireless Application Protocol for connecting wireless users to the World Wide Web.*

wireless LAN (WLAN) (p. 311) LAN that uses radio frequencies rather than physical wires to connect computers and other devices. Why it's important: *Wireless networks provide an inexpensive and easy way to share a single Internet connection among several computers.*

wireless USB (WUSB) (p. 341) Wireless standard with a typical range of 32 feet and a maximum data rate of 110–480 megabits per second. Why it's important: *Wireless USB is used in game controllers, printers, scanners, digital cameras, MP3 players, hard disks, and flash drives. USB is the de facto standard in the personal computing industry.*

worm (p. 348) Program that repeatedly copies itself into a computer's memory or onto a disk or flash drive or USB device drive until no space is left. Why it's important: *Worms can shut down computers and networks.*

zombie (p. 349) Computer taken over covertly and programmed to respond to instructions sent remotely. Why it's important: *Unbeknown to their owners, who have accidentally clicked on a malicious link or file, their infected computers become part of a botnet that cybercriminals use to crash websites, swipe passwords, bring down websites, or steal consumer financial data. (See* ***botnet.****)*

CHAPTER REVIEW

stage 1 LEARNING MEMORIZATION

"I can recognize and recall information."

Self-Test Questions

1. A(n) __________ converts digital signals into analog signals for transmission over phone lines.
2. A(n) __________ network covers a wide geographic area, such as a state or a country.
3. __________ cable transmits data as pulses of light rather than as electricity.
4. __________ refers to waves continuously varying in strength and/or quality; __________ refers to communications signals or information in a binary form.
5. Someone who posts intentionally hateful comments on a website is a(n) __________.
6. A(n) __________ is a private network that uses a public network (usually the Internet) to connect remote sites.
7. A(n) __________ is a computer that acts as a disk drive, storing programs and data files shared by users on a LAN.
8. The __________ is the system software that manages the activities of a network.
9. Modem is short for __________.
10. __________ is a short-range wireless digital standard aimed at linking cellphones, computers, and peripherals up to distances of 30 feet; it is often used for hands-free smartphone calls.
11. Your computer has been taken over by a(n) __________ and is now a(n) __________ under the control of hackers in remote places.
12. The __________ consists of the main highway—including gateways, routers, and other communications equipment—that connects all computer networks.

13. The most commonly used wired connection standard for local area networks is _________.
14. Any device that is attached to a network is called a(n) _________.
15. A set of conventions governing the exchange of data between hardware and software components in a communications network is called a(n) _________.
16. In a(n) _________ network topology, messages sent to the destination can take any possible shortest, easiest route to reach its destination; the Internet uses this topology.

Multiple-Choice Questions

1. Which of these best describes the regular telephone line that is used in most homes today?
   a. coaxial cable
   b. modem cable
   c. twisted-pair wire
   d. fiber-optic cable
   e. LAN
2. Which of these do local area networks enable?
   a. sharing of peripheral devices
   b. sharing of programs and data
   c. better communications
   d. access to databases
   e. all of these
3. Which of these is *not* a type of server?
   a. file server
   b. print server
   c. mail server
   d. disk server
   e. RAM server
4. Which of the following is *not* a short-distance wireless standard?
   a. Bluetooth
   b. PDA
   c. Wi-Fi
   d. WAP
5. Which type of local area network connects all devices through a central switch?
   a. bus network
   b. star network
   c. mesh network
   d ring network
   e. router
6. Which is the type of local area network in which all microcomputers on the network communicate directly with one another without relying on a server?
   a. client-server
   b. domain
   c. peer to peer
   d. MAN
   e. WAN
7. How do fiber-optic cables transmit data?
   a. via copper wire
   b. via infrared
   c. via AC electric current
   d. via radio waves
   e. via pulsating beams of light
8. A(n) _________ is a system of hardware and/or software that protects a computer or a network from intruders.
   a. bridge
   b. firewall
   c. gateway
   d. router
   e. switch

True-False Questions

T F 1. In a LAN, a bridge is used to connect the same type of networks, whereas a gateway is used to enable dissimilar networks to communicate.

T F 2. Frequency and amplitude are two characteristics of analog carrier waves.

T F 3. A range of frequencies is called a *spectrum*.

T F 4. Twisted-pair wire commonly connects residences to external telephone systems.

T F 5. Wi-Fi signals can travel up to about 230 feet.

T F 6. Microwave transmissions are a line-of-sight medium.

T F 7. 2G is the newest cellphone standard.

T F 8. Wi-Fi is formally known as an 802.11 network.

T F 9. A Trojan horse copies itself repeatedly into a computer's memory or onto a hard drive.

T F 10. Using Ethernet to alter readable data into unreadable form can prevent unauthorized access to transmitted messages.

2 LEARNING COMPREHENSION

"I can recall information in my own terms and explain it to a friend."

Short-Answer Questions

1. What is the difference between an intranet and an extranet?
2. What is the difference between a LAN and a WAN?
3. Why is bandwidth a factor in data transmission?
4. What is a firewall?
5. What do *2G*, *3G*, and *4G* mean?
6. Explain the differences between ring, bus, and star networks.
7. What is the electromagnetic spectrum?
8. What does a protocol do?
9. What are three or more basic rules for creating passwords?
10. What do we need encryption for?

3 LEARNING **APPLYING, ANALYZING, SYNTHESIZING, EVALUATING**

"I can apply what I've learned, relate these ideas to other concepts, build on other knowledge, and use all these thinking skills to form a judgment."

Knowledge in Action

1. Are the computers at your school connected to a network? If so, what kind of network(s)? What types of computers are connected? What hardware and software allows the network to function? What department(s) did you contact to find the information you needed to answer these questions?
2. Using current articles, publications, and/or the web, research cable modems. Where are they being used? What does a residential user need to hook up to a cable modem system?
3. Research the role of the Federal Communications Commission in regulating the communications industry. How are new frequencies opened up for new communications services? How are the frequencies determined? Who gets to use new frequencies?
4. Research the Telecommunications Act of 1996. Do you think it has had a positive or a negative effect? Why?
5. Would you like to have a job for which you telecommute instead of "going in to work"? Why or why not?
6. From your experience with cellphones, do you think it is wise to continue also paying for a "landline" POTS phone line, or is cellphone service reliable enough and clear enough to use as your sole means of telephony? Does the quality of cellphone clarity depend on where you live? Why or why not? As cell service advances, how do you think the POTS infrastructure will be used?

Web Exercises

1. Compare digital cable and satellite TV in your area. Which offers more channels? Which offers more features? How much do the services cost? Do both offer Internet connectivity? What are the main differences between the two types of service?
2. Calculate the amount of airborne data transmission that travels through your body. To do this, research the amount of radio and television station broadcast signals in your area, as well as the estimated number of mobile phone users. Imagine what the world would look like if you could see all the radio-wave signals the way you can see the waves in the ocean.
3. On the web, go to *www.trimble.com/gps/index.shtml* and work through some of the tutorial on GPS technology. Then write a short report on the applications of a GPS system.
4. Trolling can be very harmful, both to victims of trolling and to the troller; it can become a form of stalking and/or bullying. List at least four ways a troller can be stopped:

   www.businessblogshub.com/2012/10/trolling-can-damage-your-personal-life-and-get-you-fired-just-ask-michael-brutsch/

   www.osnews.com/story/25540/

   www.wikihow.com/Deal-with-an-Internet-Troll/

   http://socialmediatoday.com/adamn/1221201/trolling-age-old-problem-s-not-getting-better/

   What are patent trolls? Do a keyword search and explain why patent trolling is a problem.
5. Test your ports and shields. Is your Internet connection secure, or is it inviting intruders to come in? Use the buttons at the bottom of the page at *https://grc.com/x/ne.dll?bh0bkyd2* to test your port security and your shields and receive a full report on how your computer is communicating with the Internet.
6. Learn about the method of triangulation. This method helps when you use your cellphone to locate, for example, the nearest movie theater or restaurant. Visit the sites below to learn more. Run your own search on *triangulation.*

   http://wrongfulconvictionsblog.org/2012/06/01/cell-tower-triangulation-how-it-works/

   www.qrg.northwestern.edu/projects/vss/docs/navigation/1-what-is-triangulation.html

   http://searchnetworking.techtarget.com/sDefinition/0,,sid7_gci753924,00.html

   www.al911.org/wireless/triangulation_location.htm

   www.ehow.com/how_2385973_triangulate-cell-phone.html

   How do you ping a cellphone?

   www.ehow.com/how_5942191_ping-cell-phone.html

   www.ehow.com/how_7292559_ping-cell-phone-number.html

   http://cellphones.lovetoknow.com/How_to_Ping_a_Cell_Phone
7. GSM and CDMA: Why do you need to know what these terms mean?

   www.pcmag.com/article2/0,2817,2407896,00.asp

   http://reviews.ebay.com/Cell-Phone-technologies-GSM-CDMA-TDMA-iDEN_W0QQugidZ10000000003636609

   http://osxdaily.com/2012/11/15/determine-iphone-gsm-or-cdma/

   www.diffen.com/difference/CDMA_vs_GSM
8. Security issue—Wi-Fi security issues: As Wi-Fi becomes more widespread, how will users protect their networks? Wi-Fi is hacked almost as a harmless hobby to detect its vulnerabilities. Visit these websites to learn about Wi-Fi security.

   www.makeuseof.com/tag/combat-wifi-security-risks-connecting-public-network/

   www.wi-fi.org/discover-and-learn/security/

   http://en.kioskea.net/contents/805-risks-related-to-wireless-wifi-networks-802-11-or-wi-fi/

   www.pcmag.com/article2/0,2817,2420002,00.asp

   www.eweek.com/security/slideshows/public-wifi-security-10-things-to-remember-before-signing-on/

9. How important is your privacy to you? Are you truly aware of how your privacy is being destroyed?

   www.aclu.org/technology-and-liberty/internet-privacy/

   http://douthat.blogs.nytimes.com/2013/06/11/power-and-privacy-on-the-internet/

   http://howto.cnet.com/8301-11310_39-57590304-285/simple-ways-to-enhance-your-internet-privacy/

   www.privacyrights.org/fs/fs18-cyb.htm

   http://business.time.com/2013/06/20/the-anonymous-internet-privacy-tools-grow-in-popularity-following-nsa-revelations/

   www.humanrightsfirst.org/our-work/business-and-human-rights/internet-freedom-and-privacy/

   www.nbcnews.com/id/3078835/t/online-privacy-fears-are-real/#.UddqYdjbsS4

How about buying cut-rate drugs from online pharmacies based in Canada or Thailand?[63] Only 3% of such websites abide by federal or state laws, a study finds, and you may well risk getting fake drugs that are contaminated or even toxic. Finally, what about going online to buy some official San Francisco 49ers jerseys, Louis Vuitton bags, or upscale Beats by Dr. Dre headphones?[64] You'll probably wind up with counterfeit goods. In sum, the amount of fakery and thievery involving information technology and networks almost knows no bounds. ■

6.6 CYBERATTACKS & MALWARE

Networks and computer systems are susceptible to attacks by all kinds of malware. Some common cyberthreats are denial-of-service attacks; viruses; worms; Trojan horses; rootkits and backdoors; blended threats; zombies; ransomware; and time, logic, and email bombs.

Internet users, especially home users, are not nearly as safe as they believe, according to a study by McAfee and the nonprofit National Cyber Security Alliance.[65] Of 378 adults studied, 92% believed that they were safe from viruses; however, only 51% had up-to-date virus software. And 73% thought they had a firewall installed, but only 64% actually had it enabled. Little more than half had antispyware protection, and only about 12% had phishing protection. Such protections are essential in the Wild West world of today's Internet.

In Chapter 2 (p. 96) we described some common cyberthreats—snooping, spamming, spoofing, phishing, pharming, cookies, spyware, and viruses. But that list wasn't exhaustive. Here we consider other threats: denial-of-service attacks; worms; Trojan horses; rootkits and backdoors; blended threats; zombies; ransomware; and time, logic, and email bombs.

DENIAL-OF-SERVICE ATTACKS A denial-of-service (DoS) attack, or *distributed denial-of-service (DDoS) attack,* consists of making repeated requests of a computer system or network, thereby overloading it and denying legitimate users access to it. Because computers are limited in the number of user requests they can handle at any given time, a DoS onslaught will tie them up with fraudulent requests that cause them to shut down. The assault may come from a single computer or from hundreds or thousands of computers that have been taken over by those intending harm.

US-CERT
UNITED STATES COMPUTER EMERGENCY READINESS TEAM

HOME | PUBLICATIONS | ALERTS AND TIPS | RELATED RESOURCES | ABOUT US | GFIRST

Security Tip (ST04-015)
Understanding Denial-of-Service Attacks

View Previous Tips

Original release date: November 04, 2009 | Last revised: February 06, 2013

Print | Tweet | Send | Share

What is a denial-of-service (DoS) attack?

In a denial-of-service (DoS) attack, an attacker attempts to prevent legitimate users from accessing information or services. By targeting your computer and its network connection, or the computers and network of the sites you are trying to use, an attacker may be able to prevent you from accessing email, websites, online accounts (banking, etc.), or other services that rely on the affected computer.

You may have heard of denial-of-service attacks launched against websites, but you can also be a victim of these attacks. Denial-of-service attacks can be difficult to distinguish from common network activity, but there are some indications that an attack is in progress.

The most common and obvious type of DoS attack occurs when an attacker "floods" a network with information. When you type a URL for a particular website into your browser, you are sending a request to that site's computer server to view the page. The server can only process a certain number of requests at once, so if an attacker overloads the server with requests, it can't process your request. This is a "denial of service" because you can't access that site.

An attacker can use spam email messages to launch a similar attack on your email account. Whether you have an email account supplied by your employer or one available through a free service such as Yahoo or Hotmail, you are assigned a specific quota, which limits the amount of data you can have in your account at any given time. By sending many, or large, email messages to the account, an attacker can consume your quota, preventing you from receiving legitimate messages.

What is a distributed denial-of-service (DDoS) attack?

In a distributed denial-of-service (DDoS) attack, an attacker may use your computer to attack another computer. By taking advantage of security vulnerabilities or weaknesses, an attacker could take control of your computer. He or she could then force your computer to send huge amounts of data to a website or send spam to particular email addresses. The attack is "distributed" because the attacker is using multiple computers, including yours, to launch the denial-of-service attack.

How do you avoid being part of the problem?

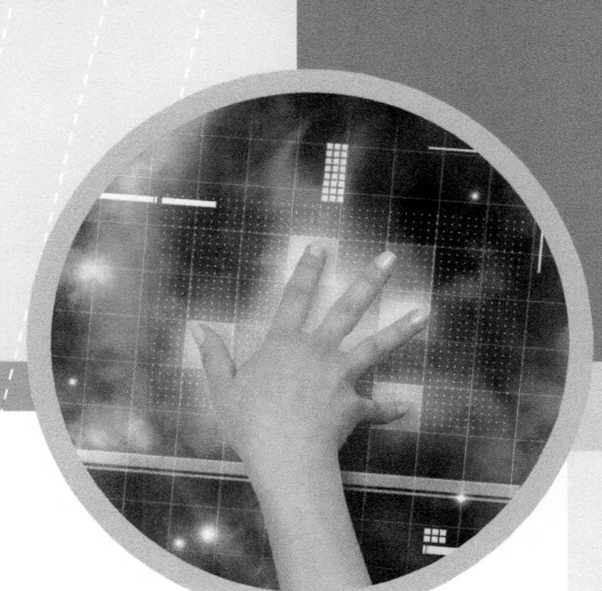

PERSONAL TECHNOLOGY

The Future Is You

Chapter Topics & Key Questions

UNIT 7A: *Personal Devices for Improving Productivity at School & Work*

7.1 **Convergence, Portability, & Personalization**
What are some of the pros and cons of the major trends in personal technology?

7.2 **Smartphones: More Than Talk**
How are smartphones different from basic cellphones?

7.3 **Tablets & E-Readers**
What are tablets and e-books superior at doing?

7.4 **Portable Media Players**
What should I know about portable media players?

UNIT 7B: *Personal Devices for Enriching Leisure & Life*

7.5 **Digital Cameras: Changing Photography**
What are some of the things I can do with digital cameras?

7.6 **High-Tech Radio: Satellite, Hybrid Digital, & Internet**
How do the three forms of high-tech radio differ?

7.7 **Digital Television**
What's new about the new television?

7.8 **Videogame Systems: The Ultimate Convergence Machine?**
What are the principal videogame consoles?

Download the free UIT 11e App for key term flash cards quizzes and a game, *Over the Edge*

CHAPTER FORECAST In Unit 7A, we begin by considering how trends in the evolving Internet—convergence, portability, and personalization—are affecting us. We then consider personal technology that can help your productivity at school and work: smartphones, tablets, e-readers, and portable media players. Smartphones have advanced operating systems and touch screens, unlike cell-phones, which are designed mostly just for calls and perhaps texting. Tablets are useful as multipurpose devices, but e-book readers are usually better for reading. The e-book reader can hold a library that you can take almost anywhere. Portable media players include music players, media players, and some mobile phones.

In Unit 7B, we discuss devices that can further enrich your leisure and life: digital cameras, high-tech radio, digital television, and videogame systems. A digital camera takes video and photographs and digitally converts the analog data by recording images via an electronic image sensor. High-tech radio uses satellite, hybrid digital, and the Internet. We also describe podcasting. New varieties of digital television include interactive, Internet, and Internet-ready TV. The principal videogame consoles—Xbox, PlayStation, and Wii—are having to adapt to competition from mobile games.

UNIT 7A: *Personal Devices for Improving Productivity at School & Work*

"The war is over," says Scott Snyder. "Mobile is the new platform. And it is changing our behavior. We are using it for everything, because we like doing things in the easiest way possible."[1]

Mobile devices such as the smartphone and the tablet have made large inroads against laptop computers and are changing the competitive landscape for all companies, no matter what the industry. The "new normal," says Scott Snyder, president of a mobile app developer, is "exposed identity" and constant sharing, because a smartphone always knows its holder's location. Seen this way, smartphones, tablets, and other mobile electronic gadgets can provide wide-ranging benefits to us in school and in business, as well as to our leisure pursuits. But, as we have seen in the last chapter, they also carry grave risks to our security and privacy.

We are well on our way toward what Yahoo! founders Jerry Yang and David Filo call the Internet's "second act."[2] The Internet's first period, they say, involved shifting real-world activities such as shopping and dating into a virtual world, one dominated by the personal computer. In the second act, in which broadband extends to every electronic gadget, especially mobile ones, creative power will shift into the hands of individuals, predicts one report, who, it suggests, "will be just as likely to generate and share their own content as to consume someone else's."[3]

This is the force, for example, behind the phenomenon known as the mashup, part of the ongoing shift toward a more interactive and participatory web. **The mashup is a creative combination of content or elements from different sources,** such as a web page that blends data from two or more sources to create new services or content. For instance, Housingmaps.com is a mashup that takes real estate information from Craigslist, such as homes for sale or apartments for rent, and blends them with Google Maps. The mashup result: an interactive map that shows you what homes and apartments are available, sorted by price and location.[4]

Let us consider how the major trends of the Internet's "second act"—convergence, portability, and personalization—are affecting us.

Mashup Sites

Information on various types of mashups:

http://blog.aids.gov/downloads/toolkit_mashups.pdf

www.mashup-charts.com/

www.programmableweb.com/mashups/

http://netforbeginners.about.com/od/m/f/What-Is-an-Internet-Mashup.htm

www.videomashups.ca/

www.last.fm/tag/mashup/

7.1 CONVERGENCE, PORTABILITY, & PERSONALIZATION

Three major trends in information technology continue to be convergence, portability, and personalization.

A smartphone seems to embody three principal results of the fusion of computers and communications that we mentioned in Chapter 1—*convergence, portability,* and *personalization.*

Convergence

The busiest area of convergence today is the merging of computers and consumer electronics.

As we said in Chapter 1, **convergence, or *digital convergence,* describes the combining of several industries—computers, communications, consumer electronics, entertainment, and mass media—through various devices that exchange data in digital form.** Long predicted but not fulfilled, convergence is now a reality. More and more households throughout the world have been going to broadband, with the faster Internet connections changing the computer, cable, phone, music, movie, and other businesses. Convergence, as we've pointed out, has led to electronic products that perform multiple functions, such as TVs with Internet access, cellphones that are also digital cameras and GPS units, and cars with various types of digital connection ports. And mashups are a convergent technology.

Of course, hybrid convergence devices have pros and cons, some of which are as follows.

CONVERGENCE: THE UPSIDE Over the past two decades, as computing and communications have migrated from expensive desktop computers, which were used mainly by upper-income people, to easier-to-use and more affordable smartphones, users have also changed, with a much greater diversity of people being involved. And they are using their handhelds for many more nonvoice data applications, such as taking pictures, accessing the Internet, playing music, retrieving email, watching movies, visiting social networking sites, and texting. Indeed, engineers have succeeded in designing the smartphone so you can use it as a universal remote to control your music, your TV, your PowerPoint presentation, or whatever.

All these capabilities have become accepted conveniences, keeping people connected to one another and to many kinds of business and educational resources, information sources, and entertainment. But these conveniences carry some problems.

CONVERGENCE: THE DOWNSIDE Not all hybrid devices are necessarily practical. For one thing, any device whose primary feature is compromised by converged technologies is not necessarily a good device. For another thing, the more hardware capabilities that one loads onto one device, the more applications one uses it for—and the more apps and types of connections—the higher the risk of security breaches, ID theft, outsiders tracking personal data and locations, and the loss of focus on face-to-face communication.

Convergence. Home entertainment centers bring together several electronic functions to access music, video, TV, and the Internet, as well as support some computer functions.

Portability

A device that is portable is small, lightweight, and easy to carry.

Portability **means the state or quality of being portable—that is, capable of being carried or moved about.** Not all too long ago, having a phone in your car was a badge of affluence, affordable mainly by Hollywood movie producers and big-city real estate developers. Now, thanks to increasing miniaturization, faster speeds, and declining costs, nearly everyone has a portable phone and, of course, a host of other devices that are also portable: laptop computers, tablets, e-book readers, portable media players, digital cameras, and the like.

Portability also has its upside and downside.

Serious portability: The Apple iPod Shuffle has 2 gigabytes of USB flash drive storage for hundreds of songs.

PORTABILITY: THE UPSIDE The advantages of portability seem obvious: being able to do phone calls and emails from anywhere that you can make a connection, keeping up with your social networks, listening to hundreds of songs on a digital music player such as an iPod, taking photos or video anywhere on a whim, and watching TV anywhere anytime. One reason that manufacturers have targeted turning cellphones into hybrids, incidentally, is that people carry them wherever they go, unlike laptop computers, portable media players, and digital cameras.

PORTABILITY: THE DOWNSIDE The same portable technology that enables you to access information and entertainment anytime anywhere often means that others can find *you* equally conveniently (for them). Thus, you have to become disciplined about preventing others from wasting your time, as by screening your cellphone calls with *Caller ID,* a feature that shows the name and/or number of the calling party on the phone's display when you receive an incoming call. You may also find yourself bombarded throughout the day by unnecessary incoming emails, text messages, and web services known as RSS aggregators that automatically update you on new information from various sites.

Nonstop connectivity may rain digital information on you, but it can also have the paradoxical result of removing you from real human contact. Consequently, the professor whose recommendation you may need someday for an employment or graduate school reference may never get to know you, because your interaction will never be face to face, for example, during his or her normal office hours. Businesses, incidentally, have recently had to deal with recurring complaints from employees about their inability to reach coworkers to get critical information they need—because their coworkers don't respond in timely fashion via email.

Also, miniaturization of electronic devices can make readability an issue.

Personalization

Is personalization of media content possible without loss of privacy and restriction of information?

As we said in Chapter 1, **personalization is the creation of information tailored to your preferences,** such as programs that automatically cull recent news and information from the Internet on just those topics you have designated. "With the world going digital so quickly," predicts one marketing executive, "consumers will soon expect each of their online experiences (on the Web, mobile, email, . . . and so forth) to be 100% relevant to them—and here's the rub—while not infringing on their privacy."[5]

PERSONALIZATION: THE UPSIDE As a consumer, you may have downloaded hundreds or thousands of songs, so that you have your own personalized library of music on your phone, tablet, and/or portable media player. You may also have created your own list of "favorites" or "bookmarks" so that you can readily access your favorite websites. And you may have accessed or contributed to certain blogs, or personalized online diaries. In addition, of course, PC software and apps can be used to create all kinds of personal projects, ranging from artwork to finances to genealogy.

PERSONALIZATION: THE DOWNSIDE One of the downsides of personalization is that people may feel overburdened with *too much choice.* Indeed, Swarthmore College psychology professor Barry Schwartz, author of *The Paradox of Choice: Why More Is Less,* has identified several factors by which choice overload hurts us: regret, inaction, excessive expectations, and self-blame.[6] These are explained in the Practical Action box on page 372.

Popular Personal Technologies

Personal electronic devices can make your educational and work life more productive, but they also can cause some problems.

Where are you, technologically speaking, with the personal electronic devices you use every day? Do they provide amusement and distraction but also waste your time? Let's explore how you can use the tools of personal technology—smartphones, tablets and e-books, and portable media players—to be more productive in your educational and work life.

7.2 SMARTPHONES: More Than Talk

A smartphone is a cellular telephone with software applications and Internet access.

"There's a digital land rush going on," says *New York Times* technology writer Steve Lohr, "driven by rapid advances in technology

15 Website Personalization and Recommendations Software Tools

Dave Chaffey
April 23, 2013. 27 comments
Quick Guide: Product page optimisation

Tweet

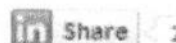

Share 2

These website personalisation tools enable you to segment visitors and then deliver personalised messages within containers as with the classic Amazon personalized recommendations – read their published methodology from this fascinating whitepaper from 2003.

Personalization integrated with web analytics

- Coremetrics Intelligent Offer IBM Coremetrics is widely used by retailers for analytics – and increasingly personalization for cross and up-selling.
- Adobe Test and Target One of the best established personalization engines evolving from the original Touch Clarity back in 2004.
- BT Buckets Lower cost option that integrates with Google Analytics.

Independent personalization engines

- Magiq dynamic personalization software – read our interview about the benefits of Maqiq
- Convert Marketing Optimization Platform
- Ecommerce recommendation engine Currently in Beta – retail personalization
- WP Greet Box Many WordPress blogging users, including me, use this personalisation plug-in to deliver a welcome message to first time users depending on their referrers. It's amazing this approach isn't used more on commercial sites.

Personalization of customer service

- eStara from atg eStara Click to Call and Click to Chat engage visitors proactively and selectively offer them the opportunity to contact a live agent from any page on any Web site, whether powered by the ATG platform or not.

E-Commerce Personalization Software as Service (SaaS)

Website personalization programs

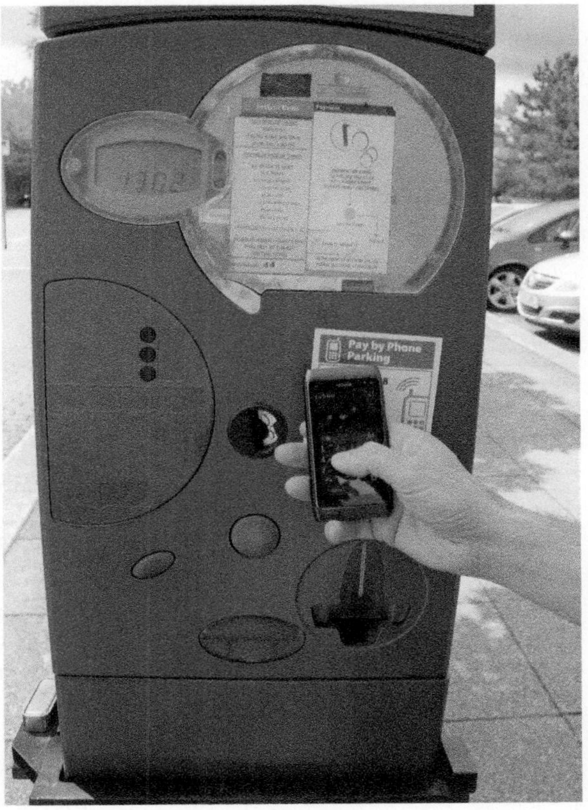

Paying for parking by smartphone

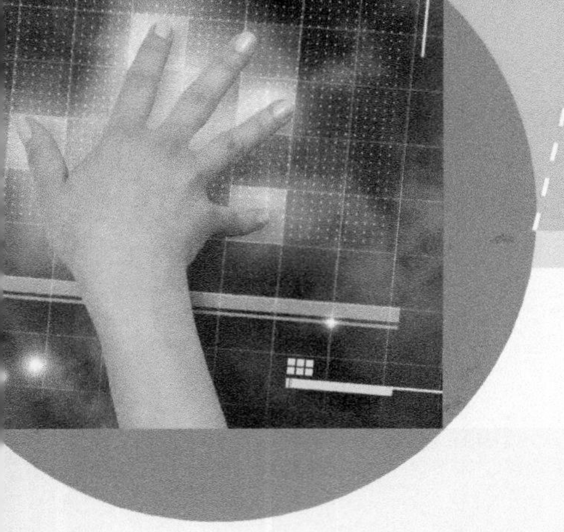

PRACTICAL ACTION

The Consequences of Choice Overload

As available options increase, says Swarthmore College psychology professor Barry Schwartz, the following may happen:[7]

- **Regret:** People are more likely to regret their decisions.
- **Inaction:** People are more likely to anticipate regretting decisions, and the anticipated regret prevents people from actually deciding.
- **Excessive expectations:** Expectations about how good the decision will be go up. Thus, reality has a hard time living up to the expectations.
- **Self-blame:** When decisions have disappointing results, people tend to blame themselves, because they feel the unsatisfying results must be their fault.

Other possible problems caused by too much choice and "overpersonalization" of media devices and media content include these:

- **Paralysis over too many choices:** Ever become paralyzed by the prospect of too many choices? Whatever you select, you fear the other option would have been better, so you choose nothing. Of course the Internet holds out the possibility of endless choices. But seeking the perfect choice, even in big decisions, like picking a college, "is a recipe for misery," Schwartz says.[8] Thus, he suggests, when looking for a new camera or a hotel, for example, limit yourself to just three websites. "It is not clear," says research scientist Benjamin Scheibehenne, "that more choice gives you more freedom. It could decrease our freedom if we spend so much time trying to make choices."[9]
- **Unwanted personalization, or filtering, of content:** Eli Pariser, of MoveOn fame, gave a talk on "the insidious encroachment of invisible filters on the Web content we see and consume." Consider, he said, his own Facebook feed. Pariser has "a number of friends who are liberal," says one report, "and a number of friends who are conservative. One day, though, he noticed that his conservative friends' comments weren't showing up in his News Feed anymore. Facebook, in its infinite wisdom, had determined that, because Eli is more likely to click on a link from a liberal friend than on one from a conservative one, it would be easier for everybody concerned to show Eli links *only* from liberal friends. Without consulting Eli, the algorithm quietly hid all the apparently unwanted messages."[10] What happened to Pariser was a case of *unwanted* personalization.
- **Choosing of facts to reinforce our worldview:** The news is the news, and it should reflect the world, not our own narrow views. "One of the key requirements for a functioning democracy is a well-informed citizenry," points out one commentator. "A democracy demands that its people are active and informed from a variety of perspectives. As one of the most recent online fads, personalization poses a rather large threat to this."[11] Many consumers of online information customize content to reinforce what they basically already "know." However, your interests should not define what news you are exposed to.

that make it possible to put more and more tools of higher and higher quality into phones."[12] Lohr is referring to *smartphones,* cellphones with built-in applications, multimedia capability, and Internet access (Chapter 1, p. 2).

There seems to be no end of features existing and forthcoming for mobile phones. New smartphones have powerful graphics chips and good screen quality that allow three-dimensional images, fast computing capabilities, realistic graphics, and fast-moving action that translate into powerful on-screen games. In the United States, students at the University of California, Santa Barbara, pay for parking stalls by charging the fee to an account through their cellphones. In Japan, customers can pay for purchases not with cash or credit cards but by making electronic payments through a smartphone. Also in Japan, mobile phones have been turned into controllers for model racing cars, for use as television remotes, and as devices for fingerprint recognition. In South Korea, smartphones have been modified to allow diabetics to check their blood-sugar levels, and the data can be sent to their physicians.

Let us see where this exciting technology is taking us.

How Do Cellphones & Smartphones Differ?

Cellphones are designed for calls and perhaps texting; smartphones have advanced operating systems and touch screens.

Smartphones differ from conventional cellphones in these ways.[13]

CELLPHONES: DESIGNED FOR CALLS & PERHAPS TEXTING The lower-priced option ($20–$150, but often free with a two-year phone company contract), cellphones are compact, have a straightforward keypad, let you receive and send text messages, and allow you to store frequently used phone numbers. Cellphones were originally designed for calls, and perhaps texting, but many have cameras, can access high-speed data networks, and support Bluetooth headsets for hands-free communication. For users who care about privacy, cellphones are usually harder to track than GPS-equipped smartphones.

SMARTPHONES: DESIGNED WITH ADVANCED OPERATING SYSTEMS & TOUCH SCREENS The arrival of smartphones, which have advanced operating systems and touch screens, has roiled the telephone industry. Phone makers such as Nokia and Motorola have stumbled over the transition from cellphones to smartphones, and are now far down the list of smartphone manufacturers.[14]

Smartphones are more expensive (generally $200–$350, with a two-year phone company contract) than cellphones, have advanced operating systems (Apple's iOS, Google's Android, Windows Phone 8) that give them access to thousands of apps, have larger touch-screen displays and more advanced cameras than those on conventional phones, feature GPS navigation technology, have Wi-Fi capabilities, and support higher mobile wireless data speeds, which gives users better web browsing, search functions, and streaming media. They can also have a sophisticated organizer and allow you to do text messaging, handle multiple email accounts, review and edit documents, and create and edit spreadsheets. Many have media players that let you view videos and sort and listen to music tracks. We expand on the features of smartphones throughout the rest of this section.

Seven useful smartphones are the iPhone 5 (which uses the Apple iOS operating system); HTC One, Nexus 5, Samsung Galaxy Note II, Samsung Galaxy S4, and LG Optimus G (all using the Android operating system); and HTC 8X (Windows Phone 8 operating system).[15]

The HTC One X+ Android smartphone weighs only 4.75 ounces and has a quad-core processor.

How a Mobile Phone Works

A cellphone is actually a radio.

In Chapter 6 (p. 336) we described how wireless services use their networks of cell towers to send voice and data over the airwaves in digital form to your cellphone or smartphone, which is basically a sophisticated radio, handing off your call from one cell to another as you move through a series of geographically overlapping cells. The cellphone or smartphone contains many of the same attributes as a personal computer: processor, memory, input/output devices, and operating system.

THE OPERATING SYSTEM & THE AVAILABILITY OF APPS The OS, which is stored in read-only memory (ROM) and is run by the processor, provides you with the interface that allows you to store data, change settings, and so on. As mentioned, the principal smartphone operating systems are the Apple iOS, Google's Android, and Windows Phone 8. All have the ability to handle email, browse the web, do social networking, and run apps.

Apps (Chapter 1, p. 34) are small, specialized programs that can be downloaded onto mobile devices. The number and variety of apps, which can range from free to a dollar or two (and some up to hundreds of dollars), vary according to the OS. The greatest in volume and diversity are apps designed for the iOS (close to 800,000 apps), which are available online from iTunes and the App Store. Also plentiful are the number of apps for the Android OS (about 900,000), which are available online from the Google Play Store.

Smartphone OS Comparison

www.geek.com/smartphone-buyers-guide/operating-system/

www.cnn.com/2012/11/05/tech/mobile/smartphone-operating-systems

http://cell-phones.toptenreviews.com/smartphones/

http://community.giffgaff.com/t5/Blog/Mobile-Operating-Systems-Compared-iOS-Android-and-Windows-Phone/ba-p/2776337/

The Windows Phone 8 offers the fewest number of apps (about 100,000), found at the Windows store. Apps for the BlackBerry smartphone, available at BlackBerry World, number about 70,000.

DISPLAY AREA, SHAPE, & SIZE Most screen sizes range from just over 2 inches to 5 inches, although more smartphones are getting larger: the Apple iPhone 5 has a 4-inch display area; the Huawei Ascend Mate is 6.1 inches. Larger sizes are helpful if you're viewing lots of web pages or watching video. "Phones that fold, slide, or swivel are typically more compact when closed," says Consumer Reports. "Phones shaped like candy bars can be used without first being opened. The best choice depends on personal preference."[16]

STORAGE The data you store in your phone, such as telephone numbers, is stored on flash memory cards, which means that when you turn off the phone, the data does not disappear. Smartphones come with as much as 64 gigabytes of memory in which you can store your music, photos, videos, contact information, applications, and the like. An 8-gigabyte phone memory card can store about 2,000 songs. Some phones also can expand their storage capacity with micro SD cards.

INPUT: TACTILE KEYBOARDS, TOUCH-SCREEN KEYBOARDS, & VOICE COMMANDS At minimum, mobile phones have a keypad for entering numbers and text (and doing text messaging), with some phones having a keyboard that slides out from behind the phone and others with the keyboard in plain sight or available when the phone is opened up. Phones also, of course, have and a microphone for picking up your voice. There are a number of variations, as follows:

BlackBerry phone with physical keyboard

- **Tactile versus touch-screen keyboards:** Also known as *physical keyboards,* tactile keyboards have raised keys and are perceptible to the sense of touch, which make them easier to type on without looking. This is the keyboard available on most BlackBerry phones. Also called *virtual keyboards,* touch-screen keyboards are those in which the image of a keyboard is displayed on a touch screen. This is the keyboard found on the majority of mobile phones, which makes them less bulky although harder to type on.
- **QWERTY versus "condensed" keyboards:** A full QWERTY keyboard, similar to a computer keyboard, is best for writing and editing text and email messages. A "condensed" keyboard crams several letters, numbers, and symbols onto a single key to save space, but is not as easy to use.
- **Voice commands:** In addition to the standard microphone, most mobile phones have a speakerphone, which gives you a hands-free option. Some smartphones allow you to use voice commands to call phone book contacts simply speaking their names. Apps are also available that enable you to get directions, search the web, make calls, and the like using natural language.

Smartphone with touch-screen keyboard

OUTPUT A cellphone includes a receiver or speaker, of course, for picking up voice calls. Mobile phones also have displays ranging from LCD to full-color, high-resolution plasma, suitable for watching TV and playing videogames, as we'll describe. Some other output technologies are these:

- **Media player:** Some phones act as media players, letting you view videos and listen to music tracks. Music companies make songs and music video downloads available to watch on mobile video screens. In addition, phone users can listen to FM radio and stereo sound.
- **Headset connector:** This permits the user to attach a headset to the mobile phone.
- **Bluetooth:** Bluetooth (Chapter 6, p. 220) enables a phone to work with wireless headsets for hands-free operation.

GPS LOCATION-BASED TECHNOLOGY All mobile phones have location-based technology that will access 911 emergency services. Some are able to use the Global Positioning System (GPS) navigation (as we described in Chapter 6, p. 332) to access maps and search engines that give you driving directions or locate nearby business services, such as all pizza restaurants in a particular neighborhood.

WI-FI CONNECTION More and more mobile phones offer the ability to connect to Wi-Fi hotspots (Chapter 2, p. 58) and home networks, giving users faster Internet and email access. For instance, some BlackBerry phones automatically detect when they are near a preset Wi-Fi network and use that network for voice calling or data instead of the common carrier's cellphone connections. Phone calls started in the cellular network will switch over to Wi-Fi and vice versa.

CAMERAS Mobile phone cameras have made the spontaneous snapshot an everyday part of life, thereby, says one observer, "turning ordinary citizens into documentarians, fine-art photographers, and, in cases such as hit-and-run accidents, community watchdogs."[17] Camera phone manufacturers have learned that consumers will take more pictures if the quality is improved and the printing made easier. Thus, there are now available 8-megapixel phone cameras or even more megapixels if you intend to print the scenes you shoot. (Megapixels are the millions of electronic dots that make up an image.) Camera phones are also made with memory card slots, so that images stored on a memory card can then be used directly to have prints made.

DOWNLOADED RINGTONES A phone's *ringtone,* the audible sound a phone makes to announce that a call is coming in, no longer needs to be an old-fashioned "ring, ring." Now your phone could be vibrating, flashing a photo of the caller across the phone's screen, and playing music. Ringtones include a variety of sound effects and melodies used to alert a phone owner of an incoming call. Most manufacturers design their phones so that users can not only choose from many musical ringtones but also program their own for a very personalized ringtone. Some ringtones may be had for free; others, which you may download from your wireless carrier (such as Verizon Wireless, Sprint, AT&T, and T-Mobile), may cost anywhere from about $1.25 to $4 per tune (not per ring).

TV & VIDEO TV programs and movies/videos made for handheld mobile devices pose particular challenges. For one thing, although smartphone screen quality has gotten better, there are still limitations in battery life, processing power, and storage capacity. In addition, most viewers don't have the patience to watch a 90-minute feature film on a small screen. Whether it's a sitcom, news show, or sports highlights, TV programs designed for smartphones have to rely heavily on close-ups, more static shots, and little movement within the frame—the opposite of MTV video. In the end, then, the producers of such fare have to rely more on writing and storytelling.

What happens if you break or lose your phone (as people do all the time)? How do you replace your built-in telephone numbers and contacts? Some carriers and technology companies offer services that, for free or a small monthly fee, back up such data wirelessly.

Text Messaging

Text messaging is the sending of short messages to others' handheld devices as well as desktop computers.

Text messaging, **or *texting* or *SMS* (for short message service), is the sending of short messages, generally no more than 160 characters in length (including spaces), to a smartphone or other handheld device,** including notebook computers. Text messages can also be sent to desktop computers and landline phones. Originally text messaging appeared during the days of mainframe computers, when workers sitting at terminals would send short text messages to one another. In the Internet world, these evolved into

Downloading Ringtones

Some are free. Check if your phone is compatible with the site.

www.zedge.net/ringtones/

www.myxer.com/ringtones/

www.phonezoo.com/ringtones-home.do

www.mycricket.com/community/ringtones/

Download a QR Reader

QR codes (*above*) are a type of matrix bar code (two-dimensional code, Chapter 5, p. 263) designed to be read by smartphones and commonly used for consumer advertising; in other words, it is a "mobile bar code." Most new smartphones have a QR code reader already installed. If your phone doesn't have a QR reader, you can download the reader and install it yourself—for example, from:

www.quickmark.cn/en/basic/downloadmain.asp

Be sure to check on the compatibility of QR readers with your phone—some readers work only on iPhones or Android phones. Some readers work on the Symbian OS, found on Nokia phones, and Java, found on lower-end smartphones.

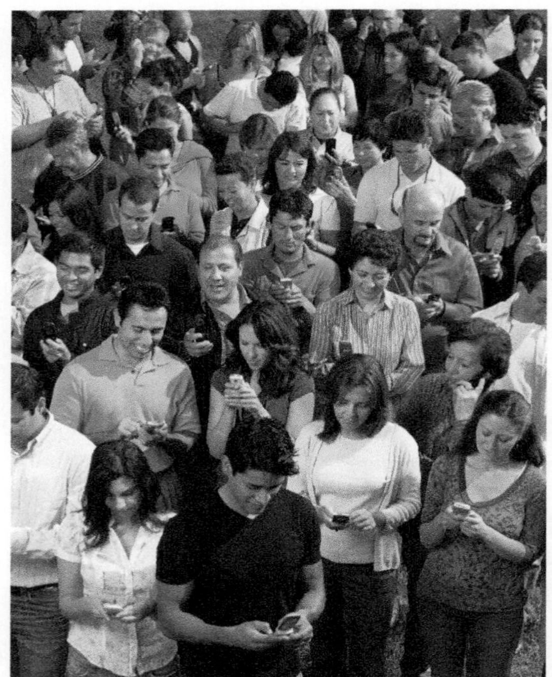
Smartphones: The everywhere device

instant messaging and live text chat sessions. Today text messaging combines the portability of cellphones with the convenience of email and instant messaging. Text messaging is particularly appropriate for situations in which making a cellphone call is intrusive, as when you want to tell someone "I'm 15 minutes late."

Incidentally, texters need to be aware that it's unwise to assume that when they hit the Delete button, the messages are gone forever. Like email and instant messages, text messages are often saved on servers, at least for a while.

Using Mobile Phones in College

Smartphones are useful in college—and careers—for managing your time and tracking your projects.

Mobile phones can be time wasters. It's hard, when you have an idle moment, to resist lighting up your phone to text, check messages, or play Angry Birds. But portable phones can also be tremendous productivity tools. For instance, many of the personal organizing functions formerly found in personal digital assistants—such as address book, schedule planner, and to-do list—are now on smartphones.

Want to keep track of what you're doing? Use a phone app for making and managing lists. Want to see how you're using your time? There's a time tracker app for that. Some apps for both smartphones and tablets that can enhance your ability to get more done in less time are shown at right. *(• See Panel 7.1.)*

Texting While Driving

More dangerous than you think . . . Texting while driving makes a crash 23 times more likely:

www.onlineschools.com/in-focus/driving-while-intexticated/

See also:

www.nationwide.com/newsroom/dwd-facts-figures.jsp

http://stoptextsstopwrecks.org/#home

www.fcc.gov/guides/texting-while-driving/

http://newyork.cbslocal.com/2013/05/09/study-texting-and-driving-kills-more-teens-annually-than-drinking-and-driving/

The Societal Effects of Mobile Phones

The effects of cellphones and smartphones are mixed.

We discussed some of the advantages, drawbacks, and dangers of smartphones in Chapter 6, and we noted that the effects of these phones are mixed. The positive attributes are many: parents can more easily monitor the safety of their children, police dispatchers can help people who are lost, information and amusements of all kinds are readily available, you can phone your apologies when you'll be late for an appointment, and so on.

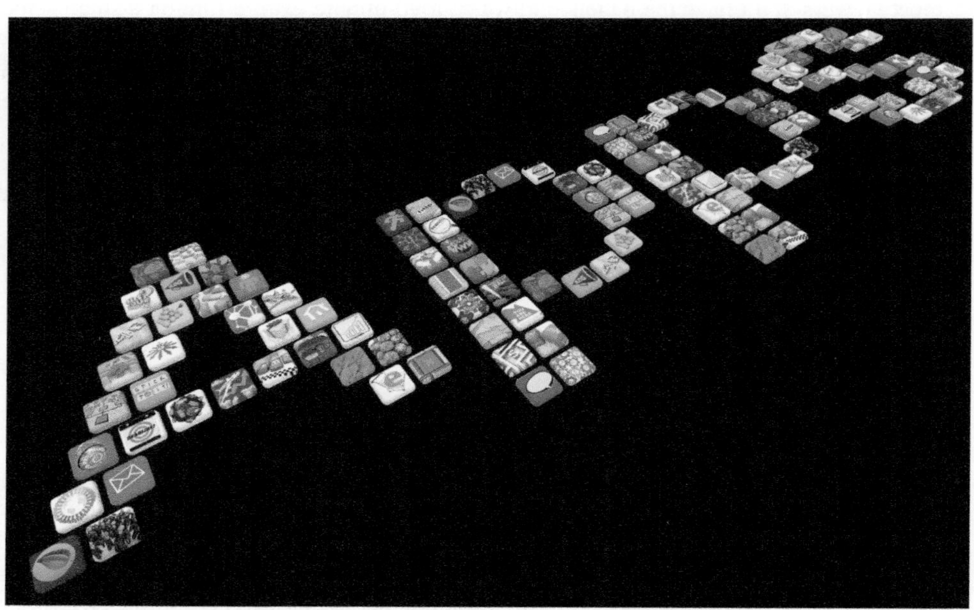
Yes, there is an app for that . . .

- **Wunderlist:** Free iOS and Android app for list management; controlled by gestures and taps.
- **Eternity Time Log Lite:** Free iOS app to log time management of your activities.
- **Timesheet-Time Tracker:** Free Android app to log time management.
- **Simple Repeat Timer:** Free iOS alarm timer that prompts you to look away from your screen.
- **Yata! Yet Another Timer:** Free Android alarm timer.
- **Swype, SwiftKey 3, Path Input Pro:** Makes typing on a smartphone or touch-screen tablet faster and more accurate; some of these even make corrections as you type.
- **Evernote:** Write, type, or speak your ideas to Evernote, which helps you stay organized.
- **Pocket:** Lets you save content you like, so you can read it later.

panel 7.1

Apps for smartphones and tablets to help college productivity

However, people's personal behavior in using such phones has not necessarily been improved. Mobile phones regularly ring—and are answered—in theaters, despite movie screen advisories. Bus and train travelers become enraged by the loud conversations of fellow passengers. The serenity of nature's wonders in national parks is disrupted by people yakking on their phones. Bosses feel obliged to rebuke their employees whose cellphones ring in meetings.

Phone use by car drivers makes even young people drive erratically, moving and reacting more slowly and increasing their risk of accidents. People inadvertently dial numbers in their phone's address book when they've had too much to drink (a phenomenon known as "drunk dialing"). Camera-equipped phones have been used to take pictures of people in bathroom stalls and clothing stores' changing rooms, to cheat on school tests, and to allow thieves to capture credit card numbers. Pornography companies see cellphones as a new frontier. Employers can hire companies that can keep track of their employees' out-of-office locations through GPS tracking of their cellphones.

But just as technology can create unforeseen problems, perhaps technology can also provide solutions. Some countries—but not the United States yet—are permitting the use of radio-jamming equipment that keeps nearby cellphones from working whether the phone user likes it or not. This would certainly allow restaurants, theaters, and the like to impose a "cone of silence" that would provide relief to long-suffering members of the public who have been forced to unwillingly share in others' cell conversations.

Hand-Free Devices Don't Solve Distracted Driving Dangers

Be careful with hands-free setups!

http://dc.streetsblog.org/2013/06/17/aaa-hands-free-devices-dont-solve-distracted-driving-dangers/

www.npr.org/blogs/health/2013/06/12/190949902/hands-free-gadgets-in-car-dont-mean-driving-is-risk-free/

www.focusdriven.org/dangers-of-conversation/

http://exchange.aaa.com/safety/distracted-driving/the-risks-of-distracted-driving/

7.3 TABLETS & E-READERS

Tablets are useful as multipurpose devices, but e-readers are usually better for reading.

As we mentioned in Chapter 1 (p. 2) and Chapter 4 (p. 196), a *tablet computer* is a general-purpose computer contained in a single panel. More than 4 out of 10 (44%) Americans now own a tablet, up from 30% in 2012. Among people between the ages of 18 and 34, the ownership rate is even higher, reaching 54%.[18] Shipments of tablets from manufacturers surpassed those of laptops in 2013 and were predicted to outpace the combined laptop-and-desktop PC market by 2015.[19]

Tablets have already become popular multipurpose devices on college campuses. E-book readers are also much in use, despite being single-purpose devices, because they are so good at one thing: displaying e-book content.[20]

The Tablet: What It Is, What It Does

Tablets are lightweight, thin, web-enabled, and portable and yet powerful enough to provide the functionality of a laptop.

A tablet is a wireless, portable personal computer with a 7- to 12-inch multitouch screen (one can manipulate the screen contents directly with one's hand). Tablets are lightweight, thin, web-enabled, and portable and yet powerful enough to do most of the things a laptop can do. The majority have a virtual on-screen keyboard, and a few have an extendable keyboard. Tablets can also work with wireless external keyboards. Most have some form of wireless connectivity to the Internet via 3G or 4G cellular, Wi-Fi, or both. The devices support multimedia (music and movies), download e-books, access the Internet, play

Apple iPad online app store

Apple Apps on the App Store

Make a picture perfect. Edit an HD movie. Read a novel or write one. Present your big idea. Or create and send a card. Apple apps from the App Store are designed specifically for iPad. Which means they give you the power and versatility to do more than you ever thought possible.

iLife

With iPhoto, iMovie, and GarageBand for iPad, you can do all the fun, creative things you love to do. Like making movies, making music, or making your photos look their best. All with a touch of your finger.

 iMovie

You can shoot 1080p HD movies from your iPad. And with iMovie, you can turn that footage into a thrilling trailer or mini feature film. Edit, add Hollywood-style themes, and fine-tune your soundtrack. No matter where you are, you're always in the director's chair.
Learn more about iMovie ›

 iPhoto

It's everything you love about viewing, editing, and sharing photos — but with the power and simplicity of Multi-Touch. You can quickly organize and compare photos. Brush adjustments onto an image with your finger. Apply professional-quality effects in a single tap. And create beautiful photo journals to share with family and friends.
Learn more about iPhoto ›

 GarageBand

GarageBand lets you play a collection of highly expressive Touch and Smart Instruments that sound just like their r counterparts — but let you do things y never could on a real instrument. You c record, mix, and share your songs, too
Learn more about GarageBand ›

With Pages, Keynote, and Numbers, you have everything you need to create beautiful documents, stellar presentations, and impressive spreadsheets, in ways you've never imagined.

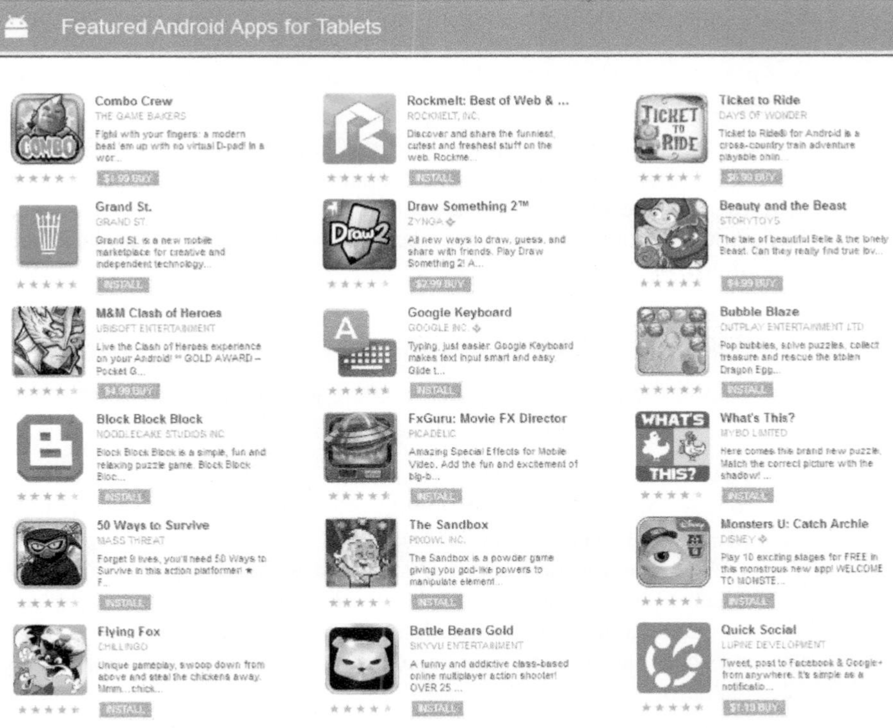

Android tablet app store

games, support email, and create and send documents. (• *See Panel 7.2.*) A tablet screen can be used both horizontally and vertically. Some screens will also work with a digital pen or stylus instead of fingertip touch.

Like smartphones, many tablets also have online access to a huge variety of apps, allowing you to purchase, download, and then use them.

panel 7.2

Android tablet

The principal tablet operating systems are Apple's iOS and Google's Android, along with Microsoft Windows RT, a tablet version of Windows 8. Android devices are owned by 59% of tablet owners, about the same as for Apple iPads and iPad Minis, which means that some homes have more than one type of tablet. The Windows RT was designed primarily for tablets and other devices that use less powerful processors, and so the system does not have certain features found in Windows 8, such as Windows Media Player and Remote Desktop.[21]

Tablets basically range in price from $199 for Google's Nexus 7, which is thin, light, and responsive to the touch, to $1,500 for the Lenovo Horizon, which, with its 27-inch screen, basically doubles as a desktop computer (running Windows 8) and, when laid flat, as a tabletop game device that several people can use simultaneously.[22] Tablets with fast processors and high-resolution screens are also being marketed for gamers, such as the Kobo Arc, the Sony Xperia Tablet S, the Google Nexus 10, and the Asus Transformer Pad Infinity TF700.[23] A great many tablets are available with fewer features than a $329 iPad Mini but for as little as $50–$200 that are designed for children ages 3–12, including Android tablets Kurio 7, MEEP, Tabeo, MG, and Nabi 2.[24] Finally, for users who have to expose their tablets to watery conditions, there is a "ruggedized" model from Sony and the Galaxy S4 Active from Samsung.

TECH TALES The Ruggedized Tablet for Splashes & Spills

"I took a tablet computer and submerged it in a bowl of water for several minutes," writes *USA Today* technology columnist Edward Baig. "I then poured more liquid onto it from a pitcher. Later I gave the machine a cold shower."[25] The tablet, the Sony Xperia Tablet Z, survived all the dousing, something not possible with other tablet PCs. The machine is resistant to dust as well.

Survival Tip

You Dropped Your Phone in Water? What to Do Next

Go to *www.wikihow.com/Save-a-Wet-Cell-Phone* to find out.

Sony doesn't claim the tablet is waterproof, only water-resistant. It will survive in water up to 3 feet for up to 30 minutes, the company says. Another technology reviewer who tested the machine, the *Wall Street Journal*'s Katherine Boehret, first made sure all the tablet's ports were covered, then submerged the device, with music playing from it, in a deep sink filled with water for 10 minutes. The Xperia Z (Sony also has a smartphone by that name) suffered no ill effects.[26]

"Most people won't go for a swim with their tablets," says Boehret, "but they will use them in places where splashes and spills are a regular occurrence, like the kitchen and the bathroom. Even with wet fingertips, gestures and selections on the Xperia screen were still recognized, however inconsistently." ■

The E-Reader: The Reading Machine

The e-book reader can hold a library that you can take almost anywhere.

How much content could you comfortably read online on a desktop or laptop? A few paragraphs from a Wikipedia entry? Some gossip about a celebrity? An entire novel? A textbook?

Many people find it difficult to read at length on a computer screen, which is why printed textbooks, for instance, remain more popular than online versions of the same thing. In recent years, however, e-books and e-readers have begun to gain some ground over paper-and-print versions of the book.

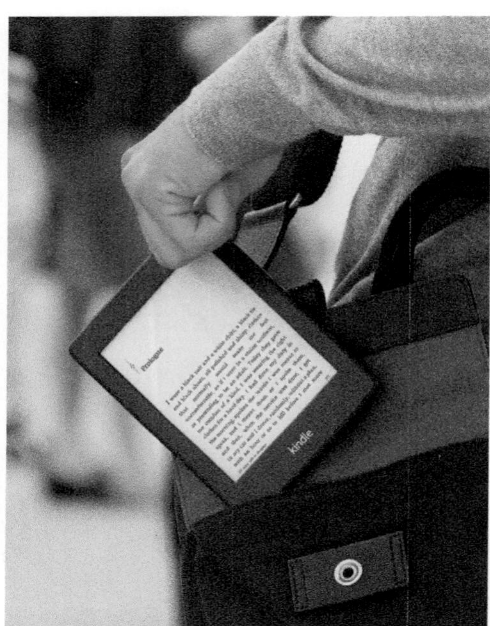

The Kindle Paperwhite, a basic e-reader model

An **e-book, or *electronic book,* is an electronic text, the digital-media equivalent of a conventional printed book.** You can read an e-book on your personal computer, tablet, or smartphone. Or you can read it on a specialized piece of hardware known as an e-reader.

As we stated in Chapter 1, an **e-reader, or *e-book reader,* is an electronic device that can download e-books**—digital versions of regular books, articles, and magazines from various suppliers. The most well-known e-readers are Amazon's Kindle and Barnes & Noble's Nook, but there are others, such as Kobo Glo and Sony Reader PRS-T2.

To get e-books into your e-reader, you most likely download them from an online e-book store maintained by the device's manufacturer, although you can also borrow e-books from public libraries or from *www.gutenberg.org/* or *booklending.com.* Almost all e-readers allow Wi-Fi access, which take about a minute to download an e-book, but some e-book readers require connecting to a computer for downloading. You can also buy magazines and newspapers, either as subscriptions or as single issues.

The Benefits of E-Readers

E-readers are better than tablets for reading e-books in terms of price, screen quality, simplicity and portability.

Tablets are multipurpose devices, more full featured and more versatile than the single-purpose e-reader, and you can certainly read e-books on them. But there are arguments in favor of using the (generally) single-purpose e-readers as well:[27]

PRICE Tablets tend to cost \$200 to about \$400 and up, e-readers range from \$80 to about \$300. E-books typically range from free to \$30, about the price of a hardcover book (though not textbooks). Both tablets and e-readers can hold thousands of titles.

SCREENS Tablets have screens that are 7–12 inches, measured diagonally, whereas e-reader screens are 5–10 inches, with 6 inches generally being an adequate size. Tablets also have color screens, and so do some e-readers, but they cost more. Most e-readers are monochrome (one color). Although color is helpful for reading magazines, most book

PRACTICAL ACTION

Multitasking—Good for Productivity?

One thing that tablets invite is **multitasking—performing several tasks at once, shifting focus from one task to another in rapid succession,** as we described in the Experience Box at the end of Chapter 1 (p. 39).

You may think you're one of those people who has no trouble juggling many tasks at once, but medical and learning experts say the brain has limits and can do only so much at one time. For instance, it has been found that people who do two demanding tasks simultaneously—drive in heavy traffic and talk on a cellphone, for example—do neither task as well as they do each alone.

Indeed, the result of constantly shifting attention is a sacrifice in quality for any of the tasks with which one is engaged. The phenomenon of half-heartedly talking to someone on the phone while simultaneously surfing the web, reading emails, or texting has been called "surfer's voice." Experts who study these things call it "absent presence."[28]

Research suggests many ways in which multitasking is inefficient or even harmful:[29]

- There is evidence that multitasking degrades short-term memory, not just for the topics being multitasked but possibly by affecting areas of the brain. Multitasking creates stress; stress invokes the more primitive parts of the brain that are concerned with personal safety, pulling energy from the more modern parts concerned with higher level thinking. Stress can also damage cells needed for new memories.
- We are more prone to errors when we multitask, so the quality of our work results goes down.
- Some parts of the brain are sequential processors, able to accept only one input at a time.
- The prefrontal cortex, the part of the brain most used for complex cognition and decision making, is the biggest energy consumer in the brain. The load from multitasking can lead to a quicker depletion of cognitive ability and more frequent need for recovery time.

readers find color irrelevant. The battery life on a tablet might be 9.5 hours (in the case of the Google Nexus 7) ; for an e-reader, it's more apt to be around 30-plus days (for the Barnes & Noble Nook).

CONNECTIVITY Some tablets offer Wi-Fi connection only, but some offer cellular service, which costs more. Similarly, some e-readers offer wireless 3G access, but those with just Wi-Fi connections cost less. Regardless, advises Consumer Reports, "don't expect to use an e-book reader's Internet access for much except downloading content from the e-book reader's dedicated store."[30]

FEATURES & PORTABILITY Tablets offer lots of features, whereas e-readers are single purpose. Some e-readers have capabilities such as being able to play music, but their basic function is for reading. The absence of multiple features, therefore, means the e-book can be smaller, lighter, and more generally portable.

How an E-Reader Works

E-readers use E Ink, which is composed of millions of tiny particles that display text.

What makes e-books on e-readers easier to read than e-books viewed on your laptop or tablet? Most monochrome e-readers use E Ink, a technology using positively charged white particles and negatively charged black particles. "The application of a positive or negative electric field," explains Consumer Reports, "forces the corresponding particles to the top, making the surface in that spot appear either white or black."[31] The principal benefit of this technology is that images on the screen remain even after the power is turned off; the power is used only when you turn the page, which is why e-readers have long battery life. A second benefit is that e-readers rely on reflected ambient light, not the backlight used by computers and phone screens. Reflected light can be hard to read in dim light, however. To compensate for this—in other words, to read in the dark, as with the Amazon Kindle Paperwhite and the Barnes & Noble's Nook Simple Touch with Glowlight—the e-reader needs to be equipped with built-in lights that turn on in dim light.

E-books allow you to adjust the type size and some even let you change fonts. To turn pages, you use an on-screen tap or swipe. There are also control buttons for accessing menus, doing highlighting, and so on. The e-book will automatically open to the page where you left off. Text can be searched automatically and cross-referenced. You can bookmark pages, search within your library, look up definitions, and annotate text. Text-to-speech software can produce an audio version of an e-book.

The Drawbacks of E-Readers

As do all electronic devices, e-readers have some drawbacks.

Consumers have to weigh the risk of buying a reading appliance that may be easily lost, damaged, stolen, or hacked compared to buying a regular book at a tenth or less of its price (and that may be resold). One also has to consider that the reader doesn't actually own the e-books that are downloaded to the e-reader; rather, they are like licensing a piece of software—you can run them only on certain designated devices, and they usually can't be resold or passed on to someone else.

One writer also found fault with the way photographs, charts, diagrams, foreign characters, and tables appeared on the gray screen of the Kindle. The beautiful illustrations and drawings in the print version of one science book turned out to be hard to make out in the electronic version. Tables in a medical book were garbled, and the color coding was lost. An elaborate chart in a highly expensive engineering book was totally illegible in its electronic form.[32]

Many students, both high school and college, are reportedly not always pleased with e-books as textbooks. Some complain that the e-texts cost too much at the outset, that they are awkward and inconvenient, that publishers make them difficult to share and print, that they can't be kept for future reference, and that they can't be resold.

Peter Fader, co-director of the Wharton Interactive Media Initiative, believes the e-reader will probably go the way of other single-use machines. In an age in which mobile phones double as cameras, music players, and computers, he suggests, it is only a matter of time before electronic readers will be embedded on mobile devices, such as smartphones and tablets.[33] At this time, you can download the Kindle application to phones and other devices.

Survival Tip

E-Reader & E-Book Cautions

Additional possible drawbacks of e-readers:

- They require electric power; the battery can run down.
- They are more fragile than paper books.
- They can malfunction (hardware/software problems).
- They are more likely to be stolen than paper books.
- They can be easily hacked.
- Some publishers don't produce e-book versions of their printed books.
- The placement of illustrations can be problematic; it is not possible to place pictures exactly where they should be.
- Not all book formats are compatible with every e-reader.

7.4 PORTABLE MEDIA PLAYERS

Portable media players include music players, media players, and some mobile phones.

"I've called the iPod the first cultural icon of the 21st century," says Michael Bull, an instructor in media and cultural studies at the University of Sussex in England. Bull has spent years researching the societal effects of portable audio devices, starting with Sony's Walkman portable cassette player and extending to Apple's iPod, which was introduced in 2001. The iPod, he says, "permits you to join the rhythm of your mind with the rhythm of the world," causing a cultural shift away from large communal areas—such as a cathedral, "a space we could all inhabit"—to the world of the iPod, "which exists in our heads."[34]

The iPod is an example of a **portable media player (PMP), or MP3 player, a small portable device that enables you to play digital audio, video, or image files.** PMPs are mostly of two types—*music players* and *media players*—but much of what they do can also be done on today's *smartphones*.[35]

- **Music players:** *Music players* are small portable devices, typically weighing around 3 ounces, that are designed primarily for playing music. They feature controls for enhancing sound and adjusting playback, and their 1- to 2-inch screens are best used to view playlists and menus. Music is downloaded from music stores such as Apple's iTunes Music Store, which has 26 million songs.[36] Alternatives are on-demand services such as Spotify and Rhapsody.[37] Many young people listen to music on YouTube, which 1 billion people access every month.[38] Storage in music players ranges from 512 megabytes to 64 gigabytes, which can hold about 120 to 160,000 songs. Some have memory cards, with capacities ranging from 2 megabytes to 32 gigabytes.

- **Media players:** *Media players* allow you not only to listen to music but also to view videos, play games, browse the web, check email, access social networks, read ebooks, and even make phone calls (using Skype). Users get downloads of music, books, movies, and videogames not only from iTunes and other music stores but also from subscription services such as Netflix, Amazon, and Hulu.[39] Most media players have Wi-Fi connections for downloading streaming content. Storage ranges from 8 gigabytes to 64 gigabytes, with some players also providing memory card slots for expanded storage capacity.
- **Smartphones:** Some mobile phones have controls and enough storage, as well as wireless connections, to rival the capabilities of music players and media players for downloading content.

PMPs are also known as *MP3 players.* Short for MPEG Audio Layer 3, an audio compression technology, **MP3 is a format that allows audio files to be compressed so they are small enough to be sent over the Internet or stored as digital files.** MP3 files are about one-tenth the size of uncompressed audio files. For example, a 4-minute song on a CD takes about 40 megabytes, but an MP3 version of that song takes only about 4 megabytes.

Principal Features of MP3 Players

MP3 players are small handheld devices that generally use small hard drives and/or solid-state flash memory for storing files.

The most famous of MP3 players are Apple's iPods (such as the iPod Touch, the iPod Nano, and the iPod Classic), although there are many others, such as the Samsung Galaxy, the Sony Walkman, and the Cowan X7 and X9. The principal characteristics of MP3 players are as follows.

MP3 Players

For reviews:

http://reviews.cnet.com/mp3-player-buying-guide/

www.pcmag.com/reviews/mp3-players/

http://mp3-players.toptenreviews.com/

STORAGE METHODS MP3 players use two methods of storage:

- **Flash memory drive:** MP3 players with flash memory drives are smaller in size, lighter weight, with longer playback time, longer battery life, and no moving parts, which means fewer parts failures. This makes them appropriate for use during physical activity such as jogging. An 8-gigabyte flash memory drive can hold about 2,000 songs.
- **Hard-disk drive:** MP3 players with hard-disk drives can hold many more songs than a flash memory drive—40,000 songs, in the case of a 160-gigabyte drive. Thus, if you have a large collection of music, a hard-disk drive may make a better choice, although it takes longer to search through menus or directories to find what you want.

A compromise might be to get a MP3 player with a flash memory drive that can also accept external memory cards, to which you can add extra songs.

SAMPLING RATE How many songs your MP3 player holds is affected not only by the storage capacity but also by the sound quality selected, which you can determine yourself when you're downloading songs from your computer to your MP3 player (what's called *ripping).* If you want high-quality sound when you're ripping (converting), the files will be relatively large, which means your player will hold fewer songs. If you're willing to have lower-quality sound, perhaps for the device you use while jogging or recording only voice in lectures, you can carry more files on your player. The quality

Wearable mobile devices. Sony Walkman Sports MP3 player in the earpieces

is determined by the **sampling rate, the number of times, expressed in kilobits per second (kbps), that a song (file) is measured (sampled) and converted to a digital value** (p. 308). For instance, a song sampled at 192 kilobits per second is three times the size of a song sampled at 64 kilobits per second and is of better sound quality. Sampling choices that range from 32 kbps to 320 kbps will give good results. Many people simply use the highest sampling rate that their device allows.

TRANSFERRING FILES When you buy an MP3 player, it comes with software that allows you to transfer files to it from your personal computer, using a high-speed port such as a FireWire or USB port, Bluetooth, or via Wi-Fi from a compatible website.

BATTERY LIFE Battery life varies depending on player settings, but some will last only 9 hours, while others can go on for 60 hours. You might get about 36 hours of music playback but only 11 hours of video. Flash memory players tend to give longer playback times than hard-disk players. Some machines will take off-the-shelf standard or rechargeable AA or AAA batteries; others have built-in, nonremovable batteries.

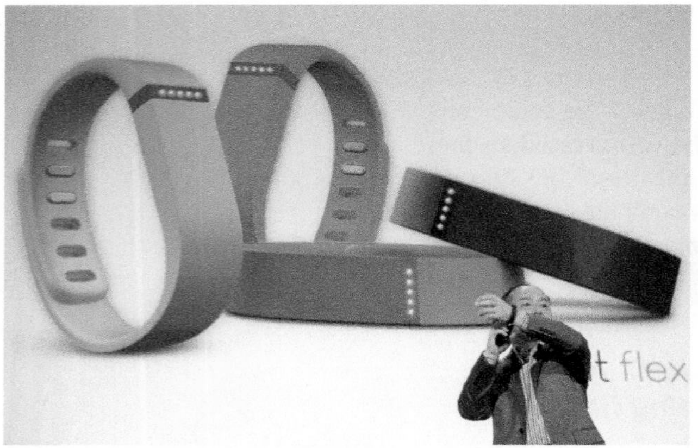

Wearables. (*left*) Masayoshi Son, president of SoftBank Corp., demonstrates a FitBit Inc. Fitbit Flex wearable fitness device, a wireless activity and sleep tracker. (*right*) These sunglasses, called Thump, plug into your computer's USB jack so that you can download MP3s from the computer to the glasses. Then, just put on the glasses, put the earbuds in your ears, and enjoy the music.

DISPLAY SCREENS The smallest MP3 players' screens are about 1.8–2 inches; midsize 2–3.5 inches (these seem to be the most popular); and larger 4 inches or more. Most MP3 screens are color.

OTHER FEATURES All players come with earphones ("earbuds"). Many MP3s, particularly flash memory devices, offer FM radio reception. Many players also are able to make high-quality music recordings, using an external microphone. Some also have a small internal microphone for voice recording, appropriate for capturing conversation or a lecture but usually unsuitable for music.

MP3 IN YOUR CAR It's dangerous, and in most places illegal, to use earphones while driving. However, most new cars now come with ports/jacks, as well as Bluetooth and Wi-Fi capabilities, for hands-free devices, including MP3 players.

The Societal Effects of MP3 Players

MP3 players are used almost everywhere by many people, but they do have the ability to damage hearing, so users should be careful with the volume controls.

Unlike television watchers and commercial radio listeners, MP3 listeners can control their own environment, expressing their individuality without intrusions from advertisements, and sharing music files with friends, creating a sense of community.

But is the increase in the use of these devices really a good thing? Many people believe that personalized digital media are making us all more isolated, with less and less face-to-face interaction, that they cut off individuals from the world. On the bus or train, at the gym, at work, at the grocery store, people are shutting out the world around them and are beginning to feel that each of them is the only person in the world. Some users also illegally download songs, effectively robbing creators of income.

In addition, hearing experts are concerned about the effect of hours of listening to audio players. Because earbuds are placed directly in the ear, they can boost the sound signal by as much as 6 to 9 decibels. Although listening with earbuds for 90 minutes a day at 80% volume is probably safe for long-term hearing, according to one study, softer is even better: you can safely tune in at 70% volume for about 4½ hours a day. The risk of permanent hearing loss can increase with just 5 minutes of exposure a day to music at full volume. Over time, the noise can damage the delicate hair cells in the inner ear that transform sound waves to the electrical signals that the brain understands as sound.[40] A Northwestern University audiologist and professor found hearing loss in younger people with the use of iPods and earbuds that is similar to that found in aging adults. To avoid permanent hearing loss in the middle ranges—the range required to hear conversation in a noisy restaurant, for example—researchers recommend the older style, larger headphones that rest over the ear opening.[41]

Using MP3 Players in College

Music players and media players are useful for recording and replaying lectures, among other things.

College instructors and students have found ways to expand the uses of the iPod beyond just the enjoyment of music. For instance, portable media players can be used to store schedules, phone number lists, and other personal information management software. "One of the most popular current uses of portable media players for educational purposes centers on the practice of recording and disseminating lectures," says one writer. "Through enabling students to use portable media players to store and play back digital copies of lectures, the intention is to make the lecture format more accessible for students and support student mobility and flexibility in their learning activities."[42]

There are also plenty of other ways in which MP3 players can be used to reinforce learning. *(• See Panel 7.3, next page.)*

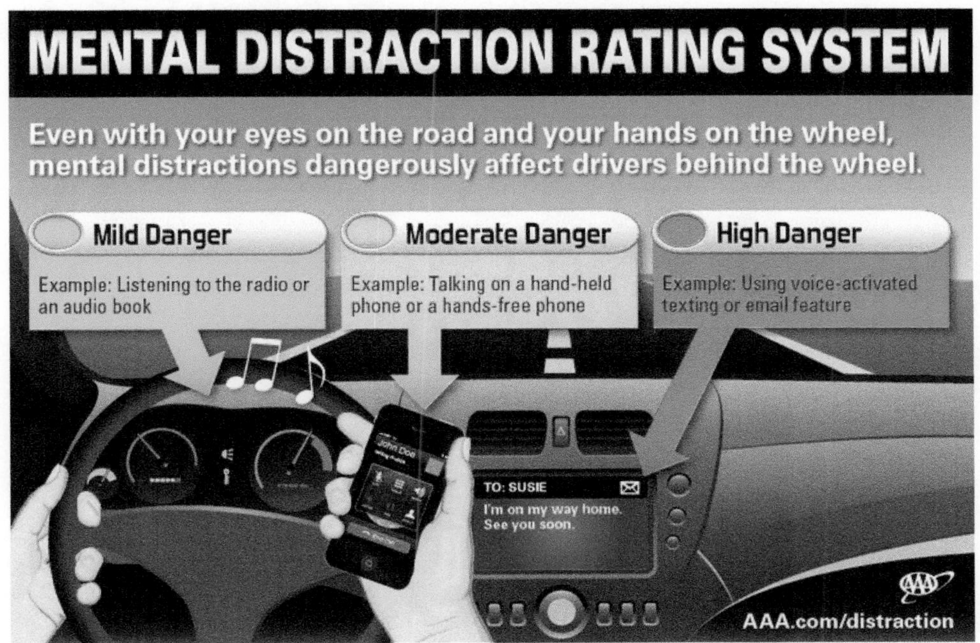

panel 7.3

Some college uses for portable media players

- Professors record lectures and post them online for students to download for later review, as when students have dead time (such as riding the bus).
- Interviews with guest speakers and messages from administrators may also be sent straight to students' portable media players.
- Some classes, such as those in music, foreign languages, or radio broadcasting, can especially benefit from use of audio players.
- Students record their own study group sessions and interviews, using their music players with microphones.
- Students record "audio blogs" during off-campus jobs to connect with people on campus.
- Students subscribe to feeds of frequently updated audio content from podcasts; students produce their own audio shows and podcast them. A "podpage" website can be created that is devoted to such podcasts.
- Students can come to class to work on projects, collaborate with others, and so forth and listen to lectures in their own time instead of in class (called "flipping" the class).

UNIT 7B: *Personal Devices for Enriching Leisure & Life*

If you have a smartphone, tablet, and portable media player, why would you need anything else, especially personal technology intended principally for one purpose? The answer: because special-purpose devices can do it better. Here we consider digital cameras, high-tech radio, digital television, and videogame systems.

7.5 DIGITAL CAMERAS: Changing Photography

A digital camera takes video and photographs and digitally converts the analog data by recording images via an electronic image sensor.

By now both professional and amateur photographers alike have pretty much abandoned film. "The evolution is having profound and unforeseen effects on society," says one analysis, "from changing the way that people record their daily lives to making it harder to trust the images we see."[43]

Parts of a digital camera

How Digital Cameras Work

Instead of film, a digital camera has a sensor that converts light into electric charges.

We described general principles of digital cameras in Chapter 5. Here we consider the subject in more detail.

The most obvious statement to make about digital cameras is this: they do not use film. Instead, a digital camera uses a light-sensitive processor chip to capture images in digital form and store them on a flash memory card. You can review your just-shot picture on the camera's LCD monitor, the little screen that displays what the camera lens sees, and decide whether to keep it or to try another angle in your next shot.

In general, digital cameras seem to be getting smaller, thinner (the size but not the thickness of a credit card), and less expensive, but they are also capable of performing more tricks. Product releases occur so frequently that it is impossible to present an up-to-date picture of the various models. However, we can outline certain general guidelines.

POINT-AND-SHOOT VERSUS SINGLE-LENS REFLEX (SLR) Point-and-shoot cameras are easy to carry around, but SLR cameras produce a brighter and crisper picture.

- **Point-and-shoot:** A *point-and-shoot camera,* or *basic camera,* is a camera, either film or digital, that automatically adjusts settings such as exposure and focus. Generally such cameras cost $75–$500. Manufacturers of digital point-and-shoots include Canon, Casio, Fujifilm, Hewlett-Packard, Kodak, Konika, Leica, Nikon, Olympus, Panasonic, Pentax, Samsung, Sony, and Vivitar. Point-and-shoots vary in size from subcompacts to compacts to superzooms.

  Although a point-and-shoot autofocus will do most of the work for you automatically, you may find it useful to get a camera that also has manual controls, so that you can take over if you want. There are also disposable point-and-shoot cameras, such as the Kodak Plus Digital, selling for about $20–$40, which are useful if you're afraid you might leave an expensive camera behind on the beach (and if you don't need high-quality images).

- **Single-lens reflex:** A *single-lens reflex (SLR) camera,* or *advanced camera,* is a camera, either film or digital, that has a reflecting mirror that reflects the incoming light in such a way that the scene viewed by the viewer through the viewfinder is the same as what's framed by the lens. There are also *SLR-likes,* which are lighter and smaller than SLRs but lack a through-the-lens (or even any) viewfinder. A digital SLR (DSLR), which may cost anywhere from $400 to $8,000, is the choice of "prosumers" (professional consumers, such as professional photographers and serious amateurs)

more info!

Point-and-Shoot vs. SLR

For more details on the differences between these two types of camera:

http://electronics.howstuffworks.com/camera5.htm

http://photo.stackexchange.com/questions/9467/what-is-the-difference-between-point-and-shoot-and-slr-cameras

Shop Point & Shoot Cameras

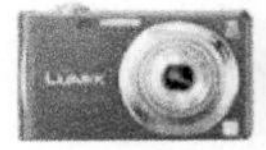

Shop DSLR Cameras

Point-and-shoot cameras (*top*) are less expensive than DSLR cameras (*bottom*). DSLR cameras are more sophisticated than point-and-shoot cameras.

because they provide more manual options and better image quality and allow the use of interchangeable lenses, from wide angle to telephoto. Manufacturers in this category include Canon, Fujifilm, Leica, Nikon, Olympus, Panasonic, Pentax, Ricoh, Samsung, Sigma, and Sony.

Megapixels

Why a higher number of mexapixels is not always best:

www.photography101.org/basics/megapixels_explained.html

www.digital-slr-guide.com/compare-digital-slr-megapixels.html

RESOLUTION: MEGAPIXELS & SENSORS *Resolution* refers to image sharpness. A digital camera's resolution is expressed in **megapixels (mp), or millions of picture elements, the electronic dots making up an image.** The more megapixels a digital camera has, the better the resolution and the higher the quality of the image, and so the higher the price of the camera. The millions of pixels are tightly packed together on the camera's image sensor, a half-inch-wide silicon chip. When light strikes a pixel, it generates an electric current that is converted into the digital data that becomes your photograph.

- **How many megapixels are best?** Megapixels measure the maximum resolution of an image taken by the camera at its *top settings.* Megapixels are in the range of 10–16 for subcompact point-and-shoot and compact cameras, and 10–24 for single-lens reflex cameras. If you shoot mainly 4 × 6s and rarely crop pictures, most cameras, which have at least 8–10 megapixels, are fine. But if you print poster-size shots or do major cropping, a 14-megapixel camera makes more sense.

In each pair, the left photo was shot with fewer megapixels than the photo on the right. (The shine on the kernels and the bowl is more apparent in the shots on the right.)

Sensor Size

"If there's a single factor that predicts the quality of the photos you'll get from a camera, a single letter grade that lets you compare cameras, it's this: the sensor size"(*http://sensor-size.com/*).

- **Don't forget sensor size:** But there's another consideration besides megapixels: sensor size. The best overall predictor of image quality is not megapixels but the size of the sensor inside the camera. "Big sensors absorb more light, so you get better color and sharper low-light images," points out one technology writer. "Small sensors pack too many light-absorbing pixels into too little space, so heat builds up, creating digital 'noise' (random speckles) on your photos."[44] Sensors in SLR digital cameras, such as those used by professional photographers, use sensors the size of a 35-mm negative, so they can easily handle more than 12 megapixels. However, even point-and-shoots, most of which have at least 10 megapixels, are getting better all the time in terms of sensors.

LENSES You also need to have a lens that ensures that your picture is properly focused and that pulls in enough light to get good exposure.

As for zoom lenses, you should be aware of the difference between digital zoom and optical zoom:

- **Digital zoom:** *Digital zoom* is just another way of saying "we'll crop the image for you in the camera." Indeed, it actually lowers the resolution and often can produce a grainier photo. "Digital zoom is not really zoom, in the strictest definition of the term," says one account. "What digital zoom does is enlarge a portion of the image, thus 'simulating' optical zoom. In other words, the camera crops a portion of the image and then enlarges it back to size. In so doing, you lose image quality."[45]
- **Optical zoom:** Only an *optical zoom* will bring you closer to your subject without your having to move. That is, the lens actually extends to make distant objects seem larger and closer. Optical zooms may be of the telescoping type or internal (untelescoping) type; the latter allows a camera to start up fast.

Digital camera memory card storage capacity (64 MB–2 GB) according to image file size and camera megapixel rating

Image Resolutions	File Size*	64 MB	128 MB	256 MB	512 MB	1 GB	2 GB
2 megapixel	0.9 MB	71**	142	284	568	1,137	2,275
3 megapixel	1.2 MB	53	106	213	426	853	1,706
4 megapixel	2.1 MB	30	60	121	243	487	975
5 megapixel	3.2 MB	20	40	80	160	320	640
6 megapixel	3.5 MB	18	36	73	146	292	585
7 megapixel	3.7 MB	17	34	69	138	276	553
8 megapixel	3.9 MB	16	32	65	131	262	525

*Average size of compressed JPG format image with best image quality settings.
**Number of images.
Source: From "Choosing the Right Memory Card for Your Digital Camera," *www.newegg.com/product/CategoryIntelligenceArticle.aspx?articleId=61* (accessed October 19, 2013).

Most subcompact and compact point-and-shoot cameras come with a 3 × to 7 × optical zoom, which is good for wide-angle, normal, and telephoto shots. If you're an experienced photographer, you should look for a superzoom camera with 10 × to 20 × optical zoom.

STORAGE Instead of being stored on film, the camera's digital images are stored on flash memory cards inside the camera. *(• See Panel 7.4.)* Cards come in a variety of formats, including Secure Digital (SD), the most widely used format; Compact Flash, mostly used on SLRs; and Memory Stick Duo. There are also high-capacity versions of SD cards, such as SDHC and SDXC (which can accept as many as 2 terabytes) that can be used with some cameras.

Most cameras come with lower-capacity "starter" cards, which hold only a handful of photos. You'll need a card (which is reusable) with at least 512 megabytes to 1 gigabyte, and you should carry 2 or 3 memory cards (professional photographers carry 6–10 cards). Digital camera memory card storage capacity varies according to image file size and camera megapixel rating. Most memory cards are 32–64 GB.

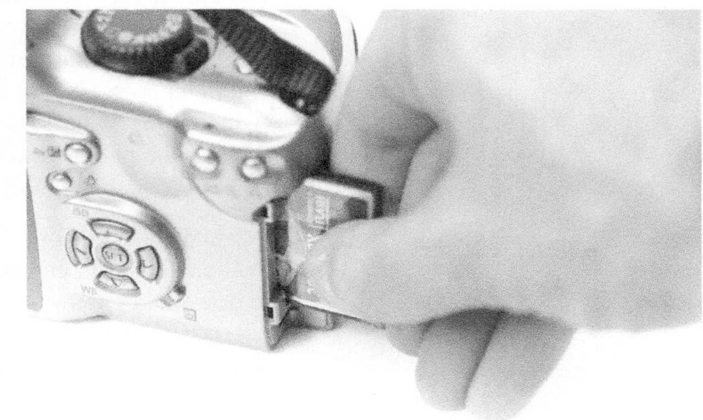

panel 7.4
Digital camera's flash memory card

OPTICAL VIEWFINDERS & LCD VIEWERS/VIEWFINDERS The original digital cameras had tiny screens, which made it difficult to review photos before deciding whether to save or delete them. Now more cameras come with both optical viewfinders and LCD viewers or viewfinders.

- **Optical viewfinders:** The *optical viewfinder* is the eye-level optical glass device on the camera that, when you look through it, shows the image to be photographed. Some digital cameras omit the viewfinder, forcing you to use only the LCD, which forces you to hold the camera with arms extended, making you more apt to shake the camera. Today hardly any subcompacts or compacts have optical viewfinders; they've been replaced by color LCD viewers, which are larger and sharper.
- **LCD viewers/viewfinders:** The *LCD (liquid crystal display) viewers/viewfinders* usually measure 2 inches or more diagonally—some are as large as 3.5 inches—and allow you to review the photos you take. It's best to get a camera with an LCD that can be seen well in daylight if you do a lot of outdoor shooting. LCDs are offered on nearly all SLRs.

"A camera with both an optical and LCD viewfinder is more versatile," says Consumer Reports, "especially when you shoot in bright light or need to conserve battery power."[46]

START-UP TIME, SHUTTER LAG, & CONTINUOUS SHOOTING A digital camera, like a PC, needs time to start up. You should look for one that takes no longer than a second or two, so that you won't miss that one-of-a-kind shot that suddenly appears out of nowhere. Another recommendation: You should look for a digicam with the least shutter lag, that annoying delay between the time you press the shutter-release button and the time the exposure is complete. Many digital cameras have a special setting called "burst" or "continuous" mode, which allows you to squeeze off a limited number of shots without pausing—helpful if you're taking pictures at sports events.

What Kind of Battery Is Best?

www.dummies.com/how-to/content/the-different-types-of-batteries-for-your-digital-.html

www.digitaltrends.com/photography/digital-camera-buying-guide/

http://reviews.cnet.com/digital-camera-buying-guide/

BATTERY LIFE Some cameras come with rechargeable batteries, although they aren't always replaceable at the nearest drugstore (and replacements can be expensive, perhaps $40–$60). Some require you to recharge the battery inside the camera, by putting the camera in a charging unit; others, in both ways. Some cameras also require proprietary batteries, which also aren't as readily available.

Regardless, you should be sure you have lots of batteries before setting out on a trip. Battery life varies depending on the size and quality of the images, how much of the time you use the flash, and whether you keep the LCD screen on all the time or use it sparingly. Be sure to charge up a spare battery and keep it on hand when you set off for a day's shooting.

TRANSFERRING IMAGES Let's assume you've spent a day taking pictures. How do you get them out of your camera? Here are the principal methods:

- **Use a direct connection between your camera and your computer:** You'll need the installation CD included with your digital camera to install the drivers and software on your PC. Then you can connect your camera to the computer using the USB or FireWire cable that came with it. (One end attaches to a slot on the camera, the other end to an open USB or FireWire port on the computer.) After connecting the camera (which must be turned on during the process), you open its software and use it to transfer the photos into the PC, typically placing the pictures into a default folder, such as My Pictures in the My Documents folder.
- **Wireless connection:** You can also connect your digital camera wirelessly, using the built-in Wi-Fi capability, often to a photo-sharing website. This makes it possible to download photos, saving photos directly to a computer while you shoot, or print wirelessly. You can also connect to a cellphone network and share photos, just as you would with a camera smartphone. To enable your camera to work wirelessly, if you do not have built-in Wi-Fi capability, you need a wireless memory card, such as Eye-Fi, and a wireless-ready digital camera.
- **Insert the memory card into your computer or a card reader:** Assuming your PC has a built-in slot for your memory card (USB card) or has a card reader attached to a USB port, you can remove the memory card from the camera and insert it into the slot. External card readers cost $20 or so.
- **Put your camera in a cradle attached to your PC:** Many camera manufacturers include cradles ("docks") into which you can set your camera and use it to transfer photos to your PC. Some cradles also are able to charge your camera, if it has rechargeable batteries.
- **Use an online photo service:** After downloading your photo to your computer, you can go online and send your images to an online photo service, such as Shutterfly, Flickr, or others mentioned in the Practical Action box. You may also be able to use the Wi-Fi transmission in your camera to upload to these services.
- **Use a photo printer with a built-in card slot:** If you've bought one of the newer photo printers, you can skip using a PC entirely and insert the memory card from your camera into a slot in the printer.
- **Use a photo-printing kiosk:** Various photo-printing kiosks are available at fast-food restaurants, big retailers, amusement parks, scrapbook-making stores, cruise ships, hospitals, and other high-traffic areas and can produce a standard 4 × 6 print in 4 seconds.

PRACTICAL ACTION

Online Viewing & Sharing of Digital Photos

You have a great photo of the sunset at Lake Tahoe. How do you share it with others? You could always print it out and mail it via U.S. mail. Or you could try the following alternatives.

- ***Send as an email attachment:*** You can download your photos to a PC and then send them as attached computer files to an email message. The drawback, however, is that if you have a lot of photos, it can quickly fill up the recipient's email inbox or take a lot of time if you are sending multiple images to multiple people. And some image files may be too large to send as email attachments.
- ***Use an online photo-sharing service:*** Web-based photo-sharing services provide online storage space for your photos and make it easier to share, especially if they are high-resolution files. Examples are Shutterfly, Flickr, Instagram, PhanFare, SmugMug, Photobucket, Picasa, Snapfish, Photobox, Kodak Gallery, and WebShots. No special software is required for you to upload from your computer, but a broadband connection is strongly recommended. If you're near a Wi-Fi hotspot, you can use the Wi-Fi transmitter in your camera (which most cameras now have) to post the pictures.

  Some photo-sharing services charge fees; some do not. Shutterfly, for instance, makes money by turning snapshots into tangible things, such as custom photo books, calendars, greeting cards, and wedding invitations.[47] Be sure to find out whether you have to renew membership in a photo-sharing service or make a purchase in order to keep your photos from being deleted after a certain amount of time.

  Competing with the photo-sharing services are Walmart, Hewlett-Packard, Eastman Kodak, and Yahoo!. Mobile apps such as Pinwheel, GroupShot, Kicksend, Pic Stitch, and StillShot allow you to make collages or otherwise manipulate your photos, and you can then get them printed out at your neighborhood Walgreens.[48]
- ***Post it to Instagram or Pinterest:*** Instagram is an online photo-sharing and video-sharing service plus social-networking service that you can send your smartphone and tablet photos or videos to, apply digital filters to them, and then share them on Facebook, Twitter, Tumblr, and other social-networking services. (Twitter's Vine is also a video-sharing application.) Pinterest is a pinboard-like photo-sharing website that enables users to create and manage theme-based image collections (known as "pinboards"), such as events or hobbies, adding other images (known as "pins") from other sources.

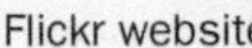

Flickr website

- **Use a photo lab:** Photo stores and labs, as well as Costco, Kinko's, Target, Walgreens, and Walmart, often sell inexpensive services (perhaps \$3–\$7) in which they will transfer the images on a memory card onto a CD and then clear the card for reuse. They will also print photos for you.
- **Bring along your own card reader and CDs and use others' computers:** If you bring along your own card reader and blank CDs, you can use other people's computers to store your images. These PCs could belong to friends, of course, but also to hotel business centers and Internet cafés.

The Societal Effects of Digital Cameras

Digital cameras have made it easier to take pictures and share them, but they have also devalued images and increased the ease of dishonestly manipulating images, the invasion of people's privacy, and the occurrence of voyeurism.

The near-universal use of digital cameras, both as stand-alone devices and as built-in parts of smartphones, means there is almost no single moment that remains unphotographed. Of course there are some beneficial results to this, as in cameras frequently being used to document crimes in progress, as well as to record animal abuses, human rights violations, revolutionary upheavals, and other important matters. But there also some other, possibly unintended effects that most people may not be aware of.

PHOTOS ARE NO LONGER JUST OF SPECIAL EVENTS People take far more pictures than they used to—perhaps 20 or more of a single scene, instead of three or four—since they don't have to worry about the cost of film and processing, and with digital it's easy to simply delete bad shots. A second consequence may be that photography has become more casual, with more off-the-cuff snapshots being taken instead of subjects being asked to pose for formal portraits. "Taking pictures used to be an event of sorts," one essay points out. Now people take or receive photos, "look at them once, and trash them. The image is not what it used to be. The value of the image is no longer what it was."[49] This raises the question of whether people will save these images for future generations, the same way they used to with old prints. Or will those that are saved be so doctored to improve reality, with the help of photo-altering programs such as Apple's iPhoto or Adobe's Photoshop Elements, that tomorrow's generations may question their authenticity? Muses one writer, will future anthropologists wonder, "Why do all those people look so good?"[50]

DOES TOO MUCH PHOTO GAZING GIVE US SKEWED IMPRESSIONS OF OTHERS? We're not keeping all those photos to ourselves. A great many are being uploaded onto social media (and thus are available to the world just about forever). On Facebook alone, 350 million photos are uploaded every day, and the total number of Facebook photos amounts to 240 billion.[51] People spend 17% of their time on the site looking at photos, according to a 2012 study.[52] All this photo gazing may skew our perceptions. For example, a Utah Valley University study found that "those spending more time on Facebook each week agreed more that others were happier and had better lives."[53]

"How many photos do we take not for ourselves," asks writer Katrina Trinko, "but to wow our hundreds or even thousands of online buddies, with a particular eye toward impressing that ex, that snotty colleague, that sibling who said we'd never make it?" When we're principally taking pictures not to document our lives but to post on social media platforms, "we're no longer taking photos to remember, but to refashion public perception."[54] One consequence of this is the surge in popularity of the *selfie,* the name given to the self-portrait photograph taken with a handheld digital camera or camera phone, usually for the purpose of posting it to social networking websites and image-sharing sites.

Cellphones in School

Are cellphones disruptive in educational settings?

www.schoolsecurity.org/trends/cell_phones.html

www.theatlantic.com/national/archive/2012/05/do-cell-phones-belong-in-the-classroom/257325/

www.facultyfocus.com/articles/teaching-professor-blog/tough-questions-on-texting-in-the-classroom/

TECH TALES The Rise of the Selfie: What Does It Mean?

"The raunchy, goofy, poignant, sexy, or drunken self-portrait," points out Associated Press writer Leanne Italie, "has become a common sight since phone camera met social media."[55] Here's singer Justin Bieber, yet again appearing on Instagram with his shirt off to show a self-taken photo of his tats and abs. Here's reality star Kim Kardashian, who went on a rant about preserving her privacy, posting selfies on Twitter.[56]

"If we're not taking them, we're certainly looking," says Italie. "We're . . . enjoying the high jinks of co-workers and friends and mooning over celebrities, who have fast learned the marketing value—and scandalous dangers—of capturing their more intimate unpolished selves."

Although self-portraits shot with cellphones began as what was once called a "MySpace pic" from 2006 to 2009, they did not really take off until Facebook profile photos, with their clean, well-lit look, became popular. Also, in 2010, the iPhone 4 with front-facing camera appeared, which meant that you could take a self-portrait while looking at the screen, allowing better framing and focus. Finally, Instagram and Snapchat (a phone app that deletes photos after 10 seconds) allowed social-media users to readily post themselves while on the go.[57] There is certainly nothing wrong with selfies per se, but Katrina Trinko, referred to above, makes the point that constantly managing our image to impress others does not advance making true human connections, which are bonds built on vulnerability and honesty.

"When we make the camera a constant presence, we make our lives a reality show, and ourselves no more than actors," she says. "That is the way to experience a permanent photo-op, not a life."[58] ■

Ethics & Digital Photography

Here is an article written by an online student of photography:

http://onlinestudentofphotography.blogspot.com/2010/04/ethics-of-digital-photography.html

And here is one about a university class on cellphone camera ethics:

www.ecampusnews.com/technologies/students-learn-the-ethics-of-cell-phone-snapshots/

See also:

www.globalethics.org/newsline/2003/10/20/camera-phones-and-public-privacy-can-evanescence-be-required/

And who really owns the photos you post on social sites?

www.pbs.org/mediashift/2013/01/who-really-owns-your-photos-in-social-media-updated-2013-edition025

www.telegraph.co.uk/technology/social-media/10028168/Instagram-Act-could-see-social-media-users-lose-ownership-of-their-own-photos.html

7.6 HIGH-TECH RADIO: Satellite, Hybrid Digital, & Internet

High-tech radio uses satellite, digital transmission on FM stations (HD radio), and the Internet. We also describe podcasting.

The number of people in the United States 12 and older listening to radio each week now reaches an estimated 242.5 million, or 92% of Americans in that age group.[59] As listeners grow, the radio industry has been transformed by a number of technological trends—satellite radio, HD radio, and Internet radio.

Satellite Radio

Satellite radio is commercial-free digital radio transmitted via satellite and paid for by subscribers.

Satellite radio **is a radio service in which digital signals are broadcast from satellites to special radios, primarily in cars.** The advantages are that the radio signal can be broadcast over a much wider area than those from terrestrial (conventional) radio stations,

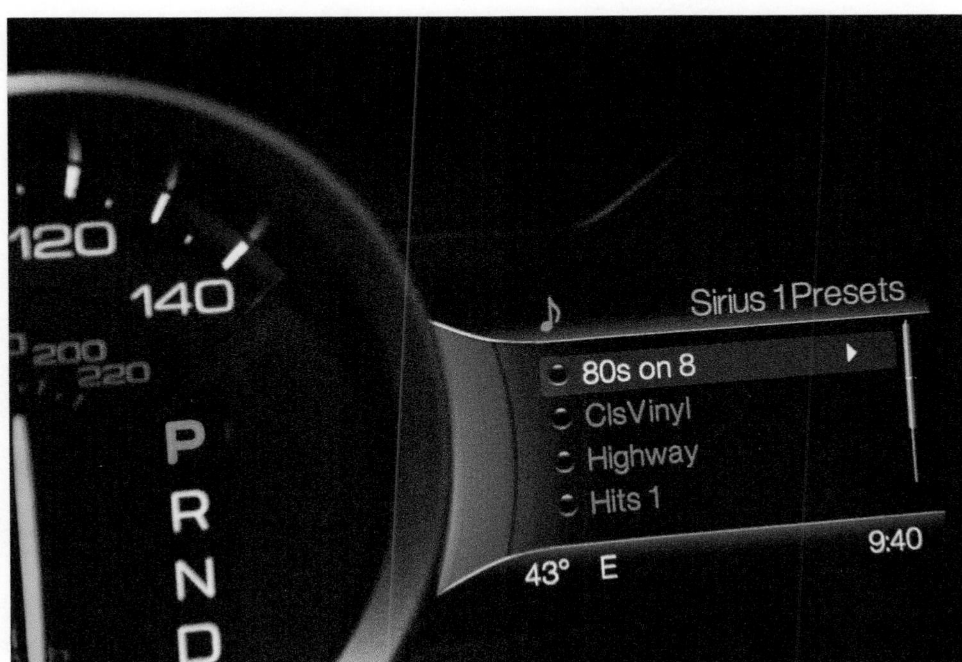

Sirius satellite radio

and, because satellite radio is available by subscription, it is mostly commercial-free and offers a wider variety of programming than terrestrial radio does. The major U.S. satellite radio company is SiriusXM, which offers more than 150 channels on a subscriber's satellite radio and over 155 channels on his or her computer, tablet, and smartphone. Subscription fees start at $14.49 a month.

HD Radio

HD radio, or hybrid digital radio, provides the digital technology for AM/FM stations in the United States.

more info!

HD Radio Stations

Check HD radio availability in your state at:

www.hdradio.com/stations/

Unlike HDTV, in which the HD stands for "high definition," the HD in **HD radio stands for *hybrid digital radio,* a technology that provides CD-quality sound and allows broadcasters to squeeze one analog and two digital stations on the same frequency.** (• *See Panel 7.5.)* That is, HD radio combines digital and analog broadcast signals, enabling stations to offer an analog main channel and digital "sidebands," so that multiple types of content can be broadcast from the same position on the dial.

HD channels (which are called HD2/HD3 channels) are located on the FM dial. Like AM radio, but unlike satellite radio, HD radio is free. HD radio is available in certain cars, as portable units for home use, and as add-ons for portable media players.

Internet Radio

Internet radio streams audio programs over the Internet.

Internet radio is the continuous streaming of audio over the Internet. Internet radio broadcasts can be played on desktop computers as well as wireless mobile devices—laptops, smartphones, tablets, and portable media players. They can also be played on dedicated hardware devices called Internet radios, web radios, or Wi-Fi radios, which are connected to home Wi-Fi networks that, of course, are themselves connected to the Internet.

POPULAR RADIO SITES The most popular online radio service is Pandora Internet Radio (200 million registered users), a free personalized radio service that streams music to your

panel 7.5

How HD radio works

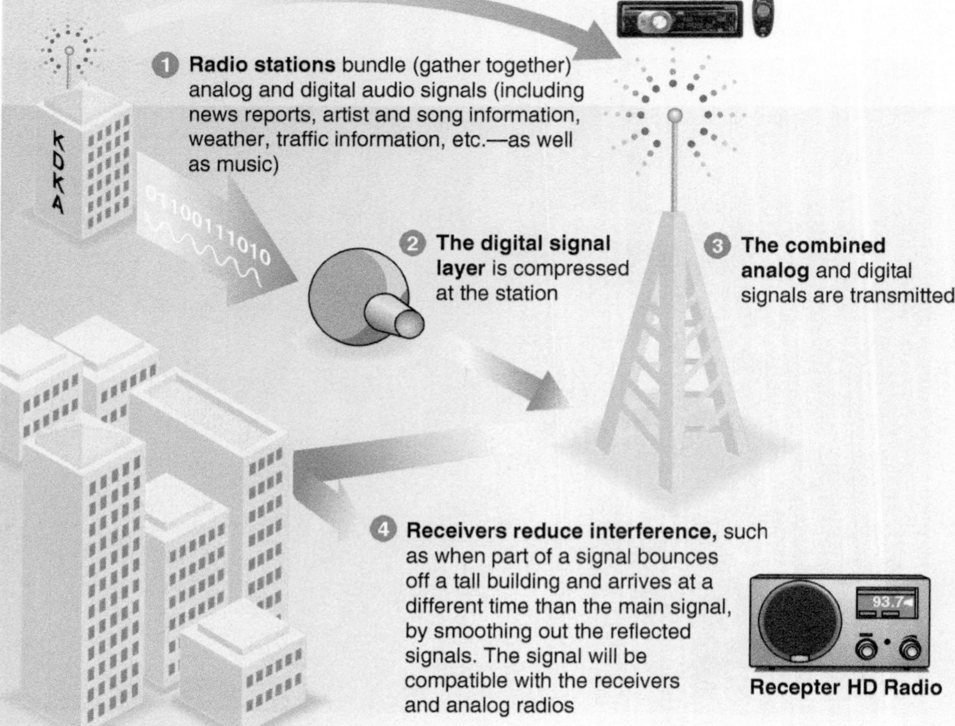
KDKA
1 Radio stations bundle (gather together) analog and digital audio signals (including news reports, artist and song information, weather, traffic information, etc.—as well as music)
01100111010
2 The digital signal layer is compressed at the station
3 The combined analog and digital signals are transmitted
4 Receivers reduce interference, such as when part of a signal bounces off a tall building and arrives at a different time than the main signal, by smoothing out the reflected signals. The signal will be compatible with the receivers and analog radios
93.7
Recepter HD Radio

phone or other devices. This is followed by Clear Channel's iHeartRadio (170 million) and, way behind in third place, by Slacker (35 million). Slacker offers a tool, FineTune, that lets consumers move sliders up or down to adjust the mix of related artists, favorite songs, and new or older songs.[60]

Free Aggregators

Free podcast-receiving software (podcatcher) is available at:

www.blogtalkradio.com

www.ziepod.com/

http://download.cnet.com/1770-20_4-0.html?query=podcast+catcher&searchtype=downloads

www.buzzmaven.com/podcast-software-list.html

A tutorial on how to create a podcast is available at:

http://radio.about.com/od/podcastin1/a/aa030805a.htm

www.smartpassiveincome.com/how-to-start-a-podcast-podcasting-tutorial/

TECH TALES Pandora's Music Genome Project

At Pandora Radio's Music Genome Project, a team of musician-analysts listens to music, one song at a time, trying to keep up with the flow of new music coming from studios, garages, and other sources, They collect hundreds of musical details on every track—melody, harmony, instrumentation, rhythm, vocals, lyrics, and so on.

As a Pandora registered user, you could specify the name of one of your favorite songs, artists, or genres—on your computer, media player, iPad, smartphone, or the like. The Music Genome Project "will quickly scan its entire world of analyzed music, almost a century of popular recordings . . . to find songs with interesting musical similarities to your choice," says the company's website. "You can create up to 100 unique 'stations.' And you can even refine them. If it's not quite right you can tell it so and it will get better for you."[61]

Can the Music Genome Project help a performer get rich? Probably not. A musician whose song gets played 1 million times on Pandora earns just $16.89.[62] ■

Listen to Pandora on your mobile device

In the car, at the gym, on the train — listen wherever and whenever you're in the mood for great music.

Enjoy all of your stations right from your mobile phone, tablet, or e-reader. You can also create new stations, and rate songs using thumbs up and thumbs down. Pandora on mobile devices is fully integrated with Pandora on the web, so everything you create and personalize on your device appears next time you're back on the web.

Pandora Internet radio website

INTERNET RADIO APPS A new way to listen to digitally stored music is streamed from a cloud-technology music service via an app. Pandora and Spotify (which has 6 million subscribers) are two popular apps, but there also others such as Rdio, TuneInRadio Pro, SHOUTcast, and Songza.[63] In 2013, Twitter launched its new #Music service, which allows you "to listen to music or artists that people you follow are discussing in tweets, for a real-time view of what's trending," in one description.[64]

PODCASTING After being fired from a radio job, comedian Marc Maron was financially bankrupt and, with few other options, decided to give podcasting a try, launching his *WTF with Marc Maron* podcast out of his garage. As we stated in Chapter 2, **podcasting involves**

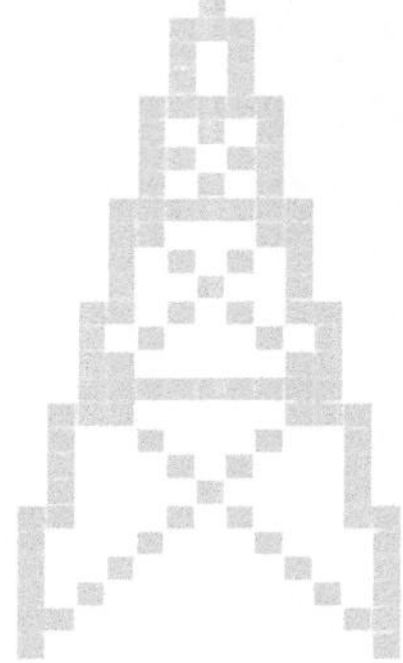

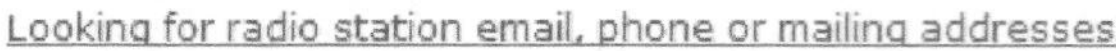

delivering Internet music, radio, or movie files from the Internet to a computer. After landing big-name guests like comedians Robin Williams and Louis C.K., Maron's podcast grew to become one of iTunes's most popular, attracting more than 1 million listeners a month.[65]

Unlike traditional radio, podcasting requires no studio or broadcast tower, and there's no Federal Communications Commission regulation, so hosts can say whatever they want. (The word *podcast* is a play on the word *broadcast* combined with the word *iPod.*) Podcasting software allows amateur deejays and hobbyists to create their own radio shows and offer them free over the Internet. Listeners can download shows onto their portable players or computer. Basically, in podcasting, providers create audio files that are available on their website, which people can then subscribe to and download to their mobile devices and listen to. With podcasts, which are delivered through RSS feeds, you choose what you want to listen to.

Podcast audio files can be automatically received from the Internet and then synced to your portable media player. Website users install a media *aggregator* program in their computers or media players, such as iTunes or Juice. Also called a "podcatcher," the application captures the audio feeds from the Internet for downloading to the music player.

7.7 DIGITAL TELEVISION

New varieties of television include interactive TV, Internet TV, & Internet-ready TV.

It's called the "TV everywhere" approach, says one writer: "Letting folks watch on their iPads. Giving access to primo content from HBO and ESPN on pretty much everything—tablets, smartphones, laptops, and Xbox 360." This is what cable and satellite TV could become—especially if the companies would lower their monthly bill to subscribers from $175 and stop forcing people to accept hundreds of channels they don't want.[66]

Interactive, Internet, & Internet-Ready TV: What's the Difference?

The HDTV screen is formatted much more closely than analog TV to the way we see.

All kinds of other technologies are putting pressure on traditional methods of delivering TV, some of the more interesting of which are the following:

INTERACTIVE TV *Interactive TV* (*iTV*) lets viewers interact with their television sets, so that, for instance, they can request information about a product or play along with a game show. We see interactive TV used with viewer voting with *American Idol, Dancing with the Stars,* and similar shows. In one form of interactive television, a technology called Clickable TV displays an icon on screen that indicates that the programming or advertisement they are watching is interactive, and viewers can then press OK/Select on their remote to receive email with more information. Many hotels are upgrading their in-room TV sets to something you can interact with, so that, as one article puts it, "you can log on to Facebook or Skype, get information about local attractions, browse the room-service menu, and even sync the TV set with your smartphone or tablet."[67]

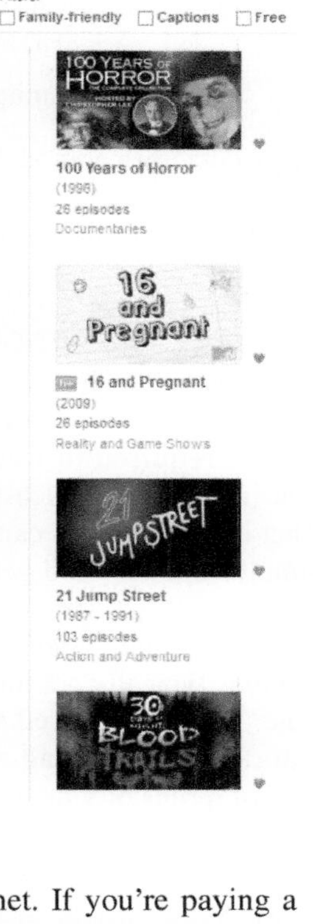

Free Internet TV from Hulu's website

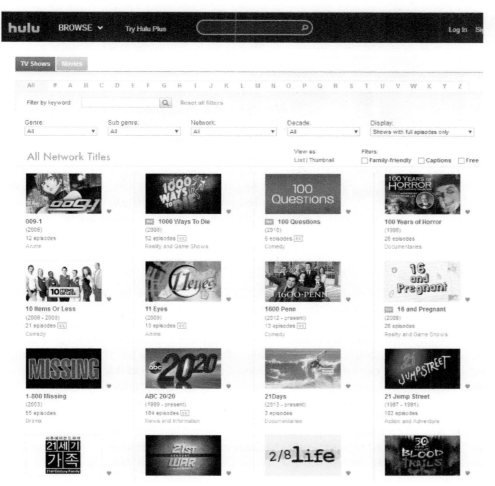

INTERNET TV *Internet TV* is television distributed via the Internet. If you're paying a monthly charge to a cable or satellite TV distribution service, you can often see the same network television shows—from ABC, CBS, NBC, and Fox—for free on Hulu or uStream, online video services that offer a selection of hit shows, clips, movies, and more. This means that Internet TV can be distributed via broadband, Wi-Fi, cable, or satellite, and you can see programs on all kinds of mobile devices, from laptops to smartphones, to tablets, to videogame systems.

INTERNET-READY TV *Internet-ready TV* is the term applied to television sets with broadband connections that allow viewers not only to watch TV shows but also go online to get news, stream movies, view photos, and the like. Many models feature a built-in Ethernet port, so that you can plug an Ethernet cable into the back of the TV. If you don't own an Internet-ready TV but want to send videos or photos from your PC screen onto your TV set's screen, you can do so by buying a box called SlingCatcher.

Three Kinds of Television: DTV, HDTV, SDTV

Analog TV has been completely supplanted by three new forms of TV.

Before 1996, most TV was analog television, a system of varying signal amplitude and frequency that represents picture and sound elements. Since then, however, things have become more complicated.

DIGITAL TELEVISION (DTV) In 1996, broadcasters and their government regulator, the Federal Communications Commission (FCC), adopted a standard called **digital television (DTV), which uses a digital signal, or series of 0s and 1s.** DTV is much clearer and less

Analog TV

HDTV

prone to interference than the old analog TV, which disappeared on June 12, 2009, requiring viewers with older sets to acquire a converter box.

HIGH-DEFINITION TELEVISION (HDTV) A form of digital TV, **high-definition television (HDTV) works with digital broadcasting signals and has a wider screen and higher resolution than analog television had.** Whereas standard analog TV has a width-to-height ratio, or *aspect ratio,* of 4 to 3, HDTV has an aspect ratio of 16 to 9, which is similar to the wide-screen approach used in movies. In addition, compared to analog display screens, an HDTV display has 10 times more pixels on a screen—1,920 × 1,080 pixels or more. Thus, HDTV could have 1,080 lines on a screen, compared with 525-line resolution for analog TV.

Choosing a TV

For HDTV FAQs, go to:

www.techhive.com/article/183095/hdtv_buying_guide_flat_panel_technology.html

www.digitaltrends.com/home-theater/tv-buying-guide-how-to-buy-a-tv/

www.pcmag.com/article2/0,2817,2344237,00.asp

STANDARD-DEFINITION TELEVISION (SDTV) HDTV takes a lot of bandwidth that broadcasters could use instead for **standard-definition television (SDTV), which has a lower resolution, a minimum of 480 vertical lines, and a picture quality similar to that required to watch DVD movies.** What's important about the SDTV standard is that it enables broadcasters to transmit more information within the HDTV bandwidth. That is, broadcasters can *multicast* their products, transmitting up to five SDTV programs simultaneously—and getting perhaps five times the revenue—instead of just one HDTV program. "Multicast services piggyback on digital signals from local stations," says one report, "including those offering HDTV versions of ABC, CBS, Fox, NBC, and PBS. . . . Stations typically get multicast programming for free and sell five minutes an hour of air time. The networks sell an additional five minutes to national advertisers."[68] With so many extra channels, having enough content becomes a problem. Thus, we will no doubt see tons of reruns of vintage TV shows, from *The Lone Ranger* to *The Addams Family.*

The Societal Effects of the New TV

New technology has changed the way people experience television.

"The ethos of New TV can be captured in a single sweeping mantra," says Steven Levy, *"anything you want to see, any time, on any device"* (his emphasis).[69]

TIME SHIFTING: CHANGING WHEN YOU WATCH TV Digital video recorders (DVRs) such as those marketed by TiVo and by cable and satellite providers allow viewers to watch favorite shows at their own convenience rather than following a broadcast schedule. They also enable viewers to freeze-frame action sequences and to skip commercials. (What this could eventually do to advertising as the economic underpinning for free-to-viewers television can only be guessed at.)

Several manufacturers make TiVo sets, including TiVo itself, but they all have one thing in common—a hard drive. The hard drive is connected to the outside world through a variety of jacks on the back of the TV set, usually the typical connections that you would use to hook up, say, a cable box (for which you pay a subscription fee). The television signal comes into the TiVo set's built-in tuner usually through cable or satellite. Some TiVo sets have more than one tuner, which means the set can record programming from two channels at the same time. Then the signal is sent to the hard drive for storage. Digital cable customers will need a CableCARD for each tuner. CableCARDs are adapters that let your TiVo receive the digital signal from the cable company. Most cable companies require a technician to install the CableCARD in your TiVo.

Another technology affecting the "when" is **video on demand *(VOD* or *VoD),* which consists of a wide set of technologies that enable viewers to select videos or TV programs from a central server to watch when they want,** rather than when TV programmers offer them (*http://home.vod.com/*). Service providers such as Comcast allow subscribers to use VOD through Internet-enabled devices.

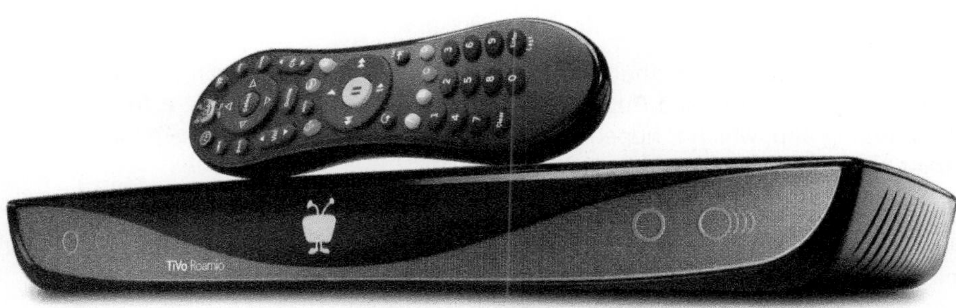

(*top*) TiVo TV; (*bottom*) TiVo box and remote

SPACE SHIFTING: CHANGING WHERE YOU WATCH TV Consumers can now download or receive TV programs, either stored or real time, and watch them on some sort of handheld device. For instance, the SlingCatcher and the SlingPlayer Mobile from Sling Media enable you to watch a program playing on your living room TV on your laptop computer—anywhere in the world.

Slingbox makes it easy to watch and control your home TV from virtually anywhere, anytime on your desktop, laptop, tablet, or mobile phone.

CONTENT SHIFTING: CHANGING THE NATURE OF TV PROGRAMS Perhaps the most important development is the movement of television to the Internet. This is made possible by *IPTV,* short for *Internet Protocol Television,* in which television and video signals are sent to viewers using Internet protocols (*http://technews.tmcnet.com/*). Cable and satellite channels have limited capacity, but the Internet has room for everything. As a consequence, you may be able to cram even *more* programs on your screen simultaneously—and what does that do to the human attention span? (Multiple-channel TV sets are available with what are known as "mosaic" screens that allow sports fans, for instance, to watch eight separate games on one screen.)

7.8 VIDEOGAME SYSTEMS: The Ultimate Convergence Machine?

The principal videogame consoles—Xbox, PlayStation, and Wii—are having to adapt to competition from mobile games.

Today more than 211 million people, or nearly two-thirds of Americans, play videogames in the United States, up from 150 million in 2005.[70] However, not all of them play on Microsoft's Xbox, Sony's PlayStation, and Nintendo's Wii—**videogame consoles or *gameboxes,* specialized computers powered by operating systems and CPUs different from those in desktop computers.**

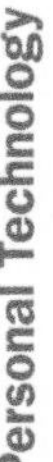

Indeed, says one report, "the lure of free, easy-to-play Facebook games and free or lower-price games such as *Angry Birds* on smartphones and tablets has expanded the game-playing populace."[71] Another challenge to console makers: the establishment of casino-style online gambling, betting games that can be played on mobile devices or PCs.[72] And still another challenge: women account for nearly 60% of players on mobile devices and are more likely than men to play games with a social bent, such as Words with Friends.[73]

Despite these changes, Microsoft, Sony, and Nintendo haven't given up. Let's see how their consoles compare.

MICROSOFT'S XBOX Because of the gaming market's shifting away from consoles, Microsoft's goal with its newest videogame player, the Xbox One, is to "move its system decisively beyond gaming," says one report, "and transform the Xbox into an entertainment hub for users' televisions." [74] The device has an 8-gigabyte system memory, a 500-gigabyte hard drive, accepts both Blu-ray and DVD drive media, features a Kinect motion-control camera, and can be directed by voice commands tied to a specific user's voice.

TECH TALES Using Your Xbox to Order Pizza

Microsoft wants to expand the reach of its Xbox beyond the gaming world into the physical world, and Pizza Hut sees opportunity—by offering a free pizza-ordering app, which it hopes will help it connect with the hard-to-reach market of men ages 18–24.

No one knows whether the concept will work, but it could be huge. "The very last thing a [game-playing] kid wants to do is look for a phone to order a pizza," says one expert. With this innovation, "the Xbox is no longer just a place to play games."[75]

As part of its strategy, Microsoft has made it so the Xbox can be customized to keep each person in a household happy. The Kinect sensor, says one writer, "can tell mom, dad, and the kids apart and arrange or push games, movies, TV shows, and music to suit each person's tastes."[76]

Thus, in ordering pizza—or anything else—you are not limited to operating with just the game controllers. You can also use Kinect hand motions and even voice commands. In addition, you can run apps simultaneously, using your voice, for instance, to switch between games, music—and restaurant menus.

Microsoft Xbox Day One Edition

Microsoft's pricing strategy associated with Xbox One carries some risks. At $399 or even $499, the new machine is about $100 above its competitors.[77] "The ultimate verdict on next-generation home consoles," says one writer, "is far from being delivered."[78]

SONY'S PLAYSTATION 4 PlayStation 4, or PS4, is described by Sony as essentially a "supercharged PC," much like the Xbox. It has a souped-up eight-core processor, 8-gigabyte system memory, 500-gigabyte hard drive, Blu-ray/DVD drive, and a new controller "designed in tandem with a stereo camera that can sense the depth of the environment in front of it," according to one account.[79] It also has a special touchpad to give the controller additional control options, enhanced graphics, and the ability to play games even as they are being downloaded.

In addition, there are new features involving social networking and remote access. You can broadcast video of your game play for friends elsewhere to watch. You can run a game that will stream over the Internet to Sony's mobile gaming device, the PlayStation Vita.[80] In this regard, Sony represents the videogame industry shift from the model of playing games on disks or cartridges in dedicated machines toward playing games on any mobile device.[81]

NINTENDO'S WII U When Nintendo started selling its Wii U videogame console in fall 2012 (basic price: $299), the company hoped the new version of its device would keep customers who had been turning to smartphones and tablets for gaming.[82]

The Wii U has a GamePad controller that includes a 6.2-inch touch screen that allows users to play games on two screens. The device also features the motion-sensor capabilities that were breakthrough innovations of the original Wii console. For Nintendo, the basic strategy is to make new installments of its well-known games, such as Legend of Zela, Super Mario Bros., and Donkey Kong, only for its own devices, despite pressure to produce them for smartphones and tablets made by others.[83]

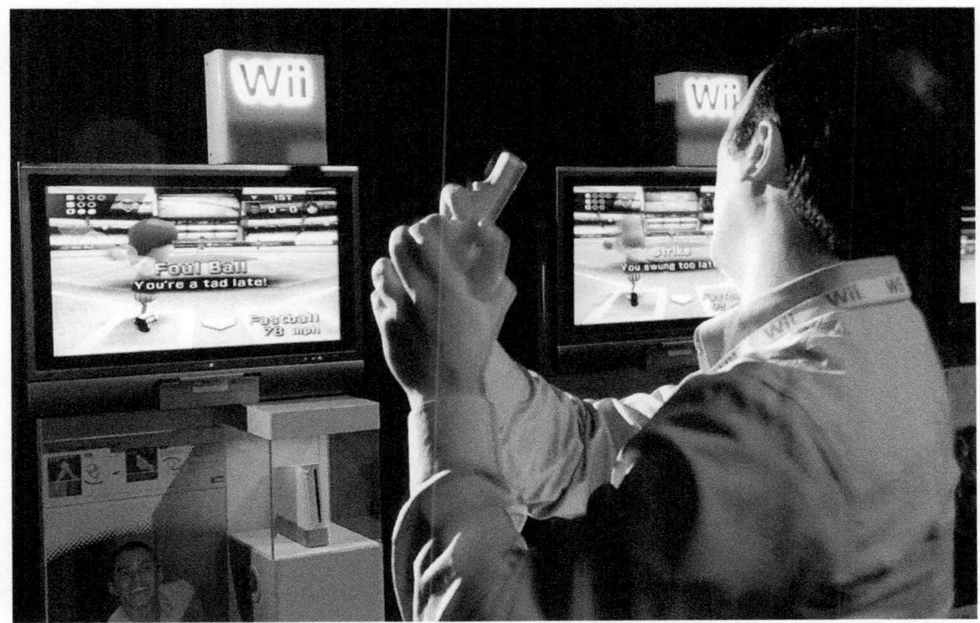

Playing baseball on the Nintendo Wii

With all these personal digital devices, it's no wonder that anyone born since 1982 is called a member of the "Always On" generation. They are the generation that has for their entire lives been surrounded by and using the toys and tools of the Digital Age. If you belong to this group, does it make you different from previous generations? We consider this question in the Experience Box.

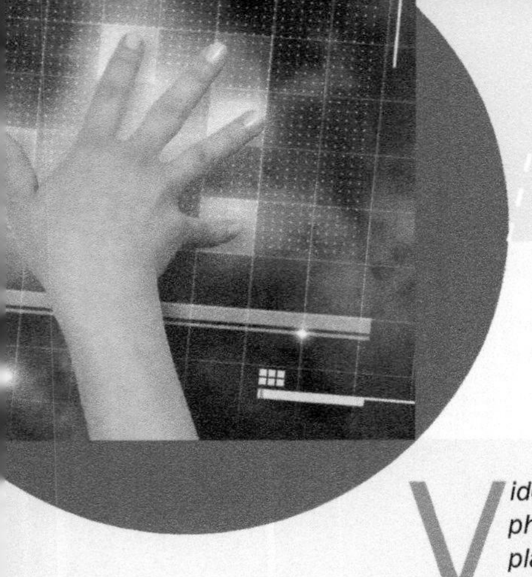

EXPERIENCE BOX

The "Always On" Generation

Videogames, computers, cellphones, portable music players, email, the Internet, instant messaging, texting, the web, tweeting, and similar personal technology: is this what you grew up with? Then you're a member of the Always On generation, also known as NetGeners *(for "Net Generation") and* Millennials *(for "Millennial Generation").*

Members of this cohort "have never known life without computers and the Internet," says one report. "To them the computer is not a technology—it is an assumed part of life."[84] As a result, say observers such as Marc Prensky, "today's students *think and process information fundamentally differently* from their predecessors."[85] (Indeed, some students grew up using cellphones as part of their classroom lessons.[86])

Unlike older students, Millennials tend to exhibit distinct learning styles. "Their learning preferences tend toward teamwork, experiential activities, structure, and the use of technology," says Diana Oblinger, executive director of higher education for Microsoft Corporation.[87] With such students, listening to music, sending instant messages, chatting on the phone, and doing homework all at the same time is second nature.

Let's consider some of the characteristics of these students.

Staying Connected Is Essential

After a college class lets out, students step into the hallway and immediately activate their smartphones, tablets, or laptops, texting friends or checking their tweets and text messages and email. At rock concerts, when the lights dim, one may see the glow of tiny blue screens, as concert goers text-message friends or have them listen to music via their phones—or observe the action through the cameras in their phones.

Connecting is what this generation of students is all about. Besides maintaining social contacts, students get homework assignments and lecture outlines online and participate in class discussions. They text friends to brainstorm class projects and other assignments. They email professors with questions at any time. The lines between work, social life, and studying are blurred.

Multitasking Is a Way of Life

Even though it may not be efficient, multitasking is second nature, as in doing homework while also watching TV, texting, or listening to music. "Attending to multiple streams of information and entertainment while studying, doing homework, or even sitting in class has become common behavior" among students, says one report. Indeed, it's so common "that many of them rarely write a paper or complete a problem set any other way."[88] Mobile is having the biggest impact on how they apportion their screen time, with students spending more time on cell- or smartphones and tablets and less on TV.[89] "Students are way too convinced that multitasking is a great way to work," says one professor summarizing studies on the subject. "They think they can do two or three tasks simultaneously and not compromise the quality of what they produce. Research says that [only] about 5% of us multitask effectively."[90]

Students Are Impatient & Results-Oriented

Today's students have grown up on the "twitch speed" of videogames, instant messaging, MTV, and a customer-service kind of culture. They have learned how to use and manage a large database of information, to take in many sources of information at once, and to incorporate peripheral information.[91] Thus, they "have a strong demand for immediacy and little tolerance for delays," says one analysis. "They expect that services will be available 24 × 7 in a variety of modes (web, phone, in person) and that responses will be quick."[92]

One result of being accustomed to receiving information really fast is that when doing reading many students prefer to see their graphics *before* the text, and when taking notes they prefer typing to handwriting. Another result: Students expect to be engaged, which is why online forums, blogs, and use of RSS aggregators to update subjects are popular.[93] They don't want to be preached to, ignored, or bored. They are also experiential learners—they prefer to learn by doing rather than learn by listening.[94]

They Respect Differences & Gravitate toward Group Activity

NetGeners are racially and ethnically diverse and consequently "accept differences that span culture, ability—or disability—and style," says one report. Indeed, it continues, they "are more comfortable with their learning differences than any other generation has been."[95] They also gravitate toward group and team activities, owing to their group-gaming experiences and their constant communication with friends through smartphones, texting, and email.

TERMS & EXPLANATIONS

convergence (p. 369) Also known as *digital convergence;* the combining of several industries—computers, communications, consumer electronics, entertainment, and mass media—through various devices that exchange data in digital form. Why it's important: *Convergence has led to electronic products that perform multiple functions, such as TVs with Internet access; cellphones that are also digital cameras, GPS units, and video players; and cars with digital connection ports.*

digital television (DTV) (p. 397) Television standard adopted in 1996 that uses a digital signal, or series of 0s and 1s. It uses digital cameras, digital transmission, and digital receivers and is capable of delivering movie-quality pictures and CD-quality sound. Why it's important: *DTV is much clearer and less prone to interference than analog TV. It may allow viewers to receive various kinds of information services, such as announcements from public safety and fire departments.*

e-book (p. 380) *Electronic book;* electronic text (and images), the digital-media equivalent of a conventional printed book or magazine. Why it's important: *Some of the advantages of e-books: e-books are searchable; you can carry an entire library on one e-reader (or tablet); e-books can be delivered almost instantly (and wirelessly too); e-books are cheaper to buy than most regular books and can be annotated without harming the original work; text can be resized for people who are visually impaired, and screens can be lit for reading in the dark; e-books can be hyperlinked, for easy access to additional information; e-books can read aloud to you; many e-books allow readers to change the font style, font size, page size, margin size, colors, and more.*

e-reader (p. 380) Handheld device specifically designed to allow people to read electronic texts. Why it's important: *Allows users to download electronic books and the like, wired or wirelessly, and read them as conveniently as printed materials.*

HD (hybrid digital) radio (p. 394) Form of radio that provides CD-quality sound and allows broadcasters to squeeze one analog and two digital stations on the same frequency. Why it's important: *HD radio combines digital and analog broadcast signals, enabling stations to offer an analog main channel and digital "sidebands," so that multiple types of content can be broadcast from the same position on the dial.*

high-definition television (HDTV) (p. 398) A form of television that works with digital broadcasting signals. Why it's important: *HDTV has a wider screen and higher resolution than analog television had. Whereas analog TV has a width-to-height ratio, or aspect ratio, of 4 to 3, HDTV has an aspect ratio of 16 to 9, which is similar to the wide-screen approach used in movies. In addition, compared to analog display screens, an HDTV display has 10 times more pixels on a screen—1,920 × 1,080 pixels or more. Thus, HDTV could have 1,080 lines on a screen, compared with 525-line resolution for analog TV.*

Internet radio (p. 394) Continuous streaming of audio over the Internet; listeners have no control over the stream—just as with regular radio. Why it's important: *Dedicated hardware devices, commonly called web radio or Internet radio appliances, can be purchased that connect to a home network and then to the Internet to play audio streams. Internet radio can also be played on computers and on portable devices, such as smartphones and media players, connected wirelessly to the Internet.*

mashup (p. 368) A creative combination of content or elements from different sources, such as a web page that blends data from two or more sources to create new services or content. Why it's important: *Mashups can increase innovation and present a broader perspective than the individual works can do on their own. However, copyright violation must be avoided when others' work is used in mashups.*

megapixels (mp) (p. 388) Millions of picture elements; the electronic dots making up an image. Why it's important: *A megapixel a unit of storage that describes the amount of data captured by a camera. It can be written to internal memory or to a removable card.*

MP3 (p. 383) MPEG Audio Layer 3; format that allows audio files to be compressed. Why it's important: *MP3 files are about one-tenth the size of uncompressed audio files. For example, a 4-minute song on a CD takes about 40 megabytes of space, but an MP3 version of that song takes only about 4 megabytes. MP3 allows audio files to be made small enough to be sent over the Internet or stored as digital files. (MP4 is the format used for video.)*

MP3 player (p. 382) (See **portable media player.**)

multitasking (p. 381) Performing several tasks at once, such as studying while eating, listening to music, talking on the phone, and handling email. Why it's important: *Medical and learning experts say the brain has limits and can do only so much at one time. For instance, it has been found that people who do two demanding tasks simultaneously, such as driving in heavy traffic and talking on a cellphone, do neither task as well as they do each alone. Indeed, the result of constantly shifting attention is a sacrifice in quality for any of the tasks with which one is engaged.*

personalization (p. 371) The creation of information tailored to your preferences. Why it's important: *An example of personalization is programs that automatically cull recent news and information from the Internet on just those topics you have designated. Consumers can expect their online experiences to be 100% relevant to them.*

podcasting (p. 395) The recording and downloading of Internet radio or similar Internet audio programs. Why it's important: *Podcasting software allows amateur deejays and hobbyists to create their own radio shows and offer them free over the Internet. Listeners can then download shows onto their MP3 players, such as the iPod, or other media players and computers.*

portability (p. 370) The state or quality of being portable—that is, capable of being carried or moved about. Why it's important: *Now nearly everyone has a portable phone and many other portable devices: laptop computers, tablets, e-readers, portable media players, digital cameras, and so on.*

portable media players (PMPs) (p. 382) Small portable devices that enable you to play digital audio, video, and/or image files. Why it's important: *MP3 players play digital audio files. Media players play not only audio but also video and image files, and they support other functions, such as web browsing, email, and social networking.*

sampling rate (p. 384) The number of times, expressed in kilobits per second, that a song is measured (sampled) and converted to a digital value when it is being recorded as a digital file. Why it's important: *The sampling rate affects the audio quality. For instance, a song sampled at 192 kilobits per second is three times the size of a song sampled at 64 kilobits per second and will be of better sound quality.*

satellite radio (p. 393) Radio service in which signals are sent from satellites in orbit around the earth or by earth-based repeaters to subscribers owning special radios that can decode the encrypted signals. Why it's important: *The CD-quality sound is much better than that of regular radio, and because the signals are digital, there are many more channels available than on traditional radio. It is mostly commercial-free and is available by subscription.*

standard-definition television (SDTV) (p. 398) TV standard that has a lower resolution than HDTV, a minimum of 480 vertical lines, and a picture quality similar to that required to watch DVD movies. Why it's important: *The SDTV standard enables broadcasters to transmit more information within the HDTV bandwidth, allowing them to multicast their products, transmitting up to five SDTV programs simultaneously—and getting perhaps five times the revenue—instead of just one HDTV program. (Analog broadcasts only one program at a time.) Thus, instead of beaming high-definition pictures, some broadcasters are splitting their digital streams into several SDTV channels.*

text messaging (p. 375) Also known as *texting;* the sending of short messages, generally no more than 160 characters in length, to a pager, smartphone, or other handheld device, including notebook computer, as well as to desktop computers and landline phones. Why it's important: *Text messaging combines the portability of cellphones with the convenience of email and instant messaging. Text messaging is particularly appropriate for situations in which making a cellphone call is intrusive.*

videogame consoles (p. 399) Also called *gameboxes;* specialized computers powered by operating systems and CPUs different from those in desktop computers. Why it's important: *Console gaming is very popular and is a lucrative business.*

video on demand (VOD or VoD) (p. 398) Set of technologies that enable viewers to select videos or TV programs from a central server to watch when they want. Why it's important: *VOD allows viewers to watch programs when they want rather than when TV programmers offer them.*

CHAPTER REVIEW

MEMORIZATION

"I can recognize and recall information."

Self-Test Questions

1. The combining of several industries through various devices that exchange data in digital form is called __________.
2. __________ allows amateur deejays and hobbyists to create their own radio shows and offer them free over the Internet.
3. __________ means capable of being carried or moved about.
4. The sending of short messages generally no longer than 160 characters is called __________.
5. The millions of electronic dots that make up a digital camera image are called __________.
6. Performing several tasks at once is called __________.
7. The number of times, expressed in kilobits per second, that a song is measured and converted to a digital value when it is being recorded as a digital file is called the __________.
8. The digital-media equivalent of a conventional printed book is called a(n) __________.
9. __________ is a format that is commonly used to compress audio files so they are small enough to be sent over the Internet as digital files.
10. __________ are small portable devices that enable you to play/display digital audio, video, and/or image files.
11. __________ works with digital broadcasting signals and has a wider screen and higher resolution than standard TV.
12. A(n) __________ digital camera is one that automatically adjusts settings such as exposure and focus.
13. The principal smartphone operating systems are __________, __________, and __________.

Multiple-Choice Questions

1. The number of times that a song is measured and converted to a digital value is called
   a. SLR
   b. ripping
   c. sampling rate
   d. mashup
2. A digital camera's resolution is expressed in
   a. dpi
   b. rpm
   c. pda
   d. megapixels
   e. betapixels

3. Smartphones have
   a. a microprocessor
   b. a display screen
   c. memory
   d. a modem
   e. all of these
4. Which of the following concerns does *not* apply to smartphone use?
   a. often causes erratic driving
   b. people can track users' movements without their knowledge
   c. users can take photos in inappropriate situations
   d. signals can open locked car doors
   e. loud conversations and ringtones can irritate people in the user's vicinity
5. MPEG Layer 3, used on MP3 players, is an audio __________ technology that allows files to be easily sent over the Internet.
   a. streaming
   b. analog
   c. amplifying
   d. compression

True-False Questions

T F 1. The increased availability of broadband connections slowed down the process of digital convergence.

T F 2. MP3 increases the size of digital audio files in order to improve the sound quality.

T F 3. If you shoot mainly 4 × 6 photos and rarely crop them, most digital cameras' megapixel memory should be adequate.

T F 4. Convergence is a creative combination of content or elements from different sources,

T F 5. Sending photos as email attachments to many people is more efficient than using an online photo-sharing service.

T F 6. One cannot transfer files from a smartphone to a desktop computer.

T F 7. HDTV uses analog signals.

T F 8. Cellphones are radios.

LEARNING COMPREHENSION

"I can recall information in my own terms and explain it to a friend."

Short-Answer Questions

1. What could you use a mashup for?
2. Why are MP3 files smaller than regular audio files, such as a purchased CD?
3. Why would you use an online photo-sharing service?
4. How does sampling rate relate to the size of MP3 files?
5. What is the difference between satellite radio and high-definition radio?
6. Which digital camera would you choose: point-and-shoot or single-lens reflex? Why?

LEARNING APPLYING, ANALYZING, SYNTHESIZING, EVALUATING

"I can apply what I've learned, relate these ideas to other concepts, build on other knowledge, and use all these thinking skills to form a judgment."

Knowledge in Action

1. Does almost everyone you know download and listen to MP3 files? Describe a few ways in which the iPod users whom you have observed are being distracted from certain activities and some responsibilities. Do you perceive a problem?
2. List five situations in which you often find yourself multitasking. How many things have you done at once? How do you think your manner of multitasking affects the quality of what you achieve?
3. What questions would you ask a friend in order to determine which digital camera, with which characteristics, you would advise her or him to buy?
4. Describe the ways that one can transfer images from a digital camera to a computer.
5. Do mashups violate copyright? Many people believe that music on the Internet should be downloadable for free. But what if a person *makes her living* from writing music (or other creative activities) only to see other people use it for free for their own gain or pleasure?

   http://lawprofessors.typepad.com/media_law_prof_blog/2012/03/mashups-and-copyright.html

   http://smallbusiness.findlaw.com/intellectual-property/fair-use-and-public-domain.html?DCMP=GOO-BUS_Copyright-FairUse&HBX_PK=what+is+fair+use

   http://188ip.wordpress.com/2010/11/30/mashups-copyright-infringement-without-a-fair-use-defense/

   www.zdnet.com/blog/btl/mashups-and-the-law/2614

Web Exercises

1. Current rules of both the FCC and the U.S. Federal Aviation Administration ban in-flight cellular calling., although some airlines now allow the use of Wi-Fi. The primary FCC concern has been possible disruption of cellphone communication on the ground. The FAA's worry is how cellphones might interfere with a plane's navigation and electrical systems. However, plans are in the works to assign new bandwidths to allow cellphone use in the air.

   Do an Internet search on the pros and cons of using cellphones during flights. Are you in favor of such use?

2. Many states prohibit drivers from using handheld cellphones while driving. Do an Internet search, and find out what the law says about driving and cellphone use in the state where you are going to school and in the state where you come from. Start here:

   www.ncsl.org/issues-research/transport/cellular-phone-use-and-texting-while-driving-laws.aspx

   The rules on driving and cellphone use in many other countries are much stricter than they are in the United States; for more information, go to *www.distracteddrivinghelp.com/international-distracted-driving-laws* and *http://seniortravel.about.com/od/travelsafety/qt/Cell-Phone-Driving-Laws-By-Region.htm.*

   According to the Automobile Association of America (AAA), hands-free phones are not risk-free. The hands-free feature is simply a convenience: it does not increase safety. Studies show that hands-free cellphones distract drivers the same as handheld phones do. Why? Because it's the conversation that distracts the driver, not the device. Search the Internet, and find some reports that support this view.

   Why do you think people don't just turn off their cellphones while they are driving and let voice mail collect messages to be retrieved later?

3. The Convergence Center (*http://dcc.syr.edu/digital-convergence/*) supports research on and experimentation with media convergence. The center is a joint effort of the Syracuse University School of Information Studies and the Newhouse School of Public Communications. Its mission is to understand the future of digital media and to engage students and faculty in the process of defining and shaping that future. Go to its site, and click on items listed under What's New, Digital Convergence; choose one article to read; then write a couple of paragraphs that summarize the article.

4. Camera voyeurism is becoming a problem. The U.S. Video Voyeurism Prevention Act of 2004 made this behavior a federal offense. This act prohibits photographing or videocapturing (including with cellphones) a naked person without his or her consent in any place where there can be "a reasonable expectation of privacy." Punishment includes fines of up to $100,000 or up to a year in prison, or both.

   Cellphone vendors say this law may be hard to enforce and may even be a deterrent to promising technology and create a false sense of security. Some cellphone manufacturers deny that voyeurs are any more likely to snoop using a cellphone camera than using other technologies such as digital cameras. But other people say that the opportunity differs and that most people don't carry digital cameras around with them. With a cellphone camera there is more opportunity to take snapshots of interesting images, and unfortunately this can include images that can threaten privacy. Voyeurs using cellphone cameras could easily pretend to be doing something else, such as dialing or talking.

   Some state legislators have proposed legislation requiring camera phones sold to emit an audible noise or flash a light when users press the shutter. But such noise and light would disturb happy occasions, such as weddings, where people use cellphone cameras to take pictures and send them instantly to loved ones who couldn't attend.

   Research the camera phone voyeurism problem on the Internet. How can you protect your privacy in public situations?

5. The Cellular Telecommunications & Internet Association (CTIA) reminds us that text messaging can be a fast, efficient, and reliable way to communicate in the event of an emergency. And if more wireless users rely on text messaging in crisis situations, the people who need to make voice calls the most—emergency responders and 911 callers—can get through more easily.

   "Everyone should have a plan for communicating in times of emergencies, and text messaging can be an efficient way to reach your friends, family or loved ones. In the time it takes one person to make a 1-minute voice call, hundreds of thousands of text messages can be exchanged," said a president and CEO of CTIA. "In these days of increased terrorist threats and heightened awareness, learning all the options on your wireless phone is an important piece of being prepared."

   In the frantic days leading up to the landfall of Hurricane Rita in September 2005, Houston radio station KRBE offered to deliver hurricane alerts via text messaging across cellphones to listeners, enabling information to be delivered anytime, anywhere, regardless of whether a person was near a radio or a computer. At a time when traditional media networks experienced coverage issues from storm damage, power lines were down, and cars were running out of gas, KRBE was able to provide a continuous two-way stream of information via the cellphone. Many listeners expressed gratitude for information on road closures, fuel availability, evacuation orders, and storm damage during a frightening experience.

   However, after giant storm Sandy in 2012, mobile communications services were knocked out for days. The problem? The companies that provide them had successfully resisted Federal Communications Commission calls to make emergency preparations, leaving New Yorkers to rely on the carriers' voluntary efforts; those that sell network connections in the United States are claiming a constitutional right to operate without any federal oversight (*www.bloomberg.com/news/2012-11-15/why-cell-phones-went-dead-after-hurricane-sandy.html*).

   Do an Internet search on how text messaging has been used recently to help in various types of emergencies around the world. What types of suppliers have provided the messages? Using what types of systems? How do cellphone users know where/how to retrieve the messages? How should the federal government regulate cellphone carriers' ability to provide service during emergencies, especially now that so many people no longer have landlines.

THE ERA OF BIG DATA

Databases, Information Systems, & Artificial Intelligence

Chapter Topics & Key Questions

UNIT 8A: *Files & Databases*

8.1 **Managing Files: Basic Concepts** What are the data storage hierarchy, the key field, types of files, and some methods of data access and storage?

8.2 **Database Management Systems** What are the benefits of database management systems, and what are the main types of database access?

8.3 **Database Models** What are the main types of database models?

8.4 **Data Mining** How does data mining work, and how could it be useful?

UNIT 8B: *Big Data, Information Systems, & Artificial Intelligence*

8.5 **The Evolving World of Big Data** What is revolutionary about Big Data?

8.6 **Information Systems in Organizations: Using Databases to Help Make Decisions** How does information flow within an organization, and what are different types of information systems?

8.7 **Artificial Intelligence** What are the main areas of artificial intelligence?

8.8 **Artificial Life, the Turing Test, & the Singularity** What are the signs to look for that computer intelligence has truly exceeded human intelligence?

Download the free UIT 11e App for key term flash cards quizzes and a game, *Over the Edge*

CHAPTER FORECAST We begin the chapter by considering files and databases and then consider Big Data and artificial intelligence.

In Unit 8A, we start with the basics of managing files, describing the data storage hierarchy, the key field, types of files, and some methods of data access and storage. We then discuss the benefits of database management systems and what the main types of database access are. Next we consider the main types of database models. We conclude by describing how data mining works and how it can be useful.

In Unit 8B, we discuss Big Data, information systems, artificial intelligence, as well as artificial life, the Turing test, and the Singularity. We consider what is revolutionary about Big Data. We then discuss how information flows within an organization and what different types of information systems are. We next describe the main areas of artificial intelligence. Finally, we consider what signs to look for that computer intelligence has truly exceeded human intelligence.

UNIT 8A: *Files & Databases*

"Some expect data to grow on the planet by 20 times between 2012 and 2020."

So says Mark Hurd, copresident of Oracle, the $100 billion California database giant.[1] Every day, 2.5 quintillion bytes of data are created, with a typical American office worker generating about 5,000 megabytes a day, including downloaded movies, Word files, e-mail, and the bits generated by computers.[2]

Not only is the sheer mass of data overwhelming, the data is also *unstructured.* This makes up what people are calling *Big Data,* data that is so large and complex that it cannot be processed using conventional methods, such as ordinary database management software. Thus, says Hurd, "the challenge is how do [we] deal with this massive amount of data and turn it into meaningful information?"

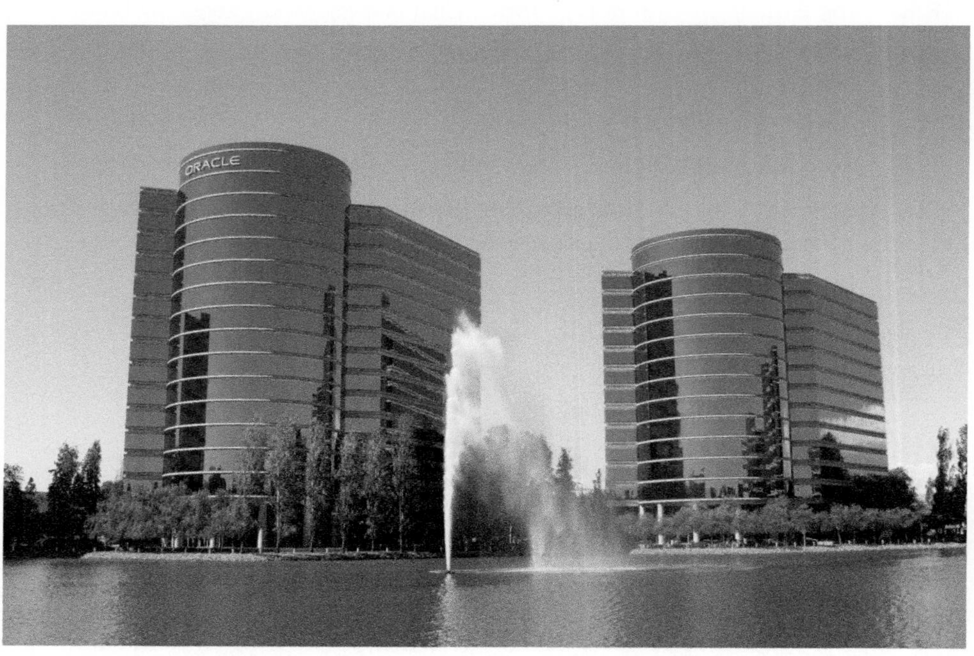

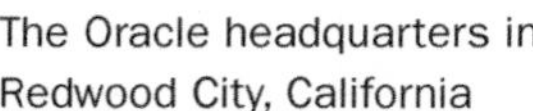

The Oracle headquarters in Redwood City, California

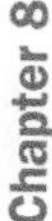

One problem is *storing* the data, No wonder there are so many huge power-gobbling cloud computing storage centers by Microsoft, Yahoo!, and others located near the electricity-generating dams of Washington's Columbia River.[3] Another problem is *organizing* the data and making it useful. That is the subject of this chapter.

In the first part of this chapter, we consider the basic concepts behind file management and data storage, the benefits of database management systems, the main types of database models, how data mining works, and databases in relation to e-business and e-commerce. In Unit 8B, we discuss the evolving role of Big Data, information systems used in organizations and how they help us make decisions, the main areas of artificial intelligence, and detailed aspects of robotics.

8.1 MANAGING FILES: Basic Concepts

A database is a computer-based collection of related data organized so that it can be conveniently accessed, managed, and updated.

An electronic database is not just the computer-based version of what used to go into cardboard folders and filing cabinets. As we said in Chapter 1 (p. 11), a **database is a collection of interrelated data and files.** More specifically, it is a logically organized collection of related data designed and built for a specific purpose, a technology for pulling together facts that allows the slicing and dicing and mixing and matching of unprocessed data in all kinds of ways and turning it into useful information.

TECH TALES Databases Everywhere

A database can be of any size and of any degree of complexity. Traditional electronic databases include those that handle airline reservation systems, many library catalogs, magazine subscriptions for large publishing companies, patient tracking in large hospitals, and inventories for supermarkets and big-box stores such as Walmart. These databases typically use text- and numeric-based data. Newer types of databases include multimedia data and formulas for data analysis.

Wikipedia (*www.wikipedia.org*) is a web-based, free-content, multilingual encyclopedia that anyone can log on to and add to or edit as he or she sees fit; it has more than 13 million articles in approximately 250 languages.[4]

The National Geographic Society and IBM's Watson Research Labs launched a massive database called the Genographic Project (*https://genographic.nationalgeographic.com/genographic/index.htm*) that is cataloging genetic markers and is capable of tracing the geographic origins of your and other people's ancestors back more than 10,000 years.

Google has created a database consisting of millions of digitally scanned books from several university libraries (*http://books.google.com/*). ■

Library of Congress Database

Practice using the Library of Congress website:

www.loc.gov

In the Search box at the top of the page, choose a category you are interested in and then click Go. Then choose another category on the left and click on it; continue to narrow your search.

Before we discuss traditional types of databases and recent innovations in database management, we need to discuss some basic concepts of file management.

How Data Is Organized: The Data Storage Hierarchy

"Hierarchy" refers to a graded series of ordered groupings—usually a pyramid-like ranking, with the most important entities on the top.

Data in a traditional database can be grouped into a hierarchy of categories, each increasingly more complex. **The data storage hierarchy consists of the levels of data stored in a computer database: bits, characters (bytes), fields, records, and tables (files).** *(• See Panel 8.1, next page).* An alternative design is the *hypertext database,* in which any object, whether it be a piece of text, a picture, or a film, can be linked to any other object. Hypertext databases are great for organizing large amounts of disparate information, but not for numerical analysis.

panel 8.1

How data is organized

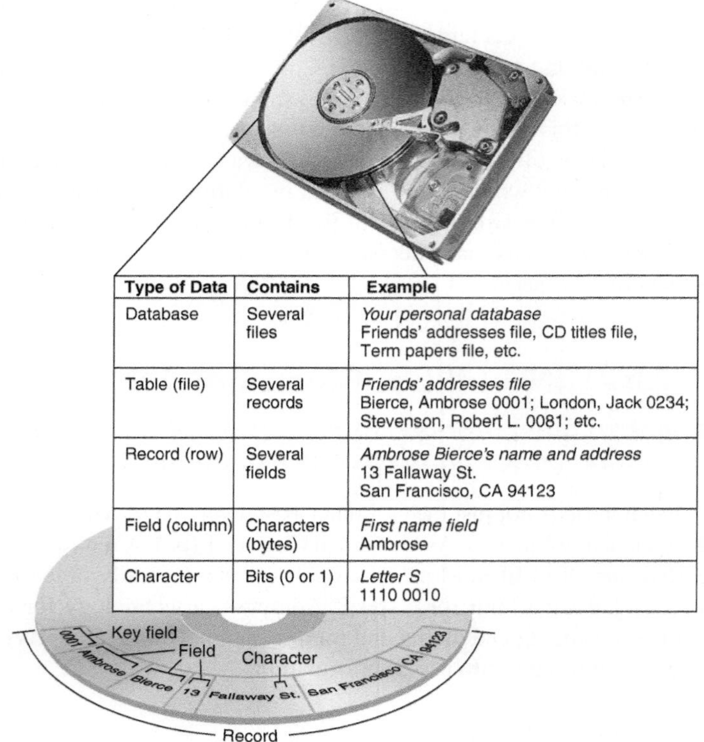

Type of Data	Contains	Example
Database	Several files	*Your personal database* Friends' addresses file, CD titles file, Term papers file, etc.
Table (file)	Several records	*Friends' addresses file* Bierce, Ambrose 0001; London, Jack 0234; Stevenson, Robert L. 0081; etc.
Record (row)	Several fields	*Ambrose Bierce's name and address* 13 Fallaway St. San Francisco, CA 94123
Field (column)	Characters (bytes)	*First name field* Ambrose
Character	Bits (0 or 1)	*Letter S* 1110 0010

Let's consider the data storage hierarchy.

BITS Computers, as we have said, are based on the principle that electricity may be on or off (Chapter 4, p. 197). Thus, the *bit* is the smallest unit of data the computer can store in a database—represented by 0 for off or 1 for on. Next is the byte.

CHARACTERS **A character *(byte)* is a letter, number, or special character.** Examples of single characters are *A, B, C, 1, 2, 3, #, $,* and *%*. A combination of bits represents a character.

Bits and bytes are the building blocks for representing data, whether it is being processed, telecommunicated, or stored in a database. The computer deals with the bits and bytes; you, however, will need to deal mostly with fields (columns), records (rows), and tables (files).

FIELD **A field *(column)* is a unit or category of data consisting of one or more characters (bytes).** It is the smallest unit of meaningful information in a database. Each field has a *field name* that describes the kind of data that should be entered into the field. An example of a field is your first name, *or* your street address, *or* your Social Security number.

Fields can be designed to be a certain maximum length or a variable length, and they can also be designed to hold different types of data, such as text only, numbers only, dates only, time, a "yes" or "no" answer only, web links only, or pictures, sound, or video.

RECORD **A record *(row)* is a collection of related fields;** it represents one entry in a table. Each record stores data about only one entity, which can be a person, a place, a thing, an occurrence, or a phenomenon. An example of a record would be your name *and* address *and* Social Security number.

FILE **A file (often called *table*) is a collection of related records.** An example of a table is data collected on everyone employed in the same department of a company, including all names, addresses, and Social Security numbers. You use tables a lot because the table is the collection of data or information that is treated as a unit by the computer.

The table is at the top of the data hierarchy. A collection of related tables forms the database. A company database might include tables on all past and current employees in all departments. There would be various records for each employee in various tables: payroll, retirement benefits, sales quotas and achievements (if in sales), and so on.

No characters or fields? Searchers of images on the ImageNet database don't rely on labels (characters and fields) to find what they want. The computer recognizes images just the way people do (*http://www.smartplanet.com/blog/bulletin/worlds-largest-image-database-to-help-computers-learn-to-see/6271*).

World's largest image database to help computers learn to see

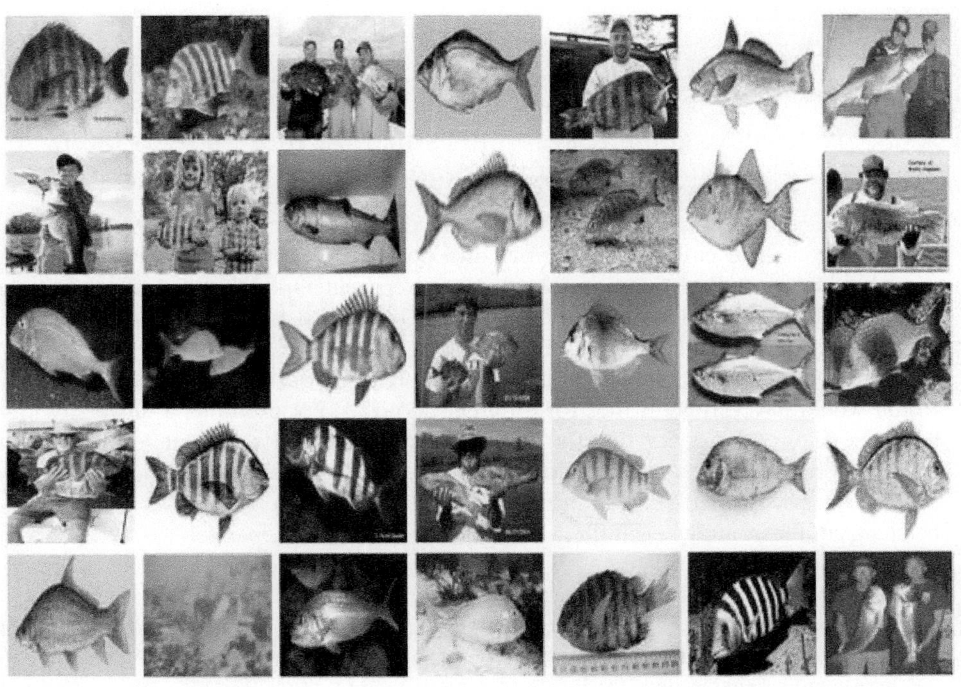

While there are images all over the Internet, there are very few good ways of searching for them.

The way it works now is that you type in a word, and if you're lucky and a person somewhere online has uploaded an image labeled with your search word, then you'll see that image in your search results.

But what if the search engine didn't have to rely on people labeling images correctly? What if the computer could just recognize images itself, the way people do?

To develop a system that can do that, Stanford computer scientist Fei-Fei Li created the world's largest visual database, ImageNet, which holds 14 million labeled images.

The Key Field

A key field (primary key) is a field (or fields) in a record that holds unique data that identifies that record from all the other records in the table and in the database.

An important concept in data organization is that of the key field. *(• See Panel 8.1.)* As we said in Chapter 3 in the section on database applications, a *primary key* (*key field*) is, in general, a field (or fields) that is chosen to uniquely identify a record so that it can be easily retrieved and processed. The primary key is often an identification number, Social Security number, customer account number, or the like or a combination of letters and numbers set up as a meaningful code. The primary characteristic of the key field is that it is *unique.* Thus, numbers are clearly preferable to names as primary keys, because there are many people with common names such as James Johnson, Susan Williams, Ann Wong, or Roberto Sanchez, whose records might be confused. Student records are often identified by student ID numbers used as primary keys.

As we also mentioned in Chapter 3, the *foreign key* (p. 163) is a field (or fields) in a table that matches the primary key of another table; in other words, it points to the primary

Survival Tip

Guard Your Social Security Number

The Social Security number is an important key field to records about you. Don't carry it with you. Don't use it as an ID password. Don't give it out unless really necessary. See also *www.ssa.gov/pubs/10064.html* regarding Social Security numbers and ID theft.

key of another table. Foreign keys thus can be used to cross-reference tables. For example, in a Student table (containing general data about all students), the primary key could be Student ID, because each student has a unique ID number. But in the Courses table, many students would be listed many times, because most students take many courses. Their Student IDs would be the foreign keys that would link each student to the primary key in the master Student table.

8.2 DATABASE MANAGEMENT SYSTEMS

A database management system is software that enables users to store, modify, and extract information from a database.

As we've said, a database is an organized collection of interrelated files. A database may be small, contained entirely within your own personal computer, or it may be massive, available through online connections or on supercomputers. Such massive databases are of particular interest, as we will see, because they offer phenomenal resources that until recently were unavailable to most ordinary computer users.

In the 1950s, when commercial use of computers was just beginning, a large organization would have different files for different purposes. For example, a university might have one file, called a *flat file,* for course grades, another for student records, another for tuition billing, and so on. In a corporation, people in the accounting, order-entry, and customer-service departments all had their own separate files. Thus, if an address had to be changed, for example, each file would have to be updated separately. The files—which are now called tables or relations—were stored on magnetic tape and had to be accessed in sequence in what was called a *file-processing system.*

Later, magnetic-disk technology came along, allowing any file to be accessed randomly (out of sequence). This permitted the development of new technology and new software: the database management system. **A database management system (DBMS), also called *database software* or *database manager,* is software written specifically to control the structure of a database and access to the data.** In a DBMS an address change need be entered only once, and the updated information is then available in any relevant table (file). (Strictly speaking, the *database* is the collection of the data, and the *database management system* is the software—but many professionals use "database" to cover both the data and the software.)

The Benefits of Database Management Systems

Information technology has dramatically improved the creation and management of data and information systems.

The advantages of database management systems are these:

REDUCED DATA REDUNDANCY *Data redundancy,* or *repetition,* means that the same data fields (a person's address, say) appear over and over again in different files and often in different formats. In the old file-processing system, separate files would repeat the same data, wasting storage space. In a database management system, the information appears just once, freeing up more storage capacity. In the old data storage systems, if one field needed to be updated, someone had to make sure that it was updated in *all* the places it appeared—an invitation to error and to wasted time.

This process of structuring data to minimize duplication and inconsistencies is called *normalization.*

SPEED Modern DBMSs are obviously much faster than manual data-organization systems and faster than older computer-based data storage arrangements.

IMPROVED DATA INTEGRITY *Data integrity* means that data is accurate, consistent, and up to date. In the old system, when a change was made in one file, it might not have been made in other necessary files. The result was that some reports were produced with erroneous information. In a DBMS, reduced redundancy increases the likelihood of data integrity—the chances that the data is accurate, consistent, and up to date—because each updating change is made in only one place.

Also, many DBMSs provide built-in check systems that help ensure the accuracy of the data that is input. The expression "garbage in, garbage out" (*GIGO*) refers to the fact that a database with incorrect data cannot generate correct information.

TIMELINESS The speed and the efficiency of DBMSs generally ensure that data can be supplied in a timely fashion—when people need it.

EASE OF SHARING The data in a database belongs to and is shared, usually over a network, by an entire organization. The data is independent of the programs that process the data, and it is easy for nontechnical users to access data (if they have authorization to do so). Individual computer users can also develop their own small databases, using a database application package (Chapter 3, p. 164).

EASE OF DATA MAINTENANCE Database management systems offer standard procedures for adding, editing, and deleting records, as well as validation checks to ensure that the appropriate type of data is being entered properly and completely into each field type. Data backup utilities ensure availability of data in case of primary system failure.

FORECASTING CAPABILITIES DBMSs can hold massive amounts of data that can be manipulated, studied, and compared in order to forecast behaviors in markets and other areas. Such improved forecasting can affect sales and marketing managers' decisions as well as the decisions of administrators of educational institutions, hospitals, and other organizations.

INCREASED SECURITY Although various departments may share data, access to specific information can be limited to selected users—called *authorization control.* Thus, for example, through the use of passwords, a student's financial, medical, and grade information in a university database is made available only to those who have a legitimate need to know.

TECH TALES How Amazon.com Used Databases to Become the World's Largest Online Bookstore

In 1994, seeing the potential for electronic retailing on the World Wide Web, Jeffrey Bezos left a successful career on Wall Street to launch an online bookstore called Amazon.com. Why the name "Amazon"? "Earth's biggest river, Earth's biggest bookstore," said Bezos in an interview. "The Amazon River is ten times as large as the next largest river, which is the Mississippi, in terms of volume of water. Twenty percent of the world's fresh water is in

Database Disadvantages

Some drawbacks of databases (depending on their size) can be these:

- Database systems are complex, difficult, and time-consuming to design.
- The hardware and software start-up costs are substantial.
- Damage to a database affects virtually all applications programs.
- Conversion costs when changing database systems can be extensive.
- Initial training is required for all programmers and users.
- If a hacker gets into the database, all data may be stolen or compromised.

the Amazon River Basin, and we have six times as many titles as the world's largest physical bookstore." A more hardheaded reason is that, according to consumer tests, words starting with "A" show up on search engine lists first.

Bezos realized that no bookstore with four walls could possibly stock the more than the 2.5 million titles that were active and in print. Moreover, he saw that an online bookstore relying on database management software wouldn't have to make the same investment in retail clerks, store real estate, or warehouse space (in the beginning, Amazon.com ordered books from the publisher *after* it took the book buyer's order), so it could pass savings along to customers in the form of discounts.

In addition, he appreciated that a database would provide Amazon with opportunities to obtain demographic information about customers in order to offer personalized services. For example, Amazon could let customers know of books that might be of interest to them. Such personalized attention is difficult for traditional large bookstores. Finally, Bezos saw that there could be a good deal of online interaction: customers could post reviews of books they read and could reach authors by email to provide feedback. All this was made possible on the web by the recording of information on giant databases.

Amazon.com sold its first book in July 1995, and by 2008 was No. 1 in the Internet Retailer Top 500 Guide, with sales of $4.06 billion. It was still No. 1 in 2013. What began as Earth's biggest bookstore also has rapidly become Earth's biggest anything store, offering CDs, DVDs, videos, electronics, toys, tools, home furnishings, clothing, prescription drugs, film-processing services, and more. ■

This is only one Amazon.com fulfillment center—out of 49 Amazon fulfillment centers in 8 countries (*www.ordoro.com/blog/2013/05/23/how-many-fulfillment-centers-does-amazon-have-and-where-are-they-located/*)

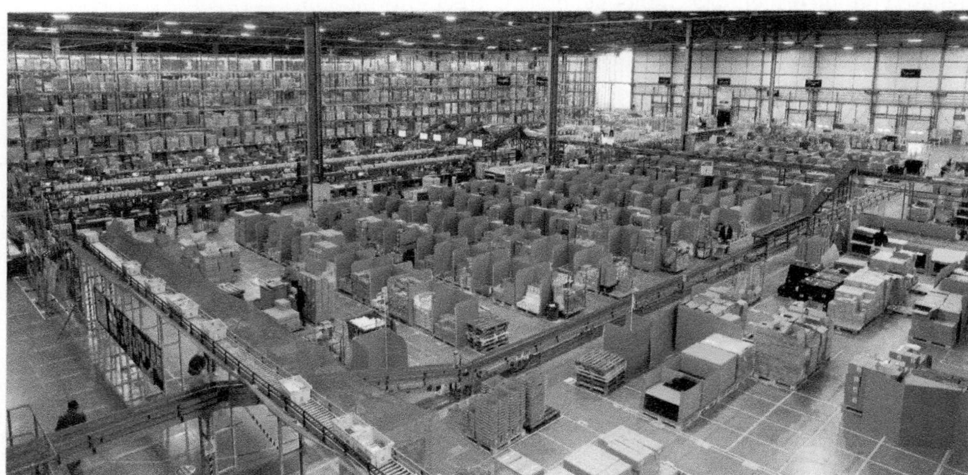

Three Database Components

A database management system may have three components integrated into the software—a data dictionary, DBMS utilities, and a report generator.

DATA DICTIONARY: FOR DEFINING DATA DEFINITIONS & STRUCTURE **A data dictionary, also called a *repository* or *database schema,* is a document or file that stores the data definitions and descriptions of the structure of data used in the database.** Data dictionaries contain no actual data from the database, only information for managing it. Without a data dictionary, however, a DBMS cannot access data from the database.

The data dictionary contains the **metadata, data that describes other data,** such as the field name, the data type (text, numeric, and so on), and the field size (expected length of each data for each field). The data dictionary defines the basic organization of the database and contains a list of all tables in the database, and the number of records in each file, and may indicate who has the right to access it. Most DBMSs keep the data dictionary hidden from users to prevent them from accidentally destroying its contents.

PRACTICAL ACTION

Accuracy & Completeness

As we have mentioned, databases—including online databases—can provide you with more facts and faster facts but not always better facts. A former professor of broadcast journalism at Buffalo State College in New York suggests five limitations to bear in mind when using databases for research:[5]

- **You Can't Get the Whole Story:** For some purposes, databases are only a foot in the door. There may be many facts or facets of the topic that are not in a database. Reporters, for instance, find a database is a starting point. It may take intensive investigation to get the rest of the story.
- **It's Not the Gospel:** Just because you see something on a computer screen doesn't mean it's accurate. Numbers, names, and facts must be verified in other ways. For instance, because in the past nearly anyone could contribute to Wikipedia, physicians have questioned the reliability of medical entries on that site.[6]
- **Know the Boundaries:** One database service doesn't necessarily have it all. For example, you might find full text articles from *The New York Times* on one service, from *The Wall Street Journal* on another, and from *The Los Angeles Times* on yet another, but no service carrying all three.
- **Find the Right Words:** You have to know which keywords (search words) to use when searching a database for a topic.
- **History Is Limited:** Most public databases have information going back to 1980, and a few into the 1970s, but this may pose problems if you're trying to research something that happened—or was written about—earlier.

Google runs some of the largest data centers in the world; take a tour through one of its centers at *www.google.com/about/datacenters/inside/streetview/*.

UTILITIES: FOR MAINTAINING THE DATABASE **DBMS utilities are programs that allow you to maintain the database by creating, editing, and deleting data, records, and files.** The utilities enable you to monitor the types of data being input and to sort your database by key fields, making searching and organizing information much easier.

REPORT GENERATOR: FOR PRODUCING DOCUMENTS A DBMS may include a **report generator, which is a program for producing an on-screen or printed document from all or part of a database.** You can specify the format of the report in advance—row headings, column headings, page headers, and so on. With a report generator, even non-experts can create attractive, readable reports on short notice.

The Database Administrator

Database administrators are specialists who manage database software.

Large databases are managed by a specialist called **the database administrator (DBA), who coordinates all related activities and needs for an organization's database.** The goal of the DBA is to ensure the database's recoverability, integrity, security, availability, reliability, and performance.

Database administrators determine user access privileges; set standards, guidelines, and control procedures; assist in establishing priorities for requests; prioritize conflicting user needs; and develop user documentation and input procedures. They are also concerned with security—establishing and monitoring ways to prevent unauthorized access and making sure data is backed up and recoverable should a failure occur—and to establish and enforce policies about user privacy.

8.3 DATABASE MODELS

A database model determines the information a database will contain and how it will be used and how the items in the database relate to one another.

Organizations may use one kind of DBMS for daily processing of transactions (such as sales figures) and then move the processed data into another DBMS that's better suited for random inquiries and analysis. Older DBMS models, introduced in the 1960s, are *hierarchical* and *network.* Commonly used new models are *relational, object-oriented, and multidimensional.* (• *See Panel 8.2.)*

Hierarchical Database

The hierarchical database model was one of the first models to be widely used.

In a *hierarchical database,* fields or records are arranged in related groups resembling a family tree, with child (lower-level) records subordinate to parent (higher-level) records. The parent record at the top of the database is called the *root record* or *root parent.* (• *See Panel 8.3, page 418.)*

The hierarchical database is the oldest and simplest of the five models. It lent itself well to the tape storage systems used by mainframes in the 1960s–1970s. It is still used in some

panel 8.2

Timeline: Developments in database technology

4000–1200 BCE	3000 BCE–1400 CE	1086	1621	1642	1666
Inhabitants of the first known civilization in Sumer keep records of commercial transactions on clay tablets	Inca civilization creates the khipu coding system to store the results of mathematical calculations	Domesday Book: William I orders a survey of England to assess value for taxing purposes	Slide rule invented (Edmund Gunther)	First mechanical adding machine (Blaise Pascal)	First mechanical calculator that can add and subtract (Samuel Morland)

Entry Level Database Administrator Job

Date: Jul 24, 2013
Location: Columbia, MD, US

Entry Level Database Administrator (Job Number:330195)

Description:

The Intelligence Systems Group of SAIC has a career opening for an Entry Level Database Administrator, with a TS/SCI and Polygraph security clearance in Columbia, Maryland.

JOB SUMMARY:
The Entry Level Database Administrator will work on a team and provide front line customer support for all information technology related problems and issues. This crucial position in cyber technology will support a 24X7 operations center that characterizes and responds to network threats to multiple government customers.

PRIMARY RESPONSIBILIES:
•Review, evaluate, design, implement and maintain databases design artifacts (e.g., schema, security, interfaces, etc.) under supervision.
•Identify data sources, construct data decomposition diagrams, provide data flow diagrams and document the process.
•Write codes for database access, modifications and constructions including stored procedures.

Qualifications:
REQUIRED QUALIFICATIONS:
•Fifteen (15) undergraduate credit hours in computer science, computer engineering, and/or information systems or related discipline or two (2) years related experience.
•Demonstrated experience and/or training in two (2) or more or the following for either relational or cloud-based databases:
a) Database development and software engineering/development;
b) Database Design and Data Modeling;
c) Writing Java code to access a database using JDBC or Open Database Connectivity (ODBC);
d) Requirements analysis/generation;
•DoD 8570 compliance – at minimum, IAT Category, Level I.
•A current TS/SCI with Polygraph security clearance.

DESIRED QUALIFICATIONS:
Prior experience working in a fast paced Government program.

Portions of SAIC to be renamed Leidos, Inc., subject to stockholder approval and consummation of a separation transaction if approved by SAIC board of directors. SAIC is pursuing a plan to separate into two independently traded companies; one that provides technical, engineering and enterprise information technology services primarily to the U.S. government (new SAIC), and one that delivers technical solutions in national security, engineering and health (Leidos, Inc).

SAIC Overview:

SAIC is a FORTUNE 500® scientific, engineering, and technology applications company that uses its deep domain knowledge to solve problems of vital importance to the nation and the world, in national security, energy & environment, health and cybersecurity. The company's approximately 41,000 employees serve customers in the U.S. Department of Defense, the intelligence community, the U.S. Department of Homeland Security, other U.S. Government civil agencies and selected commercial markets. Headquartered in McLean, Va., SAIC had annual revenues of approximately $10.6 billion for its fiscal year ended January 31, 2012. For more information, visit www.saic.com. SAIC: From Science to Solutions®

Job listing for an entry-level database administrator (DBA) for Science Applications International Corporation (SAIC), an American defense company headquartered in Tysons Corner, Virginia

types of passenger reservation systems and for inventory and accounting systems by many banks, insurance companies, hospitals, and government departments.

In hierarchical databases, accessing or updating data is very fast, because the relationships have been predefined. However, because the structure must be defined in advance, it is quite rigid. There can be only one parent per child, and no relationships among the child records are possible. Moreover, adding new fields to database records requires that the entire database be redefined. A new database model was needed to address the problems of data redundancy and complex data relationships.

1820 The first mass-produced calculator, the Thomas Arithnometer

1843 World's first computer programmer, Ada Lovelace, publishes her notes

1854 George Boole publishes "An Investigation on the Laws of Thought," a system for symbolic and logical reasoning that will become the basis for computer design

1890 Hollerith's automatic census-tabulating machine (used punched cards) tabulates U.S. Census in 2–3 months (compared to 7 years needed previously)

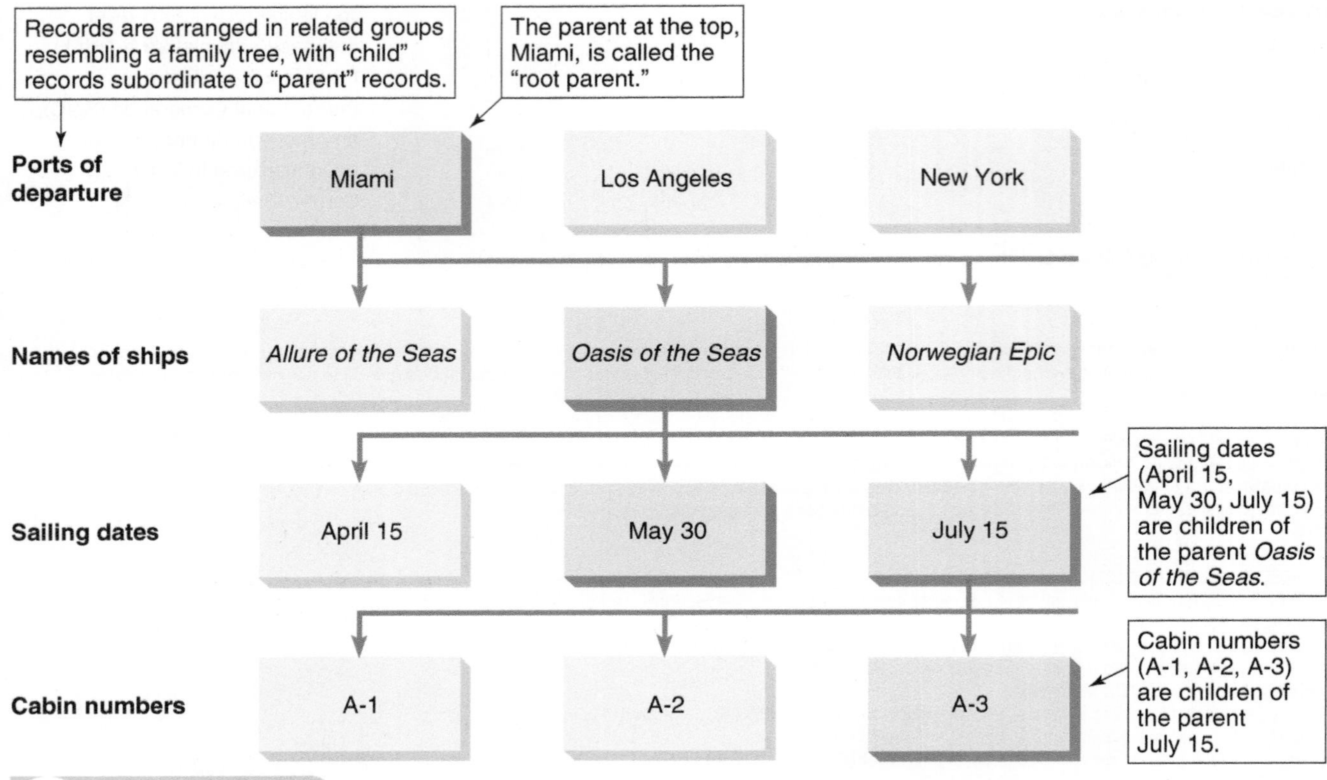

Records are arranged in related groups resembling a family tree, with "child" records subordinate to "parent" records.
The parent at the top, Miami, is called the "root parent."
Ports of departure
Miami
Los Angeles
New York
Names of ships
Allure of the Seas
Oasis of the Seas
Norwegian Epic
Sailing dates
April 15
May 30
July 15
Sailing dates (April 15, May 30, July 15) are children of the parent Oasis of the Seas.
Cabin numbers
A-1
A-2
A-3
Cabin numbers (A-1, A-2, A-3) are children of the parent July 15.

panel 8.3

Hierarchical database
Example of a cruise ship reservation system

Network Database

The network database model was created to represent a more complex data relationship effectively, improve database performance, and impose a database standard.

The *network database* was in part developed to solve some of the problems of the hierarchical database model. A network database is similar to a hierarchical database, but each child record can have more than one parent record. *(• See Panel 8.4.)* Thus, a child record, which in network database terminology is called a *member,* may be reached through more than one parent, which is called an *owner.*

Established in 1971, and also used principally with mainframes, the network database is more flexible than the hierarchical arrangement, because different relationships may be established between different branches of data. However, it still requires that the structure be defined in advance, and, as with the hierarchical model, the user must be familiar with the structure of the database. Moreover, there are limits to the number of possible links among records, and to examine a field, one must retrieve the entire record.

Although the network database was an improvement over the hierarchical database, some people in the database community believed there had to be a better way to manage large amounts of data.

1960	1961	1962	1967	1967–1968	1969	1970
Evolution of the database concept	Prototype of first DBMS—IBM developed hierarchical model	Stanford and Purdue Universities establish the first departments of computer science	Hand-held calculator	National Crime Information Center (NCIC) goes online with 95,000 pieces of information in five databases, handling 2 million transactions in its first year	ARPANet established, leads to Internet	Microprocessor chips come into use; floppy disk introduced for storing data; E.F. Codd develops the relational database, which evolves into IBM's System R project, which in turn evolves into SQL

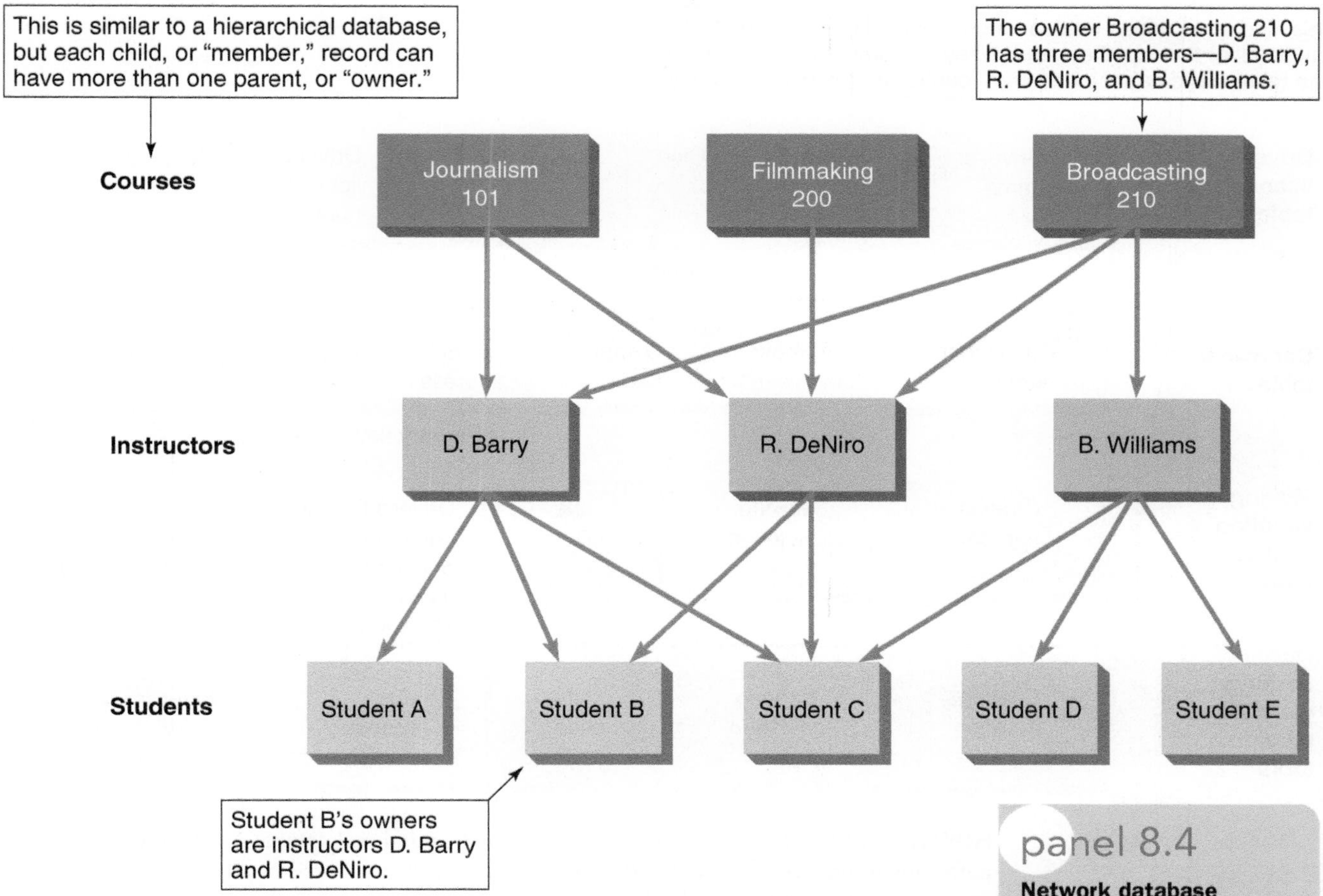

This is similar to a hierarchical database, but each child, or "member," record can have more than one parent, or "owner."

The owner Broadcasting 210 has three members—D. Barry, R. DeNiro, and B. Williams.

Courses

Journalism 101 | Filmmaking 200 | Broadcasting 210

Instructors

D. Barry | R. DeNiro | B. Williams

Students

Student A | Student B | Student C | Student D | Student E

Student B's owners are instructors D. Barry and R. DeNiro.

panel 8.4

Network database

Example of college class-scheduling system

Relational Database

The relational database model grew out of the hierarchical and network database models.

The relational database was born in 1970 when E. F. Codd, a researcher at IBM, wrote a paper outlining the model. Since then, relational databases grew in popularity in the 1980s to become the standard today. More flexible than hierarchical and network database models, the **relational database relates, or connects, data in different tables of rows and columns through the use of primary keys, or common data elements;** the tables are also called relations—tables of related data. (• *See Panel 8.5, next page.*) The data in different tables can be assembled and reassembled in many different ways without having to reorganize the database tables. A typical large database, such as Amazon.com's, contains hundreds or thousands of tables all used together to quickly find the exact information needed at any given time. Examples of relational microcomputer DBMS programs are Access and QuickBase. Examples of relational models used on larger computer systems are Oracle, Informix, MS SQL Server, and Sybase.

Who Was E. F. Codd?

To learn about him and others who influenced database technology, go to:

www.ida.liu.se/~juhta/publications/famous_cs_related_to_iislab.pdf

1971	1975	1976	1976	1978	1980	1981
First pocket calculator; all U.S. states and Washington, D.C., can access NCIC criminal data; network database model	First microcomputer (MITS Altair 8800)	Queen Elizabeth sends the first royal email	Apple I computer (first personal computer sold in assembled form)	Introduction of SQL (structured query language); publication of OSI model by the International Standards Organization	dBASE II, the first database program for personal computers; during the 1980s, the hierarchical and network database models fade into the background and the relational model becomes popular	IBM introduces personal computer

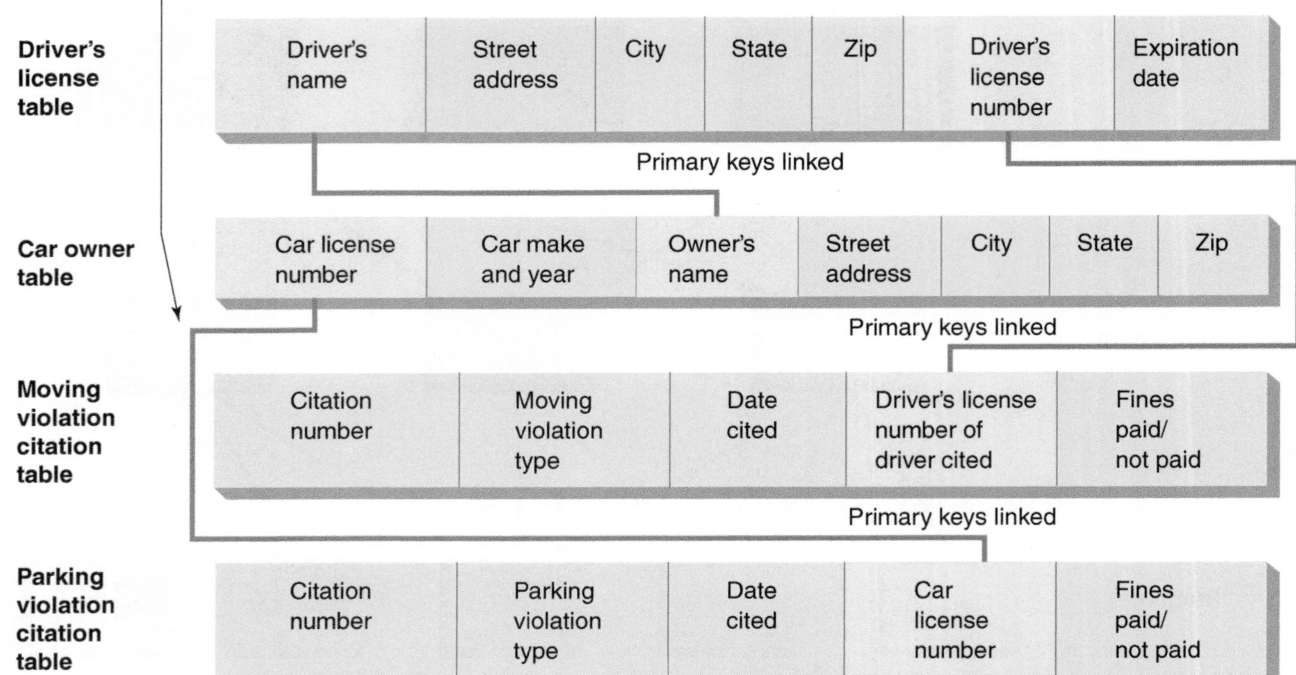

panel 8.5

Relational database

Example of a state department of motor vehicles database

HOW A RELATIONAL DATABASE WORKS In the relational database, there are no access paths down through a hierarchy. Instead, data elements are stored in different tables made up of rows and columns. In database terminology, the tables are called *relations* (files), the rows are called *tuples* (records), and the columns are called *attributes* (fields).

Two characteristics of a relational database are as follows:

- **Data is arranged by content:** Whereas in the hierarchical and network database models data is arranged according to physical address (location in storage), in the relational model data is arranged logically, by content. Hence, the physical order of the records or fields in a table is completely immaterial.
- **Each record is identified by a primary key:** Each record in the table is identified by a field—the primary key—that contains a unique value.

1984	1985	1990s	1994	2003	2006	2008	2013
Apple Macintosh; first personal laser printer; release of Ashton-Tate dBase III	Object-oriented database model	Development of the multi-dimensional database	Apple and IBM introduce PCs with full-motion video built in; wireless data transmission for small portable computers; web browser first invented	Human Genome Project completes mapping all 90,000 or so genes for massive database	Google claims a searchable database of 25 billion web pages	Google reaches 1 trillion searchable pages	World's largest databases: 1. The World Data Centre for Climate (Germany) 2. U.S. National Energy Research Scientific Computing Center 3. AT&T 4. Google 5. Sprint 6. LexisNexis 7. YouTube 8. Amazon 9. U.S. Central Intelligence Agency (CIA) 10. U.S. Library of Congress

These two characteristics allow the data in a relational database to exist independently of the way it is physically stored on the computer. Thus, unlike with the older models, a user is not required to know the physical location of a record in order to retrieve its data. And a database search does not have to go through an entire string of data before reaching the wanted data.

USING STRUCTURED QUERY LANGUAGE To retrieve data in a relational database, you specify the appropriate fields and the tables to which they belong in a query to the database, using a query language. **Structured query language (SQL, pronounced "sequel") is the standard query language used to create, modify, maintain, and query relational databases.** SQL is the foundation for all the popular database applications available today, from Access to Oracle.

The three components of a basic SQL query are:

- the SELECT . . . FROM statement
- the WHERE clause
- the ORDER BY clause

The fields used in the query are specified with SELECT, and the tables to which they belong are specified with FROM. Selection criteria are determined by WHERE, and the query results can be sorted in any sequence with ORDER.

Most popular database programs provide a graphical query-building tool (a "query by example," or QBE, discussed shortly), so the user does not need a thorough knowledge of SQL.

Here is an example of a SQL query:

```
SELECT PRODUCT-NUMBER, PRODUCT-NAME
FROM PRODUCT
WHERE PRICE < 100.00
ORDER BY PRODUCT-NAME;
```

This query selects all records in the product file for products that cost less than $100.00 and displays the selected records alphabetically according to product name and including the product number—for example:

C-50	Chair
A-34	Mirror
D-168	Table

QUERY BY EXAMPLE One feature of most query languages is query by example. Often a user will seek information in a database by describing a procedure for finding it. However, in **query by example (QBE), the user asks for information in a database by using a sample record form, or table, to define the qualifications he or she wants for selected records;** in other words, the user fills in a form. *(• See Panel 8.6, next page.)*

For example, a university's database of its student-loan records might have the column headings (field names) NAME, ADDRESS, CITY, STATE, ZIP, AMOUNT OWED. When you use the QBE method, the database would display an empty record with these column headings. You would then type in the search conditions that you want in the appropriate columns.

Thus, if you wanted to find all Beverly Hills, California, students with a loan balance due of $3,000 or more, you would type *BEVERLY HILLS* in the CITY column, *CA* in the STATE column, and > *=3000* ("greater than or equal to $3,000") in the AMOUNT OWED column.

Some DBMSs, such as Symantec's Q&A, use natural language interfaces, which allow users to make queries in any spoken language, such as English. With this software, you could ask your questions—either typing or speaking (if the system has voice recognition)—in a natural way, such as "How many sales reps sold more than one million dollars' worth of books in the Western Region in January?"

Database technology is crucial to managing inventory in large warehouses.

panel 8.6

Example of a simple database query *(http://blog.knowledgewave.com/msoffice/create-an-interactive-access-form-to-filter-a-query-by-date-range-2.html)*

Create an Interactive Access Form to Filter a Query by Date Range

Date ranges are a very common filter that database users want to implement in their queries. For example, let's say your company sells office supplies and your databases tracks customer orders. You want to run a monthly query that summarizes total orders.

You can save your database users time and frustration by creating a friendly, interactive form that allows them to enter a beginning order date and an ending order date. Then, with a click of a button, they can run a query that displays the order information for their specified date range.

Object-Oriented Database

An object-oriented database management system supports the modeling and creation of data as objects.

Traditional database models, including the relational model, still work well in traditional business situations. However, they fall short in areas such as engineering design and manufacturing, scientific experiments, telecommunications, geographic information systems, and multimedia. The object-oriented database model was developed to meet the needs of these applications.

An object-oriented database uses "objects," software written in small, reusable chunks, as elements within database files. An *object* consists of:

- Data in any form, including text, numbers, graphics, audio, and video.
- Instructions on the action to be taken on the data.

In this kind of DBMS the operations carried out on information items (data objects) are considered part of their definition.

Examples of object-oriented databases are FastObjects, GemStone, Objectivity DB, Jasmine Object Database, and KE Texpress. Many high-tech companies can create custom databases.

A MULTIMEDIA DATABASE An object-oriented database is a *multimedia database;* it can store more types of data than a relational database can. For example, an object-oriented student database might contain each student's photograph, a "sound bite" of his or her voice, and even a short piece of video, in addition to grades and personal data.

Moreover, the object would store operations, called *methods,* the programs that objects use to process themselves. For example, these programs might indicate how to calculate the student's grade-point average or how to display or print the student's record.

TYPES OF OBJECT-ORIENTED DATABASES Three types of object-oriented databases are these:

- **Hypertext database:** One type of object-oriented database is a *hypertext database,* or *web database,* which contains text links to other documents. This type of database, created by software such as Adobe ColdFusion, is accessible via the web.
- **Hypermedia database:** Another type is a *hypermedia database,* which contains these links as well as graphics, sound, and video. This type is also created by software such as ColdFusion.

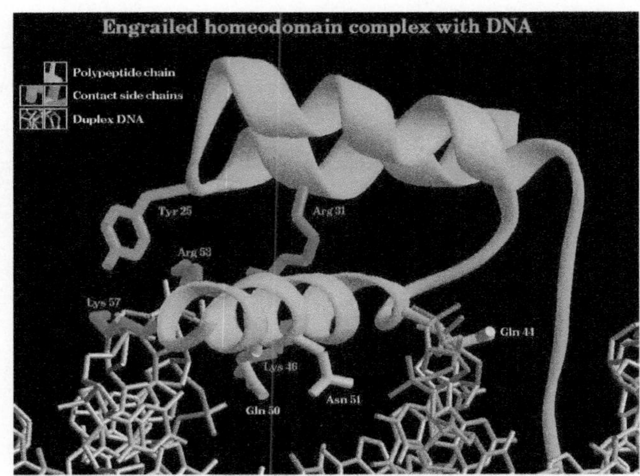

(*top*) Computer-generated model of DNA constructed from data in a multimedia database; (*bottom*) spatial and multimedia database (Google Maps) view of the St. Lucia campus at the University of Queensland, Australia

- **Object-relational database:** *Object-relational,* or *enhanced-relational,* database models handle both hierarchical and network data (structured data) and relational and object-oriented data. Examples are DB2, Cloudscape, ASE, Sybase IQ, SQL Anywhere, and Oracle.

Multidimensional Database

A multidimensional database is used to handle large amounts of data for decision-making purposes.

A **multidimensional database (MDB) models data as facts, dimensions, or numerical measures for use in the interactive analysis of large amounts of data for decision-making purposes.** Multidimensional databases are frequently created using input from existing relational databases. The multidimensional database was developed during the 1990s for analyzing data rather than performing online transactions. Examples are InterSystems Caché, ContourCube, and Cognos PowerPlay.

DATA REPRESENTED AS A CUBE A multidimensional database uses the idea of a cube to represent the dimensions of data available to a user. (• *See Panel 8.7, next page.*)

panel 8.7

Multidimensional database cube example

Sample cube capturing sales data. Data cubes support viewing of up to four dimensions simultaneously.

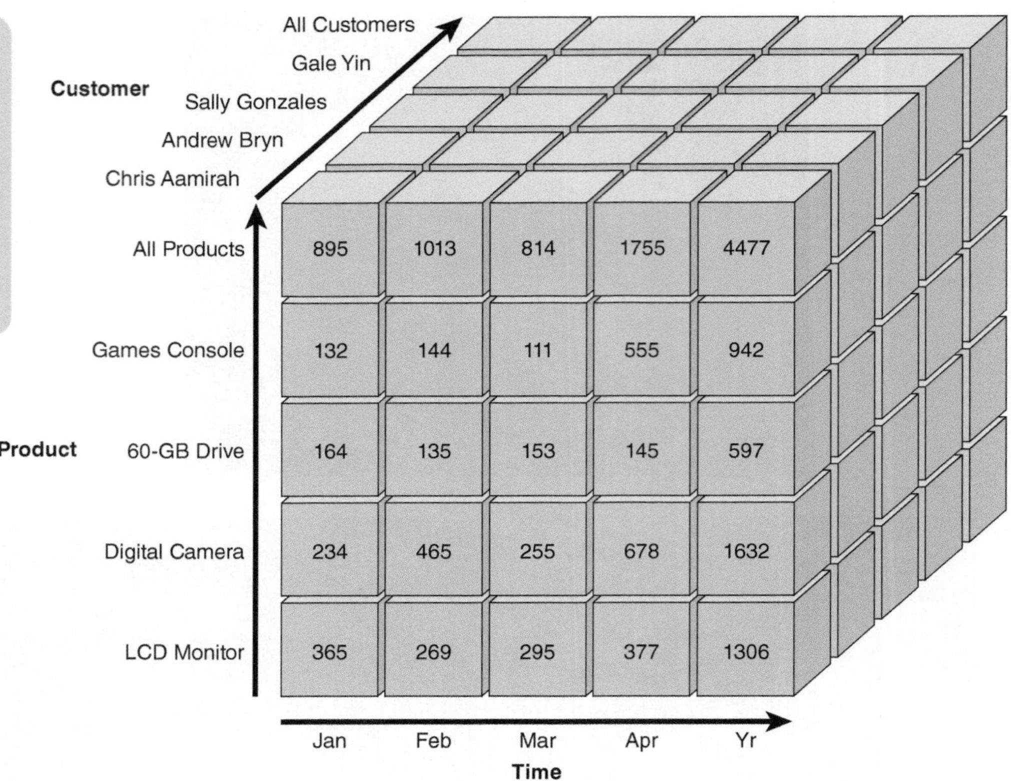

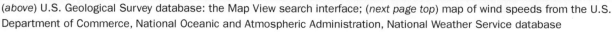

(*above*) U.S. Geological Survey database: the Map View search interface; (*next page top*) map of wind speeds from the U.S. Department of Commerce, National Oceanic and Atmospheric Administration, National Weather Service database

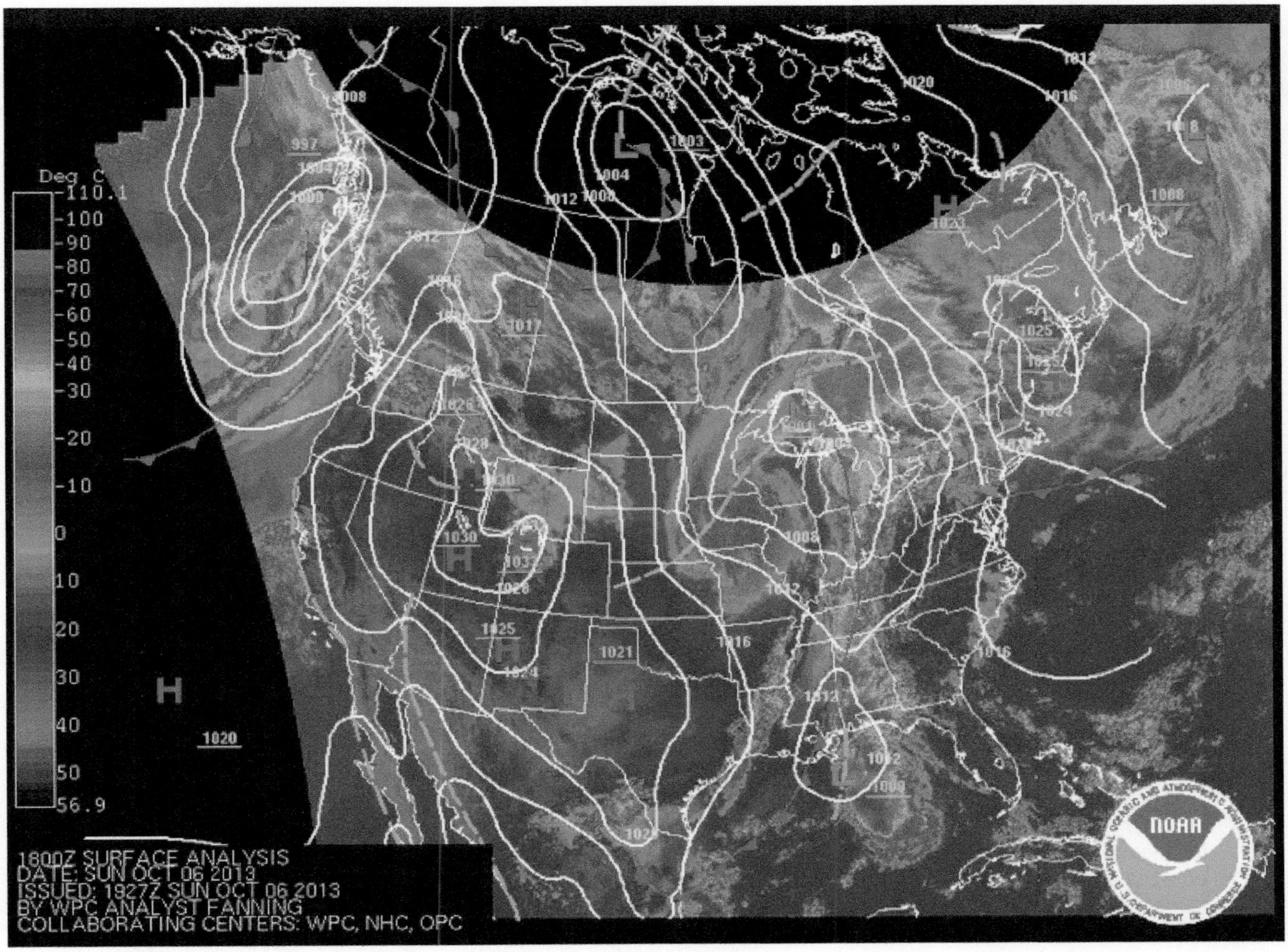

For example, "sales" could be viewed in the dimensions of (1) product model, (2) geography, (3) time, or (4) some additional dimension. In this case, "sales" is known as the main attribute (or measure) of the data cube and the other dimensions are seen as "feature" attributes. Users can pivot the data to see information from a different viewpoint, drill down to find more detailed information, or drill up to see an overview.

Cool, Clear Water?

The Environmental Protection Agency uses data on drinking water to help manage environmental programs. For public access to EPA databases, go to:

http://water.epa.gov/scitech/datait/databases/drink/

ONLINE ANALYTICAL PROCESSING (OLAP) SOFTWARE Unlike relational databases, which often require SELECT . . . FROM and other types of SQL queries to provide information, multidimensional databases allow users to ask questions in more colloquial English, such as, "How many type Z dog leashes have been sold in New Jersey so far this year?" The means for doing so is *online analytical processing (OLAP) software,* which can quickly provide answers to complex database queries. OLAP software is used in business reporting for sales, marketing, management reporting, trend analysis, and similar areas. An OLAP application that accesses data from a multidimensional database is known as a *MOLAP (multidimensional OLAP)* application.

8.4 DATA MINING

Data mining is sorting through large amounts of data to identify patterns and establish relationships.

A personal database, such as the address list of friends you have on your laptop or tablet, is generally small. But some databases are almost unimaginably vast, involving trillions of bytes of data and requiring the use of so-called massively parallel database computers each costing $1 million or more. Sorting through these databases is called **data mining (DM),**

the computer-assisted process of sifting through and analyzing vast amounts of data in order to extract hidden patterns and meaning and to discover new knowledge. Data-mining techniques are used in many research areas, including mathematics, cybernetics, genetics, and marketing, and their purpose is to describe past trends and predict future ones.

The Process of Data Mining

Data mining prepares data for a data warehouse.

In data mining, data is acquired and prepared for what is known as a "data warehouse" through the following steps. (• *See Panel 8.8.*)

1. DATA SOURCES Data may come from a number of sources: (a) point-of-sale transactions in files managed by file management systems on mainframes, (b) databases of all kinds, and (c) other—for example, news articles transmitted over newswires or online sources such as the Internet. To the mix may also be added (d) data from data warehouses, as we describe next.

panel 8.8

The data-mining process

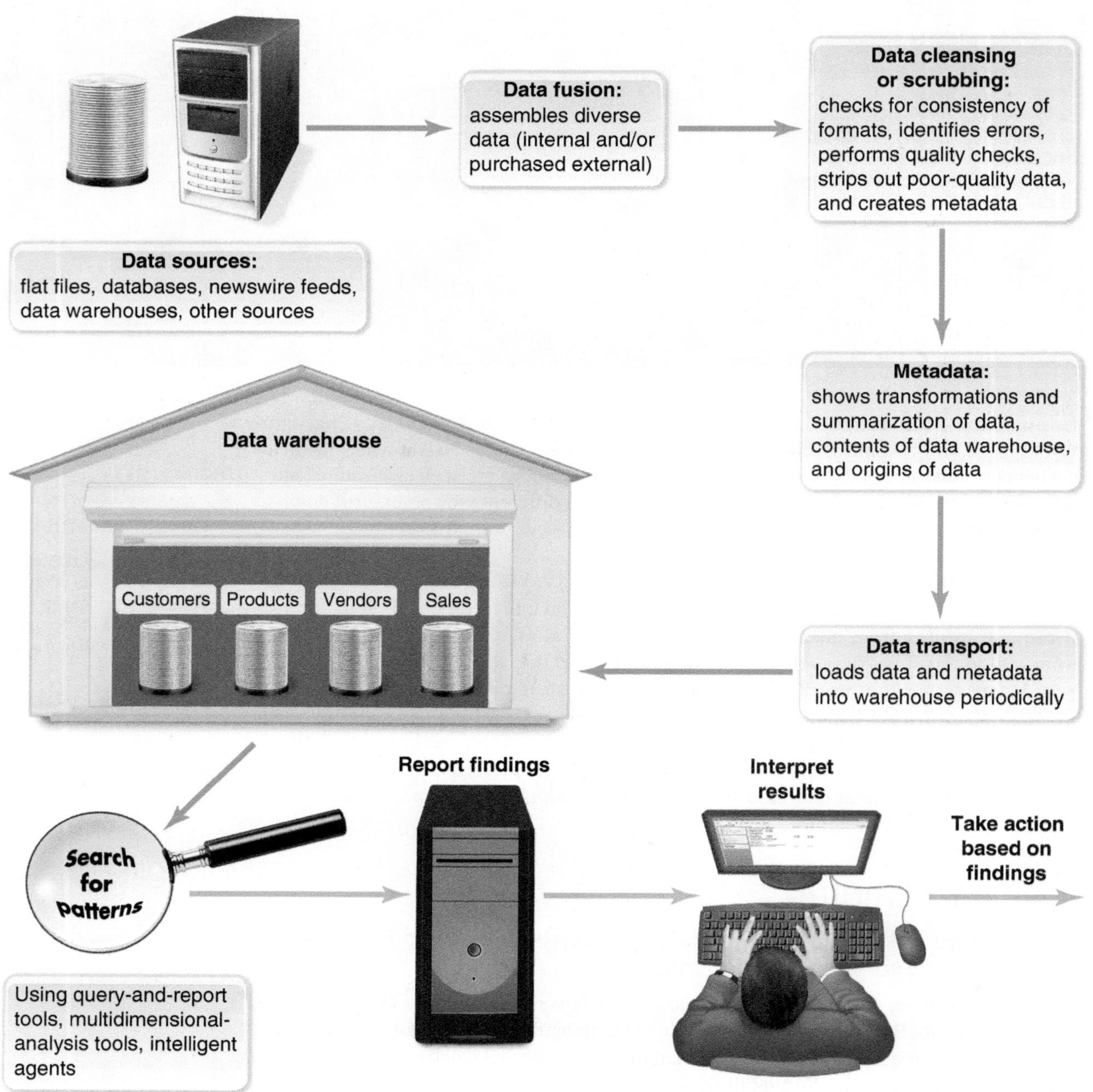

Data fusion:
assembles diverse data (internal and/or purchased external)
Data cleansing or scrubbing:
checks for consistency of formats, identifies errors, performs quality checks, strips out poor-quality data, and creates metadata
Data sources:
flat files, databases, newswire feeds, data warehouses, other sources
Metadata:
shows transformations and summarization of data, contents of data warehouse, and origins of data
Data warehouse
Customers
Products
Vendors
Sales
Data transport:
loads data and metadata into warehouse periodically
Report findings
Interpret results
Take action based on findings
Search for Patterns
Using query-and-report tools, multidimensional-analysis tools, intelligent agents

2. DATA FUSION & CLEANSING Data from diverse sources, whether from inside the company (internal data) or purchased from outside the company (external data), must be fused together and then put through a process known as *data cleansing,* or *scrubbing.* Even if the data comes from just one source, such as one company's mainframe, the data may be of poor quality, full of errors and inconsistencies. Therefore, for data mining to produce accurate results, the source data has to be "scrubbed"—that is, cleaned of errors and checked for consistency of formats.

Database of Culturally Significant Plants

What are "culturally significant plants"? Go to:

http://plants.usda.gov/java/factSheet?cultural=yes

3. DATA & METADATA The cleansing process yields both the cleaned-up data and a variation of it called metadata. As we said under the data dictionary discussion (p. 414), *metadata* is essentially data about data; it describes how and when and by whom a particular set of data was collected and how the data is formatted.

Metadata is essential for understanding information stored in data warehouses. Metadata shows the origins of the data, the transformations it has undergone, and summary information about it, which makes it more useful than the cleansed but unintegrated, unsummarized data. The metadata also describes the contents of the data warehouse.

4. DATA TRANSPORT TO THE DATA WAREHOUSE Both the data and the metadata are sent to the data warehouse. **A data warehouse is a special database of cleaned-up data and metadata.** It is a replica, or close reproduction, of a mainframe's data.

The data warehouse is stored on disk using storage technology such as RAID (redundant arrays of independent disks). Small data warehouses may hold 100 gigabytes of data or less; large ones may store terabytes of data.

MINING THE DATA: SEARCHING FOR PATTERNS & INTERPRETING THE RESULTS
Data in the warehouse is usually analyzed—or mined—using one of two popular *algorithms,* or step-by-step problem-solving procedures:

- **Regression analysis:** Basically, *regression analysis* takes a particular set of numerical data and develops a mathematical formula that fits the data. This formula is then applied to new sets of data of the same type to predict future situations.
- **Classification analysis:** *Classification analysis* is a statistics pattern-recognition process that is applied to data sets with more than just numerical data.

SOME APPLICATIONS OF DATA MINING Some short-term payoffs from data mining can be dramatic. One telephone company, for instance, mined its existing billing data to identify 10,000 supposedly "residential" customers who spent more than $1,000 a month on their phone bills. When it looked more closely, the company found that these customers were really small businesses trying to avoid paying the more expensive business rates for their telephone service.

TECH TALES The Uses of Data Mining

In government, the Internal Revenue Service has a program designed to catch tax cheaters by locating inconsistencies between mortgage payments and income.[7] Counterterrorism experts analyze records "on travel habits, calling patterns, email use, financial transactions, and other data to pinpoint possible terrorist activity," according to one report.[8]

In professional sports, Toronto Raptors management has used data mining to "rack and stack" the team to try to make it more competitive against other National Basketball Association (NBA) teams. NBA executives at the Miami Heat have used data mining to find more effective means of targeting an audience than traditional mass-media marketing.[9]

In retailing, point-of-sale databases in department stores are mined for sales data about thousands of products in hundreds of geographic areas to understand customer preferences and try to cater to individual buying needs. Companies concerned that opinion among users of social networks can make or break their products use data-mining "sentiment analysis" tools to analyze what is being said online.[10]

Most Interesting Databases

According to *Popular Science,* here are some of the world's most interesting databases:

The Combined DNA Index System (DOCIS)

www.fbi.gov/about-us/lab/biometric-analysis/codis

The Encyclopedia of Life

http://eol.org/

The Genographic Project

https://genographic.nationalgeographic.com/

The International Panel on Climate Change's Data Distribution Centre

www.ipcc-data.org/

Sloan Digital Sky Survey Database

www.sdss.org/

The Wayback Machine

http://archive.org/web/web.php

WorldCat

www.worldcat.org/

In medicine, data mining is used to see what subtle factors affect success and failure in back surgery, for example, or what groups are likely to experience health costs increases or what treatment plans are most likely to be successful.

In science, DM techniques are used to find new patterns in genetic data, molecular structures, and global climate changes and to catalog more than 50 million galaxies.[11] ■

The accomplishments of data mining using conventional databases are truly impressive. But the field stands on the verge of a historic shift. The name for this shift: Big Data.

UNIT 8B: *Big Data, Information Systems, & Artificial Intelligence*

What is the difference between data mining and Big Data? After all, big corporations, such as banks and insurance companies, have been mining huge amounts of data for years.

Here's what's new: Big Data aims also to tap all that web data and other data that is *outside* corporate databases. Big Data (also called Data Analytics) typically "means applying the tools of artificial intelligence, such as machine learning, to vast new troves of data beyond that captured in standard databases," says one report. "The new data sources include web-browsing data trails, social network communications, sensor data, and surveillance data."[12]

Let us see how this revolution is changing the world of technology, including information systems and artificial intelligence (Chapter 1, pp. 37).

8.5 THE EVOLVING WORLD OF BIG DATA

Big Data is not just more data but a label that embraces major changes in technology and decision making.

"In one field after another, in science, politics, crime prevention, public health, sports, and industries as varied as energy and advertising," says technology writer Steve Lohr, "all are being transformed by data-driven discovery and decision making. . . . Big Data is the shorthand label for the phenomenon, which embraces technology, decision making, and public policy."[13]

Three Implications of Big Data

Big Data, which is derived from a bunch of old and new data sources, could lead to a revolution in measurement and to better decision making.

The term *Big Data,* says Lohr, is often loosely used. We have defined it as data that is so large and complex that it cannot be processed using conventional methods, such as use of database management software. However, Lohr suggests, the catchall phrase basically means three things.[14]

1. BIG DATA DERIVES FROM A BUNDLE OF OLD & NEW DATA SOURCES The sources of data are those both old and new—everything from web pages, sensor signals, and GPS location data from smartphones to browsing habits, genetic information, and surveillance videos. To make sense of the oceans of data, there is advanced computer processing and storage plus complex software taken from the evolving world of artificial intelligence, the branch of computer science that is devoted to the creation of computer systems that simulate human reasoning and sensation.

The software applies what are called Big Data analytics (or simply analytics). **Big Data analytics is the process of examining large amounts of data of a variety of types to uncover hidden patterns, unknown correlations, and other useful information.** A specific kind of analytics is *web analytics,* the measurement and analysis of Internet data to understand web usage.

2. BIG DATA COULD LEAD TO A REVOLUTION IN MEASUREMENT The volume and variety of data, along with the powerful smart software, could revolutionize how things are measured—just as the invention of the telescope opened up the heavens and the microscope unveiled the mysteries of biological life down to the cellular level. In business management, for example, new kinds of measurement could replace old ideas, organizations, and ways of thinking about the world.

3. BIG DATA COULD LEAD TO BETTER DECISION MAKING Not only can data-driven insights "be used to make sense of mind-bogglingly complex situations," says one writer. Big Data "can help compensate for our overconfidence in our own intuitions and can help reduce the extent to which our desires distort our perceptions."[15]

In short, however vague the term *Big Data* is, says a Cornell computer scientist, it "is a tagline for a process that has the potential to transform everything." Or as an IBM executive says, "Big Data is really about new uses and new insights, not so much the data itself."[16]

The Uses of Big Data

Big Data is finding major uses in medical research, marketing, and even entertainment programming, to name just a few areas.

What kind of people work—or will be working—with Big Data? On the one hand, there are data scientists, who look at information sets so big that they need to work with extensive computer code and to run calculations—correlations, regression analysis, classification analysis, and the like—involving multiple servers to discover the patterns they're looking for.[17] On the other hand, small businesses need to analyze voluminous information to gain insights into markets, customers, or employees.[18] In between are all kinds of other professionals who have found valuable uses for Big Data, as follows.

BIG DATA IN MEDICINE: USING VARIETIES OF OLD & NEW DATA SOURCES Big Data is beginning to be used in medicine, and particularly medical research, in a major way. Early on there was Google Flu, which tried to detect flu outbreaks, but its methods were not successful in tracking new deadly diseases that could arise anywhere. Now researchers are placing hopes in a project called BioMosaic, which looks at three sources of data—airline records, disease reports, and demographic data—to try to build a more comprehensive picture of foreign-borne disease threats.[19]

Other medical databases are Registries for All Diseases, where patients and scientists can share information about rare diseases that might lead to treatments, and Reg4All, which links clinical data with patients' responses to medical history surveys.[20] A "biobank" in San Francisco called the Genetic Epidemiology Research Study on Adult Health and Aging includes genetic information on 100,000 people whose DNA has been analyzed from saliva samples, along with hundreds of thousands of pieces on patients' lives and medical histories.[21] Minnesota-based UnitedHealth Group, an insurance company, and the Mayo Clinic are drawing on millions of health insurance claims and in-depth clinical patient records to "glean insights about care from a growing flood of data," according to one report.[22] The UnitedHealth–Mayo effort houses the health data in massive servers and uses data from the claims records of more than 109 million people over 19 years plus 5 million clinical records.

How Companies Like Amazon Use Big Data to Make You Love Them

www.fastcodesign.com/1669551/how-companies-like-amazon-use-big-data-to-make-you-love-them

What is interesting about all these endeavors is the mix of data sources used to build the records and the use of analytics tools to detect patterns—all major characteristics of Big Data.

SMARTER JUNK MAIL: REFINING MEASUREMENT It used to be that direct-mail marketers might have only 10 pieces of information about a given individual and it might take a month to assemble the facts. Now, says one report, direct marketers can "immediately comb through hundreds of sources of public and private data and assemble more specific demographics, such as young, upper middle-class families with teenage kids who like gadgets"—and they can do so in subseconds, in some cases.[23]

How does this use of Big Data change things? It means a retailer can create a direct-marketing catalog of products that have been specially built to meet certain desirable criteria—such as high-end barbecue features specifically targeted to people who have recently purchased a home, live in an upper-income neighborhood, and have several children. In other words, both the products and the direct marketing are designed around very specific characteristics turned up in the Big Data of specific populations.

NETFLIX'S ORIGINAL TV PROGRAMMING: MAKING BETTER MANAGEMENT DECISIONS At one time, Netflix was simply a distributor of television programs and movies, both through disks by mail and through online streaming, but more recently it has entered into original programming. In early 2013, Netflix's *House of Cards* series, starring Kevin Spacey and directed by David Fincher, was the most streamed piece of TV content in the United States—and Netflix executives knew in advance that it probably would be.

How? Netflix, which has 27 million U.S. subscribers and 33 million worldwide, ran the numbers on key predecessors to the series: the number of watchers of previous Kevin Spacey movies and of David Fincher's previous work (which included *The Social Network),* plus the audience share of the earlier British version of *House of Cards.* From the results of these three Big Data inquiries, Netflix knew it had an exceptional chance of being successful by producing its own original version of the series.[24] Here, then, is an example of managerial decision making use of Big Data to replace hunches and guesses.

Now let us see how data and databases are used as information systems in organizations.

8.6 INFORMATION SYSTEMS IN ORGANIZATIONS: Using Databases to Help Make Decisions

An information system is a combination of people, hardware, software, communication devices, and databases that processes data and information for a specific purpose.

The data in databases is used to build information, and information—and how it is used—lies at the heart of every organization. Of course, how useful information is depends on the quality of it, as well as the information systems used to distribute it.

The Qualities of Good Information

Having good information is critical to the success of any organization.

In general, all information to support intelligent decision making within an organization must be as follows:

- **Correct and verifiable:** This means information must be accurate and checkable.
- **Complete yet concise:** *Complete* means information must include *all* relevant data. *Concise* means it includes *only* relevant data.
- **Cost-effective:** This means the information is efficiently obtained and understandable.
- **Current:** *Current* means timely yet also time-sensitive, based on historical, present, or future information needs.
- **Accessible:** This means the information is quickly and easily obtainable.

Information Flows within an Organization

Information flows horizontally between departments and vertically between management levels.

Consider any sizable organization with which you are familiar. Its purpose is to perform a service or deliver a product. If it's nonprofit, for example, it may deliver the service of educating students or the product of food for famine victims. If it's profit-oriented, it may, for example, sell the service of fixing computers or the product of computers themselves. Information—whether computer-based or not—has to flow within an organization in a way that will help managers, and the organization, achieve their goals. To this end, organizations are often structured horizontally and vertically—horizontally to reflect functions and vertically to reflect management levels.

THE HORIZONTAL FLOW OF INFORMATION BETWEEN SIX DEPARTMENTS Depending on the services or products they provide, most organizations have departments that perform six functions: *research and development (R&D), production* (or *operations*), *marketing and sales, accounting and finance, human resources (personnel),* and *information systems (IS).* *(• See Panel 8.9, next page.)*

- **Research and development:** The research and development (R&D) department does two things: (1) It conducts basic research, relating discoveries to the organization's current or new products. (2) It does product development and tests and modifies new products or services created by researchers. Special software is available to aid in these functions.
- **Production (operations):** The production department makes the product or provides the service. In a manufacturing company, it takes the raw materials and has people or machinery turn them into finished goods. In many cases, this department uses CAD/CAM software and workstations, as well as robots (described on p. 444). In another type of company, this department might manage the purchasing, handle the inventories, and control the flow of goods and services.
- **Marketing and sales:** The marketing department oversees advertising, promotion, and sales. The people in this department plan, price, advertise, promote, package, and distribute the services or goods to customers or clients. The sales reps may use laptop computers, cellphones, wireless email, and faxes in their work while on the road.
- **Accounting and finance:** The accounting and finance department handles all financial matters. It handles cash management, pays bills and taxes, issues paychecks, records payments, makes investments, and compiles financial statements and reports. It also produces financial budgets and forecasts financial performance after receiving information from other departments.
- **Human resources:** The human resources, or personnel, department finds and hires people and administers sick leave and retirement matters. It is also concerned with compensation levels, professional development, employee relations, and government regulations.
- **Information systems (IS):** The IS department manages the organization's computer-based systems and plans for and purchases new ones.

THE VERTICAL FLOW OF INFORMATION BETWEEN MANAGEMENT LEVELS Large organizations traditionally have three levels of management—*strategic management, tactical management,* and *operational management.* These levels can be shown on an *organization chart,* a schematic drawing showing the hierarchy of formal relationships among an organization's employees. Managers on each of the three levels have different levels of responsibility and are therefore required to make different kinds of decisions. *(• See Panel 8.9, next page.)*

- **Strategic-level management:** Top managers are concerned with long-range, or strategic, planning and decisions. This top level is headed by the chief executive officer (CEO) along with several vice presidents or managers with such titles as chief financial officer (CFO), chief operating officer (COO), and chief information officer (CIO). *Strategic* decisions are complex decisions rarely based on predetermined routine procedures; they involve the subjective judgment of the decision maker. For instance, strategic decisions relate to how growth should be financed and what new markets should be tackled first. Determining the company's 5-year goals, evaluating future financial resources, and formulating a response to competitors' actions are also strategic decisions.
- **Tactical-level management:** Tactical, or middle-level managers, make tactical decisions to implement the strategic goals of the organization. A *tactical* decision is made without a base of clearly defined informational procedures; it may require detailed analysis and computations. Examples of tactical-level managers are plant manager, division manager, sales manager, branch manager, and director of personnel.

panel 8.9

Organization chart

The six functional responsibilities are shown on the opposite page at the bottom of the pyramid. The three management levels are shown along the sides.

- **Operational-level management:** Operational, or low-level (supervisory level), managers make *operational* decisions—predictable decisions that can be made by following well-defined sets of routine procedures. These managers focus principally on supervising nonmanagement employees, monitoring day-to-day events, and taking corrective action where necessary. An example of an operational-level manager is a warehouse manager in charge of inventory restocking.

Note that because there are fewer people at the level of top management and many people at the bottom, this management structure resembles a pyramid. It's also a hierarchical structure because most of the power is concentrated at the top.

NEW INFORMATION FLOW: THE DECENTRALIZED ORGANIZATION The hierarchical, pyramid-oriented structure is changing in the computer network era to a decentralized form in which employees are linked to a centralized database. Although the different responsibilities of the various types of managers remain, the pyramid is flattened somewhat owing to increased participation of all employees via computer-enabled systems.

Nowadays, for instance, organizations that have computer networks often use groupware to enable cooperative work by groups of people—what are known as *computer-supported cooperative work systems.* Through the shared use of cloud-based databases, software, videoconferencing, email, intranets, organization forms and reports, and so on, many people can work together from different locations to manage information.

Computer-Based Information Systems

Computer-based information systems are combination of hardware, software, and telecommunications networks that people build and use to collect, create, and distribute data.

The purpose of a computer-based information system is to provide managers (and various categories of employees) with the appropriate kind of information to help them make decisions. It is used to collect and analyze data from all departments and is designed to provide

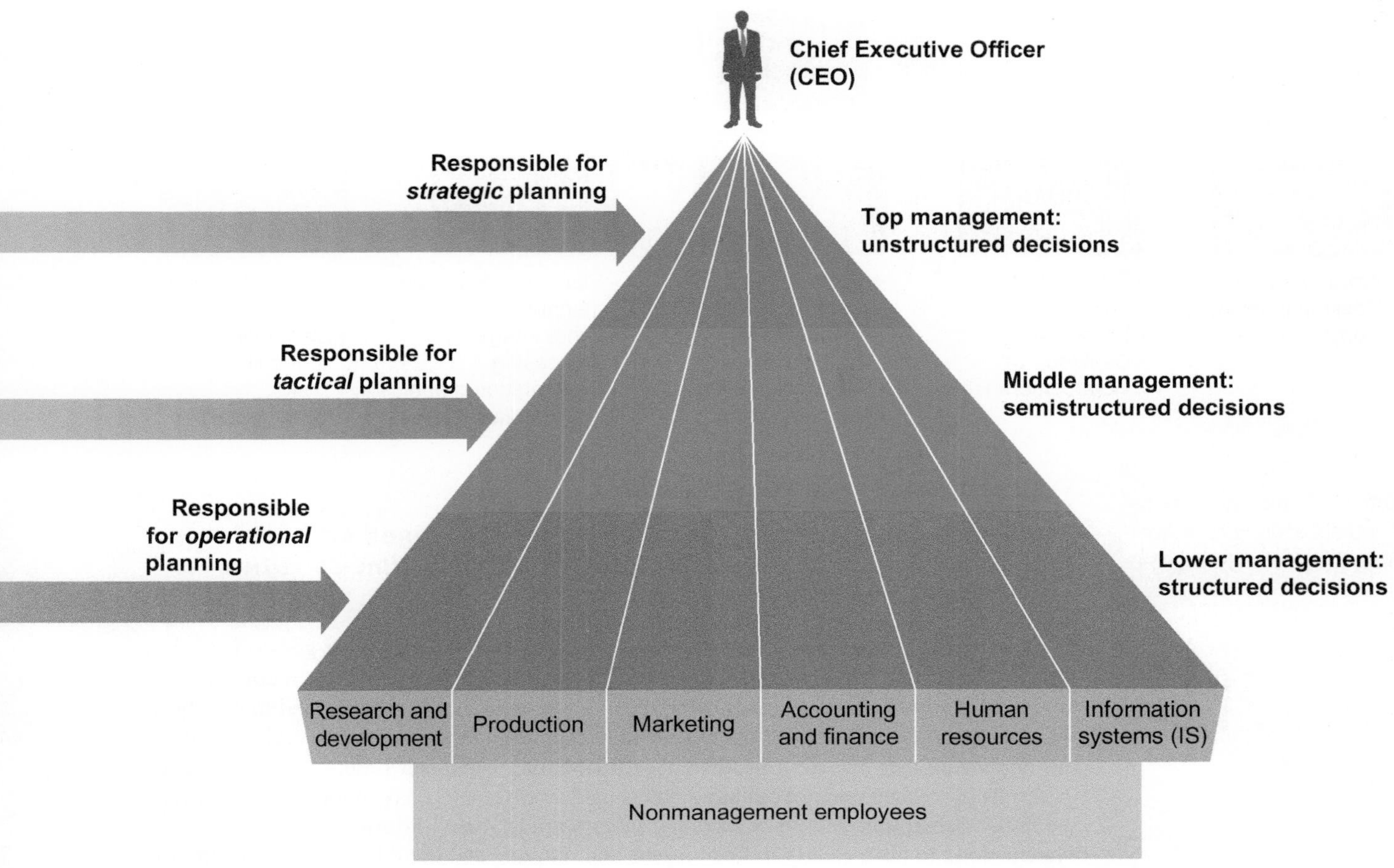

an organization's management with up-to-date information at any time. There are several types of computer-based information systems, now often housed on cloud-based servers, which assist different levels of management:

- Office information systems
- Transaction processing systems
- Management information systems
- Decision support systems
- Executive support systems
- Expert systems

Office Information Systems

Office information systems facilitate communication and collaboration between the members of an organization and between organizations.

Office information systems (OISs), also called *office automation systems (OASs)*, combine various technologies to reduce the manual labor required in operating an efficient office environment and to increase productivity. Used throughout all levels of an organization, OIS technologies include fax, voice mail, email, scheduling software, word processing, and desktop publishing, among others. *(• See Panel 8.10, next page.)*

The backbone of an OIS is a network—LAN, intranet, extranet—that connects everything. All office functions—dictation, typing, filing, copying, fax, microfilm and records management, telephone calls, and switchboard operations—are candidates for integration into the network.

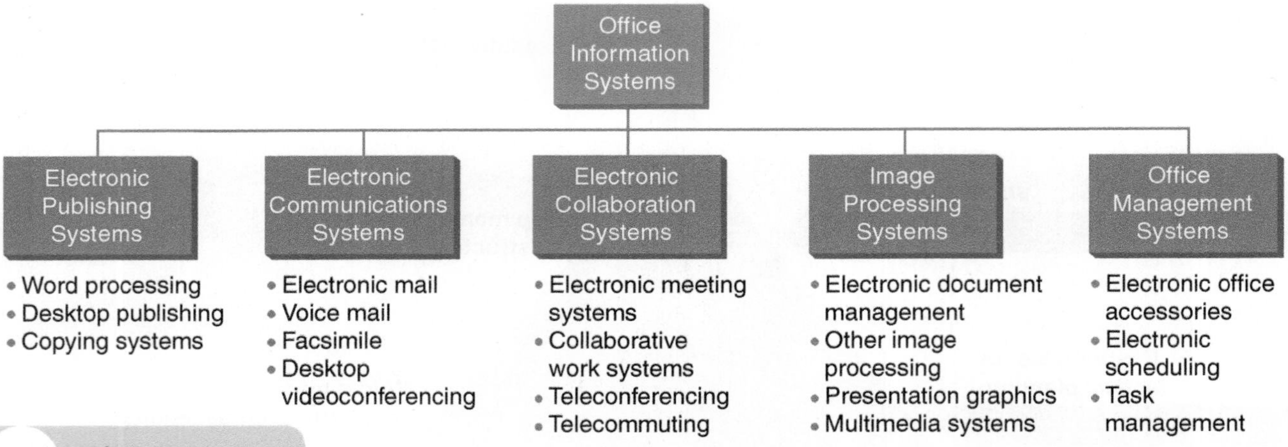

Office Information Systems

Electronic Publishing Systems	Electronic Communications Systems	Electronic Collaboration Systems	Image Processing Systems	Office Management Systems
• Word processing • Desktop publishing • Copying systems	• Electronic mail • Voice mail • Facsimile • Desktop videoconferencing	• Electronic meeting systems • Collaborative work systems • Teleconferencing • Telecommuting	• Electronic document management • Other image processing • Presentation graphics • Multimedia systems	• Electronic office accessories • Electronic scheduling • Task management

panel 8.10

Office information systems

The backbone is a network linking these technologies.

Transaction Processing Systems

Transaction processing systems are computer-based systems that take transaction-related information that is time-sensitive and immediately process it and keep it current.

In most organizations, particularly business organizations, most of what goes on consists largely of structured information known as transactions. A *transaction* is a recorded event having to do with routine business activities. A transaction may be recorded manually or via a computer system and includes everything concerning the product or service in which the organization is engaged: production, distribution, sales, and orders. It also includes materials purchased, employees hired, taxes paid, and so on. Today in most organizations, the bulk of such transactions is recorded in a computer-based information system. These systems tend to have clearly defined inputs and outputs, and there is an emphasis on efficiency and accuracy. Transaction processing systems record data but do little in the way of converting data into information.

A transaction processing system (TPS) is a computer-based information system that keeps track of the transactions needed to conduct business. The transactions can be handled via *batch processing,* also known as *offline processing*—that is, the data is gathered and processed in batches at periodic intervals, such as at the end of the day or once a week. Or they may be handled via *real-time processing,* also known as *online transaction processing (OLTP)*—that is, each transaction is processed immediately as it is entered. The data collected by a TPS is typically stored in databases.

FEATURES OF A TPS Some features of a TPS are as follows:

- **Input and output:** The inputs to the system are transaction data: bills, orders, inventory levels, and the like. The output consists of processed transactions: bills, paychecks, and so on.
- **For operational managers:** Because the TPS deals with day-to-day matters, it is principally of use to operational-level or supervisory managers, although it can also be helpful to tactical-level managers.
- **Produces detail reports:** A manager at the operational level typically receives information in the form of detail reports. A *detail report* contains specific information about routine activities. An example might be the information needed to decide whether to restock inventory.
- **One TPS for each department:** Each department or functional area of an organization usually has its own TPS (with an underlying database used by other departments). For example, the accounting and finance TPS handles order processing, accounts receivable, inventory and purchasing, accounts payable, and payroll.
- **Basis for MIS and DSS:** The database of transactions stored in a TPS provides the basis for management information systems and decision support systems, as we describe next.

Management Information Systems

Management information systems transform data into information useful in the support of decision making, principally at the tactical level.

The next level of information system after the TPS is the management information system. **A management information system (MIS)** (pronounced "em-eye-ess") **is a computer-based information system that uses data recorded by a TPS as input into programs that produce routine reports as output.**

FEATURES OF AN MIS Features of an MIS are as follows:

- **Input and output:** Inputs consist of processed transaction data, such as bills, orders, and paychecks, plus other internal data. Outputs consist of summarized, structured reports: budget summaries, production schedules, and the like.
- **For tactical managers:** An MIS is intended principally to assist tactical-level managers. It enables them to spot trends and get an overview of current business activities.
- **Draws from all departments:** The MIS draws from all six departments or functional areas, not just one.
- **Produces several kinds of reports:** Managers at this level usually receive information in the form of several kinds of reports: *summary, exception, periodic,* and *demand.*

Summary reports show totals and trends. An example is a report showing total sales by office, by product, and by salesperson, as well as total overall sales.

Exception reports show out-of-the-ordinary data. An example is an inventory report listing only those items of which fewer than 10 are in stock.

Periodic reports are produced on a regular schedule. Such daily, weekly, monthly, quarterly, or annual reports may contain sales figures, income statements, or balance sheets. They are usually produced on paper, such as computer printouts.

Demand reports produce information in response to an unscheduled demand. A director of finance might order a demand credit-background report on an unknown customer who wants to place a large order. Demand reports are often produced on a terminal or microcomputer screen, rather than on paper.

Decision Support Systems

Decision support systems are a specific class of computer-based information system that supports business and organizational decision-making activities generally at the managerial level.

A more sophisticated information system is the decision support system. **A decision support system (DSS) is a computer-based information system that provides a flexible tool for analysis and helps managers focus on the future.** A DSS aims to produce collected information known as *business intelligence,* gathering data from a wide range of sources in a way that can be interpreted by humans and used to support better business decision making. Some decision support systems come very close to acting as artificial intelligence agents (covered in the next section). DSS applications are not single information resources, such as a database or a program that graphically represents sales figures, but a combination of integrated resources working together. Whereas a TPS records data and an MIS summarizes data, a DSS analyzes data. To reach the DSS level of sophistication in information technology, an organization must have established TPSs and MISs first.

FEATURES OF A DSS Some features of a DSS are as follows:

- **Inputs and outputs:** Inputs include internal data—such as summarized reports and processed transaction data—and also data that is external to the organization. External data may be produced by trade associations, marketing research firms, the U.S. Bureau of the Census, and other government agencies. The outputs are demand reports on which a top manager can make decisions about unstructured problems.

- **Mainly for tactical managers:** A DSS is intended principally to assist tactical-level managers in making tactical decisions. Questions addressed by the DSS might be, for example, whether interest rates will rise or whether there will be a strike in an important materials-supplying industry.
- **Produces analytic models:** The key attribute of a DSS is that it uses models. A *model* is a mathematical representation of a real system. The models use a DSS database, which draws on the TPS and MIS files, as well as external data such as stock reports, government reports, and national and international news. The system is accessed through DSS software. The model allows the manager to do a simulation—play a "what-if" game—to reach decisions. Thus, the manager can simulate an aspect of the organization's environment in order to decide how to react to a change in conditions affecting it. By changing the hypothetical inputs to the model, the manager can see how the model's outputs are affected.

SOME USES OF DSSs Many DSSs are developed to support the types of decisions faced by managers in specific industries, such as airlines or real estate. Curious how airlines decide how many seats to sell on a flight when so many passengers are no-shows? American Airlines developed a DSS, the yield management system, that helps managers decide how much to overbook and how to set prices for each seat so that a plane is filled and profits are maximized. Wonder how owners of those big apartment complexes set rents and lease terms? Investors in commercial real estate have used DSSs to forecast property values up to 40 years into the future, based on income, expense, and cash-flow projections. Ever speculate about how insurance carriers set different rates or how Subway and McDonald's decide where to locate a store? Many companies use DSSs called *geographic information systems (GISs),* such as Maptitude, MapInfo, and Atlas GIS, which integrate geographic databases with other business data and display maps. (• *See Panel 8.11.)*

panel 8.11

Geographic DSS screen by Maptitude

Maptitude is a Geographic Information System (GIS) software designed to store, retrieve, manage, display, and analyze all types of geographic and spatial data. GIS software lets you produce maps and other graphic displays of geographic information for analysis and presentation. With these capabilities a GIS is a valuable tool to visualize spatial data or to build decision support systems for use in an organization. Maptitude implements a relational database.

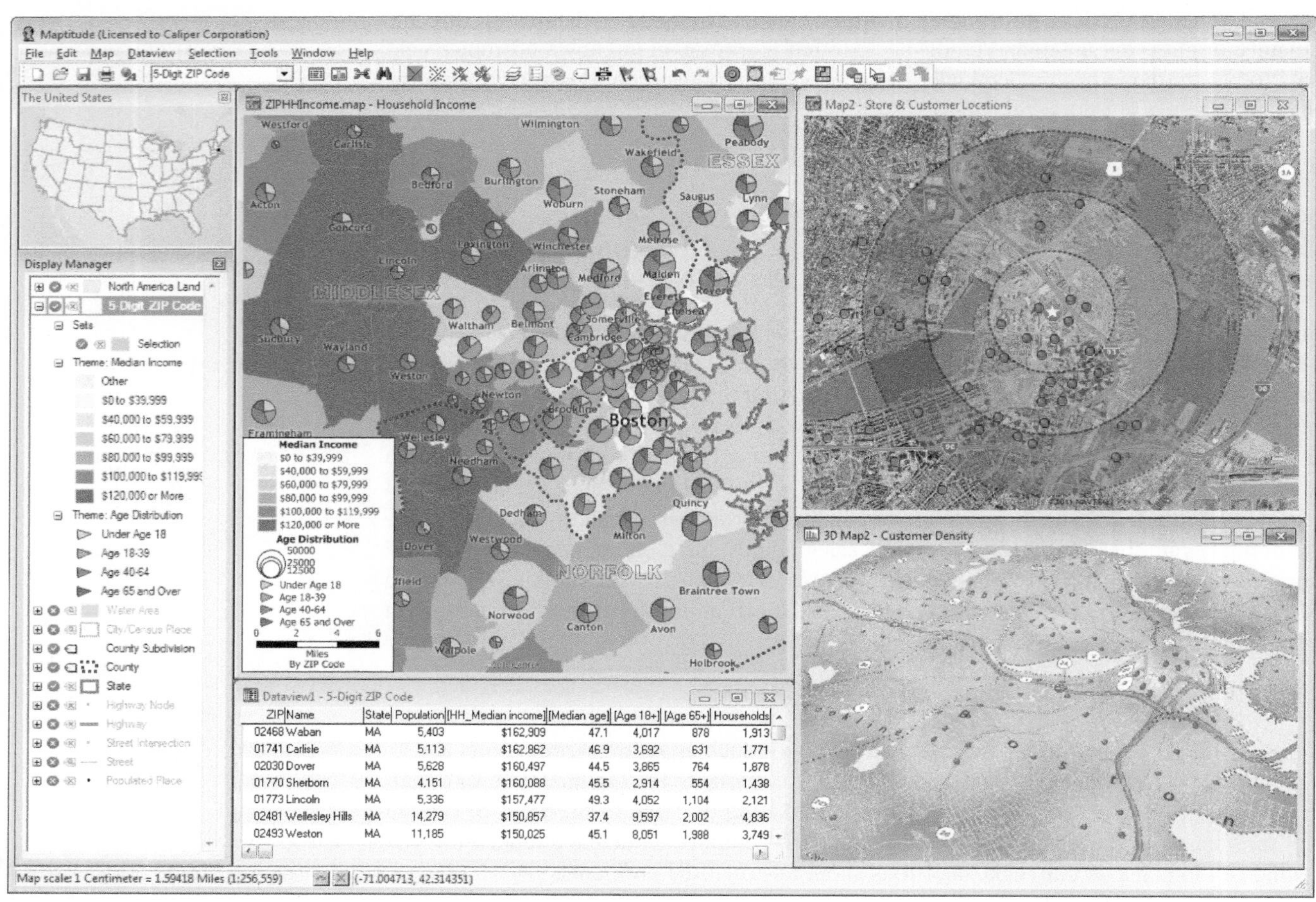

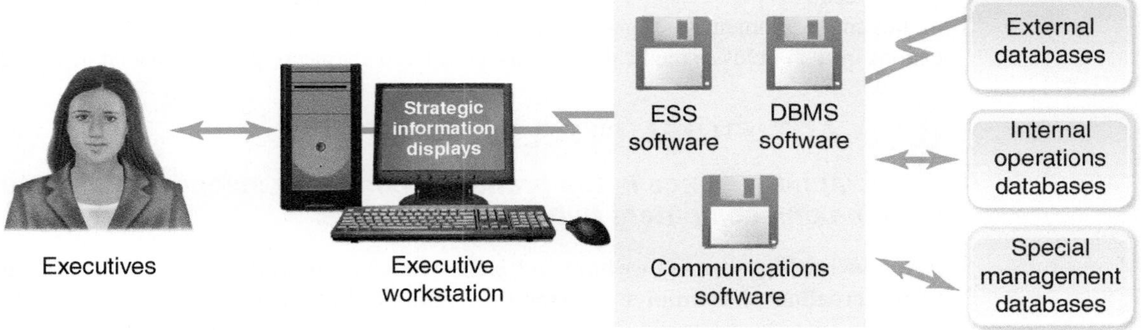

Executive Support Systems

panel 8.12

Components of an ESS

Executive support systems are reporting tools that allow organizations to turn their data into useful summarized reports. These reports are generally used by executive-level managers for quick access to reports coming from all company levels.

Also called an *executive information system (EIS),* an **executive support system (ESS) is an easy-to-use DSS made especially for strategic managers; it specifically supports strategic decision making.** It draws on data not only from systems internal to the organization but also from those outside, such as news services or market research databases. (• *See Panel 8.12.)*

An ESS might allow senior executives to call up predefined reports from their personal computers, whether desktops or laptops. They might, for instance, call up sales figures in many forms—by region, by week, by anticipated year, by projected increases. The ESS includes capabilities for analyzing data and doing what-if scenarios. ESSs also have the capability to browse through summarized information on all aspects of the organization and then zero in on ("drill down" to) detailed areas the manager believes require attention.

ESSs are relatively user-friendly and require little training to use.

Expert Systems

Expert systems are computer programs that use artificial intelligence to solve problems within a specialized domain that ordinarily requires human expertise. These expert systems represent the expert knowledge as data or rules within the computer system.

The first expert system, called Dendral, was developed in 1965 by Edward Feigenbaum and Joshua Lederberg of Stanford University and was designed to analyze chemical compounds. **An expert system, or *knowledge-based system,* is a set of interactive computer programs that helps users solve problems that would otherwise require the assistance of a human expert.** Expert systems are created on the basis of knowledge collected on specific topics from human specialists, and they imitate the reasoning process of a human being. As we describe in the next section, expert systems have emerged from the field of artificial intelligence. Expert systems are used by both management and nonmanagement personnel to solve specific problems, such as how to reduce production costs, improve workers' productivity, or reduce environmental impact. Because of their giant appetite for memory, expert systems are usually run on large computers, although some microcomputer expert systems also exist. For example, Negotiator Pro

Want to know how long you can safely keep meat in the refrigerator? Or how long to boil an egg? How about whether it's better to use wooden or plastic cutting boards?

Just ask Karen, your guide to expert knowledge on handling and storing food safely and preventing food poisoning.

Use this page to search our knowledge base of common food safety questions (available 24/7). On your mobile phone access m.askkaren.gov | En Español

Common Questions | Submit a Question | Live Chat | Help

Topics

Select a Topic

Products

Select a Product

Submit

Find the answer to your question

Knowledge based. Karen, the U.S. Food Safety and Inspection Service (FSIS) virtual representative (*www.fsis.usda.gov/wps/portal/informational/askkaren*)

helps executives plan effective negotiations by examining the personality types of the other parties and recommending negotiating strategies. These systems also have commercial applications in such fields as medical diagnosis, petroleum engineering, and financial investing.

8.7 ARTIFICIAL INTELLIGENCE

Artificial intelligence is the branch of computer science concerned with making computers behave like humans.

Artificial intelligence (AI), we have said, **is the branch of computer science that is devoted to the creation of computer systems that simulate human reasoning and sensation.** The field consists of a group of related technologies used for developing machines to emulate human qualities, such as learning, reasoning, communicating, seeing, and hearing. As will become clear, AI would not be possible without developments in database technology.

Conventional AI versus Computational Intelligence: "Neats" versus "Scruffies"

Two approaches to AI are conventional AI, based on machine learning, and computational intelligence, based on experimental and trial-and-error methods.

Artificial intelligence research is divided into two schools of thought: *conventional AI* and *computational intelligence,* sometimes characterized as "neat" versus "scruffy" approaches.[25]

CONVENTIONAL AI: BASED ON MACHINE LEARNING **Conventional AI attempts to mimic human intelligence through logic and symbol manipulation, as well as statistics.** This branch of AI is based on **machine learning, which is the development of techniques that allow a computer to simulate learning by generating rules from raw data fed into it.** Expert systems, for example, make heavy use of this kind of AI.

The researchers and designers associated with this conventional AI have often been dubbed "neats" because they believe that an intelligent system should be elegant, obvious, and based on formal logic.

Examples of Heuristics

http://examples.yourdictionary.com/examples/examples-of-heuristics.html

http://psychology.about.com/od/rindex/g/representativeness-heuristic.htm

www.indiana.edu/~p1013447/dictionary/alg_heur.htm

COMPUTATIONAL INTELLIGENCE: BASED ON HEURISTICS **Computational intelligence relies less on formal logical systems and more on experimental and trial-and-error methods.** This branch of AI is based on **heuristics ("hyu-*ris*-tiks"), or rules of thumb, for solving a problem, rather than hard-and-fast formulas or algorithms.** (An *algorithm,* as discussed in Chapter 10, is a formula or set of steps for solving a particular problem.) Fuzzy logic, which deals with imprecise data and problems with many answers (discussed on p. 446), and neural networks, which mimic the neurological structure of the human brain (discussed on p. 447), are based on this kind of AI.

Professionals associated with computational intelligence are called "scruffies" because, in the words of one writer, "the Scruffies hold that intelligence is too messy and complicated to be solved under the limitations the Neats propose."[26] As you might suspect, some good results have come about from approaches that melded both the neats and the scruffies.

Weak AI versus Strong AI

Weak AI focuses on making machines act as if they were intelligent. Strong AI focuses on making machines that really think—that represent human minds.

Two other principal approaches to artificial intelligence are *weak AI* and *strong AI.*

WEAK AI **Weak AI makes the claim that computers can be programmed to *simulate* human cognition and only *some* human cognition, to solve particular problems or reasoning tasks that do not encompass fully human intelligence.**[27] That is, weak AI suggests that some "thinking-like" features can be added to computers to make them more useful tools. We have already seen this kind of AI—call it "AI lite"—in expert systems, speech-recognition software, computer games, and the like.

TECH TALES The Brute Force of Weak AI

A useful concept for considering weak AI is that of brute force. In programming and in AI, *brute force* is a technique for solving a complex problem by using a computer's fast processing capability to repeat a simple procedure many times.

For example, a spelling checker in a word processing program doesn't really check the spelling of words; rather, it compares all the words you type into your document to a dictionary of correctly spelled words. Similarly, a chess-playing program will calculate all the possible moves that can apply to a given situation and then choose the best one; it will not analyze and strategize the way a human chess player would.

Even IBM's Deep Blue program, which defeated Russian chess master Garry Kasparov in May 1997, basically took advantage of a supercomputer's fast processing abilities to examine 200 million possible plays per second—plays that had been input via a human-knowledge-based expert system. ■

STRONG AI **Strong AI makes the claim that computers can be made to think on a level that is at least equal to humans and possibly even be conscious of themselves.** So far, most AI advances have been piecemeal and single purpose, such as factory robots. However, proponents of strong AI believe that it's possible for computers to have the kind of wide-ranging problem-solving ability that people have.

Some researchers believe that strong AI holds out a lot of promise, as evidenced by recent developments in *nanotechnology,* in which molecule-size nanostructures (nanobots) are used to create tiny machines for holding data or performing tasks.

THE AREAS OF AI Today the main areas of AI are these, which we cover next:

- Expert systems
- Natural language processing
- Intelligent agents
- Pattern recognition
- Virtual reality and simulation devices
- Robotics
- Fuzzy logic
- Neural networks

We also consider an area known as *artificial life.*

Expert Systems

An expert system has three parts: knowledge base, inference engine, and user interface.

As we said in the last section, an *expert system* is an interactive computer program used to solve problems that would otherwise require the assistance of a human specialist. As the name suggests, it is a system imbued with knowledge by human experts. Expert systems have been designed both for microcomputers and for larger computer systems with huge databases.

TECH TALES Some Interestingly Named Expert Systems

Some expert systems have straightforward names, such as Business Insight, which helps businesses find the best strategies for marketing a product. Other names are more unusual: Whale Watcher, for example, is an expert system used to identify whales.

Then there are all those all-capital-letter names: MYCIN, one of the earliest expert systems, helped diagnose infectious diseases. PROSPECTOR was

Expert systems. These software companies offer strategic-planning software that uses expert knowledge bases in various areas.

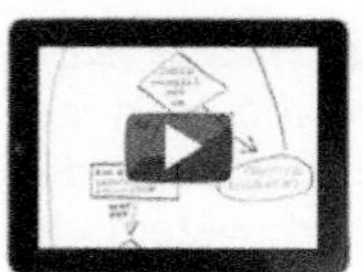

Complicated? Not so much.

Not a programmer? Not a problem. If you can draw a flowchart on a whiteboard, you can design and publish your own LogicNets application on the web. Watch the LogicNets Designer demo (on the left) to see how it's done.

Latest News

We've released a new **solution for Tech Support** organizations, adding predictive diagnostics, adaptive maintenance, and offline field service support capabilities. More...

Support Solutions

Guided. Predictive. Collaborative.

LogicNets has unleashed the full potential of Expert Systems for optimizing Tech Support and Field Service. With LogicNets, your reps, partners, and end-users access a web-based platform and are guided heuristically through the optimal diagnostic procedures. Build an expert knowledge delivery system leveraging pre-existing CRM, KM, and ERP products. Move beyond simply searching for answers. Evolve to managed knowledge delivery and predictive diagnostics. Read More...

Health and Safety Solutions

Practical. Economical. Adaptable. Painless.

LogicNets Health and Safety Solutions are designed to make the job of managing risk and complying with EHS requirements significantly easier and more effective. With a full-featured EHS decision support portal accessible by staff at their desks or in the field, LogicNets lets you cost-effectively automate and manage even the most widely distributed risk and health and safety operations. Read More...

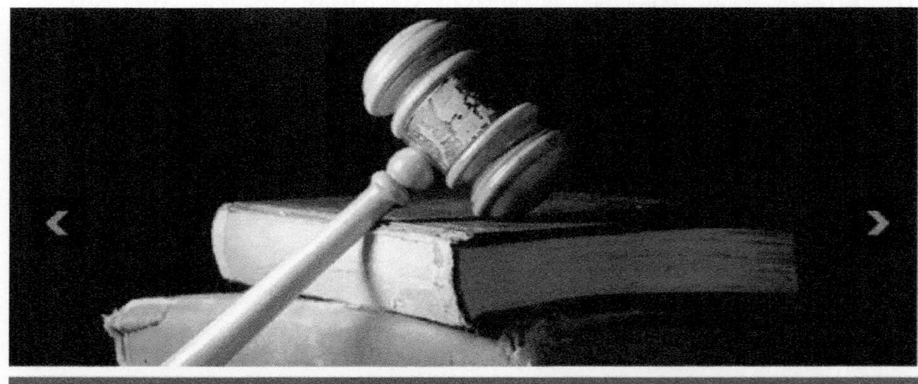

Experts

Home

Since 1986, Rieback Medical Legal Consultants, Inc. has dedicated itself to providing the most **qualified board certified physicians, nurses and other medical experts** to America's finest attorneys. Our medical expert witnesses provide medical and nursing expert reviews, depositions and trial testimony.

Rieback Medical Legal Consultants, Inc. provides attorneys with medical expert witnesses in the following areas:

Medical Malpractice	Workman's Compensation
Personal Injury	Insurance and Disability Cases
Wrongful Death	Pharmaceutical Malpractice
Product Liability	Nursing Home Malpractice and Abuse
Toxic Tort and Environmental Exposure	

for assessing geological data to locate mineral deposits. CARES (Computer Assisted Risk Evaluation System) helps nonprofit organizations evaluate risks and protect clients and staff. CLUES (Countrywide Loan Underwriting Expert System) evaluates home mortgage loan applications. CLIPS (C Language Integrated Production System), widely used in government, industry, and academia, is an expert system used to build other expert systems. STREAMES assists water managers to evaluate the effect of large stream nutrient loads on stream nutrient retention. ■

HOW EXPERT SYSTEMS DRAW ON KNOWLEDGE All these programs simulate the reasoning process of experts in certain well-defined areas. That is, professionals called *knowledge engineers* interview the experts and determine the rules and knowledge that must go into the system. For example, to develop Muckraker, an expert system to assist newspaper reporters with investigative reporting, the knowledge engineers interviewed journalists.

Programs incorporate not only the experts' surface knowledge ("textbook knowledge") but also their deep knowledge ("tricks of the trade"). What, exactly, is *deep knowledge*? "An expert in some activity has by definition reduced the world's complexity by his or her specialization," say some authorities. One result is that "much of the knowledge lies outside direct conscious awareness."[28]

THE THREE COMPONENTS OF AN EXPERT SYSTEM An expert system consists of three components. (• *See Panel 8.13.*)

- **Knowledge base:** A *knowledge base* is an expert system's database of knowledge about a particular subject, including relevant facts, information, beliefs, assumptions, and procedures for solving problems. The basic unit of knowledge is expressed as an IF-THEN-ELSE rule. ("IF this happens, THEN do this, ELSE do that.") Programs can have many thousands of rules. A system called ExperTAX, for example, which helps accountants figure out a client's tax options, consists of more than 3,000 rules. Other systems have 80,000 or 100,000 rules, which means that very large computer systems are required.
- **Inference engine:** The *inference engine* is the software that controls the search of the expert system's knowledge base and produces conclusions. It takes the problem posed by the user and fits it into the rules in the knowledge base. It then derives a conclusion from the facts and rules contained in the knowledge base.
- **User interface:** The *user interface* is the display screen. It gives the user the ability to ask questions and get answers. It also explains the reasoning behind the answer.

People fearful about machines taking over our lives need to understand that expert systems are designed to be users' assistants, not replacements. Also, the success of these systems depends on the quality of the data and rules obtained from the human experts.

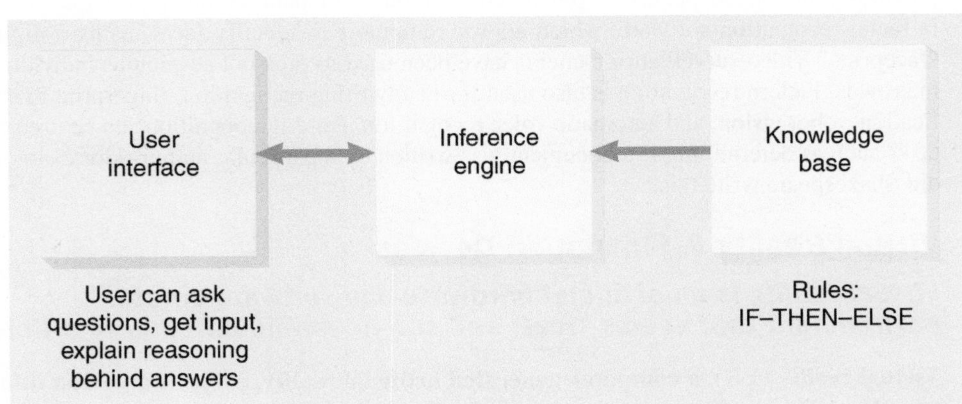

panel 8.13

Components of an expert system

Natural Language Processing

Natural language processing involves designing software that will analyze, understand, and generate human languages.

Misunderstanding . . .

Here are some English phrases that a natural language computer system might have trouble understanding.

www.transmachina.com/en/content/some-natural-language-examples-computers-may-have-trouble-understanding

Natural languages are ordinary human languages, such as English. (A second definition, discussed in Chapter 10, is that natural languages are fifth-generation programming languages.) **Natural language processing is the study of ways for computers to recognize and understand human language,** whether in spoken or written form. Major advances in natural language processing have occurred in *speech recognition,* in which computers translate spoken speech into text.

Think how challenging it is to make a computer translate English into another language. In one instance, the English sentence "The spirit is willing, but the flesh is weak" came out in Russian as "The wine is agreeable, but the meat is spoiled." The problem with human language is that it is often ambiguous; different listeners may arrive at different interpretations. Most existing language systems run on large computers, although scaled-down versions are now available for microcomputers.

Intelligent Agents

An intelligent agent is software that assists people and acts on their behalf, allowing them to delegate work to the agent.

How do you find information in the vast sea of the Internet? As one solution, computer scientists have developed so-called intelligent agents to find information on computer networks and filter it. **An intelligent agent is a form of software with built-in intelligence that monitors work patterns, asks questions, and performs work tasks on your behalf,** such as roaming networks and compiling data. Also known as *bots* or *network agents,* these intelligent agents search the Internet and online databases for information and bring the results back to you. Agents can perform repetitive tasks, remember things you forgot, intelligently summarize complex data, and even make recommendations to you.

One type of intelligent agent is a kind of electronic assistant that will filter messages, scan news services, and perform similar secretarial chores. Another kind is the *shopping bot,* or comparison engine, that helps users search the Internet for a particular product or service and then brings up price comparisons, locations, and other information. Examples of these shopping bots are Google Product Search, Nextag, Pricegrabber, Shopping.com, and Shopzilla.

Pattern Recognition

Pattern recognition is the computer-based identification of objects and images by their shape, color, texture, temperature, or other attribute.

Pattern recognition involves software that identifies recurring patterns in what it is seeing and recognize the connections between the perceived patterns and similar patterns stored in a database. Pattern recognition is used in data mining to discover previously unnoticed patterns from massive amounts of data. Another principal use is in facial-recognition software, which allows computers to identify faces, using a digital "faceprint." Video surveillance cameras have been used to pick out suspicious individuals in crowds. Pattern recognition is also used for handwriting recognition, fingerprint identification, robot vision, and automatic voice recognition. Pattern recognition can be used for tasks such as determining if a document was written by a particular author—for example, did Shakespeare write this?

Virtual Reality & Simulation Devices

Virtual reality is an artificial hardware-and-software-created environment that seems "real" and can be manipulated in real time.

Virtual reality (VR), a computer-generated artificial reality, projects a person into a sensation of three-dimensional space. (• *See Panel 8.14.)*

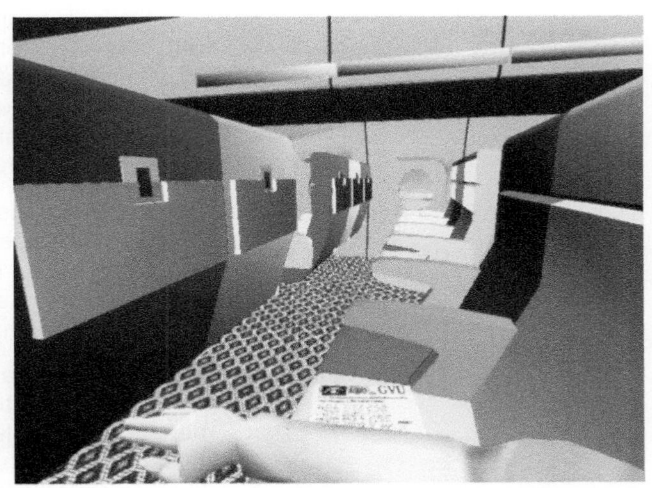

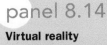

panel 8.14

Virtual reality

(*top left*) A research assistant works on a virtual reality program at the Virtual Reality in Medicine laboratory at the University of Illinois at Chicago. Surgeons use such programs to practice surgery on patients' "virtual organs" before making the first real cut. (*middle left*) Although it may look realistic, the pilot shown here is flying a conceptual aircraft. In Grumman's simulation system development laboratory, the pilot sees high-resolution images projected onto the interior of a simulation dome. (*bottom left*) This digital reconstruction, from Virginia's Institute for Advanced Technology in the Humanities, shows the steps on the back side of the Caesarean speakers' platform, the Basilica Aemilia law court at left, and the Basilica Julia law court at right, part of the ancient Roman Forum, used for the simulation of the historic city at its peak in 400 C.E. (*top right*) Ford uses 3D simulation to test car design changes in the United States, Germany, and Australia. (*above*) Passenger airline flight simulation that allows people who are afraid to fly to experience an airplane trip without leaving the ground.

more info!

Be a Train Engineer

How does it feel to drive a train? You can find out with Microsoft's Train Simulator, pretending to direct trains over routes in the United States, United Kingdom, Austria, and Japan:

www.railserve.com/Computers/

www.ea.com/rail-simulator

How does it feel to fly?

www.justflight.com/

www.gefs-online.com/

www.sciencedaily.com/releases/2011/05/110505164535.htm

www.learn4good.com/games/flying.htm

Virtual Reality Products

For more about VR products:

www.vrealities.com/main.html

www.cwonline.com/

http://nvisinc.com/products2009.php

To put yourself into virtual reality, you need software and special headgear; then you can add gloves, and later perhaps a special suit. The headgear—which is called a *head-mounted display* (marketed as a VR headset)—has two small video display screens, for each eye, to create the sense of three-dimensionality. Headphones pipe in stereophonic sound or even 3-D sound so that you think you are hearing sounds not only near each ear but also in various places all around you. The glove has sensors for collecting data about your hand movements. Once you are wearing this equipment, software gives you interactive sensory feelings similar to real-world experiences.

Virtual reality is used in arcade-type games, most recently the VR Oculus version of *SoundSelf,* but there are far more important uses—for example, in simulators for training. **Simulators are devices that represent the behavior of physical or abstract systems.** Virtual reality simulation technologies are applied a great deal in training.

TECH TALES Using Virtual Reality & Simulation for Training, Treatment, & Research

Need to learn to drive a snow plow when there's not a lot of snow to practice with? In nine states, highway officials use a sophisticated simulator for plow drivers to practice snow removal in any weather. "It works like a video game," says one writer, "recreating slick pavement, poor visibility, and even children or animals bolting across the road. In a virtual collision, drivers hear crashing noises and see a cracked windshield."[29]

Simulators are also used in drivers' education (and to discourage texting and cellphone use) and to train bus drivers, locomotive drivers, and airline pilots.[30] "Modern simulators are so realistic that a new captain can take a flight test in one and be issued a license to fly the actual aircraft without ever having gotten off the ground," says one report.[31]

Many athletes train with simulators, of course. Architects create virtual walkthroughs of the structures they are designing. Surgeons in training develop their skills through simulation on "digital patients." Virtual reality therapy has been used for autistic children and in the treatment of phobias, such as extreme fear of public speaking or of being in public places or high places, and psychotic disorders, such as paranoia, and social disorders.

Virtual reality is also being used in research. In one Stanford University study of people's feelings about conservation, subjects were immersed in a three-dimensional virtual forest and told to saw through a towering sequoia redwood tree until it crashed in front of them. Later these subjects were found to use less paper in the real world than did people who only imagined what it was like to cut down a tree. "We found that virtual reality can change how people behave," said researcher Sun Joo Ahn.[32] ■

Robotics

Robotics involves the conception, design, manufacture, and operation of robots, devices that perform humanlike functions. Robots can be classified according to locomotion or application.

In the 1956 film *Forbidden Planet,* Robby the Robot could sew, distill bourbon, and speak 187 languages. We haven't caught up with science fiction movies, but maybe we'll get there yet.

Robotics is the development and study of machines that can perform actions normally performed by living beings. The machines themselves are called *robots.* (• *See Panel 8.15.)* As we said in Chapter 1, a *robot* is an automatic device that performs functions ordinarily executed by human beings or that operates with what appears to be almost human intelligence.

Robots can be divided into two groups:[33]

ROBOTS GROUPED BY LOCOMOTION SYSTEM Robots can be classified according to their means of locomotion, which defines their shape. Thus, there are stationary, wheeled, legged, swimming, flying, rolling, swarm, modular, micro, nano, soft elastic, snake, and crawler robots. One type of flying robot that has received a lot of attention is the drone, which we consider in detail in Chapter 9.

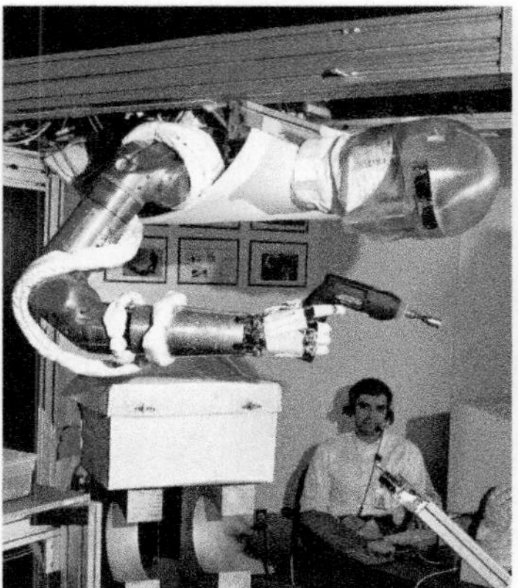

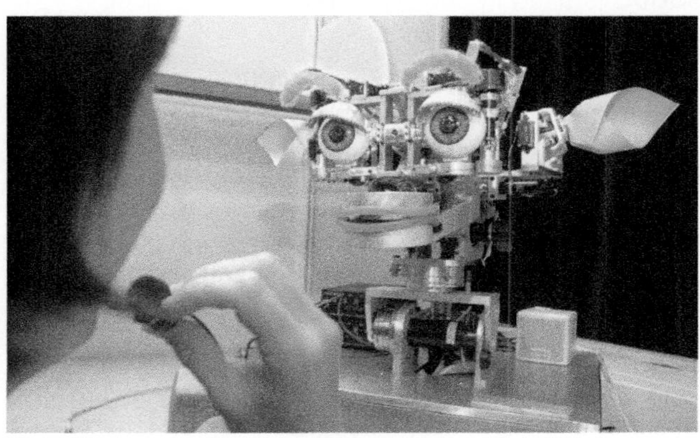
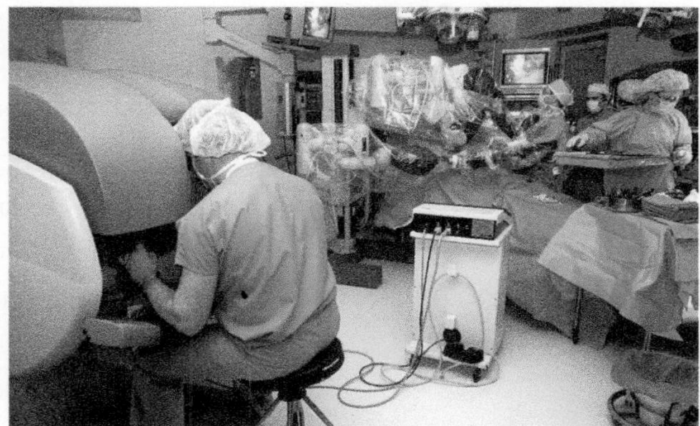

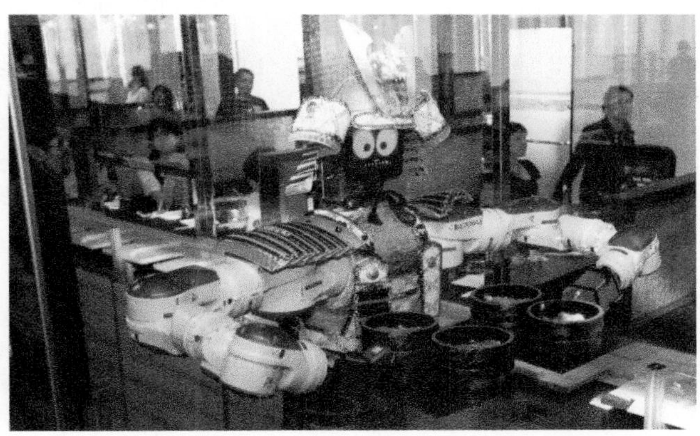

panel 8.15

Robots

(*top left*) Many Japanese people are fond of robotic pets, such as this Sega Poochi. (*top middle*) This Robonaut is a robotic system aimed at giving spacewalking astronauts a hand in space station construction. (*top right*) The Robo-Soldier is an armed, unmanned ground vehicle that never gets tired, hungry, or scared. (*middle left*) Dr. Cynthia Breazeal, at the Massachusetts Institute of Technology's Artificial Intelligence Laboratory, interacts with Kismet, a robotic head that interacts with humans in a humanlike way. (*middle right*) A robotic surgery device, called the Da Vinci Surgical System, operated by a physician, manipulates robotic arms during a gallbladder operation at a hospital in New Jersey. (*bottom left*) BigDog robot by Boston Dynamics; here it is testing hazmat gear (protective suits). (*bottom right*) A robot waiter holds a tray of food at a Japanese robot restaurant in Bangkok, Thailand. At this restaurant, all the serving waiters are robots; customers can order their food on a touch-screen display monitor on each table.

ROBOTS GROUPED BY APPLICATION Robots can be grouped according to the application they are supposed to perform, so that shape is not important. Thus, in health and medicine, there are wearable machines to help amputees walk, wheeled robots (medi-bots) that roam hospital halls and make visits to patients on behalf of their doctors, and robots used in surgery that perform actual operations.[34]

TECH TALES All Types of Robots

Shakey, developed in 1970, was the first robot to use artificial intelligence to navigate. Today Rosie and Roscoe are R2-D2-like robots that perform a variety of courier duties for hospitals, saving nurses from having to make trips to supply areas, pharmacies, and cafeterias. ScrubMate—a robot equipped with computerized controls, ultrasonic "eyes," sensors, batteries, three different cleaning and scrubbing tools, and a self-squeezing mop—can clean bathrooms. ROBODOC is used in surgery to bore the thighbone so that a hip implant can be attached.

A driverless harvester, guided by satellite signals and an artificial vision system, is used to harvest alfalfa and other crops. A robot dog named AIBO is able to learn how to sit, roll over, fetch, and do other activities. You can buy your own robot vacuum cleaner, Roomba, or the more advanced Scooba, which will not just pick up dirt but also wash, scrub, and dry the floor. At the Massachusetts Institute of Technology, a robot will water a tomato plant when the soil needs it. Roborier ("robot" + "interior") is a robot house sitter that rolls around a house and uses infrared sensors to detect suspicious movements and transmit images to absent owners.

Robots are also used for more exotic purposes such as fighting oil-well fires, doing nuclear inspections and cleanups, and checking for land mines and booby traps. An eight-legged, satellite-linked robot called Dante II was used to explore, sometimes without human guidance, the inside of Mount Spurr, an active Alaskan volcano. A six-wheeled robot vehicle called Sojourner was used in NASA's 1997 Pathfinder exploration of Mars to sample the planet's atmosphere and soil and to radio data and photos back to Earth. The robot Opportunity, which landed in 2004, is currently traversing the surface of Mars. ■

Fuzzy Logic

Fuzzy logic recognizes more than simple true and false values. It works with ranges of values, solving problems in a way that more resembles human logic.

The traditional logic behind computers is based on either-or, yes-no, true-false reasoning. Such computers make "crisp" distinctions, leading to precise decision making. **Fuzzy logic is a method of dealing with imprecise data and uncertainty, with problems that have many answers rather than one.** Unlike classical logic, fuzzy logic is more like human reasoning: It deals with probability and credibility. That is, instead of being simply true or false, a proposition is mostly true or mostly false, or more true or more false.

Fuzzy logic circuitry enables handheld autofocus video cameras to focus properly. If your hand is unsteady, the circuitry in the camera determines which parts in the visual field should stand still and which should move and makes the necessary adjustments in the image. Fuzzy logic is also used in many digital cooking appliances, such as rice cookers and some steamers. The built-in fuzzy logic system on a chip senses fluctuations in cooking and automatically adjusts operation to ensure perfect results.

TECH TALES Applying Fuzzy Logic to Elevators

How long will most people wait for an elevator before getting antsy? About a minute and a half, say researchers at the Otis Elevator Company. The Otis artificial intelligence division has thus done considerable research into how elevators may be programmed to reduce waiting time.[35]

Zojirushi fuzzy logic rice cooker. This rice cooker can "think" for itself and make fine adjustments to temperature and heating time to cook perfect rice. Rice cookers have used "fuzzy logic" for a while, but the new models include not only a microcomputer that adjusts cooking based on the rice weight, heat, and moisture but also uses artificial intelligence–it learns from each cooking experience so as to adjust to the cook's preferences.

Ordinarily, when someone on a floor in the middle of the building pushes the call button, the system will send whichever elevator is closest. However, that car might be filled with passengers, who will be delayed by the new stop (perhaps making them antsy), whereas another car that is farther away might be empty. In a fuzzy logic system, the computer assesses not only which car is nearest but also how full the cars are before deciding which one to send. ■

Neural Networks

Neural networks simulate the connections between nerve cells in the human body.

A neural network, or *neural net,* consists of a network of processors that are interconnected in a way that is similar to the connections between neurons, or nerve cells, in the human body. The neural network is able to simulate the behavior of biological neural networks, as in pattern recognition, language processing, and problem solving. A neural network is able to learn from example and does not require detailed instructions.

Neural networks have been used in machine vision, credit-card fraud detection, and diagnosis of heart attacks.

Two other forms of AI, genetic algorithms and cyborgs (cybernetic organisms), are described in the box on the next page. (• *See Panel 8.16.)*

8.8. ARTIFICIAL LIFE, THE TURING TEST, & THE SINGULARITY

Artificial intelligence leads to the question of how can we know a machine is truly intelligent, which figures in the Turing test.

What is life, and how can we replicate it in silicon chips, networks, and software? We are dealing now not with artificial intelligence but with artificial life. *Artificial life,* or *A-life,* is the field of study concerned with "creatures"—computer instructions, or pure information—that are created, replicate, evolve, and die as if they were living organisms. Thus, A-life software tries to simulate the responses of a human being.

Of course, "silicon life" does not have two principal attributes associated with true living things—it is not water- and carbon-based. Yet in other respects such creatures mimic life: If they cannot learn or adapt, then they perish.

panel 8.16

Two other types of AI: Genetic algorithms and cyborgs

Genetic Algorithms. A *genetic algorithm* is a program that uses Darwinian principles of random mutation to improve itself. The algorithms are lines of computer code that act like living organisms. Different sections of code haphazardly come together, producing programs. As in Darwin's rules of evolution, many chunks of code compete to see which can best fulfill the goal of the program. Some chunks will even become extinct. Those that survive will combine with other survivors to produce offspring programs.

Expert systems can capture and preserve the knowledge of expert specialists, but they may be slow to adapt to change. Neural networks can sift through mountains of data and discover obscure causal relationships, but if there is too much data, or too little, they may be ineffective. Genetic algorithms, by contrast, use endless trial and error to learn from experience—to discard unworkable approaches and grind away at promising approaches with the kind of tireless energy of which humans are incapable.

In 2000 scientists at Brandeis University reached a major milestone when they created a computerized robot that designs and builds other robots, automatically evolving without any significant human intervention. The "robotic life forms" are only a few inches long and are composed of a few plastic parts with rudimentary nervous systems made of wire. They do only one thing: inch themselves, wormlike, along a horizontal surface, using miniature motors. With no idea what a successful design might look like, the Brandeis computer was given the goal of moving on a horizontal surface; a list of possible parts to work with; a group of 200 randomly constructed, nonworking designs; and the physical laws of gravity and friction. Mimicking evolution through classic survival-of-the-fittest selection, the computer changed pieces in the designs, mutated the programming instructions for controlling movements, and ran simulations to test the designs. After 300–600 generations of evolution, the computer sent the design to a machine to build the robot. The robots currently have the brainpower of bacteria, say researchers, who hope to get up to insect level in a few years.

Cyborgs. *Cyborgs* are hybrids of machine and organisms. One example is a hockey-puck-size robot on wheels controlled by living tissue, an immature lamprey eel brain. The brain had been removed from the eel, kept alive in a special solution, and attached to the robot by wires. The brain is thus able to receive signals from the robot's electronic eyes and in turn can send commands to move the machine's wheels.

A number of cyborgs are in existence today—for instance, the estimated 10% of the American population with electronic heart pacemakers, artificial joints, implanted corneal lenses, and drug implant systems. Future cyborgs, however, might consist of bacteria attached to computer chips to map pollutants, insects used as parts of sensors to detect land mines and chemical weapons, and rodent brains to help identify new medicines. In his book *I, Cyborg,* British cybernetics professor Kevin Warwick described having an electrode in his arm pick up neural signals and send them to a computer, which converted them into instructions for a three-fingered robot hand elsewhere.

How Can We Know a Machine Is Truly Intelligent?

In the Turing test, a judge must decide whether a computer pretending to be human is or isn't really human.

Kevin Warwick. A professor of cybernetics at the University of Reading in the United Kingdom, Kevin Warwick takes his work seriously. So seriously, in fact, that he and his work have become one. Warwick is the founder of Project Cyborg. Using himself as the guinea pig, he's on a mission to become the world's most complete cyborg.

How can we know when we have reached the point at which computers have achieved human intelligence? How will you know, say, whether you're talking to a human being on the phone or to a computer? Clearly, with the strides made in the fields of artificial intelligence and artificial life, this question is no longer just academic.

Alan Turing, an English mathematician and computer pioneer, addressed this very question in 1950. Turing predicted that by the end of the century computers would be able to mimic human thinking and to conduct conversations indistinguishable from a person's. Out of these observations came the *Turing test,* which is intended to determine whether a computer possesses "intelligence" or "self-awareness."

In the Turing test, a human judge converses by means of a computer terminal with two entities hidden in another location—one a person typing on a keyboard, the other a computer program. Following the conversation, the judge must decide which entity is human. In this test, intelligence—the ability to think—is demonstrated by the computer's success in fooling the judge. (• *See Panel 8.17.*)

In 1990 American inventor Hugh Loebner established the Loebner Prize, which will award $100,000 to the first computer that passes the Turing test. The best the computer has done in fooling the judges came in 2008, when 3 of 12 judges, or 25%, were misled. (Turing had predicted that programs would be capable of fooling judges 30% of the time by the year 2000.)[36]

The Turing test is held every year. Go to *www.loebner.net/Prizef/loebner-prize.html* for more information and for transcripts of the human-computer interactions.

Alan Turing (*right*) in 1951, working on the Mark I computer

TECH TALES A Scene from the Turing Test

Judith Anne Gunther participated as one of eight judges in the third annual Loebner Prize Competition, which is based on Turing's ideas. The "conversations"—each limited to 15 minutes—are restricted to predetermined topics, such as baseball, because even today's best programs have neither the databases nor the syntactical ability to handle an unlimited number of subjects.

Gunther found that she wasn't fooled by any of the human-mimicking programs, which are called *chatbots.* The winning program, for example, relied as much on deflection and wit as it did on responding logically and conversationally. (For example, to a judge trying to discuss a federally funded program, the computer said: "You want logic? I'll give you logic: shut up, shut up, shut up, shut up, shut up, now go away! How's that for logic?") However, Gunther *was* fooled by one of the five humans, a

panel 8.17

Example of the Turing test

"**Computer:** As a psychoanalyst, I am familiar with discussing such marital troubles with you as the patient on the couch. If you don't have a bad marriage just pretend that you do. Please start with 'My wife . . .' or 'My husband . . .'.
Judge: OK, I'll pretend I have a bad marriage. Let's say the reason is because he never picks up his dirty underwear. Is this marriage irreparable?
Computer: Well, if you think I'm hopeless, you can always just swear at me."

—Judith Anne Gunther, "An Encounter with A.I.," *Popular Science,* June 1994.

real person discussing abortion. "He was so uncommunicative," wrote Gunther, "that I pegged him for a computer."[37]

Another participant says chatbots betray themselves in many ways. "They're unlikely to gracefully interrupt or be interrupted," he writes. "Their responses, often cobbled together out of fragments of stored conversations, make sense at a local level but lack long-term coherence. A bot I once chatted with claimed at one point to be 'happily married' and at another 'still looking for love.'"[38] ■

Human or Computer?

Make your guess as to whether it's from a human or a computer:

http://knopfdoubleday.com/2011/04/07/human-or-not-read-this-turing-test-script-and-take-a-guess/

A newer sort of "reverse" Turing test, one that's simple for humans but that can baffle sophisticated computer programs, has been devised in the form of cognitive puzzles called a *Captcha,* an acronym for "*c*ompletely *a*utomated *p*ublic Turing test to *t*ell *c*omputers and *h*umans *a*part." Captchas are most commonly used to prevent rogue bots from spamming comments or signing up for web services. Yahoo!, for example, uses a Captcha for screening when a user signs up for an account. Before being allowed to perform an action on the website, the user is presented with alphanumerical characters in a distorted graphic image (a Captcha) and asked to type them into an on-screen box. This works to prevent automated systems from abusing the site, because software does not yet exist that can read and reproduce the distorted image accurately (or such software is not available to the average user); so if the reading of and typing in of the distorted graphic are accurate, the user is likely to be a human.

Take a Few Captcha Tests

To get a feel for Captchas and learn more about what Captcha can do, go to:

www.captcha.net

The program reCaptcha is a new version of Captcha; besides doing what Captcha does, it helps clarify scrambled scanned files of poor-quality old books:

www.google.com/recaptcha/

Examples of captchas

"The Singularity": The Concept of Smarter-Than-Human Computers

The Singularity is the moment when humans will have created self-aware, smarter-than-human machines capable of designing computers better than humans can today.

Several research projects are under way that have the aim of making computers think and act more like humans. The U.S. military, for example, is spending billions to develop robots that aid or replace human soldiers. Other efforts concentrate on making driverless cars, software-based personal assistants, and an artificial brain that mimics the actions of 100 million brain neurons. All these seem to be part of a march toward a theoretical future point that scientist and science fiction writer Vernor Vinge called, in 1993,

the Singularity, or *the technological singularity,* a moment when humans would have created self-aware, smarter-than-human machines that are capable of designing computers and robots that are better than humans can make today. At this point, Vinge suggested, technological progress would have accelerated so much that machine intelligence would dominate, and the "human era would be ended."[39] Vinge thought that computers would become powerful enough by 2030 to allow the rise of such superintelligent, self-aware machines.

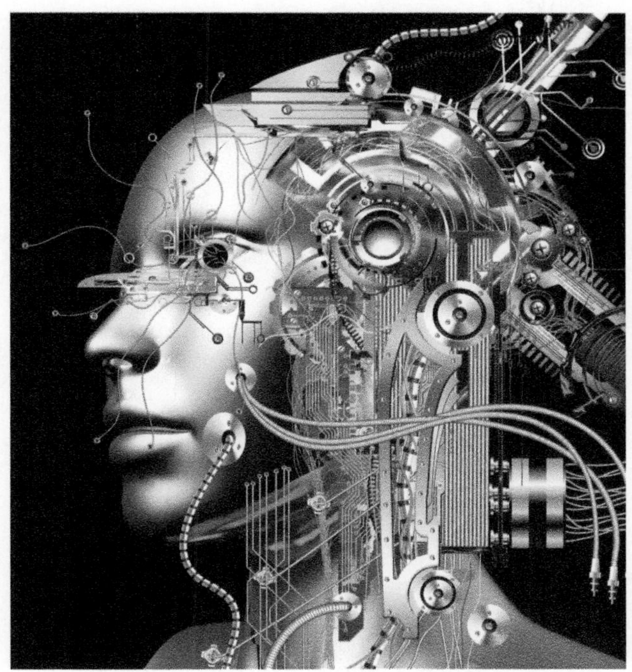

Others, such as Raymond Kurzweil, have taken the Singularity idea a great leap further, envisioning transferring the contents of human brains and thought processes into a computing environment, making a form of immortality possible. Thinkers such as Kevin Kelly take another tack, visualizing "the emergence of a global brain—the idea that the planet's interconnected computers might someday act in a coordinated fashion and perhaps exhibit intelligence," in one description.[40]

Will the machines take over the world? "Science is nowhere close to understanding what human intelligence is," notes one writer, "much less coming up with a formula to repeat it in silicon and electrons." We can program computers to say "I'm sorry" when they hear certain words, he points out, but they remain rigidly logical, unable to match the human mind "in its uniquely holistic and sometimes illogical ways."[41]

Ethics in AI

Ethics underlies everything having to do with AI.

Behind everything to do with artificial intelligence and artificial life—just as it underlies everything we do—is the whole matter of ethics. In his book *Ethics in Modeling,* William A. Wallace, professor of decision sciences at Rensselaer Polytechnic Institute, pointed out that computer software, including expert systems, is often subtly shaped by the ethical judgments and assumptions of the people who create it.[42] In one instance, he noted, a bank had to modify its loan evaluation software on discovering that the software rejected certain applications because it unduly emphasized old age as a negative factor.

More on AI & Ethics

www.nickbostrom.com/ethics/ai.html

www.cs.swarthmore.edu/~eroberts/cs91/projects/ethics-of-ai/index.html

www.aaai.org/aitopics/pmwiki/pmwiki.php/AITopics/Ethics/

http://ethics.csc.ncsu.edu/risks/ai/

www.ethicsofthefuture.com/2010/09/at-what-point-does-artificial.html

Many computer scientists are also concerned that developments in artificial intelligence might lead to loss of human control over computer systems, causing profound social disruptions, destruction of jobs, and even dangerous consequences.[43]

Clearly, there is no such thing as completely "value-free" technology. Human beings build it, use it, and have to live with the results.

We discuss ethical problems in more detail in Chapter 9.

Databases: Concerns about Privacy & Identity Theft

Databases have facilitated loss of privacy and identity theft, which have become significant concerns for many people.

If you're under 30, maybe you're at ease in sharing your activities and locations with your friends, as through Facebook or Twitter. But are you comfortable about having your movements tracked, as through GPS-locator phones, E-ZPasses, and satellite high-definition imagery (Google Earth)? Do you care if you're leaving a digital trail behind you that may wind up in corporate or government databases—or that that data might be widely disseminated, used for advertising, or stolen?

EXPERIENCE BOX

How the Rise of the Robots Will Affect Future Employment

Will there be any good jobs left for new college graduates?[44]

Americans are rightly concerned about the changing jobs picture, brought about not only by the lingering effects of the Great Recession but also by offshoring work to low-wage countries such as China, India, and the Philippines. And now we have robots that seem to be getting better and better at doing human tasks. How will they affect work in both the near and distant future?

The Changing Workforce

"If you can describe a job precisely, or write rules for doing it, it's unlikely to survive," says Fred Levy, a Massachusetts Institute of Technology economist. "Either we'll program a computer to do it, or we'll teach a foreigner to do it."[45]

Andrew McAfee, also of MIT and coauthor of *Race against the Machine,* points out that automation has currently propelled profits toward all-time highs, while wages as a share of gross domestic product is at a postwar low.[46] "The jobs that are going away aren't coming back," he says. "I have never seen a period where computers demonstrated as many skills and abilities as they have over the past seven years."[47] The result has been a "hollowing out" of the middle-class workforce that promises to continue as machines become more sophisticated and reach deeper into our lives.

Factory robots. Surgical assistants. Driverless cars. Mail-sorting machines. Self-propelling vacuum cleaners. Legal document readers. Foreign language translators. Machines are not only learning specific jobs, but they will learn to perform whole categories of traditional human jobs, suggests Carnegie Mellon robotics professor Illah Reza Nourbakhsh.[48] Even "knowledge work" will be affected. Of course, some technical occupations—software engineers, app designers, and others we describe in Chapter 9—will benefit from the march of technology. "Overall, though," says one report, "technology is eliminating far more jobs than it is creating."[49]

What Kind of Jobs Are Safer in the Short Term?

Some of the U.S. jobs that are susceptible to being taken over at some point by robots are also those that today are easily offshored—sent to foreign countries where the work can be done more cheaply. But there are jobs that are not easily sent overseas and, at present, not easily done by a machine, such as those that share the following traits, regardless of the industry they serve:

- **Face to face:** Some jobs involve *face-to-face contact,* such as being a salesperson with a specific territory or an emergency room doctor.
- **Physical contact:** Other jobs involve *physical contact,* such as those of dentists, nurses, massage therapists, gardeners, and nursing home aides.
- **Making high-end products:** *High-end products* that involve intensive research, precision assembly, and complex technology requiring skilled workers are good candidates for the U.S. labor market, says Eric Spiegel, CEO of the Siemens Corp. Low-end, low-technology products, such as textiles and furniture, will doubtless continue to be offshored.[50] And later, probably, be handled by robots.
- **Recognizing complex patterns:** Others involve the human ability to *recognize complex patterns,* which are hard to computerize, such as a physician's ability to diagnose an unusual disease. This also describes such jobs as teaching first grade or jobs that demand an intimate knowledge of the United States, such as marketing to American teenagers or lobbying Congress.[51]

What Kind of Jobs Are Safer in the Long Term?

Financial journalist Matthew Lynn suggests there are five possible strategies for future-proofing your career from the rise of the robots:[52]

- **Move upmarket:** Many customers appreciate the cheaper prices that come with automation (such as grocery checkout scanners). However, many people will pay for human service—"and the more refined that service is," says Lynn, "the more willing they will be to pay for it."
- **Find a new industry:** New technology and robots may certainly destroy some industries (travel agents, newspapers, bookstores), but it may take a while for them to take over other industries. "If you move fast," says Lynn, "you can stay ahead of the onslaught of automation."
- **Be creative:** Professions such as law, accounting, and medicine, which depend on the ability to retain and apply lots of complex information, are already being targeted by computers and robots. But there are areas that robots are not able to make creative connections in, such as spotting unusual precedents (law) or symptom clusters (medicine). The more creatively you can apply your training, the easier it will be to avoid being replaced by a robot.

Staying Flexible

"Jobs used to change very little or not at all over the course of several generations," says Jim Spohrer of the IBM Almaden Research Center in San Jose, California. "Now, they might change three or four times in a single lifetime." Flexibility—as in being willing to undergo retraining—thus becomes important.[53]

Fortunately, as the late management theorist Peter Drucker pointed out, the United States is "the only country that has a very significant continuing education system. This doesn't exist anywhere else." The United States is also the only country, he said, in which it is easy for younger people to move from one area at work to another.[54]

artificial intelligence (AI) (p. 438) Group of related technologies used for developing machines to emulate human qualities, such as learning, reasoning, communicating, seeing, and hearing. Why it's important: *Today the main areas of AI are expert systems, natural language processing, intelligent agents, pattern recognition, fuzzy logic, virtual reality and simulation devices, and robotics.*

Big Data analytics (p. 428) The process of examining large amounts of data of a variety of types to uncover hidden patterns, unknown correlations, and other useful information. Why it's important: *The primary goal of Big Data analytics is to help companies make better business decisions by enabling data specialists and other users to analyze huge volumes of transaction data as well as other data sources that may be left untapped by conventional business intelligence programs. A specific kind of analytics is* web analytics, *the measurement and analysis of Internet data to understand web usage.*

character (byte) (p. 410) A single letter, number, or special character. Why it's important: *Characters—such as A, B, C, 1, 2, 3, #, $, %—are part of the data storage hierarchy.*

computational intelligence (p. 438) AI that relies less on formal logical systems and more on experimental and trial-and-error methods. This branch of AI is based on *heuristics,* or rules of thumb, for solving a problem, rather than hard-and-fast formulas or algorithms. Why it's important: *Computational intelligence is at the center of many new technological developments*

conventional AI (p. 438) Branch of AI that attempts to mimic human intelligence through logic and symbol manipulation, as well as statistics. This branch of AI is based on *machine learning,* the development of techniques that allow a computer to simulate learning by generating rules from raw data fed into it. Why it's important: *Expert systems make heavy use of this kind of AI.*

data dictionary (p. 414) Also called *repository* or *database schema;* a procedures document or disk file that stores data definitions and descriptions of database structure. It may also monitor new entries to the database as well as user access to the database. Why it's important: *The data dictionary monitors the data being entered to make sure it conforms to the rules defined during data definition. The data dictionary may also help protect the security of the database by indicating who has the right to gain access to it.*

data mining (DM) (p. 425) Computer-assisted process of sifting through and analyzing vast amounts of data in order to extract hidden patterns and meaning and to discover new knowledge. Why it's important: *The purpose of DM is to describe past trends and predict future trends. Thus, data-mining tools might sift through a company's immense collections of customer, marketing, production, and financial data and identify what's worth noting and what's not.*

data storage hierarchy (p. 409) The levels of data stored in a computer database: bits, bytes (characters), fields (columns), records (rows), and tables (files). Why it's important: *Understanding the data storage hierarchy is necessary to understand how to use a database.*

data warehouse (p. 427) A database containing cleaned-up data and metadata (information about the data) stored using high-capacity-disk storage technology. Why it's important: *Data warehouses combine vast amounts of data from many sources in a database form that can be searched, for example, for patterns not recognizable with smaller amounts of data.*

database (p. 409) Logically organized collection of related data designed and built for a specific purpose, a technology for pulling together facts that allows the slicing and dicing and mixing and matching of data. Why it's important: *Businesses and organizations build databases to help them keep track of and manage their affairs. In addition, online database services put enormous research resources at the user's disposal.*

database administrator (DBA) (p. 416) Person who coordinates all related activities and needs for an organization's database. Why it's important: *The DBA determines user access privileges; sets standards, guidelines, and control procedures; assists in establishing priorities for requests; prioritizes conflicting user needs; develops user documentation and input procedures; and oversees the system's security.*

database management system (DBMS) (p. 412) Also called *database manager;* software that controls the structure of a database and access to the data. It allows users to manipulate more than one file at a time. Why it's important: *This software enables sharing of data (same information is available to different users); economy of files (several departments can use one file instead of each individually maintaining its own file, thus reducing data redundancy, which in turn reduces the expense of storage media and hardware); data integrity (changes made in the files in one department are automatically made in the files in other departments); and security (access to specific information can be limited to selected users).*

DBMS utilities (p. 416) Programs that allow users to maintain databases by creating, editing, and deleting data, rows (records), and tables (files). Why it's important: *DBMS utilities allow people to establish what is acceptable input data, to monitor the types of data being input, and to adjust display screens for data input.*

decision support system (DSS) (p. 435) Computer-based information system that helps managers with nonroutine decision-making tasks. Inputs consist of some summarized reports, some processed transaction data, and other internal data plus data from sources outside the organization. The outputs are flexible, on-demand reports. Why it's important: *A DSS is installed to help top managers and middle managers make strategic decisions about unstructured problems.*

executive support system (ESS) (p. 437) Also called an *executive information system (EIS);* DSS made especially for top managers. It draws on data from both inside and outside the organization. Why it's important: *The ESS includes capabilities for analyzing data and doing what-if scenarios to help with strategic decision making.*

expert system (p. 437) Also called *knowledge-based system;* set of interactive computer programs that helps users solve problems that would otherwise require the assistance of a human expert. Expert systems are created on the basis of knowledge collected on specific topics from human specialists, and they imitate the reasoning process of a human being. Why it's important: *Expert systems are used by both management and nonmanagement personnel to solve specific problems, such as how to reduce production costs, improve workers' productivity, or reduce environmental impact.*

field (column) (p. 410) Unit of data consisting of one or more characters (bytes). Examples of fields are your first name, your street address, or your Social Security number. Why it's important: *A collection of fields makes up a record.*

file (table) (p. 410) Collection of related records; the file is at the top of the data hierarchy. An example of a file is a stored listing of everyone employed in the same department of a company, including all names, addresses, and Social Security numbers. Why it's important: *A file is the collection of data or information that is treated as a unit by the computer; a collection of related files makes up a database.*

fuzzy logic (p. 446) Method of dealing with imprecise data and uncertainty, with problems that have many answers rather than one. Why it's important: *Unlike "crisp," yes-no digital logic, fuzzy logic deals with probability and credibility.*

heuristics (p. 438) Rules of thumb (aids) for solving a problem, rather than hard-and-fast formulas or algorithms. (The term derives from the Greek for "find" or "discover.") Why it's important: *A heuristic is a mental shortcut that allows people to solve problems and make judgments quickly and efficiently. Heuristic strategies shorten decision-making time.*

intelligent agent (p. 442) Software with built-in intelligence that monitors work tasks, asks questions, and performs work tasks, such as roaming networks, on the user's behalf. Why it's important: *An intelligent agent can filter messages, scan news services, travel over communications lines to databases, and collect files to add to a personal database.*

machine learning (p. 438) The development of techniques that allow a computer to simulate learning by generating rules from raw data fed into it. Why it's important: *Machine learning is a branch of AI focused on getting computers to act without being explicitly programmed.*

management information system (MIS) (p. 435) Computer-based information system that uses data recorded by TPS as input into programs that produce summary, exception, periodic, and on-demand reports of the organization's performance. Why it's important: *An MIS principally assists middle managers, helping them make tactical decisions—spotting trends and getting an overview of current business activities.*

metadata (p. 414) Data that describes other data, such as the field name, the data type (text, numeric, and so on), and the field size (expected length of each data for each field). Why it's important: *Metadata is included in the database's data dictionary; it defines the basic organization of the database and contains a list of all tables in the database, the number of records in each file, and may indicate who has the right to access it. Metadata summarizes basic information about data, which makes finding and working with specific data items easier.*

multidimensional database (MDB) (p. 423) Type of database that models data as facts, dimensions, or numerical measures for use in the interactive analysis of large amounts of data for decision-making purposes. A multidimensional database uses the idea of a cube to represent the dimensions of data available to a user. Why it's important: *A multidimensional database allows users to ask questions in colloquial English.*

natural language processing (p. 442) Study of ways for computers to recognize and understand human language, whether in spoken or written form. Why it's important: *Natural languages make it easier to work with computers.*

neural network (p. 447) An area of AI; a network of processors that are interconnected in a way that is similar to the connections between neurons, or nerve cells, in the human body. Why it's important: *The neural network is able to simulate the behavior of biological neural networks, as in pattern recognition, language processing, and problem solving; it is able to learn from example and does not require detailed instructions. Neural networks have been used in machine vision, credit-card fraud detection, and diagnosis of heart attacks.*

object-oriented database (p. 422) Database that uses "objects," software written in small, reusable chunks, as elements within database files. An object consists of (1) data in any form, including graphics, audio, and video, and (2) instructions for the action to be taken on the data. Why it's important: *A hierarchical or network database might contain only numeric and text data. By contrast, an object-oriented database might also contain photographs, sound bites, and video clips. Moreover, the object would store operations, called* methods, *the programs that objects use to process themselves.*

office information system (OIS) (p. 433) Also called *office automation system (OAS);* computer information system that combines various technologies to reduce the manual labor needed to operate an office efficiently and increase productivity; used at all levels of an organization. Why it's important: *An OIS uses a network to integrate such technologies as fax, voice mail, email, scheduling software, word processing, and desktop publishing, among others, and make them available throughout the organization.*

pattern recognition (p. 442) Use software to identify recurring patterns and to recognize the connections between the perceived patterns and similar patterns stored in a database. Why it's important: *Pattern recognition is used in data mining to discover previously unnoticed patterns; in facial-recognition software to identify faces; and in handwriting recognition, fingerprint identification, robot vision, and automatic voice recognition.*

query by example (QBE) (p. 421) Feature of query language programs whereby the user asks for information in a database by using a sample record to define the qualifications he or she wants for selected records. Why it's important: *QBE simplifies database use.*

record (row) (p. 410) Collection of related fields. An example of a record is your name and address and Social Security number. Why it's important: *Related records make up a table (file).*

relational database (p. 419) Database that relates, or connects, data in different tables of rows and columns through the use of primary keys, or common data elements. In this arrangement there are no access paths down through a hierarchy. In database terminology, the tables are called *relations* (files), the rows are called *tuples* (records), and the columns are called *attributes* (fields). Why it's important: *The relational database is now the most common database structure; it is more flexible than hierarchical and network database models.*

report generator (p. 416) In a database management system, a program users can employ to produce on-screen or printed-out documents from all or part of a database. Why it's important: *Report generators allow users to easily produce finished-looking reports.*

robotics (p. 444) Development and study of machines that can perform actions normally done by living beings. Why it's important: *Commercial and industrial robots perform jobs more cheaply or with greater accuracy and reliability than humans. They are also used for jobs that are too dirty, dangerous, or dull to be suitable for humans. Robots are widely used in manufacturing, assembly and packing, transport, earth and space exploration, surgery, weaponry, laboratory research, and mass production of consumer and industrial goods.*

simulator (p. 444) Device that represents the behavior of physical or abstract systems. Why it's important: *Virtual reality simulation technologies are widely applied for training purposes.*

the Singularity (p. 451) Also called *the technological singularity,* a moment when humans would have created self-aware, smarter-than-human machines that are capable of designing computers and robots that are better than humans can make today. Why it's important: *According to this concept, technological progress would have accelerated so much that machine intelligence would dominate, transferring the contents of human brains and thought processes into a computing environment, making a form of immortality possible.*

strong AI (p. 439) The branch of AI that makes the claim that computers can be made to think on a level that is at least equal to humans and possibly even be conscious of themselves. Why it's important: *Proponents of strong AI believe that it's possible for computers to have the kind of wide-ranging problem-solving ability that people have; the development of this kind of computer could help human beings to study intelligence.* (*Compare with* **weak AI.**)

structured query language (SQL) (p. 421) Standard language used to create, modify, maintain, and query relational databases. Why it's important: *SQL simplifies database use.*

table (See **file.**)

transaction processing system (TPS) (p. 434) Computer-based information system that keeps track of the transactions needed to conduct business. Inputs are transaction data (such as bills or orders). Outputs are processed transactions (such as bills or paychecks). Why it's important: *The TPS helps supervisory managers in making operational decisions. The data collected by a TPS is typically stored in databases.*

virtual reality (VR) (p. 442) Computer-generated artificial reality that projects a person into a sensation of three-dimensional space. Why it's important: *VR is employed in simulators for training programs.*

weak AI (p. 438) The branch of AI that makes the claim that computers can be programmed to *simulate* human cognition and only *some* human cognition, to solve particular problems or reasoning tasks that do not encompass fully human intelligence. Why it's important: *Weak AI suggests that some "thinking-like" features can be added to computers to make them more useful tools.* (*Compare with* **strong AI.**)

CHAPTER REVIEW

stage 1 LEARNING MEMORIZATION

"I can recognize and recall information."

Self-Test Questions

1. According to the data storage hierarchy, databases are composed of (small to large) __________, __________, __________, __________, and __________.
2. An individual piece of data within a record is called a(n) __________.
3. A(n) __________ coordinates all activities related to an organization's database.
4. The process of examining large amounts of data of a variety of types to uncover hidden patterns, unknown correlations, and other useful information is called __________.
5. The five types of database models are __________, __________, __________, __________, and ______.
6. A single letter or number is a(n) __________.
7. A(n) __________ is a logically organized collection of related data designed and built for a specific purpose.
8. A(n) __________ is a collection of related fields (columns).
9. A(n) __________ is an automatic device that performs functions ordinarily performed by human beings.
10. The goal of __________ is to enable the computer to communicate with the user in the user's native language.
11. __________ is a group of related technologies used for developing machines to emulate human qualities such as learning, reasoning, communicating, seeing, and hearing.

12. Devices that represent the behavior of physical or abstract systems are called ________.
13. When unauthorized persons use your name to get cash and buy things, it is called ________.
14. Most organizations have six departments: ________, ________, ________, ________, ________, and ________.
15. ________ is used to create, modify, maintain, and query relational databases.
16. Data that describes other data is called ________.

Multiple-Choice Questions

1. Which of the following is *not* an advantage of a DBMS?
   a. file sharing
   b. reduced data redundancy
   c. increased data redundancy
   d. improved data integrity
   e. increased security
2. Which of the following qualities are necessary for information to be "good"?
   a. concise
   b. complete
   c. verifiable
   d. current
   e. all of these
3. Which of the following database models relates, or connects, data in different files through the use of a key, or common data element?
   a. hierarchical
   b. network
   c. object-oriented
   d. relational
   e. offline
4. Which of the following areas of study is *not* included in AI?
   a. pattern recognition
   b. fuzzy logic
   c. transaction processing systems
   d. natural language processing
   e. robotics
5. Which of the following levels is *not* a management level?
   a. strategic
   b. tactical
   c. hierarchical
   d. operational
   e. all of these are management levels

True-False Questions

T F 1. The use of key fields makes it easier to locate a record in a database.

T F 2. The field of weak AI is working on making a computer-based machine that will think and feel just like a human being.

T F 3. A database is an organized collection of integrated files.

T F 4. Data mining is used only for small databases.

T F 5. A character is smaller than a field.

T F 6. A report generator is a machine that produces electricity by calculating complex algorithms.

T F 7. A data dictionary defines the basic organization of the database and contains a list of all files in the database.

T F 8. The most common type of database is the multidimensional model.

T F 9. Expert systems are not interactive.

T F 10. You need only software to create virtual reality.

T F 11. A knowledge base is part of a natural language system.

stage 2 LEARNING COMPREHENSION

"I can recall information in my own terms and explain it to a friend."

Short-Answer Questions

1. Name three responsibilities of a database administrator.
2. What is data mining?
3. Briefly explain what a data warehouse is.
4. List four basic advantages provided by database management systems.
5. What are expert systems used for?
6. What is SQL? QBE? Oracle? Access? DB2?
7. What are intelligent agents used for?
8. What do you need to experience virtual reality?
9. What is the main difference between weak AI and strong AI?
10. What are the four main areas of artificial intelligence?
11. What is a DSS used for? An ESS?

"I can apply what I've learned, relate these ideas to other concepts, build on other knowledge, and use all these thinking skills to form a judgment."

Knowledge in Action

1. Interview someone who works with or manages an organization's database. What types of records make up the database? Which departments use it? What database structure is used? What are the types and sizes of storage devices? How many servers are used? Where are they? Was the database software custom-written?
2. Are you comfortable with giving away some of your privacy for increased security? Why or why not? How far would you let the government go in examining people's private lives?
3. If you could design a robot, what kind would you create? What would it do?
4. If you could build an expert system, what would it do? What kinds of questions would you ask experts in order to elicit the appropriate information?
5. Should Internet-purchased products or services have a sales tax (like items purchased in regular stores)? Why or why not?
6. Do you know someone who refuses to use the Internet in any manner that requires entering any personal information whatsoever? Give some reasons for disagreeing and for agreeing with this person.

Web Exercises

1. Visit these sites about data mining, and the search for meaningfulness in large quantities of data:

   www.buzzle.com/articles/advantages-of-data-mining.html

   www.zentut.com/data-mining/advantages-and-disadvantages-of-data-mining/

   http://ethics.csc.ncsu.edu/privacy/mining/study.php

   http://highbrowmagazine.com/2558-hold-ethics-surveillance-data-mining-and-destruction-personal-privacy/

   www.dmbenchmarking.com/

   www.dmg.org/

   www.expertstown.com/data-mining-examples/

   How does data mining affect you directly? How could it be used in your planned profession? What are some of the ethical implications of data mining?
2. Store loyalty cards ask consumers to trade detailed personal information in return for the promise of savings—which may in fact not exist. Some experts say the reason that stores offer cards is so that they can profile and target their customers more accurately—not to give you savings but to increase their bottom line. Also, your personal information can be sold or traded to third parties.

   One way that stores create customer profiles is by the use of data mining. There are positive aspects to data mining, such as fraud detection, but there is a darker side to data mining too.

   Stores may use the address information from your loyalty card application to match up your shopping history with data from other databases or public records (income, how much you paid for your house) so that the store knows what kinds of specials to offer you. Information about your shopping habits can be accessed with a subpoena or warrant and used against you in court proceedings. In a "trip-and-fall" case in California, a man shopping at a Southern California grocery store sued after falling in one of the aisles. It was reported (although the store denied it) that the store threatened to use his shopping history—which included large amounts of alcohol—against him in the proceedings.

   Some states limit the types of information that a grocery store can collect from you when you register for a loyalty card. For example, California state law prohibits a grocery store from requiring that you turn over your Social Security card or your driver's license number. However, data matching techniques mean that this provides very little protection of your privacy rights.

   Find out more about loyalty cards. Read the articles at:

   http://alameda.patch.com/groups/opinion/p/have-grocery-loyalty-cards-gone-too-far-3b5e7889

   http://couponsinthenews.com/2013/04/04/store-says-requiring-loyalty-card-at-self-checkout-is-for-our-own-good/

   www.news-gazette.com/news/local/2012-05-16/loyalty-cards-extra-savings-or-invasion-privacy.html

   www.timesunion.com/business/article/About-store-loyalty-cards-4102197.php

   www.bostonglobe.com/business/2013/07/05/cutting-loyalty-cards-shaw-exception-supermarket-industry/2bVJOBNdOQBQmOeGOvzEzH/story.html

   Find a few more articles, and then write a short report on the ethical aspects and the practical aspects of using loyalty cards.
3. How much information about you is out there? Run various search strings about yourself to see just how private your life is. Also read a few articles about how social-networking sites commodify users' personal information and sell it to all sorts of entities.
4. An extensive database featuring photographs of and detailed information on each inmate of the Florida Department of Corrections can be found at this website:

   www.dc.state.fl.us/inmateinfo/inmateinfomenu.asp

Click on Search All Corrections Offenders Databases. Then, in the text boxes, type in a common last name and a common first name, and anything else you care to enter, and click on Submit Request.

Click on any of the following links to see the offender records that matched your search criteria:

Inmate Population Search Results

Inmate Release Search Results

Supervised Population Search Results

Absconder/Fugitive Search Results

What kind of databases do you think these are? Do you think such databases are useful? Ethical? If you think they are useful, give your reasons.

5. What is a DNA database? Visit the following websites to learn more:

   www.fbi.gov/about-us/lab/biometric-analysis/codis

   www.economist.com/debate/overview/141

   http://ndbserver.rutgers.edu/

   www.isogg.org/wiki/DNA_databases

   www.globalresearch.ca/challenging-liberty-the-danger-of-dna-databases/5340517

   Would you want to be included in a DNA database?

6. Read about the Homeland Security database:

   www.hsdl.org/

   www.hssd.us/

   http://publicsafety.utah.gov/emergencymanagement/homeland.html

   What is your opinion of the efficacy of such a database? Have you any concerns about the ethics or constitutionality of any aspects of this database?

7. Virtual reality is being used in some surprising areas. Visit:

   www.vrs.org.uk/virtual-reality-applications/index.html

   www.youtube.com/watch?v=idHKRWtk6dg

   www.vrac.iastate.edu/press/detail.php?s=press&r=325

   www.sciencedaily.com/news/computers_math/virtual_reality/

   Which area might you be interested in, and why?

THE CHALLENGES OF THE DIGITAL AGE

Society & Information Technology Today

Chapter Topics & Key Questions

UNIT 9A: *Security, Privacy, & Surveillance Concerns*

9.1 **Security Issues: Threats to Computers & Communications Systems** What are some key threats to computers?

9.2 **Security Safeguards: Protecting Computers & Communications** What are the characteristics of the five components of security?

9.3 **Privacy & Surveillance: Data Collectors & Spies** How do we find a balance between privacy and safety with the uses of information technology?

UNIT 9B: *Other Social, Economic, & Political Issues*

9.4 **Truth Issues: Manipulating Digital Data** What are some ways digitized output can be manipulated to fool people?

9.5 **Quality-of-Life Issues: The Environment, Mental Health, Child Protection, & the Workplace** How does information technology create environmental, mental health, pornography, and workplace problems?

9.6 **Economic & Political Issues: Employment & the Haves/Have-Nots** How may technology affect employment and the gap between rich and poor?

Download the free UIT 11e App for key term flash cards quizzes and a game, *Over the Edge*

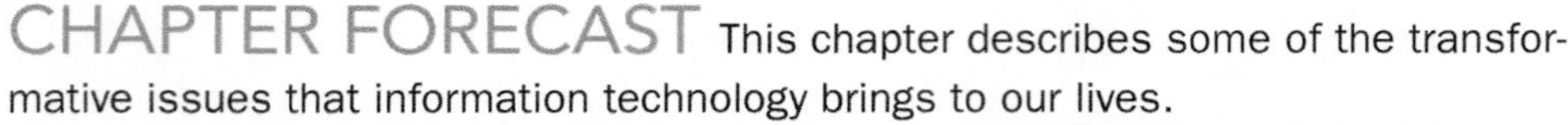

CHAPTER FORECAST This chapter describes some of the transformative issues that information technology brings to our lives.

Unit 9A discusses security, privacy, and surveillance concerns. We first discuss some key threats to computer systems, such as errors, accidents, and natural hazards. We then describe computer crimes, such as theft of hardware, software, intellectual property, time and services, and information, as well as Internet-related crimes and crimes of malice (crashing of entire systems). We next cover security safeguards: deterrents to computer crime, identification and access, encryption, protection of software and data, and disaster-recovery plans. We conclude the unit by considering privacy and surveillance, including continuing threats to privacy from business organizations, domestic and foreign governments, and criminal groups.

In Unit 9B, we discuss other social, economic, and political issues. First we consider truth issues and the manipulation or falsification of all sorts of data, including text, sound, and images, which has led to problems with truth and credibility. We then consider quality-of-life issues, such as how information technology adversely affects the environment, mental health, the welfare of children, and workplace productivity. Finally, we consider economic and political issues, including the ongoing debate about whether information technology is reducing job availability and widening the gap between the rich and the poor.

UNIT 9A: *Security, Privacy, & Surveillance Concerns*

"We have a technology that isn't waiting for you to ask it a question, but is anticipating what you need and when is the best time to deliver that."[1]

So says the CEO of a firm whose technology is used to develop *predictive search apps*—applications that know what you want before you do.

These are "new tools that act as robotic personal assistants, anticipating what you need before you ask for it," according to one description. Such personal assistant apps as Google Now "guess what you want to know based on the digital breadcrumbs you leave, like calendar entries, e-mails, social network activity, and the places you take your phone."[2]

This is something new under the sun. Predictive search apps, which are tailored to specific mobile devices, do not require you to enter a search query. Using machine learning to get to know you over time, they operate from context—your location, time of day, and digital activity.

Predictive apps are intended to help us deal with the constant inundation of digital information, much of it cloud-based. Some people, however, see the new technology as just the latest intrusion into our private lives, mining digital personal information about us whose uses we cannot always foresee. "Computers have invaluable uses for specialized work," says San Francisco historian and commentator Harold Gilliam, "but we need to question the assumption that whatever ails modern society can be cured by more information." Indeed, Gilliam goes on, many users "are hypnotized by the computer's power to summon endless arrays of facts—information without context, data without values, knowledge without perspective."[3]

Such matters have taken on more urgency since the beginning of the war on terrorism that started on September 11, 2001, when terrorist-hijacked planes destroyed the World Trade Center Twin Towers in New York City and part of the Pentagon in Washington, D.C. Will the resulting tougher security rules imposed everywhere (including on the use of information technology) be beneficial? How can we evaluate the effect of more names in more databases, for instance, on lost privacy and even lost liberty? We consider these matters in this chapter.

Is More Information Better?

www.huffingtonpost.com/don-tapscott/technology-promises-a-bet_b_2542025.html

www.aeonmagazine.com/living-together/do-we-have-a-privacy-instinct-or-are-we-wired-to-share/

http://iorgforum.org/

www.boston.com/bostonglobe/ideas/articles/2010/11/28/information_overload_the_early_years/

9.1 SECURITY ISSUES: Threats to Computers & Communications Systems

A computer connected to the Internet can encounter a breathtaking number of security threats.

Internet users just don't have "street smarts" about online safety, a survey found, and that makes them vulnerable.[4] We may think we can recognize when we're being manipulated (legally or illegally), but in fact we are often wrong. Security issues, then, go right to the heart of the workability and usefulness of computer systems. Here we discuss the following threats. *(• See Panel 9.1.)*

- Errors, accidents, and natural hazards
- Computer crimes
- Computer criminals

- Human errors
- Procedural errors
- Software errors
- "Dirty data" problems
- Electromechanical problems
- Natural hazards
- Theft of hardware
- Theft of software
- Theft of intellectual property
- Theft of time and services
- Theft of information
- Internet-related fraud
- Crimes of malice: crashing entire systems

panel 9.1

Examples of threats to computers and communications systems

Errors, Accidents, & Natural Hazards

Human, procedural, and software errors, as well as "dirty data" and electromechanical problems and certainly natural hazards, are constant threats to computer systems.

Which would you trust—human or computer? If you were a pilot and your plane's collision-avoidance computer told you to ascend but a human air traffic controller told you to descend, which order would you follow? In 2001 a Russian pilot near the Swiss-German border ignored his computer (against mandatory regulations) and complied with erroneous human orders, resulting in a collision with another plane.[5] Conversely, in 2013, pilots for a South Korean airliner attempting a computer-controlled approach to landing in San Francisco crashed after hitting a seawall at the beginning of the runway, killing two people. The event triggered concerns by some aviation experts that "pilots for foreign carriers can fail to master basic skills due to a reliance on automated instrument systems," according to a newspaper report.[6] Clearly, neither the computer's judgment nor human judgment is infallible.

HUMAN ERRORS Human errors can be of several types. Quite often, when experts speak of the "unintended effects of technology," what they are referring to are the unexpected things people do with it. Among the ways in which people can complicate the workings of a system are the following:[7]

- **Humans often are not good at assessing their own information needs:** For example, many users acquire a computer system that either is not sophisticated enough or is far more complex than they need.
- **Human emotions affect performance:** For instance, one frustrating experience with some aspect of a computer is enough to make some people abandon the whole system. But smashing your keyboard isn't going to get you any closer to learning how to use it better.
- **Humans act on their perceptions, which may not be fast enough to keep up:** In modern information environments, human perceptions are often too slow to keep up with all the signals, as happens all the time with people trying to text from their cellphones while driving.

TECH TALES How Slow Perceptions Lead to Errors: Texting While Driving

In July 2013 in Spain, the driver of a passenger train was talking on his phone when the train, traveling at 119 miles per hour, went into a sharp bend with a posted speed limit of 49 mph. The crash left 79 people dead.[8]

There have been years-long national campaigns against texting while driving, yet 68% of drivers ages 18–29 still report engaging in the practice (compared with 34% of all drivers).[9] But human perception often isn't fast enough to react to driving challenges while thus distracted. Indeed, people who drive while texting are 23 times more likely to have an accident than a nondistracted driver.[10] Texting behind the wheel can be even more dangerous than driving drunk.

Sending text messages while driving has been found to be dangerous even with hands-free devices, according to a Texas study.[11] "Drivers took about twice as long to react as when they weren't texting," says an account of the study, "and spent less time looking at the road no matter what texting method they used," whether manually or using a voice-to-text smartphone app.[12]

Texting is hazardous even when you're *not* doing it in a car. A study suggests that "distracted walking is leading to a soaring number of pedestrian injuries among 16- to 19-year-olds.[13] Texting, plus listening to music or talking on the phone, seems to be leading to increased pedestrian deaths nationwide.[14]

Think we're good at assessing our information environment? ■

PROCEDURAL ERRORS Some spectacular computer failures have occurred because someone didn't follow procedures. In 1999, for instance, the $125 million Mars Climate Orbiter was fed data expressed in pounds, the English unit of force, instead of newtons, the metric unit (about 22% of a pound). As a result, the spacecraft flew too close to the surface of Mars and broke apart. In 2009 a highly confidential document listing the U.S. nuclear sites was inadvertently posted on the Government Printing Office's website.[15]

SOFTWARE ERRORS We often hear about "software glitches" or "software bugs." A *software bug* is an error in a program that causes it not to work properly. For example, in 2008 experts found a software glitch that would have allowed attackers to gain control of water treatment plants, natural gas pipelines, and other utilities.[16] In 2012, a programming error caused more than 90% of the people chosen to receive a U.S. Permanent Resident Card in the so-called Green Card Lottery to be selected from only the first 2 of the 30 days of the registration period, which "did not represent a fair random selection of the entrants, as required by U.S. law," according to a government website.[17]

"DIRTY DATA" PROBLEMS The expression "garbage in, garbage out" (GIGO) describes what happens when *dirty data*—erroneous, incomplete, or outdated data—is input to a computer system, as when you make typing errors and then don't spell-check or grammar-check them. A lot of database problems result from dirty data entered by data-entry people around the world (perhaps because they are dealing with text or spreadsheet files from different countries). Although databases are a time-saving resource for information seekers, they can also speed up and magnify bad data.

Some common causes of dirty data are wrong or inconsistent data formats, wrong field sizes, logical inconsistency (as in spelling the same name different ways), and user errors resulting from lack of training or misunderstanding of procedures.[18] Clearly, then, there are good reasons for checking your school, credit, and medical records from time to time so you can make corrections before they cause complications.

ELECTROMECHANICAL PROBLEMS Mechanical systems, such as printers, and electrical systems, such as circuit boards, don't always work. They may be faultily constructed, get dirty or overheated, wear out, or become damaged in some other way.

TECH TALES Glitches in the System: How Electrical & Mechanical Problems Can Make Computers Fail

Power failures (brownouts and blackouts) can shut down a system. Power surges can also burn out equipment. One major area of concern is that as consumers fill their houses with iPhones, plasma TVs, and other electronics connected to outlets vulnerable to lightning strikes, electrical storms can cause far more harm. Indeed, the average cost of insurance claims for lightning damage rose from $2,646 in 2004 to $6,400 in 2012.[19]

One of many companies that fix organizations' dirty data

ComResource

Your Technology Solutions Provider

HOME | WHO WE ARE | OUR SERVICES | WORK FOR US | NEWS & EVENTS | CO

The High Cost of Treating a Dirty Data Infection

Jun 25, 2013 12:37 pm

You notice a few mistakes at first – outdated contact information for someone, irreconcilable reports, a strange customer name that's infiltrated your favorite database. The Help Desk has a recorded message stating "...technicians are looking into system performance issues, and an update will be posted in one hour." After stepping through the prompts, you speak to a real person, and politely get brushed off.

The problems may be resolved in an hour, maybe in a day. Or, you may be witnessing the first stage of a dirty data outbreak. Dirty data functions as an infection, and at ComResource, we treat the problem accordingly. If dirty data has infiltrated your environment, you need to deal with it before it gets out of hand.

One of the biggest problems with dirty data is that it looks similar to "good" data. Dirty data appears alongside the clean data that you rely on to make solid business decisions. Just one misplaced character may not seem like a big deal when you are dealing with petabytes of data, but that single character can lead directly to decreased customer satisfaction and lost revenue.

Years of mergers and acquisitions, with their requisite system integrations, help to propagate the risk of infection. As information systems become more complex, the chances of any one person understanding how a data element flows throughout the organization decreases. This means that your chances of identifying the source of the outbreak and vulnerable systems are greatly diminished. Even if the source is identified, can you successfully locate, isolate and remove all signs of the infection? A single piece of isolated dirty data in your systems may not be a problem today, or even tomorrow; while it exists, there is a chance that it will escape isolation, and the infection will begin.

Flaws in paper-based voting machines, such as jammed printers or poorly designed touch-screen ballots, have caused voters to make mistakes that invalidated their votes.[20] These failures have been used as an argument for using electronic voting systems, such as that used by 46,000 military voters in the 2010 election.[21] However, there are equally good arguments for *not* letting people vote electronically, such as the risk of outsiders taking over the system and changing results.[22] ■

Modern systems are made up of thousands of parts, all of which interrelate in ways that are impossible to anticipate. Because of that complexity, "normal accidents" are inevitable, asserts sociologist Charles Perrow.[23] That is, it is almost certain, he says, that some combinations of minor failures will eventually amount to something catastrophic. Indeed, it is just such collections of small failures that led to catastrophes such as the blowing up of the *Challenger* space shuttle in 1986 and the near meltdown of the Three Mile Island nuclear power plant in 1979. In the Digital Age, "normal accidents" are not anomalies, experts say, but are to be expected. They can also be more global in their impact.[24]

Such considerations suggest that we need to take a hard look at the concept of storing all our information "in the cloud"—that is, online instead of on our own desktop and mobile devices. Putting all our information online means our data could be at constant risk to exposure to errors, accidents, and natural hazards.

In October 2012, high winds and water from Hurricane Sandy caused devastation to northeastern New Jersey and areas around New York City.

NATURAL HAZARDS Whatever is harmful to property (and people) is harmful to computer systems, and this certainly includes natural disasters and weather extremes. Ice storms (as in eastern Canada), hurricanes (Katrina on the Gulf Coast, Sandy on the Atlantic Seaboard), earthquakes (as in New Zealand and Japan), tsunamis (Thailand and Japan), and giant wildfires (Texas and Colorado) are natural disasters that can disable all the electronic systems we take for granted. So can heat, storms, and drought brought about by the rise in weather extremes triggered by climate change and challenge not only the concrete, steel, and engineering undergirding the roads and levees in the United States but also the nation's power grid.[25] In fact, the U.S. energy supply is ill-prepared for the effects of climate change, according to the Energy Department, with hot weather lowering river levels and reducing hydroelectric power.[26]

more info!

What Is Computer Forensics?

Forensics is the process of using scientific knowledge for collecting, analyzing, and presenting evidence to the courts. (*Forensics* means "to bring to the court" or "suitable to a court of law.") Computer forensics combines elements of law and computer science to collect and analyze data from computer systems, networks, wireless communications, and storage devices in a way that is admissible as evidence in a court of law.

www.computer-forensics.net/

http://computer.howstuffworks.com/computer-forensic.htm

www.computerforensicsworld.com/

http://staff.washington.edu/dittrich/forensics.html

www.isfce.com/

Information about a career in computer forensics:

http://career-advice.monster.com/job-search/company-industry-research/careers-in-computer-forensics/article.aspx

http://jobsearchtech.about.com/od/computerjob13/a/comp_forensics_2.htm

www.legal-criminal-justice-schools.com/Criminal-Justice-Degrees/How-to-Become-a-Computer-Forensics-Investigator.html

www.computer-forensics-recruiter.com/careers.html

TECH TALES The Risks of Natural Hazards: How Bad Can It Get?

Electrical blackouts seem to be an ongoing fact of life in the United States—although none yet compete with the 2012 blackout in India, the largest in history, which affected 670 million people, or roughly 10% of the world's people. It's speculated the failure was brought about in part because of low monsoon rains, which placed excessive demands on the electric grid.[27]

"The U.S. grid contains 160,000 miles of high-voltage lines, 5 million miles of distribution lines, thousands of generators and transformers, and tens of thousands of other pieces of equipment," says Carnegie Mellon engineering professor Jay Apt. "It is difficult to imagine hardening so massive a structure against random, natural disturbances."[28]

Although new tools are being installed to stop some future electricity failures, without power and communications connections, not just computers but cellphones, automated teller machines, credit-card verifiers, and bank computers are useless.[29]

The biggest danger, of course, is that if global warming continues at its current rate through 2100, rising seas will put 1,100 cities and towns (including Miami, Virginia Beach, and Jacksonville) mostly underwater at high tide.[30] ■

Computer Crimes

There are many types of crimes that involve computers, but they fall into basically two types: the computer is the target or the computer is the tool.

Because of the opening of borders, the growth of low-cost international transportation, and the rise of the Internet, crime in general has become globalized, and computer crime is a big part of it. **A computer crime can be of two types. (1) It can be an illegal act perpetrated against computers or telecommunications, such as hardware theft, or (2) it can be the use of computers or telecommunications to accomplish an illegal act, such as identity theft.** For instance, although not all computer crime is committed by organized crime members, a good deal of it is, and they not only steal hardware, software, and data; they also use spam, phishing, and the like to commit identity theft and online fraud. Even street gangs now have their own websites, most of them perfectly legal, but some could possibly be used as chat rooms for drug distribution. In addition, gangs use computers the way legal businesses do—as business tools—but they use them for illegal purposes, such as keeping track of gambling debts and stolen goods.

THEFT OF HARDWARE Hardware theft can range from shoplifting an accessory in a computer store to removing a laptop or cellphone from someone's car. Professional criminals may steal shipments of microprocessor chips off a loading dock; steal desktop computers, laptops, and other devices for their parts; or even pry cash machines out of shopping center walls.

You can make hardware theft of your electronic items harder by following some guidelines, such as those shown below. (• *See Panel 9.2.*)

THEFT OF SOFTWARE Software theft can be large scale, on the level of industrial espionage, as when in 2013 China's biggest wind turbine company was accused of conspiring with the employee of a Massachusetts wind company to steal the American firm's software for controlling the flow of electricity.[31] Or it can be on the level at which some college students operate, such as pirating software (see Chapter 3), as in making an illegal copy of a commercial videogame.

Pirating software is so commonplace that software makers secretly prowl the Internet in search of purloined products and then try to get a court order to shut down the seller sites. They also look for organizations that "softlift"—companies, colleges, or other institutions that buy one copy of a program and make copies for many computers. In addition, software pirates often operate in China, Taiwan, Mexico, Russia, and various parts of Asia and Latin America, where the copying or counterfeiting of well-known software programs is practiced on a large scale. In some countries, most of the U.S. microcomputer software in use is thought to be illegally copied.

Many software pirates are reported by coworkers or fellow students to such organizations as the Software and Information Industry Association, the Interactive Digital Software Association, and the Business Software Alliance.

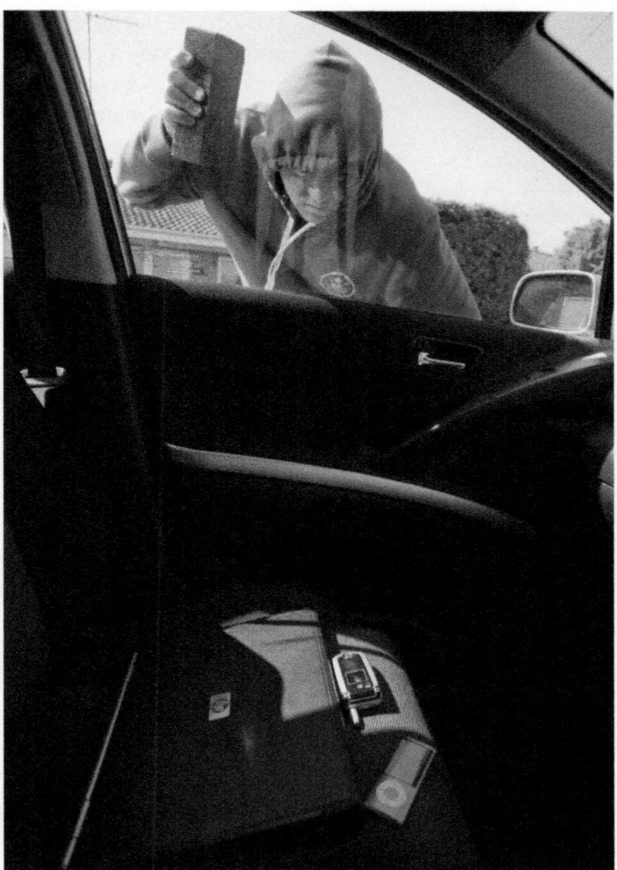

Laptop on a car seat. Computers left in cars are temptations for smash-and-grab thieves.

panel 9.2

Keeping your mobile devices safe

- Never leave your laptop, smartphone, or tablet unattended.
- Do not use obvious or flashy carrying cases on public transportation.
- Do not publicly show off items.
- Do not leave laptops and other devices in your car or in other exposed places.
- Pay attention in airports. Keep your eye on your laptop as you go through security. Hold onto it until the person in front of you has gone through the metal detector—and keep an eye out when it emerges on the other side of the screener.
- Be careful in hotels. If you stay in hotels, a security cable may not be enough. Try not to leave your laptop out in your room; use the safe in your room if there is one. If you're using a security cable to lock down your laptop, hang the "do not disturb" sign on your door.
- Lock devices so that others cannot activate them.
- Secure their storage area (laptops should always be equipped with security cables and locked away when not in use).
- Use ID labels.
- Use a permanent marker or engraving on a metal, tamper-resistant tag on the device's outer case to record your ownership (don't use your phone number or address); ultraviolet markers are available at business supply stores.
- Register the device with its manufacturer.
- Record the serial numbers/model numbers immediately after purchasing them, and keep these numbers in a safe place, not with the devices.
- Use laptop-locating software, such as LoJack for Laptops by Absolute Software, which enables you to remotely locate, lock, and/or delete the data on your computer before it falls into the wrong hands. Also LoJack for Laptops has a dedicated theft recovery team that works with local law enforcement to recover stolen laptops and return them to the owners.
- Use log-in passwords on all your devices. Back up all your data on something that is kept in a different place from the devices.

Survival Tip

Keeping Track of Your Smartphone

Here are some ways to avoid losing your smartphone:

- Tape your name and some kind of contact info (but not your home address) to your phone.
- Use a phone case that clips to your clothes or hangs around your neck; don't just stick your phone in your pocket or keep it in your hand when not using it.
- When traveling, check seats (plane, bus) and hotel rooms when leaving.
- Consider paying for a device-finding service in case you lose it, or install a phone-tracking app on your phone.
- When going through airport security, put your phone in your carry-on bag.
- Back up your phone's directory to another electronic device or with your cellphone carrier.

Survival Tip

Reporting Software Pirates

Software pirates can be reported to:

www.ic3.gov/default.aspx

https://reporting.bsa.org/r/report/add.aspx?

www.siia.net/piracy/report/report.asp

www.ehow.com/how_5266659_report-software-piracy.html

THEFT OF INTELLECTUAL PROPERTY Competing companies or individuals may break into a company's computer system to conduct industrial espionage—obtain trade secrets that they can use for competitive advantage. This, of course, is a criminal act.

However, many people may believe that illegally downloading music and movies is a victimless crime. To the entertainment industry, though, such stealing of their intellectual property is just plain piracy or theft. When you download or share a copyrighted song, movie, or software without the permission of the copyright holder, you are in violation of the copyright, for which you could face fines and be sued by the copyright holder. For instance, under federal law, people who download music illegally are liable for damages as high as $150,000 per song, even if they never distribute the music. (However, you are allowed to convert songs on an original CD that you own to digital files for personal use, which qualifies as "fair use" under U.S. copyright law. The point is that you are not allowed to distribute such copyrighted material to others.)

TECH TALES Stealing Music & Movies

People, especially students, were quick to discover the Internet music service Napster, founded in 1999, which in its original form allowed millions of people to exchange songs for free. Then illegal file swapping shifted from client-server services such as Napster to peer-to-peer services such as Kazaa, Grokster, Limeware, and StreamCast. Music CD sales shrank, and the music companies decided to go after downloaders. They did so by getting their names and addresses from Internet access providers and by monitoring traffic on file-swapping networks to obtain their IP addresses.

Once the thieves were identified, the record industry started filing copyright infringement lawsuits, principally against students illegally downloading songs on file-sharing networks at 21 college campuses. Some settled, at fees ranging from $2,000 to $10,000 and fines of $12,000 to $17,500.[32]

The government also became involved. In 2005, the U.S. Supreme Court ruled against a pair of file-sharing networks, and two days later record companies sued 784 people for illegally distributing songs from the networks.[33] In 2009 a Minnesota woman was compelled by a federal jury to pay record companies $80,000 for each of 24 songs ($1.92 million total) that she illegally shared on a file-sharing site.[34]

As for movies, the film industry has also taken aggressive aim at pirated products, such as those playing on YouTube.[35] For instance, in 2005 the government announced an 11-nation crackdown on organizations called "warez" (pronounced "wares"), groups that are sort of underground Internet co-ops set up to trade in copyrighted materials. Four men were charged with conspiring to violate copyright laws for operating an Internet site that offered stolen movies. Still, illegal movie downloads by digital pirates continue to cost the film industry billions every year. The vast majority of pirated movie download sites are movie file-sharing (P2P) sites, and they are constantly monitored by different agencies with the capability to trace illegal activity back to the server from which you downloaded. As a violator you could face a large fine or even jail time for piracy, as well as putting your system at risk for being infected with viruses or spyware borne by the pirate copies. ■

Film Theft

For information on the different types of movie theft, go to the Motion Picture Association of America's website:

www.mpaa.org/contentprotection/types-of-content-theft

This site also gives information on legal film downloading sites.

Piracy of intellectual property, whether software, music, or movies, ultimately harms everyone, directly or indirectly, because, says one writer, "thieves do not invest in research, design, production, development, or advertising." The result is "fewer advances in science, fewer new products, fewer new music CDs, fewer new movies, less new software, and higher prices for whatever is created."[36] Much better, then, to use websites offering video streaming legally, such as Netflix, Blockbuster, and Disney Video.

THEFT OF TIME & SERVICES The theft of computer time is more common than you might think. Probably the biggest instance is people using their employer's computer time to play games, do online shopping, or dip into web pornography. Some people even operate sideline businesses.

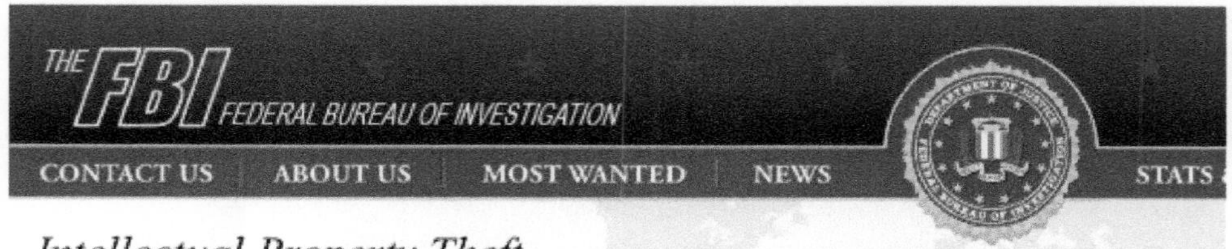

Intellectual Property Theft

Home • About Us • What We Investigate • White-Collar Crime • Intellectual Property Theft

It's an age-old crime: stealing.

But it's not about picking a pocket or holding up a bank. It's robbing people of their ideas, inventions, and creative expressions—what's called intellectual property—everything from trade secrets and proprietary products and parts to movies and music and software.

It's a growing threat—especially with the rise of digital technologies and Internet file sharing networks. And much of the theft takes place overseas, where laws are often lax and enforcement more difficult. All told, intellectual property theft costs U.S. businesses billions of dollars a year and robs the nation of jobs and lost tax revenues.

Preventing intellectual property theft is a priority of the FBI's criminal investigative program. We specifically focus on the theft of trade secrets and infringements on products that can impact consumers' health and safety, such as counterfeit aircraft, car, and electronic parts. Key to our success is linking the considerable resources and efforts of the private sector with law enforcement partners on local, state, federal, and international levels.

For years "phone phreaks" have bedeviled the telephone companies. For example, they have found ways to get into company voice mail systems and then use an extension to make long-distance calls at the company's expense. They have also found ways to tap into cellular phone networks and dial for free. Satellite-TV piracy has also grown at an alarming rate.

THEFT OF INFORMATION Bank robberies of the "stick 'em up" kind are on the decline, as criminals have discovered that bank holdups just don't pay—and there are greater rewards in online theft.[37]

In 2009 a black-hat hacker or cracker stole more than 500,000 patient records from a state-run database that tracked prescriptions in Virginia and demanded ransom for the return of the information.[38] In 2010 a young American and two Russian accomplices were convicted for carrying out the largest computer data theft in history, charged with stealing data from more than 130 million credit and debit cards, costing banks, companies, and insurers about $200 million.[39] Often cybercriminals sniff out vulnerable small firms. In 2012, a Brooklyn, New York, mannequin maker and importer had $1.2 million stolen out of its bank account in just hours through online transactions.[40]

Information thieves have infiltrated the files of the Social Security Administration, stolen confidential personal records, and sold the information. On college campuses, they have snooped on or stolen private information such as grades. They have broken into computers of the major credit bureaus and stolen credit information and have then used the information to charge purchases or have resold it to other people. They have plundered the credit-card numbers of millions of Americans and sold stolen identity data to conspirators in other countries.

INTERNET-RELATED FRAUD The U.S. Federal Trade Commission (FTC) received more than 2 million consumer complaints during 2012, with identity theft complaints making up the largest number (18%) of reports, followed by complaints about debt collection (10%),

FEDERAL TRADE COMMISSION

ESPAÑOL

CONSUMER INFORMATION

Search

Email Print SHARE

Vea esta página en español

MONEY & CREDIT

HOMES & MORTGAGES

HEALTH & FITNESS

JOBS & MAKING MONEY

PRIVACY & IDENTITY

BLOG

VIDEO & MEDIA

SCAM ALERTS

IDENTITY THEFT

Identity theft happens when someone steals your personal information and uses it without your permission. It's a serious crime that can wreak havoc with your finances, credit history, and reputation — and can take time, money, and patience to resolve.

What to Do Right Away

Immediate Steps to Repair Identity Theft

Here's how to begin to limit the harm from identity theft.

What to Do Next

Extended Fraud Alerts and Credit Freezes

Placing both extended fraud alerts and credit freezes on your credit reports can make it more difficult for an identity thief to open new accounts in your name.

Repairing Your Credit After Identity Theft

Here are step-by-step instructions for disputing fraudulent charges and accounts related to identity theft.

Lost or Stolen Credit, ATM, and Debit Cards

Federal law limits your liability if your credit, ATM, or debit card is lost or stolen, but your liability may depend on how quickly you report the loss or theft.

Specific Types of Identity Theft

Tax-Related Identity Theft

Do you know the warning signs that an identity thief is using your Social Security number?

Child Identity Theft

Here's how to protect your child's personal information against theft.

Medical Identity Theft

An identity thief can use your personal information to get medical care or services. Find out how to respond.

Protecting Your Identity

Signs of Identity Theft

If identity thieves have your personal information, they can drain your bank account, run up charges on your credit cards, open new utility accounts, or get medical treatment on your health insurance. Here's how to act quickly to limit the damage.

How to Keep Your Personal Information Secure

Safeguard your personal information, whether it is on paper, online, or on your computers and mobile devices.

Sample Letters and Forms

Sample Letters and Forms for Victims of Identity Theft

Use these samples to help write your own letters to limit damage caused by identity theft.

Related Items

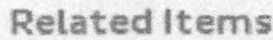

What is Identity Theft?

FREE RESOURCES

GUIDE TO ASSISTING IDENTITY THEFT VICTIMS

BUSINESS INFO

Need guidance on DATA SECURITY?

Related Blog Posts

- Talking Through Identity Theft: A Program for the Blind and Visually Impaired
  July 23, 2013
- Visit Us at the NCLR Annual Conference in New Orleans
  July 15, 2013
- Can We Talk?
  July 5, 2013

banks and lenders (6%), and shop-at-home and catalog sales (6%). About 38% of the reported fraud cases started with an email contact, the FTC said.[41] At the Internet Crime Complaint Center, the most common complaints were nondelivery of merchandise and/or payment, FBI impersonation email scams (13.2%), and identity theft.[42]

TECH TALES The Nigerian Letter, a Classic Internet Scam

A classic—and persistent—kind of confidence fraud is the *Nigerian letter scam,* also known as the *advance-fee* or *419 scam.* The fraud begins with you receiving an email in the form of a letter, in which the sender claims to have discovered an inactive or delinquent government account that holds a vast amount of money ready to be claimed. You are told you will receive money from the "Government of Nigeria" in return for your help in paying an up-front fee to effect the transfer of the money to an overseas account. Once you send that "transfer fee," which is usually in the hundreds or thousands of dollars, you never hear from the scammer again. ■

Survival Tip

Fraud Baiters

The following websites tell stories about outwitting online fraud artists; "419" refers to a section of the Nigerian legal code.

www.fbi.gov/scams-safety/fraud

www.scamvictimsunited.com/419_advance_fee.htm

The majority of Internet scams involve ruses such as those we described in Chapters 2 and 6. Examples are *pharming,* in which malicious software implanted in your computer redirects you to an impostor web page, and *Trojan horses,* programs (such as screen savers) that carry viruses that perpetuate mischief without your knowledge. Another technique is *phishing,* the sending of emails that appear to come from a trusted source but direct you to a website where you're asked to reveal personal information.

A variant we have not mentioned before is Wi-Fi phishing, also known as the **evil twin attack, in which an evil doer sets up a Wi-Fi hot spot that your computer thinks offers safe access to a secure public network and then monitors your communications and steals data you input.** To guard against your wireless data being

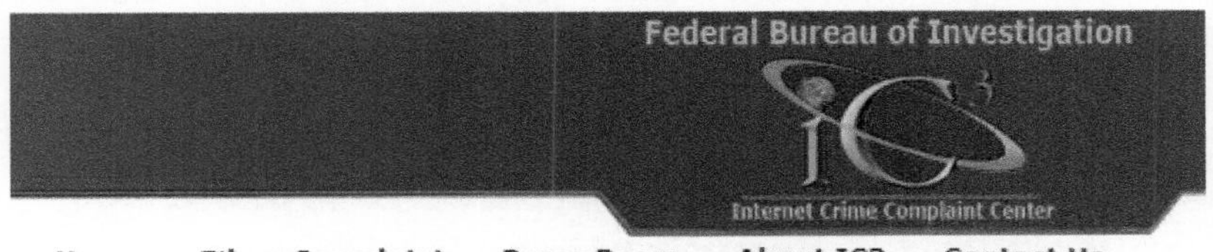

If you suspect that an Internet-related crime has occurred, you can report it on the FBI website.

stolen in this way, you should enter private information only into sites that protect data with encryption technology, as represented on the site by the image of a padlock at the bottom of the page.[43]

CRIMES OF MALICE: CRASHING ENTIRE SYSTEMS Sometimes criminals are more interested in abusing or vandalizing computers and telecommunications systems than in profiting from them. It may be a single act perpetrated by a single person, as when a Wisconsin student deliberately and repeatedly shut down his university's computer system, destroying final projects for dozens of students. Or it may be an entire class of malevolent acts; the Food and Drug Administration, for example, has warned makers of heart monitors, mammogram machines, and other medical devices that their equipment is at risk of being infected with computer viruses that can endanger patients.[44] The possible effects of other attacks could be even more dire, as follows.

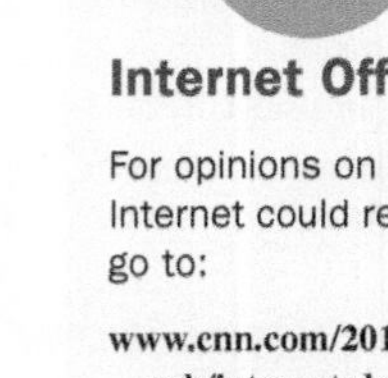

Internet Off?

For opinions on whether the Internet could really crash, go to:

www.cnn.com/2012/07/10/tech/web/internet-down-eagleman

www.computerhope.com/issues/ch000085.htm

http://mashable.com/2013/03/18/internet-crash-danny-hillis/

www.scientificamerican.com/article.cfm?id5could-internet-ever-be-destroyed

http://gizmodo.com/5912383/how-to-destroy-the-internet

- **Attacks on infrastructure:** The Department of Homeland Security reported 198 attacks on critical U.S. infrastructure in fiscal year 2012, compared to only 9 in 2009. These included 6 attacks on nuclear power plants and penetrations of 23 oil and natural gas pipelines.[45] Critical infrastructure firms such as power grids and oil refineries are said to be facing "staggering" level of cyberattacks and are not adequately prepared to defend themselves.[46]
- **Attacks on the Internet—could the entire net crash?** In March 2013, a conflict between two European groups—one fighting spam, the other said to be sending spam—escalated "into one of the largest computer attacks on the Internet, causing widespread congestion and jamming crucial infrastructure around the world," reported *The New York Times.*[47] Although the slowdown was brief, some engineers worried that if such attacks (called *distributed denial of service,* or *DDOS*) became more frequent, they would interrupt basic services, such as email and online banking. Critics point out that the notion that any cyberattack could interfere with the Internet on a massive scale is far-fetched—"a mind-bogglingly complicated task," said one. Nevertheless, it could be done because of certain vulnerabilities in the way the net connects.[48]

9.2 SECURITY SAFEGUARDS: Protecting Computers & Communications

Everyone using computers and networks must use security safeguards.

The ongoing dilemma of the Digital Age is balancing convenience against security. **Security is a system of safeguards for protecting information technology against disasters, system failures, and unauthorized access that can result in damage or loss.**

We consider five components of security.

- Deterrents to computer crime
- Identification and access
- Encryption
- Protection of software and data
- Disaster-recovery plans

Deterrents to Computer Crime

Are computer-related crimes increasing faster than the ability to deal with them? What can be done?

As information technology crime has become more sophisticated, so have the people charged with preventing it and disciplining its outlaws.

ENFORCING LAWS Campus administrators are no longer being quite as easy on offenders and are turning them over to police. Industry organizations such as the Software Publishers Association are going after software pirates large and small. Many police departments now have officers patrolling a "cyberbeat"; they regularly cruise online bulletin boards and chat rooms looking for pirated software, stolen trade secrets, child molesters, and child pornography. Interpol (the world's largest international police organization) has set up the "I-24/7" communication system to enable information technology crime units around the world to contact Interpol 24 hours a day, 7 days a week, to report cybercrimes.

More on Interpol & Cybercrime

www.interpol.int/
www.interpol.int/Crime-areas/Cybercrime/Cybercrime/
www.nyu.edu/intercep/lapietra/Interpol_Cyber.pdf

CERT: THE COMPUTER EMERGENCY RESPONSE TEAM In 1988, after one widespread Internet break-in, the U.S. Defense Department created the Computer Emergency Response Team (CERT, *www.us-cert.gov/*). Although it has no power to arrest or prosecute, CERT provides round-the-clock international information and security-related support services to users of the Internet. Whenever it gets a report of an electronic snooper, whether on the Internet or on a corporate email system, CERT stands ready to lend assistance. It counsels the party under attack, helps thwart the intruder, and evaluates the system afterward to protect against future break-ins.

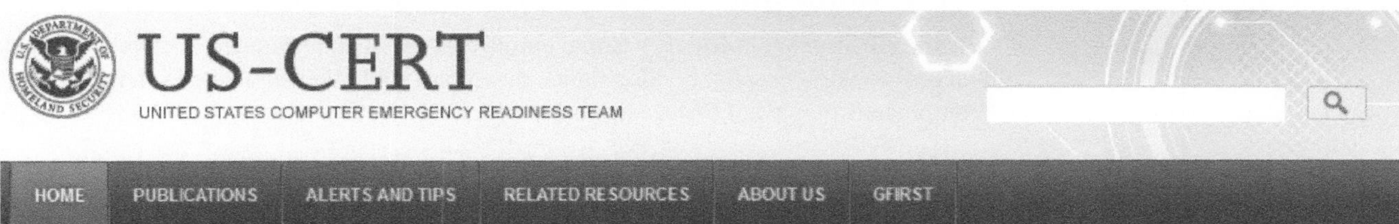

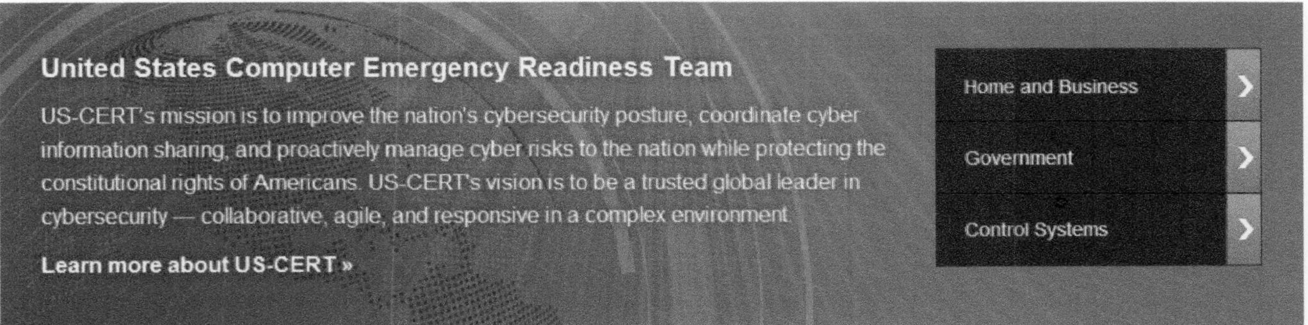

United States Computer Emergency Readiness Team
US-CERT's mission is to improve the nation's cybersecurity posture, coordinate cyber information sharing, and proactively manage cyber risks to the nation while protecting the constitutional rights of Americans. US-CERT's vision is to be a trusted global leader in cybersecurity — collaborative, agile, and responsive in a complex environment.
Learn more about US-CERT »
Home and Business
Government
Control Systems

Current Activity

Microsoft Releases Security Advisory

Published Thursday, August 15, 2013

Microsoft has released Security Advisory 2862973 impacting applications and services using certificates with the MD5 hashing algorithm. Usage of the MD5 hash algorithm in certificates could allow an attacker to spoof content, perform phishing attacks, or perform man-in-the-middle attacks.

Read Full Entry »

Microsoft Releases August 2013 Security Bulletin

Published Friday, August 9, 2013

Microsoft has released updates to address vulnerabilities in Microsoft Windows, Internet Explorer, and Microsoft Server Software as part of the Microsoft Security Bulletin Summary for August 2013. These vulnerabilities could allow remote code execution, elevation of privilege, denial of service, or information disclosure.

Read Full Entry »

Announcements

US-CERT Year In Review CY 2012

This report details US-CERT's CY 2012 accomplishments, critical mission activities, key initiatives and programs.

2013 GFIRST Conference Canceled

Visit the GFIRST page for more information.

Vulnerability Summary for the Week of May 20, 2013

US-CERT has released a Bulletin.

South Korean Malware Attack

This paper describes the recent attack by malware known as DarkSeoul and gives guidance on defensive measures.

Common Risks of Using Business Apps in the Cloud

This paper describes the risks to look for when partnering with cloud providers and how to mitigate these risks.

Cybersecurity: What Every CEO Should Be Asking

The top five questions every Chief Executive Officer should be asking when managing cyber risk at their company.

TOOLS FOR FIGHTING FRAUDULENT & UNAUTHORIZED ONLINE USES Among the tools used to detect fraud are the following:

- **Rule-based detection software:** In this technique, users such as merchants create a "negative file" that states the criteria each transaction must meet. These criteria include not only stolen credit-card numbers but also price limits, matches of the cardholder's billing address and shipping address, and warnings if a large quantity of a single item is ordered.
- **Predictive statistical model software:** In this technique, tons of data from previous transactions are examined to create mathematical descriptions of what a typical fraudulent transaction is like. The software then rates incoming orders according to a scale of risk based on their resemblance to the fraud profile. Thus, for example, if some thief overhears you giving out your phone company calling-card number and he or she makes 25 calls to a country that you never have occasion to call, AT&T's software may pick up the unusual activity and call you to ask if you are actually making the calls.
- **Employee Internet management (EIM) software:** Programs made by Websense, SmartFilter, and Pearl Echo-Suite are used to monitor how much time workers spend on the web and even block access to gambling and porn sites.
- **Internet filtering software:** Some employers use special filtering software to block access to pornography, bootleg music download, and other unwanted Internet sites that employees may want to access.
- **Electronic surveillance:** As we mentioned, employers use various kinds of electronic surveillance that includes visual and audio monitoring technologies, reading of email and blogs, and recording of keystrokes. Some companies even hire undercover agents to pretend to be coworkers.

Identification & Access

There are three main ways of authenticating a computer user's identity.

Are you who you say you are? The computer wants to know.

There are three ways a computer system can verify that you have legitimate right of access. Some security systems use a mix of these techniques. The systems try to authenticate your identity by determining (1) what you have, (2) what you know, or (3) who you are.

WHAT YOU HAVE—CARDS, KEYS, SIGNATURES, & BADGES Credit cards, debit cards, and cash-machine cards all have magnetic strips or built-in computer chips that identify you to the machine. Many require that you display your signature, which may be compared with any future signature you write. Computer rooms are always kept locked, requiring a key. Many people also keep a lock on their personal computers. A computer room may also be guarded by security officers, who may need to see an authorized signature or a badge with your photograph before letting you in.

Of course, credit cards, keys, and badges can be lost or stolen. Signatures can be forged. Badges can be counterfeited.

WHAT YOU KNOW—PINS & PASSWORDS To gain access to your bank account through an automated teller machine (ATM), you key in your PIN. A *PIN (personal identification number)* is the security number known only to you that is required to access the system. Telephone credit cards also use a PIN. If you carry either an ATM or a phone card, never carry the PIN written down elsewhere in your wallet (even disguised).

As we stated earlier in the book, *passwords* are special words, codes, or symbols required to access a computer system. Passwords are one of the weakest security links, and most can be easily guessed or stolen. We gave some suggestions on passwords in Chapters 2 and 6. There are also several technical solutions, such as the following.

- **Software with encrypted file:** You can save all your passwords in a single, easily accessible encrypted file. Two popular free programs for this are Passpack (*www.passpack.com/en/home/*) and PasswordSafe (*http://passwordsafe.sourceforge.net*).
- **Fingerprint readers for master password:** Microsoft offers fingerprint readers for Windows, and other fingerprint scanners are available such as BioMouse that are able to encrypt and keep track of all your various user names, passwords, and PINs. The fingerprint readers work only with the computer they are connected to, and the security of your various web accounts, bank accounts, frequent-flyer accounts, and so on depends on how unbreakable your passwords are. But at least you no longer have to memorize them.
- **Callback systems:** Some computer security systems have a "callback" provision. In a callback system, the user calls the computer system, punches in the password, and hangs up. The computer then calls back a certain preauthorized number. This measure will block anyone who has somehow gotten hold of a password but is calling from an unauthorized telephone.

WHO YOU ARE—PHYSICAL TRAITS Some forms of identification can't be easily faked—such as your physical traits. **Biometrics, the science of measuring individual body characteristics,** tries to use these in security devices, as we pointed out in Chapter 6. *Biometric authentication devices* authenticate a person's identity by comparing his or her physical or behavioral characteristics with a digital code stored in a computer system.

There are several kinds of devices for verifying such characteristics, as follows. (• *See Panel 9.3.*)

- **Hand-geometry systems:** Also known as *full-hand palm scanners,* these are devices to verify a person's identity by scanning the entire hand, which, for each person, is as unique as a fingerprint and changes little over time.
- **Fingerprint scanners:** These range from optical readers, in which you place a finger over a window, to swipe readers, such as those built into laptops and some handhelds, which allow you to run your finger across a barlike sensor. Microsoft offers optical fingerprint readers to go with Windows.
- **Iris-recognition systems:** Because no two people's eyes are alike, iris scans are very reliable identifiers. In Europe, some airports are using iris-scanning systems as a way of speeding up immigration controls. The Nine Zero, an upscale hotel in Boston, has experimented with letting guests enter one of its more expensive suites by staring into a camera that analyzes iris patterns.
- **Face-recognition systems:** Casinos have used facial-recognition technology for years as part of their never-ending quest to identify and catch cheaters. The technology, which compares a live face image with a digitized image stored in a computer, is used now as a security system for some notebook computers. With 230 million photos from passports and visas in its database, the U.S. State Department could clearly become the biggest user of facial-recognition systems.

panel 9.3

Biometric devices

(*left*) HT Systems Patient Secure Biometric Patient Identification System, which links the patient to his or her unique medical record, allowing healthcare providers to accurately identify the patient, improving patient safety, preventing medical identity theft and insurance fraud, and accelerating registration process. (*right*) The iPhone 5s has fingerprint ID protection.

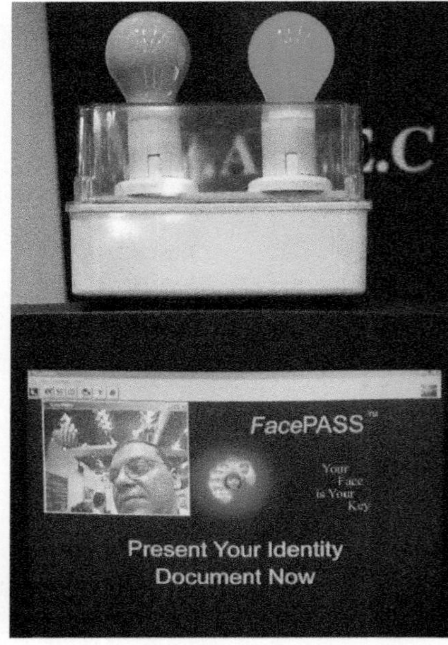

Facial-recognition. *(left)* Sigmatek's facial identification technology for corporate security at the International Security & Defense Exhibition in Tel Aviv, Israel. *(right)* Unattractive passport photos have become mandatory. Why? Because computers do not like smiles. A UN agency that sets standards for passports wants all countries to switch to a document that includes a digital representation of the bearer's face recorded on an embedded computer chip. In airports and at border crossings, a machine will read the chip—but the machine can be fooled by smiles, which introduce teeth, wrinkles, lines, and other distortions. (About half of all UN member states are now issuing biometric e-passports, according to data from the International Civil Aviation Organization, the UN agency that oversees international air travel.)

- **Voice-recognition systems:** These systems compare a person's voice with digitized voice prints stored in a computer, which the individual has previously "trained" to recognize his or her speech patterns.

Encryption

Could the use of encryption lead to invasion of privacy?

SECURITY

As we said in Chapter 6 (p. 352), **encryption is the process of altering readable data into unreadable form to prevent unauthorized access.** Available with every late-model web browser, encryption provides secure communications over the Internet and has given people confidence to do online shopping and banking. Encryption is especially necessary for organizations concerned with military matters, trade secrets, and other sensitive data.

Protection of Software & Data

Software and data can be protected by more than antivirus programs and firewalls.

Organizations go to tremendous lengths to protect their programs and data. As might be expected, this includes educating employees about making backup disks, protecting against viruses, using firewalls, and so on. Other security procedures include these:

CONTROL OF ACCESS Access to online files is restricted to those who have a legitimate right to access—because they need them to do their jobs. Many organizations have a system for user authentication and of transaction logs for recording all accesses or attempted accesses to data.

AUDIT CONTROLS Many networks have audit controls for tracking which programs and servers were used, which files opened, and so on. This creates an audit trail, a record of how a transaction was handled from input through processing and output.

PEOPLE CONTROLS Because people are the greatest threat to a computer system, security precautions begin with screening job applicants. Résumés are checked to see if people did what they said they did. Another control is to separate employee functions, so that people are not allowed to wander freely into areas not essential to their jobs. Manual and automated controls—input controls, processing controls, and output controls—are used to check if data is handled accurately and completely during the processing cycle. Printouts and other waste that may reveal passwords and trade secrets to outsiders are disposed of through shredders or locked trash barrels.

Disaster-Recovery Plans

A disaster-recovery plan enables an organization to continue operating after a natural or other type of disaster.

A disaster-recovery plan is a method of restoring information-processing operations that have been halted by destruction or accident. "Among the countless lessons that computer users have absorbed in the hours, days, and weeks after the [1993 New York] World Trade Center bombing," wrote one reporter, "the most enduring may be the need to have a disaster-recovery plan. The second most enduring lesson may be this: even a well-practiced plan will quickly reveal its flaws."[49] Although the second (2001) attack on the World Trade Center reinforced these lessons in a spectacular way, as did Hurricane Katrina in New Orleans four years later and Hurricane Sandy on the East Coast in 2012, interestingly many companies have not gotten the message. For example, the March 2011 earthquake and tsunami disaster in Japan forced 145 companies to either go bankrupt or effectively fail.[50]

Disaster. A massive tsunami engulfs a residential area after a powerful earthquake in Natori, Miyagi Prefecture, northeastern Japan, in March 2011.

Mainframe computer systems are operated in separate departments by professionals, who tend to have disaster plans. Whereas mainframes are usually backed up, many personal computers, and even entire local area networks, are not, with potentially disastrous consequences. It has been reported that, on average, a company loses as much as 3% of its gross sales within eight days of a sustained computer outage.

A disaster-recovery plan is more than a big fire drill. It includes a list of all business functions and the hardware, software, data, and people that support those functions, as well as arrangements for alternative locations. The disaster-recovery plan also includes ways for backing up and storing programs and data in another location, ways of alerting necessary personnel, and training for those personnel.

9.3 PRIVACY & SURVEILLANCE: Data Collectors & Spies

Trying to find a balance between privacy and safety with the uses of information technology is one of our greatest challenges.

There is no explicit right to privacy in the United States Constitution. Still, the U.S. Supreme Court has ruled that there is a limited constitutional right of privacy based on several provisions in the Bill of Rights. This includes a right to privacy from government surveillance into an area where a person has a "reasonable" expectation of privacy and also in matters relating to marriage, procreation, contraception, sexual activity, family relationships, child rearing, and education. The Supreme Court has also recognized a right of anonymity and the right of political groups to prevent disclosure of their members' names to government agencies.

In addition, over the years, concerns about privacy have led to the enactment of a number of federal laws to protect individuals from various kinds of invasions of privacy. (• *See Panel 9.4, next page.*) Some states within the United States have also incorporated explicit privacy protections into their constitutions.

Right to Privacy?

For more details, go to:

www.privacyinternational.org/article.shtml?cmd[347]=x-347-559478

panel 9.4

Important federal privacy laws

For further information on these laws, go to *https.epic.org* (this is an opinionated website, but it includes a lot of useful information) or *http://en.wikipedia.org/wiki/Privacy_laws_of_the_United_States.*

Americans with Disabilities Act (ADA)
Cable Communications Policy Act of 1984
California Senate Bill 1386 (SB 1386)
Children's Internet Protection Act of 2001 (CIPA)
Children's Online Privacy Protection Act of 1998 (COPPA)
Communications Assistance for Law Enforcement Act of 1994 (CALEA)
Computer Fraud and Abuse Act of 1986 (CFAA)
Computer Security Act of 1987—(superseded by the Federal Information Security Management Act (FISMA)
Consumer Credit Reporting Reform Act of 1996 (CCRRA)—modifies the Fair Credit Reporting Act (FCRA)
Controlling the Assault of Non-solicited Pornography and Marketing (CAN-SPAM) Act of 2003
Driver's Privacy Protection Act of 1994
Electronic Communications Privacy Act of 1986 (ECPA)
Electronic Freedom of Information Act of 1996 (E-FOIA)
Electronic Funds Transfer Act (EFTA)
Fair and Accurate Credit Transactions Act (FACTA) of 2003
Fair Credit Reporting Act of 1999 (FCRA)
Family Education Rights and Privacy Act of 1974 (FERPA)
Federal Information Security Management Act (FISMA)
Federal Trade Commission Act (FTCA)
Gramm-Leach-Bliley Financial Services Modernization Act of 1999 (GLBA)
Privacy Act of 1974
Privacy Protection Act of 1980 (PPA)
Right to Financial Privacy Act of 1978 (RFPA)
Telecommunications Act of 1996
Telephone Consumer Protection Act of 1991 (TCPA)
Uniting and Strengthening America by Providing Appropriate Tools Required to Intercept and Obstruct Terrorism Act of 2001 (USA PATRIOT Act)
Video Privacy Protection Act of 1988

Checking Your Personal Records

Browse the full text of FBI documents and files released under the Freedom of Information Act at:

http://blogs.justice.gov/oip/archives/1239/

For instructions on how to check and repair your personal credit reports, go to:

www.consumer.ftc.gov/articles/0058-credit-repair-how-help-yourself

www.transunion.com/personal-credit/credit-reports/update-my-credit-report.page

www.consumer.ftc.gov/articles/0151-disputing-errors-credit-reports

http://money.cnn.com/2013/06/01/pf/credit-report.moneymag/index.html

Despite these protections, the explosion in information technology—in the world-girdling Internet, in the proliferation of mobile devices, in the rise of Big Data—has led to continuing threats to privacy from three giant sources:

- From business organizations
- From governments, local to federal
- From foreign governments and criminal groups

Business & Cyberspying

Almost everything we do online is being scooped up and recorded for use by marketers, and it's difficult to know what parts of our own lives still belong to us.

"Our browsing habits, search terms, e-mail communication—even our offering of our ZIP codes at the supermarket checkout—reveal bits of information that can be assembled by data companies," points out a technology writer, "usually for the purpose of knowing what sorts of products we're likely to buy."[51] Such data is used by a host of industries.

HOW BUSINESSES OBTAIN & USE DATA ABOUT US Our past decisions and mistakes can follow us for years because of the widespread business use of databases. Mistakes like a bounced check or a small overdraft, for instance, have blacklisted more than a million low-income citizens from America's mainstream financial system for as long as seven years as a result of private databases used by the nation's major banks.[52] Google, which now accounts for about 25% of all consumer Internet traffic in North America—more than

Facebook, Netflix, and Instagram combined—compiles enough data to build comprehensive portfolios of most users, including who they are, where they go, and what they do.[53] (You can find everything that Google has collected about you at *google.com/dashboard.*)

Retailers analyzing consumer shopping habits can often predict a pregnancy, and researchers have been able to use Facebook to determine your probable gender, ethnicity, religion, and other personal information.[54] Stores use Wi-Fi trackers targeting your cellphone, as well as cameras, to monitor your movements and learn your shopping techniques.[55] Other researchers have shown what is possible by using webcam pictures of students and identifying a third of them with facial recognition software. (They also found out enough of about a fourth of them to guess part of their Social Security numbers.)[56]

"Our mobile carriers know our locations: where our phones travel during working hours and leisure time, where they reside overnight when we sleep," writes one reporter. "Verizon Wireless even sells demographic profiles of customer groups—including ZIP codes for where they 'live, work, shop, and more'—to marketers." (But wireless providers won't share their customers' own location logs with them without a subpoena.)[57] Businesses have used apps popular with children to collect data and send details to other businesses.[58] The Federal Trade Commission found that seven computer rental companies secretly collected "confidential and personal information about consumers," says a report, "including medical records, bank statements, and even webcam pictures of couples engaged in sex."[59]

Google's Dashboard

Learn more about Dashboard:

http://online.wsj.com/article/SB10001424127887324170004578635812623154242.html

WHO OWNS YOUR DATA & WHAT ARE YOUR RIGHTS? A critical procedure in medicine is for doctors and nurses to wash their hands to prevent infection. So, if you were on a hospital's staff, how would you feel about video monitors and radio-frequency ID chips being used to check if you were performing this kind of hygiene?[60] And what do you think of retailers (such as Target, CVS, and Family Dollar) assembling "vast databases of workers accused of stealing and . . . using that information to keep employees from working again in the industry," as *The New York Times* reported?[61] How about the notion of research groups, including the government, mining large DNA databases for genetic (genomic) data—including yours—as powerful tools to combat disease?[62]

Whatever the impact on your personal privacy, it seems unlikely that you can claim ownership of a lot of data that's being collected about you. At work, for instance, you basically have no rights, which is why employees are fired all the time for using a company computer or smartphone for personal business, including questionable web surfing and emailing. "Your First Amendment right to free speech," says computer columnist Kim Komando, "protects you against the government—not private employers."[63]

In addition, your ownership of text, files, images, photos, video, and the like ("content") that you post on social media depends on the terms of use (terms of service) of the company involved. For instance, Instagram, the photo- and video-sharing social-networking site, does not claim ownership of your material. Facebook, however, tells users that they own their own data, but their "likes" can be used in a certain type of advertising known as "Sponsored Stories." In other words, you might own your own data, but you do not always control its use.[64]

Government & Cyberspying

Governments at all levels spy on their citizens, sometimes encouraged by the law, sometimes in spite of the law, often unknown to us.

Since the September 11, 2001, terrorist attacks on New York's World Trade Center, our world has become a less private place—not only because we as individuals have revealed more about ourselves through our smartphones and social networking programs but also because governments, from local to federal, have been more empowered to spy on us. Consider the following:

LOCAL POLICE DATA COLLECTION Slowly, and almost without notice, a growing number of law enforcement agencies have moved into collection of data such as digital photos of car license plates and records of DNA and amassed significant databases about individual citizens, mostly without their knowing it.

PRACTICAL ACTION

Is the Boss Watching You? Trust in the Workplace

Once an employee of Wells Fargo launched an Internet blog chronicling his life, friends, and job handling mail and the front desk at a certain division—and he probably would have been all right until he began criticizing a few people he worked with, and he was fired.[65] That's when he learned that his employers had been monitoring his online activity. (Today most people are more cautious. In one poll, 57% of respondents said they would consider what their boss might think when they posted comments, photos, and the like on social-networking websites, versus 37% who said they would not.)[66]

More and more employers are using surveillance techniques to monitor their employees, from using cameras and phone taps to recording website visits, checking social media sites, and visiting the files that employees delete. About 78% of major U.S. companies keep tabs on employees by checking their email, Internet activity, phone calls, and computer files, or by videotaping them at work.[67] In most states, the companies don't have to inform employees of this fact. In addition, software is available to measure the performance and activities of independent workers such as those working from home across the country.[68]

What are employers looking for that you should be aware of? Here are the principal areas.

Surveillance

How do employers monitor employees' Internet usage?

www.wisegeek.com/how-do-employers-monitor-internet-usage-at-work.htm

www.twc.state.tx.us/news/efte/monitoring_computers_internet.html

www.workforce50.com/Content/Articles/Art0012_Employers_Monitor_Email.cfm

www.nolo.com/legal-encyclopedia/monitoring-employee-communications-29853.html

And don't forget: many employers check social-networking profiles—for example, on Facebook—to see what employees are up to and to see what they are saying about their jobs, as well as to run background checks before hiring people.

Less Productivity

There's a word for all those hours employees spend each workday talking on the phone with friends, getting coffee, or gossiping—"undertime." Some such goofing off is tolerated in the name of workplace morale. The Internet, however, has created whole new ways to slack off at work. A company with 1,000 Internet users could lose more than $35 million in productivity annually from just one hour of daily web surfing by employees; non-work-related Internet surfing results in up to a 40% loss in productivity each year at American businesses. On average, office workers spend 21 hours per week online at the office, as opposed to only 9.5 hours at home.[69]

Misleading Résumés

Employers are carrying out more rigorous background checks on prospective workers since the September 11, 2001, terrorist attacks in New York City and Washington, D.C. Among the problems with (or omitted from) résumés or application forms that turned up in one study: up to 30% of applications contain false material/information; 40% of information on résumés is misrepresented; 45% of potential employees have either a criminal record, bad driving record, workers' compensation claim, or a bad credit history.[70]

Risk of Lawsuits & Viruses

One reason corporate executives are becoming more aggressive about spying on employees is that, besides ferreting out job shirkers and office supply thieves, "they have to worry about being held accountable for the misconduct of their subordinates," says one report. "Even one offensive email message circulated around the office by a single employee can pose a liability risk for a company" under federal anticorruption and corporate governance laws.[71]

In addition, employers are worried about workers using company computers to download copyrighted music and movies, because these acts not only are a drain on corporate resources but also expose employers to the risk of lawsuits from record and movie companies as well as open company networks to viruses.

What Employers Must Do: Shred Personal Data

On the other hand, employees caught a break under part of the Fair and Accurate Credit Transactions Act passed in late 2003. If employers got employees' personal information from a credit report they must destroy the information—by "shredding or burning" or "smashing or wiping"—before they throw it out.[72]

In addition, employees transmitting text messages from devices supplied by their employer caught a break in 2008 when the Ninth U.S. Circuit Court of Appeals in San Francisco ruled that companies transmitting those messages can't disclose their contents without the recipient's consent.[73]

TECH TALES Police Use of License Plate Scanners

"Welcome to Tiburon! *Snap,*" begins a newspaper piece. "Thanks for visiting! *Snap.*"

Auto thefts have virtually disappeared from this upscale California town. That's because every car that enters or leaves Tiburon, according to *USA Today,* is photographed by a police camera, and the license plates in the digital photos are then scanned into a database that compares them with those of stolen vehicles.[74]

But in San Leandro, another California suburban town, computer security consultant Michael Katz-Lacabe was shocked to learn that a single patrol car bearing a plate-reading camera had photographed his two cars on 112 occasions, once a week on average, documenting the time and location. The discovery left him "frightened and concerned about the magnitude of police surveillance and data collection," he reports. Such frequent recordings of his movements, he says, are too revealing about someone who has done nothing wrong.[75]

As a local government official asked, "Do we really want to maintain a database that tracks personal movements of law-abiding citizens in perpetuity? That's the fundamental question here."[76] ■

Amassing DNA databases has also become a major trend in police work.[77] If your home were burglarized and the police swabbed a door handle hoping to track the suspect, would you give them a sample of your own DNA to eliminate yourself as the source? Then how would you feel if the police kept the DNA permanently and used it to investigate you for other crimes? Concerns about police restraint in data gathering are also expressed about the use of more video cameras.[78] Finally, there is always the concern that data generated locally might wind up being used by federal government agencies that are supposedly prohibited from domestic spying, such as the Central Intelligence Agency, but have been caught violating that restriction, as happened with CIA members with ties to the New York Police Department.[79]

A NATIONAL IDENTITY CARD? Unlike some European countries, the United States presently has no national ID card, or internal passport. Critics from conservatives to civil liberties defenders so dislike the idea that even efforts to get state governments to standardize driver's licenses have been met with extreme resistance.

Most supporters of a national ID card are those worried about illegal immigration. Thus, what we have instead is a program called E-Verify, which is now used voluntarily by about 7% of employers in the United States.[80] With *E-Verify,* employers send information supplied by job applicants to be matched against databases in the Social Security Administration or the Department of Homeland Security. One drawback of E-Verify is that the burden of administering the program falls on employers, such as farmers and restaurant owners, who say it increases their employee recruiting costs.[81] Another is that 54% of unauthorized workers who submitted E-Verify paperwork were able to trick the system with stolen or fraudulent documents, according to a 2009 study.[82]

One suggestion for a national ID is that it be a Social Security card embedded with biometric information, such as a fingerprint, an eye scan, or a digital photo, that an employer could swipe and match to the real you. In this format, the information would not need to go in a database and the card would be useless to a thief because it would contain your unique identifier.[83]

THE NATIONAL SECURITY AGENCY: THE RISE OF THE SURVEILLANCE STATE? The *National Security Agency (NSA)* is the official organization in charge of cryptographic design and decryption for the U.S. government. In June 2013, a contract employee for the NSA named Edward Snowden used a thumb drive to smuggle highly classified documents out of an NSA facility in Hawaii. He then gave two news organizations details of a huge NSA surveillance program to obtain a record of every phone call made in the United States. He also leaked news of another secret program, called Prism, that uses online data from nine U.S. Internet and technology companies, including Google, Facebook, and Apple,

U.S. Citizenship and Immigration Services

Home | Español

Search

FORMS NEWS RESOURCES LAWS OUTREAC

- What is E-Verify?
  - Instant Verification of Work Authorization
  - Companion to Form I-9
  - Business-Friendly Features
  - Attend an Information Session
- Getting Started
- About the Program
  - E-Verify Webinars
- Customer Support
- For Employers
- For Employees
- For Federal Contractors
- Publications
  - Questions and Answers

Home > E-Verify > What is E-Verify? Printer Friendly

What is E-Verify?

E-Verify is an Internet-based system that compares information from an employee's Form I-9, Employment Eligibility Verification, to data from U.S. Department of Homeland Security and Social Security Administration records to confirm employment eligibility.

Why E-Verify?

Why do people come to the United States illegally? They come here to work. The public can, and should, choose to reward companies that follow the law and employ a legal workforce.

The U.S. Department of Homeland Security is working to stop unauthorized employment. By using E-Verify to determine the employment eligibility of their employees, companies become part of the solution in addressing this problem.

Employment eligibility verification is good business and it's the law.

Who Uses E-Verify?

More than 409,000 employers, large and small, across the United States use E-Verify to check the employment eligibility of their employees, with about 1,300 new businesses signing up each week.

While participation in E-Verify is voluntary for most businesses, some companies may be required by state law or federal regulation to use E-Verify. For example, most employers in Arizona and Mississippi are required to use E-Verify. E-Verify is also mandatory for employers with federal contracts or subcontracts that contain the Federal Acquisition Regulation E-Verify clause.

This page provides general information about E-Verify and is meant to provide an overview of the program. For instructions and policy guidance, visit the For Employers and For Employees sections of the website.

about the online activity of customers, and disclosed broad details about NSA spying on foreign nations.[84] Later he revealed the existence of yet another NSA program, XKeyscore, that allows analysts to search with no prior authorization through vast databases containing emails, online chats, and the browsing histories of millions of individuals.[85]

National security officials insisted that Snowden didn't have access to the more secure parts of NSA and protested that their intrusions were modest, that their approach had helped disrupt potential terrorist events, and that there was sufficient oversight provided by congressional intelligence committees and other safeguards. Still, the revelations prompted a nearly successful attempt by Congress to restrain the federal government's authority to mine Americans' secrets in its hunt for terrorism.[86]

Some key facts emerging from this are the following:

- **NSA and FBI operations:** The NSA has two operations. One gathers intelligence by targeting the computers and communications of foreign entities, both friends and foes. The other protects the NSA's own computers and communications and those of the U.S. military.[87] The agency is particularly focused on the threat of cyberattack against the United States—against power plants and water systems, the military's command and control structure, and the smooth running of the Internet, on which so much of our economy depends.[88] The NSA is prohibited by law from spying on people or entities within the United States, including noncitizens, or on snooping on U.S. citizens abroad—unless they are in communication with suspected terrorists. The bombshell in Snowden's revelations was that, beginning under the Bush administration and continuing under the Obama presidency, the NSA was collecting far more information than most people thought.[89]

Under the USA Patriot Act, passed by Congress in the wake of the September 11, 2001, terrorist attacks on the World Trade Center and Pentagon, Federal Bureau of Investigation (FBI) counterterrorism agents may issue secret and warrantless (they don't require a judge's approval) so-called national security letters demanding sensitive customer data. The letters, which are issued to telecommunication companies, Internet service providers, banks, and others, are used to collect unlimited kinds of sensitive, private information, such as financial and phone records. (When Google resisted the FBI's demands, a federal judge ruled the company must comply.)[90]

- **The FISA court:** The basis for the NSA's ability to gather data hinges on two things: (1) the existence of a secret *Foreign Intelligence Surveillance Act (FISA) court,* a group of 11 judges responsible for making decisions about government surveillance in national security cases, and (2) a ruling by that court that redefined a single word—"relevant"—to mean that the NSA could search the phone records of the majority of Americans rather than only some of those records.[91]

  Created by Congress in 1978, the FISA court originally had only the power to approve electronic surveillance of Americans and foreigners in the United States believed to be acting on behalf of foreign powers or terrorist organizations, but in 2008 the judges were given oversight of data mining procedures as well. All FISA judges are appointed by one man, the chief of the U.S. Supreme Court; generally only one of the judges hears cases; and only the government is allowed to present its side, with no one representing the interests of those being monitored. In addition, "Americans do not know about its rulings so cannot challenge them," points out one editorial.[92] Finally, critics say the court is a rubber stamp, since none of the government's 1,789 requests for surveillance were denied in 2012, although 40 were modified.[93]

- **The Privacy and Civil Liberties Oversight Board:** Another supposed check on government overreach by the NSA and FBI is the Privacy and Civil Liberties Oversight Board, which is staffed by five presidential appointees. But "hamstrung by Congress and ignored by two presidents, the board has been powerless," says a business reporter.[94]

- **Secret mining of metadata:** Because the NSA is not supposed to snoop on the contents of communications by ordinary Americans, the agency has focused on collecting "metadata" logs of Internet and telephone communications—their time, location, and senders/recipients—and then to analyze the links between people in an attempt to identify networks of suspected terrorists. Typically networks were analyzed with "two degrees of separation (two hops)," according to one report, from a known suspect to create leads that could be investigated by the FBI and the Central Intelligence Agency.[95]

  Metadata mining is the practice of using computer algorithms (formulas) to search vast collections of data for patterns. Although targeted data mining can be a useful tool for tracing terrorists, says one scholar, there is no evidence that sucking up large amounts of everyday data and analyzing it for suspicious behavior is effective.[96]

Defenders say the government's secret programs are necessary because, first, there are still determined enemies out to attack the United States and, second, the programs have worked, preventing about 50 attacks.[97] However, lawmakers of all political persuasions have expressed alarm about programs that collect data on millions of innocent Americans "based on a secret legal interpretation of a statute that does not on its face appear to authorize this type of bulk collection," as Senate Judiciary Committee chair Patrick Leahy expressed it.[98] The government insists that as long as agents don't read your emails or listen to your calls, there is no danger to privacy. However, as law professor Jonathan Turley points out, "If basic information about who, when, and from where you call and email is available, it doesn't take much imagination to figure out things about you that are hidden from all but your closest friends and now a few thousand government monitors."[99]

DRONES: SNOOPING FROM THE SKIES? The courts have already ruled we have no right to privacy in a public place, and so we are all fair game for video cameras on light poles and anyone practicing smartphone photography—and even Google Earth, the website that allows people to get a satellite view of your yard. So does the use of a robot aircraft known as a *drone,* or unmanned aerial vehicle (UAV), an aircraft without a human pilot on board, differ in terms of invading your privacy?

Used as U.S. airborne weapons platforms against terrorists in Afghanistan, Pakistan, Yemen, and Somalia, drones are now being adopted for domestic use, as for surveilling oil spills, monitoring wildlife, scanning for illegal dump sites, scouting wildfires, and looking for lost hikers.[100] Some are also being considered (as unmanned helicopters) for spraying pesticides on crops.[101] All must be approved by the Federal Aviation Administration (FAA), which allows them to fly as long as their operators keep them in sight.[102]

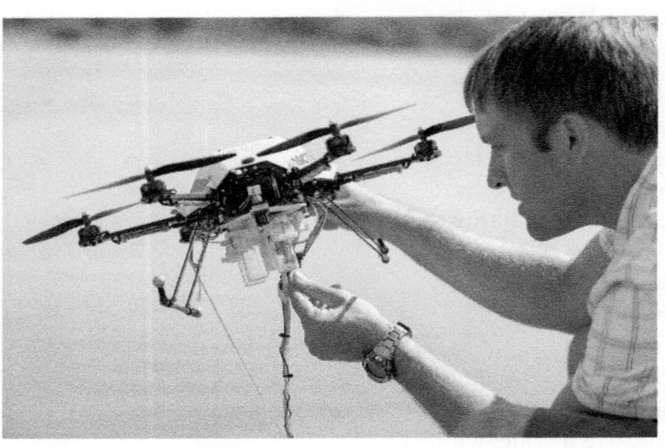

University of Nebraska assistant professor Dr. Carrick Detweiler examines a water collecting drone with its three containers at a testing site. A team led by Nebraska university scientists has won a federal grant to further develop aerial drones that could hover over and sample water from lakes, ponds, and streams that people can't easily reach and perfect algorithms to improve its safety and reliability.

Law enforcement agencies of all kinds are enthusiastic prospective users, since drones cost far less than conventional aircraft. Indeed, U.S. Customs and Border Protection has already loaned out some of its military-grade drones to other government agencies for such tasks as investigating fishing violations, searching for missing persons, and inspecting river levees.[103] However, many people worry about UAVs being used for invasive types of surveillance. Civil libertarians warn that drones may "profoundly change the character of public life," ushering in an era in which we could be watched every time we step outside—not just by police but also by Peeping Toms.[104]

Spying, Hacking, & Cyberwarfare by Foreign Governments & Groups

The world is so interconnected that it is a constant struggle for technology managers to keep us secure against cyberinvasions of all sorts.

It's one thing to be spied on, which, as we have seen, people in the United States worry that U.S. businesses and their own government are doing. It's another thing to be spied on *and* to have your data stolen or destroyed—that is, hacked—by a foreign nation or foreign criminals. And it is a huge concern when foreign governments and our own government get involved in *cyberwarfare*—warfare involving computers and the Internet in which one nation attacks another's information systems. Let's consider these matters.

CYBERSPYING BY FOREIGN—& THE U.S.—GOVERNMENTS "Malware from China has inundated the Internet," says a *Bloomberg Businessweek* article, "targeting Fortune 500 companies, tech startups, government agencies, news organizations, embassies, universities, law firms, and anything else with intellectual property to protect."[105] The main purpose of this kind of cyberspying is to mine the databases of U.S. companies and organizations for product details, trade secrets, and other intellectual property, some of which might be put to use in Chinese industry. In addition, President Barack Obama has worried that cyberattacks are not just intended to steal corporate secrets but also to "sabotage our power grid, our financial institutions, our air traffic control systems."[106] Often, apparently, the dirty work of cyberspying is done by hackers backed by the People's Liberation Army, although the Chinese have furiously denied it. Meanwhile, the Chinese accuse the U.S. government of having attacked their networks for years.[107]

Of course, the United States does its own cyberspying on enemies and even on allies.[108] The NSA's supersecret Tailored Access Operations (TAO) unit apparently harvests an astonishing 2.1 million gigabytes (2 petabytes) *an hour* from overseas computer networks. The TAO "gathers vast amounts of intelligence on terrorist financial networks, international money laundering and drug operations, the readiness of foreign militaries, even the internal political squabbles of potential adversaries," *Bloomberg Businessweek* reports.[109]

The United States takes the position that some kinds of spying are more acceptable than others and that, unlike the Chinese government, the NSA does not attempt espionage on private corporations. Still, critics argue that the NSA's involvement of nine large American tech companies, including Google, Facebook, and Apple, in gathering information could end up poisoning their reputations and harming their business.[110] As you might suspect, China and the United States are not alone in doing cyberspying; others include the French and British governments and probably several others.[111]

CYBERATTACKS & CYBERWARFARE Cyberspying, or cyberespionage, is disturbing enough. But cyberattacks—especially those intended to destroy, not merely disrupt—are the bane of the Internet and can even lead to cyberwarfare. This is the difference between *espionage* and *sabotage.* Sometimes the cyberattacks are perpetrated by gangsters (with or without state backing), sometimes by governments, and sometimes by nongovernmental terrorists.

TECH TALES Cyberattacks That Challenge Governments & Corporations

A common refrain in the computer security world is, "It's always the Chinese," that are behind cyberintrusions, according to one expert.[112] So imagine his surprise when investigators started finding typical Indian names instead of Chinese inside software designed to steal data. Hackers in India used decoy emails and documents to trick targets ranging from the Chicago Mercantile Exchange to Pakistan's National Disaster Management Authority. There was no evidence that the attacks were sponsored by the Indian government.

Other attacks have been traced to Iran, where government-backed hackers launched a campaign of cyberassaults against the computer networks of American oil, gas, and electricity companies. The hackers "were able to gain access to control-system software that could allow them to manipulate oil or gas pipelines," says one report.[113] The intent, apparently, was sabotage.[114] Earlier Iran hackers also attacked American financial firms and banks, who called on the U.S. government to help, saying they couldn't be expected to fend off attacks from a foreign government.[115]

There seems to be no end to cyberattacks like these. In Asia, South Korea and Japan worry about computer network attacks from North Korea.[116] Cambodia has been targeted by a hacker group called NullCrew, which also has attacked government websites in Ukraine.[117] In the Middle East, a hacking group called the Syrian Electronic Army has broken into Associated Press Twitter accounts and planted false tales about White House explosions, so unsettling the U.S. stock market that it nearly crashed.[118] ■

Cyberwarfare, or *cyberwar,* is warfare involving computers and the Internet in which one nation attacks another's information systems. Attacks on U.S. government computer networks increased 40% in 2008, according to the U.S. Computer Emergency Readiness team.[119] In April 2009 the Pentagon reported it spent more than $100 million in the previous six months responding to and repairing damage from cyberattacks and other computer network problems.[120] Computer spies even broke into the Pentagon's Joint Strike Fighter project.[121]

Cyberwar may be conducted on the level of psychological warfare, as has happened in the Middle East, for instance, where Israeli and Palestinian opponents in the Gaza war have used cellphones to warn the other side of impending attacks.[122] Or it may be conducted as a tactical maneuver in which one side hacks into the other side's computers and alters information that drives them into the first side's gun sights, as the Americans did with members of Al Qaeda in Iraq.[123] Or it may be on the scale of widespread cyberattacks on government websites, such as those North Korea inflicted on South Korea and the United States (where Treasury Department and Federal Trade Commission websites were shut down).[124] Cyberattacks include "terrorism, espionage, crime, protest, vandalism, and more," says one analyst. "Lines between categories are often blurred, and it is usually difficult to identify the perpetrators or understand their motives. For instance, there is still debate in the cybersecurity community over whether the 2007 cyberattacks that targeted Estonian government networks (UPI) constitute cyberwarfare by Russian intelligence or acts of political protest by hackers."[125]

Recognizing the dangers of cyberattacks, the U.S. government made online security a high priority, with President Barack Obama appointing a cybersecurity coordinator within the White House and introducing a plan for stemming cyberthreats.[126] The Pentagon also created a new agency called the Cyber Command to centralize and elevate cybersecurity.[127] A decade behind China, the United States is also now officially focused on using cyberwarfare offensively as well as defensively.[128]

A series of high-profile events in 2010 and 2011 further increased concerns about the threat of cyberattacks. These include the espionage hacks on Google and Western energy companies, the Stuxnet malware infiltration of Iranian nuclear sites, and the targeting of government networks in South Korea. "U.S. cybersecurity policy continues to evolve to meet these challenges, but critical gaps remain, including the incomplete protection of digital infrastructure vital to national security, such as power grids and financial networks."[129]

The new cybersecurity strategies implemented by President Obama supposedly will provide protections for personal privacy and civil liberties. However, Pentagon officials say these will be difficult to implement.[130]

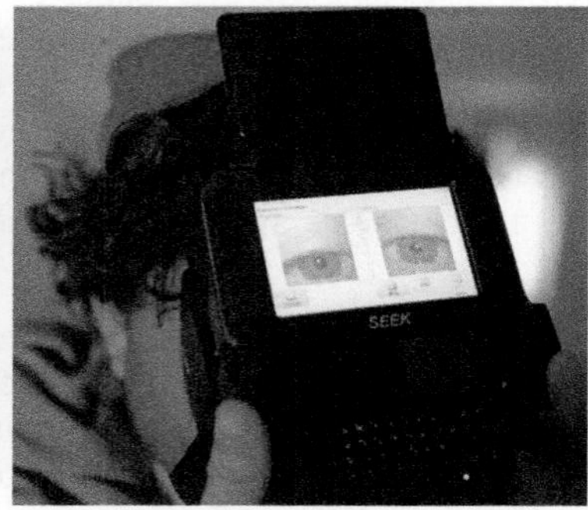

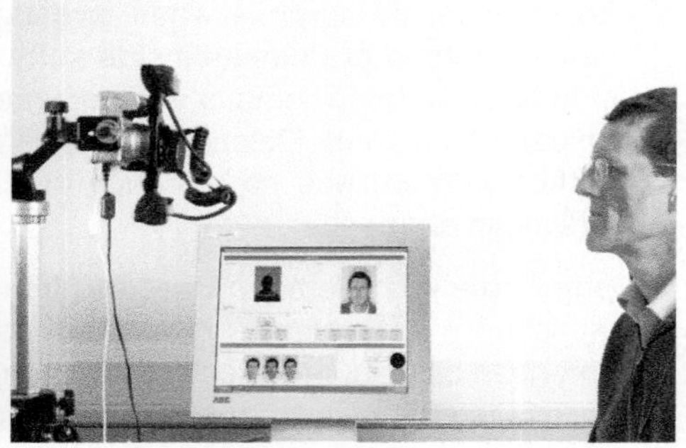

(*left*) A member of the Dutch bomb squad with a security robot at Schiphol Airport terminal 1 after examining a suspicious suitcase found in the luggage department. (*middle*) A U.S. soldier makes a biometric scan of an Afghan villager during a clearance patrol in Kandahar province. (*right*) Man having his face screened by a biometric scanner. This scanner is being used to identify him from the contours of his head and face. The computer monitor is showing a match between the person being scanned and his profile held in the computer's records.

UNIT 9B: *Other Social, Economic, & Political Issues*

Information technology is the major disrupter of just about everything. The dating culture? Texting has altered courtship more radically than anything since the automobile. Family history research? Combining a DNA sample with social networking and mapping technology may turn up family members you didn't even know you had. Resurrecting extinct species? Unbelievably, computer cloning technologies could bring the passenger pigeon and the mammoth back to life.

But the changes brought about by technology are not all to the good. Here we consider some relevant social, economic, and political issues.

9.4 TRUTH ISSUES: Manipulating Digital Data

Information technology allows the manipulation or falsification of all sorts of data, including text, sound, and image, which has led to problems with truth and credibility.

The enormous capacities of today's storage devices have given photographers, graphics professionals, and others a new tool—the ability to manipulate images at the pixel level. For example, photographers can easily do *morphing*—transforming one image into another—using image-altering software such as Adobe Photoshop (p. 172). In morphing, a film or video image is displayed on a computer screen and altered pixel by pixel, or dot by dot. As a result, the image metamorphoses into something else—a pair of lips morphs into the front of a Toyota, for example, or an owl into a baby.

The ability to manipulate digitized output—images and sounds—has brought a wonderful new tool to art. However, it has created some big new ethical problems. How can we know that what we're seeing or hearing is the truth? Consider the following areas of concern.

Manipulation of Sound

When does sound manipulation cross the line from improvement to misrepresentation?

In recent times, pop music vocals have been sounding "note and pitch perfect," and even some hip-hop singers have been hitting their notes with exaggerated precision, points out one writer. How is this done? Through a technology called Auto-Tune that "can take a vocal and instantly nudge it onto the proper note or move it to the correct pitch. . . . [I]t can transform wavering performance into something technically flawless."[131] Unfortunately, when most songs seem to have perfect pitch, they are harder to differentiate from one another, leading to bland sameness.

TECH TALES Is It Fraudulent to Manipulate Sound?

Technological manipulation of music is not new. In 2004 country music artist Anita Cochran released some new vocals, including a duet, "(I Wanna Hear) a Cheatin' Song," with Conway Twitty—who had died a decade before the song was written. The producers pulled snippets of Twitty's voice from his recording sessions, put them on a computer hard drive in digital form, and used software known as Pro Tools to patch the pieces together.

Ten years earlier Frank Sinatra's 1994 album *Duets* paired him through technological tricks with such singers as Barbra Streisand, Liza Minnelli, and Bono of U2. Sinatra recorded solos live in a recording studio. His singing partners, while listening to his taped performance on earphones, dubbed in their own voices. These second voices were recorded not only at different times but often from different places. The illusion in the final recording is that the two singers are standing together in the same room. Many people think the practice of assembling bits and pieces in a studio like this drains the music of its essential flow and unity. But is this fraud? ■

Sound Manipulation

Radio Television Digital News Association Guidelines

www.rtdna.org/content/guidelines_for_ethical_video_and_audio_editing#.Ugv4atgx18E

"Fair Use"

This term refers to the conditions under which you can use, and manipulate, material that is copyrighted by someone else without paying royalties. When can you do this?

www.nieman.harvard.edu/reports/article/102763/Detecting-the-Truth-in-Photos.aspx

www.copyright.gov/fls/fl102.html

http://fairuse.stanford.edu/Copyright_and_Fair_Use_Overview/chapter9/9-a.html

http://whatis.techtarget.com/definition/0,,sid9_gci1089600,00.html

Manipulation of Photos

And when does photo manipulation cross the line from improvement to misrepresentation?

Whatever the problems of misrepresentation in art, they pale beside those in journalism. What if, for example, a magazine or TV news station were to edit a photo or stream of video to misrepresent what actually happened?

TECH TALES Is It Fraudulent to Manipulate Photos?

In one famous case, an employee of a Danish computer company created an image purporting to show a photo from a 1954 issue of *Popular Mechanics* of what a future home computer was expected to look like. (• *See Panel 9.5, next page.*) During a 2004 speech, the manipulated photo was misused by the CEO of a computer technology company, who believed the image was real.

Digital image manipulation

panel 9.5

Photo manipulation

A manipulated photo of a typical 1950s nuclear-powered submarine console was passed off as a 1950s projection of the 2004 home computer. A well-known CEO of a computer technology company actually used the photo, believing it was real, during a speech in 2004. The image was created by a Danish hardware and software distributor, who used the submarine shot, doctored it, and entered it in a photo-manipulation contest. He said he had not intended to create a believable fake.

Scientists from the RAND Corporation have created this model to illustrate how a "home computer" could look like in the year 2004. However the needed technology will not be economically feasible for the average home. Also the scientists readily admit that the computer will require not yet invented technology to actually work, but 50 years from now scientific progress is expected to solve these problems. With teletype interface and the Fortran language, the computer will be easy to use.

When ex–sports star O. J. Simpson was arrested in 1994 on suspicion of murder, a *Time* artist working with a computer modified the police department mug shot and darkened the image so that O. J.'s face had a sinister cast to it (go to *https://webspace.utexas.edu/cherwitz/www/ie/samples/stavchansky.pdf*, p. 3, to see these photos). (*Newsweek* ran the mug shot unmodified.)

When in 2005 editors at *Newsweek* ran a cover photo of style guru Martha Stewart, who had been sent to prison for lying to federal investigators about insider trading on a stock investment, they put the image of her face on someone else's body, making the 63-year-old look terrific after five months behind bars.

In May 2011, after the killing of Taliban leader Osama bin Laden by U.S. Navy Seals, Hasidic newspapers *Der Tzitung* and *Dee Voch* "photoshopped" U.S. Secretary of State Hillary Clinton and Director for Counterterrorism Audrey Tomason out of the White House–released situation room photo that accompanied the story—ostensibly because they were women and violated the papers' "modesty guidelines."[132] (• See Panel 9.6.) ■

Should magazines and newspapers that report the news be taking such artistic license? At the least, shouldn't magazines be running credit lines (as *The New York Times Magazine* often does) that say something such as "Photographic illustration by X" or "Photomontage by Y, with digital manipulation by Z"?[133]

panel 9.6

"Photoshopping"

In May 2011 at least two newspapers used software to erase the pictures of two important people (who happened to be women; see *right*) who were present in U.S. President Obama's "situation room" during the actions against terrorist Osama bin Laden (see *left*) (*FailedMessiah.typepad.com*).

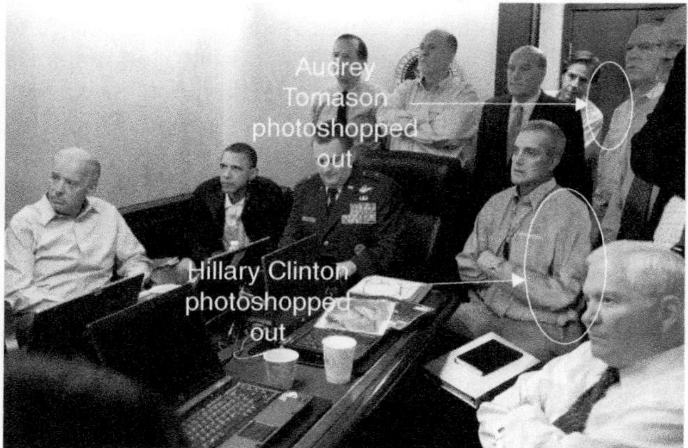

Jon Knoll, who created the image-editing program Photoshop (pp. 172, 484) in 1989, said later, "Mostly we saw the possibilities, the cool things, not how it would be abused."[134] But, as we have seen, Photoshop and similar programs designed to edit ("morph") digital images can obviously also be used to distort and falsify them.

Fortunately, some steps are being taken to combat this kind of digital deception. For example, Corbis, the online stock photo agency, places an imperceptible digital watermark on the more than 100 million images it makes available, which encodes information about the owner of the image within the pixels of the photograph and can be traced even if the image has been modified. In another technique, Dartmouth College computer science professor Hany Farid has codeveloped a program called PhotoDNA that can detect changes in photographic images.

Manipulation of Video & Television

Any user of YouTube is already aware of how regularly software is used to edit videos.

The technique of morphing, used in photos, takes a massive jump when used in TV news videos and television commercials. For example, a Baltimore television reporter lost his job after acknowledging that he doctored a video to make it appear that a rival host had made a racial slur.[135] A daily news show caught another news show and one of its hosts in what appeared to be a blatant example of doctoring a report with inappropriate video to enhance an argument.[136]

And, of course, digital image manipulation has had a tremendous impact on filmmaking. It can be used to erase jet contrails from the sky in a western and to make digital planes do impossible stunts. It is used for all sorts of special effects. It can even be used to add and erase actors. And it is possible to create virtual images during live television events. These images—such as a Coca-Cola logo in the center of a soccer field—don't exist in reality but millions of viewers see them on their TV screens.

Does Photoshopping = False Advertising, Especially for Beauty Products?

"Photoshopping and manipulating photos has become such a regular occurrence that we often see many distorted images on a daily basis without questioning them. . . . Issues that have risen with the increased use of Photoshop are seen to occur mostly in journalism and advertisment[s] and have placed an immense amount of pressure on young females to achieve the look of the technologically altered ideal . . . women" ("Maybe She's Born with It, Maybe It's Photoshop," *http://techlifepost.com/2009/02/13/photo-manipulation-false-advertising/*).

www.businessinsider.com/us-moves-toward-banning-use-of-photoshop-in-cosmetics-ads-2011-12

http://fiusm.com/2012/01/09/photoshop-creates-unrealistic-expectations-for-products/

9.5 QUALITY-OF-LIFE ISSUES: The Environment, Mental Health, Child Protection, & the Workplace

As we know, information technology is not without problems.

In this chapter and earlier ones we have discussed some of the worrisome effects of technology on intellectual property rights, on truth in art and journalism, on censorship issues, on health matters and ergonomics, and on privacy and security. In the following sections we briefly explore some other quality-of-life issues related to information technology.

Survival Tip

Is It True?

Snopes.com, a website for debunking urban legends and hoaxes, includes a section on composite photos, some true, some fake. Go to: **www.snopes.com**

Environmental Problems

Among other problems, information technology leaves a larger environmental "footprint" than we might think.

The data servers that make the Internet run are huge energy hogs. In 2010, data centers, their servers, and their associated cooling and auxiliary infrastructure used roughly 2% of the U.S. total electricity consumption.[137] Moreover, on average, data centers use only 6–12% of the electricity powering their servers to perform computations, the rest being used to keep the servers idling and ready.[138] Indeed, online sucks up enough energy to rank the Internet, if it were a country, fifth in the world for electricity use—more power than Russia uses.[139] Thus, many companies are taking steps to redesign their data centers to reduce the energy drain. Manufacturers of personal computers are also tackling the energy problem, adding green features such as speeding up going into power-saving sleep mode. You can also save a good deal on your household electricity bill by simply unplugging your computer when you're sleeping or not working.

Other environmental challenges remain—specifically, manufacturing and usage by-products, disposal by-products, environmental blight, and possible risks of nanotechnology.

Image Analysis Software

http://lifehacker.com/5644259/how-to-detect-a-photoshopped-image/

http://internet.wonderhowto.com/how-to/photo-forensics-check-if-picture-has-been-photoshopped-not-0138649/

www.imaging-resource.com/news/2012/06/12/detecting-photoshopped-images-part-art-part-science

MANUFACTURING & USAGE BY-PRODUCTS Many communities are eager to have computer and chip manufacturers locate there because they perceive them to be "clean"

Composition of a Desktop Microcomputer

Plastics Lead Aluminum Germanium Gallium Iron Tin Copper Barium Nickel Zinc Tantalum Indium Vanadium Terbium Beryllium Gold Europium Titanium Ruthenium Cobalt Palladium Manganese Silver Antimony Bismuth Chromium Cadmium Selenium Niobium Yttrium Rhodium Platinum Mercury Arsenic Silica. . . .

For more information, go to:

www.it-environment.org/

www.ehow.com/about_6396759_do-pollute-earth-can-it_.html

www.google.com/search?q=computers+and+pollution&client=firefox-a&hs=dG5&rls=org.mozilla:en-US:official&channel=np&tbm=isch&tbo=u&source=univ&sa=X&ei=gv0LUvm2C-IiviQKmxoD4CA&ved=0CGw-QsAQ&biw=1920&bih=965

Donating Old PCs & Cellphones

Want to get rid of your old electronic stuff? For guidance, try:

www.epa.gov/epawaste/conserve/materials/ecycling/index.htm

http://ww2.pcdisposal.com/

www.worldcomputerexchange.org/technology/

http://earth911.com/recycling/electronics/

www.bestbuy.com/site/Global-Promotions/Recycling-Electronics/pcmcat149900050025.c?id=pcmcat149900050025

http://electronicrecyclers.com/

For unwanted cellphones:

www.crserecycling.com/main.php?p=electronics

www.shelteralliance.net/?gclid=CMGLyN3ekKkCFQkSbAoda15koQ

www.e-cycle.com/how-it-works/environmental-responsibility/

www.recellular.com/

www.recyclingforcharities.com/index.php

industries. But there have been lawsuits charging that the semiconductor industry has knowingly exposed workers to a variety of hazardous toxins, some of which were linked to miscarriages, and there is speculation that others may be linked to cancer and birth defects. Wireless systems can disrupt pacemakers and other lifesaving devices in hospitals. The world's data centers are projected to surpass the airline industry as greenhouse gas polluters by 2020.[140]

DISPOSAL BY-PRODUCTS Technologies are quickly going obsolete. What to do with the "e-waste"—about the 400 million electronic products Americans discard per year?

- The U.S. Environmental Protection Agency (EPA) reports that over 112,000 computers are discarded every single day. That's 41.1 million desktops and laptop computers per year. And that's just in the United States (and does not include computer monitors).
- 20 million TVs are trashed in the United States every year.
- And we toss over 100 million cellphones in the trash every year.
- A ton of used cellphones (6,000 phones) yields $15,000 in precious metals.
- To manufacture one computer and monitor, it takes 530 pounds of fossil fuels, 48 pounds of chemicals, and 1.5 tons of water.
- Only 13% of electronic waste is disposed of and recycled properly.[141]

Much of the electronic waste that winds up in the nation's 2,200 landfills contains large amounts of lead and other toxins that can leach into groundwater or produce dioxins and other cancer-causing agents when burned. (• *See Panel 9.7.*) The problem is worsening as new computer models are introduced on faster cycles. *ABC News* did a secret investigation of one e-waste recycler in Denver. This company, which claimed to safely recycle e-waste, wasn't recycling at all. It was loading all those computer monitors, laptops, TVs, and cellphones into shipping containers and sending them to the Far East, mainly rural China and Hong Kong. This is illegal in the United States. But according to *ABC News,* shipping e-waste off to developing countries is not only happening; it's common. Most of our e-waste ends up in such places as Guiyu, China. The entire town has become polluted with toxins as a result of all this garbage.[142]

Many people believe that the United States should follow the lead of Europe and Japan and pass laws forcing manufacturers to reduce the use of toxic materials in new products and take back old computers for recycling.

Don't always assume you can get a school or local charity to take your old personal computer; some will, but many are tired of being stuck with junk. But there are organizations, such as the Electronic Industries Alliance Consumer Education Initiative and Electronics Recycling Services International, that help consumers locate donation programs and recycling companies. Dell, Gateway, and Hewlett-Packard have all created programs whereby users can send unwanted computer gear for donation, refurbishing, or recycling.

Chemical	Source
Lead	• Circuit boards, cathode-ray tubes; discarded electronics account for 30–40% of lead in the waste stream.
Cadmium	• Circuit boards, semiconductors.
Mercury	• Switches, batteries, fluorescent bulbs in liquid-crystal displays.
Chromium	• Circuit boards, corrosion protection in steel.
PVC plastics	• Connectors, cables, housings, plastic covers.
Brominated flame retardants	• Circuit boards and other components.

panel 9.7

Some problem chemicals in PCs

(*left*) German worker sorting electronic garbage along a conveyer at a processing center. Electronic equipment, everything from cellphones to deep freezers, is collected and disposed of separately from regular trash bins. (According to recent European Union legislation, all EU member states must increase their collection of e-waste, whether or not they already meet the current flat-rate target of 8.8 pounds per person per year.) (*right*) A worker in a crane uses a grappler to grab electronic scrap at a plant of a Swiss recycling company.

Cellphones may also be turned in for recycling or reuse. Staples takes back old printer cartridges for recycling. Hewlett-Packard makes new printers from recycled material.

ENVIRONMENTAL BLIGHT Call it "techno-blight." This is the visual pollution represented by the forest of wireless towers, roof antennas, satellite dishes, and all the utility poles topped with transformers and strung with electric, phone, cable TV, and other wires leading off in all directions. As the nation's electric grid becomes more pervasive, so, people worry, will the obtrusive, ugly technology in our physical environment.

Environmentalists worry about the impact on vegetation and wildlife, such as the millions of birds and bats that collide with cellular towers. Residents worry about the effect on views and property values, although antennas can be made into "stealth towers"—fake water towers, flagpoles, trees, and the like—to blend in better with the environment.[143] Some people worry that there may be unknown health effects. Few of the thousands of miles of lines are buried underground, and most of those are in large cities. Ultimately the decision to approve or deny wireless towers resides with the Federal Communications Commission.

Fighting techno-blight. (*left*) Environmentally friendly cellphone towers are disguised as cacti. (*right*) In Upland, California, young palm trees surround a fake palm, which is concealing a cellphone antenna.

POSSIBLE RISKS OF NANOTUBES Some environmentalists worry that the spread of nanotechnology—manipulating materials such as carbon, zinc, and gold at the molecular level—could create contaminants whose tiny size makes them especially hazardous. Many animal studies involving carbon nanotubes, superstrong carbon fibers that are now used in products such as tennis rackets and that might replace silicon in ever tinier transistors, have not found them to be risky. However, research in which nanotubes were injected into the abdomens of mice found that they developed lesions on the lungs similar to those induced by the inhalation of asbestos, which can lead to a deadly cancer. Most people are probably not endangered by nanotubes, scientists concluded, but those working with them in laboratories or at nanotube manufacturers are advised to take extra precautions.

Mental Health Problems

Overuse of computers can increase the risk of depression and insomnia, among other health problems.

Some of the mental health problems linked to information technology are the following ones.

DOES THE INTERNET LEAD TO ISOLATION? Automation allows us to go for days without actually speaking with or touching another person, from buying gas to playing games. Some studies have found that, as people spend more time online, they have less time for real-life relationships with family and friends. For example, a poll of 2,030 people ages 12 and older found that 28% of Americans in 2008 said they had been spending less time with members of their household as compared to 11% who said that two years earlier, a change coinciding with the rise of social networks.[144] And some studies have suggested that excessive dependence on cellphones and the Internet is like an addiction.[145] "The deeper a technology is woven into the patterns of everyday life," says technology writer Nicholas Carr, "the less choice we have about whether and how we use that technology."[146] With the large amount of time being spent online, some argue that although "the social media boom is clearly on its upswing, real life social skills are ironically falling off in dramatic fashion."[147]

However, a study done by the Pew Internet & American Life Project suggests that the Internet does *not* contribute to social isolation. Instead, many Internet technologies are used as much for local contact as they are for distant communication. "Internet use does not pull people away from public places," Pew found. "Rather, it is associated with engagement in places such as parks, cafés, and restaurants, the kinds of locales where research shows that people are likely to encounter a wider array of people and diverse points of view."[148]

more info!

"Warning Sign of Tech Overload"

Take this short quiz (scroll down the left side to find it):

www.nytimes.com/2010/06/07/technology/07brainside.html

ARE VIDEOGAMES HARMFUL? Parents and mental health professionals long have worried that the popularity of videogames has a dark side. When Grand Theft Auto IV was announced in spring 2008, one student at the University of Northern Colorado said he was planning to spend $90 to get the collector's edition. Even though it severely pinched his budget, he said there were things he would sacrifice for a great videogame. "I'd probably give up my cellphone," he said. "Probably not food. That's really tough. I like food."[149]

Earlier, Stanford University researchers showed that areas of the brain responsible for generating feelings of addiction and reward are activated during videogame play.[150] Almost 1 in 10 American children, ages 8 to 18, are said to be addicted to videogames, in the same way that people are addicted to drugs and gambling.[151] Although videogame addiction is not yet officially recognized as a diagnosable disorder by the American Medical Association, "there is increasing evidence that people of all ages, especially teens and pre-teens, are facing very real, sometimes severe consequences associated with compulsive use of video and computer games," says one analysis.[152]

Another issue that many people have with videogames is the violence that many of them seem to celebrate. The debate over whether this "imaginary violence," as one game designer calls it, increases the incidence of real-life violence continues.[153] In any case, the Entertainment Software Rating Board has a videogame ratings system that is linked to children's ages. (• *See Panel 9.8.)*

GAMBLING Gambling is already widespread in North America, but information technology makes it almost unavoidable. Instead of driving to a casino, for example, gamblers can find slots, roulette, and blackjack just a quick mouse click away—and just as quickly find themselves in debt.

ESRB ratings | publishers | retailers | privacy certified | about E

ratings guide | ratings process | enforcement | resources | faq |

ESRB Ratings Guide

The Entertainment Software Rating Board (ESRB) ratings provide concise and objective information about the content in video games and apps so consumers, especially parents, can make informed choices. ESRB ratings have three parts:

- Rating Categories suggest age appropriateness
- Content Descriptors indicate content that may have triggered a particular rating and/or may be of interest or concern
- Interactive Elements inform about interactive aspects of a product, including users' ability to interact, the sharing of users' location with other users, or the fact that personal information may be shared with third parties

As a supplementary source of information, boxed video games have Rating Summaries that provide a more detailed description of the content that factored into the rating assigned.

Rating Categories

EARLY CHILDHOOD
Content is intended for young children.

EVERYONE
Content is generally suitable for all ages. May contain minimal cartoon, fantasy or mild violence and/or infrequent use of mild language.

EVERYONE 10+
Content is generally suitable for ages 10 and up. May contain more cartoon, fantasy or mild violence, mild language and/or minimal suggestive themes.

TEEN
Content is generally suitable for ages 13 and up. May contain violence, suggestive themes, crude humor, minimal blood, simulated gambling and/or infrequent use of strong language.

MATURE
Content is generally suitable for ages 17 and up. May contain intense violence, blood and gore, sexual content and/or strong language.

ADULTS ONLY
Content suitable only for adults ages 18 and up. May include prolonged scenes of intense violence, graphic sexual content and/or gambling with real currency.

RATING PENDING
Not yet assigned a final ESRB rating. Appears only in advertising, marketing and promotional materials related to a game that is expected to carry an ESRB rating, and should be replaced by a game's rating once it has been assigned.

Back to Top

NOTE: Rating Category assignments can also be based upon a game or app's minimum age requirement.

panel 9.8

Videogame industry's rating system
These ratings are supposed to appear on videogame packages. To search for game ratings, go to *www.esrb.org/index-js.jsp* and type in the name of a game you are considering buying.

TECH TALES Gambling in the New IT World

In May 2013, online poker became legal to players in Nevada, New Jersey, and Delaware, legitimizing gambling over the Internet, with 10 other states considering some kind of similar legalization.[154] In addition, host computers for Internet casinos and sports books have been established in Caribbean tax havens and other places, with offshore companies taking bets from Americans for poker and casino games.

Technology has provided some interesting wrinkles in relation to gambling. "Casinos in several states are forbidding gamblers from wearing Google Glass, the tiny eyeglasses-mounted device capable of shooting photos, filming video, and surfing the Internet," reports the Associated Press. "Regulators say the gadget could be used to cheat at card games."[155]

On a more positive side, to help try to reduce gambling addiction, researchers are beginning to track the betting habits of some frequent gamblers, using casino customer-tracking information, "to create computerized models that can spot and warn people with high risk profiles," according to one report. The researchers work with the industry's own data, which is often used in conjunction with loyalty cards to pamper the best customers, to "look for risky betting patterns such as intensive play over long periods, significant shifts in behavior, or chasing losses—betting more heavily in an attempt to recoup prior losses."[156] Flagged gamblers may be given analyses of their behavior or educational tools or even be barred from casino play. ■

STRESS Information technology can bring all kinds of stress. Spending evenings in front of a glowing smartphone, computer, or TV screen can put you at risk for depression.[157] Using smartphone and tablets before bed can cut into your sleep hours.[158] Some people even work while *in* bed, trying to stay on top of their email; indeed, 20% of some British workers studied spent 2–10 hours a week working from bed, according to one study.[159]

Twitter is a time trap, what you check while you're in the elevator or waiting in line. "The constant feed gobbles up all the in-between moments," observes one writer.[160] Mobile devices can bring the workplace to you 24/7, which is why 7 in 10 U.S. workers say technology has allowed work to move into their personal life and two-thirds of U.S. employees work even during their vacations.[161] Technological advances have caused work to flood into "more hours of the day and more days of the week—curiously, as a matter of people's own behavior and choices," says Rick Segal, chair of a worldwide advertising agency.[162]

In addition, for many people, having just one mobile device is not enough. Some consumers, for example, may have an Android phone for business, an Apple iPhone for fun, and, of course, a tablet, creating competition for Wi-Fi connections at major events and swollen phone bills. One result is that some $50 billion is wasted every year in the United States on unused voice, texts, and data, according to one market research firm.[163]

So, could you use a little less self-induced stress?

Survival Tip

Alleviating Info-Mania

Hewlett-Packard offers a six-page "Guide to Avoiding Info-Mania" at:

http://demo.ort.org.il/clickit2/files/forums/920455712/548653262.pdf

Also:

www.biomedcentral.com/1471-244X/12/176

http://availabletechnology.blogspot.com/2012/08/computer-related-stress-and-how-to.html

Protecting Children: Pornography, Sexual Predators, & Online Bullies

Children are the most vulnerable members of society; protecting them is a top priority.

Since computers are simply another way of communicating, it is no surprise that they are used to communicate about pornography, sexual solicitations, and threats and violence. Let's consider these.

PORNOGRAPHY One of the biggest cultural changes in the United States of the past quarter century has been the widespread distribution of sexually explicit material. There are nearly 25 million porn sites worldwide, according to one estimate, and they make up 12% of all websites.[164] In the past, at least, pornography has been such a profitable business that even some of America's most well-known companies, such as General Motors, Time Warner, and Marriott, were said to make millions selling pornography, as on closed-circuit TV channels in hotels.[165] Audio files called "porncasts" are available for downloading for adult podcasts. On the highways, motorists have complained of "dirty driving" as they found themselves looking at X-rated fare playing in other cars outfitted with DVD players. It's also an issue on trains and planes and in libraries, cafés, and gyms—anywhere computers, laptops, and smartphones appear—giving rise "to a growing source of friction," as *The New York Times* describes it, "public displays of pornographic content."[166]

Children, of course, are among those exposed to such material. Following are some steps being taken to try to shield them.

Survival Tip

Beware!

Online pornography sites are infamous for injecting malware into users' browsers.

- **Online blocking software:** Some software developers have discovered a golden opportunity in making programs such as Websense, Cybersitter, Cyber Patrol, and Net Nanny. These blocking programs are designed to screen out objectionable material, typically by identifying certain unapproved keywords in a user's request or comparing the user's request for information against a list of prohibited sites. The leading online access providers also offer software filters.
- **DVD filters:** ClearPlay uses filtering technology that allows parents to edit out the inappropriate parts of films on DVDs—such as disturbing images, violence, nudity, swear words, and ethnic and social slurs.
- **The V-chip:** The 1996 Telecommunications Law officially launched the era of the *V-chip,* a device that is required equipment in all new television sets with screen size of 13 inches or larger sold after January 2000 (*www.fcc.gov/guides/v-chip-putting-restrictions-what-your-children-watch*). The V-chip allows parents to automatically block programs that have been labeled as high in violence, sex, or other objectionable material. Unfortunately, to turn on the controls, owners have to follow complicated instructions and menu settings, and then they have to remember their passwords when they want to watch reruns of *The Sopranos, X Factor, 1,000 Ways to Die,* and *Criminal Minds.*
- **"xxx" web addresses:** In 2011 the agency that controls domain names (ICANN, p. 62) voted to add *.xxx* to the list of suffixes people and companies can pick when establishing their identities online. The purpose of the new generic top-level domain would be to enable parents to more easily apply filtering software and so more effectively block access to at least some porn sites, those that voluntarily adopted the *xxx.*

SEXTING **Sexting is use of a smartphone or other mobile device to send sexually explicit photos or videos; sometimes it also refers to sexually charged text messages.** Sexting made big news in 2013 when New York mayoral candidate Anthony Weiner confessed he had tweeted pornographic photos of himself to women not his wife.[167] Teen sexting may worry a lot of parents, but only 2.5% of children ages 10–17 admit to creating or appearing in such photos or videos, according to one study, and even fewer produce images that amount to pornography.[168] Another study found, however, that those who admit to sexting are significantly more likely to also say they engage in sexual intercourse.[169] And earlier research found that 20% of teens (and a third of young adults 20–26) say they've sent or posted naked or seminaked photos or videos of themselves, mostly to be "fun or flirtatious," according to one survey.[170] Another survey found that at least a quarter of the teenagers polled had posted something they later regretted.[171]

The smartphone app Snapchat, which makes "snaps" automatically self-destruct after a few seconds, has developed a reputation among both young people and adults sharing photos who don't want others (such as their parents) to see them.[172]

panel 9.9

Parent prevention strategies for keeping children safe

- **Monitor Internet use:** Parents are advised to monitor their children's Internet use and to install filters.
- **Be candid:** Parents should also make children aware that having sex with an adult is a crime and explain that molesters capitalize on teenagers' needs for acceptance.
- **Caution about revealing too much:** Children, particularly teenagers, reveal far too much about themselves online, which can make them targets for predators or bullies.

Some suggested prevention strategies are shown in the panel above. *(• See Panel 9.9.)*

CYBERBULLIES In yet another example of how information technology can negatively affect the social lives of children, there have been numerous reports of **cyberbullying, in which—generally but not exclusively—children in the 9–18 age range use information technologies, including the Internet, to unleash merciless taunting, nasty rumors, humiliating pictures, and other put-downs of fellow adolescents.** The tactics include stealing one another's screen names, forwarding private material to people for whom it was not intended, and posting derogatory material on blogs.

"Bullies have gotten more complex and malicious as Internet access becomes more accessible with the rise of cheap, Internet-enabled mobile devices and as social networking becomes more intertwined with students' everyday lives," says one reporter.[173] A 2011 Pew report found that 15% of social media users between ages 12 and 17 said they'd been harassed online in the previous year.[174]

Some suggested tactics for dealing with cyberbullies are shown below. *(• See Panel 9.10.)* Incidentally, cyberbullying is also a problem on campus and in the workplace. It may even rise to the level of *cyberstalking*—an attacker harasses a victim using email, instant messaging, or communications posted on the web, hiding behind the anonymity afforded by the Internet to stalk the victim undetected.[175] (Note that cyberbullying is a felony in some U.S. states.)

Workplace Problems: Impediments to Productivity

Three types of workplace problems are misuse of technology, fussing with computers, and information overload.

MISUSE OF TECHNOLOGY Employees may look busy, as they stare into their computer screens with brows crinkled. But sometimes they're just hard at work playing videogames. Or browsing online malls (forcing corporate mail rooms to cope with a deluge of privately ordered parcels). Or looking at their investments or pornography sites.

FUSSING WITH COMPUTERS Another reason for so much wasted time is all the waiting that computer users endure or the fussing that they do with hardware, software, and connection problems. Computer users average about 13 minutes each day just waiting for their technology to load or catch up to them and up to 30 minutes each day waiting for their PCs to load or reboot.[176] Billions of hours a year are also wasted checking computer output for accuracy, helping coworkers use their applications, making online connections work, and untangling complications wrought by spam, phishing, viruses, and other Internet problems.

panel 9.10

Tactics for dealing with cyberbullies

- **Save the evidence:** Children should print out offending messages and show them to their parents, who should then contact parents of the bully as well as inform school officials.
- **Block messages:** Victims should use the Block function to block further online communication from the bully. Parents should also contact email services and change the victim's screen name (and the victim should tell only his or her friends the new name).
- **Contact an attorney or police:** If there are threats of violence or sexual harassment, parents should contact a lawyer or the police.

INFORMATION OVERLOAD Information technology is definitely a two-edged sword. Cellphones, pagers, and laptops may untether employees from the office, but these employees tend to work longer hours under more severe deadline pressure than do their tethered counterparts who stay at the office. Moreover, the devices that once promised to do away with annoying business travel by ushering in a new era of communications have done the opposite. They have created the office-in-a-bag that allows businesspeople to continue to work from airplane seats, hotel desks, and their own kitchen tables. The diminishing difference between work and leisure is what has been called the "blurring of life segments."[177]

Some studies have found an increase in labor productivity in the early years of the 21st century, most of it attributed to more investment in information technology and efficiency improvements made possible by this technology.[178] However, says one writer, "the dirty little secret of the information age is that an increasingly large slice of work goes on outside the official work hours the government recognizes. . . . The '24/7' culture of nearly round-the-clock work is endemic to the wired economy. . . . But improving productivity is not about working longer; it's about adding more value per unit of work time."[179] An additional interesting wrinkle in the Internet age is how much work is done that is voluntary or donated work, as in all the user-generated content that is contributed to YouTube, Wikipedia, the Spore's Creature Creator universe simulation game, and so on.[180]

Some people are concerned that "our workload and speed [do] not leave room for thoughtful reflection."[181] Adds Bill McKibben, author of *Enough: Staying Human in an Engineered Age,* "There is a real danger that one is absorbing and responding to bursts of information, rather than having time to think."[182]

The first recorded use of the phrase "information overload" was used by the futurologist Alvin Toffler in 1970, when he predicted that the rapidly increasing amounts of information being produced would eventually cause people problems. The root of the problem is that, although computer processing and memory speed and capacity are increasing all the time, the brain that humans must use to process the information is not getting any faster. Effectively, the human mind acts as a bottleneck in the process.[183] Trying to deal with all the information that bombards us is like trying to drink from a firehose.

What are some of the signs of information overload?[184]

- Increased cardiovascular stress owing to a rise in blood pressure.
- Weakened vision.
- Confusion and frustration.
- Impaired judgment based on overconfidence.
- Irritation with others owing to an environmental input glut (which may also account for part of the "brusqueness" that is commonly attributed to big-city dwellers).

What can be done about information overload? Some suggestions:

- Spend less time on information that is nice to know and more time on information that you need to know now.
- Focus on getting relevant information, not on getting information faster, and focus on quality of information, rather than quantity.
- Learn how to create better information. Be direct in what you ask people, so that they can provide short precise answers.
- Understand the tools you have and don't switch tasks very often (single-tasking keeps the mind focused on one issue at a time).
- Avoid interruptions.
- Have quiet periods, when you disconnect.
- Take breaks.

9.6 ECONOMIC & POLITICAL ISSUES: Employment & the Haves/Have-Nots

There is an ongoing debate about whether information technology is reducing job availability and widening the gap between the rich and the poor.

In recent times, a number of critics have provided a counterpoint to the hype and overselling of information technology to which we have long been exposed. Some critics find that the benefits of information technology are balanced by a real downside. Other critics make the alarming case that technological progress is actually no progress at all—indeed, it is a curse. The two biggest charges (which are related) are, first, that information technology is killing jobs and, second, that it is widening the gap between the rich and the poor.

Technology, the Job Killer?

Increasingly intelligent machinery and automation have caused a reduction in several types of jobs.

Certainly ATMs do replace bank tellers, E-ZPass electronic systems do replace turnpike toll takers, and Internet travel agents do lure customers away from small travel agencies. Hundreds of companies are replacing service representatives with voice software. In new so-called lights-out factories, machines make things—for example, the tiny cutting devices you see mounted on dental-floss containers—even when no one is there; as much as possible is done with no labor. The contribution of technological advances to economic progress is steady, but the contribution to social progress is not purely positive.

Kiva Systems is a subsidiary of Amazon.com. Kiva uses automation technology for distribution centers that helps companies simplify operations and reduce costs while increasing strategic flexibility. Using hundreds of autonomous mobile robots (orange) and sophisticated control software, the Kiva Mobile-Robotic Fulfillment System enables extremely fast cycle times with reduced labor requirements, from receiving to picking to shipping. Such factories usually have little lighting, because no or few humans work there.

But is it true, as technology critic Jeremy Rifkin has said, that intelligent machines are replacing humans in countless tasks, "forcing millions of blue-collar and white-collar workers into temporary, contingent, and part-time employment and, worse, unemployment"?[185]

This is too large a question to be fully considered in this book. We can say for sure that the U.S. economy is undergoing powerful structural changes, brought on not only by the widespread diffusion of technology but also by greater competition, increased global trade, the sending of jobs offshore, the shift from manufacturing to service employment, the weakening of labor unions, more flexible labor markets, more rapid immigration, partial deregulation, and certainly the great recession of 2008–2010. One futurist argues that by 2100 perhaps 2% of the U.S. non-farm workforce will be needed to handle white-collar "know-how" functions, such as those of most of today's office workers, but that "hyper-human" service workers, who will be required for creativity, social skills, conscious perception, positive feelings, hypothesizing, and the like, will zoom to over 90%.[186]

A counterargument is that jobs don't disappear—they just change. According to some observers, the jobs that do disappear represent drudgery. "If your job has been replaced by a computer," says Stewart Brand, "that may have been a job that was not worthy of a human."[187] Of course, that means little to someone who has no job at all.

Digital Divide between Rich & Poor

Advances in information technology seem to lead to a widening gap between the rich and the poor.

We seem to be living through one of those difficult periods in which technology doesn't produce widely shared economic gains but instead widens the gap—often called the digital divide—between those who have the right skills and those who don't.

According to the Organization for Economic Cooperation and Development (OECD), income inequality is increasing in most industrialized countries as a result of globalization and technological progress that requires greater skills from workers.[188] The gap between rich and poor is widening in countries that traditionally have a high level of inequality, such as the United States. It also is rising in countries that have been more equal, such as Denmark, Germany, and Sweden.[189] And although computer hardware is getting cheaper, high-speed Internet connections can be prohibitively expensive for poor and working-class families.

As *New York Times* columnist Thomas Friedman has written, in *The World Is Flat,* the world is "flattening," becoming more interconnected as the result of the Internet, wireless technology, search engines, file sharing, digital photography, and other cutting-edge technologies.[190] This may be good for many advanced nations. But half the world—Africa, much of Latin America, and rural areas of India and China—isn't flattening at all. And the future may be risky for America as well, because the fiber-optic cables that have been laid across the Pacific Ocean have made it easy to send offshore the jobs of all kinds of workers—accountants, radiologists, illustrators, and so on—whose work is knowledge-based.[191]

According to the International Monetary Fund, "better access to education would allow less-skilled and lower-income groups to capitalize on the opportunities from both technological progress and the ongoing process of globalization. Similarly, broadening access to finance, for instance, by improving institutions that promote pro-poor lending, could help improve the overall distribution of income even as financial development broadly continues to support overall growth."[192]

Whom Does the Internet Serve?

Do all people have equal access to the Internet?

Because of its unruly nature, perhaps the Internet truly serves no one—and that is both its blessing and its curse. Many business executives, for instance, find the public Internet so unreliable that they have moved their most critical applications to semiprivate networks, such as intranets and extranets (p. 314). That means that more of the network is increasingly brought under commercial control, which for consumers might mean more fees for special services and the stifling of cultural empowerment and free speech. Despite early euphoria that the Internet would unleash a democratic spirit, nonprofit uses, and progressive websites, some see increasing corporate consolidation, at least in the United States.

For many restrictive governments outside the United States—China, Saudi Arabia, Iran, Singapore, United Arab Emirates, Bahrain, for example—that try to control Internet access by their citizens, the net poses threats to their authority. China, for instance, leads the United States in the number of people online; its nondemocratic government has cracked down on some kinds of Internet political activism but tolerated others—largely because there is so much online chatter that it can't censor it all.[193] (Some of the more than 1,000 words and phrases filtered by the Chinese instant-messaging service include "democracy," "human rights," and "oppose corruption.") But if such governments want to join the global economy, an important goal for most, perhaps they will find that less control and regulation will translate into greater e-commerce.

In a World of Breakneck Change, Can You Still Thrive?

Technological change is inevitable; our being able to adapt is critical.

Clearly, information technology is driving the new world of jobs, services, and leisure, and nothing is going to stop it. People pursuing careers find the rules are changing very rapidly. Up-to-date skills are becoming ever more crucial. Job descriptions of all kinds are metamorphosing, and even familiar jobs are becoming more demanding.

Where will you be in all this? Today, experts advise, you must be willing to continually upgrade your skills, to specialize, and to market yourself. In a world of breakneck change, you can still thrive.

EXPERIENCE BOX

Student Use of Computers: Some Controversies

Information technology is very much a part of the college experience, of course. Elsewhere we discussed such matters as distance learning, web research, online plagiarism, and Internet addiction. Here we describe some other issues regarding students' computer use.

Using Computers in the Classroom

Although they're more expensive than desktop computers, laptops are useful because you can take them not only to libraries, to help with reading or term paper notes, but also to class to use in taking lecture notes. You might even try using a tablet computer; be aware, however, small or virtual keyboards may pose a problem, and tablets do not support full-fledged productivity applications, such as Microsoft Office. With laptop or tablet, battery life may also be a factor.

The use of computers in classrooms is still controversial in certain quarters. Some campuses allow students to bring laptops and other electronic items to class but are imposing rules about what they are allowed to do. Too many students text one another, check their smartphones, browse the web, and visit social-networking sites.

Notes Posted on the Web

Wouldn't it be nice, when you're out sick, to be able to go to a website and get the notes of lectures for the classes you missed? This is possible on campuses served by some commercial firms. Many such services are free, since the firms try to generate revenue by selling online advertising, but some charge a fee.

Such services can be a real help to students who learn best by reading rather than by hearing. They also provide additional reinforcement to students who feel they have not been able to grasp all of a professor's ideas during the lecture. However, they are no substitute for the classroom experience, with its spontaneous exchange of ideas. Moreover, "the very act of taking notes—not reading somebody else's notes, no matter how stellar—is a way of engaging the material, wrestling with it, struggling to comprehend or take issue."[194] In other words, you'll be better able to remember the lecture if you've reinforced the ideas by writing them down yourself.

Some faculty members have no problem with note-taking operations. Others disapprove, however. Among the criticisms: (1) Note-taking services don't always ask permission. (2) Instructors are reluctant to share their unpublished research in class if they think their ideas might end up posted in a public place and ripped off. (3) They might not wish to share controversial opinions with students if their views might be criticized in a worldwide forum. (4) Students might not come to class, especially if they think the lectures are boring or if they are given to chronic oversleeping or hangovers. (5) The notes may be sloppy, inaccurate, or incomplete.

Bottom line: These websites may be helpful, but they are certainly no substitute for going to class.

Online Student Evaluations

Student evaluations of courses and professors on the Internet can be useful. But since such evaluations are often expressed anonymously, they can also be inaccurate and unfair—even vicious, if students receiving poor grades take revenge by vilifying their instructors online. Many people don't understand how hard instructors work and believe that students should not be able to bash teachers in a public forum.

In reading teacher evaluations, it's useful to pay close attention to how civil and fair-minded the reports seem. And, of course, you should try to be as considerate and fair and objective as possible when writing them. Most students are not experts on teaching.

TERMS & EXPLANATIONS

biometrics (p. 473) Science of measuring individual body characteristics. Why it's important: *Biometric technology is used in some computer security systems to restrict user access. Biometric devices, such as those that use fingerprints, eye scans, palm prints, and face recognition, authenticate a person's identity by verifying his or her physical or behavioral characteristics.*

computer crime (p. 464) Crime of two types: (1) an illegal act perpetrated against computers or telecommunications; (2) the use of computers or telecommunications to accomplish an illegal act. Why it's important: *Crimes against information technology include theft—of hardware, of software, of computer time, of cable or telephone services, or of information. Other illegal acts are crimes of malice and destruction. Computer crimes have very real and damaging consequences.*

cyberbullying (p. 494) Abusive behavior whereby (usually but not always) adolescents use information technologies, including the Internet, to unleash merciless taunting, nasty rumors, humiliating pictures, and other put-downs of fellow adolescents. The tactics include stealing one another's screen names, forwarding private material to people for whom it was not intended, and posting derogatory material on blogs. Why it's important: *Cyberbullying may rise to the level of a misdemeanor or felony charge. Cyberbullying can greatly harm targeted people.*

cyberwarfare (p. 483) The use of computers and the Internet by one nation to attack another nation's information systems. Why it's important: *Attacks may be conducted as tactical maneuvers against an opponent or on the scale of widespread cyberattacks to impair government and military information systems.*

disaster-recovery plan (p. 475) Method of restoring information-processing operations that have been halted by destruction or accident. Why it's important: *Such a plan is important if an organization desires to resume computer operations quickly.*

encryption (p. 474) Process of altering readable data so that it is not usable unless the changes are undone. Why it's important: *Encryption can prevent unauthorized access and is useful to many organizations, especially those concerned with trade secrets, military matters, and other sensitive data. Some people maintain that encryption will determine the future of e-commerce, because transactions cannot flourish over the Internet unless they are secure.*

evil twin attack (p. 469) A variant on conventional phishing, in which a hacker or cracker sets up a Wi-Fi hot spot or access point that makes your computer think it's accessing a safe public network or your home network and then monitors your communications. Why it's important: *The hacker can steal data you enter into a website, if it doesn't have the right security measures.*

security (p. 470) System of safeguards for protecting information technology against disasters, system failures, and unauthorized access that can result in damage or loss. Five components of security are deterrents to computer crime, identification and access, encryption, protection of software and data, and disaster-recovery plans. Why it's important: *With proper security, organizations and individuals can minimize information technology losses from disasters, system failures, and unauthorized access.*

sexting (p. 493) The act of sending sexually revealing pictures of oneself through smartphone text messages or email. Why it's important: *It may lead to embarrassments later in life—for example, when one is applying for a job—cause legal troubles, or draw the attention of predators.*

CHAPTER REVIEW

LEARNING MEMORIZATION

"I can recognize and recall information."

Self-Test Questions

1. So that information-processing operations can be restored after destruction or accident, organizations should adopt a(n) __________.
2. __________ is the altering of readable data so that it is not usable unless the changes are undone.
3. __________ is incomplete, outdated, or otherwise inaccurate data.
4. The use of computers and the Internet by one nation to attack another nation's information systems is called __________.
5. CERT, created by the U.S. Department of Defense, stands for __________.
6. Software obtained illegally is called __________ software.
7. A variant on phishing in which someone sets up a Wi-Fi hot spot or access point that makes your computer think it's accessing a safe public network or your home network and then monitors your communications is called a(n) __________.
8. The term __________ refers to a system of safeguards for protecting information technology against disasters, system failures, and unauthorized access that can result in damage or loss.
9. __________ is the science of measuring individual body characteristics.

Multiple-Choice Questions

1. Which of these may be a felony?
   a. natural hazards
   b. profile theft
   c. cyberbullying
   d. software bugs
   e. procedural errors
2. Which of these methods or means is used to safeguard computer systems?
   a. facial recognition
   b. zombie
   c. adware
   d. worms
   e. Internet2
3. Which of the following are threats to computer systems?
   a. zombies
   b. evil twins
   c. crackers
   d. Trojan horses
   e. all of these
4. Which of these is an example of advance-fee fraud?
   a. zombie
   b. botnet
   c. phish
   d. evil twin attack
   e. Nigerian letter scam

True-False Questions

T F 1. The category of computer crimes includes dirty data problems.

T F 2. Software bugs include procedural errors.

T F 3. A disaster-recovery plan is a method of encryption.

T F 4. It is impossible to detect when a photo has been morphed ["photoshopped"].

T F 5. Humans are generally very good at assessing their own information needs.

stage 2 LEARNING COMPREHENSION

"I can recall information in my own terms and explain it to a friend."

Short-Answer Questions

1. Give some examples of dirty data.
2. Briefly describe how encryption works.
3. What is a procedural error?
4. Name five threats to computers and communications systems.
5. The definition of *computer crime* distinguishes between two types. What are they?
6. What is phishing?
7. If your employer is checking on you, what might he or she be watching for?
8. What are three ways of verifying legitimate right of access to a computer system?
9. Name four environmental problems caused by computers.

stage 3 LEARNING APPLYING, ANALYZING, SYNTHESIZING, EVALUATING

"I can apply what I've learned, relate these ideas to other concepts, build on other knowledge, and use all these thinking skills to form a judgment."

Knowledge in Action

1. What, in your opinion, are the most significant disadvantages of using computers? What do you think can be done about these problems?
2. What's your opinion about the issue of free speech on an electronic network? Research some recent legal decisions in various countries, as well as some articles on the topic. Should the contents of messages be censored? If so, under what conditions?
3. Research the problems of stress and isolation experienced by computer users in the United States, Japan, and one other country. Write a brief report on your findings.
4. How can you ensure that information is accurate and complete? Make a list of things to remember when you are doing research on the Internet for a term paper.

Web Exercises

1. What is 128-bit encryption? Is your browser equipped? Visit the following websites to learn more about browser security:

   www.veracode.com/blog/2013/03/browser-security-settings-for-chrome-firefox-and-internet-explorer/

   http://netsecurity.about.com/od/webbrowsersecurity/Web_Browser_Security_Information_and_Resources.htm

   www.it.cornell.edu/security/safety/malware/hardening.cfm

   http://its.ucsc.edu/software/release/browser-secure.html

   http://daol.aol.com/articles/how-to-tighten-your-browsers-security/
2. Here's a way to semi-encrypt an email message to a friend. In Word, type out your message; then press Ctrl+A (for *Select All*). Next go to the Format menu

(or the Home tab), and select a typeface such as Wingdings that doesn't use letters. When your friend receives your message, he or she need only change the font back to an understandable one (such as Times New Roman) in order to read it. This certainly isn't high-level encryption, but it's a fun activity to try.

3. Visit the following websites, which discuss general Internet addiction:

   www.helpguide.org/mental/internet_cybersex_addiction.htm

   www.mentalhelp.net/poc/center_index.php?id=66

   www.forbes.com/sites/alicegwalton/2012/10/02/the-new-mental-health-disorder-internet-addiction/

   www.mapsofworld.com/poll/is-internet-addiction-real-facts-infographic.html

   Do you have an Internet problem? Take a test:

   http://netaddiction.com/internet-addiction-test/

   What do you plan to do about it?

4. If you're spending too much time indoors using a computer or watching TV, you might want to consider going outside. Visit the following websites to learn about indoor air versus outdoor air:

   www.epa.gov/iaq/ia-intro.html

   www.epa.gov/iaq/pubs/insidestory.html

   http://home.howstuffworks.com/home-improvement/household-safety/tips/indoor-air-pollution.htm

   www.who.int/phe/health_topics/outdoorair/en/

   Also, to read more about Internet addiction that may cause isolation from the real world, visit:

   www.empowher.com/emotional-health/content/how-internet-affects-social-isolation/

   http://cogsciblog.wordpress.com/2009/11/04/internet-use-does-not-increase-social-isolation-study-finds/

   www.pewinternet.org/Reports/2009/18–Social-Isolation-and-New-Technology.aspx

   http://digitaljournal.com/article/322982/

   www.usatodayeducate.com/staging/index.php/campuslife/social-media-doesnt-mean-social-isolation/

   What's your opinion on this issue?

   The following websites discuss computer health and safety:

   www.osha.gov/SLTC/etools/computerworkstations/

   www.youtube.com/watch?v=m38cADo7cZY

   www.ors.od.nih.gov/sr/dohs/HealthAndSafety/Ergonomics/atwork/Pages/ergo_computers.aspx

5. How much do you know about the U.S. Department of Homeland Security's rules and policies concerning computer users' privacy? Go to *www.dhs.gov* and find out how you are affected.

6. Research the rules/laws regarding the use of smartphone cameras. Do we have to accept the fact that some people will take pictures of everything—including us—almost everywhere we go?

10

BUILDING SYSTEMS & APPLICATIONS Software Development, Programming, & Languages

Chapter Topics & Key Questions

UNIT 10A: *Systems Development & Programming*

10.1 **Systems Development & the Life Cycle of a Software Project** What are the six phases of the systems development life cycle?

10.2 **Programming: Traditionally a Five-Step Procedure** What is programming, and what are the five steps in accomplishing it?

UNIT 10B: *Programming Languages*

10.3 **Five Generations of Programming Languages** What are the five generations of programming languages?

10.4 **Programming Languages Used Today** What are some third-generation languages, and what are they used for?

10.5 **Object-Oriented & Visual Programming** How do OOP and visual programming work?

10.6 **Markup & Scripting Languages** What do markup and scripting languages do?

Download the free UIT 11e App for key term flash cards quizzes and a game, *Over the Edge*

CHAPTER FORECAST This chapter covers the tools that systems analysts, software engineers, and programmers work with.

In Unit 10A we explain systems development and the six phases of the systems development life cycle: preliminary investigation, systems analysis, systems design, systems development, systems implementation, and systems maintenance. We then explain the five-step process of programming: clarifying the programming needs, designing the program, coding the program, testing the program, and documenting and maintaining the program.

In Unit 10B we discuss five generations of programming languages: machine language, assembly language, third-generation languages (high-level languages—procedural and object-oriented languages), fourth-generation languages (very-high-level languages—problem-oriented languages), and fifth-generation languages (natural languages). We then discuss programming languages used today, beginning with FORTRAN, COBOL, and BASIC, and describe object-oriented and visual programming. We conclude with a discussion of markup and scripting languages.

UNIT 10A: *Systems Development & Programming*

"We think of computers as smart and powerful machines," says Jason Fried. "But your goldfish is smarter."

"Unlike a goldfish," continues Fried, CEO of 37signals, a Chicago project management software company, "a computer can't really do anything without you telling it exactly what you want it to do."[1]

Learning to tell a computer what to do—that is, learning systems development and programming, the subject of this chapter—can be a great career booster. Here's how:

- **You can do some computer-related projects yourself—including apps:** Fried, who is a designer, began taking a course on programming, studying Ruby on Rails, a programming framework that powers websites worldwide, because he wanted to be able to build software projects on his own, without having to bother a programmer. Such projects also include writing apps—software applications for mobile devices such as smartphones and tablets. (Of course, not everyone is suited to be a programmer; often it is better to hire someone who is an expert.)
- **You can become a better communicator:** In taking the course, Fried found that learning to program a computer also taught him how to be a better communicator—not just with the programmers he had to work with but with everyone, including customers.

  "When programming a computer, you can't assume a whole lot. It knows next to nothing," Fried points out. "Learning how to program has taught me that I need to explain things more clearly—and not only to machines. I used to assume a lot and rush through things. But now, when I describe something new to someone, I find myself slowing down, breaking the idea down in my mind and explaining it piece by piece."

10.1 SYSTEMS DEVELOPMENT & THE LIFE CYCLE OF A SOFTWARE PROJECT

Systems development involves several steps of systems analysis and design.

It's called the "app economy," a boom that has inspired a new class of entrepreneurs of all ages who are turning apps for smartphones and tablets "into tools for discovering, organizing, and controlling the world, spawning a multibillion-dollar industry virtually overnight," according to *The New York Times*.[2] In mid-2013, online ads for application software developers reached a new high, and demand for software developer jobs in general grew more than 190% from four years previously.[3]

Reports of instant fortunes have inspired people to quit their jobs to become freelance app writers, produced some ambitious mobile software start-up companies (such as 52apps, begun by University of South Carolina students), and even led a number of colleges to create app-writing courses and app-related business incubators.[4] Although the idea of acquiring fast riches from app writing may be illusory, nevertheless learning software development can be a valuable part of a 21st-century college graduate's toolkit. The education begins with learning about systems and systems analysis and design.

The Purpose of Systems Analysis & Design

Systems analysis and design tries to determine how a system works and how to make it better.

A system is defined as a collection of related components that interact to perform a task in order to accomplish a goal. A system may not work very well, but it is nevertheless a system. The purpose of systems analysis and design is to determine how a system works and then to take steps to make it better.

An organization's computer-based information system consists of hardware, software, people, procedures, and data, as well as communications setups. These components work together to provide people with information for running the organization.

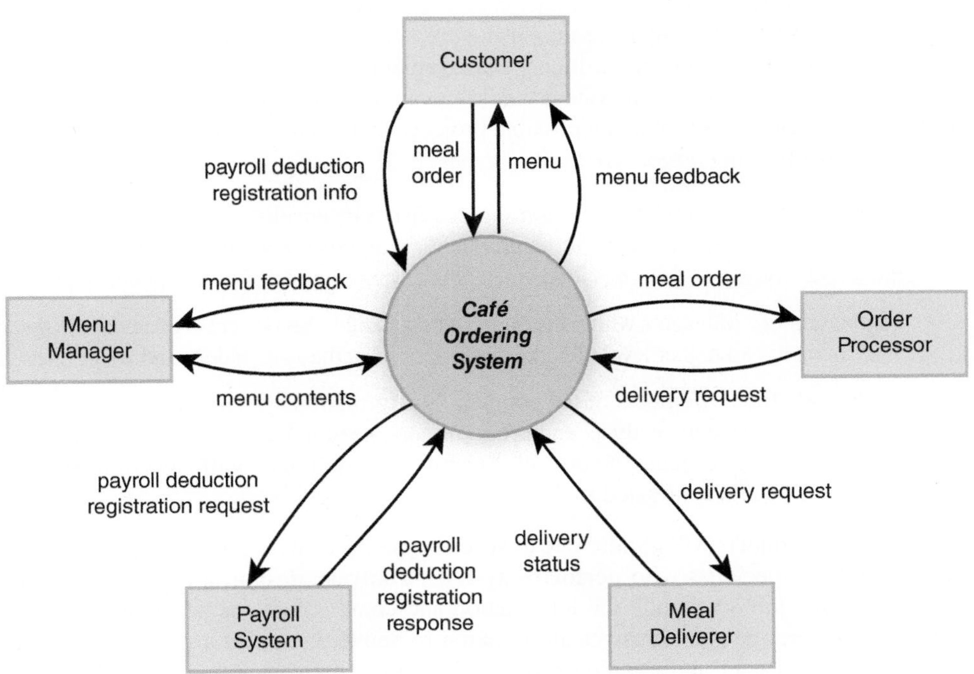

One example of a system: Café ordering system

Another example of a system: Basic elements of the human digestive system

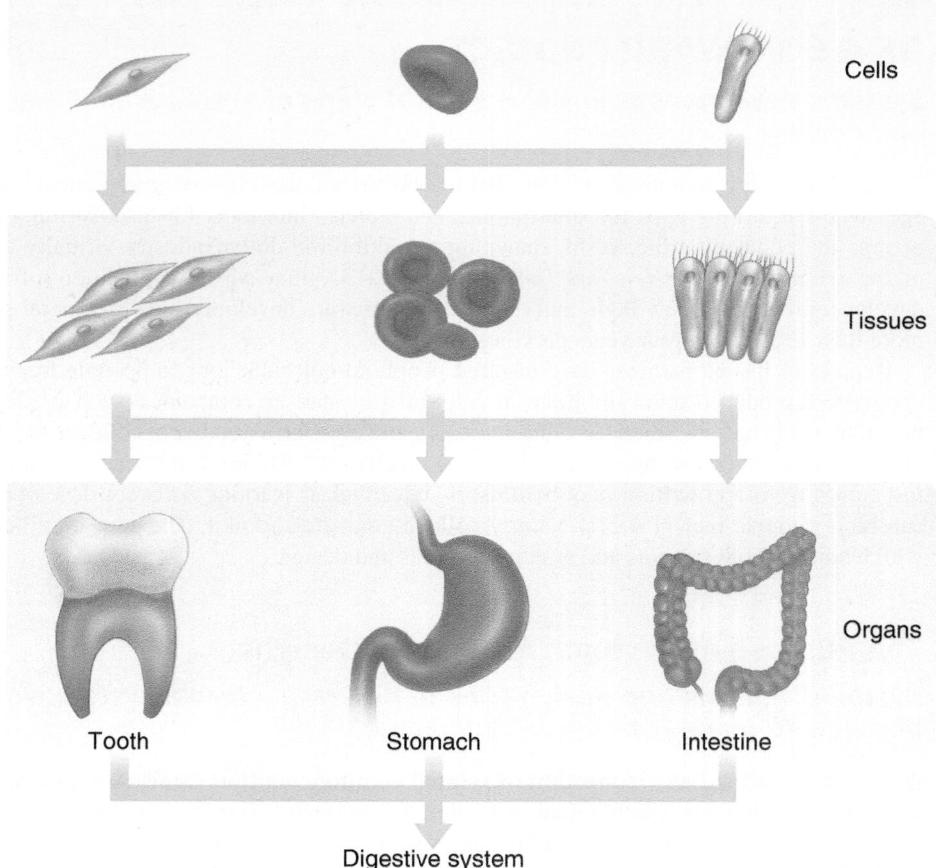

Adapted from http://en.wikibooks.org/wiki/Anatomy_and_Physiology_of_Animals/Body_Organisation.

Getting the Project Going: How It Starts, Who's Involved

Several types of people are involved in getting a project going.

A single individual who believes that something badly needs changing is all it takes to get the project rolling. An employee may influence a supervisor. A customer or supplier may get the attention of someone in higher management. Top management may decide independently to take a look at a system that seems inefficient. A steering committee may be formed to decide which of many possible projects should be worked on.

Participants in the project are of three types:

- **Users:** The system under discussion should *always* be developed in consultation with users, whether floor sweepers, research scientists, or customers. Indeed, if user involvement in analysis and design is inadequate, the system may fail for lack of acceptance.
- **Management:** Managers within the organization should also be consulted about the system. They often have a higher level of understanding of what the system does and why it is used.
- **Technical staff:** Members of the company's information systems (IS) department, consisting of systems analysts and programmers, need to be involved. For one thing, they may have to execute the project. Even if they don't, they will have to work with outside IS people contracted to do the job.

Complex projects will require one or several systems analysts. **A systems analyst is an information specialist who performs systems analysis, design, and implementation.** The analyst's job is to study the information and communications needs of an organization and determine what changes are required to deliver better information to the people who need it. "Better" information means information that is summarized in the acronym *CART*—complete, *a*ccurate, *r*elevant, and *t*imely. The systems analyst achieves this goal through the problem-solving method of systems analysis and design.

The Six Phases of Systems Analysis & Design

Although there are different names for the stages, systems analysis and design can be broken down into six basic phases.

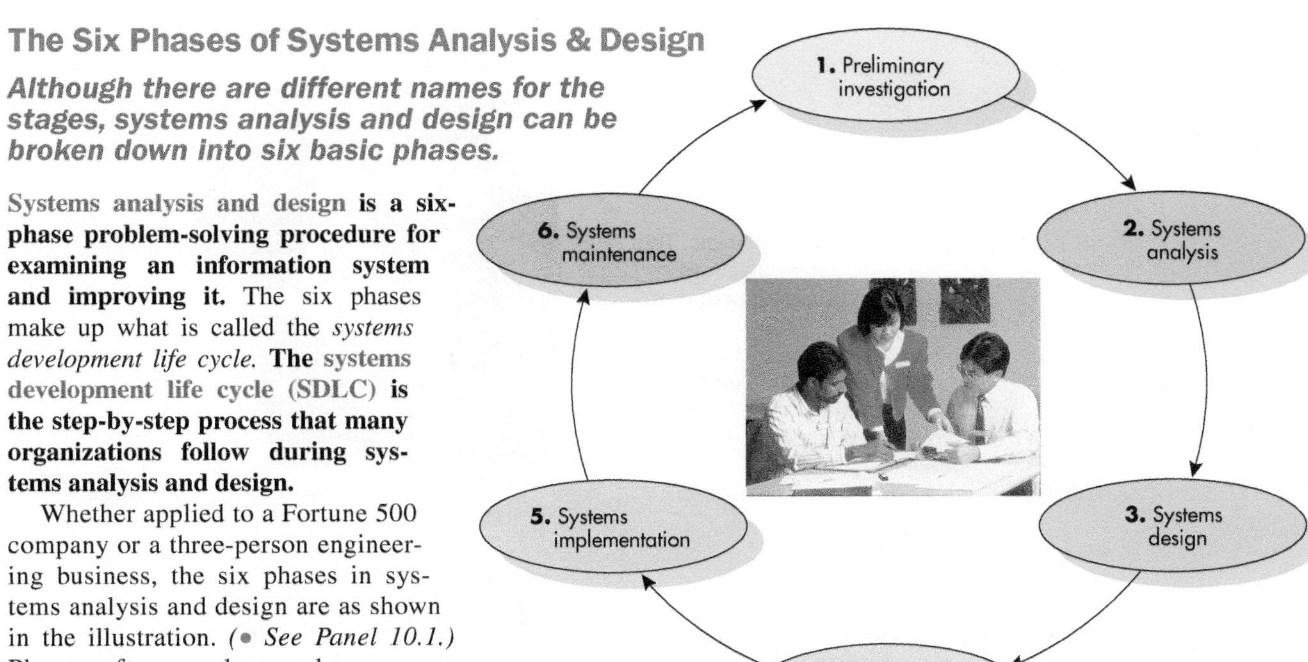

Systems analysis and design **is a six-phase problem-solving procedure for examining an information system and improving it.** The six phases make up what is called the *systems development life cycle.* **The** systems development life cycle (SDLC) **is the step-by-step process that many organizations follow during systems analysis and design.**

Whether applied to a Fortune 500 company or a three-person engineering business, the six phases in systems analysis and design are as shown in the illustration. (• *See Panel 10.1.*) Phases often overlap, and a new one may start before the old one is finished, or a particular phase might not be working out well, so the analysts and designers may return to a previous phase and make adjustments. After the first four phases, management must decide whether to proceed to the next phase. User input and review are a critical part of each phase.

panel 10.1

Systems development life cycle

An SDLC typically includes six phases.

TECH TALES "Bring Your Own Device" to Work: Applying Systems Analysis & Design to the BYOD Trend

As the prices have dropped for mobile devices—smartphones and tablets—many employees who have purchased their own have asked their bosses to support them so they can stay connected to office resources, such as email, files, and mobile applications. This trend is called "bring your own device," or BYOD. Often, however, employees have different devices with different capabilities. How should they all be integrated within one business?

"Undertaking a businesswide plan to utilize mobile devices requires planning," says Steve Cerocke, founder/president of software development firm IQ Systems of Reno, Nevada. "Without a BYOD plan or appropriate policies, organizations can incur significant support costs and be exposed to security risks."[5]

This is the kind of situation for which systems analysis and design can be of help, as we will try to show. ■

The First Phase: Preliminary Investigation

The first phase results in a preliminary plan.

The objective of **Phase 1,** preliminary investigation**, is to conduct a preliminary analysis, propose alternative solutions, describe costs and benefits, and submit a preliminary plan with recommendations.** (• *See Panel 10.2, next page.*)

1. CONDUCT THE PRELIMINARY ANALYSIS In this step, you need to find out what the organization's objectives are and the nature and scope of the problem under study. Even if a problem pertains only to a small segment of the

Many employees now bring their own electronic devices to work.

panel 10.2

First phase: Preliminary investigation

1. Conduct preliminary analysis. This includes stating the objectives, defining the nature and scope of the problem.
2. Propose alternative solutions: leave system alone, make it more efficient, or build a new system.
3. Describe costs and benefits of each solution.
4. Submit a preliminary plan with recommendations.

BYOD Can Threaten an Organization's Security

www.zdnet.com/dont-adapt-old-it-security-policies-for-byod-ibm-7000018714/

http://redmondmag.com/articles/2013/05/01/byod-empowers-users.aspx

www.usatoday.com/story/cybertruth/2013/06/21/how-byod-brings-security-risks-into-corporate-networks/2443299/

www.zdnet.com/five-security-risks-of-moving-data-in-byod-era-7000010665/

organization, you cannot study it in isolation. You need to find out what the objectives of the organization itself are. Then you need to see how the problem being studied fits in with them.

In the BYOD case, your analysis may show that employees want specific features that one device has but others do not, and you need to determine which suit the organization's best interests. "Your business requirements for connectivity, reliability, and functionality should be the major considerations when defining a mobility solution," Cerocke suggests.

2. PROPOSE ALTERNATIVE SOLUTIONS In delving into the organization's objectives and the specific problem, you may have already discovered some solutions. Other possible solutions can come from interviewing people inside the organization, clients or customers affected by it, suppliers, and consultants. You can also study what competitors are doing. With this data, you then have three choices. You can leave the system as is, improve it, or develop a new system.

All the employee mobile devices being considered in the BYOD problem will handle email, voice communication, and remote connectivity—the most common requirements for mobile users, Cerocke points out. But, he says, "they might have different prerequisites for integrating specific features into your business systems."

3. DESCRIBE THE COSTS & BENEFITS Whichever of the three alternatives is chosen, it will have costs and benefits. In this step, you need to indicate what these are. Costs may depend on benefits, which may offer savings. A broad spectrum of benefits may be derived. A process may be speeded up, streamlined through elimination of unnecessary steps, or combined with other processes. Input errors or redundant output may be reduced. Systems and subsystems may be better integrated. Users may be happier with the system. Customers' or suppliers' interactions with the system may be more satisfactory. Security may be improved. Costs may be cut.

Cerocke notes that adding additional functionality to BYOD devices, such as mobile applications that connect with company databases, might require custom programming—programming that can be incompatible between each mobile device. Thus, the costs and benefits of adding such mobile applications need to be described, including the costs of monthly connection and data plan fees.

4. SUBMIT A PRELIMINARY PLAN Now you need to wrap up all your findings in a written report. The readers of this report will be the executives who are in a position to decide in which direction to proceed—make no changes, change a little, or change a lot—and how much money to allow for the project. You should describe the potential solutions, costs, and benefits and indicate your recommendations.

A BYOD-integration implementation plan should include "programming requirements, connectivity options, security designs, and business software upgrades," Cerocke points out. It should also outline a pilot project for testing how mobility solutions can be integrated into business processes such as sales and service and discuss how to train users on proper use.

All the BYOD steps considered under Phase 1, preliminary investigation, become the basis for further exploration under the subsequent phases discussed below: 2, systems analysis; 3, systems design; 4, systems development; 5, systems implementation; and 6, systems maintenance.

1. Gather data, using tools of written documents, interviews, questionnaires, and observations.
2. Analyze the data, using modeling tools: grid charts, decision tables, data flow diagrams, systems flowcharts, connectivity diagrams.
3. Write a report.

panel 10.3

Second phase: Systems analysis

The Second Phase: Systems Analysis

The second phase involves gathering and analyzing data.

The objective of **Phase 2, systems analysis, is to gather data, analyze the data, and write a report.** *(• See Panel 10.3.)* In this second phase of the SDLC, you follow the course that management has indicated after having read your Phase 1 feasibility report. We are assuming that management has ordered you to perform Phase 2—to do a careful analysis or study of the existing system in order to understand how the new system you proposed would differ. This analysis will also consider how people's positions and tasks will have to change if the new system is put into effect.

1. GATHER DATA In gathering data, you review written documents, interview employees and managers, develop questionnaires, and observe people and processes at work.

2. ANALYZE THE DATA Once the data has been gathered, you need to come to grips with it and analyze it. Many analytical tools, or modeling tools, are available. **Modeling tools are analytical tools such as charts, tables, and diagrams used by systems analysts to present graphic, or pictorial, representations of a system.** An example of a modeling tool is a **data flow diagram (DFD), which graphically shows the flow of data through a system**—that is, the essential processes of a system, along with inputs, outputs, and files. *(• See Panel 10.4.)*

panel 10.4

Data flow diagram

(*bottom*) Symbols; (*next page*) examples of a data flow diagram (adapted from *http://visualcase.com/tutorials/about-data-flow-diagram.htm* and *www.hit.ac.il/staff/leonidm/information-systems/ch24.html#Heading6*)

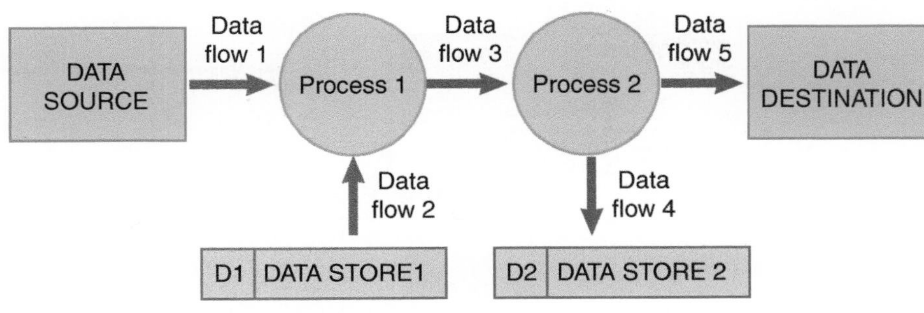

Explanation of standard data flow diagram symbols

Name or Name

Terminator Symbols (entity name) (person or organization outside the system boundaries)

File Name or File Name

Data Store Symbol

Name or Name

Process Symbol

Name

Data Flow Symbol (inputs and outputs)

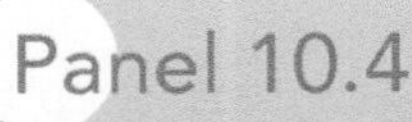

Panel 10.4

Data flow diagram

(continued)

Student
Progress report
Applies to university
Application
Approval
Denial letter
Student information
Acceptance letter
Registration
Student information
Student Database

Financial System
Cash flow
9 Report cash flow
Cash flow
D1 Sales
Invoice
Invoice
D3 Team Sold
D2 Vendor
Sales data
Item sold
Item sold
Item sold
Item sold
Supplier
Reorder
Item ordered
D4 Item Ordered
Customer
Order
Invoice
2 Sell appliance
3 Update inventory
4 Reorder stock
Advertising
Customer data
Customer data
Stock number description selling price
Stock number quantity sold
Stock number stock on hand reorder quantity
Manager
2 Maintain customer data
Customer data
D5 Customer Data
D6 Inventory
Stock number stock on hand
Customer data
8 Mail advertising
Stock number stock on hand
5 Identify sale items
Stock number quantity received
1 Process shipment
Supplier
Order
Vendor data
6 Physical inventory
Stock number stock on hand
Item ordered
D4 Item ordered
D2 Vendor

more info!

Examples of Software Used to Document Data Flows & Create Diagrams

MS Project, Visio, Visual Paradigm, Cacoo

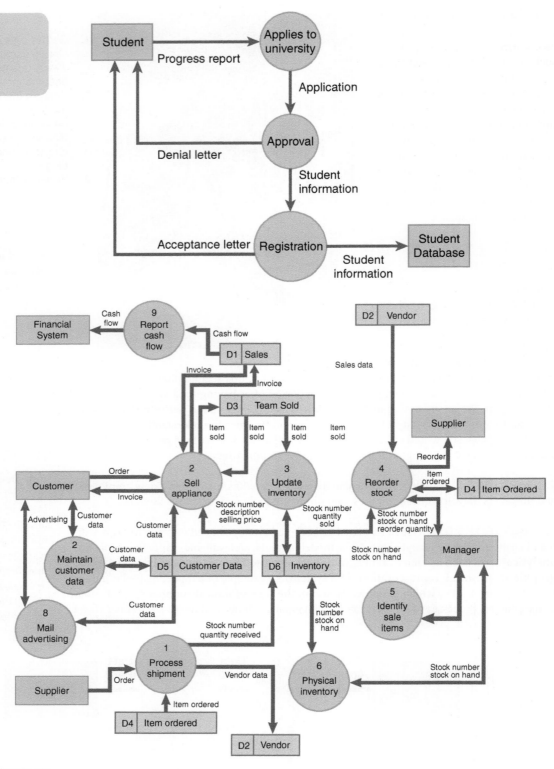

CASE tools may also be used during the analysis phase, as well as in most other phases. **CASE (computer-aided software engineering) tools are computer-automated means of designing and changing systems.** This technology is intended to speed up the process of developing systems and to improve the quality of the resulting systems. Such tools can generate and store diagrams, produce documentation, analyze data relationships, generate computer code, produce graphics, and provide project management functions. (Project management software, discussed in Chapter 3, consists of programs used to plan, schedule, and control the people, costs, and resources required to complete a project on time.)

So-called lightweight (more flexible), or "agile," team-based software and project development methodologies are also used to speed up system development; examples are Crystal Clear, Extreme Programming, Scrum, and Feature Driven Development. The agile approach supplies guiding practices that provide a framework within which to design and build a system and manage it, rather than supplying a set of rigid instructions (*http://ccpace.com/Resources/documents/AgileProjectManagement.pdf*).

Unified Modeling Language (UML) is also used to develop systems. UML is a standard language used for constructing visual models of software systems, as well as for business modeling. (In this case, modeling is the designing of software applications before coding.)

3. WRITE A REPORT Once you have completed the analysis, you need to document this phase. This report to management should have three parts. First, it should explain how the existing system works. Second, it should explain the problems with the existing system. Finally, it should describe the requirements for the new system and make recommendations on what to do next.

At this point, not a lot of money will have been spent on the systems analysis and design project. If the costs of going forward seem prohibitive, this is a good time for the managers reading the report to call a halt. Otherwise, you will be asked to move to Phase 3.

more info!

CASE Tools & UML

CASE tools and UML are important. For more information, try:

http://blog.salamtura.com/post/computer-aided-software-engineering/

www.visual-paradigm.com/product/vpuml/

http://searchcio-midmarket.techtarget.com/definition/CASE/

www.cs.nott.ac.uk/~cah/G53QAT/Report08/mxr06u%20-%20WebPage/Types%20of%20CASE%20tools.html

www.pcmag.com/encyclopedia/term/53392/uml/

For information on agile methodologies, go to:

http://agilemethodology.org/

www.ontimenow.com/scrum/learn-agile?gclid=CJHT1Y682rgCFbCDQgodfXMAIw

The Third Phase: Systems Design

In the third phase, the design is refined.

The objective of **Phase 3, systems design, is to do a preliminary design and then a detail design and to write a report.** (• *See Panel 10.5.*) In this third phase of the SDLC, you will essentially create a "rough draft" and then a "detail draft" of the proposed information system.

1. DO A PRELIMINARY DESIGN A *preliminary design* describes the general functional capabilities of a proposed information system. It reviews the system requirements and then considers major components of the system. Usually several alternative systems (called *candidates*) are considered, and the costs and the benefits of each are evaluated.

Tools used in the design phase may include CASE tools and project management software.

Prototyping is often done at this stage. **Prototyping refers to using CASE tools, UML, and other software applications to build working models of system components so that they can be quickly tested and evaluated.** Thus, a **prototype is a limited working system, or part of one, developed to test design concepts.** A prototype, which may be constructed in just a few days, allows users to find out immediately how a change in the system might benefit them. For example, a systems analyst might develop a menu as a possible screen display, which users could try out. The menu can then be redesigned or fine-tuned, if necessary.

1. Do a preliminary design, using CASE tools, prototyping tools, and project management software, among others.
2. Do a detail design, defining requirements for output, input, storage, and processing and system controls and backup.
3. Write a report.

panel 10.5

Third phase: Systems design

2. DO A DETAIL DESIGN A *detail design* describes how a proposed information system will deliver the general capabilities described in the preliminary design. The detail design usually considers the following parts of the system in this order: output requirements, input requirements, storage requirements, processing requirements, and system controls and backup.

3. WRITE A REPORT All the work of the preliminary and detail designs will end up in a large, detailed report. When you hand over this report to senior management, you will probably also make some sort of presentation or speech.

The Fourth Phase: Systems Development

In the fourth phase, the system is actually built.

In **Phase 4, systems development, the systems analyst or others in the organization develop or acquire the software, acquire the hardware, and then test the system.** (• *See Panel 10.6.*) Depending on the size of the project, this phase will probably involve the organization spending substantial sums of money. It could also involve spending a lot of time. However, at the end you should have a workable system.

1. DEVELOP OR ACQUIRE THE SOFTWARE During the design stage, the systems analyst may have had to address what is called the "make-or-buy" decision, but that decision certainly cannot be avoided now. In the *make-or-buy decision,* you decide whether you have to create a program—have it custom-written—or buy it, meaning simply purchase an existing software package. Sometimes programmers decide they can buy an existing program and modify it rather than write it from scratch.

If you decide to create a new program, then the question is whether to use the organization's own staff programmers or to hire outside contract programmers (outsource it). Whichever way you go, the task could take many months.

Programming is an entire subject unto itself, which we discuss later in this chapter, along with programming languages.

2. ACQUIRE HARDWARE Once the software has been chosen, the hardware to run it must be acquired or upgraded. It's possible your new system will not require any new hardware. It's also possible that the new hardware will cost millions of dollars and involve many items: microcomputers, mainframes, monitors, modems, and many other devices. The organization may find it's better to lease than to buy some equipment, especially since, as we mentioned (Moore's law), chip capability has traditionally doubled every 18 months.

3. TEST THE SYSTEM With the software and hardware acquired, you can now start testing the system. Testing is usually done in two stages: unit testing, then system testing.

- **Unit testing:** In *unit testing,* the performance of individual parts is examined, using test (made-up or sample) data. If the program is written as a collaborative effort by multiple programmers, each part of the program is tested separately.

panel 10.6

Fourth phase: Systems development

1. Develop or acquire the software.
2. Acquire the hardware.
3. Test the system.

- **System testing:** In *system testing,* the parts are linked together, and test data is used to see if the parts work together. At this point, actual organization data may be used to test the system. The system is also tested with erroneous data and massive amounts of data to see if the system can be made to fail ("crash").

At the end of this long process, the organization will have a workable information system, one ready for the implementation phase.

The Fifth Phase: Systems Implementation

The fifth phase involves moving everything from the old system over to the new system.

Whether the new information system involves a few handheld computers, an elaborate telecommunications network, or expensive mainframes, the fifth phase will involve some close coordination in order to make the system not just workable but successful. **Phase 5, systems implementation, consists of converting the hardware, software, and files to the new system and training the users.** (• *See Panel 10.7.)*

1. CONVERT TO THE NEW SYSTEM Conversion, the process of transition from an old information system to a new one, involves converting hardware, software, and files. There are four strategies for handling conversion: direct, parallel, phased, and pilot.

- **Direct implementation:** This means that the user simply stops using the old system and starts using the new one. The risk of this method should be evident: What if the new system doesn't work? If the old system has truly been discontinued, there is nothing to fall back on.
- **Parallel implementation:** This means that the old and new systems are operated side by side until the new system has shown it is reliable, at which time the old system is discontinued. Obviously there are benefits in taking this cautious approach. If the new system fails, the organization can switch back to the old one. The difficulty with this method is the expense of paying for the equipment and people to keep two systems going at the same time.
- **Phased implementation:** This means that parts of the new system are phased in separately—either at different times (parallel) or all at once in groups (direct).
- **Pilot implementation:** This means that the entire system is tried out, but only by some users. Once the reliability has been proved, the system is implemented with the rest of the intended users. The pilot approach still has its risks, since all the users of a particular group are taken off the old system. However, the risks are confined to a small part of the organization.

2. TRAIN THE USERS Various tools are available to familiarize users with a new system—from documentation (instruction manuals) to video to live classes to one-on-one, side-by-side teacher-student training. Sometimes training is done by the organization's own staffers; at other times it is contracted out.

1. Convert hardware, software, and files through one of four types of conversions: direct, parallel, phased, or pilot.
2. Train the users.

panel 10.7

Fifth phase: Systems implementation

The Sixth Phase: Systems Maintenance

All systems must be maintained and updated.

Phase 6, systems maintenance, adjusts and improves the system by having system audits and periodic evaluations and by making changes based on new conditions. (• *See Panel 10.8.*) Even with the conversion accomplished and the users trained, the system won't just run itself. There is a sixth—and continuous—phase in which the information system must be monitored to ensure that it is successful. Maintenance includes not only keeping the machinery running but also updating and upgrading the system to keep pace with new products, services, customers, government regulations, and other requirements.

After some time, maintenance costs will accelerate as attempts continue to keep the system responsive to user needs. At some point, these maintenance costs become excessive, indicating that it may be time to start the entire SDLC again. (This stage is sometimes called *termination.*)

Systematics

Do a search: Who wrote this, and when? "Systems are seductive. They promise to do a hard job faster, better, and more easily than you could do it by yourself. But if you set up a system, you are likely to find your time and effort now being consumed in the care and feeding of the system itself. New problems are created by its very presence. Once set up, it won't go away, it grows and encroaches. It begins to do strange and wonderful things. Breaks down in ways you never thought possible. It kicks back, gets in the way, and opposes its own proper function. Your own perspective becomes distorted by being in the system. You become anxious and push on it to make it work. Eventually you come to believe that the misbegotten product it so grudgingly delivers is what you really wanted all the time. At that point encroachment has become complete . . . you have become absorbed . . . you are now a systems person!"

Hint: Check out "The Systems Bible" and the "Laws of Systemantics."

TECH TALES Stumbles on the Road to Progress: When Big Systems Fail

Applying the procedures of system development and design are *intended* to solve problems, and they often work. But solution is not inevitable—especially if the project is huge.

In the private sector, expensive software projects can end unhappily because of unforeseen complexities, as Ford Motor found when it received poor quality ratings from customers who complained about glitches in the MyFord Touch infotainment system, which uses voice commands to let drivers place phone calls and operate other controls.[6] Expensive failures can also occur during mergers, when companies make "acquisitions of entire companies with software assets that turn out to be far less valuable than thought," as one writer put it.[7]

But failures in the public sector can be especially dramatic, perhaps because the systems that government is trying to deal with are often so colossal and so unbearably complex. In July 2012, for instance, the FBI finally switched on Sentinel, a gigantic software system that is to be used by multiple intelligence agencies that work on terrorism cases, after spending 12 years and $600 million.[8] In another instance, the U.S. Air Force canceled a complex logistics management system after spending 6 years and $1 billion because the way the effort was conceived was flawed. "We started with a Big Bang approach and put every possible requirement into the program, which made it very large and complex," said a Defense Department manager.[9]

panel 10.8

Sixth phase: Systems maintenance

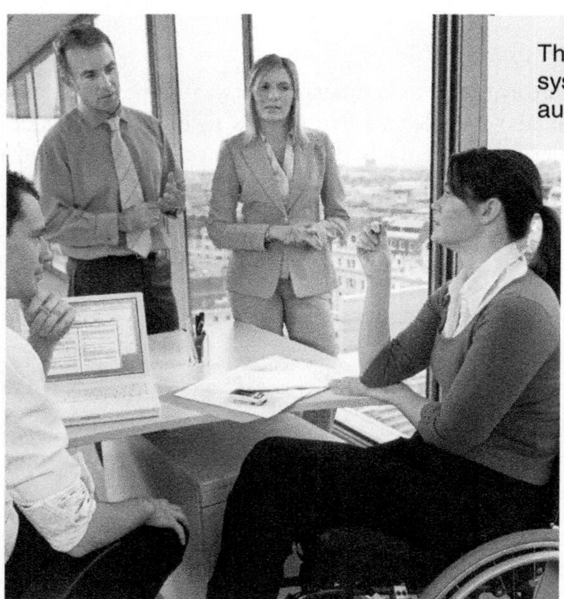

The sixth phase is to keep the system running through system audits and periodic evaluations.

For a glimpse of why big software projects can go awry, consider the classic case of California's Department of Motor Vehicles. In the 1990s, the state realized that the DMV databases needed to be modernized, and Tandem Computers (today part of Hewlett-Packard) said it could do it. "The fact that the DMV's database system, designed around an old IBM-based platform, and Tandem's new system were as different as night and day seemed insignificant at the time to the experts involved," said one writer who investigated the project.[10]

The massive driver's license database, containing the driving records of more than 30 million people, first had to be "scrubbed" of all information that couldn't be translated into the language used by Tandem computers. One such scrub yielded 600,000 errors. Then the DMV had to translate all its IBM programs into the Tandem language. "Worse, DMV really didn't know how its current IBM applications worked anymore," said the writer, "because they'd been custom-made decades before by long departed programmers and rewritten many times since."

Eventually the project became a staggering $44 million loss to California's taxpayers. ■

Needless to say, not all systems mistakes are as huge as those described above. Computer foul-ups can range from minor to catastrophic. But the examples show how important planning is, especially when an organization is trying to launch a new kind of system. The best way to avoid such mistakes is to employ systems analysis and design.

10.2 PROGRAMMING: Traditionally a Five-Step Procedure

Programming is a five-step process of software engineering.

To see how programming works, we must understand what constitutes a program. **A program is a list of instructions that the computer must follow to process data into information.** The instructions consist of statements used in a programming language (an artificial language used to write instructions that can be translated into machine language [Chapter 4, p. 200]). Examples are programs that do word processing, desktop publishing, or payroll processing.

The decision whether to buy or create a program forms part of Phase 4 in the systems development life cycle. Once the decision is made to develop a new system, the programmer goes to work.

A program, we said, is a list of instructions for the computer. **Programming is a five-step process for creating that list of instructions.** Programming is sometimes called *software engineering;* however, the latter term includes in its definition the use of best-practice processes to create and/or maintain software, whether for groups or individuals, in an attempt to get rid of the usual haphazard methods that have plagued the software industry. Software engineering involves the establishment and use of recognized engineering principles to obtain software that is reliable and works efficiently. It requires the application of a systematic, disciplined, quantifiable approach to the development, operation, and maintenance of software.

The five steps in the programming process are as follows:

1. Clarify/define the problem—include needed output, input, and processing requirements.
2. Design a solution—use modeling tools to chart the program.
3. Code the program—use a programming language's syntax, or rules, to write the program.
4. Test the program—get rid of any logic errors, or "bugs," in the program ("debug" it).
5. Document and maintain the program—include written instructions for users, explanation of the program, and operating instructions.

"Computer programming is an art, because it applies
accumulated knowledge to the world, because it
requires skill and ingenuity, and especially because
it produces objects of beauty."

Coding—sitting at the keyboard and typing words into a computer—is how many people view programming. As we will see, however, it is only one of the five steps.

FBI Flop

What happens when an organization does not properly define program objectives? In 2003 the FBI started the coding for its new Virtual Case File program—and spending $170 million of taxpayers' money and creating more than 700,000 lines of error-prone commands. Later, it canceled the project. Why? Because it had not adequately defined the program requirements.

www.washingtonpost.com/wp-dyn/content/article/2006/08/17/AR2006081701485.html

http://spectrum.ieee.org/computing/software/who-killed-the-virtual-case-file

The First Step: Clarify the Programming Needs

The first step in programming involves six smaller tasks.

The problem clarification (definition) step consists of six mini-steps—clarifying program objectives and users, outputs, inputs, and processing tasks; studying the feasibility of the program; and documenting the analysis. *(• See Panel 10.9.)*

1. CLARIFY OBJECTIVES & USERS You solve problems all the time. A problem might be deciding whether to take a required science course this term or next, or selecting classes that allow you also to fit a job into your schedule. In such cases, you are specifying your objectives. Programming works the same way. You need to write a statement of the objectives you are trying to accomplish—the problem you are trying to solve. If the problem is that your company's systems analysts have designed a new computer-based payroll processing proposal and brought it to you as the programmer, you need to clarify the programming needs.

You also need to make sure you know who the users of the program will be. Will they be people inside the company, outside, or both? What kind of skills will they bring?

2. CLARIFY DESIRED OUTPUTS Make sure you understand the outputs—what the system designers want to get out of the system—before you specify the inputs. For example, what kind of reports and other forms of communication are wanted? What information should the outputs include? This step may require several meetings with systems designers and users to make sure you're creating what they want.

panel 10.9

First step: Clarify programming needs

1. Clarify objectives and users.
2. Clarify desired outputs.
3. Clarify desired inputs.
4. Clarify desired processing.
5. Double-check feasibility of implementing the program.
6. Document the analysis.

3. CLARIFY DESIRED INPUTS Once you know the outputs required, you can then think about input. What kind of input data is needed? In what form should it appear? What is its source?

4. CLARIFY THE DESIRED PROCESSING Here you make sure you understand the processing tasks that must occur in order for input data to be processed into output data.

5. DOUBLE-CHECK THE FEASIBILITY OF IMPLEMENTING THE PROGRAM Is the kind of program you're supposed to create feasible within the present budget? Will it require hiring a lot more staff? Will it take too long to accomplish?

Occasionally programmers suggest to managers that they buy an existing program and modify it rather than having one written from scratch.

6. DOCUMENT THE ANALYSIS Throughout program clarification, programmers must document everything they do. This includes writing objective specifications of the entire process being described.

The Second Step: Design the Program

Algorithms must be developed before the program can be designed.

Assuming the decision is to make, or custom-write, the program, you then move on to design the solution specified by the systems analysts. To design the solution, you first need to create algorithms. **An algorithm is a formula or set of steps for solving a particular problem.** *(• See Panel 10.10.)* To be an algorithm, a set of rules must be unambiguous and have a clear stopping point. We use algorithms every day. For example, a recipe for baking bread is an algorithm. Most programs, with the exception of some artificial intelligence applications, consist of algorithms. In computer programming, there are often different algorithms to accomplish any given task, and each algorithm has specific advantages and disadvantages in different situations. Inventing elegant algorithms—algorithms that are simple and require the fewest steps possible—is one of the principal challenges in programming.

Algorithms can be expressed in various ways. **In the program design step, the software is designed in two mini-steps. First, the program logic is determined through a top-down approach and modularization, using a *hierarchy chart*. Then it is designed in detail, either in narrative form, using *pseudocode*, or graphically, using *flowcharts*.** *(• See Panel 10.11, next page.)*

How Does One Go about Solving a Problem?

According to Gary Hadler, who lectures on this subject, one way is to follow four stages: recognize and define the problem, determine possible solutions, choose the best solution, and implement the solution:

www.tuition.com.hk/the-stages-of-problem-solving.htm

http://jobs.monster.com/v-quality-assurance-q-software-tester-jobs.aspx

www.indeed.com/q-Software-Tester-jobs.html

In general, problems are not solved just by pondering them; specific problem-solving skills are required. For more information, try:

www.math.wichita.edu/history/men/polya.html

www.bizmove.com/skills/m8d.htm

www.wikihow.com/Solve-a-Problem

www.mindtools.com/pages/article/newTMC_00.htm

panel 10.10

Example of an algorithm

Source: Adapted from *www.cs.pitt.edu/~jmisurda/teaching/cs4/2064/cs0004-2064-algorithm.htm.*

Algorithm: Calling a friend on the telephone

Input: The telephone number of your friend

Output: None

Steps:

1. Pick up the phone and listen for a dial tone.
2. Press each digit of the phone number on the phone.
3. If busy, hang up phone, wait 5 minutes, jump to step 2.
4. If no one answers, leave a voice mail message, then hang up.
5. If no voice mail, hang up and wait 2 hours, then jump to step 2.
6. Talk to friend.
7. Hang up phone.

Assumptions:

- Step 1 assumes that you live alone and no one else could be on the phone.
- The algorithm assumes the existence of a working phone and active service.
- The algorithm assumes you are not deaf or mute.
- The algorithm assumes a phone with voice mail.

Algorithm: What's the Origin of This Word?

The word *algorithm* originates in the name of an Arab mathematician, al-Khwarizmi, of the court of Mamun in Baghdad in the 800s. His treatises on Hindu arithmetic and on algebra made him famous. He is also said to have given algebra its name. Much of the mathematical knowledge of medieval Europe was derived from Latin translations of his works.

panel 10.11

Second step: Program design

1. Determine program logic through top-down approach and modularization, using a hierarchy chart.
2. Design details using pseudocode and/or flowcharts, preferably involving control structures.

It used to be that programmers took a kind of seat-of-the-pants approach to programming. Programming was considered an art, not a science. Today, however, most programmers use a design approach called *structured programming.* **Structured programming takes a top-down approach that breaks programs into modular forms.** It also uses standard logic tools called *control structures (sequence, selection, case,* and *iteration).*

The point of structured programming is to make programs more efficient (with fewer lines of code) and better organized (more readable) and to have better notations so that they have clear and correct descriptions.

The two mini-steps of program design are as follows.

1. DETERMINE THE PROGRAM LOGIC, USING A TOP-DOWN APPROACH Determining the program logic is like outlining a long term paper before you proceed to write it. **Top-down program design proceeds by identifying the top element, or module, of a program and then breaking it down in hierarchical fashion to the lowest level of detail.** The top-down program design is used to identify the program's processing steps, or modules. After the program is designed, the actual coding proceeds from the bottom up, using the modular approach.

- **Modularization:** The concept of modularization is important. Modularization dramatically simplifies program development, because each part can be developed and tested separately. **A module is a processing step of a program. Each module is made up of logically related program statements.** (Sometimes a module is called a *subprogram, subroutine, function,* or *method.*) An example of a module might be a programming instruction that simply says "Open a file, find a record, and show it on the display screen." It is best if each module has only a single function, just as an English paragraph should have a single, complete thought. This rule limits the module's size and complexity.
- **Top-down program design:** Top-down program design can be represented graphically in a hierarchy chart. **A hierarchy chart, or *structure chart,* illustrates the overall purpose of the program, by identifying all the modules needed to achieve that purpose and the relationships among them.** *(• See Panel 10.12.)* It works from the general down to the specific, starting with the top-level (high-level) view of what the program is to do. Then each layer refines and expands the previous one until the bottom layer can be made into specific programming modules. The program must move in sequence from one module to the next until all have been processed. There must be three principal modules corresponding to the three principal computing operations—input, processing, and output. (In Panel 10.12 they are "Read input," "Calculate pay," and "Generate output.")

2. DESIGN DETAILS, USING PSEUDOCODE AND/OR FLOWCHARTS Once the essential logic of the program has been determined, through the use of top-down programming and hierarchy charts, you can go to work on the details.

There are two basic ways to show details—write them or draw them; for example, use *pseudocode* or use *flowcharts.* Most projects use both methods.

- **Pseudocode: Pseudocode is a method of designing a program using normal human-language statements to describe the logic and the processing flow.** *(• See Panel 10.13.)* Pseudocode is like an outline or summary form of the program you will write.

panel 10.12

A hierarchy chart

This represents a top-down design for a payroll program. Here the modules, or processing steps, are represented from the highest level of the program down to details. The three principal processing operations—input, processing, and output—are represented by the modules in the second layer: "Read input," "Calculate pay," and "Generate output." Before tasks at the top of the chart can be performed, all the ones below must be performed. Each module represents a logical processing step.

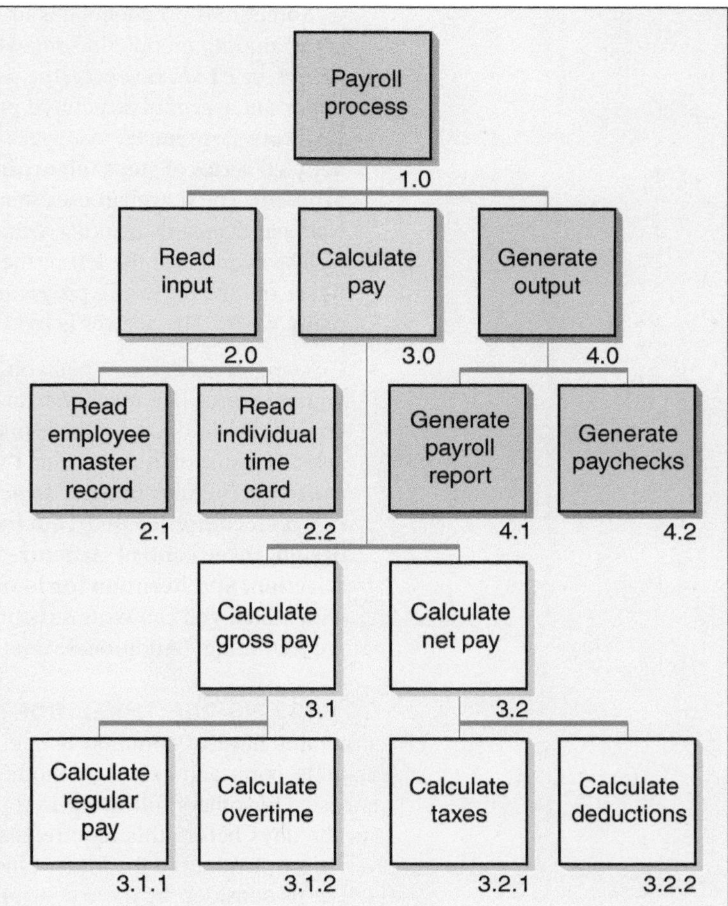

1. Each module must be of manageable size.
2. Each module should be independent and have a single function.
3. The functions of input and output are clearly defined in separate modules.
4. Each module has a single entry point (execution of the program module always starts at the same place) and a single exit point (control always leaves the module at the same place).
5. If one module refers to or transfers control to another module, the latter module returns control to the point from which it was "called" by the first module.

panel 10.13

Pseudocode

```
START
DO WHILE (so long as) there are records
     Read a customer billing account record
     IF today's date is greater than 30 days from
     date of last customer payment
          Calculate total amount due
          Calculate 5% interest on amount due
          Add interest to total amount due to calculate
          grand total
          Print on invoice overdue amount
     ELSE
          Calculate total amount due
     ENDIF
     Print out invoice
END DO
END
```

Sometimes pseudocode is used simply to express the purpose of a particular programming module in somewhat general terms. With the use of such terms as *IF, THEN,* or *ELSE,* however, the pseudocode follows the rules of *control structures,* an important aspect of structured programming, as we shall explain.

- **Program flowcharts: A program flowchart is a chart that graphically presents the detailed series of steps (algorithm, or logical flow) needed to solve a programming problem.** The flowchart uses standard symbols—called *ANSI symbols,* after the American National Standards Institute, which developed them. *(• See Panel 10.14.)*

  The symbols at the left of the drawing might seem clear enough. But how do you figure out the logic of a program? How do you reason the program out so that it will really work? The answer is to use control structures, as explained next.

- **Control structures:** When you're trying to determine the logic behind something, you use words like *if* and *then* and *else.* (For example, without using these exact words, you might reason along these lines: "If she comes over, then we'll go out to a movie, else I'll just stay in and watch TV.") Control structures make use of the same words. **A control structure, or *logic structure,* is a structure that controls the logical sequence in which computer program instructions are executed. In structured program design, three control structures are used to form the logic of a program: sequence, selection, and iteration (or loop).** *(• See Panel 10.15, page 522.)* These are the tools with which you can write structured programs and take a lot of the guesswork out of programming. (Additional variations of these three basic structures are also used.)

COMPARING THE THREE CONTROL STRUCTURES One thing that all three control structures have in common is *one entry* and *one exit.* The control structure is entered at a single point and exited at another single point. This helps simplify the logic so that it is easier for others following in a programmer's footsteps to make sense of the program. (In the days before this requirement was instituted, programmers could have all kinds of variations, leading to the kind of incomprehensible program known as *spaghetti code.*)

Let us consider the three control structures:

- **Sequence control structure:** In the *sequence control structure,* one program statement follows another in logical order. For instance, in the example shown in Panel 10.15, there are two boxes ("Statement" and "Statement"). One box could say "Open file," the other "Read a record." There are no decisions to make, no choices between "yes" or "no." The boxes logically follow one another in sequential order.

- **Selection control structure:** The *selection control structure*—also known as an IF-THEN-ELSE *structure*—represents a choice. It offers two paths to follow when a decision must be made by a program. An example of a selection structure is as follows:

  IF a worker's hours in a week exceed 40
  THEN overtime hours equal the number of hours exceeding 40
  ELSE the worker has no overtime hours.

  A variation on the usual selection control structure is the *case control structure.* This offers more than a single yes-or-no decision. The case structure allows several alternatives, or "cases," to be presented. ("IF Case 1 occurs, THEN do thus-and-so. IF Case 2 occurs, THEN follow an alternative course. . . ." And so on.) The case control structure saves the programmer the trouble of having to indicate a lot of separate IF-THEN-ELSE conditions.

- **Iteration control structure:** In the *iteration,* or *loop, control structure,* a process may be repeated as long as a certain condition remains true. There are two types of iteration structures—DO UNTIL and DO WHILE.

  An example of a DO UNTIL structure is this:

  DO read in employee records UNTIL there are no more employee records.

  Here is an example of a DO WHILE structure:
  DO read in employee records WHILE [that is, as long as] there continue to be employee records.

Start
Input Price
Input Tax Rate
Calculate Sales Tax = Price × Rate
Print Tax
Stop

Start
Input Property Value
Value >100,000 ?
NO
YES
Calculate Tax = Value × .12
Calculate Tax = Value × .15
Print Property Tax
Stop

Start
Input Name
Name = "End" ?
NO
YES
Print Name
Input Name
Stop

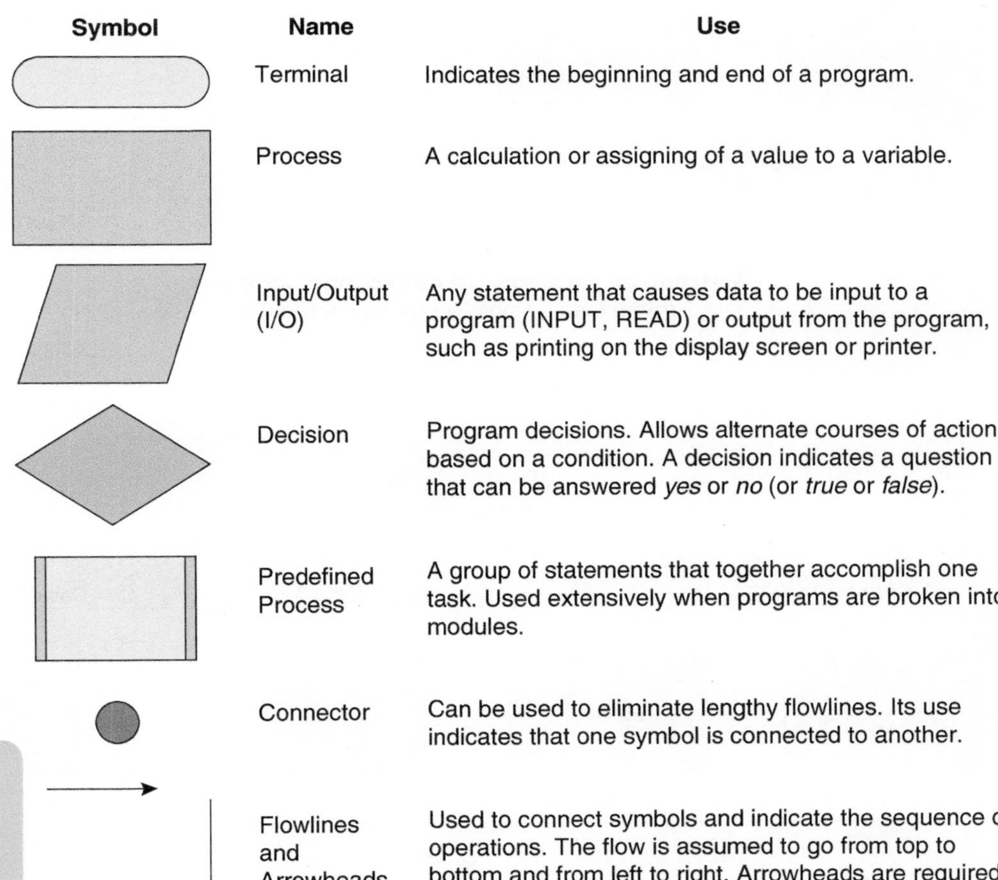

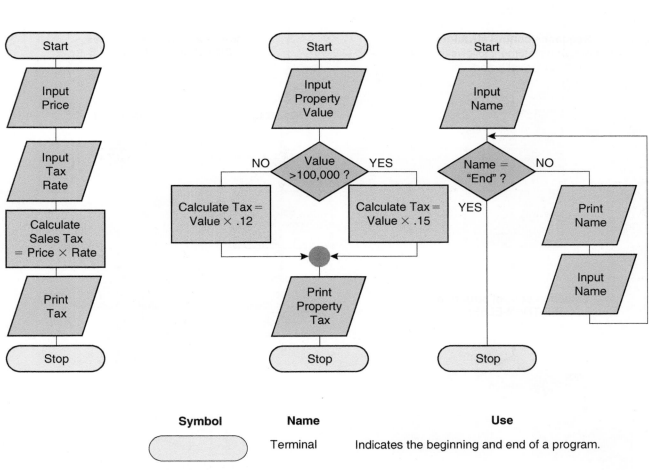

Symbol	Name	Use
	Terminal	Indicates the beginning and end of a program.
	Process	A calculation or assigning of a value to a variable.
	Input/Output (I/O)	Any statement that causes data to be input to a program (INPUT, READ) or output from the program, such as printing on the display screen or printer.
	Decision	Program decisions. Allows alternate courses of action based on a condition. A decision indicates a question that can be answered *yes* or *no* (or *true* or *false*).
	Predefined Process	A group of statements that together accomplish one task. Used extensively when programs are broken into modules.
	Connector	Can be used to eliminate lengthy flowlines. Its use indicates that one symbol is connected to another.
	Flowlines and Arrowheads	Used to connect symbols and indicate the sequence of operations. The flow is assumed to go from top to bottom and from left to right. Arrowheads are required only when the flow violates the standard direction.

panel 10.14

Example of a traditional program flowchart and explanation of flowchart symbols

This example represents a flowchart for a payroll program.

Sequence control structure
(one program statement follows another in logical order)

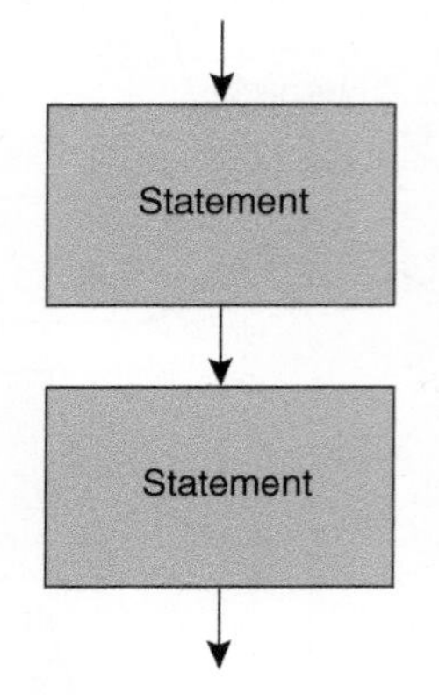

Iteration control structures: DO UNTIL and DO WHILE

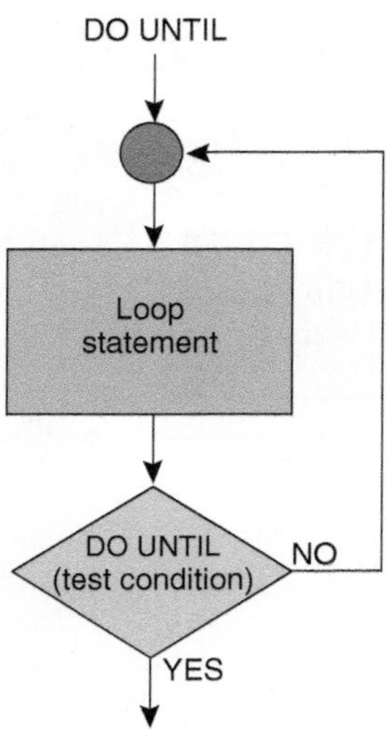

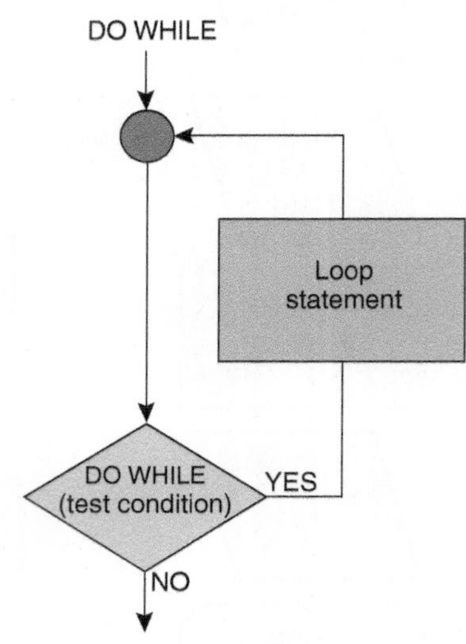

Selection control structure
(IF-THEN-ELSE)

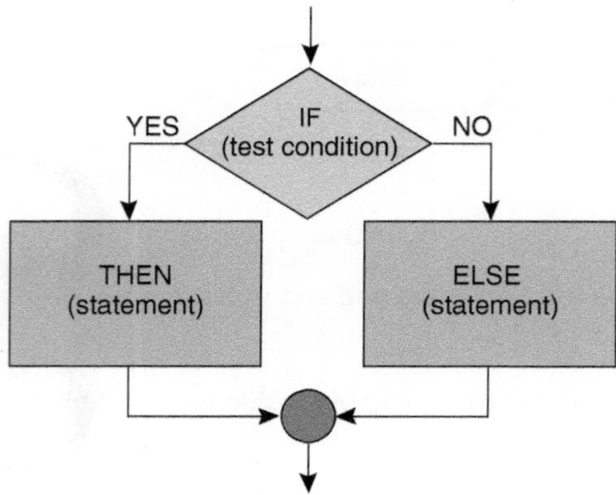

Variation on selection: the case control structure
(more than a single yes-or-no decision)

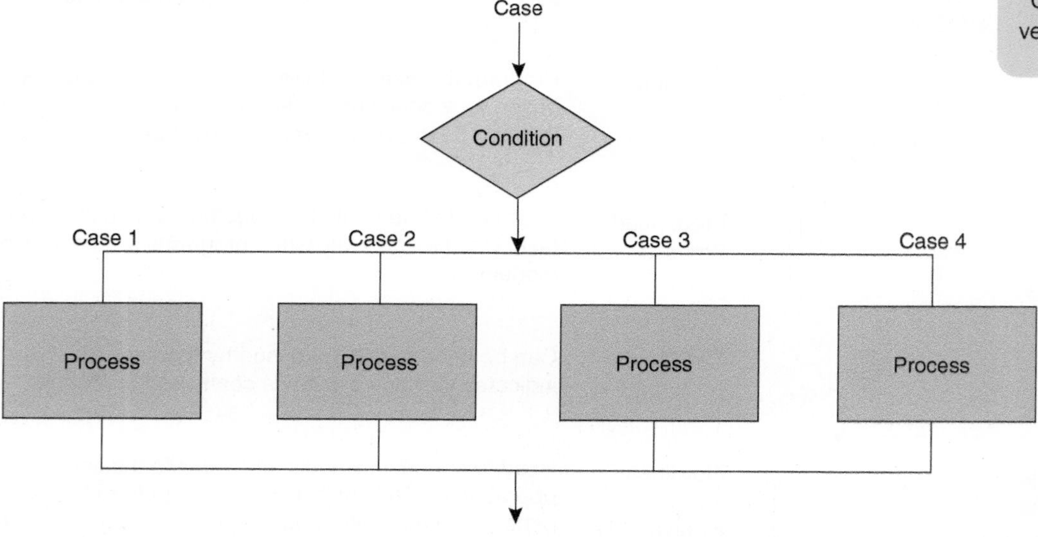

panel 10.15

The three control structures and a variation
The three structures used in structured program design to form the logic of a program are sequence, selection, and iteration. "Case" is an important version of selection.

What is the difference between the two iteration structures? It is simply this: If several statements need to be repeated, you must decide when to stop repeating them. You can decide to stop them at the beginning of the loop, using the DO WHILE structure. Or you can decide to stop them at the end of the loop, using the DO UNTIL structure. The DO UNTIL iteration means that the loop statements will be executed at least once, because in this case the iteration statements are executed before the program checks whether to stop.

Sequence, Selection, Iteration

In the 1960s it was mathematically proved that any problem that can be solved with a computer can be defined using sequence, selection, and iteration. Do an Internet search to find out who determined this and when.

The Third Step: Code the Program

Now the program is actually written.

Once the design has been developed, the actual writing, or coding, of the program begins *(• See Panel 10.16).* Coding is what many people think that programming is, although it is only one of the five steps. **Coding consists of translating the logic requirements from pseudocode or flowcharts into a programming language**—the letters, numbers, and symbols that make up the program.

1. SELECT THE APPROPRIATE HIGH-LEVEL PROGRAMMING LANGUAGE **A programming language is a set of rules that tells the computer what operations to do.** Examples of well-known programming languages are C, C++, Visual BASIC, and Java. These are called *high-level languages,* as we explain in a few pages.

Not all languages are appropriate for all uses. Some, for example, have strengths in mathematical and statistical processing. Others are more appropriate for database management or support a specific operating system, such as Unix. Some languages take more storage space than others; if you are writing code for an embedded processor (Chapter 1), for example, you would choose a language that is space efficient. And some languages are faster than others. Thus, in choosing the language, you need to consider what purpose the program is designed to serve and what languages are already being used in your organization or in your field. We consider these matters shortly in Section 10.3.

2. CODE THE PROGRAM IN THAT LANGUAGE, FOLLOWING THE SYNTAX For a program to work, you have to follow the **syntax, the rules of the programming language.** Programming languages have their own grammar just as human languages do. But computers are probably a lot less forgiving if you use these rules incorrectly.

The Fourth Step: Test the Program

Program testing involves both good data and bad data.

Program testing involves running various tests and then running real-world data to make sure the program works. *(• See Panel 10.17, next page.)* Two principal activities are desk-checking and debugging. These steps are called *alpha testing.*

1. PERFORM DESK-CHECKING **Desk-checking is simply reading through, or checking, the program to make sure that it's free of errors and that the logic works.** In other words, desk-checking is like proofreading. This step should be taken before the program is actually run on a computer.

1. Select the appropriate high-level programming language.
2. Code the program in that language, following the syntax carefully.

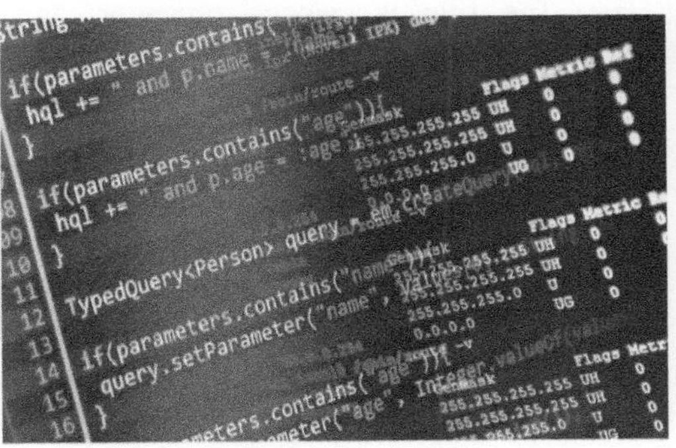

panel 10.16

Third step: Program coding

The third step in programming is to translate the logic of the program worked out from pseudocode or flowcharts into a high-level programming language, following its grammatical rules.

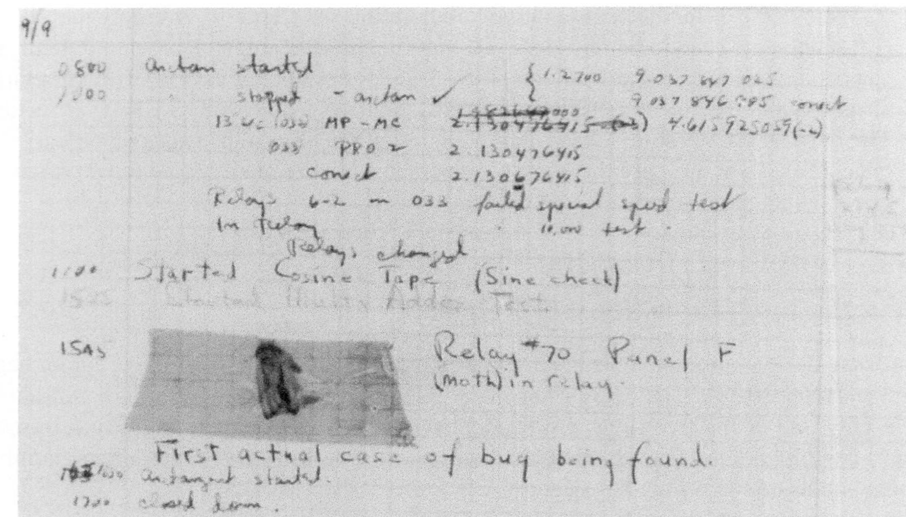

panel 10.17

Fourth step: Program testing

The fourth step is to test the program and "debug" it of errors so that it will work properly. The word "bug" dates from 1945, when a moth was discovered lodged in a relay of the Mark I computer. The moth disrupted the execution of the program.

2. DEBUG THE PROGRAM Once the program has been desk-checked, further errors, or "bugs," will doubtlessly surface. **To debug means to detect, locate, and remove all errors in a computer program.** Mistakes may be syntax errors or logic errors. **Syntax errors are caused by typographical errors and incorrect use of the programming language. Logic errors are caused by incorrect use of control structures.** Programs called *diagnostics* exist to check program syntax and display syntax-error messages. Diagnostic programs thus help identify and solve problems. (*Run-time errors* may also occur when certain conditions cause the code to abort.)

Sometimes debugging is partially done in the third step, program coding, using the "buddy system," or pair programming. In this system, two people sit side by side; while one person (the "driver") codes, the other person (the "navigator") checks the code, corrects it, and offers suggestions for improvement.[11]

3. RUN REAL-WORLD DATA After desk-checking and debugging, the program may run fine—in the laboratory. However, it needs to be tested with real data; this is called *beta testing.* Indeed, it is even advisable to test the program not only with "good" data but also with bad data—data that is faulty, incomplete, or in overwhelming quantities—to see if you can make the system crash. Many users, after all, may be far more heavy-handed, ignorant, and careless than programmers have anticipated.

Several trials using different test data may be required before the programming team is satisfied that the program can be released. Even then, some bugs may persist, because there comes a point where the pursuit of errors is uneconomical. This is one reason why many users are nervous about using the first version (version 1.0) of a commercial software package.

Testing is done module by module and then as a whole, integrated program.

more info!

More about Software Testing

Go to *www.softwareqatest.com* and read the FAQs about software testing. Would you like to be a software tester? Find some job information at:

www.essortment.com/*all*/software-testing_rxng.htm

TECH TALES Who Decides When Programs Are Okay to Go? The Release Engineer

The title is *release engineer,* and he or she is the person "tasked with gathering up all the code written by a company's many [software] engineers and making sure it works together as a whole," according to one description.[12] At Facebook in Menlo Park, California, the release engineer, Chuck Rossi, looks over code for bugs, talks to the engineers about their work, and decides which features are kept for the final product that goes up on the Facebook website. His work comes after several software tools have been applied in a first round of checks.

"It's like plumbing," Rossi says about his job "It's not the most glamorous thing in the world, but I realized that if you're good at it, you could go to any software company in the world and they would say: 'When can you start?' "[13]

Rossi is able to pull up a profile of each engineer to see what code that person submitted. Everyone starts with four stars, but if Rossi has an issue with someone's work, he can take them down half a star. If engineers drop to two stars, they're not allowed to make changes in programs until they've completed a review and retraining process. On the other hand, if they catch an error before the program goes up on the website, they can earn a half-star back.

"People here are pretty freaked out about losing their stars," says Rossi, "but not in a bad way. It's all done in good fun." ■

Programming Tools

Programming tools are used for software development or system maintenance. Any program or utility that helps programmers or users develop applications or maintain their computers can be called a tool. Where can you get programming tools?

www.freewarefiles.com/category/programming.php

www.literateprogramming.com/tools.html

http://protools.winasm.net/

The Fifth Step: Document & Maintain the Program

Preliminary documentation should have been conducted throughout the entire programming process.

Writing the program documentation is the fifth step in programming. The resulting documentation consists of written descriptions of what a program is and how to use it. Documentation is not just an end-stage process of programming. It has been (or should have been) going on throughout all programming steps. Documentation is needed for people who will be using or be involved with the program in the future. (• *See Panel 10.18.*)

Documentation should be prepared for several different kinds of readers—users, operators, and programmers.

1. WRITE USER DOCUMENTATION When you buy a commercial software package, such as a spreadsheet, you normally get a manual with it. This is user documentation. Today manuals are usually on the software CD.

2. WRITE OPERATOR DOCUMENTATION The people who run large computers are called *computer operators.* Because they are not always programmers, they need to be told what to do if the program malfunctions. The *operator documentation* gives them this information.

3. WRITE PROGRAMMER DOCUMENTATION Long after the original programming team has disbanded, the program may still be in use. If, as is often the case, a fifth of the programming staff leaves every year, after five years there could be a whole new bunch of programmers who know nothing about the software. *Program documentation* helps train these newcomers and enables them to maintain the existing system.

4. MAINTAIN THE PROGRAM A word about maintenance: *Maintenance* includes any activity designed to keep programs in working condition, error-free, and up to date—adjustments, replacements, repairs, measurements, tests, and so on. The rapid changes in modern organizations—in products, marketing strategies, accounting systems, and so on—are bound to be reflected in their computer systems. Thus, maintenance is an important matter, and documentation must be available to help programmers make adjustments in existing systems.

The five steps of the programming process are summarized in the table on the next page. (• *See Panel 10.19.*)

1. Write user documentation.
2. Write operator documentation.
3. Write programmer documentation.
4. Maintain the program.

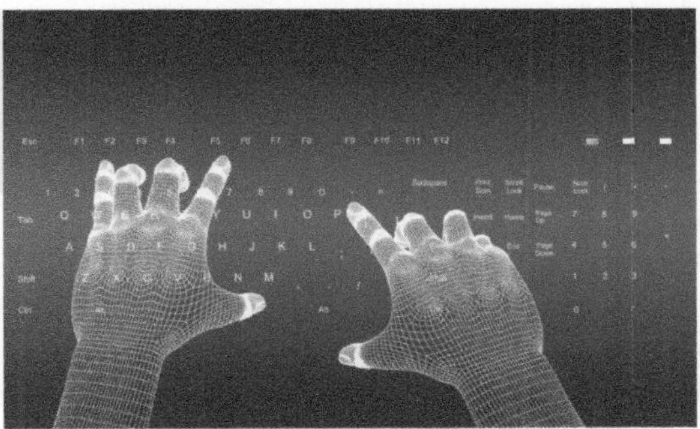

panel 10.18

Fifth step: Program documentation and maintenance

The fifth step is really the culmination of activity that has been going on through all the programming steps—documentation. Written descriptions and procedures about a program and how to use it need to be developed for different people—users, operators, and programmers. Maintenance is an ongoing process.

panel 10.19

Summary of the five programming steps

Step	Activities
Step 1: Problem clarification	**1.** Clarify program objectives and program users. **2.** Clarify desired outputs. **3.** Clarify desired inputs. **4.** Clarify desired processing. **5.** Double-check feasibility of implementing the program. **6.** Document the analysis.
Step 2: Program design	**1.** Determine program logic through top-down approach and modularization, using a hierarchy chart. **2.** Design details using pseudocode and/or using flowcharts, preferably on the basis of control structures. **3.** Test design with structured walkthrough.
Step 3: Program coding	**1.** Select the appropriate high-level programming language. **2.** Code the program in that language, following the syntax carefully.
Step 4: Program testing	**1.** Desk-check the program to discover errors. **2.** Run the program and debug it (alpha testing). **3.** Run real-world data (beta testing).
Step 5: Program documentation and maintenance	**1.** Finalize user documentation. **2.** Finalize operator documentation. **3.** Finalize programmer documentation. **4.** Maintain the program.

UNIT 10B: *Programming Languages*

Software developers are in "absolute explosive demand," says the engineering vice president of a San Francisco cloud computing firm, "We're seeing a gap between the number of software engineers we need and the number the education system is generating. . . . This is a terrific area to invest oneself."[14] Indeed, the Bureau of Labor Statistics projects 27.6% employment growth for software developers between 2010 and 2020, much faster than average for all occupations.

One of the first requirements for being a software developer or engineer is to learn not just the steps in programming but also programming languages. Some young people ages 8–18 have gotten a head start by learning languages such as Lua, Alice, and Scratch (available through online gaming sites such as Roblox), which help them learn skills that translate to other languages such as Java, Ruby, and C++.[15] Others pick up coding skills from online programming classes in two- and four-year colleges, plus courses offered by Udacity, Codecademy, and Coursera.

The following sections present an overview of the principal programming languages.

10.3 FIVE GENERATIONS OF PROGRAMMING LANGUAGES

So far, there have been five basic generations of programming languages.

As we've said, a programming language is a set of rules that tells the computer what operations to do. Programmers, in fact, use these languages to create other kinds of software. Many programming languages have been written, some with colorful names (SNOBOL, HEARSAY, DOCTOR, ACTORS, SCRATCH, PYTHON, ALICE, JOVIAL). Each is suited to solving particular kinds of problems. What do all these languages have in common? Simply this: ultimately they must be reduced to digital form—a 1 or 0, electricity on or off—because that is all the computer can work with.

To see how this works, one must consider the current five levels, or generations, of programming languages, ranging from low level to high level. **The five generations of programming languages start at the lowest level with (1) machine language** (pp. 200, 528). **They then range up through (2) assembly language, (3) high-level languages (procedural languages and object-oriented languages), and (4) very-high-level languages (problem-oriented languages). At the highest level are (5) natural languages.** Programming languages are said to be *lower level* when they are closer to the language that the computer itself uses—the 1s and 0s. They are called *higher level* when they are closer to the language people use—more like English, for example.

Beginning in 1945, the five levels, or generations, have evolved over the years, as programmers gradually adopted the later generations. The births of the generations are as follows. *(• See Panel 10.20.)*

- First generation, 1945—*machine language*
- Second generation, mid-1950s—*assembly language*
- Third generation, mid-1950s to early 1960s—*high-level languages (procedural languages and object-oriented);* for example, FORTRAN, COBOL, BASIC, C, and C++
- Fourth generation, early 1970s—*very-high-level languages (problem-oriented languages);* for example, SQL, Intellect, NOMAD, FOCUS
- Fifth generation, early 1980s—*natural languages*

Let's consider these five generations.

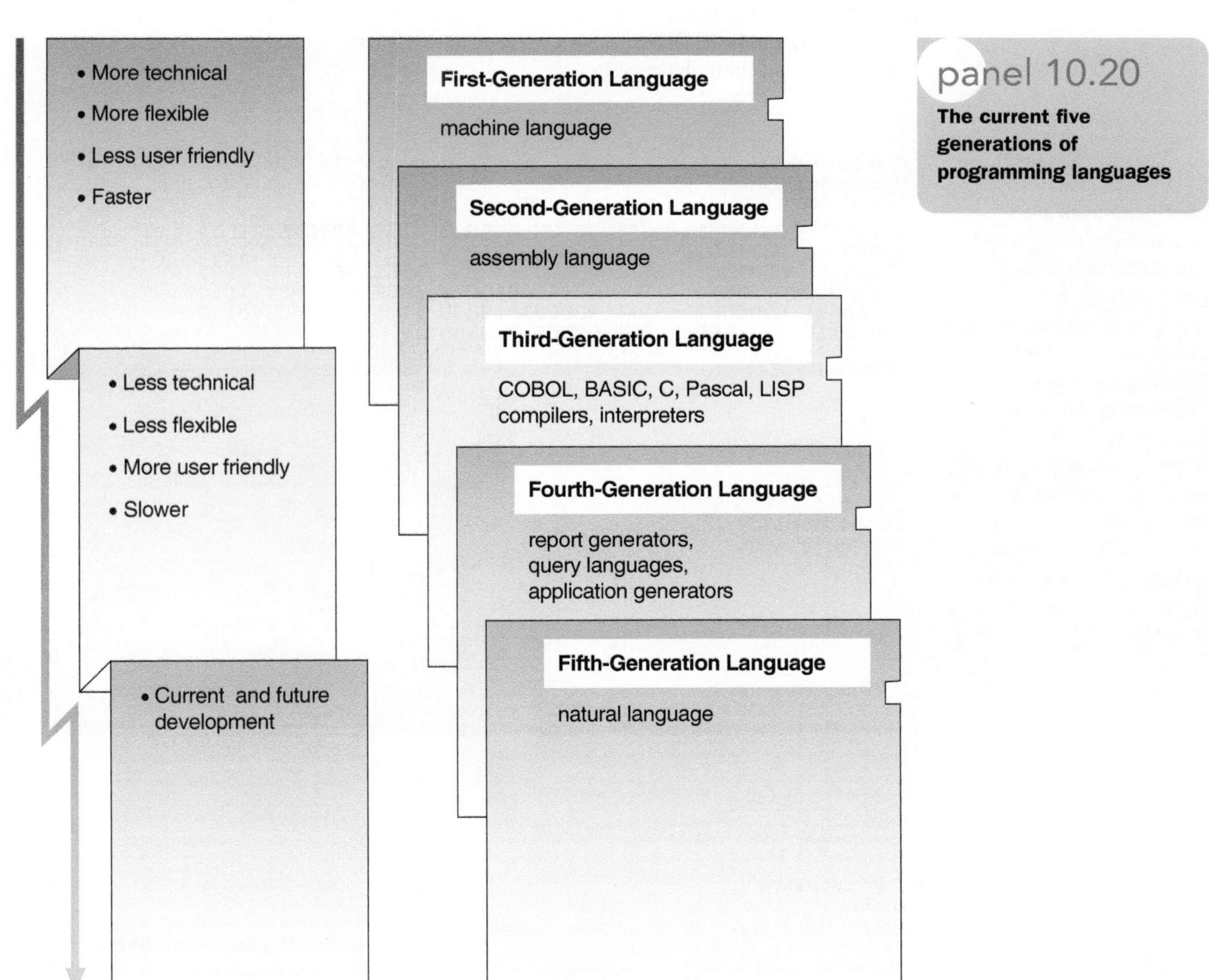

panel 10.20

The current five generations of programming languages

First Generation: Machine Language

Machine code is the computer's "native language," the only language that a computer can "understand."

Machine language is the basic language of the computer, representing data as 1s and 0s. (• *See Panel 10.21.*) Each CPU model has its own machine language. Machine-language programs vary from computer model to computer model; that is, they are *machine-dependent.*

Machine-language binary digits, which correspond to the on and off electrical states of the computer, are clearly not convenient for people to read and use. Believe it or not, though, programmers *did* work with these mind-numbing digits. There must have been great sighs of relief when the next generation of programming languages—assembly language—came along.

Second Generation: Assembly Language

Assembly language uses symbolic instruction codes.

Assembly language is a low-level programming language that allows a programmer to write a program using abbreviations or more easily remembered words instead of numbers, as in machine language; essentially, assembly language is a mnemonic version of machine language. *(Refer to Panels 10.20 and 10.21.)* For example, the letters *MP* could be used to represent the instruction "multiply" and *STO* to represent "store."

As you might expect, a programmer can write instructions in assembly language more quickly than in machine language. Nevertheless, it is still not an easy language to learn, and it is so tedious to use that mistakes are frequent. Moreover, assembly language has the same drawback as machine language in that it varies among processor (computer) brands—it is machine-dependent.

panel 10.21

Three generations of programming languages

(*top*) Machine language is all binary 0s and 1s—difficult for people to work with. (*middle*) Assembly language uses abbreviations for major instructions (such as *MP* for "multiply"). This is easier for people to use, but still challenging. (*bottom*) COBOL, a third-generation language, uses English words that people can understand.

First generation
Machine language

```
11110010 01110011 1101 001000010000 0111 000000101011
11110010 01110011 1101 001000011000 0111 000000101111
11111100 01010010 1101 001000010010 1101 001000011101
11110000 01000101 1101 001000010011 0000 000000111110
11110011 01000011 0111 000001010000 1101 001000010100
10010110 11110000 0111 000001010100
```

Second generation
Assembly language

```
PACK  210(8,13),02B(4,7)
PACK  218(8,13),02F(4,7)
MP    212(6,13),21D(3,13)
SRP   213(5,13),03E(0),5
UNPK  050(5,7),214(4,13)
OI    054(7),X'F0'
```

Third generation
COBOL

```
MULTIPLY HOURS-WORKED BY PAY-RATE GIVING GROSS-PAY ROUNDED.
```

We now need to introduce the concept of a *language translator.* Because a computer can execute programs only in machine language, a translator or converter is needed if the program is written in any other language. **A language translator is a type of system software that translates a program written in a second-, third-, or higher-generation language into machine language.**

Language translators are of three types:

- Assemblers
- Compilers
- Interpreters

An assembler, or *assembler program,* is a program that translates the assembly-language program into machine language. We describe compilers and interpreters in the next section.

Third Generation: High-Level or Procedural Languages

High-level languages are more like human language.

A high-level, or *procedural/object-oriented,* language resembles a human language such as English; an example is COBOL, which is used for business applications. *(Refer to Panels 10.20 and 10.21.)* A procedural language allows users to write in a familiar notation, rather than numbers or abbreviations. Also, unlike machine and assembly languages, most are not machine-dependent—that is, they can be used on more than one kind of computer. There are hundreds of high-level languages; however, only a few are widely used in industry. Familiar languages of this sort include FORTRAN, COBOL, and C. (We cover object-oriented languages shortly.)

For a procedural language to work on a computer, it needs a language translator to translate it into machine language. Depending on the procedural language, either of two types of translators may be used—a *compiler* or an *interpreter.*

COMPILER—EXECUTE LATER **A compiler is a language-translator program that converts the entire program of a high-level language into machine language *before* the computer executes the program.** The programming instructions of a procedural language are called the *source code.* The compiler translates it into machine language, which in this case is called the *object code.* The important point here is that the object code can be saved and thus can be executed later (as many times as desired), rather than run right away. *(• See Panel 10.22.)* These executable files—the output of compilers—have the *.exe* extension on many systems.

Examples of procedural languages using compilers are COBOL, FORTRAN, Pascal, and C. *(• See Panel 10.23, next page.)*

INTERPRETER—EXECUTE IMMEDIATELY **An interpreter is a language-translator program that converts each procedural language statement into machine language and executes it *immediately,* statement by statement.** In contrast to the compiler, an interpreter does not save object code. Therefore, interpreted code generally runs more slowly than compiled code. However, the code can be tested line by line. BASIC and Perl are procedural languages using an interpreter.

WHY DOES IT MATTER? Who cares, you might say, whether you can run a program now or later? (After all, "later" could be only a matter of seconds or minutes.) Here's the significance: When a compiler is used, it requires two steps (the source code and the

panel 10.22

Compiler

This language translator converts the procedural language *(source code)* into machine language *(object code)* before the computer can execute the program.

panel 10.23

Some third-generation languages compared
This shows how five languages handle the same statement. The statement specifies that a customer gets a discount of 7% of the invoice amount if the invoice is greater than $500; if the invoice is lower, there is no discount.

FORTRAN

```
IF (XINVO .GT. 500.00) THEN
     DISCNT = 0.07 * XINVO
ELSE
     DISCNT = 0.0
ENDIF
XINVO = XINVO – DISCNT
```

COBOL

```
OPEN-INVOICE-FILE.
       OPEN I-O INVOICE FILE.

READ-INVOICE-PROCESS.
       PERFORM READ-NEXT-REC THROUGH READ-NEXT-REC-EXIT UNTIL END-OF-FILE.
       STOP RUN.

READ-NEXT-REC.
       READ INVOICE-REC
             INVALID KEY
                   DISPLAY 'ERROR READING INVOICE FILE'
                   MOVE 'Y' TO EOF-FLAG
                   GOTO READ-NEXT-REC-EXIT.
       IF INVOICE-AMT > 500
             COMPUTE INVOICE-AMT = INVOICE-AMT – (INVOICE-AMT * .07)
             REWRITE INVOICE-REC.

READ-NEXT-REC-EXIT.
       EXIT.
```

BASIC

```
10  REM      This Program Calculates a Discount Based on the Invoice Amount
20  REM          If Invoice Amount is Greater Than 500, Discount is 7%
30  REM          Otherwise Discount is 0
40  REM
50  INPUT "What is the Invoice Amount"; INV.AMT
60  IF INV.AMT > 500 THEN LET DISCOUNT = .07 ELSE LET DISCOUNT = 0
70  REM          Display results
80  PRINT "Original Amt", "Discount", "Amt after Discount"
90  PRINT INV.AMT, INV.AMT * DISCOUNT, INV.AMT – INV.AMT * DISCOUNT
100 END
```

Pascal

```
if INVOICEAMOUNT > 500.00 then
  DISCOUNT := 0.07 * INVOICEAMOUNT
else
  DISCOUNT := 0.0;
INVOICEAMOUNT := INVOICEAMOUNT – DISCOUNT
```

C

```
if (invoice_amount > 500.00)
  discount = 0.07 * invoice_amount;
else
  discount = 0.00;
invoice_amount = invoice_amount – discount;
```

object code) before the program can be executed. The interpreter, however, requires only *one* step. The advantage of a compiler language is that, once you have obtained the object code, the program executes faster. The advantage of an interpreter language, on the other hand, is that programs are easier to develop. Some language translators can both compile and interpret.

SQL Example

If you were to update the data on a salesperson for all customers in a particular region, the procedural-language way might look something like this:

```
do until eof
  if rs("state") = "NH" then
    rs("salesperson") = "Mike"
  end if
  rs.next
loop
```

The SQL way would be:

```
UPDATE customers SET
salesperson = "Mike"
WHERE state = "NH"
```

Source: www.paragoncorporation.com/ArticleDetail.aspx?ArticleID=27.

Fourth Generation: Very-High-Level or Problem-Oriented Languages

Fourth-generation languages are even closer to human language than 3GLs; most of them are used to access databases.

Third-generation languages tell the computer *how* to do something. Fourth-generation languages, in contrast, tell the computer *what* to do. **Very-high-level, or *problem-oriented* or *nonprocedural,* languages, also called *fourth-generation languages (4GLs),* are much more user-oriented and allow users to develop programs with fewer commands compared with procedural languages,** although they require more computing power. These languages are called *problem-oriented* because they are designed to solve specific problems, whereas procedural languages are more general-purpose languages.

Three types of problem-oriented languages are *report generators, query languages,* and *application generators.*

REPORT GENERATORS A *report generator,* also called a *report writer,* is a program for end users that produces a report. The report may be a printout or a screen display. It may show all or part of a database file. You can specify the format in advance—columns, headings, and so on—and the report generator will then produce data in that format. Report generators (an example is RPGIV) were the precursors to today's query languages.

What Can SQL Do?

- Execute queries against a database.
- Retrieve data from a database.
- Insert records in a database.
- Update records in a database.
- Delete records from a database.
- Create new databases.
- Create new tables in a database.
- Create stored procedures in a database.
- Create views in a database.
- Manipulate tables.

Source: www.w3schools.com/SQl/sql_intro.asp.

QUERY LANGUAGES A *query language* is an easy-to-use language for accessing and manipulating data from a database management system. The query may be expressed in the form of a sentence or near-English command. Or the query may be obtained from choices on a menu.

Examples of query languages are SQL (for "Structured Query Language") and Intellect. For example, with Intellect, which is used with IBM mainframes, you can make an English-language request such as, "Tell me the number of employees in the sales department."

APPLICATION GENERATORS An *application generator* is a programmer's tool consisting of modules that have been preprogrammed to accomplish various tasks. The benefit is that the programmer can generate application programs from descriptions of the problem rather than by traditional programming, in which he or she has to specify how the data should be processed.

Programmers use application generators to help them create parts of other programs. For example, the software is used to construct on-screen menus or types of input and output screen formats. NOMAD and FOCUS, two database management systems, include application generators.

Fifth Generation: Natural Languages

Fifth-generation languages are used mainly for artificial intelligence and neural networks.

Natural languages are of two types. The first comprises ordinary human languages: English, Spanish, and so on. The second type comprises programming languages that use human language to give people a more natural connection with computers.

With a problem-oriented language, you can type in some rather routine inquiries, such as (in the language known as FOCUS) the following:

SUM SHIPMENTS BY STATE BY DATE.

Programming Language Popularity

Which are the most commonly used languages?

www.tiobe.com/index.php/content/paperinfo/tpci/index.html

more info!

Government in Action

In 2009, the governor of California fired about 10,000 temporary and part-time workers and reduced the pay levels of about 200,000 permanent employees. However, a week later, the state controller pointed out that the state payroll records could not be changed to accommodate the cuts, because they were written in COBOL—and the only state employees who knew the code were among the fired part-time employees (*www.funnytimes.com/*, February 2009).

"It is estimated that over 80% of the world's business still runs on COBOL. It is also estimated that 310 billion lines of software are in use today, of which 200 billion lines are COBOL (65% of the total software), and that 5 billion lines of new COBOL are developed every year. COBOL legacy applications process over 80% of all daily business transactions, and mainframe platforms store 70% of all the data" (*www.marblecomputer.com/dcd-IV-COBOL-Legacy-Modernization.html*).

Natural languages, by contrast, allow questions or commands to be framed in a more conversational way or in alternative forms—for example:

I WANT THE SHIPMENTS OF PERSONAL DIGITAL ASSISTANTS FOR ALABAMA AND MISSISSIPPI BROKEN DOWN BY CITY FOR JANUARY AND FEBRUARY. ALSO, MAY I HAVE JANUARY AND FEBRUARY SHIPMENTS LISTED BY CITIES FOR PERSONAL COMMUNICATORS SHIPPED TO WISCONSIN AND MINNESOTA.

Natural languages are part of the field of study known as *artificial intelligence* (discussed in Chapter 8). As we stated, artificial intelligence (AI) is a group of related technologies that attempt to develop machines capable of emulating human qualities, such as learning, reasoning, communicating, seeing, and hearing.

The dates of the principal programming languages are shown in the time line running along the bottom of these pages. *(• See Panel 10.24.)*

10.4 PROGRAMMING LANGUAGES USED TODAY

Third-level computer languages are still the major means of communication between the digital computer and its user.

We now turn back and consider some of the third-generation, or high-level, languages in use today.

FORTRAN

The language of mathematics and the first high-level language.

Developed from 1954 to 1956 by John Backus and others at IBM, *FORTRAN* (for *FORmula TRANslator*) was the first high-level language. *(Refer back to Panel 10.23, page 530.)* Originally designed to express mathematical formulas, it is still the most widely used language for mathematical, scientific, and engineering problems. It is also useful for complex business applications, such as forecasting and modeling. However, because it cannot handle a large volume of input/output operations or file processing, it is not used for more typical business problems and has become basically a legacy language. (A "legacy language" is still used by many companies, but it is an older language that is generally no longer updated or developed.)

COBOL

The first language of business.

Developed under the auspices of the U.S. Department of Defense, with Grace Murray Hopper as a major contributor, and formally adopted in 1960, *COBOL* (for *COmmon Business-Oriented Language*) is the most frequently used business programming language for large computers. *(Refer again to Panel 10.23.)* Its most significant attribute is that it is extremely readable. For example, a COBOL line might read:

MULTIPLY HOURLY-RATE BY HOURS-WORKED GIVING GROSS-PAY

panel 10.24

Timeline: Brief history of the development of programming languages and formatting tools

- 1843 World's first computer programmer, Ada Lovelace, publishes her notes
- 1950 **EDSAC**—assembly language
- 1951-1952 Grace Murray Hopper develops A-O, the first compiler
- 1954 **FORTRAN**—the language of mathematics
- 1958 **ALGOL-58**
- 1958 **LISP**—for artificial intelligence programs
- 1960 **COBOL**—the language of business
- 1964 **RPG**—the easy language for business reports
- 1964 **PL/1**—the best of FORTRAN and COBOL?
- 1965 **BASIC**—the easy language
- 1967 **Simula**—the first conceptual object-oriented language (also, the term *software engineering* is introduced)
- 1970 **Pascal**—the simple language

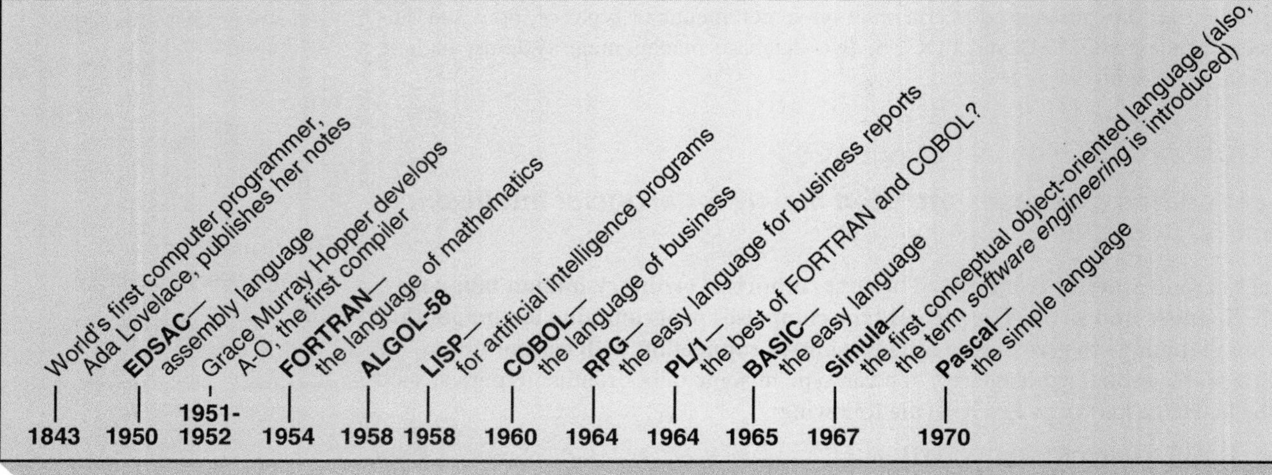

Writing a COBOL program resembles writing an outline for a research paper. The program is divided into four divisions—Identification, Environment, Data, and Procedure. The divisions in turn are divided into sections, which are divided into paragraphs, which are further divided into statements. The Identification Division identifies the name of the program and the author (programmer) and perhaps some other helpful comments. The Environment Division describes the computer on which the program will be compiled and executed. The Data Division describes what data will be processed. The Procedure Division describes the actual processing procedures.

Some people believe that COBOL is becoming obsolete. However, others disagree. Few things that were around in the IT industry in 1960 are still around today, except perhaps in museums and in basements. Yet the COBOL language, albeit highly evolved from its origins, remains relevant. The corporate assets represented by the billions of lines of COBOL code still running on commercial computers aren't about to be abandoned. Nor should they be. New tools that help integrate legacy (read: COBOL) systems with PC applications, web services, new data formats, and protocols have been available since distributive systems emerged years ago. As today's application environment has evolved, so has COBOL's capability to link to it, merge with it, and interact with it. Stretching the life span of an enterprise's legacy systems increases the value and productivity of its IT development staff and of the assets they produce.[16]

Grace Hopper

Augusta Ada King (Countess of Lovelace)

more info!

Who Was Grace Hopper?

Rear Admiral Grace Murray Hopper (1906–1992) was a pioneer computer scientist and a developer of software concepts and the first compiler. Read about Hopper and other women in computer science:

http://women.cs.cmu.edu/ada/Resources/Women/

www.history.navy.mil/photos/pers-us/uspers-h/g-hoppr.htm

www.sdsc.edu/ScienceWomen/hopper.html

www.thocp.net/biographies/hopper_grace.html

http://women.acm.org/

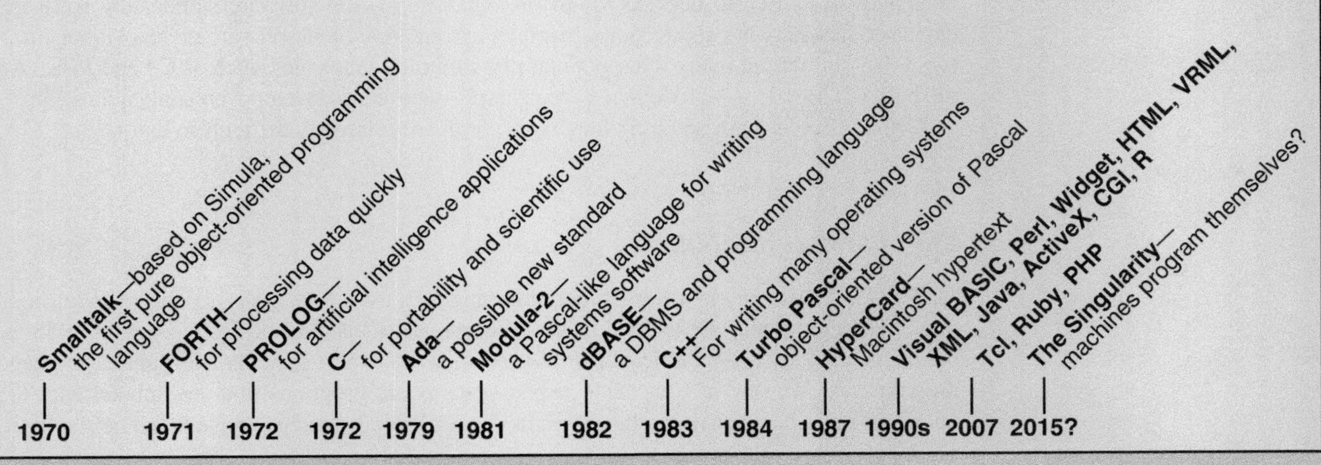
Smalltalk—based on Simula, the first pure object-oriented programming language
1970
FORTH—for processing data quickly
1971
PROLOG—for artificial intelligence applications
1972
C—for portability and scientific use
1972
Ada—a possible new standard
1979
Modula-2—a Pascal-like language for writing systems software
1981
dBASE—a DBMS and programming language
1982
C++—For writing many operating systems
1983
Turbo Pascal—object-oriented version of Pascal
1984
HyperCard—Macintosh hypertext
1987
Visual BASIC, Perl, Widget, HTML, VRML, XML, Java, ActiveX, CGI, R
1990s
Tcl, Ruby, PHP
2007
The Singularity—machines program themselves?
2015?

BASIC

The easy language.

BASIC was developed by John Kemeny and Thomas Kurtz in 1964 for use in training their students at Dartmouth College. By the late 1960s, it was widely used in academic settings on all kinds of computers, from mainframes to PCs.

BASIC (*Beginner's All-purpose Symbolic Instruction Code*) used to be the most popular microcomputer language and is considered the easiest programming language to learn. *(Refer to Panel 10.23, page 530.)* Although it is available in compiler form, the interpreter form is more popular with first-time and casual users. This is because it is interactive, meaning that user and computer can communicate with each other during the writing and running of the program. Today there is no one version of BASIC. One of the popular current evolutions is Visual BASIC (VB.net), discussed shortly.

99 Bottles of Beer

This website holds a collection of the song "99 Bottles of Beer" programmed in 1,500 different programming languages:

www.99-bottles-of-beer.net/

. . . and the number keeps growing.

Pascal

The simple language

Named after the 17th-century French mathematician Blaise Pascal and developed in 1970 by Niklaus Wirth, *Pascal* is an alternative to BASIC as a language for teaching purposes and is relatively easy to learn. *(Refer to Panel 10.23, page 530.)* Pascal is a simple language, and it helps introduce beginners to other languages, such as C, C++, and Java.

C

For portability, operating systems, and scientific use.

C is the successor of B, which was the successor of BCPL, which was the successor of CPL (Computer Programming Language), an early programming language that was not implemented. Developed by Dennis Ritchie at Bell Laboratories in the early 1970s, *C* is a general-purpose, compiled language that was developed for midrange computers (minicomputers) but that works well for microcomputers and is portable among many computers. It was originally developed for writing system software. The first major program written in C was the Unix operating system, and for many years C was considered to be inextricably linked with Unix. Now, however, C is an important language independent of Unix. Today it is widely used for creating operating systems and writing applications, including word processing, spreadsheets, games, robotics, and graphics programs. It is considered a necessary language for programmers to know.

C++

Enhancement of C.

C++ (for *increased C,* pronounced "see-plus-plus"), an object-oriented language (covered shortly) developed by Bjarne Stroustrup at Bell Labs, is one of the most popular programming languages; it is used to develop Microsoft Windows system software, application software, device drivers, network applications, graphics, and entertainment software such as videogames. C++ has influenced many other popular programming languages, such as C# and Java. (An offshoot of C++, C#—pronounced "see-sharp"—is used to develop web applications.)

C and C++ are not teaching languages; both are relatively difficult to learn.

LISP

For artificial intelligence programs.

LISP (*LISt Processor*) is a third-generation language used principally to construct artificial intelligence programs. Developed at the Massachusetts Institute of Technology in 1958 by mathematician John McCarthy, LISP is used to write expert systems and natural language programs. As we saw in Chapter 8, expert systems are programs that are imbued with the knowledge of a human expert; the programs can walk you through a problem and help solve it.

10.5 OBJECT-ORIENTED & VISUAL PROGRAMMING

Procedural languages focus on static data and the procedures and functions that need to be performed on the data; object-oriented languages focus on the "things" or classes of objects in a system and use the classes as a way to organize what needs to be done; visual programming uses graphics, drawings, animation, and/or icons.

Consider how it was for the computer pioneers, programming in machine language or assembly language. Novices programming with C, for example, can breathe a collective sigh of relief that they weren't around at the dawn of the Computer Age. Even some of the simpler third-generation languages present challenges because they are procedure-oriented, forcing the programmer to follow a predetermined path.

Fortunately, two developments have made things easier—object-oriented programming and visual programming.

Conventional Programs

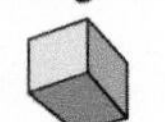

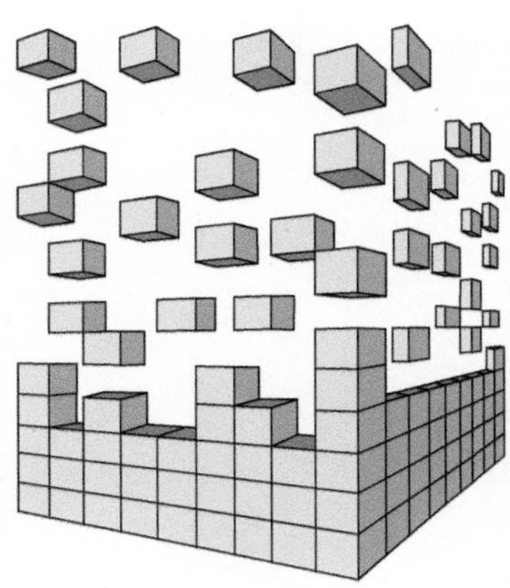

Object-Oriented Programming (OOP)

Programming by building with "classes."

Imagine you're programming in a traditional third-generation language, such as BASIC, creating your coded instructions one line at a time. As you work on some segment of the program (such as how to compute overtime pay), you may think, "I'll bet some other programmer has already written something like this. Wish I had it. It would save a lot of time." Fortunately, a kind of recycling technique exists. This is object-oriented programming, an improved version of 3GLs.

HOW OOP WORKS: OBJECT, MESSAGE, & METHOD Object-oriented programming consists of the following components:

1. ***What OOP is:*** **In object-oriented programming (*OOP,* pronounced "oop"), data and the instructions for processing that data are combined into a self-sufficient "object" that can be used in other programs.** The important thing here is the object.
2. ***What an "object" is:*** **An object is a self-contained module consisting of preassembled programming code.** The module contains, or encapsulates, both (1) a chunk of data and (2) the processing instructions that may be performed on that data.
3. ***When an object's data is to be processed—sending the "message":*** Once the object becomes part of a program, the processing instructions may or may not be activated. A particular set of instructions is activated only when the corresponding "message" is sent. A *message* is an alert sent to the object when an operation involving that object needs to be performed.
4. ***How the object's data is processed—the "methods":*** The message need only identify the operation. How it is actually to be performed is embedded within the processing instructions that are part of the object. These processing instructions within the object are called the *methods.*

Object-Oriented Programs

RECYCLING BLOCKS OF PROGRAM CODE Once you've written a block of program code (that computes overtime pay, for example), it can be reused in any number of programs. Thus, with OOP, unlike traditional programming, you don't have to start from scratch—that is, reinvent the wheel—each time.

Object-oriented programming takes longer to learn than traditional programming, because it means training oneself to a different way of thinking. However, the beauty of OOP is that an object can be used repeatedly in different applications and by different programmers, speeding up development time and lowering costs.

THREE IMPORTANT CONCEPTS OF OOP Object-oriented programming has three important concepts, which go under the jaw-breaking names of *encapsulation, inheritance,* and *polymorphism.* Actually, these are not as fearsome as they look:

- **Encapsulation:** *Encapsulation* means an object contains (encapsulates) both (1) data and (2) the relevant processing instructions, as we have seen. Once an object has been created, it can be reused in other programs. An object's uses can also be extended through the concepts of *class* and *inheritance.*
- **Inheritance:** Once you have created an object, you can use it as the foundation for similar objects that have the same behavior and characteristics. All objects that are derived from or related to one another are said to form a *class.* Each class contains specific instructions (methods) that are unique to that group.

  Classes can be arranged in hierarchies—classes and subclasses. *Inheritance* is the method of passing down traits of an object from classes to subclasses in the hierarchy. Thus, new objects can be created by inheriting traits from existing classes.

  Writer Alan Freedman gives this example: "The object MACINTOSH could be one instance of the class PERSONAL COMPUTER, which could inherit properties from the class COMPUTER SYSTEMS."[17] If you were to add a new computer, such as DELL, you would need to enter only what makes it different from other computers. The general characteristics of personal computers would be inherited.
- **Polymorphism:** Polymorphism means the presence of "many shapes." In object-oriented programming, *polymorphism* means that a message (generalized request) produces different results based on the object that it is sent to.

  Polymorphism has important uses. It allows a programmer to create procedures about objects whose exact type is not known in advance but will be at the time the program is actually run on the computer. Freedman gives this example: "A screen cursor may change its shape from an arrow to a line depending on the program mode." The processing instructions "to move the cursor on screen in response to mouse movement would be written for 'cursor,' and polymorphism would allow that cursor to be whatever shape is required at runtime." It would also allow a new cursor shape to be easily integrated into the program.

EXAMPLES OF OOP LANGUAGES: C++ & JAVA Two important examples of OOP languages are C++ and Java.

- **C++:** *C++* combines the traditional C programming language with object-oriented capability. With C++, programmers can write standard code in C without the object-oriented features, use object-oriented features, or do a mixture of both.
- **Java:** A high-level programming language developed by Sun Microsystems in 1995, *Java,* also an object-oriented language, is used to write compact programs that can be downloaded over the Internet and immediately executed on many kinds of computers. Java is similar to C++ but is simplified to eliminate language features that cause common programming errors. It is often used to collect information from networked computers and for web applications.

  Small Java applications are called Java *applets* and can be downloaded from a web server and run on your computer by a Java-compatible web browser, such as Mozilla Firefox or Microsoft Internet Explorer. Java applets make websites more interactive and attractive, adding features such as animation and calculators—but only if a browser is capable of supporting Java. Users also can download free Java applets from various sites on the internet.

Phone Apps

People buy a lot of phone apps, so developing programs for the new generation of smartphones can be a moneymaker if you do it right:

www.udemy.com/blog/making-an-app/

www.nytimes.com/2012/11/18/business/as-boom-lures-app-creators-tough-part-is-making-a-living.html?pagewanted=all&_r=0

www.bluecloudsolutions.com/blog/cost-develop-app/

www.crazyandroid.com/how-to-make-money-from-android-apps/

TECH TALES Student Entrepreneurs Create a New App in Five Days with "Premade Programming Lego Blocks"

52apps is a small software start-up founded in 2012 by two 22-year-old seniors at the University of South Carolina whose business plan is to produce 52 apps in a year for iPhones and iPads by programming an app within five days, and to sell the software through iTunes. Sometimes the apps are based on ideas acquired from members of the general public, with whom the firm shares royalties.

According to the founders, Christopher Thibault and Brendan Lee, the basis for creating an app in less than a week—far less time than is usually required—is a proprietary module framework—what has been described figuratively as "premade programming Lego blocks."[18]

"There's a lot of grunt work in creating apps," says Lee. "For example, it can take three to five hours to fully implement all features in a device's GPS system. So we developed a bunch of reusable modules that we can plug into any app we write."[19]

One of the 52app products is Canary, a smartphone app that can send an alarm to parents when their teens are doing dangerous things while driving, such as texting. ■

What's an Applet?

An applet is typically a small, limited program designed to be executed within another application. Applets are often embedded inside a web page and run in the context of the browser. Check out this applet tutorial:

http://java.sun.com/docs/books/tutorial/deployment/applet/

http://java.sun.com/applets/

Visual Programming: The Example of Visual BASIC

Visual programming allows programming via menus, buttons and other graphic elements that are selected from a palette.

Essentially, visual programming takes OOP to the next level. The goal of visual programming is to make programming easier for programmers and more accessible to nonprogrammers by borrowing the object orientation of OOP languages but exercising it in a graphical or visual way. Visual programming enables users to think more about the problem solving than about handling the programming language.

Visual programming is a method of creating programs in which the programmer makes connections between objects by drawing, pointing, and clicking on diagrams and icons and by interacting with flowcharts. Thus, the programmer can create programs by clicking on icons that represent common programming routines.

An example of visual programming is *Visual BASIC,* now available through Microsoft's .NET framework (VB.net), a Windows-based, object-oriented programming language from Microsoft that lets users develop Windows and Office applications by (1) creating command buttons, textboxes, windows, and toolbars, which (2) then may be linked to small BASIC programs that perform certain actions. Visual BASIC is *event-driven,* which means that the program waits for the user to do something (an "event"), such as click on an icon, and then the program responds. At the beginning, for example, the user can use drag-and-drop tools to develop a graphical user interface, which is created automatically by the program. Because of its ease of use, Visual BASIC allows even novice programmers to create impressive Windows-based applications.

What is .NET?

Microsoft's .NET software framework runs primarily on Windows and allows developers to use code from several programming languages:

www.microsoft.com/net/overview.aspx

http://msdn.microsoft.com/library/zw4w595w.aspx

Since its launch in 1990, the Visual BASIC approach has become the norm for programming languages. Now there are visual environments for many programming languages, including C, C++, Pascal, and Java. Visual BASIC is sometimes called a *rapid application development (RAD)* system because it enables programmers to quickly build prototype applications.

10.6 MARKUP & SCRIPTING LANGUAGES

A markup language is a set of tags that are used to "mark up" text documents so that sections of text can be logically identified and arranged. Scripting languages are simple programming languages commonly used to add functionality to web pages.

A markup language is a kind of coding, or "tags," inserted into text that embeds details about the structure and appearance of the text. Markup languages have codes for indicating layout and styling (such as boldface, italics, paragraphs, insertion of graphics, and so on) within a text file—for example, HTML. The name "markup" is derived from the traditional publishing practice of "marking up" a manuscript, that is, adding printer's instructions in the margins of a paper manuscript.

Some early examples of markup languages available outside the publishing industry could be found in typesetting tools on Unix systems. In these systems, formatting commands were inserted into the document text so that typesetting software could format the text according to the editor's specifications. After a time it was seen that most markup

Visual programming, using Blockly, compared to some other program languages *(continues next page)*

Google Blockly – A Visual Programming Language

June 12, 2012

By admin

In a week when Apple continued to go thermonuclear against anything Google and Microsoft continued to steer Windows 8 astray, Google announces Blockly a visual programming language and computer programming learning tool. Here is a screenshot of Blockly in action:

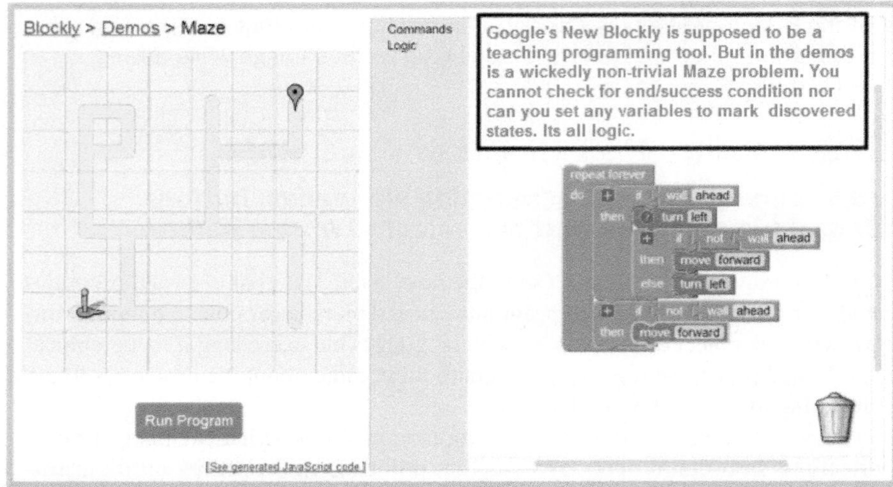

The Blockly demo of a Maze solver is a wickedly tough programming task because users have available neither a test for success/end condition nor do they have any variables to use to mark the state of the Maze traversal. Have a go at this problem – the solution appears to use levels of logic to encapsulate the four states of each block.$100 to the first user who delivers in the comments a solution to the maze problem.

Equally interesting is the Code example where a more complete set of Blockly commands and syntax is available. What is interesting is the Blockly code can be instantly turned into JavaScript, Dart [Google's new programming language], Python, or XML [but see the garrulous XML code - at least triple the size of any of the other 3 languages].

Here is a sample[Yes, Blockly has the look of Lego blocks snapped together, kids should love it]:

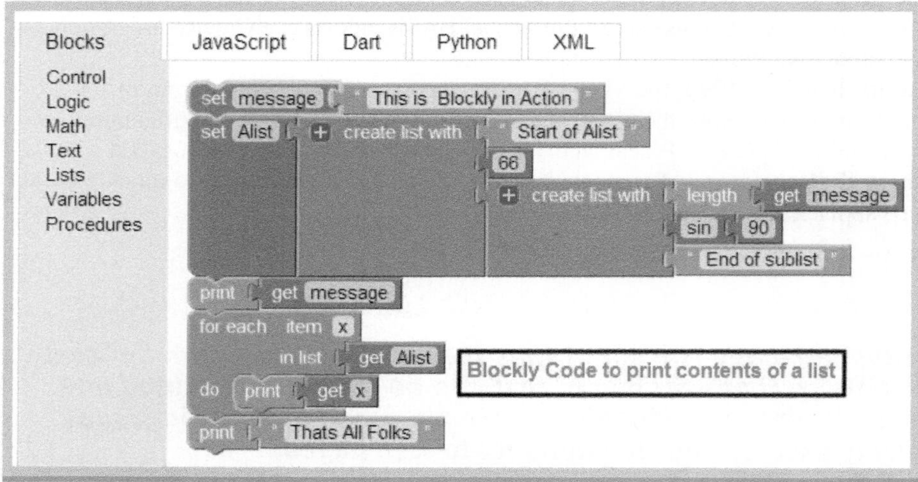

Above is the Blockly code

```
var message;
var Alist;
var x;

message = 'This is  Blockly in Action';
Alist = ['Start of Alist', 66, [message.length, Math.sin(90 / 180 * Math.PI), ':
window.alert(message);
for (var x_index in  Alist) {
  x = Alist[x_index];
  window.alert(x);
}
window.alert('Thats All Folks');
```

And if you click on the JavaScript tab here is the corresponding JavaScript code.

(continued)

```
var message;
var Alist;
var x;

main() {
  message = 'This is  Blockly in Action';
  Alist = ['Start of Alist', 66, [message.length, Math.sin(90 / 180 * Math.PI),
  print(message);
  for (var x_index in  Alist) {
    x = Alist[x_index];
    print(x);
  }
  print('Thats All Folks');
}
```

And if you click on the Dart tab above is the corresponding Dart code.

```
message = None
Alist = None
x = None
import math

message = 'This is  Blockly in Action'
Alist = ['Start of Alist', 66, [len(message), math.sin(90 / 180 * Math.PI), 'En
print message
for x in Alist:
  print x

print 'Thats All Folks'
```

And if you click on the Python tab above is the corresponding Python code.

languages had many features in common. This led to the creation of *SGML (Standard Generalized Markup Language),* which specified a syntax for including the markup in documents, as well as another system (a so-called *metalanguage*) for separately describing what the markup meant. This allowed authors to create and use any markup they wished, selecting tags that made the most sense to them. SGML was developed and standardized by the International Organization for Standards (ISO) in 1986.

SGML is used widely to manage large documents that are subject to frequent revisions and need to be printed in different formats. Because it is a large and complex system, it was not yet widely used on personal computers. This changed dramatically when Tim Berners-Lee used some of the SGML syntax, without the metalanguage, to create HTML (Hypertext Markup Language, Chapter 2, p. 66). HTML may be the most used document format in the world today.

For some people, the term *script* may conjure up images of actors and actresses on a sound stage practicing lines from a book of text. In web terms, however, a **script is a short list of self-executing commands embedded in a web page that perform a specific function or routine.** Scripts are similar to the macros used in Microsoft Word or the batch files used in the early days of DOS (p. 133), both of which performed functions ranging from generating text to displaying the date and time. Because they are self-executing, scripts can perform their work without user involvement, although some are initiated by an action on the part of the user (such as a mouse click) and others require user input to complete a task. In general, script languages are easier and faster to code in than the more structured, compiled languages such as C and C++ and are ideal for programs of very limited capability or that can reuse and tie together existing compiled programs.[20]

On web pages, scripting languages are used to perform many duties. For example, they create traffic counters and scrolling text, set cookies so that websites can remember user preferences, and switch out graphics and text when users click buttons or pass their mouse over items. They are also used for processing forms that the user fills out on screen. Any time you see something interesting occurring on a website, there is a good chance that a script is involved. Scripting languages are often designed for interactive use.

Following are some popular markup and scripting languages.

HTML Tutorial

For easy-to-follow tutorials on using HTML, go to:

http://computer.howstuffworks.com/web-page2.htm

www.tizag.com/htmlT/

www.w3schools.com/html/

After you work through a tutorial, create a sample HTML-tagged document for what could become your personal website.

HTML5

To see what HTML5 looks like go to:

www.w3schools.com/html/html5_intro.asp

What's a Widget?

Widgets are compact, single-purpose programs. Typical widgets include GUI buttons, dialog boxes, pull-down menus, etc. Among other things, widgets can be used to enhance blogs. For widget info, go to:

www.apple.com/downloads/dashboard/

www.techterms.com/definition/widget

www.pcmag.com/encyclopedia_term/0,2542,t=widget&i=54456,00.asp

Want to make your own widget?

www.widgetbox.com/widgets/make/

www.apple.com/ca/findouthow/mac/#createwidget

What Are Lateral Thinking Tools?

Lateral thinking tools help people think clearly, logically, and creatively. Do a keyword search and find out what they are.

For a more detailed description of XML, try:

http://searchsoa.techtarget.com/definition/XML

www.pcmag.com/encyclopedia/term/55048/xml

http://cplus.about.com/od/glossar1/g/xmldefn.htm

HTML

For creating 2-D web documents and links.

As we discussed in Chapter 2 (p. 66), **HTML (Hypertext Markup Language) is a markup language that lets people create on-screen documents for the Internet that can easily be linked by words and pictures to other documents.** HTML is a type of code that embeds simple commands within standard ASCII (p. 200) text documents to provide an integrated, two-dimensional display of text and graphics. In other words, a document created in any word processor and stored in ASCII format can become a web page with the addition of a few HTML commands.

One of the main features of HTML is the ability to insert hypertext links into a document. *Hypertext links* enable you to display another web document simply by clicking on a link area—usually underlined or highlighted—on your current screen (Chapter 2, p. 66). One document may contain links to many other related documents. The related documents may be on the same server as the first document, or they may be on a computer halfway around the world. A link may be a word, a group of words, or a picture.

HTML is often used with *CSS* (*Cascading Style Sheet*), which is used to describe the look of a document written in a markup language. (A style sheet is a set of instructions that tell a browser how to draw a particular element on a page.) CSS is designed primarily to enable the separation of document content (written in HTML or a similar markup language) from document presentation, including elements such as the layout, colors, and typeface sizes and styles.

The fifth revision of HTML is HTML5, which is becoming a core web technology for developing and using online applications ("web apps"). HTML is cross-platform, meaning that it can be used for mobile devices and computers, and with any operating system.

VRML

For creating 3-D web pages.

Mark Pesce and Tony Parisi created VRML at Silicon Graphics in 1994. *VRML* rhymes with "thermal." **VRML (Virtual Reality Modeling [or Markup] Language) is a type of programming language used to create three-dimensional web pages including interactive animation.** Even though VRML's designers wanted to let nonprogrammers create their own virtual spaces quickly and painlessly, it's not as simple to describe a three-dimensional scene as it is to describe a page in HTML. However, many existing modeling and CAD tools now offer VRML support, and new VRML-centered software tools are arriving. An example of a VRML scene might be a virtual room where the viewer can use controls to move around inside the room (or move the room itself) as though she or he were walking through it in real space.

To view VRML files, users need a special VRML browser (in addition to an Internet connection and a web browser). The VRML browser is what interprets VRML commands and lets the user interact with the virtual world. VRML browsers typically work as plug-ins for traditional web browsers, but newer browsers may already have the appropriate VRML browser plug-in installed. There are several VRML browsers available for Windows users, such as Cosmo and Cortona.

Web designers use software such as WireFusion to create 3-D web page components that no longer require a plug-in for users to view them with their browser. (The successor to VRML is called *X3D*.)

XML

For making the web work better.

Another newer and widely used markup language is XML, a standard maintained by the World Wide Web Consortium for creating special-purpose markup languages. **XML (eXtensible Markup Language) is a metalanguage (a language used to manipulate or define another language) written in SGML that allows one to facilitate the easy interchange of documents on the Internet.**

Unlike HTML, which uses a set of "known" tags, XML allows you to create any tags you wish (thus it's extensible) and then describe those tags in a metalanguage known as the *DTD (Document Type Definition)*. XML is similar to the concept of SGML, and in fact XML is a subset of SGML in general terms. The main purpose of XML (as opposed to

SGML) is to keep the system simpler by focusing on a particular problem—documents on the Internet and the exchange of information among websites.

Whereas HTML makes it easy for humans to read websites, XML makes it easy for machines to read websites by enabling web developers to add more "tags" to a web page. At present, when you use your browser to locate a website, search engines can turn up too much, so it's difficult to find the specific site you want—say, one with a recipe for a low-calorie chicken dish for 12. XML makes websites smart enough to tell other machines whether they're "looking at." XML lets website developers put "tags" on their web pages that describe information in, for example, a food recipe as "ingredients," "calories," "cooking time," and "number of portions." Thus, your browser no longer has to search the entire web for a low-calorie poultry recipe for 12.

Following are examples of XML and HTML tags. Note that the XML statements define data content, whereas the HTML lines deal with fonts and display (boldface). XML defines "what it is," and HTML defines "how it looks."

```
XML
<firstName>Maria</firstName>
<lastName>Roberts</lastName>
<dateBirth>10-29-52</dateBirth>
```

```
HTML
<font size="3">Maria Roberts</font>
<b>October 29, 1952</b>
```

JavaScript

For dynamic web pages.

JavaScript uses some of the same ideas found in Java, the compiled object-oriented programming language derived from C++. **JavaScript is a popular object-oriented scripting language that is widely supported in web browsers. It adds interactive functions to HTML pages,** which are otherwise static, since HTML is a display language, not a programming language. JavaScript is embedded in HTML pages and interpreted by the web browser. Like other scripting languages, JavaScript cannot be used to create stand-alone programs.

JavaScript was originally developed by Netscape Communications under the name "LiveScript" but was then renamed to "JavaScript" and given a syntax closer to that of Sun Microsystems' Java language. The change of name happened at about the same time Netscape was including support for Java technology in its Netscape Navigator browser. Consequently, the change proved a source of much confusion. There is no real relation between Java and JavaScript; their only similarities are some syntax and the fact that both languages are used extensively on the World Wide Web.

Many companies' computers and mobile devices support JavaScript for interactive multimedia use in web applications. Apple also uses HTML5 and CSS3, but so far it has refused to use Flash, which we cover next.

JavaScript Tutorial

For tutorials and information about using JavaScript, go to:

www.w3schools.com/js/js_intro.asp

www.javabeginner.com/

www.java2s.com/Tutorial/Java/CatalogJava.htm

Flash

Also for creating dynamic web pages.

Adobe Flash Player, like JavaScript also a browser "add-on," uses Adobe Flash, a scripting language based on ActionScript, to support web animation, streaming audio and video, and games. Flash is used on most computers and mobile devices—but not Apple iPads, iPhones, and iTouch devices. Apple maintains that Flash is less secure than JavaScript—that is, it's easier to introduce malware via Flash than with JavaScript; other companies disagree. Flash is designed for desktop and laptop PCs, which means it is designed for keyboards and mice; it does not work as well on touch-based devices; for this reason Adobe is now supporting HTML5 over Flash.

ActiveX

For creating interactive web pages.

ActiveX was developed by Microsoft mainly as an alternative to Java for creating interactivity on web pages. Indeed, Java and ActiveX are the two major contenders in the web war for transforming the World Wide Web into a complete interactive environment. (One big difference between Java applets and ActiveX controls is that Java applets are used on all platforms, whereas ActiveX controls are generally limited to Windows environments.)

ActiveX is a set of prewritten, reusable object-oriented components that enable programs or content of almost any type to be embedded within a web page. This provides a simple way for programmers to add extra functionality to their software or website without needing to write code from scratch. (ActiveX is not a programming language but rather a set of rules for how applications should share information.) Software add-ons created with ActiveX are called ActiveX controls. These controls can be implemented in all types of programs, but they are most commonly distributed as small web applications, such as sound and animation.

Whereas Java requires that you download an applet each time you visit a website, with ActiveX the component is downloaded only once (to a Windows-based computer) and then stored on your hard drive for later and repeated use. ActiveX is built into Microsoft's Internet Explorer and is available as a plug-in for Mozilla Firefox.

ActiveX controls have full access to the Windows operating system, and the component can be reused by an attacker to run malicious code and gain access to critical files. Thus, although they are more powerful than Java applets, ActiveX controls can be risky in that they may damage software or data on your machine. To control this risk, Microsoft developed a registration system so that browsers can identify and authenticate an ActiveX control before downloading it.

Programmers can create ActiveX controls or components in a variety of programming languages, including C, C++, Visual BASIC, and Java. Thousands of ready-made ActiveX components are now commercially available from numerous software development companies.

Survival Tip

How to Disable Add-Ons (Plug-Ins or Extensions)

Computer and device users may not want to use certain add-ons with their browsers. To disable add-ons in Internet Explorer, tap or click the Tools button, and then tap or click Manage add-ons. Under Show, click All add-ons, and then to disable an add-on, click it and then click Disable; to enable an add-on, click it and then click Enable. Tap or click Close.

In Chrome, click the Chrome menu on the browser toolbar. Click Tools, select Extensions, and click the trash can icon by the extension you'd like to completely remove. A confirmation dialog appears; click Remove. (You can also temporarily turn off an extension by disabling it on the Extensions page.)

In Firefox, click on the Add-ons icon at the bottom of the Home page; then click on Disable next to the Add-ons that you don't want.

CGI (Common Gateway Interface)

For web servers.

CGI is a standard protocol for interfacing external application software with a web server; it manages the exchange of information between a web server and computer programs that are external to it. The external programs can be written in any programming language that is supported by the operating system on which the web server is running. Forms, counters, and guestbooks are common examples of CGI scripts that process data taken from the user. CGI programs can help make web pages more interactive. They can be written in any programming language, although scripting languages are often used.

Perl

For CGI scripts.

Perl (*Practical Extraction and Report Language*) is a general-purpose programming language developed for text manipulation and now used for web development, network programming, system administration, GUI development, and other tasks. Perl is widely used to write web server programs for such tasks as automatically updating user accounts and newsgroup postings, processing removal requests, synchronizing databases, and generating reports. The major features of Perl are that it is easy to use and it supports both procedural and object-oriented programming.

Perl was developed in 1987 by Larry Wall, and it combines syntax from several Unix utilities and languages. Perl has also been adapted to non-Unix platforms.

Perl

Visit the Perl language page at:

www.perl.org/

PHP (Personal Home Page, or PHP Hypertext Preprocessor)

For interacting with databases

PHP allows web developers to create dynamic content that interacts with databases. PHP applications are normally found on Linux servers and in conjunction with MySQL databases. Originally designed for producing dynamic web pages, PHP is a widely used free, general-purpose scripting language that is especially suited for web development and can be embedded into HTML and also enable the automated writing of HTML pages. It generally runs on a web server, taking PHP code as its input and creating web pages as output.

EXPERIENCE BOX

Critical Thinking Tools

Clear thinkers aren't born that way. They work at it.

The systems development life cycle is basically an exercise in clear thinking—critical thinking. Critical thinking is fundamental to systems analysis and design—particularly in the first phase, preliminary analysis. Reaching for the truth may not come easily; it is a stance toward the world, developed with practice. To achieve this, we have to wrestle with obstacles that are mostly of our own making: *mindsets*. By the time we are grown, our minds have become "set" in various patterns of thinking that affect the way we respond to new situations and new ideas. Such mindsets determine what ideas we think are important and, conversely, what ideas we ignore.

To break past mindsets, we need to learn to think critically. *Critical thinking* means sorting out conflicting claims, weighing the evidence for them, letting go of personal biases, and arriving at reasoned conclusions. Critical thinking means actively seeking to understand, analyze, and evaluate information in order to solve specific problems.

Learning to identify fallacious (incorrect) arguments will help you avoid patterns of faulty thinking in your own writing and thinking and identify these in others'.

Jumping to Conclusions

In the fallacy called *jumping to conclusions,* also known as *hasty generalization,* a decision maker reaches a conclusion before all the facts are available. *Example:* A company instituted the strategy of total quality management (TQM) 12 months ago. As a new manager of the company, you see that TQM has not improved profitability over the past year, and you order TQM junked, in favor of more traditional business strategies. However, what you don't know is that the traditional business strategies employed prior to TQM had an even worse effect on profitability.

Irrelevant Reason or False Cause

In the faulty reasoning known as *non sequitur* (Latin for "it does not follow"), which might better be called *false cause* or *irrelevant reason,* the conclusion does not follow logically from the supposed reason or reasons stated earlier. There is no causal relationship. *Example:* You receive an A on a test. However, because you felt you hadn't been well prepared, you attribute your success to your friendliness with the professor. Or to your horoscope. Or to wearing your "lucky shirt." None of these supposed reasons had anything to do with the result.

Irrelevant Attack on a Person or Opponent

Known as an *ad hominem* argument (Latin for "to the person"), the irrelevant attack on an opponent attacks a person's reputation or beliefs rather than his or her argument. *Example:* Your boss insists you may not hire a certain person as a programmer because he or she has been married and divorced nine times, although the person's marital history plainly has no bearing on his or her skills as a programmer.

Slippery Slope

Slippery slope is a failure to see that the first step in a possible series of steps does not lead inevitably to the rest. *Example:* The "domino theory," under which the United States waged wars against communism for half a century, was a slippery-slope argument. It assumed that if communism triumphed in one country (for example, Nicaragua), then it would inevitably triumph in other regions (the rest of Central America), finally threatening the borders of the United States itself.

Appeal to Authority

The *appeal-to-authority* argument (known in Latin as *argumentum ad verecundiam*) uses authority in one area in an effort to validate claims in another area where the person is not an expert. *Example:* You see the appeal-to-authority argument used all the time in advertising. But how qualified is a professional golfer to speak about headache remedies?

Circular Reasoning

In *circular reasoning,* a statement to be proved true is rephrased, and then the new formulation is offered as supposed proof that the original statement is in fact true. *Example:* You declare that you can drive safely at high speeds with only inches separating you from the car ahead because you have driven this way for years without an accident.

Straw Man Argument

In the *straw man* argument, you misrepresent your opponent's position to make it easier to attack, or you attack a weaker position while ignoring a stronger one. In other words, you sidetrack the argument from the main discussion. *Example:* Politicians use straw man arguments all the time. If you attack a legislator for being "fiscally irresponsible" in supporting funds for a gun control bill, when what you really object to is the fact of gun control, you're using a straw man argument.

Appeal to Pity

In the *appeal-to-pity* argument, the advocate appeals to mercy rather than making an argument on the merits of the case itself. *Example:* Begging the dean not to expel you for cheating because your parents are poor and made sacrifices to put you through college would be a blatant appeal to pity.

Questionable Statistics

Statistics can be misused in many ways as supporting evidence. The statistics may be unknowable, drawn from an unrepresentative sample, or otherwise suspect. *Example:* Stating how much money is lost to taxes because of illegal drug transactions is speculation because such transactions are hidden or unrecorded.

TERMS & EXPLANATIONS

ActiveX (p. 542) A set of prewritten, reusable object-oriented controls, or components, that enable programs or content of almost any type to be embedded within a web page. Why it's important: *ActiveX features reusable components—small modules of software code that perform specific tasks, such as a spelling checker, which may be plugged seamlessly into other applications.*

algorithm (p. 517) Formula or set of steps for solving a particular problem. Why it's important: *All programs consist of algorithms.*

assembler (p. 529) Also called *assembler program;* language-translator program that translates assembly-language programs into machine language. Why it's important: *Language translators are needed to translate all upper-level languages into machine language, the language that actually runs the computer.*

assembly language (p. 528) Second-generation programming language; it allows a programmer to write a program using abbreviations instead of the 0s and 1s of machine language. Why it's important: *A programmer can write instructions in assembly language faster than in machine language.*

CASE (computer-aided software engineering) tools (p. 510) Software that provides computer-automated means of designing and changing systems. Why it's important: *CASE tools make systems design easier and can be used in almost any phase of the SDLC.*

coding (p. 523) In the programming process, the third step, consisting of translating logic requirements from pseudocode or flowcharts into a programming language. Why it's important: *Coding is the actual writing of a computer program, although it is only the third of five steps in programming.*

compiler (p. 529) Language translator that converts the entire program of a high-level language (called the *source code*) into machine language (called the *object code*) for execution later. Examples of compiler languages: COBOL, FORTRAN, Pascal, and C. Why it's important: *Unlike other language translators (assemblers and interpreters), a compiler program enables the object code to be saved and executed later rather than run right away. The advantage of a compiler is that, once the object code has been obtained, the program executes faster.*

control structure (p. 520) Also called *logic structure;* in structured program design, the programming structure that controls the logical sequence in which computer program instructions are executed. Three control structures are used to form the logic of a program: sequence, selection, and iteration (or loop). Why it's important: *One thing that all three control structures have in common is one entry and one exit. The control structure is entered at a single point and exited at another single point. This helps simplify the logic so that it is easier for others following in a programmer's footsteps to make sense of the program.*

data flow diagram (DFD) (p. 509) Modeling tool that graphically shows the flow of data through a system—essential processes, including inputs, outputs, and files. Why it's important: *A DFD diagrams the processes that change data into information.*

debug (p. 524) Part of program testing; the detection, location, and removal of syntax and logic errors in a program. Why it's important: *Debugging may take several trials using different data before the programming team is satisfied the program can be released. Even then, some errors may remain, because trying to remove them all may be uneconomical.*

desk-checking (p. 523) Form of program testing; programmers read through a program to ensure it's error-free and logical. Why it's important: *Desk-checking should be done before the program is actually run on a computer.*

documentation (p. 525) Written descriptions of what a program is and how to use it; supposed to be done during all programming steps. Why it's important: *Documentation is needed for all the people who will be using or be involved with the program—users, operators, programmers, and future systems analysts.*

Flash Player (Adobe) (p. 541) Like JavaScript, Flash is also a browser "add-on"; it uses Adobe Flash, a scripting language based on ActionScript, to support web animation, streaming audio and video, and games. Why it's important: *Flash is used on most computers and mobile devices—but not Apple iPads, iPhones, and iTouch devices.*

generations of programming languages (p. 527) Five increasingly sophisticated levels (generations) of programming languages: (1) machine language, (2) assembly language, (3) high-level languages, (4) very-high-level languages, (5) natural languages. Why it's important: *Programming languages are said to be lower level when they are closer to the language used by the computer (0s and ls) and higher level when closer to the language used by people. High-level languages are easier for most people to use than are lower-level languages.*

hierarchy chart (p. 518) Also called *structure chart;* a diagram used in programming to illustrate the overall purpose of a program, identifying all the modules needed to achieve that purpose and the relationships among them. Why it's important: *In a hierarchy chart, the program must move in sequence from one module to the next until all have been processed. There must be three principal modules corresponding to the three principal computing operations—input, processing, and output.*

high-level languages (p. 529) Also known as *procedural or object-oriented languages;* third-generation programming languages (3GLs). They somewhat resemble human languages. Examples: FORTRAN, COBOL, BASIC, Pascal, and C. Why it's important: *High-level languages allow programmers to write in a familiar notation rather than numbers or abbreviations. Most can also be used on more than one kind of computer.*

HTML (Hypertext Markup Language) (p. 540) Markup language that lets people create on-screen documents for the Internet that can easily be linked by words and pictures to other documents. Why it's important: *HTML is used to create web pages.*

interpreter (p. 529) Language translator that converts each high-level language statement into machine language and executes it immediately, statement by statement. An example of a high-level language using an interpreter is BASIC. Why it's important: *Unlike a compiler translator, an interpreter does not save object code. The advantage of an interpreter is that programs are easier to develop.*

JavaScript (p. 541) Object-oriented scripting language used, for example, to write small interactive functions that are embedded in HTML pages and interact with the browser to perform certain tasks not possible in static HTML alone. (There is no real relationship between JavaScript and Java.) Why it's important: *JavaScript is used to create dynamic web applications.*

language translator (p. 529) Type of system software that translates a program written in a second-, third-, or higher-generation language into machine language. Language translators are of three types: (1) assemblers, (2) compilers, and (3) interpreters. Why it's important: *Because computers run only using machine language, all higher-level languages must be translated.*

logic errors (p. 524) Programming errors caused by incorrect use of control structures. Why it's important: *Logic errors prevent a program from running properly.*

machine language (p. 528) Lowest-level (first-generation) programming language; the language of the computer, representing data as 1s and 0s. Most machine-language programs vary from computer to computer—they are machine-dependent. Why it's important: *Machine language is the language that actually runs the computer.*

markup language (p. 537) A kind of coding, or "tags," inserted into text that embeds details about the structure and appearance of the text within a text file—for example, HTML. The word "markup" is derived from the traditional publishing practice of "marking up" a manuscript, that is, adding printer's instructions in the margins of a paper manuscript. An example of a markup language is SGML (Standard Generalized Markup Language). Why it's important: *Markup languages have codes for indicating layout and styling, such as boldface, italics, paragraphs, and insertion of graphics.*

modeling tools (p. 509) Analytical tools such as charts, tables, and diagrams that are used by systems analysts. Examples are data flow diagrams, decision tables, systems flowcharts, and object-oriented analysis. Why it's important: *Modeling tools enable a systems analyst to present graphic, or pictorial, representations of a system.*

module (p. 518) Sometimes called *subprogram* or *subroutine;* a processing step of a program. Each module is made up of logically related program statements. Why it's important: *Each module has only a single function, which limits the module's size and complexity.*

natural languages (p. 531) (1) Ordinary human languages (for instance, English, Spanish); (2) fifth-generation programming languages that use human language to give people a more natural connection with computers. Why it's important: *Natural languages are part of the field of artificial intelligence; these languages are approaching the level of human communication.*

object (p. 535) In object-oriented programming, block of preassembled programming code that is a self-contained module. The module contains (encapsulates) both (1) a chunk of data and (2) the processing instructions that may be called on to be performed on that data. Once the object becomes part of a program, the processing instructions may be activated only when a "message" is sent. Why it's important: *The object can be reused and interchanged among programs, thus making the programming process much easier, more flexible and efficient, and faster.*

object-oriented programming (OOP) (p. 535) Programming method in which data and the instructions for processing that data are combined into a self-sufficient *object*—a piece of software that can be used in other programs. Why it's important: *Objects can be reused and interchanged among programs, producing greater flexibility and efficiency than is possible with traditional programming methods.*

preliminary investigation (p. 507) Phase 1 of the SDLC; the purpose is to conduct a preliminary analysis (determine the organization's objectives and determine the nature and scope of the problem), propose alternative solutions (leave the system as is, improve the efficiency of the system, or develop a new system), describe costs and benefits, and submit a preliminary plan with recommendations. Why it's important: *The preliminary investigation lays the groundwork for the other phases of the SDLC.*

problem clarification (definition) (p. 516) Step 1 in the programming process. The problem-definition step requires performing six mini-steps: specifying objectives and users, outputs, inputs, and processing tasks and then studying the feasibility of the program and documenting the analysis. Why it's important: *Problem definition is the forerunner to step 2, program design, in the programming process.*

program (p. 515) List of instructions the computer follows to process data into information. The instructions consist of statements written in a programming language (for example, BASIC). Why it's important: *Without programs, computers could not process data into information.*

program design (p. 517) Step 2 in the programming process; programs are designed in two mini-steps: (1) the program logic is determined through a top-down approach and modularization, using a hierarchy chart; (2) the program is designed in detail, using pseudocode or flowcharts with logical tools called *control structures.* Why it's important: *Program design is the forerunner to step 3, writing (coding), in the programming process.*

program flowchart (p. 520) Chart that graphically presents the detailed series of steps needed to solve a programming problem; it uses standard symbols called *ANSI symbols.* Why it's important: *The program flowchart is an important program design tool.*

program testing (p. 523) Step 4 in the programming process; running various tests and then running real-world data to make sure the program works. Why it's important: *The program must be tested before it is released to be sure that it works properly.*

programming (p. 515) Five-step process for creating software instructions: (1) Clarify/define the problem; (2) design a solution; (3) write (code) the program; (4) test the program; (5) document and maintain the program. Why it's important: *Programming is one step in the systems development life cycle.*

programming language (p. 523) Set of rules (words and symbols) that allow programmers to tell the computer what operations to follow. The five levels (generations) of programming languages are (1) machine language, (2) assembly language, (3) high-level (procedural) languages, (4) very-high-level (nonprocedural) languages, and (5) natural languages. Why it's important: *Not all programming languages are appropriate for all uses. Thus, languages must be chosen to suit the purpose of the program and to be compatible with other languages being used.*

prototype (p. 511) A limited working system, or part of one, developed to test design concepts. Why it's important: *A prototype, which may be constructed in just a few days, allows users to find out immediately how a change in the system might benefit them.*

prototyping (p. 511) Using workstations, CASE tools, and other software applications to build working models of system components so that they can be quickly tested and evaluated. Why it's important: *Prototyping is part of the preliminary design stage of Phase 3 of the SDLC.*

pseudocode (p. 518) Tool for designing a program in narrative form using normal human-language statements to describe the logic and processing flow. Using pseudocode is like doing an outline or summary form of the program to be written. Why it's important: *Pseudocode provides a type of outline or summary of the program.*

script (p. 539) A short list of self-executing commands embedded in a web page that perform a specific function or routine, often without user involvement. Why it's important: *Because they are self-executing, scripts can perform their work without user involvement.*

structured programming (p. 518) Method of programming that takes a top-down approach, breaking programs into modular forms and using standard logic tools called *control structures* (sequence, selection, case, iteration). Why it's important: *Structured programming techniques help programmers write better-organized programs, using standard notations with clear, correct descriptions.*

syntax (p. 523) "Grammar" rules of a programming language. Why it's important: *Each programming language has its own syntax, just as human languages do.*

syntax errors (p. 524) Programming errors caused by typographical errors and incorrect use of the programming language. Why it's important: *If a program has syntax errors, it will not run correctly or perhaps not run at all.*

system (p. 505) Collection of related components that interact to perform a task in order to accomplish a goal. Why it's important: *Understanding a set of activities as a system allows one to look for better ways to reach the goal.*

systems analysis (p. 509) Phase 2 of the SDLC; the purpose is to gather data (using written documents, interviews, questionnaires, and observation), analyze the data, and write a report. Why it's important: *The results of systems analysis determine whether the system should be redesigned.*

systems analysis and design (p. 507) Problem-solving procedure for examining an information system and improving it; consists of the six-phase systems development life cycle. Why it's important: *The point of systems analysis and design is to ascertain how a system works and then take steps to make it better.*

systems analyst (p. 506) Information specialist who performs systems analysis, design, and implementation. Why it's important: *The systems analyst studies the information and communications needs of an organization to determine how to deliver information that is complete, accurate, timely, and useful. The systems analyst achieves this goal through the problem-solving method of systems analysis and design.*

systems design (p. 511) Phase 3 of the SDLC; the purpose is to do a preliminary design and then a detail design and to write a report. Why it's important: *Systems design is one of the most crucial phases of the SDLC.*

systems development (p. 512) Phase 4 of the SDLC; consists of acquiring and testing hardware and software for the new system. This phase begins once management has accepted the report containing the design and has approved the way to development. Why it's important: *This phase may involve the organization investing substantial time and money.*

systems development life cycle (SDLC) (p. 507) Six-phase process that many organizations follow during systems analysis and design: (1) preliminary investigation; (2) systems analysis; (3) systems design; (4) systems development; (5) systems implementation; (6) systems maintenance. Phases often overlap, and a new one may start before the old one is finished. After the first four phases, management must decide whether to proceed to the next phase. User input and review are a critical part of each phase. Why it's important: *The SDLC is a comprehensive tool for solving organizational problems, particularly those relating to the flow of computer-based information.*

systems implementation (p. 513) Phase 5 of the SDLC; consists of converting the hardware, software, and files to the new system and training the users. Why it's important: *This phase involves putting design ideas into operation.*

systems maintenance (p. 514) Phase 6 of the SDLC; consists of keeping the system working by having system audits and periodic evaluations and by making changes based on new conditions. Why it's important: *This phase is important for keeping a new system operational and useful.*

top-down program design (p. 518) Method of program design; a programmer identifies the top or principal processing step, or module, of a program and then breaks it down in hierarchical fashion to the lowest level of detail. Why it's important: *This design enables an entire program to be more easily developed, because the parts can be developed and tested separately.*

very-high-level languages (p. 531) Also known as *problem-oriented* and *nonprocedural languages* and *fourth-generation languages (4GLs);* more user-oriented than third-generation languages, 4GLs require fewer commands. 4GLs consist of report generators, query languages, and application generators. Why it's important: *Programmers can write programs that need to tell the computer only what they want done, not all the procedures for doing it, which saves them the time and the labor of having to write many lines of code.*

visual programming (p. 537) Method of creating programs in which the programmer makes connections between objects by drawing, pointing, and clicking on diagrams and icons and by interacting with flowcharts. Programming is made easier because the orientation of object-oriented programming is used in a graphical or visual way. Why it's important: *Visual programming enables users to think more about the problem solving than about handling the programming language.*

VRML (Virtual Reality Modeling [Markup] Language) (p. 540) Type of programming language used to create three-dimensional web pages. Why it's important: *VRML expands the information-delivering capabilities of the web.*

writing the program documentation (p. 525) Step 5 in the programming process; programmers write procedures explaining how the program was constructed and how it is to be used. Why it's important: *Program documentation is the final stage in the five-step programming process, although documentation should also be an ongoing task accompanying all steps.*

XML (eXtensible Markup Language) (p. 540) Metalanguage used to make it easy for machines to read websites by allowing web developers to add more "tags" to a web page. Why it's important: *XML is more powerful than HTML, allowing information on a website to be described by general tags—for example, identifying one piece of information in a recipe as "cooking time" and another as "ingredients."*

CHAPTER REVIEW

stage 1 LEARNING MEMORIZATION

"I can recognize and recall information."

Self-Test Questions

1. The __________ comprises six phases of examining an information system and improving it.
2. The first major program written in C was the __________ operating system.
3. The basic language of the computer, 0s and 1s is called __________.
4. __________ is a method of creating programs in which the programmer makes connections between objects by drawing, pointing, and clicking on diagrams and icons and by interacting with flowcharts.
5. __________ is the problem-solving procedure for examining an information system and improving it.
6. Software engineering, or __________, refers to creating instructions for computers.
7. A(n) __________ is a formula or a set of steps for solving a particular problem.
8. A(n) __________ is a collection of related components that interact to perform a task in order to accomplish a goal.
9. A(n) __________ is a short list of self-executing commands embedded in a web page that perform a specific function or routine, often without user involvement.

Multiple-Choice Questions

1. One of the following activities is *not* an objective of Phase 1 of the SDLC, preliminary investigation. Which one?
   a. conduct preliminary analysis
   b. describe costs and benefits
   c. acquire new software and hardware
   d. submit a preliminary plan
   e. propose alternative solutions
2. One of the following activities is *not* an objective of Phase 4 of the SDLC, systems development. Which one?
   a. convert files to the new system
   b. acquire software
   c. acquire hardware
   d. test the system
   e. address the make-or-buy decision
3. Third-generation programming languages include all the following languages *except* which one?
   a. FORTRAN
   b. BASIC
   c. COBOL
   d. XML
   e. C
4. All these are website markup or scripting languages *except* which one?
   a. Flash
   b. JavaScript
   c. HTML
   d. XML
   e. Visual BASIC
5. There are four basic ways of converting from an old system to a new system; which of these is *not* one of them?
   a. parallel
   b. direct
   c. preliminary
   d. pilot
   e. phased

True-False Questions

T F 1. Programming errors caused by incorrect use of control structures are called *logic errors.*

T F 2. CASE tools—programs that automate various activities of the SDLC—are used only in Phase 3.

T F 3. Four methods of systems implementation are direct, parallel, phased, and pilot.

T F 4. User training takes place during Phase 1 of the SDLC.

T F 5. JavaScript is an object-oriented scripting language used in web browsers to add interactive functions to HTML pages.

T F 6. There are four generations of programming languages.

T F 7. BYOD means "bring your own data."

LEARNING **COMPREHENSION**

"I can recall information in my own terms and explain it to a friend."

Short-Answer Questions

1. What is the straw man argument? Appeal to pity? What are some of the other elements of critical thinking?
2. What does a systems analyst do?
3. What are the five steps in the programming process?
4. What are the six phases of the SDLC?
5. What is a software bug?
6. What is a prototype, and what does it do?

LEARNING **APPLYING, ANALYZING, SYNTHESIZING, EVALUATING**

"I can apply what I've learned, relate these ideas to other concepts, build on other knowledge, and use all these thinking skills to form a judgment."

Knowledge in Action

1. Alice is a 3-D programming environment that makes it easy to create animation for telling a story, playing an interactive game, or making a video to share on the web. Alice is also a teaching tool for learning object-oriented programming. It allows you to learn fundamental programming concepts in the context of creating animated movies and simple videogames.

   In Alice, you drag and drop graphic tiles to create a program, where the instructions correspond to standard statements in a programming language such as Java or C++. Alice allows you to immediately see how your animation programs run, enabling you to easily understand the relationship between the programming statements and the behavior of objects in their animation. By manipulating the objects in their virtual world, you gain experience with all the programming constructs typically taught in an introductory programming course.

   Download Alice 2.2 from:

   www.alice.org/index.php?page=downloads/download_alice3.1

   Then watch the demonstration videos at:

   www.alice.org/index.php?page=what_is_alice/what_is_alice

   Next, give Alice a try! (Following are Alice tutorials.)

   www.youtube.com/watch?v=iMyLrKuvjZc

   www.youtube.com/watch?v=DPQe4sYS7Xs

   http://alicetutorials.blogspot.com/2013/02/getting-started-with-alice.html

2. Design a system that would handle the input, processing, and output of a simple form of your choice. Use a data flow diagram to illustrate the system.
3. Have you participated in a project that failed? Why did it fail? Based on what you know now, what might you have done to help the project succeed?
4. Which step of the SDLC do you find most interesting? Why?
5. Are you interested in learning how to program? Which languages would you choose to learn? Why?
6. Create a prototype invention (of anything) and have classmates test and evaluate it. Once the evaluations are received, write a detailed report, as you would at the end of Phase 3 in the SDLC process.

Web Exercises

1. The waterfall model and the spiral model are variations of the SDLC. Do keyword searches to find out how these models differ from the basic approach.
2. Compare the SDLC process to the scientific method. How are they alike? How do they differ? If you need to be refreshed on the scientific method, you can visit

   http://scijinks.nasa.gov/scientific-method,

   http://teacher.pas.rochester.edu/phy_labs/appendixe/appendixe.html

   http://physics.ucr.edu/~wudka/Physics7/Notes_www/node6.html

   Or run a search on "scientific method."
3. Using an Internet search tool, identify a company that develops CASE tools. In a few paragraphs, describe what this company's CASE tools are used for.
4. One of the most beneficial courses you can take in college is critical thinking. The Experience Box in this chapter has an introduction to fallacious arguments. A background in logic and identification of fallacies is

essential not only for making valid arguments but for life in general. After reading the Experience Box, visit the following websites:

www.unc.edu/depts/wcweb/handouts/fallacies.html

www.skepdic.com/refuge/ctlessons/lesson5.html

http://philosophy.hku.hk/think/fallacy/fallacy-list.php

After familiarizing yourself with the types of fallacies, watch TV for an hour (especially commercials) and identify 10 fallacies. Write them down, and discuss them with your class the next day. Are our collective reality assumptions valid and cohesive? Command of logic and critical thinking will help you tremendously in any line of work.

5. Curious about the educational requirements for a systems designer/analyst? Go to:

   http://educationcareerarticles.com/career-information/job-descriptions/computer-systems-analyst-education-requirements-and-job-description/

   www.bls.gov/ooh/Computer-and-Information-Technology/Computer-systems-analysts.htm

   http://careerplanning.about.com/od/occupations/p/compsysanalyst.htm

6. Do a keyword search for "programming" and "jobs." Which languages are most in demand now? Which of the jobs seems most interesting to you?

Extra exercise: Here is another simple example of an algorithm. Choose another simple statement and develop an algorithm for it.

Algorithm: Sorting by colors

This is an example of an algorithm for sorting cards with colors on them into piles of the same color:

1. Pick up all the cards.
2. Pick a card from your hand and look at the color of the card.
3. If there is already a pile of cards of that color, put this card on that pile.
4. If there is no pile of cards of that color, make a new pile of just this card.
5. If there is still a card in your hand, go back to the second step.
6. If there is not still a card in your hand, then the cards are sorted; you are done.

Source: http://simple.wikipedia.org/wiki/Algorithm.

Thinking about Majoring in Information Science, Information Technology, or Computer Engineering?

ACM (Association for Computing Machinery), the world's largest educational and scientific computing society, provides resources that advance computing as a science and a profession.

www.acm.org/

What is the difference between these three fields of computer study?

http://online.king.edu/information-technology/difference-between-a-computer-science-information-technology-degree/

http://forums.udacity.com/questions/47927/what-is-the-difference-between-computer-science-and-information-technology

Notes

Chapter 1

1. Michael Saylor, *The Mobile Wave: How Mobile Intelligence Will Change Everything* (New York: Vanguard Press, 2012), p. 211.
2. Nick Bilton, "How My Smartphone Emptied My Pockets," *The New York Times,* December 10, 2012, p. B7. Bilton is also author of *I Live in the Future & Here's How It Works* (New York: Random House/Crown, 2010).
3. James Temple, "Mobile Pushes Us to 'Post-PC' World of Future," *San Francisco Chronicle,* December 23, 2012, pp. G1, G7.
4. Study by Council for Research Excellence, reported in Brian Stelter, "8 Hours a Day Spent on Screens, Study Finds," *The New York Times,* March 27, 2009, p. B6.
5. Anthropologist Susan D. Blum, quoted in Christine Rosen, "It's Not Theft, It's Pastiche," *The Wall Street Journal,* April 16, 2009, p. A13.
6. Aaron Smith, Lee Rainie, and Kathryn Zickuhr, "College Students and Technology," July 19, 2011, Pew Internet & American Life Project, *http://pewinternet.org/Reports/2011/College-students-and-technology/Report.aspx* (accessed January 15, 2013).
7. Data from BCG/Barkley, reported in Shelly Banjo, "Shopping's Great Age Divide," *The Wall Street Journal,* November 27, 2012, pp. B1, B4.
8. Data from Christine Barton, Boston Consulting Group, reported in Banjo, 2012.
9. Tom Peters, "A Brawl with No Rules," *Forbes ASAP,* February 21, 2000, p. 155.
10. Ben Horowitz of venture capital firm Andreessen Horowitz, quoted in James Temple and Benny Evangelista, "Why 'Software Is Eating the World,' " *San Francisco Chronicle,* September 11, 2012, pp. D1, D5.
11. "A World Transformed: What Are the Top 30 Innovations of the Last 30 Years?" *Knowledge@Wharton,* February 18, 2009, *http://knowledge.wharton.upenn.edu/article.cfm?articleid=2163* (accessed January 15, 2013). See also "Life Changers," *The New York Times,* March 8, 2009, p. BU-2.5; Larry Keeley, "History's Greatest Innovations," *BusinessWeek,* February 6, 2007, *www.businessweek.com/innovate/content/feb2007/id20070216_377845.htm* (accessed January 15, 2013).
12. Randall Stross, "When the Price Is Right, the Future Can Wait," *The New York Times,* July 12, 2009, Business section, p. 3.
13. Josh Cantrell, "The Death of the Personal Computer," *Claris Networks,* December 8, 2010, *http://clarisnetworks.com/Blog/December-2010/The-Death-of-the-Personal-Computer* (accessed January 19, 2011).
14. Data from NPD Group, reported in Brett Molina, "Survey: U.S. Web-Connected Devices Outnumber People," *USA Today,* January 3, 2013, *www.usatoday.com/story/technologylive/2013/01/03/internet-connected-devices-usa/1806565* (accessed January 15, 2013).
15. U.S. Department of Labor, cited in Ben Casselman, "The Cost of Dropping Out," *The Wall Street Journal,* November 23, 2012, pp. A1, A6. See also David B. Grusky, Beth Red Bird, Natassia Rodriguez, and Christopher Wimer, *How Much Protection Does a College Degree Afford? The Impact of the Recession on Recent College Graduates,* Pew Charitable Trusts, Economic Mobility Project, January 10, 2013, *www.pewstates.org/uploadedFiles/PCS_Assets/2013/Pew_college_grads_recession_report.pdf* (accessed January 15, 2013).
16. See, for example, Sue Shellenbarger, "When Curious Parents See Math Grades in Real Time," *The Wall Street Journal,* October 3, 2012, pp. D1, D3; Brian Shane, "Smart Devices Make for Smart Kids," *USA Today,* January 1, 2013, p. 1B; and Mary Beth Marklein, "Online-Education Trend Expands," *USA Today,* November 19, 2012, p. 3A.
17. Sara Rimer, "At M.I.T., Large Lectures Are Going the Way of the Blackboard," *The New York Times,* January 13, 2009, p. A12.
18. Ron Barnett, "Rise of Internet Education Leaves Schools Behind," *Reno Gazette-Journal,* February 18, 2013, p. 2C, reprinted from *The Greenville News.*
19. Les Smith, "Technology Can Be Useful in the Classroom," *Reno Gazette-Journal,* March 10, 2009, p. 2D. For a brilliant discussion on the use of technology in the classroom in the service of teaching science, see Carl Wieman, "Why Not Try a Scientific Approach to Science Education?" *Scientific Blogging,* March 10, 2009, and his subsequent articles, *www.scientificblogging.com/carl_wieman/why_not_try_scientific_approach_science_education* (accessed January 15, 2013).
20. Steve Jones, *Pew Internet & American Life Project: The Internet Goes to College,* September 15, 2002, *www.pewInternet.org/pdfs/PIP_College_Report.pdf* (accessed January 15, 2013).
21. 2012 Survey of Online Learning conducted by the Babson Survey Research Group, reported in Barbara Spies Blair, "New Study: Over 6.7 Million Students Learning Online," *The Sloan Consortium,* January 8, 2013, *http://sloanconsortium.org/news_press/january2013_new-study-over-67-million-students-learning-online* (accessed January 15, 2013).
22. Melissa Korn and Jenifer Levitz, "Online Courses Look for a Business Model," *The Wall Street Journal,* January 2, 2013, p. B8. See also Laura Pappano, "Suddenly, Millions Have Started Taking U.S. University Classes Online," *International Herald Tribune,* November 5, 2012, p. 15; Tamar Lewin and John Markoff, "California to Give Web Courses a Big Trial," *The New York Times,* January 15, 2013, pp. B1, B3; and Betsy Corcoran, "Internet on Verge of Toppling the Academy's Ivory Towers," *San Francisco Chronicle* and SFGate.com, February 17, 2013, pp. E5–E6.
23. Dan Carnevale, "Many Online Courses Work Best at No Distance at All," *The Chronicle of Higher Education,* July 30, 2004, p. A22.
24. "The Digital Doctor," *The New York Times,* October 9, 2012, p. D1.
25. Michael Wolff, "Paging ZocDoc for the Future of Medicine," *USA Today,* December 21, 2012, pp. 1B, 2B. See also Karen Barrow, "The Doctor Can See You Now. Really, Right Now," *The New York Times,* October 16, 2012, p. D5; and Kevin Pho, "The Doctor Will See You Now—on the Internet," *USA Today,* January 14, 2013, p. 6A.
26. Jennifer Alsever, "Point, Click, Cough: The Benefits of Virtual Doctor Visits—for Employers and Employees Alike," *Inc.,* December 2012–January 2013, pp. 100, 102.
27. Stephanie Nano, "Computers Seen as Aid in X-Ray Reading," *San Francisco Chronicle,* October 2, 2008, p. A2.
28. Christopher Weaver, "Health in the Palm of Your Hand," *The Wall Street Journal,* December 29–30, 2012, p. C2.
29. Anne Eisenberg, "When Robotic Surgery Leaves Just a Scratch," *The New York Times,* November 18, 2012, p. BU-3.
30. Jesse Ellison, "A New Grip on Life," *Newsweek,* December 15, 2008, p. 64; and Pam Belluck, "In New Procedure, Artificial Arm Listens to Brain," *The New York Times,* February 11, 2001, pp. A1, A17.
31. Rebecca Boyle, "New Electric Skin Could Bring the Human Touch to Robots, Artificial Limbs," *PopSci,* September 13, 2010, *www.popsci.com/technology/*

article/2010-09/new-electric-skin-could-bring-human-touch-robots-and-artificial-limbs (accessed January 15, 2013).
32. Drew Halley, "Computer Chip Implant to Program Brian Activity, Treat Parkinson's," *Singularity Hub,* July 21, 2010, *http://singularityhub.com/2010/07/21/computer-chip-implant-to-program-brain-activity-treat-parkinsons/* (accessed January 15, 2013).
33. Susannah Fox and Maeve Duggan, "Health Online 2013," January 15, 2013, Pew Internet & American Life Project, *http://pewinternet.org/Reports/2013/Health-online.aspx* (accessed January 15, 2013).
34. Victoria Colliver, " 'Crowd Funding' Helps Woman in Her Expensive Cancer Fight," *San Francisco Chronicle,* September 21, 2012, pp. A1, A12.
35. Cynthia G. Wager, "Money's Digital Future," *The Futurist,* January–February 2003, pp. 14–15.
36. Hadley Malcolm, "Smartphones to Play Bigger Role in Shopping," *USA Today,* November 16, 2012, pp. 1B, 2B; and Stephanie Clifford and Claire Cain Miller, "A Smartphone Loaded with Tools to Find Bargains," *The New York Times,* November 21, 2012, pp. B1, B3.
37. Dana Mattioli, "Holiday Price War Rages in Real Time," *The Wall Street Journal,* November 24, 2012, pp. A1, A2; and Stephanie Clifford, "Follow the Bouncing Prices," *The New York Times,* January 28, 2013, pp. B1, B4.
38. Jennifer Valentino-DeVries, Jeremy Singer-Vine, and Ashkan Soltani, "Online Retailers Vary Prices Based on a User's Location," *The Wall Street Journal,* December 24, 2012, pp. A1, A10.
39. Accenture Interactive survey of 1,000 people ages 20 to 40, reported in "Compare Prices Using Smartphone," *USA Today,* December 17, 2012, p. 1B.
40. David Pogue, "Pay by Voice? So Long, Wallet," *The New York Times,* July 19, 2012, pp. B1, B8; Jon Swartz, "Starbucks Gets a Square Deal," *USA Today,* October 5, 2012, pp. 1B, 2B; and "Starbucks Goes Square for Mobile Payments," *San Francisco Chronicle,* October 6, 2012, pp. D1, D3.
41. Douglas MacMillan and Danielle Kucera, "PayPal Enters Mobile Market," *San Francisco Chronicle,* March 15, 2012, p. D5.
42. Peter Mateyka, quoted in Haya El Nasser, "Home Is Where the Job Is," *USA Today,* October 5, 2012, p. 1B.
43. U.S. Census Bureau, *American Community Survey,* 2010, reported in Mateyka, 2012.
44. Katherine Boehret, "Help Wanted: Moonlighters for Mobile Apps," *The Wall Street Journal,* August 8, 2012, p. D2; Kim Komando, "Turn Extra Time into Cash with Smartphone," *Reno Gazette-Journal,* November 18, 2012, p. 4F, and "Use Digital Tools to Earn Extra Dollars," *Reno Gazette-Journal,* January 13, 2013, p. 6E.
45. "App Detects Potholes, Alerts Boston City Officials," *Nevada Appeal,* July 22, 2012, pp. C1, C3; and Gavin Newsom, interviewed by Belinda Luscombe, "10 Questions," *Time,* February 25, 2013, p. 60.
46. Henry K. Lee, "Video Link a New Way to Call Cops," *San Francisco Chronicle,* July 18, 2012, pp. A1, A10.
47. Terry Collins, "Police Agencies Embrace Emerging Social Media Tool," *Reno Gazette-Journal,* August 12, 2012, p. 2B; and Kirk Johnson, "Hey, @SeattlePD: What's the Latest from the Nabe?" *The New York Times,* October 2, 2012, p. A17.
48. Douglas Belkin, "Chicago Hunts for Answers to Gang Killings," *The Wall Street Journal,* July 13, 2012, p. A3.
49. Adam Silverman, "Getting Official Word Out via Social Media," *USA Today,* August 17, 2012, p. 3A.
50. "No Long Lines to Vote in Estonia," *Reno Gazette-Journal,* November 10, 2012, p. 1B.
51. Caleb Garling, "Online Voting OK Only in Disaster," *San Francisco Chronicle,* November 6, 2012, pp. D1, D4. See also Martha T. Moore, "Internet Voting Systems at Risk," *USA Today,* July 25, 2012, p. 5A; Michael Agresta, "Will the Next Election Be Hacked?" *The Wall Street Journal,* August 18, 2012, p. C2; and Nick Bilton, "Voting Booth in the Hands of Everyone," *The New York Times,* November 12, 2012, pp. B1, B4.
52. Byron Acohido, "More Voters Register Online," *USA Today,* October 15, 2012, p. 1B.
53. David Carr, "Hashtag Activism, and Its Limits," *The New York Times,* March 26, 2012, pp. B1, B4; Julie Bykowicz, "Social Media's Big Role in Election Campaigns," *San Francisco Chronicle,* September 6, 2012, p. D2; John Markoff, "Social Networks Can Affect Voter Turnout, Study Says," *The New York Times,* September 13, 2012, p. A17; Jenna Wortham, "Winning Social Media Votes," *The New York Times,* October 12, 2012, pp. B1, B3; and Joe Garofoli, "Labor's Social Media Muscle Reaching Young Voters," *San Francisco Chronicle,* December 26, 2012, pp. A1, A13.
54. Sam Wang, "The Great Gerrymander of 2012," *The New York Times,* February 3, 2013, pp. SR1, SR5.
55. Philip Meyer, "Computers Could Steal Election," *USA Today,* August 29, 2012, p. 7A.
56. Susan Ricker, CareerBuilder.com, "Find a Job in a Fast Growing Field," *Reno Gazette-Journal,* December 23, 2012, p. 1G.
57. Ibid. See also Susan Ricker, CareerBuilder.com, "Jobs on Rise in High-Demand Fields," *Reno Gazette-Journal,* November 11, 2012, p. G1.
58. Walter Russell Mead, "Find the Jobs of the Future," *The American Interest,* July 15, 2012, *http://blogs.the-american-interest.com/wrm/2012/07/15/finding-the-jobs-of-the-future* (accessed February 22, 2013).
59. Olga Kharif, "Hirers Turning to Social Networks," *San Francisco Chronicle,* December 26, 2012, pp. D1, D2; and Phyllis Korkki, "How to Say 'Look at Me!' to an Online Recruiter," *The New York Times,* January 27, 2013, p. BU-8.
60. Benny Evangelista, "Facebook Job Search," *San Francisco Chronicle,* November 15, 2012, pp. D1, D5.
61. Debra Auerbach, CareerBuilder.com, "Follow the New Résumé Trends," *Reno Gazette-Journal,* January 27, 2013, p. 9E.
62. Lauren Weber, "Your Résumé vs. Oblivion," *The Wall Street Journal,* January 24, 2012, *http://online.wsj.com/article/SB10001424052970204624204577178941034941330.html* (accessed February 23, 2013).
63. Bruce Horovitz, "Tweet for This Job—and It Could Be Yours," *USA Today,* February 18, 2013, p. 3A.
64. Olga Kharif, "Finding Job Candidates Who Aren't Looking," *Bloomberg Businessweek,* December 17–December 23, 2012, pp. 41–42. See also Evelyn M. Rusli, "LinkedIn Profit Soars as Site Caters to Corporate Recruiters, Adds Members," *The Wall Street Journal,* February 5, 2013, p. B5.
65. Anita Bruzzese, "Effectively Promote Yourself, Brand Online," *Reno Gazette-Journal,* May 24, 2012, p. 6A.
66. Sharon Jayson, "Say Grace, and Pass Grandma," *USA Today,* November 21, 2012, pp. 1A, 8A.
67. Kim Severson, "When Phones Come Out Long before the Turkey," *The New York Times,* November 22, 2012, pp. A22, A25.
68. Diane Cole, "When Romance Is a Click Away," *The Wall Street Journal,* July 16, 2012, p. R4; Eli J. Finkel, Paul W. Eastwick, Benjamin R. Karney, Harry T. Reis, and Susan Sprecher, "Dating in a Digital World," *Scientific American Mind,* September–October 2012, pp. 26–33; Alex Williams, "The End of Courtship," *The New York Times,* January 13, 2013, pp. ST-1, ST-11; Dan Slater, *Love in the Time of Algorithms: What Technology Does to Meeting and Mating* (New York: Current, 2013); and Brian K. Williams, Stacey C. Sawyer, and Carl M. Wahlstrom, *Marriages, Families, & Intimate Relationship: A Practical Introduction,* 3rd ed. (Upper Saddle River, NJ: Pearson, 2013), pp. 128–129.
69. Sharon Jayson, "New to the Web: Look-Alike Love," *USA Today,* June 21, 2012, p. 1A.
70. Scott Martin, "Facebook Shoots into Cupid Mode with Graph Search," *USA Today,* January 18, 2013, p. 1B.
71. Tim Bajarin, CEO of Creative Strategies, quoted in James Temple, "Mobile Pushes Us to 'Post-PC' World of Future," *San Francisco Chronicle,* December 23, 2012, pp. G1, G7.
72. Anne Knowles, "Entrepreneur: Smartphones Can Protect against Assaults," *Nevada Appeal,* February 10, 2013, p. C1.
73. Thomas Gryta, "The Latest Fitness Gadgets to Gauge and Goad," *The Wall Street Journal,* January 9, 2013, p. D3.
74. Claire Cain Miller, "Apps and Devices Assist New Mothers," *The New York Times,* January 24, 2013, p. B6.
75. Laura Petrecca, "Mourning 2.0," *USA Today,* May 30, 2012, pp. 1A, 2B; and Ellen Lee, "When Timeline Is Up, Digital Spirit Lives

On," *San Francisco Chronicle,* July 15, 2012, pp. D1, D6. See also Kelly Greene, "Passing Down Digital Assets," *The Wall Street Journal,* September 1–2, 2012, p. B8.
76. Mobile Phones to Match Globe's Population in 2014, *IndustryWeek,* February 28, 2013, *www.industryweek.com/technology/mobile-phones-match-globes-population-2014.*
77. Pew Internet, "Digital Differences:The Power of Mobile," *http://pewinternet.org/Reports/2012/Digital-differences/Main-Report/The-power-of-mobile.aspx,* April 13, 2012 (accessed May 9, 2013).
78. Michael Specter, "Your Mail Has Vanished," *The New Yorker,* December 6, 1999, pp. 96–103.
79. "Internet 2012 in Numbers," *pingdom,* January 16, 2013, *http://royal.pingdom.com/2013/01/16/internet-2012-in-numbers* (accessed February 25, 2013).
80. Robert Rossney, "E-Mail's Best Asset—Time to Think," *San Francisco Chronicle,* October 5, 1995, p. E7.
81. Adam Gopnik, "The Return of the Word," *The New Yorker,* December 6, 1999, pp. 49–50.
82. Sidney Jones and Susannah Fox, Pew Internet & American Life Project, "Generations Online in 2009," January 28, 2009, *www.pewinternet.org/~/media//Files/Reports/2009/PIP_Generations_2009.pdf* (accessed February 26, 2013).
83. Gopnik, "The Return of the Word," 1999.
84. Tamar Lewin, "Informal Style of Electronic Messages Is Showing Up in Schoolwork, Study Finds," *The New York Times,* April 25, 2008, p. A12.
85. Study by McKinsey Global Institute, reported in Kim Komando, "Eradicate Email to Achieve Efficiency," *Reno Gazette-Journal,* September 9, 2012, p. 5F.
86. Jim Giuliano, "What? Ban Email? This CEO Did It," *BusinessBrief.com,* December 11, 2012, from *Information Technology Advisor,* November 16, 2012, *www.businessbrief.com/what-ban-email-this-ceo-did-it* (accessed February 25, 2012).
87. Seth Godin, "Email Checklist," June 5, 2008, *http://sethgodin.typepad.com/seths_blog/2008/06/email-checklist.html* (accessed February 25, 2013); Komando, "Eradicate Email to Achieve Efficiency," 2012; and Alina Tugend, "What to Think before You Hit 'Send,' " *The New York Times,* April 21, 2012, p. B5.
88. Sriram Chellappan and Raghavendra Kotikalapudi, "Associating Internet Usage with Depressive Behavior among College Students," *IEEE Technology & Society Magazine,* Winter 2012, pp. 73–80.
89. Gloria Mark, Stephen Voida, and Armand V. Cardello, " 'A Pace Not Dictated by Electrons': An Empirical Study of Work without Email," paper presented May 7, 2012, at the Association for Computing Machinery's Computer-Human Interaction Conference in Austin, Texas, *www.ics.uci.edu/~gmark/Home_page/Research_files/CHI%202012.pdf* (accessed February 25, 2013). See also Nick Bilton, "Life's Too Short for So Much Email," *The New York Times,* July 9, 2012, p. B4.
90. Mike Rosenwald, " 'Reply All' Infuriates, Embarrasses Many," *San Francisco Chronicle,* December 17, 2012, pp. D1, D4, reprinted from *Bloomberg Businessweek.*
91. Demographic of Internet Users, *http://pewinternet.org/Static-Pages/Trend-Data-%28Adults%29/Whos-Online.aspx* (accessed May 9, 2013).
92. Kevin Maney, "The Net Effect: Evolution or Revolution?" *USA Today,* August 9, 1999, pp. 1B, 2B.
93. Kim Komando, "Essential Apps for Your Shiny New Tablet," *Reno Gazette-Journal,* January 6, 2013, p. 5F.
94. Darlene Storm, "Meet the Fastest, Most Powerful Science Machine in the World: Titan Supercomputer," November 1, 2012, *Computer World, http://blogs.computerworld.com/high-performance-computing/21260/meet-fastest-most-powerful-science-machine-world-titan-supercomputer* (accessed May 9, 2013).
95. Ibid.
96. Walter Mossberg, "2013: Talk Gets Cheaper, TV Gets Smarter," *The Wall Street Journal,* January 2, 2013, pp. D1, D3.
97. David Einstein, "Only a Question of Time till 'Phablets' Hit Market," *San Francisco Chronicle,* April 2, 2012, pp. D1, D2.
98. J. P. Mangalindan, "Replacing the Mouse," *Fortune,* July 2, 2012, p. 25.
99. John Markoff, "Nanotubes Seen as Alternative When Silicon Chips Hit Their Limits," *The New York Times,* February 20, 2013, p. B4.
100. Laurence Hooper, "No Compromises," *The Wall Street Journal,* November 16, 1992, p. R8.
101. John Markoff, "By and for the Masses," *The New York Times,* June 29, 2005, pp. C1, C5.
102. Robert D. Hof, "The Power of Us," *BusinessWeek,* June 20, 2005, pp. 74–82.
103. Verne Kopytoff, "Citizen Journalism Takes Root Online," *San Francisco Chronicle,* June 6, 2005, pp. E1, E5.
104. For a discussion of meanings of "cloud computing," see Ben Worthen, "Overuse of the Term 'Cloud Computing' Clouds Meaning of the Tech Buzz Phrase," *The Wall Street Journal,* September 23, 2008, p. B8; Daniel Lyons, "Today's Forecast: Cloudy," *Newsweek,* November 10, 2008, p. 24; Geoffrey A. Fowler and Ben Worthen, "The Internet Industry Is on a Cloud—Whatever That May Mean," *The Wall Street Journal,* March 26, 2009, pp. A1, A9; and "No Man Is an Island: The Promise of Cloud Computing," *Knowledge@Wharton,* April 1, 2009, *http://knowledge.wharton.upenn.edu/article.cfm?articleid=2190* (accessed February 25, 2013).
105. David Lagesse, "Taking a Walk in 'the Cloud,' " *U.S. News & World Report,* March 2009, pp. 71–73; "Up in the Cloud: Hype and High Expectations for Cloud Computing," *Knowledge@Wharton,* January 16, 2013, *http://knowledge.wharton.upenn.edu/article.cfm?articleid=3171* (accessed February 28, 2013); and Mark Veverka, "To Save IT Costs, the Cloud Is the Limit," *USA Today,* February 19, 2013, p. 3B.
106. James Temple, "Google's Pixel—a Big Bet on Cloud," *San Francisco Chronicle,* February 22, 2013, pp. A1, A14.
107. "Bringing Big Data to the Enterprise," IBM website, *www-01.ibm.com/software/data/bigdata* (accessed February 28, 2013).
108. Steve Lohr, "Searching for Origins of the Term 'Big Data,' " *The New York Times,* February 4, 2013, p. B4.
109. Ashlee Vance, "A Golden Age as Data Storage Evolves," *San Francisco Chronicle,* July 1, 2012, p. D2.
110. Quentin Hardy, "Microsoft Well Prepared to Profit from Big Data," *International Herald Tribune,* October 30, 2012, p. 16.
111. Christopher Steiner, "Automatons Get Creative," *The Wall Street Journal,* August 18–19, 2012, p. C3.
112. Tom Forester and Perry Morrison, *Computer Ethics: Cautionary Tales and Ethical Dilemmas in Computing* (Cambridge, MA: MIT Press, 1990), pp. 1–2.
113. Psychiatrist Edward M. Hallowell, quoted in Alma Tugend, "Multitasking Can Make You Lose . . . Um . . . Focus," *The New York Times,* October 25, 2008, p. B7. Hallowell is the author of *CrazyBusy: Overstretched, Overbooked, and About to Snap!* (New York: Ballantine, 2006).
114. John Tierney, "Ear Plugs to Lasers: The Science of Concentration," *The New York Times,* May 5, 2009, p. D2.
115. Winifred Gallagher, cited in Tierney, "Ear Plugs to Lasers." Gallagher is the author of *Rapt* (New York: Penguin Press, 2009).
116. Winifred Gallagher, quoted in book review, David G. Myers, "Please Pay Attention," *The Wall Street Journal,* April 20, 2009, p. A13.
117. Pam Belluck, "To Really Learn, Quit Studying and Take a Test," *The New York Times,* January 21, 2011, *www.nytimes.com/2011/01/21/science/21memory.html?partner=rss&emc=rss* (accessed January 22, 2011).
118. Francis P. Robinson, *Effective Study,* 4th ed. (New York: Harper & Row, 1970).
119. Bruce K. Broumage and Richard E. Mayer, "Quantitative and Qualitative Effects of Repetition on Learning from Technical Text," *Journal of Educational Psychology, 78,* 1982, 271–278.
120. Robin J. Palkovitz and Richard K. Lore, "Note Taking and Note Review: Why Students Fail Questions Based on Lecture Material," *Teaching of Psychology, 7,* 1980, 159–161.

Chapter 2

1. Graham T. T. Molitor, "Five Forces Transforming Communications," *The Futurist,* September–October 2001, pp. 32–37.
2. "Internet World Stats: Usage and Population Statistics," June 12, 2012, *www.internetworldstats.com/stats.htm* (accessed March 5, 2013).

3. PenPlusBytes, "Five Billion People Will Be Connected to the Internet by 2015," December 13, 2007, *http://penplusbytes.blogspot.com/2007/12/five-billion-people-will-be-connected.html* (accessed March 5, 2013).
4. Anne Neville, "NTIA Explores Broadband Availability in New Report Series," May 13, 2013, *www.ntia.doc.gov/blog/2013/ntia-explores-broadband-availability-new-report-series* (accessed May 20, 2013).
5. Terry Allison, "Got Broadband? Access Now Extends to 94 Percent of Americans," *The Christian Science Monitor,* August 24, 2012, *www.csmonitor.com/USA/Society/2012/0824/Got-broadband-Access-now-extends-to-94-percent-of-Americans* (accessed March 5, 2013); Anne Neville, "NTIA Explores Broadband Availability."
6. Chuck Sherwood, "How to Actually Get Americans Online," *CTIA—The Wireless Association Blog,* January 31, 2013, *http://blog.ctia.org/2013/01/31/how-to-actually-get-americans-online* (accessed March 5, 2013).
7. Fact Checker, "Calling It 4G Isn't Enough to Make It Faster," *Reno Gazette-Journal,* January 16, 2011, p. 3A.
8. Julius Genachowski, "The Broadband Engine of Economic Growth," *The Wall Street Journal,* March 6, 2013, p. A21.
9. "About Internet2," *www.internet2.edu/about* (accessed March 8, 2013).
10. For a short history of the development of the Internet and protocols, see Stephen D. Crocker, "How the Internet Got Its Rules," *The New York Times,* April 7, 2009, p. A25.
11. Peter Rachal, "Internet Officially Runs Out of Addresses," PCmag.com, February 3, 2011, *www.pcmag.com/article2/0%2C2817%2C2379327%2C00.asp* (accessed March 9, 2013).
12. Internet Corporation for Assigned Names and Numbers, *www.icann.org/en/about* (accessed March 9, 2013).
13. StatCounter Global Stats, "Top 5 Browsers on Jan. 2013," *http://gs.statcounter.com/#browser-ww-monthly-201301-201301-bar* (accessed March 8, 2013).
14. Claire Cain Miller, "Browser Wars Flare Again, on Little Screens," *The New York Times,* December 10, 2012, pp. B1, B6.
15. "The Size of the World Wide Web (The Internet)," WorldWideWebSize.com, March 8, 2013, *www.worldwidewebsize.com/* (accessed March 8, 2013).
16. Miller, "Browser Wars Flare Again."
17. Melanie Hanes-Ramos, "Bare Bones 101: A Basic Tutorial on Searching the Web," University of South Carolina, Beaufort Library, February 5, 2009, *www.sc.edu/beaufort/library/pages/bones/bones.shtml* (accessed March 8, 2013).
18. Chris Taylor, "It's a Wiki, Wiki World," *Time,* June 6, 2005, pp. 40–42. See also Stacy Schiff, "The Interactive Truth," *The New York Times,* June 15, 2005, p. A29.
19. Ben Eisen, "Cornell Profs Slam Use of Wikipedia," *The Cornell Daily Sun,* February 20, 2007, *www.cornellsun.com/node/21501* (accessed March 8, 2013).
20. Daniel Terdiman, "A Tool for Scholars Who Like to Dig Deep," *The New York Times,* November 25, 2004, p. B6. See also Jeffrey R. Young, "Google Unveils a Search Engine Focused on Scholarly Materials," *The Chronicle of Higher Education,* December 3, 2004, p. A34.
21. "Google's Book Scanning Project Runs into Legal Hurdles," domain-b.com, June 10, 2009, *www.domain-b.com/companies/companies_g/google/20090610_book_scanning_project.html* (accessed March 21, 2013).
22. Ellen Chamberlain, "Bare Bones 101: A Basic Tutorial on Searching the Web," University of South Carolina, Beaufort Library, September 7, 2006, *www.sc.edu/beaufort/library/pages/bones/lesson5.shtml* (accessed March 8, 2013).
23. Janet Hogan, "The ABCDs of Evaluating Internet Resources," Binghamton University Libraries, November 2, 2004, *http://library.lib.binghamton.edu/search/evaluation.html*; Hope N. Tillman, "Evaluating Quality on the Net," Babson College, March 28, 2003, *www.hopetillman.com/findqual.html*; and Esther Grassian, "Thinking Critically about World Wide Web Resources," UCLA College Library, September 6, 2000, *www.library.ucla.edu/libraries/college/help/critical/index.htm* (all accessed March 21, 2013).
24. See Jenna Wortham, "Online Emotions, in Hundreds of New Flavors," *The New York Times,* March 10, 2013, p. BU-3; Nick Bilton, "Thanks? Don't Bother," *The New York Times,* March 11, 2013, pp. B1, B6; and Anita Bruzzese, "Grammar Matters in Business World, Even in Email," *Reno Gazette-Journal,* March 14, 2013, p. 6A.
25. Nick Bilton, "The End Nears for Google Reader," *The New York Times,* March 18, 2013, p. B7.
26. Sky Stepniki, "Alternative News Readers to Google Reader," *Aereus,* March 14, 2013, *www.aereus.com/blog/posts/alternative-news-readers-to-google-reader* (accessed March 31, 2013).
27. Stephen H. Wildstrom, "Google's Magic Carpet Ride," *BusinessWeek,* July 18, 2005, p. 22.
28. Steven Levy, "The Earth Is Ready for Its Close-up," *Newsweek,* June 6, 2005, p. 13. See also James Fallows, "An Update on Stuff That's Cool (Like Google's Photo Maps)," *The New York Times,* April 17, 2005, sec. 3, p. 5; Verne Kopytoff, "Google's Free 3-D Service Brings Views of Earth Down to the PC," *San Francisco Chronicle,* June 29, 2005, pp. A1, A16; John Markoff, "Marrying Maps to Data for a New Web Service," *The New York Times,* July 18, 2005, pp. C1, C8; and Verne Kopytoff, "Microsoft, Google in Sky Fight," *San Francisco Chronicle,* July 26, 2005, pp. D1, D2.
29. Verne Koptoff, "Google Peeks beneath the Waves," *San Francisco Chronicle,* February 3, 2009, pp. A1, A14.
30. "Google Earth's Street View: Public Boon or Privacy Invasion?" EngineeringDaily.net, *www.engineeringdaily.net/google-earths-street-view-public-boon-or-privacy-invasion* (accessed March 21, 2013).
31. Jason Bellini, "Behind the Making of a Mobile Game," *The Wall Street Journal,* March 5, 2013, p. B7.
32. Chris Taylor, "Let RSS Go Fetch," *Time,* May 30, 2005, p. 82.
33. Janet Kornblum, "Welcome to the Blogosphere," *USA Today,* July 8, 2003, p. 7D.
34. Andrew Sullivan, "Why I Blog," *The Atlantic,* November 2008, pp. 106–113.
35. Michael Agger, Slate.com, reported in "Blogging for Fun and Profit," *The Week,* October 17, 2008, p. 44.
36. Daniel Lyons, "Time to Hang Up the Pajamas," *Newsweek,* February 16, 2009, p. 19; and Douglas Quenqua, "Blogs Falling in an Empty Forest," *The New York Times,* June 7, 2009, Sunday Styles, pp. 1, 7.
37. Target CEO Gregg Steinhafel and executive vice president Kathee Tesija, quoted in Ann Zimmerman, "Showdown over Showrooms," *The Wall Street Journal,* January 23, 2012, pp. B1, B5.
38. Nick Wingfield, "Shedding Light on 'Showroomers,' " *The New York Times,* March 4, 2013, p. B6.
39. Tim Berners-Lee, cited in Brian Getting, "Basic Definitions: Web 1.0, Web 2.0, Web 3.0," *Practical Ecommerce,* April 18, 2007, *www.practicalecommerce.com/articles/464-Basic-Definitions-Web-1-0-Web-2-0-Web-3-0* (accessed March 23, 2013).
40. "Web 2.0—the Social Web," About.com, *http://webtrends.about.com/od/web20/a/what-is-web20.htm* (accessed March 23, 2013).
41. "How Many People Use the Top Social Media, Apps, & Services?" Digital Marketing Ramblings," May 2103, *http://expandedramblings.com/index.php/resource-how-many-people-use-the-top-social-media/* (accessed May 16, 2013).
42. Brad Stone, "Friends May Be the Best Guide through the Noise," *The New York Times,* May 4, 2008, business sec., p. 4.
43. Jonathan Strickland, "How Web 3.0 Will Work," *How Stuff Works, http://computer.howstuffworks.com/web-30.htm/printable* (accessed March 23, 2013).
44. Getting, "Basic Definitions: Web 1.0, Web 2.0, Web 3.0"; and Strickland, "How Web 3.0 Will Work."
45. Stanley Fish, "Anonymity and the Dark Side of the Internet," *The New York Times,* January 3, 2011, *http://opinionator.blogs.nytimes.com/2011/01/03/anonymity-and-the-dark-side-of-the-internet/* (accessed March 23, 2013).
46. Jacqui Cheng, "Popular Facebook Apps Found to Be Collecting, Selling User Info," arstechnica.com, *http://arstechnica.com/tech-policy/news/2010/10/many-facebook-apps-found-to-be-collecting-selling-user-info.ars* (accessed March 23, 2013).
47. Emily Steele and Geoffrey A. Fowler, "Facebook in Privacy Breech," October 18, 2010, *http://online.wsj.com/article/SB1000*

142405270230477280457555848407523 6968.html (accessed March 23, 2013).

48. Martha Nussbaum, reported in Fish, "Anonymity and the Dark Side of the Internet."
49. TLNT: The Business of HR, Should Employers Ask Candidates for Their Facebook Passwords? *www.tlnt.com/2013/05/07/should-employers-ask-candidates-for-their-facebook-passwords/* (accessed May 16, 2013).
50. Kevin Kelly, "Achieving Techno-Literacy," *The New York Times,* September 16, 2010, *www.nytimes.com/2010/09/19/magazine/19FOB-WWLN-Kelly-t.html* (accessed March 23, 2013).
51. Timothy L. O'Brien and Saul Hansell, "Barbarians at the Digital Gate," *The New York Times,* September 19, 2004, sec. 3, pp. 1, 4.
52. "Egregious Email," *Smart Computing,* October 2002, pp. 95–97.
53. Pingdom, January 16, 2013, "Internet 2012 in Numbers," *http://royal.pingdom.com/2013/01/16/internet-2012-in-numbers/* (accessed May 16, 2013).
54. Riva Richmond, "Companies Target E-Mail 'Spoofing,' " *The Wall Street Journal,* June 9, 2004, p. D9; and Amey Stone, "How to Avoid the 'Phish' Hook," *BusinessWeek online,* May 24, 2004, *www.businessweek.com/technology/content/may2004/tc20040524_8133_tc024.htm* (accessed March 23, 2013).
55. "Email Spoofing," SearchSecurity.com Definitions, November 20, 2003, *http://searchsecurity.techtarget.com/sDefinition/0,,sid14_gci840262,00.html* (accessed March 23, 2013).
56. Kim Komando, "5 Tips for Spurning Spyware and Browser Hijackers," *Microsoft Small Business Center,* 2005, *www.microsoft.com/smallbusiness/issues/marketing/privacy_spam/5_tips_for_spurning_spyware_and_browser_hijackers.mspx* (accessed March 23, 2013).
57. David Kesmodel, "Marketers Seek to Make Cookies More Palatable," *The Wall Street Journal,* June 17, 2005, pp. B1, B2.
58. "What Is Browser Hijacking?" Microsoft Safety and Security Center, *www.microsoft.com/security/resources/hijacking-whatis.aspx* (accessed March 23, 2013).
59. Joseph Telafici, quoted in Vincent Kiernan, "The Next Plague," *The Chronicle of Higher Education,* January 28, 2005, pp. A36–A38.
60. "Speak, Friend, and Enter," *The Economist,* March 24, 2012, pp. 81–82; David Einstein, "Why Theft of Any Password Cause for Concern," *San Francisco Chronicle,* June 18, 2012, pp. D1, D3; Nicole Perlroth, "How to Devise Passwords That Drive Hackers Away," *The New York Times,* November 8, 2012, p. B8; Anick Jasdanun, "Strong Passwords and Other Security Tips," *Reno Gazette-Journal,* March 3, 2013, p. 5F; and "Worst Passwords of 2012—and How to Fix Them," SplashData, *http://splashdata.com/press/PR121023.htm* (accessed March 28, 2013).
61. David Rothenberg, "How the Web Destroys the Quality of Students' Research Papers," *The Chronicle of Higher Education,* August 15, 1997, *http://chronicle.com/article/How-the-Web-Destroys-the/7521* (accessed March 23, 2013).

Chapter 3

1. James McQuivey, *Digital Disruption: Unleashing the Next Wave of Innovation* (Seattle: Amazon, 2013).
2. McQuivey, reported in Alan Murray, "Built Not to Last," *The Wall Street Journal,* March 18, 2013, p. A11.
3. Quentin Hardy, "Google Apps Challenging Microsoft in Business," *The New York Times,* December 26, 2012, pp. B1, B6.
4. Don Clark, "Microsoft, Intel Brave a Mobile World," *The Wall Street Journal,* April 15, 2013, p. B2.
5. Associated Press, "PC Market Grim as Mobile Devices Lure Consumers," *San Francisco Chronicle,* April 12, 2013, p. C4; Ian Sherr and Shira Ovide, "H-P, Microsoft Hit by PC Worries," *The Wall Street Journal,* April 12, 2013, p. B5; Spencer Jakab, "Microsoft's Failure to Launch Is No Joke," *The Wall Street Journal,* April 18, 2013, p. C1; and Sharon Telep, Shira Ovide, and David Benoit, "PC Slide Doomed Blackstone-Dell Tie," *The Wall Street Journal,* April 20–21, 2013, pp. B1, B4.
6. John Paczkowski and Peter Kafka, "Mozilla Will Debut Firefox OS in June," *The Wall Street Journal,* April 17, 2013, p. B4.
7. Juro Osawa, "Alibaba to Promote Its Own Mobile Operating System," *The Wall Street Journal,* April 16, 2013, p. B5.
8. John Paczkowski and Peter Kafka, "Google's Android Goal: 'To Reach Everyone,' " *The Wall Street Journal,* April 17, 2013, p. B4.
9. Ron Harris, "Chrome PCs Provide Internet-Centric Option," *Reno Gazette-Journal,* July 29, 2012, p. 5F.
10. "Speak, Friend, and Enter," pp. 81–82.
11. John Underkoffler, quoted in J. P. Mangalindan, "Replacing the Mouse," *Fortune,* July 2, 2012, p. 25.
12. Mike Elgan, "How Microsoft Lost the Future of Gesture Control," *ComputerWorld,* March 30, 2013, *www.computerworld.com/s/article/9238001/How_Microsoft_lost_the_future_of_gesture_control* (accessed April 12, 2013).
13. Roberto Baldwin, "Why the Leap Is the Best Gesture-Control System We've Ever Tested," *Wired,* May 23, 2012, *www.wired.com/gadgetlab/2012/05/why-the-leap-is-the-best-gesture-control-system-weve-ever-tested* (accessed April 12, 2013); and Elgan, 2013.
14. Bill Weir, David Miller, Justin Bare, and Mark Monroy, "LEAP Motion Gesture Control May Replace Mouse," *Yahoo! News,* March 21, 2013, *http://news.yahoo.com/blogs/this-could-be-big-abc-news/leap-motion-gesture-control-may-replace-mouse-164159890.html* (accessed April 12, 2013).
15. Mingming Fan, quoted in Hal Hodson, "Leap Motion Hacks Show What 3D Gesture Sensing Can Do," *New Scientist,* April 8, 2013, *www.newscientist.com/article/mg21829116.100-leap-motion-hacks-show-what-3d-gesture-sensing-can-do.html* (accessed April 12, 2013).
16. Mangalindan, "Replacing the Mouse," 2012.
17. Edward C. Baig, "Apple's Mountain Lion for Macs Roars," *USA Today,* July 26, 2012, p. 3b; Katherine Boehret, "Apple's New System for Mac Borrows from iPhone," *The Wall Street Journal,* July 26, 2012, pp. D2, D3; and David Pogue, "The Payout in an Apple Upgrade," *The New York Times,* July 26, 2012, pp. B1, B8.
18. Netwind.com, "Desktop Operating System Market Share as of January, 2013," *http://visual.ly/desktop-operating-system-market-share-january-2013* (accessed April 28, 2013).
19. Jeremy A. Kaplan, "Review: Windows 8 a Daring Vision of the Future—but Are You Ready?" FoxNews.com, October 25, 2012, *www.foxnews.com/tech/2012/10/25/review-windows-8-daring-vision-future-but-are-ready* (accessed April 28, 2013).
20. "Definition of: Windows 8," PCMag.com, *www.pcmag.com/encyclopedia/term/62224/windows-8* (accessed April 28, 2013).
21. David Murphy, "Windows 8 Review: Microsoft Straps a Tablet Operating System to Windows 8. Should Enthusiasts Make the Big Upgrade?" *Maximum PC,* March 16, 2013, *www.maximumpc.com/article/features/windows_8_Review* (accessed April 28, 2013).
22. David Pogue, "Windows, Revamped and Split in 2," *The New York Times,* October 24, 2012, *www.nytimes.com/2012/10/25/technology/personaltech/microsofts-windows-revamped-and-split-in-2.html?pagewanted=all&_r=0* (accessed April 28, 2012).
23. Kaplan, "Review: Windows 8," 2012.
24. "Android and iOS Combine for 91.1% of the Worldwide Smartphone OS Market in 4Q12 and 87.6% for the Year, According to IDC," IDC press release, February 14, 2013, *www.idc.com/getdoc.jsp?containerId=prUS23946013* (accessed May 1, 2013).
25. Katherine Boehret, "The BlackBerry of BlackBerry Users' Dreams," *The Wall Street Journal,* April 24, 2013, p. D2; and Will Connors, "BlackBerry Keypad's Return," *The Wall Street Journal,* April 24, 2013, p. B4.
26. Edward C. Baig, "Windows Phone 8 Deserves Applause," *USA Today,* November 14, 2012, p. 4B.
27. Marshall Honorof, "How Video Game Costs Could Crash the Industry," *TechNewsDaily,* March 26, 2013, *www.technewsdaily.com/17477-development-costs-crash-industry.html* (accessed April 6, 2013).
28. Jennifer Daniel, "Video Games: Blastin' Aliens Since 1975," *Bloomberg Businessweek,* December 10–16, 2012, pp. 50–51.

29. M2 Research, reported in Honorof, "How Video Game Costs Could Crash the Industry," 2013.
30. "With Free Software, Caution Is in Order," *The New York Times,* August 30, 2012, p. B7.
31. Marc Saltzman, "Cash-Strapped Students Can Find Free Software," *USA Today,* August 21, 2012, p. 5B.
32. Katherine Noyes, "Can Apache OpenOffice Still Compete with LibreOffice?" *PC World,* May 9, 2012, *www.pcworld.com/article/255308/can_apache_openoffice_still_compete_with_libreoffice_.html* (accessed April 8, 2013).
33. Steven J. Vaughan-Nichols, "LibreOffice 4: A New, Better Open-Source Software Suite," *ZDNet,* February 7, 2013, *www.zdnet.com/libreoffice-4-a-new-better-open-source-office-suite-7000011016* (accessed April 8, 2013).
34. Rolfe Winkler, "An 'Out of Office' Message for iPads," *The Wall Street Journal,* April 29, 2013, p. C6.
35. Study by Kent Norman, Laboratory of Automation Psychology and Decision Processes, University of Maryland, cited in Katherine Seligman, "Computer Crashes Booming Business," *San Francisco Chronicle,* April 17, 2005, pp. A1, A21.

Chapter 4

1. Steve Jobs, cited in Nick Winfield, "PC Sales Still in a Slump, Despite New Offerings," *The New York Times,* April 11, 2013, p. B5.
2. Scott Martin and Jon Swartz, "Newest Dinosaur: The PC-osaurus," *USA Today,* March 7, 2013, pp. 1B, 2B; and Ian Sherr and ShiraOvide, "Computer Sales in Free Fall," *The Wall Street Journal,* April 11, 2013, pp. B1, B4.
3. Shara Tibken, "Smartphones Challenge Chip Limits," *The Wall Street Journal,* August 28, 2012, p. B7.
4. Ashlee Vance, "Chips on Shoulder of Both Samsung, Apple," *San Francisco Chronicle,* April 4, 2013, p. C3.
5. Margaret Rouse, "Tablet Computer," WhatIs.com, December 2010, *http://searchmobilecomputing.techtarget.com/definition/tablet-PC* (accessed May 11, 2013); Walter S. Mossberg, "Sometimes They're Tablets, Sometimes They're Not," *The Wall Street Journal,* January 23, 2013, pp. D1, D2; Walter S. Mossberg, "Laptop Guide: Timing the Market and the Machines," *The Wall Street Journal,* May 1, 2013, pp. D1, D2; and Choe Albanesius, "Tablets to Outshine PCs, but Touch-Based Notebooks Might Help," *PC Magazine,* May 6, 2013, *www.pcmag.com/article2/0,2817,2418585,00.asp* (accessed May 11, 2013).
6. Ernest Scheyder, "Save Some Cash, Get Unplugged," *Reno Gazette-Journal,* April 11, 2009, p. 8A.
7. Ibid.
8. Report by 1E and Alliance to Save Energy, 2009 Energy Report, reported in Jon Swartz, "Leaving PCs on Overnight Costs Companies $2.8B a Year," *USA Today,* March 25, 2009, p. 4B.
9. Ian Paul, "The End of Moore's Law Is on the Horizon, Says AMD," PCWorld.com, April 3, 2013, *www.pcworld.com/article/2032913/the-end-of-moores-law-is-on-the-horizon-says-amd.html*; and Raj Sabhlok, "Moore's Law Is Just Beginning (for Apps)," *Forbes,* April 25, 2013, *www.forbes.com/sites/rajsabhlok/2013/04/25/moores-law-is-just-beginning-for-apps* (both accessed May 14, 2013). See also Ben Worth and Don Clark, "Chip Makers Face Limits in Storing Ever More Data," *The Wall Street Journal,* August 17, 2012, p. A2.
10. Stephen H. Wildstrom, "Chips with Two Brains," *BusinessWeek,* August 1, 2005, p. 20.
11. Don Clark, "Intel Tailors 3-D Chip Process to Build Cell, Tablet Devices," *The Wall Street Journal,* December 11, 2012, p. B6.
12. IBM spokeswoman Kristin Bryson, quoted in Craig Wolf, "As Sales Heat Up, IBM Servers Stay Cool," *USA Today,* January 2, 2013, p. 2B, reprinted from *Poughkeepsie Journal.*
13. Jonathan Koomey, Stanford University, quoted in Michal Lev-Ram, "The Next Great Chip Clash," *Fortune,* December 24, 2012, pp. 37, 39.
14. Alex Williams, "From the Old to the New: Data Centers Rise Along the Columbia River," *readwrite,* November 1, 2010, *http://readwrite.com/2010/11/01/from-the-old-economy-to-the-ne* (accessed May 23, 2013).
15. James Glanz, "For Data Centers, a Place to Plug In," *The New York Times,* May 14, 2013, pp. B1, B4.
16. James Glanz, "EBay Plans Data Center That Will Run on Alternative Energy Fuel Cells," *The New York Times,* June 21, 2012, p. B3.
17. "Spyware Infection rates," March 2010, *www.plycomp.co.uk/virus-statistics-worldwide.html* (accessed May 23, 2013).
18. Alan Luber, "Hard Drive Backup & Restore Basics, Part 1," *Smart Computing,* August 2004, p. 96; Rachel Dodes, "Terminating Spyware with Extreme Prejudice," *The New York Times,* December 30, 2004, pp. E1, E6; Rachel Dodes, "Tools to Make Your Hard Drive Forget Its Past," *The New York Times,* December 30, 2004, p. E6; Jeff Dodd, "How to Install Operating Systems," *Smart Computing,* February 2005, pp. 60–63; Nigel Powell, "Archive Your Drive," *Popular Science,* March 2005, pp.73–74; Kim Komando, "Fixes for Common Computer Problems," *Reno Gazette-Journal,* December 30, 2012, p. 4F; and Kim Komando, "How to Clean and Revive Your Computer," *Reno Gazette-Journal,* April 7, 2013, p. 5F.
19. "Consumers Fail to Properly Back Up Large Digital Libraries, Says CEA," Reuters, March 18, 2008, *www.reuters.com/article/pressRelease/idUS157293+18-Mar-2008+BW20080318* (accessed May 23, 2013).
20. "10% Now Back Up Daily, 90% to Go!" *Backblaze Blog,* June 12, 2012, *http://blog.backblaze.com/2012/06/12/10-now-back-up-daily-90-to-go* (accessed May 23, 2013).
21. "What Does 'Region Free' Mean?" *wiseGEEK,* March 26, 2013, *www.wisegeek.org/what-does-region-free-mean.htm* (accessed May 21, 2013).
22. Brandon Butler, "Gartner: Top 10 Cloud Storage Providers," *Network World,* January 3, 2013, *www.networkworld.com/news/2013/010313-gartner-cloud-storage-265459.html* (accessed May 22, 2013).
23. Cicely K. Dyson, "Lofty Hopes for Cloud Users," *The Wall Street Journal,* January 10, 2013, p. B7.
24. Olga Kharif, "A Bug's Life in the Trenches," *Bloomberg Businessweek,* July 2–8, 2012, p. 34.
25. John Markoff, "I.B.M. Claims Advance in Shrinking Chips," *International Herald Tribune,* October 30, 2012, p. 15; and John Markoff, "Nanotubes Seen as Alternative When Silicon Chips Hit Their Limits," *The New York Times,* February 20, 2013, p. B4.
26. Dan Vergano, "Mini Movie Carries a Lot of (Atomic) Weight," *USA Today,* May 1, 2013, p. 3A. See also "A Boy and His Atom: The World's Smallest Movie," IBM, *www.research.ibm.com/articles/madewithatoms.shtml* (accessed May 23, 2013).
27. Robert Lee Hotz, "Future of Data: Encoded in DNA," *The Wall Street Journal,* August 17, 2012, pp. A1, A2; and Karen Weintraub, "The Newest Storage Device for Data? DNA," *USA Today,* January 24, 2013, p. 2B.
28. Mitra Basu, quoted in "Molecular Robots on the Rise," National Science Foundation press release, May 12, 2010, *www.nsf.gov/news/news_summ.jsp?cntn_id=116957* (accessed May 23, 2013).
29. Kenneth Chang, "IBM Researchers Inch toward Quantum Computer," *The New York Times,* February 28, 2012, p. B2.
30. Quentin Hardy, "A Big Leap to Quantum Computing," *The New York Times,* May 13, 2013, p. B11.
31. K. Naughton, "Now We're Cooking with Batteries," *Newsweek,* December 1, 2008, pp. 42–46.
32. Daniel Lyons, "Hurry Up and Type," *Newsweek,* June 29, 2009, p. 27.
33. See, for example, Kate Murphy, "Mobile Chargers Ease That Feeling of Powerlessness," *The New York Times,* January 10, 2013, p. B7; and Chris Hoffman, "No More Cables: How Wireless Charging Works and How You Can Use It Today," *How-To Geek,* May 6, 2013, *www.howtogeek.com/162483/no-more-cables-how-wireless-charging-works-and-how-you-can-use-it-today* (accessed May 23, 2013).
34. "The Search for a Better Battery," *The Week,* May 10, 2013, p. 9.
35. Katie Fehrenbacher, "Ultrathin Batteries Could Transform Gadget Design," *San Francisco Chronicle,* January 9, 2013, pp. D1, D2.
36. Wendy Koch, "Batteries Up! Stored-Energy Research Buzzes," *USA Today,* May 13, 2013, pp. 1B, 4B.
37. Don Clark, "Marvell Bets on 'Plug Computers,' " *The Wall Street Journal,* February 23, 2009, p. B4.

38. Bill Joy, "Why the Future Doesn't Need Us," *Wired,* April 2000, *www.wired.com/wired/archive/8.04/joy.html* (accessed May 23, 2013).
39. Mark Hachman, "The Bottomless DVD," *PC Magazine Digital Edition,* July 2009, p. 9.
40. John Markoff, "Scientists Develop Device for Image Compression," *The New York Times,* January 18, 2013, p. B4.
41. Walt Mossberg, "How to Buy a Laptop," *Newser,* April 29, 2010, *www.newser.com/story/87365/how-to-buy-a-laptop.html* (accessed June 1, 2011); Walt Mossberg, "Picking Out a Laptop in the Brave, New World of Tablets," April 20, 2011, *http://allthingsd.com/20110420/picking-out-a-laptop-in-the-brave-new-world-of-tablets/* (accessed June 1, 2011).
42. Kim Komando, "How PCs, Macs Stack Up against Each Other," *Reno Gazette-Journal,* September 23, 2012, p. 5F.
43. Brian Lam, "In Choosing a Tablet, First Try It on for Size," *The New York Times,* January 17, 2013, p. B7.

Chapter 5

1. Apple CEO Tim Cook, interviewed by Walt Mossberg and Kara Swisher, "Is Apple in Trouble?" *The Wall Street Journal,* June 3, 2013, p. D2.
2. Scott Gerber, "How Will Wearable Tech Impact the Startup World?" *Mashable,* May 27, 2013, *http://mashable.com/2013/05/27/wearable-tech-startups* (accessed June 3, 2013).
3. Scott Martin, "Is the World Really Ready for This?" *USA Today,* April 9, 2013, p. 8B.
4. Scott Martin, "Google Glasses: Computing on the Nose," *USA Today,* June 28, 2012, p. 3B.
5. "Video Shows How Google Glass Works," *USA Today,* February 21, 2013, p. 5B; Claire Cain Miller, "Google Searches for Style," *The New York Times,* February 21, 2013, pp. B1, B4; Caleb Garling, "This Hardware Is Everyday Wear," *San Francisco Chronicle,* April 7, 2013, pp. D1, D6; Kevin Sintumuang, "Google Glass: An Etiquette Guide," *The Wall Street Journal,* May 4–5, 2013, pp. B1, B2; and Evelyn M. Rusli, "Talk of Tech: Wearable Computers," *The Wall Street Journal,* May 31, 2013, p. B8.
6. John Doerr, quoted in Douglas MacMillan, "Google, Investors Join to Spur Apps for Glass," *San Francisco Chronicle,* April 12, 2013, pp. C1, C8.
7. For discussion of the viability of Google Glass, see Martin, "Is the World Really Ready for This?"; James Temple, "Cloudy Outlook for Glass Wearers," *San Francisco Chronicle,* May 19, 2013, pp. D1, D6; and "Google Glass: Can 'Tech Cool' Become 'Market Cool'?" *Knowledge@Wharton,* May 22, 2013, *http://knowledge.wharton.upenn.edu/article.cfm?articleid=3266* (accessed June 3, 2013).
8. Discussion of keyboards in David Einstein, "LED TVs Brighter, Not Necessarily Better," *San Francisco Chronicle,* April 1, 2013, pp. D1, D3.
9. Katherine Boehret, "From QWERTY to Quirky: New Ways to Type," *The Wall Street Journal,* January 16, 2013, p. D2.
10. "Thumbs Up for Speed," *The Wall Street Journal,* April 20–21, 2013, p. C4.
11. Boehret, "From QWERTY to Quirky."
12. Sarah Nassauer, "Screens Get a Place at the Table," *The Wall Street Journal,* May 31, 2012, pp. D1, D2.
13. Jessica E. Lessin, "High Priest of App Design, at Home in Philly," *The Wall Street Journal,* March 18, 2013, pp. B1, B5. See also Alex Heath, "Tweetie and Letterpress Creator Loren Brichter Helping Design Team at Facebook," *Cult of Mac,* April 16, 2013, *www.cultofmac.com/223676/tweetie-and-letterpress-creator-loren-brichter-helping-design-team-at-facebook* (accessed May 31, 2013).
14. David Pogue, "Let a Stylus, Not a Finger, Tap the Glass," *The New York Times,* August 12, 2012, pp. B1, B9.
15. Edward C. Baig, "Sing a Song of Scanners—a Pocketful, That Is," *USA Today,* May 1, 2013, p. 4B.
16. Walter S. Mossberg, "A Dragon That Takes Dictation and Controls a Mac by Voice," *The Wall Street Journal,* October 10, 2012, pp. D1, D2.
17. David B. Yoffie, quoted in Steve Lohr, "Rise of Data from Sensors," *The New York Times,* January 7, 2013, p. B6. On jet engine sensors, see, for example, Rachel King, "Industrial Internet Will End Downtime, GE Hopes," *The Wall Street Journal,* November 29, 2012, p. B7.
18. Jessica E. Vascellaro, "Alert: Your Plant Needs Water," *The Wall Street Journal,* September 11, 2012, p. B4; Roxie Hammill and Mike Hendricks, "Gadgets to Help Tend a Garden," *The New York Times,* September 25, 2012, pp. B1, B8; and Brian Dumaine, "The House of Tomorrow," *Fortune,* March 18, 2013, p. 73.
19. Ian Lovett, "To Fight Gridlock, a City Synchronizes Every Red Light," *The New York Times,* April 2, 2013, p. A11. For other traffic uses, see Larry Copeland, "Project Will Help Drivers Go More with Traffic Flow," *USA Today,* June 13, 2008, p. 1A; and Larry Copeland, "Test Project Will Gather Highway Traffic Data," *USA Today,* June 13, 2008, p. 6A.
20. "Bad Air at State and Main," *The Wall Street Journal,* December 29, 2012, p. C4.
21. Drew Joseph, "Stanford Football Field a Lab to Study Injuries," *San Francisco Chronicle,* November 21, 2012, pp. D1, D5.
22. Alicia Chang, "Sensors to Keep Tabs on Fault," *Reno Gazette-Journal,* March 29, 2009, pp. 1B, 3B.
23. Jeff Vining, Jerry Mechling, and Steve Bittinger, "Japan Earthquake and Tsunami Reaffirm the Need for Sensors," March 17, 2011, *www.gartner.com/DisplayDocument?id=1594915* (accessed June 3, 2013).
24. "The Biometrics Boom," *The Week,* June 7, 2013, p. 11.
25. Drake Bennett, "Computing That Makes You Feel," *Bloomberg Businessweek,* March 4–10, 2013, pp. 34–36.
26. Anick Jesdanun, "Mobile Payment Needs Better Compatibility," *Reno Gazette-Journal,* September 9, 2012, p. 5F; Hadley Malcolm, "Smartphones to Play Bigger Role in Shopping," *USA Today,* November 16, 2012, pp. 1B, 2B; Angus Loten and Emily Maltby, "Mobile Payments Brighten Cash Flows," *The Wall Street Journal,* February 28, 2013, p. B5; and Rhonda Abrams, "More Businesses Look at Mobile Payment Options," *Reno Gazette-Journal,* May 7, 2013, p. 5A.
27. David Pogue, "Pay by Voice? So Long, Wallet," *The New York Times,* July 19, 2012, pp. B1, B8.
28. Robert Lee Hotz, "Device Helps Eyes Do the Write Thing," *The Wall Street Journal,* July 27, 2013, p. A2; and Sven Grundberg, "Computing Looks to the Eyes," *The Wall Street Journal,* March 26, 2013, p. B5.
29. Bennett, "Computing That Makes You Feel."
30. Natasha Singer, "The Human Voice, as Game Changer," *The New York Times,* April 1, 2012, pp. BU-1, BU-6.
31. Mike Snider and Chris Woodyard, "Wave a Hand, Turn on Radio or Make Call," *USA Today,* January 8, 2013, pp. 1B, 2B. See also Matt Vella, "Rebooting the Dashboard," *Fortune,* March 18, 2013, p. 68.
32. Brian Shane, "Palm Scanners Get Thumbs Up," *USA Today,* November 26, 2012, p. 3A.
33. Timothy Hay, "Mind-Controlled Videogames Become Reality," *The Wall Street Journal,* May 29, 2012, pp. B1, B5; Benny Evangelista, "NeuroSky Expands Games with Your Mind," *San Francisco Chronicle,* April 1, 2013, pp. D1, D2; and Nick Bilton, "No Words, No Gestures, Just Your Brain as the Control Pad," *The New York Times,* April 29, 2013, pp. B1, B7.
34. David Pogue, "Out with the Real," *Scientific American,* February 2013, p. 29.
35. Lev Grossman, "Should the Virtual World Try to Look Like the Real One?" *Time,* June 3, 2013, pp. 50, 52.
36. Pogue, "Out with the Real."
37. Mike Snider and Chris Woodyard, "Wave a Hand, Turn on Radio or Make Call," *USA Today,* January 11, 2013, pp. 1B, 2B.
38. Joseph B. White, "A Car That Takes Your Pulse," *The Wall Street Journal,* November 28, 2012, pp. D1, D2.
39. Greg Bensinger, "A Computer for Your Car's Windshield," *The Wall Street Journal,* December 4, 2012, p. B7; and Matt Vella, "Rebooting the Dashboard."
40. Joan Lawy, "Cars Avoid Crashes by Talking to Each Other," *Reno Gazette-Journal,* June 17, 2012, p. 5F.
41. Joseph B. White, "Get Ready: Driverless Cars Should Go Mainstream by 2025," *The Wall Street Journal,* April 18, 2013, p. B1.
42. Jeff Bennett and Mike Ramsey, "Drivers Seek Help with Techie Cars," *The Wall Street Journal,* October 15, 2012, p. B8.
43. Ashlee Vance, "Google's Robot Cars Drive Motorists Nuts Despite Perfect Skills," *San Francisco Chronicle,* April 7, 2013, p. D6.
44. Claire Cain Miller and Matthew L. Wald, "Self-Driving Cars for Testing Are Supported by U.S.," *The New York Times,*

May 31, 2013, pp. B1, B4. See also Clifford Winston, "Paving the Way for Driverless Cars," *The Wall Street Journal,* July 18, 2012, p. A15; Dan Neil, "Who's Behind the Wheel? Nobody," *The Wall Street Journal,* September 24, 2012, pp. R1, R2; Dan Strumpf, "Liability Issues Create Potholes on the Road to Driverless Cars," *The Wall Street Journal,* January 27, 2013, pp. B1, B7; and Angela Greiling Keane, "Self-Driving Cars Get Map to U.S. Policy for Testing," *San Francisco Chronicle,* May 31, 2013, pp. C1, C5.

45. Janet Colvin, Nancy Tobler, and James A. Anderson, "Productivity and Multi-Screen Displays," *Rocky Mountain Communication Review,* Summer 2004, pp. 31–53.
46. James A. Anderson, University of Utah, quoted in "Multiple Monitor Computing Demonstrates Tangible Benefits for Corporate Workforce," NEC press release, October 6, 2003, *www.necus.com/necus/media/press_releases/template.cfm?DID=1947* (accessed June 4, 2013).
47. Farhad Manjoo, "Boss, I Need a Bigger Screen; for Work Efficiency, of Course," *The New York Times,* January 15, 2009, p. B9.
48. John Markoff, "Device from Israeli Start-Up Gives the Visually Impaired a Way to Read," *The New York Times,* June 4, 2013, p. A7.
49. Ashlee Vance, "Gadget Monitors Personal Environment," *San Francisco Chronicle,* April 22, 2013, p. D4.
50. Katy Steinmetz, "Dollars and Scents," *Time,* March 18, 2013, p. 58.
51. Daisuke Wakabayashi, "What's Next: Mirrors That Turn into Computers, Too," *The Wall Street Journal,* September 25, 2012, pp. B1, B4.
52. Elizabeth Lopatto, "Insects' Sight Modeled for Mini Cameras," *San Francisco Chronicle,* May 8, 2013, p. D3.
53. IDC, cited in Lohr, "Rise of Data from Sensors." See also *The Digital Universe in 2020,* IDC, December 2012, *www.emc.com/leadership/digital-universe/iview/index.htm* (accessed June 4, 2013).
54. Christopher Weaver, "Amputees Face New Reality," *The Wall Street Journal,* April 18, 2013, p. A7.
55. Edward C. Baig, "Will Glasses-Free Viewing Help 3-D Finally Take Off?" *USA Today,* January 13, 2013, p. 1B.
56. Paul Davidson, "More Goods Come from 3-D Printing," *USA Today,* July 11, 2012, pp. 1B, 2B; Andrew Winterbotham, "The Next Productivity Revolution," *The Bull,* October 24, 2012, p. 7; Carrie Kirby, "Boon to Entrepreneurs," *San Francisco Chronicle,* November 26, 2012, pp. D1, D2; and Elizabeth Royte, "The Printed World," *Smithsonian,* May 2013, pp. 50–57.
57. James R. Hagerty and Kate Linebaugh, "Next 3-D Frontier: Printed Plane Parts," *The Wall Street Journal,* June 14–15, 2012, pp. B1, B3; Davidson, 2012; Ashlee Vance, "3-D Design Surprise," *San Francisco Chronicle,* October 15, 2012, pp. D1, D4; John Markoff, "New Level of Micro Manufacturing," *The New York Times,* April 9, 2013, pp. D1, D7; and Clint Boulton, "Barbies, Auto Parts Hot Off the Press," *The Wall Street Journal,* June 6, 2013, pp. B1, B5.
58. "3-D Printers Can Make Parts for Weapons," *San Francisco Chronicle,* December 23, 2012, p. G3; Mark Hachman, "3D-Printed Guns: Your Questions Answered," *PC Magazine,* May 6, 2013, *www.pcmag.com/slideshow/story/311150/3d-printed-guns-your-questions-answered* (accessed June 4, 2013); and Henry Fountain, "Tools of Modern Gunmaking: Plastic and a 3-D Printer," *The New York Times,* January 30, 2013, pp. A12, A18.
59. Robert Lee Hotz, "Printing Evolves: An Inkjet for Living Tissue," *The Wall Street Journal,* September 18, 2012, pp. D1, D3; and Juro Osawa, "3-D Printing, Under the Knife," *The Wall Street Journal,* April 9, 2013, p. B5.
60. Liz Szabo, "Michigan Doctors Use a 3-D Printer to Custom-Design Baby's Implant," *USA Today,* May 28, 2013, p. 3D.
61. "3-D Printing Stem Cells," *The Week,* February 22, 2013, p. 21.
62. Christopher Mims, "The Audacious Plan to End Hunger with 3-D Printed Food," *Quartz,* May 21, 2013, *http://qz.com/86685/the-audacious-plan-to-end-hunger-with-3-d-printed-food* (accessed June 4, 2013).
63. Danielle Weatherbee, quoted in Steve Friess, "Laptop Design Can Be a Pain in the Posture," *USA Today,* April 13, 2005, p. 8D.
64. "Office Devices Awash in Bacteria," *San Francisco Chronicle,* June 7, 2012, p. A11.
65. Kim Komando, "Flu-Proof Your Tech Gadgets," *Reno Gazette-Journal,* October 21, 2012, p. 5F.
66. Tom Albin, quoted in Friess, "Laptop Design Can Be a Pain in the Posture."
67. Tamara James, quoted in Friess, "Laptop Design Can Be a Pain in the Posture."
68. Moshe Lewis, "How You Can Reduce RSI Risk," *San Francisco Chronicle,* August 22, 2012, pp. E1, E3.
69. Mark Saleh, "Carpal Tunnel Sufferers Need Prompt Treatment," *San Francisco Chronicle,* April 24, 2013, pp. C1, C3; and Ann Lukits, "Predicting Carpal Tunnel Syndrome," *The Wall Street Journal,* April 30, 2013, p. D4.
70. Leif Salford, quoted in Blaine Greteman, "Wireless Worries," *Time,* February 16, 2003, *www.time.com/time/magazine/article/0,9171,423487,00.html* (accessed June 4, 2013).
71. Siegal Sadetzki, Angela Chetrit, et al., "Cellular Phone Use and Risk of Benign and Malignant Parotid Gland Tumors—a Nationwide Case-Control Study," *American Journal of Epidemiology, 167* (4):, 457–467.
72. Nora Volkow, National Institutes of Health, quoted in Natalie Wolchover, "Cell Phone Radiation Spurs Brain Activity . . . But What Does It Mean?" *Live Science,* February 23, 2011, *www.livescience.com/33064-cell-phone-radiation-brain-activity.html* (accessed June 4, 2013).
73. Minouk Schoemaker, Anthony Swerdlow, et al., "Mobile Phone Use and Risk of Acoustic Neuroma: Results of the Interphone Case-Control Study in Five North European Countries," *British Journal of Cancer, 93* (7):, 842–848.
74. See Steve Lohr, "Taking a Stand for Office Ergonomics," *The New York Times,* December 2, 2012, p. BU-3; Amir Efrati, "Marching to a Vibrant Drummer," *The Wall Street Journal,* January 15, 2013, p. B5; Amy Schoenfeld, "The Posture Guru of Silicon Valley," *The New York Times,* May 12, 2013, p. BU-3; and Heidi Mitchell, "Burning Question: Why Sit Up Straight?" *The Wall Street Journal,* May 7, 2013, p. D2.
75. Survey by Ponemon Institute for Dell, reported in "How Workers Damage Laptops," *USA Today,* March 4, 2009, p. 1A.
76. Melinda Beck, "When Your Laptop Is a Big Pain in the Neck," *The Wall Street Journal,* December 16, 2008, p. D1.

Chapter 6

1. NPD Group, reported in *USA Today* and *The Week,* January 18, 2013, p. 16.
2. "What Does 'Digital' Mean in Regard to Electronics?" *Popular Science,* August 1997, pp. 91–94.
3. Charles Whealton of Delaware Technical & Community College; ms. review, April 2013.
4. Margaret Rouse, "Tree Network," *SearchNetworking,* September 2005, *http://searchnetworking.techtarget.com/definition/tree-network* (accessed June 13, 2013).
5. U.S. Census Bureau, cited in Neil Shah, "More Americans Working Remotely," *The Wall Street Journal,* March 6, 2013, pp. A3.
6. TeleworkResearchNetwork.com, reported in "At-Home Workers," *USA Today,* March 25, 2013, p. 1A.
7. Haya El Nasser, "Home Is Where the Job Is," *USA Today,* October 5, 2012, p. 1B.
8. Survey of 2,500 adults 18 and older by Richoh Americas/Harris Interactive, reported in "If Given a Choice, I'd Rather Work . . . ," *USA Today,* February 25, 2013, p. 1B.
9. Woman quoted in Claire Suddath, "Work-from-Home Truths, Half-Truths, and Myths," *Bloomberg Businessweek,* March 4–10, 2013, p. 75.
10. IDC study of 812 small and medium-sized businesses, reported in Rachel Emma Silverman, "Telecommuting Boosts Firms' Revenue Growth," *The Wall Street Journal,* April 17, 2013, p. B8.
11. David Wessel, "Out of the Office but Still on the Job," *The Wall Street Journal,* December 20, 2012, p. A4.
12. Eilene Zimmerman, "Working from Home, without the Sideshows," *The New York Times,* December 16, 2012, p. BU-8.
13. Sue Shellenbarger, " 'Working from Home' without Slacking Off," *The Wall Street Journal,* July 11, 2012, p. D3.
14. Elizabeth Weise, "Telecommuters to Yahoo: Boo," *USA Today,* February 26, 2013, p. 1A; and Lawrence Axil Comras, "Rounding Up the Yahoos," *San Francisco Chronicle,*

February 26, 2013, *www.triplepundit.com/2013/02/marissa-mayer-is-right* (accessed June 15, 2013).

15. Carolyn Said, "Work Is Where You Hang Your Coat," *San Francisco Chronicle,* July 18, 2005, p. E5.
16. Laura Petrecca, "Always Working," *USA Today,* March 7, 2013, pp. 1A, 2A.
17. Pew Research Center, cited in Petrecca, "Always Working."
18. Sue Shellenbarger, "More Work Goes 'Undercover,' " *The Wall Street Journal,* November 14, 2012, pp. D1, D5.
19. Aaron Smith, *Smartphone Ownership 2013 Update,* Pew Research Center, Internet & American Life Project, June 5, 2013, *www.pewinternet.org/~/media//Files/Reports/2013/PIP_Smartphone_adoption_2013.pdf* (accessed June 15, 2013).
20. Kathryn Zickuhr, *Tablet Ownership 2013,* Pew Research Center, Internet & American Life Project, June 10, 2013, *http://pewinternet.org/~/media//Files/Reports/2013/PIP_Tablet%20ownership%202013.pdf* (accessed June 15, 2013).
21. Joanna Brenner, *Pew Internet: Mobile,* Pew Research Center, Internet & American Life Project, June 6, 2013, *http://pewinternet.org/Commentary/2012/February/Pew-Internet-Mobile.aspx* (accessed June 15, 2013).
22. Akamai, cited in Eduardo Porter, "Yanking Broadband from Slow Lane," *The New York Times,* May 8, 2013, pp. B1, B9.
23. Richard Bennett, "No Country for Slow Broadband," *The New York Times,* June 16, 2013, p. BU-4.
24. Broadband for America, *Leading America into the Future: American Broadband,* June 10, 2013, *www.broadbandforamerica.com/blog/leading-america-future-american-broadband;* and David L. Cohen, "The Leader on Broadband," *Philly.com,* May 24, 2013, *http://articles.philly.com/2013-05-24/news/39478428_1_broadband-connectivity-mbps-access* (both accessed June 15, 2013).
25. Federal Communications Commission, Public Safety and Homeland Security Bureau, "9-1-1 Service," *www.fcc.gov/pshs/services/911-services* (accessed June 15, 2013).
26. Joseph Goldstein, "Police to Put GPS Devices in Pill Bottles to Stop Theft," *The New York Times,* January 16, 2013, p. A18.
27. Jack Healy, "Cash for Hay Driving Thieves to Move Bundles," *The New York Times,* January 10, 2013, pp. A11, A12.
28. Katharine Q. Seelye, "What Do Sharks Do in the Deep? Device May Tell," *The New York Times,* September 25, 2012, pp. A13, A15; and Zack Parisa, "Seeing the Forest for the Trees," *Bloomberg Businessweek,* July 9–July 15, 2012, p. 36.
29. Chris Woodyard, "Car Navigation Options Growing More Affordable," *USA Today,* October 10, 2012, p. 5B.
30. David Einstein, "BackTrack—When You Can't Find Parked Car," *San Francisco Chronicle,* July 30, 2012, p. D1.
31. Harris Interactive survey, reported in Jayne Clark, "GPS Has Steered Drivers Wrong," *USA Today,* June 21, 2013, p. 4D.
32. Tom Stienstra, "Sometimes, Maps Are Better Than GPS," *San Francisco Chronicle,* July 31, 2012, *www.sfgate.com/outdoors/article/Sometimes-maps-are-better-than-GPS-372575.php* (accessed June 16, 2013).
33. Randall Stross, "When GPS Confuses, You May Be to Blame," *The New York Times,* September 2, 2012, p. BU-3. See also Donna Leinwand, "Caution: Watch Where You're Going," *USA Today,* March 12, 2009, p. 3A.
34. Kevin Maney, "A Very Different Future Is Calling—on Billions of Cellphones," *USA Today,* July 27, 2005, p. 3B.
35. Mathew Ingram, "Mary Meeker: Mobile Internet Will Soon Overtake Fixed Internet," *Gigadom,* April 12, 2010, *http://gigaom.com/2010/04/12/mary-meeker-mobile-internet-will-soon-overtake-fixed-internet/* (accessed June 15, 2013).
36. International Telecommunications Union, Radiocommunication Sector, "ITU Global Standard for International Mobile Communications—'IMT Advanced,' " January 17, 2013, *www.itu.int/ITU-R/index.asp?category=information&rlink=imt-advanced&lang=en* (June 15, 2013).
37. Lilly Vitorovich, "Europe Plays Catch-Up in 4G Race," *The Wall Street Journal,* June 4, 2013, p. B4.
38. PricewaterhouseCoopers, *Entertainment & Media Outlook 2013–2017,* reported in Mike Snider, "Mobile Users Cast a Wider Internet," *USA Today,* June 5, 2013, p. 1B.
39. Kim Komando, "Are Latest Routers Worth Buying?" *Reno Gazette-Journal,* June 9, 2013, p. 5F.
40. Douglas Louie, quoted in Emily Maltby, "Many Gadgets, Many Risks," *The Wall Street Journal,* November 12, 2012, p. R6.
41. "Enhancing Information and Data Security: A Never Ending Quest," *Knowledge@SMU,* June 4, 2008, *http://smu.edu.sg/perspectives/2008/06/04/enhancing-information-and-data-security-never-ending-quest#.UcC2hMbn9aQ* (accessed June 17, 2013).
42. Mike McConnell, quoted in Ben Worthen, "Watching and Waiting," *The Wall Street Journal,* April 2, 2012, p. R7.
43. "The Trolls of the Internet," *The Week,* June 1, 2012, p. 11.
44. Study by Krux Digital Inc., reported in Jennifer Valentino-DeVries, "Data Tracking Slows a Bit," *The Wall Street Journal,* May 7, 2013, p. B4.
45. Valentino-DeVries, "Data Tracking Slows a Bit."
46. Evelyn M. Rusli, "Buy Signal: Facebook Widens Data Targeting," *The Wall Street Journal,* April 10, 2013, p. B4.
47. Spencer E. Ante, "Online Ads Can Now Follow You Home," *The Wall Street Journal,* April 30, 2013, p. B4.
48. Natasha Singer, "When Your Data Wonders to Places You've Never Been," *The New York Times,* April 28, 2013, p. BU-3.
49. Chris Woodyard and Jayne O'Donnell, "Watch That Lead Foot: Your Car Is Watching," *USA Today,* March 25, 2013, pp. 1B, 2B.
50. Ben Quinn, "Anonymous-Linked Groups Publish EDL Supporters' Personal Information," *guardian.co.uk,* May 28, 2013, *www.guardian.co.uk/technology/2013/may/28/anonymous-edl-supporters-information* (accessed June 17, 2013). See also Peter Ludlow, "Hacktivists as Gadflies," *The New York Times,* April 24, 2013, p. SR-5.
51. Federal Bureau of Investigation, quoted in TechTarget Security Media, "Glossary," *http://searchsecurity.techtarget.com/gDefinition/0,294236,sid14_gci771061,00.html* (accessed June 17, 2013).
52. Christopher Drew and John Markoff, "Contractors Vie for Plum Work, Hacking for U.S.," *The New York Times,* May 31, 2009, pp. News-1, News-4; Sarah Frier, "Consultants Hack Servers to Anticipate Data Breaches," *San Francisco Chronicle,* April 5, 2012, p. D2; Anita Bruzzese, "To Snuff Out a Hacker, Think Like One," *Reno Gazette-Journal,* September 13, 2012, p. 5A; Byron Acohido, "To Beat a Hacker, You'd Better Be Sneaky," *USA Today,* February 28, 2013, pp. 1B, 2B; and Geoffrey A. Fowler, "You Won't Believe How Adorable This Kitty Is! Click for More!" *The Wall Street Journal,* March 27, 2013, pp. A1, A14.
53. Katie Moussouris, senior security strategist at Microsoft Security Response Center, quoted in Byron Acohido, "Analysis: Why Is Microsoft Willing to Pay Bug Bounties?" *USA Today,* June 21, 2013, p. 6B.
54. Dinei Florencio and Cormac Herley, "The Cybercrime Wave That Wasn't," *The New York Times,* April 15, 2012, p. SR-5.
55. Jordan Robertson, "Citibank ATM Breach Reveals Password Security Problems," *Reno Gazette-Journal,* July 2, 2008, p. 6A.
56. Neal J. Riley, "Transit Riders Distracted by Gadgets Become Easy Targets as Thefts Surge, " *San Francisco Chronicle,* February 8, 2013, pp. A1, A12.
57. "Mobile Devices and Cybercrime: Is Your Phone the Weakest Link?" *Knowledge@Wharton,* June 5, 2013, *http://knowledge.wharton.upenn.edu/article.cfm?articleid=3273* (accessed June 21, 2013).
58. Brian X. Chen and Malia Wollan, "Cellphone Thefts Grow, but the Industry Looks the Other Way," *The New York Times,* May 2, 2013, pp. A1, A3; Malia Wollan, "Outsmarting Smartphone Thieves," *The New York Times,* May 9, 2013, p. B9; Kevin Fagan, "S.F., N.Y. Press Phone Makers to Battle Thefts," *San Francisco Chronicle,* June 5, 2013, pp. D1, D2; Jaxon Van Derbeken, "Apple to Add 'Kill Switches' to Help Combat iPhone Theft," *San Francisco Chronicle,* June 11, 2013, pp. A1, A6; and Emily Gogolak, "Coalition Will Seek to Curb the Theft of Smartphones," *The New York Times,* June 14, 2013, p. B2.
59. Edward C. Baig, "Phone Stolen? Lookout Can Snap a Mug Shot of Thief," *USA Today,* January 23, 2013, p. 3B.

60. Patricia Cohen, "A Picasso Online for Just $450? Yes, It Is a Steal," *The New York Times,* September 3, 2012, pp. A1, A3.
61. Carolyn Said, "Brazen Schemes Proliferate," *San Francisco Chronicle,* October 10, 2012, pp. E1, E6.
62. Susan Tompor, "Used Car Scams Easier to Pull Off Online," *USA Today,* August 16, 2012, p. 5B.
63. Linda A. Johnson, "FDA: Online Pharmacies Could Pose Risks," *Reno Gazette-Journal,* September 30, 2012, p. 4F; and Christopher Weaver and Jeanne Whalen, "Crackdown on Web Drugs," *The Wall Street Journal,* October 5, 2012, pp. B1, B2.
64. Benny Evangelista, "Counterfeit Goods Proliferate Online," *San Francisco Chronicle,* July 13, 2012, pp. D1, D4.
65. McAfee/NCSA Cyber Security Survey, Newsworthy Analysis, October 2007, *http://download.mcafee.com/products/manuals/en-us/McAfeeNCSA_Analysis09-25-07.pdf?cid=36665* (accessed June 21, 2013).
66. Graham Cluley, "German Ministry Replaced Brand New PCs Infected with Conficker Worm, Rather Than Disinfect Them," *NakedSecurity,* May 1, 2013, *http://nakedsecurity.sophos.com/2013/05/01/german-replaced-pcs-conficker* (accessed June 21, 2013).
67. Byron Acohido and Jon Swartz, "Are Hackers Using Your PC to Spew Spam and Steal?" *USA Today,* September 8, 2004, pp. 1B, 4B.
68. Ben Sisario, "Concert Industry Struggles with 'Bots' That Siphon Off Tickets," *The New York Times,* May 27, 2013, pp. B1, B4.
69. Larry Magid, quoted in Kim Painter, "Teens Using Social Media Show Savvy about Privacy Even as They Share More," *USA Today,* May 22, 2013, p. 4D. The article reports on a Pew Research Center survey about teenagers and privacy.
70. Anton Troianovski, "Phone Firms Sell Data on Customers," *The Wall Street Journal,* May 22, 2013, pp. B1, B2.
71. Somini Sengupta, "Letting Down Our Guard," *The New York Times,* March 31, 2013, pp. SR-1, SR-6.
72. Alessandro Acquisti, quoted in Sengupta, "Letting Down Our Guard."
73. Sengupta, "Letting Down Our Guard."
74. Deborah Yao, "Web-Monitoring Software Gathers Data from Kids' Private Chats—Then Sells It," *San Francisco Chronicle,* September 8, 2009, p. D2.
75. Jessica E. Vascellaro and Emily Steel, "Something New Gains with Something Borrowed," *The Wall Street Journal,* June 5, 2009, p. B6; and Miguel Helft, "Google to Offer Ads Based on Interests, with Privacy Rights," *The New York Times,* March 11, 2009, p. B3.
76. Saul Hansell, "Agency Skeptical of Internet Privacy Policies," *The New York Times,* February 13, 2009, p. B5.
77. Kim Komando, "The State of Your Digital Rights," *Reno Gazette-Journal,* July 20, 2012, p. 5F.
78. David Jackson, Susan Davis, and Kevin Johnson, "Obama's Spy Plan Includes Internet," *USA Today,* June 7–9, 2013, pp. 1A, 2A.
79. Evan Perez and Siobhan Gorman, "Phones Leave a Telltale Trail," *The Wall Street Journal,* June 15–16, 2013, pp. A1, A4.
80. Bob Sullivan, "ID Theft on the Rise Again: 12.6 Million Victims in 2012, Study Shows," *NBC News Technology, www.nbcnews.com/technology/id-theft-rise-again-12-6-million-victims-2012-study-1C8448021* (accessed July 1, 2013).
81. "Working to Resolve Identity Theft," Identity Theft Resource Center, *www.idtheftcenter.org/artman2/publish/m_facts/Facts_and_Statistics.shtml* (accessed June 21, 2013).
82. Kathryn Rambo, quoted in Ramon G. McLeod, "New Thieves Prey on Your Very Name," *San Francisco Chronicle,* April 7, 1997, pp. A1, A6.
83. Rambo, quoted in T. Trent Gegax, "Stick 'Em Up? Not Anymore; Now It's Crime by Keyboard," *Newsweek*, July 21, 1997, p. 14.
84. Blurb accompanying article by Ross Douthat, "Your Smartphone Is Watching You," *The New York Times,* June 9, 2013, p. SR-11.
85. Natasha Singer, "Ways to Make Your Online Tracks Harder to Follow," *The New York Times,* June 20, 2013, p. F4.
86. Kim Komando, "How to Disappear from the Internet," *Reno Gazette-Journal,* January 27, 2013, p. 6E; Kim Komando, "How to Protect Privacy on Google," *Reno Gazette-Journal,* May 19, 2013, p. 6D; Caleb Garling, "Not Leaving Digital Tracks a Challenge," *San Francisco Chronicle,* June 12, 2013, pp. D1, D5; and Singer, "Ways to Make Your Online Tracks Harder to Follow."
87. Princeton professor Edward W. Felten, quoted in Singer, "Ways to Make Your Online Tracks Harder to Follow."
88. Brian X. Chen, "How to Shield Yourself from Smartphone Snoops," *The New York Times,* April 4, 2013, p. B10; Garling, "Not Leaving Digital Tracks a Challenge"; and Singer, "Ways to Make Your Online Tracks Harder to Follow."
89. Garling, "Not Leaving Digital Tracks a Challenge."

Chapter 7

1. Scott Snyder, senior fellow at Wharton's Mack Institute for Innovation Management and president of Mobiquity, quoted in "The New Model for Innovation Is Social—and Mobile: But Are Companies Ready?" *Knowledge@Wharton*, June 19, 2013, *http://knowledge.wharton.upenn.edu/article.cfm?articleid=3286* (accessed June 25, 2013).
2. Jerry Yang and David Filo, cited in Cliff Edwards, "The Web's Future Is You," *BusinessWeek,* April 25, 2005, p. 18.
3. Edwards, "The Web's Future Is You."
4. Nathan Chandler, "Top 5 Web Mashups," *HowStuffWorks, http://science.howstuffworks.com/innovation/repurposed-inventions/5-web-mashups.htm* (accessed June 26, 2013).
5. Carlos Carvajal, "The Personalization Revolution," *Digiday:Data,* April 13, 2011, *www.digiday.com/platforms/the-personalization-revolution* (accessed June 26, 2013).
6. Barry Schwartz, *The Paradox of Choice: Why More Is Less* (New York: HarperCollins, 2005). See also Barry Schwartz, "Choice Overload Burdens Daily Modern Life," *USA Today,* January 5, 2004, p. 13A.
7. Schwartz, *The Paradox of Choice.*
8. Barry Schwartz, quoted in Alina Tugend, "Too Many Choices: A Problem That Can Paralyze," *The New York Times,* February 26, 2010, *www.nytimes.com/2010/02/27/your-money/27shortcuts.html* (accessed June 25, 2013).
9. Benjamin Scheibehenne, quoted in Tugend, "Too Many Choices."
10. Kaila Colbin, "The Danger of Personalization," *Online Spin,* March 11, 2011, *www.mediapost.com/publications/?fa=Articles.showArticle&art_aid=146543* (accessed June 25, 2013).
11. Adam Steinfield, "Why Personalization Is Dangerous for the Media," *Suite101,* March 25, 2013, *http://suite101.com/article/why-personalization-is-dangerous-for-the-media-a362728* (accessed June 26, 2013).
12. Steve Lohr, "How Much Is Too Much?" *The New York Times,* May 4, 2005, pp. E1, E9.
13. Consumer Reports, *Consumer Reports Electronics Buying Guide,* June 2013 (Yonkers, NY: Consumer Reports, 2013), pp. 100–105.
14. Peter Svensson, Associated Press, "Smartphones Overtake 'Dumb' Phones Worldwide," *abcnews.go.com*, April 26, 2013, *http://bigstory.ap.org/article/smartphones-overtake-dumb-phones-worldwide* (accessed June 28, 2013).
15. Kim Komando, "Seven Solid Options for Smartphones," *Reno Gazette-Journal,* March 31, 2013, p. 5F.
16. Consumer Reports, *Consumer Reports Electronics Buying Guide,* p. 104.
17. James Sullivan, "Time Waits for Everyone, Now That We've All Got Camera Phones," *San Francisco Chronicle,* May 20, 2004, p. E2.
18. Survey by Frank N. Magid Associates, reported in Mike Snider, "More Tablets Find a Home in U.S. Homes," *USA Today,* June 10, 2013, p. 2B.
19. Forecast from IDC, reported in Brett Molina and Jon Swartz, "Tablets on Pace to Be King by 2015," *USA Today,* May 29, 2013, p. 1B.
20. Consumer Reports, *Consumer Reports Electronics Buying Guide,* p. 77.
21. "Factors in Choosing a Windows Tablet," *The New York Times,* May 30, 2013, p. B11.
22. Edward C. Baig, "Nexus 7 Sets the Bar for Budget Tablets," *USA Today,* July 5, 2012, p. 3B; Casey Newton, "Worthy iPad Rival," *San Francisco Chronicle,* July 5, 2012, pp. E1, E4; David Pogue, "A Tablet That Doubles as a Desktop or Vice Versa,"

The New York Times, June 13, 2013, pp. B1, B11; and "First Wave of Tabletop All-in-One PCs," *San Francisco Chronicle,* June 17, 2013, p. D2.
23. "Fastest Android Tablets for Gamers," *San Francisco Chronicle,* May 6, 2013, p. D2.
24. Warren Buckleitner, "A Trove of Tablets for Young Hands," *The New York Times,* December 13, 2013, p. B7.
25. Edward C. Baig, "Sony Slate Makes a Splash," *USA Today,* June 5, 2013, p. 2B.
26. Katherine Boehret, "A Tablet Good for Living Room, Bag and Water," *The Wall Street Journal,* June 5, 2013, p. D3.
27. David Pogue, "Newly Enlightened E-Readers," *The New York Times,* October 4, 2012, pp. B1, B7; "E-Readers," *Wired,* January 2013, pp. 48–49; and Consumer Reports, *Consumer Reports Electronics Buying Guide,* pp. 77–79.
28. Consumer Reports, *Consumer Reports Electronics Buying Guide,* p. 79.
29. Dennis K. Berman, "Technology Has Us So Plugged into Data, We Have Turned Off," *The Wall Street Journal,* November 10, 2003, p. B1; and Olivia Barker, "Got That Virtual Glow?" *USA Today,* August 3, 2009, p. 1D.
30. Roger Brown, "Multitasking Gets You There Later," *InfoQ,* June 29, 2010, *www.infoq.com/articles/multitasking-problems* (accessed July 2, 2013).
31. Consumer Reports, *Consumer Reports Electronics Buying Guide,* p. 77.
32. Nicholson Baker, "A New Page," *The New Yorker,* August 3, 2009, pp. 24–30.
33. "Technological Evolution Stirs a Publishing Revolution," *Knowledge@Wharton,* August 5, 2009, *http://knowledge.wharton.upenn.edu/article.cfm?articleid=2307* (accessed July 1, 2013).
34. Michael Bull, quoted in Benny Evangelista, "The iPod Generation," *San Francisco Chronicle,* December 27, 2004, pp. E1, E6.
35. Consumer Reports, *Consumer Reports Electronics Buying Guide,* p. 109.
36. Brian X. Chen, "From Apple, an Overhaul for Mobile and the Mac," *The New York Times,* June 11, 2013, pp. B1, B6.
37. "Current and Future Options for Streaming Music," *The Wall Street Journal,* June 11, 2013, p. B5.
38. Jefferson Graham, "iTune Store Turns 10 in Cloud Shift," *USA Today,* April 25, 2013, p. 5B.
39. Kim Komando, "How to Transition with Video Services," *Reno Gazette-Journal,* May 26, 2013, p. 6F.
40. Study by Cory Portnuff, Colorado University, reported in Alice Park, "iPod Safety: Preventing Hearing Loss in Teens," *Time,* February 21, 2009, *www.time.com/time/health/article/0,8599,1881130,00.html* (accessed July 2, 2013).
41. Elizabeth Quinn,"iPods and Hearing Loss," *About.com, http://sportsmedicine.about.com/od/tipsandtricks/a/iPod_safety.htm* (accessed July 2, 2013).
42. Jocasta Williams and Michael Fardon, "Perpetual Connectivity: Lecture Recordings and Portable Media Players," *Proceedings ascilite Singapore 2007, www.ascilite.org.au/conferences/singapore07/procs/williams-jo.pdf* (accessed July 2, 2013).
43. Todd Wallack, "Torrent of Images Is Leaving Film in the Dust," *San Francisco Chronicle,* May 23, 2005, pp. A1, A5.
44. David Einstein, "For Digital Cameras, More Megapixels May Not Mean Sharper Shots," *San Francisco Chronicle,* August 4, 2008, p. D3. See also Russ Juskalian, "Pixels Are Like Cupcakes; Let Me Explain," *The New York Times,* November 13, 2008, p. B6; and David Einstein, "Cameras—Sensor Size Does Matter," *San Francisco Chronicle,* June 8, 2009, pp. C1, C2.
45. "Optical vs. Digital Zoom," *Photoxels, www.photoxels.com/digital-photography-tutorials/optical-digital-zoom* (accessed July 3, 2013).
46. Consumer Reports, *Consumer Reports Electronics Buying Guide,* p. 87.
47. Ashlee Vance, "Shutterfly's Improbably Long Lifespan," *Bloomberg Businessweek,* January 7–13, 2013, pp. 33–34.
48. Hadley Malcolm, "Walgreens Teams with App Developers on Photo Printing," *USA Today,* July 11, 2012, p. 5B.
49. "Evolution of Photos Creating Effects on Society," *Seek First, www.seekfirst.com/node/57* (accessed July 3, 2013).
50. Maria Puente, "Memories Gone in a Snap," *USA Today,* January 21, 2005, p. 1D.
51. Craig Smith, ""By the Numbers: 32 Amazing Facebook Stats," *Digital Marketing Ramblings,* June 27, 2013, *http://expandedramblings.com/index.php/by-the-numbers-17-amazing-facebook-stats* (accessed July 3, 2013).
52. comScore, *The State of Social Media,* February 2012, slide 31, *www.slideshare.net/IFslideshares/the-state-of-social-media-2012* (accessed July 3, 2013).
53. H. T. Chou and N. Edge, " 'They Are Happier and Having Better Lives Than I Am': The Impact of Using Facebook on Perceptions of Others' Lives," *Cyberpsychology Behavior and Social Networking,* February 2012, pp. 117–121, *www.ncbi.nlm.nih.gov/pubmed/22165917* (accessed July 3, 2013).
54. Katrina Trinko, "Awash in Kodak Moments," *USA Today,* July 11, 2012, p. 9A.
55. Leanne Italie, "The Instagram Effect: Selfies Go Mainstream," *San Jose Mercury News,* June 27, 2013, *www.mercurynews.com/business/ci_23553123/instagram-effect-selfies-go-mainstream* (accessed July 3, 2013).
56. Liat Kornowski, "Celebrity Selfies: Everyone Does It, but Who Does It Best?" *Huffington Post,* June 22, 2013, *www.huffingtonpost.com/2013/06/12/celebrity-selfies-photos_n_3430423.html* (accessed July 3, 2013).
57. Kate Losse, "The Return of the Selfie," *The New Yorker,* June 5, 2013, *www.newyorker.com/online/blogs/elements/2013/06/the-return-of-the-selfie.html* (accessed July 3, 2013).
58. Trinko, "Awash in Kodak Moments."
59. Arbitron, "Radio Reaches Nearly 242.5 Million People Each Week According to the June 2013 RADAR Report," *Arbitron Newsroom,* June 12, 2013, *http://arbitron.mediaroom.com/index.php?s=43&item=885* (accessed July 3, 2013).
60. Jefferson Graham, "Slacker's No Slacker: Reboot Draws Listeners," *USA Today,* May 9, 2013, p. 5B.
61. Pandora, "About Pandora," *www.pandora.com/corporate* (accessed July 5, 2013).
62. Copyright Royalty Board, U.S. Congress, reported in "The Bottom Line," *The Week,* July 5–12, 2013, p. 36.
63. Ben Sisario, "Pandora Faces Rivals for Ears and Ads," *The New York Times,* June 21, 2012, p. B5; and Kit Eaton, "The Soundtrack to Your Life, with a Stream of Discoveries," *The New York Times,* December 27, 2012, p. B5.
64. Jefferson Graham, "Twitter #Music Waiting to Trend," *USA Today,* June 20, 2013, pp. 1B, 2B.
65. Jefferson Graham, "Tinkering in Garage with Technology Opens Doors," *USA Today,* June 19, 2013, p. 5B.
66. Kevin Sintumuang, "A Year without Cable," *The Wall Street Journal,* December 15–16, 2012, pp. D1, D2.
67. Nancy Trejos, "Hotels Upgrade to More Interactive TVs," *USA Today,* July 2, 2013, p. 4B.
68. Kevin J. O'Brien, "Mobile TV Spreading in Europe and to the U.S.," *The New York Times,* May 5, 2008, p. C2.
69. Steven Levy, "Television Reloaded," *Newsweek,* May 30, 2005, p. 50.
70. Statistics from market research firm NPD Group, reported in Brett Molina and Mike Snider, "Feeding Hunger for Games," *USA Today,* January 28, 2013, pp. 1B, 2B.
71. Molina and Snider, "Feeding Hunger for Games." See also Mike Snider, "Fewer Americans Play Video Games," *USA Today,* September 6, 2012, p. 1B; Robert Levine, "Console Makers Expect to Coexist with Market for Mobile Downloads," *San Francisco Chronicle,* December 16, 2012, p. F3; and Nick Wingfield, "Next Xbox Will Face New Array of Rivals," *The New York Times,* May 22, 2013, pp. B1, B8.
72. Cliff Edwards, "Casino-Style Gambling Likely on Smartphones," *San Francisco Chronicle,* December 9, 2012, p. F3.
73. Mike Snider, "Women Display Clout in Mobile Video Games," *USA Today,* October 2, 2012, p. 1B.
74. Dina Bass and Ashlee Vance, with Cliff Edwards, "There Can Be Only One," *Bloomberg Businessweek,* May 27–June 2, 2013, pp. 44–46.
75. John Engages, chief technology officer at Rackspace, quoted in Bruce Horowitz, "Xbox to Serve Gamers a Slice of Heaven," *USA Today,* April 23, 2013, p. 1B.
76. Bass and Vance, with Edwards, "There Can Be Only One."
77. Ian Sherr and Daisuke Wakabayashi, "Xbox One to Launch at $499," *The Wall Street Journal,* June 11, 2013, p. B8.

78. Benny Evangelista, "Game on as Playstation 4, Xbox One Battle," *San Francisco Chronicle,* June 15, 2013, pp. D1, D3.
79. Brian X. Chen and David Streitfeld, "With PlayStation 4, Sony Hopes to Regain Past Glory," *The New York Times,* February 21, 2013, pp. B1, B4.
80. Barbara Ortutay, "Console Makers Sport Latest Gaming Products," *Reno Gazette-Journal,* June 2, 2013, p. D.
81. Daisuke Wakabayashi, "Sony Makes a Shift to Streaming Games," *The Wall Street Journal,* July 3, 2012, p. B3.
82. "A Game Controller, and More," *The New York Times,* June 13, 2013, p. B10.
83. Daisuke Wakabayashi, "Nintendo Resists the Lure of Mobile Games," *The Wall Street Journal,* June 12, 2013, p. B6.
84. Diana Oblinger, "Boomers, Gen-Xers, and Millennials: Understanding the New Students," *EDUCAUSE Review,* July/August 2003, pp. 37–47, *http://wiu.edu/Mobile-Computing/pdf/erm0342.pdf* (accessed July 6, 2013).
85. Marc Prensky, "Digital Natives, Digital Immigrants," from *On the Horizon,* October 2001, © 2001 Marc Prensky, *www.marcprensky.com/writing/prensky%20-%20digital%20natives,%20digital%20immigrants%20-%20part1.pdf* (accessed July 6, 2013).
86. Brian Shane, "Smart Devices Make for Smart Kids," *USA Today,* January 1, 2013, p. 1B.
87. Oblinger, "Boomers, Gen-Xers, and Millennials," 2003, p. 38. See also Harry Hurt III, "A Generation with More Than Hand-Eye Coordination," *The New York Times,* December 21, 2008, Business section, p. 5.
88. Annie Murphy Paul, "You'll Never Learn!" *Slate.com,* May 3, 2013, *www.slate.com/articles/health_and_science/science/2013/05/multitasking_while_studying_divided_attention_and_technological_gadgets.html* (accessed August 30, 2013).
89. "Multitasking College Students Keep Multiple Screens on Hand," *eMarketer,* June 25, 2013, *www.emarketer.com/Article/Multitasking-College-Students-Keep-Multiple-Screens-on-Hand/1009998* (accessed September 1, 2013).
90. Maryellen Weimer, "Students Think They Can Multitask. Here's Proof They Can't," *Faculty Focus,* September 12, 2012, *www.facultyfocus.com/articles/teaching-professor-blog/multitasking-confronting-students-with-the-facts* (accessed September 1, 2013).
91. Marc Prensky, "What Kids Learn That's POSITIVE from Playing Videogames," © 2002 Marc Presnsky, *www.marcprensky.com/writing/prensky%20-%20what%20kids%20learn%20thats%20positive%20from%20playing%20video%20games.pdf* (accessed July 6, 2013).
92. Oblinger, "Boomers, Gen-Xers, and Millennials," 2003, p. 40, citing Jason Frand, "The Information Age Mindset: Changes in Students and Implications for Higher Education," *EDUCAUSE Review,* September–October 2000, pp. 15–24.
93. Kevin J. Delaney, "Teaching Tools," *The Wall Street Journal,* January 17, 2005, pp. R4, R5. See also Qingya Wang, Wei Chen, and Yu Liang, "The Effects of Social Media on College Students," *MBA Student Scholarship,* November 1, 2011, Johnson & Wales University, *http://scholarsarchive.jwu.edu/cgi/viewcontent.cgi?article=1004&context=mba_student* (accessed September 1, 2013).
94. Diana G. Oblinger, "The Next Generation of Educational Engagement," *Journal of Interactive Media in Education,* May 21, 2004, pp. 1–18.
95. Wendy Rickard and Diana Oblinger, *The Next-Generation Student,* June 17, 2003, p. 4. See also *Millennials: Generation Next,* Pew Research Center, February 2010, *www.pewsocialtrends.org/files/2010/10/millennials-confident-connected-open-to-change.pdf* (accessed September 1, 2013).

Chapter 8

1. Mark Hurd, interviewed by Maria Bartiromo, "Oracle's Hurd: 'Big Data' Is Next Big Thing," *USA Today,* October 15, 2012, p. 4B.
2. Data from consulting firm IDC, reported in Patrick Tucker, "Has Big Data Made Anonymity Impossible?" *MIT Technology Review,* May 7, 2013, *www.technologyreview.com/news/514351/has-big-data-made-anonymity-impossible* (accessed July 12, 2013). See also BM Software, "IBM Big Data: Bringing Big Data to the Enterprise," *www.950.ibm.com/events/wwe/grp/grp030.nsf/v17_additional?openform&seminar=7AFBY4ES&locale=en_ZZ* (accessed July 12, 2013).
3. James Glanz, "Data Barns in a Farm Town, Gobbling Power and Flexing Muscle," *The New York Times,* September 24, 2012, pp. A1, A16–A17.
4. Noam Cohen, "Wikipedia," *The New York Times,* May 14, 2011, *http://topics.nytimes.com/top/news/business/companies/wikipedia/index.html* (accessed July 11, 2013).
5. Peggy Williams, "Database Dangers," *Quill,* July–August 1994, pp. 37–38.
6. Kevin Pho, "Wikipedia Isn't Really the Patient's Friend," *USA Today,* July 15, 2009, p. 11A.
7. Martin Vaughan, "IRS to Mine Payment Data on Mortgages," *The Wall Street Journal,* September 1, 2009, p. A5.
8. Eric Lichtblau, "Study of Data Mining for Terrorists Is Urged," *The New York Times,* October 8, 2008, p. A20.
9. Chen-Yueh Chen and Yi-Hsiu Lin, "A New Market Research Approach in Sport-Data Mining," *The Sport Journal, www.thesportjournal.org/article/new-market-research-approach-sport-data-mining* (accessed July 15, 2013).
10. Alex Wright, "Mining the Web for Feelings, Not Facts," *The New York Times,* August 24, 2009, pp. B1, B7.
11. Michael J. Way, "Galaxy Zoo Morphology Improves Photometric Redshifts in the Sloan Digital Sky Survey," *Data Mining for Astronomy,* May 5, 2011, *http://astrodatamining.net* (accessed July 15, 2013).
12. Steve Lohr, "Amid the Flood, a Catchphrase Is Born," *The New York Times,* August 12, 2012, p. BU-3.
13. Steve Lohr, "Sizing Up Big Data," *The New York Times,* June 20, 2013, pp. F1, F10.
14. Ibid., p. F10.
15. David Brooks, "What Data Can't Do," *The New York Times,* February 19, 2013, p. A23.
16. Jon Kleinberg, Cornell University computer scientist, and Rod A. Smith, IBM technical fellow and vice president for emerging Internet technologies, both quoted in Lohr, "Amid the Flood."
17. Aki Ito, "Data Science Job Bonanza," *San Francisco Chronicle,* June 17, 2013, pp. D1, D4.
18. Karen E. Klein, "Big Data Helping Small Business to Better Engage," *San Francisco Chronicle,* April 4, 2013, p. C4.
19. Amy O'Leary, "In New Tools to Combat Epidemics, the Key Is Context," *The New York Times,* June 20, 2013, p. F1.
20. John Tozzi, "A Global Database for Disease Research," *Bloomberg Businessweek,* March 25–March 31, 2013, p. 35.
21. Erin Allday, "100,000 Saliva Samples Feed High Hopes of Biobank," *San Francisco Chronicle,* November 21, 2013, pp. D1, D4.
22. Anna Wilde Mathews, "Researchers Mine Data from Clinic, Big Insurer," *The Wall Street Journal,* January 15, 2013, p. B3.
23. Joel Schectman, "A Smarter Way to Send Junk Mail," *The Wall Street Journal,* January 24, 2013, p. B11. See also Tanzina Vega, "New Ways Marketers Are Manipulating Data to Influence You," *The New York Times,* June 20, 2013, p. F2.
24. David Carr, "Giving Viewers What They Want," *The New York Times,* February 25, 2013, pp. B1, B8.
25. Jim Hurst, "Overview and Tutorial on Artificial Intelligence Systems," SANS Software Security, *http://software-security.sans.org/resources/paper/cissp/overview-tutorial-artificial-intelligence-systems* (accessed July 16, 2013).
26. Ibid.
27. Ibid.
28. Robert Benfer Jr., Louanna Furbee, and Edward Brent Jr., quoted in Steve Weinberg, "Steve's Brain," *Columbia Journal Review,* February 1991, pp. 50–52.
29. Norman Merchant, "Snowplow Simulator Offers Rare Chance to Practice," *Reno Gazette-Journal,* December 5, 2012, p. 5C.
30. Karen Ann Cullotta, "Updates to Drivers' Education Reflect New Dangers on the Road," *The New York Times,* June 29, 2013, p. A10.
31. Barry Schiff, "Airline Insider Clarifies What Goes into Pilot Training," *USA Today,* July 11, 2013, p. 9A.
32. "Virtual Reality Lab Focuses on Conservation," *Science Daily,* April 11, 2011, *www.sciencedaily.com/releases/2011/04/110408163908.htm* (accessed July 18, 2013).
33. Robotee.com, "All Types of Robots: What Are Types of Robots and Robot Types?"

ROBOT Developer Center, *www.robotee.com/index.php/types-of-robots* (accessed July 18, 2013).

34. Robert Langreth, "Do Robot Surgeons Do No Harm?" *Bloomberg Businessweek,* March 21, 2013, pp. 17–18; Scott Martin, "Paging R2-D2 to the ER," *USA Today,* May 24, 2013, pp. 1B, 2B; and Kristen V. Brown, "Robot Opens Up Surgical Options," *San Francisco Chronicle,* July 3, 2013, pp. E1, E4.
35. Jeanne B. Pinder, "Fuzzy Thinking Has Merits When It Comes to Elevators," *The New York Times,* September 22, 1993, pp. C1, C7; and Tim Catts, "Express Elevators to the Heavens," *Bloomberg Businessweek,* February 4–10, 2013, pp. 35–36.
36. Brian Christian, "Rise of the Chatbots," *Smithsonian,* July–August 2012, p. 14.
37. Judith Gunther, "An Encounter with AI," *Popular Science,* June 1994, p. 90.
38. Christian, "Rise of the Chatbots."
39. Vernor Vinge, "The Coming Technological Singularity," *Vision-21: Interdisciplinary Science & Engineering in the Era of Cyberspace,* Proceedings of Symposium Held at NASA Lewis Research Center, *NASA Conference Publication CP-10129,* March 30–31, 1993, *http://rohan.sdsu.du/faculty/vinge/misc/singularity.html* (accessed July 17, 2013).
40. John Markoff, "The Coming Superbrain," *The New York Times,* May 24, 2009, Week in Review, pp. 1, 4.
41. Brian E. Coggins, "Human vs. Machine: Which Brain Is Ahead?" letter, *The New York Times,* July 30, 2009, p. A24.
42. William A. Wallace, *Ethics in Modeling* (New York: Elsevier Science, 1994).
43. John Markoff, "Ay Robot! Scientists Worry Machines May Outsmart Man," *The New York Times,* July 26, 2009, pp. 1, 4.
44. Portions of this material were adapted from Angelo Kinicki and Brian K. Williams, *Management: A Practical Introduction,* 6th ed. (New York: McGraw-Hill/Irwin, 2013), pp. 108–109.
45. Fred Levy, quoted in D. Wessel, "The Future of Jobs: New Ones Arise, Wage Gap Widens," *The Wall Street Journal,* April 2, 2004, pp. A1, A5.
46. Andrew McAfee, quoted in Bernard Connor and Paul Wiseman, "AP Impact: Recession, Tech Kill Middle-Class Jobs," *AP The Big Story,* January 23, 2013, *http://bigstory.ap.org/article/ap-impact-recession-tech-kill-middle-class-jobs* (accessed July 17, 2013). See also James Temple, "How Rise of Robots Will Affect Workers in Future," *San Francisco Chronicle,* April 14, 2013, pp. D1, D5.
47. Illah Reza Nourbakhsh, reported in Matthew Lynn, "A Strategy for Keeping the Robots at Bay," *The Wall Street Journal,* July 6, 2013, p. C3.
48. Ibid.
49. Connor and Wiseman, "AP Impact: Recession."
50. Eric A. Spiegel, "America Can 'Insource' Jobs through Innovation," *USA Today,* January 25, 2012, p. 11A.
51. M. Chaker, "Where the Jobs Are," *The Wall Street Journal,* March 18, 2004, pp. D1, D3; J. Shinal, "Which Types of Jobs Will Be in Demand?" *San Francisco Chronicle,* March 25, 2004, pp. C1, C4; and D. Wessel, "The Future of Jobs: New Ones Arise, Wage Gap Widens," *The Wall Street Journal,* April 2, 2004, pp. A1, A5.
52. Matthew Lynn, "A Strategy for Keeping the Robots at Bay," *The Wall Street Journal,* July 6–July 13, 2013, p. C3.
53. James Spohrer, quoted in Shinal, "Which Types of Jobs Will Be in Demand?"

Chapter 9

1. N. Rao Machiraju, cofounder and CEO of reQall, quoted in Claire Cain Miller, "New Generation of Apps Knows What You Want, Before You Do," *The New York Times,* July 30, 2013, pp. A1, A3.
2. Ibid.
3. Harold Gilliam, "Mind over Matter," *San Francisco Chronicle,* February 9, 2003, pp. D1, D6.
4. May 2004 survey commissioned by Wells Fargo & Co., reported in Julie Dunn, "Poor 'Street Smarts' Make Web Users Vulnerable," *San Francisco Chronicle,* August 17, 2004, p. C8; reprinted from *Denver Post.*
5. Scott McCartney, "Pilots Go to 'the Box' to Avoid Midair Collisions," *The Wall Street Journal,* July 18, 2002, p. D3; and George Johnson, "To Err Is Human," *The New York Times,* July 14, 2002, sec. 4, pp. D1, D7.
6. Demian Bulwa, "Non-U.S. Pilots Urged to Use GPS for Landings," *San Francisco Chronicle,* July 29, 2013, pp. C1, C3.
7. We are grateful to Professor John Durham for contributing these ideas.
8. "Spain Train Driver 'on Phone' at Time of Deadly Crash," *BBC News Europe,* July 30, 2013, *www.bbc.co.uk/news/world-europe-23507348* (accessed August 8, 2013).
9. State Farm online of 872 licensed drivers, ages 18–29, reported in Larry Copeland, "Young Drivers Still Texting, Surfing the Web," *USA Today,* November 16, 2012, p. 3A.
10. Julius Genachowski, "Time to Put the Brakes on Texting and Driving," *USA Today,* September 24, 2012, p. 10A.
11. Study by the Texas Transportation Institute, reported in Larry Copeland, "Hands-Free Texting by Drivers Is Still Dangerous," *USA Today,* April 23, 2013, p. 2B.
12. Copeland, "Young Drivers Still Texting." See also study by AAA Foundation for Traffic Safety, reported in Larry Copeland, "AAA: Hands-Free Isn't Risk-Free," *USA Today,* June 12, 2013, p. 3A.
13. Data from Safe Kids Worldwide, reported in Greg Topo, " 'Distracted Walking' Endangers Teenagers," *USA Today,* August 30, 2012, p. 3A.
14. Kim Painter, "Texting, Music Listening Put Distracted Pedestrians at Risk," *USA Today,* December 13, 2012, p. 2A.
15. H. Josef Hebert, "Nuclear Sites Posted on Internet in Error," *San Francisco Chronicle,* June 4, 2009, p. A4.
16. Jordan Robertson, "Software Glitch Leaves Utilities Open to Attack," *San Francisco Chronicle,* June 12, 2008, p. C4.
17. Robert McMillan, "Computer Glitch Forces U.S. to Cancel Visa Lottery Results," *ComputerWorld,* May 13, 2011, *www.computerworld.com/s/article/9216721/Computer_glitch_forces_U.S._to_cancel_visa_lottery_results* (accessed July 26, 2013).
18. Mike, "The Problem of Dirty Data," August 9, 2009, *www.articlesbase.com/databases-articles/the-problem-of-dirty-data-1111299.html* (accessed July 26, 2013).
19. Steven Norton, "Thanks to Gadget Lust, Lightning Claims Surge," *Bloomberg Businessweek,* July 2–8, 2012, pp. 29–30; and Insurance Information Institute, reported in "Lightning Claims Costs Continue to Rise," *USA Today,* July 25, 2013, p. 1A.
20. Richard Wolf, "Get Out Your Pencils: Paper Ballots Make a Return," *USA Today,* February 29, 2008, p. 2A; Richard Wolf, "Flawed Ballots Cited in Study," *Reno Gazette-Journal,* July 21, 2008, p. 1B; Adam Cohen, "A Tale of Three (Electronic Voting) Elections," *The New York Times,* July 31, 2008, p. A22; Deborah Hastings, "Touch-Screen Voting Machines—Store or Scrap?" *San Francisco Chronicle,* August 25, 2008, p. D3; and Gary Fineout, "Invalid Ballots in Florida Doubled in 2008," *The New York Times,* February 26, 2009, p. A19.
21. Bob Carey, "Paper-Based System Is Broken," *USA Today,* September 20, 2012, p. 10A.
22. Nick Bilton, "Voting Booth in the Hands of Everyone," *The New York Times,* November 12, 2012, pp. B1, B4.
23. Charles Perrow, *Normal Accidents: Living with High-Risk Technologies* (New York: Basic Books, 1984).
24. Paul Virilio, reported in Alan Riding, "Expounding a New View of Accidents," *The New York Times,* December 26, 2002, pp. B1, B2.
25. Matthew L. Wald and John Schwartz, "Rise in Weather Extremes Threatens Infrastructure," *The New York Times,* July 26, 2012, p. A4.
26. *U.S. Energy Sector Vulnerabilities to Climate Change and Extreme Weather,* U.S. Department of Energy, July 2013, *http://energy.gov/sites/prod/files/2013/07/f2/20130716-Energy%20Sector%20Vulnerabilities%20Report.pdf* (accessed July 31, 2013).
27. Jim Yardley and Gardiner Harris, "India Staggered by Power Blackout; 670 Million People in Grip," *The New York Times,* August 1, 2012, pp. A1, A10.
28. Jay Apt, "Blackouts Are a Fact of Life. Let's Deal with Them," *The Wall Street Journal,* September 17, 2012, p. R4.
29. Matthew L. Wald, "New Tools for Keeping the Lights On," *The New York Times,* August 1, 2013, pp. B1, B5.
30. B. H. Strauss, "Rapid Accumulation of Committed Sea-Level Rise from Global Warming," *Proceedings of the National*

Academy of Sciences, published online July 29, 2013, *www.pnas.org/content/early/2013/07/26/1312464110.full.pdf+html* (accessed August 7, 2013). See also Wendy Koch, "Study Warns Rising Seas Could Swamp 1,400 Cities," *USA Today,* July 30, 2013, p. 3A.

31. Matthew L. Wald, "Chinese Firm Is Charged in Theft of Turbine Software," *The New York Times,* June 28, 2013, p. B2.
32. Jefferson Graham, "College Students Sued over Music Downloads," *USA Today,* March 24, 2005, p. 5B.
33. Larem Gullo, "Record Industry Sues 784 Users for Illegally Sharing Music Online," *San Francisco Chronicle,* June 30, 2005, pp. C1, C2.
34. "Music Labels Win $2 Million in Web Case," *The New York Times,* June 19, 2009, p. B2.
35. Amir Efrati, "Now Playing on YouTube: Pirated Films," *The Wall Street Journal,* February 8, 2013, pp. B1, B2. See also Nick Bilton, "Internet Pirates Will Always Win," *The New York Times,* August 5, 2012, p. SR-5; and Ben Sisario and Tanzina Vega, "Playing Whac-a-Mole with Piracy Sites," *The New York Times,* January 29, 2013, p. B3.
36. Pat Choate, quoted in Michael Lind, "Freebooters of Industry," *The New York Times Book Review,* July 10, 2005, p. 34. Choate is the author of *Hot Property: The Stealing of Ideas in an Age of Globalization* (New York: Alfred A. Knopf, 2005).
37. Jack Nicas, "Crime That No Longer Pays," *The Wall Street Journal,* February 15, 2013, p. A3.
38. Ben Worthen, "New Epidemic Fears: Hackers," *The Wall Street Journal,* August 4, 2009, p. A6.
39. Siobhan Gorman, "Arrest in Epic Cyber Crime," *The Wall Street Journal,* August 18, 2009, pp. A1, A4; and AP, "20-Year Sentence in Card Numbers," March 25, 2010, *www.nytimes.com/2010/03//26/technology/26hacker.html* (accessed August 8, 2013).
40. Sarah E. Needleman, "Cybercriminals Sniff Out Vulnerable Firms," *The Wall Street Journal,* July 5, 2012, p. B7.
41. Federal Trade Commission, *Consumer Sentinel Network Data Book for January–December 2012,* February 2013, *www.ftc.gov/sentinel/reports/sentinel-annual-reports/sentinel-cy2012.pdf* (accessed August 8, 2013).
42. Internet Crime Complaint Center, *IC3 2012 Internet Crime Report, www.ic3.gov/media/annualreport/2012_IC3Report.pdf* (accessed August 8, 2013).
43. David Bank and Riva Richmond, "Where the Dangers Are," *The Wall Street Journal,* July 18, 2005, pp. R1, R3; see also Jon Swartz, "Hackers Want to Be Your (Malicious) Friend," *USA Today,* August 13, 2008, p. 3B.
44. Christopher Weaver, "Patients Put at Risk by Computer Viruses," *The Wall Street Journal,* June 14, 2013, pp. A1, A12.
45. Data from Department of Homeland Security, reported in John Seabrook, "Network Insecurity," *The New Yorker,* May 20, 2013, pp. 64–70.
46. Matt Liebowitz and Paul Wagenseil, "Power Grids, Oil Refineries Face 'Staggering' Level of Cyberattacks," *TechNewsDaily,* April 19, 2011, *www.securitynewsdaily.com/power-grids-oil-refineries-staggering-level-cyberattacks-0710/* (accessed August 8, 2013).
47. John Markoff and Nicole Perlroth, "Dispute on Spam Stirs Big Assault on the Internet," *The New York Times,* March 27, 2013, pp. A1, A3.
48. Calbel Garling, "Major Cyber-Attack Prompts Evaluation," *San Francisco Chronicle,* March 31, 2013, p. D3.
49. John Holusha, "The Painful Lessons of Disruption," *The New York Times,* March 17, 1993, pp. C1, C5.
50. "March 11 Disaster Already Causes 145 Business Failures," *World Biz Today,* June 3, 2011, *http://mdn.mainichi.jp/mdnnews/national/news/20110603p2g00m0dm006000c.html* (accessed August 8, 2013).
51. Somini Sengupta, "Letting Down Our Guard," *The New York Times,* March 31, 2013, pp. SR-1, SR-6.
52. Jessica Silver-Greenberg, "Million Denied Bank Accounts for Past Errors," *The New York Times,* July 31, 2013, pp. A1, A3.
53. Amir Efrati, "Google's Data-Trove Dance," *The Wall Street Journal,* July 31, 2013, pp. B1, B4; and Tom Gara, "My Life, and Past, as Seen through Google's Dashboard," *The Wall Street Journal,* July 31, 2013, p. B4.
54. Don Greenbaum and Mark Gerstein, "Is Our DNA Prone to Snooping?" *USA Today,* June 28, 2013, p. 10A.
55. Stephanie Clifford and Quentin Hardy, "Attention Shopper: Stores Are Tracking Your Cell," *The New York Times,* July 15, 2013, pp. A1, A3; and "You (and Your Cellphone) on Candid Camera," editorial, *The New York Times,* July 19, 2013, p. A20. See also Brad Stone, "Turning Shoppers into Heat Maps," *Bloomberg Businessweek,* April 29–May 5, 2013, pp. 36–37.
56. Sengupta, "Letting Down Our Guard."
57. Natasha Singer, "If My Data Is an Open Book, Why Can't I Read It?" *The New York Times,* May 26, 2013, p. BU-3. See also Jessica Leber, "How Wireless Carriers Are Monetizing Your Movements," *MIT Technology Review,* April 12, 2013, *www.technologyreview.com/news/513016/how-wireless-carriers-are-monetizing-your-movements* (accessed July 29, 2013).
58. Jeremy Singer-Vine and Anton Torianovski, "Apps for Kids Are Data Magnets; FTC Rules to Kick In," *The Wall Street Journal,* June 28, 2013, pp. B1, B6.
59. Associated Press, "FTC Cracks Down on Firms in Cyber Spying," *San Francisco Chronicle,* September 27, 2012, p. D3; and Nick Bilton, "Rented Computers Spied on Users, FTC Case Says," *The New York Times,* October 1, 2012, p. B5.
60. Anemona Hartocollis, "With Money at Risk, Hospitals Push Staff to Wash Hands," *The New York Times,* May 29, 2013, pp. A18, A19.
61. Stephanie Clifford and Jessica Silver-Greenberg, "Retailers Track Employee Thefts in Vast Databases," *The New York Times,* April 3, 2013, pp. A1, A16.
62. Greenbaum and Gerstein, "Is Our DNA Prone to Snooping?"
63. Kim Komando, "The State of Your Digital Rights," *Reno Gazette-Journal,* July 20, 2012, p. 5F.
64. Somini Sengupta, "Control of Content in Social Media Remains Fuzzy," *The New York Times,* December 31, 2012, p. B5.
65. Stephanie Armour, "Beware the Blog: You May Get Fired," *Reno Gazette-Journal,* June 25, 2005, pp. 1E, 4E.
66. Deloitte's Ethics and Workplace survey, reported in "Social Networking and the Boss," *USA Today,* June 24, 2009, p. 1B.
67. Employee Computer & Internet Abuse Statistics, Snapshot Spy, *www.snapshotspy.com/employee-computer-abuse-statistics.htm*; and Computer Monitoring, *www.computer-monitoring.com/employee-monitoring/stats.htm* (accessed June 6, 2011).
68. Damon Darlin, "Software That Monitors Your Work, Wherever You Are," *The New York Times,* April 12, 2009, Business section, p. 4.
69. "Office Slacker Stats," Staff Monitoring Solutions, *www.staffmonitoring.com/P32/stats.htm* (accessed June 4, 2011).
70. American Databank, *www.americandatabank.com/statistics.htm* (accessed June 6, 2011).
71. Marci Alboher Nusbaum, "New Kind of Snooping Arrives at the Office," *The New York Times,* July 13, 2003, sec. 3, p. 12.
72. Mindy Fetterman, "Employers Must Shred Personal Data," *USA Today,* June 1, 2005, p. 3B.
73. Bob Egelko, "U.S. Appeals Court Limits Release of Text Messages," *San Francisco Chronicle,* June 19, 2008, p. B3; and Jennifer Ordonez, "They Can't Hide Their Pryin' Eyes," *Newsweek,* July 7–July 14, 2008, p. 22.
74. Elizabeth Weise and Greg Toppo, "License Plate Scanners: Love 'Em or Loathe 'Em," *USA Today,* July 19, 2013, p. 3A.
75. Mike Katz-Lacabe, quoted in Ali Winston, "Police Tracking of Cars on Rise," *San Francisco Chronicle,* June 26, 2013, pp. A1, A8. See also James R. Healey and Fred Meier, "ACLU: Government Keeping Track of Where You've Driven," *USA Today,* July 18, 2013, p. 1B.
76. Joe Simitian, quoted in Winston, "Police Tracking of Cars on Rise."
77. Joseph Goldstein, "Police Agencies Are Assembling Records of DNA," *The New York Times,* June 13, 2013, pp. A1, A3.
78. Jennifer Valentino-DeVries and Geoffrey A. Fowler, "Call for More Video Cameras Spotlights Debate on Use," *The Wall Street Journal,* April 20–21, 2013, p. A7.
79. Charlie Savage, "CIA Sees Concerns on Ties to New York Police," *The New York Times,* June 27, 2013, pp. A1, A26.
80. Eric Lipton, "Fears of National ID with Immigration Bill," *The New York Times,* June 15, 2013, *www.nytimes.com/2013/06/16/us/politics/*

as-immigration-bill-moves-forward-fear-of-an-id-system.html (accessed July 30, 2013).

81. Angus Loten, Sarah E. Needleman, and Adam Janofsky, "Small Business Has a Beef with E-Verify," *The Wall Street Journal,* July 25, 2013, p. B6. See also John H. Cochrane, "Think Government Is Intrusive? Wait until E-Verify Kicks In," *The Wall Street Journal,* August 2, 2013, p. A13.
82. Westat Inc., *Findings of the E-Verify Program Evaluation,* December 2009, report prepared for U.S. Department of Homeland Security, Washington, DC, *www.uscis.gov/USCIS/E-Verify/E-Verify/Final%20E-Verify%20Report%2012-16-09_2.pdf* (accessed July 29, 2013).
83. Bill Keller, "Show Me Your Papers," *The New York Times,* July 1, 2012, p. A15. See also Danny Yadron, "Senators in Immigration Talks Mull Federal IDs for All Workers," *The Wall Street Journal,* February 21, 2013, pp. A1, A4.
84. Mark Mazzetti and Michael S. Schmidt, "Ex-CIA Worker Says He Disclosed U.S. Surveillance," *The New York Times,* June 10, 2013, pp. A1, A13; Donna Leinwand Leger, "Contractor: Government Has Intruded on Privacy," *USA Today,* June 10, 2013, p. 6A; and Tribune Company, "Secret Data Smuggled Out of NSA on Digital Device," *San Francisco Chronicle,* June 14, 2013, p. A10.
85. Glenn Greenwald, "XKeyscore: NSA Tool Collects 'Nearly Everything a User Does on the Internet,' " *The Guardian,* July 31, 2013, *www.theguardian.com/world/2013/jul/31/nsa-top-secret-program-online-data* (accessed August 2, 2013).
86. Michael Riley, "What Snowden Doesn't Know," *Bloomberg Businessweek,* July 22–28, 2013, pp. 22–23; Jonathan Weisman, "Momentum Builds against NSA Surveillance," *The New York Times,* July 29, 2013, pp. A1, A9; and "Good Guys Lost Data Mining Vote, but They'll Be Back," editorial, *Reno Gazette-Journal,* August 2, 2013, p. 7A, reprinted from *USA Today.* See also Ryan Gallagher, "New Surveillance Law Would Curtail NSA Snooping on Americans, Increase Transparency," *Slate,* July 31, 2013, *www.slate.com/blogs/future_tense/2013/07/29/patrick_leahy_s_fisa_accountability_and_privacy_protection_act_would_curtail.html* (accessed August 2, 2013).
87. Riley, "What Snowden Doesn't Know."
88. James Bamford, "The Silent War," *Wired,* July 2013, pp. 90–99.
89. "Look Who's Listening," *The Economist,* June 15, 2013, pp. 23–24; and Siobhan Gorman and Jennifer Valentino-DeVries, "Details Emerge on NSA's Now-Ended Internet Program," *The Wall Street Journal,* June 28, 2013, p. A6.
90. Paul Elias, "Google Told to Give Data to FBI," *Reno Gazette-Journal,* June 1, 2013, p. A10.
91. Jennifer Valentino-DeVries and Siobhan Gorman, "Secret Court Ruling Expanded Spy Powers," *The Wall Street Journal,* July 8, 2013, pp. A1, A4.
92. "Liberty's Lost Decade," *The Economist,* August 3, 2013, p. 11.
93. Massimo Calabresi, "Watching the Watchers," *Time,* July 8–15, 2013, p. 12; Stewart M. Powell, "Surveillance Court Needs Makeover, Retired Judge Says," *San Francisco Chronicle,* July 14, 2013, p. A20; and "The Case for Oversight of the FISA Court," editorial, *Bloomberg Businessweek,* July 15–21, 2013, p. 12.
94. Chris Strohm, with Todd Shields, "The Big Secret about the Secrecy Board," *Bloomberg Businessweek,* July 1–7, 2013, pp. 26–28.
95. NSA inspector general, quoted in Charlie Savage and James Risen, "NSA Report Says Internet 'Metadata' Were Focus of Visit to Ashcroft," *The New York Times,* June 28, 2013, p. A6.
96. Elizabeth Goitein, codirector of the Liberty and National Security Program at the Brennan Center for Justice, New York University Law School, reported in Donna Leinwand Leger and Gary Strauss, "Metadata Mining: Why Do the Feds Do It?" *USA Today,* June 7, 2013, p. 5A.
97. Ron Sievert, "Secret Programs Keep Us Safe," *USA Today,* August 2–4, 2013, p. 10A.
98. Patrick Leahy, quoted in Kevin Johnson and David Jackson, "NSA in the Cross Hairs," *USA Today,* August 2–4, 2013, pp. 1A, 2A.
99. Jonathan Turley, "Creeping Surveillance State, Creepy Conclusions," *USA Today,* June 10, 2013, p. 8A.
100. Sean Patrick Farrell, "A Drone's-Eye View of Nature," *The New York Times,* May 7, 2013, p. D3; Felicity Barringer, "FAA's Concerns Hold Up Use of Wildfire Drones," *The New York Times,* May 22, 2013, p. A17; Henry Brean, "Drones to Spy on Nevada Wildlife, Not People," *Reno Gazette-Journal,* June 9, 2013, p. 13A, reprinted from *Las Vegas Review Journal;* and Joan Lowy, "U.S. Certifies First Two Drones for Domestic Flight," *Reno Gazette-Journal,* July 28, 2013, p. 7F.
101. Rachel King, "Drones Hit New Turf: U.S. Farmland," *The Wall Street Journal,* May 2, 2013, p. B9; and "Using Drones to Spray Pesticides Studied," *San Francisco Chronicle,* June 28, 2013, p. D7, reprinted from *Sacramento Bee.*
102. Richard Whittle, "Drone Skies," *Popular Mechanics,* September 2013, pp. 76–83.
103. Somini Sengupta, "U.S. Border Agency Allows Others to Use Its Drones," *The New York Times,* July 4, 2013, pp. B1, B4.
104. "The Drone over Your Backyard," *The Week,* June 15, 2012, p. 11. See also "The Dawning of Domestic Drones," editorial, *The New York Times,* December 26, 2012, p. A18; Judy Keen, "Critics Target Drones Buzzing over USA," *USA Today,* January 11, 2013, p. 1A; Lev Grossman, "Drone Home," *Time,* February 11, 2013, pp. 26–33; and "A Sky Full of Drones," *The Week,* June 28, 2013, pp. 36–37.
105. Dune Lawrence and Michael Riley, "A Portrait of a Chinese Hacker," *Bloomberg Businessweek,* February 18–24, 2013, pp. 54–59.
106. Barack Obama, quoted in "China's Cybergames," editorial, *The New York Times,* February 20, 2013, p. A22.
107. David E. Sanger, David Barboza, and Nicole Perlroth, "China's Army Seen as Tied to Hacking against U.S.," *The New York Times,* February 19, 2013, pp. A1, A9; Julian E. Barnes, Siobhan Gorman, and Jeremy Page, "U.S., China Ties Tested in Cyberspace," *The Wall Street Journal,* February 20, 2013, p. A11; David E. Sanger and Nicole Perlroth, "Chinese Hackers Resume Attacks on U.S. Targets," *The New York Times,* May 20, 2013, pp. A1, A3; Joe Nocera, "This Isn't How to Stop Hackers," *The New York Times,* June 15, 2013, p. A19; and Danny Yadron and Siobhan Gorman, "U.S., Firms Draw Bead on Chinese Cyberspies," *The Wall Street Journal,* July 12, 2013, pp. A1, A7.
108. Stephen Castle and Eric Schmitt, "Europeans Voice Anger over Reports of Spying by U.S. on Its Allies," *The New York Times,* July 1, 2013, p. A9; Larry Rohter, "Brazil Voices 'Deep Concern' over Gathering of Data by U.S.," *The New York Times,* July 8, 2013, p. A7; and "Crocodile Tears over Surveillance," editorial, *Bloomberg Businessweek,* July 8–14, 2013, p. 10.
109. Michael Riley, "How the U.S. Government Hacks the World," *Bloomberg Business-Week,* May 27–June 2, 2013, pp. 35–37.
110. Glenn Derene, "Surveillance Blowback," *Popular Mechanics,* September 2013, p. 74.
111. Steven Erlanger, "France, Too, Is Sweeping Up Data, Newspaper Reports," *The New York Times,* July 5, 2013, p. A4; and "How They See Us: Europe Is Complicit in Spying," *The Week,* July 19, 2013, p. 12.
112. Snorre Fagerland, of computer security firm Norman Shark, quoted in Geoffrey A. Fowler and Jennifer Valentino-DeVries, "A Series of Cyberattacks Points to Sites inside India," *The Wall Street Journal,* June 24, 2013, pp. B1, B2.
113. Siobhan Gorman and Danny Yadron, "Iran Hacks Energy Firms, U.S. Says," *The Wall Street Journal,* May 24, 2013, p. A4.
114. Nicole Perlroth and David E. Sanger, "New Computer Attacks Traced to Iran," *The New York Times,* May 25, 2013, p. A7.
115. Siobhan Gorman and Danny Yadron, "Banks Seek U.S. Help on Iran Cyberattacks," *The Wall Street Journal,* January 16, 2013, p. A6.
116. Nicole Perlroth and David E. Sanger, "Cyberattacks Seem Meant to Destroy, Not Just Disrupt," *The New York Times,* March 29, 2013, pp. B1, B2; and Thom Shanker and David E. Sanger, "U.S. Helps Allies Trying to Battle Iranian Hackers," *The New York Times,* June 9, 2013, pp. 1, 11.
117. James Hookway, "Computer Hackers Target Cambodia," *The Wall Street Journal,* September 6, 2012, p. B4.
118. Joe Magee, "The Hacker of Damascus," *Bloomberg Businessweek,* November 19–25, 2012, pp. 70–76; Nicole Perlroth, "Hunting for Syrian Hackers' Chain of

Command," *The New York Times,* May 18, 2013, pp. B1, B6; and Steven Stalinsky, "China Isn't the Only Source of Cyberattacks," *The Wall Street Journal,* May 22, 2013, p. A17.

119. U.S. Computer Emergency Readiness team, reported in "U.S. Computers Vulnerable," *The Week,* February 27, 2009, p. 6.
120. Lolita C. Baldor, "Pentagon Says It Spent $100 Million Fending Off 6 Months of Cyberattacks," *San Francisco Chronicle,* April 8, 2009, p. C3.
121. Jack Goldsmith, "Defend America, One Laptop at a Time," *The New York Times,* July 2, 2009, p. A21.
122. Jim Michaels, "Cellphones Put to 'Unnerving' Use in Gaza," *USA Today,* January 14, 2009, p. 4A.
123. David E. Sanger, John Markoff, and Thom Shanker, "U.S. Plans Attack and Defense in Web Warfare," *The New York Times,* April 28, 2009, pp. A1, A14.
124. "U.S. Officials Eye N. Korea in Cyber Attack," *Reno Gazette-Journal,* July 9, 2009, p. 1B.
125. Jonathan Masters, "Confronting the Cyber Threat," Council on Foreign Relations, May 23, 2011, *www.cfr.org/technology-and-foreign-policy/confronting-cyber-threat/p15577* (accessed June 6, 2011).
126. David E. Sanger, "Pentagon Plans New Arm to Wage Computer Wars," *The New York Times,* May 29, 2009, pp. A1, A17; Byron Acohido, "Obama Vows to Prioritize Cybersecurity," *USA Today,* June 1, 2009, p. 4B; and Chloe Albanesius, "Obama's Cyberspace Crackdown," *PC Magazine,* digital edition, July 2009, pp. 7–8.
127. Siobhan Gorman and Yochi Dreazen, "Military Command Is Created for Cyber Security," *The Wall Street Journal,* July 24, 2009, p. A6.
128. L. Gordon Crovitz, "Obama and Cyber Defense," *The Wall Street Journal,* June 29, 2009, p. A11.
129. Masters, "Confronting the Cyber Threat."
130. Thom Shanker and David E. Shanker, "Privacy May Be a Victim in Cyberdefense Plan," *The New York Times,* June 13, 2009, pp. A1, A3; and Siobhan Gorman, "Troubles Plague Cyberspy Defense," *The Wall Street Journal,* July 3, 2009, pp. A1, A10.
131. Josh Tyrangiel, "Singer's Little Helper," *Time,* February 16, 2009, pp. 49–51.
132. Sydney Smith, "Two Hasidic Outlets Cut Hilary Clinton, Audrey Tomason from Photo?" *iMediaEthics,* May 10, 2011, *www.imediaethics.org/News/1438/Two_hasidic_outlets_cut_hillary_clinton__audrey_tomason_from_photo.php* (accessed July 23, 2013). *Der Tzitung* apologized for causing any offense, claiming its photo editor hadn't read the White House guidelines to not manipulate the photo, and stated that modesty guidelines barred the newspaper from publishing any photos of women.
133. Byron Calame, "Pictures, Labels, Perception and Reality," *The New York Times,* July 3, 2005, sec. 4, p. 10.
134. John Knoll, quoted in Katie Hafner, "The Camera Never Lies, but the Software Can," *The New York Times,* March 11, 2004, pp. E1, E7.
135. Howard Kurtz, "Reporter Loses Job over Altered Video of Fox's Gibson," *Washington Post,* February 25, 2009, *www.washingtonpost.com/wp-dyn/content/article/2009/02/24/AR2009022403215.html.*
136. "Hannity to Address Protest Video Question," November 11, 2009, *http://mediadecoder.blogs.nytimes.com/2009/11/11/hannity-to-address-protest-video-questions-tonight/* (accessed August 7, 2013).
137. Data based on an analysis by Jonathan G. Koomey, Stanford University research fellow, cited in James Glanz, "Power, Pollution, and the Internet," *The New York Times,* September 23, 2012, pp. 1, 20, 21.
138. McKinsey & Company analysis, cited in Glanz, "Power, Pollution, and the Internet."
139. "Cloud Computing and Internet Use Suck Energy, Emit CO2, Says Greenpeace," *High Technology Resource,* April 29, 2011, *http://mardiutomo.com/publication-news/2011/04/cloud-computing-and-internet-use-suck-energy-emit-co2-says-greenpeace* (accessed August 7, 2013).
140. Steve Lohr, "Data Centers as Polluters," *The New York Times,* May 5, 2008, p. C6.
141. Heather Levin, "Electronic Waste (E-Waste) Recycling and Disposal—Fact, Statistics, & Solutions," March 25, 2011, *http://blog.macroaxis.com/2011/03/25/electronic-waste-e-waste-recycling-and-disposal-%e2%80%93-facts-statistics-solutions/* (accessed June 7, 2011); and *www.electronicstakeback.com/wp-content/uploads/Facts_and_Figures_on_EWaste_and_Recycling.pdf* (accessed August 2013).
142. Ibid.
143. See, for example, Carolyn Jones, "T-Mobile Tower Gets Makeover to Look More Like a Tree," *San Francisco Chronicle,* July 28, 2012, pp. C1, C2.
144. Study by Annenberg Center for the Digital Future, University of Southern California, reported in "Is the Internet Behind Less Family Face Time?" *USA Today,* June 16, 2009, p. 6D. See also Brad Stone, "Coffee Can Wait. The Day's First Stop Is Online," *The New York Times,* August 10, 2009, pp. A1, A3.
145. John D. Sutter, "Is 'Gaming Addiction' a Real Disorder?" CNN.com, August 6, 2012, *www.cnn.com/2012/08/05/tech/gaming-gadgets/gaming-addiction-dsm* (accessed August 4, 2013); and In-Soo Nam, "Rising Addiction Among Teens: Smartphones," *The Wall Street Journal,* July 23, 2013, p. D2.
146. Nicholas Carr, quoted in Tara Parker-Pope, "An Ugly Toll of Technology: Impatience and Forgetfulness," *The New York Times,* June 6, 2010, *www.nytimes.com/2010/06/07/technology/07brainside.html?ref=yourbrainoncomputers* (accessed August 4, 2013).
147. Jensen Carlsen, "Social Media Breeds Antisocial Interactions," *Daily Trojan,* February 2, 2010, *http://dailytrojan.com/2010/02/02/social-media-breeds-anti-social-interactions* (accessed August 4, 2013).
148. Keith Hampton, Laura Sessions Goulet, Eun Ja Herr, and Lee Rainie, *Social Isolation and New Technology,* November 4, 2009, Pew Internet & the American Life Project, *www.pewinternet.org/Reports/2009/18-Social-Isolation-and-New-Technology.aspx* (accessed August 4, 2013).
149. Matt Richtel, "For Gamers, the Craving Won't Quit," *The New York Times,* April 29, 2008, pp. C1, C4.
150. Jennifer Seter Wagner, "When Play Turns to Trouble," *U.S. News & World Report,* May 19, 2008, pp. 51–52.
151. Study by Iowa State University, reported in Staci Hupp, "1 in 10 Kids Addicted to Video Games," *Reno-Gazette-Journal,* April 21, 2009, p. 1B. See also Sutter, "Is 'Gaming Addiction' a Real Disorder?"
152. "Video Game Addiction," CRC Health Group, *www.video-game-addiction.org/* (accessed August 6, 2013).
153. Benny Evangelista, "Real Violence vs. Imaginary," *San Francisco Chronicle,* March 31, 2013, pp. D1, D6.
154. Alexandra Berzon, "Internet Gambling Scores Its Biggest Win," *The Wall Street Journal,* February 27, 2013, pp. A1, A4; Reid Cherner, "Legal Online Poker Begins," *Reno Gazette-Journal,* May 1, 2013, p. 1A; and Wayne Parry, "Nation's Casinos Brace for Internet Gaming's Impact," *Nevada Appeal,* May 5, 2013, pp. C1, C2.
155. Wayne Parry, Associated Press, "Casinos Ban Gamblers from Using Google Glass," *Reno Gazette-Journal,* June 6, 2013, p. 5A. See also Claire Cain Miller, "Privacy Officials Press Google on Its Glasses," *The New York Times,* June 24, 2013, p. B7.
156. Alexander Berzon and Mark Maremont, "Researchers Bet Casino Data Can Identify Gambling Addicts," *The Wall Street Journal,* August 3–4, 2012, pp. A1, A10.
157. T. A. Bedrosian, Z. M. Weil, and R. J. Nelson, "Chronic Dim Light at Night Provokes Reversible Depression-like Phenotype: Possible Role for TNF," *Molecular Psychiatry,* July 24, 2012, pp. 930–936. See also "Screen-Viewing Blues," *The Week,* August 10, 2012, p. 19.
158. Mayo Clinic, "Are Smartphones Disrupting Your Sleep?" *Science Daily,* August 6, 2013, *www.sciencedaily.com/releases/2013/06/130603163610.htm* (accessed August 6, 2013).
159. Credant Technologies 2009 poll of 329 British workers, reported in Sue Shellenbarger, "More Work Goes 'Undercover,' " *The Wall Street Journal,* November 14, 2012, pp. D1, D5.
160. Caleb Garling, "Learning to Tune Out Effectively Takes Work," *San Francisco Chronicle,* June 23, 2013, pp. D1, D8. See also Joe Nocera, "A Case against Twitter," *The New York Times,* July 16, 2013, p. A19.
161. Data from Accenture, reported in Laura Petrecca, "Always Working," *USA Today,* March 7, 2013, pp. 1A, 2A.

162. Rick Segal, "Mayer v. Branson: The Work from Home War," *Forbes,* February 27, 2013, *www.forbes.com/sites/gyro/2013/02/27/mayer-v-branson-the-work-from-home-war* (accessed August 6, 2013).
163. Validas, cited in Jon Swartz, "Like Chips, You Can't Have Just 1 Gadget," *USA Today,* June 27, 2013, p. 2B.
164. "Going Deep Inside the Adult Entertainment Industry," *Arbitrage Magazine,* April 15, 2013, *www.arbitragemagazine.com/features/adult-entertainment-industry-recession-proof/2* (accessed August 6, 2013).
165. "Porn in the USA," *60 Minutes,* CBS, September 5, 2004.
166. Matt Richtel, "He's Watching That, in Public? Pornography Takes the Next Seat," *The New York Times,* July 21, 2012, pp. A1, A3.
167. David W. Chen and Javier C. Hernandez, "Weiner Admits Web Dalliance after Resigning," *The New York Times,* July 24, 2013, pp. A1, A18; and "The Danger of Anthony Weiner," editorial, *USA Today,* July 26, 2013, p. 10A.
168. Kimberly J. Mitchell, David Finkelhor, Lisa M. Jones, and Janis Wolak, "Prevalence and Characteristics of Youth Sexting: A National Study," *Pediatrics,* published online December 5, 2011, *http://pediatrics.aappublications.org/content/early/2011/11/30/peds.2011-1730* (accessed August 7, 2013).
169. Eric Rice, Harmony Rhoades, Hailey Winetrobe, Monica Sanchez, Jorge Montoya, Aaron Plant, and Timothy Kordic, "Sexually Explicit Cell Phone Messaging Associated with Sexual Risk among Adolescents," *Pediatrics,* published online September 17, 2012, *http://pediatrics.aappublications.org/content/130/4/667.full?sid=e043fc50-b66b-494f-812f-bb07963249d5* (accessed August 7, 2013).
170. *Sex and Tech: Results from a Survey of Teens and Young Adults,* The National Campaign to Prevent Teen and Unplanned Pregnancy; and CosmoGirl.com, survey by Teenage Research Unlimited of 1,280 teens and young adults online, September 25–October 3, 2008, *www.thenationalcampaign.org/sextech/PDF/SexTech_Summary.pdf* (accessed August 7, 2013). See also Sharon Jayson, "Flirting Goes High-Tech, Low-Taste," *USA Today,* December 10, 2008, p. 1A; and Irene Sege, "Nude Photos of Teens Getting Unexpected Play," *San Francisco Chronicle,* December 12, 2008, p. A28. Another survey by Harris Interactive also found that one in five teens had "sexted"; see Donna Leinwand, "Survey: 1 in 5 Teens 'Sext' Despite Risks," *USA Today,* June 24, 2009, p. 3A.
171. Survey by Common Sense Media, reported in Jill Tucker, "Teens Show, Tell Too Much Online," *San Francisco Chronicle,* August 10, 2009, pp. A1, A6.
172. Jennifer Van Grove, "Snapchat Snapshot: App Counts 8M Adult Users in U.S.," *CNET News,* June 25, 2013, *http://news.cnet.com/8301-1023_3-57590968-93/snapchat-snapshot-app-counts-8m-adult-users-in-u.s* (accessed August 7, 2013).
173. Jason Koebler, "Cyber Bullying Growing More Malicious, Experts Say," *U.S. News,* June 3, 2011, *www.usnews.com/education/blogs/high-school-notes/2011/06/03/cyber-bullying-growing-more-malicious-experts-say* (accessed August 7, 2013).
174. Amanda Lenhart, Mary Madden, Aaron Smith, Kristen Purcell, Kathryn Zickuhr, and Lee Rainie, "Teens, Kindness, and Cruelty on Social Network Sites," *Pew Internet,* November 9, 2011, *http://pewinternet.org/Reports/2011/Teens-and-social-media/Summary.aspx* (accessed August 7, 2013). See also Cynthia G. Wagner, "Beating the Cyberbullies," *The Futurist,* September–October 2008, pp. 14–15; Sue Shellenbarger, "Cyberbully Alert: Web Sites Make It Easier to Flag Trouble," *The Wall Street Journal,* December 17, 2008, p. D1; and Emily Bazelon, "How to Stop the Bullies," *The Atlantic,* March 2013, pp. 82–90.
175. Cari Tuna, "Lawyers and Employers Take the Fight to 'Workplace Bullies,' " *The Wall Street Journal,* August 4, 2008, p. B6; and "My Cyberstalker," *The Week,* May 31, 2013, pp. 40–41, originally adapted for *The Chronicle Review* from James Lasdun, *Give Me Everything You Have: On Being Stalked* (New York: Farrar, Straus and Giroux, 2013).
176. Data from Sophie Chang and Martin Anderson, "A Waste of Time and Money?" *1E,* October 2010, *www.1e.com/download/WhitePapers/A_Waste_of_Time_and_Money.pdf* (accessed September 5, 2013).
177. Kevin Maney, "No Time Off? It's Tech Giants' Fault," *USA Today,* July 21, 2004, p. 4B. See also Michael Sanserino, "Suits Question After-Hours Demands of Email and Cellphones," *The Wall Street Journal,* August 10, 2009, pp. B1, B2.
178. U.S. Labor Department, reported in Sue Kirchoff, "Worker Productivity Rises at Fastest Rate since 1950," *USA Today,* February 7, 2003, p. 5B. See also Janet Rue-Dupree, "Innovation Should Mean More Jobs, Not Less," *The New York Times,* January 4, 2009, Business section, p. 3.
179. Stephen S. Roach, "Working Better or Just Harder?" *The New York Times,* February 14, 2000, p. A27.
180. N'Gai Croal, "The Internet Is the New Sweatshop," *Newsweek,* July 7–14, 2008, p. 54.
181. David Levy, quoted in Joseph Hart, "Technoskeptic Techie," *Utne,* January–February 2005, pp. 28–29.
182. Bill McKibben, quoted in Jeffrey R. Young, "Knowing When to Log Off," *The Chronicle of Higher Education,* April 22, 2005, pp. A34–A35.
183. "Understanding Information Overload," *infogineering, www.infogineering.net/understanding-information-overload.htm* (accessed June 7, 2011).
184. William Van Winkle, "Information Overload," *www.gdrc.org/icts/i-overload/infoload.html* (accessed June 7, 2011).
185. Jeremy Rifkin, "Technology's Curse: Fewer Jobs, Fewer Buyers," *San Francisco Examiner,* December 3, 1995, p. C19.
186. Richard W. Samson, "How to Succeed in the Hyper-Human Economy," *The Futurist,* September–October 2004, pp. 38–43.
187. Stewart Brand, in "Boon or Bane for Jobs?" *The Futurist,* January–February 1997, pp. 13–14.
188. Sebastian Moffett, "Technology Widens Gap Between Rich and Poor," May 4, 2011, *http://online.wsj.com/article/SB10001424052748703922804576301154008155570.html* (accessed June 8, 2011).
189. Ibid.
190. Thomas L. Friedman, *The World Is Flat: A Brief History of the Twenty-First Century* (New York: Farrar, Straus & Giroux, 2005).
191. Paul Magnusson, "Globalization Is Great—Sort Of," *BusinessWeek,* April 25, 2005, p. 25. See also Fareed Zakaria, "The Wealth of Yet More Nations," *The New York Times Book Review,* May 1, 2005, pp. 10–11; Russ L. Juskalian, "Prospering in Brave New World Takes Adaptation," *USA Today,* May 2, 2005, p. 4B; and Roberto J. Gonzalez, "Falling Flat," *San Francisco Chronicle,* May 15, 2005, pp. B1, B4.
192. Moffett, "Technology Widens Gap."
193. Charles Hutzler, "Yuppies in China Protest via the Web—and Get Away with It," *The Wall Street Journal,* March 10, 2004, pp. A1, A8; Howard W. French, "Despite an Act of Leniency, China Has Its Eye on the Web," *The New York Times,* June 27, 2004, p. 6; Charles Hutzler, "China Finds New Ways to Restrict Access to the Internet," *The Wall Street Journal,* September 1, 2004, pp. B1, B2; Tom Zeller Jr., "Beijing Loves the Web until the Web Talks Back," *The New York Times,* December 6, 2004, p. C15; Jim Yardley, "A Hundred Cellphones Bloom, and Chinese Take to the Streets," *The New York Times,* April 25, 2005, pp. A1, A6; Bruce Einhorn and Heather Green, "Blogs under Its Thumb," *BusinessWeek,* August 8, 2005, pp. 42–43; Michael Wines and Andrew Jacobs, "To Shut Off Tiananmen Talk, China Blocks More Web Sites," *The New York Times,* June 3, 2009, p. A13; Jeannie Nuss, "Web Site Tracks Online Censorship Reports," *San Francisco Chronicle,* August 24, 2009, p. D2; and Jonathan Ansfield, "China Adds Layer of Web Surveillance with a Rule Seeking Users' Names," *The New York Times,* September 6, 2009, p. 4.
194. Todd Gitlin, quoted in Dora Straus, "Lazy Teachers, Lazy Students" [letter], *The New York Times,* September 12, 1999, sec. 4, p. 18.

Chapter 10

1. Jason Fried, "Here's One Way to Be a Better Communicator: Start Treating People More Like Computers," *Inc.,* December 2012–January 2013, p. 39.

2. David Streitfeld, "Making Living Can Be Tough in Making App," *The New York Times,* November 18, 2012, pp. A1, A19.
3. Wanted Analytics, reported in Nathan Eddy, "Application Software Developers in Demand," *eWeek,* May 17, 2013, *www.eweek.com/small-business/application-software-developers-in-demand* (accessed July 20, 2013).
4. Kathleen Chaykowski, "App Making 101," *San Francisco Chronicle,* July 12, 2012, pp. D1, D5; Streitfeld, "Making Living Can Be Tough"; and "Developing Apps Opens Pathways to Jobs, Riches," *San Francisco Chronicle,* November 26, 2012, pp. D1, D4.
5. Steve Cerocke, " 'BYOD' Trend Has Pluses, but Beware of the Risks," *Reno Gazette-Journal,* February 23, 2013, p. 7A.
6. Christ Woodyard, "Software Update Aimed to Mute MyFord Criticism," *USA Today,* December 3, 2012, p. 5B.
7. Randall Stross, "Billion-Dollar Flop: Air Force Stumbles on Software Plan," *The New York Times,* December 9, 2012, p. BU-3.
8. Evan Perez, "FBI Files Go Digital, After Years of Delays," *The Wall Street Journal,* August 1, 2012, p. A3.
9. Elizabeth McGrath, quoted in Stross, "Billion-Dollar Flop."
10. Gary Webb, "Potholes, Not 'Smooth Transition,' Mark Project," *San Jose Mercury News,* July 3, 1994, p. 18A.
11. Jim Remsik, "For Software Writing, a Buddy System," *The New York Times,* September 20, 2009, p. 8.
12. Ashlee Vance, "Code Checker Engineers Facebook to Succeed," *San Francisco Chronicle,* October 9, 2012, pp. D1, D3, originally printed in *Bloomberg Businessweek.*
13. Chuck Rossi, quoted in Vance, "Code Checker Engineers Facebook."
14. Bryan Cantrill, vice president of engineering at the San Francisco–based cloud computing company Joyent, and a member of the advisory board of *ACM Queue,* a computer magazine for software engineers published by the Association for Computing Machinery, quoted in "Best Technology Jobs: Software Developer," *Money/U.S.* News.com *Careers, http://money.usnews.com/careers/best-jobs/software-developer* (accessed July 19, 2013).
15. Chris Stephenson, quoted in Kathleen Chaykowski, "Kid Programmers," *San Francisco Chronicle,* August 31, 2012, pp. D1, D6, originally printed in *Bloomberg Businessweek.*
16. Jerome Garfunkel, "COBOL: Still Relevant after All These Years," February 17, 2003 *www.jeromegarfunkel.com/authored/stillrelevent2003.html* (accessed July 21, 2013).
17. Alan Freedman, *The Computer Glossary,* 6th ed. (New York: AMACOM, 1993), p. 370.
18. Unpaid CEO and nonstudent Steve Leicht, quoted in Kathleen Chaykowski, "App Making 101," *San Francisco Chronicle,* July 12, 2012, pp. D1, D5, originally printed in *Bloomberg Businessweek.*
19. Brendan Lee, quoted in "New Company, 52apps, Turns User Ideas into an App a Week," PRWeb, June 21, 2012, *www.prweb.com/releases/2012/6/prweb9625324.htm* (accessed July 21, 2013).
20. "Tcl/Tk (Tool Command Language)," SearcEnterpriseLinux, *http://searchenterpriselinux.techtarget.com/sDefinition/0,,sid39_gci213098,00.html#* (accessed July 21, 2013).

Photo Credits

Chapter 1

Page 1: Laurence Mouton/PhotoAlto/Corbis; **3:** Edward Bock/Corbis; **5:** Bob Daemmrich/The Image Works; **6** (*left*): Jean Claude MOSCHETTI/REA/Redux; **6** (*right*): Basheera Hassanali/Alamy; **7:** Laurence Mouton/PhotoAlto/Corbis; **8** (*top left*): Courtesy of IBM; **8** (*top right*): David Silverman/Getty Images; **8** (*bottom*): © Volker Steger/Science Source; **9** (*top right*): John W. Adkisson for *The New York Times*/Redux; **9** (*left*): Fujifotos/The Image Works; **9** (*bottom*): Shizuo Kambayashi/AP Images; **11:** Jeff Greenberg/The Image Works; **13** (*bottom*): Syracuse Newspapers/Jim Commentucci/The Image Works; **13** (*top left*): Alistair Berg/Getty Images; **13** (*top right*)Denis Balibouse/Reuters/Corbis; **15** (*left*): Courtesy of Unisys Archives; **15** (*right*): Lannis Waters/ZUMA Press/Corbis; **16** (*left*): Courtesy of Apple; **16** (*middle*): Marian Stanca/Alamy; **16** (*right*): Courtesy of Google; **17:** *The Star-Ledger*/Mitsu Yasukawa/The Image Works; **18:** Laurence Mouton/PhotoAlto/Corbis; **21:** Kumar Sriskandan/Alamy; **23:** HANDOUT/Reuters/Landov; **24** (*top*): Courtesy of IBM; **24** (*middle*): Courtesy of Hewlett-Packard; **24** (*bottom*): Courtesy of Gateway Computer; **24** (*middle bottom*): Courtesy of Lenovo; **25** (*top left*): Courtesy of Apple Computer; **25** (*top right*): Courtesy of Apple; **25** (middle right): Courtesy of Lenovo; **25** (*middle*): Courtesy of Apple; **25** (*middle left*): Rex Features via AP Images; **25** (*bottom left*): Courtesy of Amazon; **25** (*bottom left*): Shutterstock; **25** (*bottom right*): Courtesy of Barnes & Noble; **25** (*top right bottom*): Courtesy of Google; **26** (*top left*): Courtesy of Wipro; **26** (*middle*): Tony Avelar/The *Christian Science Monitor*/Getty Images; **26** (*top right*): David Friedman/Getty Images; **26** (*bottom*): epa european pressphoto agency b.v./Alamy; **30** (*middle left*): Courtesy of Intel; **30** (*right*): Corbis Flirt/Alamy; **32** (*top left*): Courtesy of Seagate; **34** (*top*): Courtesy of Apple; **34** (*bottom*): Courtesy of Adobe Systems Inc.; **34** (*middle*): Courtesy of Microsoft Corporation: **35** (*bottom*): Courtesy of Ford Motor Company; **35** (*top left*): Rex Features via AP Images; **35** (*top right*): Fred Greaves/AP Images; **37:** John Foxx/Getty Images; **39:** Laurence Mouton/PhotoAlto/Corbis.

Chapter 2

Page 49: EyeSee/Fotosearch; **56:** amana images inc./Alamy; **57:** Courtesy of DirectTV; **58:** Courtesy of HTC; **61:** Courtesy of Chris Harrison; **63:** Noah Seelam/AFP/Getty Images; **75:** EyeSee/Fotosearch; **76:** EyeSee/Fotosearch; **92:** Web 20/Fotosearch; **93:** Dylan Martinez/Reuters/Landov ; **94:** EyeSee/Fotosearch; **100:** EyeSee/Fotosearch; **102:** EyeSee/Fotosearch.

Chapter 3

Page 113: John Foxx/Getty Images; **122** (*top*): John Foxx/Getty Images; **122** (*bottom*): Courtesy of Symantec; **138:** Dan Lamont/Corbis; **140:** Courtesy of Microsoft; **143** (*top*): Stanca Sanda/Alamy; **143** (*middle left*): Courtesy of Apple; **143** (*middle right*): Courtesy of Apple; **143** (*bottom right*): Courtesy of Blackberry: **143** (*bottom left*): Courtesy of Microsoft; **173:** Tom Wagner; **177:** John Foxx/Getty Images; **179:** Courtesy of SolidWorks; **179:** Courtesy of Solid-Works; **180:** John Foxx/Getty Images.

Chapter 4

Page 191: © Stockbyte/Getty Images; **193** (*left*): Courtesy of IBM Archives; **193** (*top right*): Jovani Carlo/BigStock; **193** (*bottom right*): GIPhotoStock/Science Source; **195** (*top*): Courtesy of ESA: **195** (*bottom left*): Courtesy of Intel; **195** (*bottom right*): Courtesy of Intel; **196** (*top*): Courtesy of Lian Li Co.Ltd; **196** (*bottom left*): Courtesy of Apple; **196** (*bottom right*): Courtesy of Toshiba; **196** (*middle*): Courtesy of Dell; **197** (*top*): Courtesy of Microsoft; **197** (*bottom*): Courtesy of Sony; **199:** Courtesy of Google; **201** (*top*): Courtesy of Apple; **201** (*bottom*): Courtesy of iGo, Inc.; **203** (*top*): Courtesy of www.apc.com; **203** (*bottom*): Mark Dierker/McGraw-Hill; **204** (*top*): ImageBroker.net/SuperStock; **204** (*bottom*): Corbis RF/Alamy; **205:** © Stockbyte/Getty Images; **207** (*top*): Beth Dixson/Alamy; **207** (*bottom*): Courtesy of nVidia; **208:** Bob Sacha/Corbis; **213:** Courtesy of Kingston Technology Company; **215:** Paul Velgos/Getty Images; **216:** Editorial Image, LLC/Alamy; **217** (*bottom*): Getty Images; **217** (*top*): Courtesy of Satechi; **218** (*top*): Courtesy of Hewlett-Packard: **218** (*middle right*): Radius Images/Corbis; **218** (*bottom left*): Courtesy of Alan Palmer; **218** (*bottom right*): Courtesy of Lenovo; **219** (*top*): Editorial Image, LLC/Alamy; **219** (*middle left*): Courtesy of Apple; **219** (*bottom right*): Robert Lehmann/Alamy; **219** (*bottom left*): Ellen Isaacs/Alamy; **220** (*middle*): Courtesy of Plantronics; **220** (*bottom*): Courtesy of Toyota; **220** (*top left*): Art Directors & TRIP/Alamy; **220** (*top right*): Courtesy of Lacie; **221** (*top*): Courtesy of StarTech.com; **221** (*top middle right*): David Paul Morris/Bloomberg via Getty Images; **221** (*middle left*): Courtesy of Akai; **221** (*bottom*): Courtesy of IBM; **222** (*bottom*): David Gee 3/Alamy; **223** (*top*): Courtesy of IBM; **223** (*bottom*): Courtesy of Lacie; **224:** © Stockbyte/Getty Images; **225** (*top*): Artur Marciniec/Alamy; **225** (*bottom*): Courtesy of Kprateek88; **227** (*bottom*): Courtesy of Samsung; **227** (*top*): Lawrence Manning/Corbis; **228** (*top*): Tony Cenicola/New York Times/Redux Pictures; **228** (*bottom left*): Fabian Bimmer/AP Images; **228** (*bottom right*): David Taylor Photography/Alamy; **229** (*top left*): Tony Craddock/Science Source; **229** (*top right*): GIPhotoStock/Science Source; **229** (*bottom*): USCIS/AP Images; **230:** © Stockbyte/Getty Images; **232** (*left*): Paul Wootton/Science Source; **232** (*right*): Christian Darkin/Science Source; **233** (*top left*): Courtesy of Saw-Wai Hla and Kendal Clark, Ohio University; **237:** © Stockbyte/Getty Images; **246:** Courtesy of Intel.

Chapter 5

Page 247: Steve Allen/Getty Images; **248:** Courtesy of Google; **250** (*left*): Tom Rittenhouse; **250** (*right*): McGraw-Hill Education/photographer, Mark Dierker; **251** (*top*): Courtesy of Max Planck Institute for Informatics; **251** (*bottom*): Brookstone; **252:** Courtesy of Targus; **253** (*top left*): Andrey Kekyalyaynen/Alamy; **253** (*middle left*): Courtesy of NCR; **253** (*middle right*): Todd Korol/Getty Images; **253** (*bottom*): McGraw-Hill Education/photographer, Mark Dierker; **253** (*top right*): Mary Altaffer/AP Images; **254** (*top right*): McGraw-Hill Education/photographer, Mark Dierker; **254** (*top left*): McGraw-Hill Education/photographer, Mark Dierker; **254** (*middle left*): McGraw-Hill Education/photographer, Mark Dierker; **254** (*middle right*): McGraw-Hill Education/photographer, Mark Dierker; **254** (*bottom*): Courtesy of Bellco Ventures; **255** (*top left*): Courtesy of Logitech; **255** (*middle left*): Cosmin-Constantin Sava/Alamy; **255** (*top right*): Courtesy of Logitech; **255** (*middle right*): David Gee/Alamy; **255** (*bottom*): Ali Mir/Flickr Vision/Getty Images; **256** (*bottom left*): Alex Segre/Alamy; **256** (*bottom right*): Giorgio Cosulich/Getty Images; **256** (*top*): Courtesy of Digital Obscura; **257:** Courtesy of MultiTouch Ltd.; **258** (*top*): Courtesy of Modbook Inc.; **258** (*middle*): Courtesy of Toshiba; **258** (*bottom*): Edward Rozzo/Corbis; **259** (*top*): Courtesy of Wacom Technology; **259** (*middle*): Courtesy of Livescribe; **261** (*top right*): Courtesy of Epson; **261** (*top middle*): Courtesy of ION; **261** (*top left*): Paul Hudson/Getty Images; **261** (*bottom left*): H. Mark Weidman Photography/Alamy; **261** (*bottom right*): Courtesy of NextEngine; **262** (*top*): Courtesy of Intermec Technologies; **262** (*bottom*): Caro/Alamy; **263:** Courtesy of Nikon Metrology; **264** (*top right*): GIPhotoStock/Science Source; **264** (*top left*): Elaine Thompson/AP Images; **264** (*bottom*): Stuart Walker/Alamy; **265** (*top*): Junior Gonzalez/Getty Images; **265** (*bottom*): Courtesy of Sony; **266** (*bottom left*): U.S. Geological Survey, California Water Science Center. Photographer: Owen Baynham, Hydrologic Technician, USGS; **266** (*bottom right*): Courtesy of Lenovo; **266** (*top*): John Lund/Getty Images; **270** (*left*): William Thomas Cain/Getty Images; **270** (*right*): Courtesy of Speedinfo, Inc; **270** (*middle*): Eye Ubiquitous/Alamy; **271:** Andrew Aitchison/In Pictures/Corbis; **272** (*top left*): CBP/Alamy; **272** (*bottom left*): Ed Jones/AFP/Getty Images; **272** (*top *right*): John Moore/Getty Images; **272** (*bottom right*): Saad Shalash/Reuters/Corbis; **273** (*top left*): Mark Thiessen/National Geographic Society/Corbis; **273** (*top right*): John Gress/Corbis; **273** (*bottom*): Ali Lutfi/ZUMA Press/Corbis; **274** (*bottom*): SPL/Science Source; **274** (*top*): Rick Friedman; **276:** Tony Cenicola/New York Times/Redux Pictures; **277** (*bottom*): Vladislav Kochelaevskiy/Alamy; **279** (*left*): Courtesy of LG; **279** (*right*): Courtesy of LG; **280** (*top*): Oleksiy Maksymenko/Alamy; **281:** Ted Foxx/Alamy; **282:** Courtesy of Zebra Technologies; **283** (*middle*): Courtesy of Epson; **283** (*bottom left*): Peter Thompson/New York Times/Redux Pictures; **283** (*bottom right*): Peter Thompson/New York Times/Redux Pictures; **284** (*top*): Courtesy of Zebra Technologies; **284** (*bottom*): Courtesy of Epson; **284** (*middle*): Courtesy of VuPoint Solutions; **285** (*top left*): Courtesy of Hewlett-Packard; **285** (*top right*): Courtesy of Epson; **285** (*middle*): Courtesy of Epson; **285** (*bottom left*): Steven Senne/AP Images; **285** (*bottom right*): Courtesy of Epson; **286:** Steve Allen/Getty Images; **287:** Courtesy of OrCam; **289** (*top*): Courtesy of E-Ink Corp.; **293:** Steve Allen/Getty Images.

Chapter 6

Page 303: Mehau Kulyk/Getty Images; **309:** Science Photo Library/Alamy; **311:** Ahmad Yusni/Corbis Images; **316** (*top*): Courtesy of Belkin; **316** (*top middle*): Courtesy of Sling Media; **316** (*bottom middle*): Courtesy of HMS Industrial Networks; **316** (*bottom*): Courtesy of Linksys; **318** (*bottom left*): Tetra Images/Getty Images; **318** (*bottom right*): artpartner-images.com/Alamy; **320:** PETER FOLEY/epa/Corbis; **322**: digerati/Alamy; **323:** Mehau Kulyk/Getty Images; **324** (*bottom left*): Corbis; **324** (*top left*): Sergey Galushko/Alamy; **324** (*top right*): Dorling Kindersley/Getty Images; **324** (*bottom right*): Don Farrall/Getty Images; **325** (*top left*): Steve Allen/Brand X Pictures/Corbis; **325** (*bottom left*): Andy Whale/Getty Images; 325 (*right*): Seth Resnick/Science Faction/Corbis; **330** (*right*): Brian Williams; **330** (*left*): Bob Rowan; Progressive Image/Corbis; **331** (*top right*): Olivier Prevosto/Corbis; **331** (*top left*): HO/AP Images; **331** (*bottom*): Pallava Bagla/Corbis; **332** (*top*): frans lemmens/Alamy; **332** (*bottom left*): ra photography/Getty Images; **332** (*bottom right*): Patrick Pleul/dpa/Corbis; **334:** Guy Spangenberg/Transtock/Corbis; **337** (*bottom*): Brian Jackson/Alamy; **337** (*top*): McGraw-Hill Education/photographer, Mark Dierker; **337** (*top*): McGraw-Hill Education/photographer, Mark Dierker; **342:** Mehau Kulyk/Getty Images; **344:** Sitade/Getty Images; **346:** spinetta/Shutterstock; **352:** Chad Hunt/Corbis; **357:** Mehau Kulyk/Getty Images.

Chapter 7

Page 367: Maciej Frolow/Getty Images; **369:** Sergey150770/Shutterstock; **370** (*top*): Shizuo Kambayashi/AP Images; **370** (*bottom*): Paul Sakuma/AP Images; **371:** macana/Alamy; **372:** Maciej Frolow/Getty Images; **373:** Courtesy of HTC; **374** (*top*): Courtesy of Blackberry; **374** (*bottom*): picturelibrary/Alamy; **376** (*top*): Ryan McVay/Getty Images; **376** (*bottom*): iQoncept/Shutterstock; **379:** Courtesy of Samsung; **380:** Courtesy of Amazon.com; **381:** Maciej Frolow/Getty Images; **383:** Courtesy of Sony; **384** (*right*): Courtesy of Sony Corp.; **384** (*left*): Kiyoshi Ota/Bloomberg via Getty Images; **384** (*right*): Tomohiro Ohsumi/Bloomberg via Getty Images; **386:** D-BASE/Getty Images; **388:** McGraw-Hill Education/photographer, Mark Dierker; **389:** Woodygraphs/Alamy; **391:** Maciej Frolow/Getty Images; **393:** Texas Stock Photo/Alamy; **399** (*top*): Enigma/Alamy; **399** (*bottom*): Courtesy of Sling Media; **399** (*bottom*): Courtesy of Sling Media; **399** (*middle*): Courtesy of Tivo; **400:** Al Powers/Invision/AP Images; **401:** CP, Aaron Harris/AP Images; **402:** Maciej Frolow/Getty Images.

Chapter 8

Page 407: Simone Brandt/Alamy; **408:** Christoph Dernbach/dpa/Corbis; **413:** Courtesy of Forbes.com; **414:** Simon Dawson/Bloomberg via Getty Images; **415:** Simone Brandt/Alamy; **421:** Jim Craigmyle/Corbis; **423** (*top*): Corbis; **436:** Courtesy of Caliper Corporation; **443** (*middle right*): Bob Mahoney/The Image Works; **443** (*top left*): M.Spencer Green/AP Images; **443** (*top right*): Courtesy of Ford Motor Company; **443** (*middle left*): AP Images; **443** (*bottom*): Courtesy of Bernard Frischer of Virginia's Institute for Advanced Technology in the Humanities/AP Images; **445** (*bottom left*): BigDog Robot image courtesy of Boston Dynamics; **445** (*top right*): Kim Jae-Hwan/AFP/Getty Images; **445** (*middle left*): Lisa Poole/AP Images; **445** (*top left*): Bertil Ericson/AP Images; **445** (*top middle*): Brett Coomer/AP Images; **445** (*bottom right*): Narong Sangnak/epa/Corbis; **445** (*middle right*): Mike Derer/AP Images; **447** (*left*): Courtesy of Zojirushi; **448:** Courtesy of Kevin Warwick; **449** (*top*): Science Museum/SSPL/The Image Works; **449** (*bottom right*): Tetra Images/Getty Images; **449** (*top*): Jeff McIntosh/AP Images; **451:** 3QuarksMedia/Alamy; **452:** Simone Brandt/Alamy.

Chapter 9

Page 459: Corbis; **464:** Orjan F. Ellingvag/Corbis; **465:** Everyday Images/Alamy; **473** (*left*): PRNewsFoto/HT Systems, LLC/AP Images; **473** (*right*): Courtesy of Apple; **474** (*left*): Ricki Rosen/Corbis; **474** (*right*): Tony Cenicola/New York Times/Redux Pictures; **475:** Kyodo/XinHua/Xinhua Press/Corbis; **478:** Corbis; **482:** Nati Harnik/AP Images; **484** (*left*): Ted S. Warren/AP Images; **484** (*middle*): Erik de Castro/Reuters/Corbis; **484** (*right*): Andrew Brookes, National Physical Laboratory/Science Source; **485** (*left*): John Turner/Corbis; **485** (*right*): Don Farrall/Getty Images; **486** (*top*): Courtesy of Troels Eklund Andersen; **486** (*bottom*): Pete Souza/The White House/MCT via Getty Images; **488:** Gabe Palmer/Corbis; **489** (*bottom left*): Courtesy of Larson, a DMB Company; **489** (*top right*): Arnd Wiegmann/Reuters/Corbis; **489** (*top left*): Bernd Thissen/dpa/Corbis; **489** (*bottom right*): David Butow/Corbis SABA; **491** (*bottom right*): Comstock/PictureQuest; **492:** Vladimir Maravic/Getty Images; **496:** © 2013, Dawghaus Photography; **499:** Corbis.

Chapter 10

Page 503: Max Delson Martins Santos/Getty Images; **507** (*top*): PhotoDisc/Getty Images; **507** (*bottom*): Tetra Images/Alamy; **508:** Sam Edwards/age fotostock; **509:** Photodisc/Getty Images; **511:** Photodisc/Getty Images; **512:** Alexander A. Kataytsev/Alamy; **513:** Blend Images/Alamy; **514:** Image Source/PunchStock; **516** (*bottom*): Squaredpixels/Getty Images; **516** (*top*): Steve Jurvetson/Creative Commons; **518:** nullplus/Getty Images; **523:** isak55/Shutterstock; **524:** PhotoDisc/Getty Images; **525:** tawan/Shutterstock; **526:** Carol and Mike Werner/Alamy; **533** (*left*): Cynthia Johnson//Time Life Pictures/Getty Images; **533** (*right*): Science Source; **543:** Max Delson Martins Santos/Getty Images.

Index

Boldface *page numbers indicate pages on which key terms are defined.*

A

Abandonware, 146
Accelerometer, 274
Access points, **58, 103,** 339
Access security
  biometrics and, **473**–474
  control of access and, 474
  techniques used for, 472–474
Accounting and finance department, 431
Acronyms, 40
Acrostics, 40
Active display area, 277
Active matrix LCDs, 279
Active RFID tags, 263
ActiveX controls, 541–**542, 544**
Addiction, 490, 492, 502
Add-ons, disabling, 542
Address-book feature, 79
Addresses
  email, 78–79
  web page, 64–65
Adobe Acrobat, 178
Adobe Flash Player, **541**
Adobe InDesign, 170, 172
Advance-fee scam, 469
Adware, **99, 103**
Aerial maps, 86–87
Agents, 71
Aggregator programs, 395, 396
Agile system development, 511
AGP (accelerated graphics port) bus, 217
Air mouse, 254
Airplay Mirroring feature, 136
Albin, Tom, 291
Algorithms, **37**–38, **41,** 427, 438, **517, 544,** 549
Alpha testing, 523
Always On generation, 402
Amazon.com, 413–414
AMD chips, 206, 207
AM radio, 329
Analog cellphones, 335–336
Analog signals, **305**–306, **359**
  converting into digital signals, 308
  modem conversion of, 306–307
Analog-to-digital converter, 308
Analytical graphics, **160**–161, **182**
Analyzing systems. *See* Systems analysis
Android operating system, **143**
Animation, **87, 103, 173**–174, **182**
Animation files, 150
Animation software, 173–174
Anonymous FTP sites, 83
ANSI symbols, 520
Antispyware programs, 99
Antivirus software, **100, 103,** 122, 350–351
Appeal-to-authority argument, 543
Appeal-to-pity argument, 543
Applets, **86, 103,** 536, 537
Application generators, 531
Application software, **34, 41, 114,** 144–179, **182**
  animation software, 173–174
  audio editing software, 173
  computer-aided design programs, **178**–179
  database software, **161**–163
  desktop publishing software, 170–172
  documentation for, 148–149
  file types and, 150–151
  financial software, **168**–169
  illustration programs, 172
  installation of, 149–150
  integrated packages of, **164**
  IT timeline and, 164–171
  licenses for, 145–146
  methods for obtaining, 145–148
  multimedia authoring software, **174**
  personal information managers, **164**–165, 166
  presentation graphics software, **166**–168
  project management software, **176**–177
  review questions/exercises on, 187–190
  specialty software, 165–179
  spreadsheet programs, **158**–161
  suites of, 164–165
  tech support for, 180–181
  tutorials for, 148
  types of, 149
  video editing software, 172
  web page design/authoring software, **174**–175
  word processing software, **153**–158
Application virtualization, 231
Apps, 373
  Apple, 136, 378
  availability of, 373–374
  choosing necessary, 20–21
  college productivity, 377
  development of, 536
  Google, 149, 379
  Internet radio, 395
  predictive, 460
  UIT 11e, 1
  web, 147
Apt, Jay, 464
Archival copy, 145
Arithmetic/logic unit (ALU), 210, **211, 239**
Arithmetic operations, 211
ARPANET, 50
Artifacts, 173
Artificial intelligence (AI), **37**–38, **41, 438**–451, **453,** 532
  approaches to, 438
  cyborgs, 448
  ethics and, 451
  expert systems, 439–441
  fuzzy logic, **446**–447
  genetic algorithms, 448
  intelligent agents, **442**
  machine learning, 37
  natural language processing, 38, **442**
  neural networks, **447**
  pattern recognition, 38, **442**
  review questions/exercises on, 455–458
  robotics, 38, **444**–446
  simulators, **444**
  the Singularity and, 450–**451**
  Turing test and, 448–450
  virtual reality, 38, **442**–444
  weak vs. strong, 438–439
Artificial life (A-life), 447
Art programs, 172
ASCII coding scheme, **200, 239**
ASCII files, 151
Aspect ratio, 277, 398
Assemblers, **529, 544**
Assembly language, **528**–529, **544**
Association for Computing Machinery (ACM), 549
Attachments, email, 81, 82
Auctions, web, 91–92
Audio
  digital sampling of, 308
  input devices, 268–269

Audio—*Cont.*
MP3 format, **383**
output devices, 287
search tools for, 74
software for editing, 173
streaming, **88,** 394
web-based, 74, 88
Audioconferencing, 342
Audio files, 150, 151
Audio-input devices, **268**–269, **296**
Audit controls, 474
Authentication process, 60
Authorization control, 413
Autocorrect function, 155
Automated teller machines (ATMs), **252,** 472
Avatars, **6, 41**

B

B2B (business-to-business) commerce, **91, 103**
B2C (business-to-consumer) commerce, **91, 103**
Back and neck pains, 291, 294
Backbone, **317, 359**
Internet, 59, **60,** 317
network, 317, 318
Backdoors, 349
Backups
application software, 145
cloud storage vs., 231
data file, 224, 226
Backup utility, 122
Backus, John, 532
Baig, Edward, 379
Bandwidth, **52, 103, 327**–328, **359**
Banking, online, 91
Bar charts, 161
Bar-code readers, 261–**262, 296**
Bar codes, **261**–262, 263, **296**
Baseband transmission, 52
BASIC programming language, 530, 534
Basu, Mitra, 234
Batch processing, 434
Bathroom mirror technology, 288
Batteries
digital camera, 390
future of, 235
laptop, 237
portable media player, 384
Bays, 201
Beepers, 335
Berners-Lee, Tim, 62, 63, 92, 539
Beta testing, 524
Bezos, Jeffrey, 413–414
Big Data, **37, 41,** 288, 408, 428–430
three implications of, 428–429
uses of, 429–430
Big Data analytics, **428, 453**
Bilton, Nick, 2
Binary coding schemes, 199–200
Binary system, **197**–200, **239**
Bing web portal, 70
Biometric devices, 271, 272, 274, 352
Biometrics, **271,** 272, **296,** 351–352, **473**–474, **500**
BIOS programs, 116
Bit depth, 261, 278
Bit-mapped images, 172
Bitmaps, 261
Bits (binary digits), **198, 239,** 410
Bits per second (bps), **52, 103**
BlackBerry OS, 143
Black-hat hackers, 344
Blended threats, **349, 359**
Blocking software, 493
Blogosphere, **88, 103**
Blogs, **14, 41,** 88–89
Bloom, Benjamin, 44
Bluetooth technology, **220**–221, **239,** 330, **340, 359,** 374
Blu-ray optical format, **227, 239**
Boehret, Katherine, 380
Booker, Cory, 11
Bookmarks, 67, 69
Boolean operators, 76
Bootcamp utility, 135
Boot disk, 116–117
Booting, **116**–118, **182**
Botnets, **349, 359**
Bots, 71, 442
Brainwave devices, 275
Brand, Stewart, 497
Breazeal, Cynthia, 445
Brichter, Loren, 257
Bricklin, Daniel, 158
Bridges, **316, 359**
Broadband connections, **52,** 54, **103, 327**–328, **359**
Broadband wireless services, 337
Broadcast radio, **329**–330, **359**
Brooks, Cathy, 93
Browser hijackers, **99, 103**
Browser software. *See* Web browsers
Brute force technique, 439
BSD operating system, 141
Buffer, 118
Bugs, software, 462
Bull, Michael, 382
Bullying, Internet, 94
Buses, 210, **211**–212, 216–217, **239**
Businesses
cyberspying by, 476–477
electronic commerce by, 90–92
Business graphics, 160–161
Business intelligence, 435
Business start-ups, 12–13
Business-to-business (B2B) commerce, **91, 103**
Business-to-consumer (B2C) commerce, **91, 103**
Bus network, **320**–321, **359**
Buying considerations
for laptop computers, 236, 237–238
for monitors, 280
for printers, 286
BYOD considerations, 507, 508
Bytes, 31, **198, 239,** 410

C

C programming language, 530, 534
C++ programming language, 534, 536
C2C (consumer-to-consumer) commerce, **91**–92, **103**
Cable modems, **56**–57, **103**
Cache memory, **213**–214, **239**
CAD programs, 178–179
CAD/CAM programs, 178
Callback systems, 473
Caller ID, 370
Camera phones, 375
Cameras. *See* Digital cameras
Cantu, Homaro, 283
Captchas, 450
Career information, 12–14
See also Employment
Carpal tunnel syndrome (CTS), **291, 296**
Carr, Nicholas, 490
Cars
GPS units in, 334
hands-free devices in, 377
self-driving, 275–276
Cascading menus, 130
Case (system cabinet), **30, 41,** 201, 202
Case control structure, 520, 522
CASE tools, **510,** 511, **544**
Cashless society, 10
Cathode-ray tube (CRT) displays, 280
CD drive, **32, 41**
CDMA standard, 337
CD-R disks, **226, 239**
CD-ROM disks, **225, 239**
CD-ROM drives, 225
CD-RW disks, **226, 239**
Cell pointer, 159
Cells, spreadsheet, **159, 182**
Cellular radio, **330, 359**
Cellular telephones, 15–16, 335–338
analog, 335–336
broadband, 337
comparison sites, 337
digital, 336–337
E911 capability, 334
features of, 373–375
health issues and, 292
LTE standard for, 338
malware protection for, 101
recycling/donating, 488, 489
school settings and, 392
smartphones vs., 373
societal effects of, 376–377
texting with, 375–376
tracking of, 334
See also Smartphones
Central processing unit (CPU), 30, 195, **209**–212, **239–240**
components on, 210–212
internal management of, 118
Cerocke, Steve, 507, 508
CGI (Common Gateway Interface), 542

Channel capacity, 52
Character (byte), **410, 453**
Character-recognition devices, 264–265
Charge-coupled devices (CCDs), 266
Charts, 160–161
Cheating, 102
Children
cyberbullying of, **494**
protection of, 492–494
Chips, **194**–195, **239**
CMOS, 214
flash memory, 214
making of, 194
memory, **30,** 212
microprocessor, **195,** 205–209
RAM, 212–213
ROM, 214
Chipsets, **206, 239**
Choice overload, 371, 372
Chrome OS, 118
Circuit, 192
Circular reasoning, 543
Citing web sources, 74
Clamshells, 196
Classes, 536
Classification analysis, 427
Classrooms, computer use in, 499
Clean install, 150
Client operating systems, 134
Clients, **26, 41, 59, 103,** 312
Client-server networks, 26, **312**–313, **359**
Clinton, Hillary, 486
Clip art, 168
Clipboard, 154–155
Clock speed, 208
Closed architecture, 215
Closed-circuit television, 342
Cloud computing, **36**–37, **41,** 118
Cloud storage, **231, 239**
Cloud suites, 164
Cloze app, 19
Clusters, 222
CMOS chips, **214, 239**
Coaxial cable, **324, 359**
COBOL programming language, 528, 529, 530, 532–533
Cochran, Anita, 485
Codd, E. F., 419
Codecs, 152
Coding, **523, 544**
Cognitive Tutor, 6
Cold boot, 116
Collaboration, 36
Colleges
online education through, 5–6
uses of information technology in, 5
Color depth, 261, **278, 296**
Column charts, 161
Columns
spreadsheet, 159
text, 157
Command-driven interface, 126
Command-line interface, 133, 135
Commerce, electronic. *See* E-commerce
Commercial software, 145
Communications, 28, 29
Communications hardware, 33
Communications media, **324, 359–360**
wired, 324–326
wireless, 327–343
Communications satellites, **57, 103, 330**–331, **360**
Communications technology, **4, 41,** 303–366
bandwidth and, **327**–328
cellular telephones, 335–338
contemporary examples of, 4–15
electromagnetic spectrum and, **327,** 328
Global Positioning System (GPS), **332**–334
networks, **308**–322
pagers, **335**
radio-frequency spectrum and, **327,** 328–329
recent developments in, 35–36
review questions/exercises on, 363–366
satellites and, 330–331
security issues and, 343–358
telecommuting/telework and, 323
timeline of progress in, 16–24, 304–307
virtual meetings and, 342
wired, 324–326
wireless, 327–343
See also Information technology
Compilers, **529, 544**
Comprehension, 44
Compression, **152**–153, **182**
lossless vs. lossy, 153
new technology for image, 236
utility programs for, 122–123
video and audio, 173
Computational intelligence, **438, 453**
Computer-aided design (CAD) programs, **178**–179, **182**
Computer-aided design/computer-aided manufacturing (CAD/CAM) programs, 178
Computer-aided software engineering (CASE) tools, **510,** 511
Computer animation, 173–174
Computer-based information systems, 432–438
decision support systems, **435**–436
executive support systems, **437**
expert systems, **437**–438
management information systems, **435**
office information systems, **433**–434
review questions/exercises on, 455–457
transaction processing systems, **434**
Computer crime, **464**–472, **500**
deterrents to, 470–472
types of, 345–347, 464–470
Computer Emergency Response Team (CERT), 471
Computer Ethics (Forester and Morrison), 38
Computer forensics, 464
Computer Fraud and Abuse Act (CFAA), 345
Computer operators, 525
Computers, **4, 41**
basic operations of, 27–28, 29
crimes related to, 464–470
custom-built, 28
environmental issues related to, 487–490
guarding against theft, 293
hardware of, **27,** 28–33
health issues related to, 290–292, 294–295
purpose of, 27
recycling/donating, 38, 488, 489
software of, **27,** 33–34
student use of, 499
types of, 22–26
warfare using, 483–484
work area setup, 295
See also Personal computers
Computer-supported cooperative work systems, 432
Computer technology, 4
contemporary examples of, 4–15
future developments in, 232–236
information resources on, 196
overview of developments in, 34–35
timeline of progress in, 16–24, 304–307
See also Information technology
Computer vision syndrome (CVS), **291, 296**
Con artists, 346
Concentration, 39
Concurrent-use license, 146
Conficker worm, 348
Connectivity, **35, 41**
Consumer-to-consumer (C2C) commerce, **91**–92, **103**
Contactless smart cards, 231
Contact smart cards, 231
Content templates, 168
Context-sensitive help, 133
Control structures, 518, **520,** 522, 523, **544**
Control unit, **210, 239**
Conventional AI, **438, 453**
Convergence, 36, 304–305, **369**–370, **403**
Conversion
signal, 306–307
system, 513
Convertible tablets, 196–197
Cook, Tim, 248
Cookies, **98, 103,** 357

Copy command, 154
Copyright, 145, 466
Cordless mouse, 254
Counterfeiters, 346
Counterterrorism, 427
Course-management software (CMS), 5
CPU. *See* Central processing unit
Crackers, **344**–345, **360**
Cramming, 39
Crawlers, 71
Credit bureaus, 356, 358
Critical thinking, 44, 543, 548–549
CRITIC guidelines, 75
Crowdfunding, 9
CSS (Cascading Style Sheet), 540
Cunningham, Ward, 73
Cursor, **153, 182**
Custom-built PCs, 28
Custom software, **145, 182**
Cut command, 154
Cyberattacks, **343, 360,** 483–484
Cyberbullying, **494, 500**
Cybercrime. *See* Computer crime
Cyberintruders, 343–347
Cyberspace, **17,** 19, **41**
Cyberspying, 476–482
  by businesses, 476–477
  by governments, 477, 479–483
Cyberstalking, 494
Cyberterrorists, 344–345
Cyberthreats, 343, 347–350
Cyberwarfare, 482, **483**–484, **500**
Cyborgs, 448
Cycles, 208

D

Daniel, Jennifer, 145
Dashboard
  Google, 477
  Mac OS X, 135
Data, **27, 41**
  accuracy of, 415
  analog vs. digital, 305–306
  analyzing, 163, 509–511
  backing up, 122, 224, 226
  Big Data, **37, 41,** 288, 408
  completeness of, 415
  compressing, 122–123
  gathering, 509
  hierarchical organization of, 409–410
  importing and exporting, 152
  longevity of, 230
  manipulation of, 484–487
  network sharing of, 309
  permanent storage of, 28, 30–32
  preservation of, 230
  privacy issues, 353, 477
  protecting, 293–294, 474–475
  recovering, 223
Data access area, 222
Database administrator (DBA), **416,** 417, **453**
Database files, 150
Database management system (DBMS), **412**–416, **453**
  administrator of, 416
  benefits of, 412–413
  components of, 414, 416
Databases, **11, 41, 161, 182, 409**–428, **453**
  accessed through networks, 309
  accuracy of information in, 415
  components of, 414, 416
  data mining and, **425**–428
  data storage hierarchy and, **409**–410
  decision-making process and, 430–438
  disadvantages of, 414
  ethics related to, 451
  hierarchical, 416–418
  identity theft and, 355
  IT timeline and, 416–420
  key field in, **163,** 411–412
  list of interesting, 428
  management systems for, 412–416
  multidimensional, **423**–425
  network, 418–419
  object-oriented, **422**–423
  privacy issues and, 353, 477
  querying, 421–422, 425
  relational, **162, 419**–422
  review questions/exercises on, 455–458
  security of, 413
Database servers, 312
Database software, **161**–163, **182**
  benefits of, 161–162
  features of, 162–163
  illustrated overview of, 162
  personal information managers, **164**–165, 166
Data centers, **207**–208, **240**
Data cleansing, 427
Data compression utilities, 122–123
Data dictionary, **414, 453**
Data files, **150**–151, **182**
Data flow diagram (DFD), **509**–510, **544**
Data integrity, 412–413
Data mining (DM), **425**–428, **453**
  applications of, 427–428
  process of, 426–427
Data-recovery utility, 122
Data redundancy, 412
Data scrubbing, 427
Data storage hierarchy, **409**–410, **453**
Data transmission speeds, 52–53
Data warehouse, **427, 453**
Dating, online, 14–15
DBMS utilities, **416, 453**
  See also Database management system
DDR-SDRAM chips, 213
Debugging programs, **524, 544**
Decentralized organizations, 432
Decision making
  Big Data and, 429, 430
  computer-based information systems for, 435–436
  make-or-buy decisions, 512
  management levels and, 431–432, 433
Decision support system (DSS), **435**–436, **453**
Dedicated ports, 217
Deep knowledge, 441
Default settings, **157, 182**
Defragmenter, 123
Deleting text, 154
Demand reports, 435
Democracy, electronic, 10–11
Denial-of-service (DoS) attacks, **347, 360**
Departments, organizational, 431
Design templates, 168
Desk-checking programs, **523, 544**
Desktop, **128, 182**
Desktop operating system, 134–140
Desktop PCs, **24, 41,** 196
Desktop publishing (DTP), **170**–172, **182–183**
Desktop scanners, 260
Desktop Windows, 137–138, 139
Detachable PCs, 197
Detail design, 512
Detweiler, Carrick, 482
Developing information systems. *See* Systems development
Device drivers, 34, 115, **121, 183**
Dextr keyboard, 251
Diagnostic programs, 524
Diagnostic routines, 116
Dial-up connections, **53,** 55, **103**
Dictation feature, 136
Digital cameras, **265**–266, **296,** 386–393
  batteries for, 390
  ethics related to, 393
  how they work, 266, 387–391
  lenses of, 388–389
  phones as, 375
  point-and-shoot, 387
  resolution of, 388
  sharing photos from, 391
  single-lens reflex, 387–388
  societal effects of, 392–393
  storage media for, 389
  transferring images from, 390–391
  viewfinders and screens for, 389
Digital convergence, **304**–305, **360,** 369–370
Digital natives, 3
Digital pens, **259, 296**
Digital radio, 393–394
Digital signals, **306, 360**
  converting analog signals into, 308
  modem conversion of, 306–307
Digital television (DTV), **397**–398, **403**
Digital-to-analog converter, 308
Digital video recorders (DVRs), 398

Digital wireless services, **336, 360**
Digital zoom, 388
Digitizers, **258, 296**
Digitizing tablets, **258,** 259, **296**
DIMMs, 213
Direct implementation, 513
Direct-mail marketing, 429–430
Directories, 118, 119
Dirty data problems, 462, 463
Disabilities, computer users with
Disaster-recovery plans, **475, 500**
Discussion groups, 83
Disk cleanup utility, 123
Display screens, **276**–280, **296**
  clarity of, 277–278
  features of, 276–278
  future developments in, 289
  health issues related to, 291, 294
  how they work, 279
  laptop computer, 238
  multitouch screens, **256**–257
  portable media player, 384
  resolution standards for, 278
  size and aspect ratio of, 277
  smartphone, 374
  touch screens, **256**
  types of, 278–280
  using multiple, 280
Distance learning, **5**–6, **41**
Distracted driving, 385
Distributed denial of service (DDOS), 470
DNA computing, 234–235
DNA databases, 479
Documentation, 148–149, **525, 544**
Document files, 150
  creating, 153–154
  editing, 154–156
  formatting, 156–157
  illustrated overview of, 154
  navigating to, 130
  printing, 157
  saving, 157–158
  tracking changes in, 156
  web formatted, 157
Document Type Definition (DTD), 540
Domain names, 64–65, 79
Domains, **64,** 79, **103**
DOS (Disk Operating System), 133, 135
Dot-matrix printers, 280
Dot pitch (dp), **277, 296**
Dots per inch (dpi), **261,** 277, 280, **296**
Dotted quad, 61
Downlinking, 330
Downloading, **20, 41,** 53
Draft quality output, 280
DRAM chips, **212**–213
Drawing programs, 172
Drivers. *See* Device drivers
Drones, 482
Drop-down menu, 128
Drum scanners, 260
DSL (digital subscriber line), **54,** 57, **103**
Dual-core processors, 207
Dual-scan monitors, 279
Dumb terminals, **252, 296**
DVD drive, **32**
DVD filters, 493
DVD-ROM disks, **226**–227, **240**
DVD zones, 227–228
DVI ports, 219
Dvorak keyboard, 251
Dye-sublimation printers, 284
Dynamic IP address, 61
Dynamic range, 261

E

E911 (Enhanced 911), 334
Earbuds, dangers of, 385
EBCDIC coding scheme, **200, 240**
E-book readers, **25, 42, 380**–382, **403**
  benefits of, 380–381
  drawbacks of, 382
  how they work, 381–382
E-books, **380, 403**
E-commerce (electronic commerce), **90**–92, **104**
Economic issues, 496–498
E-Democracy website, 11
Editing documents, 154–156
Education
  distance learning and, 5–6
  information technology and, 4–6
  plagiarism issues and, 102
  software for, 149, 179
  See also Learning
E Ink technology, 381–382
E-learning, 5–6
Electrical power issues, 201, 203, 205, 462, 464
Electromagnetic fields (EMFs), **291, 296**
Electromagnetic spectrum of radiation, **327,** 328, **360**
Electromechanical problems, 462–463
Electronic imaging, 260, 265
Electronic spreadsheets. *See* Spreadsheet programs
Electronic surveillance, 472
Electrostatic plotters, 284
Email (electronic mail), **5,** 16–17, **42,** 77–81
  addresses, 78–79
  attachments, 81, 82
  fake, 97
  filters for, 81
  how to use, 78–81
  junk or spam, 97
  mailing lists, **83**
  managing, 18–19
  netiquette, **81**
  organizing, 81
  privacy of, 96, 357
  reactionary nature of, 17
  remote access to, 81
  replying to, 80
  sending and receiving, 78, 80
  software programs for, 78
  web-based, 78
Email bombs, 350
Email programs, **78, 104**
Embedded computers, 26, 195
Embedded Linux, 143–144
Embedded operating systems, **142**–144, **183**
Emoji, 81
Emoticons, 81
Emotion recognition, 274
Employee crime, 345
Employee Internet management (EIM) software, 472
Employee monitoring, 472, 478
Employment
  computer skills for, 12, 13, 14
  contemporary changes in, 496–497
  robots and the future of, 452
  searching for, 13–14
  social networking and, 94
  See also Workplace
Encapsulation, 536
Encryption, **352, 360, 474, 500**
Enhanced keyboards, 250
Enhanced-relational databases, 423
ENIAC computer, 15, 192, 205
Enough: Staying Human in an Engineered Age (McKibben), 495
Entertainment software, 149
Environmental problems, 487–490
Environmental Protection Agency (EPA), 425
E-personality, 93
Erasable optical disk, 226
Erasable paper, 289
E-readers, **25, 42**
Ergonomics, **292,** 294–295, **296**
Errors
  human, 461–462
  procedural, 462
  software, 462, 524
eSATA ports, **220, 240**
Ethernet, **219, 240, 321,** 322, 325, **360**
Ethical hackers, 345
Ethics, **38, 42**
  AI and, 451
  databases and, 451
  media manipulation and, 484–487
  nanotechnology and, 235
  netiquette and, 81
  plagiarism and, 102
  privacy and, 96, 353
  RFID tags and, 264
Ethics in Modeling (Wallace), 451
Event-driven program, 537
E-Verify program, 479
Evil twin attack, **469, 500**
Exabyte (EB), 31, **199, 240**
Exception reports, 435
Executable files, **152, 183**

Executive information system (EIS), 437
Executive support system (ESS), **437, 453**
Expansion, **204,** 215, **240**
Expansion buses, 216
Expansion cards, 204, **215**–216, **240**
Expansion slots, **30, 42, 215, 240**
Expert systems, **437**–438, 439–441, **453–454**
Exporting data, **152, 183**
Exposed identity, 368
ExpressCards, 216
Extensible hypertext markup language (XHTML), 66
Extensible markup language (XML), **88, 108, 540**–541, **547**
Extension names, 150
External cache, 213
External hard disks, 223
Extranets, **314, 360**
Eyestrain, 291, 294

F

Facebook, 14, 92, 93, 392
Face recognition, 272, 274, 473, 474
Fader, Peter, 382
Fair and Accurate Credit Transactions Act (2003), 478
Fair use, 485
Fake email, 97
False cause argument, 543
Farid, Hany, 487
Fast Ethernet, 321
Favorites, 67, 69
Feathering, 282
Federal Bureau of Investigation (FBI), 469, 481, 516
Federal Communications Commission (FCC), 292, 327, 397
Federal Trade Commission (FTC), 354, 355, 467
Feigenbaum, Edward, 437
Fiber-optic cable, 318, **324**–325, **360**
Field (column), 162, **410, 454**
File names, **150, 183**
File-processing system, 412
Files, **118,** 150, **183**
  backing up, 122
  compressing, **152**–153
  converting, 513
  data, **150**–151
  database, **410, 454**
  exporting, **152**
  importing, **152**
  managing, 118–119
  program, **152**
  transferring, 390–391
  types of, 150–151
File servers, 312
File-sharing networks, 466
Filo, David, 368
Filters, email, 81
Finance, online, 10
Financial information, 10
Financial software, **168**–169, **183**
Find command, 154
Fingerprint readers, 473
Firewalls, **314**–315, **360**
FireWire bus, 217
FireWire port, **219, 240**
First-generation (1G) technology, 335–336
FISA court, 481
Fixed disks, 223
Flaming, **81, 104**
Flash memory, 214
Flash memory cards, **228, 240,** 389
Flash memory chips, **214, 240**
Flash memory drives, 383
Flash memory sticks, **228, 240**
Flash Player (Adobe), **541, 544**
Flash scripting language, 541
Flatbed scanners, **260, 297**
Flat-panel displays, **279, 296–297**
Flops, 23
Florencio, Dinei, 345
Flowcharts, 517, 520, 521
FM radio, 329
Focusing, 39
Folders, 118, 119, 128
Fonts, 157, 281
Footers, 157
Foreign Intelligence Surveillance Act (FISA) court, 481
Foreign keys, 163, 411–412
Forensics, computer, 464
Forester, Tom, 38
Formatting
  documents, 156–157
  hard drives, 224
Formulas, **160,** 163, **183**
FORTRAN programming language, 530, 532
Forums, web, 83
4G technology, **58, 104,** 337–338
Fourth-generation languages (4GLs), 531
Fragmentation, 123
Frame-grabber video card, 267
Frames, **69–70, 104**
Fraud
  Internet-related, 467–470
  tools for detecting, 472
Freedman, Alan, 536
Freedom of Information Act, 476
Freeware, **147, 183**
Frequency, 327
Fried, Jason, 504
Friedman, Thomas, 497
FriendFeed, 93, 95
Frontside bus, 216
FTP (File Transfer Protocol), **83**–84, **104**
Full-motion video (FMV) card, 267–268
Function keys, **125, 183**
Functions, **160, 183**
Fuzzy logic, **446**–447, **454**

G

Gambling, online, 490, 492
Gameboxes, 399–401
Games
  consoles for playing, 399–401
  input devices for, 257
Gaming software, 179
Garden area networks, 311
Gateways, **316, 360**
Generations of programming languages, **527, 544**
Genetic algorithms, 448
Genographic Project, 409
Geocaching, 332
Geographic information system (GIS), 436
Geostationary Earth orbit (GEO), 330–331
Geschke, Charles, 169
Gesture interface, 29, 125–126
Gesture recognition, 274, 275
Gibson, William, 17
GIF animation, 174
Gigabit Ethernet, 321
Gigabits per second (Gbps), **53, 104**
Gigabyte (G, GB), 31, **198**–199, **240**
Gigahertz (GHz), 30, **208, 240**
Gilliam, Harold, 460
Global Positioning System (GPS), **332**–334, **360–361,** 375
Golden-i headset, 35
Google, 74, 76, 325
Google Android, **143, 183**
Google Apps, 149
Google Books Library Project, 74, 409
Google Chrome, 63, 66–67, 141
Google Earth, 86–87
Google Glass, 248
Google Scholar, 74
Google Sites, 177
Government
  domestic spying by, 353, 477, 479–482
  foreign spying by, 482–483
  information technology and, 10–11
GPS. *See* Global Positioning System
Grammar checker, 155
Graphical user interface (GUI), **126**–133, **183**
Graphics
  analytical, **160**–161
  presentation, 166–168
Graphics cards, **215, 240,** 278
Graphics files, 150, 151, 172
Graphics ports, **219**
Graphics processing unit (GPU), **207, 240**
Groupware, 149
GSM standard, 337
Gunther, Judith Anne, 449–450
Gutenberg, Johannes, 230

H

Hackers, **344**–345, **361**
Hacktivists, 344

Hadler, Gary, 517
Hand-geometry systems, 473
Handheld scanners, 260
Handheld system units, 197
Hands-free device setups, 377
Handshaking process, 60, 316
Handwriting recognition, **258, 297**
Hardcopy output, **276, 297**
Hard-disk cartridges, 223
Hard-disk drive, **32, 42**
Hard disks, 32, **221**–224, **240**
  crashing of, 222–223
  defragmenting, 123
  external, 223
  higher-density, 223, 225
  large computer system, 223
  MP3 player, 383
  nonremovable, 223
  starting over with, 224
Hard goods, 90
Hardware, **27,** 28–33, **42,** 191–246
  communications, 33
  computer case, 30, 196, 201, 202
  converting, 513
  CPU, 195, **209**–212
  ergonomics and, **292,** 294–295
  expandability of, 215–217
  firewall protection using, 315
  future developments in, 232–236, 271–275, 288–290
  health issues related to, 290–292, 294–295
  input, 28–29, **248,** 249–275
  IT timeline and, 194–204, 254–260
  memory, 30, 212–214
  microchips, **194**–195
  miniaturization of, 195
  mobility of, 195
  motherboard, 203–204
  network sharing of, 309
  obsolescence of, 230
  obtaining for systems, 512
  output, 32–33, **248,** 249, 275–290
  ports, **217**–221
  power supply, **201,** 203
  processing, 30, 205–207
  protecting, 293, 294
  review questions/exercises on, 243–246, 300–302
  secondary storage, 30–32, **221**–229
  system unit, 30, **196**–197, 201, 202
  theft of, 293, 346, 464–465
  transistors, **193**
Hasty generalization, 543
HD (hybrid digital) radio, **394, 403**
HDMI ports, **221, 240**
Headaches, 291, 294
Head crash, 223
Headers, 157
Head-mounted display, 444
Health issues
  cellphones and, 292
  computer use and, 290–292, 294–295
  data mining and, 428
  medical technology and, 6, 8–9
  online information about, 8
Hearing loss, 385
Help command, **133,** 134, **183**
Help programs, 180
Hepatic systems, 274
Herley, Cormac, 345
Hertz (Hz), 278, 327
Heuristics, **438, 454**
Hexa-core processors, 207
Hierarchical databases, 416–418
Hierarchy chart, 517, **518,** 519, **544**
High-definition television (HDTV), **398, 403**
High-level programming languages, 523, **529**–531, **544**
High-speed phone lines, 53–56
HIIDE scanner, 352
History list, 67, 68
Hits, **72, 104**
Holographic technology, 235
Home area networks, **311, 361**
Home automation networks, 311, 338, 341, 343
Home entertainment centers, 370
Home page, **63,** 64, 67, **104**
HomePlug technology, 325, 326
HomePNA (HPNA) technology, 325, 326
Honorof, Marshall, 144
Hopper, Grace Murray, 532, 533
Host computer, 59, **315, 361**
Hotspots, **58, 104,** 340
How-to books, 180
HTML (Hypertext Markup Language), **66, 104,** 174, 539, **540, 544**
HTTP (Hypertext Transfer Protocol), **64,** 65, **104**
Hubs, 217
Hughes, Shayne, 18
Human-centric computing, 274
Human errors, 461–462
Human resources department, 431
Hurd, Mark, 408
Hybrid digital (HD) radio, **394, 403**
Hybrid tablets/PCs, 197
Hyperlinks, 66, 69
Hypermedia database, 422
Hypertext database, 409, 422
Hypertext links, **66, 104,** 540
Hypertext Markup Language (HTML), **66, 104,** 174, 539, **540, 544**
Hypertext Transfer Protocol (HTTP), **64,** 65, **104**
Hyperthreading, 207

I

ICANN (Internet Corporation for Assigned Names and Numbers), **62, 104**
Icons, **128, 183**
Identity theft, **354**–356, 358, **361,** 467, 468
IF-THEN-ELSE structure, 520, 522
Illustration software, 172
Image analysis software, 487
Image-compression technology, 236
Image-editing software, 172, 487
Image files
  search tools for, 74
  transferring, 390–391
  web-based, 74, 86
ImageNet database, 411
Imagery, 40
Impact printers, **280**–281, **297**
Implementing systems. *See* Systems implementation
Importing data, **152, 183**
Income inequality, 497
Individual search engines, **71**–72, **104**
Inference engine, 441
Info-mania, 492
Information, **27, 42**
  accuracy of, 415
  completeness of, 415
  evaluation of, 71, 75
  flow within organizations, 430–432
  manipulation of, 484–487
  privacy issues, 353, 477
  problem with quantity of, 460
  qualities of good, 430
  security of, 309–310
  theft of, 345, 467
  See also Data
Information overload, 495
Information systems (ISs)
  organizational department for managing, 431
  See also Computer-based information systems
Information technology (IT), **3,** 4, **42**
  business and, 10
  contemporary trends in, 34–38
  crime related to, 345–347, 464–470
  cyberwarfare and, 483–484
  economic issues and, 496–498
  education and, 4–6
  employment resources and, 13–14
  ethics and, 38
  finances and, 10
  government and, 10–11
  health/medicine and, 6, 8–9
  innovations in, 3–4
  jobs/careers and, 12–14
  majoring in, 549
  media manipulation and, 484–487
  modern examples of, 4–15
  personal life and, 14–15
  privacy/surveillance and, 475–483
  quality-of-life issues and, 487–495
  security issues and, 461–475
  timeline of progress in, 16–24
  See also Communications technology; Computer technology
Infrared wireless keyboards, 252
Infrared wireless transmission, **329, 361**

Infrastructure attacks, 470
Inheritance, 536
Inkjet printers, **281**–282, 283, **297**
Input, **27,** 29, **42,** 249
Input hardware, 28–29, **248,** 249–275, **297**
audio-input devices, **268**–269
biometric devices, 271, 272, 274
brainwave devices, 275
digital cameras, **265**–266
digital pens, **259**
digitizers, **258,** 259
ergonomics and, **292,** 294–295
future of, 271–275
gesture recognition and, 274, 275
health issues related to, 290–292, 294–295
image-capture devices, 265–268
IT timeline and, 254–260
keyboards, **28–29, 249**–252
light pens, **258**
mouse, **29, 253**–255
multitouch screens, **256**–257
pen-based computer systems, **258**–259
pointing devices, **252**–259
remote locations and, 272
review questions/exercises on, 300–302
scanning and reading devices, 260–265
sensors, **270**–271
source data-entry devices, **260**–271
speech-recognition systems, **268**–270, 274
terminals, 252, 253
touch screens, **256**
types of, 249, 250
users with disabilities 273, 275
webcams, **266**–268
In Search of Excellence (Peters), 3
Inserting text, 154
Instagram, 391
Installing software, 33–34, 114, 149–150
Instant messaging (IM), **81,** 83, **104**
Insteon technology, 341
Instruction manuals, 180
Integrated circuits, 34, **193, 240–241**
Integrated packages, **164, 183**
Intellectual property theft, 466, 467
Intelligence, artificial. *See* Artificial intelligence
Intelligent agents, **442, 454**
Intelligent terminals, **252, 297**
Intelligent tutoring systems, 6
Intel-type chips, **206,** 207, **241**
Interactive education, 5
Interactive TV (iTV), 396
Interactivity, **35, 42**
Internal cache, 213
Internal Revenue Service (IRS), 427
International Telecommunications Union (ITU), 15, 327
Internet, **19, 42,** 49–112
attacks on, 470
bandwidth and, **52**
brief history of, 20
business conducted on, 90–92
citing sources from, 74
connection speed information, 54, 57
control and regulation of, 497–498
cyberwarfare using, 483–484
discussion groups, 83
distance learning via, **5**–6
domain abbreviations on, 65
email and, 77–81, 82
evaluating information on, 71, 75
examples of uses for, 51
fraud on, 467–470
FTP sites on, 83–84
global users of, 50
government resources on, 10–11
how it works, 59–62
influence of, 19–20
instant messaging on, 81, 83
intrusiveness of, 96–101
ISPs and, 58–59
job searching on, 13–14
netiquette, 81
organizations overseeing, 62
physical connections to, 52–58
plagiarism issues, 102
programming for, 537–542
protocol used on, 60
review questions/exercises on, 108–112
shopping safely on, 98
smartphone access to, 375
telephone calls via, 84–85
timeline of telecommunications and, 50–56
tips for searching, 76
See also World Wide Web
Internet2, **60, 105**
Internet access providers, 53, 58–59
Internet Architecture Board (IAB), 62
Internet backbone, 59, **60, 104,** 317
Internet Corporation for Assigned Names and Numbers (ICANN), **62, 104**
Internet Engineering Task Force, 62
Internet Exchange Points (IXPs), 59, **60, 104**
Internet Explorer (IE), 63
Internet filtering software, 472
Internet Message Access Protocol (IMAP), 77
Internet Protocol (IP) addresses, **61, 104**
Internet Protocol Television (IPTV), 399
Internet radio, **394**–396, **403**
Internet-ready TV, 397
Internet service providers (ISPs), **58**–59, **104–105**
Internet Society, 62
Internet telephony, **84**–85, **105**
Internet Traffic Report, 60
Internet TV, 397
Interpol, 471
Interpreters, **529, 544–545**
Intranets, **314, 361**
iOS operating system, **143**
iPods. *See* Portable media players
IPTV (Internet Protocol Television), 399
IPv4 and IPv6 addresses, 61
IrDA ports, **221, 241,** 329
Iris-recognition systems, 473
Irrelevant attack, 543
Irrelevant reason, 543
Isolation, 490
ISPs. *See* Internet service providers
Italie, Leanne, 392
Iteration control structure, 520, 522, 523

J

Java programming language, **86, 105,** 536
JavaScript, **541, 545**
Jobs, Steve, 192
Job searching, 13–14
See also Employment
Joules, 203
Jumping to conclusions, 543
Junk email, 97
Justification, 157

K

KALQ keyboard, 251
Kasparov, Garry, 439
Katz-Lacade, Michael, 479
Kelly, Kevin, 94, 451
Kemeny, John, 534
Kernel, 118
Keyboards, **28–29, 42, 249**–252, **297**
ergonomic use of, 294, 295
features/layout, 125, 126–127
laptop computer, 237
repetitive stress injuries from, 291, 294
smartphone, 374
tactile vs. touch-screen, 251
traditional and its variants, 250–251
wired vs. wireless, 252
Keyboard shortcuts, 125, 138
Keyes, Anna, 8
Key field, **163, 183,** 411–412
Key loggers, **99, 105**
Keypads, 250
Keywords, **70**
Kilby, Jack, 193
Kilobits per second (Kbps), **52, 105**
Kilobyte (K, KB), 31, **198, 241**
Kinder, Lexie, 9
Kinect controller, 125
Knoll, John, 487
Knowledge base, 441
Knowledge-based system, 437
Knowledge engineers, 441

Kochanowski, Ed, 285
Komando, Kim, 98, 290, 477
Kurtz, Thomas, 534
Kurzweil, Raymond, 37, 451

L

Labels
mailing, 163
spreadsheet, 159
Languages, programming. *See* Programming languages
Language translators, 115, 200, **529, 545**
Lanier, Jaron, 230
LANs. *See* Local area networks
Laptop computers, **25**
buying, 236, 237–238
classroom use of, 499
durability of, 293
guarding against theft, 293, 465
health issues related to, 290–291
system unit for, 196
See also Tablet computers
Large-format plotters, 284
LaserCard technology, 229
Laser printers, **281,** 282, **297**
Last-mile problem, 56, 324
Latency (lag time), 257
Lateral thinking tools, 540
Laws
personal privacy, 476
software piracy, 471
Lawsuits, 478
LCD viewers/viewfinders, 389
Leahy, Patrick, 481
Leap Motion sensor, 125–126
Learning
critical-thinking skills for, 44
distance, **5**–6, 7
information technology and, 4–6
lectures and, 40
memorization and, 39, 40
note taking and, 40
prime study time for, 39
reading method for, 39–40
See also Education
Lectures, 40
Lederberg, Joshua, 437
Lee, Brendan, 537
Legacy systems, 133, 135
Lenses, camera, 388–389
Levy, Fred, 452
Levy, Steven, 398
Library of Congress, 409
LibreOffice suite, 148
License plate scanners, 479
Licenses, software, 145–146
Life, artificial, 447
Light pens, **258, 297**
Lights-out factories, 496
Line graphs, 161
Line-of-sight systems, 252, 329
Line printers, 280
LinkedIn, 92, 93
Links. *See* Hyperlinks
Linux, **141**–142, **183**
Liquid crystal display (LCD), **279, 297**
LISP programming language, 534
Local area networks (LANs), **24, 42, 311, 361**
client-server, 312–313
Ethernet technology, 321, 322
operating systems for, 140–142, 317
peer-to-peer, 312, 313
wireless, 338–340
Location memory, 40
Loebner, Hugh, 449
Logical operations, 211
Logic bomb, 350
Logic errors, **524, 545**
Logic structures, 520
Lohr, Steve, 371, 428
Long-distance wireless communications, 332–338
one-way communication, 332–335
two-way communication, 335–338
Longevity calculator, 9
Loop control structure, 520
Lossless compression, 153
Lossy compression, 153
Lost clusters, 222
Love Bug virus, 348
Low-Earth orbit (LEO), 331
LTE standard, **338, 361**
Lycos, 177
Lynn, Matthew, 452

M

M2A Imaging Capsule, 35
Machine cycle, 210–211, **241**
Machine language, **200, 241, 528, 545**
Machine learning, 37, **438, 454**
Macintosh operating system (Mac OS), **135**–136, **183–184**
Macros, **125, 184**
Magid, Larry, 353
Magnetic-ink character recognition (MICR), **264, 297**
Magnetic-stripe cards, 228–229
Mail, electronic. *See* Email
Mailing labels, 163
Mailing lists, **83, 105**
Mail servers, 77, 313
Mainframes, **24, 42**
Main memory, 210, 212
Maintenance
data, 413
program, 525
system, 514–515
Make-or-buy decision, 512
Malware, **100**–101, **105,** 348–350
cellphone, 101, 350
ransomware, 350
reducing the risk of, 100–101
rootkits, **349**
Trojan horses, **349**
viruses, **100,** 348
worms, **348**
Management
CPU, 118
database, 412–416
file, 118–119
memory, 118
security, 120
task, 119–120
Management information system (MIS), **435, 454**
Managers
computer-based information systems for, 432–438
levels and responsibilities of, 431–432, 433
participation in systems development by, 506
Maney, Kevin, 20, 335
Maps, aerial, 86–87
Margins, 157
Marketing
Big Data related to, 429–430
organizational department for, 431
Markoff, John, 36
Mark-recognition devices, 264–265
Markup languages, **537,** 539, 540–541, **545**
Maron, Marc, 395
Mashups, **368,** 369, **403**
Massive open online courses (MOOCs), 5
Matthies, Brad, 75
Mayer, Marissa, 323
McAfee, Andrew, 452
McCarthy, John, 534
McConnell, Mike, 343
McCready, Mike, 38
McKibben, Bill, 495
McQuivey, James, 114
Mead, Walter Russell, 12
Mechanical mouse, 253
Media manipulation, 484–487
Media players. *See* Portable media players
Media players, 383
Media-sharing websites, **93,** 95, **105**
Medical technology, 6, 8–9
Medicine
Big Data in, 429
data mining in, 428
robots in, 445, 446
See also Health issues
Medium-Earth orbit (MEO), 331
Meeker, Mary, 336
Meetings, virtual, 342
Megabits per second (Mbps), **53, 105**
Megabyte (M, MB), 31, 53, **198, 241**
Megahertz (MHz), 30, **208, 241**
Megapixels (mp), **388, 403**
Memorization, 39, 40, 44
Memory, 28, 212–214
cache, 213–214
flash, 214

Memory—*Cont.*
main, 212
managing, 118
RAM, 212–213
ROM, **214**
virtual, 118, **214**
Memory chips, **30, 42,** 212–214
Memory modules, 213
Memory stick, 228
Mental health problems, 490–492
Mental imagery, 40
Menu, **128, 184**
Menu bar, **131, 184**
Menu-driven interface, 126
Mesh network, **321,** 322, **361**
Mesh technologies, 341
Message, 535
Message boards, **83, 105**
Messaging feature, 136
Metadata, **414,** 427, **454**
Metadata mining, 481
Metalanguage, 539, 540
Metamaterials, 236
Metasearch engines, **72,** 73, **105**
Methods, 535
Metropolitan area networks (MANs), **310, 361**
Microblogging, 88
Microchips. *See* Chips
Microcomputers, **24**–25, **42**
networking, 24
types of, 24–25
See also Personal computers
Microcontrollers, **26, 42,** 195
Microholographic disks, 235
Microphones, 268
Microprocessors, 22, **195,** 205–209, **241**
Microreplication, 289
Microsoft Access, 162
Microsoft Excel, 159, 160
Microsoft Internet Explorer, 63
Microsoft .NET framework, 537
Microsoft Outlook, 166
Microsoft PowerPoint, 167
Microsoft Windows, **136**–140, **184**
Microsoft Windows 7, **137,** 138, **184**
Microsoft Windows 8, **137**–140, **184**
Microsoft Windows Server 2012, 140
Microsoft Word, 153, 154, 155, 158
Microsoft Xbox One, 400–401
Microwave radio, **330, 361**
Middle-level managers, 431
MIDI board, **268, 297**
MIDI ports, **221, 241**
Midsize computers, 24
Millennial generation, 3, 402
Mindsets, 543
Miniaturization, 34–35
Minicomputers, 24
Mobile blogs, 88
Mobile browsers, 66–67
Mobile data terminals (MDTs), **252**
Mobile devices, **25, 42**
Mobile operating systems, 116, 142–144
Mobile phones. *See* Cellular telephones; Smartphones
Mobile-telephone switching office (MTSO), 336
Mobile Wave, The (Saylor), 2
Mobility, 195
Modeling tools, **509, 545**
Models, 436
Modems, **33, 42, 105, 306, 361**
cable, **56**–57
dial-up, 53, 55
signal conversion by, 306–307
Modules, **518, 545**
MOLAP applications, 425
Molecular electronics, 235–236
Molitor, Graham, 50
Money
information technology and, 10
software for managing, 168–169
Monitors, **32, 42,** 276–280
See also Display screens
Moore, Gordon, 206, 232
Moore's law, 206, 232
More info! icons, 5
Morphing, 484
Morrison, Perry, 38
Mossberg, Walter, 237
Motherboard, **30, 42,** 203–204
Mountain Lion (Mac OS 10.8), 135–136
Mouse, **29, 42,** 125, **253**–255, **297**
ergonomic options for, 294
functions performed by, 127
laptop computer, 237–238
repetitive stress injuries from, 291
setting properties for, 255
variant forms of, 254–255
See also Pointing devices
Mouse pointer, 125, 253
Movies, theft of, 466
Mozilla Firefox, 63
MP3 format, **383, 403**
MP3 players, 382–386
features of, 383–384
societal effects of, 384–385
using in college, 385–386
MRAM chips, 213
Multicasting, 398
Multicore processors, **206–207, 241**
Multidimensional databases (MDBs), **423**–425, **454**
Multidimensional spreadsheets, 161
Multifunction printers, **284, 297**
Multimedia, 19, **35–36, 43**
databases for storing, 422
portable media players and, 382–386
search tools for, 74
social networks for sharing, 93, 95
software for creating, 174
tools for developing, 86
World Wide Web and, 62, 74, 85–88
Multimedia authoring software, **174, 184**
Multiple-user license, 146
Multitasking, 39, **119**–120, **184, 381,** 402, **403**
Multitouch screens, **256**–257, **297**
Music
MP3 players and, 383–384
online sources of, 88
search tools for, 74
smartphones and, 374
streaming, 88
theft of, 466
Music Genome Project, 395
Music players, 382–383
My Documents icon, 130
MySpace, 92

N

Nagle, Matt, 274
Name migration, 353
Nanotechnology, **23, 43,** 232–233, 235, 439, 489–490
Narrowband connections, **53, 105, 327, 361**
National Cyber Security Alliance, 347
National ID cards, 479
National Science Foundation (NSF), 318
National Security Agency (NSA), 353, 479–481, 482
National Telecommunications and Information Administration (NTIA), 327
Natural hazards, 464
Natural language processing, 38, **442, 454**
Natural languages, **531**–532, **545**
NBIC technology, 235
Near-letter-quality (NLQ) output, 280
Neck and back pains, 291, 294
Negrin, Liat, 287
Netbooks, **25, 43,** 196
Netflix, 430
NetGeners, 402
Netiquette, **81, 105**
NetWare, 140
Network agents, 442
Network architecture, **312**–313, **361**
Network databases, 418–419
Network interface cards (NICs), **216, 241,** 317
Network operating system (NOS), 317
Networks, **4, 43, 308**–322, **361**
benefits of, 308–310
client-server, 26, **312**–313
components of, 315–318
Ethernet, **321,** 322, 325
extranets, **314**
firewalls for, **314**–315
home area, **311**
home automation, 311, 338, 341, 343
intranets, **314**
local area, **311,** 338–340
metropolitan area, **310**
operating systems for, 140–142, 317

peer-to-peer, 312, **313**
personal area, 311, 338, 340–341
security for, 314–315
structures for, 312–313
topologies of, **318**–321
tutorials on, 313
types of, 310–311
virtual private, **314**
wide area, **310**
wireless, **58**
Neural networks, **447, 454**
Neuromancer (Gibson), 17
Newsgroups, **83, 105**
Newsreader program, 83
Nigerian letter scam, 469
Nintendo Wii U, 401
Nodes, **315, 361**
Noise-cancellation technology, 269
Noise pollution, 292
Nonimpact printers, 280, **281**–284, **297–298**
Nonremovable hard disks, 223
Normal accidents, 463
Normalization, 412
Notebook computers, **25, 43**
See also Laptop computers
Note taking
tips for students, 40
web-based services for, 499
Nourbakhsh, Rez, 452
Novak, Ben, 38
Novell OES, 140
NSFNET backbone, 318
Nussbaum, Martha, 94

O

Obama, Barack, 482, 484
Object, **535, 545**
Object code, 529
Object-oriented databases, **422**–423, **454**
Object-oriented programming (OOP), **535**–537, **545**
Object-relational databases, 423
Oblinger, Diana, 402
Octa-core processors, 207
Odor-producing devices, 288
OEM operating systems, 137
Office automation systems (OASs), 433
Office information systems (OISs), **433**–434, **454**
Office suites, 149, 164
Offline processing, 434
OLAP software, 425
OLED displays, 279
One-way communications, 332–335
Online, **4, 43**
Online analytical processing (OLAP) software, 425
Online behavior, 81
Online classified ads, 91
Online learning, 5–6, 7
Online office suites, 164
Online relationships sites, **14**–15, **43**
Online services. *See* Internet service providers
Online snooping, 353, 357
Online storage, 231
Online students, 7
Online transaction processing (OLTP), 434
Online voting, 11
Open architecture, 215
Open Enterprise Server (OES), 140
OpenOffice suite, 148
Open-source software, **141, 184**
Opera browser, 63
Operating systems (OSs), 34, **115**–120, 133–144, **184**
comparisons of, 142
DOS, 133
embedded, 142–144
functions of, 115–120
Linux, **141**–142
Macintosh, **135**–136
mobile, 116, 142–144
network, 140–142, 317
Open Enterprise Server, 140
reinstalling, 224
rules for upgrading, 142
smartphone, 116, 142–144, 373
stand-alone, **134**–140
tablet, 142–144, 379
Unix, **140**–141
Windows, **136**–140
See also System software
Operational-level management, 432
Operator documentation, 525
Operators, Boolean, 76
Optical character recognition (OCR), **265, 298**
Optical computing, 233–234
Optical density, 261
Optical disks, **225,** 226–228, **241**
future developments in, 235
how they work, 225, 226
types of, 225, 226–227
Optical mark recognition (OMR), **264**–265, **298**
Optical mouse, 254
Optical scanners, 260–261
Optical viewfinders, 389
Optical zoom, 388–389
OrCam glasses, 287
Organization chart, 431, 432
Organizations
decentralized, 432
departments in, 431
flow of information within, 430–432
management levels in, 431–432, 433
review questions/exercises on, 455–457
Organized crime, 464
Outline View feature, 153–154
Output, **28,** 29, **43,** 275, 276
Output hardware, 32–33, **248,** 275–290, **298**
display screens, **276**–280
ergonomics and, **292,** 294–295
future of, 288–290
health issues related to, 290–292, 294–295
IT timeline and, 254–260
printers, **280**–286
review questions/exercises on, 300–302
sound-output devices, **287**
types of, 249, 276
video, **287**–288
voice-output devices, **287**
Overlearning, 39
Over the Edge game, 1

P

Packaged software, **145**–146, **184**
Packets, **60**–61, **105, 316, 362**
Packet switching, 316
Padlock icon, 97
Page description language (PDL), **281, 298**
Pagers, **335, 362**
Painting programs, 172
Pairing, Bluetooth, 340
Palm-scanning technology, 275
Pandora Internet Radio, 394, 395
Paradox of Choice: Why More Is Less, The (Schwartz), 371
Parallel implementation, 513
Parallel ports, **220, 241**
Parallel processing, 207
Parent folders, 119
Pariser, Eli, 372
Parisi, Tony, 540
Pascal, Blaise, 534
Pascal programming language, 530, 534
Passive matrix LCDs, 279
Passive RFID tags, 263
Passport photos, 474
Passwords, **60, 105,** 351
access, 120, 472–473
creating strong, 101, 120
list of worst, 101
phishing for, **97**
Paste command, 154–155
Pathnames, 119
Pattern recognition, 38, 274, **442,** 452, **454**
PC cards, **216, 241**
PCI bus, 216
PCIe (PCI Express) bus, 217
PCs. *See* Personal computers
PDAs. *See* Personal digital assistants
PDF files, 151, 177–178
Peer-to-peer (P2P) networks, 312, **313, 362**
Pen-based computer systems, **258**–259, **298**
Pen plotters, 284
People controls, 474–475
Periodic reports, 435
Peripheral devices, **32, 43**

Perl (Practical Extraction and Report Language), 542
Perpendicular recording technology, 223, 225
Perrow, Charles, 463
Personal area networks, 311, 338, 340–341
Personal browsers, 94, 96
Personal computers (PCs)
chemical composition of, 488
custom-built, 28
environmental issues related to, 487–490
guarding against theft, 293
health issues related to, 290–292, 294–295
recycling/donating, 38, 488, 489
system unit for, 196
tune-ups for, 123
types of, 24–25
work area setup, 295
See also Computers; Laptop computers
Personal digital assistants (PDAs), **25, 43**
See also Smartphones
Personal-finance managers, **168**–169, **184**
Personal information managers (PIMs), **164**–165, 166, **184**
Personalization, 36, **371, 403**
Personal life, 14–15
Personal software, 149
Personal technology, 367–406
convergence and, **369**–370
digital cameras, 386–393
digital television, 396–399
e-book readers, **380**–382
high-tech radio, 393–396
multitasking and, **381,** 402
Netgeners and, 402
personalization and, **371**
portability and, **370**–371
portable media players, **382**–386
review questions/exercises on, 404–406
smartphones, 371–377
tablet computers, 377–380
videogame systems, 399–401
Person-to-person auctions, 91
Pervasive computing, 4, 274
Pesce, Mark, 540
Petabyte (P, PB), 31, **199, 241**
Peters, Tom, 3
Phablets, 25
Pharming, **97–98, 105,** 469
Phased implementation, 513
Phishing, **97, 105–106,** 469
Phone line networks, 325
Phonemes, 269
Photography
camera phones and, 375
digital cameras and, **265**–266, 386–393
ethics related to, 393
societal effects of, 392–393
Photo manipulation, 485–487
Photo printers, 284
Photo-sharing services, 391
Photoshop program, 487
PHP programming language, 542
Physical connections, 52–58
broadband, 52
cable modems, 56–57
dial-up modems, 53, 55
high-speed phone lines, 53–56
wireless systems, 57–58
Physical keyboards, 374
Piconets, 340
Pie charts, 161
Pilot implementation, 513
PIN (personal identification number), 472
Pinterest, 391
Pirated software, **146, 184,** 465
Pixels, **277, 298**
Plagiarism, 102
Plasma displays, **280, 298**
Platforms, **133, 184**
PlayStation 4 (PS4), 401
Plotters, **284,** 285, **298**
Plug and Play, **215, 241**
Plug-ins, 85–**86, 106**
Podcasting, **90, 106, 395**–396, **403**
Point-and-shoot cameras, 387
Pointer, **125, 184**
Pointing devices, **252**–259, **298**
laptop computer, 237–238
mouse and its variants, 253–255
multitouch screens, **256**–257
pen input devices, 258–259
touch screens, **256**
users with disabilities, 273
Pointing stick, **255, 298**
Point of presence (POP), **60, 106**
Point-of-sale (POS) terminals, **252**
Police data collection, 477, 479
Politics, 11
Polygons, 289
Polymer memory, 236
Polymorphism, 536
Pop-up ads, **99, 106**
Pop-up generators, 99
Pornography, 493
Portability, 36, **370**–371, **403**
Portable computers. *See* Laptop computers; Tablet computers
Portable Document Format (PDF), **177**–178, **184–185**
Portable hard-drive systems, 223
Portable media players (PMPs), **382**–386, **404**
features of, 383–384
smartphones as, 374
societal effects of, 384–385
using in college, 385–386
Ports, 30, **217**–221, **241**
Post Office Protocol version 3 (POP3), 77
POTS connection, **53, 106**
Power line networks, 325
Power Nap feature, 136
Power supply, **201,** 203, **241**
Predictive search apps, 460
Predictive statistical model software, 472
Preliminary design, 511
Preliminary investigation, **507**–509, **545**
Prensky, Marc, 402
Presentation graphics software, 5, **166**–168, **185**
Previewing documents, 157
Primary key, 163, 411
Primary storage, **28,** 30, **43,** 212
Prime study time, 39
Printers, **33, 43, 280**–286, **298**
buying considerations, 286
dot-matrix, 280
future developments in, 289
impact, **280**–281
inkjet, **281**–282, 283
laser, **281,** 282
multifunction, **284**
nonimpact, 280, **281**–284
photo, 284
plotter, **284,** 285
specialty, 285
thermal, **282,** 284
three-dimensional, 289–290
Printing documents, 157
Print Scrn key, 281
Print servers, 312–313
Privacy, **353, 362,** 475–476
commercial spying and, 476–477
databases and, 353, 451, 477
email and text, 96
federal laws on, 476
government spying and, 353, 477, 479–482
information on guarding, 353, 357
social networking and, 92, 94
threats to, 353, 476
Privacy and Civil Liberties Oversight Board, 481
Probe storage, 236
Problem clarification/definition, **516**–517, **545**
Problem-oriented programming languages, 531
Problem solving, 517
Procedural errors, 462
Procedural languages, 529–531
Processing, **28,** 29, **43**
future developments in, 232–236
hardware components for, 30
IT timeline and, 194–204
speed of, 35, 208–209
Processor chips, **30, 43,** 195, 205–207
Production department, 431
Productivity issues, 478

Productivity software, **149, 185**
Productivity suites, **164, 185**
Program design, **517**–523, **545**
Program documentation, 525
Program files, **152, 185**
Program flowchart, **520,** 521, **545**
Programming, **515**–526, **545**
  Internet, 537–542
  languages used for, 523, 526–542
  object-oriented, 535–537
  obtaining tools for, 525
  review questions/exercises on, 547–549
  steps in process of, 515–526
  structured, **518**
  visual, **537,** 538
Programming languages, **523, 546**
  assembly language, **528**–529
  contemporary examples of, 532–534
  generations of, **527**
  high-level or procedural, **529**–531
  historical development of, 532–533
  machine language, **200, 528**
  markup, **537,** 539, 540–541
  natural, **531**–532
  scripting, 539, 541–542
  very-high-level or problem-oriented, **531**
  website development, 537–542
  See also names of specific languages
Programming process, 515–526
  clarifying programming needs, 516–517
  coding the program, 523
  designing the program, 517–523
  documenting the program, 525
  maintaining the program, 525
  summary of steps in, 526
  testing the program, 523–525
Programs, 27, 114, **515, 545**
  creating, 515–526
  utility, 115, 121, 122–123
  See also Software
Program testing, **523**–525, **545**
Project management software, **176**–177, **185**
PROM (programmable read-only memory), 214
Proprietary software, 145
Protocols, **60, 106, 316, 362**
Prototypes, **511, 546**
Prototyping, **511, 546**
Pseudocode, 517, **518,** 519, 520, **546**
Public-domain software, **146**–147, **185**
Pull-down menu, 128
Pull technology, 88
Pull-up menu, 130
Push technology, **88, 106**

Q

QR codes, 263, 375
Quad-core processors, 207
Quality-of-life issues, 487–495
  environmental problems, 487–490
  mental health problems, 490–492
  protection of children, 492–494
  workplace problems, 494–495
Quantum computing, 235
Queries, database, 163, 421–422, 425
Query by example (QBE), **421, 454**
Query languages, 531
Questionable statistics, 543
Queues, 118
QuickTime, 86
QWERTY keyboards, 250, 374
QXGA monitors, 278

R

Radio
  broadcast, **329**–330
  cellular, **330**
  HD, **394**
  Internet, **394**–396
  microwave, **330**
  satellite, **393**–394
  smartphone, 374
Radio buttons, **69, 106**
Radio-frequency (RF) spectrum, **327,** 328–329, **362**
Radio-frequency identification (RFID) tags, **263**–264, **298**
Radio-frequency wireless keyboards, 252
RAID storage system, 223
RAM (random access memory), 212–213
  See also Memory
RAM chips, 30, **212, 241**
Range, spreadsheet, **159, 185**
Ransomware, 350
Rapid application development (RAD) system, 537
Raster images, 172
RDRAM chips, 213
Reading data, **214, 241**
Reading skills, 39–40
Read-only memory (ROM), 116, **214,** 225, **242**
Read/write head, **222, 241–242**
Real-time processing, 434
Recalculation, **160, 185**
Recharging technology, 235
Record (row), 162, **410, 454**
Recycling computers, 38, 488, 489
Red Flag Software Company, 142
Reference software, 149
Reformatting hard drives, 224
Refresh rate, **278, 298**
Registers, 210, **211, 242**
Regression analysis, 427
Reinstalling software, 224
Relational databases, **162, 185, 419**–422, **454–455**
Relationships, online, 14–15
Release engineer, 524–525
Remote input, 272
Rentalware, **147, 185**
Repetitive stress injuries (RSIs), **291,** 294, **298**
Replace command, 154
Report generators, **416, 455,** 531
Research
  database, 415
  web-based, 102
Research and development (R&D) department, 431
Resolution, **261, 277,** 278, **298,** 388
Response time, 278
Résumés
  misleading information on, 478
  posting on the Internet, 14
  privacy issues and, 353
Review questions/exercises, 44
  on application software, 187–190
  on artificial intelligence, 455–458
  on communications technology, 363–366
  on computer-based information systems, 455–457
  on databases, 455–458
  on hardware, 243–246, 300–302
  on information technology, 45–48
  on the Internet, 108–112
  on organizations, 455–457
  on personal technology, 404–406
  on programming, 547–549
  on security, 500–502
  on systems analysis and design, 547–549
  on system software, 187–190
Rifkin, Jeremy, 496
Ring network, **319**–320, **362**
Ringtones, 375
Ripping process, 383
Ritchie, Dennis, 534
Robotics, 38, **444**–446, **455**
Robots, **8**–9, **43,** 444–446, 452
Rollover feature, **128, 185**
ROM (read-only memory), 116, **214,** 225, **242**
ROM chips, 214
Root directory, 118
Rootkits, **349, 362**
Root record, 416
Rossi, Chuck, 524–525
Rothenberg, David, 102
Routers, **316,** 318, **362**
Row headings, 159
RSS newsreaders, **88, 106**
Rule-based detection software, 472
Runtime libraries, 152

S

Safari browser, 63
Safe Mode, 116
Salary information, 12
Salford, Lief, 292
Sampling process, 308
Sampling rate, **384, 404**
Sanger, Larry, 73
Satellite radio, **393**–394, **404**

Satellites, communications, **57, 330**–331
Saving files, **157**–158, **185**
Saylor, Michael, 2
Scammers, 346
Scanners, **260**–261, **298**
Scanning and reading devices, 260–265
  bar-code readers, **261**–262
  character-recognition devices, 264–265
  mark-recognition devices, 264–265
  optical scanners, 260–261
  RFID tags and, **263**–264
Scatter charts, 161
Scheibehenne, Benjamin, 372
Schmidt, Eric, 116
Scholarly works, 74
Schwartz, Barry, 371, 372
Science, data mining in, 428
Sciolla, Gabriella, 5
Screens. *See* Display screens
Scripting languages, 539, 541–542
Script kiddies, 344
Scripts, **539, 546**
Scroll arrows, **69,** 70, **106**
Scrolling, **69, 106, 153, 185**
SDLC. *See* Systems development life cycle
SDRAM chips, 212–213
Search box, 69
Search command, 154
Search engines, **71, 106**
  individual, **71**–72
  lists of, 73
  metasearch, **72,** 73
  multimedia, 74
  specialized, 72, 73
Search hijackers, **99, 106**
Searching the web, 70–74
  multimedia content and, 74
  serious techniques for, 76
  strategies for, 73–74
  tools for, 71–73
Search services, **70**–71, **106**
Secondary storage, **28,** 30–32, **43,** 212, 221–232
  cloud storage as, 231
  future developments in, 235–236
  hardware used for, 221–229
  longevity of data and, 230
  online, 231
Secondary storage hardware, 30–32, **221**–229, **242**
  flash memory cards, **228**
  hard disks, **221**–224, 224
  life span of, 230
  optical disks, **225,** 226–228
  smart cards, 228–**229**
  solid-state drives, **228**
  USB flash drives, **228**
Sectors, **222, 242**
Security, **343**–358, **362,** 461–475, **470, 500**
  access rights and, 472–474
  biometric, **271,** 351–352, **473**–474
  blended threats to, **349**
  broadband connections and, 54
  components of, 470
  computer crime and, 345–347, 464–472
  cyberwarfare and, **483**–484
  database, 413
  denial-of-service attacks and, **347**
  disaster-recovery plans and, **475**
  employee monitoring and, 472, 478
  encryption and, **352, 474**
  errors/accidents and, 461–463
  firewalls for, **314**–315
  fraud detection tools for, 472
  free online check of, 348
  general procedures for, 474–475
  hackers and, **344**–345
  identification systems and, 472–474
  identity theft and, **354**–356, 358
  malware attacks and, 348–350
  natural hazards and, 464
  network, 314–315
  OS management of, 120
  password, 351
  privacy and, 96, 353, 357
  review questions/exercises on, 500–502
  RFID tags for, 263–264
  software for, 350–351
  spies and, 344
  thieves and, 345–347
  trolls and, **343**–344
  types of threats to, 461
  website indicators of, 97
  WiFi connections and, 340, 469–470
  zombies and, 349–350
Segal, Rick, 492
Selection control structure, 520
Self-driving cars, 275–276
Self-scanning checkout, 262
Self-taken photos, 392–393
Semantic markup, 93–94
Semiconductors, **194, 242**
Sengupta, Somini, 353
Sensors, **270**–271, **298–299**
  digital camera, 388
  gesture recognition, 125–126
Sentiment analysis, 427
Sequence control structure, 520, 522
Serial ports, **219**–220, **242**
Server farms, 207–208
Servers, **26, 43, 59, 106,** 312
Service programs, 121
Services, theft of, 467
Sexting, **493, 500**
SGML (Standard Generalized Markup Language), 539
Shareware, **147, 185**
Sheet-fed scanners, 260
Shopping bots, 442
Short-range wireless, 338–343
Showrooming, 10, **90**–91, **106**
Signal words, 40
Silicon, 34, **194, 242**
SIM cards, 337
Simpson, O. J., 486
Simulators, **444, 455**
Sinatra, Frank, 485
Single-lens reflex (SLR) cameras, 387–388
Single-user license, 146
Singularity, the, 450–**451, 455**
Site license, 146
Skeuomorphism, 275
Slate tablets, 196
Slider PCs, 197
Slide shows, 166
Slippery slope, 543
Smart cards, 228–**229, 242**
Smartphones, **2,** 16, **43,** 371–377
  apps for, 373–374
  college students and, 376, 377
  dangers of, 338
  developing apps for, 536
  features of, 373–375
  keeping track of, 465
  malware attacks on, 350, 351
  media player capability of, 383
  operating systems for, 116, 142–144, 373
  privacy tips for, 357
  protecting, 78, 293, 294, 351
  shopping via, 10
  societal effects of, 376–377
  texting with, 375–376
  used as webcams, 267
  wireless services for, 337–338
  See also Cellular telephones
Smishing, 97
Smithsonian Museum, 290
SMTP server, 77
Snapchat app, 493
Snapkeys Si keyboard, 251
Snopes.com website, 487
Snowden, Edward, 479–480
Snyder, Scott, 369
Social-bookmarking websites, 74, 75
Social-network aggregators, **93, 106**
Social networking, 92–93
  content aggregators, 93
  dating and, 15
  downside of, 94
  media sharing and, 93, 95
  privacy in, 92, 357
  software for managing, 176
Social-networking websites, **92, 106**
Social networks, **3, 43**
Social Security number, 163, 356, 412
Softcopy output, **276, 299**
Soft goods, 90
Software, **27,** 33–34, **43,** 114
  abandonware, 146
  antivirus, **100,** 122, 350–351
  blocking, 493
  compatibility requirements, 116
  converting, 513
  creating, 515–526

custom, **145**
documentation, 148–149, 525
errors in, 462
firewall, 315
freeware, **147,** 148
installing, 33–34, 114, 149–150
IT timeline and, 164–171
list of best-selling, 176
make-or-buy decision for, 512
network sharing of, 309
obsolescence of, 230
open-source, **141**
origins of term, 114
packaged, **145**–146
pirated, **146,** 465
productivity, **149**
protecting, 293, 474–475
public-domain, **146**–147
reinstalling, 224
rentalware, **147**
security, 350–351
shareware, **147**
tech support for, 180–181
theft of, 465
tutorials, 148
utility, 115, **121,** 122–123
web application, **147**
See also Application software; System software
Software engineering, 515
See also Programming
Software license, **145, 185**
Software Publishers Association (SPA), 471
Software suites, **164**–165, **185**
Solaris, 141
Solid-state device, **193, 242**
Solid-state drive (SSD), **228, 242**
Son, Masayoshi, 384
Sony PlayStation 4 (PS4), 401
Sorting
database records, 163
email messages, 81
Sound board, **268, 299**
Sound card, **32, 43, 215**–216, **242,** 287
Sound manipulation, 485
Sound-output devices, **287, 299**
Source code, 529
Source data-entry devices, **260**–271, **299**
Source program files, 152
Southers, Jennifer, 5
Spacing, text, 157
Spaghetti code, 520
Spam, **97, 106**
Speakers, **32, 43**
Spear-phishing, 97
Specialized search engines, 72, 73
Special-purpose keys, **125, 185**
Specialty printers, 285
Specialty software, 149, 165–179
Specific Absorption Rate (SAR), 292
Speech-recognition systems, **268**–270, 274, **299,** 442
Speed
data transmission, 52–53
Internet connection, 54, 57
processing, 35, 208–209
Spelling checker, 155
Spiders, **71, 106**
Spiegel, Eric, 452
Spies, online, 344
Spohrer, Jim, 452
Spoofing, **97, 106**
Spooling, 118
Sports, data mining in, 427
Spotlight search, 135
Spreadsheet programs, 158–161, **185–186**
chart creation, 160–161
how they work, 158–160
illustrated overview of, 159
worksheet templates in, 160
Spying. *See* Cyberspying
Spyware, 98–**99,** 100, **107**
SQ3R reading method, 39–40
SQL (Structured Query Language), 531
SRAM chips, 213
Stand-alone operating system, **134**–140, **186**
Standard-definition television (SDTV), **398, 404**
Star network, **319, 362**
Start button, 130
Static IP address, 61
Statistics, questionable, 543
Stewart, Martha, 486
Storage, 28, 29
cloud, **231**
digital camera, 389
future of, 235–236
history of, 223
IT timeline and, 194–204
MP3 player, 383
online, 231
primary, **28,** 30, 212
secondary, **28,** 30–32, 212, 221–232, 235–236
smartphone, 374
volatile, **212**
Strategic-level management, 431
Straw man argument, 543
Streaming audio, **88, 107,** 394
Streaming video, **87, 107**
Stress, 492
Strong AI, **439, 455**
Stroustrup, Bjarne, 534
Structured programming, **518, 546**
Structured query language (SQL), **421, 455**
Students
classroom computer use by, 499
distance learning for, **5**–6, 7
online evaluations by, 499
plagiarism issues for, 102
portable media player use by, 385–386
smartphone use by, 376, 377
study and learning tips for, 7, 39–40
Study skills, 39–40
Stuxnet worm, 348
Stylus, 258
Subfolders, 118, 119
Subject directories, **72,** 73, **107**
Subprograms/subroutines, 518
Summary reports, 435
Supercomputers, **23, 44**
Superconductors, 233
Supervisor, **118, 186**
Supervisory managers, 432
Surfing the web, **63, 107**
Surge protector, 201, 205
Surveillance, employee, 472, 478
Switches, **316,** 318, **362**
SXGA monitors, 278
Syntax, **523, 546**
Syntax errors, **524, 546**
System, **505**–506, **546**
Systemantics, 514
System board. *See* Motherboard
System cabinet, 30, 201, 202
System clock, **208, 242**
System crashes, 236
System Restore, 117
Systems analysis, **509**–511, **546**
Systems analysis and design, **507, 546**
participants in, 506
purpose of, 505
review questions/exercises on, 547–549
six phases of, 507–515
See also Systems development life cycle
Systems analyst, **506, 546**
Systems design, **511**–512, **546**
Systems development, **512**–513, **546**
Systems development life cycle (SDLC), **507**–515, **546**
analyzing the system, 509–511
designing the system, 511–512
developing/acquiring the system, 512–513
implementing the system, 513
maintaining the system, 514–515
overview of phases in, 507
preliminary investigation, 507–509
termination stage of, 514
Systems implementation, **513, 546**
Systems maintenance, **514**–515, **546**
System software, **34, 44, 114**–144, **186**
components of, 115
device drivers, 115, **121**
Help command, **133,** 134
IT timeline and, 164–171
language translators, 115, 200
operating systems, **115**–120, 133–144
review questions/exercises on, 187–190
tech support for, 180–181
user interface, **124**–133
utility programs, 115, **121,** 122–123

System testing, 513
System unit, 30, **196**–197, 201, 202, **242**

T

T1 line, **54**–56, **107**
Tables, database, 410
Tablet computers, **2, 25, 44, 196, 242,** 377–380
classroom use of, 499
features of, 378–379
guarding against theft, 293, 465
health issues related to, 290–291
operating systems for, 142–144, 379
ruggedized versions of, 379–380
system units for, 196–197
Tactical-level management, 431
Tactile keyboards, **251, 299,** 374
Tags, **75, 107**
Taskbar, **131, 186**
Task management, 119–120
Taxonomy of Educational Objectives (Bloom), 44
Tax software programs, 169
Technical staff, 506
Techno-blight, 489
Technological singularity, 451
Tech smart, 20–22
Tech support, 180–181
Telecommunications, 4
timeline on the development of, 50–56
See also Communications technology
Telecommuting, 10, 323
Teleconferencing, 342
Telemedicine, 6, 8
Telephones
conferencing via, 342
Internet telephony and, 84–85
modems connected to, 53, 306–307
See also Cellular telephones; Smartphones
Television, 396–399
closed-circuit, 342
manipulation of content on, 487
new technologies for, 396–397
smartphones and, 375
societal effects of new, 398–399
three types of, 397–398
V-chips and, 493
Telework, 323
Temp file removal, 123, 124
Templates, **156, 186**
document, 156–157
presentation graphics, 168
worksheet, 160
Terabyte (T, TB), 31, **199, 242**
Terminals, **24, 44,** 252, 253
Termination stage of SDLC, 514
Term papers, 102
Terrorism, 460, 477, 480–481
Testing
information systems, 512–513
Internet connection speed, 57
program code, 523–525
Text boxes, **69, 107**
Texting (text messaging), **17, 44, 375**–376, **404**
driving and, 376, 461–462
instant messaging vs., 83
mobile phones for, 375–376
privacy of, 96
Text-to-speech (TTS) systems, 287
Theft, 345–347
hardware, 293, 346, 464–465
identity, **354**–356, 358, 467, 468
information, 345, 467
intellectual property, 466, 467
music and movie, 466
preventing with GPS, 334
software, 465
time and services, 466–467
Thermal printers, **282,** 284, **299**
Thermal wax-transfer printers, 284
Thesaurus, 156
Thibault, Christopher, 537
Thieves, 345–347
Thin-film transistor (TFT) displays, 279
Thinking skills, 44, 543
Thread, **83, 107**
3-D output, 289–290
3G technology, **58, 107,** 337
Thrill-seeker hackers, 345
Tile-Based Windows, 138, 139
Time, theft of, 466
Time bomb, 350
Titan supercomputer, 23
Title bar, **131, 186**
TiVo systems, 398, 399
Toffler, Alvin, 495
Token Ring Network, 320
Tomason, Audrey, 486
Tomlinson, Ray, 79
Toner cartridges, 281
Toolbar, **131, 186**
Tooltips, 128
Top-down program design, **518, 546**
Top-level domain, 79
Top managers, 431
Topology of networks, **318**–321, **362**
Tor software, 357
Torvalds, Linus, 141
Touchpad, 237, **255, 299**
Touch screen, 25, 29, **256, 299**
Touch-screen keyboards, **251, 299,** 374
Touch systems, 274
Tower PCs, **24, 44,** 196, 201, 202
Trackball, **254**–255, **299**
Tracking document changes, 156
Tracks, **222, 242**
Transaction processing system (TPS), **434, 455**
Transceivers, 329
Transferring files
from digital cameras, 390–391
to portable media players, 384
Transistors, 34, **193,** 205–206, **242**
Transmission Control Protocol/ Internet Protocol (TCP/IP), **60, 107**
Tree network, **321, 362**
Trinko, Katrina, 392, 393
Trojan horses, **349, 363,** 469
Trolls, **343**–344, **362**
TSA scanners, 294
Tufte, Edward, 257
Tukey, John, 114
Tumblr, 88
Turing, Alan, 448, 449
Turing test, 448–450
Turley, Jonathan, 481
Tutorials, 148
TWAIN technology, 260
Tweeting, 83
Twisted-pair wire, **324, 363**
Twitter, 88, 90
instant messaging vs., 83
job interviews via, 14
Twitty, Conway, 485
2G technology, 336–337
Two-way communications, 335–343
long-distance wireless, 335–338
short-range wireless, 338–343

U

Ubiquitous computing, 4
UIT 11e App, 1
Ultrabooks, 196
Ultra-wideband (UWB) technology, **340**–341, **363**
Underkoffler, John, 125
Undo command, 154
Unicode, **200, 242**
Unified Modeling Language (UML), 511
Uninstall utility, 135
Unit testing, 512
Unix, **140**–141, **186,** 534
Unmanned aerial vehicles (UAVs), 482
Upgrading, **204,** 215, **242–243**
hardware, 204
software, 150
Uplinking, 330
Uploading, **20, 44,** 53
UPS (uninterruptible power supply), 201, 203, 205
URL (Uniform Resource Locator), 63, **64**–65, **107**
USB (Universal Serial Bus), 217
USB flash drives, **228, 243**
USB hubs, 217
USB ports, **217,** 219, **243**
Usenet, 83
User guides, 180
User interface, **124**–133, **186**
expert system, 441
gesture-driven, 125–126
GUI features, 126–133
Help command, **133,** 134
keyboard, 125, 126–127
mouse and pointer, 125
Username (user ID), **60,** 79, **107**

Users
participation in systems development by, 506
preparing documentation for, 525
training on new systems, 513
Utility programs, 115, **121,** 122–123, **186**
UXGA monitors, 278

V

Vacuum tubes, 192
Values, spreadsheet, **159, 186**
Vance, Ashlee, 194
Vandalism, computer, 470
V-chip technology, 493
Vector images, 172
Veligdan, Ben, 205
Vendor-based auctions, 91
Vertical portals, 70
Very-high-level languages, **531, 546**
VGA ports, 219
Video, **287, 299**
future developments in, 289
manipulation of, 487
search tools for, 74
smartphones and, 375
software for editing, 172
streaming, **87**
web-based, 74, 87
Video blogs, 88
Video cards, **32, 44,** 215, 267–268, 278
Videoconferencing, **287**–288, **299,** 342
Video display terminals (VDTs), 252
See also Display screens
Video files, 150, 151
Videogame consoles, **399**–401, **404**
Microsoft XBox One, 400–401
Nintendo Wii U, 401
Sony PlayStation 4, 401
Videogames
evolution of, 144–145
hardware systems for, 399–401
mental health issues with, 490
rating system for, 490, 491
Video on demand (VOD), **398, 404**
Videophones, 342
Video RAM (VRAM), 215, 278
Vinge, Vernor, 450–451
Virtual, meaning of, **10, 44**
Virtual File Allocation Table (VFAT), 222
Virtual keyboards, 251, 374
Virtual meetings, 342
Virtual memory, 118, **214, 243**
Virtual private networks (VPNs), **314, 363**
Virtual reality (VR), 38, **442**–444, **455**
Virtual Reality Modeling Language (VRML), **540, 547**
Viruses, **100, 107,** 348
cellphone, 101, 350
downloaded by employees, 478
free online check for, 348
software for protecting against, 122, 350–351
tips on preventing, 122
See also Malware
Visual BASIC, 537
Visual programming, **537,** 538, **547**
Vocal references, 269
Voiceband communications, 327
Voice commands, 374
Voice-output devices, **287, 299**
Voice-recognition systems, 474
VoIP phoning, 84–85
Volatile storage, **212, 243**
Volkow, Nora, 292
Voltage regulator, 201
Von Neumann, John, 22
Vortals, 70
Voting technology, 11, 463
VRML (Virtual Reality Modeling Language), **540, 547**

W

Wales, Jimmy, 74
Wall, Larry, 542
Wallace, William A., 451
Warm boot, 116
Warnock, John, 169
Warwick, Kevin, 448
Wavetable synthesis, 216
Weak AI, **438**–439, **455**
Wearable technology, 248, 384
Weatherbee, Danielle, 290
Web 2.0, **92, 107**
Web 3.0, 92, 93–96
Web analytics, 428
Web applications, **147, 186**
Web auctions, 91–92
Web-based email, 78, **107**
Web browsers, **63, 107**
features of, 67–69
mobile, 66–67
navigating with, 66–69
personal, 94, 96
privacy settings, 357
Webcams, **266**–268, **299,** 342
Webcasting, **88, 107–108**
Web conferencing, 342
Web database, 422
Web documents, 157
Web exercises
on application software, 190
on communications technology, 365–366
on databases, 457–458
on hardware, 245–246, 301–302
on information technology, 47–48
on the Internet, 111–112
on personal technology, 406
on quality-of-life issues, 502
on security issues, 501–502
on systems analysis and design, 548–549
on system software, 190
on virtual reality, 458
See also Review questions/exercises
Web files, 151
Web forums, 83
Webmail, 78
Web page design/authoring software, **174**–175, **186**
Web pages, **63, 108**
finding things on, 70
hyperlinks on, 66, 69
interactivity of, 69
multimedia effects on, 85–88
resources on designing and building, 175, 177
software for creating, 174–175
See also Websites
Web portals, **70, 108**
Web servers, 313
Websites, **63, 108**
bookmarking, 67, 69
favorite, 67, 69
history of visited, 67, 68
job listing, 14
media-sharing, 93, 95
secure, 97
social-networking, 92–93
verifying valid, 97
See also Web pages; World Wide Web
Weiner, Anthony, 493
What-if analysis, **160, 186**
White-hat hackers, 345
White House website, 11
Whois Database, 62
Wide area networks (WANs), **310, 363**
Widgets, 540
Wi-Fi, **58, 108**
network examples, 339
security issues, 340, 469–470
smartphones and, 375
standards for, 58, 338, 340
Wi-Fi phishing, 469
Wii U console, 401
Wikipedia, 73–74, 409, 415
Wikis, 36, **73, 108**
Wildcards, 76
Wildstrom, Stephen, 206
WiMax standard, **340, 363**
Window (computer display), **81, 108, 131**–133, **186**
Windows operating systems, **136**–140
Windows 7, **137,** 138
Windows 8, **137**–140
Windows Phone 8, 143
Windows RT, 138–139
Windows Server 2012, 140
Wired communications media, 324–326
Wireless access point (WAP), 315
Wireless Application Protocol (WAP), **329, 363**
Wireless communications, 327–343
bandwidth and, **327**–328
digital cameras and, 390
electromagnetic spectrum and, **327,** 328

Wireless communications—*Cont.*
Internet connections and, 57–58
laptop computers and, 238
long-distance, 332–338
protocol used for, 329
radio-frequency spectrum and, **327,** 328–329
short-range, 338–343
tutorials about, 341
types of, 329–331
Wireless Internet service providers (WISPs), **58**–59, **108**
Wireless keyboards, 252
Wireless LANs (WLANs), **311,** 338–340, **363**
Wireless mouse, 254
Wireless network cards, **216, 243**
Wireless networks, **58, 108,** 311
Wireless portals, 70
Wireless USB (WUSB), **341, 363**
Wirth, Niklaus, 534
Wolff, Michael, 8
Word games, 40
Word processing software, **153**–158, **186**
creating documents, 153–154
default settings, 157
editing documents, 154–156
formatting documents, 156–157
illustrated overview of, 154
printing documents, 157
saving documents, 157–158
tracking document changes, 156
web documents and, 157
Word size, **212, 243**
Word wrap, **153, 186**
Workbook files, 150, 158
Workgroup computing, 342
Workplace
computer skills for, 12, 13, 14
email privacy in, 96
monitoring employees in, 472, 478
new technologies in, 496–497
quality-of-life issues and, 494–495
See also Employment
Worksheets, **158**–161
chart creation, 160–161
how they work, 158–160
illustrated overview, 159
templates, 160
Workstations, **24, 44**
World Is Flat, The (Friedman), 497
World Wide Web (the "web"), **19, 44,** 62–76
addresses used on, 64–65
blogs on, 88–89
browser software, **63,** 66–69
business conducted on, 90–92
citing sources from, 74
domain abbreviations on, 65
evaluating information on, 71, 75
government resources on, 10–11
HTML and, 66
hyperlinks on, 66
intrusiveness of, 96–101
job searching on, 13–14
lecture notes posted on, 499
multimedia on, 62, 74, 85–88
navigating, 66–69
plagiarism issues, 102
podcasting and, **90**
portal sites on, 70
programming for, 537–542
push technology and, **88**
review questions/exercises on, 108–112
RSS newsreaders on, **88**
searching, 70–74, 76
shopping safely on, 98
social networking on, 92–93
telephone calls via, 84–85
terminology associated with, 62–63
tips for searching, 76
See also Internet; Websites
World Wide Web Consortium (W3C), 62, 63
Worms, **348, 363**
Writing data, **214, 243**
Writing program documentation, **525, 547**
Writing skills, 17
WSXGA+ monitors, 278
WUXGA monitors, 278
WXGA monitors, 278

X

Xbox One console, 400–401
XGA monitors, 278
XHTML (extensible hypertext markup language), 66
XML (extensible markup language), **88, 108, 540**–541, **547**

Y

Yahoo!, 177, 323
Yang, Jerry, 368
Yoffie, David B., 270
YouTube, 93, 95

Z

Zettabyte (ZB), 31
ZigBee technology, 343
ZocDoc program, 8
Zoho applications, 148
Zombie computers, **349**–350, **363**
Z-Wave technology, 343